SOCIAL THEORY

ROOTS AND BRANCHES

Readings

Third Edition

Peter Kivisto
Augustana College

D0073835

New York   Oxford
OXFORD UNIVERSITY PRESS
2008

Oxford University Press, Inc., publishes works that further Oxford University's
objective of excellence in research, scholarship, and education.

Oxford   New York
Auckland   Cape Town   Dar es Salaam   Hong Kong   Karachi
Kuala Lumpur   Madrid   Melbourne   Mexico City   Nairobi
New Delhi   Shanghai   Taipei   Toronto

With offices in
Argentina   Austria   Brazil   Chile   Czech Republic   France   Greece
Guatemala   Hungary   Italy   Japan   Poland   Portugal   Singapore
South Korea   Switzerland   Thailand   Turkey   Ukraine   Vietnam

Copyright © 2008 by Oxford University Press, Inc.

Published by Oxford University Press, Inc.
198 Madison Avenue, New York, New York 10016
http://www.oup.com

Oxford is a registered trademark of Oxford University Press

ISBN 978-0-19-533243-8

Printing number: 9 8 7 6 5 4 3 2 1

Printed in the United States of America
on acid-free paper

Contents

Part One: The Roots—Classical Social Theory

I. Karl Marx

II. Émile Durkheim

*New in the Third Edition.

iii

IV. Georg Simmel

V. Neglected Voices

---

*New in the Third Edition.

VI. Voices Outside the Discipline

Part Two: The Branches—Contemporary Social Theory

IX. Symbolic Interactionism

X. Phenomenology and Ethnomethodology

XI. Exchange Theory and Rational Choice Theory

*New in the Third Edition.

*New in the Third Edition.

XIII. Critical Theory

*New in the Third Edition.

XIV. Contemporary Theories of Modernity

XV. Structuralism, Poststructuralism, and Postmodernism

*New in the Third Edition.

*New in the Third Edition.

XVII. New Directions/Creative Syntheses

*New in the Third Edition.

*New in the Third Edition.

Preface

New to the Third Edition

There are 14 new selections in this edition of *Social Theory: Roots and Branches,* including four substitutions for entries appearing in the previous edition and 10 new readings. These include the following: (1) Karl Marx's "The German Ideology"; (2) Georg Simmel's "Philosophy of Money"; (3) Harold Garfinkel's "Studies of the Routine Grounds of Everyday Activities"; (4) Harrison White's "Persons"; (5) Candace West and Don Zimmerman's "Doing Gender"; (6) Walter Benjamin's "Art in the Age of Mechanical Reproduction"; (7) Guy Debord's "Spectacular Time"; (8) Anthony Giddens' "The Reflexivity of Modernity"; (9) Roland Robertson's "Mapping the Global Condition"; (10) Arjun Appadurai's "Disjuncture and Difference in the Global Cultural Economy"; (11) Douglas Kellner's "Theorizing Globalization"; (12) Alain Touraine's "The Subject and Societal Movements"; (13) Randall Collins' "Interaction Ritual Theory"; and (14) John Urry's "Mobile Sociology."

Acknowledgments

I have been teaching social theory for nearly a quarter of a century. First and foremost I would like to thank all of the students who have passed through my classes during that time. In particular, I would like to thank three exceptional students: Dan Pittman, Chad McPherson, and Sonia Hanson. In addition, I would like to thank a number of former professors who in rather different ways and with different results shaped my ability to think like a theorist. They include from my undergraduate days Max Heirich and Stephen Berkowitz and from my graduate school days David Apter, Norman Birnbaum, Niklas Luhmann, Stanford Lyman, Benjamin Nelson, Arthur Vidich, and R. Stephen Warner.

The reviewers for this edition of the text were generous with their comments and helpful with their suggestions. I would like to thank: Andy Abels, Keene State College; Donna Abrams, Kennesaw State University; Gabriel Acevedo, University of Texas, San Antonio; Deborah B. Berman, Framingham State College; Kelly A. Dagan, Illinois College; M. Gilbert Dunn, Roanoke College; Mary J. Gallant, Rowan College; Phoebe Godfrey, Eastern Connecticut State University; Barbara Heisler, Gettysburg College; Lynn Schlesinger, Plattsburgh State University of New York; Barbara Vann, Loyola College in Maryland; and Yong Wang, Montclair State University.

Jim Ballinger and I have worked together on all three editions of this anthology. Over the course of several years, I have learned again and again that his judgment is always sound, and he is a pleasure to work with. Scott Carter, a more recent arrival on the team, has kept us focused and on task. I want to thank Claude Teweles for initiating this project at the outset and for sticking with it. I also want to thank my new Editor at Oxford, Sherith Pankratz, whom I have worked with in the past and look forward to working with in the future.

About the Editor

Dr. Peter Kivisto is the Richard Swanson Professor of Social Thought and Chair of Sociology at Augustana College. He is the author or editor of 21 books, including *Key Ideas in Sociology, Illuminating Social Life, Americans All,* and *Citizenship: Discourse, Theory, and Transnational Prospects.* ✦

Introduction
What Is Social Theory?

Peter Kivisto

A few years ago, Alan Sica, the director of the Graduate Program in Social Thought at Pennsylvania State University and a well-known scholar of classical social theory, convened a panel of prominent scholars to probe the question, "What is social theory?" The result of the gathering was a book whose title posed that very question (Sica 1998). Thus it is that a question inevitably raised by undergraduate sociology majors entering a required course in social theory is also a question that scholars who have made theory their vocation continue to ask.

Those who have asked this question repeatedly over the course of their careers are well aware of the fact that one of the reasons it remains germane is that sociologists are far from arriving at a consensus in articulating a reply. At a very general level, most would concur with various depictions of social theory. Thus, few would object to those who characterize theories, variously, as tools of analysis, or lenses into aspects of social reality. All would concur that theories offer something more than description or broad generalizations based on composites of cases.

But it is here that theorists of various persuasions begin to part company. Some advance theories that are interpretive, while others construct theories to explain. Some theorists prefer to focus on structure, while others concentrate on the agency of social actors. Indeed, some theorists begin with the individual while others think it quite all right to dispense altogether with individuals. Some theorists think the proper object of investigation ought to be social structures, while others are equally convinced that culture should be the main focus. In another theoretical divide, one side is intent on keeping social theory closely linked to social philosophy, while the other side urges the construction of formal mathematical models patterned after the natural sciences. Finally, for some theorists the purpose of theory extends no further than to understand some patch of reality, a view that was articulated by Erving Goffman (1982) in his presidential address to the American Sociological Association, where he contended that the reason one studies the social world is simply "because it is there." Others—indeed, if Goffman is right, a majority of the profession—think that theories ought to have some practical or applied import or, to use Marxist terminology, theory ought to be related to praxis (or, in other words, concrete social practices).

Given such widely divergent assessments of the nature and functions of theory, it's reasonable to ask what counts as theory and what doesn't. It is also reasonable to ask whether the fragmented and contested discipline of sociology will ever move beyond being what George Ritzer (1975) has called a "multiple paradigm science." There are those who dream of the time that sociology will "mature" sufficiently to develop a commonly shared paradigm that serves to shape inquiry. To lay my cards on the table, I am not convinced that we are moving or someday will move toward consensus nor do I think it is necessary to do so. Indeed, part of the vitality of the discipline derives from the fact that it is engaged in attempting to make sense of what is invariably "contested knowledge" (Seidman 1998). Sociology is a big-tent discipline. It relies on a wide range of research methodologies as well as a broad spectrum of theoretical approaches.

This fact, of course, poses challenges to anybody seeking to introduce students to social theory, for being as comprehensive as possible can make it difficult for students to be able to see the forest for the trees. Moreover, the need to be selective means that some theorists are being privileged over others. It is this issue that I want to address by explaining the structure and rationale for this particular collection of articles. Social theory encompasses a body of writing dating from the early nineteenth century that has informed and continues to inform the discipline of sociology. This anthology has a simple objective, which is to assist students in social theory classes to acquire an appreciation of its range and scope. A casual perusal of the 78 entries in this collection will reveal the remarkable variety of work that falls under the rubric "social theory." Looking a bit further, readers will find ample indications that social theory is indeed a contested terrain abounding in intellectual debates and controversies.

As with the first two editions of this book, I have selected Peter Xiao's painting titled "Intellectual Pursuits" for the cover, because I think it manages to humorously convey the sense of urgency and importance that thinkers attach to ideas. While it is not often that intellectual disputes lead scholars to throw books at one another, it is true that social theorists are capable of being quite feisty! They take ideas seriously, and as such do not enter lightly into debates with those who have a different sense of the nature and purpose of theory.

Although the selection process necessarily excluded many significant theorists, I have tried to identify and include representatives of those theoretical approaches that have had the greatest impact on sociology. The history of sociology has been an ongoing process of defining disciplinary boundaries while remaining open to interdisciplinary dialogues. The readings I have selected reflect an attempt to show how sociology has developed as a distinctive enterprise while also revealing the ways in which voices from outside the discipline have continued to enrich it.

What Is a Classic?

This reader is divided into two sections, which I have termed "roots" and "branches." The former comprises the period from roughly 1840 to 1920, a time when sociology emerged as a distinctive enterprise, distinguishing itself from philosophy and the other social sciences. During this time, the first explicit advocates of this new field of inquiry appeared on the scene and created what might be seen as the infrastructure needed to sustain it, particularly the carving out of a legitimate place in the university system, with all that implies. This time frame represents sociology's classical period. The individuals associated with this era were responsible, even when they were not trying to do so, for giving sociology its initial identity.

How does one become a classic, and, related to this question, how does a text become part of the canon? There is no simply answer to either of these questions. The reputations of early sociologists have often waxed and waned over time. Likewise, the canon, being a social construct, is subject to challenges and to change. There is no central sociological authority that lays claim to being the final arbiter regarding who counts as a classic figure and who doesn't and, similarly, which texts are canonical and which are not. Nevertheless, it is clear that influential and well-positioned sociological elites play a key role in making these determinations, acting as brokers.

This situation is no different than in other fields. Thus, in literature, the literary establishment—English professors at elite universities and critics writing for national newspapers and the most influential literary journals—once excoriated James Joyce, and his masterpiece, *Ulysses*, was prevented from entering the United States because it was considered pornographic. Today Joyce is comfortably located in the pantheon of the twentieth century's greatest authors of fiction. Contemporary novelists such as Philip Roth and John Updike are highly regarded today, but exactly how they will be viewed in the long run is still to be determined—their precise place in the canon can only be surmised. On the other hand, today's literary gatekeepers disparage Danielle Steele's oeuvre, viewing it as nothing more than drivel for the masses. Given that this assessment is not likely to be overturned by subsequent critics, Steele will no doubt remain forever outside the canon, her only consolation being the fortune she has amassed as a result of her pandering.

While the financial stakes and prestige have never been quite so high in sociology, a similar process has been and continues to be at play. The gatekeepers are not all that different from those in the literary world. Professors at elite universities, journal editors, and the editorial decision makers at publishing houses have had a say in deciding which works enter the canon and which are excluded. This is at best an imperfect process, as honest considerations of the particular merits and weaknesses of any work inevitably mingle with the intellectual predilections and cultural prejudices of the critics in question. Nowhere are the latter more evident than in matters related to the gender and racial backgrounds of specific authors.

One way of determining whether someone ought to be considered a contender for the sociological pantheon is whether his or her work continues to be read today and in some fashion still informs the varied ways in which sociologists frame their patterns of inquiry. Early in the twenty-first century, there is fairly widespread consensus that four scholars have played especially significant roles in shaping what has come to be contemporary sociology: (1) Karl Marx (1818–1883), who never claimed to be a sociologist or suggested he wanted to advance sociology's cause (he did, however, criticize the earliest proponent of sociology, Auguste Comte); (2) Émile Durkheim (1858–1917), who was single-minded in his determination to promote sociology as a science clearly distinct from competing social sciences; (3) Max Weber (1864–1920), who became a sociologist later in life but never gave up also considering himself to be a historian and economist; and (4) Georg Simmel (1858–1918), who until fairly recently was not considered in the league of the preceding trio but whose reputation in recent years has finally landed him in the pantheon of founding figures.

What exactly does it mean to say that this quartet is viewed as foundational to the discipline? Suffice it to say that all of them are widely read today, with all of their major works still in print in many languages. Moreover, in all cases there are virtual cottage industries devoted to exegeses, analyses, and assessments of their works. Parenthetically, the fact that we maintain such interest in individuals who were dead by 1920 and that we continue to read them indicates that sociologists disagree with Alfred North Whitehead's (1938) claim that a science cannot progress unless it forgets its founders. We read them

because whatever their shortcomings and however different our world is from theirs, they provide insights that continue to inform the discipline.

In other words, we examine these theorists because they get us thinking in intellectually productive ways. Their works are not construed as ends in themselves. If sociologists were to treat any or all of these scholars as providing something akin to revealed truth, they would be approaching works such as *Capital, The Division of Labor in Society, The Protestant Ethic and the Spirit of Capitalism,* and *The Philosophy of Money* in a manner analogous to the way Christian fundamentalists view the Bible—as inerrant and complete. Fortunately, few sociologists operate with such a perspective—and those who do tend to be adherents of an orthodox Marxism that is fast fading from the scene.

The appropriate reason for reading these canonical figures is that sociological theory does not arise out of nowhere, without context or history. Rather, it is always the product of responding to a tradition of thought, and in this regard theorists are no different from other writers who both look forward to what they want to produce and backward to whence they came. Much theoretical work is intended to be revisionist, by which I mean that it seeks to simultaneously build upon and correct those who came before. It sometimes wants to amend, while at other times to challenge, to embrace and refine, or to dismiss. Whatever the particular nature of the relationship with past theorists, all are motivated in part by what literary scholar Harold Bloom (1997) has called the "anxiety of influence."

When did Marx, Durkheim, Weber, and Simmel become classics? Certainly after their deaths, since death would appear to be a prerequisite. While this is not the place for intellectual history, I note simply that Durkheim and Weber were accorded classic status first. While the process of becoming part of the canon began rather quickly after their deaths, a most important point occurred with the publication of Talcott Parsons' *The Structure of Social (SSA)* in 1937. Therein the young Harvard theorist, sensing an unappreciated convergence in their writing, placed them in the center of sociological theory. His book was to have a singularly important impact on their subsequent reputations. However, it was not altogether determinative in shaping the received wisdom of various theorists, for he also included two other theorists who are largely unread today: Alfred Marshall and Vilfredo Pareto. At the same time, it is worth mentioning that Parsons appeared to be ambivalent about Simmel. On the one hand, he treated him as a sufficiently compelling theorist to draft a chapter for the book. On the other hand, in the end he decided not to publish that particular chapter.

Marx was never considered for inclusion into Parsons' first major work. Moreover, Marx's move into the canon was stymied by the association of his work with the events surrounding the Russian Revolution and subsequent Marxist-inspired revolutions. During the Cold War, and especially during the McCarthy era, embracing Marx's ideas could be a risky enterprise. Nonetheless, even before the events of the 1960s—the civil rights movement, the anti-Vietnam war movement, and the counterculture—Marx's reputation was on the rise among sociologists. As Alvin Gouldner (1973) pointed out, two of the most significant theorists of the post-World War II era, Robert Merton and C. Wright Mills "kept open an avenue of access to Marxist theory" (pp. x–xi). This meant that two of the three major theory schools of the period—functionalism and conflict theory—made room for Marxist thought.

Finally, Simmel's claim to canonical status occurred only in the late 1960s and early 1970s. In no small part, this was due to the promotional efforts of a small number of scholars, most notably the émigré scholar Kurt Wolfe and University of Chicago theorist Donald Levine. It is fair to say that, just like during his lifetime when he was highly regarded by many influential sociologists ranging from Weber to the key figures associated with the early years of the Chicago School of sociology but still remained marginalized, so it is today. Indeed, if theorists continue to debate whether any of these four should be considered central founders of social theory, Simmel is clearly the one whose status is most insecure.

If these individuals have made the grade, who didn't? I could provide a long list of also-rans, but among the more obvious are Auguste Comte, Herbert Spencer, William Graham Sumner, and Vilfredo Pareto. Comte was a prolific writer who bequeathed to us the name of our discipline, creating "sociology" out of two stems, the Latin *socius* and Greek *logos*. He had an impact, not the least on someone included in this collection: Harriett Martineau. Nonetheless, he is little read today, and when he is it is more out of historical curiosity than a desire to import his ideas into contemporary sociological discourse. A similar fate befell Spencer, who was widely read and respected during his lifetime. Nevertheless, by the time Parsons wrote *SSA*, he was increasingly ignored, in no small part because of his association with Social Darwinian ideology. Parsons (1937) famously began his book with the following sentence: "Who now reads Spencer?" A similar fate befell Sumner, who introduced sociology to Yale and was one of the first presidents of the American Sociological Society, and he was left out for similar reasons, as his politics were in main respects similar to those of Spencer. Pareto was an acerbic and lacerating critic of other theorists, including Marx and Durkheim, which made him controversial in his lifetime. Over time, his ideas (perhaps fairly, perhaps unfairly) became associated with Italian fascism, which did his reputation no good. In addition, many subsequent theorists concluded that in the end he really wasn't a theorist. It should be noted that periodically calls have been made to reconsider the contribution of one or another of these largely ignored thinkers, as when Jonathan Turner (1985) proposed a reevaluation of Spencer's legacy. It should also be noted that those calls have largely gone unheeded.

In recent decades the discipline at large has increasingly come to the realization that some scholars from the nineteenth and early twentieth centuries were not given their due during their lifetimes. These neglected figures are the products of the dual legacies of racism and sexism. In several instances, concerted efforts have been made to redress this situation, beginning with the civil rights and women's movements in the 1960s. While many of the neglected voices made valuable contributions to one or another of sociology's various subfields, they were not necessarily interested in advancing social theory.

In this collection, I have identified a few particularly significant individuals who because of their race or gender were marginalized from the mainstream of the emerging sociological profession and as a result failed to influence developments in theory the way they might have. The earliest such neglected voice that I have included is the British writer Harriet Martineau, whose thought, as noted earlier, was shaped by Comte. Viewed for decades as an entertaining travel writer and essayist, she has only recently—due in no small part to the efforts of historical sociologists such as Michael Hill and Susan Hoecker-Drysdale (2001)—been viewed as someone who made a contribution to social theory. The marginalization of W. E. B. DuBois is perhaps even more curious given that he was trained as a sociologist, becoming the first black to obtain a Ph.D. from Harvard (where he studies with such luminaries as William James), and the author of *The Philadelphia Negro* (1899), considered to be the first major empirical research study published by an American sociologist. Part of the reason that he was frequently forgotten as a sociologist is that he left academe (his job options were limited to historically black colleges) to become one of the founding members of the NAACP and spent his life, in the United States—and later, when he embraced Pan-Africanism, in Ghana—as a civil rights and political activist. Nonetheless, as has become clear due to renewed attention to his writings (see, for example, Zuckermann 2004), it is well worth the effort to explore how Du Bois can contribute to social theory—particularly, in an age of multiculturalism, to the ongoing salience of racial and ethnic identities.

For her part, Jane Addams, the founder of Hull House and recipient of the Nobel Peace Prize, had an ongoing relationship with the members of the Chicago School of sociology and as such was well positioned to be viewed as a sociologist in her own right, despite a lack of explicit training in the field. She is appropriately known as one of the most important founding figures of contemporary social work and as an activist supporting a variety of progressive causes, and these activities clearly overshadowed her contribution to sociology in general and theory in particular. Nevertheless, as Mary Jo Deegan (1988) and others have made clear, it is worth the effort to return to her work, particularly in coming to terms with changing gender roles brought about by the newly emerging industrial society and the birth of the welfare state.

And thus it goes with other neglected figures. Charlotte Perkins Gilman, a student of early American sociologist Lester Ward, is better known today as an early feminist; whether she had anything to offer social theorists has only recently been explored. Somewhat differently, Elsie Clews Parsons was acclaimed as an anthropologist during her lifetime, being elected president of the American Anthropological Association, but her specific contribution to theory was then and is today not fully appreciated.

Whether or not in the end what I have referred to here as neglected voices will be fully included in the canon cannot be determined at this point. What is clear, however, is that the canon developed slowly and fitfully and that the construction of a canon is an ongoing process. While it would appear from the vantage of the present that four scholars are firmly located in the pantheon of founding figures of modern social theory, there is also an appreciation of the fact that they are not the only intellectuals from the past who ought to inform present and future trends in social theory.

A Multiple-Paradigm Science

No unified theoretical paradigm shapes sociology today. Nor is one looming on the horizon. In fact, many inside and outside the world of social theory would describe the situation as a cacophony of competing approaches. Some bemoan this reality, others embrace it as salutary, and still others simply see it as a fact of life. This is not to suggest that efforts have not been made to create a unified and singular theoretical paradigm. However, the experience of the past seven decades has led most sociologists to be rather circumspect about the prospects of becoming other than a multiple-paradigm science.

The boldest attempt to forge a one-paradigm science commenced with the publication of Parsons' *SSA*. The central claim of that work was that those classic theorists he was prepared to place in the canon, particularly Durkheim and Weber, had more in common than first met the eye. Indeed, in articulating what he was to call a "theory of action," Parsons explicitly intended to stress the commonalities of these figures (Camic 1989). He thought that none had managed to develop an entirely satisfactory basis for a unified theoretical approach, but they had set the stage. Parsons then turned his attention to a sustained effort to establish that unified theory. Indeed, his goal in *Toward a General Theory of Action* (1951), which he edited with Edward Shils, was to create a theoretical paradigm that would serve to unite the various social sciences, particularly sociology, anthropology, and psychology. He found that paradigm in what was first defined as functionalism and later as structural functionalism (he shifted to systems theory during the later phase of his life). Given his missionary zeal and his ecumenical outlook on those theory camps that differed from his approach (particularly symbolic interactionism and phenomenology), he managed for a time to establish a hegemonic theoretical stance, though not one without significant dissent. During the 1950s and 1960s, functionalism was the reigning orthodoxy. However, it never managed to eliminate all theoretical competitors. Rather, two competing schools during this time came to characterize what might be described as the loyal opposition: conflict theories and symbolic interactionism. Thus it is that the first three sections of the "branches" part of this book represent each of these theoretical orientations.

Conflict theories comprise a variety of approaches that share one thing in common: the assumption that functionalism tended to gloss over the tensions, fissions, and problems—in short the conflictual tendencies and realities—in contemporary social life. That functionalism thought it could account for conflict is evident in the first selection in the conflict section, for Lewis Coser's focus on the "functions" of conflict was an attempt to illustrate how functionalism could incorporate conflict. Such was disputed, in differing ways, by the three theorists used to exemplify the conflict stance: C. Wright Mills, Ralf Dahrendorf, and Randall Collins. Collins, it should be noted, was responsible for the first significant effort to provide a systematic conflict theory.

Symbolic interaction theory was deeply indebted to the work of philosopher George Herbert Mead, though it was sociologist Herbert Blumer who was responsible, in the selection included herein, for spelling out what a symbolic interactionist perspective might look like. Blumer rejected Parsons' claim that this theoretical stance could readily be incorporated into Parsons' own theoretical edifice. Symbolic interactionists became closely associated with ethnographic research methods and with the presentation of thick descriptions in attempts to uncover the interpretive work of actors creating their lives and their social worlds. Anselm Strauss was one of the key figures associated with the formative years of symbolic interaction, while for his part Erving Goffman would probably have resisted being so labeled. Indeed, although in many respects he ought to be seen as offering a distinctive approach to theory, it is clear that subsequent symbolic interactionists like to claim Goffman as one of their own, and it is fair to conclude that if one has to categorize him, this is the most appropriate label to apply. The same can be said of Stanford Lyman, who was also influenced by phenomenology, ethnomethodology, and existentialist theory and in fact defined his own work as a "sociology of the absurd."

If symbolic interaction is a distinctly American theoretical branch, phenomenology's roots are European, located in particular in the philosopher Edmund Husserl's work. Among the most important scholars to bring phenomenology into sociology was the Austrian-born émigré scholar Alfred Schutz, who along with other European exile scholars taught at New York's New School for Social Research. Unlike Blumer, he actually sought to engage Parsons in an ongoing dialogue, but in the end he was frustrated by where it was leading. Aron Gurwitsch is less well known than Schutz, but he, too, played an invaluable role in developing this particular theoretical perspective. Certainly not to be confused with phenomenology, but bearing what might be called a family resemblance, ethnomethodology emerged, like symbolic interactionism, on American soil. Harold Garfinkel is the founding figure of ethnomethodology, and thus it is appropriate that an excerpt from his landmark book, *Studies in Ethnomethodology* (1967), be included in the section. Given the interest of many ethnomethodologists in conversational analysis, it is also appropriate that one of the early proponents of such a focus, Harvey Sacks, also be included.

The following section, Exchange, Rational Choice, and Network Theories, like the preceding one, links three theoretical camps that are distinct but nonetheless are in some respects related or offer overlapping perspectives. Exchange theory is the oldest, generally associated with Parsons's Harvard colleague and theoretical rival, George Homans. He was an exponent of methodological individualism and a behavioralist approach to the social sciences and thus disagreed profoundly with Parsons's work. Indeed, in his autobiography, *Coming to My Senses* (1984) Homans wrote that Parsons asked him to read *SSA*. He went on the say, "I conscientiously read it, but did not criticize it, I hated it so much" (p. 323). Exchange theory was taken up by Richard Emerson, who utilized laboratory experiments to ground his theoretical work on "power-dependence relations." Peter Blau's contribution to exchange theory in this collection occurs in his effort to link the micro-level analysis characteristic of exchange theory to macro-level issues.

Two of the selections in this section were penned by rational choice theorists, James S. Coleman and Michael Hechter. Coleman's selection derives from his magnum opus, *Foundations of Social Theory* (1990), wherein he sought to do nothing less than point social theory in a new direction, specifically one that in many respects abandoned Parsons. Like exchange theorists, Coleman embraced methodological individualism. His excerpt sketches some of the fundamental grounding principles of the approach.

Meanwhile, Hechter's selection reveals how rational choice moves from individual actors to the creation of social institutions. The representative of network theory, Harrison White, was no less ambitious in his aspirations than Coleman, for he, too, thought that social theory had gone off the tracks and needed to be set right. Doing so, in his view, necessitated the turn to network analysis, a flavor of which can be derived from the enclosed entry from his work.

If the preceding two sections contain theoretical orientations that operate at fairly high levels of abstraction and at a remove from political engagements, such is not the case with the next two sections. Beginning with the first, feminist theories, a great outpouring of theoretical work developed during and in the wake of the 1960s women's movement. Feminist theories often have their origins in other theoretical perspectives, including but not limited to Marxism, neo-Freudianism, structuralism, symbolic interactionism, and postmodernism. This section provides readers with some indication of the range of feminist theories, beginning with Candace West and Don Zimmerman's symbolic interactionist-grounded article and including Judith Butler's postmodern interest in transgression, Patricia Hill Collins' attempt to link race and gender in outlining an Afrocentric feminist epistemology, Dorothy Smith's explanation of what "standpoint" means for a theoretical approach that begins with the concrete experiences of women, and finally Nancy Chodorow's effort to rethink the relevance of Freud for feminist theorizing.

The next section contains selections from the key figures associated with the Frankfurt School of sociology who advanced a "critical theory" that was at once deeply indebted to Marx and also profoundly influenced (even when not explicitly acknowledged) by Weber. Although different from one another in many ways, what linked these individuals was an abiding critique of capitalism and a concern with the consequences of rationalization. This section includes an excerpt from Walter Benjamin's extremely influential article "Art in the Age of Mechanical Reproduction," Herbert Marcuse's account of the philosophical underpinnings of critical theory in Kant and Hegel, and Max Horkheimer's comparison of traditional and critical theory. All three of these individuals were contemporaries and associated with the founding of the Frankfurt School. In contrast, Jürgen Habermas is the current heir of these founding figures. His work on systematically distorted communication is a reflection of his concern with the relationship between communication and power and reveals something of the range of influences shaping his thought.

The following section offers an array of articles by theorists seeking to account for aspects of the causes and consequences of modernity. It begins with an excerpt from Norbert Elias, a scholar who worked in relative obscurity for decades on the "civilizing process" but who by the 1970s was finally recognized as a major theorist of the rise of modernity. Guy Debord, a key figure of the French Situationist International, is an original thinker, though his work resembles in some respects both critical theory and postmodernism. His contribution to the collection provides a brief introduction to his concept of "the society of the spectacle." Anthony Giddens, one of the most influential theorists in the world during the past three decades, rejects the notion that we have entered a postmodern epoch, instead contending that we have moved to a higher stage of modernity. His focus in the selection contained here is on the reflexive character of modernity. This essay is followed by a selection from German theorist Ulrich Beck, who is a colleague of Giddens at the London School of Economics. Beck is one of the key exponents of the idea that contemporary societies should be characterized as risk societies.

Three distinct but often related theoretical strands define the next section: structuralism, poststructuralism, and postmodernism. In his discussion of structures and habitus, the late French theorist Pierre Bourdieu builds on both Marxism and structuralism in developing his own distinctive theoretical perspective. A sketch of that perspective is offered in a selection from his *Outline of a Theory of Practice* (1977). Michel Foucault is the poststructuralist representative in the collection. His analysis of Jeremy Bentham's notion of the panopticon reveals something of his understanding of the relationship between knowledge, power, and control. Postmodernism has been a highly influential theoretical perspective in the social sciences and humanities, but because it is defined so variably by different advocates, it is often difficult to specify what one means in using the term. Two rather different representatives of postmodernism are included in order to illustrate this fact: the radical postmodernist Jean Baudrillard and the more moderate version of postmodernism associated with the writings of Zygmunt Bauman. The section is rounded out with an essay by Mike Featherstone that does a nice job of comparatively defining and analyzing the modern and the postmodern.

Few would dispute the fact that we live in an increasingly interconnected world where what geographer David Harvey (1996) calls "time-space compression" has led to an emerging global economy, the increasing significance of transnational politics, and the ascendance of a global culture. It has become incumbent on theorists to increasingly frame their work with globalization in mind. The four authors in the section on world systems and globalization theory are among the most prominent exemplars of current developments. Immanuel Wallerstein's major project on world systems theory offers a Marxist-inspired approach to the emergence of a capitalist system that no longer operates primarily at the national level but has over several centuries managed to become a worldwide phenomenon. If his work is more explicitly associated with world systems theory, the other three authors in the section are globalization theorists, including Roland Robertson, who distinguishes his perspective from that of Wallerstein or traditional theorists of modernity. While Arjun Appadurai is primarily interested in the cultural aspects of globalization, Douglas Kellner focuses his lens on the intersections of political and economic globalization, with a keen eye to the reconfigurations of power.

The final section contains selections from three particularly prominent contemporary theorists whose current work does not fit neatly into any of the existing section headings. In rather different ways, they point to new potential directions for theory development. Bryan Turner, known as a critical exegete of Weber and a theorist of citizenship, has turned his gaze to the sociology of the body, a long ignored topic within the discipline, and advances that as a starting point we ought to appreciate the "ontological fragility" of all humans. French theorist Alain Touraine offers a theoretical account of the role of social movements in shaping the contours of change in post-industrial society. In his work, the subject is conceived in collective rather than individual terms. Randall Collins, whose contribution to conflict sociology appears earlier in the collection, has recently built on the work of Durkheim and Goffman to advance what he calls "interaction ritual theory." Manuel Castells offers a version of network theory quite different from that advanced by Harrison White. Castells offers a macro-sociological theoretical account of the contours of a network society in an information age. Finally, John Urry proposes that sociology ought to shift its focus from the study of society, which encourages a static approach to social life, to the study of mobility—or more specifically, mobilities.

Conclusion

As this overview reveals, social theory is a remarkably broad and diverse enterprise. I, quite frankly, would have liked to include far more theorists than I was able to within the confines of a single volume. Many of the reviewers of the second edition offered suggested theorists and readings, and in some instances I followed their advice. In the end, there were many excellent suggestions that I simply could not make room for. The choice of entries is further complicated by the fact that deciding what to include and what to exclude was partially dependent on any particular work's accessibility to student readers—an inherently difficult matter for all social theory anthologies. While I make no claim that the readings are easy, I do believe that careful attention has been paid to including seminal readings that can be made comprehensible to most students. Confidence in my judgment was reinforced by the fact that I received valuable advice from a number of people who currently teach theory courses in a variety of institutional settings.

It is my firm conviction that students cannot get a feel for what theory is or how theorists think without reading them in their own words. There are a number of fine textbooks on the market that can assist students in understanding the intellectual and social contexts that shaped various theoretical projects. These texts can also provide cogent and helpful overviews of the key issues motivating particular theorists and the characteristic elements of their respective theoretical approaches. However, these ought to be viewed as complementary—modes of assistance as one engages with the texts themselves. It is only after engaging the original works that one is in a position to begin to offer a compelling, if tentative, answer to the question, What is social theory?

References

Bloom, Harold. 1997. *The Anxiety of Influence: A Theory of Poetry,* 2nd edition. New York: Oxford University Press.

Bourdieu, Pierre. 1977. *Outline of a Theory of Practice.* Cambridge, UK: Cambridge: University Press.

Camic, Charles. 1989. "Structure After 50 Years: The Anatomy of a Charter." *American Journal of Sociology,* 95(1): 38–107.

Coleman, James S. 1990. *Foundations of Social Theory.* Cambridge, MA: The Belknap Press of Harvard University Press.

Deegan, Mary Jo. 1988. *Jane Addams and the Men of the Chicago School, 1892–1918.* New Brunswick, NJ: Transaction Books.

DuBois, W. E. B. 1999 [1899]. *The Philadelphia Negro: A Social Study.* Philadelphia: University of Pennsylvania Press.

Goffman, Erving. 1982. "The Interaction Order." *American Sociological Review,* 48(1): 1–17.

Gouldner, Alvin. 1973. "Forward." Pp. ix-xiv in Ian Taylor, Paul Walton, and Jock Young (eds.), *The New Criminology: For a Social Theory of Deviance.* London: Routledge and Kegan Paul.

Harvey, David. 1996. *Justice, Nature, and the Geography of Difference.* Malden, MA: Blackwell Publishing.

Hill, Michael R. and Susan Hoecker-Drysdale. 2001. *Harriet Martineau: Theoretical and Methodological Perspectives.* New York: Routledge.

Homans, George. 1984. *Coming to My Senses: The Autobiography of a Sociologist.* New Brunswick, NJ: Transaction Books.

Parsons, Talcott. 1937. *The Structure of Social Action,* vols. I and II. Glencoe, IL: The Free Press.

Parsons, Talcott and Edward A. Shils (eds.). 1951. *Toward a General Theory of Action.* Cambridge, MA: Harvard University Press.

Ritzer, George. 1975. *Sociology: A Multiple Paradigm Science.* Boston: Allyn and Bacon.

Seidman, Steven. 1998. *Contested Knowledge: Social Theory in a Postmodern Era.* Malden, MA: Blackwell Publishers.

Sica, Alan, ed. 1998. *What Is Social Theory? The Philosophical Debates.* Malden, MA: Blackwell Publishers.

Turner, Jonathan. 1985. *Herbert Spencer: A Renewed Appreciation.* Newbury Park, CA: Sage.

Whitehead, Alfred North. 1938. *Science and the Modern World.* New York: Penguin.

Zuckerman, Phil (ed.). 2004. *The Social Theory of W. E. B. DuBois.* Thousand Oaks, CA: Pine Forge Press. ✦

Part One

The Roots:
Classical Social Theory

I. Karl Marx

1
Alienated Labor

Karl Marx

Unpublished during Marx's lifetime (1818–1883), *The Economic and Philosophic Manuscripts* of 1844 provide key insights into the early period of his intellectual development. This excerpt concerns alienated labor; it allows the reader to see the Hegelian-inspired philosopher begin to link philosophy to the realm of economics. In this early critique of capitalism, alienation becomes the focus of Marx's analysis. He contends that as a result of a loss of control of the means of production, workers end up alienated not only from the goods that they produce and the process of work itself but from fellow humans, from themselves, and from nature. Wage labor means that workers are reduced to the level of a commodity—an object.

. . . We started from the presuppositions of political economy. We accepted its vocabulary and its laws. We presupposed private property, the separation of labour, capital, and land, and likewise of wages, profit, and ground rent; also division of labour; competition; the concept of exchange value, etc. Using the very words of political economy we have demonstrated that the worker is degraded to the most miserable sort of commodity; that the misery of the worker is in inverse proportion to the power and size of his production; that the necessary result of competition is the accumulation of capital in a few hands, and thus a more terrible restoration of monopoly; and that finally the distinction between capitalist and landlord, and

that between peasant and industrial worker disappears and the whole of society must fall apart into the two classes of the property owners and the propertyless workers.

Political economy starts with the fact of private property, it does not explain it to us. It conceives of the material process that private property goes through in reality in general abstract formulas which then have for it a value of laws. It does not understand these laws, i.e. it does not demonstrate how they arise from the nature of private property. Political economy does not afford us any explanation of the reason for the separation of labour and capital, of capital and land. When, for example, political economy defines the relationship of wages to profit from capital, the interest of the capitalist is the ultimate court of appeal, that is, it presupposes what should be its result. In the same way competition enters the argument everywhere. It is explained by exterior circumstances. But political economy tells us nothing about how far these exterior, apparently fortuitous circumstances are merely the expression of a necessary development. We have seen how it regards exchange itself as something fortuitous. The only wheels that political economy sets in motion are greed and war among the greedy, competition.

It is just because political economy has not grasped the connections in the movement that new contradictions have arisen in its doctrines, for example, between that of monopoly and that of competition, freedom of craft and corporations, division of landed property and large estates. For competition, free trade, and the division of landed property were only seen as fortuitous circumstances created by will and force, not developed and comprehended as necessary, inevitable, and natural results of monopoly, corporations, and feudal property.

So what we have to understand now is the essential connection of private property, selfishness, the separation of labour, capital, and landed property, of exchange and competition, of the value and degradation of man, of monopoly and competition, etc.—the connection of all this alienation with the money system.

Let us not be like the political economist who, when he wishes to explain something, puts himself in an imaginary original state of affairs. Such an original stage of affairs explains nothing. He simply pushes the question back into a grey and nebulous distance. He presupposes as a fact and an event what he ought to be deducing, namely the necessary connection between the two things, for example, between the division of labour and exchange. Similarly, the theologian explains the origin of evil through the fall, i.e. he presupposes as an historical fact what he should be explaining.

We start with a contemporary fact of political economy:

The worker becomes poorer the richer is his production, the more it increases in power and scope. The worker becomes a commodity that is all the cheaper the more commodities he creates. The depreciation of the human world progresses in direct proportion to the increase in value of the world of things. Labour does not only produce commodities; it produces itself and the labourer as a commodity and that to the extent to which it produces commodities in general.

What this fact expresses is merely this: the object that labour produces, its product, confronts it as an alien being, as a power independent of the producer. The product of labour is labour that has solidified itself into an object, made itself into a thing, the objectification of labour. The realization of labour is its objectification. In political economy this realization of labour appears as a loss of reality for the worker, objectification as a loss of the object or slavery to it, and appropriation as alienation, as externalization.

The realization of labour appears as a loss of reality to an extent that the worker loses his reality by dying of starvation. Objectification appears as a loss of the object to such an extent that the worker is robbed not only of the objects necessary for his life but also of the objects of his work. Indeed, labour itself becomes an object he can only have in his power with the greatest of efforts and at irregular intervals. The appropriation of the object appears as alienation to such an extent that the more objects the worker produces, the less he can possess and the more he falls under the domination of his product, capital.

All these consequences follow from the fact that the worker relates to the product of his labour as to an alien object. For it is evident from this presupposition that the more the worker externalizes himself in his work, the more powerful becomes the alien, objective world that he creates opposite himself, the poorer he becomes himself in his inner life and the less he can call his own. It is just the same in religion. The more man puts into God, the less he retains in himself. The worker puts his life into the object and this means that it no longer belongs to him but to the object. So the greater this activity, the more the worker is without an object. What the product of his labour is, that he is not. So the greater this product the less he is himself. The externalization of the worker in his product implies not only that his labour becomes an object, an exterior existence but also that it exists outside him, independent and alien, and becomes a self-sufficient power opposite him, that the life that he has lent to the object affronts him, hostile and alien.

Let us now deal in more detail with objectification, the production of the worker, and the alienation, the loss of the object, his product, which is involved in it.

The worker can create nothing without nature, the sensuous exterior world. It is the matter in which his labour realizes itself, in which it is active, out of which and through which it produces.

But as nature affords the means of life for labour in the sense that labour cannot live without objects on which it exercises itself, so it affords a means of life in the narrower sense, namely the means for the physical subsistence of the worker himself.

Thus the more the worker appropriates the exterior world of sensuous nature by his labour, the more he doubly deprives himself of the means of subsistence, firstly since the exterior sensuous world increasingly ceases to be an object belonging to his work, a means of subsistence for his labour; secondly, since it increasingly ceases to be a means of subsistence in the direct sense, a means for the physical subsistence of the worker.

Thus in these two ways the worker becomes a slave to his object: firstly he receives an object of labour, that is he receives labour, and secondly, he receives the means of subsistence. Thus it is his object that permits him to exist first as a worker and secondly as a physical subject. The climax of this slavery is that only as a worker can he maintain himself as a physical subject and it is only as a physical subject that he is a worker.

(According to the laws of political economy the alienation of the worker in his object is expressed as follows: the more the worker produces the less he has to consume, the more values he creates the more valueless and worthless he becomes, the more formed the product the more deformed the worker, the more civilized the product, the more barbaric the worker, the more powerful the work the more powerless becomes the worker, the more cultured the work the more philistine the worker becomes and more of a slave to nature.)

Political economy hides the alienation in the essence of labour by not considering the immediate relationship between the worker (labour) and production. Labour produces works of wonder for the rich, but nakedness for the worker. It produces palaces, but only hovels for the worker; it produces beauty, but cripples the worker; it replaces labour by machines but throws a part of the workers back to a barbaric labour and turns the other part into machines. It produces culture, but also imbecility and cretinism for the worker.

The immediate relationship of labour to its products is the relationship of the worker to the objects of his production. The relationship of the man of means to the objects of production and to production itself is only a consequence of this first relationship. And it confirms it. We shall examine this other aspect later.

So when we ask the question: what relationship is essential to labour, we are asking about the relationship of the worker to production.

Up to now we have considered only one aspect of the alienation or externalization of the worker, his relationship to the products of his labour. But alienation shows itself not only in the result, but also in the act of production, inside productive activity itself. How would the worker be able to affront the product of his work as an alien being if he did not alienate himself in the act of production itself? For the product is merely the summary of the activity of production. So if the product of labour is externalization, production itself must be active externalization, the externalization of activity, the activity of externalization. The alienation of the object of labour is only the résumé of the alienation, the externalization in the activity of labour itself.

What does the externalization of labour consist of then?

Firstly, that labour is exterior to the worker, that is, it does not belong to his essence. Therefore he does not confirm himself in his work, he denies himself, feels miserable instead of happy, deploys no free physical and intellectual energy, but mortifies his body and ruins his mind. Thus the worker only feels a stranger. He is at home when he is not working and when he works he is not at home. His labour is therefore not voluntary but compulsory, forced labour. It is therefore not the satisfaction of a need but only a means to satisfy needs outside itself. How alien it really is is very evident from the fact that when there is no physical or other compulsion, labour is avoided like the plague. External labour, labour in which man externalizes himself, is a labour of self-sacrifice and mortification. Finally, the external character of labour for the worker shows itself in the fact that it is not his own but someone else's, that it does not belong to him, that he does not belong to himself in his labour but to someone else. As in religion the human imagination's own activity, the activity of man's head and his heart, reacts independently on the individual as an alien activity of gods or devils, so the activity of the worker is not his own spontaneous activity. It belongs to another and is the loss of himself.

The result we arrive at then is that man (the worker) only feels himself freely active in his animal functions of eating, drinking, and procreating, at most also in his dwelling and dress, and feels himself an animal in his human functions.

Eating, drinking, procreating, etc. are indeed truly human functions. But in the abstraction that separates them from the other round of human activity and makes them into final and exclusive ends they become animal.

We have treated the act of alienation of practical human activity, labour, from two aspects. (1) The relationship of the worker to the product of his labour as an alien object that has power over him. This relationship is at the same time the relationship to the sensuous exterior world and to natural objects as to an alien and hostile world opposed to him. (2) The relationship of labour to the act of production inside labour. This relationship is the relationship of the worker to his own activity as something that is alien and does not belong to him; it is activity that is passivity, power that is weakness, procreation that is castration, the worker's own physical and intellectual energy, his personal life (for what is life except activity?) as an activity directed against himself, independent of him and not belonging to him. It is self-alienation, as above it was the alienation of the object.

We now have to draw a third characteristic of alienated labour from the two previous ones.

Man is a species-being not only in that practically and theoretically he makes both his own and other species into his objects, but also, and this is only another way of putting the same thing, he relates to himself as to the present, living species, in that he relates to himself as to a universal and therefore free being.

Both with man and with animals the species-life consists physically in the fact that man (like animals) lives from inorganic nature, and the more universal man is than animals the more universal is the area of inorganic nature from which he lives. From the theoretical point of view, plants, animals, stones, air, light, etc. form part of human consciousness, partly as objects of natural science, partly as objects of art; they are his intellectual inorganic nature, his intellectual means of subsistence, which he must first prepare before he can enjoy and assimilate them. From the practical point of view, too, they form a part of human life and activity. Physically man lives solely from these products of nature, whether they appear as food, heating, clothing, habitation, etc. The universality of man appears in practice precisely in the universality that makes the whole of nature into his inorganic body in that it is both (i) his immediate means of subsistence and also (ii) the material object and tool of his vital activity. Nature is the inorganic body of a man, that is, in so far as it is not itself a human body. That man lives from nature means that nature is his body with which he must maintain a constant interchange so as not to die. That man's physical and intellectual life depends on nature merely means that nature depends on itself, for man is a part of nature.

While alienated labour alienates (1) nature from man, and (2) man from himself, his own active function, his vital activity, it also alienates the species from man; it turns his species-life into a means towards his individual life. Firstly it alienates species-life and individual life, and secondly in its abstraction it makes the latter into the aim of the former which is also conceived of in its abstract and alien form. For firstly, work, vital activity, and productive life itself appear to man only as a means to the satisfaction of a need, the need to preserve his physical existence. But productive life is species-life. It is life producing life. The whole character of a species, its generic character, is contained in its manner of vital activity, and free conscious activity is the species-characteristic of man. Life itself appears merely as a means to life.

The animal is immediately one with its vital activity. It is not distinct from it. They are identical. Man makes his vital activity itself into an object of his will and consciousness. He has a conscious vital activity. He is not immediately identical to any of his characterizations. Conscious vital activity differentiates man immediately from animal vital activity. It is this and this alone that makes man a species-being. He is only a conscious being, that is, his own life is an object to him, precisely because he is a species-being. This is the only reason for his activity being free activity. Alienated labour reverses the relationship so that, just because he is a conscious being, man makes his vital activity and essence a mere means to his existence.

The practical creation of an objective world, the working-over of inorganic nature, is the confirmation of man as a conscious species-being, that is, as a being that relates to the species as to himself and to himself as to the species. It is true that the animal, too, produces. It builds itself a nest, a dwelling, like the bee, the beaver, the ant, etc. But it only produces what it needs immediately for itself or its offspring; it produces one-sidedly whereas man produces universally; it produces only under the pressure of immediate physical need, whereas man produces freely from physical need and only truly produces when he is thus free; it produces only itself whereas man reproduces the whole of nature. Its product belongs immediately to its physical body whereas man can freely separate himself from his product. The animal only fashions things according to the standards and needs of the species it belongs to, whereas man knows how to produce according to the measure of every species and knows everywhere how to apply its inherent standard to the object; thus man also fashions things according to the laws of beauty.

Thus it is in the working over of the objective world that man first really affirms himself as a species-being. This production is his active species-life. Through it nature appears as his work and his reality. The object of work is therefore the objectification of the species-life of man; for he duplicates himself not only intellectually, in his mind, but also actively in reality and thus can look at his image in a world he has created. Therefore when alienated labour tears from man the object of his production, it also tears from him his species-life, the real objectivity of his species and turns the advantage he has over animals into a disadvantage in that his inorganic body, nature, is torn from him.

Similarly, in that alienated labour degrades man's own free activity to a means, it turns the species-life of man into a means for his physical existence.

Thus consciousness, which man derives from his species, changes itself through alienation so that species-life becomes a means for him.

Therefore alienated labour:

(3) makes the species-being of man, both nature and the intellectual faculties of his species, into a being that is alien to him, into a means for his individual existence. It alienates from man his own body, nature exterior to him, and his intellectual being, his human essence.

(4) An immediate consequence of man's alienation from the product of his work, his vital activity and his species-being, is the alienation of man from man. When man is opposed to himself, it is another man that is opposed to him. What is valid for the relationship of a man to his work, of the product of his work and himself, is also valid for the relationship of man to other men and of their labour and the objects of their labour.

In general, the statement that man is alienated from his species-being, means that one man is alienated from another as each of them is alienated from the human essence.

The alienation of man and in general of every relationship in which man stands to himself is first realized and expressed in the relationship with which man stands to other men.

Thus in the situation of alienated labour each man measures his relationship to other men by the relationship in which he finds himself placed as a worker.

We began with a fact of political economy, the alienation of the worker and his production. We have expressed this fact in conceptual terms: alienated, externalized labour. We have analysed this concept and thus analysed a purely economic fact.

Let us now see further how the concept of alienated, externalized labour must express and represent itself in reality.

If the product of work is alien to me, opposes me as an alien power, whom does it belong to then?

If my own activity does not belong to me and is an alien, forced activity to whom does it belong then?

To another being than myself.

Who is this being?

The gods? Of course in the beginning of history the chief production, as for example, the building of temples etc. in Egypt, India, and Mexico was both in the service of the gods and also belonged to them. But the gods alone were never the masters of the work. And nature just as little. And what a paradox it would be if, the more man mastered nature through his work and the more the miracles of the gods were rendered superfluous by the miracles of industry, the more man had to give up his pleasure in producing and the enjoyment in his product for the sake of these powers.

The alien being to whom the labour and the product of the labour belongs, whom the labour serves and who enjoys its product, can only be man himself. If the product of labour does not belong to the worker but stands over against him as an alien power, this is only possible in that it belongs to another man apart from the worker.

If his activity torments him it must be a joy and a pleasure to someone else. This alien power above man can be neither the gods nor nature, only man himself.

Consider further the above sentence that the relationship of man to himself first becomes objective and real to him through his relationship to other men. So if he relates to the product of his labour, his objectified labour, as to an object that is alien, hostile, powerful, and independent of him, this relationship implies that another man is the alien, hostile, powerful, and independent master of this object. If he relates to his own activity as to something unfree, it is a relationship to an activity that is under the domination, oppression, and yoke of another man.

Every self-alienation of man from himself and nature appears in the relationship in which he places himself and nature to other men distinct from himself. Therefore religious self-alienation necessarily appears in the relationship of layman to priest, or, because here we are dealing with a spiritual world, to a mediator, etc. In the practical, real world, the self-alienation can only appear through the practical, real relationship to other men. The means through which alienation makes progress are themselves

practical. Through alienated labour, then, man creates not only his relationship to the object and act of production as to alien and hostile men; he creates too the relationship in which other men stand to his production and his product and the relationship in which he stands to these other men. Just as he turns his production into his own loss of reality and punishment and his own product into a loss, a product that does not belong to him, so he creates the domination of the man who does not produce over the production and the product. As he alienates his activity from himself, so he hands over to an alien person an activity that does not belong to him.

Up till now we have considered the relationship only from the side of the worker and we will later consider it from the side of the non-worker.

Thus through alienated, externalized labour the worker creates the relationship to this labour of a man who is alien to it and remains exterior to it. The relationship of the worker to his labour creates the relationship to it of the capitalist, or whatever else one wishes to call the master of the labour. Private property is thus the product, result, and necessary consequence of externalized labour, of the exterior relationship of the worker to nature and to himself.

Thus private property is the result of the analysis of the concept of externalized labour, i.e. externalized man, alienated work, alienated life, alienated man.

We have, of course, obtained the concept of externalized labour (externalized life) from political economy as the result of the movement of private property. But it is evident from the analysis of this concept that, although private property appears to be the ground and reason for externalized labour, it is rather a consequence of it, just as the gods are originally not the cause but the effect of the aberration of the human mind, although later this relationship reverses itself.

It is only in the final culmination of the development of private property that these hidden characteristics come once more to the fore, in that firstly it is the product of externalized labour and secondly it is the means through which labour externalizes itself, the realization of this externalization.

This development sheds light at the same time on several, previously unresolved contradictions.

1. Political economy starts from labour as the veritable soul of production, and yet it attributes nothing to labour and everything to private property. Proudhon has drawn a conclusion from this contradiction that is favourable to labour and against private property. But we can see that this apparent contradiction is the contradiction of alienated labour with itself and that political economy has only expressed the laws of alienated labour.

We can therefore also see that wages and private property are identical: for wages, in which the product, the object of the labour, remunerates the labour itself, are just a necessary consequence of the alienation of labour. In the wage system the labour does not appear as the final aim but only as the servant of the wages. We will develop this later and for the moment only draw a few consequences.

An enforced raising of wages (quite apart from other difficulties, apart from the fact that, being an anomaly, it could only be maintained by force) would only mean a better payment of slaves and would not give this human meaning and worth either to the worker or to his labour.

Indeed, even the equality of wages that Proudhon demands only changes the relationship of the contemporary worker to his labour into that of all men to labour. Society is then conceived of as an abstract capitalist.

Wages are an immediate consequence of alienated labour and alienated labour is the immediate cause of private property. Thus the disappearance of one entails also the disappearance of the other.

2. It is a further consequence of the relationship of alienated labour to private property that the emancipation of society from private property, etc., from slavery, is expressed in its political form by the emancipation of the workers. This is not because only their emancipation is at stake but because general human emancipation is contained in their emancipation. It is contained within it because the whole of human slavery is involved in the relationship of the worker to his product and all slave relationships are only modifications and consequences of this relationship.

Just as we have discovered the concept of private property through an analysis of the concept of alienated, externalized labour, so all categories of political economy can be deduced with the help of these two factors. We shall recognize in each category of market, competition, capital, money, only a particular and developed expression of these first two fundamental elements.

However, before we consider this structure let us try to solve two problems:

1. To determine the general essence of private property as it appears as a result of alienated labour in its relationship to truly human and social property.

2. We have taken the alienation and externalization of labour as a fact and analysed this fact. We now ask, how does man come to externalize, to alienate his labour? How is this alienation grounded in human development? We have already obtained much material for the solution of this problem, in that we have turned the question of the origin of private property into the question of the relationship of externalized labour to the development of human history. For when we speak of private property we think we are dealing with something that is exterior to man. When we speak of labour then we are dealing directly with man. This new formulation of the problem already implies its solution.

To take point 1, the general nature of private property and its relationship to truly human property.

Externalized labour has been broken down into two component parts that determine each other or are only different expressions of one and the same relationship. Appropriation appears as alienation, as externalization, and externalization as appropriation, and alienation as true enfranchisement. We have dealt with one aspect, alienated labour as regards the worker himself, that is, the relationship of externalized labour to itself. As a product and necessary result of this relationship we have discovered the property relationship of the nonworker to the worker and his labour.

As the material and summary expression of alienated labour, private property embraces both relationships, both that of the worker to his labour, the product of his labour and the non-worker, and that of the non-worker to the worker and the product of his labour.

We have already seen that for the worker who appropriates nature through his work, this appropriation appears as alienation, his own activity as activity for and of someone else, his vitality as sacrifice of his life, production of objects as their loss to an alien power, an alien man: let us now consider the relationship that this man, who is alien to labour and the worker, has to the worker, to labour and its object.

The first remark to make is that everything that appears in the case of the worker to be an activity of externalization, of alien-

ation, appears in the case of the non-worker to be a state of externalization, of alienation.

Secondly, the real, practical behaviour of the worker in production and towards his product (as a state of mind) appears in the case of the non-worker opposed to him as theoretical behaviour. Thirdly, the non-worker does everything against the worker that the worker does against himself but he does not do against himself what he does against the worker.

Let us consider these three relationships in more detail. . . . [The manuscript breaks off unfinished here.]

2
The German Ideology

Karl Marx and
Friedrich Engels

The German Ideology is a sprawling work of over 700 pages, written largely between the fall of 1845 and the summer of 1846. It picks up where *The Economic and Philosophic Manuscripts* left off. In its pages one sees not only the continued settling of accounts with the German philosophic tradition, but the beginnings of what would become a distinctly Marxist vision of the social world created by industrial capitalism. In this particular selection Marx and Engels take aim at certain exponents of Hegelian idealism, and they do so with a certain acerbic flair, referring to Max Stirner as "the Blessed Max Stirner" and Bruno Bauer as "St. Bruno." In their discussion of the production of consciousness, they begin to lay the foundations for an alternative, materialist theory of historical development. In so doing, they part company with Ludwig Feuerbach's version of materialism, which they find wanting because it is rooted in nature and not history.

Communism is for us not a stable state which is to be established, an *ideal* to which reality will have to adjust itself. We call communism the *real* movement which abolishes the present state of things. The conditions of this movement result from the premises now in existence. Besides, the world-market is presupposed by the mass of propertyless workers labour-power cut off as a mass from capital or from even a limited satisfaction—and therefore no longer by the mere precariousness of labour, which, not giving an assured livelihood, is often lost through competition. The proletariat can thus only exist *world-historically,* just as communism, its movement, can only have a "world-historical" existence. World-historical existence of

individuals, i.e. existence of individuals which is directly linked up with world history.

The form of intercourse determined by the existing productive forces at all previous historical stages, and in its turn determining these, is *civil society.* . . . This, as is clear from what we have said above, has as its premises and basis the simple family and the multiple, the so-called tribe, the more precise determinants of which are enumerated in our remarks above. Already here we see how this civil society is the true source and theatre of all history, and how nonsensical is the conception of history held hitherto, which neglects the real relationships and confines itself to high-sounding dramas of princes and states. Civil society embraces the whole material intercourse of individuals within a definite stage of the development of productive forces. It embraces the whole commercial and industrial life of this stage and, in so far, transcends the State and the nation though, on the other hand again, it must assert itself towards foreign peoples as nationality, and inwardly must organize itself as State. The word "civil society" emerged in the eighteenth century, when property relationships had already extricated themselves from the ancient and medieval communal society. Civil society as such only develops with the bourgeoisie; the social organization evolving directly out of production and commerce, which in all ages forms the basis of the State and of the rest of the idealistic superstructure, has, however, always been designated by the same name.

(b) Concerning the Production of Consciousness.

In history up to the present it is certainly an empirical fact that separate individuals have, with the broadening of their activity into world-historical activity, become more and more enslaved under a power alien to them (a pressure which they have conceived of as a dirty trick on the part of the so-called universal spirit), a power which has become more and more enormous and, in the last instance, turns out to be the *world-market.* But it is just as empirically established that, by the overthrow of the existing state of society by the communist revolution (of which more below) and the abolition of private property which is identical with it, this power, which so baffles the German theoreticians, will be dissolved; and that then the liberation of each single individual will be accomplished in the measure in which history becomes transformed into world-history. From the above it is clear that the real intellectual wealth of the individual depends entirely on the wealth of his real connections. Only then will the separate individuals be liberated from the various national and local barriers, be brought into practical connection with the material and intellectual production of the whole world and be put in a position to acquire the capacity to enjoy this all-sided production of the whole earth (the creations of man). Universal dependence, this natural form of the world-historical co-operation of individuals, will be transformed by this communist revolution into the control and conscious mastery of these powers, which, born of the action of men on one another, have till now overawed and governed men as powers completely alien to them. Now this view can be expressed again in speculative-idealistic, i.e. fantastic, terms as "spontaneous generation of the species," ("society as the subject"), and thereby the series of inter-related individuals can be conceived as a single individual, which accomplishes the mystery of generating itself. It is clear here that individuals certainly make one another, physically and mentally, but do not make themselves either in the non-sense of Saint Bruno, nor in the sense of the "unique," of the "made" man. . . .

Our conception of history depends on our ability to expound the real process of production, starting out from the simple material production of life, and to comprehend the form of intercourse connected with this and created by this (i.e. civil society in its various stages), as the basis of all history; further, to show it in its action as State; and so, from this starting-point, to explain the whole mass of different theoretical products and forms of consciousness, religion, philosophy, ethics etc., etc., and trace their origins and growth, by which means, of course, the whole thing can be shown in its totality (and therefore, too, the reciprocal action of these various sides on one another). It has not, like the idealistic view of history, in every period to look for a category, but remains constantly on the real ground of history; it does not explain practice from the idea but explains the formation of ideas from material practice; and accordingly it comes to the conclusion that all forms and products of consciousness cannot be dissolved by mental criticism, by resolution into "self-consciousness" or transformation into "apparitions," "spectres," "fancies," etc., but only by the practical overthrow of the actual social relations which gave rise to this idealistic humbug; that not criticism but revolution is the driving force of history, also of religion, of philosophy and all other types of theory. It shows that history does not end by being resolved into "self-consciousness" as "spirit of the spirit," but that in it at each stage there is found a material result: a sum of productive forces, a historically created relation of individuals to nature and to one another, which is handed down to each generation from its predecessor; a mass of productive forces, different forms of capital, and conditions, which, indeed, is modified by the new generation on the one hand, but also on the other prescribes for it its conditions of life and gives it a definite development, a special character. It shows that circumstances make men just as much as men make circumstances.

This sum of productive forces, forms of capital and social forms of intercourse, which every individual and generation finds in existence as something given, is the real basis of what the philosophers have conceived as "substance" and "essence of man," and what they have deified and attacked: a real basis which is not in the least disturbed, in its effect and influence on the development of men, by the fact that these philosophers revolt against it as "self-consciousness" and "the unique." These conditions of life, which different generations find in existence, decide also whether or not the periodically recurring revolutionary convulsion will be strong enough to overthrow the basis of all existing forms. And if these material elements of a complete revolution are not present (namely, on the one hand the existence of productive forces, on the other the formation of a revolutionary mass, which revolts not only against separate conditions of society up till then, but against the very "production of life" till then, the "total activity" on which it was based), then, as far as practical development is concerned, it is absolutely immaterial whether the "idea" of this revolution has been expressed a hundred times already; as the history of communism proves.

In this whole conception of history up to the present this real basis of history has either been totally neglected or else considered as a minor matter quite irrelevant to the course of history. History must therefore always be written according to an extraneous standard; the real production of life seems to be beyond history, while the truly historical appears to be separated from ordinary life, something extra-super terrestrial. With this the relation of man to nature is excluded from history and hence the antithesis of nature and history is created. The exponents of this conception of history have consequently only been able to see in history the political actions of princes and States religious and all sorts of theoretical struggles, and in particular in each historical epoch have had to share the *illusion of that epoch*. For instance, if an epoch imagines itself to be actuated by purely "political" or "religious" motives, although "religion" and "politics" are only forms of its true motives, the historian accepts this opinion. The "idea," the "conception" of these conditioned men about their real practice, is transformed into the sole determining, active force, which controls and determines their practice. When the crude form in which the division of labor appears with the Indians and Egyptians calls forth the caste-system in their State and religion, the historian believes that the caste-system is the power which has produced this crude social form. While the French and the English at least hold by the political illusion, which is moderately close to reality, "the Germans move the realm of the "pure spirit," and make religious illusion the driving force of history.

The Hegelian philosophy of history is the last consequence, reduced to its "final expression," of all this German historiography, for which it is not a question of real, nor even

of political, interests, but of pure thoughts, which inevitably appear, even to Saint Bruno, as a series of "thoughts" that devour one another and are finally swallowed up in "self-consciousness." And equally inevitably, and more logically, the course of history appears to the Blessed Max Stirner, who knows not a thing about real history, as a mere tale of "knights," robbers and ghosts, from whose visions he can, of course, only save himself by "unholiness." This conception is truly religious: it postulates religious man as the primitive man, and in its imagination puts the religious production of fancies in the place of the real production of the means of subsistence and of life itself. This whole conception of history, together with its dissolution and the scruples and qualms resulting from it, is a purely *national* affair of the Germans and has only *local* interest for the Germans, as for instance the important question treated several times of late: how really we "pass from the realm of God to the realm of man"—as if this "realm of God" had ever existed anywhere save in the imagination, and the learned gentlemen, without being aware of it, were not constantly living in the "realm of man" to which they are now seeking the way; and as if the learned pastime (for it is nothing more) of explaining the mystery of this theoretical bubble-blowing did not on the contrary lie in demonstrating its origin in actual earthly conditions.

Always, for these Germans, it is simply a matter of resolving the nonsense of earlier writers into some other freak, i.e. of presupposing that all this nonsense has a special meaning which can be discovered; while really it is only a question of explaining this theoretical talk from the actual existing conditions. The real, practical dissolution of these phrases, the removal of these notions from the consciousness of men, will, as we have already said, be effected by altered circumstances, not by theoretical deductions. For the mass of men, i.e. the proletariat, these theoretical notions do not exist and hence do not require to be dissolved, and if this mass ever had any theoretical notions, e.g. religion, etc., these have now long been dissolved by circumstances. The purely national character of these questions and solutions is shown again in the way these theorists believe in all seriousness that chimeras like "the God-Man," "Man," etc., have presided over individual epochs of history (Saint Bruno even goes so far as to assert that "only criticism and critics have made history") and when they themselves construct historical systems, they skip over all earlier periods in the greatest haste and pass immediately from Mongolism to history "with meaningful content," that is to say, to the history of the Halle and German Annals . . . and the dissolution of the Young-Hegelian school into a general squabble. They forget all other nations, all real events, and the *theatrum mundi* . . . is confined to the Leipzig Book Fair and the mutual quarrels of "Criticism," "Man," and "the Unique."

If these theorists treat really historical subjects, as for instance the eighteenth century, they merely give a history of the ideas of the times, torn away from the facts and the practical development fundamental to them; and even then they only give these ideas in order to represent them as an imperfect preliminary stage, the as yet limited predecessor of the real historical age[i.e. the period of the German philosophic struggle from 1840 to 1844. As might be expected when the history of an earlier period is written with the aim of accentuating the brilliance of an unhistoric person and his fantasies, all the really historic events, even the really historic invasions of politics into history, receive no mention. Instead we get a narrative based on systematic constructions and literary gossip, such as Saint Bruno provided in his now forgotten history of the eighteenth century. . . . These high-falutin, bombastic hucksters of ideas, who imagine themselves infinitely exalted above all national prejudices, are thus in practice far more national than the beer-quaffing German philistines who dream of a united Germany. They do not recognize the deeds of other nations as historical: they live in Germany, to Germany, and for Germany; they turn the Rhine-song into a religious hymn and conquer Alsace-Lorraine by robbing French philosophy instead of the French State, by Germanizing French ideas instead of French provinces. Herr Venedey is a cosmopolitan compared with the Saints Bruno

and Max, who, in the universal dominance of theory, proclaim the universal dominance of Germany.

It is also clear from these arguments how grossly Feuerbach is deceiving himself, when (*Wigand's Quarterly* 1845, Vol. 2) by virtue of the qualification "common man" he declares himself a communist, transforms the latter into a predicate of *"man,"* and thereby thinks it possible to change the word "communist," which in the real world means the follower of a definite revolutionary party, into a mere category. Feuerbach's whole deduction with regard to the relation of men to one another goes only so far as to prove that men need and always have needed each other. He wants to establish consciousness of this fact, that is to say, like the other theorists, merely to produce a correct consciousness about an existing fact; whereas for the real communist it is a question of overthrowing the existing state of things. We thoroughly appreciate, moreover, that Feuerbach, in endeavouring to produce consciousness of just *this* fact, is going as far as a theorist possibly can, without ceasing to be a theorist and philosopher. It is characteristic, however, that Saint Bruno and Saint Max seize on Feuerbach's conception of the communist and put it in place of the real communist—which occurs, partly, merely in order that they can combat communism too as "spirit of the spirit," as a philosophical category, as an equal opponent and, in the case of Saint Bruno, partly also for pragmatic reasons.

Like our opponents, Feuerbach still accepts and at the same time misunderstands existing reality. We recall the passage in the *Philosophy of the Future,* . . . where he develops the view that the existence of a thing or a man is at the same time its or his essence, that the conditions of existence, the mode of life and particular activity of an animal or human individual are those, in which its "essence" feels itself satisfied. Here every exception is expressly conceived as an unhappy chance, as an abnormality which cannot be altered. Thus if millions of proletarians feel themselves by no means contented in their conditions of life, if their existence [is in contradiction with their "essence," then it is certainly an abnormality, but not an unhappy chance; an historical fact based on quite definite social relationships. Feuerbach is content to affirm this fact; he only interprets the existing sensuous world, has only the relation of a theorist to it], . . . while in reality for the practical materialist, i.e. the communist, it is a question of revolutionizing the existing world, of practically attacking and changing existing things. When occasionally we find such views with Feuerbach, they are never more than isolated surmises and have much too little influence on his general outlook to be considered here as anything else than embryos capable of development.

Feuerbach's "interpretation" of the sensuous world is confined on the one hand to mere contemplation of it and on the other to mere feeling; he says "man" instead of "real, historical men." "Man" is really "the German." In the first case, the contemplation of the sensuous world, he necessarily lights on things which contradict his consciousness and feeling, which upset the harmony of all parts of the sensuous world and especially of man and nature, a harmony he presupposes. . . . To push these on one side, he must take refuge in a double perception, a profane one which only perceives the "flatly obvious" and a higher more philosophical one which perceives the "true essence" of things. He does not see how the sensuous world around him is, not a thing given direct from all eternity, ever the same, but the product of industry and of the state of society; and, indeed, in the sense that it is an historical product, the result of the activity of a whole succession of generations, each standing on the shoulders of the preceding one, developing its industry and its intercourse, modifying its social organization according to the changed needs. Even the objects of the simplest "sensuous certainty" are only given him through social development, industry and commercial intercourse. The cherry-tree, like almost all fruit-trees, was, as is well known, only a few centuries ago transplanted by commerce into our zone, and therefore only by this action of a definite society in a definite age provided for the evidence of Feuerbach's "senses." Actually, when we conceive things thus, as they really are and happened, every profound philosophical problem is resolved, as will be seen even more clearly later, quite simply into an empirical fact.

For instance, the important question of the relation of man to nature (Bruno goes so far as to speak of "the antitheses in nature and history," as though these were two separate "things" and man did not always have before him an historical nature and a natural history) out of which all the "unfathomably lofty works" on "substance" and "self-consciousnes" were born, crumbles of itself when we understand that the celebrated "unity of man with nature" has always existed in industry and has existed in varying forms in every epoch according to the lesser or greater development of industry, just like the "struggle" of man with nature, right up to the development of his productive powers on a corresponding basis. Industry and commerce, production and the exchange of the necessities of life, themselves determine distribution, the structure of the different social classes and are, in turn, determined by these as to the mode in which they are earned on; and so it happens that in Manchester for instance, Feuerbach sees only factories and machines where a hundred years ago only spinning-wheels and weaving-looms were to be seen, or in the Campagna of Rome he finds only pasture lands and swamps, where in the time of Augustus he would have found nothing but the vineyards and villas of Roman capitalists. Feuerbach speaks in particular of the perception of natural science; he mentions secrets which are disclosed only to the eye of the physicist and chemist: but where would natural science be without industry and commerce? Even this "pure" natural science is provided with an aim, as with its material, only through trade and industry, through the sensuous activity of men. So much is this activity, this unceasing sensuous labour and creation, this production, the basis of the whole sensuous world as it now exists, that, were it interrupted only for a year, Feuerbach would not only find an enormous change in the natural world, but would very soon find that the whole world of men and his own perceptive faculty, nay his own existence, were missing.

Of course, in all this the priority of external nature remains unassailed, and all this has no application to the original men produced by "generatio æquivoca" (spontaneous generation); but this differentiation has meaning only in so far as man is considered to be distinct from nature. For that matter, nature, the nature that preceded human history, is not by any means the nature in which Feuerbach lives, nor the nature which today no longer exists anywhere (except perhaps on a few Australian coral-islands of recent origin) and which, therefore, does not exist for Feuerbach. . . .

Certainly Feuerbach has a great advantage over the "pure" materialists in that he realizes how man too is an "object of the senses." But apart from the fact that he only conceives him as a "sensuous object," not as "sensuous activity," because he still remains in the realm of theory and conceives of men not in their given social connection, not under their existing conditions of life, which have made them what they are, he never arrives at the really existing active men, but stops at the abstraction "man," and gets no further than recognizing "the true, individual, corporeal man" emotionally, i.e. he knows no other "human relationships" "of man to man" than love and friendship, and

even then idealized. He gives no criticism of the present conditions of life. Thus he never manages to conceive the sensuous world as the total living sensuous activity of the individuals composing it; and therefore when, for example, he sees instead of healthy men a crowd of scrofulous over-worked and consumptive starvelings, he is compelled to take refuge in the "higher perception" and in the ideal "compensation in the species," and thus to relapse into idealism at the very point where the communist materialist sees the necessity, and at the same time the condition, of a transformation both of industry and of the social structure.

As far as Feuerbach is a materialist he does not deal with history, and as far as he considers history he is not a materialist. With him materialism and history diverge completely, a fact which explains itself from what has been said. . . .

Reprinted by permission from *The German Ideology, Parts I and III*, by Karl Marx and Friedrich Engels, edited by R. Pascal, pp. 26–38. Copyright © 1947 by International Publishers (New York). ✦

3
Manifesto of the Communist Party

Karl Marx and
Friedrich Engels

The *Communist Manifesto*, coauthored by Marx and his close ally Friedrich Engels (1820–1895) in 1847 and published the following year, is one of the most important political tracts of all time. A stirring call to arms, the essay begins with the claim that all history is the history of class conflict, and it concludes with the injunction, "Workers of the world unite! You have nothing to lose but your chains." Thus, it is an appeal to workers to engage in the revolutionary overthrow of capitalism. However, the *Manifesto* is much more than this, for it offers a succinct and insightful analysis of the nature of the conflictual relationship between the two central classes in a capitalist class structure, the bourgeoisie and the proletariat. Moreover, as a part of this excerpt reveals, Marx and Engels maintained a keen appreciation of the historically progressive character of the bourgeoisie, who, they contend, have created a dynamic, innovative, and highly productive economic system that is capable of laying the groundwork for a post-scarcity society in which alienation and economic exploitation are overcome.

A spectre is haunting Europe—the spectre of Communism. All the Powers of old Europe have entered into a holy alliance to exorcise this spectre: Pope and Czar, Metternich and Guizot, French Radicals and German police-spies.

Where is the party in opposition that has not been decried as Communistic by its opponents in power? Where the Opposition that has not hurled back the branding reproach of Communism, against the more advanced opposition parties, as well as against its reactionary adversaries?

Two things result from this fact.

I. Communism is already acknowledged by all European Powers to be itself a Power.

II. It is high time that Communists should openly, in the face of the whole world, publish their views, their aims, their tendencies, and meet this nursery tale of the Spectre of Communism with a Manifesto of the party itself.

To this end, Communists of various nationalities have assembled in London, and sketched the following Manifesto, to be published in the English, French, German, Italian, Flemish and Danish languages.

Bourgeois and Proletarians[1]

The history of all hitherto existing society[2] is the history of class struggles.

Freeman and slave, patrician and plebian, lord and serf, guild-master[3] and journeyman, in a word, oppressor and oppressed, stood in constant opposition to one another, carried on an uninterrupted, now hidden, now open fight, a fight that each time ended, either in a revolutionary re-constitution of society at large, or in the common ruin of the contending classes.

In the earlier epochs of history, we find almost everywhere a complicated arrangement of society into various orders, a manifold gradation of social rank. In ancient Rome we have patricians, knights, plebeians, slaves; in the Middle Ages, feudal lords, vassals, guild-masters, journeymen, apprentices, serfs; in almost all of these classes, again, subordinate gradations.

The modern bourgeois society that has sprouted from the ruins of feudal society has not done away with class antagonisms. It has but established new classes, new conditions of oppression, new forms of struggle in place of the old ones.

Our epoch, the epoch of the bourgeoisie, possesses, however, this distinctive feature: it has simplified the class antagonisms: Society as a whole is more and more splitting up into two great hostile camps, into two great classes directly facing each other: Bourgeoisie and Proletariat.

From the serfs of the Middle Ages sprang the chartered burghers of the earliest towns. From these burgesses the first elements of the bourgeoisie were developed.

The discovery of America, the rounding of the Cape, opened up fresh ground for the rising bourgeoisie. The East-Indian and Chinese markets, the colonisation of America, trade with the colonies, the increase in the means of exchange and in commodities generally, gave to commerce, to navigation, to industry, an impulse never before known, and thereby, to the revolutionary element in the tottering feudal society, a rapid development.

The feudal system of industry, under which industrial production was monopolised by closed guilds, now no longer sufficed for the growing wants of the new markets. The manufacturing system took its place. The guild-masters were pushed on one side by the manufacturing middle class; division of labour between the different corporate guilds vanished in the face of division of labour in each single workshop.

Meantime the markets kept ever growing, the demand ever rising. Even manufacture no longer sufficed. Thereupon, steam and machinery revolutionised industrial production. The place of manufacture was taken by the giant, Modern Industry, the place of the industrial middle class, by industrial millionaires, the leaders of whole industrial armies, the modern bourgeois. Modern industry has established the world-market, for which the discovery of America paved the way. This market has given an immense development to commerce, to navigation, to communication by land. This development has, in its turn, reacted on the extension of industry; and in proportion as industry, commerce, navigation, railways extended, in the same proportion the bourgeoisie developed, increased its capital, and pushed into the background every class handed down from the Middle Ages.

We see, therefore, how the modern bourgeoisie is itself the product of a long course of development, of a series of revolutions in the modes of production and of exchange.

Each step in the development of the bourgeoisie was accompanied by a corresponding political advance of that class. An oppressed class under the sway of the feudal nobility, an armed and self-governing association in the mediaeval commune;[4] here independent urban republic (as in Italy and Germany), there taxable "third estate" of the monarchy (as in France), afterwards, in the period of manufacture proper, serving either the semi-feudal or the absolute monarchy as a counterpoise against the nobility, and, in fact, corner-stone of the great monarchies in general, the bourgeoisie has at last, since the establishment of Modern Industry and of the world-market, conquered for itself, in the modern representative State, exclusive political sway. The executive of the modern State is but a committee for managing the common affairs of the whole bourgeoisie.

The bourgeoisie, historically, has played a most revolutionary part.

The bourgeoisie, wherever it has got the upper hand, has put an end to all feudal, patriarchal, idyllic relations. It has pitilessly torn asunder the motley feudal ties that bound man to his "natural superiors," and has left remaining no other nexus between man and man than naked self-interest, than callous "cash payment." It has drowned the most heavenly ecstasies of religious fervour, of chivalrous enthusiasm, of philistine sentimentalism, in the icy water of egotistical calculation. It has resolved personal worth into exchange value, and in place of the numberless indefeasible chartered freedoms, has set up that single, unconscionable freedom— Free Trade. In one word, for exploitation, veiled by religious and political illusions, it has substituted naked, shameless, direct, brutal exploitation.

The bourgeoisie has stripped of its halo every occupation hitherto honoured and looked up to with reverent awe. It has converted the physician, the lawyer, the priest, the poet, the man of science, into its paid wage-labourers.

The bourgeoisie has torn away from the family its sentimental veil, and has reduced the family relation to a mere money relation.

The bourgeoisie has disclosed how it came to pass that the brutal display of vigour in the Middle Ages, which Reactionists so much admire, found its fitting complement in the most slothful indolence. It has been the first to show what man's activity can bring about. It has accomplished wonders far surpassing Egyptian pyramids, Roman aqueducts, and Gothic cathedrals; it has conducted expeditions that put in the shade all former Exoduses of nations and crusades.

The bourgeoisie cannot exist without constantly revolutionising the instruments of production, and thereby the relations of production, and with them the whole relations of society. Conservation of the old modes of production in unaltered form, was, on the contrary, the first condition of existence for all earlier industrial classes. Constant revolutionising of production, uninterrupted disturbance of all social conditions, everlasting uncertainty and agitation distinguish the bourgeois epoch from all earlier ones. All fixed, fast-frozen relations, with their train of ancient and venerable prejudices and opinions, are swept away, all new-formed ones become antiquated before they can ossify. All that is solid melts into air, all that is holy is profaned, and man is at last compelled to face with sober senses, his real conditions of life, and his relations with his kind.

The need of a constantly expanding market for its products chases the bourgeoisie over the whole surface of the globe. It must nestle everywhere, settle everywhere, establish connexions everywhere.

The bourgeoisie has through its exploitation of the world-market given a cosmopolitan character to production and consumption in every country. To the great chagrin of Reactionists, it has drawn from under the feet of industry the national ground on which it stood. All old-established national industries have been destroyed or are daily being destroyed. They are dislodged by new industries, whose introduction becomes a life and death question for all civilised nations, by industries that no longer work up indigenous raw material, but raw material drawn from the remotest zones; industries whose products are consumed, not only at home, but in every quarter of the globe. In place of the old wants, satisfied by the productions of the country, we find new wants, requiring for their satisfaction the products of distant lands and climes. In place of the old local and national seclusion and self-sufficiency, we have intercourse in every direction, universal inter-dependence of nations. And as in material, so also in intellectual production. The intellectual creations of individual nations become common property. National one-sidedness and narrow-mindedness become more and more impossible, and from the numerous national and local literatures, there arises a world literature.

The bourgeoisie, by the rapid improvement of all instruments of production, by the immensely facilitated means of communication, draws all, even the most barbarian, nations into civilisation. The cheap prices of its commodities are the heavy artillery with which it batters down all Chinese walls, with which it forces the barbarians' intensely obstinate hatred of foreigners to capitulate. It compels all nations, on pain of extinction, to adopt the bourgeois mode of production; it compels them to introduce what it calls civilisation into their midst, *i.e.*, to become bourgeois themselves. In one word, it creates a world after its own image.

The bourgeoisie has subjected the country to the rule of the towns. It has created enormous cities, has greatly increased the urban population as compared with the rural, and has thus rescued a considerable part of the population from the idiocy of rural life. Just as it has made the country dependent on the towns, so it has made barbarian and semi-barbarian countries dependent on the civilised ones, nations and peasants on nations of bourgeois, the East on the West.

The bourgeoisie keeps more and more doing away with the scattered state of the population, of the means of production, and of property. It has agglomerated population, centralised means of production, and has concentrated property in a few hands. The necessary consequence of this was political centralisation. Independent, or but loosely connected provinces, with separate interests, laws, governments and systems of taxation, became lumped together into one nation, with one government, one code of laws, one national class-interest, one frontier and one customs-tariff.

The bourgeoisie, during its rule of scarce one hundred years, has created more massive and more colossal productive forces than have all preceding generations together. Subjection of Nature's forces to man, machinery, application of chemistry to industry and agriculture, steam-navigation, railways, electric telegraphs, clearing of whole continents for cultivation, canalisation of rivers, whole populations conjured out of the ground—what earlier century had even a presentiment that such productive forces slumbered in the lap of social labour?

We see then: the means of production and of exchange, on whose foundation the bourgeoisie built itself up, were generated in feudal society. At a certain stage in the development of these means of production and of exchange, the conditions under which feudal society produced and exchanged, the feudal organisation of agriculture and manufacturing industry, in one word, the feudal relations of property became no longer compatible with the already developed productive forces; they became so many fetters. They had to be burst asunder; they were burst asunder.

Into their place stepped free competition, accompanied by a social and political constitution adapted to it, and by the economical and political sway of the bourgeois class.

A similar movement is going on before our own eyes. Modern bourgeois society with its relations of production, of exchange and of property, a society that has conjured up such gigantic means of production and of exchange, is like the sorcerer, who is no longer able to control the powers of the nether world whom he has called up by his spells. For many a decade past the history of industry and commerce is but the history of the revolt of modern productive forces against modern conditions of production, against the property relations that are the conditions for the existence of the bourgeoisie and of its rule. It is enough to mention the commercial crises that by their periodical return put on its trial, each time more threateningly, the existence of the entire bourgeois society. In these crises a great part not only of the existing products, but also of the previously created productive forces, are periodically destroyed. In these crises there breaks out an epidemic that, in all earlier epochs, would have seemed an absurdity—the epidemic of over-production. Society suddenly finds itself put back into a state of momentary barbarism; it appears as if a famine, a universal war of devastation had cut off the supply of every means of subsistence; industry and

commerce seem to be destroyed; and why? Because there is too much civilisation, too much means of subsistence, too much industry, too much commerce. The productive forces at the disposal of society no longer tend to further the development of the conditions of bourgeois property; on the contrary, they have become too powerful for these conditions, by which they are fettered, and so soon as they overcome these fetters, they bring disorder into the whole of bourgeois society, endanger the existence of bourgeois property. The conditions of bourgeois society are too narrow to comprise the wealth created by them. And how does the bourgeoisie get over these crises? On the one hand by enforced destruction of a mass of productive forces; on the other, by the conquest of new markets, and by the more thorough exploitation of the old ones. That is to say, by paving the way for more extensive and more destructive crises, and by diminishing the means whereby crises are prevented.

The weapons with which the bourgeoisie felled feudalism to the ground are now turned against the bourgeoisie itself.

But not only has the bourgeoisie forged the weapons that bring death to itself; it has also called into existence the men who are to wield those weapons—the modern working class—the proletarians.

In proportion as the bourgeoisie, *i.e.*, capital, is developed, in the same proportion is the proletariat, the modern working class, developed—a class of labourers, who live only so long as they find work, and who find work only so long as their labour increases capital. These labourers, who must sell themselves piece-meal, are a commodity, like every other article of commerce, and are consequently exposed to all the vicissitudes of competition, to all the fluctuations of the market.

Owing to the extensive use of machinery and to division of labour, the work of the proletarians has lost all individual character, and consequently, all charm for the workman. He becomes an appendage of the machine, and it is only the most simple, most monotonous, and most easily acquired knack, that is required of him. Hence, the cost of production of a workman is restricted, almost entirely, to the means of subsistence that he requires for his maintenance, and for the propagation of his race. But the price of a commodity, and therefore also of labour,[5] is equal to its cost of production. In proportion, therefore, as the repulsiveness of the work increases, the wage decreases. Nay more, in proportion as the use of machinery and division of labour increases, in the same proportion the burden of toil also increases, whether by prolongation of the working hours, by increase of the work exacted in a given time or by increased speed of the machinery, etc.

Modern industry has converted the little workshop of the patriarchal master into the great factory of the industrial capitalist. Masses of labourers, crowded into the factory, are organised like soldiers. As privates of the industrial army they are placed under the command of a perfect hierarchy of officers and sergeants. Not only are they slaves of the bourgeois class, and of the bourgeois State; they are daily and hourly enslaved by the machine, by the over-looker, and, above all, by the individual bourgeois manufacturer himself. The more openly this despotism proclaims gain to be its end and aim, the more petty, the more hateful and the more embittering it is.

The less the skill and exertion of strength implied in manual labour, in other words, the more modern industry becomes developed, the more is the labour of men superseded by that of women. Differences of age and sex have no longer any distinctive social validity for the working class. All are instruments of labour, more or less expensive to use, according to their age and sex.

No sooner is the exploitation of the labourer by the manufacturer, so far, at an end, that he receives his wages in cash, than he is set upon by the other portions of the bourgeoisie, the landlord, the shopkeeper, the pawnbroker, etc.

The lower strata of the middle class—the small tradespeople, shopkeepers, and retired tradesmen generally, the handicraftsmen and peasants—all these sink gradually into the proletariat, partly because their diminutive capital does not suffice for the scale on which Modern Industry is carried on, and is swamped in the competition with the large capitalists, partly because their specialised skill is rendered worthless by new methods of production. Thus the proletariat is recruited from all classes of the population.

The proletariat goes through various stages of development. With its birth begins its struggle with the bourgeoisie. At first the contest is carried on by individual labourers, then by the workpeople of a factory, then by the operatives of one trade, in one locality, against the individual bourgeois who directly exploits them. They direct their attacks not against the bourgeois conditions of production, but against the instruments of production themselves; they destroy imported wares that compete with their labour, they smash to pieces machinery, they set factories ablaze, they seek to restore by force the vanished status of the workman of the Middle Ages.

At this stage the labourers still form an incoherent mass scattered over the whole country, and broken up by their mutual competition. If anywhere they unite to form more compact bodies, this is not yet the consequence of their own active union, but of the union of the bourgeoisie, which class, in order to attain its own political ends, is compelled to set the whole proletariat in motion, and is moreover yet, for a time, able to do so. At this stage, therefore, the proletarians do not fight their enemies, but the enemies of their enemies, the remnants of absolute monarchy, the landowners, the non-industrial bourgeois, the petty bourgeoisie. Thus the whole historical movement is concentrated in the hands of the bourgeoisie; every victory so obtained is a victory for the bourgeoisie. But with the development of industry the proletariat not only increases in number; it becomes concentrated in greater masses, its strength grows, and it feels that strength more. The various interests and conditions of life within the ranks of the proletariat are more and more equalised, in proportion as machinery obliterates all distinctions of labour, and nearly everywhere reduces wages to the same low level. The growing competition among the bourgeois, and the resulting commercial crises, make the wages of the workers ever more fluctuating. The unceasing improvement of machinery, ever more rapidly developing, makes their livelihood more and more precarious; the collisions between individual workmen and individual bourgeois take more and more the character of collisions between two classes. Thereupon the workers begin to form combinations (Trades Unions) against the bourgeois; they club together in order to keep up the rate of wages; they found permanent associations in order to make provision beforehand for these occasional revolts. Here and there the contest breaks out into riots.

Now and then the workers are victorious, but only for a time. The real fruit of their battles lies, not in the immediate result, but in the ever-expanding union of the workers. This union is helped on by the improved means of communication that are created by modern industry and that place the workers of different localities in contact with one another. It was just this contact that was needed to centralise the numerous local struggles, all of the same character, into one national struggle between classes. But every class struggle is a political struggle. And that union, to attain which the burghers of the Middle Ages, with their miserable highways, required centuries, the modern proletarians, thanks to railways, achieve in a few years.

This organisation of the proletarians into a class, and consequently into a political party, is continually being upset again by the competition between the workers themselves. But it ever rises up again, stronger, firmer, mightier. It compels legislative recognition of particular interests of the workers, by taking advantage of the divisions among the bourgeoisie itself. Thus the ten-hours' bill in England was carried.

Altogether collisions between the classes of the old society further, in many ways, the course of development of the proletariat. The bourgeoisie finds itself involved in a constant battle. At first with the aristocracy; later on, with those portions of the bourgeoisie itself, whose interests have become antagonistic to the progress of industry; at all times, with the bourgeoisie of foreign countries. In all these battles it sees itself compelled to appeal to the proletariat, to ask for its help, and thus, to drag it into the political arena. The bourgeoisie itself, therefore, sup-

plies the proletariat with its own elements of political and general education, in other words, it furnishes the proletariat with weapons for fighting the bourgeoisie.

Further, as we have already seen, entire sections of the ruling classes are, by the advance of industry, precipitated into the proletariat, or are at least threatened in their conditions of existence. These also supply the proletariat with fresh elements of enlightenment and progress.

Finally, in times when the class struggle nears the decisive hour, the process of dissolution going on within the ruling class, in fact within the whole range of society, assumes such a violent, glaring character, that a small section of the ruling class cuts itself adrift, and joins the revolutionary class, the class that holds the future in its hands. Just as, therefore, at an earlier period, a section of the nobility went over to the bourgeoisie, so now a portion of the bourgeoisie goes over to the proletariat, and in particular, a portion of the bourgeois ideologists, who have raised themselves to the level of comprehending theoretically the historical movement as a whole.

Of all the classes that stand face to face with the bourgeoisie today, the proletariat alone is a really revolutionary class. The other classes decay and finally disappear in the face of Modern Industry; the proletariat is its special and essential product. The lower middle class, the small manufacturer, the shopkeeper, the artisan, the peasant, all these fight against the bourgeoisie, to save from extinction their existence as fractions of the middle class. They are therefore not revolutionary, but conservative. Nay more, they are reactionary, for they try to roll back the wheel of history. If by chance they are revolutionary, they are so only in view of their impending transfer into the proletariat, they thus defend not their present, but their future interests, they desert their own standpoint to place themselves at that of the proletariat.

The "dangerous class," the social scum, that passively rotting mass thrown off by the lowest layers of old society, may, here and there, be swept into the movement by a proletarian revolution; its conditions of life, however, prepare it far more for the part of a bribed tool of reactionary intrigue.

In the conditions of the proletariat, those of old society at large are already virtually swamped. The proletarian is without property; his relation to his wife and children has no longer anything in common with the bourgeois family-relations; modern industrial labour, modern subjection to capital, the same in England as in France, in America as in Germany, has stripped him of every trace of national character. Law, morality, religion, are to him so many bourgeois prejudices, behind which lurk in ambush just as many bourgeois interests.

All the preceding classes that got the upper hand, sought to fortify their already acquired status by subjecting society at large to their conditions of appropriation. The proletarians cannot become masters of the productive forces of society, except by abolishing their own previous mode of appropriation, and thereby also every other previous mode of appropriation. They have nothing of their own to secure and to fortify; their mission is to destroy all previous securities for, and insurances of, individual property.

All previous historical movements were movements of minorities, or in the interests of minorities. The proletarian movement is the self-conscious, independent movement of the immense majority, in the interests of the immense majority. The proletariat, the lowest stratum of our present society, cannot stir, cannot raise itself up, without the whole superincumbent strata of official society being sprung into the air.

Though not in substance, yet in form, the struggle of the proletariat with the bourgeoisie is at first a national struggle. The proletariat of each country must, of course, first of all settle matters with its own bourgeoisie.

In depicting the most general phases of the development of the proletariat, we traced the more or less veiled civil war, raging within existing society, up to the point where that war breaks out into open revolution, and where the violent overthrow of the bourgeoisie lays the foundation for the sway of the proletariat.

Hitherto, every form of society has been based, as we have already seen, on the antagonism of oppressing and oppressed classes.

But in order to oppress a class, certain conditions must be assured to it under which it can, at least, continue its slavish existence. The serf, in the period of serfdom, raised himself to membership in the commune, just as the petty bourgeois, under the yoke of feudal absolutism, managed to develop into a bourgeois. The modern labourer, on the contrary, instead of rising with the progress of industry, sinks deeper and deeper below the conditions of existence of his own class. He becomes a pauper, and pauperism develops more rapidly than population and wealth. And here it becomes evident, that the bourgeoisie is unfit any longer to be the ruling class in society, and to impose its conditions of existence upon society as an overriding law. It is unfit to rule because it is incompetent to assure an existence to its slave within his slavery, because it cannot help letting him sink into such a state, that it has to feed him, instead of being fed by him. Society can no longer live under this bourgeoisie, in other words, its existence is no longer compatible with society.

The essential condition for the existence, and for the sway of the bourgeois class, is the formation and augmentation of capital; the condition for capital is wage-labour. Wage-labour rests exclusively on competition between the labourers. The advance of industry, whose involuntary promoter is the bourgeoisie, replaces the isolation of the labourers, due to competition, by their revolutionary combination, due to association. The development of Modern Industry, therefore, cuts from under its feet the very foundation on which the bourgeoisie produces and appropriates products. What the bourgeoisie, therefore, produces, above all, is its own grave-diggers. Its fall and the victory of the proletariat are equally inevitable. . . .

Endnotes

1. By bourgeoisie is meant the class of modern Capitalists, owners of the means of social production and employers of wage-labour. By proletariat, the class of modern wage-labourers who, having no means of production of their own, are reduced to selling their labour-power in order to live. [*Engels, English edition of 1888*]

2. That is, all *written* history. In 1847, the pre-history of society, the social organisation existing

previous to recorded history, was all but un-known. Since then, Haxthausen discovered com-mon ownership of land in Russia, Maurer proved it to be the social foundation from which all Teu-tonic races started in history, and by and by village communities were found to be, or to have been the primitive form of society everywhere from India to Ireland. The inner organisation of this primi-tive Communistic society was laid bare, in its typi-cal form, by Morgan's crowning discovery of the true nature of the *gens* and its relation to the *tribe*. With the dissolution of these primaeval commu-nities society begins to be differentiated into separate and finally antagonistic classes. I have attempted to retrace this process of dissolu-tion in: "Der Ursprung der Familie, des Pri-vateigenthums und des Staats" [*The Origin of the Family, Private Property and the State*], 2nd edi-tion, Stuttgart 1886. [*Engels, English edition of 1888*]

3. Guild-master, that is, a full member of a guild, a master within, not a head of a guild. [*Engels, Eng-lish edition of 1888*]

4. "Commune" was the name taken, in France, by the nascent towns even before they had con-quered from their feudal lords and masters local self-government and political rights as the "Third Estate." Generally speaking, for the economical development of the bourgeoisie, England is here taken as the typical country; for its political devel-opment, France. [*Engels, English edition of 1888*]

This was the name given their urban communi-ties by the townsmen of Italy and France, after they had purchased or wrested their initial rights of self-government from their feudal lords. [*Engels, German edition of 1890*]

5. Subsequently Marx pointed out that the worker sells not his labour but his labour power.

4
Commodities

Karl Marx

During many years of intellectual labor in the British Museum, Marx produced a huge body of work designed to uncover and explicate the underlying dynamics of capitalism. These works include *The Grundrisse* (1857–58), the multi-volume *Theories of Surplus Value* (1862–63), and the three-volume Capital (1867, 1885, 1894). The first volume of this latter work is generally seen as his most important critique of capitalism. In this selection from that book, Marx presents his understanding of what is meant by the term commodity, discussing its dual-edged character as both a source of use-value and value. This discussion is an essential building block in the further elaboration of his economic theory of capitalism.

Section 1. The Two Factors of a Commodity: Use-Value and Value (The Substance of Value and the Magnitude of Value)

The wealth of those societies in which the capitalist mode of production prevails, presents itself as "an immense accumulation of commodities,"[1] its unit being a single commodity. Our investigation must therefore begin with the analysis of a commodity.

A commodity is, in the first place, an object outside us, a thing that by its properties satisfies human wants of some sort or another. The nature of such wants, whether, for instance, they spring from the stomach or from fancy, makes no difference.[2] Neither are we here concerned to know how the object satisfies these wants, whether directly as means of subsistence, or indirectly as means of production.

Every useful thing, as iron, paper, &c., may be looked at from the two points of view of quality and quantity. It is an assemblage of many properties, and may therefore be of use in various ways. To discover the various uses of things is the work of history.[3] So also is the establishment of socially-recognised standards of measure for the quantities of these useful objects. The diversity of these measures has its origin partly in the diverse nature of the objects to be measured, partly in convention.

The utility of a thing makes it a use-value.[4] But this utility is not a thing of air. Being limited by the physical properties of the commodity, it has no existence apart from that commodity. A commodity, such as iron, corn, or a diamond, is therefore, so far as it is a material thing, a use-value, something useful. This property of a commodity is independent of the amount of labour required to appropriate its useful qualities. When treating of use-value, we always assume to be dealing with definite quantities, such as dozens of watches, yards of linen, or tons of iron. The use-values of commodities furnish the material for a special study, that of the commercial knowledge of commodities.[5] Use-values become a reality only by use or consumption: they also constitute the substance of all wealth, whatever may be the social form of that wealth. In the form of -society we are about to consider, they are, in addition, the material depositories of exchange-value.

Exchange-value, at first sight, presents itself as a quantitative relation, as the proportion in which values in use of one sort are exchanged for those of another sort,[6] a relation constantly changing with time and place. Hence exchange-value appears to be something accidental and purely relative, and consequently an intrinsic value, *i.e.*, an exchange-value that is inseparably connected with, inherent in commodities, seems a contradiction in terms.[7] Let us consider the matter a little more closely.

A given commodity, *e.g.*, a quarter of wheat is exchanged for x blacking, y silk, or z gold, &c.—in short, for other commodities in the most different proportions. Instead of one exchange-value, the wheat has, therefore, a great many. But since x blacking, y silk, or z gold, &c., each represent the exchange-value of one quarter of wheat, x blacking, y silk, z gold, &c., must, as exchange-values, be replaceable by each other, or equal to each other. Therefore, first: the valid exchange-values of a given commodity express something equal; secondly, exchange-value, generally, is only the mode of expression, the phenomenal form, of something contained in it, yet distinguishable from it.

Let us take two commodities, e.g., corn and iron. The proportions in which they are exchangeable, whatever those proportions may be, can always be represented by an equation in which a given quantity of corn is equated to some quantity of iron: *e.g.*, 1 quarter corn = x cwt. iron. What does this equation tell us? It tells us that in two different things—in 1 quarter of corn and x cwt. of iron, there exists in equal quantities something common to both. The two things must therefore be equal to a third, which in itself is neither the one nor the other. Each of them, so far as it is exchange-value, must therefore be reducible to this third.

A simple geometrical illustration will make this clear. In order to calculate and compare the areas of rectilinear figures, we decompose them into triangles. But the area of the triangle itself is expressed by something totally different from its visible figure, namely, by half the product of the base into the altitude. In the same way the exchange-values of commodities must be capable of being expressed in terms of something common to them all, of which thing they represent a greater or less quantity.

This common "something" cannot be either a geometrical, a chemical, or any other natural property of commodities. Such properties claim our attention only in so far as they affect the utility of those commodities, make them use-values. But the exchange of commodities is evidently an act characterised by a total abstraction from use-value. Then one use-value is just as good as another, provided only it be present in sufficient quantity. Or, as old Barbon says, "one sort of wares are as good as another, if the values be equal. There is no difference or distinction in things of equal value. . . . An hundred pounds' worth of lead or iron, is of as great value as one hundred pounds' worth of silver or gold." As use-values, commodities are, above all, of different qualities, but as

exchange-values they are merely different quantities, and consequently do not contain an atom of use-value.

If then we leave out of consideration the use-value of commodities, they have only one common property left, that of being products of labour. But even the product of labour itself has undergone a change in our hands. If we make abstraction from its use-value, we make abstraction at the same time from the material elements and shapes that make the product a use-value; we see in it no longer a table, a house, yarn, or any other useful thing. Its existence as a material thing is put out of sight. Neither can it any longer be regarded as the product of the labour of the joiner, the mason, the spinner, or of any other definite kind of productive labour. Along with the useful qualities of the products themselves, we put out of sight both the useful character of the various kinds of labour embodied in them, and the concrete forms of that labour; there is nothing left but what is common to them all; all are reduced to one and the same sort of labour, human labour in the abstract.

Let us now consider the residue of each of these products; it consists of the same unsubstantial reality in each, a mere congelation of homogeneous human labour, of labour-power expended without regard to the mode of its expenditure. All that these things now tell us is, that human labour-power has been expended in their production, that human labour is embodied in them. When looked at as crystals of this social substance, common to them all, they are—Values.

We have seen that when commodities are exchanged, their exchange-value manifests itself as something totally independent of their use-value. But if we abstract from their use-value, there remains their Value as defined above. Therefore, the common substance that manifests itself in the exchange-value of commodities, whenever they are exchanged, is their value. The progress of our investigation will show that exchange-value is the only form in which the value of commodities can manifest itself or be expressed. For the present, however, we have to consider the nature of value independently of this, its form.

A use-value, or useful article, therefore, has value only because human labour in the abstract has been embodied or materialised in it. How, then, is the magnitude of this value to be measured? Plainly, by the quantity of the value-creating substance, the labour, contained in the article. The quantity of labour, however, is measured by its duration, and labour-time in its turn finds its standard in weeks, days, and hours.

Some people might think that if the value of a commodity is determined by the quantity of labour spent on it, the more idle and unskillful the labourer, the more valuable would his commodity be, because more time would be required in its production. The labour, however, that forms the substance of value, is homogeneous human labour, expenditure of one uniform labour-power. The total labour-power of society, which is embodied in the sum total of the values of all commodities produced by that society, counts here as one homogeneous mass of human labour-power, composed though it be of innumerable individual units. Each of these units is the same as any other, so far as it has the character of the average labour-power of society, and takes effect as such; that is, so far as it requires for producing a commodity, no more time than is needed on an average, no more than is socially necessary. The labour-time socially necessary is that required to produce an article under the normal conditions of production, and with the average degree of skill and intensity prevalent at the time. The introduction of power-looms into England probably reduced by one-half the labour required to weave a given quantity of yarn into cloth. The hand-loom weavers, as a matter of fact, continued to require the same time as before; but for all that, the product of one hour of their labour represented after the change only half an hour's social labour, and consequently fell to one-half its former value.

We see then that that which determines the magnitude of the value of any article is the amount of labour socially necessary, or the labour-time socially necessary for its production.[8] Each individual commodity, in this connexion, is to be considered as an average sample of its class.[9] Commodities, therefore, in which equal quantities of la-bour are embodied, or which can be produced in the same time, have the same value. The value of one commodity is to the value of any other, as the labour-time necessary for the production of the one is to that necessary for the production of the other. "As values, all commodities are only definite masses of congealed labour-time."

The value of a commodity would therefore remain constant, if the labour-time required for its production also remained constant. But the latter changes with every variation in the productiveness of labour. This productiveness is determined by various circumstances, amongst others, by the average amount of skill of the workmen, the state of science, and the degree of its practical application, the social organisation of production, the extent and capabilities of the means of production, and by physical conditions. For example, the same amount of labour in favourable seasons is embodied in 8 bushels of corn, and in unfavourable, only in four. The same labour extracts from rich mines more metal than from poor mines. Diamonds are of very rare occurrence on the earth's surface, and hence their discovery costs, on an average, a great deal of labour-time. Consequently much labour is represented in a small compass. Jacob doubts whether gold has ever been paid for at its full value. This applies still more to diamonds. According to Eschwege, the total produce of the Brazilian diamond mines for the eighty years, ending in 1823, had not realised the price of one-and-a-half years' average produce of the sugar and coffee plantations of the same country, although the diamonds cost much more labour, and therefore represented more value. With richer mines, the same quantity of labour would embody itself in more diamonds, and their value would fall. If we could succeed at a small expenditure of labour, in converting carbon into diamonds, their value might fall below that of bricks. In general, the greater the productiveness of labour, the less is the labour-time required for the production of an article, the less is the amount of labour crystallised in that article, and the less is its value; and *vice versa*, the less the productiveness of labour, the greater is the labour-time required for the production of an article, and the greater is its value. The value of a commodity, therefore, varies directly as the quantity, and inversely as the productiveness, of the labour incorporated in it.

A thing can be a use-value, without having value. This is the case whenever its utility to man is not due to labour. Such are air, virgin soil, natural meadows, &c. A thing can be useful, and the product of human labour, without being a commodity. Whoever directly satisfies his wants with the produce of his own labour, creates, indeed, use-values, but no commodities. In order to produce the latter, be must not only produce use-values, but use-values for others, social use-values. (And not only for others, without more. The mediaeval peasant produced quit-rent-corn for his feudal lord and tithe-corn for his parson. But neither the quit-rent-corn nor the tithe-corn became commodities by reason of the fact that they had been produced for others. To become a commodity a product must be transferred to another, whom it will serve as a use-value, by means of an exchange.)[10] Lastly nothing can have value, without being an object of utility. If the thing is useless, so is the labour contained in it; the labour does not count as labour, and therefore creates no value.

Section 2. The Two-Fold Character of the Labour Embodied in Commodities

At first sight a commodity presented itself to us as a complex of two things—use-value and exchange-value. Later on, we saw also that labour, too, possesses the same two-fold nature; for, so far as it finds expression in value, it does not possess the same characteristics that belong to it as a creator of use-values. I was the first to point out and to examine critically this two-fold nature of the labour contained in commodities. As this point is the pivot on which a clear comprehension of Political Economy turns, we must go more into detail.

Let us take two commodities such as a coat and 10 yards of linen, and let the former be double the value of the latter, so that, if 10 yards of linen = W, the coat = 2W.

The coat is a use-value that satisfies a particular want. Its existence is the result of a special sort of productive activity, the nature of which is determined by its aim, mode of operation, subject, means, and result. The labour, whose utility is thus represented by the value in use of its product, or which manifests itself by making its product a use-value, we call useful labour. In this connexion we consider only its useful effect.

As the coat and the linen are two qualitatively different use-values, so also are the two forms of labour that produce them, tailoring and weaving. Were these two objects not qualitatively different, not produced respectively by labour of different quality, they could not stand to each other in the relation of commodities. Coats are not exchanged for coats, one use-value is not exchanged for another of the same kind.

To all the different varieties of values in use there correspond as many different kinds of useful labour, classified according to the order, genus, species, and variety to which they belong in the social division of labour. This division of labour is a necessary condition for the production of commodities, but it does not follow, conversely, that the production of commodities is a necessary condition for the division of labour. In the primitive Indian community there is social division of labour, without production of commodities. Or, to take an example nearer home, in every factory the labour is divided according to a system, but this division is not brought about by the operatives mutually exchanging their individual products. Only such products can become commodities with regard to each other, as result from different kinds of labour, each kind being carried on independently and for the account of private individuals.

To resume, then: In the use-value of each commodity there is contained useful labour, *i.e.*, productive activity of a definite kind and exercised with a definite aim. Use-values cannot confront each other as commodities, unless the useful labour embodied in them is qualitatively different in each of them. In a community, the produce of which in general takes the form of commodities, *i.e.*, in a community of commodity producers, this qualitative difference between the useful forms of labour that are carried on independently by individual producers, each on their own account, develops into a complex system, a social division of labour.

Anyhow, whether the coat be worn by the tailor or by his customer, in either case it operates as a use-value. Nor is the relation between the coat and the labour that produced it altered by the circumstance that tailoring may have become a special trade, an independent branch of the social division of labour. Wherever the want of clothing forced them to it, the human race made clothes for thousands of years, without a single man becoming a tailor. But coats and linen, like every other element of material wealth that is not the spontaneous produce of Nature, must invariably owe their existence to a special productive activity, exercised with a definite aim, an activity that appropriates particular nature-given materials to particular human wants. So far therefore as labour is a creator of use-value, is useful labour, it is a necessary condition, independent of all forms of society, for the existence of the human race; it is an eternal nature-imposed necessity, without which there can be no material exchanges between man and Nature, and therefore no life.

The use-values, coat, linen, &c., i.e., the bodies of commodities, are combinations of two elements—matter and labour. If we take away the useful labour expended upon them, a material substratum is always left, which is furnished by Nature without the help of man. The latter can work only as Nature does, that is by changing the form of matter. Nay more, in this work of changing the form he is constantly helped by natural forces. We see, then, that labour is not the only source of material wealth, of use-values produced by labour. As William Petty puts it, labour is its father and the earth its mother.

Let us now pass from the commodity considered as a use-value to the value of commodities.

By our assumption, the coat is worth twice as much as the linen. But this is a mere quantitative difference, which for the present does not concern us. We bear in mind, however, that if the value of the coat is double that of 10 yds. of linen, 20 yds. of linen must have the same value as one coat. So far as they are values, the coat and the linen are things of a like substance, objective expressions of essentially identical labour. But tailoring and weaving are, qualitatively, different kinds of labour. There are, however, states of society in which one and the same man does tailoring and weaving alternately, in which case these two forms of labour are mere modifications of the labour of the same individual, and no special and fixed functions of different persons; just as the coat which our tailor makes one day, and the trousers which he makes another day, imply only a variation in the labour of one and the same individual. Moreover, we see at a glance that, in our capitalist society, a given portion of human labour is, in accordance with the varying demand, at one time supplied in the form of tailoring, at another in the form of weaving. This change may possibly not take place without friction, but take place it must.

Productive activity, if we leave out of sight its special form, viz., the useful character of the labour, is nothing but the expenditure of human labour-power. Tailoring and weaving, though qualitatively different productive activities, are each a productive expenditure of human brains, nerves, and muscles, and in this sense are human labour. They are but two different modes of expending human labour-power. Of course, this labour-power, which remains the same under all its modifications, must have attained a certain pitch of development before it can be expended in a multiplicity of modes. But the value of a commodity represents human labour in the abstract, the expenditure of human labour in general. And just as in society, a general or a banker plays a great part, but mere man, on the other hand, a very shabby part,[11] so here with human labour. It is the expenditure of simple labour-power, i.e., of the labour-power which, on an average, apart from any special development, exists in the organism of every ordinary individual. Simple average labour, it is true, varies in character in different countries and at different times, but in a particular society it is given. Skilled labour counts only as simple labour intensified, or rather, as multiplied simple labour, a given quantity of skilled being considered equal to a greater quantity of simple labour. Experience shows that this reduction is constantly being made. A commodity may be the product of the most skilled labour, but its value, by equating it to the product of simple unskilled labour, represents a definite quantity of the latter labour alone.[12] The different proportions in which different sorts of labour are reduced to unskilled labour as their standard, are established by a social process that goes on behind the backs of the producers, and, consequently, appear to be fixed by custom. For simplicity's sake we shall henceforth account every kind of labour to be unskilled, simple labour; by this we do no more than save ourselves the trouble of making the reduction.

Just as, therefore, in viewing the coat and linen as values, we abstract from their different use-values, so it is with the labour represented by those values: we disregard the difference between its useful forms, weaving and tailoring. As the use-values, coat and linen, are combinations of special productive activities with cloth and yarn, while the values, coat and linen, are, on the other hand, mere homogeneous congelations of undifferentiated labour, so the labour embodied in these latter values does not count by virtue of its productive relation to cloth and yarn, but only as being expenditure of human labour-power. Tailoring and weaving are necessary factors in the creation of the use-values, coat and linen, precisely because these two kinds of labour are of different qualities; but only in so far as abstraction is made from their special qualities, only in so far as both possess the same quality of being human labour, do tailoring and weaving form the substance of the values of the same article.

Coats and linen, however, are not merely values, but values of definite magnitude, and according to our assumption, the coat is worth twice as much as the ten yards of linen. Whence this difference in their values? It is owing to the fact that the linen contains only half as much labour as the coat, and consequently, that in the production of the latter, labour-power must have been expended during twice the time necessary for the production of the former.

While, therefore, with reference to use-value, the labour contained in a commodity counts only qualitatively, with reference to value it counts only quantitatively, and must first be reduced to human labour pure and simple. In the former case, it is a question of How and What, in the latter of How much? How long a time? Since the magnitude of the value of a commodity represents only the quantity of labour embodied in it, it follows that all commodities, when taken in certain proportions, must be equal in value.

If the productive power of all the different sorts of useful labour required for the production of a coat remains unchanged, the sum one coat represents x days' labour, two coats represent 2x days' labour, and so on. But assume that the duration of the labour necessary for the production of a coat becomes doubled or halved. In the first case, one coat is worth as much as two coats were before; in the second case, two coats are only worth as much as one was before, although in both cases one coat renders the same service as before, and the useful labour embodied in it remains of the same quality. But the quantity of labour spent on its production has altered.

An increase in the quantity of use-values is an increase of material wealth. With two coats two men can be clothed, with one coat only one man. Nevertheless, an increased quantity of material wealth may correspond to a simultaneous fall in the magnitude of its value. This antagonistic movement has its origin in the two-fold character of labour. Productive power has reference, of course, only to labour of some useful concrete form, the efficacy of any special productive activity during a given time being dependent on its productiveness. Useful labour becomes, therefore, a more or less abundant source of products, in proportion to the rise or fall of its productiveness. On the other hand, no change in this productiveness affects the labour represented by value. Since productive power is an attribute of the concrete useful forms of labour, of course it can no longer have any bearing on that labour, so soon as we make abstraction from those concrete useful forms. However then productive power may vary, the same labour, exercised during equal periods of time, always yields equal amounts of value. But it will yield, during equal periods of time, different quantities of values in use; more, if the productive power rise, fewer, if it fall. The same change in productive power, which increases the fruitfulness of labour, and, in consequence, the quantity of use-values produced by that labour, will diminish the total value of this increased quality of use-values, provided such change shorten the total labour-time necessary for their production; and *vice versa*.

On the one hand all labour is, speaking physiologically, an expenditure of human labour-power, and in its character of identical abstract human labour, it creates and forms the value of commodities. On the other hand, all labour is the expenditure of human labour-power in a special form and with a definite aim, and in this, its character of concrete useful labour, it produces use-values.

Endnotes

1. Karl Marx, "Zur Kritik der Politischen Oekonomie." Berlin, 1859, p. 3. [*Marx*]

2. "Desire implies want; it is the appetite of the mind, and as natural as hunger to the body. . . . The greatest number (of things) have their value from supplying the wants of the mind." Nicholas Barbon: "A Discourse Concerning Coining the New Money Lighter. In Answer to Mr. Locke's Considerations," &c., London, 1696, pp. 2, 3. [*Marx*]

3. "Things have an intrinsick vertue" (this is Barbon's special term for value in use) "which in all places have the same vertue; as the loadstone to attract iron" (1. c., p. 6). The property which the magnet possesses of attracting iron, became of use only after by means of that property the polarity of the magnet had been discovered. [*Marx*]

4. "The natural worth of anything consists in its fitness to supply the necessities, or serve the conveniences of human life." (John Locke, "Some Considerations on the Consequences of the Lowering of Interest, 1691," in Works Edit. Lond., 1777, Vol. II., p. 28.) In English writers of the 17th century we frequently find "worth" in the sense of value in use, and "value" in the sense of exchange-value. This is quite in accordance with the spirit of a language that likes to use a Teutonic word for the actual thing, and a Romance word for its reflexion. [*Marx*]

5. In bourgeois societies the economic fictio juris prevails, that every one, as a buyer, possesses an encyclopaedic knowledge of commodities. [*Marx*]

6. "La valeur consiste dans le rapport d'échange qui se trouve entre telle chose et telle autre, entre telle mesure d'une production, et telle mesure d'une autre." (Le Trosne: "De l'Intérêt Social. Physiocrates," ed. Daire. Paris, 1846 P. 889.) [*Marx*]

7. "Nothing can have an intrinsick value." (N. Barbon, 1. c., p. 6); or as Butler says—"The value of a thing is just as much as it will bring." [*Marx*]

8. "The value of them (the necessaries of life), when they are exchanged the one for another, is regulated by the quantity of labour necessarily required and commonly taken in producing them." ("Some Thoughts on the Interest of Money in General, and Particularly in the Publick Funds, &c." Lond., p. 36.) This remarkable anonymous work, written in the last century, bears no date. It is clear, however, from internal evidence, that it appeared in the reign of George II, about 1739 or 1740. [*Marx*]

9. "Toutes les productions d'un même genre ne forment proprement qu'une masse, dont le prix se détermine en général et sans égard aux circonstances particulières." (Le Trosen, 1. c., p. 893.) [*Marx*]

10. I am inserting the parenthesis because its omission has often given rise to the misunderstanding that every product that is consumed by some one other than its producer is considered in Marx a commodity. [*Engels, 4th German edition*]

11. Comp. Hegel, "Philosophie des Rechts." Berlin, 1840. P. 250, § 190. [*Marx*]

12. The reader must note that we are not speaking here of the wages or value that the labourer gets for a given labour-time, but of the value of the commodity in which that labour-time is materialised. Wages is a category that, as yet, has no existence at the present stage of our investigation. [*Marx*]

5
The General Formula for Capital

Karl Marx

In this selection from *Capital*, volume 1 (1867), Marx sketches a general formula to account for the distinctive way that commodities circulate in capitalism. In a simple version of commodity circulation, C—M—C, one commodity is exchanged for another, and money becomes a medium that allows one to compare corn and clothes. However, in capitalism, another form is evident: M—C—M', where M' is greater than M. In the first example, a transaction occurs that provides the seller with a good that he or she did not possess before, and that has personal use-value. With the second formula, the individual who has money puts it into circulation with the anticipation of having the money returned along with an additional increment, which Marx calls "surplus value." What, then, is the actual source of surplus value? Answering this question is a focal concern of Marx's subsequent work.

The circulation of commodities is the starting-point of capital. The production of commodities, their circulation, and that more developed form of their circulation called commerce, these form the historical groundwork from which it rises. The modern history of capital dates from the creation in the 16th century of a world-embracing commerce and a world-embracing market.

If we abstract from the material substance of the circulation of commodities, that is, from the exchange of the various use-values, and consider only the economic forms produced by this process of circulation, we find its final result to be money: this final product of the circulation of commodi-

ties is the first form in which capital appears. As a matter of history, capital, as opposed to landed property, invariably takes the form at first of money; it appears as moneyed wealth, as the capital of the merchant and of the usurer. But we have no need to refer to the origin of capital in order to discover that the first form of appearance of capital is money. We can see it daily under our very eyes. All new capital, to commence with, comes on the stage, that is, on the market, whether of commodities, labour, or money, even in our days, in the shape of money that by a definite process has to be transformed into capital.

The first distinction we notice between money that is money only, and money that is capital, is nothing more than a difference in their form of circulation. The simplest form of the circulation of commodities is C—M—C, the transformation of commodities into money, and the change of the money back again into commodities; or selling in order to buy. But alongside of this form we find another specifically different form: M—C—M, the transformation of money into commodities, and the change of commodities back again into money; or buying in order to sell. Money that circulates in the latter manner is thereby transformed into, becomes capital, and is already potentially capital.

Now let us examine the circuit M—C—M a little closer. It consists, like the other, of two antithetical phases. In the first phase, M—C, or the purchase, the money is changed into a commodity.

In the second phase, C—M, or the sale, the commodity is changed back again into money. The combination of these two phases constitutes the single movement whereby money is exchanged for a commodity, and the same commodity is again exchanged for money; whereby a commodity is bought in order to be sold, or, neglecting the distinction in form between buying and selling, whereby a commodity is bought with a commodity. The result, in which the phases of the process vanish, is the exchange of money for money, M—M. If I purchase 2,000 lbs. of cotton for £100, and resell the 2,000 lbs. of cotton for £110, I have, in fact, exchanged £100 for £110, money for money.

Now it is evident that the circuit M—C—M would be absurd and without meaning if the intention were to exchange by this means two equal sums of money, £100 for £100. The miser's plan would be far simpler and surer; he sticks to his £100 instead of exposing it to the dangers of circulation. And yet, whether the merchant who has paid £100 for his cotton sells it for £110, or lets it go for £100, or even £50, his money has, at all events, gone through a characteristic and original movement, quite different in kind from that which it goes through in the hands of the peasant who sells corn, and with the money thus set free buys clothes. We have therefore to examine first the distinguishing characteristics of the forms of the circuits M—C—M and C—M—C, and in doing this the real difference that underlies the mere difference of form will reveal itself.

Let us see, in the first place, what the two forms have in common.

Both circuits are resolvable into the same two antithetical phases, C—M, a Sale, and M—C, a purchase. In each of these phases the same material elements—a commodity, and money, and the same economic dramatis personæ, a buyer and a seller—confront one another. Each circuit is the unity of the same two antithetical phases, and in each case this unity is brought about by the intervention of three contracting parties, of whom one only sells, another only buys, while the third both buys and sells.

What, however, first and foremost distinguishes the circuit C—M—C from the circuit M—C—M, is the inverted order of succession of the two phases. The simple circulation of commodities begins with a sale and ends with a purchase, while the circulation of money as capital begins with a purchase and ends with a sale. In the one case both the starting-point and the goal are commodities, in the other they are money. In the first form the movement is brought about by the intervention of money, in the second by that of a commodity.

In the circulation C—M—C, the money is in the end converted into a commodity, that serves as a use-value; it is spent once for all. In the inverted form, M—C—M, on the contrary, the buyer lays out money in order that, as a seller, he may recover money. By the purchase of his commodity he throws money into circulation, in order to withdraw it again by the sale of the same commodity. He lets the money go, but only with the sly intention of getting it back again. The money, therefore, is not spent, it is merely advance.

In the circuit C—M—C, the same piece of money changes its place twice. The seller gets it from the buyer and pays it away to another seller. The complete circulation, which begins with the receipt, concludes with the payment, of money for commodities. It is the very contrary in the circuit M—C—M. Here it is not the piece of money that changes its place twice, but the commodity. The buyer takes it from the hands of the seller and passes it into the hands of another buyer. Just as in the simple circulation of commodities the double change of place of the same piece of money effects its passage from one hand into another, so here the double change of place of the same commodity brings about the reflux of the money to its point of departure.

Such reflux is not dependent on the commodity being sold for more than was paid for it. This circumstance influences only the amount of the money that comes back. The reflux itself takes place, so soon as the purchased commodity is resold, in other words, so soon as the circuit M—C—M is completed. We have here, therefore, a palpable difference between the circulation of money as capital, and its circulation as mere money.

The circuit C—M—C comes completely to an end, so soon as the money brought in by the sale of one commodity is abstracted again by the purchase of another.

If, nevertheless, there follows a reflux of money to its starting-point, this can only happen through a renewal of repetition of the operation. If I sell a quarter of corn of £3, and with this £3 buy clothes, the money, so far as I am concerned, is spent and done with. It belongs to the clothes merchant. If I now sell a second quarter of corn, money indeed flows back to me, not however as a sequel to the first transaction, but in consequence of its repetition. The money again leaves me, so soon as I complete this second transaction by a fresh purchase. Therefore, in the circuit C—M—C, the expenditure of money has nothing to do with its reflux. On the other hand, in M—C—M, the reflux of the money is conditioned by the very mode of its expenditure. Without this reflux, the operation fails, or the process is interrupted and incomplete, owing to the absence of its complementary and final phase, the sale.

The circuit C—M—C starts with one commodity, and finishes with another, which falls out of circulation and into consumption. Consumption, the satisfaction of wants, in one word, use-value, is its end and aim. The circuit M—C—M, on the contrary, commences with money and ends with money. Its leading motive, and the goal that attracts it, is therefore mere exchange-value.

In the simple circulation of commodities, the two extremes of the circuit have the same economic form. They are both commodities, and commodities of equal value. But they are also use-values differing in their qualities, as, for example, corn and clothes. The exchange of products, of the different materials in which the labour of society is embodied, forms here the basis of the movement. It is otherwise in the circulation M—C—M, which at first sight appears purposeless, because tautological. Both extremes have the same economic form. They are both money, and therefore are not qualitatively different use-values; for money is but the converted form of commodities, in which their particular use-values vanish. To exchange £100 for cotton, and then this same cotton again for £110, is merely a roundabout way of exchanging money for money, the same for the same, and appears to be an operation just as purposeless as it is absurd. One sum of money is distinguishable from another only by its amount. The character and tendency of the process M—C—M, is therefore not due to any qualitative difference between its extremes, both being money, but solely to their quantitative difference. More money is withdrawn from circulation at the finish than was thrown into it at the start. The cotton that was bought for £100 is perhaps resold for £100+£10 or £110. The exact form of this process is therefore M—C—M′, where M′ = M+ ΔM = the original sum advanced, plus an increment. This increment or excess over the original value I call "surplus-value." The value originally advanced, therefore, not only remains intact while in circulation, but adds to itself a surplus-value or expands

itself. It is this movement that converts it into capital.

Of course, it is also possible, that in C—M—C, the two extremes G—C, say corn and clothes, may represent different quantities of value. The farmer may sell his corn above its value, or may buy the clothes at less than their value. He may, on the other hand, "be done" by the clothes merchant. Yet, in the form of circulation now under consideration, such differences in value are purely accidental. The fact that the corn and the clothes are equivalents, does not deprive the process of all meaning, as it does in M—C—M. The equivalence of their values is rather a necessary condition to its normal course.

The repetition or renewal of the act of selling in order to buy, is kept within bounds by the very object it aims at, namely, consumption or the satisfaction of definite wants, an aim that lies altogether outside the sphere of circulation. But when we buy in order to sell, we, on the contrary, begin and end with the same thing, money, exchange-value; and thereby the movement becomes interminable. No doubt, M becomes M+ΔM, £100 become £110. But when viewed in their qualitative aspect alone, £110 are the same as £100, namely money; and considered quantitatively, £110 is, like £100, a sum of definite and limited value. If now, the £110 be spent as money, they cease to play their part. They are no longer capital. Withdrawn from circulation, they become petrified into a hoard, and though they remained in that state till doomsday, not a single farthing would accrue to them. If, then, the expansion of value is once aimed at, there is just the same inducement to augment the value of the £110 as that of the £100; for both are but limited expressions for exchange-value, and therefore both have the same vocation to approach, by quantitative increase, as near as possible to absolute wealth. Momentarily, indeed, the value originally advanced, the £100, is distinguishable from the surplus-value of £10, that is annexed to it during circulation; but the distinction vanishes immediately. At the end of the process, we do not receive with one hand the original £100, and with the other, the surplus-value of £10. We simply get a value of £110, which is in exactly the same condition and fitness for commencing the expanding process, as the original £100 was. Money ends the movement only to begin it again.[1] Therefore, the final result of every separate circuit, in which a purchase and consequent sale are completed, forms of itself the starting-point of a new circuit. The simple circulation of commodities—selling in order to buy—is a means of carrying out a purpose unconnected with circulation, namely, the appropriation of use-values, the satisfaction of wants. The circulation of money as capital is, on the contrary, an end in itself, for the expansion of value takes place only within this constantly renewed movement. The circulation of capital has therefore no limits.[2]

As the conscious representative of this movement, the possessor of money becomes a capitalist. His person, or rather his pocket, is the point from which the money starts and to which it returns. The expansion of value, which is the objective basis or main-spring of the circulation M—C—M, becomes his subjective aim, and it is only in so far as the appropriation of ever more and more wealth in the abstract becomes the sole motive of his operations, that he functions as a capitalist, that is, as capital personified and endowed with consciousness and a will. Use-values must therefore never be looked upon as the real aim of the capitalist; neither must the profit on any single transaction. The restless never-ending process of profit-making alone is what he aims at. This boundless greed after riches, this passionate chase after exchange-value, is common to the capitalist and the miser; but while the miser is merely a capitalist gone mad, the capitalist is a rational miser. The never-ending augmentation of exchange-value, which the miser strives after, by seeking to save his money from circulation, is attained by the more acute capitalist, by constantly throwing it afresh into circulation.

The independent form, *i.e.*, the money-form, which the value of commodities assumes in the case of simple circulation, serves only one purpose, namely, their exchange, and vanishes in the final result of the movement. On the other hand, in the circulation M—C—M, both the money and the commodity represent only different modes of existence of value itself, the money its general

mode, and the commodity its particular, or, so to say, disguised mode. It is constantly changing from one form to the other without thereby becoming lost, and thus assumes an automatically active character. If now we take in turn each of the two different forms which self-expanding value successively assumes in the course of its life, we then arrive at these two propositions: Capital is money: Capital is commodities. In truth, however, value is here the active factor in a process, in which, while constantly assuming the form in turn of money and commodities, it at the same time changes in magnitude, differentiates itself by throwing off surplus-value from itself; the original value, in other words, expands spontaneously. For the movement, in the course of which it adds surplus-value, is its own movement, its expansion, therefore, is automatic expansion. Because it is value, it has acquired the occult quality of being able to add value to itself. It brings forth living offspring, or, at the least, lays golden eggs.

Value, therefore, being the active factor in such a process, and assuming at one time the form of money, at another that of commodities, but through all these changes preserving itself and expanding, it requires some independent form, by means of which its identity may at any time be established. And this form it possesses only in the shape of money. It is under the form of money that value begins and ends, and begins again, every act of its own spontaneous generation. It began by being £100, it is now £110, and so on. But the money itself is only one of the two forms of value. Unless it takes the form of some commodity, it does not become capital. There is here no antagonism, as in the case of boarding, between the money and commodities. The capitalist knows that all commodities, however scurvy they may look, or however badly they may smell, are in faith and in truth money, inwardly circumcised Jews, and what is more, a wonderful means whereby out of money to make more money.

In simple circulation, C—M—C, the value of commodities attained at the most a form independent of their use-values, *i.e.*, the form of money; but that same value now in the circulation M—C—M, or the circulation of capital, suddenly presents itself as an independent substance, endowed with a motion of its own, passing, through a life-process of its own, in which money and commodities are mere forms which it assumes and casts off in turn. Nay, more: instead of simply representing the relations of commodities, it enters now, so to say, into private relations with itself. It differentiates itself as original value from itself as surplus-value; as the father differentiates himself from himself quâ the son, yet both are one and of one age: for only by the surplus-value of £10 does the £100 originally advanced become capital, and so soon as this takes place, so soon as the son, and by the son, the father, is begotten, so soon does their difference vanish, and they again become one, £110.

Value therefore now becomes value in process, money in process, and, as such, capital. It comes out of circulation, enters into it again, preserves and multiplies itself within its circuit, comes back out of it with expanded bulk, and begins the same round ever afresh. M—M, money which begets money, such is the description of Capital from the mouths of its first interpreters, the Mercantilists.

Buying in order to sell, or, more accurately, buying in order to sell dearer, M—C—M, appears certainly to be a form peculiar to one kind of capital alone, namely merchants' capital. But industrial capital too is money, that is changed into commodities, and by the sale of these commodities, is re-converted into more money. The events that take place outside the sphere of circulation, in the interval between the buying and selling, do not affect the form of this movement. Lastly, in the case of interest-bearing capital, the circulation M—C—M appears abridged. We have its result without the intermediate stage, in the form M—M "en style lapidaire" so to say, money that is worth more money, value that is greater than itself.

M—C—M' is therefore in reality the general formula of capital as it appears prima facie within the sphere of circulation.

Endnotes

1. "Capital is divisible . . . into the original capital and the profit, the increment to the capital . . . although in practice this profit is immediately turned into capital, and set in motion with the original." (F. Engels, "Umrisse zu einer Kritik der Nationalökonomie," in the "Deutsch-Französische Jahrbücher," edited by Arnold Ruge and Karl Marx. Paris, 1844, p. 99.) [*Marx*]

2. Aristotle opposes Oeconomic to Chrematistic. He starts from the former. So far as it is the art of gaining a livelihood, it is limited to procuring those articles that are necessary to existence, and useful either to a household or the state. "True wealth consists of such values in use; for the quantity of possessions of this kind, capable of making life pleasant, is not unlimited. There is, however, a second mode of acquiring things, to which we may by preference and with correctness give the name of Chrematistic, and in this case there appear to be no limits to riches and possessions. Trade (literally retail trade, and Aristotle takes this kind because in it values in use predominate) does not in its nature belong to Chrematistic, for here the exchange has reference only to what is necessary to themselves (the buyer or seller)." Therefore, as he goes on to show, the original form of trade was barter, but with the extension of the latter, there arose the necessity for money. On the discovery of money, barter of necessity developed into trading in commodities, and this again, in opposition to its original tendency, grew into Chrematistic, into the art of making money. Now Chrematistic is distinguishable from Oeconomic in this way, that "in the case of Chrematistic circulation is the source of riches. And it appears to revolve about money, for money is the beginning and end of this kind of exchange. Therefore also riches, such as Chrematistic strives for, are unlimited. Just as every art that is not a means to an end, but an end in itself, has no limit to its aims, because it seeks constantly to approach nearer and nearer to that end, while those arts that pursue means to an end, are not boundless, since the goal itself imposes a limit upon them, so with Chrematistic, there are no bounds to its aims, these aims being absolute wealth. Oeconomic not Chrematistic has a limit . . . the object of the former is something different from money, of the latter the augmentation of money. . . . By confounding these two forms, which overlap each other, some people have been led to look upon the preservation and increase of money ad infinitum as the end and aim of Oeconomic." (Aristoteles, "De-rep." edit. Bekker. lib. I. c. 8, 9. passim.) [*Marx*]

6

On Mechanical and Organic Solidarity

Émile Durkheim

Émile Durkheim (1858–1917) used two metaphors to describe the different bases of solidarity, or social order, in traditional preindustrial and modern industrial societies. He saw traditional society as characterized by mechanical solidarity and modern society as defined in terms of organic solidarity. In this excerpt from his first major book, *The Division of Labor in Society* (1893), Durkheim poses a fundamental question about modern society: How can it facilitate individual autonomy while people are increasingly more dependent on others? As the title of the book might suggest, the answer has to do with the ever more complex and differentiated division of labor in industrial societies.

… This work had its origins in the question of the relations of the individual to social solidarity. Why does the individual, while becoming more autonomous, depend more upon society? How can he be at once more individual and more solidary? Certainly, these two movements, contradictory as they appear, develop in parallel fashion. This is the problem we are raising. It appeared to us that what resolves this apparent antinomy is a transformation of social solidarity due to the steadily growing development of the division of labor. That is how we have been led to make this the object of our study. . . .

Introduction

The Problem

The division of labor is not of recent origin, but it was only at the end of the eighteenth century that social cognizance was taken of the principle, though, until then, unwitting submission had been rendered to it. To be sure, several thinkers from earliest times saw its importance;[1] but Adam Smith was the first to attempt a theory of it. Moreover, he adopted this phrase that social science later lent to biology.

Nowadays, the phenomenon has developed so generally it is obvious to all. We need have no further illusions about the tendencies of modern industry; it advances steadily towards powerful machines, towards great concentrations of forces and capital, and consequently to the extreme division of labor. Occupations are infinitely separated and specialized, not only inside the factories, but each product is itself a specialty dependent upon others. Adam Smith and John Stuart Mill still hoped that agriculture, at least, would be an exception to the rule, and they saw it as the last resort of small-scale industry. Although one must be careful not to generalize unduly in such matters, nevertheless it is hard to deny today that the principal branches of the agricultural industry are steadily being drawn into the general movement.[2] Finally, business itself is ingeniously following and reflecting in all its shadings the infinite diversity of industrial enterprises; and, while this evolution is realizing itself with unpremeditated spontaneity, the economists, examining its causes and appreciating its results, far from condemning or opposing it, uphold it as necessary. They see in it the supreme law of human societies and the condition of their progress. . . .

***

. . . [T]he relations governed by co-operative law with restitutive sanctions and the solidarity which they express, result from the division of social labor. We have explained, moreover, that, in general, co-operative relations do not convey other sanctions. In fact, it is in the nature of special tasks to escape the action of the collective conscience, for, in order for a thing to be the object of common sentiments, the first condition is that it be common, that is to say, that it be present in all consciences and that all can represent it in one and the same manner. To be sure, in so far as functions have a certain generality, everybody can have some idea of them. But the more specialized they are, the more circumscribed the number of those cognizant of each of them. Consequently, the more marginal they are to the common conscience. The rules which determine them cannot have the superior force, the transcendent authority which, when offended, demands expiation. It is also from opinion that their authority comes, as is the case with penal rules, but from an opinion localized in restricted regions of society.

Moreover, even in the special circles where they apply and where, consequently, they are represented in people, they do not correspond to very active sentiments, nor even very often to any type of emotional state. For, as they fix the manner in which the different functions ought to concur in diverse combinations of circumstances which can arise, the objects to which they relate themselves are not always present to consciences. We do not always have to administer guardianship trusteeship,[3] or exercise the rights of creditor or buyer, etc., or even exercise them in such and such a condition. But the states of conscience are strong only in so far as they are permanent. The violation of these rules reaches neither the common soul of society in its living parts, nor even, at least not generally, that of special groups, and, consequently, it can determine only a very moderate reaction. All that is necessary is that the functions concur in a regular manner. If this regularity is disrupted, it behooves us to re-establish it. Assuredly, that is not to say that the development of the division of labor cannot be affective of penal law. There are, as we already know, administrative and governmental functions in which certain relations are regulated by repressive law, because of the particular character which the organ of common conscience and everything that relates to it has. In still other cases, the links of solidarity which unite certain social functions can be such that from their break quite general repercussions result invoking a penal sanction. But, for the reason we have given, these counter-blows are exceptional.

This law definitely plays a role in society analogous to that played by the nervous system in the organism. The latter has as its task, in effect, the regulation of the different functions of the body in such a way as to make them harmonize. It thus very naturally expresses the state of concentration at which the organism has arrived, in accordance with the division of physiological labor. Thus, on different levels of the animal scale, we can measure the degree of this concentration according to the development of the nervous system. Which is to say that we can equally measure the degree of concentration at which a society has arrived in accordance with the division of social labor according to the development of co-operative law with restitutive sanctions. We can foresee the great services that this criterion will render us. . . .

***

Since negative solidarity does not produce any integration by itself, and since, moreover, there is nothing specific about it, we shall recognize only two kinds of positive solidarity which are distinguishable by the following qualities:

1. The first binds the individual directly to society without any intermediary. In the second, he depends upon society, because he depends upon the parts of which it is composed.

2. Society is not seen in the same aspect in the two cases. In the first, what we call society is a more or less organized totality of beliefs and sentiments common to all the members of the group: this is the collective type. On the other hand, the society in which we

are solidary in the second instance is a system of different, special functions which definite relations unite. These two societies really make up only one. They are two aspects of one and the same reality, but none the less they must be distinguished.

3. From this second difference there arises another which helps us to characterize and name the two kinds of solidarity.

The first can be strong only if the ideas and tendencies common to all the members of the society are greater in number and intensity than those which pertain personally to each member. It is as much stronger as the excess is more considerable. But what makes our personality is how much of our own individual qualities we have, what distinguishes us from others. This solidarity can grow only in inverse ratio to personality. There are in each of us, as we have said, two consciences: one which is common to our group in its entirety, which, consequently, is not ourself, but society living and acting within us; the other, on the contrary, represents that in us which is personal and distinct, that which makes us an individual.[4] Solidarity which comes from likenesses is at its maximum when the collective conscience completely envelops our whole conscience and coincides in all points with it. But, at that moment, our individuality is nil. It can be born only if the community takes smaller toll of us. There are, here, two contrary forces, one centripetal, the other centrifugal, which cannot flourish at the same time. We cannot, at one and the same time, develop ourselves in two opposite senses. If we have a lively desire to think and act for ourselves, we cannot be strongly inclined to think and act as others do. If our ideal is to present a singular and personal appearance, we do not want to resemble everybody else. Moreover, at the moment when this solidarity exercises its force, our personality vanishes, as our definition permits us to say, for we are no longer ourselves, but the collective life.

The social molecules which can be coherent in this way can act together only in the measure that they have no actions of their own, as the molecules of inorganic bodies. That is why we propose to call this type of solidarity mechanical. The term does not signify that it is produced by mechanical and artificial means. We call it that only by analogy to the cohesion which unites the elements of an inanimate body, as opposed to that which makes a unity out of the elements of a living body. What justifies this term is that the link which thus unites the individual to society is wholly analogous to that which attaches a thing to a person. The individual conscience, considered in this light, is a simple dependent upon the collective type and follows all of its movements, as the possessed object follows those of its owner. In societies where this type of solidarity is highly developed, the individual does not appear, as we shall see later. Individuality is something which the society possesses. Thus, in these social types, personal rights are not yet distinguished from real rights.

It is quite otherwise with the solidarity which the division of labor produces. Whereas the previous type implies that individuals resemble each other, this type presumes their difference. The first is possible only in so far as the individual personality is absorbed into the collective personality; the second is possible only if each one has a sphere of action which is peculiar to him; that is, a personality. It is necessary, then, that the collective conscience leave open a part of the individual conscience in order that special functions may be established there, functions which it cannot regulate. The more this region is extended, the stronger is the cohesion which results from this solidarity. In effect, on the one hand, each one depends much more strictly on society as labor is more divided; and, on the other, the activity of each is much more personal as it is, more specialized. Doubtless, as circumscribed as it is, it is never completely original. Even in the exercise of our occupation, we conform to usages, to practices which are common to our whole professional brotherhood. But, even in this instance, the yoke that we submit to is much less heavy than when society completely controls us, and it leaves much more place open for the free play of our initiative. Here, then, the individuality of all grows at the same time as that of its parts. Society becomes more capable of collective movement, at the same time that each of its elements has more freedom of movement. This solidarity resembles that which we observe among the higher animals. Each organ, in effect, has its special physiognomy, its autonomy. And, moreover, the unity of the organism is as great as the individuation of the parts is more marked. Because of this analogy, we propose to call the solidarity which is due to the division of labor, organic. . . .

***

Not only, in a general way, does mechanical solidarity link men less strongly than organic solidarity, but also, as we advance in the scale of social evolution, it grows ever slacker.

The force of social links which have this origin vary with respect to the three following conditions:

1. The relation between the volume of the common conscience and that of the individual conscience. The links are as strong as the first more completely envelops the second.

2. The average intensity of the states of the collective conscience. The relation between volumes being equal, it has as much power over the individual as it has vitality. If, on the other hand, it consists of only feeble forces, it can but feebly influence the collective sense. It will the more easily be able to pursue its own course, and solidarity will be less strong.

3. The greater or lesser determination of these same states. That is, the more defined beliefs and practices are, the less place they leave for individual divergencies. They are uniform moulds into which we all, in the same manner, couch our ideas and our actions. The *consensus* is then as perfect as possible; all consciences vibrate in unison. Inversely, the more general and indeterminate the rules of conduct and thought are, the more individual reflection must intervene to apply them to particular cases. But it cannot awaken without upheavals occurring, for, as it varies from one man to another in quality and quantity, everything that it produces has the same character. Centrifugal tendencies thus multiply at the expense of social cohesion and the harmony of its movements.

On the other hand, strong and defined states of the common conscience are the roots of penal law. But we are going to see that the number of these is less today than heretofore, and that it diminishes, progressively, as societies approach our social type. . . .

To prove this, it would avail us nothing to compare the number of rules with repressive sanctions in different social types, for the number of rules does not vary exactly with the sentiments the rules represent. The same sentiment can, in effect, be offended in several different ways, and thus give rise to several rules without diversifying itself in so doing. Because there are now more ways of acquiring property, there are also more ways of stealing, but the sentiment of respect for the property of another has not multiplied itself proportionally. . . .

This is not to say, however, that the common conscience is threatened with total disappearance. Only, it more and more comes to consist of very general and very indeterminate ways of thinking and feeling, which leave an open place for a growing multitude of individual differences. There is even a place where it is strengthened and made precise: that is the way in which it regards the individual. As all the other beliefs and all the other practices take on a character less and less religious, the individual becomes the object of a sort of religion. We erect a cult in behalf of personal dignity which, as every strong cult, already has its superstitions. It is thus, if one wishes, a common cult, but it is possible only by the ruin of all others, and, consequently, cannot produce the same effects as this multitude of extinguished beliefs. There is no compensation for that. Moreover, if it is common in so far as the community partakes of it, it is individual in its object. If it turns all wills towards the same end, this end is not social. It thus occupies a completely exceptional place in the collective conscience. It is still from society that it takes all its force, but it is not to society that it attaches us; it is to ourselves. Hence, it does not constitute a true social link. That is why we have been justly able to reproach the theorists who have made this sentiment exclusively basic in their moral doctrine, with the ensuing dissolution of society. We can then conclude by saying that all social links which result from likeness progressively slacken.

This law, in itself, is already enough to show the tremendous grandeur of the role of the division of labor. In sum, since mechanical solidarity progressively becomes enfeebled, life properly social must decrease or another solidarity must slowly come in to take the place of that which has gone. The choice must be made. In vain shall we contend that the collective conscience extends and grows stronger at the same time as that of individuals. We have just proved that the two terms vary in a sense inverse to each other. Social progress, however, does not consist in a continual dissolution. On the contrary, the more we advance, the more profoundly do societies reveal the sentiment of self and of unity. There must, then, be some other social link which produces this result; this cannot be any other than that which comes from the division of labor.

If, moreover, one recalls that even where it is most resistant, mechanical solidarity does not link men with the same force as the division of labor, and that, moreover, it leaves outside its scope the major part of phenomena actually social, it will become still more evident that social solidarity tends to become exclusively organic. It is the division of labor which, more and more, fills the role that was formerly filled by the common conscience. It is the principal bond of social aggregates of higher types.

This is a function of the division of labor a good deal more important than that ordinarily assigned to it by economists.

Endnotes

1. Aristotle, *Nichomachean Ethics*, E1133a, 16.

2. *Journal des Economistes*, November 1884, p. 211.

3. That is why the law which governs the relations of domestic functions is not penal, although these functions are very general.

4. However, these two consciences are not in regions geographically distinct from us, but penetrate from all sides.

7

What Is a Social Fact?

Émile Durkheim

Durkheim was intent on staking out a distinctive place for sociology among the human sciences. He took particular pains to indicate the ways in which sociology and psychology differ. In *The Rules of Sociological Method* (1895), his famous methodological treatise, he begins making his case by defining what he refers to as "social facts." These, he proceeds to argue, are the proper subject matter of sociology and are what serve to distinguish it from the other sciences. Central to his understanding of the proper domain of sociological inquiry is his claim that social facts are forces that have an impact on the behavior of individuals. This focus on the constraining character of social facts has led subsequent critics to charge that Durkheim's overemphasis on social structure resulted in a devaluation of agency. In other words, he failed to appreciate that although people are shaped by their social circumstances, they can affect those circumstances.

Before inquiring into the method suited to the study of social facts, it is important to know which facts are commonly called "social." This information is all the more necessary since the designation "social" is used with little precision. It is currently employed for practically all phenomena generally diffused within society, however small their social interest. But on that basis, there are, as it were, no human events that may not be called social. Each individual drinks, sleeps, eats, reasons; and it is to society's interest that these functions be exercised in an orderly manner. If, then, all these facts are counted as "social" facts, sociology would have no subject matter exclusively its own, and its domain would be confused with that of biology and psychology.

But in reality there is in every society a certain group of phenomena which may be differentiated from those studied by the other natural sciences. When I fulfil my obligations as brother, husband, or citizen, when I execute my contracts, I perform duties which are defined, externally to myself and my acts, in law and in custom. Even if they conform to my own sentiments and I feel their reality subjectively, such reality is still objective, for I did not create them; I merely inherited them through my education. How many times it happens, moreover, that we are ignorant of the details of the obligations incumbent upon us, and that in order to acquaint ourselves with them we must consult the law and its authorized interpreters! Similarly, the church-member finds the beliefs and practices of his religious life ready-made at birth; their existence prior to his own implies their existence outside of himself. The system of signs I use to express my thought, the system of currency I employ to pay my debts, the instruments of credit I utilize in my commercial relations, the practices followed in my profession, etc., function independently of my own use of them. And these statements can be repeated for each member of society. Here, then, are ways of acting, thinking, and feeling that present the noteworthy property of existing outside the individual consciousness.

These types of conduct or thought are not only external to the individual but are, moreover, endowed with coercive power, by virtue of which they impose themselves upon him, independent of his individual will. Of course, when I fully consent and conform to them, this constraint is felt only slightly, if at all, and is therefore unnecessary. But it is, nonetheless, an intrinsic characteristic of these facts, the proof thereof being that it asserts itself as soon as I attempt to resist it. If I attempt to violate the law, it reacts against me so as to prevent my act before its accomplishment, or to nullify my violation by restoring the damage, if it is accomplished and reparable, or to make me expiate it if it cannot be compensated for otherwise.

In the case of purely moral maxims the public conscience exercises a check on every act which offends it by means of the surveillance it exercises over the conduct of citizens, and the appropriate penalties at its disposal. In many cases the constraint is less violent, but nevertheless it always exists. If I do not submit to the conventions of society, if in my dress I do not conform to the customs observed in my country and in my class, the ridicule I provoke, the social isolation in which I am kept, produce, although in an attenuated form, the same effects as a punishment in the strict sense of the word. The constraint is nonetheless efficacious for being indirect. I am not obliged to speak French with my fellow countrymen nor to use the legal currency, but I cannot possibly do otherwise. If I tried to escape this necessity, my attempt would fail miserably. As an industrialist, I am free to apply the technical methods of former centuries; but by doing so, I should invite certain ruin. Even when I free myself from these rules and violate them successfully, I am always compelled to struggle with them. When finally overcome, they make their constraining power sufficiently felt by the resistance they offer. The enterprises of all innovators, including successful ones, come up against resistance of this kind.

Here, then, is a category of facts with very distinctive characteristics: it consists of ways of acting, thinking, and feeling, external to the individual, and endowed with a power of coercion, by reason of which they control him. These ways of thinking could not be confused with biological phenomena, since they consist of representations and of actions; nor with psychological phenomena, which exist only in the individual consciousness and through it. They constitute, thus, a new variety of phenomena; and it is to them exclusively that the term "social" ought to be applied. And this term fits them quite well, for it is clear that, since their source is not in the individual, their substratum can be no other than society, either the political society as a whole or some one of the partial groups it includes, such as religious denominations, political, literary, and occupational associations, etc. On the other hand, this term "social" applies to them exclusively, for it has a distinct meaning only if it designates exclusively the phenomena which are not included in any of the categories of facts that have already been established and classified.

These ways of thinking and acting therefore constitute the proper domain of sociology. It is true that, when we define them with this word "constraint," we risk shocking the zealous partisans of absolute individualism. For those who profess the complete autonomy of the individual, man's dignity is diminished whenever he is made to feel that he is not completely self-determinant. It is generally accepted today, however, that most of our ideas and our tendencies are not developed by ourselves but come to us from without. How can they become a part of us except by imposing themselves upon us? This is the whole meaning of our definition. And it is generally accepted, moreover, that social constraint is not necessarily incompatible with the individual personality.[1]

Since the examples that we have just cited (legal and moral regulations, religious faiths, financial systems, etc.) all consist of established beliefs and practices, one might be led to believe that social facts exist only where there is some social organization. But there are other facts without such crystallized form which have the same objectivity and the same ascendency over the individual. These are called "social currents." Thus the great movements of enthusiasm, indignation, and pity in a crowd do not originate in any one of the particular individual consciousnesses. They come to each one of us from without and can carry us away in spite of ourselves. Of course, it may happen that, in abandoning myself to them unreservedly, I do not feel the pressure they exert upon me. But it is revealed as soon as I try to resist them. Let an individual attempt to oppose one of these collective manifestations, and the emotions that he denies will turn against him. Now, if this power of external coercion asserts itself so clearly in cases of resistance, it must exist also in the first-mentioned cases, although we are unconscious of it. We are then victims of the illusion of having ourselves created that which actually forced itself from without. If the complacency with which we permit ourselves to be carried along conceals the pressure undergone, nevertheless it does not abolish it. Thus, air is no less heavy because we do not detect its weight. So, even if we ourselves have spontaneously contributed to the production of the common emotion, the impression we have received differs markedly from that which we would have experienced if we had been alone. Also, once the crowd has dispersed, that is, once these social influences have ceased to act upon us and we are alone again, the emotions which have passed through the mind appear strange to us, and we no longer recognize them as ours. We realize that these feelings have been impressed upon us to a much greater extent than they were created by us. It may even happen that they horrify us, so much were they contrary to our nature. Thus, a group of individuals, most of whom are perfectly inoffensive, may, when gathered in a crowd, be drawn into acts of atrocity. And what we say of these transitory outbursts applies similarly to those more permanent currents of opinion on religious, political, literary, or artistic matters which are constantly being formed around us, whether in society as a whole or in more limited circles.

To confirm this definition of the social fact by a characteristic illustration from common experience, one need only observe the manner in which children are brought up. Considering the facts as they are and as they have always been, it becomes immediately evident that all education is a continuous effort to impose on the child ways of seeing, feeling, and acting which he could not have arrived at spontaneously. From the very first hours of his life, we compel him to eat, drink, and sleep at regular hours; we constrain him to cleanliness, calmness, and obedience; later we exert pressure upon him in order that he may learn proper consideration for others, respect for customs and conventions, the need for work, etc. If, in time, this constraint ceases to be felt, it is because it gradually gives rise to habits and to internal tendencies that render constraint unnecessary; but nevertheless it is not abolished, for it is still the source from which these habits were derived. It is true that, according to Spencer, a rational education ought to reject such methods, allowing the child to act in complete liberty; but as this pedagogic theory has never been applied by any known people, it must be accepted only as an expression of personal opinion, not as a fact which can contradict the aforementioned observations. What makes these facts particularly instructive is that the aim of education is, precisely, the socialization of the human being; the process of education, therefore, gives us in a nutshell the historical fashion in which the social being is constituted. This unremitting pressure to which the child is subjected is the very pressure of the social milieu which tends to fashion him in its own image, and of which parents and teachers are merely the representatives and intermediaries.

It follows that sociological phenomena cannot be defined by their universality. A thought which we find in every individual consciousness, a movement repeated by all individuals, is not thereby a social fact. If sociologists have been satisfied with defining them by this characteristic, it is because they confused them with what one might call the reincarnation in the individual. It is, however, the collective aspects of the beliefs, tendencies, and practices of a group that characterize truly social phenomena. As for the forms that the collective states assume when refracted in the individual, these are things of another sort. This duality is clearly demonstrated by the fact that these two orders of phenomena are frequently found dissociated from one another. Indeed, certain of these social manners of acting and thinking acquire, by reason of their repetition, a certain rigidity which on its own account crystallizes them, so to speak, and isolates them from the particular events which reflect them. They thus acquire a body, a tangible form, and constitute a reality in their own right, quite distinct from the individual facts which produce it. Collective habits are inherent not only in the successive acts which they determine but, by a privilege of which we find no example in the biological realm, they are given permanent expression in a formula which is repeated from mouth to mouth, transmitted by education, and fixed even in writing. Such is the origin and nature of legal and moral rules, popular aphorisms and proverbs, articles of faith wherein religious or political groups condense their beliefs, standards of taste established by literary schools, etc. None of these can be found entirely reproduced in the applications made of them by individuals, since they can exist even without being actually applied.

No doubt, this dissociation does not always manifest itself with equal distinctness, but its obvious existence in the important and numerous cases just cited is sufficient to prove that the social fact is a thing distinct from its individual manifestations. Moreover, even when this dissociation is not immediately apparent, it may often be disclosed by certain devices of method. Such dissociation is indispensable if one wishes to separate social facts from their alloys in order to observe them in a state of purity. Currents of opinion, with an intensity varying according to the time and place, impel certain groups either to more marriages, for example, or to more suicides, or to a higher or lower birthrate, etc. These currents are plainly social facts. At first sight they seem inseparable from the forms they take in individual cases. But statistics furnish us with the means of isolating them. They are, in fact, represented with considerable exactness by the rates of births, marriages, and suicides, that is, by the number obtained by dividing the average annual total of marriages, births, suicides, by the number of persons whose ages lie within the range in which marriages, births, and suicides occur.[2] Since each of these figures contains all the individual cases indiscriminately, the individual circumstances which may have had a share in the production of the phenomenon are neutralized and, consequently, do not contribute to its determination. The average, then, expresses a certain state of the group mind (*l'âme collective*).

Such are social phenomena, when disentangled from all foreign matter. As for their individual manifestations, these are indeed, to a certain extent, social, since they partly reproduce a social model. Each of them also depends, and to a large extent, on the organopsychological constitution of the individual and on the particular circumstances in which he is placed. Thus they are not sociological phenomena in the strict sense of the word. They belong to two realms at once; one could call them sociopsychological. They interest the sociologist without constituting the immediate subject matter of sociology. There exist in the interior of organisms similar phenomena, compound in their nature, which form in their turn the subject matter of the "hybrid sciences," such as physiological chemistry, for example.

The objection may be raised that a phenomenon is collective only if it is common to all members of society, or at least to most of them—in other words, if it is truly general. This may be true; but it is general because it is collective (that is, more or less obligatory), and certainly not collective because general. It is a group condition repeated in the individual because imposed on him. It is to be found in each part because it exists in the whole, rather than in the whole because it exists in the parts. This becomes conspicuously evident in those beliefs and practices which are transmitted to us ready-made by previous generations; we receive and adopt them because, being both collective and ancient, they are invested with a particular authority that education has taught us to recognize and respect. It is, of course, true that a vast portion of our social culture is transmitted to us in this way; but even when the social fact is due in part to our direct collaboration, its nature is not different. A collective emotion which bursts forth suddenly and violently in a crowd does not express merely what all the individual sentiments had in common; it is something entirely different, as we have shown. It results from their being together, a product of the actions and reactions which take place between individual consciousnesses; and if each individual consciousness echoes the collective sentiment, it is by virtue of the special energy resident in its collective origin. If all hearts beat in unison, this is not the result of a spontaneous and pre-established harmony but rather because an identical force propels them in the same direction. Each is carried along by all.

We thus arrive at the point where we can formulate and delimit in a precise way the domain of sociology. It comprises only a limited group of phenomena. A social fact is to be recognized by the power of external coercion which it exercises or is capable of exercising over individuals, and the presence of this power may be recognized in its turn either by the existence of some specific sanction or by the resistance offered against every individual effort that tends to violate it. One can, however, define it also by its diffusion within the group, provided that, in conformity with our previous remarks, one takes care to add as a second and essential characteristic that its own existence is independent of the individual forms it assumes in its diffusion. This last criterion is perhaps, in certain cases, easier to apply than the preceding one. In fact, the constraint is easy to ascertain when it expresses itself externally by some direct reaction of society, as is the case in law, morals, beliefs, customs, and even fashions. But when it is only indirect, like the constraint which an economic organization exercises, it cannot always be so easily detected. Generality combined with externality may, then, be easier to establish. Moreover, this second definition is but another form of the first; for if a mode of behavior whose existence is external to individual consciousnesses becomes general, this can only be brought about by its being imposed upon them.[3]

But these several phenomena present the same characteristic by which we defined the others. These "ways of existing" are imposed on the individual precisely in the same fashion as the "ways of acting" of which we have spoken. Indeed, when we wish to know how a society is divided politically, of what these divisions themselves are composed, and how complete is the fusion existing between them, we shall not achieve our purpose by physical inspection and by geographical observations; for these phenomena are social, even when they have some basis in physical nature. It is only by a study of public law that a comprehension of this organization is possible, for it is this law that determines the organization, as it equally determines our domestic and civil relations. This political organization is, then, no less obligatory than the social facts mentioned above. If the population crowds into our cities instead of scattering into the country, this is due to a trend of public opinion, a collective drive that imposes this concentration upon the individuals. We can no more choose the style of our houses than of our clothing—at least, both are equally obligatory. The channels of communication prescribe the direction of internal migrations and commerce, etc., and even

their extent. Consequently, at th... it should be necessary to add... phenomena which we have e... presenting the distinctive criterion of a so... cial fact only one additional category, "ways of existing"; and, as this enumeration was not meant to be rigorously exhaustive, the addition would not be absolutely necessary.

Such an addition is perhaps not necessary, for these "ways of existing" are only crystallized "ways of acting." The political structure of a society is merely the way in which its component segments have become accustomed to live with one another. If their relations are traditionally intimate, the segments tend to fuse with one another, or, in the contrary case, to retain their identity. The type of habitation imposed upon us is merely the way in which our contemporaries and our ancestors have been accustomed to construct their houses. The methods of communication are merely the channels which the regular currents of commerce and migrations have dug, by flowing in the same direction. To be sure, if the phenomena of a structural character alone presented this permanence, one might believe that they constituted a distinct species. A legal regulation is an arrangement no less permanent than a type of architecture, and yet the regulation is a "physiological" fact. A simple moral maxim is assuredly somewhat more malleable, but it is much more rigid than a simple professional custom or a fashion. There is thus a whole series of degrees without a break in continuity between the facts of the most articulated structure and those free currents of social life which are not yet definitely molded. The differences between them are, therefore, only differences in the degree of consolidation they present. Both are simply life, more or less crystallized. No doubt, it may be of some advantage to reserve the term "morphological" for those social facts which concern the social substratum, but only on condition of not overlooking the fact that they are of the same nature as the others. Our definition will then include the whole relevant range of facts if we say: *A social fact is every way of acting, fixed or not, capable of exercising on the individual an external constraint;* or again, *every way of acting which is general throughout a*

en society, while at the same time existing
in its own right independent of its individual
manifestations.[4]

Endnotes

1. We do not intend to imply, however, that all constraint is normal. We shall return to this point later.

2. Suicides do not occur at every age, and they take place with varying intensity at the different ages in which they occur.

3. It will be seen how this definition of the social fact diverges from that which forms the basis of the ingenious system of M. Tarde. First of all, we wish to state that our researches have nowhere led us to observe that preponderant influence in the genesis of collective facts which M. Tarde attributes to imitation. Moreover, from the preceding definition, which is not a theory but simply a résumé of the immediate data of observation, it seems indeed to follow, not only that imitation does not always express the essential and characteristic features of the social fact, but even that it never expresses them. No doubt, every social fact is imitated; it has, as we have just shown, a tendency to become general, but that is because it is social, i.e., obligatory. Its power of expansion is not the cause but the consequence of its sociological character. If, further, only social facts produced this consequence, imitation could perhaps serve, if not to explain them, at least to define them. But an individual condition which produces a whole series of effects remains individual nevertheless. Moreover, one may ask whether the word "imitation" is indeed fitted to designate an effect due to a coercive influence. Thus, by this single expression, very different phenomena, which ought to be distinguished, are confused.

4. This close connection between life and structure, organ and function, may be easily proved in sociology because between these two extreme terms there exists a whole series of immediately observable intermediate stages which show the bond between them. Biology is not in the same favorable position. But we may well believe that the inductions on this subject made by sociology are applicable to biology and that, in organisms as well as in societies, only differences in degree exist between these two orders of facts.

8

Anomic Suicide

Émile Durkheim

Durkheim has been depicted as a physician of society because of his interest in diagnosing the problems of contemporary society and offering prescriptions to remedy social ills. This approach is nowhere more evident than in his landmark empirical study of self-destruction, *Suicide* (1897). One reason for undertaking this particular study was Durkheim's desire to meet psychology on what might seem to be its own turf, by examining a phenomenon that lends itself to psychological interpretations. As such, the book is a polemic in which he argues that sociology can offer unique insights beyond the access of psychological concepts. In this excerpt, Durkheim discusses what he means by anomic suicide, one of four types of suicide he identifies. He contends that anomie, which is often translated as "rulelessness" or "normlessness," is a characteristic social pathology of modern society.

. . . If anomy never appeared except . . . in intermittent spurts and acute crisis, it might cause the social suicide rate to vary from time to time, but it would not be a regular, constant factor. In one sphere of social life, however—the sphere of trade and industry—it is actually in a chronic state.

For a whole century, economic progress has mainly consisted in freeing industrial relations from all regulation. Until very recently, it was the function of a whole system of moral forces to exert this discipline. First, the influence of religion was felt alike by workers and masters, the poor and the rich. It consoled the former and taught them contentment with their lot by informing them of the providential nature of the social order, that the share of each class was assigned by God himself, and by holding out the hope for just compensation in a world to come in return for the inequalities of this world. It gov-

erned the latter, recalling that worldly interests are not man's entire lot, that they must be subordinate to other and higher interests, and that they should, therefore, not be pursued without rule or measure. Temporal power, in turn, restrained the scope of economic functions by its supremacy over them and by the relatively subordinate role it assigned them. Finally, within the business world proper, the occupational groups, by regulating salaries, the price of products and production itself, indirectly fixed the average level of income on which needs are partially based by the very force of circumstances. However, we do not mean to propose this organization as a model. Clearly it would be inadequate to existing societies without great changes. What we stress is its existence, the fact of its useful influence, and that nothing today has come to take its place.

Actually, religion has lost most of its power. And government, instead of regulating economic life, has become its tool and servant. The most opposite schools, orthodox economists and extreme socialists, unite to reduce government to the role of a more or less passive intermediary among the various social functions. The former wish to make it simply the guardian of individual contracts; the latter leave it the task of doing the collective bookkeeping, that is, of recording the demands of consumers, transmitting them to producers, inventorying the total revenue and distributing it according to a fixed formula. But both refuse it any power to subordinate other social organs to itself and to make them converge toward one dominant aim. On both sides nations are declared to have the single or chief purpose of achieving industrial prosperity; such is the implication of the dogma of economic materialism, the basis of both apparently opposed systems. And as these theories merely express the state of opinion, industry, instead of being still regarded as a means to an end transcending itself, has become the supreme end of individuals and societies alike. Thereupon the appetites thus excited have become freed of any limiting authority. By sanctifying them, so to speak, this apotheosis of well-being has placed them above all human law. Their restraint seems like a sort of sacrilege.

For this reason, even the purely utilitarian regulation of them exercised by the industrial world itself through the medium of occupational groups has been unable to persist. Ultimately, this liberation of desires has been made worse by the very development of industry and the almost infinite extension of the market. So long as the producer could gain his profits only in his immediate neighborhood, the restricted amount of possible gain could not much overexcite ambition. Now that he may assume to have almost the entire world as his customer, how could passions accept their former confinement in the face of such limitless prospects?

Such is the source of the excitement predominating in this part of society, and which has thence extended to the other parts. There, the state of crisis and anomy is constant and, so to speak, normal. From top to bottom of the ladder, greed is aroused without knowing where to find ultimate foothold. Nothing can calm it, since its goal is far beyond all it can attain. Reality seems valueless by comparison with the dreams of fevered imaginations; reality is therefore abandoned, but so too is possibility abandoned when it in turn becomes reality. A thirst arises for novelties, unfamiliar pleasures, nameless sensations, all of which lose their savor once known. Henceforth one has no strength to endure the least reverse. The whole fever subsides and the sterility of all the tumult is apparent, and it is seen that all these new sensations in their infinite quantity cannot form a solid foundation of happiness to support one during days of trial. The wise man, knowing how to enjoy achieved results without having constantly to replace them with others, finds in them an attachment to life in the hour of difficulty. But the man who has always pinned all his hopes on the future and lived with his eyes fixed upon it, has nothing in the past as a comfort against the present's afflictions, for the past was nothing to him but a series of hastily experienced stages. What blinded him to himself was his expectation always to find further on the happiness he had so far missed. Now he is stopped in his tracks; from now on nothing remains behind or ahead of him to fix his gaze upon. Weariness alone, moreover, is enough to bring disillusionment, for he cannot in the end escape the futility of an endless pursuit.

We may even wonder if this moral state is not principally what makes economic catastrophes of our day so fertile in suicides. In societies where a man is subjected to a healthy discipline, he submits more readily to the blows of chance. The necessary effort for sustaining a little more discomfort costs him relatively little, since he is used to discomfort and constraint. But when every constraint is hateful in itself, how can closer constraint not seem intolerable? There is no tendency to resignation in the feverish impatience of men's lives. When there is no other aim but to outstrip constantly the point arrived at, how painful to be thrown back! Now this very lack of organization characterizing our economic condition throws doors wide to every sort of adventure. Since imagination is hungry for novelty, and ungoverned, it gropes at random. Setbacks necessarily increase with risks and thus crises multiply, just when they are becoming more destructive. Yet these dispositions are so inbred that society has grown to accept them and is accustomed to think them normal. It is everlastingly repeated that it is man's nature to be eternally dissatisfied, constantly to advance, without relief or rest, toward an indefinite goal. The longing for infinity is daily represented as a mark of moral distinction, whereas it can only appear within unregulated consciences which elevate to a rule the lack of rule from which they suffer. The doctrine of the most ruthless and swift progress has become an article of faith. But other theories appear parallel with those praising the advantages of instability, which, generalizing the situation that gives them birth, declare life evil, claim that it is richer in grief than in pleasure and that it attracts men only by false claims. Since this disorder is greatest in the economic world, it has most victims there.

Industrial and commercial functions are really among the occupations which furnish the greatest number of suicides (see Table 8-1). Almost on a level with the liberal professions, they sometimes surpass them; they are especially more afflicted than agriculture, where the old regulative forces still make their appearance felt most and where

Table 8-1

Suicides per Million Persons of Different Occupations

	Trade	Transportation	Industry	Agriculture	Liberal* Professions
France (1878–87) †	440	—	340	240	300
Switzerland (1876)	664	1,514	577	304	558
Italy (1866–76)	277	152.6	80.4	26.7	618‡
Prussia (1883–90)	754	—	456	315	832
Bavaria (1884–91)	465	—	369	153	454
Belgium (1886–90)	421	—	160	160	100
Wurttemberg (1873–78)	273	—	190	206	—
Saxony (1878)		341.59§		71.17	—

* When statistics distinguish several different sorts of liberal occupations, we show as a specimen the one in which the suicide-rate is highest.
† From 1826 to 1880 economic functions seem less affected (see *Compte-rendu* of 1880); but were occupational statistics very accurate?
‡ This figure is reached only by men of letters.
§ Figure represents Trade, Transportation and Industry combined for Saxony.—Ed.

Table 8-2

Comparison of European States From the Point of View of Both Divorce and Suicide

	Annual Divorces per 1,000 Marriages	Suicides per Million Inhabitants
I. Countries Where Divorce and Separation Are Rare		
Norway	0.54 (1875–80)	73
Russia	1.6 (1871–77)	30
England and Wales	1.3 (1871–79)	68
Scotland	2.1 (1871–81)	—
Italy	3.05 (1871–73)	31
Finland	3.9 (1875–79)	30.8
Averages	2.07	46.5
II. Countries Where Divorce and Separation Are of Average Frequency		
Bavaria	5.0 (1881)	90.5
Belgium	5.1 (1871–80)	68.5
Holland	6.0 (1871–80)	35.5
Sweden	6.4 (1871–80)	81
Baden	6.5 (1874–79)	156.6
France	7.5 (1871–79)	150
Wurttemberg	8.4 (1871–78)	162.4
Prussia	—	133
Averages	6.4	109.6
III. Countries Where Divorce and Separation Are Frequent		
Kingdom of Saxony	26.9 (1876–80)	299
Denmark	38.0 (1871–80)	258
Switzerland	47.0 (1876–80)	216
Averages	37.3	257

our owner demographics [handwritten]

the fever of business has least penetrated. Here is best recalled what was once the general constitution of the economic order. And the divergence would be yet greater if, among the suicides of industry, employers were distinguished from workmen, for the former are probably most stricken by the state of anomy. The enormous rate of those with independent means (720 per million) sufficiently shows that the possessors of most comfort suffer most. Everything that enforces subordination attenuates the effects of this state. At least the horizon of the lower classes is limited by those above them, and for this same reason their desires are more modest. Those who have only empty space above them are almost inevitably lost in it, if no force restrains them.

Anomy, therefore, is a regular and specific factor in suicide in our modern societies; one of the springs from which the annual contingent feeds. So we have here a new type to distinguish from the others. It differs from them in its dependence, not on the way in which individuals are attached to society, but on how it regulates them. Egoistic suicide results from man's no longer finding a basis for existence in life; altruistic suicide, because this basis for existence appears to man situated beyond life itself. The third sort of suicide, the existence of which has just been shown, results from man's activity's lacking regulation and his consequent sufferings. By virtue of its origin we shall assign this last variety the name of *anomic suicide*.

Certainly, this and egoistic suicide have kindred ties. Both spring from society's insufficient presence in individuals. But the sphere of its absence is not the same in both cases. In egoistic suicide it is deficient in truly collective activity, thus depriving the latter of object and meaning. In anomic suicide, society's influence is lacking in the basically individual passions, thus leaving them without a check-rein. In spite of their relationship, therefore, the two types are independent of each other. We may offer society everything social in us, and still be unable to control our desires; one may live in an anomic state without being egoistic, and vice versa. These two sorts of suicide therefore do not draw their chief recruits from the same

social environments; one has its principal field among intellectual careers, the world of thought—the other, the industrial or commercial world.

But economic anomy is not the only anomy which may give rise to suicide. The suicides occurring at the crisis of widowhood . . . are really due to domestic anomy resulting from the death of husband or wife. A family catastrophe occurs which affects the survivor. He is not adapted to the new situation in which he finds himself and accordingly offers less resistance to suicide.

But another variety of anomic suicide should draw greater attention, both because it is more chronic and because it will serve to illustrate the nature and functions of marriage.

In the *Annales de demographie internationale* (September 1882), Bertillon published a remarkable study of divorce, in which he proved the following proposition: throughout Europe the number of suicides varies with that of divorces and separations. If the different countries are compared from this twofold point of view, this parallelism is apparent (see Table 8-2). Not only is the relation between the averages evident, but the single irregular detail of any importance is that of Holland, where suicides are not as frequent as divorces.

The law may be yet more vigorously verified if we compare not different countries but different provices of a single country. Notably, in Switzerland the agreement between phenomena is striking (see Table 8-3). The Protestant cantons have the most divorces and also the most suicides. The mixed cantons follow, from both points of view, and only then come the Catholic cantons. Within each group the same agreements appear. Among the Catholic cantons Solothurn and Inner Appenzell are marked by the high number of their divorces; they are likewise marked by the number of their suicides. Freiburg, although Catholic and French, has a considerable number of both divorces and suicides. Among the Protestant German cantons none has so many divorces as Schaffhausen; Schaffhausen also leads the list for suicides. Finally, the mixed cantons, with the one exception of Argau, are classed in exactly the same way in both respects.

Anomic vs Egoist [handwritten]

Table 8-3

Comparison of Swiss Cantons From the Point of View of Divorce and Suicide

	Divorces and Separations per 1,000 Marriages	Suicides per Million		Divorces and Separations per 1,000 Marriages	Suicides per Million
I. Catholic Cantons					
French and Italian					
Tessina	7.6	57	Freiburg	15.9	119
Valais	4.0	47			
Averages	5.8	50	Averages	15.9	119
German					
Uri	—	60	Solothurn	37.7	205
Upper Unterwalden	4.9	20	Inner Appenzell	18.9	158
Lower Unterwalden	5.2	1	Zug	14.8	87
Schwyz	5.6	70	Luzern	13.0	100
Averages	3.9	37.7	Averages	21.1	137.5
II. Protestant Cantons					
French					
Neufchâtel	42.4	560	Vaud	43.5	352
German					
Bern	47.2	229	Schaffhausen	106.0	602
Basel (city)	34.5	323	Outer Appenzell	100.7	213
Basel (country)	33.0	288	Glaris	83.1	127
			Zurich	80.0	288
Averages	38.2	280	Averages	92.4	307
III. Cantons Mixed as to Religion					
Argau	40.0	195	Geneva	70.5	360
Grisons	30.9	116	Saint Goll	57.6	179
Averages	36.9	155	Averages	64.0	269

The same comparison, if made between French departments, gives the same result. Having classified them in eight categories according to the importance of their suicidal mortality, we discovered that the groups thus formed were arranged in the same order as with reference to divorces and separations (see Table 8-4):

Having shown this relation, let us try to explain it.

We shall mention only as a note the explanation Bertillon summarily suggested. According to that author, the number of suicides and that of divorces vary in parallel manner because both depend on the same factor: the greater or less frequency of peo-

Table 8.4

	Suicides per Million	Average of Divorces and Separations per 1,000 Marriages
1st group (5 departments)	Below 50	2.6
2nd group (18 departments)	From 51 to 75	2.9
3rd group (15 departments)	76 to 100	5.0
4th group (19 departments)	101 to 150	5.4
5th group (10 departments)	151 to 200	7.5
6th group (9 departments)	201 to 250	8.2
7th group (4 departments)	251 to 300	10.0
8th group (5 departments)	Above 300	12.4

ple with unstable equilibrium. There are actually, he says, more divorces in a country the more incompatible married couples it contains. The latter are recruited especially from among people of irregular lives, persons of poor character and intelligence, whom this temperament predisposes to suicide. The parallelism would then be due, not to the influence of divorce itself upon suicide, but to the fact that these two phenomena derive from a similar cause which they express differently. But this association of divorce with certain psychopathic flaws is made arbitrarily and without proof. There is no reason to think that there are 15 times as many unbalanced people in Switzerland as in Italy and from 6 to 7 times as many as in France, and yet in the first of these countries divorces are 15 times as frequent as in the second and about 7 times as frequent as in the third. Moreover, so far as suicide is concerned, we know how far purely individual conditions are from accounting for it. Furthermore, all that follows will show the inadequacy of this theory.

One must seek the cause of this remarkable relation not in the organic predispositions of people but in the intrinsic nature of divorce. As our first proposition here we may assert: in all countries for which we have the necessary data, suicides of divorced people are immensely more numerous than those of other portions of the population.

Thus, divorced persons of both sexes kill themselves between three and four times as often as married persons, although younger (40 years in France as against 46 years), and considerably more often than widowed persons in spite of the aggravation resulting for the latter from their advanced age. What is the explanation?

There is no doubt that the change of moral and material regimen which is a consequence of divorce is of some account in this result. But it does not sufficiently explain the matter. Widowhood is indeed as complete a disturbance of existence as divorce; it usually even has much more unhappy results, since it was not desired by husband and wife, while divorce is usually a deliverance for both. Yet divorced persons who, considering their age, should commit suicide only one half as often as widowed persons, do so more often everywhere, even twice as often in certain countries. This aggravation, to be represented by a coefficient between 2.5 and 4, does not depend on their changed condition in any way.

Let us refer to one of the propositions established above to discover the causes of this fact. . . . [I]n a given society the tendency of widowed persons to suicide was a function of the corresponding tendency of married

Suicides in a Million

	Unmarried Above 15 Years		Married		Widowed		Divorced	
	Men	Women	Men	Women	Men	Women	Men	Women
Prussia (1887–1889) *	360	120	430	90	1,471	215	1,875	290
Prussia (1883–1890) *	388	129	498	100	1,552	194	1,952	328
Baden (1885–1893)	45	93	460	85	1,172	171	1,328	—
Saxony (1847–1858)	—	—	481	120	1,242	240	3,102	312
Saxony (1876)	555.18†		821	146	—	—	3,252	389
Wurttemberg (1846–1860)	—	—	226	52	530	97	1,298	281
Wurttemberg (1873–1892)	251	—	218 †		405 †		796 †	

* There appears to be some error in the figures for Prussia here.—Ed
†Men and women combined.—Ed.

persons. While the latter are highly protected, the former enjoy an immunity less, to be sure, but still considerable, and the sex best protected by marriage is also that best protected in the state of widowhood. Briefly, when conjugal society is dissolved by the death of one of the couple, the effects which it had with reference to suicide continue to be felt in part by the survivor. . . . Then, however, is it not to be supposed that the same thing takes place when the marriage is interrupted, not by death, but by a judicial act, and that the aggravation which afflicts divorced persons is a result not of the divorce but of the marriage ended by divorce? It must be connected with some quality of the matrimonial society, the influence of which the couple continue to experience even when separated. If they have so strong an inclination to suicide, it is because they were already strongly inclined to it while living together and by the very effect of their common life.

Admitting so much, the correspondence between divorces and suicides becomes explicable. Actually, among the people where divorce is common, this peculiar effect of marriage in which divorce shares must necessarily be very wide-spread; for it is not confined to households predestined to legal separation. If it reaches its maximum intensity among them, it must also be found among the others, or the majority of the others, though to a lesser degree. For just as where there are many suicides, there are many attempted suicides, and just as mortality cannot grow without morbidity increasing simultaneously, so wherever there are many actual divorces there must be many households more or less close to divorce. The number of actual divorces cannot rise, accordingly, without the family condition predisposing to suicide also developing and becoming general in the same degree, and thus the two phenomena naturally vary in the same general direction.

9
Primitive Classification

Émile Durkheim and
Marcel Mauss

In his later writings, Durkheim showed an interest in those preindustrial peoples that had become the object of anthropology. Indeed, in *Primitive Classification* (1903), which he co-authored with his student and nephew Marcel Mauss, as well as in his later writings, he showed a familiarity with and made extensive use of the burgeoning body of anthropological research conducted around the turn of the century. The purpose of this particular book, as this summary selection indicates, is to show that the way we structure our world into classificatory schemas is determined by social relations. In other words, classifications derive from, and indeed are reflections of, preexisting forms of social organization. Here the power of society to provide the form and content through which we experience social life is revealed.

Primitive classifications are therefore not singular or exceptional, having no analogy with those employed by more civilized peoples; on the contrary, they seem to be connected, with no break in continuity, to the first scientific classifications. In fact, however different they may be in certain respects from the latter, they nevertheless have all their essential characteristics. First of all, like all sophisticated classifications, they are systems of hierarchized notions. Things are not simply arranged by them in the form of isolated groups, but these groups stand in fixed relationships to each other and together form a single whole. Moreover, these systems, like those of science, have a purely speculative purpose. Their object is not to facilitate action, but to advance understanding, to make intelligible the relations which

exist between things. Given certain concepts which are considered to be fundamental, the mind feels the need to connect to them the ideas which it forms about other things. Such classifications are thus intended, above all, to connect ideas, to unify knowledge; as such, they may be said without inexactitude to be scientific, and to constitute a first philosophy of nature.[1] The Australian does not divide the universe between the totems of his tribe with a view to regulating his conduct or even to justify his practice; it is because, the idea of the totem being cardinal for him, he is under a necessity to place everything else that he knows in relation to it. We may therefore think that the conditions on which these very ancient classifications depend may have played an important part in the genesis of the classificatory function in general.

Now it results from this study that the nature of these conditions is social. Far from it being the case, as Frazer seems to think, that the social relations of men are based on logical relations between things, in reality it is the former which have provided the prototype for the latter. According to him, men were divided into clans by a pre-existing classification of things; but, quite on the contrary, they classified things because they were divided by clans.

We have seen, indeed, how these classifications were modelled on the closest and most fundamental form of social organization. This, however, is not going far enough. Society was not simply a model which classificatory thought followed; it was its own divisions which served as divisions for the system of classification. The first logical categories were social categories; the first classes of things were classes of men, into which these things were integrated. It was because men were grouped, and thought of themselves in the form of groups, that in their ideas they grouped other things, and in the beginning the two modes of grouping were merged to the point of being indistinct. Moieties were the first genera; clans, the first species. Things were thought to be integral parts of society, and it was their place in society which determined their place in nature. We may even wonder whether the schematic manner in which genera are ordinarily conceived may not have depended in part on the same influences. It is a fact of current observation that the things which they comprise are generally imagined as situated in a sort of ideational milieu, with a more or less clearly delimited spatial circumscription. It is certainly not without cause that concepts and their interrelations have so often been represented by concentric and eccentric circles, interior and exterior to each other, etc. Might it not be that this tendency to imagine purely logical groupings in a form contrasting so much with their true nature originated in the fact that at first they were conceived in the form of social groups occupying, consequently, definite positions in space? And have we not in fact seen this spatial localization of genus and species in a fairly large number of very different societies?

Not only the external form of classes, but also the relations uniting them to each other, are of social origin. It is because human groups fit one into another—the sub-clan into the clan, the clan into the moiety, the moiety into the tribe—that groups of things are ordered in the same way. Their regular diminution in span, from genus to species, species to variety, and so on, comes from the equally diminishing extent presented by social groups as one leaves the largest and oldest and approaches the more recent and the more derivative. And if the totality of things is conceived as a single system, this is because society itself is seen in the same way. It is a whole, or rather it is the unique whole to which everything is related. Thus logical hierarchy is only another aspect of social hierarchy, and the unity of knowledge is nothing else than the very unity of the collectivity, extended to the universe.

Furthermore, the ties which unite things of the same group or different groups to each other are themselves conceived as social ties. We recalled in the beginning that the expressions by which we refer to these relations still have a moral significance; but whereas for us they are hardly more than metaphors, originally they meant what they said. Things of the same class were really considered as relatives of the individuals of the same social group, and consequently of each other. They are of "the same flesh", the same family. Logical relations are thus, in a sense, domestic

relations. Sometimes, too, as we have seen, they are comparable at all points with those which exist between a master and an object possessed, between a chief and his subjects. We may even wonder whether the idea of the pre-eminence of genus over species, which is so strange from a positivistic point of view, may not be seen here in its rudimentary form. Just as, for the realist, the general idea dominates the individual, so the clan totem dominates those of the sub-clans and, still more, the personal totems of individuals; and wherever the moiety has retained its original stability it has a sort of primacy over the divisions of which it is composed and the particular things which are included in them. Though he may be essentially Wartwut and partially Moiwiluk, the Wotjobaluk described by Howitt is above all a Krokitch or a Gamutch. Among the Zuñi, the animals symbolizing the six main clans are set in sovereign charge over their respective sub-clans and over creatures of all kinds which are grouped with them.

But if the foregoing has allowed us to understand how the notion of classes, linked to each other in a single system, could have been born, we still do not know what the forces were which induced men to divide things as they did between the classes. From the fact that the external form of the classification was furnished by society, it does not necessarily follow that the way in which the framework was used is due to reasons of the same origin. *A priori* it is very possible that motives of a quite different order should have determined the way in which things were connected and merged, or else, on the contrary, distinguished and opposed.

The particular conception of logical connexions which we now have permits us to reject this hypothesis. We have just seen, in fact, that they are represented in the form of familial connexions, or as relations of economic or political subordination; so that the same sentiments which are the basis of domestic, social, and other kinds of organization have been effective in this logical division of things also. The latter are attracted or opposed to each other in the same way as men are bound by kinship or opposed in the vendetta. They are merged as members of the same family are merged by common sentiment. That some are subordinate to others is analogous in every respect to the fact that an object possessed appears inferior to its owner, and likewise the subject to his master. It is thus states of the collective mind (*âme*) which gave birth to these groupings, and these states moreover are manifestly affective. There are sentimental affinities between things as between individuals, and they are classed according to these affinities.

We thus arrive at this conclusion: it is possible to classify other things than concepts, and otherwise than in accordance with the laws of pure understanding. For in order for it to be possible for ideas to be systematically arranged for reasons of sentiment, it is necessary that they should not be pure ideas, but that they should themselves be products of sentiment. And in fact, for those who are called primitives, a species of things is not a simple object of knowledge but corresponds above all to a certain sentimental attitude. All kinds of affective elements combine in the representation made of it. Religious emotions, notably, not only give it a special tinge, but attribute to it the most essential properties of which it is constituted. Things are above all sacred or profane, pure or impure, friends or enemies, favourable or unfavourable;[2] i.e. their most fundamental characteristics are only expressions of the way in which they affect social sensibility. The differences and resemblances which determine the fashion in which they are grouped are more affective than intellectual. This is how it happens that things change their nature, in a way, from society to society; it is because they affect the sentiments of groups differently. What is conceived in one as perfectly homogeneous is represented elsewhere as essentially heterogeneous. For us, space is formed of similar parts which are substitutable one for the other. We have seen, however, that for many peoples it is profoundly differentiated according to regions. This is because each region has its own affective value. Under the influence of diverse sentiments, it is connected with a special religious principle, and consequently it is endowed with virtues *sui generis* which distinguish it from all others. And it is this emotional value of notions which plays the preponderant part in the manner in which ideas

are connected or separated. It is the dominant characteristic in classification. It has quite often been said that man began to conceive things by relating them to himself. The above allows us to see more precisely what this anthropocentrism, which might better be called *sociocentrism*, consists of. The centre of the first schemes of nature is not the individual; it is society.[3] It is this that is objectified, not man. Nothing shows this more clearly than the way in which the Sioux retain the whole universe, in a way, within the limits of tribal space; and we have seen how universal space itself is nothing else than the site occupied by the tribe, only indefinitely extended beyond its real limits. It is by virtue of the same mental disposition that so many peoples have placed the centre of the world, "the navel of the earth", in their own political or religious capital,[4] i.e. at the place which is the centre of their moral life. Similarly, but in another order of ideas, the creative force of the universe and everything in it was first conceived as a mythical ancestor, the generator of the society.

This is how it is that the idea of a logical classification was so hard to form, as we showed at the beginning of this work. It is because a logical classification is a classification of concepts. Now a concept is the notion of a clearly determined group of things; its limits may be marked precisely. Emotion, on the contrary, is something essentially fluid and inconsistent. Its contagious influence spreads far beyond its point of origin, extending to everything about it, so that it is not possible to say where its power of propagation ends. States of an emotional nature necessarily possess the same characteristic. It is not possible to say where they begin or where they end; they lose themselves in each other, and mingle their properties in such a way that they cannot be rigorously categorized. From another point of view, in order to be able to mark out the limits of a class, it is necessary to have analysed the characteristics by which the things assembled in this class are recognized and by which they are distinguished. Now emotion is naturally refractory to analysis, or at least lends itself uneasily to it, because it is too complex. Above all when it has a collective origin it defies critical and rational examination. The pressure exerted by the group on each of its members does not permit individuals to judge freely the notions which society itself has elaborated and in which it has placed something of its personality. Such constructs are sacred for individuals. Thus the history of scientific classification is, in the last analysis, the history of the stages by which this element of social affectivity has progressively weakened, leaving more and more room for the reflective thought of individuals. But it is not the case that these remote influences which we have just studied have ceased to be felt today. They have left behind them an effect which survives and which is always present; it is the very cadre of all classification, it is the ensemble of mental habits by virtue of which we conceive things and facts in the form of co-ordinated or hierarchized groups.

This example shows what light sociology throws on the genesis, and consequently the functioning, of logical operations. What we have tried to do for classification might equally be attempted for the other functions or fundamental notions of the understanding. We have already had occasion to mention, in passing, how even ideas so abstract as those of time and space are, at each point in their history, closely connected with the corresponding social organization. The same method could help us likewise to understand the manner in which the ideas of cause, substance, and the different modes of reasoning, etc. were formed. As soon as they are posed in sociological terms, all these questions, so long debated by metaphysicians and psychologists, will at last be liberated from the tautologies in which they have languished. At least, this is a new way which deserves to be tried.

Endnotes

1. As such they are very clearly distinguished from what might be called technological classifications. It is probable that man has always classified, more or less clearly, the things on which he lived, according to the means he used to get them: for example, animals living in the water, or in the air or on the ground. But at first such groups were not connected with each other or systematized. They were divisions, distinctions of ideas, not schemes of classification. Moreover, it is evident that these distinctions are closely linked to practical concerns, of which they merely express certain aspects. It is for this reason that we have not spoken of them in this work, in which we have tried above all to throw some light on the origins of the logical procedure which is the basis of scientific classifications.

2. For the adherent of many cults, even now, foodstuffs are classified first of all into two main classes, fat and lean, and we know to what extent this classification is subjective.

3. De la Grasserie has developed ideas fairly similar to our own, though rather obscurely and above all without evidence (1899, chap. III).

4. Something understandable enough for the Romans and even the Zuñi, but less so for the inhabitants of Easter Island, called Te Pito-te Henua (navel of the earth); but the idea is perfectly natural everywhere.

10
The Human Meaning of Religion

Émile Durkheim

In his final—and what some take to be his most important—work, *The Elementary Forms of the Religious Life* (1912), Durkheim looks to "primitive" religions in order to ascertain the significance of religion for social life. The earliest manifestations of religious belief and practice are seen as the building blocks for later, more complex expressions of religious phenomena. Thus, if we want to get at the essence of religion, Durkheim thought it appropriate to go to the least complex articulation of the religious. In this passage, he offers a definition of religion that emphasizes not simply the socially constructed nature of the religious but makes the more controversial claim that religion is a mirror of society and that in fact what people take to be the realm of the sacred is society itself.

At the beginning of this work we announced that the religion whose study we were taking up contained within it the most characteristic elements of the religious life. The exactness of this proposition may now be verified. Howsoever simple the system which we have studied may be, we have found within it all the great ideas and the principal ritual attitudes which are at the basis of even the most advanced religions: the division of things into sacred and profane, the notions of the soul, of spirits, of mythical personalities, and of a national and even international divinity, a negative cult with ascetic practices which are its exaggerated form, rites of oblation and communion, imitative rites, commemorative rites and expia-

tory rites; nothing essential is lacking. We are thus in a position to hope that the results at which we have arrived are not peculiar to totemism alone, but can aid us in an understanding of what religion in general is.

It may be objected that one single religion, whatever its field of extension may be, is too narrow a base for such an induction. We have not dreamed for a moment of ignoring the fact that an extended verification may add to the authority of a theory, but it is equally true that when a law has been proven by one well-made experiment, this proof is valid universally. If in one single case a scientist succeeded in finding out the secret of the life of even the most protoplasmic creature that can be imagined, the truths thus obtained would be applicable to all living beings, even the most advanced. Then if, in our studies of these very humble societies, we have really succeeded in discovering some of the elements out of which the most fundamental religious notions are made up, there is no reason for not extending the most general results of our researches to other religions. In fact, it is inconceivable that the same effect may be due now to one cause, now to another, according to the circumstances, unless the two causes are at bottom only one. A single idea cannot express one reality here and another one there, unless the duality is only apparent. If among certain peoples the ideas of sacredness, the soul and God are to be explained sociologically, it should be presumed scientifically that, in principle, the same explanation is valid for all the peoples among whom these same ideas are found with the same essential characteristics. Therefore, supposing that we have not been deceived, certain at least of our conclusions can be legitimately generalized. The moment has come to disengage these. And an induction of this sort, having at its foundation a clearly defined experiment, is less adventurous than many summary generalizations which, while attempting to reach the essence of religion at once, without resting upon the careful analysis of any religion in particular, greatly risk losing themselves in space.

***

The theorists who have undertaken to explain religion in rational terms have generally seen in it before all else a system of ideas, corresponding to some determined object. This object has been conceived in a multitude of ways: nature, the infinite, the unknowable, the ideal, etc.; but these differences matter but little. In any case, it was the conceptions and beliefs which were considered as the essential elements of religion. As for the rites, from this point of view they appear to be only an external translation, contingent and material, of these internal states which alone pass as having any intrinsic value. This conception is so commonly held that generally the disputes of which religion is the theme turn about the question whether it can conciliate itself with science or not, that is to say, whether or not, there is a place beside our scientific knowledge for another form of thought which would be specifically religious.

But the believers, the men who lead the religious life and have a direct sensation of what it really is, object to this way of regarding it, saying that it does not correspond to their daily experience. In fact, they feel that the real function of religion is not to make us think, to enrich our knowledge, nor to add to the conceptions which we owe to science others of another origin and another character, but rather, it is to make us act, to aid us to live. The believer who has communicated with his god is not merely a man who sees new truths of which the unbeliever is ignorant; he is a man who is *stronger*. He feels within him more force, either to endure the trials of existence, or to conquer them. It is as though he were raised above the miseries of the world, because he is raised above his condition as a mere man; he believes that he is saved from evil, under whatever form he may conceive this evil. The first article in every creed is the belief in salvation by faith. But it is hard to see how a mere idea could have this efficacy. An idea is in reality only a part of ourselves; then how could it confer upon us powers superior to those which we have of our own nature? Howsoever rich it might be in affective virtues, it could add nothing to our natural vitality; for it could only release the motive powers which are within us, neither creating them nor increasing them. From the mere fact that we consider an object worthy of being loved and

sought after, it does not follow that we feel ourselves stronger afterwards; it is also necessary that this object set free energies superior to these which we ordinarily have at our command and also that we have some means of making these enter into us and unite themselves to our interior lives. Now for that, it is not enough that we think of them; it is also indispensable that we place ourselves within their sphere of action, and that we set ourselves where we may best feel their influence; in a word, it is necessary that we act, and that we repeat the acts thus necessary every time we feel the need of renewing their effects. From this point of view, it is readily seen how that group of regularly repeated acts which form the cult get their importance. In fact, whoever has really practiced a religion knows very well that it is the cult which gives rise to these impressions of joy, of interior peace, of serenity, of enthusiasm which are, for the believer, an experimental proof of his beliefs. The cult is not simply a system of signs by which the faith is outwardly translated; it is a collection of the means by which this is created and recreated periodically. Whether it consists in material acts or mental operations, it is always this which is efficacious.

Our entire study rests upon this postulate that the unanimous sentiment of the believers of all times cannot be purely illusory. Together with a recent apologist of the faith[1] we admit that these religious beliefs rest upon a specific experience whose demonstrative value is, in one sense, not one bit inferior to that of scientific experiments, though different from them. We, too, think that "a tree is known by its fruits,"[2] and that fertility is the best proof of what the roots are worth. But from the fact that a "religious experience," if we choose to call it this, does exist and that it has a certain foundation—and, by the way, is there any experience which has none?—it does not follow that the reality which is its foundation conforms objectively to the idea which believers have of it. The very fact that the fashion in which it has been conceived has varied infinitely in different times is enough to prove that none of these conceptions express it adequately. If a scientist states it as an axiom that the sensations of heat and light which we feel correspond to some objective cause, he does not conclude that this is what it appears to the senses to be. Likewise, even if the impressions which the faithful feel are not imaginary, still they are in no way privileged intuitions; there is no reason for believing that they inform us better upon the nature of their object than do ordinary sensations upon the nature of bodies and their properties. In order to discover what this object consists of, we must submit them to an examination and elaboration analogous to that which has substituted for the sensuous idea of the world another which is scientific and conceptual. This is precisely what we have tried to do, and we have seen that this reality, which mythologies have represented under so many different forms, but which is the universal and eternal objective cause of these sensations *sui generis* out of which religious experience is made, is society. We have shown what moral forces it develops and how it awakens this sentiment of a refuge, of a shield and of a guardian support which attaches the believer to his cult. It is that which raises him outside himself; it is even that which made him. For that which makes a man is the totality of the intellectual property which constitutes civilization, and civilization is the work of society. Thus is explained the preponderating rôle of the cult in all religions, whichever they may be. This is because society cannot make its influence felt unless it is in action, and it is not in action unless the individuals who compose it are assembled together and act in common. It is by common action that it takes consciousness of itself and realizes its position; it is before all else an active co-operation. The collective ideas and sentiments are even possible only owing to these exterior movements which symbolize them, as we have established.[3] Then it is action which dominates the religious life, because of the mere fact that it is society which is its source.

In addition to all the reasons which have been given to justify this conception, a final one may be added here, which is the result of our whole work. As we have progressed, we have established the fact that the fundamental categories of thought, and consequently of science, are of religious origin. We have seen that the same is true for magic and con-

sequently for the different processes which have issued from it. On the other hand, it has long been known that up until a relatively advanced moment of evolution, moral and legal rules have been indistinguishable from ritual prescriptions. In summing up, then, it may be said that nearly all the great social institutions have been born in religion.[4] Now in order that these principal aspects of the collective life may have commenced by being only varied aspects of the religious life, it is obviously necessary that the religious life be the eminent form and, as it were, the concentrated expression of the whole collective life. If religion has given birth to all that is essential in society, it is because the idea of society is the soul of religion.

Religious forces are therefore human forces, moral forces. It is true that since collective sentiments can become conscious of themselves only by fixing themselves upon external objects, they have not been able to take form without adopting some of their characteristics from other things: they have thus acquired a sort of physical nature; in this way they have come to mix themselves with the life of the material world, and then have considered themselves capable of explaining what passes there. But when they are considered only from this point of view and in this rôle, only their most superficial aspect is seen. In reality, the essential elements of which these collective sentiments are made have been borrowed by the understanding. It ordinarily seems that they should have a human character only when they are conceived under human forms;[5] but even the most impersonal and the most anonymous are nothing else than objectified sentiments.

It is only by regarding religion from this angle that it is possible to see its real significance. If we stick closely to appearances, rites often give the effect of purely manual operations: they are anointings, washings, meals. To consecrate something, it is put in contact with a source of religious energy, just as today a body is put in contact with a source of heat or electricity to warm or electrify it; the two processes employed are not essentially different. Thus understood, religious technique seems to be a sort of mystic mechanics. But these material manœuvres are only the external envelope under which the mental operations are hidden. Finally, there is no question of exercising a physical constraint upon blind and, incidentally, imaginary forces, but rather of reaching individual consciousnesses of giving them a direction and of disciplining them. It is sometimes said that inferior religions are materialistic. Such an expression is inexact. All religions, even the crudest, are in a sense spiritualistic: for the powers they put in play are before all spiritual, and also their principal object is to act upon the moral life. Thus it is seen that whatever has been done in the name of religion cannot have been done in vain: for it is necessarily the society that did it, and it is humanity that has reaped the fruits.

But, it is said, what society is it that has thus made the basis of religion? Is it the real society, such as it is and acts before our very eyes, with the legal and moral organization which it has laboriously fashioned during the course of history? This is full of defects and imperfections. In it, evil goes beside the good, injustice often reigns supreme, and the truth is often obscured by error. How could anything so crudely organized inspire the sentiments of love, the ardent enthusiasm and the spirit of abnegation which all religions claim of their followers? These perfect beings which are gods could not have taken their traits from so mediocre, and sometimes even so base a reality.

But, on the other hand, does someone think of a perfect society, where justice and truth would be sovereign, and from which evil in all its forms would be banished forever? No one would deny that this is in close relations with the religious sentiment; for, they would say, it is towards the realization of this that all religions strive. But that society is not an empirical fact, definite and observable; it is a fancy, a dream with which men have lightened their sufferings, but in which they have never really lived. It is merely an idea which comes to express our more or less obscure aspirations towards the good, the beautiful and the ideal. Now these aspirations have their roots in us; they come from the very depths of our being; then there is nothing outside of us which can account for them. Moreover, they are already reli-

gious in themselves; thus it would seem that the ideal society presupposes religion, far from being able to explain it.[6]

But, in the first place, things are arbitrarily simplified when religion is seen only on its idealistic side: in its way, it is realistic. There is no physical or moral ugliness, there are no vices or evils which do not have a special divinity. There are gods of theft and trickery, of lust and war, of sickness and of death. Christianity itself, howsoever high the idea which it has made of the divinity may be, has been obliged to give the spirit of evil a place in its mythology. Satan is an essential piece of the Christian system; even if he is an impure being, he is not a profane one. The anti-god is a god, inferior and subordinated, it is true, but nevertheless endowed with extended powers; he is even the object of rites, at least of negative ones. Thus religion, far from ignoring the real society and making abstraction of it, is in its image; it reflects all its aspects, even the most vulgar and the most repulsive. All is to be found there, and if in the majority of cases we see the good victorious over evil, life over death, the powers of light over the powers of darkness, it is because reality is not otherwise. If the relation between these two contrary forces were reversed, life would be impossible; but, as a matter of fact, it maintains itself and even tends to develop.

But if, in the midst of these mythologies and theologies we see reality clearly appearing, it is nonetheless true that it is found there only in an enlarged, transformed and idealized form. In this respect, the most primitive religions do not differ from the most recent and the most refined. For example, we have seen how the Arunta place at the beginning of time a mythical society whose organization exactly reproduces that which still exists today; it includes the same clans and phratries, it is under the same matrimonial rules and it practises the same rites. But the personages who compose it are ideal beings, gifted with powers and virtues to which common mortals cannot pretend. Their nature is not only higher, but it is different, since it is at once animal and human. The evil powers there undergo a similar metamorphosis: evil itself is, as it were, made sublime and idealized. The question now raises itself of whence this idealization comes.

Some reply that men have a natural faculty for idealizing, that is to say, of substituting for the real world another different one, to which they transport themselves by thought. But that is merely changing the terms of the problem; it is not resolving it or even advancing it. This systematic idealization is an essential characteristic of religions. Explaining them by an innate power of idealization is simply replacing one word by another which is the equivalent of the first; it is as if they said that men have made religions because they have a religious nature. Animals know only one world, the one which they perceive by experience, internal as well as external. Men alone have the faculty of conceiving the ideal, of adding something to the real. Now where does this singular privilege come from? Before making it an initial fact or a mysterious virtue which escapes science, we must be sure that it does not depend upon empirically determinable conditions.

The explanation of religion which we have proposed has precisely this advantage, that it gives an answer to this question. For our definition of the sacred is that it is something added to and above the real: now the ideal answers to this same definition; we cannot explain one without explaining the other. In fact, we have seen that if collective life awakens religious thought on reaching a certain degree of intensity, it is because it brings about a state of effervescence which changes the conditions of psychic activity. Vital energies are over-excited, passions more active, sensations stronger; there are even some which are produced only at this moment. A man does not recognize himself; he feels himself transformed and consequently he transforms the environment which surrounds him. In order to account for the very particular impressions which he receives, he attributes to the things with which he is in most direct contact properties which they have not: exceptional powers and virtues which the objects of everyday experience do not possess. In a word, above the real world where his profane life passes he has placed another which, in one sense, does not exist except in thought, but to which he attributes a higher sort of dignity than to the first. Thus, from a double point of view it is an ideal world.

The formation of the ideal world is therefore not an irreducible fact which escapes science; it depends upon conditions which observation can touch; it is a natural product of social life. For a society to become conscious of itself and maintain at the necessary degree of intensity the sentiments which it thus attains, it must assemble and concentrate itself. Now this concentration, brings about an exaltation of the mental life which takes form in a group of ideal conceptions where is portrayed the new life thus awakened; they correspond to this new set of psychical forces which is added to those which we have at our disposition for the daily tasks of existence. A society can neither create itself nor recreate itself without at the same time creating an ideal. This creation is not a sort of work of supererogation for it, by which it would complete itself, being already formed; it is the act by which it is periodically made and remade. Therefore when some oppose the ideal society to the real society, like two antagonists which would lead us in opposite directions, they materialize and oppose abstractions. The ideal society is not outside of the real society; it is a part of it. Far from being divided between them as between two poles which mutually repel each other, we cannot hold to one without holding to the other. For a society is not made up merely of the mass of individuals who compose it, the ground which they occupy, the things which they use and the movements which they perform, but above all is the idea which it forms of itself. It is undoubtedly true that it hesitates over the manner in which it ought to conceive itself; it feels itself drawn in divergent directions. But these conflicts which break forth are not between the ideal and reality, but between two different ideals, that of yesterday and that of today, that which has the authority of tradition and that which has the hope of the future. There is surely a place for investigating whence these ideals evolve; but whatever solution may be given to this problem, it still remains that all passes in the world of the ideal. Thus the collective ideal which religion expresses is far from being due to a vague innate power of the individual, but it is rather at the school of collective life that the individual has learned to idealize. It is in assimilating the ideals elaborated by society that he has become capable of conceiving the ideal. It is society which, by leading him within its sphere of action, has made him acquire the need of raising himself above the world of experience and has at the same time furnished him with the means of conceiving another. For society has constructed this new world in constructing itself, since it is society which this expresses. Thus both with the individual and in the group, the faculty of idealizing has nothing mysterious about it. It is not a sort of luxury which a man could get along without, but a condition of his very existence. He could not be a social being, that is to say, he could not be a man, if he had not acquired it. It is true that in incarnating themselves in individuals, collective ideals tend to individualize themselves. Each understands them after his own fashion and marks them with his own stamp; he suppresses certain elements and adds others. Thus the personal ideal disengages itself from the social ideal in proportion as the individual personality develops itself and becomes an autonomous source of action. But if we wish to understand this aptitude, so singular in appearance, of living outside of reality, it is enough to connect it with the social conditions upon which it depends.

Therefore it is necessary to avoid seeing in this theory of religion a simple restatement of historical materialism: that would be misunderstanding our thought to an extreme degree. In showing that religion is something essentially social we do not mean to say that it confines itself to translating into another language the material forms of society and its immediate vital necessities. It is true that we take it as evident that social life depends upon its material foundation and bears its mark, just as the mental life of an individual depends upon his nervous system and in fact his whole organism. But collective consciousness is something more than a mere epiphenomenon of its morphological basis, just as individual consciousness is something more than a simple efflorescence of the nervous system. In order that the former may appear, a synthesis *sui generis* of particular consciousnesses is required. Now this synthesis has the effect of disengaging a whole world of sentiments, ideas and images which, once born, obey laws all their own. They attract each other, repel each other, unite, divide themselves, and multiply, though these combinations are not commanded and necessitated by the condition of the underlying reality. The life thus brought into being even enjoys so great an independence that it sometimes indulges in manifestations with no purpose or utility of any sort, for the mere pleasure of affirming itself. We have shown that this is often precisely the case with ritual activity and mythological thought.[7]

But if religion is the product of social causes, how can we explain the individual cult and the universalistic character of certain religions? If it is born *in foro externo*, how has it been able to pass into the inner conscience of the individual and penetrate there ever more and more profoundly? If it is the work of definite and individualized societies, how has it been able to detach itself from them, even to the point of being conceived as something common to all humanity? In the course of our studies, we have met with the germs of individual religion and of religious cosmopolitanism, and we have seen how they were formed; thus we possess the more general elements of the reply which is to be given to this double question. We have shown how the religious force which animates the clan particularizes itself, by incarnating itself in particular consciousnesses. Thus secondary sacred beings are formed; each individual has his own, made in his own image associated to his own intimate life, bound up with his own destiny; it is the soul, the individual totem, the protecting ancestor, etc. These beings are the object of rites which the individual can celebrate by himself, outside of any group; this is the first form of the individual cult. To be sure, it is only a very rudimentary cult; but since the personality of the individual is still only slightly marked, and but little value is attributed to it, the cult which expresses it could hardly be expected to be very highly developed as yet. But as individuals have differentiated themselves more and more and the value of an individual has increased, the corresponding cult has taken a relatively greater place in the totality of the religious life and at the same time it is more fully closed to outside influences.

Thus the existence of individual cults implies nothing which contradicts or embarrasses the sociological interpretation of religion; for the religious forces to which it addresses itself are only the individualized forms of collective forces. Therefore, even when religion seems to be entirely within the individual conscience, it is still in society that it finds the living source from which it is nourished. We are now able to appreciate the value of the radical individualism which would make religion something purely individual: it misunderstands the fundamental conditions of the religious life. If up to the present it has remained in the stage of theoretical aspirations which have never been realized, it is because it is unrealizable. A philosophy may well be elaborated in the silence of the interior imagination, but not so a faith. For, before all else, a faith is warmth, life, enthusiasm, the exaltation of the whole mental life, the raising of the individual above himself. Now how could he add to the energies which he possesses without going outside himself? How could he surpass himself merely by his own forces? The only source of life at which we can morally reanimate ourselves is that formed by the society of our fellow beings; the only moral forces with which we can sustain and increase our own are those which we get from others. Let us even admit that there really are beings more or less analogous to those which the mythologies represent. In order that they may exercise over souls the useful direction which is their reason for existence, it is necessary that men believe in them. Now these beliefs are active only when they are partaken by many. A man cannot retain them any length of time by a purely personal effort; it is not thus that they are born or that they are acquired; it is even doubtful if they can be kept under these conditions. In fact, a man who has a veritable faith feels an invincible need of spreading it: therefore he leaves his isolation, approaches others and seeks to convince them, and it is the ardour of the convictions which

he arouses that strengthens his own. It would quickly weaken if it remained alone.

It is the same with religious universalism as with this individualism. Far from being an exclusive attribute of certain very great religions, we have found it, not at the base, it is true, but at the summit of the Australian system. Bunjil, Daramulum or Baiame are not simple tribal gods; each of them is recognized by a number of different tribes. In a sense, their cult is international. This conception is therefore very near to that found in the most recent theologies. So certain writers have felt it their duty to deny its authenticity, howsoever incontestable this may be.

And we have been able to show how this has been formed.

Neighboring tribes of a similar civilization cannot fail to be in constant relations with each other. All sorts of circumstances give an occasion for it: besides commerce, which is still rudimentary, there are marriages; these international marriages are very common in Australia. In the course of these meetings, men naturally become conscious of the moral relationship which united them. They have the same social organization, the same division into phratries, clans and matrimonial classes; they practise the same rites of initiation, or wholly similar ones. Mutual loans and treaties result in reinforcing these spontaneous resemblances. The gods to which these manifestly identical institutions were attached could hardly have remained distinct in their minds. Everything tended to bring them together and consequently, even supposing that each tribe elaborated the notion independently, they must necessarily have tended to confound themselves with each other. Also, it is probable that it was in inter-tribal assemblies that they were first conceived. For they are chiefly the gods of initiation, and in the initiation ceremonies, the different tribes are usually represented. So if sacred beings are formed which are connected with no geographically determined society, that is not because they have an extra-social origin. It is because there are other groups above these geographically determined ones, whose contours are less clearly marked: they have no fixed frontiers, but include all sorts of more or less neighbouring and related tribes. The particular social life thus created tends to spread itself over an area with no definite limits. Naturally the mythological personages who correspond to it have the same character; their sphere of influence is not limited; they go beyond the particular tribes and their territory. They are the great international gods.

Now there is nothing in this situation which it peculiar to Australian societies. There is no people and no state which is not a part of another society, more or less unlimited, which embraces all the peoples and all the states with which the first comes in contact, either directly or indirectly; there is no national life which is not dominated by a collective life of an international nature. In proportion as we advance in history, these international groups acquire a greater importance and extent. Thus we see how, in certain cases, this universalistic tendency has been able to develop itself to the point of affecting not only the higher ideas of the religious system, but even the principles upon which it rests. . . .

Endnotes

1. William James, *The Varieties of Religious Experience*.

2. Quoted by James, *op. cit.*, p. 20.

3. See above, pp. 262 ff.

4. Only one form of social activity has not yet been expressly attached to religion: that is economic activity. Sometimes processes that are derived from magic have, by that fact alone, an origin that is indirectly religious. Also, economic value is a sort of power or efficacy, and we know the religious origins of the idea of power. Also, richness can confer *mana;* therefore it has it. Hence it is seen that the ideas of economic value and of religious value are not without connection. But the question of the nature of these connections has not yet been studied.

5. It is for this reason that Frazer and even Preuss set impersonal religious forces outside of, or at least on the threshold of religion, to attach them to magic.

6. Boutroux, *Science et Religion*, pp. 206–207.

7. See above, pp. 423 ff. On this same question, see also our article, "Représentations individuelles et représentations collectives," in the *Revue de Métaphysique*, May, 1898.

III. Max Weber

11

'Objectivity' in Social Science and Social Policy

Max Weber

Max Weber's (1864–1920) quest for the construction of an empirical science of social life differed from Durkheim's. Trained in both history and economics, Weber did not abandon these disciplines when he turned to sociology; instead, he sought to weave them into sociology. Thus, whereas Durkheim wanted to differentiate sociology from other disciplines, Weber was interested in interconnections among disciplines. Moreover, as this essay (first published in 1904) illustrates, his idea of an objective science was shaped by his conviction about the perspectival nature of knowledge and the relativity of values. He advocated a sociology concerned not merely with causal explanation, but with interpretation, or *Verstehen*. What the sociologist wants to learn, Weber suggests here, entails both explanation and interpretation. For Weber, causal analysis is a preliminary to inquiring into matters related to what he refers to in this passage as the cultural significance of social phenomena.

There is no absolutely "objective" scientific analysis of culture—or put perhaps more narrowly but certainly not essentially differently for our purposes—of "social phenomena" independent of special and "one-sided" viewpoints according to which—expressly or tacitly, consciously or unconsciously—they are selected, analyzed and organized for expository purposes. The reasons for this lie in the character of the cognitive goal of all research

in social science which seeks to transcend the purely formal treatment of the legal or conventional norms regulating social life.

The type of social science in which we are interested is an *empirical science* of concrete *reality* (*Wirklichkeitswissenschaft*). Our aim is the understanding of the characteristic uniqueness of the reality in which we move. We wish to understand on the one hand the relationships and the cultural significance of individual events in their contemporary manifestations and on the other the causes of their being historically *so* and not *otherwise*. Now, as soon as we attempt to reflect about the way in which life confronts us in immediate concrete situations, it presents an infinite multiplicity of successively and coexistently emerging and disappearing events, both "within" and "outside" ourselves. The absolute infinitude of this multiplicity is seen to remain undiminished even when our attention is focused on a single "object," for instance, a concrete act of exchange, as soon as we seriously attempt an exhaustive description of *all* the individual components of this "individual phenomena," to say nothing of explaining it casually. All the analysis of infinite reality which the finite human mind can conduct rests on the tacit assumption that only a finite portion of this reality constitutes the object of scientific investigation, and that only it is "important" in the sense of being "worthy of being known." But what are the criteria by which this segment is selected? It has often been thought that the decisive criterion in the cultural sciences, too, was in the last analysis, the "regular" recurrence of certain causal relationships. The "laws" which we are able to perceive in the infinitely manifold stream of events must—according to this conception—contain the scientifically "essential" aspect of reality. As soon as we have shown some causal relationship to be a "law," i.e., if we have shown it to be universally valid by means of comprehensive historical induction or have made it immediately and tangibly plausible according to our subjective experience, a great number of similar cases order themselves under the formula thus attained. Those elements in each individual event which are left unaccounted for by the selection of their elements subsumable under the "law" are considered as scientifically unintegrated residues which will be taken care of in the further perfection of the system of "laws." Alternatively they will be viewed as "accidental" and therefore scientifically unimportant *because* they do not fit into the structure of the "law"; in other words, they are not typical of the event and hence can only be the objects of "idle curiosity." Accordingly, even among the followers of the Historical School we continually find the attitude which declares that the ideal which all the sciences, including the cultural sciences, serve and towards which they should strive even in the remote future is a system of propositions from which reality can be "deduced." As is well known, a leading natural scientist believed that he could designate the (factually unattainable) ideal goal of such a treatment of cultural reality as a sort of *"astronomical"* knowledge.

Let us not, for our part, spare ourselves the trouble of examining these matters more closely—however often they have already been discussed. The first thing that impresses one is that the "astronomical" knowledge which was referred to is not a system of laws at all. On the contrary, the laws which it presupposes have been taken from other disciplines like mechanics. But it too concerns itself with the question of the *individual* consequence which the working of these laws in an unique *configuration* produces, since it is these individual configurations which are *significant* for us. Every individual constellation which it "explains" or predicts is causally explicable only as the consequence of another equally individual constellation which has preceded it. As far back as we may go into the grey mist of the far-off past, the reality to which the laws apply always remains equally *individual*, equally *undeducible* from laws. A cosmic "primeval state" which had no individual character or less individual character than the cosmic reality of the present would naturally be a meaningless notion. But is

there not some trace of similar ideas in our field in those propositions sometimes derived from natural law and sometimes verified by the observation of "primitives," concerning an economic-social "primeval state" free from historical "accidents," and characterized by phenomena such as "primitive agrarian communism," sexual "promiscuity," etc., from which individual historical development emerges by a sort of fall from grace into concreteness?

The social-scientific interest has its point of departure, of course, in the *real*, i.e., concrete, individually-structured configuration of our cultural life in its universal relationships which are themselves no less individually structured, and in its development out of other social cultural conditions, which themselves are obviously likewise individually structured. It is clear here that the situation which we illustrated by reference to astronomy as a limiting case (which is regularly drawn on by logicians for the same purpose) appears in a more accentuated form. Whereas in astronomy, the heavenly bodies are of interest to us only in their *quantitative* and exact aspects, the *qualitative* aspect of phenomena concerns us in the social sciences. To this should be added that in the social sciences we are concerned with psychological and intellectual (*geistig*) phenomena the empathic understanding of which is naturally a problem of a specifically different type from those which the schemes of the exact natural sciences in general can or seek to solve. Despite that, this distinction in itself is not a distinction in principle, as it seems at first glance. Aside from pure mechanics, even the exact natural sciences do not proceed without qualitative categories. Furthermore, in our own field we encounter the idea (which is obviously distorted) that at least the phenomena characteristic of a money-economy—which are basic to our culture—are quantifiable and on that account subject to formulation as "laws." Finally it depends on the breadth or narrowness of one's definition of "law" as to whether one will also include regularities which because they are not quantifiable are not subject to numerical analysis. Especially insofar as the influence of psychological and intellectual (*geistig*) factors is concerned, it does not in any case exclude the establishment of *rules* governing rational conduct. Above all, the point of view still persists which claims that the task of psychology is to play a role comparable to mathematics for the *Geisteswissenschaften* in the sense that it analyzes the complicated phenomena of social life into their psychic conditions and effects, reduces them to their most elementary possible psychic factors and then analyzes their functional interdependences. Thereby, a sort of "chemistry" if not "mechanics" of the psychic foundations of social life would be created. Whether such investigations can produce valuable and—what is something else—useful results for the cultural sciences, we cannot decide here. But this would be irrelevant to the question as to whether the aim of social-economic knowledge in our sense, i.e., knowledge of *reality* with respect to its cultural *significance* and its causal relationships can be attained through the quest for recurrent sequences. Let us assume that we have succeeded by means of psychology or otherwise in analyzing all the observed and imaginable relationships of social phenomena into some ultimate elementary "factors," that we have made an exhaustive analysis and classification of them and then formulated rigorously exact laws covering their behavior. What would be the significance of these results for our knowledge of the *historically* given culture or any individual phase thereof, such as capitalism, in its development and cultural significance? As an analytical tool, it would be as useful as a textbook of organic chemical combinations would be for our knowledge of the biogenetic aspect of the animal and plant world. In each case, certainly an important and useful preliminary step would have been taken. In neither case can concrete reality be deduced from "laws" and "factors." This is not because some higher mysterious powers reside in living phenomena (such as "dominants," "entelechies," or whatever they might be called). This, however, is a problem in its own right. The real reason is that the analysis of reality is concerned with the *configuration* into which those (hypothetical!) "factors" are arranged to form a cultural phenomenon which is historically significant to us. Furthermore, if we wish to "explain" this individual configuration "causally" we must invoke other equally individual configurations on the basis of which we will explain it with the aid of those (hypothetical!) "laws."

The determination of those (hypothetical) "laws" and "factors" would in any case only be the first of the many options which would lead us to the desired type of knowledge. The analysis of the historically given individual configuration of those "factors" and their *significant* concrete interaction, conditioned by their historical context and especially the *rendering intelligible* of the basis and type of this significance would be the next task to be achieved. This task must be achieved, it is true, by the utilization of the preliminary analysis but it is nonetheless an entirely new and *distinct* task. The tracing as far into the past as possible of the individual features of these historically evolved configurations which are *contemporaneously* significant, and their historical explanation by antecedent and equally individual configurations would be the third task. Finally the prediction of possible future constellations would be a conceivable fourth task.

For all these purposes, clear concepts and the knowledge of those (hypothetical) "laws" are obviously of great value as heuristic means—but only as such. Indeed they are quite indispensable for this purpose. But even in this function their limitations become evident at a decisive point. In stating this, we arrive at the decisive feature of the method of the cultural sciences. We have designated as "cultural sciences" those disciplines which analyze the phenomena of life in terms of their cultural significance. The *significance* of a configuration of cultural phenomena and the basis of this significance cannot however be derived and rendered intelligible by a system of analytical laws (*Gesetzesbegriffen*), however perfect it may be, since the significance of cultural events presupposes a *value-orientation* towards these events. The concept of culture is a *value-concept*. Empirical reality becomes "culture" to us because and insofar as we relate it to *value-ideas*. It includes those segments and only those segments of reality which have become significant to us because of this value-relevance. Only a small portion of existing concrete reality is colored by our value-conditioned interest and it alone is significant to us. It is significant because it reveals relationships which are important to us due to their connection with our values. Only because and to the extent that this is the case is it worthwhile for us to know it in its individual features. We cannot discover, however, what is meaningful to us by means of a "presuppositionless" investigation of empirical data. Rather perception of its meaningfulness to us is the presupposition of its becoming an *object* of investigation. Meaningfulness naturally does not coincide with laws as such, and the more general the law the less the coincidence. For the specific meaning which a phenomenon has for us is naturally *not* to be found in those relationships which it shares with many other phenomena.

The focus of attention on reality under the guidance of values which lend it significance and the selection and ordering of the phenomona which are thus affected in the light of their cultural significance is entirely different from the analysis of reality in terms of laws and general concepts. Neither of these two types of the analysis of reality has any necessary logical relationship with the other. They can coincide in individual instances but it would be most disastrous if their occasional coincidence caused us to think that they were not distinct *in principle*. The *cultural significance* of a phenomenon, e.g., the significance of exchange in a money economy, can be the fact that it exists on a mass scale as a fundamental component of modern culture. But the historical fact that it plays this role must be causally explained in order to render its cultural significance understandable. The analysis of the *general* aspects of exchange and the technique of the market is a—highly important and indispensable—*preliminary task*. For not only does this type of analysis leave unanswered the question as to how exchange historically acquired its fundamental significance in the modern world; but above all else, the fact with which we are primarily concerned, namely, the *cultural significance* of the money-economy, for the sake of which we are interested in the description of exchange technique and for the sake of which alone a science exists which deals with that tech-

nique—is not derivable from any "law." The *generic features* of exchange, purchase, etc., interest the jurist—but we are concerned with the analysis of the *cultural significance* of the concrete *historical* fact that today exchange exists on a mass scale. When we require an explanation, when we wish to understand what distinguishes the social-economic aspects of our culture for instance from that of antiquity in which exchange showed precisely the same generic traits as it does today and when we raise the question as to where the significance of "money economy" lies, logical principles of quite heterogeneous derivation enter into the investigation. We will apply those concepts with which we are provided by the investigation of the general features of economic mass phenomena—indeed, insofar as they are relevant to the meaningful aspects of our culture, we shall use them as *means* of exposition. The *goal* of our investigation is not reached through the exposition of those laws and concepts, precise as it may be. The question as to what should be the object of universal conceptualization cannot be decided "presuppositionlessly" but only with reference to the *significance* which certain segments of that infinite multiplicity which we call "commerce" have for culture. We seek knowledge of an historical phenomenon, meaning by historical: significant in its individuality (*Eigenart*). And the decisive element in this is that only through the presupposition that a finite part alone of the infinite variety of phenomena is significant, does the knowledge of an individual phenomenon become logically meaningful. Even with the widest imaginable knowledge of "laws," we are helpless in the face of the question: how is the *causal explanation* of an *individual* fact possible—since a *description* of even the smallest slice of reality can never be exhaustive? The number and type of causes which have influenced any given event are always infinite and there is nothing in the things themselves to set some of them apart as alone meriting attention. A chaos of "existential judgments" about countless individual events would be the only result of a serious attempt to analyze reality "without presuppositions." And even this result is only seemingly possible, since every single perception discloses on closer examination an infinite number of constituent perceptions which can never be exhaustively expressed in a judgement. Order is brought into this chaos only on the condition that in every case only a *part* of concrete reality is interesting and *significant* to us, because only it is related to the *cultural values* with which we approach reality. Only certain sides of the infinitely complex concrete phenomenon, namely those to which we attribute a general *cultural significance*—are therefore worthwhile knowing. They alone are objects of causal explanation. And even this causal explanation evinces the same character; an *exhaustive* causal investigation of any concrete phenomenon in its full reality is not only practically impossible—it is simply nonsense. We select only those causes to which are to be imputed in the individual case, the "essential" feature of an event. Where the *individuality* of a phenomenon is concerned, the question of causality is not a question of *laws* but of concrete causal *relationships;* it is not a question of the subsumption of the event under some general rubric as a representative case but of its imputation as a consequence of some constellation. It is in brief a *question of imputation*. Wherever the causal explanation of a "cultural phenomenon"—a "historical individual"[1]—is under consideration, the knowledge of causal *laws* is not the *end* of the investigation but only a *means*. It facilitates and renders possible the causal imputation to their concrete causes of those components of a phenomenon the individuality of which is culturally significant. So far and only so far as it achieves this, is it valuable for our knowledge of concrete relationships. And the more "general," i.e., the more abstract the laws, the less they can contribute to the causal imputation of *individual* phenomena and, more indirectly, to the understanding of the significance of cultural events.

What is the consequence of all this?

Naturally, it does not imply that the knowledge of *universal* propositions, the construction of abstract concepts, the knowledge of regularities and the attempt to formulate *"laws"* have no scientific justification in the cultural sciences. Quite the contrary, if the causal knowledge of the historians con-

sists of the imputation of concrete effects to concrete causes, a *valid* imputation of any individual effect without the application of *"nomological" knowledge*—i.e., the knowledge of recurrent causal sequences—would in general be impossible. Whether a single individual component of a relationship is, in a concrete case, to be assigned causal responsibility for an effect, the causal explanation of which is at issue, can in doubtful cases be determined only by estimating the effects which we *generally* expect from it and from the other components of the same complex which are relevant to the explanation. In other words, the *"adequate"* effects of the causal elements involved must be considered in arriving at any such conclusion. The extent to which the historian (in the widest sense of the word) can perform this imputation in a reasonably certain manner with his imagination sharpened by personal experience and trained in analytic methods and the extent to which he must have recourse to the aid of special disciplines which make it possible, varies with the individual case. Everywhere, however, and hence also in the sphere of complicated economic processes, the more certain and the more comprehensive our general knowledge the greater is the *certainty* of imputation. This proposition is not in the least affected by the fact that even in the case of all so-called "economic laws" without exception, we are concerned here not with "laws" in the narrower exact natural science sense, but with *adequate* causal relationships expressed in rules and with the application of the category of "objective possibility." The establishment of such regularities is not the *end* but rather the *means* of knowledge. It is entirely a question of expediency, to be settled separately for each individual case, whether a regularly recurrent causal relationship of everyday experience should be formulated into a "law." Laws are important and valuable in the exact natural sciences, in the measure that those sciences are *universally valid*. For the knowledge of historical phenomena in their concreteness, the most general laws, because they are most devoid of content are also the least valuable. The more comprehensive the validity—or scope—of a term, the more it leads us away from the richness of reality since in order to include the common elements of the largest possible number of phenomena, it must necessarily be as abstract as possible and hence *devoid* of content. In the cultural sciences, the knowledge of the universal or general is never valuable in itself.

The conclusion which follows from the above is that an "objective" analysis of cultural events, which proceeds according to the thesis that the ideal of science is the reduction of empirical reality to "laws," is meaningless. It is not meaningless, as is often maintained, because cultural or psychic events for instance are "objectively" less governed by laws. It is meaningless for a number of other reasons. Firstly, because the knowledge of social laws is not knowledge of social reality but is rather one of the various aids used by our minds for attaining this end; secondly, because knowledge of *cultural* events is inconceivable except on a basis of the *significance* which the concrete constellations of reality have for us in certain *individual* concrete situations. In *which* sense and in *which* situations this is the case is not revealed to us by any law; it is decided according to the *value-ideas* in the light of which we view "culture" in each individual case. "Culture" is a finite segment of the meaningless infinity of the world process, a segment on which *human beings* confer meaning and significance. This is true even for the human being who views a *particular* culture as a mortal enemy and who seeks to "return to nature." He can attain this point of view only after viewing the culture in which he lives from the standpoint of his values, and finding it "too soft." This is the purely logical-formal fact which is involved when we speak of the logically necessary rootedness of all historical entities (*historische Individuen*) in "evaluative ideas." The transcendental presupposition of every *cultural science* lies not in our finding a certain culture or any

"culture" in general to be *valuable* but rather in the fact that we are *cultural beings*, endowed with the capacity and the will to take a deliberate attitude towards the world and to lend it *significance*. Whatever this significance may be, it will lead us to judge certain phenomena of human existence in its light and to respond to them as being (positively or negatively) meaningful. Whatever may be the content of this attitude—these phenomena have cultural significance for us and on this significance alone rests its scientific interest. Thus when we speak here of the conditioning of cultural knowledge through *evaluative* ideas (*Wertideen*) (following the terminology of modern logic), it is done in the hope that we will not be subject to crude misunderstandings such as the opinion that cultural significance should be attributed only to *valuable* phenomena. Prostitution is a *cultural* phenomenon just as much as religion or money. All three are cultural phenomena *only* because and *only* insofar as their existence and the form which they historically assume touch directly or indirectly on our cultural *interests* and arouse our striving for knowledge concerning problems brought into focus by the evaluative ideas which give *significance* to the fragment of reality analyzed by those concepts. . . .

Endnote

1. We will use the term which is already occasionally used in the methodology of our discipline and which is now becoming widespread in a more precise forumlation in logic.

12
The Spirit of Capitalism

Max Weber

Weber's most famous and widely read work is *The Protestant Ethic and the Spirit of Capitalism* (1904–05). In this essay, he seeks to account for what he describes as an elective affinity between capitalism and Protestantism. The spirit of capitalism, according to Weber, encouraged a distinctive mentality that proved to be vital during the early stages of capitalist development. The capitalist was an ascetic—a rational miser—who was devoted to the task of making money, not in order to enjoy its fruits but to reinvest it to make more money. The question Weber poses is: Why would someone act in such a manner? The answer he develops hinges on the idea that a distinctly Protestant ethic served to provide a rationale for such conduct. While the thrust of the essay is to focus on the formative period of capitalism, Weber concludes with a pessimistic account of the future wrought by capitalism, depicted most graphically and poignantly by his metaphor of the "iron cage."

In the title of this study is used the somewhat pretentious phrase, the *spirit* of capitalism. What is to be understood by it? The attempt to give anything like a definition of it brings out certain difficulties which are in the very nature of this type of investigation.

If any object can be found to which this term can be applied with any understandable meaning, it can only be an historical individual, i.e., a complex of elements associated in historical reality which we unite into a conceptual whole from the standpoint of their cultural significance.

Such an historical concept, however, since it refers in its content to a phenomenon significant for its unique individuality, cannot be defined according to the formula *genus proximum, differentia specifica*, but it must be gradually put together out of the individual parts which are taken from historical reality to make it up. Thus the final and definitive concept cannot stand at the beginning of the investigation, but must come at the end. We must, in other words, work out in the course of the discussion, as its most important result, the best conceptual formulation of what we here understand by the spirit of capitalism, that is the best from the point of view which interests us here. This point of view (the one of which we shall speak later) is, further, by no means the only possible one from which the historical phenomena we are investigating can be analysed. Other standpoints would, for this as for every historical phenomenon, yield other characteristics as the essential ones. The result is that it is by no means necessary to understand by the spirit of capitalism only what it will come to mean to *us* for the purposes of our analysis. This is a necessary result of the nature of historical concepts which attempt for their methodological purposes not to grasp historical reality in abstract general formulæ, but in concrete genetic sets of relations which are inevitably of a specifically unique and individual character.[1]

Thus, if we try to determine the object, the analysis and historical explanation of which we are attempting, it cannot be in the form of a conceptual definition, but at least in the beginning only a provisional description of what is here meant by the spirit of capitalism. Such a description is, however, indispensable in order clearly to understand the object of the investigation. For this purpose we turn to a document of that spirit which contains what we are looking for in almost classical purity, and at the same time has the advantage of being free from all direct relationship to religion, being thus, for our purposes, free of preconceptions.

"Remember, that *time* is money. He that can earn ten shillings a day by his labour, and goes abroad, or sits idle, one half of that day, though he spends but sixpence during his diversion or idleness, ought not to reckon *that* the only expense; he has really spent, or rather thrown away, five shillings besides.

"Remember, that *credit* is money. If a man lets his money lie in my hands after it is due, he gives me the interest, or so much as I can make of it during that time. This amounts to a considerable sum where a man has good and large credit, and makes good use of it.

"Remember, that money is of the prolific, generating nature. Money can beget money, and its offspring can beget more, and so on. Five shillings turned is six, turned again it is seven and threepence, and so on, till it becomes a hundred pounds. The more there is of it, the more it produces every turning, so that the profits rise quicker and quicker. He that kills a breeding-sow, destroys all her offspring to the thousandth generation. He that murders a crown, destroys all that it might have produced, even scores of pounds."

"Remember this saying, *The good paymaster is lord of another man's purse*. He that is known to pay punctually and exactly to the time he promises, may at any time, and on any occasion, raise all the money his friends can spare. This is sometimes of great use. After industry and frugality, nothing contributes more to the raising of a young man in the world than punctuality and justice in all his dealings; therefore never keep borrowed money an hour beyond the time you promised, lest a disappointment shut up your friend's purse for ever.

"The most trifling actions that affect a man's credit are to be regarded. The sound of your hammer at five in the morning, or eight at night, heard by a creditor, makes him easy six months longer; but if he sees you at a billiard-table, or hears your voice at a tavern, when you should be at work, he sends for his money the next day; demands it, before he can receive it, in a lump.

"It shows, besides, that you are mindful of what you owe; it makes you appear a careful as well as an honest man, and that still increases your credit.

"Beware of thinking all your own that you possess, and of living accordingly. It is a mistake that many people who have credit fall into. To prevent this, keep an exact account for some time both of your expenses and your income. If you take the pains at first to mention particulars, it will have this good effect: you will discover how wonderfully small, trifling expenses mount up to large sums, and will discern what might have been, and may for the future be saved, without occasioning any great inconvenience."

"For six pounds a year you may have the use of one hundred pounds, provided you are a man of known prudence and honesty.

"He that spends a groat a day idly, spends idly above six pounds a year, which is the price for the use of one hundred pounds.

"He that wastes idly a groat's worth of his time per day, one day with another, wastes the privilege of using one hundred pounds each day.

"He that idly loses five shillings worth of time, loses five shillings, and might as prudently throw five shillings into the sea.

"He that loses five shillings, not only loses that sum, but all the advantage that might be made by turning it in dealing, which by the time that a young man becomes old, will amount to a considerable sum of money."[2]

It is Benjamin Franklin who preaches to us in these sentences, the same which Ferdinand Kürnberger satirizes in his clever and malicious *Picture of American Culture*[3] as the supposed confession of faith of the Yankee. That it is the spirit of capitalism which here speaks in characteristic fashion, no one will doubt, however little we may wish to claim that everything which could be understood as pertaining to that spirit is contained in it. Let us pause a moment to consider this passage, the philosophy of which Kürnberger sums up in the words, "They make tallow out of cattle and money out of men." The peculiarity of this philosophy of avarice appears to be the ideal of the honest man of recognized credit, and above all the idea of a duty of the individual toward the increase of his capital, which is assumed as an end in itself. Truly what is here preached is not simply a means of making one's way in the world, but a peculiar ethic. The infraction of its rules is treated not as foolishness but as forgetfulness of duty. That is the essence of the matter. It is not mere business astuteness, that sort of thing is common enough, it is an ethos. *This* is the quality which interests us.

When Jacob Fugger, in speaking to a business associate who had retired and who wanted to persuade him to do the same, since he had made enough money and should let others have a chance, rejected that as pusillanimity and answered that "he (Fugger) thought otherwise, he wanted to make money as long as he could,"[4] the spirit of his statement is evidently quite different from that of Franklin. What in the former case was an expression of commercial daring and a personal inclination morally neutral,[5] in the latter takes on the character of an ethically coloured maxim for the conduct of life. The concept spirit of capitalism is here used in this specific sense,[6] it is the spirit of modern capitalism. For that we are here dealing only with Western European and American capitalism is obvious from the way in which the problem was stated. Capitalism existed in China, India, Babylon, in the classic world, and in the Middle Ages. But in all these cases, as we shall see, this particular ethos was lacking.

Now, all Franklin's moral attitudes are coloured with utilitarianism. Honesty is useful, because it assures credit; so are punctuality, industry, frugality, and that is the reason they are virtues. A logical deduction from this would be that where, for instance, the appearance of honesty serves the same purpose, that would suffice, and an unnecessary surplus of this virtue would evidently appear to Franklin's eyes as unproductive waste. And as a matter of fact, the story in his autobiography of his conversion to those virtues,[7] or the discussion of the value of a strict maintenance of the appearance of modesty, the assiduous belittlement of one's own deserts in order to gain general recognition later,[8] confirms this impression. According to Franklin, those virtues, like all others, are virtues only in so far as they are actually useful to the individual, and the surrogate of mere appearance is always sufficient when it accomplishes the end in view. It is a conclusion which is inevitable for strict utilitarianism. The impression of many Germans that the virtues professed by Americanism are pure hypocrisy seems to have been confirmed by this striking case. But in fact the matter is not by any means so simple. Benjamin Franklin's own character, as it appears in the really unusual candidness of his autobiography, belies that suspicion. The circumstance that he ascribes his recognition of the utility of virtue to a divine revelation which was intended to lead him in the path of righteousness, shows that something more than mere garnishing for purely egocentric motives is involved.

In fact, the *summum bonum* of this ethic, the earning of more and more money, combined with the strict avoidance of all spontaneous enjoyment of life, is above all completely devoid of any eudæmonistic, not to say hedonistic, admixture. It is thought of so purely as an end in itself, that from the point of view of the happiness of, or utility to, the single individual, it appears entirely transcendental and absolutely irrational.[9] Man is dominated by the making of money, by acquisition as the ultimate purpose of his life. Economic acquisition is no longer subordinated to man as the means for the satisfaction of his material needs. This reversal of what we should call the natural relationship, so irrational from a naïve point of view, is evidently as definitely a leading principle of capitalism as it is foreign to all peoples not under capitalistic influence. At the same time it expresses a type of feeling which is closely connected with certain religious ideas. If we thus ask, *why* should "money be made out of men," Benjamin Franklin himself, although he was a colourless deist, answers in his autobiography with a quotation from the Bible, which his strict Calvinistic father drummed into him again and again in his youth: "Seest thou a man diligent in his business? He shall stand before kings" (Prov. xxii. 29). The earning of money within the modern economic order is, so long as it is done legally, the result and the expression of virtue and proficiency in a calling; and this virtue and proficiency are, as it is now not difficult to see, the real Alpha and Omega of Franklin's ethic, as expressed in the passages we have quoted, as well as in all his works without exception.[10]

And in truth this peculiar idea, so familiar to us today, but in reality so little a matter of course, of one's duty in a calling, is what is most characteristic of the social ethic of capitalistic culture, and is in a sense the fundamental basis of it. It is an obligation which the individual is supposed to feel and does feel towards the content of his professional[11] activity, no matter in what it consists, in particular no matter whether it appears on the surface as a utilization of his personal powers, or only of his material possessions (as capital).

Of course, this conception has not appeared only under capitalistic conditions. On the contrary, we shall later trace its origins back to a time previous to the advent of capitalism. Still less, naturally, do we maintain that a conscious acceptance of these ethical maxims on the part of the individuals, entrepreneurs or labourers, in modern capitalistic enterprises, is a condition of the further existence of present-day capitalism. The capitalistic economy of the present day is an immense cosmos into which the individual is born, and which presents itself to him, at least as an individual, as an unalterable order of things in which he must live. It forces the individual, in so far as he is involved in the system of market relationships, to conform to capitalistic rules of action. The manufacturer who in the long run acts counter to these norms, will just as inevitably be eliminated from the economic scene as the worker who cannot or will not adapt himself to them will be thrown into the streets without a job. . . .

One of the fundamental elements of the spirit of modern capitalism, and not only of that but of all modern culture: rational conduct on the basis of the idea of the calling, was born—that is what this discussion has sought to demonstrate—from the spirit of Christian asceticism. One has only to re-read the passage from Franklin, quoted at the beginning of this essay, in order to see that the essential elements of the attitude which was there called the spirit of capitalism are the same as what we have just shown to be the content of the Puritan worldly asceticism,[12] only without the religious basis, which by Franklin's time had died away. The idea that modern labour has an ascetic character is of course not new. Limitation to specialized work, with a renunciation of the Faustian universality of man which it involves, is a condition of any valuable work in the modern world; hence deeds and renunciation inevitably condition each other today. This fundamentally ascetic trait of middle-class life, if it attempts to be a way of life at all, and not

simply the absence of any, was what Goethe wanted to teach, at the height of his wisdom, in the *Wander-jahren*, and in the end which he gave to the life of his *Faust*.[13] For him the realization meant a renunciation, a departure from an age of full and beautiful humanity, which can no more be repeated in the course of our cultural development than can the flower of the Athenian culture of antiquity.

The Puritan wanted to work in a calling; we are forced to do so. For when asceticism was carried out of monastic cells into everyday life, and began to dominate worldly morality, it did its part in building the tremendous cosmos of the modern economic order. This order is now bound to the technical and economic conditions of machine production which to-day determine the lives of all the individuals who are born into this mechanism, not only those directly concerned with economic acquisition, with irresistible force. Perhaps it will so determine them until the last ton of fossilized coal is burnt. In Baxter's view the care for external goods should only lie on the shoulders of the "saint like a light cloak, which can be thrown aside at any moment."[14] But fate decreed that the cloak should become an iron cage.

Since asceticism undertook to remodel the world and to work out its ideals in the world, material goods have gained an increasing and finally an inexorable power over the lives of men as at no previous period in history. To-day the spirit of religious asceticism—whither finally, who knows?—has escaped from the cage. But victorious capitalism, since it rests on mechanical foundations, needs its support no longer. The rosy blush of its laughing heir, the Enlightenment, seems also to be irretrievably fading, and the idea of duty in one's calling prowls about in our lives like the ghost of dead religious beliefs. Where the fulfilment of the calling cannot directly be related to the highest spiritual and cultural values, or when, on the other hand, it need not be felt simply as economic compulsion, the individual generally abandons the attempt to justify it at all. In the field of its highest development, in the United States, the pursuit of wealth, stripped of its religious and ethical meaning, tends to become associated with purely mundane passions, which often actually give it the character of sport.[15]

No one knows who will live in this cage in the future, or whether at the end of this tremendous development entirely new prophets will arise, or there will be a great rebirth of old ideas and ideals, or, if neither, mechanized petrification, embellished with a sort of convulsive self-importance. For of the last stage of this cultural development, it might well be truly said: "Specialists without spirit, sensualists without heart; this nullity imagines that it has attained a level of civilization never before achieved."

But this brings us to the world of judgments of value and of faith, with which this purely historical discussion need not be burdened. The next task would be rather to show the significance of ascetic rationalism, which has only been touched in the foregoing sketch, for the content of practical social ethics, thus for the types of organization and the functions of social groups from the conventicle to the state. Then its relations to humanistic rationalism,[16] its ideals of life and cultural influence; further to the development of philosophical and scientific empiricism, to technical development and to spiritual ideals would have to be analysed. Then its historical development from the mediæval beginnings of worldly asceticism to its dissolution into pure utilitarianism would have to be traced out through all the areas of ascetic religion. Only then could the quantitative cultural significance of ascetic Protestantism in its relation to the other plastic elements of modern culture be estimated.

Here we have only attempted to trace the fact and the direction of its influence to their motives in one, though a very important point. But it would also further be necessary to investigate how Protestant Asceticism was in turn influenced in its development and its character by the totality of social conditions, especially economic.[17] The modern man is in general, even with the best will, unable to give religious ideas a significance for culture and national character which they deserve. But it is, of course, not my aim to substitute for a one-sided materialistic an equally one-sided spiritualistic causal interpretation of culture and of history. Each is equally possible,[18] but each, if it does not serve

as the preparation, but as the conclusion of an investigation, accomplishes equally little in the interest of historical truth.[19]

Endnotes

1. These passages represent a very brief summary of some aspects of Weber's methodological views. At about the same time that he wrote this essay he was engaged in a thorough criticism and revaluation of the methods of the Social Sciences, the result of which was a point of view in many ways different from the prevailing one, especially outside of Germany. In order thoroughly to understand the significance of this essay in its wider bearings on Weber's sociological work as a whole it is necessary to know what his methodological aims were. Most of his writings on this subject have been assembled since his death (in 1920) in the volume *Gesammelte Aufsätze zur Wissenschaftslehre*. A shorter exposition of the main position is contained in the opening chapters of *Wirtschaft und Gesellschaft, Grundriss der Sozialökonomik, III.*— TRANSLATOR'S NOTE.

2. The final passage is from *Necessary Hints to Those That Would Be Rich* (written 1736, Works, Sparks edition, 11, p. 80), the rest from *Advice to a Young Tradesman* (written 1748, Sparks edition, II, pp. 87 ff.). The italics in the text are Franklin's.

3. *Der Amerikamüde* (Frankfurt, 1855), well known to be an imaginative paraphrase of Lenau's impressions of America. As a work of art the book would to-day be somewhat difficult to enjoy, but it is incomparable as a document of the (now long since blurred over) differences between the German and the American outlook, one may even say of the type of spiritual life which, in spite of everything, has remained common to all Germans, Catholic and Protestant alike, since the German mysticism of the Middle Ages, as against the Puritan capitalistic valuation of action.

4. Sombart has used this quotation as a motto for his section dealing with the genesis of capitalism (*Der moderne Kapitalismus*, first edition, I, p. 193. See also p. 390).

5. Which quite obviously does not mean either that Jacob Fugger was a morally indifferent or an irreligious man, or that Benjamin Franklin's ethic is completely covered by the above quotations. It scarcely required Brentano's quotations (*Die Anfänge des modernen Kapitalismus*, pp. 150 ff.) to protect this well-known philanthropist from the misunderstanding which Brentano seems to attribute to me. The problem is just the reverse: how could such a philanthropist come to write these particular sentences (the especially characteristic

form of which Brentano has neglected to reproduce) in the manner of a moralist?

6. This is the basis of our difference from Sombart in stating the problem. Its very considerable practical significance will become clear later. In anticipation, however, let it be remarked that Sombart has by no means neglected this ethical aspect of the capitalistic entrepreneur. But in his view of the problem it appears as a result of capitalism, whereas for our purposes we must assume the opposite as an hypothesis. A final position can only be taken up at the end of the investigation. For Sombart's view see *op. cit.*, pp. 357, 380, etc. His reasoning here connects with the brilliant analysis given in Simmel's *Philosophie des Geldes* (final chapter). Of the polemics which he has brought forward against me in his *Bourgeois* I shall come to speak later. At this point any thorough discussion must be postponed.

7. "I grew convinced that truth, sincerity, and integrity in dealings between man and man were of the utmost importance to the felicity of life; and I formed written resolutions, which still remain in my journal book to practise them ever while I lived. Revelation had indeed no weight with me as such; but I entertained an opinion that, though certain actions might not be bad because they were forbidden by it, or good because it commanded them, yet probably these actions might be forbidden because they were bad for us, or commanded because they were beneficial to us in their own nature, all the circumstances of things considered." *Autobiography* (ed. F. W. Pine, Henry Holt, New York, 1916), p. 112.

8. "I therefore put myself as much as I could out of sight and started it"—that is the project of a library which he had initiated—"as a scheme of a *number of friends*, who had requested me to go about and propose it to such as they thought lovers of reading. In this way my affair went on smoothly, and I ever after practised it on such occasions; and from my frequent successes, can heartily recommend it. The present little sacrifice of your vanity will afterwards be amply repaid. If it remains awhile uncertain to whom the merit belongs, someone more vain than yourself will be encouraged to claim it, and then even envy will be disposed to do you justice by plucking those assumed feathers and restoring them to their right owner." *Autobiography*, p. 140.

9. Brentano (*op. cit.*, pp. 125, 127, note 1) takes this remark as an occasion to criticize the later discussion of "that rationalization and discipline" to which worldly asceticism* has subjected men. That he says, is a rationalization toward an irrational mode of life. He is, in fact, quite correct. A thing is never irrational in itself, but only from a particular rational point of view. For the unbeliever every religious way of life is irrational, for the hedonist every ascetic standard, no matter whether measured with respect to its particular basic values. If this essay makes any contribution at all, may it be to bring out the complexity of the only superficially simple concept of the rational.

10. In reply to Brentano's (*Die Anfänge des modernen Kapitalismus*, pp. 150 ff.) long and somewhat inaccurate apologia for Franklin, whose ethical qualities I am supposed to have misunderstood, I refer only to this statement which should, in my opinion, have been sufficient to make that apologia superfluous.

11. The two terms profession and calling I have used in translation of the German *Beruf* whichever seemed best to fit the particular context. Vocation does not carry the ethical connotation in which Weber is interested. It is especially to be remembered that profession in this sense is not contrasted with business, but it refers to a particular attitude toward one's occupation, no matter what that occupation may be. This should become abundantly clear from the whole of Weber's argument.—TRANSLATOR'S NOTE.

12. That those other elements, which have here not yet been traced to their religious roots, especially the idea that honesty is the best policy (Franklin's discussion of credit), that are also of Puritan origin, must be proved in a somewhat different connection. . . . Here I shall limit myself to repeating the following remark of J. A. Rowntree (*Quakerism, Past and Present*, pp. 95–6), to which E. Bernstein has called my attention: "Is it merely a coincidence, or is it a consequence, that the lofty profession of spirituality made by the Friends has gone hand in hand with shrewdness and tact in the transaction of mundane affairs? Real piety favours the success of a trader by insuring his integrity and fostering habits of prudence and forethought, important items in obtaining that standing and credit in the commercial world, which are requisites for the steady accumulation of wealth.". . . "Honest as a Huguenot" was as proverbial in the seventeenth century as the respect for law of the Dutch which Sir W. Temple admired, and a century later, that of the English as compared with those Continental peoples that had not been through this ethical schooling.

13. Well analysed in Bielschowsky's *Goethe*, II, chap. xviii. For the development of the scientific cosmos Windelband, at the end of his *Blütezeit der deutschen Philosophie* (Vol. II of the *Gesch. d. Neueren Philosophie*), has expressed a similar idea.

14. *Saints' Everlasting Rest*, chap. xii.

15. "Couldn't the old man be satisfied with his $75,000 a year and rest? No! The frontage of the

store must be widened to 400 feet. Why? That beats everything, he says. In the evening when his wife and daughter read together, he wants to go to bed. Sundays he looks at the clock every five minutes to see when the day will be over—what a futile life!" In these terms the son-in-law (who had emigrated from Germany) of the leading dry-goods man of an Ohio city expressed his judgment of the latter, a judgment which would undoubtedly have seemed simply incomprehensible to the old man. A symptom of German lack of energy.

16. This remark alone (unchanged since his criticism) might have shown Brentano (*op. cit.*) that I have never doubted its independent significance. That humanism was also not pure rationalism has lately again been strongly emphasized by Borinski in the *Abhandl. der Münchener Akad. der Wiss.*, 1919.

17. The academic oration of V. Below, *Die Ursachen der Reformation* (Freiburg, 1919), is not concerned with this problem, but with that of the Reformation in general, especially Luther. For the question dealt with here, especially the controversies which have grown out of this study, I may refer finally to the work of Hermelink, *Reformation und Gegenreformation*, which, however, is also primarily concerned with other problems.

18. For the above sketch has deliberately taken up only the relations in which an influence of religious ideas on the material culture is really beyond doubt. It would have been easy to proceed beyond that to a regular construction which logically deduced everything characteristic of modern culture from Protestant rationalism. But that sort of thing may be left to the type of dilettante who believes in the unity of the group mind and its reducibility to a single formula. Let it be remarked only that the period of capitalistic development lying before that which we have studied was everywhere in part determined by religious influences, both hindering and helping. Of what sort these were belongs in another chapter. Furthermore, whether, of the broader problems sketched above, one or another can be dealt with in the limits of this Journal [the essay first appeared in the *Archiv für Sozialwissenschaft und Sozialpolitik*—TRANSLATOR'S NOTE] is not certain in view of the problems to which it is devoted. On the other hand, to write heavy tomes, as thick as they would have to be in this case, and dependent on the work of others (theologians and historians), I have no great incli-

nation (I have left these sentences unchanged).

For the tension between ideals and reality in early capitalistic times before the Reformation, see now Strieder, *Studien zur Geschichte der kapit. Organizationformen*, 1914, Book II. (Also as against the work of Keller, cited above, which was utilized by Sombart.)

19. I should have thought that this sentence and the remarks and notes immediately preceding it would have sufficed to prevent any misunderstanding of what this study was meant to accomplish, and I find no occasion for adding anything. Instead of following up with an immediate continuation in terms of the above programme, I have, partly for fortuitous reasons, especially the appearance of Troeltsch's *Die Soziallehren der christlichen Kirchen und Gruppen*, which disposed of many things I should have had to investigate in a way in which I, not being a theologian, could not have done it; but partly also in order to correct the isolation of this study and to place it in relation to the whole of cultural development determined, first, to write down some comparative studies of the general historical relationship of religion and society. These follow. Before them is placed only a short essay in order to clear up the concept of sect used above, and at the same time to show the significance of the Puritan conception of the Church for the capitalistic spirit of modern times.

Translator's Note [for Endnote 9]

*This seemingly paradoxical term has been the best translation I could find for Weber's *innerweltliche Askese*, which means asceticism practised within the world as contrasted with *ausserweltliche Askese*, which withdraws from the world (for instance into a monastery). Their precise meaning will appear in the course of Weber's discussion. It is one of the prime points of his essay that asceticism does not need to flee from the world to be ascetic. I shall consistently employ the terms worldly and otherworldly to denote the contrast between the two kinds of asceticism.

13
Bureaucracy

Max Weber

Weber was the first scholar to assess the impact of modern bureaucratic organizations, which he saw as an integral aspect of industrial capitalism, parallel in significance to the machine. He thought this to be the case because he understood that a successful capitalist had to make decisions based on such criteria as efficiency, calculability, predictability, and control. Bureaucracy, like the machine, was a reflection of a scientific and rational worldview. Bureaucracy was thus essential if capitalism was to expand productive capacity. In Weber's estimation, this novel form of modern bureaucracy was becoming so pervasive that it was appropriate to define the present era as the age of bureaucracy. In this selection from his magnum opus, *Economy and Society* (1921), Weber presents an ideal typical portrait of the most salient features of bureaucracy, paying particular attention to the nature and basis of authority in bureaucracy.

Modern officialdom functions in the following specific manner:

I.

There is the principle of fixed and official jurisdictional areas, which are generally ordered by rules, that is, by laws or administrative regulations.

1. The regular activities required for the purposes of the bureaucratically governed structure are distributed in a fixed way as official duties.

2. The authority to give the commands required for the discharge of these duties is distributed in a stable way and is strictly delimited by rules concerning the coercive means, physical, sacerdotal, or otherwise, which may be placed at the disposal of officials.

3. Methodical provision is made for the regular and continuous fulfilment of these duties and for the execution of the corresponding rights; only persons who have the generally regulated qualifications to serve are employed.

In public and lawful government these three elements constitute 'bureaucratic authority.' In private economic domination, they constitute bureaucratic 'management.' Bureaucracy, thus understood, is fully developed in political and ecclesiastical communities only in the modern state, and, in the private economy, only in the most advanced institutions of capitalism. Permanent and public office authority, with fixed jurisdiction, is not the historical rule but rather the exception. This is so even in large political structures such as those of the ancient Orient, the Germanic and Mongolian empires of conquest, or of many feudal structures of state. In all these cases, the ruler executes the most important measures through personal trustees, table-companions, or court-servants. Their commissions and authority are not precisely delimited and are temporarily called into being for each case.

II.

The principles of office hierarchy and of levels of graded authority mean a firmly ordered system of super- and subordination in which there is a supervision of the lower offices by the higher ones. Such a system offers the governed the possibility of appealing the decision of a lower office to its higher authority, in a definitely regulated manner. With the full development of the bureaucratic type, the office hierarchy is monocratically organized. The principle of hierarchical office authority is found in all bureaucratic structures: in state and ecclesiastical structures as well as in large party organizations and private enterprises. It does not matter for the character of bureaucracy whether its authority is called 'private' or 'public.'

When the principle of jurisdictional 'competency' is fully carried through, hierarchical subordination—at least in public office—does not mean that the 'higher' authority is simply authorized to take over the business of the 'lower.' Indeed, the opposite is the rule. Once established and having fulfilled its task, an office tends to continue in existence and be held by another incumbent.

III.

The management of the modern office is based upon written documents ('the files'), which are preserved in their original or draught form. There is, therefore, a staff of subaltern officials and scribes of all sorts. The body of officials actively engaged in a 'public' office, along with the respective apparatus of material implements and the files, make up a 'bureau.' In private enterprise, 'the bureau' is often called 'the office.'

In principle, the modern organization of the civil service separates the bureau from the private domicile of the official and, in general, bureaucracy segregates official activity as something distinct from the sphere of private life. Public monies and equipment are divorced from the private property of the official. This condition is everywhere the product of a long development. Nowadays, it is found in public as well as in private enterprises; in the latter, the principle extends even to the leading entrepreneur. In principle, the executive office is separated from the household, business from private correspondence, and business assets from private fortunes. The more consistently the modern type of business management has been carried through the more are these separations the case. The beginnings of this process are to be found as early as the Middle Ages.

It is the peculiarity of the modern entrepreneur that he conducts himself as the 'first official' of his enterprise, in the very same way in which the ruler of a specifically modern bureaucratic state spoke of himself as 'the first servant' of the state.[1] The idea that the bureau activities of the state are intrinsically different in character from the management of private economic offices is a continental European notion and, by way of contrast, is totally foreign to the American way.

IV.

Office management, at least all specialized office management—and such management is distinctly modern—usually presupposes thorough and expert training. This increasingly holds for the modern executive and employee of private enterprises, in the same manner as it holds for the state official.

V.

When the office is fully developed, official activity demands the full working capacity of the official irrespective of the fact that his obligatory time in the bureau may be firmly delimited. In the normal case, this is only the product of a long development, in the public as well as in the private office. Formerly, in all cases, the normal state of affairs was reversed: official business was discharged as a secondary activity.

VI.

The management of the office follows general rules, which are more or less stable, more or less exhaustive, and which can be learned. Knowledge of these rules represents a special technical learning which the officials possess. It involves jurisprudence, or administrative or business management.

The reduction of modern office management to rules is deeply embedded in its very nature. The theory of modern public administration, for instance, assumes that the authority to order certain matters by decree—which has been legally granted to public authorities—does not entitle the bureau to regulate the matter by commands given for each case, but only to regulate the matter abstractly. This stands in extreme contrast to the regulation of all relationships through individual privileges and bestowals of favor, which is absolutely dominant in patrimonialism, at least in so far as such relationships are not fixed by sacred tradition.

The Position of the Official

All this results in the following for the internal and external position of the official:

I.

Office holding is a 'vocation.' This is shown, first, in the requirement of a firmly prescribed course of training, which demands the entire capacity for work for a long period of time, and in the generally prescribed and special examinations which are prerequisites of employment. Furthermore, the position of the official is in the nature of a duty. This determines the internal structure of his relations, in the following manner: Legally and actually, office holding is not considered a source to be exploited for rents or emoluments, as was normally the case during the Middle Ages and frequently up to the threshold of recent times. Nor is office holding considered a usual exchange of services for equivalents, as is the case with free labor contracts. Entrance into an office, including one in the private economy, is considered an acceptance of a specific obligation of faithful management in return for a secure existence. It is decisive for the specific nature of modern loyalty to an office that, in the pure type, it does not establish a relationship to a *person*, like the vassal's or disciple's faith in feudal or in patrimonial relations of authority. Modern loyalty is devoted to impersonal and functional purposes. Behind the functional purposes, of course, 'ideas of culture-values' usually stand. These are *ersatz* for the earthly or supra-mundane personal master: ideas such as 'state,' 'church,' 'community,' 'party,' or 'enterprise' are thought of as being realized in a community; they provide an ideological halo for the master.

The political official—at least in the fully developed modern state—is not considered the personal servant of a ruler. Today, the bishop, the priest, and the preacher are in fact no longer, as in early Christian times, holders of purely personal charisma. The supra-mundane and sacred values which they offer are given to everybody who seems to be worthy of them and who asks for them. In former times, such leaders acted upon the personal command of their master; in principle, they were responsible only to him. Nowadays, in spite of the partial survival of the old theory, such religious leaders are officials in the service of a functional purpose, which in the present-day 'church' has become routinized and, in turn, ideologically hallowed.

II.

The personal position of the official is patterned in the following way:

1. Whether he is in a private office or a public bureau, the modern official always strives and usually enjoys a distinct *social esteem* as compared with the governed. His social position is guaranteed by the prescriptive rules of rank order and, for the political official, by special definitions of the criminal code against 'insults of officials' and 'contempt' of state and church authorities.

The actual social position of the official is normally highest where, as in old civilized countries, the following conditions prevail: a strong demand for administration by trained experts; a strong and stable social differentiation, where the official predominantly derives from socially and economically privileged strata because of the social distribution of power; or where the costliness of the required training and status conventions are binding upon him. The possession of educational certificates—to be discussed elsewhere[2]—are usually linked with qualification for office. Naturally, such certificates or patents enhance the 'status element' in the social position of the official. For the rest this status factor in individual cases is explicitly and impassively acknowledged; for example, in the prescription that the acceptance or rejection of an aspirant to an official career depends upon the consent ('election') of the members of the official body. This is the case in the German army with the officer corps. Similar phenomena, which promote this guild-like closure of officialdom, are typically found in patrimonial and, particularly, in prebendal officialdoms of the past. The desire to resurrect such phenomena in changed forms is by no means infrequent among modern bureaucrats. For instance, they have played a role among the demands of the quite proletarian and expert officials (the *tretyj* element) during the Russian revolution.

Usually the social esteem of the officials as such is especially low where the demand for expert administration and the dominance of status conventions are weak. This is especially the case in the United States; it is often the case in new settlements by virtue of their wide fields for profit-making and the great instability of their social stratification.

2. The pure type of bureaucratic official is *appointed* by a superior authority. An official elected by the governed is not a purely bureaucratic figure. Of course, the formal existence of an election does not by itself mean that no appointment hides behind the election—in the state, especially, appointment by party chiefs. Whether or not this is the case does not depend upon legal statutes but upon the way in which the party mechanism functions. Once firmly organized, the parties can turn a formally free election into the mere acclamation of a candidate designated by the party chief. As a rule, however, a formally free election is turned into a fight, conducted according to definite rules, for votes in favor of one of two designated candidates.

In all circumstances, the designation of officials by means of an election among the governed modifies the strictness of hierarchical subordination. In principle, an official who is so elected has an autonomous position opposite the superordinate official. The elected official does not derive his position 'from above' but 'from below,' or at least not from a superior authority of the official hierarchy but from powerful party men ('bosses'), who also determine his further career. The career of the elected official is not, or at least not primarily, dependent upon his chief in the administration. The official who is not elected but appointed by a chief normally functions more exactly, from a technical point of view, because, all other circumstances being equal, it is more likely that purely functional points of consideration and qualities will determine his selection and career. As laymen, the governed can become acquainted with the extent to which a candidate is expertly qualified for office only in terms of experience, and hence only after his service. Moreover, in every sort of selection of officials by election, parties quite naturally give decisive weight not to expert considerations but to the services a follower renders to the party boss. This holds for all kinds of procurement of officials by elections, for the designation of formally free,

elected officials by party bosses when they determine the slate of candidates, or the free appointment by a chief who has himself been elected. The contrast, however, is relative: substantially similar conditions hold where legitimate monarchs and their subordinates appoint officials, except that the influence of the followings are then less controllable.

Where the demand for administration by trained experts is considerable, and the party followings have to recognize an intellectually developed, educated, and freely moving 'public opinion,' the use of unqualified officials falls back upon the party in power at the next election. Naturally, this is more likely to happen when the officials are appointed by the chief. The demand for a trained administration now exists in the United States, but in the large cities, where immigrant votes are 'corraled,' there is, of course, no educated public opinion. Therefore, popular elections of the administrative chief and also of his subordinate officials usually endanger the expert qualification of the official as well as the precise functioning of the bureaucratic mechanism. It also weakens the dependence of the officials upon the hierarchy. This holds at least for the large administrative bodies that are difficult to supervise. The superior qualification and integrity of federal judges, appointed by the President, as over against elected judges in the United States is well known, although both types of officials have been selected primarily in terms of party considerations. The great changes in American metropolitan administrations demanded by reformers have proceeded essentially from elected mayors working with an apparatus of officials who were appointed by them. These reforms have thus come about in a 'Caesarist' fashion. Viewed technically, as an organized form of authority, the efficiency of 'Caesarism,' which often grows out of democracy, rests in general upon the position of the 'Caesar' as a free trustee of the masses (of the army or of the citizenry), who is unfettered by tradition. The 'Caesar' is thus the unrestrained master of a body of highly qualified military officers and officials whom he selects freely and personally without regard to tradition or to any other considerations. This 'rule of the personal genius,' however, stands in contradiction to the formally 'democratic' principle of a universally elected officialdom.

3. Normally, the position of the official is held for life, at least in public bureaucracies; and this is increasingly the case for all similar structures. As a factual rule, *tenure for life* is presupposed, even where the giving of notice or periodic reappointment occurs. In contrast to the worker in a private enterprise, the official normally holds tenure. Legal or actual life-tenure, however, is not recognized as the official's right to the possession of office, as was the case with many structures of authority in the past. Where legal guarantees against arbitrary dismissal or transfer are developed, they merely serve to guarantee a strictly objective discharge of specific office duties free from all personal considerations. In Germany, this is the case for all juridical and, increasingly, for all administrative officials.

Within the bureaucracy, therefore, the measure of 'independence,' legally guaranteed by tenure, is not always a source of increased status for the official whose position is thus secured. Indeed, often the reverse holds, especially in old cultures and communities that are highly differentiated. In such communities, the stricter the subordination under the arbitrary rule of the master, the more it guarantees the maintenance of the conventional seigneurial style of living for the official. Because of the very absence of these legal guarantees of tenure, the conventional esteem for the official may rise in the same way as, during the Middle Ages, the esteem of the nobility of office[3] rose at the expense of esteem for the freemen, and as the king's judge surpassed that of the people's judge. In Germany, the military officer or the administrative official can be removed from office at any time, or at least far more readily than the 'independent judge,' who never pays with loss of his office for even the grossest offense against the 'code of honor' or against social conventions of the salon. For this very reason, if other things are equal, in the eyes of the master stratum the judge is considered less qualified for social intercourse than are officers and administrative officials, whose greater dependence on the master is a greater guarantee of their conformity with status conventions. Of course, the average official strives for a civil-service law, which would materially secure his old age and provide increased guarantees against his arbitrary removal from office. This striving, however, has its limits. A very strong development of the 'right to the office' naturally makes it more difficult to staff them with regard to technical efficiency, for such a development decreases the career-opportunities of ambitious candidates for office. This makes for the fact that officials, on the whole, do not feel their dependency upon those at the top. This lack of a feeling of dependency, however, rests primarily upon the inclination to depend upon one's equals rather than upon the socially inferior and governed strata. The present conservative movement among the Badenia clergy, occasioned by the anxiety of a presumably threatening separation of church and state, has been expressly determined by the desire not to be turned 'from a master into a servant of the parish.'[4]

4. The official receives the regular pecuniary compensation of a normally fixed salary and the old age security provided by a pension. The salary is not measured like a wage in terms of work done, but according to 'status,' that is, according to the kind of function (the 'rank') and, in addition, possibly, according to the length of service. The relatively great security of the official's income, as well as the rewards of social esteem, make the office a sought-after position, especially in countries which no longer provide opportunities for colonial profits. In such countries, this situation permits relatively low salaries for officials.

5. The official is set for a 'career' within the hierarchical of the public service. He moves from the lower, less important, and lower paid to the higher positions. The average official naturally desires a mechanical fixing of the conditions of promotion: if not of the offices, at least of the salary levels. He wants these conditions fixed in terms of 'seniority,' or possibly according to grades achieved in a developed system of expert examinations. Here and there, such examinations actually form a character indelebilis of the official and have lifelong effects on his career. To this is joined the desire to qualify the right to office and the increasing tendency toward status group closure and economic security. All of this makes for a tendency to consider the offices as 'prebends' of those who are qualified by educational certificates. The necessity of taking general personal and intellectual qualifications into consideration, irrespective of the often subaltern character of the educational certificate, has led to a condition in which the highest political offices, especially the positions of 'ministers,' are principally filled without reference to such certificates. . . .

Endnotes

1. Frederick II of Prussia.
2. Cf. *Wirtschaft und Gesellschaft*, pp. 73 ff. and part II. (German Editor.)
3. *Ministerialan.'*
4. Written before 1914. (German editor's note.)

Reprinted from "Bureaucracy," from *From Max Weber: Essays in Sociology* by Max Weber, edited by H. H. Gerth & C. Wright Mills, translated by H. H. Gerth & C. Wright Mills. Translation copyright © 1946, 1958 by H. H. Gerth & C. Wright Mills. Used by permission of Oxford University Press, Inc. ✦

14
The Nature of Charismatic Domination

Max Weber

In his political sociology, Weber identified three bases for legitimate authority or domination: traditional, charismatic, and legal-rational. In this selection from *Economy and Society* (1921), he discusses the characteristic features of charismatic authority. Borrowing the term from Rudolph Sohm's depiction of religious leadership in early Christianity, he locates this type of authority in the perceived extraordinary character of the individual, who is viewed by followers as being endowed with grace. Charismatic leadership involves a profoundly emotional bond between the leader and followers, and in its purest form it is construed as being potentially disruptive, revolutionary, and anti-institutional, and thus a source of far-reaching social upheaval.

Bureaucracy, like the patriarchal system which is opposed to it in so many ways, is a structure of 'the everyday', in the sense that stability is among its most important characteristics. Patriarchal power, above all, is rooted in the supply of the normal, constantly recurring needs of everyday life and thus has its basis in the economy—indeed, in just those sections of the economy concerned with the supply of normal everyday requirements. The patriarch is the 'natural leader' in everyday life. In this respect, bureaucracy is the counterpart of patriarchalism, only expressed in more rational terms. Bureaucracy, moreover, is a permanent structure and is well adapted, with its system of rational rules, for the satisfaction of calculable long-term needs by normal methods. On the other hand, the supply of all needs which go beyond the economic requirements of everyday life is seen, the further back we go in history, to be based on a totally different principle, that of *charisma*. In other words, the 'natural' leaders in times of spiritual, physical, economic, ethical, religious or political emergency were neither appointed officials nor trained and salaried specialist 'professionals' (in the present-day sense of the word 'profession'), but those who possessed specific physical and spiritual gifts which were regarded as supernatural, in the sense of not being available to everyone.

In this context, the concept of 'charisma' is being used in a completely 'value-free' way. The ability of the Nordic 'Berserker' to work himself up into an heroic trance, in which he bites his shield and his person like a rabid dog, eventually dashing off in a raving blood-lust (like the Irish hero Cuculain or Homer's Achilles) is a form of manic attack, artificially induced, according to a theory long held about the Berserkers, by acute poisoning: in Byzantium, indeed, a number of 'blond beasts' with a talent for inducing such attacks were kept, in much the same way as war elephants had previously been. Shamanic trances, likewise, are connected with constitutional epilepsy, the possession of which, once confirmed, constitutes the charismatic qualification. Thus, both kinds of trance have nothing 'uplifting' about them to our way of thinking, any more than does the kind of 'revelation' to be found in the sacred book of the Mormons which must, at least in terms of its value, be considered a crude swindle. Such questions, however, do not concern sociology: the Mormon leader, like the heroes and magicians already referred to, is certified as charismatically gifted by the beliefs of his followers. It was in virtue of possessing this gift or 'charisma' and (if a clear concept of god had already been formed) in virtue of the divine mission embodied therein that they practised their art and exercised their domination. This was as true of healers and prophets as of judges or leaders in war or great hunting expeditions. We have to thank Rudolph Sohm for having worked out the sociological features of this type of power-structure in relation to one particular case of great historical importance (the historical development of the power of the Christian Church in its early stages) in a way which is intellectually coherent and so, from a purely historical point of view, necessarily one-sided. But the same situation in all its essentials is repeated everywhere, even though often expressed in its purest form in the religious domain.

In contrast with all forms of bureaucratic administrative system, the charismatic structure recognises no forms or orderly procedures for appointment or dismissal, no 'career', no 'advancement', no 'salary'; there is no organised training either for the bearer of charisma or his aides, no arrangements for supervision or appeal, no allocation of local areas of control or exclusive spheres of competence, and finally no standing institutions comparable to bureaucratic 'governing bodies' independent of persons and of their purely personal charisma. Rather, charisma recognises only those stipulations and limitations which come from within itself. The bearer of charisma assumes the tasks appropriate to him and requires obedience and a following in virtue of his mission. His success depends on whether he finds them. If those to whom he feels himself sent do not recognise his mission, then his claims collapse. If they do recognise him, then he remains their master for as long as he is able to retain their recognition by giving 'proofs'. His right to rule, however, is not dependent on their will, as is that of an elected leader; on the contrary, it is the duty of those to whom he is sent to recognise his charismatic qualification. When the Emperor's right to rule is said, in the Chinese theory, to depend on recognition by the people, that is no more a case of the acceptance of popular sovereignty than is the requirement of the early Christian Church that prophets should be 'recognised' by the faithful. Rather, it is a sign of the charismatic character of the monarch's office, based as it is on personal qualification and proof. Charisma may be, and obviously often is, qualitatively specialised, in which case qualitative limitations are imposed on the mission and power of its bearer by the internal character of his charisma, not by external regulation. The meaning and content of the mission may be (and normally are) directed to a human group which is defined geographically, ethnically, socially, politically, occupationally, or in some other way; its limits are then set by the boundaries of that group.

Charismatic domination is diametrically opposed to bureaucratic in all respects, and hence in its economic sub-structure. Bureaucracy depends on constancy of income, and so *a fortiori* on a money economy and money taxation, while charisma lives in the world, but is certainly not of it. The true meaning of this remark needs to be understood. Frequently there is a completely conscious sense of horror at the possession of money and at money incomes as such, as in the case of St. Francis and many like him. But of course this is not the general rule. The domination exercised even by a gifted pirate may be 'charismatic' in the value-free sense of that term used here, and charismatic political heroes seek booty, above all in the form of money. But the important point is that charisma rejects as dishonourable all rational planning in the acquisition of money, and in general all rational forms of economy. In this it is sharply contrasted also with all 'patriarchal' structures, which are based on the orderly foundation of the 'household'. In its 'pure' form, charisma is not a private source of income for its bearer, either in the sense of being economically exploited in the fashion of an exchange of services or in the other sense of being salaried; equally, it is without any organised levying of tribute to provide for the material needs of the mission. Rather, if its mission is a peaceful one, its requirements are economically provided either by individual patrons or by the donations, contributions or other voluntary services given by those to whom it is directed. Alternatively, in the case of charismatic war heroes, booty furnishes both one of the goals of the mission and a means of supplying its material needs. 'Pure' charisma is opposed to all forms of regulated economy—in contrast with all kinds of 'patriarchal' domination in the sense of that term used here: it is a, indeed *the*, anti-economic force, even (indeed precisely) when it seeks to obtain possession of material goods, as in the case of the charismatic war hero. This is possible because charisma, by its very essence, is not a permanent 'institutional' structure, but rather, when it is functioning in its 'pure' form, the exact opposite. Those who possess charisma—not only the master himself but his disciples and followers—must, in order to fulfil their mission, keep themselves free of all worldly ties, free from everyday occupations as well as from everyday family responsibilities. The prohibition against accepting payment for ecclesiastical office laid down in the statutes of the Jesuit order, the prohibition against owning property imposed on members of an order, or even, as in the original rule of the Franciscans, on the order itself, the rule of celibacy for priests and members of knightly orders, the actual celibacy of many bearers of prophetic or artistic charisma—all express the necessary 'alienation from the world' of those who have a share ('κλῆρος') in charisma. The economic conditions of having such a share may, however, seem from the outside to be opposed to each other, depending on the kind of charisma and the way of life which expresses its meaning (religious or artistic, for example). When modern charismatic movements of artistic origin suggest 'those of independent means' (or, putting it in plainer language, *rentiers*) as the persons normally best qualified to be followers of someone with a charismatic mission, this is just as logical as was the vow of poverty taken by the medieval monastic orders, which had precisely the opposite economic implications.

The continued existence of charismatic authority is, by its very nature, characteristically *unstable:* the bearer may lose his charisma, feel himself, like Jesus on the cross, to be 'abandoned by his God', and show himself to his followers as 'bereft of his power', and then his mission is dead, and his followers must hopefully await and search out a new charismatic leader. He himself, however, is abandoned by his following, for pure charisma recognises no 'legitimacy' other than that conferred by personal power, which must be constantly re-confirmed. The charismatic hero does not derive his authority from ordinances and statutes, as if it were an official 'competence', nor from customary usage or feudal fealty, as with patrimonial power: rather, he acquires it and retains it only by proving his powers in real life. He

must perform miracles if he wants to be a prophet, acts of heroism if he wants to be a leader in war. Above all, however, his divine mission must 'prove' itself in that those who entrust themselves to him must prosper. If they do not, then he is obviously not the master sent by the gods. This very serious conception of genuine charisma obviously stands in stark contrast with the comfortable pretensions of the modern theory of the 'divine right of kings', with its references to the 'inscrutable' decrees of God, 'to whom alone the monarch is answerable': the genuinely charismatic leader, by contrast, is answerable rather to his subjects. That is, it is for that reason and that reason alone that precisely he personally is the genuine master willed by God.

Someone who holds power in a way which still has important residual charismatic elements, as the Chinese monarchs did (at least in theory), will blame himself if his administration does not succeed in exorcising some calamity which has befallen his subjects, whether a flood or a defeat in war: openly, before the whole people, he will condemn his own sins and shortcomings, as we have seen even in the last few decades. If even this penitence does not appease the gods, then he resigns himself to dismissal and death, which is often the method of atonement. This is the very specific meaning of the proposition found, for instance, in Mencius that the voice of the people is 'the voice of God' (according to Mencius, this is the *only* way in which God speaks!): once he is no longer recognised by the people, the master becomes (as is expressly said) a simple private citizen, and, if he aspires to anything more, he is a usurper and deserves to be punished. The situation expressed in these phrases, with their extremely revolutionary resonance, can also be found, in forms which carry no hint of pathos, in primitive societies, where authority has the charismatic character to be found in almost all primitive authority, with the exception of domestic power in the strictest sense, and the chief is often simply deserted if success deserts him.

The purely *de facto* 'recognition', whether active or passive, of his personal mission by the subjects, on which the power of the charismatic lord rests, has its source in submission by faith to the extraordinary and un-heard-of, to that which does not conform to any rule or tradition and is therefore re-garded as divine—a submission born from distress and enthusiasm. In genuine charis-matic domination, therefore, there are no abstract legal propositions and regulations and no 'formalised' legal judgments. 'Objec-tive' law, in such a case, flows from concrete and intensely personal experience of heav-enly grace and a semi-divine heroic stature: it means the rejection of the bonds of exter-nal organisation in favour of nothing but the ecstasy of the true prophet and hero. It thus leads to a revolutionary revaluation of every-thing and a sovereign break with all tradi-tional or rational norms: 'it is written, but I say unto you'. The specifically charismatic method of settling disputes is a revelation through the prophet or oracle, or the 'Solomonic' judgments of a charismatically qualified sage based on evaluations which, while extremely concrete and individual, yet claim absolute validity. This is the true home of 'Kadi-justice', in the proverbial rather than the historical sense of that word. For, as an actual historical phenomenon, the judg-ments of the Islamic *Kadi* were bound up with sacred traditions and their often ex-tremely formalistic interpretation: they amounted in some situations, to be sure, to specific, rule-free evaluations of the individ-ual case, but only where these sources of knowledge had failed. Genuinely charismatic justice is always rule-free in this sense: in its pure form it is completely opposed to all the bonds of formalism and tradition and is as free in its attitude to the sanctity of tradition as to rationalistic deductions from abstract concepts. There will be no discussion here of the relation of the reference to '*aequum et bonum*' in Roman Law and the original sense of the term 'equity' in English law to charismatic justice in general and the theo-cratic Kadi-justice of Islam in particular. However, both are products in part of a sys-tem of justice which is already highly ration-alised and in part of the abstract concepts of Natural Law: the phrase '*ex fide bona*' con-tains in any case an allusion to good com-mercial 'morality' and so has as little to do with genuinely irrational justice as does our own 'free judicial opinion'. To be sure, all

forms of trial by ordeal are derived from charismatic justice. But to the extent that they substitute for the personal authority of a bearer of charisma a rule-bound mechanism for the formal determination of the divine will, they already belong to the domain of that 'bringing down to earth' of charisma which is shortly to be discussed.

As we saw, bureaucratic rationalisation can also be, and often has been, a revolution-ary force of the first order in its relation to tradition. But its revolution is carried out by *technical* means, basically 'from the outside' (as is especially true of all economic reor-ganisation); first it revolutionises things and organisations, and then, in consequence, it changes people, in the sense that it alters the conditions to which they must adapt and in some cases increases their chances of adapt-ing to the external world by rational determi-nation of means and ends. The power of cha-risma, by contrast, depends on beliefs in revelation and heroism, on emotional con-victions about the importance and value of a religious, ethical, artistic, scientific, political or other manifestation, on heroism, whether ascetic or military, or judicial wisdom or magical or other favours. Such belief revolu-tionises men 'from within' and seeks to shape things and organisations in accor-dance with its revolutionary will. This con-trast must, to be sure, be rightly understood. For all the vast differences in the areas in which they operate, the psychological ori-gins of ideas are essentially the same, whether they are religious, artistic, ethical, scientific or of any other kind: this is espe-cially true of the organising ideas of social and political life. Only a purely subjective, 'time-serving' evaluation could attribute one sort of idea to 'understanding' and another to 'intuition' (or whatever other pair of terms one might care to use): the mathematical 'imagination' of a Weierstrass is 'intuition' in exactly the same sense as that of any artist, prophet or, for that matter, of any dema-gogue: that is not where the difference lies.[1] If we are to understand the true meaning of 'rationalism', we must emphasise that the difference does not lie in general in the per-son or in the inner 'experiences' of the cre-ator of the ideas or the 'work', but in the man-ner in which it is inwardly 'appropriated' or 'experienced' by those whom he rules or leads. We have already seen that, in the process of rationalisation, the great majority of those who are led merely appropriate the external technical consequences which are of practical importance to their interests, or else adapt themselves to them (in the same way that we 'learn' our multiplication tables or as all too many jurists learn the techniques of the law): the actual content of their creator's ideas remains irrelevant to them. This is the meaning of the assertion that rationalisation and rational organisation revolutionise 'from the outside', whereas charisma, wherever its characteristic influence is felt, on the contrary exerts its revolutionary power from within, by producing a fundamental change of heart ('*metanoia*') in the ruled. The bureaucratic form of organisation merely replaces the belief in the holiness of what has always been—the traditional standards—with submission to deliberately created rules: everyone knows that anyone with sufficient power can always replace these rules with others, equally deliberately created, and so that they are not in any sense 'sacred'. By contrast, charisma, in its highest forms, bursts the bonds of rules and tradition in general and overturns all ideas of the sacred. Instead of the pious following of time-hallowed custom, it enforces inner subjection to something which has never before existed, is absolutely unique and is therefore considered divine. It is in this purely empirical and value-free sense the characteristically 'creative' revolutionary force in history.

Although both charismatic and patriarchal power rest on personal submission to 'natural leaders' and personal exercise of authority by them (in contrast with the 'appointed' leaders of bureaucratic systems), the submission and the authority take very different forms in the two cases. The patriarch, like the bureaucratic official, holds his authority in virtue of a certain established order: the difference between this order and the laws and regulations of the bureaucracy is that it is not deliberately created by men but has been accepted as inviolably valid from time immemorial. The bearer of charisma holds his authority in virtue of a mission held to be incarnate in his person: this

mission need not always or necessarily be of a revolutionary nature, dedicated to the subversion of all hierarchies of value and the overthrow of existing morality, law and tradition, but it certainly has been in its highest forms. However unstable the existence of patriarchal power may be in the case of any particular individual, it is nevertheless the structure of social domination which is appropriate to the demands of everyday life and which, like everyday life itself, continues to function without regard to changes in the individual holder of power or in the environment. In these respects it may be contrasted with the charismatic structure which is born of extraordinary situations of emergency and enthusiasm. Both kinds of structure may, in themselves, be suited to any sphere of life: many of the old German armies, for instance, fought patriarchally, divided into families each under the leadership of its head. The ancient colonising armies of Eastern monarchs and the contingents of small farmers in the Frankish army, marching under the leadership of their '*seniores*', were patrimonially organised. The religious function of the head of the household and religious worship within the household persist alongside the official community cult on the one hand and the great movements of charismatic prophecy, which in the nature of the case are almost always revolutionary, on the other. Along with the peacetime leader who deals with the everyday economic business of the community, and the popular levy in times of war involving the whole community, there is found nevertheless, among the Germans as well as the Indians, the charismatic war hero, who takes the field with his volunteer force of followers; even in official national wars the normal peacetime authorities are very often replaced by the war-prince, proclaimed as '*Herzog*' on an *ad hoc* basis because he has proved himself as a hero in such adventures.

In the political sphere, as in the religious, it is traditional, customary, everyday needs which are served by the patriarchal structure, resting as it does on habit, respect for tradition, piety towards elders and ancestors and bonds of personal loyalty, in contrast with the revolutionary role of charisma. This holds likewise in the economic sphere. The economy, as an organised permanent system of transactions for the purpose of planned provision for the satisfaction of material needs, is the specific home of the patriarchal structure of domination, and of the bureaucratic structure as it becomes increasingly rationalised to the level of the 'enterprise'. Nevertheless, even here there may be room for charisma. In primitive societies, charismatic features are often found in the organisation of hunting, which was at that time an important branch of the provision of material needs, even if it became less important as material culture increased: hunting was organised in a similar way to war, and even at a later stage was long treated in much the same way as war (even up to the time of the Assyrian royal inscriptions). But even in specifically capitalist economies the antagonism between charisma and the everyday can be found, except that here it is not charisma and 'household', but charisma and 'enterprise' which are opposed. When Henry Villard, with the aim of pulling off a coup on the stock exchange involving the shares of the Northern Pacific Railroad, arranged the famous 'blind pool', asked the public, without stating his purpose, for fifty million pounds for an undertaking which he refused to specify any further, and got the loan without security on the basis of his reputation, his action was an example of grandiose booty-capitalism and economic brigandage which, like other similar examples, was fundamentally different in its whole structure and spirit from the rational management of a normal large capitalist 'enterprise', while on the other hand resembling the large financial undertakings and projects for colonial exploitation, or the 'occasional trade' combined with piracy and slave-hunting expeditions, which have been known since earliest times. One can only understand the double nature of what one might call 'the spirit of capitalism', and equally the specific features of the modern, professionalised, bureaucratic form of everyday capitalism if one learns to make the conceptual distinction between these two structural elements, which are thoroughly entangled with one another, but are in the last analysis distinct.

Although a 'purely' charismatic authority in the sense of the word used here cannot, to the extent that it preserves its purity, be understood as an 'organisation' in the usual sense of an ordering of men and things according to the principle of ends and means, nevertheless its existence implies, not an amorphous, unstructured condition, but a well-defined form of social structure with personal organs and a suitable apparatus for providing services and material goods for the mission of the bearer of charisma. The leader's personal aides and, among them, a certain kind of charismatic aristocracy represent a narrower group of followers within the group, formed on principles of discipleship and personal loyalty and chosen according to personal charismatic qualification. The provision of material goods, though in theory voluntary, non-statutory and fluctuating, is regarded as a bounden duty of the charismatic ruler's subjects to an extent sufficient to cover what is required, and such services are offered according to need and capacity. The more the purity of the charismatic structure is maintained, the less the followers or disciples receive their material means of support or social position in the form of prebends, stipends, or any form of remuneration or salary, or in the form of titles or places in an ordered hierarchy. As far as material needs are concerned, to the extent that individuals have no other means of support, the master, in a community under authoritarian leadership, shares with his followers, without any form of deduction or contract, the wealth which flows in, according to circumstances, in the form of donations, booty or bequests; in some cases, therefore, they have rights of commensality and claims to equipment and donations which he bestows on them. As for non-material needs, they have a right to share in the social, political and religious esteem and honour which is paid to the master himself. Every deviation from this sullies the purity of the charismatic structure and marks a step towards other structural forms.

Together with the household community (though distinct from it), charisma is thus the second great historical example of communism, if that term is taken to mean a lack of 'calculation' in the *consumption* of goods, rather than the rational organisation of the *production* of goods for some kind of common benefit (which might be called 'social-ism'). Every form of 'communism' in this sense which is known to history finds its true home either in traditional or patriarchal societies (household communism)—the only form in which it has been or is now a phenomenon of the everyday—or amongst charismatic modes of thought far removed from the everyday: in the latter case, when complete, it is either the camp-communism of the robber band or the love-communism of the monastery in all its varied forms and its tendency to degenerate into mere 'charity' or alms-giving. Camp-communism (in varying degrees of purity) can be found in charismatic warrior societies in all periods, from the pirate-state of the Ligurian islands to the organisation of Islam under the Caliph Omar and the warrior orders of Christendom and of Japanese Buddhism. Love-communism in one form or another is found at the origins of all religions, and lives on amongst the professional followers of the god, or monks; it is also to be found in the many pietistic sects (Labadie, for instance) and other extremist religious communities. Both the genuine heroic disposition and genuine sanctity, as it seems to their true advocates, can only be preserved by maintenance of the communistic basis and absence of the urge towards individual private property. In this they are right: charisma is a force which is essentially outside the everyday and so necessarily outside economics. It is immediately threatened in its innermost being when the economic interests of everyday life prevail, as always tends to happen: the first stage in its decline is the 'prebend', the 'allowance' granted in place of the earlier communistic mode of provision from the common store. Every possible means is used by the proponents of true charisma to set limits to this decline. All specifically warrior states—Sparta is a typical example—retained remnants of charismatic commu-nism and sought (no less than religious orders) to protect the heroes from the 'temptations' presented by a concern for possessions, rational industry, and family cares. The adjustments achieved between these remnants of the older charismatic principles and individual economic interests, which enter with the introduction of prebends and are constantly hammering at the doors, take the most varied forms. In all cases, however, the limitless freedom to found families and acquire wealth which is finally given marks the end of the domination of true charisma. It is only the shared dangers of the military camp or the loving disposition of disciples who are withdrawn from the world which can hold communism together, and it is only communism in its turn which can ensure the purity of charisma against the interests of the everyday.

All charisma, however, in every hour of its existence finds itself on this road, from a passionate life in which there is no place for the economic to slow suffocation under the weight of material interests, and with every hour of its existence it moves further along it. . . .

Endnote

1. And incidentally they correspond completely with each other also in the 'value-sphere,' which does not concern us here, in that they all—even artistic intuition—in order to make themselves objective and so in general to prove their reality, imply 'grasping', or, if it is preferred, being 'grasped' by the claims of the 'work', and not a subjective 'feeling' or 'experience' like any other.

15
Class, Status, Party

Max Weber

[handwritten: Class Status Party]

Albert Salomon once wrote that Weber's sociology constitutes "a long and intense dialogue with the ghost of Marx." While this is something of an overstatement, Weber was in significant ways responding to Marxist theory. In this passage from *Economy and Society* (1921), Weber articulates at the conceptual level the basis of a critique of the economic determinism that he thought infected Marx's work. He identifies three discrete but interrelated realms: the economic, where class is the key concept; the social order (or culture), where status is the central notion; and power (or the political), where the party is the key associational mode. Weber was actually in agreement with Marx insofar as he believed that the economy has a particularly determinative impact on the social order and power, but he sought to correct what he thought was Marx's tendency to deny a relative autonomy to culture and politics.

Economically Determined Power and the Social Order

Law exists when there is a probability that an order will be upheld by a specific staff of men who will use physical or psychical compulsion with the intention of obtaining conformity with the order, or of inflicting sanctions for infringement of it.[1] The structure of every legal order directly influences the distribution of power, economic or otherwise, within its respective community. This is true of all legal orders and not only that of the state. In general, we understand by 'power' the chance of a man or of a number of men to realize their own will in a communal action even against the resistance of others who are participating in the action.

'Economically conditioned' power is not, of course, identical with 'power' as such. On the contrary, the emergence of economic power may be the consequence of power existing on other grounds. Man does not strive for power only in order to enrich himself economically. Power, including economic power, may be valued 'for its own sake.' Very frequently the striving for power is also conditioned by the social 'honor' it entails. Not all power, however, entails social honor: The typical American boss, as well as the typical big speculator, deliberately relinquishes social honor. Quite generally, 'mere economic' power, and especially 'naked' money power, is by no means a recognized basis of social honor. Nor is power the only basis of social honor. Indeed, social honor, or prestige, may even be the basis of political or economic power, and very frequently has been. Power, as well as honor, may be guaranteed by the legal order, but, at least normally, it is not their primary source. The legal order is rather an additional factor that enhances the chance to hold power or honor; but it cannot always secure them.

The way in which social honor is distributed in a community between typical groups participating in this distribution we may call the 'social order.' The social order and the economic order are, of course, similarly related to the 'legal order.' However, the social and the economic order are not identical. The economic order is for us merely the way in which economic goods and services are distributed and used. The social order is of course conditioned by the economic order to a high degree, and in its turn reacts upon it. Now: 'classes,' 'status groups,' and 'parties' are phenomena of the distribution of power within a community.

Determination of Class-Situation by Market-Situation

In our terminology, 'classes' are not communities; they merely represent possible, and frequent, bases for communal action. We may speak of a 'class' when (1) a number of people have in common a specific causal component of their life chances, in so far as (2) this component is represented exclusively by economic interests in the possession of goods and opportunities for income, and (3) is represented under the conditions of the commodity or labor markets. [These points refer to 'class situation,' which we may express more briefly as the typical chance for a supply of goods, external living conditions, and personal life experiences, in so far as this chance is determined by the amount and kind of power, or lack of such, to dispose of goods or skills for the sake of income in a given economic order. The term 'class' refers to any group of people that is found in the same class situation.]

It is the most elemental economic fact that the way in which the disposition over material property is distributed among a plurality of people, meeting competitively in the market for the purpose of exchange, in itself creates specific life chances. According to the law of marginal utility this mode of distribution excludes the non-owners from competing for highly valued goods; it favors the owners and, in fact, gives to them a monopoly to acquire such goods. Other things being equal, this mode of distribution monopolizes the opportunities for profitable deals for all those who, provided with goods, do not necessarily have to exchange them. It increases, at least generally, their power in price wars with those who, being propertyless, have nothing to offer but their services in native form or goods in a form constituted through their own labor, and who above all are compelled to get rid of these products in order barely to subsist. This mode of distribution gives to the propertied a monopoly on the possibility of transferring property from the sphere of use as a 'fortune,' to the sphere of 'capital goods;' that is, it gives them the entrepreneurial function and all chances to share directly or indirectly in returns on capital. All this holds true within the area in which pure market conditions prevail. 'Property' and 'lack of property' are, therefore, the basic categories of all class situations. It does not matter whether these two categories become effective in price wars or in competitive struggles.

Within these categories, however, class situations are further differentiated: on the one hand, according to the kind of property that is usable for returns; and, on the other hand, according to the kind of services that can be offered in the market. Ownership of domestic buildings; productive establish-ments; warehouses; stores; agriculturally usable land, large and small holdings—quantitative differences with possibly qualitative consequences—; ownership of mines; cattle; men (slaves); disposition over mobile instruments of production, or capital goods of all sorts, especially money or objects that can be exchanged for money easily and at any time; disposition over products of one's own labor or of others' labor differing according to their various distances from consumability; disposition over transferable monopolies of any kind—all these distinctions differentiate the class situations of the propertied just as does the 'meaning' which they can and do give to the utilization of property, especially to property which has money equivalence. Accordingly, the propertied, for instance, may belong to the class of rentiers or to the class of entrepreneurs.

Those who have no property but who offer services are differentiated just as much according to their kinds of services as according to the way in which they make use of these services, in a continuous or discontinuous relation to a recipient. But always this is the generic connotation of the concept of class: that the kind of chance in the *market* is the decisive moment which presents a common condition for the individual's fate. 'Class situation' is, in this sense, ultimately 'market situation.' The effect of naked possession *per se*, which among cattle breeders gives the non-owning slave or serf into the power of the cattle owner, is only a forerunner of real 'class' formation. However, in the cattle loan and in the naked severity of the law of debts in such communities, for the first time mere 'possession' as such emerges as decisive for the fate of the individual. This is very much in contrast to the agricultural communities based on labor. The creditor-debtor relation becomes the basis of 'class situations' only in those cities where a 'credit market,' however primitive, with rates of interest increasing according to the extent of dearth and a factual monopolization of credits, is developed by a plutocracy. Therewith 'class struggles' begin.

Those men whose fate is not determined by the chance of using goods or services for themselves on the market, e.g., slaves, are not, however, a 'class' in the technical sense of the term. They are, rather, a 'status group.'

Communal Action Flowing From Class Interest

According to our terminology, the factor that creates 'class' is unambiguously economic interest, and indeed, only those interests involved in the existence of the 'market.' Nevertheless, the concept of 'class-interest' is an ambiguous one: even as an empirical concept it is ambiguous as soon as one understands by it something other than the factual direction of interests following with a certain probability from the class situation for a certain 'average' of those people subjected to the class situation. The class situation and other circumstances remaining the same, the direction in which the individual worker, for instance, is likely to pursue his interests may vary widely, according to whether he is constitutionally qualified for the task at hand to a high, to an average, or to a low degree. In the same way, the direction of interests may vary according to whether or not a *communal* action of a larger or smaller portion of those commonly affected by the 'class situation,' or even an association among them, e.g., a 'trade union,' has grown out of the class situation from which the individual may or may not expect promising results. [Communal action refers to that action which is oriented to the feeling of the actors that they belong together. Societal action, on the other hand, is oriented to a rationally motivated adjustment of interests.] The rise of societal or even of communal action from a common class situation is by no means a universal phenomenon.

The class situation may be restricted in its effects to the generation of essentially *similar* reactions, that is to say, within our terminology, of 'mass actions.' However, it may not have even this result. Furthermore, often merely an amorphous communal action emerges. For example, the 'murmuring' of the workers known in ancient oriental ethics: the moral disapproval of the work-master's conduct, which in its practical significance was probably equivalent to an increasingly typical phenomenon of precisely the latest industrial development, namely, the 'slow down' (the deliberate limiting of work effort) of laborers by virtue of tacit agreement. The degree in which 'communal action' and possibly 'societal action,' emerges from the 'mass actions' of the members of a class is linked to general cultural conditions, especially to those of an intellectual sort. It is also linked to the extent of the contrasts that have already evolved, and is especially linked to the *transparency* of the connections between the causes and the consequences of the 'class situation.' For however different life chances may be, this fact in itself, according to all experience, by no means gives birth to 'class action' (communal action by the members of a class). The fact of being conditioned and the results of the class situation must be distinctly recognizable. For only then the contrast of life chances can be felt not as an absolutely given fact to be accepted, but as a resultant from either (1) the given distribution of property, or (2) the structure of the concrete economic order. It is only then that people may react against the class structure not only through acts of an intermittent and irrational protest, but in the form of rational association. There have been 'class situations' of the first category (1), of a specifically naked and transparent sort, in the urban centers of Antiquity and during the Middle Ages; especially then, when great fortunes were accumulated by factually monopolized trading in industrial products of these localities or in foodstuffs. Furthermore, under certain circumstances, in the rural economy of the most diverse periods, when agriculture was increasingly exploited in a profit-making manner. The most important historical example of the second category (2) is the class situation of the modern 'proletariat.'

Types of Class Struggle

Thus every class may be the carrier of any one of the possibly innumerable forms of 'class action,' but this is not necessarily so. In any case, a class does not in itself constitute a community. To treat 'class' conceptually as having the same value as 'community' leads to distortion. That men in the same class situation regularly react in mass actions to such tangible situations as economic ones in the direction of those interests that are most adequate to their average number is an important and after all simple fact for the understanding of historical events. Above all, this fact must not lead to that kind of pseudo-scientific operation with the concepts of 'class' and 'class interests' so frequently found these days, and which has found its most classic expression in the statement of a talented author, that the individual may be in error concerning his interests but that the 'class' is 'infallible' about its interests. Yet, if classes as such are not communities, nevertheless class situations emerge only on the basis of communalization. The communal action that brings forth class situations, however, is not basically action between members of the identical class; it is an action between members of different classes. Communal actions that directly determine the class situation of the worker and the entrepreneur are: the labor market, the commodities market, and the capitalistic enterprise. But, in its turn, the existence of a capitalistic enterprise presupposes that a very specific communal action exists and that it is specifically structured to protect the possession of goods *per se*, and especially the power of individuals to dispose, in principle freely, over the means of production. The existence of a capitalistic enterprise is preconditioned by a specific kind of 'legal order.' Each kind of class situation, and above all when it rests upon the power of property *per se*, will become most clearly efficacious when all other determinants of reciprocal relations are, as far as possible, eliminated in their significance. It is in this way that the utilization of the power of property in the market obtains its most sovereign importance.

Now 'status groups' hinder the strict carrying through of the sheer market principle. In the present context they are of interest to us only from this one point of view. Before we briefly consider them, note that not much of a general nature can be said about the more specific kinds of antagonism between 'classes' (in our meaning of the term). The great shift, which has been going on continuously in the past, and up to our times, may be summarized, although at the cost of some precision: the struggle in which class situations are effective has progressively shifted from consumption credit toward, first, com-

petitive struggles in the commodity market and, then, toward price wars on the labor market. The 'class struggles' of antiquity—to the extent that they were genuine class struggles and not struggles between status groups—were initially carried on by indebted peasants, and perhaps also by artisans threatened by debt bondage and struggling against urban creditors. For debt bondage is the normal result of the differentiation of wealth in commercial cities, especially in seaport cities. A similar situation has existed among cattle breeders. Debt relationships as such produced class action up to the time of Cataline. Along with this, and with an increase in provision of grain for the city by transporting it from the outside, the struggle over the means of sustenance emerged. It centered in the first place around the provision of bread and the determination of the price of bread. It lasted throughout antiquity and the entire Middle Ages. The propertyless as such flocked together against those who actually and supposedly were interested in the dearth of bread. This fight spread until it involved all those commodities essential to the way of life and to handicraft production. There were only incipient discussions of wage disputes in antiquity and in the Middle Ages. But they have been slowly increasing up into modern times. In the earlier periods they were completely secondary to slave rebellions as well as to fights in the commodity market.

The propertyless of antiquity and of the Middle Ages protested against monopolies, pre-emption, forestalling, and the withholding of goods from the market in order to raise prices. Today the central issue is the determination of the price of labor.

This transition is represented by the fight for access to the market and for the determination of the price of products. Such fights went on between merchants and workers in the putting-out system of domestic handicraft during the transition to modern times. Since it is quite a general phenomenon we must mention here that the class antagonisms that are conditioned through the market situation are usually most bitter between those who actually and directly participate as opponents in price wars. It is not the rentier, the share-holder, and the banker who suffer the ill will of the worker, but almost exclusively the manufacturer and the business executives who are the direct opponents of workers in price wars. This is so in spite of the fact that it is precisely the cash boxes of the rentier, the share-holder, and the banker into which the more or less 'unearned' gains flow, rather than into the pockets of the manufacturers or of the business executives. This simple state of affairs has very frequently been decisive for the role the class situation has played in the formation of political parties. For example, it has made possible the varieties of patriarchal socialism and the frequent attempts—formerly, at least—of threatened status groups to form alliances with the proletariat against the 'bourgeoisie.'

Status Honor

In contrast to classes, *status groups* are normally communities. They are, however, often of an amorphous kind. In contrast to the purely economically determined 'class situation' we wish to designate as 'status situation' every typical component of the life fate of men that is determined by a specific, positive or negative, social estimation of *honor*. This honor may be connected with any quality shared by a plurality, and, of course, it can be knit to a class situation: class distinctions are linked in the most varied ways with status distinctions. Property as such is not always recognized as a status qualification, but in the long run it is, and with extraordinary regularity. In the subsistence economy of the organized neighborhood, very often the richest man is simply the chieftain. However, this often means only an honorific preference. For example, in the so-called pure modern 'democracy,' that is, one devoid of any expressly ordered status privileges for individuals, it may be that only the families coming under approximately the same tax class dance with one another. This example is reported of certain smaller Swiss cities. But status honor need not necessarily be linked with a 'class situation.' On the contrary, it normally stands in sharp opposition to the pretensions of sheer property.

Both propertied and propertyless people can belong to the same status group, and frequently they do with very tangible consequences. This 'equality' of social esteem may,

however, in the long run become quite precarious. The 'equality' of status among the American 'gentlemen,' for instance, is expressed by the fact that outside the subordination determined by the different functions of 'business,' it would be considered strictly repugnant—wherever the old tradition still prevails—if even the richest 'chief,' while playing billiards or cards in his club in the evening, would not treat his 'clerk' as in every sense fully his equal in birthright. It would be repugnant if the American 'chief' would bestow upon his 'clerk' the condescending 'benevolence' marking a distinction of 'position,' which the German chief can never dissever from his attitude. This is one of the most important reasons why in America the German 'clubby-ness' has never been able to attain the attraction that the American clubs have. . . .

frontier heritage

Parties

Whereas the genuine place of 'classes' is within the economic order, the place of 'status groups' is within the social order, that is, within the sphere of the distribution of 'honor.' From within these spheres, classes and status groups influence one another and they influence the legal order and are in turn influenced by it. But 'parties' live in a house of 'power.'

Their action is oriented toward the acquisition of social 'power,' that is to say, toward influencing a communal action no matter what its content may be. In principle, parties may exist in a social 'club' as well as in a 'state.' As over against the actions of classes and status groups, for which this is not necessarily the case, the communal actions of 'parties' always mean a societalization. For party actions are always directed toward a goal which is striven for in planned manner. This goal may be a 'cause' (the party may aim at realizing a program for ideal or material purposes), or the goal may be 'personal' (sinecures, power, and from these, honor for the leader and the followers of the party). Usually the party action aims at all these simultaneously. Parties are, therefore, only possible within communities that are societalized, that is, which have some rational order and a staff of persons available who are ready to enforce it. For parties aim precisely at influencing this staff, and if possible, to recruit it from party followers.

In any individual case, parties may represent interests determined through 'class situation' or 'status situation,' and they may recruit their following respectively from one or the other. But they need be neither purely 'class' nor purely 'status' parties. In most cases they are partly class parties and partly status parties, but sometimes they are neither. They may represent ephemeral or enduring structures. Their means of attaining power may be quite varied, ranging from naked violence of any sort to canvassing for votes with coarse or subtle means: money, social influence, the force of speech, suggestion, clumsy hoax, and so on to the rougher or more artful tactics of obstruction in parliamentary bodies.

The sociological structure of parties differs in a basic way according to the kind of communal action which they struggle to influence. Parties also differ according to whether or not the community is stratified by status or by classes. Above all else, they vary according to the structure of domination within the community. For their leaders normally deal with the conquest of a community. They are, in the general concept which is maintained here, not only products of specially modern forms of domination. We shall also designate as parties the ancient and medieval 'parties,' despite the fact that their structure differs basically from the structure of modern parties. By virtue of these structural differences of domination it is impossible to say anything about the structure of parties without discussing the structural forms of social domination *per se*. Parties, which are always structures struggling for domination, are very frequently organized in a very strict 'authoritarian' fashion. . . .

Concerning 'classes,' 'status groups,' and 'parties,' it must be said in general that they necessarily presuppose a comprehensive societalization, and especially a political framework of communal action, within which they operate. This does not mean that parties would be confined by the frontiers of any individual political community. On the contrary, at all times it has been the order of the day that the societalization (even when it aims at the use of military force in common) reaches beyond the frontiers of politics. This has been the case in the solidarity of interests among the Oligarchs and among the democrats in Hellas, among the Guelfs and among Ghibellines in the Middle Ages, and within the Calvinist party during the period of religious struggles. It has been the case up to the solidarity of the landlords (International Congress of Agrarian Landlords), and has continued among princes (Holy Alliance, Karlsbad Decrees), socialist workers, conservatives (the longing of Prussian conservatives for Russian intervention in 1850). But their aim is not necessarily the establishment of new international political, i.e. *territorial*, dominion. In the main they aim to influence the existing dominion.[2]

Endnotes

1. *Wirtschaft und Gesellschaft*, part III, chap. 4, pp. 631–40. The first sentence in paragraph one and the several definitions in this chapter which are in brackets do not appear in the original text. They have been taken from other contexts of *Wirtschaft und Gesellschaft*.

2. The posthumously published text breaks off here. We omit an incomplete sketch of types of 'warrior estates.'

IV. Georg Simmel

16
Fashion

Georg Simmel

Georg Simmel (1858–1918) was the first classical figure in sociology to turn his attention to the realms of leisure and consumption. This interest is nowhere more evident than in this 1904 essay on fashion, in which he discusses the reason that fashions come into vogue and go out of style with such rapidity in modern social life. On the one hand, he explains this phenomenon in terms of the collective psyche of the times: We live, he says, in a "more nervous age" than the past. On the other hand, Simmel attributes changes in fashion to the wide expansion of consumer choices industrial society makes possible and to the fact that people increasingly seek to use fashions as ways to differentiate themselves from others. He also points out, however, that fashions are not merely reflections of individual choices but are structured by class and other social divisions.

The vital conditions of fashion as a universal phenomenon in the history of our race are circumscribed by these conceptions. Fashion is the imitation of a given example and satisfies the demand for social adaptation; it leads the individual upon the road which all travel, it furnishes a general condition, which resolves the conduct of every individual into a mere example. At the same time it satisfies in no less degree the need of differentiation, the tendency towards dissimilarity, the desire for change and contrast, on the one hand by a constant change of contents, which gives to the fashion of to-day an individual stamp as opposed to that of yesterday and of to-morrow, on the other hand because fashions differ for different classes—the fashions of the upper stratum of society are never identical with those of the lower; in fact, they are abandoned by the former as soon as the latter prepares to appropriate them. Thus fashion represents nothing more than one of the many forms of life by the aid of which we seek to combine in uniform spheres of activity the tendency towards social equalization with the desire for individual differentiation and change. Every phase of the conflicting pair strives visibly beyond the degree of satisfaction that any fashion offers to an absolute control of the sphere of life in question. If we should study the history of fashions (which hitherto have been examined only from the view-point of the development of their contents) in connection with their importance for the form of the social process, we should find that it reflects the history of the attempts to adjust the satisfaction of the two counter-tendencies more and more perfectly to the condition of the existing individual and social culture. The various psychological elements in fashion all conform to this fundamental principle.

Fashion, as noted above, is a product of class distinction and operates like a number of other forms, honor especially, the double function of which consists in revolving within a given circle and at the same time emphasizing it as separate from others. Just as the frame of a picture characterizes the work of art inwardly as a coherent, homogeneous, independent entity and at the same time outwardly severs all direct relations with the surrounding space, just as the uniform energy of such forms cannot be expressed unless we determine the double effect, both inward and outward, so honor owes its character, and above all its moral rights, to the fact that the individual in his personal honor at the same time represents and maintains that of his social circle and his class. These moral rights, however, are frequently considered unjust by those without the pale. Thus fashion on the one hand signifies union with those in the same class, the uniformity of a circle characterized by it, and, *uno actu*, the exclusion of all other groups.

Union and segregation are the two fundamental functions which are here inseparably united, and one of which, although or because it forms a logical contrast to the other, becomes the condition of its realization. Fashion is merely a product of social demands, even though the individual object which it creates or recreates may represent a more or less individual need. This is clearly proved by the fact that very frequently not the slightest reason can be found for the creations of fashion from the standpoint of an objective, aesthetic, or other expediency. While in general our wearing apparel is really adapted to our needs, there is not a trace of expediency in the method by which fashion dictates, for example, whether wide or narrow trousers, colored or black scarfs shall be worn. As a rule the material justification for an action coincides with its general adoption, but in the case of fashion there is a complete separation of the two elements, and there remains for the individual only this general acceptance as the deciding motive to appropriate it. Judging from the ugly and repugnant things that are sometimes in vogue, it would seem as though fashion were desirous of exhibiting its power by getting us to adopt the most atrocious things for its sake alone. The absolute indifference of fashion to the material standards of life is well illustrated by the way in which it recommends something appropriate in one instance, something abstruse in another, and something materially and aesthetically quite indifferent in a third. The only motivations with which fashion is concerned are formal social ones. The reason why even aesthetically impossible styles seem *distingué*, elegant, and artistically tolerable when affected by persons who carry them to the extreme, is that the persons who do this are generally the most elegant and pay the greatest attention to their personal appearance, so that under any circumstances we would get the impression of something *distingué* and aesthetically cultivated. This impression we

credit to the questionable element of fashion, the latter appealing to our consciousness as the new and consequently most conspicuous feature of the *tout ensemble*.

Fashion occasionally will affect objectively determined subjects such as religious faith, scientific interests, even socialism and individualism; but it does not become operative as fashion until these subjects can be considered independent of the deeper human motives from which they have risen. For this reason the rule of fashion becomes in such fields unendurable. We therefore see that there is good reason why externals—clothing, social conduct, amusements—constitute the specific field of fashion, for here no dependence is placed on really vital motives of human action. It is the field which we can most easily relinquish to the bent towards imitation, which it would be a sin to follow in important questions. We encounter here a close connection between the consciousness of personality and that of the material forms of life, a connection that runs all through history. The more objective our view of life has become in the last centuries, the more it has stripped the picture of nature of all subjective and anthropomorphic elements, and the more sharply has the conception of individual personality become defined. The social regulation of our inner and outer life is a sort of embryo condition, in which the contrasts of the purely personal and the purely objective are differentiated, the action being synchronous and reciprocal. Therefore wherever man appears essentially as a social being we observe neither strict objectivity in the view of life nor absorption and independence in the consciousness of personality.

Social forms, apparel, aesthetic judgment, the whole style of human expression, are constantly transformed by fashion, in such a way, however, that fashion—*i.e.*, the latest fashion—in all these things affects only the upper classes. Just as soon as the lower classes begin to copy their style, thereby crossing the line of demarcation the upper classes have drawn and destroying the uniformity of their coherence, the upper classes turn away from this style and adopt a new one, which in its turn differentiates them from the masses; and thus the game goes merrily on. Naturally the lower classes look and strive towards the upper, and they encounter the least resistance in those fields which are subject to the whims of fashion; for it is here that mere external imitation is most readily applied. The same process is at work as between the different sets within the upper classes, although it is not always as visible here as it is, for example, between mistress and maid. Indeed, we may often observe that the more nearly one set has approached another, the more frantic becomes the desire for imitation from below and the seeking for the new from above. The increase of wealth is bound to hasten the process considerably and render it visible, because the objects of fashion, embracing as they do the externals of life, are most accessible to the mere call of money, and conformity to the higher set is more easily acquired here than in fields which demand an individual test that gold and silver cannot affect.

We see, therefore, that in addition to the element of imitation the element of demarcation constitutes an important factor of fashion. This is especially noticeable wherever the social structure does not include any superimposed groups, in which case fashion asserts itself in neighboring groups. Among primitive peoples we often find that closely connected groups living under exactly similar conditions develop sharply differentiated fashions, by means of which each group establishes uniformity within, as well as difference without, the prescribed set. On the other hand, there exists a widespread predilection for importing fashions from without, and such foreign fashions assume a greater value within the circle, simply because they did not originate there. The prophet Zephaniah expressed his indignation at the aristocrats who affected imported apparel. As a matter of fact the exotic origin of fashions seems strongly to favor the exclusiveness of the groups which adopt them. Because of their external origin, these imported fashions create a special and significant form of socialization, which arises through mutual relation to a point without the circle. It sometimes appears as though social elements, just like the axes of vision, converge best at a point that is not too near.

The currency, or more precisely the medium of exchange among primitive races, often consists of objects that are brought in from without. On the Solomon Islands, and at Ibo on the Niger, for example, there exists a regular industry for the manufacture of money from shells, etc., which are not employed as a medium of exchange in the place itself, but in neighboring districts, to which they are exported. Paris modes are frequently created with the sole intention of setting a fashion elsewhere.

This motive of foreignness, which fashion employs in its socializing endeavors, is restricted to higher civilization, because novelty, which foreign origin guarantees in extreme form, is often regarded by primitive races as an evil. This is certainly one of the reasons why primitive conditions of life favor a correspondingly infrequent change of fashions. The savage is afraid of strange appearances; the difficulties and dangers that beset his career cause him to scent danger in anything new which he does not - understand and which he cannot assign to a familiar category. Civilization, however, transforms this affectation into its very opposite. Whatever is exceptional, bizarre, or conspicuous, or whatever departs from the customary norm, exercises a peculiar charm upon the man of culture, entirely independent of its material justification. The removal of the feeling of insecurity with reference to all things new was accomplished by the progress of civilization. At the same time it may be the old inherited prejudice, although it has become purely formal and unconscious, which, in connection with the present feeling of security, produces this piquant interest in exceptional and odd things. For this reason the fashions of the upper classes develop their power of exclusion against the lower in proportion as general culture advances, at least until the mingling of the classes and the leveling effect of democracy exert a counter-influence.

Fashion plays a more conspicuous *rôle* in modern times, because the differences in our standards of life have become so much more strongly accentuated, for the more numerous and the more sharply drawn these differences are, the greater the opportunities for emphasizing them at every turn. In innumerable instances this cannot be accomplished by passive inactivity, but only by the development of forms established by fashion; and this has become all the more pronounced since legal restrictions prescribing various forms of apparel and modes of life for different classes have been removed.

***

Two social tendencies are essential to the establishment of fashion, namely, the need of union on the one hand and the need of isolation on the other. Should one of these be absent, fashion will not be formed—its sway will abruptly end. Consequently the lower classes possess very few modes and those they have are seldom specific; for this reason the modes of primitive races are much more stable than ours. Among primitive races the socializing impulse is much more powerfully developed than the differentiating impulse. For, no matter how decisively the groups may be separated from one another, separation is for the most part hostile in such a way that the very relation the rejection of which within the classes of civilized races makes fashion reasonable, is absolutely lacking. Segregation by means of differences in clothing, manners, taste, etc., is expedient only where the danger of absorption and obliteration exists, as is the case among highly civilized nations. Where these differences do not exist, where we have an absolute antagonism, as for example between not directly friendly groups of primitive races, the development of fashion has no sense at all.

It is interesting to observe how the prevalence of the socializing impulse in primitive peoples affects various institutions, such as the dance. It has been noted quite generally that the dances of primitive races exhibit a remarkable uniformity in arrangement and rhythm. The dancing group feels and acts like a uniform organism; the dance forces and accustoms a number of individuals, who are usually driven to and fro without rime or reason by vacillating conditions and needs of life, to be guided by a common impulse and a single common motive. Even making allowances for the tremendous difference in the outward appearance of the dance, we are

dealing here with the same element that appears in socializing force of fashion. Movement, time, rhythm of the gestures, are all undoubtedly influenced largely by what is worn: similarly dressed persons exhibit relative similarity in their actions. This is of especial value in modern life with its individualistic diffusion, while in the case of primitive races the effect produced is directed within and is therefore not dependent upon changes of fashion. Among primitive races fashions will be less numerous and more stable because the need of new impressions and forms of life, quite apart from their social effect, is far less pressing. Changes in fashion reflect the dulness of nervous impulses: the more nervous the age, the more rapidly its fashions change, simply because the desire for differentiation, one of the most important elements of all fashion, goes hand in hand with the weakening of nervous energy. This fact in itself is one of the reasons why the real seat of fashion is found among the upper classes. . . .

The very character of fashion demands that it should be exercised at one time only by a portion of the given group, the great majority being merely on the road to adopting it. As soon as an example has been universally adopted, that is, as soon as anything done only by a few has really come to be practiced by all—as is the case in certain portions of our social conduct—we no longer speak of fashion. As fashion spreads, it gradually goes to its doom. The distinctiveness which in the early stages of a set fashion assures for it a certain distribution is destroyed as the fashion spreads, and as this element wanes, the fashion also is bound to die. By reason of this peculiar play between the tendency towards universal acceptation and the destruction of its very purpose to which this general adoption leads, fashion includes a peculiar attraction of limitation, the attraction of a simultaneous beginning and end, the charm of novelty coupled to that of transitoriness. The attractions of both poles of the phenomena meet in fashion, and show also here that they belong together unconditionally, although, or rather because, they are contradictory in their very nature. Fashion always occupies the dividing-line between the past and the future, and consequently conveys a stronger feeling of the present, at least while it is at its height, than most other phenomena. What we call the present is usually nothing more than a combination of a fragment of the past with a fragment of the future. Attention is called to the present less often than colloquial usage, which is rather liberal in its employment of the word, would lead us to believe.

Few phenomena of social life possess such a pointed curve of consciousness as does fashion. As soon as the social consciousness attains to the highest point designated by fashion, it marks the beginning of the end for the latter. This transitory character of fashion, however, does not on the whole degrade it, but adds a new element of attraction. At all events an object does not suffer degradation by being called fashionable, unless we reject it with disgust or wish to debase it for other, material reasons, in which case, of course, fashion becomes an idea of value. In the practice of life anything else similarly new and suddenly disseminated is not called fashion, when we are convinced of its continuance and its material justification. If, on the other hand, we feel certain that the fact will vanish as rapidly as it came, then we call it fashion. We can discover one of the reasons why in these latter days fashion exercises such a powerful influence on our consciousness in the circumstance that the great, permanent, unquestionable convictions are continually losing strength, as a consequence of which the transitory and vacillating elements of life acquire more room for the display of their activity. The break with the past, which, for more than a century, civilized mankind has been laboring unceasingly to bring about, makes the consciousness turn more and more to the present. This accentuation of the present evidently at the same time emphasizes the element of change, and a class will turn to fashion in all fields, by no means only in that of apparel, in proportion to the degree in which it supports the given civilizing tendency. It may almost be considered a sign of the increased power of fashion, that it has overstepped the bounds of its original domain, which comprised only personal externals, and has acquired an increasing influ-

ence over taste, over theoretical convictions, and even over the moral foundations of life.

***

From the fact that fashion as such can never be generally in vogue, the individual derives the satisfaction of knowing that as adopted by him it still represents something special and striking, while at the same time he feels inwardly supported by a set of persons who are striving for the same thing, not as in the case of other social satisfactions, by a set actually doing the same thing. The fashionable person is regarded with mingled feelings of approval and envy; we envy him as an individual, but approve of him as a member of a set or group. Yet even this envy has a peculiar coloring. There is a shade of envy which includes a species of ideal participation in the envied object itself. An instructive example of this is furnished by the conduct of the poor man who gets a glimpse of the feast of his rich neighbor. The moment we envy an object or a person, we are no longer absolutely excluded from it; some relation or other has been established—between both the same psychic content now exists—although in entirely different categories and forms of sensations. This quiet personal usurpation of the envied property contains a kind of antidote, which occasionally counter-acts the evil effects of this feeling of envy. The contents of fashion afford an especially good chance of the development of this conciliatory shade of envy, which also gives to the envied person a better conscience because of his satisfaction over his good fortune. This is due to the fact that these contents are not, as many other psychic contents are, denied absolutely to any one, for a change of fortune, which is never entirely out of the question, may play them into the hands of an individual who had previously been confined to the state of envy.

From all this we see that fashion furnishes an ideal field for individuals with dependent natures, whose self-consciousness, however, requires a certain amount of prominence, attention, and singularity. Fashion raises even the unimportant individual by making him the representative of a class, the embodiment of a joint spirit. And here again we observe the curious intermixture of antagonistic values. Speaking broadly, it is characteristic of a standard set by a general body, that its acceptance by any one individual does not call attention to him; in other words, a positive adoption of a given norm signifies nothing. Whoever keeps the laws the breaking of which is punished by the penal code, whoever lives up to the social forms prescribed by his class, gains no conspicuousness or notoriety. The slightest infraction or opposition, however, is immediately noticed and places the individual in an exceptional position by calling the attention of the public to his action. All such norms do not assume positive importance for the individual until he begins to depart from them. It is peculiarly characteristic of fashion that it renders possible a social obedience, which at the same time is a form of individual differentiation. Fashion does this because in its very nature it represents a standard that can never be accepted by all. While fashion postulates a certain amount of general acceptance, it nevertheless is not without significance in the characterization of the individual, for it emphasizes his personality not only through omission but also through observance. In the dude the social demands of fashion appear exaggerated to such a degree that they completely assume an individualistic and peculiar character. It is characteristic of the dude that he carries the

elements of a particular fashion to an extreme; when pointed shoes are in style, he wears shoes that resemble the prow of a ship; when high collars are all the rage, he wears collars that come up to his ears; when scientific lectures are fashionable, you cannot find him anywhere else, etc., etc. Thus he represents something distinctly individual, which consists in the quantitative intensification of such elements as are qualitatively common property of the given set of class. He leads the way, but all travel the same road. Representing as he does the most recently conquered heights of public taste, he seems to be marching at the head of the general procession. In reality, however, what is so frequently true of the relation between individuals and groups applies also to him: as a matter of fact, the leader allows himself to be led. . . .

Reprinted from *On Individuality & Social Forms*, by Georg Simmel, edited by Donald Levine. From the series *The Heritage of Sociology*, edited by Morris Janowitz. Copyright © 1971 by The University of Chicago. Reprinted from "Fashion," *American Journal of Sociology* 62 (May 1957); originally published in *International Quarterly* (New York), 10 (1904). Translator unknown. Published in German as *Philosophie der Mode* (Berlin: Pan-Verlag, 1905), and in slightly revised and enlarged form in *Philosophische Kultur* (Leipzig: W. Klinkhardt, 1911). Reprinted with permission of The University of Chicago Press. ✦

17
The Problem of Sociology

Georg Simmel

In this 1908 essay Simmel articulates his understanding of the proper object of sociological inquiry: sociation, or (a term that would become the focus of some of his intellectual heirs) social interaction. Although sociation is rooted in individual psychological predispositions, the realm of psychology is nonetheless separate from that of sociology, whose proper focus should be the forms and types of interaction. Whereas many of Simmel's discussions of interaction deal with the micro level, this essay makes clear that he was equally interested in the "web" of social life. Simmel makes frequent reference to geometry in his writings, and in this essay he suggests that a parallel can be drawn between it and sociology.

Society exists where a number of individuals enter into interaction. This interaction always arises on the basis of certain drives or for the sake of certain purposes. Erotic, religious, or merely associative impulses; and purposes of defense, attack, play, gain, aid, or instruction—these and countless others cause man to live with other men, to act for them, with them, against them, and thus to correlate his condition with theirs. In brief, he influences and is influenced by them. The significance of these interactions among men lies in the fact that it is because of them that the individuals, in whom these driving impulses and purposes are lodged, form a unity, that is, a society. For unity in the empirical sense of the word is nothing but the interaction of elements. An organic body is a unity because its organs maintain a more intimate exchange of their energies with each other than with any other organism; a state is a unity because its citizens show similar mutual effects. In fact, the whole world could not be called one if each of its parts did not somehow influence every other part, or, if at any one point the reciprocity of effects, however indirect it may be, were cut off.

This unity, or sociation, may be of very different degrees, according to the kind and the intimacy of the interaction which it obtains. Sociation ranges all the way from the momentary getting together for a walk to the founding of a family, from relations maintained "until further notice" to membership in a state, from the temporary aggregation of hotel guests to the intimate bond of a medieval guild. I designate as the content—the materials, so to speak—of sociation everything that is present in individuals (the immediately concrete loci of all historical reality)—drive, interest, purpose, inclination, psychic state, movement—everything that is present in them in such a way as to engender or mediate effects upon others or to receive such effects. In themselves, these materials which fill life, these motivations which propel it, are not social. Strictly speaking, neither hunger nor love, work nor religiosity, technology nor the functions and results of intelligence, are social. They are factors in sociation only when they transform the mere aggregation of isolated individuals into specific forms of being with and for one another, forms that are subsumed under the general concept of interaction. Sociation is the form (realized in innumerably different ways) in which individuals grow together into a unity and within which their interests are realized. And it is on the basis of their interests—sensuous or ideal, momentary or lasting, conscious or unconscious, causal or teleological—that individuals form such unities.

In any given social phenomenon, content and societal form constitute one reality. A social form severed from all content can no more attain existence than a spatial form can exist without a material whose form it is. Any social phenomenon or process is composed of two elements which in reality are inseparable: on the one hand, an interest, a purpose, or a motive; on the other, a form or mode of interaction among individuals through which, or in the shape of which, that content attains social reality.

It is evident that that which constitutes society in every current sense of the term is identical with the kinds of interaction discussed. A collection of human beings does not become a society because each of them has an objectively determined or subjectively impelling life-content. It becomes a society only when the vitality of these contents attains the form of reciprocal influence; only when one individual has an effect, immediate or mediate, upon another, is mere spatial aggregation or temporal succession transformed into society. If, therefore, there is to be a science whose subject matter is society and nothing else, it must exclusively investigate these interactions, these kinds and forms of sociation. For everything else found within "society" and realized through it and within its framework is not itself society. It is merely a content that develops or is developed by this form of coexistence, and it produces the real phenomenon called "society" in the broader and more customary sense of the term only in conjunction with this form. To separate, by scientific abstraction, these two factors of form and content which are in reality inseparably united; to detach by analysis the forms of interaction or sociation from their contents (through which alone these forms become social forms); and to bring them together systematically under a consistent scientific viewpoint—this seems to me the basis for the only, as well as the entire, possibility of a special science of society as such. Only such a science can actually treat the facts that go under the name of sociohistorical reality upon the plane of the purely social.

Abstractions alone produce science out of the complexity or the unity of reality. Yet however urgently such abstractions may be demanded by the needs of cognition itself, they also require some sort of justification of their relation to the structure of the objective world. For only some functional relation to actuality can save one from sterile inquiries or from the haphazard formulation of scientific concepts. Certainly, naïve naturalism errs in assuming that the given itself contains the analytic or synthetic arrangements through which it becomes the content of a science. Nevertheless, the characteristics of the given are more or less susceptible to such arrangements. An analogy may help here. A portrait fundamentally transforms the natural human appearance, but one face is better suited than another to such a transformation into something radically alien. Remembering this helps us to appraise the greater or lesser appropriateness of various scientific problems and methods. The right to subject sociohistorical phenomena to an analysis in terms of form and content (and to synthesize the forms) rests upon two conditions which must be verified on a factual basis. On the one hand, we must demonstrate that the same form of sociation can be observed in quite dissimilar contents and in connection with quite dissimilar purposes. On the other hand, we must show that the content is realized in using quite dissimilar forms of sociation as its medium or vehicle. A parallel is found in the fact that the same geometric forms may be observed in the most heterogeneous materials and that the same material occurs in the most heterogeneous spatial forms. Similar relations obtain between logical forms and the material contents of cognition.

Both of these conditions are undeniable facts. We do find that the same form of interaction obtains among individuals in societal groups that are the most unlike imaginable in purpose and significance. Superiority, subordination, competition, division of labor, formation of parties, representation, inner solidarity coupled with exclusiveness toward the outside, and innumerable similar features are found in the state as well as in a religious community, in a band of conspirators as in an economic association, in an art school as in a family. However diverse the interests that give rise to these sociations, the forms in which the interests are realized are identical. On the other hand, the identical interest may take on form in very different sociations. Economic interest is realized both in competition and in the planned organization of producers, in isolation from other groups and in fusion with them. Although the religious contents of life remain identical, at one time they demand an unregulated, at another time a centralized, form of community. The interests upon which the relations between the sexes are based are satisfied by an almost endless variety of family forms. The educational interest may lead to a liberal or to a despotic relation between teacher and pupil, to individualistic interaction between them, or to a more collectivistic type of interaction between the teacher and the totality of his pupils. Hence, not only may the form in which the most widely different contents are realized be identical, but a content too may persist while its medium—the interactions of the individuals—moves in a variety of forms. We see, then, that the analysis in terms of form and content transforms the facts—which in their immediacy present form and content as an indissoluble unity of social life—in such a way as to furnish the legitimation of the sociological problem. This problem demands that the pure forms of sociation be identified, ordered systematically, explained psychologically, and studied from the standpoint of their historical development. . . .

This conception of society implies a further proposition: A given number of individuals may be a society to a greater or a smaller degree. With each formation of parties, with each joining for common tasks or in a common feeling or way of thinking, with each articulation of the distribution of positions of submission and domination, with each common meal, with each self-adornment for others—with every growth of new synthesizing phenomena such as these, the same group becomes "more society" than it was before. There is no such thing as society "as such"; that is, there is no society in the sense that it is the condition for the emergence of all these particular phenomena. For there is no such thing as interaction "as such"—there are only specific kinds of interaction. And it is with their emergence that society too emerges, for they are neither the cause nor the consequence of society but are, themselves, society. The fact that an extraordinary multitude and variety of interactions operate at any one moment has given a seemingly autonomous historical reality to the general concept of society. Perhaps it is this hypostatization of a mere abstraction that is the reason for the peculiar vagueness and uncertainty involved in the concept of society and in the customary treatises in general sociology. We are here reminded of the fact that not much headway was made in formulating a concept of "life" as long as it was conceived of as an immediately real and homogeneous phenomenon. The science of life did not establish itself on a firm basis until it investigated specific processes within organisms—processes whose sum or web life is; not until, in other words, it recognized that life consists of these particular processes.

Only if we follow the conception here outlined can we grasp what in "society" really *is* society. Similarly, it is only geometry that determines what the spatiality of things in space really is. Sociology, the discipline that deals with the purely social aspects of man (who, of course, can be an object of scientific inquiry in innumerable other respects), is related to the other special science of man as geometry is related to the physicochemical sciences. Geometry studies the forms through which any material becomes an empirical body, and these forms as such exist, of course, in abstraction only, precisely like the forms of sociation. Both geometry and sociology leave to other sciences the investigation of the contents realized in the forms, that is, the total phenomena whose forms they explore.

It is hardly necessary to point out that this analogy with geometry does not go beyond the clarification of the fundamental problem of sociology. It was only in attempting this clarification that we made use of this analogy. Above all, geometry has the advantage of having at its disposal extremely simple structures into which it can resolve the more complicated figures. Geometry can construe the whole range of possible formations from a relatively few fundamental definitions. Not even a remotely similar resolution into simple elements is to be hoped for in the foreseeable future as regards the forms of sociation. Sociological forms, if they are to be even approximately definite, can apply only to a limited range of phenomena. Even if we say, for instance, that superordination and subordination are forms found in almost every human sociation, we gain very little from this general knowledge. What is needed is the study of specific kinds of superordination and subordination, and of the specific forms in which they are realized. Through such a study, of course, these forms would lose in applicability what they would gain in definiteness.

In our day, we are used to asking of every science whether it is devoted to the discovery of timelessly valid laws or to the presentation and conceptualization of real, unique historical processes. Generally, this alternative ignores innumerable intermediate phenomena dealt with in the actual practice of science. It is irrelevant to our conception of the problem of sociology because this conception renders a choice between the two answers unnecessary. For, on the one hand, in sociology the object abstracted from reality may be examined in regard to laws entirely inhering in the objective nature of the elements. These laws must be sharply distinguished from any spatiotemporal realization; they are valid whether the historical actualities enforce them once or a thousand times. On the other hand, the forms of sociation may be examined, with equal validity, in regard to their occurrence at specific places and at specific times, and in regard to their historical development in specific groups. In this latter case, ascertaining them would be in the service of history, so to speak; in the former case, it would provide material for the induction of timeless uniformities. About competition, for instance, we learn something from a great many fields—political science, economics, history of religion, history of art, and so on. The point is to ascertain from all the facts what competition is as a pure form of human behavior; under what circumstances it emerges and develops; how it is modified by the particular character of its object; by what contemporaneous formal and material features of a society it is increased or reduced; and how competition between individuals differs from that between groups. In short, we must ascertain what competition is as a form of relation among individuals. This form may involve all sorts of contents. But in spite of the great variety of these contents, the form maintains its own identity and proves that it belongs to a sphere which is governed by its own laws and which may legitimately be abstracted from other spheres or from total reality. What we are suggesting, in brief, is that similar elements be singled out of the complex phenomena so as to secure a cross-section, whereby dissimilar elements—in our case the contents—reciprocally paralyze each other, as it were.

We have to proceed in this fashion with respect to all the great situations and interactions that form society—the formation of parties; imitation; the formation of classes and circles; secondary subdivisions; the embodiment of types of social interaction in special structures of an objective, personal, or ideal nature; the growth and the role of hierarchies; the representation of groups by individuals; the bearing of common hostility on the inner solidarity of the group. In addition to such major problems, there are others which no less regularly involve the form of the group and which are either more specialized or more complex than these. Among the more specialized questions, there are those such as the significance of the nonpartisan, the role of the poor as organic members of society, the numerical determination of group elements, and the phenomena of *primus inter pares* and *tertius gaudens*. Among more complex processes are the intersection of various social circles in the individual; the special significance of the secret for the formation of groups; the modification of the character of groups by a membership composed of individuals who belong together geographically, or by the addition of elements who do not; and innumerable other processes.

In this whole discussion, as I have already indicated, I waive the question of whether there ever occurs an *absolute* identity of forms along with a difference in content. The *approximate* identity that forms exhibit under materially dissimilar circumstances (and vice versa) is enough to conceive, in principle, of an affirmative answer to this question. The fact that absolute identity is not actually realized shows the difference between historical-psychological and geometrical phenomena. Historical-psychological processes, in their fluctuations and complexities, can never be completely rationalized. Geometry, by contrast, does have the power to isolate absolutely pure forms out of their material realizations. It should always be remembered that this identity of the kinds of interaction in the face of the simultaneously existing variety of human or objective material (and vice versa) is nothing primarily but a device to make and legitimate the scientific discrimination between form and content in the treatment of empirical phenomena. Methodologically speaking, this discrimination would be required even if the actual constellations did not call for the inductive procedure of crystallizing the like out of the unlike. In the same way, the geometrical abstraction of the spatial form of a body would be justified even if a body with such a particular form occurred only once empirically.

It cannot be denied, however, that this discussion suggests a difficulty in methodology. For instance, toward the end of the Middle Ages, extended trade relations forced certain guild masters to employ apprentices and to adopt new ways of obtaining materials and attracting customers. All of this was inconsistent with traditional guild principles, according to which every master was to have the same living as every other. Through these innovations, every master sought to place himself outside this traditional narrow unity. Now, what about the purely sociological form which is abstracted from the special content of this whole process? The process seems to indicate that the expansion of the circle with which the individual is connected through his actions is accompanied by a greater articulation of individuality, an expansion of the freedom of the individual, and a greater differentiation of the members of the circle. Yet, as far as I can see, there is no sure method of distilling this sociological significance out of our complex fact which is, after all, real only along with all its contents. In other words, there is no sure method for answering the question of what purely sociological configurations and what specific interactions of individuals (irrespective of the interests and impulses residing in the individual, and of purely objective conditions) are involved in the historical process. On the contrary, all this can be interpreted in more than one way and, furthermore, the historical facts that attest to reality of the specific sociological forms must be presented in their material totality. In brief, there is no means of teaching and, under certain conditions, even of performing, the analysis of form and content into sociological elements.

The case is comparable to the proof of a geometrical theorem by means of figures drawn in the unavoidably accidental and crude way of all drawings. The mathematician can feel quite safe in assuming that, in spite of the imperfect drawing, the concept of the ideal geometrical figure is known and understood, and that it is regarded as the essential significance of the chalk or ink marks. The sociologist, however, may not make the corresponding assumption; the isolation of truly pure sociation out of the complex total phenomenon cannot be forced by logical means.

Here we must take upon ourselves the odium of talking about intuitive procedures (however far these are removed from speculative, metaphysical intuition). We admit that we are discussing a particular viewpoint that helps to make the distinction between form and content. This viewpoint, for the time being, can be conveyed only by means of examples. Only much later may it be possible to grasp it by methods that are fully conceptualized and are sure guides to research. The difficulty is increased by two factors. Not only is there no perfectly clear technique for applying the fundamental sociological concept itself (that is, the concept of sociation), but, in addition, where this concept can be effectively applied, there are still many elements in the phenomena to be studied whose subsumption under the concept or form and content remains arbitrary. There will be contrary opinions, for instance, concerning the extent to which the phenomenon of the poor is a matter of form or content; the extent to which it is a result of formal relations within the group, a result which is determined by general currents and shifts that are the necessary outcome of contacts among human beings; or the extent to which poverty is to be regarded as a merely material characteristic of certain individuals, a characteristic that must be studied exclusively from the viewpoint of economic interests (that is, as regards its content)....

To this extent, any history or description of a social situation is an exercise of psychological knowledge. But it is of extreme methodological relevance even of decisive importance to the principles of human studies in general to note that the scientific treatment of psychic data is not thereby automatically psychological. Even where we constantly use psychological rules and knowledge, even where the explanation of every single fact is possible only psychologically (as is true in sociology), the sense and intent of our activities do not have to be psychological. They do not have to aim, that is, at an understanding of the law of the psychic process itself (which, to be sure, has its content), but can aim rather at this content and its configurations. There is only a difference in degree between the studies of man and the sciences of external nature. After all, the natural sciences too, inasmuch as they are phenomena of the intellectual life, have their locus in the mind. The discovery of every astronomical or chemical truth, as well as the rethinking of each of them, is an event occurring in consciousness, an event which a perfect psychology could deduce without residue from physical conditions and developments alone. The procedure followed by the natural sciences in choosing the contents and interrelations of psychological processes—rather than the processes themselves—for their subject matter is similar to the procedure which determines the significance of a painting from its aesthetic relevance and from its place in the history of art, rather than from the physical oscillations which produce its colors and which constitute and carry its whole, actual existence. There is always one reality and we cannot grasp it scientifically in its immediacy and wholeness but must consider it from a number of different viewpoints and thereby make it into a plurality of mutually independent scientific subject matters. This applies, too, to those psychological phenomena whose contents fail to combine into an autonomous spatial world and which are not strikingly set apart from their psychic reality. Language, for instance, is certainly constructed out of psychological forces and for psychological purposes. But its forms and laws are treated by the science of linguistics with complete neglect of the realization (a realization which alone is given) that this is the object; they are treated exclusively through the presentation and analysis of the construction of the content and the forms that result from it.

The facts of sociation offer a similar picture. That people influence one another—that an individual does something, suffers something, shows his existence or his development because there are others who express themselves, act, or feel—is, of course, a psychological phenomenon. And the only way to grasp the historical emergence of each particular instance of this general phenomenon is to re-create it psychologically, to construct plausible psychological series, to interpret the externally observable by means of psychological categories. Yet from the particular scientific viewpoint conceived by the notion of sociation, this psychological phenomenon as such may be entirely ignored, and attention may be focused rather upon tracing, analyzing, and connecting its contents. Suppose, for example, that it is noted that the relation of a stronger to a weaker individual, which has the form of *primus inter pares*, tends to lead to a possession of absolute power by the stronger party and a gradual elimination of any elements of equality. This, in terms of historical reality, is certainly a psychological process. Yet from the sociological viewpoint, we are interested only in such questions as: How do the various phases of superordination and subordination follow one another? To what extent is superordination in a given relation compatible with co-ordination in other relations? How much superordination is required in the initial phase of the relation to destroy coordination completely? Has combination or co-operation a greater chance to occur in an earlier or in a later stage of such a development? Or, as a further example, let us suppose it is noted that those hostilities are the bitterest that arise on the basis of a previous and somehow still felt communion or solidarity (hatred between blood relatives has been called the most burning hatred). As an occurrence, this can only be understood, or even described, psychologically. However, looking at this phenomenon as a sociological formation, we are not interested in the psychological processes that occur in each of the two individuals but in their subsumption under the categories of union and discord. We are interested in such problems as: Up to what point can the relation between two individuals or parties contain hostility and solidarity before depriving the relation of the character of solidarity or giving it that of hostility? What sort of solidarity—that which arises from remembered communion or that which is based on inextinguishable instinct—furnishes the means for more cruel, more profoundly wounding injury than is ever possible when the original relation was one of relatively great distance? In brief, how is our observation to be presented as the realization of forms of relation between people—what specific combination of social categories does it present? This is the point, and it is so in spite of the fact that the concrete description of the process, or the description of it as a typical process, can be nothing but psychological. Returning to an earlier illustration, we may (ignoring all differences) compare the procedure of sociology with the performance of a geometrical deduction using a figure drawn on a blackboard. All that is given and seen here is the physically produced chalk marks, but it is not in them that we are interested but in their significance from the viewpoint of geometry, which has nothing whatever to do with that physical figure as a deposit of chalk particles. (On the other hand, this figure, precisely as a physical structure, may be brought under scientific categories; its physiological genesis, its chemical composition, or its optical impression may become the object of special investigations.)

In this sense, then, the givens of sociology are psychological processes whose immediate reality presents itself first of all under psychological categories. But these psychological categories, although indispensable for the description of the facts, remain outside the purpose of sociological investigation. It is to this end that we direct our study to the objective reality of sociation, a reality which, to be sure, is embodied in psychic processes and can often be described only by means of them. Similarly, a drama, from beginning to end, contains only psychological processes and can be understood only psychologically; but its purpose is not to study psychological cognitions but to examine the syntheses which result when the contents of the psychic processes are considered from the viewpoints of tragedy and artistic form, or as symbolic of certain aspects of life.

Reprinted from *On Individuality & Social Forms*, by Georg Simmel, edited by Donald Levine. From the series *The Heritage of Sociology*, edited by Morris Janowitz. Copyright © 1971 by The University of Chicago. Reprinted from "The Problem of Sociology," translated by Kurt H. Wolff, in *Georg Simmel, 1858–1918: A Collection of Essays, with Translations and a Bibliography*, edited by Kurt H. Wolff. Copyright © 1959 by the Ohio State University Press. All rights reserved. Originally published in German as "Das Problem der Soziologie," in *Soziologie* (Munich and Leipzig: Duncker & Humblot, 1908). Reprinted with permission of The University of Chicago Press. ✦

18
Conflict as the Basis of Group Formation

Georg Simmel

As this selection from 1908 attests, Simmel was keenly interested in the role of social conflict; indeed, he was one of the earliest students of conflict sociology. The tone of this essay is indicative of his writings on the topic, characterized by a rather formal and dispassionate analysis of the phenomenon. His central claim is that contrary to the tendency to see conflict as a source of divisiveness, we should look for ways in which conflict serves to bind individuals and groups together. Having shared enemies, or those perceived to be "social others," plays a significant role in forging solidarity, whether or not overt conflicts occur. Such solidarity might be a feature of enduring relationships (as in the relationship between workers and their employers) or might occur in rather fleeting social encounters with relative strangers sharing certain common characteristics. In either event, conflict can be seen playing a role in facilitating group creation and preservation.

. . . The last example leads to cases of an intensified cohesive function of conflict. Conflict may not only heighten the concentration of an existing unit, radically eliminating all elements which might blur the distinctness of its boundaries against the enemy; it may also bring persons and groups together which have otherwise nothing to do with each other. The powerful effect of conflict in this respect emerges probably most clearly in the fact that the connection between conflict situation and unification is strong enough to become significant even in the reverse process. Psychological associations generally show their strength in their retroactive effect. If, for instance, we imagine a given person under the category of "hero," the connection between the representation of the person and of the hero is most intimate if we cannot think of the category of hero without the automatic, simultaneous emergence of the image of that personality.

In similar fashion, unification for the purpose of fighting is a process which is experienced so often that sometimes the mere collation of elements, even when it occurs for no purpose of aggression or other conflict, appears in the eyes of others as a threatening and hostile act. The despotism of the modern state was directed above all against the medieval idea of unification. Eventually, every association as such—whether between cities, estates, knights, or any other elements of the state—appeared to the government as a rebellion, as a latent fight against it. Charlemagne prohibited guilds as sworn associations and explicitly permitted them for charitable purposes, without oath. The emphasis of the prohibition lies on the sworn obligation even for legitimate purposes, because these legitimate purposes can easily combine with others which are dangerous to the state. Thus, the Moravian land order of 1628 says: "Accordingly, to enter or erect federations or unions, for whatever purpose and against whomever they may be conceived, is not permitted to anybody but the king." The fact that the ruling power itself sometimes favors or even launches such associations does not contradict this connection, but confirms it. This is so not only if the association is to counteract an existing opposition party (where it is obvious), but also in the more interesting case when it is designed harmlessly to distract the general tendency to associate. After the Romans dissolved all political associations of the Greeks, Hadrian created an organization of all Hellenes (*koinón synédrion ton Hellénon*) for ideal purposes: games and commemorations—for the maintenance of an ideal, wholly unpolitical pan-Hellenism.

For the direction taken by the relationship under discussion, historical cases are so close at hand that the only point worth insisting upon is the observation of the *degrees* of unification which are possible through conflict. Uppermost is the establishment of the unified state. Essentially, France owes the consciousness of its national unity only to its fight against the English, and only the Moorish war made the Spanish regions into one people. The next lower grade of unification is constituted by confederacies and federations of states, with additional numerous gradations according to their cohesion and the measure of power of their central authorities. The United States needed the War of Independence; Switzerland, the fight against Austria; the Netherlands, rebellion against Spain; the Achaean League, the struggle against Macedonia; and the founding of the new German Empire furnishes a parallel to all of these instances.

Here also belongs the formation of unified estates. The element of conflict (latent and open contrasts) is of such evident significance for them that I only mention a negative example. The fact that Russia has no proper aristocracy as a closed estate would seem to be bound to favor the broad and unrestrained development of a bourgeoisie. In reality, the opposite is the case. If, as elsewhere, there had been a powerful aristocracy, it certainly would have put itself in frequent opposition to the prince, who in turn would have depended upon an urban bourgeoisie. Evidently, among the princes such a conflict situation would have aroused an interest in developing a unified bourgeois class. The bourgeois themselves found no militant stimulus (in this case, no stimulus at all) to close ranks as an estate. If they had, they could have gained from the conflict by joining one or the other side.

In all positive cases of this type, it is characteristic that the unity, while it originates in conflict and for purposes of conflict, maintains itself beyond the period of struggle. It comes to have additional interests and associative forces which no longer have any relation to the initial militant purpose. In fact, the significance of conflict consists in the articulation of the latent relationship and unity; conflict is more the occasion of unifications which are required internally than it is the purpose of these unifications. To be sure, within the collective interest in conflict, there is a further gradation, namely,

according to whether the unification for the purpose of conflict refers to attack *and* defense or to defense only. Unification for the exclusive purpose of defense probably occurs in most coalitions of extant groups, especially when the groups are numerous and heterogeneous. This defense purpose is the collectivistic minimum, because even for the single group and the single individual it constitutes the least avoidable test of the drive for self-preservation. Evidently, the more numerous and varied are the elements which associate, the smaller is the number of interests in which they coincide—in the extreme case, the number is reduced to the most primitive urge, the defense of one's existence. Thus, in reply to the entrepreneurs' fear that all English trade unions might unite one day, one of their most ardent adherers pointed out that even if it came to that, it could only be for purposes of defense.

In comparison with these cases in which the collectivizing effect of conflict transcends the moment and the immediate purpose of the group (and this may happen even in regard to the minimum just mentioned), the extent of this effect is slighter when the unification occurs only *ad hoc*. Two types must be distinguished here. On the one hand, there is association for a single action. Frequently, especially in wars properly speaking, this claims the total energies of its elements. It creates a unit without residue; but after achieving or failing to achieve its immediate objective, this unit lets its parts go back to their former separate existence— as, for instance, did the Greeks after eliminating the danger from the Persians. In the second type, the unity is less complete but also less transitory. Here, the elements are grouped around a war aim which is singular, not so much in terms of time as in terms of content, and which does not cause any contact among them other than in this one respect. Thus there has been in England a Federation of Associated Employers of Labour, founded in 1873 to fight the influence of trade unions; and a few years later, a similar association was formed in the United States in order to counteract strikes, no matter in what branch of industry.

The character of both types of unification appears of course most pointed when it is composed of elements who at other times or in respects other than the one at issue are not only indifferent but hostile toward one another. The unifying power of the principle of conflict nowhere emerges more strongly than when it manages to carve a temporal or contentual area out of competitive or hostile relationships. Under certain circumstances, the contrast between ordinary antagonism and momentary association for purposes of fight can be so pointed that it is precisely the depth of the mutual hostility of the parties which forms the direct cause of their joining up. In the English parliament, the Opposition has sometimes been formed when the extreme partisans of the ministerial policy were not satisfied with the administration and joined their radical opponents with whom they were connected by the common antagonism against the ministry. For instance, under Pulteney, the Ultra-Whigs united with the High-Tories against Robert Walpole. It was precisely the radicalism of the principle of enmity against the Tories which united its adherents with the Tories: had their anti-Toryism not been so fundamental, they would not have joined their enemies in order to bring about the fall of the Whig minister who for them was not Whiggish enough.

This case is so extreme because the common adversary brings otherwise mutual enemies together; in the view of each of these enemies, he, their common adversary, leans too much toward the other side. But this extreme case is only the purest example of the trivial experience that even the bitterest enmities do not prevent an association if this association is directed against a *common* enemy. This is particularly true if both or at least one of the parties now cooperating has very concrete and immediate goals, and all that is needed to attain them is the removal of particular adversaries. French history from the Huguenots to Richelieu shows that it was sufficient for one of the internal parties to increase its hostility to Spain or England, Savoy or the Netherlands, and the other at once joined this foreign power— without regard to the harmony or disharmony between that power and its own positive aims. These parties in France, however, had very concrete goals and only needed

"room," freedom from the opponent. They were thus ready to join up with any opponent of that opponent if only he had the same intention, in utter disregard of their usual relations with him. The more purely negative or destructive a given enmity is, the more easily will it bring about a unification of those who ordinarily have no motive for any community.

The lowest step in this scale of unifications on the basis of conflict, their least acute form, is constituted by associations which are held together only by a common mood. In such cases, members know that they belong together in so far as they have a similar aversion or similar practical interest against a third party. This interest, however, does not necessarily lead to a common aggression against that party. Here too, two types must be distinguished. The first is illustrated by the opposition between masses of workers and few employers in large-scale industry. In the struggle for working conditions, this situation evidently produces not only particular, really effective coalitions among the laborers, but also the quite general feeling that they all belong together somehow because they all are united in the basically identical struggle against the employers. To be sure, at certain points this feeling is crystallized in particular actions of political party formation or wage struggles. Yet as a whole, it can by its own nature not become practical. It remains the mood of an abstract belonging-together by virtue of common opposition to an abstract adversary. Here, then, the feeling of unity is abstract but lasting.

In the second type, it is concrete but temporary. This second type is exemplified when persons who are not acquainted with each other but who share the same level of education or sensitivity, find themselves together, perhaps in a railroad car or under similar circumstances, with others of crude and vulgar behavior. Without any scene, without so much as exchanging a word or glance with each other, they still feel like a party, held together by their common aversion to the vulgarity (which is aggressive at least in the ideal sense) of those others. This unification, with its extremely tender and delicate, though wholly unambiguous character, marks the extreme on the scale of unifications of completely alien elements through a common antagonism.

The synthetic strength of a common opposition may be determined, not by the number of shared points of interest, but by the duration and intensity of the unification. In this case, it is especially favorable to the unification if instead of an actual fight with the enemy, there is a permanent *threat* by him. In regard to the first period of the Achaean League, that is, around 270 B.C., it is emphasized that Achaea was surrounded by enemies, all of whom, however, had something else to do than attack it. It is said that such a period of danger which always threatened but never materialized, was especially apt to strengthen the feeling of unity.

This is a case of a peculiar type: a certain distance between the elements to be united, on the one hand, and the point and interest uniting them, on the other, is a particularly favorable constellation for unification, notably in large groups. Religious relations are a case in point. In contrast to tribal and national deities, the world-spanning God of Christianity has an infinite distance from the believers. He is entirely without features related to the specific character of the individual. In compensation, however, he can comprise even the most heterogeneous peoples and personalities in an incomparable religious community. Another illustration: dress always characterizes certain social strata as belonging together; and it seems to fulfill this social function best when it is imported from abroad. To dress as one dresses in Paris, means to have a close and exclusive association with a certain social stratum in other countries—already the prophet Zephaniah speaks of noblemen as wearing foreign clothes.

The very manifold meanings connoted by the symbol "distance" have much psychological affinity with one another. For instance, an image the object of which is in any sense represented as "distant" seems almost always to have a more impersonal effect. If accompanied by such a representation, the individual reaction following from immediate closeness and touch is less poignant, has a less immediately subjective character, and thus can be the same for a larger number of

individuals. The general concept which covers a number of particulars is the more abstract (that is, the more distant from each of the particulars), the more numerous and different from each other these particulars are. Just so, a point of social unification at a greater distance from the elements to be unified (both in a spatial and in a figurative sense) likewise appears to have specifically unifying and comprehensive effects. Unification by a more chronic than acute danger, by an always latent but never exploding conflict, will be most effective where the problem is the lasting unification of somehow divergent elements. This was true of the Achaean League I already mentioned. In the same vein, Montesquieu remarks that while peace and confidence are the glory and security of monarchies, republics need somebody they fear. This observation is apparently based on a feeling for the constellation discussed. Monarchy itself sees to it that possibly antagonistic elements are held together. But when such elements have nobody above them to enforce their unity but instead enjoy relative sovereignty, they will easily break apart unless a danger shared by all forces them together. Evidently, such a danger can last and can guarantee a permanent group structure only by a permanent threat of conflict, rather than through a single, open fight.

While this is more a question of degree, the basic connection between collectivity and hostility requires the following additional comments. From their very origin, aggressive, much more than peaceful, enterprises tend to solicit the cooperation of the largest possible number of elements which would otherwise remain scattered and would not have started action on their own account. On the whole, people engaging in peaceful actions usually limit themselves to those who are close to them in other respects as well. For "allies," however—and linguistic usage has indeed given a warlike color to this intrinsically neutral concept—one often enough accepts elements with whom one hardly has, or even wants to have, anything in common. There are several reasons for this. First, war, and not only political war, often constitutes an emergency in which one cannot be choosy about friends. Secondly, the object of the action lies outside the territory or periphery of the allies' other immediate interests, so that after the fight is over they can return to their earlier distance. Thirdly, while gain by means of fight is dangerous, if the fight is successful, the gain usually is quick and intensive. Hence for certain elements, it has a *formal* attraction which peaceful enterprises can engender only through a particular *content*. Fourthly, in conflict, the specifically personal element in the fighter recedes; and thus the unification of otherwise wholly heterogeneous elements is possible. Finally must be noted the motive of the easy reciprocal stimulation of hostility. Even *within* a group which feuds with another, all kinds of latent or half-forgotten hostilities of its members against those of the other group come to the fore. In this way, war between two groups usually evokes in a third group much ill will and resentment against one of the two. By themselves, these feelings would not have led to an outbreak but now that another group has led the way, as it were, they cause the third group to join it in its action. It is quite in line with this that in general, convergent relations among *peoples* as *wholes*, especially in earlier times, existed only for purposes of war, while other relations, such as trade and commerce, hospitality, and intermarriage, only concerned *individuals*. Agreements between the peoples made these individual relationships possible, but did not themselves initiate them.

19
The Stranger

Georg Simmel

"The Stranger" (1908) is one of Simmel's classic essays on social types. In it he describes the type of person who lives among and yet apart from—in but not of—a society. The stranger, as he writes in one crucial passage, is a person who "comes today and stays tomorrow." The stranger is both integrally part of the society and in some fashion appended onto it. As Simmel points out, the classic example of the stranger is the Jew in European society: Although part of the economy as trader, the Jew is also marginalized from that society, living in close physical proximity to non-Jews, but in a situation where the social distance between Jews and Christians is pronounced. This social type, recast as the "marginal man," became at the hands of Simmel's former student, the American sociologist Robert E. Park, an important concept in the study of immigration and ethnic relations.

If wandering, considered as a state of detachment from every given point in space, is the conceptual opposite of attachment to any point, then the sociological form of "the stranger" presents the synthesis, as it were, of both of these properties. (This is another indication that spatial relations not only are determining conditions of relationships among men, but are also symbolic of those relationships.) The stranger will thus not be considered here in the usual sense of the term, as the wanderer who comes today and goes tomorrow, but rather as the man who comes today and stays tomorrow—the potential wanderer, so to speak, who, although he has gone no further, has not quite got over the freedom of coming and going. He is fixed within a certain spatial circle—or within a group whose boundaries are analogous to spatial boundaries—but his position within it is fundamentally affected by the fact that he does not belong in it initially and that he

brings qualities into it that are not, and cannot be, indigenous to it.

In the case of the stranger, the union of closeness and remoteness involved in every human relationship is patterned in a way that may be succinctly formulated as follows: the distance within this relation indicates that one who is close by is remote, but his strangeness indicates that one who is remote is near. The state of being a stranger is of course a completely positive relation; it is a specific form of interaction. The inhabitants of Sirius are not exactly strangers to us, at least not in the sociological sense of the word as we are considering it. In that sense they do not exist for us at all; they are beyond being far and near. The stranger is an element of the group itself, not unlike the poor and sundry "inner enemies"—an element whose membership within the group involves both being outside it and confronting it.

The following statements about the stranger are intended to suggest how factors of repulsion and distance work to create a form of being together, a form of union based on interaction.

In the whole history of economic activity the stranger makes his appearance everywhere as a trader, and the trader makes his as a stranger. As long as production for one's own needs is the general rule, or products are exchanged within a relatively small circle, there is no need for a middleman within the group. A trader is required only for goods produced outside the group. Unless there are people who wander out into foreign lands to buy these necessities, in which case they are themselves "strange" merchants in this other region, the trader *must* be a stranger; there is no opportunity for anyone else to make a living at it.

This position of the stranger stands out more sharply if, instead of leaving the place of his activity, he settles down there. In innumerable cases even this is possible only if he can live by trade as a middleman. Any closed economic group where land and handicrafts have been apportioned in a way that satisfies local demands will still support a livelihood for the trader. For trade alone makes possible unlimited combinations, and through it intelligence is constantly extended and applied in new areas, something that is much harder for the primary producer with his more limited mobility and his dependence on a circle of customers that can be expanded only very slowly. Trade can always absorb more men than can primary production. It is therefore the most suitable activity for the stranger, who intrudes as a supernumerary, so to speak, into a group in which all the economic positions are already occupied. The classic example of this is the history of European Jews. The stranger is by his very nature no owner of land—land not only in the physical sense but also metaphorically as a vital substance which is fixed, if not in space, then at least in an ideal position within the social environment.

Although in the sphere of intimate personal relations the stranger may be attractive and meaningful in many ways, so long as he is regarded as a stranger he is no "landowner" in the eyes of the other. Restriction to intermediary trade and often (as though sublimated from it) to pure finance gives the stranger the specific character of *mobility*. The appearance of this mobility within a bounded group occasions that synthesis of nearness and remoteness which constitutes the formal position of the stranger. The purely mobile person comes incidentally into contact with *every* single element but is not bound up organically, through established ties of kinship, locality, or occupation, with any single one.

Another expression of this constellation is to be found in the objectivity of the stranger. Because he is not bound by roots to the particular constituents and partisan dispositions of the group, he confronts all of these with a distinctly "objective" attitude, an attitude that does not signify mere detachment and nonparticipation, but is a distinct structure composed of remoteness and nearness, indifference and involvement. I refer to my analysis of the dominating positions gained by aliens, in the discussion of superordination and subordination,[1] typified by the practice in certain Italian cities of recruiting their judges from outside, because no native was free from entanglement in family interests and factionalism.

Connected with the characteristic of objectivity is a phenomenon that is found chiefly, though not exclusively, in the stranger who moves on. This is that he often receives the most surprising revelations and confidences, at times reminiscent of a confessional, about matters which are kept carefully hidden from everybody with whom one is close. Objectivity is by no means nonparticipation, a condition that is altogether outside the distinction between subjective and objective orientations. It is rather a positive and definite kind of participation, in the same way that the objectivity of a theoretical observation clearly does not mean that the mind is a passive tabula rasa on which things inscribe their qualities, but rather signifies the full activity of a mind working according to its own laws, under conditions that exclude accidental distortions and emphases whose individual and subjective differences would produce quite different pictures of the same object.

Objectivity can also be defined as freedom. The objective man is not bound by ties which could prejudice his perception, his understanding, and his assessment of data. This freedom, which permits the stranger to experience and treat even his close relationships as though from a bird's-eye view, contains many dangerous possibilities. From earliest times, in uprisings of all sorts the attacked party has claimed that there has been incitement from the outside, by foreign emissaries and agitators. Insofar as this has happened, it represents an exaggeration of the specific role of the stranger: he is the freer man, practically and theoretically; he examines conditions with less prejudice; he assesses them against standards that are more general and more objective; and his actions are not confined by custom, piety, or precedent.[2]

Finally, the proportion of nearness and remoteness which gives the stranger the character of objectivity also finds practical expression in the more *abstract* nature of the relation to him. That is, with the stranger one has only certain *more general* qualities in common, whereas the relation with organically connected persons is based on the similarity of just those specific traits which differentiate them from the merely universal. In fact, all personal relations whatsoever can be analyzed in terms of this scheme. They are not determined only by the existence of certain common characteristics which the individuals share in addition to their individual differences, which either influence the relationship or remain outside of it. Rather, the kind of effect which that commonality has on the relation essentially depends on whether it exists only among the participants themselves, and thus, although general within the relation, is specific and incomparable with respect to all those on the outside, or whether the participants feel that what they have in common is so only because it is common to a group, a type, or mankind in general. In the latter case, the effect of the common features becomes attenuated in proportion to the size of the group bearing the same characteristics. The commonality provides a basis for unifying the members, to be sure; but it does not specifically direct *these* particular persons to one another. A similarity so widely shared could just as easily unite each person with every possible other. This, too, is evidently a way in which a relationship includes both nearness and remoteness simultaneously. To the extent to which the similarities assume a universal nature, the warmth of the connection based on them will acquire an element of coolness, a sense of the contingent nature of precisely *this* relation—the connecting forces have lost their specific, centripetal character.

In relation to the stranger, it seems to me, this constellation assumes an extraordinary preponderance in principle over the individual elements peculiar to the relation in question. The stranger is close to us insofar as we feel between him and ourselves similarities of nationality or social position, of occupation or of general human nature. He is far from us insofar as these similarities extend beyond him and us, and connect us only because they connect a great many people.

A trace of strangeness in this sense easily enters even the most intimate relationships. In the stage of first passion, erotic relations strongly reject any thought of generalization. A love such as this has never existed before; there is nothing to compare either with the person one loves or with our feelings for that person. An estrangement is wont to set in (whether as cause or effect is hard to decide) at the moment when this feeling of uniqueness disappears from the relationship. A skepticism regarding the intrinsic value of the relationship and its value for us adheres to the very thought that in this relation, after all, one is only fulfilling a general human destiny, that one has had an experience that has occurred a thousand times before, and that, if one had not accidentally met this precise person, someone else would have acquired the same meaning for us.

Something of this feeling is probably not absent in any relation, be it ever so close, because that which is common to two is perhaps never common *only* to them but belongs to a general conception which includes much else besides, many *possibilities* of similarities. No matter how few of these possibilities are realized and how often we may forget about them, here and there, nevertheless, they crowd in like shadows between men, like a mist eluding every designation, which must congeal into solid corporeality for it to be called jealousy. Perhaps this is in many cases a more general, at least more insurmountable, strangeness than that due to differences and obscurities. It is strangeness caused by the fact that similarity, harmony, and closeness are accompanied by the feeling that they are actually not the exclusive property of this particular relation, but stem from a more general one—a relation that potentially includes us and an indeterminate number of others, and therefore prevents that relation which alone was experienced from having an inner and exclusive necessity.

On the other hand, there is a sort of "strangeness" in which this very connection on the basis of a general quality embracing the parties is precluded. The relation of the Greeks to the barbarians is a typical example; so are all the cases in which the general characteristics one takes as peculiarly and merely human are disallowed to the other. But here the expression "the stranger" no longer has any positive meaning. The relation with him is a non-relation; he is not what we have been discussing here: the stranger as a member of the group itself.

As such, the stranger is near and far *at the same time*, as in any relationship based on merely universal human similarities. Between these two factors of nearness and distance, however, a peculiar tension arises, since the consciousness of having only the absolutely general in common has exactly the effect of putting a special emphasis on that which is not common. For a stranger to the country, the city, the race, and so on, what is stressed is again nothing individual, but alien origin, a quality which he has, or could have, in common with many other strangers. For this reason strangers are not really perceived as individuals, but as strangers of a certain type. Their remoteness is no less general than their nearness.

This form appears, for example, in so special a case as the tax levied on Jews in Frankfurt and elsewhere during the Middle Ages. Whereas the tax paid by Christian citizens varied according to their wealth at any given time, for every single Jew the tax was fixed once and for all. This amount was fixed because the Jew had his social position as a *Jew*, not as the bearer of certain objective contents. With respect to taxes every other citizen was regarded as possessor of a certain amount of wealth, and his tax could follow the fluctuations of his fortune. But the Jew as taxpayer was first of all a Jew, and thus his fiscal position contained an invariable element. This appears most forcefully, of course, once the differing circumstances of individual Jews are no longer considered, limited though this consideration is by fixed assessments, and all strangers pay exactly the same head tax.

Despite his being inorganically appended to it, the stranger is still an organic member of the group. Its unified life includes the specific conditioning of this element. Only we do not know how to designate the characteristic unity of this position otherwise than by saying that it is put together of certain amounts of nearness and of remoteness. Although both these qualities are found to some extent in all relationships, a special proportion and reciprocal tension between them produce the specific form of the relation to the "stranger."

Endnotes

1. Simmel refers here to a passage which may be found in *The Sociology of Georg Simmel*, pp. 216–21.

2. Where the attacked parties make such an assertion falsely, they do so because those in higher positions tend to exculpate inferiors who previously have been in a close, solidary relationship with them. By introducing the fiction that the rebels were not really guilty, but only instigated, so they did not actually start the rebellion, they exonerate themselves by denying that there were any real grounds for the uprising.

Reprinted from *On Individuality & Social Forms*, by Georg Simmel, edited by Donald Levine. From the series *The Heritage of Sociology*, edited by Morris Janowitz. Copyright © 1971 by The University of Chicago. From "Der Fremde," in *Soziologie* (Munich and Leipzig: Duncker & Humblot, 1908), pp. 685–91. Translated by Donald N. Levine. Reprinted with permission of The University of Chicago Press. ✦

20
The Philosophy of Money

Georg Simmel

(translated by Tom Bottomore and David Frisby from a first draft by Kaethe Mengelberg)

Simmel is often remembered as a superb essayist, as someone whose métier was the short but incisive analysis of the fragments that constitute the modern world. He did, however, produce a magnum opus that offers his most sustained argument about the character of the modern world writ large: *The Philosophy of Money*, which was published in 1900 but wasn't translated into English until 1978. In this work one sees similarities in his theoretical framework to the theoretical positions advanced by both Marx and Weber. What was distinctive about his work was that he opted to focus on the varied ways that a money economy transforms culture and in turn the individual's relations with others. In this particular passage from the text, Simmel is intent on illustrating the possibilities that are generated by a money economy. Money is viewed as a tool that has no other purpose than to facilitate the exchange of goods and services. Indeed, as he puts it, money is "the purest example of the tool." One of the consequences of a money economy is that it expands the possibilities of social exchange with larger circles of people, which in turn transforms cultural expectations and ideals. Simmel concludes this passage by examining what he terms "the surplus value of wealth."

Money as the Purest Example of the Tool

Here, finally, we reach the point at which money finds its place in the interweaving of purposes. I will begin with some generally accepted facts. All economic transactions rest upon the fact that I want something that someone else owns, and that he will transfer it to me if I give him something I own that he wants. It is obvious that the final link in this two-sided process will not always be present when the first link appears; on many occasions I want the object A which A possesses, but the object or service B which I am willing to give in return does not interest A; or else the goods offered are acceptable to both parties but no agreement can be reached about the respective quantities. Thus, it is of great value in the attainment of our purposes that an intermediate link should be introduced into the chain of purposes; something into which I can change B at any time and which can itself be changed into A—in much the same way as any form of power, from water, wind, etc., can be transformed into another form of power by means of a dynamo. Just as my thoughts must take the form of a universally understood language so that I can attain my practical ends in this roundabout way, so must my activities and possessions take the form of money value in order to serve my more remote purposes. Money is the purest form of the tool, in the category mentioned above; it is an institution through which the individual concentrates his activity and possessions in order to attain goals that he could not attain directly. The fact that everyone works with it makes its character as a tool more evident than was the case in the examples given earlier. The nature and effectiveness of money is not to be found simply in the coin that I hold in my hand; its qualities are invested in the social organizations and the supra-subjective norms that make this coin a tool of endlessly diverse and extensive uses despite its material limitations, its insignificance and rigidity. It is characteristic of the State and of religious rites that, since they are constituted entirely by mental powers and do not have to compromise with any independent material objects, they can express their purpose fully in themselves. Yet they are so close to their specific purposes, indeed almost identical with them, that we often hesitate to recognize that they are tools (which would make them instruments without value in themselves, brought to life only by the will behind them) and regard them as ultimate moral values. In the case of money, its character as an instrument is very rarely obscured. By contrast with the other institutions mentioned earlier, money has no inherent relation to the specific purpose the attainment of which it aids. Money is totally indifferent to the objects because it is separated from them by the fact of exchange. What money mediates is not the possession of an object but the exchange of objects. Money in its perfected forms is an absolute means because, on the one hand, it is completely teleologically determined and is not influenced by any determination from a different series, while on the other hand it is restricted to being a pure means and tool in relation to a given end, has no purpose of its own and functions impartially as an intermediary in the series of purposes. Money is perhaps the clearest expression and demonstration of the fact that man is a 'tool-making' animal, which, however, is itself connected with the fact that man is a 'purposive' animal. The concept of means characterizes the position of man in the world; he is not dependent as is an animal upon the mechanism of instinctual life and immediate volition and enjoyment, nor does he have unmediated power, such as we attribute to a god, such that his will is identical with its realization. He stands between the two in so far as he can extend his will far beyond the present moment, but can realize it only in a roundabout way through a teleological series which has several links. Love, which according to Plato is an intermediate stage between possessing and not-possessing, is in the inner subjective life what means are in the objective external world. For man, who is always striving, never satisfied, always becoming, love is the true human condition. Means, on the other hand, and their enhanced form, the tool, symbolize the human genus. The tool illustrates or incorporates the grandeur of the human will, and at the same time its limitations. The practical necessity to introduce a series of intermediate steps between ourselves and our ends has perhaps given rise to the concept of the past, and so has endowed man with his specific sense of life, of its extent and its limits, as a watershed between past and future. Money is the purest reification of means, a concrete instrument which is absolutely identical with its abstract concept; it is a pure instrument. The tremendous importance of money

for understanding the basic motives of life lies in the fact that money embodies and sublimates the practical relation of man to the objects of his will, his power and his impotence; one might say, paradoxically, that man is an indirect being. I am here concerned with the relation of money to the totality of human life only in so far as it illuminates our immediate problem, which is to comprehend the nature of money through the internal and external relationships that find their expression, their means or their effects in money. I shall add here to the functions previously discussed one that shows with particular clarity how the abstract character of money is transposed into practical reality.

The Unlimited Possibilities for the Utilization of Money

I noted earlier that the representation and provision of means does not always depend upon an already formed purpose; the availability of materials and forces often provokes us to form certain purposes which these means will enable us to attain. Once a purpose has engendered the idea of means, the means may produce the conception of a purpose. This relationship, frequently modified but enduring, may be seen in the case of tools, which I characterized as the purest kind of means. While ordinary, simple means are entirely used up in achieving the purpose, a tool continues to exist apart from its particular application and is capable of a variety of other uses that cannot be foreseen. This is true not only for thousands of cases in daily life that need not be exemplified, but also in much more complicated situations. How often are military organizations, which were intended for external deployment, used by a dynasty for internal political ends? How often does a relationship among individuals which was originally established for a particular purpose grow beyond this and become the bearer of altogether different contents, with the result that one may say of all enduring human associations—familial, economic, religious, political or social—that they have a tendency to acquire purposes for which they were not originally conceived? It is obvious that a tool will be more significant and valuable—*ceteris paribus*—if it has various and extensive uses. At the same time, it must then become more neutral and colourless, more objective in relation to particular interests and more remote from any specific purpose. Money as the means *par excellence* fulfils this condition perfectly; from this point of view its importance is enhanced. The matter can be put as follows. The value of a given quantity of money exceeds the value of the particular object for which it is exchanged, because it makes possible the choice of any other object in an unlimited area. Of course, the money can be used ultimately only for one of the objects, but the choice that it offers is a bonus which increases its value. Since money is not related at all to a specific purpose, it acquires a relation to the totality of purposes. Money is the tool that has the greatest possible number of unpredictable uses and so possesses the maximum value attainable in this respect. The mere possibility of unlimited uses that money has, or represents, on account of its lack of any content of its own, is manifested in a positive way by the restlessness of money, by its urge to be used, so to speak. As in the case of languages such as French, which have a limited vocabulary, the need to employ the same expression for different things makes possible a wealth of allusions, references and psychological overtones, and one might almost say that their wealth results from their poverty; so the absence of any inner significance of money engenders the abundance of its practical uses, and indeed provides the impulse to fill its infinite conceptual categories with new formations, to give new content to its form, because it is never a conclusion but only a transitional point for each content. In the last analysis, the whole vast range of commodities can only be exchanged for one value, namely money; but money can be exchanged for any one of the range of commodities. By contrast with labour, which can rarely change its application, and the less easily the more specialized it is, capital in the form of money can almost always be transferred from one use to another, at worst with a loss, but often with a gain. The worker can hardly ever extricate his art and skill from his trade and invest it somewhere else. By comparison with

the owner of money he is at a disadvantage so far as free choice is concerned, just as the merchant is. Thus, the value of a given amount of money is equal to the value of any object for which it might be exchanged plus the value of free choice between innumerable other objects, and this is an asset that has no analogy in the area of commodities or labour.

This surplus value of money appears all the more important if one considers the nature of the decision to which this power of choice leads in reality. It has been asserted that a commodity that is limited in quantity and has alternative uses will be valued by its owners with respect to its most important use; all other uses will appear uneconomic and unreasonable. On the other hand, a supply of goods that is sufficient or more than sufficient for all possible uses, so that the goods compete to be used, will be valued according to its least important use. The most important use becomes the measure of the object if there are competing uses. This is most fully and effectively demonstrated by money. Since money can be used for any economic purpose, a given amount of it can be used to satisfy the most important subjective need for the moment. The choice is not limited, as is the case with all other commodities, and, because human desires know no limit, a great variety of possible uses is always competing for any given quantity of money. Since the decision will always be in favour of the good that is desired most intensely, money must be valued at any moment as equivalent to the most important interest experienced at that moment. A supply of wood or a building plot that is adequate only for one of several desired uses, and which is therefore valued according to the most valuable of those uses cannot have a significance beyond the region of things of its own kind. Money, however, has no such limitation, and so its value corresponds with the most important universal interest of the individual that can be satisfied with the available supply.

The opportunity of choice which money as an abstract instrument provides applies not only to the goods offered at any one time, but also to the date when it can be used. The value of a commodity is not determined simply by its practical significance at the moment of its use. The relative freedom of choice in timing the use is a factor that can increase or diminish considerably the value placed upon the commodity. The first of these possibilities of choice results from the coexistence of different uses, the second from the existence of alternative uses over time. Other things being equal, that commodity is more valuable which I *can* but do not *have to* use immediately. The range of commodities falls into a graduated series of values between two extremes: at one end is the commodity that can be enjoyed later but not now. If, for example, fish caught during the summer is exchanged for furs that are going to be worn in the winter, then the value of the fish is increased by the fact that I can consume it immediately, whereas the value of the furs is affected by the fact that the delay in using them involves the risk of damage, loss or devaluation. On the other hand, the value of the fish is diminished because it will no longer be fresh tomorrow, and the value of the furs is increased because they will still be serviceable at a later date. An object used as a means of exchange is most suitable for money, if it possesses both of these value-enhancing qualities. Money as a pure instrument represents their highest possible synthesis because it has no specific quality for a specific use, but is only a tool for acquiring concrete values, and because the opportunities for using it are just as great at any point of time and for any object.

The superiority of the owner of money over the owner of commodities results from this unique quality of money as being unrelated to all particular characteristics of things or moments of time, dissociated from any purpose, and a purely abstract means. There are some exceptions to this, such as the refusal to sell on ideological grounds, boycotts and cartels, but these arise only when the objects of exchange in that particular situation cannot be replaced by other objects. The freedom of choice and also the particular advantage that money confers upon its owner are then eliminated precisely because there is a single object of desire instead of a choice. In general, the owner of money enjoys this twofold liberty and he will demand a recompense if he relinquishes it in favour of the owner of goods. This is shown, for example, by the economically and psychologically interesting principle of the 'supplement'. When goods that can be measured or weighed are purchased the merchant is expected to 'measure liberally', that is to add at least one additional unit, and he usually does so. It must be taken into account that a mistake is more likely in measuring goods than in counting money, but the important feature is that the buyer has the power to enforce an interpretation of this possibility in his own favour even though the chances of advantage or disadvantage are equal for both parties. It is significant that the advantage is given to the buyer even when the other party is also dealing in money. The customer expects the banker, the insured expects the insurance company in case of a claim, to deal 'fairly', that is to give a little more, even if only in a formal way, than what is enforceable by law. The bank and the insurance company also trade only in money, but the customer for his part does not think of being 'fair' or 'liberal'; he only offers what has been agreed upon beforehand. The sums of money offered on each side have in fact quite a different significance. For the banker and the insurance company the money with which they operate is simply a commodity that they can use only in this particular way; for the customer it is 'money' in the sense with which we are here concerned, namely a value that he can, but need not necessarily, use for stock exchange business or insurance. The freedom to use the money for diverse purposes gives the customer an advantage which is compensated by the 'fairness' of the other party. Where a supplement is given by the owner of money, as in tipping waiters and taxi-drivers, this merely expresses the social superiority of the giver, which is the presupposition of tipping. Like all other monetary phenomena these are not occurrences isolated from the rest of human life; they display in a particularly clear and obvious manner a fundamental characteristic of life, namely that in every relationship the individual who has less interest in the substance of the relationship is at an advantage. This may appear paradoxical, since the more intense the desire to possess something or to establish a relationship, the more intense and passionate is the enjoyment of it. It is indeed the anticipated enjoyment that determines the strength of our desire. Yet it is just this situation that gives an advantage to the less interested party, for it is in the nature of things that the one who benefits less should be compensated by some concessions from the other party. This is apparent even in the most refined and intimate relations. In every love relationship, the one who is less involved has an advantage, because the other renounces from the very beginning any exploitation of the relationship, is more ready to make sacrifices, and offers a greater measure of devotion in exchange for the greater satisfaction that he derives. Equity is thus established: since the degree of desire corresponds with the degree of enjoyment it is right that the relationship should provide the individual who is less involved with a special gain, which he is able to exact because he is more hesitant, more reserved and more ready to make conditions. Thus the profit of the one who gives money is not altogether unfair; since he is usually less interested in the commodity—money transaction, an agreement between the two parties is brought about by the one who is more interested in the transaction giving to the other a gain over and above the objective equivalence of the exchange values. It should also be borne in mind that the owner of money has this advantage not because he possesses money, but because he is prepared to part with it.

The profit that accrues to money because it is detached from any particular content or process of the economy is also shown in other ways, and particularly in the fact that owners of money usually profit from violent and ruinous economic upheavals, often to an extraordinary extent. However many bankruptcies and business failures result from price slumps or from commodity market booms, experience has shown that the big bankers usually make a steady profit out of these dangers that confront sellers and buyers, creditors and debtors. The services of money, as the neutral tool of economic processes, have to be paid for regardless of the direction or pace of these processes. Of course, money has to pay something for this freedom; the uncommitted nature of money

means that contradictory demands are made upon the dispenser of money from different sides, and that he excites the suspicion of betrayal more easily than does the individual who deals in specific commodities. In early modern times, when the great financial powers—the Fuggers, the Welsers, the Florentine and Genoan bankers—entered the political arena, particularly during the great struggle between the Habsburgs and the French monarchy for European hegemony, they were regarded with permanent mistrust by all parties, including those to whom they had lent vast sums of money. One never could be sure of the financiers, whose money transactions did not commit them beyond the present moment; and even the enemy against whom they had lent their financial support did not regard this as an obstacle to approaching them himself with requests and propositions. Money has the very positive quality that is designated by the negative concept of lack of character. The individual whom we regard as a weak character is not directed by the inner worth of persons, things or thoughts, but by the external pressure that is brought to bear upon him. The fact that money is detached from all specific contents and exists only as a quantity earns for money and for those people who are only interested in money the quality of characterlessness. This is the almost logically necessary reverse side of the advantages of finance and of the over-valuation of money in relation to qualitative values. The superiority of money is expressed first in the fact that the seller is more interested and eager than the buyer. A very significant feature of our whole attitude towards objects is involved here; namely, when two opposing classes of values are considered as a whole, the first class may be distinctly superior to the second, while the individual objects or representatives of the second group may be superior to those of the first. Faced with a choice between the totality of material goods and the totality of ideal goods, we should probably be obliged to choose the first, because to renounce it would be to negate life, including all its ideal contents; but on the other hand, we might not hesitate to give up any single material good in exchange for an ideal good. In our relations with other people we do not question that one relationship is much more valuable and indispensable than another, when viewed as a whole; but on particular occasions and in particular aspects the less valuable relationship may be more enjoyable and attractive. This is how matters stand in the relation between money and concrete objects of value; a choice between the objects as a whole and money as a whole would immediately reveal the intrinsic valueless-ness of the latter, which provides us only with means, not with an end. Yet when a given sum of money is set against a given quantity of commodities, the exchange of the latter for the former is usually demanded much more strongly than vice-versa. This relationship exists not only between commodities and money in general, but also between money and particular categories of commodities. A single pin is almost worthless, but pins in general are almost indispensable and 'worth their weight in gold'. The case is similar with many kinds of commodities; the ease with which a single specimen can be supplied in return for money devalues it in relation to money, which now appears as a ruling power disposing over the object. But the significance of the class of object as a whole seems incommensurable with money; it has a value independent of money which is often concealed from our notice by the fact that the single specimen can so easily be replaced. However, since our practical economic interests are almost exclusively concerned with single units or with a limited number of units, our sense of the value of objects generally employs the measuring rod of money. This is evidently connected with the overriding interest in possessing money rather than commodities.

The Unearned Increment of Wealth

This leads to a more general phenomenon, which might be termed the surplus value of wealth and which resembles the unearned rent of land. The wealthy man enjoys advantages beyond the enjoyment of what he can buy with his money. The merchant supplies him more reliably and more cheaply than he does poorer people; everyone he meets, whether likely to profit from his wealth or not, is more deferential; he

moves in an ideal atmosphere of unquestioned privilege. One can observe everywhere all manner of small privileges being granted to the purchaser of expensive goods and to the first-class traveller; privileges that have as little connection with the objective value as has the friendly smile of the merchant with the more expensive goods that he is selling. These privileges are a gratuitous supplement, and their most painful feature is perhaps that the consumer of cheaper goods, who is denied them, cannot complain that he is being cheated. This can be best illustrated by a very minor instance. The streetcars in some cities have two separate classes which differ in price, although the more expensive class offers no material advantage in the way of greater comfort. What the traveller buys with his first-class ticket is the right to join the exclusive company of those who pay such a higher price in order to be separated from the second-class passengers. Thus the well-to-do individual can acquire an advantage simply by spending more money, without necessarily receiving a material equivalent for his expenditure.

Viewed from the outside, it may seem that this is the opposite of an unearned increment, because the well-to-do individual receives relatively less, not relatively more, for his money. But the unearned increment of wealth appears here in a negative, but pure, form; the rich man gains an advantage without recourse to an object and exclusively by virtue of the fact that other people cannot spend as much money as he can. Wealth, indeed, is often regarded as a kind of moral merit, as is indicated by the term 'respectability' and by popular references to the well-to-do as 'upright citizens' or 'the better-class public'. The same phenomenon is shown from the other side by the fact that the poor are treated as if they were guilty, that beggars are angrily driven away, and that even good-natured people consider themselves naturally superior to the poor. When it was decreed in 1536 that the journeyman locksmiths in Strasbourg who earned more than eight *kreuzer* should have a holiday on Monday afternoons, a bonus was given to those who were better off, when moral logic suggests that it should have been given to the needy. It is not uncommon for the unearned increment of wealth to attain such a degree of perversity: practical idealism, when it is manifested in the unpaid scientific work of a wealthy man, is generally more highly esteemed than is the work of a poor schoolteacher. This usurious interest upon wealth, these advantages that its possessor gains without being obliged to give anything in return, are bound up with the money form of value. For those phenomena obviously express or reflect that unlimited freedom of use which distinguishes money from all other values. This it is that creates the state of affairs in which a rich man has an influence not only by what he does but also by what he could do; a great fortune is encircled by innumerable possibilities of use, as though by an astral body, which extend far beyond the employment of the income from it on the benefits which the income brings to other people. The German language indicates this by the use of the word *Vermögen*, which means 'to be able to do something', for a great fortune. These possibilities, only a small number of which can be realized, are nevertheless put to account psychologically. They convey the impression of an indetermi-

nate power which is not confined to the achievement of a particular result, and this impression is all the stronger the more mobile and more easily available for any purpose the possessions are; that is to say, the more the fortune consists of money or is convertible to money, and the more distinctly money itself has become a tool and a point of transition without any purpose of its own. The pure potentiality of money as a means is distilled in a general conception of power and significance which becomes effective as real power and significance for the owner of money. It is like the attraction of a work of art, which is produced not only by its content and the associated psychological reactions, but by all the accidental, individual and indirect complexes of feeling that it makes possible. Only the indeterminate sum of these feelings circumscribes the whole value and significance of a work of art.

21

Dress and Its Victims

Harriet Martineau

A growing body of scholarly opinion has concluded that Harriet Martineau (1802–1876) ought to be seen—along with figures such as August Comte and Herbert Spencer—as one of the critical formative influences on the subsequent development of sociology. She was a prolific author; included among her most important achievements are *Society in America* (1837), which has been compared favorably with Tocqueville's *Democracy in America*, and *How to Observe Morals and Manners* (1838). Martineau's writings evince a keen appreciation of the importance of social theory, which, like many of her contemporaries, she sought to advance by employing both historical and comparative perspectives. Moreover, she sought to connect theory to both empirical research and social reform. Far more consistently than her male contemporaries, she attempted to explore the significance of gender relations. This interest is apparent in this essay, in which Martineau attacks much of women's clothing as detrimental to health and safety. She offers a critique of women's "slavishness to fashion" and of the role of men in "inducing" women to wear clothing that puts them at risk. What one finds in this selection is a reflection of both Martineau's feminism and her interest in the realms of culture and consumption. In this regard, she can be seen as a nineteenth-century precursor to both contemporary feminists and to cultural sociologists. At the same time, in contrast to Simmel's essay on fashion contained herein, it is clear that Martineau was very much a nineteenth-century moralist.

There are a good many people who cannot possibly believe that dress can have any share in the deaths of the 100,000 persons who go needlessly to the grave every year in our happy England, where there are more means of comfort for everybody than in any other country in Europe.

How can people be killed by dress, now-a-days? they ask. We must be thinking of the old times when the ladies laced so tight that "salts and strong waters" seem to have been called for to some fainting fair one, as often as numbers were collected together, whether at church, or at Ranelagh,[1] or the theatres. Or perhaps we are thinking of the accidents that have happened during particular fashions of dress, as the burning of the Marchioness of Salisbury, from her high cap nodding over the candle; or the deaths of the Ladies Bridgman two years since, from the skirts of one of them catching fire at the grate; or the number of inquests held during the fashion of gigot-sleeves, when a lady could scarcely dine in company, or play the piano at home, without peril of death by fire.

Perhaps it may be the heavy, towering head-dresses of the last century we may be thinking of, bringing in a crowd of bad symptoms, headaches, congestions, fits, palsies, with the fearful remedies of bleeding and reducing, which we read of in medical books, and in gossiping literature, like Horace Walpole's correspondence. Or we may even be thinking of the barbaric fashion of painting the face, neck, and hands, at one time carried on to the excess of enamelling the skin. That was not at so very remote a time; for I have heard from the lips of witnesses what it was like; and a friend of mine, yet living, can tell what she saw at a concert where a lady sat before her with a pair of broad shoulders which looked like tawny marble,—as smooth, as shining, and as little like anything human. These shoulders were once enamelled, and may have looked white in their day; but no life-long pains to renew their whiteness would serve after a certain lapse of time; and there they were, hopeless, tawny, and the quality of the skin destroyed. The poisonings by means of cosmetics that we read of in the history of past centuries, may have been sometimes intentional; but there was plenty of unconscious poisoning besides.

I do not, however, mean any of these things when I speak of dress, in connection with preventible mortality.

Perhaps I may be supposed to be referring to the notoriously afflicted and short-lived classes of milliners and shopworkers who are worn out and killed off in the cause of dress. No; I am not now going to bring forward their case, because it comes under a different head. At this moment I am not thinking of either the political economy or the general morality of the dress-question, or I should bring up the group of suicides who have perished, some from hopeless poverty, some from intolerable degradation, and some from the embarrassment of gambling debts incurred for the sake of dress.

If the secrets of the city were known, we might hear of more tragedies than the theatres show, from the spread of gambling among women, and especially among servant-girls and shop women, who have been carried beyond bounds by the extravagant fashion of the day. But I am not speaking of suicides, nor of the victims of the needle, whose case is too grave to be treated lightly, and whose day of deliverance, too, is at hand, if the sewing machine is the reality it appears—and not a phantom, cheating the hopes of thousands. We may possibly look into that another time. Meanwhile our business is with the injurious and sometimes murderous effect of dress which we see worn every day.

It will not seem so wonderful that the familiar clothing of our neighbours and ourselves may be of such importance when we remember the explanations of physicians— that dress may, and usually does, affect the condition and action of almost every department of the human frame;—the brain and nervous system, the lungs, the stomach, and other organs of the trunk; the eyes, the skin, the muscles, the glandular system, the nutri-

tive system, and even the bony frame, the skeleton on which all hangs. If dress can meddle mischievously with the action, or affect the condition of all these, it can be no marvel that it is responsible for a good many of the hundred thousand needless deaths which are happening around us this year.

Putting aside the ordinary associations, as far as we can, and trying for the moment to consider what is to be desired in the clothing of the human body,—what is requisite to make dress good and beautiful,—let us see what is essential.

Dress should be a covering to all the parts of the body which need warmth or coolness, as the case may be. It should be a shelter from the evils of the atmosphere, whether these be cold, or heat, or wet, or damp, or glare. This is the first requisite; for such shelter is the main purpose of clothing. In our own country the dress should easily admit of the necessary changes in degrees of warmth demanded by our changeable climate.

Dress should bear a close relation to the human form. No other principle can be permanent; no other can be durably sanctioned by sense and taste, because no other has reality in it. We may fancy that we admire the old Greek and Roman robes which look dignified in Julius Caesar on the stage, and in statues, and in our own imaginations of classical times; but we could not get through our daily business in such a costume; nor should we admire the appearance of our acquaintance in it. In fact, the wearers themselves were always tucking up or putting away their troublesome wrappers when they had anything to do: and the busy people of society appeared in their workshops and fields in garments which left their limbs free, and their whole body fit for action. On the whole, in a general way, with particular variations according to taste, the dress should follow the outline of the body. Any great deviation from this principle involves inconvenience on the one hand, and deformity on the other.

Where it follows the outline of the frame it should fit accurately enough to fulfil its intention, but so easily as not to embarrass action. It should neither compress the internal structure nor impede the external movement. An easy fit, in short, is the requisite. It is a part of this easy fit that the weight of the clothes should be properly hung and distributed.

After the peace of 1815 it was said that we gained two things from the French—gloves that would fit, and the shoulderpiece. It would make the difference of some lives out of the great number thrown away, if we made due use of the shoulderpiece, now. By the shoulder-piece, the weight of the garment is spread on the part best fitted to bear it, instead of being hung from the neck, as it was before we knew better or from the hips or the waist (in the case of women's dress) as now, when we ought to know better.

Next; dress ought to be agreeable to wear: and this includes something more than warmth and a good fit. It should be light, and subject to as few dangers and inconveniences as possible. . . .

[Women's] clothing does not protect them from cold, heat, damp, or glare. Some few uncover the chest and arms under trying circumstances of heat and draught: but they are few; and they must have heard all that can be said to them in the way of warning. The great body of Englishwomen—those of the middle and lower classes—have usually some sort of covering from the throat to the hands and feet, but it is too seldom judicious in degree or quality. The modern linsey petticoats are excellent as far as they go; but it is certain that the working-women of our country are too thoroughly weaned from the woollen clothing of their ancestors. At present, too, no woman who adopts the fashion of the hoop in any form is properly guarded against the climate. Any medical man in good practice can tell of the spread of rheumatism since women ceased to wear their clothing about their limbs, and stuck it off with frames and hoops, admitting damp and draught, with as little rationality as if they tried to make an umbrella serve the purpose of a bonnet.

Then observe the head and the feet. The eyes are unsheltered from sun and wind, and the most important region of the head is exposed by the bonnets which Englishwomen are so weak as to wear in imitation of the French. Again, the doctors have their painful tale to tell of neuralgic pains in the face and head, which abound beyond all prior experience, of complaints in the eyes, and all the consequences that might be anticipated from the practice of lodging the bonnet on the nape of the neck, and leaving all the fore part of the skull exposed.[2] Why the bonnet is worn at all is the mystery. A veil, white or black, would be considered an absurdity as a substitute for the bonnet in a climate like ours; but it would be actually more serviceable than the handful of flimsy decorations now usurping the place of the useful, cheap, and pretty straw bonnet, which suits all ages in its large variety. There are the hats, to be sure, which young ladies wear so becomingly. They are hardly simple enough in form for a permanence, but they are substantially unexceptionable for youthful wearers. Their advantages unfortunately tempt elderly ladies to put them on; but the class of mistaken wearers of hats is not a very large one, and we may let them pass. In praising the hat, however, I am thinking of the sort that has a brim. The new and brimless invention is nearly as bad as the bonnet for use, while more fantastic. A chimney-pot hat with a tall upright plume may possibly suit a volunteer rifle corps or a regiment of Amazons rehearsing for the opera, but it is not very English in taste.

The fearful spread of throat and chest diseases is ascribed, by those who should know best, mainly to the modern notion of muffling up the throat in furs and other heating substances. Before the boa came in, we heard little of any one of the tribe of throat diseases which we now meet at every turn. Some ladies carry a boa all through the summer, and many tie up their throats with a silk handkerchief whenever they go abroad, in all seasons; suffering their retribution in hoarsenesses, bronchitis, sore throat, and other ailments never endured by those who cultivate more hardy habits, reserving such wraps for very special occasions. People who use cold water in some form of bath every day of the year, and who give their faces and throats to the bracing air, under the safeguard of vigorous personal exercise, forget what colds and coughs are.

As for the other point—the feet—it is to be feared that some are still sent to the grave by thin shoes. The danger of gutta-percha and patent-leather shoes has been referred to. The Balmoral boots of the day would be admirable but for the military heels. Those heels throw the foot into an unnatural posture, by which a great strain is produced. If my readers happen to be acquainted with a respectable chiropodist, let them inquire the recent news of bunions—that severest of small maladies. They will learn that there has been an unheard-of increase and aggravation of bunions since the high-heeled boots came in. The danger of falls is also considerable: and those who have a dread of a long tumble down the stairs, had better put on their boots on the ground-floor.

If we consider the female dress of 1859 under any of the remaining conditions, what can we say of it? Does the costume, as a whole, follow the outline of the form? Does it fit accurately and easily? Is the weight made to hang from the shoulders? Are the garments of to-day convenient and agreeable in use? Is the mode modest and graceful? So far from it, that all these conditions are conspicuously violated by those who think they dress well. Here and there we may meet a sensible woman, or a girl who has no money to spend in new clothes, whose appearance is pleasing—in a straw bonnet that covers the head, in a neat gown which hangs gracefully and easily from the natural waist, and which does not sweep up the dirt: but the spectacle is now rare; for bad taste in the higher classes spreads very rapidly downwards, corrupting the morals as it goes.

The modern dress perverts the form very disagreeably. The evil still begins with the stays, in too many instances, though there is less tight-lacing than formerly. It is a pity that women do not know how little they gain by false pretences in regard to figure and complexion. Our grandmothers would not have worn paint if they had been aware that it is useless after forty to attempt to seem younger—the texture of the skin revealing at a glance the fact which paint and dyed hair cannot conceal; except perhaps in the parks, or across a theatre. In the same way, the round waist produced by tight-lacing is always distinguishable in a moment from the easy oval form of the genuine small waist. Compare the two extremes, and you will see it at once. Compare the figure of the Graces of Raffaelle, or the Venus de Medici, with the smallest and most praised waist in a factory,

and observe the difference. Before the glass, the owner of the latter sees the smallness in front, and fancies it beautiful; but it is disgusting to others. It is as stiff as the stem of a tree, and spoils the form and movement more than the armour of ancient knights ever did; and we know what is going on within. The ribs are pressed out of their places, down upon the soft organs within, or overlapping one another—the heart is compressed, so that the circulation is irregular— the stomach and liver are compressed, so that they cannot act properly: and then parts which cannot be squeezed are thrust out of their places, and grave ailments are the consequence. At the very best, the complexion loses more than the figure can be supposed to gain. It is painful to see what is endured by some young women in shops and factories, as elsewhere. They cannot stoop for two minutes over their work without gasping and being blue, or red, or white in the face. They cannot go upstairs without stopping to take breath every few steps. Their arms are half numb, and their hands red or chilblained; and they must walk as if they were all-of-a-piece, without the benefit and grace of joints in the spine and limbs. A lady had the curiosity to feel what made a girl whom she knew so like a wooden figure, and found a complete palisade extending round the body. On her remonstrating, the girl pleaded that she had "only six-and-twenty whalebones!"

Any visitor of a range of factories will be sure to find that girls are dropping in fainting-fits, here and there, however pure the air and proper the temperature; and here and there may be seen a vexed and disgusted proprietor, seeking the warehouse-woman, or some matron, to whom he gives a pair of large scissors, with directions to cut open the stays of some silly woman who had fainted. Occasional inquests afford a direct warning of the fatal effects which may follow the practice of tight-lacing; but slow and painful disease is much more common; and the register exhibits, not the stays, but the malady created by the stays as the cause of death. That such cases are common, any physician who practises among the working-classes will testify.

Do the petticoats of our time serve as anything but a mask to the human form—a perversion of human proportions? A woman on a sofa looks like a child popping up from a haycock. A girl in the dance looks like the Dutch tumbler that was a favourite toy in my infancy. The fit is so the reverse of accurate as to be like a silly hoax—a masquerade without wit: while, at the same time, it is not an easy fit. The prodigious weight of the modern petticoat, and the difficulty of getting it all into the waistband, creates a necessity for compressing and loading the waist in a way most injurious to health. Under a rational method of dress the waist should suffer neither weight nor pressure—nothing more than the girdle which brings the garment into form and folds. As to the convenience of the hooped skirts, only ask the women themselves, who are always in danger from fire, or wind, or water, or carriage wheeles, or rails, or pails, or nails, or, in short, everything they encounter. Ask the husbands, fathers, or brothers, and hear how they like being cut with the steel frame when they enter a gate with a lady, or being driven into a corner of the pew at church, or to the outside of the coach, for want of room. As for the children—how many have been swept off pathways, or footbridges, or steamboat decks by the pitiless crinoline, or hoops of some unconscious walking balloon! More children have been killed, however, by the extension of the absurd petticoat fashion to them. For many months past, it has been a rare thing to see a child under the tunic age duly clothed. The petticoats are merely for show; and the actual clothing, from the waist downwards, is nothing more than thin cotton drawers and socks, leaving a bare space between. For older boys there is a great improvement in dress—the tunic and loose trousers being preferable in every way to the stiff mannish tailed coat and tight trousers of half a century ago. But the younger children are at present scarcely clothed at all, below the arms; and the blue legs of childhood are a painful sight, whether in a beggar boy or a citizen's son. Even in such a climate as Sierra Leone there is something forlorn in thinking of the lady's maid in a great house wearing (and possessing) nothing more in the way of clothing than a muslin gown and a blue bead-necklace (on an ebony throat, of course), but in winters like ours to see children's legs covered with nothing better than thin cotton (thin, because the ornamentation is the vanity), is in fact reading the sentence of death of many victims. Let it be remembered, too, that the neuralgic, rheumatic and heart diseases thus brought on are of a hereditary character. The wearer of crinoline and invisible bonnets, in incurring such diseases herself, renders her future children liable to them; and the children now bitten by the wintry winds, if they live to be parents, may see their offspring suffer from the ignorance and vanity of their own mothers. It is universally observed that certain diseases are becoming more common every year—neuralgia and heart disease, as well as the throat ailments of which we hear so much. It would be a great benefit if we could learn how much of the form and the increase of maladies is ascribable to our modes of dress.

What is to be done? Will anything ever be done? or is feminine wilfulness and slavishness to fashion to kill off hundreds and thousands of the race, as at present? I see, with much satisfaction, that the Messrs. Courtauld, the great silk manufacturers in Essex, have put up a notice in their factories, that a fine is imposed on the wearing of crinoline by their workwomen. The ground of the regulation is, that the work cannot be done with either decency or safety in that kind of dress. I hope this example will be followed in all mills and factories where the same reason can be assigned. There are whole societies in America who do not see the necessity for such mischief, and who hope to put an end to it—in their own country at least. The Dress-Reform Association of the United States was instituted some years since by women who refused the inconvenience of Paris fashions in American homesteads: and they have been aided, not only by physicians, but by other men, on the ground of the right of women to wear what suits their occupations and their taste, without molestation. The dress which was long ago agreed upon, after careful consideration—the so-called Bloomer costume (not as we see it in caricature, but in its near resemblance to the most rational English fashion of recent times)—is extensively worn, not only in rural districts, but in many towns. It seems to fulfil the various conditions of rational, modest, and graceful dress better than any other as yet devised for temperate climates; and if so, it will spread, in spite of all opposition.

What opposition it met with here is not forgotten at home or abroad, and never will be forgotten. Some of our highest philosophers and best-bred gentlemen were more indignant and ashamed than perhaps anybody else. They said that we constantly saw Englishmen angry and scornful because of the indignities cast by Mussulman bigotry on the dress of Europeans in Damascus and Jerusalem; but here were Englishmen doing the same thing, without equal excuse, when Englishwomen proposed to adapt their dress to their health, convenience, and notions of grace. The aggressors triumphed. They induced outcast women to adopt the dress, and stamped it with disrepute before it had a chance of a trial. It was an unmanly act; and if those who were concerned in it have since suffered from the extravagance of wife and daughters, or from sickness and death in their households, which might have been averted by a sensible method of clothing old and young, they have had their retribution. Some of our newspapers are rebuking others for meddling with the women's choice of fashions . . . but it is an affair which concerns both sexes and all ages. What hinders a simple obedience to common sense in the matter? It is only for the women of those classes who really have business in life to refuse to encumber themselves with tight, or heavy, or long, or unserviceable dress, and to adhere to any mode which suits them; and then, whatever the idle and fanciful may choose to do, the useless mortality will be mainly stopped, and the general health prevented from sinking lower. It may be confidently avowed that in this way only can women win back some of the respect which they have forfeited by the culpable absurdity of their dress within the last few seasons. From the duchess to the maid-servant, the slaves of French taste have lost position; and it will require a permanent establishment of some leading points of the sense and morality of dress to restore their full dignity to the matronage and maidenhood of England.

Endnotes

1. A fashionable pleasure garden during the second half of the eighteenth century.
2. In 1859.

Reprinted from Harriet Martineau, *Health, Husbandry and Handicraft* (London: Bradbury and Evans, 1861), pp. 49–60. Published originally in *Once a Week* in 1859. ✦

22
The Conservation of Races

W. E. B. Du Bois

William Edward Burghardt Du Bois (1868–1963) was one of the monumental figures in the struggle for racial justice in America. He founded the Niagara Movement, was one of the creators of the National Association for the Advancement of Colored People (NAACP), and later became an advocate of Pan-Africanism. Du Bois was trained as a sociologist, the first African American to receive a Ph.D. from Harvard University. In "The Conservation of Races," first published in 1897, he argues that contrary to those who would contend that racial differences are inconsequential when seen in the light of the similarities that bind all humans, there are important differences that transcend the obvious physical differences. These he characterizes as spiritual and psychical differences, and out of these differences the races have contributed to civilization. With this in mind, and without resorting to such language, Du Bois argues against assimilation and in favor of cultural pluralism.

The American Negro has always felt an intense personal interest in discussions as to the origins and destinies of races: primarily because back of most discussions of race with which he is familiar, have lurked certain assumptions as to his natural abilities, as to his political, intellectual and moral status, which he felt were wrong. He has, consequently, been led to deprecate and minimize race distinctions, to believe intensely that out of one blood God created all nations, and to speak of human brotherhood as though it were the possibility of an already dawning to-morrow.

Nevertheless, in our calmer moments we must acknowledge that human beings are divided into races; that in this country the two most extreme types of the world's races have met, and the resulting problem as to the future relations of these types is not only of intense and living interest to us, but forms an epoch in the history of mankind.

It is necessary, therefore, in planning our movements, in guiding our future development, that at times we rise above the pressing, but smaller questions of separate schools and cars, wage-discrimination and lynch law, to survey the whole question of race in human philosophy and to lay, on a basis of broad knowledge and careful insight, those large lines of policy and higher ideals which may form our guiding lines and boundaries in the practical difficulties of every day. For it is certain that all human striving must recognize the hard limits of natural law, and that any striving, no matter how intense and earnest, which is against the constitution of the world, is vain. The question, then, which we must seriously consider is this: What is the real meaning of Race; what has, in the past, been the law of race development, and what lessons has the past history of race development to teach the rising Negro people?

When we thus come to inquire into the essential difference of races we find it hard to come at once to any definite conclusion. Many criteria of race differences have in the past been proposed, as color, hair, cranial measurements and language. And manifestly, in each of these respects, human beings differ widely. They vary in color, for instance, from the marble-like pallor of the Scandinavian to the rich, dark brown of the Zulu, passing by the creamy Slav, the yellow Chinese, the light brown Sicilian and the brown Egyptian. Men vary, too, in the texture of hair from the obstinately straight hair of the Chinese to the obstinately tufted and frizzled hair of the Bushman. In measurement of heads, again, men vary; from the broad-headed Tartar to the medium-headed European and the narrow-headed Hottentot; or, again in language, from the highly-inflected Roman tongue to the monosyllabic Chinese. All these physical characteristics are patent enough, and if they agreed with each other it would be very easy to classify mankind. Unfortunately for scientists, however, these criteria of race are most exasperatingly intermingled. Color does not agree with texture of hair, for many of the dark races have straight hair; nor does color agree with the breadth of the head, for the yellow Tartar has a broader head than the German; nor, again, has the science of language as yet succeeded in clearing up the relative authority of these various and contradictory criteria. The final word of science, so far, is that we have at least two, perhaps three, great families of human beings—the whites and Negroes, possibly the yellow race. That other races have arisen from the intermingling of the blood of these two. This broad division of the world's races which men like Huxley and Raetzel have introduced as more nearly true than the old five-race scheme of Blumenbach, is nothing more than an acknowledgment that, so far as purely physical characteristics are concerned, the differences between men do not explain all the differences of their history. It declares, as Darwin himself said, that great as is the physical unlikeness of the various races of men their likenesses are greater, and upon this rests the whole scientific doctrine of Human Brotherhood.

Although the wonderful developments of human history teach that the grosser physical differences of color, hair and bone go but a short way toward explaining the different roles which groups of men have played in Human Progress, yet there are differences—subtle, delicate and elusive, though they may be—which have silently but definitely separated men into groups. While these subtle forces have generally followed the natural cleavage of common blood, descent and physical peculiarities, they have at other times swept across and ignored these. At all times, however, they have divided human beings into races, which, while they perhaps transcend scientific definition, nevertheless, are clearly defined to the eye of the Historian and Sociologist.

If this be true, then the history of the world is the history, not of individuals, but of groups, not of nations, but of races, and he who ignores or seeks to override the race idea in human history ignores and overrides the central thought of all history. What, then, is a race? It is a vast family of human beings, generally of common blood and language, always of common history, traditions and impulses, who are both voluntarily and involuntarily striving together for the accomplishment of certain more or less vividly conceived ideals of life.

Turning to real history, there can be no doubt, first, as to the widespread, nay, universal, prevalence of the race idea, the race spirit, the race ideal, and as to its efficiency as the vastest and most ingenious invention for human progress. We, who have been reared and trained under the individualistic philosophy of the Declaration of Independence and the laisser-faire philosophy of Adam Smith, are loath to see and loath to acknowledge this patent fact of human history. We see the Pharaohs, Caesars, Toussaints and Napoleons of history and forget the vast races of which they were but epitomized expressions. We are apt to think in our American impatience, that while it may have been true in the past that closed race groups made history, that here in conglomerate America *nous avons changer tout cela*—we have changed all that, and have no need of this ancient instrument of progress. This assumption of which the Negro people are especially fond, can not be established by a careful consideration of history.

We find upon the world's stage today eight distinctly differentiated races, in the sense in which History tells us the word must be used. They are, the Slavs of eastern Europe, the Teutons of middle Europe, the English of Great Britain and America, the Romance nations of Southern and Western Europe, the Negroes of Africa and America, the Semitic people of Western Asia and Northern Africa, the Hindoos of Central Asia and the Mongolians of Eastern Asia. There are, of course, other minor race groups, as the American Indians, the Esquimaux and the South Sea Islanders; these larger races, too, are far from homogeneous; the Slav includes the Czech, the Magyar, the Pole and the Russian; the Teuton includes the German, the Scandinavian and the Dutch; the English include the Scotch, the Irish and the conglomerate American. Under Romance nations the widely-differing Frenchman, Italian, Sicilian and Spaniard are comprehended. The term Negro is, perhaps, the most indefinite of all, combining the Mulattoes and

Zamboes of America and the Egyptians, Bantus and Bushmen of Africa. Among the Hindoos are traces of widely differing nations, while the great Chinese, Tartar, Corean and Japanese families fall under the one designation—Mongolian.

The question now is: What is the real distinction between these nations? Is it the physical differences of blood, color and cranial measurements? Certainly we must all acknowledge that physical differences play a great part, and that, with wide exceptions and qualifications, these eight great races of to-day follow the cleavage of physical race distinctions; the English and Teuton represent the white variety of mankind; the Mongolian, the yellow; the Negroes, the black. Between these are many crosses and mixtures, where Mongolian and Teuton have blended into the Slav, and other mixtures have produced the Romance nations and the Semites. But while race differences have followed mainly physical race lines, yet no mere physical distinctions would really define or explain the deeper differences—the cohesiveness and continuity of these groups. The deeper differences are spiritual, psychical, differences—undoubtedly based on the physical, but infinitely transcending them. The forces that bind together the Teuton nations are, then, first, their race identity and common blood; secondly, and more important, a common history, common laws and religion, similar habits of thought and a conscious striving together for certain ideals of life. The whole process which has brought about these race differentiations has been a growth, and the great characteristic of this growth has been the differentiation of spiritual and mental differences between great races of mankind and the integration of physical differences.

The age of nomadic tribes of closely related individuals represents the maximum of physical differences. They were practically vast families, and there were as many groups as families. As the families came together to form cities the physical differences lessened, purity of blood was replaced by the requirement of domicile, and all who lived within the city bounds became gradually to be regarded as members of the group; *i.e.*, there was a slight and slow breaking down of physical barriers. This, however, was accompanied by an increase of the spiritual and social differences between cities. This city became husbandmen, this, merchants, another warriors, and so on. The *ideals of life* for which the different cities struggled were different. When at last cities began to coalesce into nations there was another breaking down of barriers which separated groups of men. The larger and broader differences of color, hair and physical proportions were not by any means ignored, but myriads of minor differences disappeared, and the sociological and historical races of men began to approximate the present division of races as indicated by physical researches. At the same time the spiritual and physical differences of race groups which constituted the nations became deep and decisive. The English nation stood for constitutional liberty and commercial freedom; the German nation for science and philosophy; the Romance nations stood for literature and art, and the other race groups are striving, each in its own way, to develope for civilization its particular message, its particular ideal, which shall help to guide the world nearer and nearer that perfection of human life for which we all long, that "one far off Divine event."

This has been the function of race differences up to the present time. What shall be its function in the future? Manifestly some of the great races of today—particularly the Negro race—have not as yet given to civilization the full spiritual message which they are capable of giving. I will not say that the Negro race has as yet given no message to the world, for it is still a mooted question among scientists as to just how far Egyptian civilization was Negro in its origin; if it was not wholly Negro, it was certainly very closely allied. Be that as it may, however the fact still remains that the full, complete Negro message of the whole Negro race has not as yet been given to the world: that the messages and ideal of the yellow race have not been completed, and that the striving of the mighty Slavs has but begun. The question is, then: How shall this message be delivered; how shall these various ideals be realized? The answer is plain: By the development of these race groups, not as individuals, but as races. For the development of Japanese genius, Japanese literature and art, Japanese spirit, only Japanese, bound and welded together, Japanese inspired by one vast ideal, can work out in its fullness the wonderful message which Japan has for the nations of the earth. For the development of Negro genius, of Negro literature and art, of Negro spirit, only Negroes bound and welded together, Negroes inspired by one vast ideal, can work out in its fullness the great message we have for humanity. We cannot reverse history; we are subject to the same natural laws as other races, and if the Negro is ever to be a factor in the world's history—if among the gaily-colored banners that deck the broad ramparts of civilization is to hang one uncompromising black, then it must be placed there by black hands, fashioned by black heads and hallowed by the travail of 200,000,000 black hearts beating in one glad song of jubilee.

For this reason, the advance guard of the Negro people—the 8,000,000 people of Negro blood in the United States of America—must soon come to realize that if they are to take their just place in the van of Pan-Negroism, then their destiny is *not* absorption by the white Americans. That if in America it is to be proven for the first time in the modern world that not only Negroes are capable of evolving individual men like Toussaint, the Saviour, but are a nation stored with wonderful possibilities of culture, then their destiny is not a servile imitation of Anglo-Saxon culture, but a stalwart originality which shall unswervingly follow Negro ideals.

It may, however, be objected here that the situation of our race in America renders this attitude impossible; that our sole hope of salvation lies in our being able to lose our race identity in the commingled blood of the nation; and that any other course would merely increase the friction of races which we call race prejudice, and against which we have so long and so earnestly fought.

Here, then, is the dilemma, and it is a puzzling one, I admit. No Negro who has given earnest thought to the situation of his people in America has failed, at some time in life, to find himself at these cross-roads; has failed to ask himself at some time: What, after all, am I? Am I an American or am I a Negro? Can I be both? Or is it my duty to cease to be a Negro as soon as possible and be an American? If I strive as a Negro, am I not perpetuating the very cleft that threatens and separates Black and White America? Is not my only possible practical aim the subduction of all that is Negro in me to the American? Does my black blood place upon me any more obligation to assert my nationality than German, or Irish or Italian blood would?

It is such incessant self-questioning and the hesitation that arises from it, that is making the present period a time of vacillation and contradiction for the American Negro; combined race action is stifled, race responsibility is shirked, race enterprises languish, and the best blood, the best talent, the best energy of the Negro people cannot be marshalled to do the bidding of the race. They stand back to make room for every rascal and demagogue who chooses to cloak his selfish deviltry under the veil of race pride.

Is this right? Is it rational? Is it good policy? Have we in America a distinct mission as a race—a distinct sphere of action and an opportunity for race development, or is self-obliteration the highest end to which Negro blood dare aspire?

If we carefully consider what race prejudice really is, we find it, historically, to be nothing but the friction between different groups of people; it is the difference in aim, in feeling, in ideals of two different races; if, now, this difference exists touching territory, laws, language, or even religion, it is manifest that these people cannot live in the same territory without fatal collision; but if, on the other hand, there is substantial agreement in laws, language and religion; if there is a satisfactory adjustment of economic life, then there is no reason why, in the same country and on the same street, two or three great national ideals might not thrive and develop, that men of different races might not strive together for their race ideals as well, perhaps even better, than in isolation. Here, it seems to me, is the reading of the riddle that puzzles so many of us. We are Americans, not only by birth and by citizenship, but by our political ideals, our language, our religion. Farther than that, our Americanism does not go. At that point, we are Negroes, members of a vast historic race that from the very dawn of creation has slept, but half awakening in the dark forests of its African fatherland. We are the first fruits of this new nation, the harbinger of that black to-morrow which is yet destined to soften the whiteness of the Teutonic to-day. We are that people whose subtle sense of song has given America its only American music, its only American fairy tales, its only touch of pathos and humor amid its mad money-getting plutocracy. As such, it is our duty to conserve our physical powers, our intellectual endowments, our spiritual ideals; as a race we must strive by race organization, by race solidarity, by race unity to the realization of that broader humanity which freely recognizes differences in men, but sternly deprecates inequality in their opportunities of development.

For the accomplishment of these ends we need race organizations: Negro colleges, Negro newspapers, Negro business organizations, a Negro school of literature and art, and an intellectual clearing house, for all these products of the Negro mind, which we may call a Negro Academy. Not only is all this necessary for positive advance, it is absolutely imperative for negative defense. Let us not deceive ourselves at our situation in this country. Weighted with a heritage of moral iniquity from our past history, hard pressed in the economic world by foreign immigrants and native prejudice, hated here, despised there and pitied everywhere; our one haven of refuge is ourselves, and but one means of advance, our own belief in our great destiny, our own implicit trust in our

ability and worth. There is no power under God's high heaven that can stop the advance of eight thousand thousand honest, earnest, inspired and united people. But—and here is the rub—they *must* be honest, fearlessly criticising their own faults, zealously correcting them; they must be *earnest*. No people that laughs at itself, and ridicules itself, and wishes to God it was anything but itself ever wrote its name in history; it *must* be inspired with the Divine faith of our black mothers, that out of the blood and dust of battle will march a victorious host, a mighty nation, a peculiar people, to speak to the nations of earth a Divine truth that shall make them free. And such a people must be united; not merely united for the organized theft of political spoils, not united to disgrace religion with whoremongers and ward-heelers; not united merely to protest and pass resolutions, but united to stop the ravages of consumption among the Negro people, united to keep black boys from loafing, gambling and crime; united to guard the purity of black women and to reduce that vast army of black prostitutes that is today marching to hell; and united in serious organizations, to determine by careful conference and thoughtful interchange of opinion the broad lines of policy and action for the American Negro. . . .

23
The Dependence of Women

Charlotte Perkins Gilman

Charlotte Perkins Gilman (1860–1935) is best known today as a feminist theorist and novelist. Her personal account of her own descent into madness, *The Yellow Wallpaper*, along with her futuristic novel *Herland*, continue to be read today. Less well known is the fact that Gilman was interested in sociology, having been influenced in particular by the work of one of the founders of American sociology, Frank Lester Ward. In this descriptive passage from *Women and Economics* (1898), she discusses the implications of consigning women to household labor and child rearing—which, because these forms of work are uncompensated, means that they have no impact on the economic status of women. As a consequence of this situation, wives are dependent on their husbands for their status in the larger community. As contemporary feminists have frequently pointed out, this assessment by a turn-of-the-century feminist remains relevant today.

...Grateful return for happiness conferred is not the method of exchange in a partnership. The comfort a man takes with his wife is not in the nature of a business partnership, nor are her frugality and industry. A housekeeper, in her place, might be as frugal, as industrious, but would not therefore be a partner. Man and wife are partners truly in their mutual obligation to their children, their common love, duty, and service. But a manufacturer who marries, or a doctor, or a lawyer, does not take a partner in his business, when he takes a partner in parenthood, unless his wife is also a manufacturer, a doctor, or a lawyer. In his business, she cannot even advise wisely without training and experience. To love her husband the composer, does not enable her to compose; and the loss of a man's wife, though it may break his heart, does not cripple his business, unless his mind is affected by grief. She is in no sense a business partner, unless she contributes capital or experience or labor, as a man would in like relation. Most men would hesitate very seriously before entering a business partnership with any woman, wife or not.

If the wife is not, then, truly a business partner, in what way does she earn from her husband the food, clothing, and shelter she receives at his hands? By house service, it will be instantly replied. This is the general misty idea upon the subject,—that women earn all they get, and more, by house service. Here we come to a very practical and definite economic ground. Although not producers of wealth, women serve in the final processes of preparation and distribution. Their labor in the household has a genuine economic value.

For a certain percentage of persons to serve other persons, in order that the ones so served may produce more, is a contribution not to be overlooked. The labor of women in the house, certainly, enables men to produce more wealth than they otherwise could; and in this way women are economic factors in society. But so are horses. The labor of horses enables men to produce more wealth than they otherwise could. The horse is an economic factor in society. But the horse is not economically independent, nor is the woman. If a man plus a valet can perform more useful service than he could minus a valet, then the valet is performing useful service. But, if the valet is the property of the man, is obliged to perform this service, and is not paid for it, he is not economically independent.

The labor which the wife performs in the household is given as part of her functional duty, not as employment. The wife of the poor man, who works hard in a small house, doing all the work for the family, or the wife of the rich man, who wisely and gracefully manages a large house and administers its functions, each is entitled to fair pay for services rendered.

To take this ground and hold it honestly, wives, as earners through domestic service, are entitled to the wages of cooks, housemaids, nursemaids, seamstresses, or house-keepers, and to no more. This would of course reduce the spending money of the wives of the rich, and put it out of the power of the poor man to "support" a wife at all, un-less, indeed, the poor man faced the situa-tion fully, paid his wife her wages as house servant, and then she and he combined their funds in the support of their children. He would be keeping a servant: she would be helping keep the family. But nowhere on earth would there be "a rich woman" by these means. Even the highest class of pri-vate housekeeper, useful as her services are, does not accumulate a fortune. She does not buy diamonds and sables and keep a car-riage. Things like these are not earned by house service.

But the salient fact in this discussion is that, whatever the economic value of the do-mestic industry of women is, they do not get it: The women who do the most work get the least money, and the women who have the most money do the least work. Their labor is neither given nor taken as a factor in eco-nomic exchange. It is held to be their duty as women to do this work; and their economic status bears no relation to their domestic la-bors, unless an inverse one. Moreover, if they were thus fairly paid,—given what they earned, and no more,—all women working in this way would be reduced to the eco-nomic status of the house servant. Few women—or men either—care to face this condition. The ground that women earn their living by domestic labor is instantly for-saken, and we are told that they obtain their livelihood as mothers. This is a peculiar posi-tion. We speak of it commonly enough, and often with deep feeling, but without due analysis.

In treating of an economic exchange, ask-ing what return in goods or labor women make for the goods and labor given them,—either to the rate collectively or to their hus-bands individually,—what payment women make for their clothes and shoes and furni-ture and food and shelter, we are told that the duties and services of the mother entitle her to support.

If this is so, if motherhood is an exchange-able commodity given by women in payment for clothes and food, then we must of course find some relation between the quantity or quality of the motherhood and the quantity and quality of the pay. This being true, then the women who are not mothers have no economic status at all; and the economic sta-tus of those who are must be shown to be rel-ative to their motherhood. This is obviously absurd. The childless wife has as much money as the mother of many—more; for the children of the latter consume what would otherwise be hers; and the inefficient mother is no less provided for than the efficient one. Visibly, and upon the face of it, women are not maintained in economic prosperity pro-portioned to their motherhood. Motherhood bears no relation to their economic status. Among primitive races, it is true,—in the pa-triarchal period, for instance,—there was some truth in this position. Women being of no value whatever save as bearers of chil-dren, their favor and indulgence did bear di-rect relation to maternity; and they had rea-son to exult on more grounds than one when they could boast a son. To-day, however, the maintenance of the woman is not condi-tioned upon this. A man is not allowed to dis-card his wife because she is barren. The claim of motherhood as a factor in economic exchange is false to-day. But suppose it were true. Are we willing to hold this ground, even in theory? Are we willing to consider moth-erhood as a business, a form of commercial exchange? Are the cares and duties of the mother, her travail and her love, com-modities to be exchanged for bread?

It is revolting so to consider them; and, if we dare face our own thoughts, and force them to their logical conclusion, we shall see that nothing could be more repugnant to human feeling, or more socially and individ-ually injurious, than to make motherhood a trade. Driven off these alleged grounds of women's economic independence; shown that women, as a class, neither produce nor distribute wealth; that women, as individu-als, labor mainly as house servants, are not paid as such, and would not be satisfied with such an economic status if they were so paid; that wives are not business partners or co-producers of wealth with their husbands, unless they actually practise the same pro-fession; that they are not salaried as moth-ers, and that it would be unspeakably degrading if they were,—what remains to those who deny that women are supported by men? This (and a most amusing position it is),—that the function of maternity unfits a woman for economic production, and, therefore, it is right that she should be supported by her husband.

The ground is taken that the human female is not economically independent, that she is fed by the male of her species. In denial of this, it is first alleged that she is economically independent,—that she does support herself by her own industry in the house. It being shown that there is no relation between the economic status of woman and the labor she performs in the home, it is then alleged that not as house servant, but as mother, does woman earn her living. It being shown that the economic status of woman bears no relation to her motherhood, either in quantity or quality, it is then alleged that motherhood renders a woman unfit for economic production, and that, therefore, it is right that she be supported by her husband. Before going farther, let us seize upon this admission,—that she *is* supported by her husband.

Without going into either the ethics or the necessities of the case, we have reached so much common ground: the female of genus homo is supported by the male. Whereas, in other species of animals, male and female alike graze and browse, hunt and kill, climb, swim, dig, run, and fly for their livings, in our species the female does not seek her own living in the specific activities of our race, but is fed by the male.

Now as to the alleged necessity. Because of her maternal duties, the human female is said to be unable to get her own living. As the maternal duties of other females do not unfit them for getting their own living and also the livings of their young, it would seem that the human maternal duties require the segregation of the entire energies of the mother to the service of the child during her entire adult life, or so large a proportion of them that not enough remains to devote to the individual interests of the mother.

Such a condition, did it exist, would of course excuse and justify the pitiful dependence of the human female, and her support by the male. As the queen bee, modified entirely to maternity, is supported, not by the male, to be sure, but by her co-workers, the "old maids," the barren working bees, who labor so patiently and lovingly in their branch of the maternal duties of the hive, so would the human female, modified entirely to maternity, become unfit for any other exertion, and a helpless dependant.

Is this the condition of human motherhood? Does the human mother, by her motherhood, thereby lose control of brain and body, lose power and skill and desire for any other work? Do we see before us the human race, with all its females segregated entirely to the uses of motherhood, consecrated, set apart, specially developed, spending every power of their nature on the service of their children?

We do not. We see the human mother worked far harder than a mare, laboring her life long in the service, not of her children only, but of men; husbands, brothers, fathers, whatever male relatives she has; for mother and sister also; for the church a little, if she is allowed; for society, if she is able; for charity and education and reform,—working in many ways that are not the ways of motherhood.

It is not motherhood that keeps the housewife on her feet from dawn till dark; it is house service, not child service. Women work longer and harder than most men, and not solely in maternal duties. The savage mother carries the burdens, and does all menial service for the tribe. The peasant mother toils in the fields, and the workingman's wife in the home. Many mothers, even now, are wage-earners for the family, as well as bearers and rearers of it. And the women who are not so occupied, the women who belong to rich men,—here perhaps is the exhaustive devotion to maternity which is supposed to justify an admitted economic dependence. But we do not find it even among these. Women of ease and wealth provide for their children better care than the poor woman can; but they do not spend more time upon it themselves, nor more care and effort. They have other occupation.

In spite of her supposed segregation to maternal duties, the human female, the world over, works at extra-maternal duties for hours enough to provide her with an independent living, and then is denied independence on the ground that motherhood prevents her working!

If this ground were tenable, we should find a world full of women who never lifted a finger save in the service of their children, and of men who did *all* the work besides, and waited on the women whom motherhood prevented from waiting on themselves. The ground is not tenable. A human female, healthy, sound, has twenty-five years of life before she is a mother, and should have twenty-five years more after the period of such maternal service as is expected of her has been given. The duties of grandmotherhood are surely not alleged as preventing economic independence.

The working power of the mother has always been a prominent factor in human life. She is the worker *par excellence*, but her work is not such as to affect her economic status.

Her living, all that she gets,—food, clothing, ornaments, amusements, luxuries,—these bear no relation to her power to produce wealth, to her services in the house, or to her motherhood. These things bear relation only to the man she marries, the man she depends on,—to how much he has and how much he is willing to give her. The women whose splendid extravagance dazzles the world, whose economic goods are the greatest, are often neither houseworkers nor mothers, but simply the women who hold most power over the men who have the most money. The female of genus homo is economically dependent on the male. He is her food supply.

24

Utilization of Women in City Government

Jane Addams

Jane Addams (1860–1935) was perhaps the most prominent social reformer of her generation. As the founder of Hull House in Chicago, she was a leader in the settlement house movement. She was recognized for her work as a peace activist by being awarded the Nobel Peace Prize. Addams was also a social thinker who had close connections with the members of the Chicago School of Sociology. In "Utilization of Women in City Government" (1907), this influence is evident in her discussion of the modern industrial city. But Addams takes this analysis in an original direction by first arguing for the need to create a welfare state in order to address the myriad social problems that have emerged in urban settings. Moreover, she proceeds to contend that since many of the tasks the welfare state will need to perform involve the nurturing and caring jobs heretofore consigned to women in the domestic realm, it makes sense to utilize women, with their unique expertise, in the public arena as well.

As the city itself originated for the common protection of the people and was built about a suitable centre of defense which formed a citadel such as the Acropolis at Athens or the Kremlin at Moscow, so we can trace the beginning of the municipal franchise to the time when the problems of municipal government were still largely those of protecting the city against rebellion from within and against invasion from without. A voice in city government, as it was extended from the nobles, who alone bore arms, was naturally given solely to those who were valuable to the military system. . . . It was fair that only those who were liable to a sudden call to arms should be selected to decide as to the relations which the city should bear to rival cities, and that the vote for war should be cast by the same men who would bear the brunt of battle and the burden of protection. . . .

But rival cities have long since ceased to settle their claims by force of arms, and we shall have to admit, I think, that this early test of the elector is no longer fitted to the modern city. . . .

It has been well said that the modern city is a stronghold of industrialism, quite as the feudal city was a stronghold of militarism, but the modern city fears no enemies, and rivals from without, and its problems of government are solely internal. Affairs for the most part are going badly in these great new centres in which the quickly congregated population has not yet learned to arrange its affairs satisfactorily. Insanitary housing, poisonous sewage, contaminated water, infant mortality, the spread of contagion, adulterated food, impure milk, smoke-laden air, ill-ventilated factories, dangerous occupations, juvenile crime, unwholesome crowding, prostitution, and drunkenness are the enemies which the modern city must face and overcome would it survive. Logically, its electorate should be made up of those who can bear a valiant part in this arduous contest, of those who in the past have at least attempted to care for children, to clean houses, to prepare foods, to isolate the family from moral dangers, of those who have traditionally taken care of that side of life which, as soon as the population is congested, inevitably becomes the subject of municipal consideration and control.

To test the elector's fitness to deal with this situation by his ability to bear arms, is absurd. A city is in many respects a great business corporation, but in other respects it is enlarged housekeeping. If American cities have failed in the first, partly because office holders have carried with them the predatory instinct learned in competitive business, and cannot help "working a good thing" when they have an opportunity, may we not say that city housekeeping has failed partly because women, the traditional housekeepers, have not been consulted as to its multiform activities? The men of the city have been carelessly indifferent to much of this civic housekeeping, as they have always been indifferent to the details of the household. They have totally disregarded a candidate's capacity to keep the streets clean, preferring to consider him in relation to the national tariff or to the necessity for increasing the national navy, in a pure spirit of reversion to the traditional type of government which had to do only with enemies and outsiders.

It is difficult to see what military prowess has to do with the multiform duties, which, in a modern city, include the care of parks and libraries, superintendence of markets, sewers' and bridges, the inspection of provisions and boilers, and the proper disposal of garbage. Military prowess has nothing to do with the building department which the city maintains to see to it that the basements be dry, that the bedrooms be large enough to afford the required cubic feet of air, that the plumbing be sanitary, that the gas-pipes do not leak, that the tenement-house court be large enough to afford light and ventilation, and that the stairways be fireproof. The ability to carry arms has nothing to do with the health department maintained by the city, which provides that children be vaccinated, that contagious diseases be isolated and placarded, that the spread of tuberculosis be curbed, and that the water be free from typhoid infection. Certainly the military conception of society is remote from the functions of the school boards, whose concern it is that children be educated, that they be supplied with kindergartens and be given a decent place in which to play. The very multifariousness and complexity of a city government demands the help of minds accustomed to detail and variety of work, to a sense of obligation for the health and welfare of young children, and to a responsibility for the cleanliness and comfort of others.

Because all these things have traditionally been in the hands of women, if they take no part in them now, they are not only missing the education which the natural participation in civic life would bring to them, but they are losing what they have always had. From the beginning of tribal life women

have been held responsible for the health of the community, a function which is now represented by the health department; from the days of the cave dwellers, so far as the home was clean and wholesome, it was due to their efforts, which are now represented by the bureau of tenement-house inspection; from the period of the primitive village, the only public sweeping performed was what they undertook in their own dooryards, that which is now represented by the bureau of street cleaning. Most of the departments in a modern city can be traced to woman's traditional activity, but in spite of this, so soon as these old affairs were turned over to the care of the city, they slipped from woman's hands, apparently because they then became matters for collective action and implied the use of the franchise. Because the franchise had in the first instance been given to the man who could fight, because in the beginning he alone could vote who could carry a weapon, the franchise was considered an improper thing for a woman to possess. . . .

It is so easy to believe that things that used to exist still go on long after they are passed; it is so easy to commit irreparable blunders because we fail to correct our theories by our changing experience. So many of the stumbling-blocks against which we fail are the opportunities to which we have not adjusted ourselves. Because it shocks an obsolete ideal, we keep hold of a convention which no longer squares with our genuine insight, and we are slow to follow a clue which might enable us to solace and improve the life about us.

Why is it that women do not vote upon the matters which concern them so intimately? Why do they not follow these vital affairs and feel responsible for their proper administration, even though they have become municipalized? What would the result have been could women have regarded the suffrage, not as a right or a privilege, but as a mere piece of governmental machinery without which they could not perform their traditional functions under the changed conditions of city life? Could we view the whole situation as a matter of obligation and of normal development, it would be much simplified. We are at the beginning of a prolonged effort to incorporate a progressive developing life founded upon a response to the needs of all the people, into the requisite legal enactments and civic institutions. To be in any measure successful, this effort will require all the intelligent powers of observation, all the sympathy, all the common sense which may be gained from the whole adult population. . . .

It is questionable whether women to-day, in spite of the fact that there are myriads of them in factories and shops, are doing their full share of the world's work in the lines of production which have always been theirs. Even two centuries ago they did practically all the spinning, dyeing, weaving, and sewing. They carried on much of the brewing and baking and thousands of operations which have been pushed out of the domestic system into the factory system. But simply to keep on doing the work which their grandmothers did, was to find themselves surrounded by conditions over which they have no control.

Sometimes when I see dozens of young girls going into the factories of a certain biscuit company on the West Side of Chicago, they appear for the moment as a mere cross-section in the long procession of women who have furnished the breadstuffs from time immemorial, from the savage woman who ground the meal and baked a flat cake, through innumerable cottage hearths, kitchens, and bake ovens, to this huge concern in which they are still carrying on their traditional business. But always before, during the ages of this unending procession, women themselves were able to dictate concerning the hours and the immediate conditions of their work; even grinding the meal and baking the cake in the ashes was diversified by many other activities. But suddenly, since the application of steam to the processes of kneading bread and of turning the spindle, which really means only a different motor power and not in the least an essential change in her work, she has been denied the privilege of regulating the conditions which immediately surround her. . . .

Practically one-half of the working women in the United States are girls—young women under the age of twenty-five years. This increase in the number of young girls in industry is the more striking when taken in connection with the fact that industries of to-day differ most markedly from those of the past in the relentless speed which they require. This increase in speed is as marked in the depths of sweat-shop labor as in the most advanced New England mills, where the eight looms operated by each worker have increased to twelve, fourteen, and even sixteen looms. This speed, of course, brings a new strain into industry and tends inevitably to nervous exhaustion. Machines may be revolved more and more swiftly, but the girl workers have no increase in vitality responding to the heightened pressure. An ampler and more far-reaching protection than now exists, is needed in order to care for the health and safety of woman in industry. Their youth, their helplessness, their increasing numbers, the conditions under which they are employed, all call for uniform and enforceable statutes. The elaborate regulations of dangerous trades, enacted in England and on the Continent for both adults and children, find no parallel in the United States. The injurious effects of employments involving the use of poisons, acids, gases, atmospheric extremes, or other dangerous processes, still await adequate investigation and legislation in this country. How shall this take place, save by the concerted efforts of the women themselves, those who are employed, and those other women who are intelligent as to the worker's needs and who possess a conscience in regard to industrial affairs? . . .

So far as women have been able, in Chicago at least, to help, the poorest workers in the sweatshops, it has been accomplished by women organized into trades unions. The organization of Special Order Tailors found that it was comparatively simple for an employer to give the skilled operatives in a clothing factory more money by taking it away from the wages of the seam-sewer and button-holer. The fact that it resulted in one set of workers being helped at the expense of another set did not appeal to him, so long as he was satisfying the demand of the union without increasing the total cost of production. But the Special Order Tailors, at the sacrifice of their own wages and growth, made a determined effort to include even the sweat-shop workers in the benefits they had slowly secured for themselves. By means of the use of the label they were finally able to insist that no goods should be given out for home-finishing save to women presenting union cards, and they raised the wages from nine and eleven cents a dozen for finishing garments, to the minimum wage of fifteen cents. They also made a protest against the excessive subdivision of the labor upon garments, a practice which enables the manufacturer to use children and the least skilled adults. Thirty-two persons are commonly employed upon a single coat, and it is the purpose of the Special Order Tailors to have all the machine work performed by one worker, thus reducing the number working on one coat to twelve or fourteen. As this change will at the same time demand more skill on the part of the operator, and will increase the variety and interest in his work, these garment-makers are sacrificing both time and money for the defence of Ruskinian principles—one of the few actual attempts to recover the "joy of work.". . . The poorest women are often but uncomprehending victims of this labor movement of which they understand so little, and which has become so much a matter of battle that helpless individuals are lost in the conflict.

A complicated situation occurs to me in illustration. A woman from the Hull-House Day Nursery came to me two years ago asking to borrow twenty-five dollars, a sum her union had imposed as a fine. She gave such an incoherent account of her plight that it was evident that she did not in the least understand what it was all about. A little investigation disclosed the following facts: The "Nursery Mother," as I here call her for purposes of identification, had worked for a long time in an unorganized overall factory, where the proprietor, dealing as he did in goods purchased exclusively by workingmen, found it increasingly difficult to sell his overalls because they did not bear the union label. He finally made a request to the union that the employees in his factory be organized. This was done, he was given the use of the label, and upon this basis he prospered for several months.

Whether the organizer was "fixed" or not, the investigation did not make clear; for, although the "Nursery Mother," with her fel-low-workers, had paid their union dues regularly, the employer was not compelled to pay the union scale of wages, but continued to pay the same wages as before. At the end of three months his employees discovered that they were not being paid the union scale, and demanded that their wages be raised to that amount. The employer, in the meantime having extensively advertised his use of the label, concluded that his purpose had been served, and that he no longer needed the union. He refused, therefore, to pay the union scale, and a strike ensued. The "Nursery Mother" went out with the rest, and within a few days found work in another shop, a union shop doing a lower grade of manufacturing. At that time there was no uniform scale in the garment trades, and although a trade unionist working for union wages, she received lower wages than she had under the non-union conditions in the overall factory. She was naturally much confused and, following her instinct to get the best wages possible, she went back to her old place. Affairs ran smoothly for a few weeks, until the employer discovered that he was again losing trade because his goods lacked the label, whereupon he once more applied to have his shop unionized. The organizer, coming back, promptly discovered the recreant "Nursery Mother," and, much to her bewilderment, she was fined twenty-five dollars. She understood nothing clearly, nor could she, indeed, be made to understand so long as she was in the midst of this petty warfare. Her labor was a mere method of earning money quite detached from her European experience, and failed to make for her the remotest connection with the community whose genuine needs she was supplying. No effort had been made to show her the cultural aspect of her work, to give her even the feeblest understanding of the fact that she was supplying a genuine need of the community, and that she was entitled to respect and a legitimate industrial position. It would have been necessary to make such an effort from the historic standpoint, and this could be undertaken only by the community as a whole and not by any one class in it. Protective legislation would be but the first step toward making her a more valuable producer and a more intelligent citizen. The whole effort would imply a closer connection between industry and government, and could be accomplished intelligently only if women were permitted to exercise the franchise.

A certain healing and correction would doubtless ensue could we but secure for the protection and education of industrial workers that nurture of health and morals which women have so long reserved for their own families and which has never been utilized as a directing force in industrial affairs.

When the family constituted the industrial organism of the day, the daughters of the household were carefully taught in reference to the place they would take in that organism, but as the household arts have gone outside the home, almost nothing has been done to connect the young women with the present great industrial system. This neglect has been equally true in regard to the technical and cultural sides of that system.

The failure to fit the education of women to the actual industrial life which is carried on about them has had disastrous results in two directions. First, industry itself has lacked the modification which women might have brought to it had they committed the entire movement to that growing concern for a larger and more satisfying life for each member of the community, a concern which we have come to regard as legitimate. Second, the more prosperous women would have been able to understand and adjust their own difficulties of household management in relation to the producer of factory products, as they are now utterly unable to do.

As the census of 1900 showed that more than half of the women employed in "gainful occupations" in the United States are engaged in households, certainly their conditions of labor lie largely in the hands of women employers. At a conference held at Lake Placid by employers of household labor, it was contended that future historical review may show that the girls who are today in domestic service are the really progressive women of the age; that they are those who are fighting conditions which limit their freedom, and although they are doing it blindly, at least they are demanding avenues of self-expression outside their work; and that this struggle from conditions detrimental to their highest life is the ever-recurring story of the emancipation of first one class and then another. It was further contended that in this effort to become sufficiently educated to be able to understand the needs of an educated employer from an independent standpoint, they are really doing the community a great service, and did they but receive co-operation instead of opposition, domestic service would lose its social ostracism and attract a more intelligent class of women. And yet this effort, perfectly reasonable from the standpoint of historic development and democratic tradition, receives little help from the employing housekeepers, because they know nothing of industrial development. . . .

If American women could but obtain a liberating knowledge of that history of industry and commerce which is so similar in every country of the globe, the fact that so much factory labor is performed by immigrants would help to bring them nearer to the immigrant woman. Equipped with "the informing mind" on the one hand and with experience on the other, we could then walk together through the marvelous streets of the human city, no longer conscious whether we are natives or aliens, because we have become absorbed in a fraternal relation arising from a common experience.

And this attitude of understanding and respect for the worker is necessary, not only to appreciate what he produces, but to preserve his power of production, again showing the necessity for making that substitute for war—human labor—more aggressive and democratic. We are told that the conquered races everywhere, in their helplessness, are giving up the genuine practise of their own arts. In India, for instance, where their arts have been the blossom of many years of labor, the conquered races are casting them aside as of no value in order that they may conform to the inferior art, or rather, lack of art, of their conquerors. Morris constantly lamented that in some parts of India the native arts were quite destroyed, and in many others nearly so; that in all parts they had more or less begun to sicken. This lack of respect and understanding of the primitive arts found among colonies of immigrants in a modern cosmopolitan city, produces a like result in that the arts languish and disappear. We have made an effort at Hull-House to recover something of the early industries from an immigrant neighborhood, and in a little exhibit called a labor museum, we have placed in historic sequence and order methods of spinning and weaving from a dozen nationalities in Asia Minor and Europe. The result has been a striking exhibition of the unity and similarity of the earlier industrial processes. Within the narrow confines of one room, the Syrian, the Greek, the Italian, the Russian, the Norwegian, the Dutch, and the Irish find that the differences in their spinning have been merely putting the distaff upon a frame or placing the old hand-spindle in a horizontal position. A group of women representing vast differences in religion, in language, in tradition, and in nationality, exhibit practically no difference in the daily arts by which, for a thousand generations, they have clothed their families. When American women come to visit them, the quickest method, in fact almost the only one of establishing a genuine companionship with them, is through this same industry, unless we except that still older occupation, the care of little children. Perhaps this experiment may claim to have made a genuine effort to find the basic experiences upon which a cosmopolitan community may unite at least on the industrial side. . . .

Can we learn our first lesson in modern industry from these humble peasant women who have never shirked the primitive labors upon which all civilized life is founded, even as we must obtain our first lessons in social morality from those who are bearing the brunt of the overcrowded and cosmopolitan city which is the direct result of modern industrial conditions? If we contend that the franchise should be extended to women on the ground that less emphasis is continually placed upon the military order and more upon the industrial order of society, we should have to insist that, if she would secure her old place in industry, the modern woman must needs fit her labors to the present industrial organization as the simpler woman fitted hers to the more simple industrial order. It has been pointed out that woman lost her earlier place when man usurped the industrial pursuits and created wealth on a scale unknown before. Since that time women have been reduced more and more to a state of dependency, until we see only among the European peasant women as they work in the fields, "the heavy, strong, enduring, patient, economically functional representative of what the women of our day used to be."

Cultural education as it is at present carried on in the most advanced schools, is to some extent correcting the present detached relation of women to industry but a sense of responsibility in relation to the development of industry would accomplish much more. As men earned their citizenship through their readiness and ability to defend their city, so perhaps woman, if she takes a citizen's place in the modern industrial city, will have to earn it by devotion and self-abnegation in the service of its complex needs.

The old social problems were too often made a cause of war in the belief that all difficulties could be settled by an appeal to arms. But certainly these subtler problems which confront the modern cosmopolitan city, the problems of race antagonisms and economic adjustments, must be settled by a more searching and genuine method than mere prowess can possibly afford. The first step toward their real solution must be made upon a past experience common to the citizens as a whole and connected with their daily living. As moral problems become more and more associated with our civic and industrial organizations, the demand for enlarged activity is more exigent. If one could connect the old maternal anxieties, which are really the basis of family and tribal life, with the candidates who are seeking offices, it would never be necessary to look about for other motive powers, and if to this we could add maternal concern for the safety and defence of the industrial worker, we should have an increasing code of protective legislation.

We certainly may hope for two results if women enter formally into municipal life. First, the opportunity to fulfill their old duties and obligations with the safeguard and the consideration which the ballot alone can secure for them under the changed conditions, and, second, the education which participation in actual affairs always brings. As we believe that woman has no right to allow what really belongs to her to drop away from her, so we contend that ability to perform an obligation comes very largely in proportion as that obligation is conscientiously assumed.

25
Feminism and Conventionality

Elsie Clews Parsons

Elsie Clews Parsons (1875–1941) was a cultural anthropologist who became the first woman elected president of the American Anthropological Association. In "Feminism and Conventionality" (1914), Parsons addresses themes raised by her contemporaries regarding the impact of the subordination of women brought about by confining their proper sphere to that of the private or household realm—but she does so with an anthropologist's comparative frame of reference. Moreover, she reveals how out of subordination women have come to be, as she puts it, "closer to life" than men. She also articulates a radical critique of the antifeminist apprehension of difference, using language that resonates with that of latter-day postmodernist feminists.

A few years ago there was discussion in academic circles over differentiating the college curriculum of women from that of men. Surely the curriculum for men is not so satisfactory, it was urged, that it cannot be improved. Besides, the educational needs of women may be different, if only a little, from the needs of men. "True, perhaps," was the answer of the advocates of an identical curriculum, "but even so, we can't *afford* to differentiate, as yet at least. To give women as 'good' an education as men, we must give them the *same* education. That is the only way we can keep up the standard." And hitherto in the colleges this plea, right or wrong, has governed. It is the same argument that underlies feminist effort in other fields. That women may have as *ample* opportunities throughout society as men, they must have, it is felt, more or less consciously, the *same* opportunities. Society is after all very simple

minded, one new idea at a time is its measure. Let not feminism confuse its issues. Before women can improve on men's ways, those ways, one and all, must be open to women.

Whether or not this is sound feminist doctrine, it is the clue to an understanding of much of the feminist agitation of today. It suggests, too, some of the directions still to be taken by the feminist movement. It may be profitable therefore to consider some of the differentiations[1] in habits and customs that have arisen in society for the lives of men and women, the differentiations of daily life and of life at crises, not overlooking, where we can discern them, the psychological reasons for these differentiations.

"So long as a lady shall deem herself in need of some gentleman's arm to conduct her properly out of a dining or ballroom," wrote an American publicist over half a century ago, "so long as she shall consider it dangerous or unbecoming to walk half a mile alone by night—I cannot see how the Woman's Rights' theory is ever to be anything more than a logically defensible abstraction." If this opinion of Horace Greeley is to be taken as a prediction that the Woman's Rights' platform of his time would not be enacted until another measure of freedom was secure to women, it has not been justified by the course of events. Property disqualifications have been entirely removed from women, the right of guardianship has become theirs (to the extent it was originally desired), and the days are counted to their possession, throughout the country, of the right of suffrage. These rights are theirs and yet it still embarrasses a woman to stand alone in a ballroom or sit with other women after the men have come out from the smoking-room; and it may be that the woman allured by the mystery of solitude under the stars is still rare. But perhaps what Greeley meant to say was that economic or political reform would not greatly affect women as long as the conventionalities of their daily life remained unchanged. If so, was he not, in the main, right and for his period extraordinarily discerning? Even today, many a suffragist, however ardent, is unpossessed of this insight. Anxious beyond measure for the vote, she is wholly unperturbed by the constraints of her daily life. Loath to be wholly dependent upon men in the limited number of matters which make up government, she is willing enough to be dependent upon them and upon women too in those endless details of daily life any woman might be expected to determine for herself. I recently attended a political convention at Saratoga where several women were lobbying for suffrage. One evening one of them wanted to go with a man to a dance, but she would not go, I overheard her declare, unless another woman went with them. The following afternoon another suffragist who had started to motor to New York took the train at Albany because, thanks to an unforeseen emergency, one of the two men motoring with her had to remain in Albany. "I couldn't think of getting into New York after midnight with only one man. . . ." Is not chaperonage a more important question for women, I wonder, than suffrage?

Comparative inability to choose either solitariness or their company is not characteristic merely of modern women. In no culture have women shown desire to do anything which requires running the risks of being alone. Women hermits are extremely scarce, there are few women explorers, there are no women vagabonds, even the licensed adventuress, too restricted in her activity for any real adventure, is outcasted in a group. Rarely indeed do women go off by themselves—into the corner of a ballroom, into the wilderness, to the play, to the sacred high places of the earth or to the Islands of the Blessed. Penelope stays at home. Her reasons for staying at home vary, of course. She has to help her mother; she will be raped by a licentious male, a man or perhaps a god; she owes obedience to her parents; she will lose her reputation; she will give birth to a monster or her baby will die; she has to get the dinner ready; she has to look after the baby; she will bring disgrace to her family, dishonor to her husband, shame upon her children, disaster to her clan.

Whatever the sanctions, whatever the necessities or the excuses, woman's place having been in the home, her acquaintances have been restricted to the family circle and to the segments of the other family circles it overlaps. And with these friends and relatives her intercourse is unbroken and more or less incessant. The womanly woman has ever been an available woman, "always there when you wanted her." From such "home life" there have been for all women two prime outcomes. The unfamiliar person, the stranger, has been feared and shunned, more feared and shunned by women even than by men. Women in other words are peculiarly apprehensive of people of other localities, of other tribes or nations, of other castes, of other sets; and with such outlanders or outsiders they have as little to do as possible. Women are "inhospitable." They are "snobs." They are "full of prejudices." They are not "good mixers."

But to this characteristic tendency of women to keep to themselves, there are two exceptions. Within the home itself women associate with strangers, *i.e.*, with those unlike themselves, unlike in age and in sex, and seldom, too, are the times when women do not have to put up with this association. Being "home bodies," they cannot get away, like men, from their children or their parents, they have to make the best of their brothers or their husbands. Face to face with these heterogeneities of sex or age, women have raised up barriers against them, carefully regulating their relations with their juniors and seniors and with the other sex. Their attitude is very conventional with members of different age classes and with men, more conventional, I mean, than that of men with women or with those unlike in age—and this is the second important outcome for women of their home life. Upon women age and sex taboos are heavier than upon men. And it is they who are the foremost teachers of the proprieties, of politeness, of good manners, of the amenities—all rules of conduct for life with others more or less unlike yourself and yet not to be avoided.

With beings unlike yourself the alternative to conventionality is avoidance. And that alternative is taken on the whole by men in relation both to their juniors and seniors[2] and to women. More or less unconsciously they avoid women and more or less deliberately they exclude them from their interests and their places of assembly—from their economic pursuits, from their learned professions, from their games and pastimes, from their club-houses, churches,[3] forums, council halls, universities, and play-houses. Even the initiative in the avoidance practiced within the family group is taken, I surmise, by men.[4] At home and away from it such seclusiveness and exclusiveness in men result, of course, in increasing the differences between them and women. Increased differences stimulate to greater seclusiveness or exclusiveness; we get a closed circle.

For the moment let us turn away from this closed circle to consider certain sex differentiations in customs at times of crisis. We noted that the heterogeneities of sex and of age are more constantly under the noses of women, so to speak, than of men. Women are closer to life, we sometimes say, meaning that they are face to face with birth and growth, decay and death. And so it is to be expected that they, rather than men, will play the leading parts in the policy human beings have chosen to meet the changes of life—the policy of ignoring the change until it is inevitable and then mitigating the shock of it through the diversion of ceremonial.[5] And women do play in the ceremonial of crisis the more prominent or lasting rôles. Mourning observances are far more elaborate for women than for men and far more prolonged. So are wedding and honeymoon observances, although in them of course the character of duality must preclude any great differentiation.[6] As for puberty or initiation ceremonial, that curious means of breaking the shock of realizing that the young have grown up, if women appear to take a less important part in it than men, reasons consistent with our general interpretation are not hard to find. The initiation of boys means they are leaving home. No amount of ceremonial can disguise that break. Were they to stay on at home in a different relation to it, then the women might enter more strikingly into their man-making rites.[7] As it is, all women can do is to express ceremonially their distress at "losing" their boys. Andamanese women "weep over" an initiate the morning after he breaks his turtle fast. Throughout the first night of an initiation Mita-Koodi women are expected to wail. The kinswomen of an Euahlayi initiate are sup-

posed to be so much in need of comforting that the old men bring them presents of food. In other Australian tribes we find rites to symbolize the separation imminent between the initiate and his kinswomen. Among the Kurnai he sprinkles his mother with water, among the Arunta he throws his boomerang towards her spirit camp to show her, the ethnographers suggest, that all is at an end between them.[8] But the initiates are turning their backs on their mother only to turn their faces towards their father and their father's friends. For these seniors, upon taking into their life youthful participants, an adjustment is necessary, and it is for them to get it over with as quickly and easily as possible. Naturally they resort to the usual social method, the method of ceremonial. It is plain enough why men figure rather than women in the puberty or initiation rites to celebrate a boy's growing up.

But there are other conditions in the life of men besides an adjustment to their juniors to be met with ceremonial or with conventionality. Their contacts with all their non-familial groups, the groups they resort to when they leave home, when they go out "to meet a man," all these associations have to be entered upon with ceremonial and, their membership never entirely homogeneous, safeguarded with conventionalities. Hence presentations and introductions of all kinds, the conferring of orders or degrees, the induction into office, "treating" and the "sacred laws of hospitality." Hence tribal or patriotic standards, professional etiquette, chivalry, the code of a gentleman, and many other caste taboos or rules. In all these matters women figure far less than men, of course, for the simple enough reason that they are out of touch with the different groups concerned. They have avoided them or they have been excluded from them. Then when they do begin to seek admission into these non-familial groups we may note that very often they ride roughshod over their conventionalities,[9] breaking their rules, either because they are ignorant of them or because they see in them little or no value. This procedure, whatever its explanation, is very disturbing to men, distasteful to them and even abhorrent. And often enough it is the more or less unconscious anticipation of such violations by women, of such misbehaviour, that sets men so bitterly against opening the doors to them. Merely to lessen masculine apprehensiveness and to overcome masculine antagonism women might do well to adopt quickly and unquestioningly masculine conventionalities.

But even if women develop a sense of honor and a respect for masculine routine, even if they shear their hair and dress like men, even if they keep men's hours, and work and play like men, even if they smoke and swear and get drunk like men, even if they succeed in getting from the outside the loyalty and *esprit de corps* that usually come only with participation in the life of the group, learning to swim, in other words, without going near the water, even if they conform in all these ways, differences will still exist between them and men, natural differences, urges the anti-feminist, and should not these natural differences receive appreciation and be given social expression? However we may answer this question, it does not quite meet the point of masculine exclusiveness. It is *apprehension of difference* rather than actual difference which bulks so large now and always in the social regulation of sex. It is fear of the unlike rather than the fact of it. The anti-feminist wishes to keep women apart from men not because he values sex differences, but because he fears them. He or she is not so anxious to preserve them as to get away from them, to be protected from the danger of being disturbed by them. Differences in age, in caste, in family, and in race, have filled mankind with analogous apprehensions and prompted analogous methods and plans of self-protection.

Age-class, caste group, family, and race, each has its own closed circle—from unlikeness to exclusion or seclusion, from exclusion or reclusion to unlikeness—but each of these vicious circles the modern spirit has begun to invade and break down. In the spirit of our time fear of the unlike is waning, and *pari passu* intolerance. Fear of the unlike and intolerance are due to fear of change, and that fear, whether of change wrought by life or of change threatened by the stranger, that great fear, is passing. With it are bound to go the devices of self-protection it prompted—ceremonial, conventionality, and segregation. In this general movement of the human spirit feminism was born; upon its march the hopes of feminism ultimately must depend.

Endnotes

1. Not all; feministic discussion must confine itself, for example, to the exclusiveness of men, trusting that the exclusiveness of women will some day be a matter for hominist agitation. The farseeing feminist trusts, too, that the legal rights of men will cease to be neglected—inequalities before the law in responsibility for crime, for example, and in matters of property (damages for breach of promise, alimony, or any legal obligation to support women).

2. Although classification by age is characteristic of every society, our specific data on age classes are scant and very scattered; but from what I have from others and have observed at first hand I am inclined to believe that seniority is more of a bar in daily intercourse between adult men than between women. The fact that men see comparatively little of children hardly needs mention. Seeing them seldom, they can afford, they feel, to treat them as contemporaries. This is a reason why children "take to men" and not, as a fond mother sometimes alleges, because men are novelties. Children, like women, dread the Stranger.

3. From religious exclusiveness almost all other forms of exclusiveness can be traced just as all the professions were differentiated from the priesthood and as games and the arts had religious origins. But the exclusion of women from the derivatives of ecclesiasticism is no mere historical sequence or survival. History gives it the sanction of the past in given cases, but it has an ever fresh psychological spring.

4. Among us it is the son-in-law who avoids his mother-in-law and there appears to be no evidence that it is the other way round among savages where this practice is more formal. At any rate it is the father-in-law in every society who avoids his daughter-in-law and not *vice versa*. Everywhere, too, it is "up to" the boy to stop "hanging round" his mother and playing with his sisters.

5. Under the rubric of *Ceremonial Reluctance* I am preparing a fuller statement of this shock absorber theory of ceremonial.

6. The veiling of the bride and her seclusiveness before and after the wedding are the most notable. But the bridal couple apart, the women of the family are more concerned with the marriage ceremonial than the men.

7. As they do at the nubility of girls; for the "coming out" rites of girls do not mean a break with family life.

8. The rigid separation of initiates from females is also more of a symbol of sex segregation, I think, than a practical measure against sexual intercourse. It is a concentration rite, a synopsis, so to speak, of the life ahead of them, life apart from women.

9. An infraction we recognize when we say, for example, that women have no sense of honor, or that women dislike "red tape."

Reprinted from *Women in Public Life*, by Elsie Clews Parsons. Copyright © 1914 by American Academy of Political and Social Science. Reprinted with permission. ✦

VI. Voices Outside the Discipline

26
The Madman

Friedrich Nietzsche

Friedrich Nietzsche (1844–1900) was a tormented but extremely influential German philosopher. His thought was held to be of particular consequence by Weber and Simmel in the classical period of social theory, and more recently it has been referred to by postmodernists. In these aphorisms from *The Gay Science* (first published in 1887), he proclaims his conviction that not only had the death of God occurred but that we were responsible for it. Moreover, he contends that most people have not yet begun to appreciate the full implications of the end of theistic religion—namely, that the religious grounding for a meaningful, purposeful, and moral life have disappeared. Indeed, as the final section suggests, those secularists who have turned to science as a substitute for religion fail to realize that they, too, have grounded their convictions in faith. They have not yet begun to struggle with the relativizing implications of the demise of God and the end of metaphysics.

Have you not heard of that madman who lit a lantern in the bright morning hours, ran to the market place, and cried incessantly, "I seek God! I seek God!" As many of those who do not believe in God were standing around just then, he provoked much laughter. Why, did he get lost? said one. Did he lose his way like a child? said another. Or is he hiding? Is he afraid of us? Has he gone on a voyage? or emigrated? Thus they yelled and laughed. The madman jumped into their midst and pierced them with his glances.

"Whither is God" he cried. "I shall tell you. *We have killed him*—you and I. All of us are his murderers. But how have we done this? How were we able to drink up the sea? Who gave us the sponge to wipe away the entire horizon? What did we do when we unchained this earth from its sun? Whither is it moving now? Whither are we moving now? Away from all suns? Are we not plunging continually? Backward, sideward, forward, in all directions? Is there any up or down left? Are we not straying as through an infinite nothing? Do we not feel the breath of empty space? Has it not become colder? Is not night and more night coming on all the while? Must not lanterns be lit in the morning? Do we not hear anything yet of the noise of the gravediggers who are burying God? Do we not smell anything yet of God's decomposition? Gods too decompose. God is dead. God remains dead. And we have killed him. How shall we, the murderers of all murderers, comfort ourselves? What was holiest and most powerful of all that the world has yet owned has bled to death under our knives. Who will wipe this blood off us? What water is there for us to clean ourselves? What festivals of atonement, what sacred games shall we have to invent? Is not the greatness of this deed too great for us? Must not we ourselves become gods simply to seem worthy of it? There has never been a greater deed; and whoever will be born after us—for the sake of this deed he will be part of a higher history than all history hitherto."

Here the madman fell silent and looked again at his listeners; and they too were silent and stared at him in astonishment. At last he threw his lantern on the ground, and it broke and went out. "I come too early," he said then; "my time has not come yet. This tremendous event is still on its way, still wandering—it has not yet reached the ears of man. Lightning and thunder require time, the light of the stars requires time, deeds require time even after they are done, before they can be seen and heard. This deed is still more distant from them than the most distant stars—*and yet they have done it themselves.*"

It has been related further that on that same day the madman entered divers churches and there sang his *requiem aeternam deo*. Led out and called to account, he is said to have replied each time, "What are these churches now if they are not the tombs and sepulchers of God?". . .

***

The background of our cheerfulness. The greatest recent event—that "God is dead," that the belief in the Christian God has ceased to be believable—is even now beginning to cast its first shadows over Europe. For the few, at least, whose eyes, whose *suspicion* in their eyes, is strong and sensitive enough for this spectacle, some sun seems to have set just now. . . . In the main, however, this may be said: the event itself is much too great, too distant, too far from the comprehension of the many even for the tidings of it to be thought of as having *arrived* yet, not to speak of the notion that many people might know what has really happened here, and what must collapse now that this belief has been undermined—all that was built upon it, leaned on it, grew into it; for example, our whole European morality. . . .

Even we born guessers of riddles who are, as it were, waiting on the mountains, put there between today and tomorrow and stretched in the contradiction between today and tomorrow, we firstlings and premature births of the coming century, to whom the shadows that must soon envelop Europe really *should* have appeared by now—why is it that even we look forward to it without any real compassion for this darkening, and above all without any worry and fear for *ourselves*? Is it perhaps that we are still too deeply impressed by the first consequences of this event—and these first consequences, the consequences for *us*, are perhaps the reverse of what one might expect: not at all sad and dark, but rather like a new, scarcely describable kind of light, happiness, relief, exhilaration, encouragement, dawn? Indeed, we philosophers and "free spirits" feel as if a new dawn were shining on us when we receive the tidings that "the old god is dead"; our heart overflows with gratitude, amazement, anticipation, expectation. At last the horizon appears free again to us, even granted that it is not bright; at last our ships may venture out again, venture out to face any danger; all the daring of the lover of knowledge is permitted again; the sea, *our* sea, lies open again; perhaps there has never yet been such an "open sea.". . .

***

How far we too are still pious. In science, convictions have no rights of citizenship, as is said with good reason. Only when they decide to descend to the modesty of a hypothesis, of a provisional experimental point of view, of a regulative fiction, may they be granted admission and even a certain value within the realm of knowledge—though always with the restriction that they remain under police supervision, under the police of mistrust. But does this not mean, more precisely considered, that a conviction may obtain admission to science only when it *ceases* to be a conviction? Would not the discipline of the scientific spirit begin with this, no longer to permit oneself any convictions? Probably that is how it is. But one must still ask whether it is not the case that, *in order that this discipline could begin*, a conviction must have been there already, and even such a commanding and unconditional one that it sacrificed all other convictions for its own sake. It is clear that science too rests on a faith; there is no science "without presuppositions." The question whether truth is needed must not only have been affirmed in advance, but affirmed to the extent that the principle, the faith, the conviction is expressed: "*nothing* is needed *more* than truth, and in relation to it everything else has only second-rate value."

This unconditional will to truth: what is it? . . . What do you know in advance of the character of existence, to be able to decide whether the greater advantage is on the side of the unconditionally mistrustful or of the unconditionally trusting? Yet if both are required, much trust *and* much mistrust: whence might science then take its unconditional faith, its conviction, on which it rests, that truth is more important than anything else, even than any other conviction? Just this conviction could not have come into being if both truth *and* untruth showed themselves to be continually useful, as is the case. Thus, though there undeniably exists a faith in science, it cannot owe its origin to such a utilitarian calculus but it must rather have originated *in spite* of the fact that the inutility and dangerousness of the "will to truth," of "truth at any price," are proved to it continually. . . .

Consequently, "will to truth" does *not* mean "I will not let myself be deceived" but—there is no choice—"I will not deceive, not even myself": *and with this we are on the ground of morality*. For one should ask oneself carefully: "Why don't you want to deceive?" especially if it should appear—and it certainly does appear—that life depends on appearance; I mean, on error, simulation, deception, self-deception; and when life has, as a matter of fact, always shown itself to be on the side of the most unscrupulous *polytropoi*. Such an intent, charitably inter-preted, could perhaps be a quixotism, a little enthusiastic impudence; but it could also be something worse, namely, a destructive prin-ciple, hostile to life. "Will to truth"—that might be a concealed will to death.

Thus the question "Why science?" leads back to the moral problem, "For what end any morality at all" if life, nature, and history are "not moral"? . . . But one will have gath-ered what I am driving at, namely, that it al-ways remains a *metaphysical faith* upon which our faith in science rests—that even we devotees of knowledge today, we godless ones and anti-metaphysicians, still take *our* fire too from the flame which a faith thou-sands of years old has kindled: that Christian faith, which was also Plato's faith, that God is truth, that truth is divine. . . .

27

What Pragmatism Means

William James

William James (1842–1910), the brother of novelist Henry James, was an American philosopher who, along with Charles S. Peirce and John Dewey, is considered one of the founders of a distinctly American school of philosophy called "pragmatism." In this selection from Chapter 2 of *Pragmatism* (1907), James offers in characteristically straightforward and unambiguous language what he means by the term. His argument entails a major shift from traditional philosophy's understanding of its purpose. James contends that pragmatism offers not answers, but a method of inquiry. Moreover, rather than being preoccupied with first principles that serve as the requisite basis for traditional philosophy, pragmatism is concerned from the outset with the implications or consequences of any theoretical position. Such an orientation implies that philosophy ought to be less grandiose in its aims, content to assist in obtaining insights that are both more limited and more provisional than the goal of most philosophers, yet still having the potential for actually affecting people in their everyday lives.

Some years ago, being with a camping party in the mountains, I returned from a solitary ramble to find every one engaged in a ferocious metaphysical dispute. The *corpus* of the dispute was a squirrel—a live squirrel supposed to be clinging to one side of a tree-trunk; while over against the tree's opposite side a human being was imagined to stand. This human witness tries to get sight of the squirrel by moving rapidly round the tree, but no matter how fast he goes, the squirrel moves as fast in the opposite direction, and always keeps the tree between himself and the man, so that never a glimpse of him is caught. The resultant metaphysical

problem now is this: *Does the man go round the squirrel or not?* He goes round the tree, sure enough, and the squirrel is on the tree; but does he go round the squirrel? In the unlimited leisure of the wilderness, discussion had been worn threadbare. Every one had taken sides, and was obstinate; and the numbers on both sides were even. Each side, when I appeared therefore appealed to me to make it a majority. Mindful of the scholastic adage that whenever you meet a contradiction you must make a distinction, I immediately sought and found one, as follows: "Which party is right," I said, "depends on what you *practically mean* by 'going round' the squirrel. If you mean passing from the north of him to the east, then to the south, then to the west, and then to the north of him again, obviously the man does go round him, for he occupies these successive positions. But if on the contrary you mean being first in front of him, then on the right of him, then behind him, then on his left, and finally in front again, it is quite as obvious that the man fails to go round him, for by the compensating movements the squirrel makes, he keeps his belly turned towards the man all the time, and his back turned away. Make the distinction, and there is no occasion for any farther dispute. You are both right and both wrong according as you conceive the verb 'to go round' in one practical fashion or the other."

Although one or two of the hotter disputants called my speech a shuffling evasion, saying they wanted no quibbling or scholastic hairsplitting, but meant just plain honest English 'round,' the majority seemed to think that the distinction had assuaged the dispute.

I tell this trivial anecdote because it is a peculiarly simple example of what I wish now to speak of as *the pragmatic method*. The pragmatic method is primarily a method of settling metaphysical disputes that otherwise might be interminable. Is the world one or many?—fated or free?—material or spiritual?—here are notions either of which may or may not hold good of the world; and disputes over such notions are unending. The pragmatic method in such cases is to try to interpret each notion by tracing its respective practical consequences. What difference would it practically make to any one if this notion rather than that notion were true? If no practical difference whatever can be traced, then the alternatives mean practically the same thing, and all dispute is idle. Whenever a dispute is serious, we ought to be able to show some practical difference that must follow from one side or the others' being right. A glance at the history of the idea will show you still better what pragmatism means. The term is derived from the same Greek word *pragma*, meaning action, from which our words 'practice' and 'practical' come. It was first introduced into philosophy by Mr. Charles Peirce in 1878. In an article entitled 'How to Make Our Ideas Clear,' in the *Popular Science Monthly* for January of that year, Mr. Peirce, after pointing out that our beliefs are really rules for action, said that, to develop a thought's meaning, we need only determine what conduct it is fitted to produce: that conduct is for us its sole significance. And the tangible fact at the root of all our thought-distinctions, however subtle, is that there is no one of them so fine as to consist in anything but a possible difference of practice. To attain perfect clearness in our thoughts of an object, then, we need only consider what conceivable effects of a practical kind the object may involve—what sensations we are to expect from it, and what reactions we must prepare. Our conception of these effects, whether immediate or remote, is then for us the whole of our conception of the object, so far as that conception has positive significance at all.

This is the principle of Peirce, the principle of pragmatism. It lay entirely unnoticed by any one for twenty years, until I, in an address before Professor Howison's philosophical union at the University of California, brought it forward again and made a special application of it to religion. By that date (1898) the times seemed ripe for its reception. The word 'pragmatism' spread, and at present it fairly spots the pages of the philosophic journals. On all hands we find the 'pragmatic movement' spoken of, sometimes with respect, sometimes with contumely, seldom with clear understanding. It is evident that the term applies itself conveniently to a number of tendencies that hitherto have lacked a collective name, and that it has 'come to stay.'

To take in the importance of Peirce's principle, one must get accustomed to applying it to concrete cases. I found a few years ago that Ostwald, the illustrious Leipzig chemist, had been making perfectly distinct use of the principle of pragmatism in his lectures on the philosophy of science, though he had not called it by that name.

"All realities influence our practice," he wrote me, "and that influence is their meaning for us. I am accustomed to put questions to my classes in this way: In what respects would the world be different if this alternative or that were true? If I can find nothing that would become different, then the alternative has no sense."

That is, the rival views mean practically the same thing, and meaning, other than practical, there is for us none. Ostwald in a published lecture gives this example of what he means. Chemists have long wrangled over the inner constitution of certain bodies called 'tautomerous.' Their properties seemed equally consistent with the notion that an instable hydrogen atom oscillates inside of them, or that they are instable mixtures of two bodies. Controversy raged, but never was decided. "It would never have begun," says Ostwald, "if the combatants had asked themselves what particular experimental fact could have been made different by one or the other view being correct. For it would then have appeared that no difference of fact could possibly ensue; and the quarrel was as unreal as if, theorizing in primitive times about the raising of dough by yeast, one party should have invoked a 'brownie,' while another insisted on an 'elf' as the true cause of the phenomenon."[1]

It is astonishing to see how many philosophical disputes collapse into insignificance the moment you subject them to this simple test of tracing a concrete consequence. There can *be* no difference anywhere that doesn't *make* a difference elsewhere—no difference in abstract truth that doesn't express itself in a difference in concrete fact and in conduct consequent upon that fact, imposed on somebody, somehow, somewhere, and somewhen. The whole function of philosophy ought to be to find out what definite difference it will make to you and me, at definite instants of our life, if this world-formula or that world-formula be the true one.

There is absolutely nothing new in the pragmatic method. Socrates was an adept at it. Aristotle used it methodically. Locke, Berkeley, and Hume made momentous contributions to truth by its means. Shadworth Hodgson keeps insisting that realities are only what they are 'known as.' But these forerunners of pragmatism used it in fragments: they were preluders only. Not until in our time has it generalized itself, become conscious of a universal mission, pretended to a conquering destiny. I believe in that destiny, and I hope I may end by inspiring you with my belief.

Pragmatism represents a perfectly familiar attitude in philosophy, the empiricist attitude, but it represents it, as it seems to me, both in a more radical and in a less objectionable form than it has ever yet assumed. A pragmatist turns his back resolutely and once for all upon a lot of inveterate habits dear to professional philosophers. He turns away from abstraction and insufficiency, from verbal solutions, from bad *a priori* reasons, from fixed principles, closed systems, and pretended absolutes and origins. He turns towards concreteness and adequacy, towards facts, towards action and towards power. That means the empiricist temper regnant and the rationalist temper sincerely given up. It means the open air and possibilities of nature, as against dogma, artificiality, and the pretense of finality in truth.

At the same time it does not stand for any special results. It is a method only. But the general triumph of that method would mean an enormous change in what I called in my last lecture the 'temperament' of philosophy. Teachers of the ultra-rationalistic type would be frozen out, much as the courtier type is frozen out in republics, as the ultramontane type of priest is frozen out in protestant lands. Science and metaphysics would come much nearer together, would in fact work absolutely hand in hand.

Metaphysics has usually followed a very primitive kind of quest. You know how men have always hankered after unlawful magic, and you know what a great part in magic

words have always played. If you have his name, or the formula of incantation that binds him, you can control the spirit, genie, afrite, or whatever the power may be. Solomon knew the names of all the spirits, and having their names, he held them subject to his will. So the universe has always appeared to the natural mind as a kind of enigma, of which the key must be sought in the shape of some illuminating or power-bringing word or name. That word names the universe's *principle*, and to possess it is after a fashion to possess the universe itself. 'God,' 'Matter,' 'Reason,' 'the Absolute,' 'Energy,' are so many solving names. You can rest when you have them. You are at the end of your metaphysical quest.

But if you follow the pragmatic method, you cannot look on any such word as closing your quest. You must bring out of each word its practical cash-value, set it at work within the stream of your experience. It appears less as a solution, then, than as a program for more work, and more particularly as an indication of the ways in which existing realities may be *changed*.

Theories thus become instruments, not answers to enigmas, in which we can rest. We don't lie back upon them, we move forward, and, on occasion, make nature over again by their aid. Pragmatism unstiffens all our theories, limbers them up and sets each one at work. Being nothing essentially new, it harmonizes with many ancient philosophic tendencies. It agrees with nominalism for instance, in always appealing to particulars; with utilitarianism in emphasizing practical aspects; with positivism in its disdain for verbal solutions, useless questions and metaphysical abstractions.

All these, you see, are *anti-intellectualist* tendencies. Against rationalism as a pretension and a method pragmatism is fully armed and militant. But, at the outset, at least, it stands for no particular results. It has no dogmas, and no doctrines save its method. As the young Italian pragmatist Papini has well said, it lies in the midst of our theories, like a corridor in a hotel. Innumerable chambers open out of it. In one you may find a man writing an atheistic volume; in the next some one on his knees praying for faith and strength; in a third a chemist investigating a body's properties. In a fourth a system of idealistic metaphysics is being excogitated; in a fifth the impossibility of metaphysics is being shown. But they all own the corridor, and all must pass through it if they want a practicable way of getting into or out of their respective rooms.

No particular results then, so far, but only an attitude of orientation, is what the pragmatic method means. *The attitude of looking away from first things, principles, 'categories,' supposed necessities; and of looking towards last things, fruits, consequences, facts.*

So much for the pragmatic method! You may say that I have been praising it rather than explaining it to you, but I shall presently explain it abundantly enough by showing how it works on some familiar problems. Meanwhile the word pragmatism has come to be used in a still wider sense, as meaning also a certain *theory of truth*. I mean to give a whole lecture to the statement of that theory, after first paving the way, so I can be very brief now. But brevity is hard to follow, so I ask for your redoubled attention for a quarter of an hour. If much remains obscure, I hope to make it clearer in the later lectures.

One of the most successfully cultivated branches of philosophy in our time is what is called inductive logic, the study of the conditions under which our sciences have evolved. Writers on this subject have begun to show a singular unanimity as to what the laws of nature and elements of fact mean, when formulated by mathematicians, physicists and chemists. When the first mathematical, logical, and natural uniformities, the first *laws*, were discovered, men were so carried away by the clearness, beauty and simplification that resulted, that they believed themselves to have deciphered authentically the eternal thoughts of the Almighty. His mind also thundered and reverberated in syllogisms. He also thought in conic sections, squares and roots and ratios, and geometrized like Euclid. He made Kepler's laws for the planets to follow; he made velocity increase proportionally to the time in falling bodies; he made the law of the sines for light to obey when refracted; he established the classes, orders, families and genera of plants and animals, and fixed the distances between them. He thought the ar-

chetypes of all things, and devised their variations; and when we rediscover any one of these his wondrous institutions, we seize his mind in its very literal intention.

But as the sciences have developed farther, the notion has gained ground that most, perhaps all, of our laws are only approximations. The laws themselves, moreover, have grown so numerous that there is no counting them; and so many rival formulations are proposed in all the branches of science that investigators have become accustomed to the notion that no theory is absolutely a transcript of reality, but that any one of them may from some point of view be useful. Their great use is to summarize old facts and to lead to new ones. They are only a man-made language, a conceptual shorthand, as some one calls them, in which we write our reports of nature; and languages, as is well known, tolerate much choice of expression and many dialects.

Thus human arbitrariness has driven divine necessity from scientific logic. If I mention the names of Sigwart, Mach, Ostwald, Pearson, Milhaud, Poincaré, Duhem, Ruyssen, those of you who are students will easily identify the tendency I speak of, and will think of additional names.

Riding now on the front of this wave of scientific logic Messrs. Schiller and Dewey appear with their pragmatistic account of what truth everywhere signifies. Everywhere, these teachers say, 'truth' in our ideas and beliefs means the same thing that it means in science. It means, they say, nothing but this, *that ideas (which themselves are but parts of our experience) become true just in so far as they help us to get into satisfactory relation with other parts of our experience,* to summarize them and get about among them by conceptual shortcuts instead of following the interminable succession of particular phenomena. Any idea upon which we can ride, so to speak; any idea that will carry us prosperously from any one part of our experience to any other part, linking things satisfactorily, working securely, simplifying, saving labor; is true for just so much, true in so far forth, true *instrumentally*. This is the 'instrumental' view of truth taught so successfully at Chicago, the view that truth in our ideas means their power to 'work,' promulgated so brilliantly at Oxford.

Messrs. Dewey, Schiller and their allies, in reaching this general conception of all truth, have only followed the example of geologists, biologists and philologists. In the establishment of these other sciences, the successful stroke was always to take some simple process actually observable in operation—as denudation by weather, say, or variation from parental type, or change of dialect by incorporation of new words and pronunciations—and then to generalize it, making it apply to all times, and produce great results by summating its effects through the ages.

The observable process which Schiller and Dewey particularly singled out for generalization is the familiar one by which any individual settles into *new opinions*. The process here is always the same. The individual has a stock of old opinions already, but he meets a new experience that puts them to a strain. Somebody contradicts them; or in a reflective moment he discovers that they contradict each other; or he hears of facts with which they are incompatible; or desires arise in him which they cease to satisfy. The result is an inward trouble to which his mind till then had been a stranger, and from which he seeks to escape by modifying his previous mass of opinions. He saves as much of it as he can, for in this matter of belief we are all extreme conservatives. So he tries to change first this opinion, and then that (for they resist change very variously), until at last some new idea comes up which he can graft upon the ancient stock with a minimum of disturbance of the latter, some idea that mediates between the stock and the new experience and runs them into one another most felicitously and expediently.

This new idea is then adopted as the true one. It preserves the older stock of truths with a minimum of modification, stretching them just enough to make them admit the novelty, but conceiving that in ways as familiar as the case leaves possible. An *outrée* explanation, violating all our preconceptions, would never pass for a true account of a novelty. We should scratch round industriously till we found something less excentric. The most violent revolutions in an individual's beliefs leave most of his old order standing. Time and space, cause and effect, nature and history, and one's own biography remain untouched. New truth is always a go-between, a smoother-over of transitions. It marries old opinion to new fact so as ever to show a minimum of jolt, a maximum of continuity. We hold a theory true just in proportion to its success in solving this 'problem of maxima and minima.' But success in solving this problem is eminently a matter of approximation. We say this theory solves it on the whole more satisfactorily than that theory; but that means more satisfactorily to ourselves, and individuals will emphasize their points of satisfaction differently. To a certain degree, therefore, everything here is plastic.

The point I now urge you to observe particularly is the part played by the older truths. Failure to take account of it is the source of much of the unjust criticism levelled against pragmatism. Their influence is absolutely controlling. Loyalty to them is the first principle—in most cases it is the only principle; for by far the most usual way of handling phenomena so novel that they would make for a serious re-arrangement of our preconception is to ignore them altogether, or to abuse those who bear witness for them.

You doubtless wish examples of this process of truth's growth, and the only trouble is their superabundance. The simplest case of new truth is of course the mere numerical addition of new kinds of facts, or of new single facts of old kinds, to our experience—an addition that involves no alteration in the old beliefs. Day follows day, and its contents are simply added. The new contents themselves are not true, they simply, *come* and *are*. Truth is *what we say about them*, and when we say that they have come, truth is satisfied by the plain additive formula.

But often the day's contents oblige a re-arrangement. If I should now utter piercing shrieks and act like a maniac on this platform, it would make many of you revise your ideas as to the probable worth of my philosophy. 'Radium' came the other day as part of the day's content, and seemed for a moment to contradict our ideas of the whole order of nature, that order having come to be identified with what is called the conservation of energy. The mere sight of radium paying heat away indefinitely out of its own pocket seemed to violate that conservation. What to think? If the radiations from it were nothing but an escape of unsuspected 'potential' energy, pre-existent inside of the atoms, the principle of conservation would be saved. The discovery of 'helium' as the radiation's outcome, opened a way to this belief. So Ramsay's view is generally held to be true, because, although it extends our old ideas of energy, it causes a minimum of alteration in their nature.

I need not multiply instances. A new opinion counts as 'true' just in proportion as it gratifies the individual's desire to assimilate the novel in his experience to his beliefs in stock. It must both lean on old truths and grasp new fact; and its success (as I said a moment ago) in doing this, is a matter for the individual's appreciation. When old truth grows, then, by new truth's addition, it is for subjective reasons. We are in the process and obey the reasons. That new idea is truest which performs most felicitously its function of satisfying our double urgency. It makes itself true, gets itself classed as true, by the way it works; grafting itself then upon the ancient body of truth, which thus grows much as a tree grows by the activity of a new layer of cambium.

Now Dewey and Schiller proceed to generalize this observation and to apply it to the most ancient parts of truth. They also once were plastic. They also were called true for human reasons. They also mediated between still earlier truths and what in those days were novel observations. Purely objective truth, truth in whose establishment the function of giving human satisfaction in marrying previous parts of experience with newer parts played no rôle whatever, is no-where to be found. The reason why we call things true is the reason why they *are* true, for 'to be true' *means* only to perform this marriage-function.

The trail of the human serpent is thus over everything. Truth independent; truth that we *find* merely; truth no longer malleable to human need; truth incorrigible, in a word; such truth exists indeed superabundantly—or is supposed to exist by rationalistically minded thinkers; but then it means only the dead heart of the living tree, and its being there means only that truth also has its paleontology, and its 'prescription,' and may grow stiff with years of veteran service and petrified in men's regard by sheer antiquity. But how plastic even the oldest truths nevertheless really are has been vividly shown in our day by the transformation of logical and mathematical ideas, a transformation which seems even to be invading physics. The ancient formulas are reinterpreted as special expressions of much wider principles, principles that our ancestors never got a glimpse of in their present shape and formulation. . . .

Endnote

1. 'Theorie und Praxis,' *Zeitsch. des Oesterreichischen Ingenieur u. Architecten-Vereines*, 1905, Nr. 4 u. 6. I find a still more radical pragmatism than Ostwald's in an address by Professor W. S. Franklin: "I think that the sickliest notion of physics, even if a student gets it, is that it is 'the science of masses, molecules, and the ether.' And I think that the healthiest notion, even if a student does not wholly get it, is that physics is the science of the ways of taking hold of bodies and pushing them!" (*Science*, January 2, 1903.)

28

Civilization and Its Discontents

Sigmund Freud

Sigmund Freud (1856–1939), the founder of psychoanalysis, was an intellectual giant whose influence transcended psychology and the other social sciences to shape literature, art, and the general culture. He was known to Weber, who was rather critical of Freud's work, and to Simmel, who was more appreciative. Freud's work has had a profound impact on subsequent theorists, ranging from critical theorists to Parsons, from feminists to postmodernists. In this selection from his classic work *Civilization and Its Discontents* (1930), Freud argues that, although it is worth it, we pay a steep psychological price for civilization because it demands that we repress instinctual drives circumscribing the limits of human happiness. Freud's tragic view of life is nowhere better articulated than in this passage.

Our enquiry concerning happiness has not so far taught us much that is not already common knowledge. And even if we proceed from it to the problem of why it is so hard for men to be happy, there seems no greater prospect of learning anything new. We have given the answer already . . . by pointing to the three sources from which our suffering comes: the superior power of nature, the feebleness of our own bodies and the inadequacy of the regulations which adjust the mutual relationships of human beings in the family, the state and society. In regard to the first two sources, our judgement cannot hesitate long. It forces us to acknowledge those sources of suffering and to submit to the inevitable. We shall never completely master nature; and our bodily organism, itself a part of that nature, will always remain a transient structure with a limited capacity for adaptation and achievement. This recognition does not have a paralysing effect. On the contrary, it points the direction for our activity. If we cannot remove all suffering, we can remove some, and we can mitigate some: the experience of many thousands of years has convinced us of that. As regards the third source, the social source of suffering, our attitude is a different one. We do not admit it at all; we cannot see why the regulations made by ourselves should not, on the contrary, be a protection and a benefit for every one of us. And yet, when we consider how unsuccessful we have been in precisely this field of prevention of suffering, a suspicion dawns on us that here, too, a piece of unconquerable nature may lie behind—this time a piece of our own psychical constitution.

When we start considering this possibility, we come upon a contention which is so astonishing that we must dwell upon it. This contention holds that what we call our civilization is largely responsible for our misery, and that we should be much happier if we gave it up and returned to primitive conditions. I call this contention astonishing because, in whatever way we may define the concept of civilization, it is a certain fact that all the things with which we seek to protect ourselves against the threats that emanate from the sources of suffering are part of that very civilization.

How has it happened that so many people have come to take up this strange attitude of hostility to civilization?[1] I believe that the basis of it was a deep and long-standing dissatisfaction with the then existing state of civilization and that on that basis a condemnation of it was built up, occasioned by certain specific historical events. I think I know what the last and the last but one of those occasions were. I am not learned enough to trace the chain of them far back enough in the history of the human species; but a factor of this kind hostile to civilization must already have been at work in the victory of Christendom over the heathen religions. For it was very closely related to the low estimation put upon earthly life by the Christian doctrine. The last but one of these occasions was when the progress of voyages of discovery led to contact with primitive peoples and races. In consequence of insufficient observation and a mistaken view of their manners and customs, they appeared to Europeans to be leading a simple, happy life with few wants, a life such as was unattainable by their visitors with their superior civilization. Later experience has corrected some of those judgements. In many cases the observers had wrongly attributed to the absence of complicated cultural demands what was in fact due to the bounty of nature and the ease with which the major human needs were satisfied. The last occasion is especially familiar to us. It arose when people came to know about the mechanism of the neuroses, which threaten to undermine the modicum of happiness enjoyed by civilized men. It was discovered that a person becomes neurotic because he cannot tolerate the amount of frustration which society imposes on him in the service of its cultural ideals, and it was inferred from this that the abolition or reduction of those demands would result in a return to possibilities of happiness.

There is also an added factor of disappointment. During the last few generations mankind has made an extraordinary advance in the natural sciences and in their technical application and has established his control over nature in a way never before imagined. The single steps of this advance are common knowledge and it is unnecessary to enumerate them. Men are proud of those achievements, and have a right to be. But they seem to have observed that this newly-won power over space and time, this subjugation of the forces of nature, which is the fulfilment of a longing that goes back thousands of years, has not increased the amount of pleasurable satisfaction which they may expect from life and has not made them feel happier. From the recognition of this fact we ought to be content to conclude that power over nature is not the *only* precondition of human happiness, just as it is not the *only* goal of cultural endeavour; we ought not to infer from it that technical progress is without value for the economics of our happiness. One would like to ask: is there, then, no positive gain in pleasure, no unequivocal increase in my feeling of happiness, if I can, as often as I please, hear the voice of a child of mine who is living hundreds of miles away or if I can learn in the shortest possible time after a friend has

reached his destination that he has come through the long and difficult voyage unharmed? Does it mean nothing that medicine has succeeded in enormously reducing infant mortality and the danger of infection for women in childbirth, and, indeed, in considerably lengthening the average life of a civilized man? And there is a long list that might be added to benefits of this kind which we owe to the much-despised era of scientific and technical advances. But here the voice of pessimistic criticism makes itself heard and warns us that most of these satisfactions follow the model of the 'cheap enjoyment' extolled in the anecdote—the enjoyment obtained by putting a bare leg from under the bedclothes on a cold winter night and drawing it in again. If there had been no railway to conquer distances, my child would never have left his native town and I should need no telephone to hear his voice; if travelling across the ocean by ship had not been introduced, my friend would not have embarked on his sea-voyage and I should not need a cable to relieve my anxiety about him. What is the use of reducing infantile mortality when it is precisely that reduction which imposes the greatest restraint on us in the begetting of children, so that, taken all round, we nevertheless rear no more children than in the days before the reign of hygiene, while at the same time we have created difficult conditions for our sexual life in marriage, and have probably worked against the beneficial effects of natural selection? And, finally, what good to us is a long life if it is difficult and barren of joys, and if it is so full of misery that we can only welcome death as a deliverer?

It seems certain that we do not feel comfortable in our present-day civilization, but it is very difficult to form an opinion whether and in what degree men of an earlier age felt happier and what part their cultural conditions played in the matter. We shall always tend to consider people's distress objectively—that is, to place ourselves, with our own wants and sensibilities, in *their* conditions, and then to examine what occasions we should find in them for experiencing happiness or unhappiness. This method of looking at things, which seems objective because it ignores the variations in subjective sensibility, is, of course, the most subjective possible, since it puts one's own mental states in the place of any others, unknown though they may be. Happiness, however, is something essentially subjective. No matter how much we may shrink with horror from certain situations—of a galley-slave in antiquity, of a peasant during the Thirty Years' War, of a victim of the Holy Inquisition, of a Jew awaiting a pogrom—it is nevertheless impossible for us to feel our way into such people—to divine the changes which original obtuseness of mind, a gradual stupefying process, the cessation of expectations, and cruder or more refined methods of narcotization have produced upon their receptivity to sensations of pleasure and unpleasure. Moreover, in the case of the most extreme possibility of suffering, special mental protective devices are brought into operation. It seems to me unprofitable to pursue this aspect of the problem any further.

It is time for us to turn our attention to the nature of this civilization on whose value as a means to happiness doubts have been thrown. We shall not look for a formula in which to express that nature in a few words, until we have learned something by examining it. We shall therefore content ourselves with saying once more that the word 'civilization'[2] describes the whole sum of the achievements and the regulations which distinguish our lives from those of our animal ancestors and which serve two purposes—namely to protect men against nature and to adjust their mutual relations.[3] In order to learn more, we will bring together the various features of civilization individually, as they are exhibited in human communities. In doing so, we shall have no hesitation in letting ourselves be guided by linguistic usage or, as it is also called, linguistic feeling, in the conviction that we shall thus be doing justice to inner discernments which still defy expression in abstract terms.

The first stage is easy. We recognize as cultural all activities and resources which are useful to men for making the earth serviceable to them, for protecting them against the violence of the forces of nature, and so on. As regards this side of civilization, there can be scarcely any doubt. If we go back far enough, we find that the first acts of civilization were the use of tools, the gaining of control over fire and the construction of dwellings. Among these, the control over fire stands out as a quite extraordinary and unexampled achievement,[4] while the others opened up paths which man has followed ever since, and the stimulus to which is easily guessed. With every tool man is perfecting his own organs, whether motor or sensory, or is removing the limits to their functioning. Motor power places gigantic forces at his disposal, which, like his muscles, he can employ in any direction; thanks to ships and aircraft neither water nor air can hinder his movements; by means of spectacles he corrects defects in the lens of his own eye; by means of the telescope he sees into the far distance; and by means of the microscope he overcomes the limits of visibility set by the structure of his retina. In the photographic camera he has created an instrument which retains the fleeting visual impressions, just as a gramophone disc retains the equally fleeting auditory ones; both are at bottom materializations of the power he possesses of recollection, his memory. With the help of the telephone he can hear at distances which would be respected as unattainable even in a fairy tale. Writing was in its origin the voice of an absent person; and the dwelling-house was a substitute for the mother's womb, the first lodging, for which in all likelihood man still longs, and in which he was safe and felt at ease.

These things that, by his science and technology, man has brought about on this earth, on which he first appeared as a feeble animal organism and on which each individual of his species must once more make its entry ('oh inch of nature!'[5]) as a helpless suckling—these things do not only sound like a fairy tale, they are an actual fulfillment of every—or of almost every—fairy-tale wish. All these assets he may lay claim to as his cultural acquisition. Long ago he formed an ideal conception of omnipotence and omniscience which he embodied in his gods. To these gods he attributed everything that seemed unattainable to his wishes, or that was forbidden to him. One may say, therefore, that these gods were cultural ideals. Today he has come very close to the attainment of this ideal, he has almost become a god himself. Only, it is true, in the fashion in which ideals are usually attained according to the general judgement of humanity. Not completely; in some respects not at all, in others only half way. Man has, as it were, become a kind of prosthetic[6] God. When he puts on all his auxiliary organs he is truly magnificent; but those organs have not grown on to him and they still give him much trouble at times. Nevertheless, he is entitled to console himself with the thought that this development will not come to an end precisely with the year 1930 A.D. Future ages will bring with them new and probably unimaginably great advances in this field of civilization and will increase man's likeness to God still more. But in the interests of our investigations, we will not forget that present-day man does not feel happy in his Godlike character.

We recognize, then, that countries have attained a high level of civilization if we find that in them everything which can assist in the exploitation of the earth by man and in his protection against the forces of nature—everything, in short, which is of use to him—is attended to and effectively carried out. In such countries rivers which threaten to flood the land are regulated in their flow, and their water is directed through canals to places where there is a shortage of it. The soil is carefully cultivated and planted with the vegetation which it is suited to support; and the mineral wealth below ground is assiduously brought to the surface and fashioned into the required implements and utensils. The means of communication are ample, rapid and reliable. Wild and dangerous animals have been exterminated, and the breeding of domesticated animals flourishes. But we demand other things from civilization besides these, and it is a noticeable fact that we hope to find them realized in these same countries. As though we were seeking to repudiate the first demand we made, we welcome it as a sign of civilization as well if we see people directing their care too to what has no practical value whatever, to what is useless—if for instance, the green spaces necessary in a town as playgrounds and as reservoirs of fresh air are also laid out with flower-beds, or if the windows of the houses are decorated with pots of flowers. We soon observe that this useless thing which we expect civilization to value is beauty. We require civilized man to reverence beauty wherever he sees it in nature and to create it in the objects of his handiwork so far as he is able. But this is far from exhausting our demands on civilization. We expect besides to see the signs of cleanliness and order. We do not think highly of the cultural level of an English country town in Shakespeare's time when we read that there was a big dungheap in front of his father's house in Stratford; we are indignant and call it 'barbarous' (which is the opposite of civilized) when we find the paths in the Wiener Wald[7] littered with paper. Dirtiness of any kind seems to us incompatible with civilization. We extend our demand for cleanliness to the human body too. We are astonished to learn of the objectionable smell which emanated from the *Roi Soleil*;[8] and we shake our heads on the Isola Bella[9] when we are shown the tiny washbasin in which Napoleon made his morning toilet. Indeed, we are not surprised by the idea of setting up the use of soap as an actual yardstick of civilization. The same is true of order. It, like cleanliness, applies solely to the works of man. But whereas cleanliness is not to be expected in nature, order, on the contrary, has been imitated from her. Man's observation of the great astronomical regularities not only furnished him with a model for introducing order into his life, but gave him the first points of departure for doing so. Order is a kind of compulsion to repeat which, when a regulation has been laid down once and for all, decides when, where and how a thing shall be done, so that in every similar circumstance one is spared hesitation and indecision. The benefits of order are incontestable. It enables men to use space and time to the best advantage, while conserving their psychical forces. We should have a right to expect that order would have taken its place in human activities from the start and without difficulty; and we may well wonder that this has not happened—that, on the contrary, human beings exhibit an inborn tendency to carelessness, irregularity and unreliability in their work, and that a laborious training is needed before they learn to follow the example of their celestial models.

Beauty, cleanliness and order obviously occupy a special position among the requirements of civilization. No one will maintain that they are as important for life as control over the forces of nature or as some other factors with which we shall become acquainted. And yet no one would care to put them in the background as trivialities. That civilization is not exclusively taken up with what is useful is already shown by the example of beauty, which we decline to omit from among the interests of civilization. The usefulness of order is quite evident. With regard to cleanliness, we must bear in mind that it is demanded of us by hygiene as well, and we may suspect that even before the days of scientific prophylaxis the connection between the two was not altogether strange to man. Yet utility does not entirely explain these efforts; something else must be at work besides.

No feature, however, seems better to characterize civilization than its esteem and encouragement of man's higher mental activities—his intellectual, scientific and artistic achievements—and the leading role that it assigns to ideas in human life. Foremost among those ideas are the religious systems, on whose complicated structure I have endeavoured to throw light elsewhere.[10] Next come the speculations of philosophy; and finally what might be called man's 'ideals'—his ideas of a possible perfection of individuals, or of peoples or of the whole of humanity, and the demands he sets up on the basis of such ideas. The fact that these creations of his are not independent of one another, but are on the contrary closely interwoven, increases the difficulty not only of describing them but of tracing their psychological derivation. If we assume quite generally that the motive force of all human activities is a striving towards the two confluent goals of utility and a yield of pleasure, we must suppose that this is also true of the manifestations of civilization which we have been discussing here, although this is easily visible only in scientific and aesthetic activities. But it cannot be doubted that the other activities, too, correspond to strong needs in men—perhaps to needs which are only developed in a minority. Nor must we allow ourselves to be misled by judgements of value concerning any particular religion, or

philosophic system, or ideal. Whether we think to find in them the highest achievements of the human spirit, or whether we deplore them as aberrations, we cannot but recognize that where they are present, and, in especial, where they are dominant, a high level of civilization is implied.

The last, but certainly not the least important, of the characteristic features of civilization remains to be assessed: the manner in which the relationships of men to one another, their social relationships, are regulated—relationships which affect a person as a neighbour, as a source of help, as another person's sexual object, as a member of a family and of a State. Here it is especially difficult to keep clear of particular ideal demands and to see what is civilized in general. Perhaps we may begin by explaining that the element of civilization enters on the scene with the first attempt to regulate these social relationships. If the attempt were not made, the relationships would be subject to the arbitrary will of the individual: that is to say, the physically stronger man would decide them in the sense of his own interests and instinctual impulses. Nothing would be changed in this if this stronger man should in his turn meet someone even stronger than he. Human life in common is only made possible when a majority comes together which is stronger than any separate individual, and which remains united against all separate individuals. The power of this community is then set up as 'right' in opposition to the power of the individual, which is condemned as 'brute force'. This replacement of the power of the individual by the power of a community constitutes the decisive step of civilization. The essence of it lies in the fact that the members of the community restrict themselves in their possibilities of satisfaction, whereas the individual knew no such restrictions. The first requisite of civilization, therefore, is that of justice—that is, the assurance that a law once made will not be broken in favour of an individual. This implies nothing as to the ethical value of such a law. The further course of cultural development seems to tend towards making the law no longer an expression of the will of a small community—a caste or a stratum of the population or a racial group—which, in its turn, behaves like a violent individual towards other, and perhaps more numerous, collections of people. The final outcome should be a rule of law to which all—except those who are not capable of entering a community—have contributed by a sacrifice of their instincts, and which leaves no one—again with the same exception—at the mercy of brute force.

The liberty of the individual is no gift of civilization. It was greatest before there was any civilization, though then, it is true, it had for the most part no value, since the individual was scarcely in a position to defend it. The development of civilization imposes restrictions on it, and justice demands that no one shall escape those restrictions. What makes itself felt in a human community as a desire for freedom may be their revolt against some existing injustice, and so may prove favourable to a further development of civilization; it may remain compatible with civilization. But it may also spring from the remains of their original personality, which is still untamed by civilization and may thus become the basis in them of hostility to civilization. The urge for freedom, therefore, is directed against particular forms and demands of civilization or against civilization altogether. It does not seem as though any influence could induce a man to change his nature into a termite's. No doubt he will always defend his claim to individual liberty against the will of the group. A good part of the struggles of mankind centre round the single task of finding an expedient accommodation—one, that is, that will bring happiness—between this claim of the individual and the cultural claims of the group; and one of the problems that touches the fate of humanity is whether such an accommodation can be reached by means of some particular form of civilization or whether this conflict is irreconcilable.

By allowing common feeling to be our guide in deciding what features of human life are to be regarded as civilized, we have obtained a clear impression of the general picture of civilization; but it is true that so far we have discovered nothing that is not universally known. At the same time we have been careful not to fall in with the prejudice that civilization is synonymous with perfect-

ing, that it is the road to perfection pre-ordained for men. But now a point of view presents itself which may lead in a different direction. The development of civilization appears to us as a peculiar process which mankind undergoes, and in which several things strike us as familiar. We may characterize this process with reference to the changes which it brings about in the familiar instinctual dispositions of human beings, to satisfy which is, after all, the economic task of our lives. A few of these instincts are used up in such a manner that something appears in their place which, in an individual, we describe as a character-trait. The most remarkable example of such a process is found in the anal erotism of young human beings. Their original interest in the excretory function, its organs and products, is changed in the course of their growth into a group of traits which are familiar to us as parsimony, a sense of order and cleanliness—qualities which, though valuable and welcome in themselves, may be intensified till they become markedly dominant and produce what is called the anal character. How this happens we do not know, but there is no doubt about the correctness of the finding.[11] Now we have seen that order and cleanliness are important requirements of civilization, although their vital necessity is not very apparent, any more than their suitability as sources of enjoyment. At this point we cannot fail to be struck by the similarity between the process of civilization and the libidinal development of the individual. Other instincts [besides anal erotism] are induced to displace the conditions for their satisfaction, to lead them into other paths. In most cases this process coincides with that of the *sublimation* (of instinctual aims) with which we are familiar, but in some it can be differentiated from it. Sublimation of instinct is an especially conspicuous feature of cultural development; it is what makes it possible for higher psychical activities, scientific, artistic or ideological, to play such an important part in civilized life. If one were to yield to a first impression, one would say that sublimation is a vicissitude which has been forced upon the instincts entirely by civilization. But it would be wiser to reflect upon this a little longer. In the third place,[12] finally, and this seems the most important of all, it is impossible to overlook the extent to which civilization is built up upon a renunciation of instinct, how much it presupposes precisely the non-satisfaction (by suppression, repression or some other means?) of powerful instincts. This 'cultural frustration' dominates the large field of social relationships between human beings. As we already know, it is the cause of the hostility against which all civilizations have to struggle. It will also make severe demands on our scientific work, and we shall have much to explain here. It is not easy to understand how it can become possible to deprive an instinct of satisfaction. Nor is doing so without danger. If the loss is not compensated for economically, one can be certain that serious disorders will ensue.

But if we want to know what value can be attributed to our view that the development of civilization is a special process, comparable to the normal maturation of the individual, we must clearly attack another problem. We must ask ourselves to what influences the development of civilization owes its origin, how it arose, and by what its course has been determined. . . .

Endnotes

1. [Freud had discussed this question at considerable length two years earlier, in the opening chapters of *The Future of an Illusion* (1927c).]

2. '*Kultur.*' For the translation of this word see the Editor's Note to *The Future of an Illusion*.

3. See *The Future of an Illusion*.

4. Psycho-analytic material, incomplete as it is and not susceptible to clear interpretation, nevertheless admits of a conjecture—a fantastic-sounding one—about the origin of this human feat. It is as though primal man had the habit, when he came in contact with fire, of satisfying an infantile desire connected with it, by putting it out with a stream of his urine. The legends that we possess leave no doubt about the originally phallic view taken of tongues of flame as they shoot upwards. Putting out fire by micturating—a theme to which modern giants, Gulliver in Lilliput and Rabelais' Gargantua, still hark back—was therefore a kind of sexual act with a male, an enjoyment of sexual potency in a homosexual competition. The first person to renounce this desire and spare the fire was able to carry it off with him and subdue it to his own use. By

damping down the fire of his own sexual excitation, he had tamed the natural force of fire. This great cultural conquest was thus the reward for his renunciation of instinct. Further, it is as though woman had been appointed guardian of the fire which was held captive on the domestic hearth, because her anatomy made it impossible for her to yield to the temptation of this desire. It is remarkable, too, how regularly analytic experience testifies to the connection between ambition, fire and urethral erotism.—[Freud had pointed to the connection between urination and fire as early as in the 'Dora' case history (1905e [1901]). The connection with ambition came rather later. A full list of references will be found in the Editor's Note to the later paper on the subject, 'The Acquisition and Control of Fire' (1932a).]

5. [In English in the original. This very Shakespearean phrase is not in fact to be found in the canon of Shakespeare. The words 'Poore inch of Nature' occur, however, in a novel by George Wilkins, *The Painfull Adventures of Pericles Prince of Tyre*, where they are addressed by Pericles to his infant daughter. This work was first printed in 1608, just after the publication of Shakespeare's play, in which Wilkins has been thought to have had a hand. Freud's unexpected acquaintance with the phrase is explained by its appearance in a discussion of the origins of *Pericles* in Georg Brandes's well-known book on Shakespeare, a copy of the German translation of which had a place in Freud's library (Brandes, 1896). He is known to have greatly admired the Danish critic (cf. Jones, 1957, 120), and the same book is quoted in his paper on the three caskets (1913f)].

6. [A prosthesis is the medical term for an artificial adjunct to the body, to make up for some missing or inadequate part: e.g. false teeth or a false leg.]

7. [The wooded hills on the outskirts of Vienna.]

8. [Louis XIV of France.]

9. [The well-known island in Lake Maggiore, visited by Napoleon a few days before the battle of Marengo.]

10. [Cf. *The Future of an Illusion* (1927c).]

11. Cf. my 'Character and Anal Erotism' (1908b), and numerous further contributions, by Ernest Jones [1918] and others.

12. [Freud had already mentioned two other factors playing a part in the 'process' of civilization: character-formation and sublimation.]

29

The Fusion of the 'I' and the 'Me' in Social Activities

George Herbert Mead

George Herbert Mead (1863–1931), a philosopher at the University of Chicago, was a brilliant conversationalist, preferring to present his ideas orally rather than in writing. Thus, many of his books that have had an enduring impact were actually posthumous publications compiled from former students' lecture notes. This is the case with the book from which the following selection derives: *Mind, Self, and Society* (1934). Mead distinguished two aspects of the self, which he rather prosaically referred to as the "I" and the "me." The former includes the spontaneous, dynamic, and autonomous aspects of selfhood, while the latter is the socialized self that is shaped by external social conditions and is responsive to them. The "I" is the aspect of self responsible for initiative, creativity, and novelty, while the "me" provides selfhood with stability and continuity. In this passage, Mead discusses the ways these two aspects of the self working together make possible action in social life.

In a situation where persons are all trying to save someone from drowning, there is a sense of common effort in which one is stimulated by the others to do the same thing they are doing. In those situations one has a sense of being identified with all because the reaction is essentially an identical reaction. In the case of team work, there is an identification of the individual with the group; but in that case one is doing something different from the others, even though what the others do determines what he is to do. If things move smoothly enough, there may be something of the same exaltation as in the other

situation. There is still the sense of directed control. It is where the "I" and the "me" can in some sense fuse that there arises the peculiar sense of exaltation which belongs to the religious and patriotic attitudes in which the reaction which one calls out in others is the response which one is making himself. I now wish to discuss in more detail than previously the fusion of the "I" and the "me" in the attitudes of religion, patriotism, and team work.

In the conception of universal neighborliness, there is a certain group of attitudes of kindliness and helpfulness in which the response of one calls out in the other and in himself the same attitude. Hence the fusion of the "I" and the "me" which leads to intense emotional experiences. The wider the social process in which this is involved, the greater is the exaltation, the emotional response, which results. We sit down and play a game of bridge with friends or indulge in some other relaxation in the midst of our daily work. It is something that will last an hour or so, and then we shall take up the grind again. We are, however, involved in the whole life of society; its obligations are upon us; we have to assert ourselves in various situations; those factors are all lying back in the self. But under the situations to which I am now referring that which lies in the background is fused with what we are all doing. This, we feel, is the meaning of life—and one experiences an exalted religious attitude. We get into an attitude in which everyone is at one with each other in so far as all belong to the same community. As long as we can retain that attitude we have for the time being freed ourselves of that sense of control which hangs over us all because of the responsibilities we have to meet in difficult and trying social conditions. Such is the normal situation in our social activity, and we have its problems back in our minds; but in such a situation as this, the religious situation, all seem to be lifted into the attitude of accepting everyone as belonging to the same group. One's interest is the interest of all. There is complete identification of individuals. Within the individual there is a fusion of the "me" with the "I."

The impulse of the "I" in this case is neighborliness, kindliness. One gives bread to the hungry. It is that social tendency which we all have in us that calls out a certain type of response: one wants to give. When one has a limited bank account, one cannot give all he has to the poor. Yet under certain religious situations, in groups with a certain background, he can get the attitude of doing just that. Giving is stimulated by more giving. He may not have much to give, but he is ready to give himself completely. There is a fusion of the "I" and the "me." The time is not there to control the "I," but the situation has been so constructed that the very attitude aroused in the other stimulates one to do the same thing. The exaltation in the case of patriotism presents an analogous instance of this fusion.

From the emotional standpoint such situations are peculiarly precious. They involve, of course, the successful completion of the social process. I think that the religious attitude involves this relation of the social stimulus to the world at large, the carrying-over of the social attitude to the larger world. I think that that is the definite field within which the religious experience appears. Of course, where one has a clearly marked theology in which there are definite dealings with the deity, with whom one acts as concretely as with another person in the room, then the conduct which takes place is simply of a type which is comparable to the conduct with reference to another social group, and it may be one which is lacking in that peculiar mystical character which we generally ascribe to the religious attitude. It may be a calculating attitude in which a person makes a vow, and carries it out providing the deity gives him a particular favor. Now, that attitude would normally come under the general statement of religion, but in addition it is generally recognized that the attitude has to be one that carries this particular extension of the social attitude to the universe at large. I think it is that which we generally refer to as the religious experience, and that this is the situation out of which the mystical experience of religion arises. The social situation is spread over the entire world.

It may be only on certain days of the week and at certain hours of that day that we can get into that attitude of feeling at one with everybody and everything about us. The day goes around; we have to go into the market to compete with other people and to hold our heads above the water in a difficult economic situation. We cannot keep up the sense of exaltation, but even then we may still say that these demands of life are only a task which is put on us, a duty which we must perform in order to get at particular moments the religious attitude. When the experience is attained, however, it comes with this feeling of complete identification of the self with the other.

It is a different, and perhaps higher, attitude of identification which comes in the form of what I have referred to as "team work." Here one has the sort of satisfaction which comes from working with others in a certain situation. There is, of course, still a sense of control; after all, what one does is determined by what other persons are doing; one has to be keenly aware of the positions of all the others; he knows what the others are going to do. But he has to be constantly awake to the way in which other people are responding in order to do his part in the team work. That situation has its delight, but it is not a situation in which one simply throws himself, so to speak, into the stream where he can get a sense of abandonment. That experience belongs to the religious or patriotic situation. Team work carries, however, a content which the other does not carry. The religious situation is abstract as far as the content is concerned. How one is to help others is a very complicated undertaking. One who undertakes to be a universal help to others is apt to find himself a universal nuisance. There is no more distressing person to have about than one who is constantly seeking to assist everybody else. Fruitful assistance has to be intelligent assistance. But if one can get the situation of a well-organized group doing something as a unit, a sense of the self is attained which is the experience of team work, and this is certainly from an intellectual standpoint higher than mere abstract neighborliness. The sense of team work is found where all are working toward a common end and everyone has a sense of the common end interpenetrating the particular function which he is carrying on.

The frequent attitude of the person in social service who is trying to express a fundamental attitude of neighborliness[1] may be compared with the attitude of the engineer, the organizer, which illustrates in extreme form the attitude of team work. The engineer has the attitudes of all the other individuals in the group, and it is because he has that participation that he is able to direct. When the engineer comes out of the machine shop with the bare blue print, the machine does not yet exist; but he must know what the people are to do, how long it should take them, how to measure the processes involved, and how to eliminate waste. That sort of taking the attitudes of everyone else as fully and completely as possible, entering upon one's own action from the standpoint of such a complete taking of the rôle of the others, we may perhaps refer to as the "attitude of the engineer." It is a highly intelligent attitude; and if it can be formed with a profound interest in social team work, it belongs to the high social processes and to the significant experiences. Here the full concreteness of the "me" depends upon a man's capacity to take the attitude of everybody else in the process which he directs. Here is gained the concrete content not found in the bare emotional identification of one's self with everyone else in the group.

These are the different types of expressions of the "I" in their relationship to the "me" that I wanted to bring out in order to complete the statement of the relation of the "I" and the "me." The self under these circumstances is the action of the "I" in harmony with the taking of the rôle of others in the "me." The self is both the "I" and the "me"; the "me" setting the situation to which the "I" responds. Both the "I" and "me" are involved in the self, and here each supports the other.

I wish now to discuss the fusion of the "I" and the "me" in terms of another approach, namely, through a comparison of the physical object with the self as a social object.

The "me," I have said, presents the situation within which conduct takes place, and the "I" is the actual response to that situation. This twofold separation into situation and response is characteristic of any intelligent act even if it does not involve this social mechanism. There is a definite situation which presents a problem, and then the organism responds to that situation by an organization of the different reactions that are involved. There has to be such an organization of activities in our ordinary movements among different articles in a room, or through a forest, or among automobiles. The stimuli present tend to call out a great variety of responses; but the actual response of the organism is an organization of these tendencies, not a single response which mediates all the others. One does not sit down in a chair, one does not take a book, open a window, or do a great variety of things to which in a certain sense the individual is invited when he enters a room. He does some specific thing; he perhaps goes and takes a sought paper out of a desk and does not do anything else. Yet the objects exist there in the room for him. The chair, the windows, tables, exist as such because of the uses to which he normally puts these objects. The value that the chair has in his perception is the value which belongs to his response; so he moves by a chair and past a table and away from a window. He builds up a landscape there, a scene of objects which make possible his actual movement to the drawer which contains the paper that he is after. This landscape is the means of reaching the goal he is pursuing; and the chair, the table, the window, all enter into it as objects. The physical object is, in a certain sense, what you do not respond to in a consummatory fashion. If the moment you step into a room, you drop into a chair you hardly do more than direct your attention to the chair; you do not view it as a chair in the same sense as when you just recognize it as a chair and direct your movement toward a distant object. The chair that exists in the latter case is not one you are sitting down in; but it is a something that will receive you after you do drop into it, and that gives it the character of an object as such.

Such physical objects are utilized in building up the field in which the distant object is reached. The same result occurs from a temporal standpoint when one carries out a more distant act by means of some precedent act which must be first carried through. Such organization is going on all the time in intelligent conduct. We organize the field with reference to what we are going to do. There is now, if you like, a fusion of the getting of the paper out of the drawer and the room through which we move to accomplish that end, and it is this sort of fusion that I referred to previously, only in such instances as religious experiences it takes place in the field of social mediation, and the objects in the mechanism are social in their character and so represent a different level of experience. But the process is analogous: we are what we are in our relationship to other individuals through taking the attitude of the other individuals toward ourselves so that we stimulate ourselves by our own gesture, just as a chair is what it is in terms of its invitation to sit down; the chair is something in which we might sit down, a physical "me," if you like. In a social "me" the various attitudes of all the others are expressed in terms of our own gesture, which represents the part we are carrying out in the social cooperative activity. Now the thing we actually do, the words we speak, our expressions, our emotions, those are the "I"; but they are fused with the "me" in the same sense that all the activities involved in the articles of furniture of the room are fused with the path followed toward the drawer and the taking out of the actual paper. The two situations are identical in that sense.

The act itself which I have spoken of as the "I" in the social situation is a source of unity of the whole, while the "me" is the social situation in which this act can express itself. I think that we can look at such conduct from the general standpoint of intelligent conduct; only, as I say, conduct is taking place here in this social field in which a self arises in the social situation in the group, just as the room arises in the activity of an individual in getting to this particular object he is after. I think the same view can be applied to the appearance of the self that applies to the appearance of an object in a field that constitutes in some sense a problem; only the peculiar character of it lies in the fact that it is a social situation and that this social situation involves the appearance of the "me" and the "I" which are essentially social elements. I think it is consistent to recognize this parallelism between what we call the "physical

object" over against the organism, and the social object over against the self. The "me" does definitely answer to all the different reactions which the objects about us, tend to call out in us. All such objects call out responses in ourselves, and these responses are the meanings or the natures of the objects: the chair is something we sit down in, the window is something that we can open, that gives us light or air. Likewise the "me" is the response which the individual makes to the other individuals in so far as the individual takes the attitude of the other. It is fair to say that the individual takes the attitude of the chair. We are definitely in that sense taking the attitude of the objects about us; while normally this does not get into the attitude of communication in our dealing with inanimate objects, it does take that form when we say that the chair invites us to sit down, or the bed tempts us to lie down. Our attitude under those circumstances is, of course, a social attitude. We have already discussed the social attitude as it appears in the poetry of nature, in myths, rites, and rituals. There we take over the social attitude toward nature itself. In music there is perhaps always some sort of a social situation, in terms of the emotional response involved; and the exaltation of music would have, I suppose, reference to the completeness of the organization of the response that answers to those emotional attitudes. The idea of the fusion of the "I" and the "me" gives a very adequate basis for the explanation of this exaltation. I think behavioristic psychology provides just the opportunity for such development of aesthetic theory. The significance of the response in the aesthetic experience has already been stressed by critics of painting and architecture.

The relationship of the "me" to the "I" is the relationship of a situation to the organism. The situation that presents the problem is intelligible to the organism that responds to it, and fusion takes place in the act. One can approach it from the "I" if one knows definitely what he is going to do. Then one looks at the whole process simply as a set of means for reaching the known end. Or it can be approached from the point of view of the means and the problem appears then as a decision among a set of different ends. The attitude of one individual calls out this response, and the attitude of another individual calls out another response. There are varied tendencies, and the response of the "I" will be one which relates all of these together. Whether looked at from the viewpoint of a problem which has to be solved or from the position of an "I" which in a certain sense determines its field by its conduct, the fusion takes place in the act itself in which the means expresses the end.

Endnote

1. ["Philanthropy from the Point of View of Ethics," *Intelligent Philanthropy*, edited by Faris, Lane, and Dodd.]

Part Two

The Branches:
Contemporary Social Theory

VII. Functionalism and Neofunctionalism

30

The Unanticipated Consequences of Social Action

Robert K. Merton

Appearing in the first issue of the *American Sociological Review*, Robert K. Merton's (1910–2003) "The Unanticipated Consequences of Social Action" (1936) has become one of the most frequently cited essays in the discipline. What makes this all the more remarkable is that it was composed by a 26-year-old Harvard graduate student. Merton, a student of Talcott Parsons, became one of the central figures associated with structural-functionalism. The article revealed a writer whose penetrating analyses were matched by a stylistic virtuosity quite uncharacteristic of most sociologists. Merton elevated what at one level is an obvious fact to a matter of central concern to the sociological enterprise: that our actions often turn out other than what we thought they would, or that they have, for better or worse, implications of which we were not originally aware. The sociologist is called upon to examine not only the intended outcomes of actions but those outcomes that were unanticipated, and Merton suggested a variety of factors that contribute to unintended consequences.

In some one of its numerous forms, the problem of the unanticipated consequences of purposive action has been touched upon by virtually every substantial contributor to the long history of social thought.[1] The diversity of context[2] and variety of terms[3] by which this problem has been known, however, have tended to obscure any continuity in its consideration. In fact, this diversity of context—ranging from theology to technology—has been so pronounced that not only has the substantial identity of the problem been overlooked, but no systematic, scientific analysis of it has as yet been made. The failure to subject the problem to thoroughgoing investigation has perhaps resulted in part from its having been linked historically with transcendental and ethical considerations. Obviously, the ready solution provided by ascribing uncontemplated consequences of action to the inscrutable will of God or Providence or Fate precludes, in the mind of the believer, any need for scientific analysis. Whatever the actual reasons, the fact remains that although the process has been widely recognized and its importance appreciated, it still awaits systematic treatment.

Formulation of the Problem

Although the phrase, unanticipated consequences of purposive social action, is in a measure self-explanatory, the setting of the problem demands further specification. In the first place, the greater part of this paper deals with isolated purposive acts rather than with their integration into a coherent system of action (though some reference will be made to the latter). This limitation is prescribed by expediency; a treatment of systems of action would introduce further unmanageable complications. Furthermore, *unforeseen* consequences should not be identified with consequences which are necessarily *undesirable* (from the standpoint of the actor). For though these results are unintended, they are not upon their occurrence always deemed axiologically negative. In short, undesired effects are not always undesirable effects. The intended and anticipated outcomes of purposive action, however, are always, in the very nature of the case, relatively desirable to the actor, though they may seem axiologically negative to an outside observer. This is true even in the polar instance where the intended result is "the lesser of two evils" or in such cases as suicide, ascetic mortification and self-torture which, in given situations, are deemed desirable relative to other possible alternatives.

Rigorously speaking, the *consequences* of purposive action are limited to those elements in the resulting situation that are exclusively the outcome of the action, that is, that would not have occurred had the action not taken place. Concretely, however, the consequences result from the interplay of the action and the objective situation, the conditions of action.[4] We shall be primarily concerned with a pattern of results of action under certain conditions. This still involves the problems of causal imputation (of which more later) though to a less pressing degree than consequences in the rigorous sense. These relatively concrete consequences may be differentiated into (a) consequences to the actor(s), (b) consequences to other persons mediated through the social structure, the culture, and the civilization.[5]

In considering *purposive* action, we are concerned with "conduct" as distinct from "behavior," that is, with action that involves motives and consequently a choice between alternatives.[6] For the time being, we take purposes as given, so that any theories that "reduce" purpose to conditioned reflexes or tropisms, which assert that motives are simply compounded of instinctual drives, may be considered as irrelevant. Psychological considerations of the source or origin of motives, although undoubtedly important for a more complete understanding of the mechanisms involved in the development of unexpected consequences of conduct, will be ignored.

Moreover, it is not assumed that social action always involves clear-cut, explicit pur-

pose. Such awareness of purpose may be unusual, the aim of action more often than not being nebulous and hazy. This is certainly the case with habitual action which, though it may originally have been induced by conscious purpose, is characteristically performed without such awareness. The significance of habitual action will be discussed later.

Above all, it must not be inferred that purposive action implies "rationality" of human action (that persons always use the objectively most adequate means for the attainment of their end).[7] In fact, part of my analysis is devoted to identifying those elements which account for concrete deviations from rationality of action. Moreover, rationality and irrationality are not to be identified with the success and failure of action, respectively. For in a situation where the number of *possible* actions for attaining a given end is severely limited, one acts rationally by selecting the means which, on the basis of the available evidence, has the greatest probability of attaining this goal[8] even though the goal may actually *not* be attained. . . . Contrariwise, an end may be attained by action that, on the basis of the knowledge available to the actor, is irrational (as in the case of "hunches").

Turning now to *action*, we differentiate this into two kinds: unorganized and formally organized. The first refers to actions of individuals considered distributively out of which may grow the second when like-minded individuals form an association in order to achieve a common purpose. Unanticipated consequences follow both types of action, although the second type seems to afford a better opportunity for sociological analysis since the processes of formal organization more often make for explicit statements of purpose and procedure.

Before turning to the actual analysis of the problem it is advisable to indicate two methodological pitfalls that are, moreover, common to all sociological investigations of purposive action. The first involves the problem of causal imputation, the problem of ascertaining the extent to which "consequences" can justifiably be attributed to certain actions. For example, to what extent has the recent increase in economic production in this country resulted from governmental measures? To what extent can the spread of organized crime be attributed to Prohibition? This ever-present difficulty of causal imputation must be solved for every empirical case.

The second problem is that of ascertaining the actual purposes of a given action. There is the difficulty, for instance, of discriminating between rationalization and truth in those cases where apparently unintended consequences are *ex post facto* declared to have been intended.[9] Rationalizations may occur in connection with nation-wide social planning just as in the classical instance of the horseman who, on being thrown from his steed, declared that he was "simply dismounting." This difficulty, though not completely obviated, is significantly reduced in cases of organized group action since the circumstance of organized action customarily demands explicit (though not always "true") statements of goal and procedure. Furthermore, it is easily possible to exaggerate this difficulty since in many, if indeed not in most, cases, the observer's own experience and knowledge of the situation enables him to arrive at a solution. Ultimately, the final test is this: does the juxtaposition of the overt action, our general knowledge of the actor(s) and the specific situation and the inferred or avowed purpose "make sense," is there between these, as Weber puts it, a "verständliche Sinnzusammenhang?" If the analyst self-consciously subjects these elements to such probing, conclusions about purpose can have evidential value. The evidence available will vary, and the probable error of the imputation of purpose will likewise vary.

Although these methodological difficulties are not discussed further in this paper, an effort has been made to take them into account in the substantive analysis.

Last, a frequent source of misunderstanding will be eliminated at the outset if it is realized that the factors involved in unanticipated consequences are—precisely—factors, and that none of these serves by itself to explain any concrete case.

Sources of Unanticipated Consequences

The most obvious limitation to a correct anticipation of consequences of action is provided by the existing state of knowledge. The extent of this limitation can be best appreciated by assuming the simplest case where the lack of adequate knowledge is the sole barrier to a correct anticipation.[10] Obviously, a very large number of concrete reasons for inadequate knowledge may be found, but it is also possible to summarize several classes of factors that are most important.

Ignorance

The first class derives from the type of knowledge—usually, perhaps exclusively—attained in the sciences of human behavior. The social scientist usually finds stochastic, not functional relationships.[11] This is to say, in the study of human behavior, there is found a set of different values of one variable associated with each value of the other variable(s), or in less formal language, the set of consequences of any repeated act is not constant but there is a range of possible consequences, *any one of which may follow the act in a given case*. In some instances, we have sufficient knowledge of the limits of the range of possible consequences, and even adequate knowledge for ascertaining the statistical (empirical) probabilities of the various possible consequences, but it is impossible to predict with certainty the results in any particular case. Our classifications of acts and situations never involve completely homogeneous categories nor even categories whose approximate degree of homogeneity is sufficient for the prediction of particular events.[12] We have here the paradox that whereas past experiences are the guide to our expectations on the assumption that certain past, present and future acts are sufficiently alike to be grouped in the same category, these experiences are in fact different. To the extent that these differences are pertinent to the outcome of the action and appropriate corrections for these differences are not adopted, the actual results will differ from the expected. As Poincaré has put it, ". . . small differences in the initial conditions produce very great ones in the final phenomena. . . . Prediction becomes impossible, and we have the fortuitous phenomenon."[13]

However, deviations from the usual consequences of an act can be anticipated by the actor who recognizes in the given situation some differences from previous similar situations. But insofar as these differences can themselves not be subsumed under general rules, the direction and extent of these deviations cannot be anticipated.[14] It is clear, then, that the partial knowledge in the light of which action is commonly carried on permits a varying range of unexpected outcomes of conduct.

Although we do not know the *amount* of knowledge necessary for foreknowledge, one may say in general that consequences are fortuitous when an exact knowledge of many details and facts (as distinct from general principles) is needed for even a highly approximate prediction. In other words, "chance consequences" are those occasioned by the interplay of forces and circumstances that are so numerous and complex that prediction of them is quite beyond our reach. This area of consequences should perhaps be distinguished from that of "ignorance," since it is related not to the knowledge actually in hand but to knowledge that can conceivably be obtained.[15]

The importance of ignorance as a factor is enhanced by the fact that the exigencies of practical life frequently compel us to act with some confidence even though it is manifest that the information on which we base our action is not complete. We usually act, as Knight has properly observed, not on the basis of scientific knowledge, but on that of opinion and estimate: Thus, situations that demand (or what is for our purposes tantamount to the same thing, that appear to the actor to demand) immediate action of some sort, will usually involve ignorance of certain aspects of the situation and will the more likely bring about unexpected results.

Even when immediate action is not required there is the *economic* problem of distributing our fundamental resources, time and energy. Time and energy are scarce means and economic behavior is concerned with the rational allocation of these means among alternative wants, only one of which

is the anticipation of consequences of action.[16] An economy of social engineers is no more practicable than an economy of laundrymen. It is the fault of the extreme antinoetic activists who promote the idea of action above all else to exaggerate this limit and to claim (in effect) that practically no resources be devoted to the acquisition of knowledge. On the other hand, the grain of truth in the anti-intellectualist position is that there are decided economic limits to the advisability of not acting until uncertainty is eliminated, and also psychological limits since, after the manner of Hamlet, excessive "forethought" of this kind precludes any action at all.

Error

A second major factor in unexpected consequences of conduct, perhaps as pervasive as ignorance, is error. Error may intrude itself, of course, in any phase of purposive action: we may err in our appraisal of the present situation, in our inference from this to the future, objective situation, in our selection of a course of action, or finally in the execution of the action chosen. A common fallacy is frequently involved in the too-ready assumption that actions which have in the past led to the desired outcome will continue to do so. This assumption is often fixed in the mechanism of habit and there often finds pragmatic justification. But precisely because habit is a mode of activity that has previously led to the attainment of certain ends, it tends to become automatic and undeliberative through continued repetition so that the actor fails to recognize that procedures which have been successful *in certain circumstances* need not be so *under any and all conditions*.[17] Just as rigidities in social organization often balk and block the satisfaction of new wants, so rigidities in individual behavior block the satisfaction of old wants in a changing social environment.

Error may also be involved in instances where the actor attends to only one or some of the pertinent aspects of the situation that influence the outcome of the action. This may range from the case of simple neglect (lack of thoroughness in examining the situation) to pathological obsession where there is a determined refusal or inability to consider certain elements of the problem. This last type has been extensively dealt with in the psychiatric literature. In cases of wish-fulfilment, emotional involvements lead to a distortion of the objective situation and of the probable future course of events; action predicated upon imaginary conditions must have unexpected consequences.

Imperious Immediacy of Interest

A third general type of factor, the "imperious immediacy of interest," refers to instances where the actor's paramount concern with the foreseen immediate consequences excludes consideration of further or other consequences of the same act. The most prominent elements in such immediacy of interest range from physiological needs to basic cultural values. Thus, Vico's imaginative example of the "origin of the family," which derived from the practice of men carrying their mates into caves to satisfy their sex drive out of the sight of God, might serve as a somewhat fantastic illustration of the first. Another kind of example is provided by that doctrine of classical economics in which the individual endeavoring to employ his capital where most profitable to him and thus tending to render the annual revenue of society as great as possible is, in the words of Adam Smith, led "by an invisible hand to promote an end which was no part of his intention."

However, after the acute analysis by Max Weber, it goes without saying that action motivated by interest is not antithetical to an intensive investigation of the conditions and means of successful action. On the contrary, it would seem that interest, if it is to be satisfied, requires objective analysis of situation and instrumentality, as is assumed to be characteristic of "economic man." The irony is that intense interest often tends to preclude such analysis precisely because strong concern with the satisfaction of the immediate interest is a psychological generator of emotional bias, with consequent lopsidedness or failure to engage in the required calculations. It is as much a fallacious assumption to hold that interested action necessarily entails a rational calculation of the elements in the situation[18] as to deny rationality any and all influence over such con-

duct. Moreover, action in which the element of immediacy of interest is involved may be rational in terms of the values basic to that interest but irrational in terms of the life organization of the individual. Rational, in the sense that it is an action which may be expected to lead to the attainment of the specific goal; irrational, in the sense that it may defeat the pursuit or attainment of other values not, at the moment, paramount but which nonetheless form an integral part of the individual's scale of values. Thus, *precisely because a particular action is not carried out in a psychological or social vacuum, its effects will ramify into other spheres of value and interest*. For example, the practice of birth control for "economic reasons" influences the age-composition and size of sibships with profound consequences of a psychological and social character and, in larger aggregations, of course, affects the rate of population growth.

Basic Values

Superficially similar to the factor of immediacy of interest, but differing from it in a significant theoretical sense, is that of basic values. This refers to instances where further consequences of action are not considered because of the felt necessity of the action enjoined by fundamental values. The classical analysis is Weber's study of the Protestant Ethic and the spirit of capitalism. He has properly generalized this case, saying that active asceticism paradoxically leads to its own decline through the accumulation of wealth and possessions entailed by the conjunction of intense productive activity and decreased consumption.

The process contributes much to the dynamic of social and cultural change, as has been recognized with varying degrees of cogency by Hegel, Marx, Wundt, and many others. The empirical observation is incontestable: activities oriented toward certain values release processes that so react as to change the very scale of values which precipitated them. This process can come about when a system of basic values enjoins certain *specific* actions, and adherents are concerned not with the objective consequences of these actions but with the subjective satisfaction of duty well performed. Or, action in accordance with a dominant set of values tends to be focused upon that particular value-area. But with the complex interaction that constitutes society, action ramifies. Its consequences are not restricted to the specific area in which they are intended to center and occur in interrelated fields explicitly ignored at the time of action. Yet it is because these fields are in fact interrelated that the further consequences in adjacent areas tend to *react* upon the fundamental value-system. It is this usually unlooked-for reaction that constitutes a most important element in the process of secularization, of the transformation or breakdown of basic value-systems. Here is the essential paradox of social action—the "realization" of values may lead to their renunciation. We may paraphrase Goethe and speak of "Die Kraft, die stets das Gute will, und stets das Böse schafft."

Self-Defeating Predictions

There is one other circumstance, peculiar to human conduct, that stands in the way of successful social prediction and planning. Public predictions of future social developments are frequently not sustained precisely because the prediction has become a new element in the concrete situation, thus tending to change the initial course of developments. This is not true of prediction in fields that do not pertain to human conduct. Thus the prediction of the return of Halley's comet does not in any way influence the orbit of that comet; but, to take a concrete social example, Marx' prediction of the progressive concentration of wealth and increasing misery of the masses did influence the very process predicted. For at least one of the consequences of socialist preaching in the nineteenth century was the spread of organization of labor, which, made conscious of its unfavorable bargaining position in cases of individual contract, organized to enjoy the advantages of collective bargaining, thus slowing up, if not eliminating, the developments that Marx had predicted.[19]

Thus, to the extent that the predictions of social scientists are made public and action proceeds with full cognizance of these predictions, the "other-things-being-equal" condition tacitly assumed in all forecasting is not fulfilled. Other things will not be equal just because the scientist has introduced a new "other thing"—his prediction.[20] This contingency may often account for social movements developing in utterly unanticipated directions, and it hence assumes considerable importance for social planning.

The foregoing discussion represents no more than the briefest exposition of the major elements involved in one fundamental social process. It would take us too far afield, and certainly beyond the compass of this paper, to examine exhaustively the implications of this analysis for social prediction, control, and planning. We may maintain, however, even at this preliminary juncture, that no blanket statement categorically affirming or denying the practical feasibility of *all* social planning is warranted. Before we may indulge in such generalizations, we must examine and classify the *types* of social action and organization with reference to the elements here discussed and then refer our generalizations to these essentially different types. If the present analysis has served to set the problem, even in only its paramount aspects, and to direct attention toward the need for a systematic and objective study of the elements involved in the development of unanticipated consequences of purposive social action, the treatment of which has for much too long been consigned to the realm of theology and speculative philosophy, then it has achieved its avowed purpose.

Endnotes

1. Some of the theorists, though their contributions are by no means of equal importance, are: Machiavelli, Vico, Adam Smith (and some later classical economists), Marx, Engels, Wundt, Pareto, Max Weber, Graham Wallas, Cooley, Sorokin, Gini, Chapin, von Schelting.

2. This problem has been related to such heterogeneous subjects as: the problem of evil (theodicy), moral responsibility, free will, predestination, deism, teleology, fatalism, logical, illogical and nonlogical behavior, social prediction, planning and control, social cycles, the pleasure- and reality principles, and historical "accidents."

3. Some of the terms by which the whole or certain aspects of the process have been known are: Providence (immanent or transcendental), Moira,

Paradoxie der Folgen, Schicksal, social forces, heterogony of ends, immanent causation, dialectical movement, principle of emergence and creative synthesis.

4. Cf. Frank H. Knight, *Risk, Uncertainty and Profit* (Boston and New York: Houghton Mifflin Co., 1921), pp. 201–2. Professor Knight's doctoral dissertation represents by far the most searching treatment of certain phases of this problem that I have yet seen.

5. For the distinction between society, culture and civilization, see Alfred Weber, "Prinzipielles zur Kultursoziologie: Gesellschaftsprozess, Civilisationsprozess und Kulturbewegung," *Archiv für Sozialwissenschaft und Sozialpolitik*, 47, 1920, pp. 1–49; R. K. Merton, "Civilization and Culture," *Sociology and Social Research* 21 (1936), pp.103–13.

6. Knight, *op. cit.*, p. 52.

7. Max Weber, *Wirtschaft und Gesellschaft* (Tübingen: J. C. B. Mohr, 1925), pp. 3 ff.

8. See J. Bertrand, *Calcul des probabilités* (Paris, 1889), pp. 90 ff.; J. M. Keynes, *A Treatise on Probability* (London: The Macmillan Co., 1921), Chap. XXVI.

9. This introduces the problem of "chance," which will be treated in another connection. It should be realized that the aim of an action and the circumstances that actually ensue may coincide without the latter being a consequence of the action. Moreover, the longer the interval of time between the action and the circumstances in view, the greater the probability (in the absence of contrary evidence) that these circumstances have happened "by chance." Lastly, if this interval is greatly extended, the probability that the desired circumstances will occur fortuitously may increase until virtually the point of certainty. This reasoning is perhaps applicable to the case of governmental action "restoring prosperity." Compare V. Pareto, *Traité de sociologie générale* (Paris: Payot, 1917), II, par. 1977.

10. Most discussions of unanticipated consequences limit the explanation of unanticipated consequences to this one factor of ignorance. Such a view either reduces itself to a sheer tautology or exaggerates the role of only one of many factors. In the first instance, the argument runs in this fashion: "if we had only known enough, we could have anticipated the consequences which, as it happens, were unforeseen." The evident fallacy in this *post mortem* argument rests in the word "enough" which is implicitly taken to mean "enough knowledge to foresee" the consequences of our action. It is then no difficult matter to uphold the contention. This viewpoint is basic to several schools of educational theory, just as it was to Comte's dictum, *savoir pour prevoir, prevoir pour*

pouvoir. This intellectualist stand has gained credence partly because of its implicit optimism and because of the indubitable fact that sheer ignorance does actually account for the occurrence of some unforeseen consequences *in some cases*.

11. Cf. A. A. Tschuprow, *Grundbegriffe und Grundprobleme der Korrelationstheorie* (Leipzig: B. G. Teubner, 1925), pp. 20 ff., where he introduces the term "stochastic." It is apparent that stochastic associations are obtained because we have not ascertained, or having ascertained, have not controlled the other variables in the situation that influence the final result.

12. A classification into completely homogeneous categories would, of course, lead to functional associations and would permit successful prediction, but the aspects of social action which are of practical importance are too varied and numerous to permit such homogeneous classification.

13. Henri Poincaré, *Calcul des probabilités* (Paris, 1912), p. 2.

14. The actor's awareness of his ignorance and its implications is perhaps most acute in the type of conduct which Thomas and Znaniecki attribute to the wish for "new experience." This is the case where unforeseen consequences actually constitute the purpose of action, but there is always the tacit assumption that the consequences will be desirable.

15. Cf. Keynes, *op. cit.*, p. 295. This distinction corresponds to that made by Keynes between "subjective chance" (broadly, ignorance) and "objective chance" (where even additional wide knowledge of general principles would not suffice to foresee the consequences of a particular act). Much the same distinction appears in the works of Poincaré and Venn, among others.

16. Cf. Knight, *op. cit.*, p. 348. The reasoning is also applicable to cases where the occupation of certain individuals (e.g., social engineers and scientists) is devoted solely to such efforts, since then it is a correlative question of the distribution of the resources of society. Furthermore, there is the practical problem of the communicability of knowledge so obtained, since it may be very complex; the effort to assimilate such knowledge leads back to the same problem of distribution of resources [and costs of information].

17. Similar fallacies in the field of thought have been variously designated as "the philosophical fallacy" (Dewey), the "principle of limits" (Sorokin, Bridgman) and, with a somewhat different emphasis, "the fallacy of misplaced concreteness" (Whitehead). [For an application of the general idea to the case of organizations, see . . . "Bureaucratic Structure and Personality," in Mer-

ton, *Social Theory and Social Structure* (New York: The Free Press, 1968, enlarged ed.), pp. 249–60.]

18. The assumption is tenable only in a normative sense. Obviously such calculation, within the limits specified in our previous discussion, *should* be made if the probability of satisfying the interest is to be at a maximum. The error lies in confusing norm with actuality.

19. Corrado Gini, *Prime linée di patologia economica* (Milan: A. Giuffè, 1935), pp. 72–75. John Venn uses the picturesque term "suicidal prophecies" to refer to this process and properly observes that it represents a class of con-siderations which have been much neglected by the various sciences of human conduct. See his *Logic of Chance* (London, 1888), pp. 225–26.

20. [For the correlative process, see the paper, "The Self-Fulfilling Prophecy" first published a dozen years after this one, and reprinted in Merton, *op. cit.*, 1968, pp. 475–90.]

31
The Functional Prerequisites of Social Systems

Talcott Parsons

Talcott Parsons (1902–1979) was the preeminent social theorist of his generation, and during the two decades after World War II his home institution, Harvard, became in effect the center of the sociological universe. His theoretical work has carried several labels, including functionalism, structural-functionalism, and systems theory. His first major book, *The Structure of Social Action* (1937), was an exegesis of the works of key figures in the formative years of the discipline. He examined them in order to articulate, despite their manifold differences, what Parsons saw as a theoretical convergence that set the foundation for his subsequent work. This selection derives from *The Social System* (1951), his first and perhaps most comprehensive attempt at a theoretical synthesis. Parsons' prose style, as he knew only too well, left something to be desired. It was often verbose and opaque. However, this selection reveals a Parsons quite capable of lucid writing. He sketches the interrelated character of personality, social system, and culture, identifying key elements of personalities and culture that amount to fundamental prerequisites for the viability of any social system.

Interactive relationships analyzed in terms of statuses and roles occur as we have seen in systems. If such a system is to constitute a persistent order or to undergo an orderly[1] process of developmental change, certain functional prerequisites must be met. A brief discussion of these functional prerequisites is in order because it provides the setting for a more extended analysis of the points of reference for analyzing the structure of social systems.

The problem of functional prerequisites is a protean problem because of the variety of different levels on which it may be approached. What we propose here is to start on the most general and therefore formal level of action theory and proceed to introduce specifications step by step. It should be possible to do this in a sufficiently orderly fashion.

The broadest framework of such an analysis is directly deducible from the considerations about action in general. . . . The basis of this is the insight that action systems are structured about three integrative foci, the individual actor, the interactive system, and a system of cultural patterning.[2] Each implies the others and therefore the variability of any one is limited by its compatibility with the minimum conditions of functioning of each of the other two.

Looked at from the perspective of any one integrate of action such as the social system there are in turn two aspects of this reciprocal interrelation with each of the others. First, a social system cannot be so structured as to be radically incompatible with the conditions of functioning of its component individual actors as biological organisms and as personalities, or of the relatively stable integration of a cultural system. Secondly, in turn the social system, on both fronts, depends on the requisite minimum of "support" from each of the other systems. It must, that is, have a sufficient proportion of its component actors adequately motivated to act in accordance with the requirements of its role system, positively in the fulfillment of expectations and negatively in abstention from too much disruptive, i.e., deviant, behavior. It must on the other hand avoid commitment to cultural patterns which either fail to define a minimum of order or which place impossible demands on people and thereby generate deviance and conflict to a degree which is incompatible with the minimum conditions of stability or orderly development. These problems may be briefly taken up in turn.

We have tried to make clear that there is no simple relation between personalities and social systems. Because of this fact, in the present state of knowledge it is not possible to define precisely what are the minimum needs of individual actors, so only certain rather general things can be said. From the point of view of functioning of the social system, it is not the needs of all the participant actors which must be met, nor all the needs of any one, but only a sufficient proportion for a sufficient fraction of the population. It is indeed a very general phenomenon that social forces are directly responsible for injury to or destruction of some individuals and some of the wants or needs of all individuals, and though this may be reduced it is highly probable that it cannot be eliminated under realistic conditions. To cite a very simple case, a war cannot be won without casualties, and acceptance of war is sometimes a condition of survival of a social system as a distinctive system.

The elements of this class of functional prerequisites may be said to begin with the biological prerequisites of individual life, like nutrition and physical safety. They go on to the subtler problems of the conditions of minimum stability of personality. It seems to be reasonably well established that there are minimum conditions of socialization with respect for instance to the relation between affectional support and security, without which a functioning personality cannot be built up. The present task is not to attempt to analyze these borderline problems, but only to make clear where they fit in relation to the theory of the social system. These minimum needs of individual actors constitute a set of conditions to which the social system must be adapted. If the variation of the latter goes too far in a given direction this will tend to set up repercussions which will in turn tend to produce deviant behavior in the actors in question, behavior which is either positively disruptive or involves withdrawal from functionally important activities. Such a need, as a functional prerequisite, may be likened to a spring. The less adequately it is met, the more "pressure" it will take to realize certain patterns of social action in the face of it, and hence the less energy will be available for other purposes. At certain points for certain individuals or classes of them then the pressure may become too great and the spring may break—such persons no longer participate in the interactive system of personality and social system.[3]

The obverse of the functional prerequisite of meeting a minimum proportion of the needs of the individual actors, is the need to secure adequate participation of a sufficient proportion of these actors in the social system, that is to motivate them adequately to the performances which may be necessary if the social system in question is to persist or develop. Indeed it is because it is a condition of this that the need to satisfy minimum needs of actors is a prerequisite at all.

The prerequisite of adequate motivation in turn subdivides into two main aspects, a negative and a positive. The negative is that of a minimum of control over potentially disruptive behavior. This means action which interferes with the action of others in their roles in the social system. It may involve either aggressive action toward others or merely action which has deleterious consequences for others or for an aspect of the system, without aggressive intent.

The field is highly complex but perhaps one particular aspect of it may be singled out for special mention. This is that in terms of functional significance relative to the social system, the significance of an action or class of them is to be understood not directly and primarily in terms of its motivation but of its actual or probable consequences for the system. In this sense the pursuit of "private interests" may be highly disruptive under certain circumstances even though the content of the interests, for example in religious terms, may be such as to be rather generally ethically approved. Similarly conflict as such may be highly disruptive. If it becomes sufficiently severe the functional problem for the system becomes the control of the conflict as such. In such a case the merits of the "case" of one or the other of the parties may become of quite secondary importance.

In general terms the functional problem for a social system of minimizing potentially disruptive behavior and the motivation to it, may be called the "motivational problem of order." Because of certain further features of social systems . . . the present discussion should lead up to consideration of certain relatively specific classes of potential disruption, notably the problem of opportunity, the problem of prestige allocation, and the problem of power. There is, that is to say, an immense variety of particular acts which are disruptive in that they interfere with the role-performance of one or more other actors. So long, however, as they remain nearly randomly distributed they may reduce the efficiency of the system by depressing levels of role performance, but still not constitute a threat to its stability. This latter may develop when disruptive tendencies become organized as a sub-system in such a way as to impinge on strategic points in the social system itself. It is as such strategic points that the problems of opportunity, prestige and power will be treated below.[4]

The distinction between the negative and the positive aspects of the problem of adequate motivation is relative and gradual. Both present functional problems in terms of the operation of the social system, which focus attention on the mechanisms which fit into the relevant context. But in spite of this relativity there is an important distinction between action which is positively disruptive of a going system of social relationships, and simple withdrawal of the individual from performance of his obligations. The principal criterion would be that in the latter case the only interference with others would consist in forcing them to do without the benefits expected from a person's actions. The possibility of withdrawal in fact defines one of the most important directions of deviant behavior, and enters as we shall see in most important ways into the structure of the problems and mechanisms of social control. Illness is for example one of the most important types of withdrawal behavior in our society. . . .

Again in relation to withdrawal as a type of failure to be motivated to adequate role performance, it must be made clear that the negative aspect of withdrawal is *not* defined in motivational terms but in functional terms relative to the social system. Precisely because people are dependent on each other's performances, simple withdrawal from fulfillment of expectations may, motivationally speaking, be a highly aggressive act, and may in fact injure the other severely. But in part precisely because it does not correspond to the motivational distinction the functional distinction is highly significant as will become evident. It provides a point of reference for the analysis of the directions of deviant behavior and hence places such behavior in relation to problems of the mechanisms of operation of the social system.

The prerequisite of adequate motivation gives us one of the primary starting points for building up to the concepts of role and of institutionalization. Fundamentally the problem is, will the personalities developed within a social system, at whatever stage in the life cycle, "spontaneously" act in such ways as to fulfill the functional prerequisites of the social systems of which they are parts, or is it necessary to look for relatively specific mechanisms, that is, modes of organization of the motivational systems of personalities, which can be understood in direct relation to the socially structured level or role behavior? The older "psychological" view that societies are resultants of the independently determined "traits" of individuals would take the first alternative. The modern sociological view tends to emphasize the second.

Statement of the problem of adequate motivation not only poses in general the problems of the mechanisms of socialization and of social control and their relation to the dynamics of the social system, but it provides the setting for an approach to the analysis of the relevant mechanisms. Personality psychology, as we have seen, is becoming highly oriented to the actor's relational system, that is, his orientation to objects. When this fact is combined with the fundamental place of the concept of expectations in the theory of action, it becomes clear that one central aspect of the general and especially the cathectic orientation of the actor is his set of need-dispositions toward the fulfillment of role expectations, in the first place those of other significant actors but also his own. There is, in the personality structure of the individual actor a "conformity-alienation" dimension in the sense of a disposition to conform with the expectations of others or to be alienated from them. When these relevant expectations are those relative to the fulfillment of role-obligations, this conformity-alienation balance, in general or in particular role contexts, becomes a central focus of the articulation of the motivational system of the personality with the structure of the social system.

It is furthermore in the present context of the problem of adequate motivation of role-expectation fulfillment that the basic significance for the social system of two fundamental properties of biological "human nature" may best be briefly brought to attention. The first of these is the much discussed "plasticity" of the human organism, its capacity to learn any one of a large number of alternative patterns of behavior instead of being bound by its genetic constitution to a very limited range of alternatives. It is of course within the limits of this plasticity that the independent determinant significance of cultural and social factors in action must be sought. The clear demonstration of determination in terms of the genes automatically narrows the range of relevance of the factors which are of theoretical interest in the sciences of action, except for their possible bearing on the problems of assortative mating which influence the processes of combination and recombination of genetic strains. The limits of plasticity are for the most part still unknown.[5]

The second characteristic of human nature in the biological sense is what may be called "sensitivity." By this is meant the accessibility of the human individual to influence by the attitudes of others in the social interaction process, and the resulting dependence on receiving relatively particular and specific reactions. What this provides essentially is the motivational basis for accessibility to influence in the learning process. Thus the attitudes of others are probably of first rate importance in all human learning, but are particularly crucial in motivating the acceptance of value-orientation patterns, with their legitimation of the renunciations which are essential to the achievement of a disciplined integration of personality. Without this discipline the stability of expectations in relation to their fulfillment which is essential for a functioning social system would not be possible. It is highly probable that one of the principal limitations on the social potentialities of animals on other than an instinct basis, lies in the absence or weakness of this lever. The physiological dependency of the human infant is associated with its capacity for developing emotional dependency which in turn is an essential condition of much of social learning.

It has not been common in discussions of the functional prerequisites of social systems to include explicit treatment of cultural prerequisites, but the need to do so seems to follow directly from the major premises of action theory as set forth above. The integration of cultural patterns as well as their specific content involve factors which at any given time are independent of the other elements for the action system and yet must be articulated with them. Such integration imposes "imperatives" on the other elements just as truly as is the case the other way around. This major functional problem area of the social system may be subdivided along the same lines as in the case of the motivational problem.

In the first place there are minimum social conditions necessary for the production, maintenance and development of cultural systems in general and of particular types of cultural system. It may be presumed that disruption of the communication system of a society is ultimately just as dangerous as disruption of its system of order in the above sense of motivational integration. This is an aspect of "anomie" which deserves much more explicit analysis than it has received. Perhaps the most obvious specific example is provided by the role of language. We know quite definitely that the individual does not develop language spontaneously without undergoing a socially structured learning process in relation to others. It is quite definite that this process must be part of a system of social relations which is orderly within certain limits, however difficult it may be to specify the limits in detail. It is altogether probable that many protohuman groups failed to make the transition to the human sociocultural level of action because of failure to fulfill the prerequisites of the emergence of language or of some other functionally essential aspects of culture.

Thus a social system in the present sense is not possible without language, and without certain other minimum patterns of culture, such as empirical knowledge necessary to cope with situational exigencies, and sufficiently integrated patterns of expressive symbolism and of value orientation. A social system which leads to too drastic disruption of its culture, for example through blocking the processes of its acquisition, would be exposed to social as well as cultural disintegration.

We do not accurately know the cultural limits of "human society," so exactly what the above limits may be remains to be determined. With respect to certain more specific types of cultural pattern, however, we have relatively detailed knowledge—we shall, for example, discuss modern science from this point of view below. In any case the determination of these conditions is an important field of sociological research.

One final remark in orientation to the general problem. Culture may of course be "embodied" in physical form independently of particular actors, e.g., knowledge in books, but it is a cardinal principle of the theory of action that culture is not merely "situational" relative to action but becomes directly constitutive of personalities as such through what personality psychologists now tend to call "internalization." The minimum cultural prerequisites of a social system may thus be said to operate at least in part through the functions of culture for personality. Without the requisite cultural resources to be assimilated through internalization it is not possible for a human level of personality to emerge and hence for a human type of social system to develop.

The other aspect of the problem of prerequisites on the cultural side is that of adequate cultural resources and organization for the maintenance of the social system. This has already been touched upon in the discussions above, but a few additional remarks may be made. Perhaps the most obvious type of case is instrumental knowledge. Without a minimum of technical lore which makes it possible to deal with the physical environment and with other human beings no human society would be possible. This in turn presupposes language. But similar considerations also apply to the other departments of culture, to non-empirical existential ideas, to expressive symbol systems and above all to patterns of value-orientation about which much will have to be said in what follows.

It was pointed out above that tendencies to deviant behavior on the part of the component actors pose functional "problems" for the social system in the sense that they must be counteracted by "mechanisms of control" unless dysfunctional consequences are to ensue. The parallel on the cultural side is the case where the maintenance of certain cultural patterns as integral parts of the going system of action imposes certain strains. This may be true both on the personality and the social system levels. The most obvious cases are those of a value-orientation pattern and of cognitive beliefs which are motivationally difficult to conform with. Such difficulty might be attributable to a conflict with reality. Thus within the area covered by well established medical science the maintenance of and action upon some beliefs of Christian Science may impose a serious strain on the actor especially where he cannot escape knowing the medical views. Or it may be a matter of difficulty in attaining conformative motivation, as in the case where certain types of socialization tend to generate deeply anti-authoritarian sentiments so that at least some kinds of authority cannot be tolerated by some people. In particular a utopian ideal if accepted and institutionalized imposes strains on the social system.

Though the limits in this as in the other cases are in general not known, it is safe to say not only that the social system must be able to keep a minimum of culture going, but vice versa, any given culture must be compatible with a social system to a minimum degree if its patterns are not to become extinct, and if the latter is to continue functioning unchanged. Analysis of the mediating mechanisms between the cultural patterns and the concrete action systems in its motivational aspect constitutes one of the most important problem areas of action theory and specifically of the theory of social systems. . . .

Endnotes

1. An orderly process in this sense is contrasted with the disintegration of a system. Disintegration in this sense means disappearance of the boundaries of the system relative to its environment. Cf. *Values, Motives, and Systems of Action*, Chapter I.

2. And also in a different sense about the non-action environment, the physical aspects of the situation.

3. It is, of course, highly important not to invent ad hoc generalizations about these prerequisites which allegedly explain certain classes of concrete social phenomena. This procedure is especially tempting because such an ad hoc hypothesis can serve to absolve the investigator from the difficult analysis of the internal balances and processes of the social system itself. In its cruder forms this procedure has played a very prominent part in the history of social thought, as in the currency of theories that virtually all social phenomena were determined by the genetic constitution of populations or their geographical environments. It is an index of the increasing maturity of our science that such sweeping formulae are no longer considered to merit even serious discussion. Both the positive role of such conditioning factors and of internal social processes are in general terms fully established. But the general formulae do not solve the specific problems. The task is to unravel the complex patterns of interaction between the two classes of factors.

4. It is in this kind of a context that the distinction between manifest and latent function becomes significant. In general only within limited ranges and to a limited extent are the consequences which the sociologist takes as his standard for the analysis of the systemic significance of actions explicitly intended by the actor, individual or collective. It is these unintended consequences which constitute the latent functions or dysfunctions of the actions. Cf. Robert K. Merton, *Social Theory and Social Structure*, Chapter I.

5. From the point of view of action theory and specifically that of the social system it may be said that the burden of proof rests upon him who would assert that what has been considered an action theory problem is adequately solved by invoking the role of such sub-action determinants of behavior. This will often turn out to be the case, but resort to ad hoc hypotheses on this level which have failed to stand up under criticism and further investigation, has been so prominent in the history of social science that we must insist on this burden of proof maxim.

32

Functional Differentiation

Niklas Luhmann

Niklas Luhmann (1927–1998) was perhaps the most important German thinker associated with systems theory. His work is indebted to, while seeking to go beyond, that of Talcott Parsons. In addition, Luhmann was influenced by cybernetic theories. He had an ongoing dialogue with his German contemporary Jürgen Habermas, but unlike the writings of that sociologist, which offer a neo-Marxist critique of modern capitalism, the political implications of Luhmann's work are not immediately evident. In this essay from 1986, he explores the ways complex advanced industrial societies, characterized by considerable structural and functional differentiation, address societal problems. In focusing on issues related to environmental concerns, he contends that the tendency to think that problems such as air and water pollution can be resolved by recourse to value commitments to a clean environment are overly simplistic. Instead, he suggests, we must realize that the ways we look at such issues are a consequence of the structure of a society in which we can no longer presume to speak about the unity of the system.

The preceding . . . discussed the existence of ecological problems and the ways in which they trigger resonance in the function systems of modern society. But in the analysis of particular systems the sociologist should not lose sight of the unity of society. Indeed, the comparability of function systems and certain agreements in the structures of their differentiation—we examined the differentiation of codes and programs but this is only one of many viewpoints—point to this. The unity of the entire system resides in the way it operates and the form of its differentiation. The more clearly social evolution approaches a specific kind of operation, namely, meaningful communication, and the primacy of functional differentiation *vis-à-vis* other forms of internal system-formation the more obvious its corresponding structures become. If one eliminates all anachronisms, the conceptual and theoretical means by which society describes itself in its scientific system—in this case in sociology—have to be adapted to this.

Above all, one must realize that theories of hierarchy, delegation or decentralization that begin from an apex or center are incapable of grasping contemporary society adequately. They presuppose a channelling of the communication flow that does not exist nor can even be produced. Furthermore, the attempts to describe the relation of state and economy according to the model of centralization and decentralization and then, when it is politically expedient, to praise the advantages of decentralized decision-making and to warn against its disadvantages is unrealistic. In reality, the economy is a system that is highly centralized by the money-mechanism but with a concomitant, extensive decentralization of decision-making, whereas the political system organizes the political organisation more or less centrally and handles political influences according to entirely different models, like those of social movements. These systems distinguish themselves through the way in which they try to combine and reinforce centralization and decentralization according to their respective media of communication. But their independencies cannot be understood according to the model of centralization and decentralization.

Thus it is pointless to try to conceive the unity of modern society as the organization of a network of channels of communication, steering-centers and impulse receivers. One immediately gets the impression that good intentions cannot be realized because somewhere something is directed against them[1] which frequently ends up in mythical explanations in terms of capitalism, bureaucracy or complexity. With the help of a theory of system differentiation it is evident, however, that every formation of a subsystem is nothing more than a *new expression for the unity of the whole system*.[2] Every formation of a subsystem breaks the unity of the whole system down into a specific difference of system and environment, i.e., of the subsystem and its environment within the encompassing system. Every subsystem therefore, can use such a boundary line to reflect the entire system, in its own specific way; one that leaves other possibilities of subsystem formation open. For example, a political system can interpret society as the relation of consensus and the exercise of force and then attempt to optimize its own relation to these conditions. On one hand, consensus and force are specific operations, but on the other, they are also all-encompassing formulas and horizons for social conditions and consequences that can never be made completely transparent in the political subsystem.

Every function system, together with *its* environment, reconstructs *society*. Therefore, every function system can plausibly presume to be society *for itself*, if and in so far as it is open to its *own* environment. With the closure of its own autopoiesis it serves *one* function of *the* societal system (society). With openness to environmental conditions and changes it realizes that this has to occur *in the* societal system because society cannot specialize *itself* to one function alone. This is a matter of the operationalization of a paradox. Presented as the difference of system and environment the function system is and is not society at the same time. It operates closed and open at the same time and confers exclusivity on its own claim to reality, even if only in the sense of a necessary, operative illusion. It confers bivalence upon its own code and excludes third values that lurk in the environment's opacity and the susceptibility to surprise. In this way society reproduces itself as unity and difference at the same time. Of course, this does not eliminate the paradox of *unitas multiplex*. It reappears within the system as opacities, illusions, disturbances and the need for screening-off—as transcendence in immanence, to put it in terms of the religious system's selective coding.

This systems-theoretical analysis highlights the significance and the preference of modern society for institutions like the market or democracy. Such descriptions symbolize the unity of closure and openness, of functional logic and sensibility. Of course, the market is not a real one (as it could be seen to be from the cousin's corner window)[3] and democracy no longer means that the people rule. This is a matter of a semantic coding of an ultimately paradoxical state of affairs. It explains the meaning and the illusionary components of these concepts, explains the weakness of the corresponding theories and explains why, since the beginning of the eighteenth century, a kind of self-critique has accompanied this.

Yet the unity of this order is already necessarily given by evolution, i.e., through the continual adjustment of possibilities. Evolution does not guarantee either the selection of the best of all possible worlds nor 'progress' in any sense. At first evolutionary selection produces a very improbable, highly complex order. It transforms an improbable order into a probable (functional) one. This is exactly what concepts like negentropy or complexity intend. But it does not mean that the improbability disappears or is inactualized as prehistory. It is co-transformed and *'aufgehoben'* in Hegel's famous sense. It remains a structurally precipitated risk that cannot be negated.

Stratified societies already had to deal with problematical consequences of their own structural decisions. These were expressed, for example, as the constant conflict between inherited honors and distinctions and new ones, as the unfulfillable obligation to prescribe a class-specific endogamy and not least of all as the conflicts that result from centralizing the control of access to scarce resources, above all of the ownership of land. Compared to modern society these are relatively harmless problems for which historically stable solutions were found in many cases. The transition to primarily functional differentiation leads to a completely different constellation with higher risks and more intensified problems resulting from structural achievements. Society's self-exposure to ecological dangers is therefore not a completely new problem. But it is a problem that, today, is coming dramatically to the fore.

With functional differentiation the principle of elastic adaptation through processes of substitution becomes the principle of the specification of subsystems. Its consequence is that, more than ever before, functional equivalents can be projected and actualized *but only in the context of the subsystems and their coding*. Extreme elasticity is purchased at the cost of the peculiar rigidity of its contextual conditions. Everything appears as contingent. But the realization of other possibilities is bound to specific system references. Every binary code claims universal validity, but only for its own perspective. Everything, for example, can be either true or false, but only true or false according to the specific theoretical programs of the scientific system. Above all, this means that no function system can step in for any other. None can replace or even relieve any other. Politics cannot be substituted for the economy, nor the economy for science, nor science for law or religion nor religion for politics, etc., in any conceivable intersystem relations.

Of course, this structural barrier does not exclude corresponding attempts. But they must be purchased at the price of dedifferentiation (*Entdifferenzierung*), i.e., with the surrender of the advantages of functional differentiation. This can be seen clearly in socialism's experiments with the politization of the productive sector of the economy or even in tendencies towards the 'Islamization' of politics, the economy and law. Moreover, these are carried out only partially. For example, they do not touch on money (but, at best, the purely economic calculation of capital investment and prices) and are arrested by an immune reaction of the system of the world society.

The structurally imposed non-substitutability of function systems does not exclude interdependencies of every kind. A flowering economy is also a political blessing—and vice versa. This does not mean that the economy could fulfill a political function, namely, to produce collectively binding decisions (to whose profit?). Instead, the non-substitutability of functions (i.e., the regulation of substitution by functions) is compensated by increasing interdependencies. Precisely because function systems cannot replace one another they support and burden one another reciprocally. It is their irreplace-

ability that imposes the continual displacement of problems from one system into another. The result is a simultaneous intensification of independencies and interdependencies (dependencies) whose operative and structural balance inflates the individual systems with an immense uncontrollable complexity.

This same state of affairs can be characterized as a progressive resolution and reorganization of the structural redundancies of society. The certainties that lay in multifunctional mechanisms and that specified systems for different functions and programmed them to 'not only/but also' were abandoned. This is shown very clearly by the reduction of the social relevance of the family and morality. Instead, new redundancies were created that rested on the differentiation of functional perspectives and '*ceteris paribus*' clauses. But this does not safeguard the interdependencies between the function systems and the social effects of the change of one for the other. Time, then, becomes relevant: the consequences result only after a certain amount of time and then they have to be handled with new means that are, once again, specific to the system. This is accomplished without being able to go back to the initiating causes. Complexity is temporalized[4] and so are the ideas of certainty. The future becomes laden with hopes and fears, in any event, with the expectation that it will be different. The transformation of results into problems is accelerated, and structural precautions (for example, for sufficient liquidity or for invariably functional legislation) are established so that such a reproblematization of the solution is always possible.

The rejection of substitutability has to be understood essentially as the rejection of redundancy, i.e., as the rejection of multiple safeguarding. As we know, the rejection of redundancy restricts the system's possibilities of learning from disturbances and environmental 'noises'.[5] This implies that a functionally differentiated system cannot adapt itself to environmental changes as well as systems that are constructed more simply although it increasingly initiates concomitant environmental changes. But this is only part of the truth. For, through abstract coding and the functional specification of subsystems, functional differentiation makes a large measure of sensibility and learning possible on this level. This state of affairs becomes quite complicated when many system levels have to be kept in view at the same time. Society's rejection of redundancy is compensated on the level of subsystems, and the problem is that this is the only place that this can occur. Family households, moralities and religious cosmologies are replaced by an arrangement in which highly organized capacities for substitution and recuperation remain bound to specific functions that operate at the cost of ignoring other functions. Because of this the consequences of adaptive changes are situated within a complex net of dependencies and independencies. In part, they lead to unforeseen extensions, in part they are absorbed. In such cases simple estimations and simple comparisons of the efficiency of different social formations are insufficient and inadvisable.

A further consequence of functional differentiation resides in the intensification of apparent contingencies on the structural level of all function systems. Examples of this are the replacement of natural by positive law, the democratic change of governments, the still merely hypothetical character of the validity of theories, the possibility of the free choice of a spouse and not least of all everything that is experienced as 'a market decision' (with whoever or whatever may decide) and is subjected to criticism. The result is that much of what was previously experienced as nature is presented as a decision and needs justification. Thus a need arises for new 'inviolate levels'. . . . for a more rational and justifiable a priori or, finally, for 'values'.[6] Evidently, the strangely non-binding compulsion of values correlates to a widespread discontent with contingencies as much as to the fact that decisions become more exposed to criticism through structural critique and statistical analyses than facts. Indeed, even if we cannot determine that someone has decided (for example, about the number of deaths from accidents or about the increase of the rate of unemployment) decisions are still necessary to redress these unsatisfactory conditions. To require decisions means to appeal to values, explicitly or implicitly. Consequently, struc-

tural contingency generates an order of values without considering the possibilities of concretely causing effects, i.e., without considering the attainability of the corresponding conditions.

It is probable that ecological communication will intensify this inflation of values even more. For if society has to ascribe environmental changes to itself then it is quite natural to reduce them to decisions that would have to be corrected: decisions about emissions quotas, total consumption amounts, new technologies whose consequences are still unknown, etc. . . . [S]uch ascriptions are based on simplifying, illuminating and obscuring causal attributions. This does not prevent them from being carried out and communicated, but, if nothing else, it permits values to surface.[7]

At first, one might think that the value of clean air and water, trees and animals could be placed alongside the values of freedom and equality, and since this is only a matter of lists we could include pandas, Tamils, women, etc. But viewed essentially and in the long run this would be much too simple an answer. The problematic of the inflation of values as a symbolically generalized medium of communication—an idea of Parsons's[8]—results from its influence on society's observation and description of itself.

Actually the descriptions of society are steered by the problems that result from structural decisions and, therefore, they have a tendency to evoke values and see 'crises'. Contrary to the mature phase of bourgeois-socialist theories in the first two-thirds of the nineteenth century disadvantages are deferred for a time, are read off in values and are understood as the indefinite obligation to act. In any event, they are no longer understood as digressions of the spirit or matter on the way to perfection. Instead, they are the inescapable result of evolution. According to the theory proposed here, they are consequences of the principle of system differentiation and of its making probable what is improbable.

Moreover, the critical self-observation and description that constantly accompanies society has to renounce moral judgements or end up getting lost in a factional morass.[9] Instead, a new kind of schematism, namely, manifest or latent (conscious or unconscious, intentional or unintentional) takes its place. Only manifest functions can be used to differentiate and specify because only these can be transformed into points of comparison or goal-formulas. This means that the critique is formed as a scheme of difference that also illuminates the other side, the counterpart. Straightforward striving toward a goal is viewed as naive. This even undermines the straightforward intention of enlightenment.[10] A mirror is, as it were, held up to society, assuming that it cannot look through it because that which is latent can fulfill its function only latently. This is the way sociology, too, pursues 'enlightenment' [*Aufklärung*] and explains its ineffectuality in the same process.[11] In this sense ideology, the unconscious, latent structures and functions and unintended side-effects all become themes without a clarification of the status of this shadow world—note especially the reversal of Platonic metaphysics. One can therefore use this distinction only to discover that society enlightens itself about itself.

The problem of reintroducing the unity of society within society or even of expressing it in it is extended to the forms of the system's critical self-description. Equally symptomatic are all attempts at judging and condemning society from the exalted standpoint of the subject, i.e., *ab extra*. This signifies nothing more than placing the unity of society in a principle outside itself.[12] A systems-theoretical analysis of such attempts, however, enjoys the advantage of being able to retrace this problematic back to the structure of modern society (which changes nothing about the fact that this must occur in society).

Essentially, every attempt within the system to make the unity of the system the object of a system operation encounters a paradox because this operation must exclude and include itself. As long as society was differentiated according to center/periphery or rank, positions could be established where it was possible, as it never has been since, to represent the system's unity, i.e., in the center or at the apex of the hierarchy. The transition to functional differentiation destroys this possibility when it leaves it to the many function systems to represent the unity of society through their respective subsystem/environment differences and exposes them in this respect to competition among themselves while there is no superordinate standpoint of representation for them all. To be sure, one can observe and describe this too. But the unity of society is nothing more than this difference of function systems. It is nothing more than their reciprocal autonomy and non-substitutability; nothing more than the transformation of this structure into a togetherness of inflated independence and dependence. In other words, it is the resulting complexity, which is highly improbable evolutionarily.

Endnotes

1. Cf., among others Jeffrey L. Pressman/Aaron Wildavsky, *Implementation: How Great Expectations in Washington are Dashed in Oakland*, Berkeley Ca. 1973.

2. Cf., Niklas Luhmann, *Soziale Systeme*, Frankfurt 1984, pp. 37ff.

3. According to E. T. A. Hoffmann, 'Des Vetters Eckfenster', *Werke*, Berlin-Leipzig, no date, vol. 12, pp. 142–64.

4. Cf., for a historico-semantic context Niklas Luhmann, 'Temporalisierung von Komplexitaet: Zur Semantik neuzeitlicher Zeitbegriffe', in Luhmann, *Gesellschaftsstruktur und Semantik*, vol. 1, Frankfurt 1980, pp. 235–300.

5. Cf., André Béjin, 'Différenciation, complexification, évolution des sociétés', in *Communications*, vol. 22 (1974), pp. 109–18 (114) in connection with Henri Atlan, *L'Organisation biologique et la théorie de l'information*, Paris 1972, pp. 270ff.

6. The still unclear semantic career of the concept of value (especially prior to the middle of the nineteenth century) might have one of its sources here. To be sure, it is incorrect to say that the concept of value was appropriated by morality, literature, aesthetics and philosophy from economics only in the middle of the nineteenth century. (The Abbé Morellet, *Prospectus d'un nouveau dictionnaire de commerce*, Paris 1769, reprint Munich 1980, pp. 98ff., observes a restriction to economic profit. But the entire eighteenth century used it in a much more general sense.) It is equally clear, however, that the concept of value has been used as an ultimate guarantee for meaning and therefore non-contradictably in the last hundred years.

7. This happens in any event. But it is also required in many respects and viewed as the precon-

dition for the solutions of problems. Cf., Karl-Heinz Hillmann, *Umweltkrise und Wertwandel: Die Umwertung der Werte als Strategie des Überlebens*, Frankfurt-Bern 1981.

8. Cf., Talcott Parsons, 'On the Concept of Value-Commitments', in *Sociological Inquiry*, vol. 38 (1968), pp. 135–60 (153ff.).

9. For a comparison: the self-description of stratified societies had always used a moral schematism—whether in the direct moral criticism of typical behavior in the individual strata or in the formulation of types of perfection from which everyone could measure their distance.

10. Cf., for example, Simon-Nicolas-Henri Linquet, *Le Fanatisme des philosophes*, London-Abbeville 1764; Peter Villaume, *Über das Verhältnis der Religion zur Moral und zum Staate*, Libau 1791, and of course, the widespread critique of the French Revolution as the outbreak of a naive faith in principles.

11. This led many to the conclusion of 'revolution'—with very little support for possibilities and consequences. One finds typically that the manifest/latent schema is introduced without further reflection as a description of facts and forms the basis for analyses. This has been the case especially since Robert K. Merton, 'The Unanticipated Consequences of Purposive Social Action', in *American Sociological Review*, vol. 1 (1936), pp. 894–904.

12. Jürgen Habermas judges much more sharply and leaves more room for hope. He views this as the theory-immanent *problem* of the Enlightenment's erroneous semantic guidance by the theory of the subject and its object and therefore sees the solution of the problem in the transition to a new paradigm of intersubjective agreement. Cf., *Der philosophische Diskurs der Moderne: Zwölf Vorlesungen*, Frankfurt 1985. To make this useful sociologically, one must still clarify how this erroneous guidance and the possibility of correcting it are connected with the structure of modern society.

33
After Neofunctionalism

Jeffrey Alexander

Jeffrey Alexander (b. 1947) teaches sociology at UCLA and is one of the currently active theorists chiefly responsible for a resurgence of interest in Parsonian social theory. Like Parsons, Alexander began his career with a multi-volume exegetical inquiry into his sociological predecessors, in this case a book titled *Theoretical Logic in Sociology* (1982–83). Since then, he has begun to stake out his own position, which has become known as "neofunctionalism." While not having attempted anything approaching a sustained effort at theory construction akin to Parsons' *The Social System*, Alexander has advanced the contours of neofunctionalism in a series of essays. The approach of these essays is to incorporate major features of earlier functionalist theory while correcting its various shortcomings and being open to new currents outside of the functionalist tradition. This excerpt from *After Neofunctionalism* (1998) offers a flavor of Alexander's sense of the main currents in contemporary social theory and his reaction to them.

By presuppositions (Alexander 1982, 1987a), I refer to the most general assumptions sociologists make when they encounter reality. Every social theory and every empirical work take a priori positions that allow observers to organize in the most simple categorical terms the data that enter their minds via their senses. Only on this basis can the more conscious manipulations that constitute rational or scientific thought be made. Presuppositions are subjects of discourse, and they are sometimes even discursively justified. For the most part, however, they originate in processes that precede the exercise of reason itself.

Perhaps the most obvious thing that students of social life must presuppose in their encounters with social reality is the nature of action. In the modern era, when one thinks about action, one thinks about whether it is rational or not. I do not mean to imply here that common sense equation of rational with good and smart, and non-rational with bad and stupid. Rather, in modern social science, this dichotomy refers to whether people are selfish (rational) or idealistic (nonrational), whether they are normative and moral (nonrational) or instrumental and strategic (rational), whether they act in terms of maximizing efficiency (rationally) or are governed by emotions and unconscious desires (nonrationally). In terms of empirical orientations, of course, the descriptions I have just offered—of rational action and of nonrational action—differ from one another in specific and important ways. In terms of theoretical practice, however, these orientations have, in fact, formed two ideal types. In the history of social theory these ideal types of rational and nonrational have demarcated distinctive theoretical traditions and discursive argument of the most polemical kind.[1]

How can these traditions be defined in terms that supersede but do not violate the more finely graded distinctions upon which each is based, in such a way, for example, that moralistic theories and emotionalist theories may both be seen as part of the "nonrationalist" tradition? The answer is deceptively simple; it is to see the dichotomy as relating to the internal versus external reference of action (see Alexander 1982a, pp. 17–79). Rationalistic or instrumental approaches portray actors as taking their bearings from forces outside of themselves, whereas nonrational approaches suggest that action is motivated from within. It is possible, in principle, to presuppose that action is both rational and nonrational, but it is surprising how rarely in the history of social theory this interpenetration has actually been made.

Yet to answer the central question about action is not enough. A second major issue needs to be presupposed as well. I refer here to the famous "problem of order," although I will define it somewhat differently than has typically been the case. Sociologists are sociologists because they believe there are patterns to society, structures somehow separate from the actors who compose it. Yet, while all sociologists believe such patterns exist, they often disagree sharply about how such an order is actually produced. Once again, I will cast these disagreements in terms of dichotomous ideal types because it is just this agglomerated antipathy that has characterized the empirical and discursive history of social thought (see Ekeh 1974, Lewis and Smith 1980). This dichotomy refers to the opposition between individualistic and collectivist positions.

If thinkers presuppose a collectivist position, they see social patterns as existing prior to any specific individual act, as in a sense the product of history. Social order confronts newborn individuals as an established fact outside of them. If the confusion aroused by Durkheim's (1937/1895) early formulations of this position is to be avoided, and if the necessity for "correcting" Durkheim's errors by developing equally one-sided discursive justifications on the other side is to be avoided as well, certain codas to this definition of collectivism must immediately be made.[2] If they are writing about adults, collectivists may well acknowledge that social order exists as much inside the individual as without; this is, in fact, an important qualification to which we will return. Whether it is conceptualized as inside or outside an actor, however, the collectivist position does not view order as the product of purely this-instant, this-moment considerations. According to collectivist theory every individual actor is pushed in the direction of preexisting structure; whether this direction remains only a probability or a determined fate depends on refinements in the collectivist position I will take up below.

Individualistic theories often acknowledge that there do appear to be such extraindividual structures in society, and they certainly recognize that there are intelligible patterns. They insist, however, that these patterns are the result of individual negotiation. They believe not simply that structure is "carried" by individuals but that it is actually produced by the carriers in the course of their individual interactions. The assumption is that individuals can alter the

fundaments of order at each successive moment in historical time. Individuals, in this view, do not carry order inside of them. Rather, they follow or rebel against social order—even the values that they hold within themselves—according to their individual desires.

Once again, whether it is possible to combine some elements of this contingent position with a more collectivist emphasis is a matter I will take up in the following discussion. What I wish to emphasize at this point is that the problems of action and order are not optional. Every theory must take some position on both. The logical permutations among these presuppositions form the fundamental traditions of sociology. As such, they form the most important axes around which social science discourse revolves.

Presuppositions are so central to discourse because they have implications that go well beyond the explanatory concerns I have just defined. The study of society revolves around the questions of freedom and order, and every theory is pulled between these poles. Modern men and women believe that individuals have free will and that, because of this capacity, individuals can be trusted to act in responsible ways. To one degree or another, this belief has been institutionalized in Western societies. Individuals have been set apart as privileged political and cultural units. Elaborate legal efforts have been made to protect them from the group, from the state, and from other coercive organs like an established church.

Sociological theorists, whether individualist or collectivist, are likely to be as committed to the autonomy of the individual as other citizens. Indeed, sociology emerged as a discipline as a result of this differentiation of the individual in society, for it was the independence of the individual and the growth of his or her powers to think freely about society that allowed society itself to be conceived of as an independent object of study. It is the independence of the individual that makes order problematic, and it is this problematizing of order that makes sociology possible. At the same time, sociologists acknowledge that the everyday life of an individual has a patterned quality. It is this tension between freedom and order that provides the intellectual and moral rationale for sociology. Sociologists explore the nature of social order, and discursively justify the positions they adopted in regard to this question, because they are deeply concerned about its implications for individual freedom.

Individualistic theories are attractive and powerful because they preserve individual freedom in an overt, explicit, and thoroughgoing way. Their a priori postulates assume the integrity of the rational or moral individual, taking for granted actors' abilities to act freely against their situations, which are defined either in material or cultural terms. It is because of this natural convergence between ideological and explanatory discourse that individualism has been such a powerful strand in modern thought.

Social theory emerged out of the long process of secularization and rebellion against the hierarchical institutions of traditional society. In the Renaissance, Machiavelli emphasized the autonomy of the rational prince to remake his world. English contract theorists, like Hobbes and Locke, broke free from traditional restraints by developing a discourse claiming that social order depended on individual bargaining and, ultimately, upon a social contract. The same path was followed by some of the principal thinkers of the French Enlightenment. Each of these individualistic traditions was a strongly rationalistic one. While emphasizing different kinds of individual needs—power, happiness, pleasure, security—each portrayed society as emanating from the choices of rational actors. The crucial conceptual bridge between these traditions and contemporary theorizing in the social sciences was utilitarianism, particularly classical economics, whose theory of the invisible regulation of markets provided an elegant empirical explanation of how individual decisions can be aggregated to form societies.[3] It is from quasi-economic discourse that the central justifications for rationalistic modes of individualistic theorizing are largely drawn today.

Individualistic theories have, of course, also assumed a nonrational form. In its inversion of the Enlightenment and its revulsion against utilitarianism, romanticism inspired theories about the passionate actor

(see, e.g., Abrams 1971) from Wundt to Freud. In its hermeneutic version, which stretches from Hegel (Taylor 1975) to Husserl and existentialism (Spiegelberg 1971), this antirationalist tradition takes on a moral and often cognitive form.

The advantages that an individualistic position bestows, then, are very great. Still, it can be achieved only at great theoretical cost. These costs emerge because such individualistic theories begin from a wholly unrealistic perspective about voluntarism in society. By radically neglecting the power of social structure, individualistic theory in the end does freedom no real service. It encourages the illusion that individuals have no need for others or for society as a whole. It also ignores the great sustenance to freedom that social structures can provide. It is upon such costs that the discourse against individualistic theory focuses its aim.

By acknowledging that social controls exist, collectivist theory can subject them to explicit analysis. In this sense, collectivist thought represents a real gain over the individualistic position, in moral as well as theoretical terms. The question is whether this gain, in turn, has been achieved only at an unacceptable price. What does such collectivist theorizing lose? How is the collective force it postulates related to the individual will, to the possibility of preserving voluntarism and self-control? In order to answer this decisive question, it is necessary to make explicit a point that has only been implicit in my discourse thus far. Assumptions about order do not entail any particular assumptions about action. Because of this indeterminacy, there are very different kinds of collectivist theory.

Whether collective theory is worth the cost depends on whether it presupposes the possibility for moral or expressive, that is, for nonrational, action. Many collectivist theories assume that actions are motivated by narrow, technically efficient forms of rationality. If such an assumption is made, then collective structures must be portrayed as if they were external to individuals and entirely unresponsive to their will. Political or economic institutions, for example, are said to control the actors from without, whether they like it or not. They do so by arranging punitive sanctions and positive rewards for actors who are reduced—whatever the specific nature of their personal goals—to calculators of pleasure and pain. Because such actors are assumed to respond rationally to this external situation, motives are eliminated as a theoretical concern. Such theorizing assumes that the actor's response can be predicted from analysis of the external environment alone. Rational-collectivist theories, then, explain order only by sacrificing the subject. In effect, they dispense with the very notion of an autonomous self. In classical sociology, orthodox Marxism presents the most formidable example of this development, and the coercive implications that surround its discourse—as revealed, for example, in recurring references to the "dictatorship of the proletariat" and the "laws of history"—have generated intense critical response (e.g., Van den Berg 1988). The same tendency to justify a discourse without a subject permeates every neoclassical theory that has collective ambitions, and Weber's sociology as well, as the controversy over the status of "domination" in the Weberian corpus demonstrates.

If, by contrast, collectivist theory allows that action may be nonrational, it perceives actors as guided by ideals and emotion. This internal realm of subjectivity is initially structured, it is true, by encounters with external objects—with parents, teachers, siblings, and books. In the process of socialization, however, such extraindividual structures become internal to the self. Only if this phenomenon of internalization is accepted can subjectivity become a topic for collectivist theory. According to this view, individual interaction becomes a negotiation between two "social selves." The dangers that such theorizing encounters are quite the opposite from collectivist theories of a more rationalistic kind. It tends to engage in moralistic rhetoric and idealistic justifications. As such, it often underestimates the ever-present tension between even the socialized individual and his or her social environment. This tension, of course, is most obvious when the theorist must consider an environment that is material in form, a possibility that cannot be conceptualized when collecti-

vist theory is formulated in a one-sidedly normative way.

In the discussion of recent theoretical discourse that follows, I will focus on how presuppositional commitments have shaped sociological debate since the early 1960s. They have exerted their influence, of course, even if no attempt has been made discursively to justify them. The central figures in these debates, however, have sought such discursive justification. This, indeed, is what made them influential theorists. Through their discourse these theorists developed claims about the scope and implications of their theories, claims that stipulated "truth criteria" at a supraempirical level. In the present section I have laid out my own conception of what such criteria should be. When I apply these criteria to recent theoretical debate, I will often be arguing in opposition to the truth claims of the principal participants in these debates. This, of course, is the very stuff of which social science discourse is made.

Reconsidering Micro and Macro Theory

It is perhaps because of the discipline's methodological and empirical focus that the massive renewal of individualistic theorizing in sociology has been seen as a revival of "microsociology."[4] For, strictly speaking, micro and macro are thoroughly relativistic terms, referring to part/whole relationships at every level of social organization. In the language of recent social science, however, they have been identified with the distinction between taking individual interaction as an empirical focus, on the one hand, and taking an entire social system as one's empirical focus, on the other.

When Homans (1958, 1961) introduced exchange theory, he was renewing the very utilitarian position that had constituted the basis of Parsons' (1937) earliest and most powerful critique. Not only did Homans reject the collective tradition in classical and contemporary sociology, but the interpretive strand of individualistic theorizing as well. He insisted that the elementary forms of social life were not extraindividual elements such as symbol systems but individual actors of an exclusively rationalist bent. He focused on what he called sub-institutional behavior, the behavior of "actual individuals," which he believed to be entirely independent of socially specified norms. The procedures through which individuals make calculations occupied Homans' attention. So did the balance of supply and demand in the actor's external environment. In Homans' rationalistic perspective the social forces impinging on actors could only be conceived in an objectified and external way.

Exchange theory became enormously influential in reviving the case for microsociology. Its simple and elegant model facilitated predictions; its focus on individuals made it empirically operational. It also caught hold of a fundamental insight that Parsons and, indeed, collectivist theorists of every stripe had ignored: It is through individual actors making decisions about the costs of contingent exchange that "objective social conditions" become articulated vis-à-vis the everyday life of individuals, institutions, and groups.[5] The price for such insights was high, however, even for theorists inside the paradigm itself. For example, Homans (1961, pp. 40, 54–5) was never able to define the "value" of a commodity in anything but a circular way; he was compelled to argue that it stemmed from reinforcing an orientation that was already in place. His conception of distributive justice showed similar strains (1961 chapter 12); he was forced to refer to "irrational" solidarity in order to decide just what the definition of an equitable "rational" exchange might be.

The other major strands of micro-theorizing have taken up the interpretive side. Blumer (1969) was the general theorist most responsible for the revival of Meadian theory, although the tradition that Blumer (1937) labeled *symbolic interactionism* took up pragmatism only in its radically contingent form.[6] Blumer insisted that meaning is determined by individual negotiation—indeed, by the reaction of others to the individual's act. The actor is not seen as bringing some previously defined collective order into play. It is immediate situational-relevance, not internalization, that defines attitudes. Through "self-indication" actors make objects even out of their own selves. It

is the temporally rooted "I" of the actor, not the more societally focused "me," that determines the pattern of social order described in Blumer's work.

Though powerful, Blumer's most influential writing was almost entirely discursive in form; even when it was programmatic, moreover, it focused more on promoting the methodology of direct observation than on elaborating theoretical concepts. It is Goffman who must be seen as the most important empirical theorist of the symbolic interactionist movement. To most contemporaries, Goffman's work appeared merely to point interactionist theory in a more problem-specific and dramaturgic direction. Certainly his early work tends to support this reading. In contrast to the clear collectivist strains that emerged in his later theorizing, Goffman (e.g., 1959) emphasized individuals' desires to manipulate the presentation of self in opposition to socially structured roles, and he tried (1963) to explain institutional behavior as emerging from face-to-face interaction.

Ethnomethodology, and phenomenological work more generally, presents a more complicated story. Garfinkel was a student not only of Schutz but also of Parsons, and his earliest work (e.g., 1963) accepts the centrality of internalization. What Garfinkel explored in this early writing was how actors make social norms their own; he explored, that is, their "ethno" methodology. Emphasizing the constructed character of action, he described how, through cognitive techniques like "ad hocing" (Garfinkel 1967), individuals conceived of contingent and unique events as representations, or "indexes," of socially structured rules. In the process, he showed, these rules were in actuality not simply specified but modified and changed.

As ethnomethodology became a major theoretical movement, it was forced to justify itself in general and discursive ways. In the process, its concepts became more one-sided. Presenting itself as committed to an alternative sociology, ethnomethodology emphasized "members' own practices" over and against structure. That constitutive techniques like indexicality were omnipresent, it was now argued, should be seen as evidence that order is completely emergent, and the endlessly resourceful practice of orderly activity came to be identified (Garfinkel et al. 1981) with social order itself. That this kind of individualistic reduction is somehow inherent in a phenomenological approach is belied, however, by other strains that emerged from the ethnomethodological school. Conversational analysis (Sacks et al. 1974), for example, viewed speech as subject to strong structural constraints even if it did not usually conceptualize these constraints in a systematic way.

It is certainly an ironic demonstration of the lack of linear accumulation in sociology that, concurrent with this resurgence of micro-theorizing, there emerged a strong movement toward equally one-sided kinds of macro, collectivist work. This movement began when "conflict theorists" justified themselves by defining Parsonian work as "order theory." Like the new microsociologists, these theorists, too, denied the centrality of internalization and the link between action and culture that concept implies. Rather than emphasizing individual consciousness as the basis of collective order, however, conflict theorists severed the link between consciousness and structural processes altogether. Dahrendorf (1959) gave to administrative power positions the central ordering role. Rex (1961) emphasized the allocative economic processes that gave power to the ruling class.

While conflict arguments certainly provided the most powerful justifications for structural theorizing in its initial phase, it was the Marxism of Althusser and his students (Althusser and Balibar 1970, Godelier 1967) that formulated the most sophisticated and influential discourse in its later phase. Drawing from Spinoza and as well as from modern linguistic and anthropological theory, this so-called structural Marxism analyzed historical developments as particular variations, transformations, and incarnations of fundamental structural principles. Rather than starting with the empirical and phenomenal diversity of social actions and lifeworlds, as contemporary microtheorists advised, these Marxist structuralists gave ontological and methodological primacy to the "totality." Although individual actions may deviate from structural imperatives, the objective consequences of these actions are determined by structures that exist beyond the actors' control.

While just as deterministic, this structural Marxism was less directly economic than other variants. It emphasized the political mediation of productive forces rather than their direct control (e.g., Poulantzas 1972). This discourse about mediation and structural "overdetermination" set the stage for Marxist theorizing with a distinctively Weberian cast. Critical political economists like Offe (1984/1972) and O'Connor (1978) focused on the function of the state in capitalist accumulation and tried to derive social problems and crises from "inevitable" state intervention.

While the most important discursive justifications for the new structural theory have come from Europe, its influence in America has depended on a series of influential arguments at the middle range. Moore's (1966) major work on the class origins of state formations provided the major impetus for this work, though it was much more classically Marxist than the neo-Weberian structuralist work that followed in its wake. The most imposing single work that followed Moore's was Skocpol's (1979). Skocpol not only provided what appeared to be a powerful new covering law to explain revolutions but offered a widely persuasive polemic against subjective and voluntaristic theories of revolution (in the name of her structural theory). Wright's (1978) class analysis takes up the same antimicro theme, arguing that ambiguities in a group's class consciousness come from "contradictory class locations." Treiman (1977) similarly produced what he called a "structural theory of prestige" that converted cultural into organizational control and denied to subjective understandings of stratification any independent causal role. In still another influential work, Lieberson (1980) put his explanation for racial inequality in the terms of this same highly persuasive discourse. He identified "structures of opportunity" with material environment and justified this by dismissing the focus on subjective volition as conservative and idealist.

Endnotes

1. The claim that rational and nonrational have, in fact, informed broadly distinctive traditions in the history of social thought has been advanced by a wide range of different writers, for example, Parsons (1937), Hughes (1958), and Habermas (1971).

2. It is just such an overreaction against the standard misreading of Durkheim's position that marks Giddens' position (e.g., Giddens 1976). This overreaction has led him to an overly individualistic position on the order question.

3. In his subtle essay on the origins of modern economic theory, Hirschman (1977) has shown that contract theories that emphasized market exchanges originated as part of a struggle against the arbitrary power of despots and kings. He also suggests, however, that in its early stages—for example, in the work of Montesquieu—such contract theories had a relatively social and often normative and emotional bent, for such self-interested exchanges were supposed to civilize passionate and often destructive human instincts. The initial rationale for this prototype of individualistic and rationalistic theory, then, was clearly cultural and collective. As market theory developed, however, it became more purely materialistic in orientation, and the notion that contractual exchanges had any relationship to subjective motive dropped out. This account provides a historical documentation for the theoretical criticism I make below—namely, that the whole topic of volition and will is eliminated by rationalistic and individualistic theories.

4. For a historical perspective on shifts in theorizing the micro-macro link, as well as a more detailed and systematic account of the analytic issues involved, see Alexander and Giesen (1987). I have drawn from this essay for many of the arguments that follow.

5. In explaining the success of exchange theory one would not want to underestimate the power and bombastic eloquence of Homans' discursive justifications on its behalf. He first articulated exchange theory (Homans 1958) in a purely discursive way, in his highly publicized presidential address to the American Sociological Association. In the major introduction to his collection of essays (Homans 1962), he developed new modes of biographical and ideological discourse to justify exchange theorizing. His remarkable dedication to developing discursive justifications for exchange theory continued to be revealed in his autobiography (Homans 1984), which, I have argued elsewhere (Alexander 1987b), creates a series of not entirely accurate frameworks through which the exchange perspective is presented as psychologically, morally, scientifically, and historically inevitable.

6. Lewis and Smith (1980) demonstrate this point in a powerful and systematic way in their brilliant reinterpretation of the history of pragmatic social theory in America. That upon its publication this book became extraordinarily controversial points, in my view, to the danger its argument posed to the discursive justifications of symbolic interactionism in its Blumerian mode.

References

Abrams, M. H. 1971, *Natural Supernaturalism*. New York: Norton.

Alexander, J. C. 1982, *Theoretical Logic in Sociology*, Vol. 1: *Positivism, Presuppositions, and Current Controversies*. Berkeley: University of California Press.

——. 1987a, *Twenty Lectures: Sociological Theory Since World War II*. New York: Columbia University Press.

——. 1987b, Science, sense, and sensibility. *Theory and Society*, 15, pp. 443–63.

Alexander, J. C., and Giesen, B. 1987, From reduction to linkage: The long view of the micro-macro link. In S. C. Alexander et al. (eds.), *The Micro-Macro Link*. Berkeley: University of California Press, pp. 1–42.

Althusser, L., and Balibar, E. 1970, *Reading Capital*. London: New Left Books.

Blumer, H. 1937, Social psychology. In E. D. Schmidt (ed.), *Man and Society*. Englewood Cliffs, NJ: Prentice-Hall, pp. 144–98.

——. (ed.) 1969, The methodological position of symbolic interactionism. In H. Blumer, *Symbolic Interactionism*. Englewood Cliffs, NJ: Prentice-Hall, pp. 1–60.

Dahrendorf, R. 1959, *Class and Class Conflict in Industrial Society*. Stanford, CA: Stanford University Press.

Durkheim, E. 1937 [1895], *The Rules of Sociological Method*. New York: Free Press.

Ekeh, P. K. 1974, *Social Exchange Theory: The Two Traditions*. Cambridge, MA: Harvard University Press.

Garfinkel, H. 1963, A conception of and experiments with trust as a condition of concerted stable actions. In O. J. Harvey (ed.), *Motivation and Social Interaction*. New York: Ronald Press, pp. 187–238.

——. 1967, *Studies in Ethnomethodology*. Englewood Cliffs, NJ: Prentice-Hall.

Garfinkel, H., Lynch, M., and Livingston, E. 1981, The work of discovering science construed with materials from the optically discovered pulsar. *Philosophy of Social Science*, 11, pp. 131–58.

Giddens, A. 1976, *New Rules of Sociological Method*. New York: Basic Books.

Godelier, M. 1967, System, structure, and contradition in "Capital." In R. Miliband and J. Saville (eds), *The Socialist Register*, New York: Monthly Review Press, pp. 91–119.

Goffman, E. 1959, *The Presentation of Self in Everyday Life*. Garden City, NY: Doubleday.

——. 1963, *Behavior in Public Places*. New York: Free Press.

Habermas, J. 1971, *Knowledge and Human Interests*. Boston: Beacon Press.

Hirschman, A. 1977, *The Passions and the Interests*. Princeton, NJ: Princeton University Press.

Homans, G. 1958, Social behavior as exchange. *American Journal of Sociology*, 62, pp. 597–606.

——. 1961, *Social Behavior: Its Elementary Forms*. New York: Harcourt, Brace and World.

——. (ed.) 1962, Introduction. In G. Homans, *Sentiments and Activities*. New York: Free Press.

——. 1984, *Coming to My Senses*. New Brunswick, NJ: Transaction.

Hughes, H. S. 1958, *Consciousness and Society*. New York: Random House.

Lewis, J. D., and Smith, R. L. 1980, *American Sociology and Pragmatism: Mead, Chicago Sociology and Symbolic Interactionism*. Chicago: University of Chicago Press.

Lieberson, S. 1980, *A Piece of the Pie*. Berkeley: University of California Press.

Moore, B. 1966, *The Social Origins of Dictatorship and Democracy*. Boston: Beacon Press.

O'Connor, J. 1978, *The Fiscal Crisis of the State*. New York: St Martin's.

Offe, C. 1984 [1972], *Contradictions of the Welfare State*. Cambridge, MA: MIT Press.

Parsons, T. 1937, *The Structure of Social Action*. New York. Free Press.

Poulantzas, N. 1972, *Political Power and Social Classes*. London: New Left Books.

Rex, J. 1961, *Key Problems in Sociological Theory*. London: Routledge and Kegan Paul.

Sacks, H., Schegloff, E. A., and Jefferson, G. 1974, A simplest systematics for the organization of turn-taking for conversation. *Language*, 50, pp. 696–735.

Skocpol, T. 1979, *States and Social Revolution*. New York: Cambridge University Press.

Spiegelberg, H. 1971, *The Phenomenological Movement: A Historical Introduction*. The Hague: Martinus Nijhoff.

Taylor, C. 1975, *Hegel*. New York: Oxford University Press.

Treiman, D. 1977, *Occupational Prestige in Comparative Perspective*. New York: John Wiley.

Van den Berg, A. 1988, *The Immanent Utopia: From Marxism on the State to the State of Marxism*. Princeton, NJ: Princeton University Press.

Wright, E. O. 1978, *Class, Crisis, and the State*. London: New Left Books.

Reprinted from "The New Theoretical Movement in Sociology" (chapter 8), first appearing in *Revista Brasileira de Ciencias Sociais*, vol. 4, no. 2 (1987), pp. 5–28, and later in N. J. Smelser (ed.), *Handbook of Sociology* (1988), pp. 77–101. Copyright © 1988 by Sage Publications. Reprinted by permission of Sage Publications, Inc. ✦

VIII. Conflict Theories

34
The Functions of Social Conflict

Lewis Coser

Although Lewis Coser (1913–2003) wrote this essay from a functionalist perspective, he took up a topic that critics contended was generally ignored by its Parsonian variant: conflict. In fact, Coser was indebted not only to Parsonian theory but to such classic figures as Simmel, who was concerned with the varied ways that conflict can draw antagonistic parties into webs of group affiliation. While Coser realizes that conflict can be destructive to groups and to intergroup relations, and thus agrees that attempts at conflict resolution are generally appropriate, he focuses in this essay on the functions of conflict not only in reinforcing group solidarity but in serving as a safety-valve, channeling tensions in constructive ways rather than letting them build up to such a point that when conflict is unleashed, it is unleashed with destructive force.

Conflict within a group . . . may help to establish unity or to reestablish unity and cohesion where it has been threatened by hostile and antagonistic feelings among the members. Yet, not *every* type of conflict is likely to benefit group structure, nor that conflict can subserve such functions for *all* groups. Whether social conflict is beneficial to internal adaptation or not depends on the type of issues over which it is fought as well as on the type of social structure within which it occurs. However, types of conflict and types of social structure are not independent variables.

Internal social conflicts which concern goals, values or interests that do not contradict the basic assumptions upon which the relationship is founded tend to be positively functional for the social structure. Such conflicts tend to make possible the readjustment of norms and power relations within groups in accordance with the felt needs of its individual members or subgroups.

Internal conflicts in which the contending parties no longer share the basic values upon which the legitimacy of the social system rests threaten to disrupt the structure.

One safeguard against conflict disrupting the consensual basis of the relationship, however, is contained in the social structure itself: it is provided by the institutionalization and tolerance of conflict. Whether internal conflict promises to be a means of equilibration of social relations or readjustment of rival claims, or whether it threatens to "tear apart," depends to a large extent on the social structure within which it occurs.

In every type of social structure there are occasions for conflict, since individuals and subgroups are likely to make from time to time rival claims to scarce resources, prestige or power positions. But social structures differ in the way in which they allow expression to antagonistic claims. Some show more tolerance of conflict than others.

Closely knit groups in which there exists a high frequency of interaction and high personality involvement of the members have a tendency to suppress conflict. While they provide frequent occasions for hostility (since both sentiments of love and hatred are intensified through frequency of interaction), the acting out of such feelings is sensed as a danger to such intimate relationships, and hence there is a tendency to suppress rather than to allow expression of hostile feelings. In close-knit groups, feelings of hostility tend, therefore, to accumulate and hence to intensify. If conflict breaks out in a group that has consistently tried to prevent expression of hostile feelings, it will be particularly intense for two reasons: First, because the conflict does not merely aim at resolving the immediate issue which led to its outbreak; all accumulated grievances which were denied expression previously are apt to emerge at this occasion. Second, because the total personality involvement of the group members makes for mobilization of all sentiments in the conduct of the struggle.

Hence, the closer the group, the more intense the conflict. Where members participate with their total personality and conflicts are suppressed, the conflict, if it breaks out nevertheless, is likely to threaten the very root of the relationship.

In groups comprising individuals who participate only segmentally, conflict is less likely to be disruptive. Such groups are likely to experience a multiplicity of conflicts. This in itself tends to constitute a check against the breakdown of consensus: the energies of group members are mobilized in many directions and hence will not concentrate on *one* conflict cutting through the group. Moreover, where occasions for hostility are not permitted to accumulate and conflict is allowed to occur wherever a resolution of tension seems to be indicated, such a conflict is likely to remain focused primarily on the condition which led to its outbreak and not to revive blocked hostility; in this way, the conflict is limited to "the facts of the case." One may venture to say that multiplicity of conflicts stands in inverse relation to their intensity.

So far we have been dealing with internal social conflict only. At this point we must turn to a consideration of external conflict, for the structure of the group is itself affected by conflicts with other groups in which it engages or which it prepares for. Groups which are engaged in continued struggle tend to lay claim on the total personality involvement of their members so that internal conflict would tend to mobilize all energies and affects of the members. Hence such groups are unlikely to tolerate more than limited departures from the group unity. In such groups there is a tendency to suppress conflict, where it occurs, it leads the group to break up through splits or through forced withdrawal of dissenters.

Groups which are not involved in continued struggle with the outside are less prone to make claims on total personality involvement of the membership and are more likely to exhibit flexibility of structure. The multiple internal conflicts which they tolerate may in turn have an equilibrating and stabilizing impact on the structure.

In flexible social structures, multiple conflicts crisscross each other and thereby prevent basic cleavages along one axis. The multiple group affiliations of individuals makes them participate in various group conflicts so that their total personalities are not involved in any single one of them. Thus segmental participation in a multiplicity of conflicts constitutes a balancing mechanism within the structure.

In loosely structured groups and open societies, conflict, which aims at a resolution of tension between antagonists, is likely to have stabilizing and integrative functions for the relationship. By permitting immediate and direct expression of rival claims, such social systems are able to readjust their structures by eliminating the sources of dissatisfaction. The multiple conflicts which they experience may serve to eliminate the causes for dissociation and to re-establish unity. These systems avail themselves, through the toleration and institutionalization of conflict, of an important stabilizing mechanism.

In addition, conflict within a group frequently helps to revitalize existent norms; or it contributes to the emergence of new norms. In this sense, social conflict is a mechanism for adjustment of norms adequate to new conditions. A flexible society benefits from conflict because such behavior, by helping to create and modify norms, assures its continuance under changed conditions. Such mechanism for readjustment of norms is hardly available to rigid systems: by suppressing conflict, the latter smother a useful warning signal, thereby maximizing the danger of catastrophic breakdown.

Internal conflict can also serve as a means for ascertaining the relative strength of antagonistic interests within the structure, and in this way constitute a mechanism for the maintenance or continual readjustment of the balance of power. Since the outbreak of the conflict indicates a rejection of a previous accommodation between parties, once the respective power of the contenders has been ascertained through conflict, a new equilibrium can be established and the relationship can proceed on this new basis. Consequently, a social structure in which there is room for conflict disposes of an important means for avoiding or redressing conditions of disequilibrium by modifying the terms of power relations.

Conflicts with some produce associations or coalitions with others. Conflicts through such associations or coalitions, by providing a bond between the members, help to reduce social isolation or to unite individuals and groups otherwise unrelated or antagonistic to each other. A social structure in which there can exist a multiplicity of conflicts contains a mechanism for bringing together otherwise isolated, apathetic or mutually hostile parties and for taking them into the field of public social activities. Moreover, such a structure fosters a multiplicity of associations and coalitions whose diverse purposes crisscross each other, we recall, thereby preventing alliances along one major line of cleavage.

Once groups and associations have been formed through conflict with other groups, such conflict may further serve to maintain boundary lines between them and the surrounding social environment. In this way, social conflict helps to structure the larger social environment by assigning position to the various subgroups within the system and by helping to define the power relations between them.

Not all social systems in which individuals participate segmentally allow the free expression of antagonistic claims. Social systems tolerate or institutionalize conflict to different degrees. There is no society in which any and every antagonistic claim is allowed immediate expression. Societies dispose of mechanisms to channel discontent and hostility while keeping intact the relationship within which antagonism arises. Such mechanisms frequently operate through "safety-valve" institutions which provide substitute objects upon which to displace hostile sentiments as well as means of abreaction of aggressive tendencies.

Safety-valve institutions may serve to maintain both the social structure and the individual's security system, but they are incompletely functional for both of them. They prevent modification of relationships to meet changing conditions and hence the satisfaction they afford the individual can be only partially or momentarily adjustive. The hypothesis has been suggested that the need for safety-valve institutions increases with the rigidity of the social structure, i.e., with the degree to which it disallows direct expression of antagonistic claims.

Safety-valve institutions lead to a displacement of goal in the actor: he need no longer aim at reaching a solution of the unsatisfactory situation, but merely at releasing the tension which arose from it. Where safety-valve institutions provide substitute objects for the displacement of hostility, the conflict itself is channeled away from the original unsatisfactory relationship into one in which the actor's goal is no longer the attainment of specific results, but the release of tension.

This affords us a criterion for distinguishing between realistic and nonrealistic conflict.

Social conflicts that arise from frustrations of specific demands within a relationship and from estimates of gains of the participants, and that are directed at the presumed frustrating object, can be called realistic conflicts. Insofar as they are means toward specific results, they can be replaced by alternative modes of interaction with the contending party if such alternatives seem to be more adequate for realizing the end in view.

Nonrealistic conflicts, on the other hand, are not occasioned by the rival ends of the antagonists, but by the need for tension release of one or both of them. In this case the conflict is not oriented toward the attainment of specific results. Insofar as unrealistic conflict is an end in itself, insofar as it affords only tension release, the chosen antagonist can be substituted for by any other "suitable" target.

In realistic conflict, there exist functional alternatives with regard to the means of carrying out the conflict, as well as with regard to accomplishing desired results short of conflict; in nonrealistic conflict, on the other hand, there exist only functional alternatives in the choice of antagonists.

Our hypothesis, that the need for safety-valve institutions increases with the rigidity of the social system, may be extended to suggest that unrealistic conflict may be expected to occur as a consequence of rigidity present in the social structure.

Our discussion of the distinction between types of conflict, and between types of social structures, leads us to conclude that conflict tends to be dysfunctional for a social structure in which there is no or insufficient toleration and institutionalization of conflict. The intensity of a conflict which threatens to "tear apart," which attacks the consensual basis of a social system, is related to the rigidity of the structure. What threatens the equilibrium of such a structure is not conflict as such, but the rigidity itself which permits hostilities to accumulate and to be channeled along one major line of cleavage once they break out in conflict.

35

Culture and Politics

C. Wright Mills

C. Wright Mills (1916–1962), who has been referred to as "the angry Texan," is in many respects the heir of Marx and Weber. Writing during the Cold War of the 1950s, Mills was a vocal and persistent critic of those figures in the social scientific community who thought we had entered a new age in which the old conflicts of the preceding era had been overcome. One of the first sociological theorists to use the term "post-modern," Mills contends that we have entered a new and dangerous age characterized by large unresolved questions in the economic and political realms and by the threat of future large-scale violence at a time of continual war preparedness.

We are at the ending of what is called The Modern Age. Just as Antiquity was followed by several centuries of Oriental ascendancy which Westerners provincially call The Dark Ages, so now The Modern Age is being succeeded by a post-modern period. Perhaps we may call it: The Fourth Epoch.

The ending of one epoch and the beginning of another is, to be sure, a matter of definition. But definitions, like everything social, are historically specific. And now our basic definitions of society and of self are being overtaken by new realities. I do not mean merely that we *feel* we are in an epochal kind of transition. I mean that too many of our explanations are derived from the great historical transition from the Medieval to the Modern Age; and that when they are generalized for use today, they become unwieldy, irrelevant, not convincing. And I mean also that our major orientations—liberalism and socialism—have virtually collapsed as adequate explanations of the world and of ourselves.

I

These two ideologies came out of The Enlightenment, and they have had in common many assumptions and two major values: in both, freedom and reason are supposed to coincide: increased rationality is held to be the prime condition of increased freedom. Those thinkers who have done the most to shape our ways of thinking have proceeded under this assumption; these values lie under every movement and nuance of the work of Freud: to be free, the individual must become more rationally aware; therapy is an aid to giving reason its chance to work freely in the course of an individual's life. These values underpin the main line of Marxist work: men, caught in the irrational anarchy of production, must become rationally aware of their position in society; they must become "class conscious"—the Marxian meaning of which is as rationalistic as any term set forth by Bentham.

Liberalism has been concerned with freedom and reason as supreme facts about the individual; Marxism as supreme facts about man's role in the political making of history. But what has been happening in the world makes evident, I believe, why the ideas of freedom and of reason now so often seem so ambiguous in both the capitalist and the communist societies of our time: why Marxism has so often become a dreary rhetoric of bureaucratic defense and political abuse; and liberalism, a trivial and irrelevant way of masking social reality. The major developments of our time can be adequately understood in terms of neither the liberal nor the Marxian interpretation of politics and culture. These ways of thought, after all, arose as guide-lines to reflection about types of society which do not now exist. John Stuart Mill never examined the kinds of political economy now arising in the capitalist world. Karl Marx never analyzed the kinds of society now arising in the Communist bloc. And neither of them ever thought through the problems of the so-called underdeveloped countries in which seven out of ten men are trying to exist today.

The ideological mark of The Fourth Epoch—that which sets it off from The Modern Age—is that the ideas of freedom and of reason have become moot; that increased rationality may not be assumed to make for increased freedom.

II

The underlying trends are well known. Great and rational organizations—in brief, bureaucracies—have indeed increased, but the substantive reason of the individual at large has not. Caught in the limited milieux of their everyday lives, ordinary men often cannot reason about the great structures—rational and irrational—of which their *milieux* are subordinate parts. Accordingly, they often carry out series of apparently rational actions without any ideas of the ends they serve, and there is the increasing suspicion that those at the top as well—like Tolstoy's generals—only pretend they know. That the techniques and the rationality of science are given a central place in a society does not mean that men live reasonably and without myth, fraud and superstition. Science, it turns out, is not a technological Second Coming. Universal education may lead to technological idiocy and nationalist provinciality, rather than to the informed and independent intelligence. Rationally organized social arrangements are not necessarily a means of increased freedom—for the individual or for the society. In fact, often they are a means of tyranny and manipulation, a means of expropriating the very chance to reason, the very capacity to act as a free man.

The atrocities of The Fourth Epoch are committed by men as "functions" of a rational social machinery—men possessed by an abstracted view that hides from them the humanity of their victims and as well their own humanity. The moral insensibility of our times was made dramatic by the Nazis, but is not the same lack of human morality revealed by the atomic bombing of the peoples of Hiroshima and Nagasaki? And did it not prevail, too, among fighter pilots in Korea, with their petroleum-jelly broiling of children and women and men? Auschwitz and Hiroshima—are they not equally features of the highly rational moral-insensibility of The Fourth Epoch? And is not this lack of moral sensibility raised to a higher and technically more adequate level among the brisk generals and gentle scientists who are now rationally—and absurdly—planning the weapons and the strategy of the third world war? These actions are not necessarily sadistic; they are merely businesslike; they are not emotional at all; they are efficient, rational, technically clean-cut. They are inhuman acts because they are impersonal.

III

In the meantime, ideology and sensibility quite apart, the compromises and exploitations by which the nineteenth-century world was balanced have collapsed. In this sixth decade of the twentieth century the structure of a new world is indeed coming into view.

The ascendancy of the USA, along with that of the USSR, has relegated the scatter of European nations to subsidiary status. The world of The Fourth Epoch is divided. On either side, a superpower now spends its most massive and co-ordinated effort in the highly scientific preparation of a third world war.

Yet, for the first time in history, the very idea of victory in war has become idiotic. As war becomes total, it becomes absurd. Yet in both the superstates, virtually all policies and actions fall within the perspective of war; in both, elites and spokesmen—in particular, I must say, those of the United States—are possessed by the military metaphysic, according to which all world reality is defined in military terms. By both, the most decisive features of reality are held to be the state of violence and the balance of fright.

Back of this struggle there is the world-encounter of two types of political economy, and in this encounter capitalism is losing. Some higher capitalists of the USA are becoming aware of this, and they are very much frightened. They fear, with good justification, that they are going to become an isolated and a second-rate power. They represent utopian capitalism in a world largely composed of people whose experiences with real capitalism, if any, have been mostly brutal. They profess "democracy" in a nation where it is more a formal outline than an actuality, and in a world in which the great majority of people have never experienced the bourgeois revolutions, in a world in which the values deposited by the Renaissance and the Reformation do not restrain the often brutal thrust to industrialize.

United States foreign policy and lack of foreign policy is firmly a part of the absurdity of this world scene, and it is foremost among the many defaults of the Western societies. During the last few years, confronting the brinks, I have often suspected that the world is not at the third world war largely because of the calculation and the forbearance of the Soviet elite.

IV

What kind of a society is the USA turning out to be in the middle of the twentieth century? Perhaps it is possible to characterize it as a prototype of at least "The West." To locate it within its world context in The Fourth Epoch, perhaps we may call it The Overdeveloped Society.

The *Underdeveloped Country* as you know, is one in which the focus of life is necessarily upon economic subsistence; its industrial equipment is not sufficient to meet Western standards of minimum comfort. Its style of life and its system of power are dominated by the struggle to accumulate the primary means of industrial production.

In a *Properly Developing Society*, one might suppose that deliberately cultivated styles of life would be central; decisions about standards of living would be made in terms of debated choices among such styles; the industrial equipment of such a society would be maintained as an instrument to increase the range of choice among styles of life.

But in *The Overdeveloped Nation*, the standard of living dominates the style of life; its inhabitants are possessed, as it were, by its industrial and commercial apparatus: collectively, by the maintenance of conspicuous production; individually, by the frenzied pursuit and maintenance of commodities. Around these fetishes, life, labor and leisure are increasingly organized. Focused upon

these, the struggle for status supplements the struggle for survival; a panic for status replaces the proddings of poverty.

In underdeveloped countries, industrialization, however harsh, may be seen as man conquering nature and so freeing himself from want. But in the overdeveloped nation, as industrialization proceeds, the economic emphasis moves from production to merchandizing, and the economic system which makes a fetish of efficiency becomes highly inefficient and systematically wasteful. The pivotal decade for this shift in the United States was the twenties, but it is since the ending of the second world war that the overdeveloped economy has truly come to flourish.

Surely there is no need to elaborate this theme in detail; since Thorstein Veblen formulated it, it has been several times "affluently" rediscovered. Society in brief has become a great sales-room—and a network of rackets: the gimmick of success becomes the yearly change of model, as in the mass-society fashion becomes universal. The marketing apparatus transforms the human being into the ultimately-saturated man—the cheerful robot—and makes "anxious obsolescence" the American way of life.

V

But all this—although enormously important to the quality of life—is, I suppose, merely the obvious surface. Beneath it there are institutions which in the United States today are as far removed from the images of Tocqueville as is Russia today from the classic expectations of Marx.

The power structure of this society is based upon a privately incorporated economy that is also a permanent war economy. Its most important relations with the state now rest upon the coincidence of military and corporate interests—as defined by generals and businessmen, and accepted by politicians and publics. It is an economy dominated by a few hundred corporations, economically and politically interrelated, which together hold the keys to economic decision. These dominating corporation-hierarchies probably represent the highest concentration of the greatest economic power in human history, including that of the Soviet Union. They are firmly knit to political and military institutions, but they are dogmatic—even maniacal—in their fetish of the "freedom" of their private and irresponsible power.

I should like to put this matter in terms of certain parallel developments in the USA and the USSR. The very terms of their world antagonism are furthering their similarities. Geographically and ethnically both are super-societies; unlike the nations of Europe, each has amalgamated on a continental domain great varieties of peoples and cultures. The power of both is based upon technological development. In both, this development is made into a cultural and a social fetish, rather than an instrument under continual public appraisal and control. In neither is there significant craftsmanship in work or significant leisure in the non-working life. In both, men at leisure and at work are subjected to impersonal bureaucracies. In neither do workers control the process of production or consumers truly shape the process of consumption. Workers' control is as far removed from both as is consumers' sovereignty.

In both the United States and the Soviet Union, as the political order is enlarged and centralized, it becomes less political and more bureaucratic; less the locale of a struggle than an object to be managed. In neither are there nationally responsible parties which debate openly and clearly the issues which these nations, and indeed the world, now so rigidly confront. Under some conditions, must we not recognize that the two-party state can be as irresponsible as is a one-party state?

In neither the USA nor the USSR is there a senior civil service firmly linked to the world of knowledge and sensibility and composed of skilled men who, in their careers and in their aspirations, are truly independent—in the USA of corporation interests, in the USSR of party dictation.

In neither of these superpowers are there, as central facts of power, voluntary associations linking individuals, smaller communities and publics, on the one hand, with the state, the military establishment, the economic apparatus on the other. Accordingly, in neither are there readily available vehicles for reasoned opinions and instruments for the national exertion of public will. Such voluntary associations are no longer a dominant feature of the political structure of the overdeveloped society.

The classic conditions of democracy, in summary, do not exactly flourish in the overdeveloped society; democratic formations are not now ascendant in the power structure of the United States or of the Soviet Union. Within both, history-making decisions and lack of decisions are virtually monopolized by elites who have access to the material and cultural means by which history is now powerfully being made.

VI

I stress these parallels, and perhaps exaggerate them, because of the great nationalist emphasis upon the differences between the two world antagonists. The parallels are, of course, due in each case to entirely different sources; and so are the great differences. In the capitalist societies the development of the means of power has occurred gradually, and many cultural traditions have restrained and shaped them. In most of the Communist societies they have happened rapidly and brutally and from the beginning under tightly centralized authority; and without the cultural revolutions which in the West so greatly strengthened and gave political focus to the idea of human freedom.

You may say that all this is an immoderate and biased view of America, that America also contains many good features. Indeed that is so. But you must not expect me to provide A Balanced View. I am not a sociological bookkeeper. Moreover, "balanced views" are now usually surface views which rest upon the homogeneous absence of imagination and the passive avoidance of reflection. A balanced view is usually, in the phrase of Royden Harrison, merely a vague point of equilibrium between platitudes.

I feel no need for, and perhaps am incapable of arranging for you, a lyric upsurge, a cheerful little pat on the moral back. Yet perhaps, by returning to my point of beginning, I can remind you of the kinds of problems you might want to confront. I must make two points only: one about fate and the making of history; the other about the roles many intellectuals are now enacting.

Fate has to do with events in history that are the summary and unintended results of innumerable decisions of innumerable men. Each of their decisions is minute in consequence and subject to cancellation or reinforcement by other such decisions. There is no link between any one man's intention and the summary result of the innumerable decisions. Events are beyond human decisions: history is made, behind men's backs.

So conceived, fate is not a universal fact; it is not inherent in the nature of history or in the nature of man. In a society in which the ultimate weapon is the rifle; in which the typical economic unit is the family farm and shop; in which the national-state does not yet exist or is merely a distant framework; and in which communication is by word of mouth, handbill, pulpit—in *such* a society, history is indeed fate.

But consider now the major clue to our condition, to the shape of the overdeveloped society in The Fourth Epoch. In modern industrial society the means of economic production are developed and centralized, as peasants and artisans are replaced by private corporations and government industries. In the modern nation-state the means of violence and of administration undergo similar developments, as kings control nobles and self-equipped knights are replaced by standing armies and now by fearful military machines. The *post-modern* climax of all three developments—in economics, in politics, and in violence—is now occurring most dramatically in the USA and the USSR. In the polarized world of our time, international as well as national, means of history-making are being centralized. Is it not thus clear that the scope and the chance for conscious human agency in history-making are just now uniquely available? Elites of power in charge of these means do now make history—to be sure, "under circumstances not of their own choosing"—but compared to other men and other epochs, these circumstances themselves certainly do not appear to be overwhelming.

And surely here is the paradox of our immediate situation: the facts about the newer means of history-making are a signal that men are not necessarily in the grip of fate, that men *can* now make history. But this fact stands ironically alongside the further fact that just now those ideologies which offer men the hope of making history have declined and are collapsing in the overdeveloped nation of the United States. That collapse is also the collapse of the expectations of the Enlightenment, that reason and freedom would come to prevail as paramount forces in human history. It also involves the abdication of many Western intellectuals.

VII

In the overdeveloped society, where is the intelligentsia that is carrying on the big discourse of the Western world *and* whose work as intellectuals is influential among parties and publics and relevant to the great decisions of our time? Where are the mass media open to such men? Who among those in charge of the two-party state and its ferocious military machines are alert to what goes on in the world of knowledge and reason and sensibility? Why is the free intellect so divorced from decisions of power? Why does there now prevail among men of power such a higher and irresponsible ignorance?

In The Fourth Epoch, must we not face the possibility that the human mind, as a social fact might be deteriorating in quality and cultural level, and yet not many would notice it because of the overwhelming accumulation of technological gadgets? Is not that the meaning of rationality without reason? Of human alienation? Of the absence of any role for reason in human affairs? The accumulation of gadgets hides these meanings: those who use them do not understand them; those who invent and maintain them do not understand much else. That is why we may not, without great ambiguity, use technological abundance as the index of human quality and cultural progress.

VIII

To formulate any problem requires that we state the values involved and the threat to these values. For it is the felt threat to cherished values—such as those of freedom and reason—that is the necessary moral substance of all significant problems of social inquiry, and as well of all public issues and private troubles.

The values involved in the cultural problem of freedom and individuality are conveniently embodied in all that is suggested by the ideal of The Renaissance Man. The threat to that ideal is the ascendancy among us of The Cheerful Robot, of the man with rationality but without reason. The values involved in the political problem of history-making are embodied in the Promethean ideal of its human making. The threat to that ideal is twofold: On the one hand, history-making may well go by default, men may continue to abdicate its willful making, and so merely drift. On the other hand, history may indeed be made—but by narrow elite circles without effective responsibility to those who must try to survive the consequences of their decisions and of their defaults.

I do not know the answer to the question of political irresponsibility in our time or to the cultural and political question of The Cheerful Robot; but is it not clear that no answers will be found unless these problems are at least confronted? Is it not obvious that the ones to confront them, above all others, are the intellectuals, the scholars, the ministers, the scientists of the rich societies? That many of them do not now do so, with moral passion, with intellectual energy, is surely the greatest human default being committed by privileged men in our times.

Reprinted from "Culture & Politics: The Fourth Epoch" from *Power, Politics, and People: The Collected Essays of C. Wright Mills* by C. Wright Mills, edited by Irving Louis Horowitz. Copyright © 1959 by The Estate of C. Wright Mills. Reprinted by permission of Brandt & Hochman Literary Agents, Inc. ✦

36
Conflict Groups and Group Conflicts

Ralf Dahrendorf

Ralf Dahrendorf (b. 1929) is a German-born social theorist who spent much of his academic career in England, where he rose to the directorship of the London School of Economics. Dahrendorf, like Lewis Coser, addresses the topic of the functions of social conflict, but he does so in an effort to examine the future of one particular type of conflict in advanced industrial societies: class conflict. He is also more attentive to the potential negative, or dysfunctional, consequences of conflict than Coser is. The potential for conflict, according to Dahrendorf, is contingent on the particular configurations of authority in a given society. In this essay, he sketches out some of the variables that must be considered in assessing both the potential for violence and the intensity of conflict in various situations.

The 'Functions' of Social Conflict

Classes, understood as conflict groups arising out of the authority structure of imperatively coordinated associations, are in conflict. What are—so we must ask if we want to understand the lawfulness of this phenomenon—the social consequences, intended or unintended, of such conflicts? The discussion of this question involves, almost inevitably, certain value judgments. I think that R. Dubin is right in summarizing at least one prominent attitude toward the functions of social conflict as follows:

> From the standpoint of the social order, conflict is viewed from two positions: (*a*) it may be destructive of social stability

and therefore 'bad' because stability is good; (*b*) it may be evidence of the breakdown of social control and therefore symptomatic of an underlying instability in the social order. Both positions express a value preference for social stability. (2, p. 183)

I would also agree with Dubin's own position:

> Conflict may be labeled dysfunctional or symptomatic of an improperly integrated society. The empirical existence of conflict, however, is not challenged by the stability argument. . . . The fact of the matter is that group conflict cannot be wished out of existence. It is a reality with which social theorists must deal in constructing their general models of social behaviour. (p. 184)

But I think that in two respects Dubin might have been rather less cautious. First, I should not hesitate, on the level of value judgments, to express a strong preference for the concept of societies that recognizes conflict as an essential feature of their structure and process. Secondly, and quite apart from value judgments, a strong case can be made for group conflict having consequences which, if not "functional," are utterly necessary for the social process. This case rests on the distinction between the two faces of society—a distinction which underlies our discussions throughout this study. It is perhaps the ultimate proof of the necessity of distinguishing these two faces that conflict itself, the crucial category in terms of the coercion model, has two faces, i.e., that of contributing to the integration of social "systems" and that of making for change.

Both these consequences have been admirably expressed by L. Coser. (Although, to my mind, Coser is rather too preoccupied with what he himself tends to call the "positive" or "integrative functions" of conflict.) On the one hand, Coser states in the unmistakable terminology of the integration theory of society (for which see my italics):

> Conflict may serve to remove dissociating elements in a relationship and to *reestablish* unity. Insofar as conflict is the resolution of tension between antago-

nists it has *stabilizing functions* and becomes an *integrating component* of the relationship. However, not all conflicts are *positively functional* for the relationship. . . . Loosely structured groups, and open societies, by allowing conflicts, institute safeguards against the type of conflict which would *endanger basic consensus* and thereby *minimize the danger of divergences* touching core values. The interdependence of antagonistic groups and the crisscrossing within such societies of conflicts, which *serve to 'sew the social system together'* by cancelling each other out, thus *prevent disintegration* along one primary line of cleavage. (4, p. 80)

On the other hand, Coser follows Sorel in postulating "the idea that conflict . . . prevents the ossification of the social system by exerting pressure for innovation and creativity" and states:

This conception seems to be more generally applicable than to class struggle alone. Conflict within and between groups in a society can prevent accommodations and habitual relations from progressively impoverishing creativity. The clash of values and interests, the tension between what is and what some groups feel ought to be, the conflict between vested interests and new strata and groups demanding their share of power, wealth and status, have been productive of vitality. (3, pp. 197 f.)

Conflict may, indeed, from a Utopian point of view, be conceived as one of the patterns contributing to the maintenance of the *status quo*. To be sure, this holds only for regulated conflicts, some of the conditions of which we shall try to explore presently. Coser's analysis of Simmel (4) has convincingly demonstrated that there is no need to abandon the integration theory of society simply because the phenomenon of conflict "cannot be wished away" but is a fact of observation. In this sense, conflict joins role allocation, socialization, and mobility as one of the "tolerable" processes which foster rather than endanger the stability of social systems. There seems little doubt, however, that from this point of view we can barely begin to understand the phenomenon of group conflicts. Were it only for its "positive functions," for which Coser found so many telling synonyms, class conflict would continue to be rather a nuisance which the sociologist would prefer to dispense with since it may, after all, "endanger basic consensus." So far as the present study is concerned, "continuing group conflict" will be regarded as "an important way of giving direction to social change" (Dubin, 2, p. 194). Societies are essentially historical creatures, and, because they are, they require the motive force of conflict—or, conversely, because there is conflict, there is historical change and development. The dialectics of conflict and history provide the ultimate reason of our interest in this phenomenon and at the same time signify the consequences of social conflict with which we are concerned.

Dubin's observation that conflict is a stubborn fact of social life is undoubtedly justified. Earlier, we have made the assertion explicit that social conflict is ubiquitous; in fact, this is one of the premises of our analysis. Possibly, this premise permits even further generalization. There has been in recent years some amount of interdisciplinary research on problems of conflict. In specific features the results of these interdisciplinary efforts remain as yet tentative; but one conclusion has been brought out by them with impressive clarity: it appears that not only in social life, but wherever there is life, there is conflict.[1] May we perhaps go so far as to say that conflict is a condition necessary for life to be possible at all? I would suggest, in any case, that all that is creativity, innovation, and development in the life of the individual, his group, and his society is due, to no small extent, to the operation of conflicts between group and group, individual and individual, emotion and emotion within one individual. This fundamental fact alone seems to me to justify the value judgment that conflict is essentially "good" and "desirable."

If I here assume social conflict, and the particular type of group conflict with which we are concerned in the present study, to be ubiquitous, I want this statement to be understood more rigidly than is usual. At an earlier point I have intimated what I mean by rigidity in this sense. One or two remarks in addition to these earlier hints seem in order. In summarizing earlier research,

Mack and Snyder state with some justice that by most authors "competition is not regarded as conflict or a form of conflict" (2, p. 217). The alleged difference between the two is identified differently by different authors. T. H. Marshall emphasizes common interests, rather than divergent interests, as characteristic of states of competition or conflict (1, p. 99). For Mack and Snyder,

> competition involves striving for scarce objects . . . according to established rules which strictly limit what the competitors can do to each other in the course of striving; the chief objective is the scarce object, not the injury or destruction of an opponent per se. (2, p. 217)

It seems to me, however, that it is not accidental if Mack and Snyder state a little later that "conflict arises from 'position scarcity' and 'resource scarcity,'" and that therefore "conflict relations always involve attempts to gain control of scarce resources and positions" (pp. 218 f.). Despite terminological traditions, I can see no reason why a conceptual distinction between competition and conflict should be necessary or, indeed, desirable.[2] Like competition, conflict involves a striving for scarce resources. From the point of view of linguistic usage, it is perfectly proper to say that conflicting interest groups compete for power. As far as the "established rules" of competition are concerned, they emphasize but one type of conflict, namely, regulated conflict. In the present study, the notion of conflict is intended to include relations such as have been described by many other authors as competitive.

Another distinction almost general in the literature is that between changes "within" and changes "of" or conflicts "within" and conflicts "about" the system. Many authors have been at pains to define these differences. Coser, e.g., proposes "to talk of a change *of* system when all major structural relations, its basic institutions and its prevailing value system have been drastically altered," but admits that "in concrete historical reality, no clear-cut distinctions exist" (3, p. 202). Marshall distinguishes more specifically "conflict that arises out of the division of labor, conflict, that is to say, over the terms on which cooperation is to take place, as il-

lustrated by a wage dispute between employer and employed," from "conflict over the system itself upon which the allocation of functions and the distribution of benefits are based" (1, p. 99). Thinking in terms of inclusive epochs like "feudalism" and "capitalism" as well as in terms of the existence of political parties that propose to change "the whole system" can probably explain the widespread feeling that a distinction between "changes within" and "changes of" is necessary. But apart from these, it is surely no coincidence that it was Parsons who emphasized that "it is necessary to distinguish clearly between the processes *within* the system and processes of change *of* the system." This very distinction betrays traces of the integration approach to social analysis. If conflict and change are assumed to be ubiquitous, there is no relevant difference between "changes within" and "changes of," because the "system" is no longer the frame of reference. It may be useful to distinguish more or less intense or violent conflicts and major and minor changes, but these are gradations to be accounted for in terms of intervening variables of an empirical nature. In the present study, no assumption is implied as to the type of change or conflict effected by the antagonism of conflict groups. Wage disputes as well as political conflicts "over the system itself" will be regarded as manifestations of class conflict, i.e., of clashes of interest arising out of and concerned with the distribution of authority in associations.

As with the theory of class formation, the real problems of the theory of class conflict consist in the identification of the empirical variables delimiting the range of variability of forms and types. Change and conflict are equally universal in society. But in historical reality we always encounter particular changes and specific conflicts, and these, even in the more limited sphere of class conflict, present a varied picture of manifold types and forms. Assuming the ubiquity of conflict and change, we have to try to discover some of the factors that influence its concrete shapes.

Intensity and Violence: The Variability of Class Conflict

The substance of the theory of class action, or class conflict, can be summarized in one statement: conflict groups in the sense of this study, once they have organized themselves, engage in conflicts that effect structure changes. The theory of class action presupposes the complete formation of conflict groups and specifies their interrelations. However, this tautological statement is evidently not all that can be said about group conflicts, nor is it all that one would expect a theory of group conflict to provide. Beyond a basic assumption of this kind, a theory of class conflict has to identify and systematically interrelate those variables that can be shown to influence patterns of intergroup conflict. In the present chapter several such variables will be discussed in some detail, their selection being guided by the significance they suggest for the course and outcome of class conflict. Before we embark upon this discussion, however, there is one preliminary question that has to be settled. The statement that class conflicts are empirically variable is sufficiently vague to be almost meaningless. What is it—we must ask—about class conflicts that is variable and therefore subject to the influence of factors to be identified? In this question, the categories of intensity and violence are essential. In some connection or other, the terms "intensity" and "violence" can be found present in any discussion of conflict. Here is one example. Mack and Snyder, in their summary of earlier research, on the one hand derive the proposition "a high degree of intimacy between the parties, as contrasted with a high degree of functional interdependence, will *intensify* conflict" (2, p. 225), while, on the other hand, they suggest "the more integrated into the society are the parties to conflict, the less likely will conflict be *violent*" (p. 227). The distinction between the two concepts is not perhaps entirely clear from these statements, and, indeed, many authors use them almost synonymously. Yet there is an important difference between them, as Simmel knew when he said:

It is almost inevitable that an element of commonness injects itself into . . . enmity once the stage of open *violence* yields to another relationship, even though this new relation may contain a completely undiminished sum of *animosity* between the two parties. (see 4, p. 121)

That conflict is variable means that its intensity and violence are variable; but the two may vary independently and are, therefore, distinct aspects of any conflict situation.[3]

The category of intensity refers to the energy expenditure and degree of involvement of conflicting parties. A particular conflict may be said to be of high intensity if the cost of victory or defeat is high for the parties concerned. The more importance the individual participants of a conflict attach to its issues and substance, the more intense is this conflict. For class conflict a continuum might be constructed ranging, e.g., from a conflict within a chess club which involves but a small segment of the individual personalities concerned to the overriding class conflict, in Marx's analyses, in which individuals are engaged with almost their entire personalities. In operational terms, the cost aspect is here crucial. Members of a group that strives to upset the authority structure of a chess club stand to lose less in case of defeat than members of a trade union who endeavor to change the authority structure of the enterprise (or their own social conditions by way of this authority structure).[4] The cost of defeat, and with it the intensity of conflict, differs in these cases.

By contrast to its intensity, the violence of conflict relates rather to its manifestations than to its causes; it is a matter of the weapons that are chosen by conflict groups to express their hostilities. Again, a continuum can be constructed ranging from peaceful discussions to militant struggles such as strikes and civil wars. Whether or not class conflict expresses itself in militant clashes of interest is in principle independent of the intensity of involvement of the parties. The scale of degree of violence, including discussion and debate, contest and competition, struggle and war, displays its own patterns and regularities.[5] Violent class struggles, or class wars, are but one point on this scale.

While violence and intensity of conflict vary independently, several of the factors shortly to be discussed affect both. This fact can be illustrated with reference to one factor which has been mentioned already and which need not therefore be discussed again at any length. . . . [T]he conditions of organization of interest groups continue to affect group conflict even after the complete formation of conflict groups. They are, in this sense, a factor which, among others, accounts for variations of intensity and violence. With respect to the intensity of class conflict, the political conditions of organization appear especially relevant. It may be suggested that, for the individuals concerned, involvement in conflicts decreases as the legitimacy of conflicts and, by implication, their issues become recognized. However, in the ensemble of factors affecting intensity of conflict, the specific weight of the conditions of organization is probably not very great. By contrast, it is considerable among the variables involved in determining the violence of conflict manifestations. As soon as conflict groups have been permitted and been able to organize themselves, the most uncontrollably violent form of conflict, that of guerrilla warfare, is excluded. Moreover, the very fact of organization presupposes some degree of recognition which in turn makes the most violent forms of conflict unnecessary and, therefore, unlikely. This is not to say, of course, that conflicts between organized groups cannot be highly intense and violent. The conditions of organization are but one, and not the most important, factor among many. Of these I have selected four which seem to me of particular importance and which will be dealt with separately in the following sections of this chapter.

Pluralism Versus Superimposition: Contexts and Types of Conflict

One of the crucial elements of the theory of group conflict consists in the strict relation of conflicts to particular associations. Any given conflict can be explained only in terms of the association in which it arose and, conversely, any given association can be analyzed in terms of the conflicts to which it gives rise. In theory, this approach would suggest that inclusive societies present the picture of a multitude of competing conflicts and conflict groups. The two-class model applies not to total societies but only to specific associations within societies (including, of course, the inclusive association of the state, i.e., the whole society in its political aspect). If, in a given society, there are fifty associations, we should expect to find a hundred classes, or conflict groups in the sense of the present study. Apart from these, there may be an undetermined number of conflict groups and conflicts arising from antagonisms other than those based on the authority structure of associations. In fact, of course, this extreme scattering of conflicts and conflict groups is rarely the case. Empirical evidence shows that different conflicts may be, and often are, superimposed in given historical societies, so that the multitude of possible conflict fronts is reduced to a few dominant conflicts. I suggest that this phenomenon has considerable bearing on the degree of intensity and violence of empirical conflicts.

The pluralism-superimposition scale which might thus be constructed has two distinct dimensions. One of these relates to the separation or combination of conflicts of the class type in different associations. Let us restrict ourselves, for purposes of illustration, to the three associations of the state, industry, and the church in countries in which one church dominates the sphere of religious institutions. It is conceivable that the ruling and the subjected groups of each of these associations are largely separate aggregations. The dignitaries of the church may be mere citizens of the state and may have no industrial property or authority. Similarly, the citizens of the state may be church dignitaries or industrial managers. This is the kind of situation here described as pluralistic. Within each of the three associations there are (class) conflicts, but, as between these, there is dissociation rather than congruence. Evidently, complete dissociation and pluralism are, in the case mentioned, empirically rather unlikely. It is more probable that the workers of industry are at the same time mere members of the church and mere citizens of the state. One might expect that the dignitaries of the church are in some ways connected with the rulers of the state and possibly even with the owners or managers of industry. If this is the case, (class) conflicts of different associations appear superimposed; i.e., the opponents of one association meet again—with different tides, perhaps, but in identical relations—in another association. In this case, the personnel of the conflict groups of different associations is the same.

Such congruence may also occur with conflict groups of different types. Again, a realistic example may serve to illustrate the point. We might suppose that in a given country there are three dominant types of social conflict: conflict of the class type, conflict between town and country, and conflict between Protestants and Catholics. It is of course conceivable that these lines of conflict cut across each other in a random fashion, so that, e.g., there are as many Protestants among the ruling groups of the state as there are Catholics and as many townspeople in either denomination as there are country-people. However, here, too, we might suspect that dissociation and pluralism are empirically rather unlikely to occur. One would not be surprised to find that most Protestants live in towns and most Catholics in the country, or that only one of the denominations commands the instruments of political control. If this is so, we are again faced with a phenomenon of superimposition in the sense of the same people meeting in different contexts but in identical relations of conflict.

With respect to the violence of manifestations of conflict, the pluralism-superimposition scale is not likely to be a factor of great significance. While there is a possible (negative) correlation between the degree of pluralism and the violence of conflicts in a given society, there is little reason to believe that dissociation of types and contexts of conflict makes industrial strikes, for example, impossible. Only in the inclusive association of the state would there seem to be a probability of pluralism reducing and superimposition increasing the violence of interest clashes.

At the same time, this scale is of the utmost importance for variations in the intensity of class conflict. The proposition seems plausible that there is a close positive correlation between the degree of superimposi-

tion of conflicts and their intensity. When conflict groups encounter each other in several associations and in several clashes, the energies expended in all of them will be combined and one overriding conflict of interests will emerge. The situation with which Marx dealt is a case in point. If incumbents of subjected positions in industry are also subjected in all other associations; if they are, moreover, identical with conflict groups other than those determined by authority relations, a "division of society into two large hostile classes" may indeed result—a situation, that is, in which one inclusive conflict dominates the picture of the total society. If, on the other hand, the inevitable pluralism of associations is accompanied by a pluralism of fronts of conflict, none of these is likely to develop the intensity of class conflicts of the Marxian type. There is in this case, for every member of the subjected class of one association, the promise of gratification in another association. Every particular conflict remains confined to the individual in one of his many roles and absorbs only that part of the individual's personality that went into this role.[6] The empirical analysis of pluralism and superimposition of contexts and types of conflict is one of the important problems suggested by the theory of social classes and class conflicts.

Pluralism Versus Superimposition: Authority and the Distribution of Rewards and Facilities

. . . It is evident that in the context of a theory of group conflict of the type under discussion, "class situation" is an unnecessary concept. It means no more than what we have described as the authority position of aggregates in associations. The condition of a quasi-group in terms of the distribution of authority signifies the "situation" that underlies class conflict. However, the traditional concept of class situation includes a number of elements which, while irrelevant for the formation of social classes, affect their patterns of conflict in ways to be defined. Property, economic status, and social status are no determinants of class, but they do belong to the factors influencing the empirical course of clashes of interest between conflict groups.

As with contexts and types of conflict, the problem of rewards and facilities can be seen in terms of a contrast between divergence and parallelism, or pluralism and superimposition. Thus, property can, but need not, be associated with the exercise of authority. It is conceivable that those who occupy positions of domination in industry do not own industrial property—and, indeed, that those in positions of subjection do own such property. The separation of ownership and control, and certain systems of the distribution of shares to industrial workers, are cases in point. While neither of these structural arrangements eliminates the causes of (industrial) conflict, they have an impact on its intensity and violence. Once again, a certain parallelism between authority and property ownership may seem more probable, but it is not necessary.

The same holds for the economic status of persons in different authority positions. By economic status I shall here understand status in terms of strictly occupational rewards such as income, job security, and general social security as it accrues from occupational position. It is both possible and reasonably probable that those in positions of domination enjoy a somewhat higher economic status, and that these two attributes of social position are in this sense superimposed. But numerous illustrations could also be given for divergences between the two. In the early labor unions, and for many shop stewards and local union secretaries today, authority involves a comparative loss of income and security. In the Roman Catholic church, authority is supposed, in theory if not in practice, to be accompanied by low economic status. In totalitarian countries, political authority usually conveys high incomes but also a high degree of insecurity which lowers the economic status of dominant groups. Such divergences of authority position and economic status make for a plurality of noncongruent scales of position in a society, which constitutes one of the critical facts of class analysis.

Divergences of position are even more evident if we contrast authority positions with people's social status in the sense of the prestige attached to their position by themselves and by others in relevant universes of ranking. The prestige of power is a highly precarious quantity in all societies. Unless all existing studies are wrong in their findings, there would in fact seem to be, for persons in the upper ranges of the status scale, an inverse relation between the authority and the prestige. The judge (United States), the doctor (Britain), and the university professor (Germany) enjoy a markedly higher prestige than the cabinet minister or the large-scale entrepreneur.[7] Probably, the theory of class conflict with its assumption of opposing role interests would account for this phenomenon. On the other hand, there are and have been associations in which the division of authority and the scale of prestige followed identical lines. In the industrial enterprise, this would still seem to be the case in most countries (and with the possible exception of scientifically trained staff members). Thus, we also find here an empirically variable relation that is likely to affect the course of class conflict.

All examples chosen in the preceding paragraphs serve to illustrate the phenomenon of relative deprivation, i.e., the situation in which those subjected to authority are at the same time relatively worse placed in terms of socioeconomic status. However, in nineteenth-century Europe, and in some countries even today, we encounter what by contrast may be called an absolute deprivation of groups of people in socioeconomic terms. If the social condition of industrial workers, who are as such excluded from authority, falls below a physiological subsistence minimum or "poverty line," the effects of such deprivation are likely to be different in kind from those of relative deprivation. I would suggest that in this case, and in this case only, the superimposition of scales of status and the distribution of authority is likely to increase the violence of class conflict. This is a subtle and complex relation. So far as we know, oppression and deprivation may reach a point at which militant conflict motivation gives way to apathy and lethargy. Short of this point, however, there is reason to believe that absolute deprivation coupled with exclusion from authority makes for greater violence in conflict relations.

Relative deprivation, on the other hand, tends to affect the intensity of conflict rather than its violence. If incumbents of positions of subjection enjoy the countervailing gratification of a relatively high socioeconomic status, they are unlikely to invest as much energy in class conflicts arising out of the authority structure of associations as they would if they were deprived of both authority and socioeconomic status. Dominant groups are correspondingly not so likely to be as involved in the defense of their authority unless their high socioeconomic status is simultaneously involved. In terms of the intensity of conflict, pluralism would again seem to make for a decrease, and superimposition or congruence for an increase:[8] the lower the correlation is between authority position and other aspects of socioeconomic status, the less intense are class conflicts likely to be, and vice versa. . . .

Endnotes

1. This and numerous other statements in the present chapter are based on discussions with and publications of psychologists, anthropologists, lawyers, and social psychologists at the Center for Advanced Study in the Behavioral Sciences, Stanford, California. John Bowlby, M.D., and Professor Frank Newman, LL.D., have been particularly helpful in making suggestions. In support of the statement in the text I might also refer, however, to the symposium published in *Conflict Resolution* (2), which includes contributions by economists, sociologists, social psychologists, anthropologists, and psychologists, and strongly supports my point.

2. At least, no such reason has been put forward. It might be argued, of course, that the concept of competition employed in economic theory is rather different from that defined by Marshall or Mack and Snyder, and does not carry any conflict connotation. I am not entirely sure that this argument is justified, but for purposes of the present analysis competition in a technical economic sense will be excluded.

3. All italics in the quotations of this paragraph are mine.

4. I have as yet not given a systematic exposition of the patterns of change effected by class conflict;

the formulation in the text may therefore give rise to misunderstandings. . . .

5. In terms of the distinction thus introduced, we are now able to reformulate the contrast between the conception of conflict here assumed and that of several other authors. The latter tend to confine the term "conflict" to one point on the scale of degree of violence, namely, highly violent clashes. In the present study, however, conflict is conceived as including the whole scale, i.e., any clash of interest independent of the violence of its expressions.

6. This type of analysis seems to me to provide one of the answers to the question why there is no socialism in the United States. Throughout her history, the pluralism of associations and conflicts has made inclusive conflict groups held together by quasi-religious ideologies unnecessary. There has been no single group that enjoyed universal privilege or suffered universal alienation.

7. For relevant data, cf. the studies by the National Opinion Research Center (120), Glass (107), and Bolte (103).

8. This proposition must be opposed to the assumption of integration theorists that the congruence of different scales of social position is a requisite of stable, integrated societies (cf. Parsons, in 35). The exact opposite seems true, even from the point of view of integration theory. I cannot help feeling that this is one of the points at which integration theorists display—unwillingly, to be sure—almost totalitarian convictions.

References

1. T. H. Marshall, *The Nature of Class Conflict*, in *Class Conflict and Social Stratification*, T. H. Marshall, ed., London, 1938.

2. "Approaches to the Study of Social Conflict: A Colloquium," *Conflict Resolution*, Vol. I, No. 2 (June 1957).

3. L. A. Coser, "Social Conflict and Social Change," *British Journal of Sociology*, Vol. VII, No. 3 (September 1957).

4. ——. *The Functions of Social Conflict*. London, 1956.

37

The Basics of Conflict Theory

Randall Collins

Randall Collins (b. 1941), in his book *Conflict Sociology* (1975), attempted to free conflict theory from its roots in structural functionalism while offering the first formal theoretical presentation of this paradigm. Open to the influences of a wide range of theorists, perhaps most importantly Marx, Weber, and Goffman, Collins sought to articulate an integrative theoretical approach that avoided the political polemics of someone like C. Wright Mills while establishing theoretical links between the micro level and the macro level. In this selection from his book, Collins outlines a conflict theory of stratification, looking not only at class (as Dahrendorf did), but also at the more Durkheimian concern with occupations.

The level of interpersonal interaction is all-inclusive; by the same token, it is highly abstract. To reduce its myriad complexities to causal order requires theory on another level of analysis. The most fruitful tradition of explanatory theory is the conflict tradition, running from Machiavelli and Hobbes to Marx and Weber. If we abstract out its main causal propositions from extraneous political and philosophical doctrines, it looks like the following.

Machiavelli and Hobbes initiated the basic stance of cynical realism about human society. Individuals' behavior is explained in terms of their self-interests in a material world of threat and violence. Social order is seen as being founded on organized coercion. There is an ideological realm of belief (religion, law), and an underlying world of struggles over power; ideas and morals are not prior to interaction but are socially cre-

ated, and serve the interests of parties to the conflict.

Marx added more specific determinants of the lines of division among conflicting interests, and indicated the material conditions that mobilize particular interests into action and that make it possible for them to articulate their ideas. He also added a theory of economic evolution which turns the wheels of this system toward a desired political outcome; but that is a part of Marx's work that lies largely outside his contributions to conflict sociology, and hence will receive no attention here. Put schematically, Marx's sociology states:

1. Historically, particular forms of property (slavery, feudal landholding, capital) are upheld by the coercive power of the state; hence classes formed by property divisions (slaves and slaveowners, serfs and lords, capitalists and workers) are the opposing agents in the struggle for political power—the underpinning of their means of livelihood.

2. Material contributions determine the extent to which social classes can organize effectively to fight for their interests; such conditions of mobilization are a set of intervening variables between class and political power.

3. Other material conditions—the means of mental production—determine which interests will be able to articulate their ideas and hence to dominate the ideological realm.

In all of these spheres, Marx was primarily interested in the determinants of political power, and only indirectly in what may be called a "theory of stratification." The same principles imply, however:

1. The material circumstances of making a living are the main determinant of one's style of life; since property relations are crucial for distinguishing ways of supporting oneself, class cultures and behaviors divide up along opposing lines of control over, or lack of, property.

2. The material conditions for mobilization as a coherent, intercommunicating group also vary among social classes; by implication, another major difference among class lifestyles stems from the differing organization of their communities and their differing experience with the means of social communication.

3. Classes differ in their control of the means of mental production; this produces yet another difference in class cultures—some are more articulated symbolically than others, and some have the symbolic structures of another class imposed upon them from outside.

These Marxian principles, with certain modifications, provide the basis for a conflict theory of stratification. Weber may be seen as developing this line of analysis: adding complexity to Marx's view of conflict, showing that the conditions involved in mobilization and "mental production" are analytically distinct from property, revising the fundamentals of conflict, and adding another major set of resources. Again making principles more explicit than they are in the original presentation, we may summarize Weber as showing several different forms of property conflict coexisting in the same society, and hence, by implication, the existence of multiple class divisions; elaborating the principles of organizational intercommunication and control in their own right, thereby adding a theory of organization and yet another sphere of interest conflict, this time intraorganizational factions; emphasizing that the violent coercion of the state is analytically prior to the economy, and thus transferring the center of attention to the control of the material means of violence.

Weber also opens up yet another area of resources in these struggles for control, what might be called the "means of emotional production." It is these that underlie the power of religion and make it an important ally of the state; that transform classes into status groups, and do the same to territorial communities under particular circumstances (ethnicity); and that make "legitimacy" a crucial focus for efforts at domination. Here,

Weber comes to an insight parallel to those of Durkheim, Freud, and Nietzsche: not only that man is an animal with strong emotional desires and susceptibilities, but that particular forms of social interaction designed to arouse emotions operate to create strongly held beliefs and a sense of solidarity within the community constituted by participation in these rituals. I have put this formulation in a much more Durkheimian fashion than Weber himself, for Durkheim's analysis of rituals can be incorporated at this point to show the mechanisms by which emotional bonds are created. There involves especially the emotional contagion that results from physical copresense, the focusing of attention on a common object, and the coordination of common actions or gestures. To invoke Durkheim also enables me to bring in the work of Goffman (1959, 1967), which carries on his microlevel analysis of social rituals, with an emphasis on the materials and techniques of stage-setting that determine the effectiveness of appeals for emotional solidarity.

Durkheim and Goffman are to be seen as amplifying our knowledge of the mechanisms of emotional production, but within the framework of Weber's conflict theory. For Weber retains a crucial emphasis: The creation of emotional solidarity does not supplant conflict, but is one of the main weapons used in conflict. Emotional rituals can be used for domination within a group or organization; they are a vehicle by which alliances are formed in the struggle against other groups; and they can be used to impose a hierarchy of status prestige in which some groups dominate others by providing an ideal to emulate under inferior conditions. Weber's theory of religion incorporates all of these aspects of domination through the manipulation of emotional solidarity, and thereby provides an archetype for the various forms of community stratification. Caste, ethnic group, feudal Estate *(Stand)*, educational-cultural group, or class "respectability" lines are all forms of stratified solidarities, depending on varying distributions of the resources for emotional production. The basic dynamics are captured in the hierarchy implicit in any religion between ritual leaders, ritual followers, and non-members of the community.

From this analytical version of Weber, incorporating the relevant principles of Marx, Durkheim, and Goffman, we can move into an explicit theory of stratification. It should be apparent that there are innumerable possible types of stratified societies; our aim is not to classify them, but to state the set of causal principles that go into various empirical combinations. Our emphasis is on the cutting tools of a theory, whatever the complexity of their application in the historical world.

For conflict theory, the basic insight is that human beings are sociable but conflict-prone animals. Why is there conflict? Above all else, there is conflict because violent coercion is always a potential resource, and it is a zero-sum sort. This does not imply anything about the inherence of drives to dominate; what we do know firmly is that being coerced is an intrinsically unpleasant experience, and hence that any use of coercion, even by a small minority, calls forth conflict in the form of antagonism to being dominated. Add to this the fact that coercive power, especially as represented in the state, can be used to bring one economic goods and emotional gratification—and to deny them to others—and we can see that the availability of coercion as a resource ramifies conflicts throughout the entire society. The simultaneous existence of emotional bases for solidarity—which may well be the basis of cooperation, as Durkheim emphasized—only adds group divisions and tactical resources to be used in these conflicts.

The same argument may be transposed into the realm of social phenomenology. Every individual maximizes his subjective status according to the resources available to him and to his rivals. This is a general principle that will make sense out of the variety of evidence. By this I mean that one's subjective experience of reality is the nexus of social motivation; that everyone constructs his own world with himself in it; but this reality construction is done primarily by communication, real or imaginary, with other people; and hence people hold the keys to each other's identities. These propositions will come as no surprise to readers of George Herbert Mead or Erving Goffman. Add to this an emphasis from conflict theories: that each individual is basically pursuing his own interests and that there are many situations, notably ones where power is involved, in which those interests are inherently antagonistic. The basic argument, then, has three strands: that men live in self-constructed subjective worlds; that others pull many of the strings that control one's subjective experience; and that there are frequent conflicts over control. Life is basically a struggle for status in which no one can afford to be oblivious to the power of others around him. If we assume that everyone uses what resources are available to have others aid him in putting on the best possible face under the circumstances, we have a guiding principle to make sense out of the myriad variations of stratification.[1]

The general principles of conflict analysis may be applied to any empirical area. (*1*) Think through abstract formulations to a sample of the typical real-life interactions involved. Think of people as animals maneuvering for advantage, susceptible to emotional appeals, but steering a self-interested course toward satisfactions and away from dissatisfactions. (*2*) Look for the material arrangements that affect interaction: the physical places, the modes of communication, the supply of weapons, devices for staging one's public impression, tools, and goods. Assess the relative resources available to each individual: their potential for physical coercion, their access to other persons with whom to negotiate, their sexual attractiveness, their store of cultural devices for invoking emotional solidarity, as well as the physical arrangements just mentioned. (*3*) Apply the general hypothesis that inequalities in resources result in efforts by the dominant party to take advantage of the situation; this need not involve conscious calculation but a basic propensity of feeling one's way toward the areas of greatest immediate reward, like flowers turning to the light. Social structures are to be explained in terms of the behavior following from various lineups of resources, social change from shifts in resources resulting from previous conflicts. (*4*) Ideals and beliefs likewise are to be explained in terms of the interests which have the resources to make their viewpoint prevail. (5) Compare empirical cases; test hypotheses by looking for the conditions under which certain things occur versus the conditions under which other things occur. Think causally; look for generalizations. Be awake to multiple causes—the resources for conflict are complex.

Nowhere can these principles be better exemplified than on the materials of stratification. Especially in modern societies, we must separate out multiple spheres of social interaction and multiple causes in each one. These influences may be reduced to order through the principles of conflict theory. We can make a fair prediction of what sort of status shell each individual constructs around himself if we know how he deals with people in earning a living; how he gets along in the household in which he lives; how he relates to the population of the larger community, especially as determined by its political structures; and the ways in which he associates with friends and recreational companions. The conventional variables of survey research are all reflected in this list: occupation, parental occupation, education, ethnicity, age, and sex are cryptic references to how one's associations are structured at work, in the household, and in community and recreational groups. In each sphere, we look for the actual pattern of personal interaction, the resources available to persons in different positions, and how these affect the line of attack they take for furthering their personal status. The ideals and beliefs of persons in different positions thus emerge as personal ideologies, furthering their dominance or serving for their psychological protection.

I begin with occupational situations, as the most pervasively influential of all stratification variables. They are analyzed into several causal dimensions, elaborating a modified version of Marx, Weber, and Durkheim. Other stratified milieux are treated in terms of other resources for organizing social communities; here we find parallel applications of conflict principles as well as interaction with the occupational realm. The sum of these stratified milieux makes up the concrete social position of any individual.

Occupational Influences on Class Cultures

Occupations are the way people keep themselves alive. This is the reason for their fundamental importance. Occupations shape the differences among people, however, not merely by the fact that work is essential for survival, but because people relate to each other in different ways in this inescapable area of their lives. Occupations are the major basis of class cultures; these cultures, in turn, along with material resources for intercommunication, are the mechanisms that organize classes as communities, i.e., as kind of status group. The first process is dealt with here and the second takes up a later part of this chapter. The complexity of a system of class cultures depends on how many dimensions of difference we can locate among occupations. In order of importance, these are dominance relationships, position in a network of communication, and some additional variables, including the physical nature of the work and the amount of wealth it produces.

Dominance Relationships

Undoubtedly, the most crucial difference among work situations is the power relations involved (the ways that men give or take orders). Occupational classes are essentially power classes within the realm of work. In stating this, I am accepting Ralf Dahrendorf's (1959) modification of Marx. Marx took property as the power relation par excellence. The dividing line between possessors and nonpossessors of property marked the crucial breaks in the class structure; changes among different sorts of property—slaves, land, industrial capital—made the difference among historical eras. But, although property classes might be the sharpest social distinctions in certain periods, the twentieth century has shown that other types of power can be equally important. In capitalist societies, the salaried managerial employee has remained socially distinct from the manual worker, although a strictly Marxist interpretation would put both of them in the working class. In socialist countries where conventional property classes do not exist, the same sorts of social distinctions and conflicts of interest appear among various levels of the occupational hierarchy. As Dahrendorf points out, Marx mistook an historically limited form of power for power relations in general; his theory of class divisions and class conflict can be made useful for a wider range of situations if we seek its more abstract form.[2]

Max Weber (1968:53) defined power as the ability to secure compliance against someone's will to do otherwise. This is not the only possible use of the word "power," but it is the most useful one if we are looking for ways to explain people's outlooks. There is power like the engineer's over inanimate objects; there is power like the scholar's over ideas and words; there is the power of the planner to affect future events. But, since men encountering men is the whole observable referent of "social causation," a social power that will directly affect someone's behavior is that of a man giving orders to another. It affects the behavior of the man who gives orders, for he must take a certain bearing, think certain thoughts, and speak certain formulas. It affects the man who must listen to orders, even though he may not accept too many of them or carry them out, for he accepts at least one thing—to put up with standing before someone who is giving him orders and with deferring to him at least for the moment. One animal cows another to its heels: That is the archetypal situation of organizational life and the shaper of classes and cultures.

The situations in which authority is acted out are the key experiences of occupational life. Since one cannot avoid having an occupation or being cared for by someone who does, it influences everyone. On this basis, three main classes can be distinguished: those who take orders from few or none, but give orders to many; those who must defer to some people, but can command others; and those who are order-takers only. The readily understood continuum from upper class through middle class to working class corresponds to this dimension. This is especially clear if we note how the middle-class-working-class break is commonly assigned: not so much on the basis of the cleanliness of the work, or of the income derived from it; certainly not, today, on the basis of property dis-

tinctions; but on the basis of where one stands when orders are given.

Upper middle class and lower middle class correspond to relative positions within the middle group, based on the ratio of order-giving to order-taking. Lower class can be distinguished from working class as a marginal group who work only occasionally and at the most menial positions. Farmers and farm laborers can be fitted into this categorization at a variety of middle-class and working-class levels. Prosperous farmers are similar to other businessmen; tenant farmers and laborers are not unlike the urban working class, with differences attributable to the different community structure rather than to occupational conditions per se. The power situation is similar, too, if one understands that the people who give orders are not necessarily all in the same organization and that one need not be an actual employee to be a subordinate; the small farmer or businessman meets the banker with much the same face as the foreman meets his supervisor. There are some differences too, of course. First, I want to show that the most powerful effects on a man's behavior are the sheer volume of occupational deference he gives and gets. Then I will show how some different types of situations at about the same class level can add variations on the pattern.

Dahrendorf's (1959) revision of Marx converges here with Weber's emphasis on power relations. It should be noted that this formulation brings us into the universe of Durkheimian sociology as well, at least in its Goffmanian variant. If the successful application of power is a matter of personal bearing (in which sanctions are implied but not called upon), Goffman's analysis of the ritual dramatization of status provides us with detailed evidence on the mechanism. In a sense, the apocryphal Weberian principle of the "means of emotional production" applies not only in the realm of community formation but in the heart of the occupational relationship. Hence, it happens that Weber's historical summary of the religious propensities of various classes epitomizes later evidence on class cultures.

Networks of Occupational Communication

Another dimension of occupational cultures comes from the sheer volume and diversity of personal contacts. The politician must see diverse audiences and the king receive the awe of crowds, whereas the tenant farmer and the servant rarely see outsiders, and the workman regularly deals with few besides his boss and a little-changing circle of friends and family. The greater cosmopolitanism of the higher occupational levels is one key to their outlooks. Cosmopolitanism is generally correlated with power because power is essentially the capacity to keep up relations with a fairly large number of persons in such a way as to draw others to back one up against whoever he happens to be with at the moment. But communications are also a separate variable, as we can see in the case of occupations that have greater contacts than power, such as salesmen, entertainers, intellectuals, and professionals generally. This variable accounts for horizontal variants within classes, and for their complex internal hierarchies (e.g., within professions or in the intellectual world) that stratify whole sectors over and above their actual order-giving power.

This dimension has its classic theoretical antecedents. Marx's (1963: 123–124) principle of class mobilization by differential control of the means of transportation and communication applies not only to politics but to the differentiation of class cultures themselves. Weber's extensions of this principle to the internal structure of organizations reinforces the implication, for organizational evidence not only documents the crucial distinctions in outlook and power derived from control over information and communications . . . but provides a look from a different angle at the *empirically* same phenomenon of occupational stratification. Durkheim's model of ritual interactions and their effects on the "collective conscience" provides a finer specification of the mechanisms involved. In the *Division of Labor in Society*, Durkheim shows that the content of social beliefs, and especially the pressure for group conformity and respect for symbols, varies with the intensity and diversity of social contacts. In *The Elementary Forms of the Religious Life*, Durkheim examines the mechanisms at the high-intensity end of the continuum and shows that the highly reified conception of collective symbols, and the intense loyalties to the immediate group, are produced by ceremonial interactions within a group of unchanging characters, in a situation of close physical proximity and highly concentrated attention. By abstraction, we can see that not only entire historical eras but particular occupational milieus vary along these dimensions and hence produce different sorts of cultural objects and personal loyalties. Weber's distinction between bureaucratic and patrimonial cultures captures this dimension, with its different centers of loyalty and standards of ethics; the bureaucratic and entrepreneurial sectors of the modern occupational world represent these variations across the dimension of class power.[3]

Wealth and Physical Demands

Besides the main variables of power and communications networks, occupations vary in additional ways that add to the explanation of class cultures and hence to their potential variety. One is the wealth produced and another is the kind of physical demands made. To insist on the importance of money as the main difference among social classes, of course, is vulgar Marxism. It is the organizational forms of power that produce the income that are crucial in determining basic distinctions in outlook. But money is important as one intervening link between occupational position and many aspects of lifestyle that set classes apart; as such it can have some independent effects. Income is not always commensurate with power. Some men make less or more than others of their power level. Power of position and power of money can be separate ways of controlling others, and hence have alternative or additive effects on one's outlook. Moreover, income can be saved, collected, or inherited so that an aspect of power can be passed on—and so preserve its accompanying culture—when its organizational basis is no longer present.

On the physical side, some work calls for more exertion than others; some is more dirty or more dangerous. These aspects tend to be correlated with power, since it can be used to force others to do the harder and more unpleasant labor. But physical demands do influence lifestyle, making the lower classes more immured to hardship and dirt, and allowing the upper to be more effete and fastidious. Physical demands also vary independently of class power, and help account for variations between more military and more pacific eras and occupations, and between rural and urban milieux. . . .

Endnotes

1. The proposition that individuals *maximize* their subjective status appears to contradict March and Simon's (1958) organizational principle that men operate by *satisficing*—setting minimal levels of payoff in each area of concern, and then troubleshooting where crises arise. The contradiction is only apparent. Satisficing refers to a strategy for dealing with the *cognitive* problem produced by inherent limits on the human capacity for processing information. The principle of maximizing subjective status is a *motivational* principle, telling us what are the goals of behavior. Any analysis of cognitive strategies is incomplete without some motivational principle such as the latter to tell us what are the purposes of action, and what areas of concern are most emphasized. In other words, it is one thing to predict what goals someone will pursue, another to predict what strategies he will use in pursuing them, given the inability to see very far into the future or deal with very many things at once.

2. This is not to say that Dahrendorf's (1959) position is completely satisfactory. Power organized as property, and power organized within a government or corporate structure, are not entirely equivalent. Men whose power depends on one of these forms are likely to be politically committed to maintaining it. The political differences among capitalists and socialists remain, even though the elites of both systems may have similar outlooks, in much the same way as holders of landed and industrial property have fought bitter political battles over whose organizational form should dominate. Dahrendorf's formulation is a product of the period of Cold War liberalism; he argued for decreasing international hostilities by focusing on those things that might be taken as structural convergence among all modern societies.

Ideological considerations aside, it is useful to retain both levels of analysis. Differences in power position, in whatever kind of organization, are the most fundamental determinant of mens' outlooks, and hence of where solidarity groups will form. Within the same general level of power, differences in the organizational basis of power—different forms of economic property or government organization—result in different political and ideological commitments. Men of power all resemble each other in general, but the specific source of power makes for some specific differences in political culture and creates definite political factions.

3. Patrimonial organization, most characteristic of traditional societies, centers around families, patrons and their clients, and other personalistic networks. The emphasis is on traditional rituals that demonstrate the emotional bonds among men; the world is divided into those whom one can trust because of strongly legitimated personal connections, and the rest of the world from whom nothing is to be expected that cannot be exacted by cold-blooded bargaining or force. In modern bureaucratic organization, by contrast, personal ties are weaker, less ritualized, and emotionally demonstrative; in their place is the allegiance to a set of abstract rules and positions. The different class cultures in patrimonial and bureaucratic organizations are accordingly affected. Patrimonial elites are more ceremonious and personalistic. Bureaucratic elites emphasize a colder set of ideals.

The contrast is not merely an historical one. There are many elements of bureaucracy in premodern societies, notably in China; in Europe, bureaucracy gradually set in within the heart of the aristocracy, especially in France and Germany, around the seventeenth century. Patrimonial forms of organization exist in modern society as well, alongside and within bureaucracies. They are prominent in the entrepreneurial sector of modern business, especially in volatile areas like entertainment, construction, real estate, speculative finance, and organized crime, as well as in the politics of a complex, federated governmental system like the United States. Weber (1958: 57–58) caught the contrast between the two ways of doing business when he pointed out two kinds of business ethos throughout history. One has existed in all major societies: it emphasizes trickery, cleverness, and speculation aimed at making the greatest possible immediate profit. A second form is rationalistic, ascetic capitalism, which approaches business in a methodical and routinized fashion. Work and production are more ends in themselves, a way of life, rather than a means to get rich quick. In Weber's famous theory, capitalism developed in Europe precisely because business was dominated not merely by the entrepreneurial ethic, as in ancient and oriental societies, but by a sizable group holding the ascetic business ethic. The entrepreneurial type does not disappear once the modern economy is established, of course. He survives to skim the cream off of a system he could not have created.

References

Dahrendorf, R. 1959. *Class and class conflict in industrial society*. Stanford, California: Stanford Univ. Press.

Goffman, Erving. 1959. *The presentation of self in everyday life*. Garden City, NY: Doubleday.

——. 1967. *Interaction ritual*. Garden City, NY: Doubleday.

March, J. G., and H. A. Simon. 1958. *Organizations*. New York: Wiley.

Marx, K. 1963. *The eighteenth brumaire of Louis Napoleon*. New York: International Publishers (Originally published 1852).

Weber, M. 1958. *The Protestant ethic and the spirit of capitalism*. New York: Scribner's (Originally published 1904–1905).

——. 1968. *Economy and Society*. New York: Bedminster Press (Originally published 1922).

38
Membership and History

Anselm Strauss

In this essay, Anselm Strauss (1916–1997) offers a symbolic interactionist account of the symbolic foundations of all human groups, illustrating the centrality of language as the means by which shared meaning is communicated. Group membership, whether a matter of acquired or achieved identity, results from interactional processes (and here the influence of Simmel can be seen) in which meaning becomes a collective enterprise. Strauss goes on to observe that shared meanings are precarious, as they are subject to challenge because of the diverse ways that individuals and subgroups interpret the symbols relevant to group membership. In the final section of the essay, he connects this discussion to the topic of historical memory, illustrating the ways in which symbol systems are embedded in the collective past, which is not fixed but rather is subject to ongoing reinterpretation.

Membership as a Symbolic Matter[1]

... Group life is organized around communication. Communication consists not merely in the transmission of ideas from the head of one person to that of another, it signifies shared meanings. "Shared" means more than that terms are used in ways sufficiently alike so that persons understand each other; it also means that terms arise out of and in turn permit community action. As Dewey has written, language

compels one individual to take the standpoint of other individuals and to see and inquire from a standpoint that is . . . common to them as participants or "parties" in a conjoint undertaking. . . . The physical sound gets its meaning in and by conjoint community of functional use.[2]

We might speak of a group that consisted of only two members provided they were to act conjointly, with consensus, because they shared important symbols. Popular idiom does not usually refer to groups of two persons, but the principle involved is the same whether the groups have three members, ten, one hundred, or more. The members are able to participate in various coordinated activities because they share a common terminology. Groups form around points of agreement, and then new classifications arise on the basis of further shared experience.

The constitution of any human group is thus a symbolic, not a physical fact. This is obvious, of course, when one considers such groups as the United Nations or the Democratic Party; but it is equally true of the Smith family, the American Negro, or the United States. A family is composed of more than blood members and is hardly dependent upon the face-to-face contact of all its members. A man is a Negro not merely or even necessarily because of skin color. As for a nation, 150,000,000 persons scarcely constitute a unit merely because of geographic proximity. Geographical and biological considerations may contribute to the formation of concepts and may in some sense enter into the concepts themselves—for the members of a nation conceive of themselves as occupying a common territory and sometimes as stemming from a common ancestry. But groups exist as such only because of the common symbolizations of their members. Many or most groups are easily visualized in purely symbolic terms since they are less directly connected with geography and biology than are nation and family.

The symbolic nature of groups raises intricate questions concerning membership. If one takes membership to mean only formal "joining," no great question arises concerning membership in certain kinds of groups. You either are, or are not, a Rotarian or a Senator. But clearly the formal criteria are not sufficient. In a more subtle sense, you may belong but not have much allegiance, not participate much, and you may not actually belong but participate a good deal. To ticket a man as formally holding membership in such and such groups barely suggests the nature and quality of his allegiances.

When a group is small, it is usually possible to determine the outer limits of its membership, although even then difficulties may be encountered. But when a group is large, and especially when it is not territorially fixed, then genuine practical and theoretical questions arise concerning who really does belong and upon whom the group may rely for what. Is a man a Lutheran if he has not been to church for twenty years? Is a man always a Catholic in some sense, even though he may have been excommunicated (a significant word) or have left the Church? If a gentile woman marries a Jew and embraces his faith, is she or is she not a Jewess? Suppose that she divorces him but continues to attend synagogue services regularly and raises her children as Jews, is she still Jewish? If he in turn grows unreligious and associates with fewer Jewish people than she does, who is the more Jewish or the more truly Jewish of the two? Likewise, if a Negro passes for a number of years as white, is he still a Negro, particularly if he now names or identifies himself as white? If a "white" mixes with Negroes to the extent that he thinks about most racial issues as they do, to what extent is he still, conventionally speaking, white? These are not extreme cases, for membership and allegiance often are just that elusive.

Sometimes social scientists draw distinctions between "membership" and "reference" groups, attempting to take into account two situations: membership without much participation, and participation without membership. Thus Sherif has defined a membership group as one in which an individual "is an actual member" and a reference group as one from which

> the individual's standards, attitudes and status aspiration stem. . . . In many cases his reference groups are groups of which he is an actual member. . . . But this is not always so. He may be actually a member of one group, but through his contact with the attitudes and aspirations of another he may do his best to relate himself, his standards, his aspirations to that group.[3]

The phrase "groups of which he is an actual member" can signify only formal membership, or membership in a group so well structured that its members know of each other. Membership group and reference group are, in fact, such an oversimplification of the facts of social life that it is possible to find one writer (Sherif) sharply criticizing others (Merton and Kitt) for writing that enlisted men in the Army were "positively oriented to the norms of a group of which they were not members, that is the norms of the officers." Sherif has maintained that "the army organization and its officers serve as a reference group for such enlisted men and not the informal groups that emerged among their fellow enlisted men."[4] Merton and Kitt, though committed to the distinction, themselves write that

> There is nothing fixed about the boundaries separating . . . membership-groups from non-membership groups. These change with the changing situation. Vis-à-vis civilians . . . men in the Army may regard themselves and be regarded as members of an in-group; yet, in another context, enlisted men may regard themselves and be regarded as an in-group in distinction to the out-group of officers. Since these concepts are relative to the situation, rather than absolute, there is no paradox in referring to the officers as an out-group for enlisted men in one context, and as members of the more inclusive in-group in another context.[5]

The last sentence in the Merton-Kitt quotation, particularly, suggests the entirely symbolic character of membership; but at the same time the quotation illustrates how blunt an instrument is the membership-reference distinction for handling intricacies of group belonging. Another term, "multiple group membership," has also been coined to describe the evident fact that each of us belongs simultaneously to many groups. This term also reflects the layman's and the scientist's difficulties in assessing motivation. Since people do belong to many groups, a problem arises about any given situation: "as a member of which group is he acting now, or was he acting, or will he act?" This is, of course, simply another way of inquiring about situational identity.

"Multiple group membership," "reference group membership," judgments "anchored in group standards and frames of reference"—such terms come close to but do not directly focus on what, I would maintain, is the heart of membership: that is, its symbolic character. When we participate in cooperative activities we learn, and develop, certain terminologies. Insofar as the perspectives of various groups are similar, we are able to participate simultaneously or successively in them without experiencing the need to reconcile conflicting terminologies. Some of these terminologies are, as a host of writers have observed, logically contradictory; yet we who act in accordance with them may not be aware of our inconsistency. A man may purchase a "modern home," having developed his architectural tastes through discussions with artists, other modern art enthusiasts, and his reading of magazines; but may expect his wife to cook the foods he and she learned to like while living in slum tenements as members of immigrant families. Different standards apply to home and food consumption. House buying and home living, in fact, are not widely regarded as consumption. In similar vein, sociologists sometimes use the example of a man acting as a Christian on Sunday and a businessman on Monday, and they note that many men seem to be able to "disassociate" or keep in watertight compartments the different "role demands." To ask whether someone is more an immigrant than a member of the *avant garde*, or whether he is more a businessman than a Christian, is to raise pointless questions. When a man buys a modern house, he is acting as would others who share his terminology of perception and

judgment. When he tells his wife not to experiment with the "American" recipes that stud the same magazines from whence he derived some of his best architectural ideas, then he is acting as do others who share his discriminations in food.

The members of any group necessarily experience certain areas of conceptual disagreement as well as non-communication. Groups are composed of individuals who, after all, bring with them to their participation in cooperative activity a body of symbolization derived from their other memberships. These symbols brought to the group from the outside contribute to the inevitable formation of subgroups, as for instance cliques among school teachers or those characteristic groupings of family quarrels that form along sex and age lines. Just because there exists within any group a divergency of concepts (whether imported or developed) there is frequent, not to say continual, formation and dissolution of coalitions, splinter groups, cliques, and other sub-groupings. Symbols, we may conclude, are pregnant with possibilities for convergence and divergence, for combination and permutation. Meanings, to quote John Dewey again, "breed new meanings.". . .

History: Heritage, Memorialization, and Creation

. . . [O]ne ought not to speak of group membership without painstakingly seeking to take history into account. Identities imply not merely personal histories but also social histories. The preceding statement follows rather simply from this: individuals hold memberships in groups that themselves are products of a past. If you wish to understand persons—their development and their relations with significant others—you must be prepared to view them as embedded in historical context. Psychological and psychiatric theory, at least of the American variety, underplay this context; and those sociologists and anthropologists who are interested in personal identity tend to treat historical matters more as stage settings, or backdrops, than as crucial to the study of persons. This is an oversimplification, I am certain, of the use and lack of use that is made of historical materials in social psychology. Nevertheless it allows me to state forthrightly a view of history that is implicit throughout this essay.

A man must be viewed as embedded in a temporal matrix not simply of his own making, but which is peculiarly and subtly related to something of his own making—his conception of the past as it impinges on himself. I take the liberty here of using some autobiographical comments by Sir Osbert Sitwell to make this proposition especially vivid. Do not be deceived by these comments: they are unusual merely because Sir Osbert belongs to an aristocratic world and thereby seems incredibly affected by his sense of an impinging and lively past.

The first volume of his autobiography bears the title of *Left Hand, Right Hand*[6] which Sir Osbert is at pains to explain is

> because, according to the palmists, the lines of the left hand are incised inalterably at birth, while those of the right hand are modified by our actions and environment, and the life we lead.

The left hand theme is encountered on the initial pages, which portray his father walking over the ancestral grounds, upon or near which the family has lived for seven centuries. For his father the Middle Ages "are the model for all life to follow, and his life was largely devoted to living out that model." Like others of the British aristocracy at the turn of the century "he was interested more in ancestors and descendants than in sons and fathers." During a walk—the book opens with a description of it—the father remarks to Osbert, "It's quite evident, if you read the family letters, that we've been working up toward something for a long time, for well over a century." He did not mean, and did not realize, that three of his children were to become recognized as among Great Britain's most celebrated writers; but Sir Osbert himself is concerned, in the autobiography, with the very question of how this was to come about.

> Who knows whence come the various traits of sensibility? Ancestors stretch behind a man and his nature like a fan, or the spread tail of a peacock. At every turn, in the very gesture and look, in every deci-

sion he takes, he draws on the reserves or deficits of the past.

Naturally he has countless ancestors. He makes no claim that all are important to his own character and personal history: but he has taken the trouble to record, through some seventy pages, fact and anecdote about various of his father's and mother's ancestors. They may possibly be relevant to his autobiography. What is more, it is apparent that Sir Osbert is versed in their lives. Aristocratic families leave records, letters, and diaries to their descendants, and appear on the pages and in the memoirs of contemporary authors and acquaintances. Sir Osbert knows his many ancestors as others know their immediate relatives. He is writing with restraint: he could write volumes about his kin. Once through these introductory pages, and unleashed upon the actual story of his life, Sir Osbert brings into his narrative his living kin; displaying a keen sense of what was happening to them, during the specific period that he, as a youth, was meeting and experiencing them. Personal relations are hardly ever described merely as personal, they are embroidered into an historic tapestry. In his own words: he is writing of his elders and of "people who died before I was born, but who still influence me, perhaps, in ways I do not know as well as in ways to be recognized."

You may exclaim that this is a very particular kind of memory, valued and possessed only by certain kinds of people and populations. This is not the point. Even when a man lacks knowledge of kinship history, this has bearing upon the fact and sense of his identity: to his name both in the literal sense and in the reputational sense. America was settled by immigrants who thereby cut off their children from extensive memories; memory stopping, so to speak, at our shores and reaching no further back than the ancestor who migrated. The discrepancy between the sons of migrants and those inheritors of longer American genealogies—with heirlooms, histories, and prestige to match—is still noticeable on the American scene. The attempts to maintain, repudiate and acquire such symbolic genealogies are, as is well known, important endeavors of some of our citizens. Kinship is so entwined with social class that a deficiency of kinship memories means also deficiency of class memories. American fiction and autobiography have recorded the quashing of old class memories by upwardly mobile persons, and the some-times frantic acquisition of historical and anecdotal knowledge of the social class into which they are moving.

But the impact of history upon identity in-volves much more than consciousness of kinship and placement in a social class. . . . [I]t will pay to note two further aspects of the relation between history and personal iden-tity. The first is this: a people may create an historical past which they do not possess, or discard a past and then create a new one. Thus, in the development of nationalistic movements, and in the nationalism of na-tions, the past may be recreated in the image of the desired present and future. Many his-torians have documented, Carleton Hayes among them,[7] that these imagined and glori-ous pasts are laboriously and carefully cre-ated through the various mass media. This has led George Orwell to depict the ultimate in totalitarian control, in his reverse Utopia, *Nineteen Eighty-Four*,[8] where history was completely rewritten through the creation of "newspeak," a special language which per-mitted only certain limited ideas to be con-ceived. E. C. Hughes[9] has written of another nationalistic tendency: he suggests that under conditions of tribal disintegration as in Africa, when nationalistic movements form, they and the countries which emerge from them must quite literally create new mythical national histories. They must do this in order that their heterogeneous popu-lations be brought together under one ban-ner. Thus the emerging territorial bound-aries, and the emerging collective acts, will be rationalized in terms of a symbolic past as well as a realistic present.

This leads me to a second point that actu-ally none of this is very different than occurs in the more humdrum histories of less dra-matically changing groups and organiza-tions. Each generation perceives the past in new terms, and rewrites its own history. In-sofar as there are shared group-perspectives bearing upon the past, the selves of the com-ponent members are vitally affected. Certain

groups and organizations have immensely long histories, and strong vested interests, in preserving and reviewing their histories. An American thinks immediately of the South since the Civil War. Even the writings of pro-fessional historians, white and Negro, are a reflection of each generation's successively revised posture toward the past and a contribution toward what is known and felt about that past.

In Europe, collective memories are lon-ger, and so identities may be linked with con-ceptions of ancient eras. The citizens of Nuremberg have an urban history which in-cludes a glorious sixteenth century. The signs of it are visible in the churches, in the houses, in the very street plan of the central city; so that when the center of the city was badly destroyed during the war, little or no question was raised afterwards whether it should be reconstructed in modern styles. It was deliberately rebuilt to recapture, if pos-sible, something of the atmosphere of the past, and ancient public buildings were sometimes rebuilt from the ground up at great cost. This is not to say that the identi-ties of all citizens of Nuremberg are equally involved with the city's past, nor in the same ways: but Nuremberg's past hovers over the city visibly, gets into the press and into con-versation; and must be taken into account even by those who spurn or fight it. Nuremberg's bustling business men have re-cently published a book about their city, ad-vertising its great industrial capacity and po-tential. They necessarily had to couch their slogans in opposition to the city's past, for even the outside world thinks of Nuremberg first and foremost as a treasure house of Ger-man medieval art, rather than as a progres-sive industrial city. "We are happy to present at this time a city in the bloom of a new youth. Its title [the book] might well be 'Nuremburg the living city.' "[10]. . .

Endnotes

1. Much of this section is taken from a paper titled "Concepts, Communication, Groups," published in M. Sherif and M. Wilson (eds.), *Social Relations at the Crossroads* (New York: Harper, 1953), pp. 99–105.

2. John Dewey, *Experience and Nature* (Chicago: Open Court, 1925).

3. M. Sherif, *An Outline of Social Psychology* (New York: Harper, 1948), p. 105.

4. M. Sherif and C. Sherif, *Groups in Harmony and Tension* (New York: Harper, 1953), p. 164.

5. Robert K. Merton and Alice S. Kitt, "Contributions to the Theory of Reference Group Behavior," in R. K. Merton and P. Lazarsfeld (eds.), *Continuities in Social Research* (Glencoe: The Free Press, 1950), pp. 86–87.

6. Osbert Sitwell, *Left Hand, Right Hand!* (Boston: Little and Brown, 1944).

7. Carleton J. Hayes, *Essays on Nationalism* (New York: Macmillan, 1926).

8. George Orwell, *Nineteen Eighty-Four* (New York: Harcourt Brace, 1949).

9. Everett C. Hughes, in conversation.

10. Stadtrat zu Nürnberg, *Lebendiges Nürnberg* (Nürnberg: Ulrich, 1953), p. 8.

39
Society as Symbolic Interaction

Herbert Blumer

Herbert Blumer (1900–1987) coined the term *symbolic interactionism* to describe a theoretical approach to sociology different from the reigning orthodoxies of the day, which in his view included behaviorism, functionalism, and other deterministic theoretical approaches. Noting his intellectual debt not only to the key figures associated with the Chicago School of Sociology but to social philosophers William James, John Dewey, and George Herbert Mead, in this 1962 essay Blumer urges a sociology that treats human beings as authors of their own lives insofar as they imbue their actions with meaning and purpose. He believes that competing theoretical paradigms tend to treat people as the products or effects of social forces. To the extent that they do so, they fail to take seriously the idea of the self and the interpretive work that selves do in constructing their social lives—not in isolation, but through complex processes of interaction.

A view of human society as symbolic interaction has been followed more than it has been formulated. Partial, usually fragmentary, statements of it are to be found in the writings of a number of eminent scholars, some inside the field of sociology and some outside. Among the former we may note such scholars as Charles Horton Cooley, W. I. Thomas, Robert E. Parks, E. W. Burgess, Florian Znaniecki, Ellsworth Faris, and James Mickel Williams. Among those outside the discipline we may note William James, John Dewey, and George Herbert Mead. None of these scholars, in my judgment, has presented a systematic statement of the nature of human group life from the standpoint of symbolic interaction. Mead stands out among all of them in laying bare the fundamental premises of the approach, yet he did little to develop its methodological implications for sociological study. Students who seek to depict the position of symbolic interaction may easily give different pictures of it. What I have to present should be regarded as my personal version. My aim is to present the basic premises of the point of view and to develop their methodological consequences for the study of human group life.

The term "symbolic interaction" refers, of course, to the peculiar and distinctive character of interaction as it takes place between human beings. The peculiarity consists in the fact that human beings interpret or "define" each other's actions instead of merely reacting to each other's actions. Their "response" is not made directly to the actions of one another but instead is based on the meaning which they attach to such actions. Thus, human interaction is mediated by the use of symbols, by interpretation, or by ascertaining the meaning of one another's actions. This mediation is equivalent to inserting a process of interpretation between stimulus and response in the case of human behavior.

The simple recognition that human beings interpret each other's actions as the means of acting toward one another has permeated the thought and writings of many scholars of human conduct and of human group life. Yet few of them have endeavored to analyze what such interpretation implies about the nature of the human being or about the nature of human association. They are usually content with a mere recognition that "interpretation" should be caught by the student, or with a simple realization that symbols, such as cultural norms or values, must be introduced into their analyses. Only G. H. Mead, in my judgment, has sought to think through what the act of interpretation implies for an understanding of the human being, human action and human association. The essentials of his analysis are so penetrating and profound and so important for an understanding of human group life that I wish to spell them out, even though briefly.

The key feature in Mead's analysis is that the human being has a self. This idea should not be cast aside as esoteric or glossed over as something that is obvious and hence not worthy of attention. In declaring that the human being has a self, Mead had in mind chiefly that the human being can be the object of his own actions. He can act toward himself as he might act toward others. Each of us is familiar with actions of this sort in which the human being gets angry with himself, rebuffs himself, takes pride in himself, argues with himself, tries to bolster his own courage, tells himself that he should "do this" or not "do that," sets goals for himself, makes compromises with himself, and plans what he is going to do. That the human being acts toward himself in these and countless other ways is a matter of easy empirical observation. To recognize that the human being can act toward himself is no mystical conjuration.

Mead regards this ability of the human being to act toward himself as the central mechanism with which the human being faces and deals with his world. This mechanism enables the human being to make indications to himself of things in his surroundings and thus to guide his actions by what he notes. Anything of which a human being is conscious is something which he is indicating to himself—the ticking of a clock, a knock at the door, the appearance of a friend, the remark made by a companion, a recognition that he has a task to perform, or the realization that he has a cold. Conversely, anything of which he is not conscious is, ipso facto, something which he is not indicating to himself. The conscious life of the human being, from the time that he awakens until he falls asleep, is a continual flow of self-indications—notations of the things with which he deals and takes into account. We are given, then, a picture of the human being as an organism which confronts its world with a mechanism for making indications to itself. This is the mechanism that is involved in interpreting the actions of others. To interpret the actions of another is to point out to oneself that the action has this or that meaning or character.

Now, according to Mead, the significance of making indications to oneself is of paramount importance. The importance lies along two lines. First, to indicate something is to extricate it from its setting, to hold it apart, to give it a meaning or, in Mead's language, to make it into an object. An object—that is to say, anything that an individual indicates to himself—is different from a stimulus; instead of having an intrinsic character which acts on the individual and which can be identified apart from the individual, its character or meaning is conferred on it by the individual. The object is a product of the individual's disposition to act instead of being an antecedent stimulus which evokes the act. Instead of the individual being surrounded by an environment of pre-existing objects which play upon him and call forth his behavior, the proper picture is that he constructs his objects on the basis of his ongoing activity. In any of his countless acts—whether minor, like dressing himself, or major, like organizing himself for a professional career—the individual is designating different objects to himself, giving them meaning, judging their suitability to his action, and making decisions on the basis of the judgment. This is what is meant by interpretation or acting on the basis of symbols.

The second important implication of the fact that the human being makes indications to himself is that his action is constructed or built up instead of being a mere release. Whatever the action in which he is engaged, the human individual proceeds by pointing out to himself the divergent things which have to be taken into account in the course of his action. He has to note what he wants to do and how he is to do it; he has to point out to himself the various conditions which may be instrumental to his action and those which may obstruct his action; he has to take account of the demands, the expectations, the prohibitions, and the threats as they may arise in the situation in which he is acting. His action is built up step by step through a process of such self-indication. The human individual pieces together and guides his action by taking account of different things and interpreting their significance for his prospective action. There is no instance of conscious action of which this is not true.

The process of constructing action through making indications to oneself cannot be swallowed up in any of the conventional psychological categories. This process is distinct from and different from what is spoken of as the "ego"—just as it is different from any other conception which conceives of the self in terms of composition or organization. Self-indiction is a moving communicative process in which the individual notes things, assesses them, gives them a meaning, and decides to act on the basis of the meaning. The human being stands over against the world, or against "alters," with such a process and not with a mere ego. Further, the process of self-indication cannot be subsumed under the forces, whether from the outside or inside, which are presumed to play upon the individual to produce his behavior. Environmental pressures, external stimuli, organic drives, wishes, attitudes, feelings, ideas, and their like do not cover or explain the process of self-indication. The process of self-indication stands over against them in that the individual points out to himself and interprets the appearance or expression of such things, noting a given social demand that is made on him, recognizing a command, observing that he is hungry, realizing that he wishes to buy something, aware that he has a given feeling, conscious that he dislikes eating with someone he despises, or aware that he is thinking of doing some given thing. By virtue of indicating such things to himself, he places himself over against them and is able to act back against them, accepting them, rejecting them, or transforming them in accordance with how he defines or interprets them. His behavior, accordingly, is not a result of such things as environmental pressures, stimuli, motives, attitudes, and ideas but arises instead from how he interprets and handles these things in the action which he is constructing. The process of self-indication by means of which human action is formed cannot be accounted for by factors which precede the act. The process of self-indication exists in its own right and must be accepted and studied as such. It is through this process that the human being constructs his conscious action.

Now Mead recognizes that the formation of action by the individual through a process of self-indication always takes place in a social context. Since this matter is so vital to an understanding of symbolic interaction it needs to be explained carefully. Fundamentally, group action takes the form of a fitting together of individual lines of action. Each individual aligns his action to the action of others by ascertaining what they are doing or what they intend to do—that is, by getting the meaning of their acts. For Mead, this is done by the individual "taking the role" of others—either the role of a specific person or the role of a group (Mead's "generalized other"). In taking such roles the individual seeks to ascertain the intention or direction of the acts of others. He forms and aligns his own action on the basis of such interpretation of the acts of others. This is the fundamental way in which group action takes place in human society.

The foregoing are the essential features, as I see them, in Mead's analysis of the bases of symbolic interaction. They presuppose the following: that human society is made up of individuals who have selves (that is, make indications to themselves); that individual action is a construction and not a release, being built up by the individual through noting and interpreting features of the situations in which he acts; that group or collective action consists of the aligning of individual actions, brought about by the individuals' interpreting or taking into account each other's actions. Since my purpose is to present and not to defend the position of symbolic interaction I shall not endeavor in this essay to advance support for the three premises which I have just indicated. I wish merely to say that the three premises can be easily verified empirically. I know of no instance of human group action to which the three premises do not apply. The reader is challenged to find or think of a single instance which they do not fit. I wish now to point out that sociological views of human society are, in general, markedly at variance with the premises which I have indicated as underlying symbolic interaction. Indeed, the predominant number of such views, especially those in vogue at the present time, do not see or treat human society as symbolic interaction. Wedded, as they tend to be, to some form of sociological determinism, they adopt images of human society, of individuals in it, and of group action which do not square with the premises of symbolic interaction. I wish to say a few words about the major lines of variance.

Sociological thought rarely recognizes or treats human societies as composed of individuals who have selves. Instead, they assume human beings to be merely organisms with some kind of organization, responding to forces which play upon them. Generally, although not exclusively, these forces are lodged in the make-up of the society, as in the case of "social system," "social structure," "culture," "status position," "social role," "custom," "institution," "collective representation," "social situation," "social norm," and "values." The assumption is that the behavior of people as members *of a society* is an expression of the play on them of these kinds of factors or forces. This, of course, is the logical position which is necessarily taken when the scholar explains their behavior or phases of their behavior in terms of one or another of such social factors. The individuals who compose a human society are treated as the media through which such factors operate, and the social action of such individuals is regarded as an expression of such factors. This approach or point of view denies, or at least ignores, that human beings have selves—that they act by making indications to themselves. Incidentally, the "self" is not brought into the picture by introducing such items as organic drives, motives, attitudes, feelings, internalized social factors, or psychological components. Such psychological factors have the same status as the social factors mentioned: they are regarded as factors which play on the individual to produce his action. They do not constitute the process of self-indication. The process of self-indication stands over against them, just as it stands over against the social factors which play on the human being. Practically all sociological conceptions of human society fail to recognize that the individuals who compose it have selves in the sense spoken of.

Correspondingly, such sociological conceptions do not regard the social actions of individuals in human society as being constructed by them through a process of interpretation. Instead, action is treated as a product of factors which play on and through individuals. The social behavior of people is not seen as built up by them through an interpretation of objects, situations, or the actions of others. If a place is given to "interpretation," the interpretation is regarded as merely an expression of other factors (such as motives) which precede the act, and accordingly disappears as a factor in its own right. Hence, the social action of people is treated as an outward flow or expression of forces playing on them rather than as acts which are built up by people through their interpretation of the situations in which they are placed.

These remarks suggest another significant line of difference between general sociological views and the position of symbolic interaction. These two sets of views differ in where they lodge social action. Under the perspective of symbolic interaction, social action is lodged in acting individuals who fit their respective lines of action to one another through a process of interpretation; group action is the collective action of such individuals. As opposed to this view, sociological conceptions generally lodge social action in the action of society or in some unit of society. Examples of this are legion. Let me cite a few. Some conceptions, in treating societies or human groups as "social systems," regard group action as an expression of a system, either in a state of balance or seeking to achieve balance. Or group action is conceived as an expression of the "functions" of a society or of a group. Or group action is regarded as the outward expression of elements lodged in society or the group, such as cultural demands, societal purposes, social values, or institutional stresses. These typical conceptions ignore or blot out a view of group life or of group action as consisting of the collective or concerted actions of individuals seeking to meet their life situations. If recognized at all, the efforts of people to develop collective acts to meet their situations are subsumed under the play of underlying or transcending forces which are lodged in society or its parts. The individuals composing the society or the group become "carriers," or media for the expression of such forces; and the interpretative behavior by means of which people form their actions is merely a coerced link in the play of such forces.

The indication of the foregoing lines of variance should help to put the position of symbolic interaction in better perspective. In the remaining discussion I wish to sketch somewhat more fully how human society appears in terms of symbolic interaction and to point out some methodological implications.

Human society is to be seen as consisting of acting people, and the life of the society is to be seen as consisting of their actions. The acting units may be separate individuals, collectivities whose members are acting together on a common quest, or organizations acting on behalf of a constituency. Respective examples are individual purchasers in a market, a play group or missionary band, and a business corporation or a national professional association. There is no empirically observable activity in a human society that does not spring from some acting unit. This banal statement needs to be stressed in light of the common practice of sociologists of reducing human society to social units that do not act—for example, social classes in modern society. Obviously, there are ways of viewing human society other than in terms of the acting units that compose it. I merely wish to point out that in respect to concrete or empirical activity human society must necessarily be seen in terms of the acting units that form it. I would add that any scheme of human society claiming to be a realistic analysis has to respect and be congruent with the empirical recognition that a human society consists of acting units.

Corresponding respect must be shown to the conditions under which such units act. One primary condition is that action takes place in and with regard to a situation. Whatever be the acting unit—an individual, a family, a school, a church, a business firm, a labor union, a legislature, and so on—any particular action is formed in the light of the situation in which it takes place. This leads to the recognition of a second major condition, namely, that the action is formed or constructed by interpreting the situation. The acting unit necessarily has to identify the things which it has to take into account—tasks, opportunities, obstacles, means, demands, discomforts, dangers, and the like; it has to assess them in some fashion and it has to make decisions on the basis of the assess-

ment. Such interpretative behavior may take place in the individual guiding his own action, in a collectivity of individuals acting in concert, or in "agents" acting on behalf of a group or organization. Group life consists of acting units developing acts to meet the situations in which they are placed.

Usually, most of the situations encountered by people in a given society are defined or "structured" by them in the same way. Through previous interaction they develop and acquire common understandings or definitions of how to act in this or that situation. These common definitions enable people to act alike. The common repetitive behavior of people in such situations should not mislead the student into believing that no process of interpretation is in play; on the contrary, even though fixed, the actions of the participating people are constructed by them through a process of interpretation. Since ready-made and commonly accepted definitions are at hand, little strain is placed on people in guiding and organizing their acts. However, many other situations may not be defined in a single way by the participating people. In this event, their lines of action do not fit together readily and collective action is blocked. Interpretations have to be developed and effective accommodation of the participants to one another has to be worked out. In the case of such "undefined" situations, it is necessary to trace and study the emerging process of definition which is brought into play.

Insofar as sociologists or students of human society are concerned with the behavior of acting units, the position of symbolic interaction requires the student to catch the process of interpretation through which they construct their actions. This process is not to be caught merely by turning to conditions which are antecedent to the process. Such antecedent conditions are helpful in understanding the process insofar as they enter into it, but as mentioned previously they do not constitute the process. Nor can one catch the process merely by inferring its nature from the overt action which is its product. To catch the process, the student must take the role of the acting unit whose behavior he is studying. Since the interpretation is being made by the acting unit in terms of objects designated and appraised, meanings acquired, and decisions made, the process has to be seen from the standpoint of the acting unit. It is the recognition of this fact that makes the research work of such scholars as R. E. Park and W. I. Thomas so notable. To try to catch the interpretative process by remaining aloof as a so-called "objective" observer and refusing to take the role of the acting unit is to risk the worst kind of subjectivism—the objective observer is likely to fill in the process of interpretation with his own surmises in place of catching the process as it occurs in the experience of the acting unit which uses it.

By and large, of course, sociologists do not study human society in terms of its acting units. Instead, they are disposed to view human society in terms of structure or organization and to treat social action as an expression of such structure or organization. Thus, reliance is placed on such structural categories as social system, culture, norms, values, social stratification, status positions, social roles and institutional organization. These are used both to analyze human society and to account for social action within it. Other major interests of sociological scholars center around this focal theme of organization. One line of interest is to view organization in terms of the functions it is supposed to perform. Another line of interest is to study societal organization as a system seeking equilibrium; here the scholar endeavors to detect mechanisms which are indigenous to the system. Another line of interest is to identify forces which play upon organization to bring about changes in it; here the scholar endeavors, especially through comparative study, to isolate a relation between causative factors and structural results. These various lines of sociological perspective and interest, which are so strongly entrenched today, leap over the acting units of a society and bypass the interpretative process by which such acting units build up their actions.

These respective concerns with organization on one hand and with acting units on the other hand set the essential difference between conventional views of human society and the view of it implied in symbolic interaction. The latter view recognizes the presence of organization to human society

and respects its importance. However, it sees and treats organization differently. The difference is along two major lines. First, from the standpoint of symbolic interaction the organization of a human society is the framework inside of which social action takes place and is not the determinant of that action. Second, such organization and changes in it are the product of the activity of acting units and not of "forces" which leave such acting units out of account. Each of these two major lines of difference should be explained briefly in order to obtain a better understanding of how human society appears in terms of symbolic interaction.

From the standpoint of symbolic interaction, social organization is a framework inside of which acting units develop their actions. Structural features, such as "culture," "social systems," "social stratification," or "social roles," set conditions for their action but do not determine their action. People—that is, acting units—do not act toward culture, social structure or the like; they act toward situations. Social organization enters into action only to the extent to which it shapes situations in which people act, and to the extent to which it supplies fixed sets of symbols which people use in interpreting their situations. These two forms of influence of social organization are important. In the case of settled and stabilized societies, such as isolated primitive tribes and peasant communities, the influence is certain to be profound. In the case of human societies, particularly modern societies, in which streams of new situations arise and old situations become unstable, the influence of organization decreases. One should bear in mind that the most important element confronting an acting unit in situations is the actions of other acting units. In modern society, with its increasing criss-crossing of lines of action, it is common for situations to arise in which the actions of participants are not previously regularized and standardized. To this extent, existing social organization does not shape the situations. Correspondingly, the symbols or tools of interpretation used by acting units in such situations may vary and shift considerably. For these reasons, social action may go beyond, or depart from, existing organization in any of its structural dimensions. The organization of a human society is not to be identified with the process of interpretation used by its acting units; even though it affects that process, it does not embrace or cover the process.

Perhaps the most outstanding consequence of viewing human society as organization is to overlook the part played by acting units in social change. The conventional procedure of sociologists is (a) to identify human society (or some part of it) in terms of an established or organized form, (b) to identify some factor or condition of change playing upon the human society or the given part of it, and (c) to identify the new form assumed by the society following upon the play of the factor of change. Such observations permit the student to couch propositions to the effect that a given factor of change playing upon a given organized form results in a given new organized form. Examples ranging from crude to refined statements are legion, such as that an economic depression increases solidarity in the families of working-men or that industrialization replaces extended families by nuclear families. My concern here is not with the validity of such propositions but with the methodological position which they presuppose. Essentially, such propositions either ignore the role of the interpretive behavior of acting units in the given instance of change, or else regard the interpretative behavior as coerced by the factor of change. I wish to point out that any line of social change, since it involves change in human action, is necessarily mediated by interpretation on the part of the people caught up in the change—the change appears in the form of new situations in which people have to construct new forms of action. Also, in line with what has been said previously, interpretations of new situations are not predetermined by conditions antecedent to the situations but depend on what is taken into account and assessed in the actual situations in which behavior is formed.

Variations in interpretation may readily occur as different acting units cut out different objects in the situation, or give different weight to the objects which they note, or piece objects together in different patterns. In formulating propositions of social change, it would be wise to recognize that any given line of such change is mediated by acting units interpreting the situations with which they are confronted.

Students of human society will have to face the question of whether their preoccupation with categories of structure and organization can be squared with the interpretative process by means of which human beings, individually and collectively, act in human society. It is the discrepancy between the two which plagues such students in their efforts to attain scientific propositions of the sort achieved in the physical and biological sciences. It is this discrepancy, further, which is chiefly responsible for their difficulty in fitting hypothetical propositions to new arrays of empirical data. Efforts are made, of course, to overcome these shortcomings by devising new structural categories, by formulating new structural hypotheses, by developing more refined techniques of research, and even by formulating new methodological schemes of a structural character. These efforts continue to ignore or to explain away the interpretative process by which people act, individually and collectively, in society. The question remains whether human society or social action can be successfully analyzed by schemes which refuse to recognize human beings as they are, namely, as persons constructing individual and collective action through an interpretation of the situations which confront them.

40
Performances

Erving Goffman

Erving Goffman (1922–1982) has been described as the most important American sociological theorist in the second half of the twentieth century. Moreover, because of the literary character of his writing, his influence has extended well beyond the discipline. As a dramaturgical sociologist, he is sometimes seen as a perceptive, if somewhat cynical, chronicler of the contemporary "human comedy." In this selection from *The Presentation of Self in Everyday Life*, Goffman uses the metaphor of social life as theater in outlining his dramaturgical perspective. In a play, actors attempt to convey to an audience a particular impression of both the actor and the social scene. Through the use of scripted dialogue, gestures, props, costumes, and so on, actors create a new reality for the audience to consider. Goffman is concerned here with the ways in which actors convey a sense of personal identity. He begins with an intriguing discussion about whether the individual is taken in by her role performance, embracing it with sincerity or viewing it cynically, and then moves on to an analysis of the nature and function of the "front"—which he describes as the "expressive equipment" used to convince the other about the authenticity of the individual's performance. Goffman concludes by observing that fronts—along with other theatrical props—tend to be embedded in our social worlds. Rather than social life being improvisational, much of it is predicated on routines that actors select when deemed appropriate.

Belief in the Part One Is Playing

When an individual plays a part he implicitly requests his observers to take seriously the impression that is fostered before them. They are asked to believe that the character they see actually possesses the attributes he appears to possess, that the task he performs will have the consequences that are implicitly claimed for it, and that, in general, matters are what they appear to be. In line with this, there is the popular view that the individual offers his performance and puts on his show "for the benefit of other people." It will be convenient to begin a consideration of performances by turning the question around and looking at the individual's own belief in the impression of reality that he attempts to engender in those among whom he finds himself.

At one extreme, one finds that the performer can be fully taken in by his own act; he can be sincerely convinced that the impression of reality which he stages is the real reality. When his audience is also convinced in this way about the show he puts on—and this seems to be the typical case—then for the moment at least, only the sociologist or the socially disgruntled will have any doubts about the "realness" of what is presented.

At the other extreme, we find that the performer may not be taken in at all by his own routine. This possibility is understandable, since no one is in quite as good an observational position to see through the act as the person who puts it on. Coupled with this, the performer may be moved to guide the conviction of his audience only as a means to other ends, having no ultimate concern in the conception that they have of him or of the situation. When the individual has no belief in his own act and no ultimate concern with the beliefs of his audience, we may call him cynical, reserving the term "sincere" for individuals who believe in the impression fostered by their own performance. It should be understood that the cynic, with all his professional disinvolvement, may obtain unprofessional pleasures from his masquerade, experiencing a kind of gleeful spiritual aggression from the fact that he can toy at will with something his audience must take seriously.[1]

It is not assumed, of course, that all cynical performers are interested in deluding their audiences for purposes of what is called "self-interest" or private gain. A cynical individual may delude his audience for what he considers to be their own good, or for the good of the community, etc. For illustrations of this we need not appeal to sadly enlightened showmen such as Marcus

Aurelius or Hsun Tzu. We know that in service occupations practitioners who may otherwise be sincere are sometimes forced to delude their customers because their customers show such a heartfelt demand for it. Doctors who are led into giving placebos, filling station attendants who resignedly check and recheck tire pressures for anxious women motorists, shoe clerks who sell a shoe that fits but tell the customer it is the size she wants to hear—these are cynical performers whose audiences will not allow them to be sincere. Similarly, it seems that sympathetic patients in mental wards will sometimes feign bizarre symptoms so that student nurses will not be subjected to a disappointingly sane performance.[2] So also, when inferiors extend their most lavish reception for visiting superiors, the selfish desire to win favor may not be the chief motive; the inferior may be tactfully attempting to put the superior at ease by simulating the kind of world the superior is thought to take for granted.

I have suggested two extremes: an individual may be taken in by his own act or be cynical about it. These extremes are something a little more than just the ends of a continuum. Each provides the individual with a position which has its own particular securities and defenses, so there will be a tendency for those who have traveled close to one of these poles to complete the voyage. Starting with lack of inward belief in one's role, the individual may follow the natural movement described by Park:

> It is probably no mere historical accident that the word person, in its first meaning, is a mask. It is rather a recognition of the fact that everyone is always and everywhere, more or less consciously, playing a role . . . It is in these roles that we know each other; it is in these roles that we know ourselves.[3]

In a sense, and in so far as this mask represents the conception we have formed of ourselves—the role we are striving to live up to—this mask is our truer self, the self we would like to be. In the end, our conception of our role becomes second nature and an integral part of our personality. We come into the world as individuals, achieve character, and become persons.[4]

This may be illustrated from the community life of Shetland.[5] For the last four or five years the island's tourist hotel has been owned and operated by a married couple of crofter origins. From the beginning, the owners were forced to set aside their own conceptions as to how life ought to be led, displaying in the hotel a full round of middle-class services and amenities. Lately, however, it appears that the managers have become less cynical about the performance that they stage; they themselves are becoming middle class and more and more enamored of the selves their clients impute to them.

Another illustration may be found in the raw recruit who initially follows army etiquette in order to avoid physical punishment and eventually comes to follow the rules so that his organization will not be shamed and his officers and fellow soldiers will respect him.

As suggested, the cycle of disbelief-to-belief can be followed in the other direction, starting with conviction or insecure aspiration and ending in cynicism. Professions which the public holds in religious awe often allow their recruits to follow the cycle in this direction, and often recruits follow it in this direction not because of a slow realization that they are deluding their audience—for by ordinary social standards the claims they make may be quite valid—but because they can use this cynicism as a means of insulating their inner selves from contact with the audience. And we may even expect to find typical careers of faith, with the individual starting out with one kind of involvement in the performance he is required to give, then moving back and forth several times between sincerity and cynicism before completing all the phases and turning-points of self-belief for a person of his station. Thus, students of medical schools suggest that idealistically oriented beginners in medical school typically lay aside their holy aspirations for a period of time. During the first two years the students find that their interest in medicine must be dropped that they may give all their time to the task of learning how to get through examinations. During the next two years they are too busy learning about diseases to show much concern for the persons who are diseased. It is only after their medical schooling has ended that their original ideals about medical service may be reasserted.[6]

While we can expect to find natural movement back and forth between cynicism and sincerity, still we must not rule out the kind of transitional point that can be sustained on the strength of a little self-illusion. We find that the individual may attempt to induce the audience to judge him and the situation in a particular way, and he may seek this judgment as an ultimate end in itself, and yet he may not completely believe that he deserves the valuation of self which he asks for or that the impression of reality which he fosters is valid. Another mixture of cynicism and belief is suggested in Kroeber's discussion of shamanism:

> Next there is the old question of deception. Probably most shamans or medicine men, the world over, help along with sleight-of-hand in curing and especially in exhibitions of power. This sleight-of-hand is sometimes deliberate; in many cases awareness is perhaps not deeper than foreconscious. The attitude, whether there has been repression or not, seems to be as toward a pious fraud. Field ethnographers seem quite generally convinced that even shamans who know that they add fraud nevertheless also believe in their powers, and especially in those of other shamans: they consult them when they themselves or their children are ill.[7]

Front

I have been using the term "performance" to refer to all the activity of an individual which occurs during a period marked by his continuous presence before a particular set of observers and which has some influence on the observers. It will be convenient to label as "front" that part of the individual's performance which regularly functions in a general and fixed fashion to define the situation for those who observe the performance. Front, then, is the expressive equipment of a standard kind intentionally or unwittingly employed by the individual during his performance. For preliminary purposes, it will be convenient to distinguish and label what seem to be the standard parts of front.

First, there is the "setting," involving furniture, decor, physical layout, and other background items which supply the scenery and stage props for the spate of human action played out before, within, or upon it. A setting tends to stay put, geographically speaking, so that those who would use a particular setting as part of their performance cannot begin their act until they have brought themselves to the appropriate place and must terminate their performance when they leave it. It is only in exceptional circumstances that the setting follows along with the performers; we see this in the funeral cortège, the civic parade, and the dream-like processions that kings and queens are made of. In the main, these exceptions seem to offer some kind of extra protection for performers who are, or who have momentarily become, highly sacred. These worthies are to be distinguished, of course, from quite profane performers of the peddler class who move their place of work between performances, often being forced to do so. In the matter of having one fixed place for one's setting, a ruler may be too sacred, a peddler too profane.

In thinking about the scenic aspects of front, we tend to think of the living room in a particular house and the small number of performers who can thoroughly identify themselves with it. We have given insufficient attention to assemblages of sign-equipment which large numbers of performers can call their own for short periods of time. It is characteristic of Western European countries, and no doubt a source of stability for them, that a large number of luxurious settings are available for hire to anyone of the right kind who can afford them. One illustration of this may be cited from a study of the higher civil servant in Britain:

> The question how far the men who rise to the top in the Civil Service take on the 'tone' or 'color' of a class other than that to which they belong by birth is delicate and difficult. The only definite information bearing on the question is the figures relating to the membership of the great London clubs. More than three-quarters of our high administrative officials be-

long to one or more clubs of high status and considerable luxury, where the entrance fee might be twenty guineas or more, and the annual subscription from twelve to twenty guineas. These institutions are of the upper class (not even of the upper-middle) in their premises, their equipment, the style of living practiced there, their whole atmosphere. Though many of the members would not be described as wealthy, only a wealthy man would unaided provide for himself and his family space, food and drink, service, and other amenities of life to the same standard as he will find at the Union, the Travellers', or the Reform.[8]

Another example can be found in the recent development of the medical profession where we find that it is increasingly important for a doctor to have access to the elaborate scientific stage provided by large hospitals, so that fewer and fewer doctors are able to feel that their setting is a place that they can lock up at night.[9]

If we take the term "setting" to refer to the scenic parts of expressive equipment, one may take the term "personal front" to refer to the other items of expressive equipment, the items that we most intimately identify with the performer himself and that we naturally expect will follow the performer wherever he goes. As part of personal front we may include: insignia of office or rank; clothing; sex, age, and racial characteristics; size and looks; posture; speech patterns; facial expressions; bodily gestures; and the like. Some of these vehicles for conveying signs, such as racial characteristics, are relatively fixed and over a span of time do not vary for the individual from one situation to another. On the other hand, some of these sign vehicles are relatively mobile or transitory, such as facial expression, and can vary during a performance from one moment to the next.

It is sometimes convenient to divide the stimuli which make up personal front into "appearance" and "manner," according to the function performed by the information that these stimuli convey. "Appearance" may be taken to refer to those stimuli which function at the time to tell us of the performer's social statuses. These stimuli also tell us of the individual's temporary ritual state, that is, whether he is engaging in formal social activity, work, or informal recreation, whether or not he is celebrating a new phase in the season cycle or in his life-cycle. "Manner" may be taken to refer to those stimuli which function at the time to warn us of the interaction role the performer will expect to play in the oncoming situation. Thus a haughty, aggressive manner may give the impression that the performer expects to be the one who will initiate the verbal interaction and direct its course. A meek, apologetic manner may give the impression that the performer expects to follow the lead of others, or at least that he can be led to do so.

We often expect, of course, a confirming consistency between appearance and manner; we expect that the differences in social statuses among the interactants will be expressed in some way by congruent differences in the indications that are made of an expected interaction role. This type of coherence of front may be illustrated by the following description of the procession of a mandarin through a Chinese city:

> Coming closely behind . . . the luxurious chair of the mandarin, carried by eight bearers, fills the vacant space in the street. He is mayor of the town, and for all practical purposes the supreme power in it. He is an ideal-looking official, for he is large and massive in appearance, whilst he has that stern and uncompromising look that is supposed to be necessary in any magistrate who would hope to keep his subjects in order. He has a stern and forbidding aspect, as though he were on his way to the execution ground to have some criminal decapitated. This is the kind of air that the mandarins put on when they appear in public. In the course of many years' experience, I have never once seen any of them, from the highest to the lowest, with a smile on his face or a look of sympathy for the people whilst he was being carried officially through the streets.[10]

But, of course, appearance and manner may tend to contradict each other, as when a performer who appears to be of higher estate than his audience acts in a manner that is unexpectedly equalitarian, or intimate, or apologetic, or when a performer dressed in the garments of a high position presents himself to an individual of even higher status.

In addition to the expected consistency between appearance and manner, we expect, of course, some coherence among setting, appearance, and manner.[11] Such coherence represents an ideal type that provides us with a means of stimulating our attention to and interest in exceptions. In this the student is assisted by the Journalist, for exceptions to expected consistency among setting, appearance, and manner provide the piquancy and glamor of many careers and the salable appeal of many magazine articles. For example, a *New Yorker* profile on Roger Stevens (the real estate agent who engineered the sale of the Empire State Building) comments on the startling fact that Stevens has a small house, a meager office, and no letter-head stationery.[12]

In order to explore more fully the relations among several parts of social front, it will be convenient to consider here a significant characteristic of the information conveyed by front, namely, its abstractness and generality.

However specialized and unique a routine is, its social front, with certain exceptions, will tend to claim facts that can be equally churned and asserted of other, somewhat different routines. For example, many service occupations offer their clients a performance that is illuminated with dramatic expressions of cleanliness, modernity, competence, and integrity. While in fact these abstract standards have a different significance in different occupational performances, the observer is encouraged to stress the abstract similarities. For the observer this is a wonderful, though sometimes disastrous, convenience. Instead of having to maintain a different pattern of expectation and responsive treatment for each slightly different performer and performance, he can place the situation in a broad category around which it is easy for him to mobilize his past experience and stereotypical thinking. Observers then need only be familiar with a small and hence manageable vocabulary of fronts, and know how to respond to them, in order to orient themselves in a wide variety of situations. Thus in London the current tendency for chimney sweeps[13] and perfume clerics to wear white lab coats tends to provide the client with an understanding that the delicate tasks performed by these persons will be performed in what has become a standardized, clinical, confidential manner.

There are grounds for believing that the tendency for a large number of different acts to be presented from behind a small number of fronts is a natural development in social organization. Radcliffe-Brown has suggested this in his claim that a "descriptive" kinship system which gives each person a unique place may work for very small communities, but, as the number of persons becomes large, clan segmentation becomes necessary as a means of providing a less complicated system of identifications and treatments.[14] We see this tendency illustrated in factories, barracks, and other large social establishments. Those who organize these establishments find it impossible to provide a special cafeteria, special modes of payment, special vacation rights, and special sanitary facilities for every line and staff status category in the organization, and at the same time they feel that persons of dissimilar status ought not to be indiscriminately thrown together or classified together. As a compromise, the full range of diversity is cut at a few crucial points, and all those within a given bracket are allowed or obliged to maintain the same social front in certain situations.

In addition to the fact that different routines may employ the same front, it is to be noted that a given social front tends to become institutionalized in terms of the abstract stereotyped expectations to which it gives rise, and tends to take on a meaning and stability apart from the specific tasks which happen at the time to be performed in its name. The front becomes a "collective representation" and a fact in its own right.

When an actor takes on an established social role, usually he finds that a particular front has already been established for it. Whether his acquisition of the role was primarily motivated by a desire to perform the given task or by a desire to maintain the corresponding front, the actor will find that he must do both.

Further, if the individual takes on a task that is not only new to him but also unestablished in the society, or if he attempts to change the light in which his task is viewed, he is likely to find that there are already several well-established fronts among which he must choose. Thus, when a task is given a new front we seldom find that the front it is given is itself new.

Since fronts tend to be selected, not created, we may expect trouble to arise when those who perform a given task are forced to select a suitable front for themselves from among several quite dissimilar ones. Thus in military organizations, tasks are always developing which (it is felt) require too much authority and skill to be carried out behind the front maintained by one grade of personnel and too little authority and skill to be carried out behind the front maintained by the next grade in the hierarchy. Since there are relatively large jumps between grades, the task will come to "carry too much rank" or to carry too little.

Endnotes

1. Perhaps the real crime of the confidence man is not that he takes money from his victims but that he robs all of us of the belief that middle-class manners and appearance can be sustained only by middle-class people. A disabused professional can be cynically hostile to the service relation his clients expect him to extend to them; the confidence man is in a position to hold the whole "legit" world in this contempt.

2. See Taxel, op. cit., p. 4. Harry Stack Sullivan has suggested that the tact of institutionalized performers can operate in the other direction, resulting in a kind of noblesse-oblige sanity. See his "Socio-Psychiatric Research," *American Journal of Psychiatry*, X, pp. 987–88.

"A study of 'social recoveries' in one of our large mental hospitals some years ago taught me that patients were often released from care because they had learned not to manifest symptoms to the environing persons; in other words, had integrated enough of the personal environment to realize the prejudice opposed to their delusions. It seemed almost as if they grew wise enough to be tolerant of the imbecility surrounding them, having finally discovered that it was stupidity and not malice. They could then secure satisfaction from contact with others, while discharging a part of their cravings by psychotic means."

3. Robert Ezra Park, *Race and Culture* (Glencoe, IL: The Free Press, 1950), p. 249.

4. Ibid., p. 250.

5. Shetland Isle study.

6. H. S. Becker and Blanche Greer, "The Fate of Idealism in Medical School," *American Sociological Review*, 23, pp. 50–56.

7. A. L. Kroeber, *The Nature of Culture* (Chicago: University of Chicago Press, 1952), p. 311.

8. H. E. Dale, *The Higher Civil Service of Great Britain* (Oxford: Oxford University Press, 1941), p. 50.

9. David Solomon, "Career Contingencies of Chicago Physicians" (unpublished Ph.D. dissertation, Department of Sociology, University of Chicago, 1952), p. 74.

10. J. Macgowan, *Sidelights on Chinese Life* (Philadelphia: Lippincott, 1908), p. 187.

11. Cf. Kenneth Burke's comments on the "scene-act-agent ratio," *A Grammar of Motives* (New York: Prentice-Hall, 1945), pp. 6–9.

12. E. J. Kahn, Jr., "Closings and Openings," *The New Yorker*, February 13 and 20, 1954.

13. See Mervyn Jones, "White as a Sweep," *The New Statesman and Nation*, December 6, 1952.

14. A. R. Radcliffe-Brown, "The Social Organization of Australian Tribes," *Oceania*, I, 440.

41

The Drama in the Routine: A Prolegomenon to a Praxiological Sociology

Stanford M. Lyman

Stanford M. Lyman (1933–2003) was influenced by phenomenology as well as by the symbolic interactionist tradition, and like Goffman he was sometimes described as a dramaturgical sociologist. In this essay, he took aim at those critics who claimed that the preoccupation with meaning construction and articulation so central to symbolic interactionism did not take us very far in a world where so much of everyday life is devoted to routine or habitual behavior. In this outline of a sociology of praxis, Lyman contended that such behavior was not beyond the purview of his theoretical orientation but on the contrary should be construed as a necessary prerequisite, to the extent that the taken-for-granted aspects of social life served as frameworks within which more theatrical dramas take place.

> It should be . . . kept in mind that in order to contemplate our spiritual individuality in its fullness we must free ourselves of practical life and of its routine.
>
> —Nicolas Evreinoff,
> *The Theatre in Life*

The script of life in modern societies is more and more conceived by social scientists in a dramatistic form.[1] Of course, such an approach owes an unrepayable debt to the stimulating work on dramatism by Kenneth Burke.[2] However, much of dramatism in sociology has been constrained by the limits imposed by one of its modes—theatricality. Theatricality, especially as that concept has been elaborated by Elizabeth Burns,[3] describes, I believe, but one kind of drama. Unfortunately, that kind has been reframed into a synecdoche, the part taken for the whole, and as such it exercises an all too hegemonic sovereignty over the less flamboyant elements composing the drama of social reality. Of the latter, the drama in the routine is remarkable for its neglect,[4] since, in sociological terms, routines—habits, customs, the ongoing action that is *interrupted* by a crisis in *Lebenswelt*—constitute the praxes of everyday life, the fundamental stuff of any truly praxiological sociology. In what follows I present an elaboration of the drama in the routine; my remarks are intended as a prolegomenon, looking toward the development of such a sociology, so long promised but so far unfulfilled.

Routines: Their Origins and Persistence

In an early essay that has been much neglected, W. I. Thomas formulated a psychosocial theory of routine life and its relation to social change.[5] As Thomas conceived of the matter, most of life is carried on in accordance with habits. Habits are ways of living that have arisen as sociocultural "definitions of the situation," features of the unreflected-upon world of everyday activities. Habits go unnoticed and, for the most part, uncriticized. They are the active expression of the mores, and, if they are formalized, they appear as folk wisdom, common sense, precepts, traditions, and standardized understandings; sometimes they are coded in language, carved in stone, written out in legislation, or observed and enforced in law. "And," Thomas went on to observe, "the great part of our life is lived in the region of habit. The habits, like the instincts, are safe and serviceable. They have been tried, and they are associated with a feeling of security."[6] The habits, thence, constitute and are constituted in the routines of everyday life. In their repetitions, their carefully formulated modes of action, their characteristic

259

rhetorics, and their moves on the stages of everyday life, they are inherently dramatic—but they are equally inherently devoid of histrionics, melodrama, or theatrics. Their drama resides precisely in their dullness. They do not stimulate the imagination; rather, they effect the unreflexive praxis.

Habitual routines are the stages from which the far more theatrical dramas of social change occur. Indeed, true, or fundamental, social changes—as opposed to those that occur in and as part of the *longue durée*—may be understood as occurring in an assault on established habits of life in the name of a proposed instauration of a new set of habits (or, to be more precise, habits-to-be). This perspective on social change offers a comprehensive dramatism, one that distinguishes the theatrical aspects of social life from those that are commonplace. The former are fewer in number, but greater in respect, and they make up the content of history and ideology. The latter are the more frequent, the less-noticed, the taken-for-granted, but, like their more remarkable counterparts, they partake of the entire panoply of the Burkean pentad: They occur as acts, in scenes, committed by persons who know how to do (or perform) them, and they serve a knowable purpose. What distinguishes them from theatrical dramas is their remarkable unremarkability.

How do routines come to be such? A dramatistic sociology of social change conceives of this as a by-no-means predetermined metamorphosis from innovatively theatrical to familiar and ordinary performances. Cultural phenomena partake of such a transformation, as the studies of Norbert Elias have documented so well.[7] Indeed, as Elias's studies seem to suggest, those elementary forms of everyday life, for example, the tie-signs that Erving Goffman showed to be foundations of a modern civic social order,[8] had once been innovative and perhaps bizarre forms of conduct that had to overcome their original designation as strange behavior and to become legitimate ways to shore up a sagging social relationship.[9] Moreover, as the separate and independent works of W. I. Thomas,[10] Frederick J. Teggart,[11] and Victor Turner[12] have shown, what is here being called a dramatistic ap-

proach to social change stands in sharp contrast to, and in critical refutation of, the predominant developmentalist theories of sociocultural change that take their point of departure from Comte and owe their origins to Aristotle's conception of *physis*. Against the illusion that social change occurs slowly, orderly, continuously, and teleologically, the dull drama in the routine is that established obdurate reality, that body of all-too-familiar performances against which the theatrical dramas of reform, rebellion, and revolution are enacted on an irregular and surely nonlinear time track. The success of a reform, rebellion, or revolution is ultimately represented by the routinization of its once charismatic, awesome, or outlandish ideas about conduct appropriate for everyday life. The theatrical drama has then become transformed into a nontheatrical play, a feature of the taken-for-granted *Umwelt* of its practitioners.

Routines as Habits

The ethologist Konrad Lorenz believes that the formation of habits among human groups occurs as part of a process that he calls "cultural ritualization."[13] Such habitual behaviors may arise for highly specific purposes in the early history of a group—for example, the collectively enforced prohibition on eating pork among contemporary observant Jews might have originated as part of a theocratically legislated health plan designed to prevent trichinosis from debilitating the fighting strength of the ancient Hebrew settlers of Canaan—but ultimately they achieve both autonomy—that is, transcendence from the originally impelling reason for the conduct—and routinization—that is, taken-for-grantedness that is accompanied by a vague but powerful feeling that to do otherwise is fearsome, tantamount to courting danger, or unpleasant, inviting at the very least an undesirable degree of discomfort. As autonomous and routinized modes of conduct, the habits become the fundamental stuff, the "text," to use language familiar to students of society perceived in this manner, of a people's everyday life. Habits are, hence, the praxes against which, and with respect to which, deviance, is observed and measured. And deviant conduct is, in effect, would-be or potential praxis.

In effect, we may observe a theorem at work here: no praxes, no deviance; no deviance, no new praxis. And through this theorem we have part of the answer to the Hobbesian question that became the basis for sociology as a discipline. That question—how is society possible?—is answered thus: Society is possible because people have somehow come to agree upon conformity to a body of habits. As Lorenz saw the matter, cultural ritualization performs a triple function—"suppressing fighting within the group, . . . holding the group together, and . . . setting it off, as an independent entity, against other similar units. . . ."[14] The very formation of the group in question, the formation of any true group (be it as small as Mead's self-reflective and internally interacting self, or as large as a nation-state or a *Gemeinschaft* of confederated states), is founded upon the establishment of such habits. As W. I. Thomas once observed,

> The attitudes and values, or we may say, the attitudes toward values, which reflect the personality of the individual are the result of a process of conditioning by the influences of the cultural milieu, eventuating in a body of habits.[15]

Routines as Interaction Rituals

Routines are not only (or merely) habits. They are also rituals whose expression is manifested in rites. These rites evoke in their performers and in the audience that observes them an imperative of perfectly coordinated and precisely executed actions. As Florian Znaniecki once observed, "The attitude of a collectivity toward its moral order shows the same primary desire for integral perfection which is illustrated in all the rituals of the world. Just as magical or religious rites acquire their proper virtue only when they are perfectly performed, so moral norms sanctioned by a community or a group need to be perfectly followed to be completely valid."[16] However, if perfection were really demanded for every routine performance of an interaction ritual, the actors would suffer from inordinate amounts of

stage fright.[17] In contemporary America, it appears to be sufficient for maintaining social order that, in the rituals that make up the routines of everyday life, the individual show proper deference, that is, the "appreciation an individual shows of another to that other," and an appropriate demeanor, that is,

> ceremonial behavior typically conveyed through deportment, dress, and bearing which serves to express to those in his [or her] immediate presence that he [or she] is a person of certain . . . qualities.[18]

Goffman lists the basic attributes of these qualities as

> discretion and sincerity; modesty in claims regarding self; sportsmanship; command of speech and physical movements; self-control over his [or her] emotions, . . . appetites, and . . . desires; poise under pressure; and so forth.[19]

When a person so comports him- or herself in a manner that is taken to indicate a character that possesses these attributes, there is created in the scene wherein the conduct takes place the basic conditions of trust that undergird the social contract. These conditions correspond to those signs of probity that Max Weber noticed were taken to be signaled when, in 1904 in rural America, a person submitted to immersive baptism and to public acknowledgment that he or she was a "born-again" adherent to the Calvinist variant of the Protestant faith.[20]

The contents and qualities of performances necessary to create the conditions of confidence that permit ongoing and unaggressive human association might vary over time, place, and culture, but within the context of their own established and routinized codes, they constitute a mode of conduct that has all the qualities and confers all the qualifications of a religious ritual. Nevertheless, again within the circumscribed code, less-than-perfect performance is often tolerated. Taking note of this aspect of conduct in the context of a larger discussion of the repression of crime, Znaniecki called attention to the fact that

> an objective observation of individual conduct would show at every step deviations from the standard of perfection; but

communities and groups do not observe their insiders objectively. Having a fundamentally positive, lasting prejudice toward them, they either ignore or explain away their innumerable omissions and peccadillos.[21]

Hence, departures from ritual perfection are not uncommon, and they usually do not shred the social fabric. And, as Znaniecki concludes on this point, "a collectivity may for a long time live under a half-voluntary illusion of the essential perfection of its moral order. . . ."[22] The continued performance of routine dramas—that is, the dramas that are devoid of awesomeness, charisma, melodrama, histrionics, or theatricality—make up the everyday life process and, by their very unremarkability, sew together the social fabric.

The Theatricalization of Routines

A single line of thought unites the otherwise quite disparate sociologies of Thomas, Teggart, Turner, Gramsci, Schutz, Goffman, and Garfinkel. Taking notice of the significance of what they variously refer to as habits, routines, ritualized performances, behavioral presentations of self in public and private places, the *Lebenswelt*, the taken-for-granted world, and the old civilization, these students of social order and its changes correctly perceived that the routinized charisma of everyday life, that is, the drama in the routine, was protected against any easy banishment from the stage of the legitimate theater of life by the familiarity and the comfort in the familiarity of its own scenario. For Thomas, what was required to ring down the curtain on the habitual performances of everyday life was a "crisis" so great as to force the performers and their audience to come to "attention,"[23] that is, to engage in a veritable epoche of the dramas in the routine. Teggart also supposed that the onset of a crisis, in the form of an irruptive intrusion onto the fixed stage of everyday life happenings, could, if disturbing enough, bring about the release of the performers from their commitment to the text of habitual conduct.[24] Victor Turner, taking his point of departure from the studies of Van Gennep, summarized the latter's observations on the matter thus:

He insisted that in all ritualized movement there was at least a moment when those being moved in accordance with a cultural script were liberated from normative demands, when they were, indeed, betwixt and between successive lodgments in jural political systems. In this gap between ordered worlds almost anything may happen.[25]

Gramsci, as interpreted by Dick Howard, perceived society to be "articulation" within a field of discursive politics. As Howard observes, "it constantly subverts itself, releasing the floating signifiers which present the possibility of new articulations." Moreover, "Articulation can—but need not—produce hegemonic practice." In Gramsci's terms, which without too much difficulty can be transposed into a dramatistic discourse,

> the constitution of an 'historical bloc' . . . is possible when the old civilisation loses its coherence, setting free elements which can be recombined in a new civilisation.[26]

Large-scale social change is constituted by ringing up the curtain on a new civilizational drama in the hopes that its performance will reoccur continuously on the stage of future history.

Whereas Thomas, Teggart, Turner, and Gramsci perceived these moments of disruption, liberation, and reformation of the scripts of life as macroevents, sociocultural, historical, or civilizational in scope, Goffman and Schutz noticed the microecological counterparts of similar disjunctions in the small routines of daily life. For Goffman, these are the numerous slips, gaffes, performance failures, individual or team subversions, embarrassments, and nasty surprises that threaten to bring down the props and supports of that life and to reveal the terrors of its insanity of place; however, most of these are repairable, so that the rituals of interaction persist and the conduct of daily life's dull dramaturgy goes on without suffering a destructive discreditation.[27] Schutz took special notice of those crises that disrupted the *Lebenswelten* of ordinary people, situations wherein they discovered that the recipes for living on which they had always relied no longer produced the cake of customary results for which they had in the past always been efficaciously employed. In reaction and response to such moments, individuals are in a position to perceive as it were for the first time the sense- (and the nonsense-) structures of their conscious life and to reconsider their adherence to them. The structures become visible as alterable scenarios and texts.[28] Although Garfinkel did not seem to take special note of the fact, his introduction of artificial disruptive intrusions into the daily life routines of department store shoppers, parents of college students, and participants in what appeared to be standardized psychological tests generated crises that were resolvable by forms of talk that functioned to elaborate upon, as well as to shore up, the only seemingly shaky props of modern routine dramas.[29] In all of this, however, there is a raising of the consciousness to what Turner calls "liminality," a sensory threshold.[30] That threshold bids fair to introduce theatricality into the mundane drama in the routine.

In a critique of Lyman's and Scott's *The Drama of Social Reality*, Elizabeth Burns sought to take issue with the authors' claim that the social world is inherently dramatic by pointing out that "most of life is routine, only punctuated by 'dramas.' "[31] Burns's critique fails in its intention, but it does call attention to the dialectic governing the relationship between theatrical and routine dramas. That dialectic may be described as circumscribing the transformative process by which mundane dramas in the routine are, because of a sudden burst of liminality, reconstituted as either "theatrical," that is, as those that proceed by means of exaggerated gestures and unexpected vocalizations; "histrionic," that is, as those that employ deliberately affected or overdetermined motions, movements, and tones; or "melodramatic," that is, those that rely on a heightened emotionalism and conventionally unconventional stylistics. As a hypothesis central to the validation of a dramatistic sociology of social change, it may be suggested that theatricalism (i.e., theatrics, histrionics, or melodramatics) arises in conduct when the routine dramas of everyday life are interrupted, invaded, or intruded upon by forms of action that are unexpected, unwar-

ranted, or untoward with respect to the conventional text. The dramas-in-the-routine are performed in accordance with scripts of everyday life that place the action in unprepossessing scenes, identify the performers as uninspiring agents, employ unremarkable agencies of achievement, and accomplish expected and expectable outcomes. Theatrical dramas arise when such scenes are desublimated, their agents despoiled, their agencies deprived of efficaciousness, and the outcomes frustrated or unanticipated. The liminality that finds theatricalized expression bids fair to write a new drama of social reality, to modify but not tear up the conventional scripts toward which its exaggerated gestures, histrionics, or melodramatics are directed, or to restore and, possibly, reinvigorate the drama in the routine that is under assault. Social statics, that is, the drama in the routine, and social dynamics, that is, theatrical dramas, constitute the irregular dialectic, the warp and woof of the historic process.

The Future of the Dramas in the Routine

The characteristics of society since the advent of modernity and its successor, still so indescribable that it can only be designated "postmodern," make it possible to suggest a possible future for dramas in the routine. Such suggestions are, at best, guesses based upon the probabilities of conventionality and its survival. It was Alfred Schutz who called attention to the fact that

the social world has near and far zones: the surrounding world . . . , in which you and I experience one another in spatial and temporal immediacy, may pass over into the world of my contemporaries, who are not given to me in spatial immediacy; and in multiple transitions, [he also noted that] there are the worlds of both predecessors and successors.[32]

To gauge the possibilities for routinized dramas, one must first add a corollary to Schutz's perceptive observation: Modernity is characterized, indeed, formed and reformed by the greater likelihood that interpenetrations will occur in these spatio-temporal zones. Thus, the *Umwelt* composed of my consociates is subjected to threats emanating from its unexpected collisions with the zones that contain my contemporaries as well as those that house the reconstitutable memories and histories of my predecessors and those that promise a future for my successors. Such enhanced threats in turn evoke a greater probability that theatricality will more and more overcome mundane dramas as zonal collisions and conflicts undermine established societal texts and aroused liminalities release aggressive self- and group-assertions.

Modernity finds its societal expression in the mass. Two characteristics of mass society are relevant for the dramatic modes of routine life. As Herbert Blumer has pointed out,

> In a mass society, the parts are not fused into an organic whole. . . . Instead, because of the overabundance of parts, many of these . . . are far removed from one another.[33]

One result of this unfused conglomeration of parts is the relative autonomy of each. As autonomous units in a nonintegrated society, these units—which might be as small as a lone individual or as large as an organized conectivity—are in a position to "write" their own scripts of life, to develop what for each is its conventionalized drama in the routine. Mass society is thus something like those multiplex theaters that are increasingly found in suburban malls—a number of dramas are going on at once. The difference is that the multiplex theaters have walls to prevent the dramas from penetrating into one another. Mass society guarantees no walls to separate its autonomous scenarios of mundane life. The mutual adjustment of each to the other constitutes a problem which is resolved in a drama that overlays the discrete but interconnecting routine dramas.

A second characteristic feature of mass society is "that it is caught up in a world of constant motion."[34] Such motion is not necessarily tantamount to change, but holds out the possibility, or for some, the threat, that it might introduce an intrusion, a nasty surprise, or a contradiction that is so disturbing

as to convert routine plays into theatrical dramas. More than societies founded upon castes, estates, or classes, mass societies tend to engender competition and conflicts among their parts. Such a sense of fearful disunity undermines the general conditions of trust and order, encouraging intrigues, deceptions, and interactions that are strategic rather than spontaneous. Hence, every routine drama is threatened and theatrically bids fair to become a routine in its own right.

Mass societies are not necessarily just or democratic. They entail a struggle among units—individuals and groups—for power and for the right to order the hierarchy of social status that will somehow always prevail in one form or another. These conflicts over power and status are dramas that develop their own routine dramatic forms as well as their theatrical or untheatrical cease-fires, and their histrionic, melodramatic, or unremarkable accommodations. Thus the vital order that is found in mass societies speaks not to "alienation," "anomie," "social disorganization," or imminent dissolution, but rather to an interplay of dramas in the routine and theatrical performances vying for hegemony and forming a metasocietal rhythm of macrosocial and microecological dynamics.

Endnotes

1. See, e.g., Marlis Buchmann, *The Script of Life in Modern Society: Entry into Adulthood in a Changing World* (Chicago: University of Chicago Press, 1989).

2. This debt has been acknowledged in two recent publications: Joseph R. Gusfield, ed., *Kenneth Burke on Symbols and Society* (Chicago: University of Chicago Press, 1989); and Herbert W. Simons and Trevor Melia, eds., *The Legacy of Kenneth Burke* (Madison: University of Wisconsin Press, 1989).

3. Elizabeth Burns, *Theatricality: A Study of Convention in the Theatre and in Social Life* (London: Longman, 1972).

4. The phrase "drama in the routine" was introduced in Stanford M. Lyman, "Cherished Values and Civil Rights," *The Crisis: A Record of the Darker Races* 71 (December 1964): pp. 645–54, 695.

5. W. I. Thomas, "Introductory" in idem, *Source Book for Social 0rigins: Ethnological Materials, Psychological Standpoint, Classified and Annotated Bibliographies for the Interpretation of Savage*

Societies, 6th edition (Boston: Richard G. Badger, 1909), pp. 3–28.

6. Ibid., p. 21.

7. See the following works of Norbert Elias, *The Civilizing Process: The History of Manners*, trans. Edmund Jephcott (New York: Urizen Books, 1978); *Power and Civility: The Civilizing Process*, vol. 2, trans. Edmund Jephcott (New York: Pantheon Books, 1982); *The Court Society*, trans. Edmund Jephcott (New York: Pantheon Books, 1983); *Involvement and Detachment*, trans. Edmund Jephcott (New York: Basil Blackwell, 1987); *What Is Sociology?*, trans. Stephen Mennell and Grace Morrissey (New York: Columbia University Press, 1978), esp. pp. 134–74; *The Loneliness of the Dying*, trans. Edmund Jephcott (New York: Basil Blackwell, 1985); and Norbert Elias and Eric Dunning, *Quest for Excitement: Sport and Leisure in the Civilizing Process* (New York: Basil Blackwell, 1986). See also Stephen Mennell, *Norbert Elias: Civilization and the Human Self-image* (New York: Basil Blackwell, 1989), pp. 29–112.

8. Erving Goffman, *Relations in Public: Microstudies of the Public Order* (New York: Basic Books, 1971), pp. 188–237.

9. Cf. Stanford M. Lyman, "Civilization: Contents, Discontents, Malcontents," a review essay of Erving Goffman, *Relations in Public: Microstudies of the Public Order*, *Contemporary Sociology* 2:4 (July 1973): pp. 360–66.

10. See esp. W. I. Thomas and Dorothy Swaine Thomas, *The Child in America: Behavior Problems and Programs* (New York: Alfred A. Knopf, 1928), esp. pp. 505–76; W. I. Thomas, *Primitive Behavior: An Introduction to the Social Sciences* (New York: McGraw-Hill, 1937), esp. pp. 1–48, 610–747; Edmund H. Volkhart, ed., *Social Behavior and Personality: Contributions of W. I. Thomas to Theory and Social Research* (New York: Social Science Research Council, 1951), esp. pp. 215–88; Morris Janowitz, ed., *W. I. Thomas on Social Organization and Social Personality* (Chicago: University of Chicago Press, 1966), pp. 37–56, 231–56.

11. Frederick J. Teggart, *The Theory and Processes of History* (Berkeley: University of California Press, 1941).

12. Victor Turner, *Dramas, Fields, and Metaphors: Symbolic Action in Human Society* (Ithaca, N.Y.: Cornell University Press, 1974).

13. Konrad Lorenz, "Habit, Ritual, and Magic," trans. Marjorie Kenwilson, in *Ritual, Play, and Performance: Readings in the Social Sciences/Theatre*, ed. Richard Schechner and Mady Schuman (New York: Seabury Press, 1976), pp. 18–34.

14. Ibid., p. 30.

15. W. I. Thomas, *Primitive Behavior*, p. 1.

16. Florian Znaniecki, *Social Actions* (New York: Farrar and Rinehart, 1936), p. 383.

17. See Stanford M. Lyman and Marvin B. Scott, *A Sociology of the Absurd*, 2d ed. (Dix Hills, New York: General Hall, 1989), pp. 69-89.

18. Erving Goffman, *Interaction Ritual: Essays in Face-to-Face Behavior* (Chicago: Aldine Publishing Co., 1967), p. 77.

19. Ibid.

20. Max Weber, "The Protestant Sects and the Spirit of Capitalism," in *From Max Weber: Essays in Sociology*, trans. and ed. H. H. Gerth and C. Wright Mills (New York: Oxford University Press, 1946), pp. 302–22.

21. Znaniecki, *Social Actions*, p. 384.

22. Ibid.

23. Thomas, *Source Book for Social Origins*, pp. 16–19.

24. Frederick J. Teggart, *Theory of History* (New Haven, Conn.: Yale University Press, 1925), pp. 71–223.

25. Turner, *Dramas, Fields, and Metaphors*, p. 13.

26. Dick Howard, *Defining the Political* (Minneapolis: University of Minnesota Press, 1989), p. 87.

27. Erving Goffman, *Frame Analysis: An Essay on the Organization of Experience* (New York: Harper Colophon, 1974), pp. 300–77; *Forms of Talk* (Philadelphia: University of Pennsylvania Press, 1981), pp. 1–123.

28. Alfred Schutz, *Collected Papers*, vol. 3, *Studies in Phenomenological Philosophy*, ed. I. Schutz (The Hague, Netherlands: Martinus Nijhoff, 1966), pp. 104–6, 116–32.

29. Harold Garfinkel, *Studies in Ethnomethodology* (Englewood Cliffs, NJ: Prentice-Hall, 1967).

30. Turner, *Dramas, Fields, and Metaphors*, pp. 231–70.

31. Elizabeth Burns, review of *The Drama of Social Reality* by Stanford M. Lyman and Marvin B. Scott, in *Contemporary Sociology* 7 (March 1978): p. 158.

32. Alfred Schutz, "The Problem of Transcendental Intersubjectivity in Husserl," in his *Collected Papers* vol. 3, p. 81.

33. Herbert Blumer, "The Concept of Mass Society," in Stanford M. Lyman and Arthur J. Vidich, *Social Order and the Public Philosophy: An Analysis and Interpretation of the Work of Herbert Blumer* (Fayetteville: University of Arkansas Press, 1988), p. 341.

34. Ibid., p. 343.

42
Indirect Social Relationships

Alfred Schutz

Alfred Schutz (1899–1959) was an Austrian émigré scholar who, after fleeing his native land when the Nazis invaded, found a position at the New School for Social Research in New York City. From this institution, he became an important sociological exponent of a phenomenological theory derived primarily from the work of the philosopher Edmund Husserl. In this essay, Schutz describes the characteristic features of social relationships other than those that are direct or face to face. After discussing a spectrum of possible mediate relationships, such as moving from face-to-face encounters to telephone conversations and letters, he turns to a range of types of relatedness that include people one once encountered, people one expects to encounter in the future, and people one encounters not as individuals but in the roles they play (e.g., the clerk in a store). In understanding such types of relationships, Schutz argues for the centrality of the concept of anonymity.

Derived Relationships

In none of them does the self of the other become accessible to the partner as a unity. The other appears merely as a partial self, as originator of these and those acts, which I do not share in a vivid present. The shared vivid present of the We-relation presupposes co-presence of the partners. To each type of derived social relationship belongs a particular type of time perspective which is derived from the vivid present. There is a particular quasi-present in which I interpret the mere outcome of the other's communicating—the written letter, the printed book—without having participated in the ongoing process of communicating acts. There are other time dimensions in which I am connected with contemporaries I never met, or with predecessors or with successors; another, the historical time, in which I experience the actual present as the outcome of past events; and many more. All of these time perspectives can be referred to a vivid present: my own actual or former one, or the actual or former vivid present of my fellow-man with whom, in turn, I am connected in an originary or derived vivid present and all this in the different modes of potentiality or quasi-actuality, each type having its own forms of temporal diminution and augmentation and its appurtenant style of skipping them in a direct move or "knight's move." There are furthermore the different forms of overlapping and interpenetrating of these different perspectives, their being put into and out of operation by a shift from one to the other and a transformation of one into the other, and the different types of synthesizing and combining or isolating and disentangling them. Manifold as these different time perspectives and their mutual relations are, they all originate in an intersection of *durée* and cosmic time.

In and by our social life with the natural attitude they are apprehended as integrated into one single supposedly homogeneous dimension of time which embraces not only the individual time perspectives of each of us during his wide-awake life but which is common to all of us. We shall call it the civic or *standard time*.

From Direct to Indirect Social Experience

In the face-to-face situation, directness of experience is essential, regardless of whether our apprehension of the Other is central or peripheral and regardless of how adequate our grasp of him is. I am still "Thou-oriented" even to the man standing next to me in the subway. When we speak of "pure" Thou-orientation or "pure" We-relationship, we are ordinarily using these as limiting concepts referring to the simple givenness of the Other in abstraction from any specification of the degree of concreteness involved. But we can also use these terms for the lower limits of experience obtainable in the face-to-face relationship, in other words, for the most peripheral and fleeting kind of awareness of the other person.

We make the transition from direct to indirect social experience simply by following this spectrum of decreasing vividness. The first steps beyond the realm of immediacy are marked by a decrease in the number of perceptions I have of the other person and a narrowing of the perspectives within which I view him. At one moment I am exchanging smiles with my friend, shaking hands with him, and bidding him farewell. At the next moment he is walking away. Then from the far distance I hear a faint good-by, a moment later I see a vanishing figure give a last wave, and then he is gone. It is quite impossible to fix the exact instant at which my friend left the world of my direct experience and entered the shadowy realm of those who are merely my contemporaries. As another example, imagine a face-to-face conversation, followed by a telephone call, followed by an exchange of letters, and finally messages exchanged through a third party. Here too we have a gradual progression from the world of immediately experienced social reality to the world of contemporaries. In both examples the total number of the other person's reactions open to my observation is progressively diminished until it reaches a minimum point. It is clear, then, that the world of

contemporaries is itself a variant function of the face-to-face situation. They may even be spoken of as two poles between which stretches a continuous series of experiences. . . .

In everyday life there seems to be no practical problem of where the one situation breaks off and the other begins. This is because we interpret both our own behavior and that of others within contexts of meaning that far transcend the immediate here and now. For this reason, the question whether a social relationship we participate in or observe is direct or indirect seems to be an academic one. But there is a yet deeper reason for our customary indifference to this question. Even after the face-to-face situation has receded into the past and is present only in memory, it still retains its essential characteristics, modified only by an aura of pastness. Normally we do not notice that our just-departed friend, with whom we have a moment ago been interacting, perhaps affectionately or perhaps in an annoyed way, now appears to us in a quite different perspective. Far from seeming obvious, it actually seems absurd that someone we are close to has somehow become "different" now that he is out of sight, except in the trite sense that our experiences of him bear the mark of pastness. However, we must still sharply distinguish between such memories of face-to-face situations, on the one hand, and an intentional Act directed toward a mere contemporary, on the other. The recollections we have of another bear all the marks of direct experience. When I have a recollection of you, for instance, I remember you as you were in the concrete We-relationship with me. I remember you as a unique person in a concrete situation, as one who interacted with me in the mode of "mutual mirroring" described above. I remember you as a person vividly present to me with a maximum of symptoms of inner life, as one whose experiences I witnessed in the actual process of formation. I remember you as one whom I was for a time coming to know better and better. I remember you as one whose conscious life flowed in one stream with my own. I remember you as one whose consciousness was continuously changing in content. However, now that you are out of my direct experience, you are no more than my contemporary, someone who merely inhabits the same planet that I do. I am no longer in contact with the living you, but with the you of yesterday. You, indeed, have not ceased to be a living self, but you have a "new self" now; and, although I am contemporaneous with it, I am cut off from vital contact with it. Since the time we were last together, you have met with new experiences and have looked at them from new points of view. With each change of experience and outlook you have become a slightly different person. But somehow I fail to keep this in mind as I go about my daily round. I carry your image with me, and it remains the same. But then, perhaps, I hear that you have changed. I then begin to look upon you as a contemporary— not any contemporary, to be sure, but one whom I once knew intimately.

Regions of Anonymity

We have been describing the intermediate zone between the face-to-face situation and the situation involving mere contemporaries. Let us continue our journey. As we approach the outlying world of contemporaries, our experience of others becomes more and more remote and anonymous. Entering the world of contemporaries itself, we pass through one region after another: (1) the region of those whom I once encountered face to face and could encounter again (for instance, my absent friend); then (2) comes the region of those once encountered by the person I am now talking to (for instance, your friend, whom you are promising to introduce to me); next (3) the region of those who are as yet pure contemporaries but whom I will soon meet (such as the colleague whose books I have read and whom I am now on my way to visit); then (4) those contemporaries of whose existence I know, not as concrete individuals, but as points in social space as defined by a certain function (for instance, the postal employee who will process my letter); then (5) those collective entities whose function and organization I know while not being able to name any of their members, such as the Canadian Parliament; then (6) collective entities which are by their very nature anonymous and of which I could never

in principle have direct experience, such as "state" and "nation"; then (7) objective configurations of meaning which have been instituted in the world of my contemporaries and which live a kind of anonymous life of their own, such as the interstate commerce clause and the rules of French grammar; and finally (8) artifacts of any kind which bear witness to the subjective meaning-context of some unknown person. The farther out we get into the world of contemporaries, the more anonymous its inhabitants become, starting with the innermost region, where they can almost be seen, and ending with the region where they are by definition forever inaccessible to experience.

Mediate Experience of Contemporaries

My mere contemporary (or "contemporary") . . . is one who I know coexists with me in time but whom I do not experience immediately. This kind of knowledge is, accordingly, always indirect and impersonal. I cannot call my contemporary "Thou" in the rich sense that this term has within the We-relationship. Of course, my contemporary may once have been my consociate or may yet become one, but this in no way alters his present status.

Let us now examine the ways in which the world of contemporaries is constituted and the modifications which the concepts "Other-orientation" and "social relationship" undergo in that world. These modifications are necessitated by the fact that the contemporary is only indirectly accessible and that his subjective experiences can only be known in the form of *general types* of subjective experience.

That this should be the case is easy to understand if we consider the difference between the two modes of social experience. When I encounter you face to face I know you as a person in one unique moment of experience. While this We-relationship remains unbroken, we are open and accessible to each other's intentional Acts. For a little while we grow older together, experiencing each other's flow of consciousness in a kind of intimate mutual possession.

It is quite otherwise when I experience you as my contemporary. Here you are not prepredicatively given to me at all. I do not even directly apprehend your existence (*Dasein*). My whole knowledge of you is mediate and descriptive. In this kind of knowledge your "characteristics" are established for me by inference. From such knowledge results the indirect We-relationship.

To become clear about this concept of "mediacy," let us examine two different ways in which I come to know a contemporary. The first way we have already mentioned: my knowledge is derived from a previous face-to-face encounter with the person in question. But this knowledge has since become mediate or indirect because he has moved outside the range of my direct observation. For I make inferences as to what is going on in his mind under the assumption that he remains much the same since I saw him last, although, in another sense, I know very well that he must have changed through absorbing new experiences or merely by virtue of having grown older. But, as to how he has changed, my knowledge is either indirect or nonexistent.

A second way in which I come to know a contemporary is to construct a picture of him from the past direct experience of someone with whom I am now speaking (for example, when my friend describes his brother, whom I do not know). This is a variant of the first case. Here too I apprehend the contemporary by means of a fixed concept, or type, derived ultimately from direct experience but now held invariant. But there are differences. First, I have no concrete vivid picture of my own with which to start: I must depend on what my friend tells me. Second, I have to depend on my friend's assumption, not my own, that the contemporary he is describing has not changed.

These are the modes of constitution of all the knowledge we have of our contemporaries derived from our own past experience, direct or indirect, and of all the knowledge we have acquired from others, whether through conversation or through reading. It is clear, then, that indirect social experiences derive their original validity from the direct mode of apprehension. But the instances cited above do not exhaust all the ways by which I can come to know my contemporaries. There is the whole world of cultural objects, for instance, including everything from artifacts to institutions and conventional ways of doing things. These, too, contain within themselves implicit references to my contemporaries. I can "read" in these cultural objects the subjective experiences of others whom I do not know. Even here, however, I am making inferences on the basis of my previous direct experience of others. Let us say that the object before me is a finished product. Once, perhaps, I stood by the side of a man who was manufacturing something just like this. As I watched him work, I knew exactly what was going on in his mind. If it were not for this experience I would not know what to make of the finished product of the same kind that I now see. I might even fail to recognize it as an artifact at all and would treat it as just another natural object, like a stone or a tree. For what we have called the general thesis of the alter ego, namely, that the Thou coexists with me and grows older with me, can only be discovered in the We-relationship. Even in this instance, therefore, I have only an indirect experience of the other self, based on past direct experiences either of a Thou as such or of a particular Thou. My face-to-face encounters with others have given me a deep prepredicative knowledge of the Thou as a self. But the Thou who is *merely* my contemporary is never experienced personally as a self and never prepredicatively. On the contrary, all experience (*Erfahrung*) of contemporaries is predicative in nature. It is formed by means of interpretive judgments involving all my knowledge of the social world, although with varying degrees of explicitness.

Now this is real Other-orientation, however indirect it may be.

They-Orientation

Under this indirect Other-orientation we will find the usual forms of simple Other-orientation, social behavior and social interaction. Let us call all such intentional Acts directed toward contemporaries cases of "They-orientation," in contrast to the "Thou-orientation" of the intentional Acts of direct social experience.

The term "They-orientation" serves to call attention to the peculiar way in which I apprehend the conscious experiences of my contemporaries. For I apprehend them as anonymous processes. Consider the contrast to the Thou-orientation. When I am Thou-oriented, I apprehend the other person's experiences within their setting in his stream of consciousness. I apprehend them as existing within a subjective context of meaning, as being the unique experiences of a particular person. All this is absent in the indirect social experience of the They-orientation. Here I am not aware of the ongoing flow of the Other's consciousness. My orientation is not toward the existence (*Dasein*) of a concrete individual Thou. It is not toward any subjective experiences now being constituted in all their uniqueness in another's mind nor toward the subjective configuration of meaning in which they are taking place. Rather, the object of my They-orientation is my own experience (*Erfahrung*) of social reality in general, of human beings and their conscious processes as such, in abstraction from any individual setting in which they may occur. My knowledge of my contemporaries is, therefore, inferential and discursive. It stands, by its essential nature, in an objective context of meaning and only in such. It has within it no intrinsic reference to persons nor to the subjective matrix within which the experiences in question were constituted. However, it is due to this very abstraction from subjective context of meaning that they exhibit the property which we have called their "again and again" character. They are treated as typical conscious experiences of "someone" and, as such, as basically homogeneous and repeatable. The unity of the contemporary is not constituted originally in his own stream of consciousness. . . . Rather, the contemporary's unity is constituted in my own stream of consciousness, being built up out of a synthesis of my own interpretations of his experiences. This synthesis is a synthesis of recognition in which I monothetically bring within one view my own conscious experiences of someone else. Indeed, these experiences of mine may have been of more than one person. And they may have been of definite individuals or of anonymous

"people." It is in this synthesis of recognition that the *personal ideal type* is constituted.

Personal Ideal Types

We must be quite clear as to what is happening here. The subjective meaning-context has been abandoned as a tool of interpretation. It has been replaced by a series of highly complex and systematically interrelated objective meaning-contexts. The result is that the contemporary is anonymized in direct proportion to the number and complexity of these meaning-contexts. Furthermore, the synthesis of recognition does not apprehend the unique person as he exists within his living present. Instead it pictures him as always the same and homogeneous, leaving out of account all the changes and rough edges that go along with individuality. Therefore, no matter how many people are subsumed under the ideal type, it corresponds to no one in particular. It is just this fact that justified Weber in calling it "ideal."

Let us give a few examples to clarify this point. When I mail a letter, I assume that certain contemporaries of mine, namely, postal employees, will read the address and speed the letter on its way. I am not thinking of these postal employees as individuals. I do not know them personally and never expect to. Again, as Max Weber pointed out, whenever I accept money I do so without any doubt that others, who remain quite anonymous, will accept it in turn from me. To use yet another Weberian example, if I behave in such a way as to avoid the sudden arrival of certain gentlemen with uniforms and badges, in other words, to the extent that I orient myself to the laws and to the apparatus which enforces them, here, too, I am relating myself socially to my contemporaries conceived under ideal types.

On occasions like these I am always expecting others to behave in a definite way, whether it be postal employees, someone I am paying, or the police. My social relationship to them consists in the fact that I interact with them, or perhaps merely that, in planning my actions, I keep them in mind. But they, on their part, never turn up as real people, merely as anonymous entities defined exhaustively by their functions. Only as bearers of these functions do they have any relevance for my social behavior. How they happen to feel as they cancel my letter, process my check, or examine my income tax return—these are considerations that never even enter into my mind. I just assume that there are "some people" who "do these things." Their behavior in the conduct of their duty is from my point of view defined purely through an objective context of meaning. In other words, when I am They-oriented, I have "types" for partners.

Anonymity of the Contemporary

The They-orientation is the pure form of understanding the contemporary in a predicative fashion, that is, in terms of his typical characteristics. Acts of They-orientation are, therefore, intentionally directed toward another person imagined as existing at the same time as oneself but conceived in terms of an ideal type. And just as in the cases of the Thou-orientation and the We-relationship, so also with the They-orientation can we speak of different *stages of concretization* and *actualization*.

In order to distinguish from one another the various stages of concretization of the We-relationship, we established as our criterion the degree of closeness to direct experience. We cannot use this criterion within the They-orientation. The reason is that the latter possesses by definition a high degree of remoteness from direct experience, and the other self which is its object possesses a corresponding higher degree of anonymity.

It is precisely this degree of anonymity which we now offer as the criterion for distinguishing between the different levels of concretization and actualization that occur in the They-orientation. The more anonymous the personal ideal type applied in the They-orientation, the greater is the use made of objective meaning-contexts instead of subjective ones, and likewise, we shall find, the more are lower-level personal ideal types and objective meaning-contexts pregiven. (The latter have in turn been derived from other stages of concretization of the They-orientation.)

Let us get clear as to just what we mean by the anonymity of the ideal type in the world of contemporaries. The pure Thou-orientation consists of mere awareness of the existence of the other person, leaving aside all questions concerning the characteristics of that person. On the other hand, the pure They-orientation is based on the presupposition of such characteristics in the form of a type. Since these characteristics are genuinely typical, they can in principle be presupposed again and again. Of course, whenever I posit such typical characteristics, I assume that they now exist or did once exist. However, this does not mean that I am thinking of them as existing in a particular person in a particular time and place. The contemporary alter ego is therefore anonymous in the sense that its existence is only the individuation of a type, an individuation which is merely supposable or possible. Now since the very existence of my contemporary is always less than certain, any attempt on my part to reach out to him or influence him may fall short of its mark, and, of course, I am aware of this fact.

The concept which we have been analyzing is the concept of the anonymity of the partner in the world of contemporaries. It is crucial to the understanding of the nature of the indirect social relationship.

From *The Phenomenology of the Social World* by Alfred Schutz, translated by George Walsh and Frederick Lehnert, published by Northwestern University Press in 1967. Copyright © 1967 by Northwestern University Press. All rights reserved. Reprinted with permission. ✦

43
Rules of Conversational Sequence[1]

Harvey Sacks

Harvey Sacks (1935–1975) studied sociology with Goffman at Berkeley but is generally known as one of the earliest ethnomethodologists, and thus he is typically associated more with the work of Harold Garfinkel than with that of Goffman. This essay, put together posthumously by former students from Sacks' lecture notes, is a good example of the attention ethnomethodologists pay to conversational analysis. In this particular case, Sacks is dissecting telephone conversations he recorded at a psychiatric hospital between staff and persons calling from outside the facility. What he is attempting to get at—in a fairly provisional way—are the rules or "ethnomethods" people use to achieve orderly and stable interactional exchanges.

I'll start off by giving some quotations.

(1) *A:* Hello
    B: Hello

(2) *A:* This is Mr Smith may I help you
    B: Yes, this is Mr Brown

(3) *A:* This is Mr Smith may I help you
    B: I can't hear you.
    A: This is Mr *Smith*.
    B: Smith.

These are some first exchanges in telephone conversations I collected at an emergency psychiatric hospital. They are occurring between persons who haven't talked to each other before. One of them, A, is a staff member of this psychiatric hospital. B can be either somebody calling about themselves, that is to say in trouble in one way or another, or somebody calling about somebody else.

I have a large collection of these conversations, and I got started looking at these first exchanges as follows. A series of persons who called this place would not give their names. The hospital's concern was, can anything be done about it? One question I wanted to address was, where in the course of the conversation could you tell that somebody would not give their name? So I began to look at the materials. It was in fact on the basis of that question that I began to try to deal in detail with conversations.

I found something that struck me as fairly interesting quite early. And that was that if the staff member used "This is Mr Smith may I help you" as their opening line, then overwhelmingly, any answer other than "Yes, this is Mr Brown" (for example, "I can't hear you," "I don't know," "How do you spell your name?") meant that you would have serious trouble getting the caller's name, if you got the name at all.

I'm going to show some of the ways that I've been developing of analyzing stuff like this. There will be series of ways fitted to each other, as though one were constructing a multi-dimensional jigsaw puzzle. One or another piece can be isolated and studied, and also the various pieces can be studied as to how they fit together. I'll be focussing on a variety of things, starting off with what I'll call 'rules of conversational sequence.'

Looking at the first exchange compared to the second, we can be struck by two things. First of all, there seems to be a fit between what the first person who speaks uses as their greeting, and what the person who is given that greeting returns. So that if A says "Hello," then B tends to say "Hello." If A says "This is Mr Smith may I help you," B tends to say "Yes, this is Mr Brown." We can say there's a procedural rule there, that a person who speaks first in a telephone conversation can choose their form of address, and in choosing their form of address they can thereby choose the form of address the other uses.

By 'form' I mean in part that the exchanges occur as 'units.' That is, "Hello" "Hello" is a unit, and "This is Mr Smith may I help you" "Yes, this is Mr Brown," is a unit.

They come in pairs. Saying "This is Mr Smith may I help you" thereby provides a 'slot' to the other wherein they properly would answer "Yes, this is Mr Brown." The procedural rule would describe the occurrences in the first two exchanges. It won't describe the third exchange, but we'll come to see what is involved in such materials.

Secondly, if it is so that there is a rule that the person who goes first can choose their form of address and thereby choose the other's, then for the unit, "This is Mr Smith, may I help you" "Yes, this is Mr Brown," if a person uses "This is Mr Smith . . ." they have a way of asking for the other's name—without, however, asking the question, "What is your name?" And there is a difference between saying "This is Mr Smith may I help you"—thereby providing a slot to the other wherein they properly would answer "Yes, this is Mr Brown"—and asking the question "What is your name?" at some point in the conversation. They are very different phenomena.

For one, in almost all of the cases where the person doesn't give their name originally, then at some point in the conversation they're asked for their name. One way of asking is just the question "Would you give me your name?" To that, there are alternative returns, including "No" and "Why?" If a caller says "Why?" the staff member may say something like, "I want to have something to call you" or "It's just for our records." If a caller says "No," then the staff member says "Why?" and may get something like "I'm not ready to do that" or "I'm ashamed."

Now, I'll consider many times the use of "Why?" What I want to say about it just to begin with, is that what one does with "Why?" is to propose about some action that it is an 'accountable action.' That is to say, "Why?" is a way of asking for an account. Accounts are most extraordinary. And the use of accounts and the use of requests for accounts are very highly regulated phenomena. We can begin to cut into these regularities by looking at what happens when "May I have your name?" is followed by "Why?" Then you get an account; for example, "I need something to call you." The other might then say, "I don't mind." Or you might get an account, "It's just for our records." To which

the other might say, "Well I'm not sure I want to do anything with you, I just want to find out what you do"—so that the records are not relevant.

What we can see is that there are ways that accounts seem to be dealable with. If a person offers an account, which they take it provides for the action in question being done—for example, the caller's name being given—then if the other can show that the interest of that account can be satisfied without the name being given, the name doesn't have to be given. That is, if the account is to control the action, then if you can find a way that the account controls the alternative action than it proposed to control, you can use it that way.

It seems to be quite important, then, who it is that offers the account. Because the task of the person who is offered the account can then be to, in some way, counter it. Where, alternatively, persons who offer an account seem to feel that they're somehow committed to it, and if it turns out to be, for example, inadequate, then they have to stand by it.

The fact that you could use questions—like "Why?"—to generate accounts, and then use accounts to control activities, can be marked down as, I think, one of the greatest discoveries in Western civilization. It may well be that that is what Socrates discovered. With his dialectic he found a set of procedures by which this thing, which was not used systematically, could become a systematic device. Socrates will constantly ask "Why?," there will be an answer, and he'll go on to show that that can't be the answer. And that persons were terribly pained to go through this whole business is clear enough from the Dialogues. And it's also clear in our own experiences. And in the materials I'll present.

We see, then, one dear difference between providing a slot for a name, and asking for a name. Asking for a name tends to generate accounts and counters. By providing a slot for a name, those activities do not arise.

We can also notice that, as a way of asking for the other's name, "This is Mr Smith . . ." is, in the first place, not an accountable action. By that I mean to say, it's not required that staff members use it and they don't always use it, but when they do, the caller doesn't ask why. "This is Mr Smith . . ." gets its character as a non-accountable action simply by virtue of the fact that this is a place where, routinely, two persons speak who haven't met. In such places the person who speaks first can use that object. And we could say about that kind of item that the matters discriminated by its proper use are very restricted. That is to say, a call is made; the only issue is that two persons are speaking who presumably haven't met, and this object can be used.

Furthermore, the matters are discriminated in different terms than those which the agency is constructed for. That is, they are discriminated in terms of 'two people who haven't met' rather than, for example, that an agency staff member is speaking to someone calling the agency for help. And where one has some organization of activities which sets out to do some task—and in this case it's important for the agency to get names—then if you find a device which discriminates in such a restricted fashion, you can use that device to do tasks for you.

Now, given the fact that such a greeting as "This is Mr Smith . . ." provides for the other giving his own name as an answer, one can see what the advantage of "Hello" is for someone who doesn't want to give their name. And I found in the first instance that while sometimes the staff members use "Hello" as their opening line, if it ever occurred that the persons calling the agency spoke first, they always said "Hello."

Persons calling could come to speak first because at this agency, caller and staff member are connected by an operator. The operator says "Go ahead please" and now the two parties are on an open line, and one can start talking or the other can start talking. This stands in contrast to, for example, calling someone's home. There, the rights are clearly assigned; the person who answers the phone speaks first. If they speak first, they have the right to choose their form. If they have the right to choose their form, they have the right thereby to choose the other's. Here, where the rights are not clearly assigned, the caller could move to speak first and thereby choose the form. And when callers to this agency speak first, the form they choose is the unit "Hello" "Hello." Since such

a unit involves no exchange of names, they can speak without giving their name and be going about things in a perfectly appropriate way.

Now, there are variant returns to "This is Mr Smith may I help you?" one of which is in our set of three exchanges: "I can't hear you." I want to talk of that as an 'occasionally usable' device. That is to say, there doesn't have to be a particular sort of thing preceding it; it can come at any place in a conversation. Here is one from the middle of a conversation, from a different bunch of materials.

> *A:* Hey you got a cigarette Axum. I ain't got, I ain't got a good cigarette, and I can't roll one right now. Think you can afford it maybe?
>
> *B:* I am not here to support your habits.
>
> *A:* Huh? My helplessness?
>
> *B:* I am not responsible for supporting your habits ( )
>
> *A:* My habits ((laughing))

Our third exchange from the psychiatric hospital has the device used at the beginning of the conversation,

> *A:* This is Mr Smith may I help you
>
> *B:* I can't hear you.
>
> *A:* This is Mr *Smith*.
>
> *B:* Smith.

What kind of a device is it? What you can see is this. When you say "I can't hear you," you provide that the other person can repeat what they said. Now what does that repetition do for you? Imagine you're in a game. One of the questions relevant to the game would be, is there a way in that game of skipping a move? It seems that something like "I can't hear you" can do such a job. If you introduce it you provide for the other to do some version of a repeat following which you yourself can repeat. And then it's the other's turn to talk again. What we find is that the slot where the return would go—your name in return to "This is Mr Smith . . ."—never occurs.

It is not simply that the caller ignores what they properly ought to do, but something rather more exquisite. That is, they have ways of providing that the place where the return name fits is never opened. So that their name is not absent. Their name would be absent if they just went ahead and talked. But that very rarely occurs. The rules of etiquette—if you want to call them that, though we take etiquette to be something very light and uninteresting and to be breached as you please—seem to be quite strong. Persons will use ways to not ignore what they properly ought to do by providing that the place for them to do it is never opened.

I hope it can also be seen that a device like "I can't hear you"—the repeat device, providing for a repetition of the thing that was first said, which is then repeated by the person who said "I can't hear you"—is not necessarily designed for skipping a move. It is not specific to providing a way of keeping in the conversation and behaving properly while not giving one's name. It can be used for other purposes and do other tasks, and it can be used with other items. That's why I talk about it as an 'occasional device.' But where that is what one is trying to do, it's a rather neat device.

Let me turn now to a consideration which deals with a variant return to "May I help you?" That is, not "Yes . . ." but "I don't know." I'll show a rather elaborate exchange in which the staff member opens with a version of "This is Mr Smith may I help you" but the combination gets split. The name is dealt with, and when the "can I help you" is offered, it occurs in such a way that it can be answered independent of the name.[2]

Op: Go ahead please

A: This is Mr Smith (*B:* Hello) of the Emergency Psychiatric Center can I help you.

B: Hello?

A: Hello

B: I can't hear you.

A: I see. Can you hear me, now?

B: Barely. Where are you, in the womb?

A: Where are you calling from?

B: Hollywood.

A: Hollywood.

B: I can hear you a little better.

A: Okay. Uh I was saying my name is Smith and I'm with the Emergency Psychiatric Center.

B: Your name is what?

A: Smith.

B: Smith?

A: Yes.

A: Can I help you?

B: I don't know hhheh . . . I hope you can.

A: Uh hah . . . Tell me about your problems.

B: I uh . . . Now that you're here I'm embarrassed to talk about it. I don't want you telling me I'm emotionally immature 'cause I know I am.

I was very puzzled by "I don't know" in return to "May I help you." I couldn't figure out what they were doing with it. And the reason I was puzzled was that having listened to so many of these things and having been through the scene so many times, I heard "May I help you" as something like an idiom. I'm going to call these idiom-like things 'composites.' That means you hear the whole thing as a form, a single unit. And as a single unit, it has a proper return. As a composite, "May I help you" is a piece of etiquette; a way of introducing oneself as someone who is in the business of helping somebody, the answer to which is "Yes" and then some statement of what it is one wants. We can consider this item in terms of what I'll call the 'base environment' of its use.

By 'base environment' I mean, if you go into a department store, somebody is liable to come up to you and say "May I help you." And in business-type phone calls this item is routinely used. And if you come into a place and you don't know what it's like, and somebody comes up to you and uses such an item, that's one way of informing you what kind of a place it is. So, if a new institution is being set up, then there are available in the society whole sets of ways that persons go about beginning conversations, and one could, for example, adopt one or another of a series of them as the ones that are going to be used in this place.

Now the thing about at least some composites is that they can be heard not only as composites, but as ordinary sentences, which we could call 'constructives,' which are understood by taking the pieces and adding them up in some way. As a composite, "May I help you" is a piece of etiquette, a signal for stating your request—what you want to be helped with. Alternatively, as a constructive, "May I help you" is a question. If one hears it as a question, the piece of etiquette and its work hasn't come up, and "I don't know" is a perfectly proper answer.

Further, "I don't know" may be locating a problem which "May I help you" is designed, in the first place, to avoid. In its base environment, for example a department store, it's pretty much the case that for a customer, the question of whether some person "can help" is a matter of the department store having made them the person who does that. That is to say, lots of things, like telling you whether you can find lingerie in a certain size, is something anybody can do, and as long as the department store says this person is going to do it, that's enough. But we're dealing with a psychiatric hospital. In a department store, being selected to do a job and having credentials to do it are essentially the same thing. In a psychiatric hospital and lots of other places, however, they are very different things. That is, whether somebody can help you if you have a mental disorder, is not solved or is not even presumptively solved by the fact that they've been selected by somebody to do that job. The way it's solved in this society is by reference to such things as having been trained in a particular fashion, having gotten degrees, having passed Board examinations, etc.

Now, in the base environment of the use of "May I help you?" there is, as I say, no difference essentially between having credentials and being selected. If one can formulate the matter in a psychiatric hospital such that those things come on as being the same, then one needn't start off by producing one's credentials at the beginning of the conversation. And in my materials, again and again, when "May I help you" is used the person calling says "Yes" and begins to state their troubles.

As a general matter, then, one can begin to look for kinds of objects that have a base environment, that, when they get used in that environment perform a rather simple task, but that can be used in quite different environments to do quite other tasks. So, a matter like 'credentials' can be handled by this "May I help you" device. There will be lots of other devices which have a base environment, which do some other task in some other environment.

Before moving off of "May I help you" I want to mention one other thing about it. If the base environment is something like a department store, then, when it's used in other places—for example, a psychiatric hospital—one of the pieces of information it seems to convey is that whatever it is you propose to do, you do routinely. To whomsoever that calls. That is, it's heard as standardized utterance. How is that relevant? It can be relevant in alternative ways. First of all, it can be a very reassuring thing to hear. Some persons feel that they have troubles, and they don't know if anybody else has those troubles; or, if others do have those troubles, whether anybody knows about them. If someone knows about them, then there may be a known solution to them. Also and relatedly, a lot of troubles—like mental diseases—are things that persons feel very ambivalent about. That is, they're not sure whether it's some defect of their character, or something else. That, in part, is why they're hesitant to talk about it. And it seems that one of the ways one begins to tell people that they can talk, that you know what they have and that you routinely deal with such matters, is to use manifestly organizational talk.

"May I help you," then, can be a reassuring way to begin. It can alternatively be something else. Consider the exchange I just showed, in which such standardized utterances as "May I help you" and "Tell me about your problems" are used.

A: Can I help you?

B: I don't know hhheh . . . I hope you can

A: Uh hah . . . Tell me about your problems

B: I uh . . . Now that you're here I'm embarrassed to talk about it. I don't want you telling me I'm emotionally immature 'cause I know I am

That is, the use of standardized, manifestly organizational talk can provide for the person calling that they're going to get routine treatment. But 'routine,' for them, may not be such a happy thing. Because, for example, they've been through it before. But they may have gone through it, as psychiatrists would say, part way. For example, they were in analysis for three years and ran out of money, or the psychiatrist wouldn't keep them on, or they didn't want to stay. Part way, they may have come to some point in the analysis where they 'knew what was wrong with them.' That is, they knew the diagnostic term. But that diagnostic term may have had a lay affiliate. By that I mean, if a psychiatrist says you're regressed, it's a technical term. But 'regressed' is also a lay term, and as a lay term it doesn't have a great deal of attractiveness. If one finds oneself living with a lay understanding of such a term, where the term is not a very nice thing to have in its lay sense, then when you hear someone using such an item as "May I help you," you can hear that some procedure will be gone through, the upshot of which will be the discovery of what you 'already know'—the knowing of which doesn't do you any good.

Related to that are such things as, some people seem to feel very much disturbed about the fact that their relationship to a psychiatrist or to other doctors is monetary. What they want, they say, is a personal solution. Ask them what they want, "Well, that you don't have to pay for it." When they hear "May I help you," they hear 'a professional.' But they feel that the way you get cured is by getting an affiliation to somebody which is like the affiliations that they failed to get in their lives. That is, they may already have come to learn from some other psychiatrist that the failure of love by their parents is the cause of their troubles. Then, what they come to see is that they need the love of somebody else. And they can't get that from a therapist. Because as soon as they don't pay, that's the end of the relationship.

Now let me just make a few general points. Clearly enough, things like "This is Mr Smith," "May I help you?" and "I can't hear you" are social objects. And if you begin to look at what they do, you can see that they, and things like them, provide the makings of activities. You assemble activities by using these things. And now when you, or I, or sociologists, watching people do things, engage in trying to find out what they do and how they do it, one fix which can be used is: Of the enormous range of activities that people do, all of them are done with something. Someone says "This is Mr Smith" and the other supplies his own name. Someone says "May I help you" and the other states his business. Someone says "Huh?" or "What did you say?" or "I can't hear you," and then the thing said before gets repeated. What we want then to find out is, can we first of all construct the objects that get used to make up ranges of activities, and then see how it is those objects do get used.

Some of these objects can be used for whole ranges of activities, where for different ones a variety of the properties of those objects will get employed. And we begin to see alternative properties of those objects. That's one way we can go about beginning to collect the alternative methods that persons use in going about doing whatever they have to do. And we can see that these methods will be reproducible descriptions in the sense that any scientific description might be, such that the natural occurrences that we're describing can yield abstract or general phenomena which need not rely on statistical observability for their abstractness or generality.

There was a very classical argument that it would not be that way; that singular events were singular events, given a historian's sort of argument, that they just happen and they get more or less accidentally thrown together. But if we could find that there are analytically hard ways of describing these things—where, that is, we're talking about objects that can be found elsewhere, that get placed, that have ways of being used; that are abstract objects which get used on singular occasions and describe singular courses of activity—then that's something which is exceedingly non-trivial to know.

One final note. When people start to analyze social phenomena, if it looks like things occur with the sort of immediacy we find in some of these exchanges, then, if you have to make an elaborate analysis of it—that is to say, show that they did something as involved as some of the things I have proposed—then you figure that they couldn't have thought that fast. I want to suggest that you have to forget that completely. Don't worry about how fast they're thinking. First of all, don't worry about whether they're 'thinking.' Just try to come to terms with how it is that the thing comes off. Because you'll find that they can do these things. Just take any other area of natural science and see, for example, how fast molecules do things. And they don't have very good brains. So just let the materials fall as they may. Look to see how it is that persons go about producing what they do produce.

Endnotes

1. A combination of Fall 1964, tape 1, side 2 and tape 2, side 1, with brief extract from Winter 1965, lecture (1)—the parentheses indicate that the original transcripts were unnumbered, the current numbering likely but not certain—pp. 1 and 11–12 (transcriber unknown) and Spring 1965 ('64–'65), lecture 3, pp. 6–7 (transcriber unknown). . . .

2. The fragment of data is reproduced pretty much as Sacks transcribed it, preserving his attempts to deal with simultaneous talk (i.e., *A:* This is Mr Smith (*B:* Hello) of the Emergency Psychiatric Center) and silence (e.g., *B:* I uh . . . Now that you're here. . . .). . . .

From *Lectures on Conversation*, vol. 1, pp. 3–11, by Harvey Sacks. Copyright © 1992, 1995, The Estate of Harvey Sacks. Reprinted by permission of Blackwell Publishers. ✦

44
Studies of the Routine Grounds of Everyday Activities

Harold Garfinkel

Harold Garfinkel (b. 1929) coined the term "ethnomethodology" and offered its initial portrayal as a distinctive theory school in his influential 1967 book, *Studies in Ethnomethodology*. The term refers to the methods people use to make sense of and find ways to act in the routine situations of their everyday lives. As Garfinkel notes, he was significantly influenced by Alfred Schutz, so it is not surprising that phenomenology and ethnomethodology bear a family resemblance. In his own unique way, and with his own distinctive terminology, Garfinkel urges sociologists to refrain from imposing their interpretive frames to explain the subjects of their empirical research. Instead, as an alternative he calls for attentiveness to the structured ways in which the subjects themselves use what is typically referred to as "common sense." In this particular excerpt, he stresses the importance of attempting to make visible those routine aspects of everyday life that are generally taken for granted, and thus are not really noticed.

The Problem

For Kant the moral order "within" was an awesome mystery; for sociologists the moral order "without" is a technical mystery. From the point of view of sociological theory the moral order consists of the rule governed activities of everyday life. A society's members encounter and know the moral order as perceivedly normal courses of action—familiar scenes of everyday affairs, the world of daily life known in common with others and with others taken for granted.

They refer to this world as the "natural facts of life" which for members, are through and through moral facts of life. For members not only are matters so about familiar scenes, but they are so because it is morally right or wrong that they are so. Familiar scenes of everyday activities, treated by members as the "natural facts of life," are massive facts of the members' daily existence both as a real world and as the product of activities in a real world. They furnish the "fix," the "this is it" to which the waking state returns one, and are the points of departure and return for every modification of the world of daily life that is achieved in play, dreaming, trance, theater, scientific theorizing, or high ceremony.

In every discipline, humanistic or scientific, the familiar common sense world of everyday life is a matter of abiding interest. In the social sciences, and in sociology particularly, it is a matter of essential preoccupation. It makes up sociology's problematic subject matter, enters the very constitution of the sociological attitude, and exercises an odd and obstinate sovereignty over sociologists' claims to adequate explanation.

Despite the topic's centrality, an immense literature contains little data and few methods with which the essential features of socially recognized "familiar scenes" may be detected and related to dimensions of social organization. Although sociologists take socially structured scenes of everyday life as a point of departure they rarely see,[1] as a task of sociological inquiry in its own right, the general question of how any such common sense world is possible. Instead, the possibility of the everyday world is either settled by theoretical representation or merely assumed. As a topic and methodological ground for sociological inquiries, the definition of the common sense world of everyday life, though it is appropriately a project of sociological inquiry, has been neglected. My purposes in this paper are to demonstrate the essential relevance, to sociological inquiries, of a concern for common sense activities as a topic of inquiry in its own right and, by reporting a series of studies, to urge its "rediscovery."

Making Commonplace Scenes Visible

In accounting for the stable features of everyday activities sociologists commonly select familiar settings such as familial households or work places and ask for the variables that contribute to their stable features. Just as commonly, one set of considerations are unexamined: the socially standardized and standardizing, "seen but unnoticed," expected, background features of everyday scenes. The member of the society uses background expectancies as a scheme of interpretation. With their use actual appearances are for him recognizable and intelligible as the appearances-of-familiar-events. Demonstrably he is responsive to this background, while at the same time he is at a loss to tell us specifically of what the expectancies consist. When we ask him about them he has little or nothing to say.

For these background expectancies to come into view one must either be a stranger to the "life as usual" character of everyday scenes, or become estranged from them. As Alfred Schutz pointed out, a "special motive" is required to make them problematic. In the sociologists' case this "special motive" consists in the programmatic task of treating a societal member's practical circumstances, which include from the member's point of view the morally necessary character of many of its background features, as matters of theoretic interest. The seen but unnoticed backgrounds of everyday activities are made visible and are described from a perspective in which persons live out the lives they do, have the children they do, feel the feelings, think the thoughts, enter the relationships they do, all in order to permit the sociologist to solve his theoretical problems.

Almost alone among sociological theorists, the late Alfred Schutz, in a series of classical studies[2] of the constitutive phenomenology of the world of everyday life, described many of these seen but unnoticed background expectancies. He called them the "attitude of daily life." He referred to their scenic attributions as the "world known in common and taken for granted." Schutz' fundamental work makes it possible to pursue further the tasks of clarifying their nature and operation, of relating them to the processes of concerted actions, and assigning them their place in an empirically imaginable society.

The studies reported in this paper attempt to detect some expectancies that lend commonplace scenes their familiar, life-as-usual character, and to relate these to the stable social structures of everyday activities. Procedurally it is my preference to start with familiar scenes and ask what can be done to make trouble. The operations that one would have to perform in order to multiply the senseless features of perceived environments; to produce and sustain bewilderment, consternation, and confusion; to produce the socially structured affects of anxiety, shame, guilt, and indignation; and to produce disorganized interaction should tell us something about how the structures of everyday activities are ordinarily and routinely produced and maintained.[3]

A word of reservation. Despite their procedural emphasis, my studies are not properly speaking experimental. They are demonstrations, designed, in Herbert Spiegelberg's phrase, as "aids to a sluggish imagination." I have found that they produce reflections through which the strangeness of an obstinately familiar world can be detected.

Some Essential Features of Common Understandings

Various considerations dictate that common understandings cannot possibly consist of a measured amount of shared agreement among persons on certain topics. Even if the topics are limited in number and scope and every practical difficulty of assessment is forgiven, the notion that we are dealing with an amount of shared agreement remains essentially incorrect. This may be demonstrated as follows.

Students were asked to report common conversations by writing on the left side of a sheet what the parties actually said and on the right side what they and their partners understood that they were talking about. A student reported the following colloquy between himself and his wife. (See Text Box.)

An examination of the colloquy reveals the following. (a) There were many matters

HUSBAND:	Dana succeeded in putting a penny in a parking meter today without being picked up.	This afternoon as I was bringing Dana, our four-year-old son, home from the nursery school, he succeeded in reaching high enough to put a penny in a parking meter when we parked in a meter parking zone, whereas before he has always had to be picked up to reach that high.
WIFE:	Did you take him to the record store?	Since he put a penny in a meter that means that you stopped while he was with you. I know that you stopped at the record store either on the way to get him or on the way back. Was it on the way back, so that he was with you or did you stop there on the way to get him and somewhere else on the way back?
HUSBAND:	No, to the shoe repair shop.	No, I stopped at the record store on the way to get him and stopped at the shoe repair shop on the way home when he was with me.
WIFE:	What for?	I know of one reason why you might have stopped at the shoe repair shop. Why did you in fact?
HUSBAND:	I got some new shoe laces for my shoes.	As you will remember I broke a shoe lace on one of my brown oxfords the other day so I stopped to get some new laces,
WIFE:	Your loafers need new heels badly.	Something else you could have gotten that I was thinking of. You could have taken in your black loafers which need heels badly. You'd better get them taken care of pretty soon.

that the partners understood they were talking about that they did not mention. (b) Many matters that the partners understood were understood on the basis not only of what was actually said but what was left unspoken. (c) Many matters were understood through a process of attending to the temporal series of utterances as documentary evidences of a developing conversation rather than as a string of terms. (d) Matters that the two understood in common were understood only in and through a course of understanding work that consisted of treating an actual linguistic event as "the document of," as "pointing to," as standing on behalf of an underlying pattern of matters that each already supposed to be the matters that the person, by his speaking, could be telling the other about. The underlying pattern was not only derived from a course of individual documentary evidences but the documentary evidences in their turn were interpreted on the basis of "what was known" and anticipatorily knowable about the underlying patterns.[4] Each was used to elaborate the other. (e) In attending to the utterances as events-in-the-conversation each party made references to the biography and prospects of the present interaction which each used and attributed to the other as a common scheme of interpretation and expression. (f) Each

waited for something more to be said in order to hear what had previously been talked about, and each seemed willing to wait.

Common understandings would consist of a measured amount of shared agreement if the common understandings consisted of events coordinated with the successive positions of the hands of the clock, i.e., of events in standard time. The foregoing results, because they deal with the exchanges of the colloquy as events-in-a-conversation, urge that one more time parameter, at least, is required: the role of time as it is constitutive of "the matter talked about" as a developing and developed event over the course of action that produced it, as both the process and product were known *from within* this development by both parties, each for himself as well as on behalf of the other.

The colloquy reveals additional features. (1) Many of its expressions are such that their sense cannot be decided by an auditor unless he knows or assumes something about the biography and the purposes of the speaker, the circumstances of the utterance, the previous course of the conversation, or the particular relationship of actual or potential interaction that exists between user and auditor. The expressions do not have a sense that remains identical through the changing occasions of their use. (2) The events that were talked about were specifically vague. Not only do they not frame a clearly restricted set of possible determinations but the depicted events include as their essentially intended and sanctioned features an accompanying "fringe" of determinations that are open with respect to internal relationships, relationships to other events, and relationships to retrospective and prospective possibilities. (3) For the sensible character of an expression, upon its occurrence each of the conversationalists as auditor of his own as well as the other's productions had to assume as of any present accomplished point in the exchange that by waiting for what he or the other person might have said at a later time the present significance of what had already been said would have been clarified. Thus many expressions had the property of being progressively realized and realizable through the further course of the conversation. (4) It hardly needs to be pointed out that the sense of the expressions depended upon where the expression occurred in serial order, the expressive character of the terms that comprised it, and the importance to the conversationalists of the events depicted.

These properties of common understandings stand in contrast to the features they would have if we disregarded their temporally constituted character and treated them instead as precoded entries on a memory drum, to be consulted as a definite set of alternative meanings from among which one was to select, under predecided conditions that specified in which of some set of alternative ways one was to understand the situation upon the occasion that the necessity for a decision arose. The latter properties are those of strict rational discourse as these are idealized in the rules that define an adequate logical proof.

For the purposes of *conducting their everyday affairs* persons refuse to permit each other to understand "what they are really talking about" in this way. The anticipation that persons *will* understand, the occasional-

ity of expressions, the specific vagueness of references, the retrospective-prospective sense of a present occurrence, waiting for something later in order to see what was meant before, are sanctioned properties of common discourse. They furnish a background of seen but unnoticed features of common discourse whereby actual utterances are recognized as events of common, reasonable, understandable, plain talk. Persons require these properties of discourse as conditions under which they are themselves entitled and entitle others to claim that they know what they are talking about, and that what they are saying is understandable and ought to be understood. In short, their seen but unnoticed presence is used to entitle persons to conduct their common conversational affairs without interference. Departures from such usages call forth immediate attempts to restore a right state of affairs.

Endnotes

1. The work of Alfred Schutz, cited in endnote 2, is a magnificent exception. Readers who are acquainted with his writings will recognize how heavily this paper is indebted to him.

2. Alfred Schutz, *Der Sinnhafte Aufbau Der Sozialen Welt* (Wein: Verlag von Julius Springer, 1932); *Collected Papers I: The Problem of Social Reality,* ed. Maurice Natanson (The Hague: Martinus Nijhoff, 1962); *Collected Papers II: Studies in Social Theory,* ed. Arvid Broderson (The Hague: Martinus Nijhoff, 1964); *Collected Papers III: Studies in Phenomenological Philosophy,* ed. I. Schutz (The Hague: Martinus Nijhoff, 1966).

3. Obversely, a knowledge of how the structures of everyday activities are routinely produced should permit us to tell how we might proceed for the effective production of desired disturbances.

4. Karl Mannheim, in his essay "On the Interpretation of 'Weltanschauung' " (in *Essays on the Sociology of Knowledge,* trans. and ed. Paul Kecskemeti [New York: Oxford University Press, 1952], pp. 33–83), referred to this work as the documentary method of interpretation.". . .

45
Partnership

Aron Gurwitsch

Aron Gurwitsch (1901–1973) was a phenomenological theorist, working out of the tradition of
Husserl and Schutz. In this essay he explores the situational bonds that emerge as two people engaging
in situated and coordinated actions come to constitute a partnership. Gurwitsch discusses the significance of roles as instances of "relational determinedness," contrasting such a "having-to-do-within-one-
another" with what he refers to as "external relationships." From this discussion, he moves on to a consideration of philosophical issues raised by the
German philosopher Wilhelm Dilthey related to
the understanding of the other. Gurwitsch attempts to ground his discussion sociologically by
exploring those basic forms of understanding that
occur in everyday life, concluding with a brief
assessment of the relevance of such understanding
for the human sciences.

Being Together in a Common Situation

We shall consider the being-together of
partners in a common situation as the first
dimension of the actual being-together of
fellow human beings. What this signifies can
best be made clear by the simplest possible
example of people working together.

In cobbling a street, for instance, one
worker lays the stones while the other knocks
them into place. Limiting ourselves for the
sake of simplicity of analysis to the being-together of *two* men, each stands in a situation
which is their work-situation and each orients himself to the references in that situation. But because both workers are busied
with one and the same job, they stand in a
common situation. Yet, strictly speaking, the
situation of the one is not exactly that of the
other: through his work, the one prepares

the foundation for the appropriate activity
of the other. What is common to them is for
the one a stage at the end, for the other a
stage at the beginning. They work, mutually
helping each other; each is related to the
other in his dealings and his work. *This relation makes up the meaning of fellow workers*.
Precisely because the one is entirely absorbed
in the whole work and gears into it, he encounters the other as fellow worker and,
more particularly, he encounters him with
respect to the function that he possesses in
the common, concrete work-situation. By
accident one does not meet a "stranger"
who—literally or figuratively—stands next
to the work and is superfluous in the sense of
the work-situation. Rather, the dependency
signifies that one does not do justice to the
situation and cannot fulfill his own functions in it when the other is denied in some
manner or other. One is thus dependent on
his fellow worker in the sense that his own
situational comportment is oriented to him
and to his comportment. But that signifies:
the other also belongs to the situation in
which I stand; his presence also contributes
to the constituting of the situation and to
making it what it is *in concreto*. It is necessary
that someone or other[1] be present and take on
specific functions in the situation—that is to
say, the functions which my fellow worker now
fulfills. Thus my fellow worker is an integrating
and meaningful situational moment.

What was developed in our example (in
which the working-hand-in-hand-with-one-
another is to be understood literally) obtains
only where one can speak in a transferred
sense—thus, say, a conference where it is a
matter of making concerted comportment
and action understandable and giving advice
about it—or, stated differently, the one who
does not take the other into consideration
and expresses his opinion without relating it
to what is advanced on the other side, stands
outside consultation in common even when
he sits among others.[2] The case is similar to
one who is there only passively and does not
participate in the conference, who is not
even genuinely present, whose absence does
not touch the course of the conference. Likewise, being-together has the structure described when one does not work together but
acts against the other as, e.g., in a game of

chess where each player orients his moves toward those of his opponent, trying to guess his opponent's plans and combinations and to correct his moves so that his opponent is thwarted, forestalled.

This sort of comportment, namely, in view of that which is to be expected from one's partner such that one takes his own measures and "answers in advance" by anticipating his partner, was worked out by Löwith as a general structural moment of all mutual being and speaking together.[3] But this structure of comportment only has its place in that dimension of fellow being-together pertaining to the partner which we are now considering; the structure is grounded in what is constituted in this dimension by that which is essentially in the encounters. It is lacking, therefore, in the dimension of encounters of others which is to be analyzed later. If the anticipatory "answering in advance" is to be restricted to the being-together characterized as partnership, then within this dimension the structure itself worked out and over-emphasized by Löwith really only appears in its pregnance where the partners are together because they "will something from each other," e.g., when the one wills to convince or persuade the other,[4] or when they confer in order to agree. Should one make an agreement with his partner, or come to an understanding with him about a controversy on the basis of an already existing contract, then one is together with him in a situation of negotiation and, more particularly, one is together with him for the sake of making an agreement, for the sake of the controversy, and the like. While one confers with his partner, he faces the wishes, aims, and interests of the partner which, even when not explicitly expressed, are provided by the setting of the things. In virtue of the partner's comportment during the negotiations, his aims, motivations, etc., can be discovered. One orients his comportment with respect to the position disclosed by his partner; whereas, in anticipation, one seeks to "answer in advance" his opponent, whose responses and counter-measures are foreseen and encountered such that one tries to guide them in the desired, or in the least undesirable, direction. As a result, one's own comportment in the situation is tuned in on the other and

takes account of him. Here, as in the cases mentioned earlier, one is related to his partner in one's comportment while comporting oneself in view of his partner and his partner's comportment. One notices the presence of his partner in the common situation; precisely for that reason the situation in question is determined as what it is.

In the examples just mentioned, the "pressure of the external world" already obtains—a phenomenon to which, as is known, Dilthey had given special emphasis in his theory of the experience of reality.[5] But most distinctive is the experience of pressure and resistance in that being-together for which the existence of superordinate and subordinate relations are essential. The servant becomes aware of the pressure of the master when he is together with him in a situation for which the relation of subordination holds.[6] Accordingly, he experiences his partner as the one for the sake of whose will he submits to this situation[7] toward which he is directed and which also has meaning for him when he orients himself negatively to the master. In these last cases, the master experiences the resistance of the external world; he finds himself in the common situations in which he is master, precisely as master related to his servant and oriented to him and his comportment in a way that corresponds to his role as master. As a consequence, it is essential that pressure and resistance be made apparent with respect to the situation itself and in the situation-conforming comportment of the partner.

No matter how characteristic and essential the experience of pressure, resistance, and anticipatory "answering in advance" may be for some of the examples considered (as well as for the realm of encounters of fellow human beings taken collectively), as paradigmatic representatives of which each example engaged our attention, we still have not designated the structure which persists in all encounters of the dimension observed and which allows of being shown in all the concrete cases belonging to it. Simultaneously exhibiting the viewpoint under which the encounters of the fellow human beings involved belong together, this structure consists of the *being related to the part-*

ner that we have emphasized continuously. That we are in a common situation together with the partner, whose presence and comportment in it produce an essential contribution to its constitution, signifies that we encounter him not only in the common situation but that we also encounter him *in the sense of the situation constituted in this way.* Our being-together is determined in its meaning by what we do in the situation of encounter, how we comport ourselves in it in relation to the partner and, conversely, how our partner comports himself toward us. The aims of the comportment are, obviously, also constitutive for the expression of the situation. One can describe perfectly the being-together of this dimension by the circumstance that the partner acts for the sake of a common concern. On the basis of the particular attitudes of the partner to this common concern, the sense is determined in which each of them is my partner. As a consequence, the encounter of fellow human beings within the dimension to be discussed can be defined as a consociate encounter [*gebundene Begegnung*].

On the basis of these situational bonds we can see how far the personal presence of the partner is particularly necessary for being together, although not sufficient for it. It is necessary because the relation to a fellow human being comporting himself in the situation in question, by which he becomes a partner, is constitutive for being-together. If the master gives his instructions and then goes away, he may thus still remain very "close" to the servant who now carries out the orders; even when the servant, who is now alone, directs his comportment precisely in view of the expected re-encounter with the master, we still have here only an extreme case of " 'being co-included' nearby" and perhaps even a limiting case of "co-presence." But, in any case, there is no being-together in the pregnant sense of doing-something-with-one-another. On the other hand, the personal presence is insufficient for the constitution of a partnership-encounter when personal presence only means a series of people residing in one and the same place. If many workers work at a machine, and if all of them (though each for himself) produces the same thing, they are then neither fellow workers nor are they together with one another in any genuine and pregnant sense. Because they work *next* to one another, the work of the one does not itself become observable in the work of the other—this, indeed, lies in the sense of being-next-to-one-another.

Role-Encounters

The situational encounter-bonds of fellow human beings under consideration here only reveal their full meaning when we ask as what the partner is encountered in his being-together.

By appealing to what was previously discussed with regard to becoming determined by the situation,[8] we may say that if I acquire the sense of my concrete being from the situation, then that signifies for the determination of my concrete being with respect to the other that I am also determined with regard to one or many partners. Thus I am co-determined by the relationship that I have to my partner. In my relationship to him I encounter him as the one for whom I am *hic et nunc* and come into account; and he encounters me in exactly the same way. The relationship that each of us has to the other arises from the fact that we *actually* comport ourselves to each other in a determinate way. *How* we comport ourselves, in which concrete sense we are partners, is, to be sure, determined by the situation of our being-together. Our relationship to one another is a founded relationship insofar as it has its root in the situation mentioned. In other words: the situation prescribes a *role* to us which we take over as long as we are in the situation in question. That we exist in such a place in the role assigned us and *as such a role* is indeed everywhere the sense of the situational determinedness of our concrete being. In relation to the situations of being-together with a partner with which we are concerned here, it is important to note that the mutual role of the partner is already aimed at beforehand. The mutual roles are constitutive for the sense of this role of ours which requires them according to its meaning since they can only be meaningful in relation to this role of ours. Therefore we always and necessarily have our role in view of the role of the partner. In that fact are grounded the relation and reference to the partner which . . . we developed as the characteristic of being together in a common situation.

The partners encounter each other in their partnership-situations in these roles constituted by the relationship to one another, they encounter each as the ones who are what they are in the particular common situations, e.g., as fellow workers, as buyers and sellers, as employees and employers, as masters and servants, and, more particularly, in just the roles which they have in the concrete case— as the coachman who carries the passengers on a journey, etc. Hence I do not encounter an individual in this dimension with his individual properties accruing specifically to him that constitute him as this determinate individual. As a consequence, it can be accidental and irrelevant in a certain sense—especially if one seizes upon it as a "structured life-unity" in Dilthey's sense—that the individual is now in this concrete situation and has precisely this role in it.[9] But we certainly do not encounter an absolutely other person, as it were, a second example of the genus to which I belong and which I interpret by analogy or empathy and only make comprehensible by the "transfer of my own livingness" and its structure, of my own mental processes and their concatenations such that I conceive it in an entirely determinate way as *alter ego*.[10] The other is rather encountered by me as partner in just the concrete sense of partnership in which he is my partner *hic et nunc*. For me he is considered only as the role that he represents in the particular situation of our being together on the ground of his function in this situation and, in a sense to be explained, as the role that he also *is*.[11] He appears to me as one motivated by the situation which prescribes a role and function to him. Only in this role of his do I have something to do with him. In this situation, his being is exhausted in the role whose bearer he is.[12] What I otherwise still know about my partner is, insofar as it has no material bearing on the situation, irrelevant for his behavior toward me. Likewise, in the sense of our being together it makes no difference in what measure the roles are rooted in the reciprocal "life-unities" which each of us exhibits as individual. We are indeed together only in our roles, not as individuals.

Accordingly, it also does not even follow that it is just the certain someone or other with whom I am now in this concrete partnership. This someone or other can be substituted by anyone else insofar as he assumes the function and role determined by the situation. In this sense, one can say that my partner is "someone or other in this quite determinate role." This is because it does not signify any interference in the situation when someone takes over the role of someone else.[13]

On various occasions we have considered Löwith's book, *Das Individuum in der Rolle des Mitmenschen* [*The Individual in the Role of Fellow Human Being*]. In that book, Löwith expresses the idea that people do not encounter each other as individuals, that is to say, as encapsuled "monads"; instead, they encounter each other essentially in the "roles" they have in relation to each other and hence in "relational determinedness."

> Each of the others is thus determined above all precisely *in himself* in that he can have a *relationship* to a determinate *other*. Fellow human beings do not encounter each other as a plurality of *individuals* existing for themselves but instead as *personae* who have a role within and for their fellow world on the basis of which they then are themselves determined as persons.[14]

This idea of the determination of people by their relational significance as *"personae"* is, in fact, central to Löwith's investigations. It is in this connection that Löwith arrives at the elaboration of the anticipatory "answering in advance":

> One's own comportment is . . . not only directed *to* the other, but also at the same time *according to* the other; it regulates itself beforehand according to the other. The primary ambiguity of one's own comportment towards the other is thus reflected when one in his comportment (towards the other) is *related to the relationship*. To relate oneself in his comportment towards the relationship signifies that I relate myself to another beforehand in view of his possible comportment towards me.[15]

Here we also see the reason why Löwith absolutizes this structure to the extent that he holds it to be the governing structure without restriction of all encounters with fellow human beings. Because he, furthermore, introduces no difference among the different dimensions of being-together, the encounter with fellow human beings is not limited to the realm in which *only* this sort of encounter has its place and basis ("ground"). By virtue of this radicalization, being-together occurs in the sense that "the one allows of being determined by the other in the measure that his own being [*Dasein*] receives and loses its existential meaning *primarily* from the relationship to the other."[16] Accordingly, there arises for him the problem of the "autonomy of the one for the other *in the relationship itself* as not simply an absolutized, but, instead, as an *absolute, relationship*"—a problem that leads back beyond Dilthey to Kant.[17]

No matter how fruitful, now, this idea proves to be in many respects (e.g., in the interpretation of the "moral qualities" of the individual, say, "egoism" and "altruism" as "expressions of life," as ways of comportment toward other people and not as "inner properties of an individual substance which exist for themselves" because "I and the other are not objects indifferent to one another with immanental . . . properties"[18]), it still is not sufficient to clarify the "relational significance and determination" in its own peculiarity and in its full sense in a phenomenologically satisfying way. The fault for this is *also*, but not *alone*, the circumstance that Löwith overlooks the different dimensions of being-together of fellow human beings in their difference as well as in their own peculiarity in every case.[19] The essential deficiencies of Löwith's investigations rest on the fact that he did not carry out his ideas on the basis of thorough analyses of concrete phenomena. Here, as elsewhere . . . he orients himself to the peculiarities of the German use of language which he takes so seriously that he tries to make assertions about phenomena and concatenations of phenomena with respect to investigations into the "material logic of language." Löwith allows himself to be guided by the unquestioned obviousness of language rather than examining by description and explication the "affairs" in their differences, in their

commonalities, and the founding and derivative relationships obtaining between them, in terms of the phenomenal itself, so that clarity might be created concerning them when the peculiarities of linguistic use touch upon actual phenomena and their concatenations and when linguistic use is exclusively present. Because he places on the same plane as equally justified examples of "relational determination" those of the young and the old, of servants and masters,[20] it escapes Löwith that the word "*Verhältnis*" ["relationship"] has a different meaning in each of these examples. The relationship between master and servant is characterized by both of them coming together in concrete situations and having something to do with one another, while the relationship obtaining between old and young exhibits a relationship between ages which can be, and at the most also is, entirely a phenomenal characteristic.

That is to say, that a man "in his best years" is older than a youth who only by accident sits next to him, and with whom he has nothing at all to do is suggested without one even having to take recourse to the exact numerical relationship of their ages. In the one case, the relationship is grounded in an actual comportment toward one another in concrete, common situations. In the other case, the comporting-themselves-toward-one-another is not even present: it is, instead, exclusively an objective fact which exists independently of whether or not, even accidentally, the people in question encounter each other in common situations. For this reason the relationship existing in the latter case will be called an "external relationship" just because it is not grounded in having-to-do-within-one-another. The sense in which a father "belongs" to his children is different from the sense in which an officer "belongs" to the military, and it is different, again, from the sense in which "an old man does (not) belong to young people." Only on the ground of distinguishing the relationships in which people interact from those that exist "objectively," i.e., without the compliance of his partner, can the "relational determination" be clarified in its sense. But this clarification can only be accomplished in investigations that analyze the phenomena themselves and by returning to what any "standing in a situation" whatever means. In the same way, admittedly under inclusion of dimensional differences, the different sense in which we speak of the "belongingness" of human beings to one another must and can receive their clarification.

Mutual Understanding in the Common Situation

In situations of the surrounding world, life knows itself in "implicit" ways and contains its rules for this knowledge, i.e., for knowledge about the situation.[21] As governed by an inherent knowledge, this life is "circumspective concern" in Heidegger's sense. Obviously, the characteristic of this knowledge is not altered if I am now alone in the situation, or if the sense of the situation is constituted precisely by the fact that I encounter other people. In the preceding analyses we have already made different use of this knowledge. At its most pregnant, it came to light in the anticipatory "answering in advance." In fact, this is nothing else than an entirely determinate sort of reacting to the partner guided by knowledge about the situation and the other. Because it is thus a knowledge inherent in "living in . . . ," it illuminates the situation *precisely, but also only precisely, as the situation* comes into consideration for us. In the "implicit" self-knowledge belonging to "living in. . ." we understand that with which we deal as that which is of concern to itself. Already included therein is the own specific kind of understanding of the partner in the common situation since this understanding represents a moment of "implicit" knowledge about the situation.

In the common situations under discussion *here*, we encounter the partner as a bearer of roles. Understanding gears into the concrete being inherent in this role. Thus we neither have in front of us—as the position that is the starting point of the traditional inquiry believes—a "piece of the external world"[22] in which we empathize, etc., and only when we enliven it, or animate it, or the like, by some form or other of the "transfer" of our own inwardness, do we then have present another human being, someone

else's ego; nor do we prepare the way here for something like the understanding of the *individuality* of someone else. In his posthumously published fragments on "Das Verstehen andere Personen und Lebensäußerungen" ["The Understanding of Other Persons and Life-expressions"], Dilthey distinguishes between "elementary" and "higher forms of understanding."[23] Here we are truly concerned with what he calls "elementary forms of understanding," i.e., with an understanding that "arises out of the interests of practical life." The situations of "practical life" are comprehensible with respect to their bearing on us:

> The elementary acts, by virtue of which connective activities are composed, such as picking up an object, letting the hammer fall, the sawing of wood by a saw, designate for us the presence of certain goals. In this elementary understanding, therefore, there is no recurrence to the entire nexus of life which the enduring subject of life-expressions forms . . . we also need not . . . seize upon it as a method that goes back from a given effect to some piece or other of the life-context which makes the effect possible. Certainly this latter relationship is contained in the affair-complex itself, and thus the passage from this into that is similarly always at the door: but it need not come in.[24]

If we set Dilthey's ideas into the context of our considerations, then we may say: *The knowledge immanent to the Being in the common situations understands the partner in his particular role with respect to the concrete situation.* The core of another person is neither accessible to this understanding, nor does it disclose such things as the characteristic traits of fellow human beings; nor, finally, does it confront consciousness-processes, i.e., the *cogitationes* of another ego. What exclusively comes into view here is the partner in the sense of partnership in which we have to deal with him in every case. Understanding, therefore, concerns the way in which the other plays the role assigned to him by the situation. As a consequence, this orientation characterizes this understanding not primarily because it involves other people but because it represents a moment in the knowledge about the immediately actual situation-totality. This orientation grips fellow human beings only insofar as it is a component of the situation. In other words, we are dealing with a functional understanding. Accordingly, the partner is disclosed in existence *determined by the situation:* in the role that he directly represents and "is." Expressed in all of this is the fact that this understanding of the partner disclosed forms of comportment, of modes of "living in . . . ," but not the properties which accrue to a human being as substance even when one seizes upon this substance as a "structured life-unity."

It is in this manner that in and with respect to the common work I experience my fellow worker. If he is revealed to me as a worker who is useful or clumsy, fit or unfit, then I need not reason back from the finished work to him as a person who shared in the production. While standing in the common situation with the other, I overlook this and conceive him in terms of the situation; I always already "know" about the suitability or unsuitability of his comportment. From that standpoint the sense of the fitness or unfitness of the fellow worker is determined: namely, with respect to the actual work in common. To be sure, the other is still disclosed *only* as a fellow worker, what he might otherwise be, in which sectors he might otherwise exist, in which sense he exists in them—all of this is inaccessible to this understanding immanent in being-together. . . . The considerations about fellow workers hold in a corresponding way for all forms of fellow being-together meant here. When I ask someone for something, I then experience the way in which the person asked listens to me, enters into the request, offers resistance, avoids the request, sets conditions, gives in, etc.; I do not experience something like an alien and autonomous will simpliciter. Rather a human being encounters me who comports himself in a certain way in the situation in question, who is unfriendly or complaisant, who allows this and that purpose to clearly appear or even be explicitly expressed, who lets a certain position toward the affair be known, etc. Even the one asked to do something does not experience anything like the "claim of the Thou" simpliciter.

Where it is not a matter of asking for something but instead involves a transaction, the being-together is nonetheless of a similar structure. However, here the anticipatory "answering in advance" emerges more distinctly and occasionally governs our being together. But such anticipation is only possible on the ground of "implicit" situational understanding and is ruled by that understanding. On that rests the fact that the demands of the other are provided in being together and transacting. One's own comportment is oriented toward this knowledge which is on the point of answering what is expected from the opposite side in a purposive way: just that makes up the anticipatory "answering in advance."

In common situations the partner listens deliberately. While each plays his role, he divines the purposes and tendencies of the other even when the other does not declare them—as is clear from the example of the chess player.

Expressive phenomena also arise in the encounters under consideration. While I am conversing with my partner, he shakes his head or wrinkles his brow. Shaking the head and wrinkling the brow are not in themselves unambiguous gestures, but they can mean many things. One cannot simply infer what a gesture signifies in a concrete case; it is not "inscribed" as this determinate gesture. Scheler's notion[25] that there is a "universal grammar" "that obtains for *all* languages of expression and is the highest foundation of comprehension for all kinds of mime and pantomime of living things" is justified for a certain realm. But those ordinary and daily expressive phenomena, gestures, etc., that we have in mind here will not be understood on the basis of that "universal grammar." Rather it is the case that we understand them by virtue of the whole of the common situation.

Stated differently: the comprehension of this and similar expressive phenomena smoothly arises from knowledge about the situation in which I am with others, and fits into this knowledge as one of its moments. Even where I perceive that an expressive movement is not genuine, but purposively produced, and hence creates the suspicion that my partner wishes to deceive me, this assumption need not found a disturbance of the "essential connection" between mental process and expression. In this situation and its "co-included" backgrounds this reaction of the other does not "fit" in. The not-fitting-in, the not-being-in-order, and the like, are phenomenal properties of the expressive phenomenon under consideration . . . properties, indeed, that do not accrue to this phenomenon in and of itself. Rather they are only supplied by the total situation. In this total situation alone it becomes the expressive phenomenon that it is *in concreto*, by means of it and from it the phenomenon receives its particular meaning. The "same" shaking of the head can, as we have seen, take on different meanings in different situations, and in addition still be called genuine in the one situation and artificial in the other. What an expressive phenomenon is and signifies in a particular case becomes comprehensible to me in the whole of the present situation. By means of and with respect to this situational understanding, I can penetrate behind the actual reaction of my partner in a given case. The understanding of expressive phenomena is *as* understanding by virtue of relations to the situation of exactly the same sort as the understanding of what is totally present in the situation. But that signifies that a specific problem of expressive phenomena is not given in the realm of the being-together of fellow human beings under consideration here.

The understanding of fellow human beings presented here has a meaning transcending the being-together in a common situation. When we turn from a work, as we can at any time,[26] to the people engaged in it, they likewise only come into view in the roles which they have taken over in the work-situation in question. In a carelessly made work the producer appears as a worker determined as such and such, e.g., as a watch-maker, an architect, etc., who had lacked conscientiousness, just as a scrupulous, skilled, industrious worker appears in a precision-made work. But it is always a matter of a person *in his role*. Understanding is yielded here by virtue of the situation and is, therefore, limited to what is inherent in it.

Now, in his analysis of the understanding of someone else's volitional activities,

Spranger[27] refers to the fact that the "psychical situation (the motive)" of the one who acts is "directly inaccessible" to the one who understands; but insofar as "objective cognitions also arise in this inner situation," that is, insofar as the activity is oriented toward determinate constellations ("situations" in our sense of the term), the situation is "subsequently controllable" and contains a component which, as a "rational part of the activity, is accessible to the other <scl. the one who understands> as objectively legitimated." The activity is comprehensible as activity in this whole situation with respect to what is "subsequently controllable"; on the basis of this understanding of the situation, the on-looker understands this concrete activity[28] and can make a judgment about it with respect to its suitability. The specific limitation peculiar to this understanding, which of essential necessity remains bound to the situation and its horizons, becomes distinct precisely in this understanding of the activity as activity in which the "inner psychical situation" remains "directly inaccessible."[29]

This understanding also possesses a certain meaning for the human sciences. Whenever it is a matter of a certain product, or of the concrete emergence of a historical figure, these are to be conceived with respect to the situation. On its side, this situation fits into an entirely determinate horizon of tissues of references.[30] As a consequence, the historical figure in question comes into view in his concrete role: Hence it is thus a matter not of closed and "structured life-unities," but rather of a *particular concrete existence*.[31] Nonetheless, at the most the historian would not be satisfied with this understanding of the particular situation and of the historical person in his concrete roles; even when he has not aimed at historical figures in their individuality, he asks about the underlying reasons as much of the persons in their roles as he does of the situation itself. A new book of laws, for instance, serves the needs of a certain time; the book of laws and the law-giver in his law-giving performance are to be understood in terms of the changed conditions of life, the altered economic system, etc. But, as Dilthey noted,[32] the historian can go back from the book of laws to the "spirit of the times" and investigate it. This regression does not depend on the whim of the historian; because of what Dilthey calls the "spirit of the times," the historian is required, consequently, to make comprehensible situations as well as people in their roles in a profound sense. But in this procedure of the historian it is no longer a question of an understanding in terms of the situation. . . .

Endnotes

1. On the sense of this "someone or other," see §4.

2. We find here the essential and characteristic difference between a lecture and a discussion; for that reason, a discussion in which the participant is not focused on the other, but rather expresses his point of view in a monologue, gives the impression of chaos.

3. See Löwith, *Das Individuum*, §§20 and 27.

4. Löwith correctly refers with special emphasis in this connection to the phenomenon of "conversation."

5. Dilthey, *Gesammelte Schriften* (Berlin, 1924), Vol. V ["Der Glaube an die Realität Anderer Personen"], pp. 110ff. for our context. —Because the experience of pressure and resistance constitutes our "belief in reality" as much in "inanimate" physical things as in fellow human beings, Dilthey still appeals to the inference by analogy as the logical equivalent of "interlocking apperception-processes" for what is involved in the experience of fellow human beings in their particularity ("this particular class of objects"). The unification of both these motives makes possible a one-dimensional theory of human encounters. In the experience of resistance which forms "the presupposition of each further experience," processes are attached by means of which we attain to a knowledge about the concretely present mind of someone else. We reproduce "what is internal to someone else"; but this is inseparable from "fellow feeling." While our "fellow feeling" arises by "reproducing and reliving" "of events attentively perceived from outside but relived by internal supplementations," we arrive at the "inner structure" of another person, at a "unity of life and will" which we experience in its independence and in the core-quality of its "value-filled existence." On the basis of the *experience* of the independence of another person there arises the *respect* for this independence: we recognize this other person "as a self-goal just as we ourselves are such a goal." But we experience the life-unity of someone else as like and akin to us, as homogeneous with us (which otherwise also certainly cannot be different since

we can only acquire and seize upon the "life-unity" of someone else by the "transfer of our own mental living"; see pp. 189f. and 249ff.), and therefore as having solidarity with us. "Closed core realities, akin to our own, bound up with ours in cooperation and solidarity, yet each <being> a seat of its own will that limits us, form our social horizon." Let us disregard everything said before (e.g., let us disregard the appeal to the inference by analogy and the apperception-processes, the "inseparability" of "reproducing what is internal to someone else" from "fellow feeling"; let us further disregard the fact that the traditional concept of the world stands behind Dilthey's theory and even in a sensualistic coloration: "The concept of the object is conditioned by the relation of sense-impressions to what is differentiated from the self and by the connection of these impressions to a whole which, therefore, lies independently over against the self"); let us heed instead just those dimensionally different kinds of being-together of fellow human beings that Dilthey tries to draw up. Just because we stand in a "social relation" with other people, and a "constantly faint interchange of pressure, resistance and demands allow us to feel that we are not alone," not every attitude toward fellow human beings is legitimated in which we wish to understand the "life-unity" in its structure which makes up its "core existence" as individuum. Even when we are together at one time with the "same" person in a situation of partnership, in which we perceive his pressure, and another time direct to him the intention to understand, we are nonetheless together with the "same" person in two different dimensions, and we can encounter the "same" person in still different dimensions. This in no way alters the fact that these different kinds of being-together are not founded in one another just because of their dimensional differences; they must be conceived instead as self-sufficient and in their own particular, specific characteristic. It is rather essential for the dimension of partnership that the fellow human being is *not* accessible in it as a "structured life-unity" (see §§4 and 5). —The understanding of the other as "life-unity" also does not necessarily allow "consciousness of kinship and solidarity" to arise. In a specific sense, admittedly not intended by Dilthey, solidarity is rooted in the dimension of community (see §21); but the understanding implicit in and immanent to this dimension does not, again, touch upon the individual "life-unity" (see pp. 143f.) which is also not seized upon in the being together in a "group" (§§26 and 27). In both of these last-mentioned dimensions there is neither respect for the independence of another's individuality as a self-goal, nor is an accompanying demand meaningful in the being-together of this dimension. Rather the demand for recognition and respect for another's independence have their place in certain relations of partnership (see §21), for which reason it is also completely legitimate that Löwith asks about the "autonomy of the one and the other . . ." precisely "within personal relationships" (op. cit., Chapter III). Although Löwith appeals to Dilthey and continues his lines of thought, he grounds the autonomy in question not by recourse to seizing upon the structured "life-unity," but instead by penetrating into the relationship and, in this freely effected retrospect, by recourse to the other as an other of "equal rank." For this reason Löwith's discussions also merge with an interpretation of Kant's doctrine of the autonomy of man.

6. We speak here only of a determinate province of limited relations of subordination, but not of specifically communal ones such as, e.g., the patriarchy.

7. We must mention here the horizonal "knowledge" that, outside of this being together with the master, one is free, i.e., one is his own master. See below, pp. 115f.

8. Above, Scheler, Wesen und Formen der Sympathie (Bonn, 1923) C, II [G. W. 7, pp. 228–232].

9. Whether this concrete situation and role are relevant for an individual as "structured life-unity," in what measure and in what sense they are relevant, depends on which place and what degree the situation in question and the role, as well as their type, occupy in the structure of this "life-unity," in addition to the concrete situation and role they are in the given case.

10. If, in the same situation, one were to say to his partner that he "would do such and such in your place," this would signify that the situation demands a specific comportment, namely, "to do such and such," at the place in which the partner stands in his role assigned him by the situation at this place; it also signifies that the partner, while comporting himself differently, does not completely take in and understand the situation. But it has nothing to do with what I myself confront as person, individual, and "life-unity."

11. See below, pp. 116f.

12. Because we encounter each other in our roles by being together in partnership and, more particularly, in the roles which have already been mutually attuned beforehand, the structure of anticipatory "answering in advance," worked out by Löwith, is at all possible and governs many provinces of this dimension. But for the same reasons this structure is also to be restricted to this, and only this, dimension.

13. See Heidegger, op. cit., §22. The "They" ["Man"] which Heidegger introduces in this connection is, however, not a univocal concept but rather a "predication by analogy" in the sense of Aristotle's Metaphysics, Book V, Chapter 6, 1016b34, which is differentiated in its particular meaning in accordance with the dimensions of the being together of fellow human beings. Here "They" signifies the "someone or other" in a quite determinate and concrete role (see pp. 130f).

14. Löwith, op. cit., p. 51.

15. Löwith, ibid., pp. 19f. "The essentially necessary structure of relationships consists of . . . the fact that the comporting of the one is co-determined by the other; it is reflexive in co-reflexivity. Disregarding his relationship to another, what one does and allows is incomprehensible since he does and allows, not as an encapsuled individual, but rather as a persona, i.e., as one who has a 'role,' namely, the role is eo ipso already assigned to him by his relationship to another even when one does not at all speak and act explicitly in the sense of 'we.' "

16. Löwith, ibid., pp. 22f.

17. On this variation, see above, p. 182, note 20.

18. Löwith, op. cit., p. 52; see also §3. —Here we can only call attention to the question about what then would be the ground and root of these "moral qualities" in the individual as a "structured life-unity"—qualities which not only arise and are manifested in being together with others, but to which, constitutively, the view of such a being-together belongs.

19. This oversight is also noticeable in Löwith's analysis of Pirandello's Cosi è (se vi pare), ibid., §8, where the point of the piece is just not made apparent. The point consists of the fact that outsiders want to explore by interrogation and confrontation three persons "living in a closed world" without those persons being aware that they have to do with a "closed world." In this context, "closed world" signifies that each of the three have a common history by virtue of and motivated by which they stand in a determinate way with respect to one another. Because the outsiders do not appreciate the historicality of the "world of the three," their curiosity scarcely reaches its goal. Although Löwith sees that only regress to the history of the relationship would make these themselves comprehensible, and although he sees it as a weakness of the piece that this history remains in the background, he does not note what it means for the way of being-together of the three in their "closed world," namely, that this being-together is of "historical obviousness." Because their being-together is historically rooted, it is therefore directly characterized as a being-together in the di-

mension of community (see §8). As such, however, it is *of essence* articulated differently than the dimension of the encounter of "relational" roles attuned to one another. Of course, this difference can only be made distinct in sufficiently detailed analysis.

20. Löwith, *op. cit.*, pp. 50ff.

21. See §1. . . .

22. See above, p. 26.

23. Dilthey, *Gesammelte Schriften*, Vol. VII; see especially, pp. 207f. The complexity of even contradictory thought-motives is explained by the state of this unfinished fragment (see the "Preface of the Editor," pp. 348ff.).

24. *Ibid.*, pp. 207f. Just this circumstance legitimates for Dilthey (p. 212) the difference between the "elementary" and "higher forms" of understanding. What "being at the door" signifies will be clarified below, pp. 135f.

25. See Scheler, *Wesen und Formen der Sympathie*, pp. 7f. [*G. W. 7*, pp. 22f.].

26. It is always possible to make this turn because the work, just as work, refers to people in the modes of their participation and, more particularly, in the sense of "co-inclusive" references.

27. Eduard Spranger, "Zur Theorie des Verstehens und zur geisteswissenschaftlichen Psychologie," *Festschrift für Johannes Volkelt* (München, 1918), pp. 379f.

28. In this connection, see Dilthey, *Gesammelte Schriften*, Vol. VII, p. 321; Spranger, *op. cit.*, p. 389:

"All understanding presupposes a having understood."

29. Spranger's thesis, "that we only understand the mental [*Seelische*] by the psychical [*Geistige*]," experiences here some concrete support. As "psyche" Spranger designates "the ideal meeting place" of "isolated encapsuled egos" (*op cit.*, pp. 371 and 398).

30. See Spranger, *ibid.*, pp. 389f.

31. The *concrete* existence of the "victor at Austerlitz" is obviously not identically the same as the "author of the Napoleonic Code." For the realm under consideration here it holds universally that, if the concrete existence of a person is determined with respect to the situation in which he has a role, then the identity of the "individual" persisting throughout the different roles is, as identity, hardly an unquestioned obviousness, and is a problem. . . .

32. Dilthey, *Gesammelte Schriften*, Vol. VII, pp. 320f. When Dilthey notes that "deeds happen in the drive of the will in order to bring something about, not in order to communicate something to contemporaries or successors," reference is therefore made to what we emphasized before as the necessity of a *turn* from institutions, works, etc., to the persons who, in certain ways, have a stake in them.

XI. Exchange Theory and Rational Choice Theory

46
Social Behavior as Exchange

George C. Homans

George C. Homans (1910–1989), a Boston Brahmin, was one of the key figures associated with the development of modern exchange theory, which he intended as an alternative to the grand sociological theorizing of his Harvard colleague, Talcott Parsons. Homans argues that sociological theory ought to be grounded in neoclassical economic theory and in behaviorist psychology, associated with figures such as B. F. Skinner. As such he advocates a form of psychological reductionism. In this essay, published in 1958, Homans sketches an outline of an exchange paradigm, which in its most elementary form seeks to explain social behavior in terms of costs and rewards. He sees social exchange as offering sociology a set of general propositions that, in explaining human behavior, constitute an essential starting point for examining issues related to social structure.

The Problems of Small-Group Research

This essay will hope to honor the memory of George Simmel in two different ways. So far as it pretends to be suggestive rather than conclusive, its tone will be Simmel's; and its subject, too, will be one of his. Because Simmel, in essays such as those on sociabil-

ity, games, coquetry, and conversation, was an analyst of elementary social behavior, we call him an ancestor of what is known today as small-group research. For what we are really studying in small groups is elementary social behavior: what happens when two or three persons are in a position to influence one another, the sort of thing of which those massive structures called "classes," "firms," "communities," and "societies" must ultimately be composed.

As I survey small-group research today, I feel that, apart from just keeping on with it, three sorts of things need to be done. The first is to show the relation between the results of experimental work done under laboratory conditions and the results of *quasi*-anthropological field research on what those of us who do it are pleased to call "real-life" groups in industry and elsewhere. If the experimental work has anything to do with real life—and I am persuaded that it has everything to do—its propositions cannot be inconsistent with those discovered through the field work. But the consistency has not yet been demonstrated in any systematic way.

The second job is to pull together in some set of general propositions the actual results from the laboratory and from the field, of work on small groups—propositions that at least sum up, to an approximation, what happens in elementary social behavior, even though we may not be able to explain why the propositions should take the form they do. A great amount of work has been done, and more appears every day, but what it all amounts to in the shape of a set of propositions from which, under specified conditions, many of the observational results might be derived, is not at all clear—and yet to state such a set is the first aim of science.

The third job is to begin to show how the propositions that empirically hold good in small groups may be derived from some set of still more general propositions. "Still more general" means only that empirical propositions other than ours may also be derived from the set. This derivation would constitute the explanatory stage in the science of elementary social behavior, for explanation *is* derivation.[1] (I myself suspect that the more general set will turn out to contain the propositions of behavioral psychology. I hold myself to be an "ultimate psychological reductionist," but I cannot know that I am right so long as the reduction has not been carried out.)

I have come to think that all three of these jobs would be furthered by our adopting the view that interaction between persons is an exchange of goods, material and non-material. This is one of the oldest theories of social behavior, and one that we still use every day to interpret our own behavior, as when we say, "I found so-and-so rewarding"; or "I got a great deal out of him"; or, even, "Talking with him took a great deal out of me." But, perhaps just because it is so obvious, this view has been much neglected by social scientists. So far as I know, the only theoretical work that makes explicit use of it is Marcel Mauss's *Essai sur le don*, published in 1925, which is ancient as social science goes.[2] It may be that the tradition of neglect is now changing and that, for instance, the psychologists who interpret behavior in terms of transactions may be coming back to something of the sort I have in mind.[3]

An incidental advantage of an exchange theory is that it might bring sociology closer to economics—that science of man most advanced, most capable of application, and, intellectually, most isolated. Economics studies exchange carried out under special circumstances and with a most useful built-in numerical measure of value. What are the laws of the general phenomenon of which economic behavior is one class?

In what follows I shall suggest some reasons for the usefulness of a theory of social behavior as exchange and suggest the nature of the propositions such a theory might contain.

An Exchange Paradigm

I start with the link to behavioral psychology and the kind of statement it makes about the behavior of an experimental animal such as the pigeon.[4] As a pigeon explores its cage in the laboratory, it happens to peck a target, whereupon the psychologist feeds it corn. The evidence is that it will peck the target again; it has learned the behavior, or, as my friend Skinner says, the behavior has been reinforced, and the pigeon has undergone *operant conditioning*. This kind of psychologist is not interested in how the behavior was learned: "learning theory" is a poor name for his field. Instead, he is interested in what determines changes in the rate of emission of learned behavior, whether pecks at a target or something else.

The more hungry the pigeon, the less corn or other food it has gotten in the recent past, the more often it will peck. By the same token, if the behavior is often reinforced, if the pigeon is given much corn every time it pecks, the rate of emission will fall off as the pigeon gets *satiated*. If, on the other hand, the behavior is not reinforced at all, then, too, its rate of emission will tend to fall off, though a long time may pass before it stops altogether, before it is *extinguished*. In the emission of many kinds of behavior the pigeon incurs *aversive stimulation*, or what I shall call "cost" for short, and this, too, will lead in time to a decrease in the emission rate. Fatigue is an example of a "cost." Extinction, satiation, and cost, by decreasing the rate of emission of a particular kind of behavior, render more probable the emission of some other kind of behavior, including doing nothing. I shall only add that even a hard-boiled psychologist puts "emotional" behavior, as well as such things as pecking, among the unconditioned responses that may be reinforced in operant conditioning. As a statement of the propositions of behavioral psychology, the foregoing is, of course, inadequate for any purpose except my present one.

We may look on the pigeon as engaged in an exchange—pecks for corn—with the psychologist, but let us not dwell upon that, for the behavior of the pigeon hardly determines the behavior of the psychologist at all.

Let us turn to a situation where the exchange is real, that is, where the determination is mutual. Suppose we are dealing with two men. Each is emitting behavior reinforced to some degree by the behavior of the other. How it was in the past that each learned the behavior he emits and how he learned to find the other's behavior reinforcing we are not concerned with. It is enough that each does find the other's behavior reinforcing, and I shall call the reinforcers—the equivalent of the pigeon's corn—*values*, for this, I think, is what we mean by this term. As he emits behavior, each man may incur costs, and each man has more than one course of behavior open to him.

This seems to me the paradigm of elementary social behavior, and the problem of the elementary sociologist is to state propositions relating the variations in the values and costs of each man to his frequency distribution of behavior among alternatives, where the values (in the mathematical sense) taken by these variables for one man determine in part their values for the other.[5]

I see no reason to believe that the propositions of behavioral psychology do not apply to this situation, though the complexity of their implications in the concrete case may be great indeed. In particular, we must suppose that, with men as with pigeons, an increase in extinction, satiation, or aversive stimulation of any one kind of behavior will increase the probability of emission of some other kind. The problem is not, as it is often stated, merely, what a man's values are, what he has learned in the past to find reinforcement but how much of any one value his behavior is getting him now. The more he gets, the less valuable any further unit of that value is to him, and the less often he will emit behavior reinforced by it.

The Influence Process

We do not, I think, possess the kind of studies of two-person interaction that would either bear out these propositions or fail to do so. But we do have studies of larger numbers of persons that suggest that they may apply, notably the studies by Festinger, Schachter, Back, and their associates on the dynamics of influence. One of the variables they work with they call *cohesiveness*, defined as anything that attracts people to take part in a group. Cohesiveness is a value variable; it refers to the degree of reinforcement people find in the activities of the group. Festinger and his colleagues consider two kinds of reinforcing activity: the symbolic behavior we call "social approval" (sentiment) and activity valuable in other ways, such as doing something interesting.

The other variable they work with they call *communication* and others call *interaction*. This is a frequency variable: it is a measure of the frequency of emission of valuable and costly verbal behavior. We must bear in mind that, in general, the one kind of variable is a function of the other.

Festinger and his co-workers show that the more cohesive a group is, that is, the more valuable the sentiment or activity the members exchange with one another, the greater the average frequency of interaction of the members.[6] With men, as with pigeons, the greater the reinforcement, the more often is the reinforced behavior emitted. The more cohesive a group, too, the greater the change that members can produce in the behavior of other members in the direction of rendering these activities more valuable.[7] That is, the more valuable the activities that members get, the more valuable those that they must give. For if a person is emitting behavior of a certain kind, and other people do not find it particularly rewarding, these others will suffer their own production of sentiment and activity, in time, to fall off. But perhaps the first person has found their sentiment and activity rewarding, and, if he is to keep on getting them, he must make his own behavior more valuable to the others. In short, the propositions of behavioral psychology imply a tendency toward a certain proportionality between the value to others of the behavior a man gives them and the value to him of the behavior they give him.[8]

Schachter also studied the behavior of members of a group toward two kinds of other members, "conformers" and "deviates."[9] I assume that conformers are people whose activity the other members find valuable. For conformity is behavior that coincides to a degree with some group standard or norm, and the only meaning I can assign to *norm* is "a verbal description of behavior that many members find it valuable for the actual behavior of themselves and others to conform to." By the same token, a deviate is a member whose behavior is not particularly valuable. Now Schachter shows that, as the members of a group come to see another member as a deviate, their interaction with him—communication addressed to getting him to change his behavior—goes up, the faster the more cohesive the group. The members need not talk to the other conformers so much; they are relatively satiated by the conformers' behavior: they have gotten what they want out of them. But if the deviate, by failing to change his behavior, fails to reinforce the members, they start to withhold social approval from him: the deviate gets low sociometric choice at the end of the experiment. And in the most cohesive groups—those Schachter calls "high cohesive-relevant"—interaction with the deviate also falls off in the end and is lowest among those members that rejected him most strongly, as if they had given him up as a bad job. But how plonking can we get? These findings are utterly in line with everyday experience.

Practical Equilibrium

At the beginning of this paper I suggested that one of the tasks of small-group research was to show the relation between the results of experimental work done under laboratory conditions and the results of field research on real-life small groups. Now the latter often appear to be in practical equilibrium, and by this I mean nothing fancy. I do not mean that all real-life groups are in equilibrium. I certainly do not mean that all groups must tend to equilibrium. I do not mean that groups have built-in antidotes to change: there is no homeostasis here. I do not mean that we assume equilibrium. I mean only that we sometimes *observe* it, that for the time we are with a group—and it is often short—there is no great change in the values of the variables we choose to measure. If, for instance, person A is interacting with B more than with C both at the beginning and at the end of the study, then at least by this crude measure the group is in equilibrium.

Many of the Festinger-Schachter studies are experimental, and their propositions about the process of influence seem to me to imply the kind of proposition that empirically holds good of real-life groups in practical equilibrium. For instance, Festinger *et al.* find that, the more cohesive a group is, the greater the change that members can produce in the behavior of other members. If the influence is exerted in the direction of conformity to group norms, then, when the process of influence has accomplished all the change of which it is capable, the proposition should hold good that, the more cohesive a group is, the larger the number of members that conform to its norms. And it does hold good.[10]

Again, Schachter found, in the experiment I summarized above, that in the most cohesive groups and at the end, when the effort to influence the deviate had failed, members interacted little with the deviate and gave him little in the way of sociometric choice. Now two of the propositions that hold good most often of real-life groups in practical equilibrium are precisely that the more closely a member's activity conforms to the norms the more interaction he receives from other members and the more liking choices he gets from them too. From these main propositions a number of others may be derived that also hold good.[11]

Yet we must ever remember that the truth of the proposition linking conformity to liking may on occasion be masked by the truth of other propositions. If, for instance, the man that conforms to the norms most closely also exerts some authority over the group, this may render liking for him somewhat less than it might otherwise have been.[12]

Be that as it may, I suggest that the laboratory experiments on influence imply propositions about the behavior of members of small groups, when the process of influence has worked itself out, that are identical with propositions that hold good of real-life groups in equilibrium. This is hardly surprising if all we mean by equilibrium is that all the change of which the system is, under present conditions, capable has been effected, so that no further change occurs. Nor would this be the first time that statics has turned out to be a special case of dynamics.

Profit and Social Control

Though I have treated equilibrium as an observed fact, it is a fact that cries for explanation. I shall not, as structural-functional sociologists do, use an assumed equilibrium as a means of explaining or trying to explain, why the other features of a social system should be what they are. Rather, I shall take practical equilibrium as something that is itself to be explained by the other features of the system.

If every member of a group emits at the end of, and during, a period of time much the same kinds of behavior and in much the same frequencies as he did at the beginning, the group is for that period in equilibrium. Let us then ask why any one member's behavior should persist. Suppose he is emitting behavior of value A_1. Why does he not let his behavior get worse (less valuable or reinforcing to the others) until it stands at $A_1 — \Delta A$? True, the sentiments expressed by others toward him are apt to decline in value (become less reinforcing to him), so that what he gets from them may be $S_1 — \Delta S$. But it is conceivable that, since most activity carries cost, a decline in the value of what he emits will mean a reduction in cost to him that more than offsets his losses in sentiment. Where, then, does he stabilize his behavior? This is the problem of social control.[13]

Mankind has always assumed that a person stabilizes his behavior, at least in the short run, at the point where he is doing the best he can for himself under the circumstances, though his best may not be a "rational" best, and what he can do may not be at all easy to specify, except that he is not apt to think like one of the theoretical antagonists in the *Theory of Games*. Before a sociologist rejects this answer out of hand for its horrid profit-seeking implications, he will do well to ask himself if he can offer any other answer to the question posed. I think he will find that he cannot. Yet experiments designed to test the truth of the answer are extraordinarily rare.

I shall review one that seems to me to provide a little support for the theory, though it was not meant to do so. The experiment is reported by H. B. Gerard, a member of the Festinger-Schachter team, under the title "The Anchorage of Opinions in Face-to-Face Groups."[14] The experimenter formed artificial groups whose members met to discuss a case in industrial relations and to express their opinions about its probable outcome. The groups were of two kinds: high-attraction groups, whose members were told that they would like one another very much, and low-attraction groups, whose members were told that they would not find one another particularly likable.

At a later time the experimenter called the members in separately, asked them again to express their opinions on the outcome of the case, and counted the number that had changed their opinions to bring them into accord with those of other members of their groups. At the same time, a paid participant entered into a further discussion of the case with each member, always taking, on the probable outcome of the case, a position opposed to that taken by the bulk of the other members of the group to which the person belonged. The experimenter counted the number of persons shifting toward the opinion of the paid participant.

The experiment had many interesting results, from which I choose only those summed up in Tables 46-1 and 46-2. The three different agreement classes are made up of people who, at the original sessions, expressed different degrees of agreement with the opinions of other members of their groups. And the figure 44, for instance, means that, of all members of high-attraction groups whose initial opinions were strongly in disagreement with those of other members, 44 per cent shifted their opinion later toward that of others.

Table 46-1

Percentage of Subjects Changing Toward Someone in the Group

	Agreement	Mild Disagreement	Strong Disagreement
High Attraction. . . .	0	12	44
Low Attraction. . . .	0	15	9

Table 46-2

Percentage of Subjects Changing Toward the Paid Participant

	Agreement	Mild Disagreement	Strong Disagreement
High Attraction. . . .	7	13	25
Low Attraction. . . .	20	38	8

In these results the experimenter seems to have been interested only in the differences in the sums of the rows, which show that there is more shifting toward the group, and less shifting toward the paid participant, in the high-attraction than in the low-attraction condition. This is in line with a proposition suggested earlier. If you think that the members of a group can give you much—in this case, liking—you are apt to give them much—in this case, a change to an opinion in accordance with their views—or you will not get the liking. And, by the same token, if the group can give you little of value, you will not be ready to give it much of value. Indeed, you may change your opinion so as to depart from agreement even further, to move, that is, toward the view held by the paid participant.

So far so good, but, when I first scanned these tables, I was less struck by the difference between them than by their similarity. The same classes of people in both tables showed much the same relative propensities to change their opinions, no matter whether the change was toward the group or toward the paid participant. We see, for instance, that those who change least are the high-attraction, agreement people and the low-attraction, strong-disagreement ones. And those who change most are the high-attraction, strong-disagreement people and the low-attraction, mild-disagreement ones.

How am I to interpret these particular results? Since the experimenter did not discuss them, I am free to offer my own explanation. The behavior emitted by the subjects is opinion and changes in opinion. For this behavior they have learned to expect two possible kinds of reinforcement. Agreement with the group gets the subject favorable sentiment (acceptance) from it, and the experiment was designed to give this reinforce-

ment a higher value in the high-attraction condition than in the low-attraction one. The second kind of possible reinforcement is what I shall call the "maintenance of one's personal integrity," which a subject gets by sticking to his own opinion in the face of disagreement with the group. The experimenter does not mention this reward, but I cannot make sense of the results without something much like it. In different degrees for different subjects, depending on their initial positions, these rewards are in competition with one another: they are alternatives. They are not absolutely scarce goods, but some persons cannot get both at once.

Since the rewards are alternatives, let me introduce a familiar assumption from economics—that the cost of a particular course of action is the equivalent of the foregone value of an alternative[15]—and then add the definition: Profit = Reward − Cost.

Now consider the persons in the corresponding cells of the two tables. The behavior of the high-attraction, agreement people gets them much in the way of acceptance by the group, and for it they must give up little in the way of personal integrity, for their views are from the start in accord with those of the group. Their profit is high, and they are not prone to change their behavior. The low-attraction, strong-disagreement people are getting much in integrity and they are not giving up for it much in valuable acceptance, for they are members of low-attraction groups. Reward less cost is high for them, too, and they change little. The high-attraction, strong-disagreement people are getting much in the way of integrity, but their costs in doing so are high, too, for they are in high-attraction groups and thus foregoing much valuable acceptance by the group. Their profit is low, and they are very apt to change, either toward the group or toward the paid participant, from whom they think, perhaps, they will get some acceptance while maintaining some integrity. The low-attraction, mild-disagreement people do not get much in the way of integrity, for they are only in mild disagreement with the group, but neither are they giving up much in acceptance, for they are members of low-attraction groups. Their rewards are low; their costs are low too, and their profit—the difference between the two—is also low. In their low profit they resemble the high-attraction, strong-disagreement people, and, like them, they are prone to change their opinions, in this case, more toward the paid participant. The subjects in the other two cells, who have medium profits, display medium propensities to change.

If we define profit as reward less cost, and if cost is value foregone, I suggest that we have here some evidence for the proposition that change in behavior is greatest when perceived profit is least. This constitutes no direct demonstration that change in behavior is least when profit is greatest, but if, whenever a man's behavior brought him a balance of reward and cost, he changed his behavior away from what got him, under the circumstances, the less profit, there might well come a time when his behavior would not change further. That is, his behavior would be stabilized, at least for the time being. And, so far as this were true for every member of a group, the group would have a social organization in equilibrium.

I do not say that a member would stabilize his behavior at the point of greatest conceivable profit to himself, because his profit is partly at the mercy of the behavior of others. It is a commonplace that the short-run pursuit of profit by several persons often lands them in positions where all are worse off than they might conceivably be. I do not say that the paths of behavioral change in which a member pursues his profit under the condition that others are pursuing theirs too are easy to describe or predict; and we can readily conceive that in jockeying for position they might never arrive at any equilibrium at all.

Distributive Justice

Yet practical equilibrium is often observed, and thus some further condition may make its attainment, under some circumstance, more probable than would the individual pursuit of profit left to itself. I can offer evidence for this further condition only in the behavior of subgroups and not in that of individuals. Suppose that there are two subgroups, working close together in a factory, the job of one being somewhat different from that of the other. And suppose that the members of the first complain and say: "We are getting the same pay as they are. We ought to get just a couple of dollars a week more to show that our work is more responsible." When you ask them what they mean by "more responsible," they say that, if they do their work wrong, more damage can result, and so they are under more pressure to take care.[16] Something like this is a common feature of industrial behavior. It is at the heart of disputes not over absolute wages but over wage differentials—indeed, at the heart of disputes over rewards other than wages.

In what kind of proposition may we express observations like these? We may say that wages and responsibility give status in the group, in the sense that a man who takes high responsibility and gets high wages is admired, other things equal. Then, if the members of one group score higher on responsibility than do the members of another, there is a felt need on the part of the first to score higher on pay too. There is a pressure, which shows itself in complaints, to bring the *status factors*, as I have called them, into line with one another. If they are in line, a condition of *status congruence* is said to exist. In this condition the workers may find their jobs dull or irksome, but they will not complain about the relative position of groups.

But there may be a more illuminating way of looking at the matter. In my example I have considered only responsibility and pay, but these may be enough, for they represent the two kinds of thing that come into the problem. Pay is clearly a reward: responsibility may be looked on, less clearly, as a cost. It means constraint and worry—or peace of mind foregone. Then the proposition about status congruence becomes this: If the costs of the members of one group are higher than those of another, distributive justice requires that their rewards should be higher too. But the thing works both ways: If the rewards are higher, the costs should be higher too. This last is the theory of *noblesse oblige*, which we all subscribe to, though we all laugh at it, perhaps because the *noblesse* often fails to *oblige*. To put the matter in terms of profit: though the rewards and costs of two persons or the members of two groups may be different, yet the profits of the two—the excess of reward over cost—should tend to equality. And more than "should." The less-advantaged group will at least try to attain greater equality, as, in the example I have used, the first group tried to increase its profit by increasing its pay.

I have talked of distributive justice. Clearly, this is not the only condition determining the actual distribution of rewards and costs. At the same time, never tell me that notions of justice are not a strong influence on behavior, though we sociologists often neglect them. Distributive justice may be one of the conditions of group equilibrium.

Exchange and Social Structure

I shall end by reviewing almost the only study I am aware of that begins to show in detail how a stable and differentiated social structure in a real-life group might arise out of a process of exchange between members. This is Peter Blau's description of the behavior of sixteen agents in a federal law-enforcement agency.[17]

The agents had the duty of investigating firms and preparing reports on the firms' compliance with the law. Since the reports might lead to legal action against the firms, the agents had to prepare them carefully, in the proper form, and take strict account of the many regulations that might apply. The agents were often in doubt what they should do, and then they were supposed to take the question to their supervisor. This they were reluctant to do, for they naturally believed that thus confessing to him their inability to solve a problem would reflect on their competence, affect the official ratings he made of their work, and so hurt their chances for promotion. So agents often asked other agents for help and advice, and, though this was nominally forbidden, the supervisor usually let it pass.

Blau ascertained the ratings the supervisor made of the agents, and he also asked the agents to rate one another. The two opinions agreed closely. Fewer agents were regarded as highly competent than were regarded as of middle or low competence; competence, or the ability to solve technical problems,

was a fairly scarce good. One or two of the more competent agents would not give help and advice when asked, and so received few interactions and little liking. A man that will not exchange, that will not give you what he has when you need it, will not get from you the only thing you are, in this case, able to give him in return, your regard.

But most of the more competent agents were willing to give help, and of them Blau says:

A consultation can be considered an exchange of values: both participants gain something, and both have to pay a price. The questioning agent is enabled to perform better than he could otherwise have done, without exposing his difficulties to his supervisor. By asking for advice, he implicitly pays his respect to the superior proficiency of his colleague. This acknowledgment of inferiority is the cost of receiving assistance. The consultant gains prestige, in return for which he is willing to devote some time to the consultation and permit it to disrupt his own work. The following remark of an agent illustrates this: 'I like giving advice. It's flattering, I suppose, if you feel that others come to you for advice.'[18]

Blau goes on to say: "All agents liked being consulted, but the value of any one of very many consultations became deflated for experts, and the price they paid in frequent interruptions became inflated."[19] This implies that, the more prestige an agent received, the less was the increment of value of that prestige; the more advice an agent gave, the greater was the increment of cost of that advice, the cost lying precisely in the forgone value of time to do his own work. Blau suggests that something of the same sort was true of an agent who went to a more competent colleague for advice: the more often he went, the more costly to him, in feelings of inferiority, became any further request. "The repeated admission of his inability to solve his own problems . . . undermined the self-confidence of the worker and his standing in the group."[20]

The result was that the less competent agents went to the more competent ones for help less often than they might have done if the costs of repeated admissions of inferiority had been less high and that, while many agents sought out the few highly competent ones, no single agent sought out the latter much. Had they done so (to look at the exchange from the other side), the costs to the highly competent in interruptions to their own work would have become exorbitant. Yet the need of the less competent for help was still not fully satisfied. Under these circumstances they tended to turn for help to agents more nearly like themselves in competence. Though the help they got was not the most valuable, it was of a kind they could themselves return on occasion. With such agents they could exchange help and liking, without the exchange becoming on either side too great a confession of inferiority.

The highly competent agents tended to enter into exchanges, that is, to interact with many others. But, in the more equal exchanges I have just spoken of, less competent agents tended to pair off as partners. That is, they interacted with a smaller number of people, but interacted often with these few. I think I could show why pair relations in these more equal exchanges would be more economical for an agent than a wider distribution of favors. But perhaps I have gone far enough. The final pattern of this social structure was one in which a small number of highly competent agents exchanged advice for prestige with a large number of others less competent and in which the less competent agents exchanged, in pairs and in trios, both help and liking on more nearly equal terms.

Blau shows, then, that a social structure in equilibrium might be the result of a process of exchanging behavior rewarding and costly in different degrees, in which the increment of reward and cost varied with the frequency of the behavior, that is, with the frequency of interaction. Note that the behavior of the agents seems also to have satisfied my second condition of equilibrium: the more competent agents took more responsibility for the work, either their own or others', than did the less competent ones, but they also got more for it in the way of prestige. I suspect that the same kind of explanation could be given for the structure of many "informal" groups.

Summary

The current job of theory in small-group research is to make the connection between experimental and real-life studies, to consolidate the propositions that empirically hold good in the two fields, and to show how these propositions might be derived from a still more general set. One way of doing this job would be to revive and make more rigorous the oldest of theories of social behavior—social behavior as exchange.

Some of the statements of such a theory might be the following. Social behavior is an exchange of goods, material goods but also non-material ones, such as the symbols of approval or prestige. Persons that give much to others try to get much from them, and persons that get much from others are under pressure to give much to them. This process of influence tends to work out at equilibrium to a balance in the exchanges. For a person engaged in exchange, what he gives may be a cost to him, just as what he gets may be a reward, and his behavior changes less as profit, that is, reward less cost, tends to a maximum. Not only does he seek a maximum for himself, but he tries to see to it that no one in his group makes more profit than he does. The cost and the value of what he gives and of what he gets vary with the quantity of what he gives and gets. It is surprising how familiar these propositions are; it is surprising, too, how propositions about the dynamics of exchange can begin to generate the static thing we call "group structure" and, in so doing, generate also some of the propositions about group structure that students of real-life groups have stated.

In our unguarded moments we sociologists find words like "reward" and "cost" slipping into what we say. Human nature will break in upon even our most elaborate theories. But we seldom let it have its way with us and follow up systematically what these words imply.[21] Of all our many "approaches" to social behavior, the one that sees it as an economy is the most neglected, and yet it is the one we use every moment of our lives—except when we write sociology.

Endnotes

1. See R. B. Braithwaite, *Scientific Explanation* (Cambridge: Cambridge University Press, 1953).

2. Translated by I. Cunnison as *The Gift* (Glencoe, Ill.: Free Press, 1954).

3. In social anthropology D. L. Oliver is working along these lines, and I owe much to him. See also T. M. Newcomb, "The Prediction of Interpersonal Attraction," *American Psychologist*, XI (1956), 575–86.

4. B. F. Skinner, *Science and Human Behavior* (New York: Macmillan Co., 1953).

5. *Ibid.*, pp. 297–329. The discussion of "double contingency" by T. Parsons and E. A. Shils could easily lead to a similar paradigm (see *Toward a General Theory of Action* [Cambridge, Mass.: Harvard University Press, 1951], pp. 14–16).

6. K. W. Back, "The Exertion of Influence through Social Communication," in L. Festinger, K. Back, S. Schachter, H. H. Kelley, and J. Thibaut (eds.), *Theory and Experiment in Social Communication* (Ann Arbor: Research Center for Dynamics, University of Michigan, 1950), pp. 21–36.

7. S. Schachter, N. Ellertson, D. McBride, and D. Gregory, "An Experimental Study of Cohesiveness and Productivity," *Human Relations*, IV (1951), 229–38.

8. Skinner, *op. cit.*, p. 100.

9. S. Schachter, "Deviation, Rejection, and Communication," *Journal of Abnormal and Social Psychology*, XLVI (1951), 190–207.

10. L. Festinger, S. Schachter, and K. Back, *Social Pressures in Informal Groups* (New York: Harper & Bros., 1950), pp. 72–100.

11. For propositions holding good of groups in practical equilibrium see G. C. Homans, *The Human Group* (New York: Harcourt, Brace & Co., 1950), and H. W. Riecken and G. C. Homans, "Psychological Aspects of Social Structure," in G. Lindzey (ed.), *Handbook of Social Psychology* (Cambridge, Mass.: Addison-Wesley Publishing Co., 1954), II, 786–832.

12. See Homans, *op. cit.*, pp. 244–48, and R. F. Bales, "The Equilibrium Problem in Small Groups," in A. P. Hare, E. F. Borgatta, and R. F. Bales (eds.), *Small Groups* (New York: A. A. Knopf, 1953), pp. 450–56.

13. Homans, *op. cit.*, pp. 281–301.

14. *Human Relations*, VII (1954), 313–25.

15. G. J. Stigler, *The Theory of Price* (rev. ed.; New York: Macmillan Co., 1952), p. 99.

16. G. C. Homans, "Status among Clerical Workers," *Human Organization*, XII (1953), 5–10.

17. Peter M. Blau, *The Dynamics of Bureaucracy* (Chicago: University of Chicago Press, 1955), 99–116.

18. *Ibid.*, p. 108.

19. *Ibid.*, p. 108.

20. *Ibid.*, p. 109.

21. *The White-Collar Job* (Ann Arbor: Survey Research Center, University of Michigan, 1953), pp. 115–27.

47

Power-Dependence Relations

Richard M. Emerson

Early in his career, Richard Emerson (1925–1982) sought to advance exchange theory by developing a parsimonious theory of power/dependence that was amenable to a quantitative research program. Unlike many sociologists, he considered laboratory experiments with humans to hold considerable potential in developing such a program. In so doing, he extended Homans' efforts to ground social exchange theory in behaviorist psychology. In this classic essay—one of the more widely cited articles in sociology—Emerson attempts to provide a link among the concepts of "power," "authority," "legitimacy," and "structure" by articulating a view of power that emphasizes its relational character. More specifically, he sees power as predicated on "ties of mutual dependence." At its most fundamental level, this means that B's power is proportionally related to A's dependency on B for particular rewards or resources. Power is a potential that is realized in social exchange. Much of Emerson's interest in this essay focuses on exchanges that he calls "balancing operations." These operations consist of various options that A can attempt in responding to situations in which power is unbalanced in favor of B. Moreover, these operations constitute the core focus of the research agenda he stakes out.

Judging from the frequent occurrence of such words as *power, influence, dominance* and *submission, status* and *authority*, the importance of power is widely recognized, yet considerable confusion exists concerning these concepts.[1] There is an extensive literature pertaining to power, on both theoretical and empirical levels, and in small group[2] as well as large community contexts.[3] Unfortunately, this already large and rapidly growing body of research has not achieved the cumulative character desired. Our *integrated* knowledge of power does not significantly surpass the conceptions left by Max Weber.[4]

This suggests that there is a place at this moment for a systematic treatment of social power. The underdeveloped state of this area is further suggested by what appears, to this author, to be a recurrent flaw in common conceptions of social power; a flaw which helps to block adequate theoretical development as well as meaningful research. That flaw is the implicit treatment of power as though it were an attribute of a person or group ("X is an influential person," "Y is a powerful group," etc.). Given this conception, the natural research question becomes "Who in community X are the power *holders*?" The project then proceeds to rank-order persons by some criterion of power, and this ordering is called the *power-structure*. This is a highly questionable representation of a "structure," based upon a questionable assumption of generalized power.[5]

It is commonly observed that some person X dominates Y, while being subservient in relations with Z. Furthermore, these power relations are frequently intrasensitive! Hence, to say that "X has power" is vacant, unless we specify "over whom." In making these necessary qualifications we force ourselves to face up to the obvious: power is a property of the social relation; it is not an attribute of the actor.[6]

In this paper, an attempt is made to construct a sample theory of the power aspects of social relations. Attention is focused upon characteristics of the relationship as such, with little or no regard for particular features of the persons or groups engaged in such relations. Personal traits, skills or possessions (such as wealth) which might be relevant in one relation are infinitely variable across the set of possible relations, and hence have no place in a general theory.

The Power-Dependence Relation

While the theory presented here is anchored most intimately in small groups research, it is meant to apply to more complex community relations as well. In an effort to make these conceptions potentially as broadly applicable as possible, we shall speak of relations among *actors*, where an actor can be a person or a group. Unless otherwise indicated, any relation discussed might be a person-person, group-person or group-group relation.

Social relations commonly entail *ties of mutual dependence* between the parties. A depends upon B if he aspires to goals or gratifications whose achievement is facilitated by appropriate actions on B's part. By virtue of mutual dependency, it is more or less imperative to each party that he be able to control or influence the other's conduct. At the same time, these ties of mutual dependence imply that each party is in position, to some degree, to grant or deny, facilitate or hinder, the other's gratification. Thus, it would appear that the power to control or influence the other resides in control over the things he values, which may range all the way from oil resources to ego-support, depending upon the relation in question. In short, *power resides implicitly in the other's dependency.* When this is recognized, the analysis will of necessity revolve largely around the concept of dependence.[7]

Two variables appear to function jointly in fixing the dependence of one actor upon another. Since the precise nature of this joint function is an empirical question our proposition can do no more than specify the directional relationships involved:

> *Dependence (Dab).* The dependence of actor A upon actor B is (1) directly proportional to A's *motivational investment* in goals mediated by B, and (2) inversely proportional to the *availability* of those goals outside of the A-B relation.

In this proposition "goal" is used in the broadest possible sense to refer to gratifications consciously sought as well as rewards unconsciously obtained through the relationship. The "availability" of such goals outside of the relation refers to alternative avenues of goal-achievement, most notably other social relations. The costs associated with such alternatives must be included in any assessment of dependency.[8]

If the dependence of one party provides the basis for the power of the other, that power must be defined as a potential influence:

> *Power (Pab).* The power of actor A over actor B is the amount of resistance on the part of B which can be potentially overcome by A.

Two points must be made clear about this definition. First, the power defined here will not be, of necessity, observable in every interactive episode between A and B, yet we suggest that it exists nonetheless as a potential, to be explored, tested, and occasionally employed by the participants. Pab will be empirically manifest only *if* A makes some demand, and only if this demand runs counter to B's desires (resistance to be overcome). Any operational definition must make reference to *change* in the conduct of B attributable to demands made by A.

Second, we define power as the "resistance" which can be overcome, without restricting it to any one domain of action. Thus, if A is dependent upon B for love and respect, B might then draw A into criminal activity which he would normally resist. The reader might object to this formulation, arguing that special power is in fact restricted to certain channels. If so, the reader is apparently concerned with "legitimized power" embedded in a social structure. Rather than begin at this more evolved level, we hope to derive legitimized power in the theory itself.

The premise we began with can now be stated as Pab=Dba; the power of A over B is equal to, and based upon, the dependence of B upon A.[9] Recognizing the reciprocity of social relations, we can represent a power-dependence relation as a pair of equations:

Pab=Dba

Pba=Dab.

Before proceeding further we should emphasize that these formulations have been so worded in the hope that they will apply across a wide range of social life. At a glance our conception of dependence contains two variables remarkably like supply and demand ("availability" and "motivational investment," respectively).[10] We prefer the term *dependency* over these economic terms because it facilitates broader application, for all we need to do to shift these ideas from one area of application to another is change the motivational basis of dependency. We can speak of the economic dependence of a home builder upon a loan agency as varying directly with his desire for the home, and hence capital, and inversely with the "availability" of capital from other agencies. Similarly, a child may be dependent upon another child based upon motivation toward the pleasures of collective play, the availability of alternative playmates, etc. The same generic power-dependence relation is involved in each case. The dependency side of the equation may show itself in "friendship" among playmates, in "filial love" between parent and child, in "respect for treaties" among nations. On the other side of the equation, I am sure no one doubts that mothers, lovers, children, and nations enjoy the power to influence their respective partners, within the limit set by the partner's dependence upon them.

Finally, because these concepts are meant to apply across a wide variety of social situations, operational definitions cannot be appropriately presented here. Operational definitions provide the necessary bridge between generalizing concepts on the one hand, and the concrete features of a specific research situation on the other hand. Hence, there is no one proper operational definition for a theoretical concept.[11]

Balance and Imbalance

The notion of reciprocity in power-dependency relations raises the question of equality or inequality of power in the relation. If the power of A over B (Pab) is confronted by equal opposing power of B over A, is power then neutralized or canceled out? We suggest that in such a balanced condition, power is in no way removed from the relationship. A pattern of "dominance" might not emerge in the interaction among these actors, but that does not imply that power is inoperative in either or both directions. A *balanced* relation and an *unbalanced* relation are represented respectively as follows:

$$
\begin{array}{cc}
\text{Pab=Dba} & \text{Pab=Dba} \\
\| \quad \| & \text{V} \quad \text{V} \\
\text{Pba=Dab} & \text{Pba=Dab}
\end{array}
$$

Consider two social relations, both of which are balanced, but at *different levels* of dependency (say Loeb and Leopold, as compared with two casual friends). A moment's thought will reveal the utility of the argument that balance does not neutralize power, for each party may continue to exert profound control over the other. It might even be meaningful to talk about the parties being controlled by the relation itself.

Rather than canceling out considerations of power, reciprocal power provides the basis for studying three more features of power-relations: first, a power advantage can be defined as Pab minus Pba, which can be either positive or negative (a power disadvantage);[12] second, the *cohesion* of a relationship can be defined as the average of Dab and Dba, though this definition can be refined;[13] and finally, it opens the door to the study *balancing operations* as structural changes in power-dependence relations which tend to reduce power advantage.

Discussion of balancing tendencies should begin with a concrete illustration. In the unbalanced relation represented symbolically above, A is the more powerful party because B is the more dependent of the two. Let actor B be a rather "unpopular" girl, with puritanical upbringing, who wants desperately to date; and let A be a young man who occasionally takes her out, while dating other girls as well. (The reader can satisfy himself about A's power advantage in this illustration by referring to the formulations above.) Assume further that A "discovers" this power advantage, and, in exploring for the limits of his power, makes sexual advances. In this simplified illustration, these advances should encounter resistance in B's puritanical values. Thus, when a power advantage is used, the weaker member will achieve one value at the expense of other values.

In this illustration the tensions involved in an unbalanced relation need not be long endured. They can be reduced in either of two ways: (1) the girl might reduce the psychic costs involved in continuing the relation by redefining her moral values, with appropriate rationalizations and shifts in reference group attachments; or (2) she might renounce the value of dating, develop career aspirations, etc., thus reducing A's power. Notice that the first solution does not of necessity alter the unbalanced relation. The weaker member has sidestepped one painful demand but she is still vulnerable to new demands. By contrast, the second solution alters the power relation itself, in general, it appears that an unbalanced relation is unstable for it encourages the use of power which in turn sets in motion processes which we will call (a) cost reduction and (b) balancing operations.[14]

Cost Reduction

The "cost" referred to here amounts to the "resistance" to be overcome in our definition of power—the cost involved for one party in meeting the demands made by the other. The process of cost reduction in power dependence relations shows itself in many varied forms. In the courting relation above it took the form of alteration in moral attitudes on the part of a girl who wanted to be popular; in industry it is commonly seen as the impetus for improved plant efficiency and technology in reducing the cost of production. What we call the "mark of oppression" in the character structure of members of low social castes (the submissive and "painless" loss of freedom) might well involve the same power processes, as does the "internalization of parental codes" in the socialization process. In fact, the oedipal conflict might be interpreted as a special case of the tensions of imbalance in a power-dependence relation, and cost reduction takes the form of identification and internalization classically described. "Identification with the aggressor" in any context would appear to be explainable in terms of cost reduction.

In general, *cost reduction* is a process involving change in values (personal, social, economic) which reduces the pains incurred in meeting the demands of a powerful other. It must be emphasized, however, that these adjustments do not necessarily alter the balance or imbalance of the relation, and, as a result, they must be distinguished from more fundamental *balancing operations* described below. It must be recognized that cost reducing tendencies will take place under conditions of balance, and while this is obvious in economic transactions, it is equally true of other social relations, where the "costs" involved are anchored in modifiable attitudes and values. The intense cohesion of a lasting social relation like the Locb-Leopold relation mentioned above can be attributed in part to the cost reduction processes involved in the progressive formation of their respective personalities, taking place in the interest of preserving the valued relation. We suggest that cost reducing tendencies generally will function to deepen and stabilize social relations over and above the condition of balance.

Balancing Operations

The remainder of this paper will deal with balancing processes which operate through changes in the variables which define the structure of the power-dependence relation as such. The formal notation adopted here suggests exactly four generic types of balancing operation. In the unbalanced relation

$$\begin{array}{c} Pab=Dba \\ V \qquad V \\ Pba=Dab \end{array}$$

balance can be restored either by an increase in Dab or by a decrease in Dba. If we recall that dependence is a joint function of two variables, the following alterations will move the relation toward a state of balance:

1. If B reduces motivational investment in goals mediated by A;

2. If B cultivates alternative sources for gratification of those goals;

3. If A increases motivational investment in goals mediated by B;

4. If A is denied alternative sources for achieving those goals.

While these four types of balancing operation are dictated by the logic of the scheme, we suggest that each corresponds to well known social processes. The first operation yields balance through motivational withdrawal by B, the weaker member. The second involves the cultivation of alternative social relations by B. The third is based upon "giving status" to A, and the fourth involves coalition and group formation.

In some of these processes the role of power is well known, while in others it seems to have escaped notice. In discussing any one of these balancing operations it must be remembered that a prediction of which one (or what combination) of the four will take place must rest upon analysis of conditions involved in the concrete case at hand.

In the interest of simplicity and clarity, we will illustrate each of the four generic types of balancing operation in relations among children in the context of play. Consider two children equally motivated toward the pleasures of collective play and equally capable of contributing to such play. These children, A and B, form a balanced relation if we assume further that each has the other as his only playmate, and the give-and-take of their interactions might well be imagined, involving the emergence of such equalitarian rules as "taking turns," etc. Suppose now that a third child, C, moves into the neighborhood and makes the acquaintance of A, but *not* B. The A-B relation will be thrown out of balance by virtue of A's decreased dependence upon B. The reader should convince himself of this fact by referring back to the proposition on dependence. Without any of these parties necessarily "understanding" what is going on, we would predict that A would slowly come to dominate B in the pattern of their interactions. On more frequent occasions B will find himself deprived of the pleasures A can offer, thus slowly coming to sense his own dependency more acutely. By the same token A will more frequently find B saying "yes" instead of "no" to his proposals, and he will gain increased awareness of his power over B. The growing self-images of these children will surely reflect and perpetuate this pattern.

Operation Number One: Withdrawal

We now have the powerful A making demands on the dependent B. One of the processes through which the tensions in the unbalanced A-B relation can be reduced is *motivational withdrawal* on the part of B, for this will reduce Dba and Pab. In this illustration, child B might lose some of his interest in collective play under the impact of frustrations and demands imposed by A. Such a withdrawal from the play relation would presumably come about if the other three balancing operations were blocked by the circumstances peculiar to the situation. The same operation was illustrated above in the case of the girl who might renounce the value of dating. It would seem to be involved in the dampened level of aspiration associated with the "mark of oppression" referred to above.

In general, the denial of dependency involved in this balancing operation will have the effect of moving actors away from relations which are unbalanced to their disadvantage. The actor's motivational orientations and commitments toward different areas of activity will intimately reflect this process.

Operation Number Two: Extension of Power Network

Withdrawal as a balancing operation entails subjective alterations in the weaker actor. The second operation takes place through alterations in a structure we shall call a *power network*, defined as two or more connected power-dependence relations. As we have seen in our illustration, when the C-A relation is connected through A with the A-B relation, forming a simple linear network C-A-B, the properties of A-B are altered. In this example, a previously balanced A-B relation is thrown out of balance, giving A a power advantage. This points up the general fact that while each relation in a network will involve interactions which appear to be independent of other relations in the network (e.g., A and B are seen to play together in the absence of C; C and A in the absence of B), the internal features of one relation are nonetheless a function of the entire network. Any adequate conception of a "power structure" must be based upon this fact.

In this illustration the form of the network throws both relations within it out of balance, thus stimulating one or several of the balancing operations under discussion. If balancing operation number two takes place, *the network* will be extended by the formation of new relationships. The tensions of imbalance in the A-B and A-C relations will make B and C "ready" to form new friendships (1) with additional children D and E, thus lengthening a linear network, or (2) with each other, thus "closing" the network. It is important to notice that the lengthened network balances some relations, but not the network as a whole, while the closed network is completely balanced under the limiting assumptions of this illustration. Thus, we might offer as a corollary to operation number two: Power networks tend to achieve closure.[15]

If the reader is dissatisfied with this illustration in children's play relations, let A be the loan agent mentioned earlier, and B, C, . . . be home builders or others dependent upon A for capital. This is the familiar monopoly situation with the imbalance commonly attributed to it. As a network, it is a set of relations connected only at A. Just as the children were "ready" to accept new friends, so the community of actors B, C, . . . is ready to receive new loan agencies. Balancing operation number 2 involves in all cases the *diffusion* of dependency into new relations in a network. A final illustration of this principle can be found in institutionalized form in some kinship systems involving the extended family. In the case of Hopi, for example, Dorothy Eggan has described at length the diffusion of child dependency among many "mothers," thus draining off much of the force of oedipal conflicts in that society.[16] We have already suggested that oedipal conflict may be taken as a special case of the tension of imbalance, which in this case appears to be institutionally handled in a manner resembling operation number two. This is not to be taken, however, as an assertion that the institution evolved as a balancing process, though this is clearly open for consideration.

It is convenient at this juncture to take my balancing operation number 4, leaving number 3 to the last.

Operation Number Four: Coalition Formation

Let us continue with the same illustration. When the B-C relation forms, closing the C-A-B network in the process of balancing, we have what appears to be a coalition of the two weaker against the one stronger. This, however, is not technically the case, for A is not involved in the B-C interactions; he simply exists as an alternative playmate for both B and C.

The proper representation of coalitions in a triad would be (AB)-C, (AC)-B, or (BC)-A. That is, a triadic network reduces to a coalition only if two members unite as a single actor in the process of dealing directly with the third. The difference involved here may be very small in behavioral terms and the distinction may seem overly refined, but it goes to the heart of an important conceptual problem (the difference between a closed "network" and a "group"), and it rests upon the fact that two very different balancing operations are involved. The C-A-B network is balanced through the addition of a third relation (C-B) in operation number 2, but it is still just a power network. In operation number 4 it achieves balance through collapsing the two-relational network into one group-person relation with the emergence of a "collective actor." Operation number two reduces the power of the stronger actor, while number 4 increases the power of weaker actors through collectivization. If the rewards mediated by A are such that they can be jointly enjoyed by B and C, then the tensions of imbalance in the A-B and A-C relations can be resolved in the (BC)-A coalition.

In a general way, Marx was asking for balancing operation number 4 in his call to "Workers of the world," and the collectivization of labor can be taken as an illustration of this balancing tendency as an historic process. Among the balancing operations described here, coalition formation is the one most commonly recognized as a power process. However, the more general significance of this balancing operation seems to have escaped notice, for the typical coalition is only one of the many forms this same operation takes. For this reason the next section will explore coalition processes further.

The Organized Group

We wish to suggest that the coalition process is basically involved in all organized group functioning, whether the group be called a coalition or not. We believe this illuminates the role which power processes play in the emergence and maintenance of group structure in general.

In the typical coalition pattern, (AB)-C, A and B constitute a collective actor in the sense that they act as one, presenting themselves to their common environment as a single unit. A coalition, as one *type* of group, is characterized by the fact that (a) the common environment is an actor to be controlled, and (b) its unity is historically based upon efforts to achieve that control. Now, all we need do to blend this type of group with groups in general is to *dehumanize* the environmental problem which the group collectively encounters. Thus, instead of having the control of actor C as its end, the group attempts to control C in the interest of achieving X, some "group goal." Now, if C also aspires toward X, and if C is dependent upon the group for achieving X, C might well be one of the group members—any member. Thus, in a three-member group we have three coalition structures as *intra-group* relations, each representable as ([AB]-C)-X, with A, B and C interchangeable.

The situation involved here is reminiscent of the rapidly forming and reforming coalitions in unconsolidated children's play groups. As the group consolidates, these coalitions do not drop out of the picture; they become stabilized features of group structure, and the stabilization process is identical with "norm formation." In fact, the demands made by (AB) of C in the power process within ([AB]-C) are exactly what we normally call *group norms* and *role-prescriptions*. Such norms are properly viewed as the "voice" of a collective actor, standing in coalition against the object of its demands. This reasoning suggests an idealized conception of group structure, based upon two types of collective demands:

(1) *Role-Prescriptions*. Specifications of behavior which all group members expect (demand) of one or more but not all members.

(2) *Group Norms*. Specifications of behavior which all group members expect of all group members.

Certain actions, when performed by some member or members, need not be performed by all other members to properly facilitate group functioning. These will tend to be incorporated in role-prescriptions, which, taken together, provide a division of labor in a role structure. Roles are defined and enforced through a consolidation of power in coalition formation. Likewise with group norms. Thus, the structure of a group (its norms and prescriptions) will specify the makeup of the coalition a member would face for any group-relevant act he might perform.

This conception of group structure is idealized in the sense that it describes complete consensus among members, even to the point of group identification and internalization of collective demands (members expect things of themselves in the above definitions). Balancing operations, along with cost reduction, should move group structure toward this ideal.

Authority

It should be clear that in introducing conceptions of group *structure* we have in no way digressed from our discussion of power processes, for the emergence of these structural forms is attributed directly to operation number four, closely resembling coalition formation. Even the most formalized role-prescription is properly viewed as the "voice" of all members standing as a coalition in making its demand of the occupant of the role. Whenever a specific member finds occasion to remind another member of his "proper" job in terms of such prescriptions, he speaks with the *authority* of the group behind him; he is "authorized" to speak for them. In this sense, every member has authority of a kind (as in civil arrest), but authority is usually used to refer to power vested in an office or role. The situation is basically the same, however, in either case. The occupant of such a role has simply been singled out and commissioned more explicitly to speak for the group in the group's dealings with its members. That authority is *lim-*

ited, power follows from logical necessity when role-prescriptions are treated as they are here. A dean, for example, can force faculty member A to turn in his grades on time because the demand is "legitimate," that is, supported by a coalition of all other faculty members joining with the dean in making the demand. If that dean, however, were to employ sanctions in an effort to induce that member to polish the dean's private car, the "coalition" would immediately re-form around the faculty member, as expressed in role-prescriptions defining the boundary of "legitimate power" or authority. The dean's authority is power contained and restricted through balancing operation number four, coalition formation.

The notion of legitimacy is important, for authority is more than balanced power; it is *directed* power which can be employed (legitimately) only in channels defined by the norms of the group. A person holding such authority is commissioned; he does not simply have the right to rule or govern—he is obliged to. Thus, authority emerges as a transformation of power in a process called "legitimation," and that process is one special case of balancing operation number four.[17]

Earlier in this section we referred to the common phenomenon of rapidly forming and re-forming coalitions in children's play groups. Our reasoning suggests that it is precisely through these coalition processes that unifying norms emerge. These fluctuating coalitions can be taken as the prototype of organized group life wherein the tempo of coalition realignment is accelerated to the point of being a blur before our eyes. Stated more accurately, the norms and prescriptions define implicitly the membership of the coalition which would either support or oppose any member if he were to perform any action relevant to those norms.

Operation Number Three: Emergence of Status

One important feature of group structure remains to be discussed: status and status hierarchies. It is interesting that the one remaining balancing operation provided in this theory takes us naturally to the emergence of status ordering. Operation number three increases the weaker member's power to control the formerly more powerful member through increasing the latter's motivational investment in the relation. This is normally accomplished through giving him status recognition in one or more of its many forms, from ego-gratifications to monetary differentials. The ego-rewards, such as prestige, loom large in this process because they are highly valued by many recipients while given at low cost to the giver.

The discussion of status hierarchies forces us to consider *intra*-group relations, and how this can be done in a theory which treats the group in the singular as an actor. The answer is contained in the idealized conception of group structure outlined above. That conception implies that every intra-group relation involves at once every member of the group. Thus, in a group with members A, B, C, and D, the relations A-B, A-C, etc. do not exist. Any interactions between A and B, for example, lie outside of the social system in question unless one or both of these persons "represents" the group in his actions, as in the coalition pattern discussed at length above. The relations which do exist are (ABCD)-A, (ABCD)-B, (ABCD)-C and (ABCD)-D as a minimum, plus whatever relations of the (ABCD)-(AB) type may be involved in the peculiar structure of the group in question. Thus, in a group of N members we have theoretical reason for dealing with N *group-member* relations rather than considering all of the $\frac{N(N-1)}{2}$ possible member-member relations. Each of these group-member relations can now be expressed in the familiar equations for a power-dependence relation:

$$Pgm_i = Dm_ig$$

$$Pm_ig = Dgm_i.$$

To account for the emergence of a status hierarchy within a group of N members, we start with a set of N group-member relations of this type and consider balancing operations in these relations.

Let us imagine a five member group and proceed on three assumptions: (1) *status* involves differential valuation of members (or roles) by the group, and this valuation is equivalent to, or an expression of, Dgm_i; (2) a member who is highly valued by the group is highly valued in other *similar* groups he belongs to or might freely join; and (3) all five members have the same motivational investment in the group at the outset. Assumptions 2 and 3 are empirical, and when they are true they imply that Dgm and Dmg are inversely related across the N group-member relations. This in turn implies a state of imbalance of a very precarious nature so far as group stability is concerned. The least dependent member of a group will be the first to break from the group, and these members are precisely the most valued members. It is this situation which balancing operation number three alleviates through "giving status" to the highly valued members, thus gaining the power to keep and control those members.

These ideas are illustrated with hypothetical values in Table 47-1, with imbalance represented as power advantage (PA). Balancing operations will tend to move PA toward zero, as shown in column 6 after the highly valued members A and B have come to depend upon the group for the special rewards of status, and in column 9 after the least valued members D and E have withdrawn some of their original motivational investment in the group. The table presents three stages in status crystallization, and the process of crystallization is seen as a balancing pro-

cess. The final stage (columns 7, 8, and 9) should be achieved only in groups with very low membership turnover. The middle stage might well be perpetual in groups with new members continually coming in at the lower levels. In such "open" groups, status striving should be a characteristic feature and can be taken as a direct manifestation of the tensions of imbalance. In the final stage, such strivers have either succeeded or withdrawn from the struggle.

Among the factors involved in status ordering, this theory focuses attention upon the extreme importance of the *availability factor* in dependency as a determinant of status position and the values employed in status ordering. In considering Dgm (the relative value or importance the group attaches to member roles), it is notably difficult to rely upon a functional explanation. Is the pitcher more highly valued than the center fielder because he is functionally more important or because good pitchers are harder to find? Is the physicist valued over the plumber because of a "more important" functional contribution to the social system, or because physicists are more difficult to replace, more costly to obtain, etc.? The latter considerations involve the availability factor. We suggest here that the *values* people use in ordering roles or persons express the dependence of the system upon those roles, and that the availability factor in dependency plays the decisive part in historically shaping those values.[18]

Table 47-1

Hypothetical Values Showing the Relation Between Dgm and Dmg in a Group With Five Members

| | Before Balancing | | | After Operation #3 | | | After Operation #1 | | |
| | 1 | 2 | 3 | 4 | 5 | 6 | 7 | 8 | 9 |
Member	Dgm	Dmg*	PAgm**	Dgm	Dmg	PAgm**	Dgm	Dmg	PAgm**
A	5	1	−4	5	5	0	5	5	0
B	4	2	−2	4	4	0	4	4	0
C	3	3	0	3	3	0	3	3	0
D	2	4	2	2	4	2	2	2	0
E	1	5	4	1	5	4	1	1	0

* Assuming that all members have the same motivational investment in the group at the outset, and that highly valued members (A and B) are valued in other groups as well.
** Power Advantage PAgm=Dmg–Dgm.

Conclusion

The theory put forth in this paper is in large part contained implicitly in the ties of mutual dependence which bind actors together in social systems. Its principal value seems to be its ability to pull together a wide variety of social events, ranging from the internalization of parental codes to society-wide movements, like the collectivization of labor, in terms of a few very simple principles. Most important, the concepts involved are subject to operational formulation. Two experiments testing certain propositions discussed above led to the following results:

1. Conformity (Pgm) varies directly with motivational investment in the group;

2. Conformity varies inversely with acceptance in alternative groups;

3. Conformity is high at both status extremes in groups with membership turnover (see column 5, Table 47-1);

4. Highly valued members of a group are strong conformers only if they are valued by other groups as well. (This supports the notion that special status rewards are used to hold the highly valued member who does not depend heavily upon the group, and that in granting him such rewards power is obtained over him.);

5. Coalitions form among the weak to control the strong (balancing operation number three);

6. The greatest rewards within a coalition are given to the less dependent member of the coalition (balancing operation number three, analogous to "status giving").

Once the basic ideas in this theory have been adequately validated and refined, both theoretical and empirical work must be extended in two main directions. First, the interaction process should be studied to locate carefully the factors leading to *perceived* power and dependency in self and others, and the conditions under which power, as a potential, will be employed in action. Secondly, and, in the long run, more important, will be study of *power networks* more complex than those referred to here, leading to more adequate understanding of complex power structures. The theory presented here does no more than provide the basic underpinning to the study of complex networks. There is every reason to believe that modern mathematics, graph theory in particular,[19] can be fruitfully employed in the analysis of complex networks and predicting the outcome of power plays within such networks.

Endnotes

1. See the Communications by Jay Butler and Paul Harrison on "On Power and Authority: An Exchange on Concepts," *American Sociological Review*, 25 (October, 1960), pp. 731–732. That both men can be essentially correct in the points they make yet fail to reconcile these points, strongly suggests the need for conceptual development in the domain of power relations.

2. Among many studies, see Ronald Lippitt, Norman Polansky, Fritz Redl and Sidney Rosen, "The Dynamics of Power," *Human Relations*, 5 (February, 1952), pp. 37–64.

3. Floyd Hunter, *Community Power Structure*, Chapel Hill: University of North Carolina Press, 1953.

4. Max Weber, in *The Theory of Social and Economic Organization*, New York: Oxford University Press, 1947, presents what is still a classic formulation of power, authority and legitimacy. However, it is characteristic of Weber that he constructs a typology rather than an organized theory of power.

5. Hence see Raymond E. Wolfinger, "Reputation and Reality in the Study of 'Community Power'," *American Sociological Review*, 25 (October, 1960), pp. 636–644, for a well-taken critical review of Floyd Hunter's work on these very points. The notion of "generalized power" which is not restricted to specific social relations, if taken literally, is probably meaningless. Power may indeed be generalized across a finite set of relations in a power network, but this notion too requires very careful analysis. Are you dealing with some kind of halo effect (reputations if you wish), or are the range and boundary of generalized power anchored in the power structure itself? These are questions which must be asked and answered.

6. Just as power is often treated as though it were a property of the person, so leadership, conformity, etc., are frequently referred to the personal traits of "leaders," "conformers" and so on, as if there were distinguishable types of people. In a sociological perspective such behavior should be ex-

plicitly treated as an attribute of a relation rather than a person.

7. The relation between power and dependence is given similar emphasis in the systematic treatment by J. Thibaut and H. H. Kelley, *The Social Psychology of Groups*, New York: John Wiley and Sons, 1959.

8. The notion of "opportunity costs" in economics is a similar idea. If an employee has alternative employment opportunities, and if these opportunities have low associated cost (travel, etc.), the employee's dependence upon his current employer is reduced.

9. In asserting that power is based upon the dependency of the other, it might appear that we are dealing with *one* of the bases of power ("reward power") listed by John R. P. French, Jr. and Bertram Raven, "The Bases of Social Power," *Studies in Social Power*, D. Cartwright, editor, Ann Arbor, Michigan: Institute for Social Research, 1959. However, careful attention to our highly generalized conception of dependence will show that it covers most if not all of the forms of power listed in that study.

10. Professor Alfred Kuhn, Department of Economics, University of Cincinnati, has been working on a theory for power analysis soon to be published. The scheme he develops, though very similar to the one presented here, is put together in a different way. It is anchored more tightly to economic concepts, and hence its implications lead off in different directions from those presented below.

11. Many different operational definitions can serve one theoretical concept, and there is no reason to require that they produce intercorrelated results when applied in the same research situation. While the controversies surrounding "operationalism" have now been largely resolved, there remains some confusion on this point. See, for example, Bernice Eisman, "Some Operational Measures of Cohesiveness and Their Interrelations," *Human Relations*, 12 (May, 1959), pp. 183–189.

12. J. Thibaut and H. H. Kelley, *op. cit.*, pp. 107–108.

13. This definition of cohesion, based upon dependency seems to have one advantage over the definition offered by Leon Festinger, et al., *Theory and Experiment in Social Communication*, Ann Arbor: Research Center for Group Dynamics, University of Michigan Press, 1950. The Festinger definition takes into account only one of the two variables involved in dependency.

14. The "tensions of imbalance," which are assumed to make an unbalanced relation unstable, are closely related to the idea of "distributive jus-

tice" discussed by George C. Homans, *Social Behavior: Its Elementary Forms*, New York: Harcourt, Brace and World, Inc., 1961. All of what Homans has to say around this idea could be fruitfully drawn into the present formulation.

15. The notion of closed versus open networks as discussed here can be directly related to research dealing with communication networks, such as that reported by Harold J. Leavitt, "Some Effects of Communication Patterns on Group Performance," *Journal of Abnormal and Social Psychology*, 46 (January, 1951), pp. 38–50, in which the limiting assumptions involved in this discussion are fully met by experimental controls. In discussing those experiments in terms of the concepts in this theory we would consider each actor's dependence upon other actors for information. A formal treatment of such networks is suggested by A. Bavelas, "A Mathematical Model For Group Structure," *Applied Anthropology*, 7 (Summer, 1948), pp. 16–30.

16. Dorothy Eggan, "The General Problem of Hopi Adjustment," *American Anthropologist*, 45 (July-September, 1943), pp. 357–373.

17. The process of legitimation has sometimes been described as a tactic employed by a person aspiring to power or trying to hold his power, rather than a process through which persons are granted restricted power. For example, C. Wright Mills states: "Those in authority attempt to justify their rule over institutions by linking it, as if it were a necessary consequence, with widely believed in moral symbols, sacred emblems, legal formulae. These central conceptions may refer to God or gods, the 'vote of the majority,' 'the will of the people,' 'the aristocracy of talent or wealth,' to the 'divine right of kings,' or to the allegedly extraordinary endowments of the ruler himself. Social scientists, following Weber, call such conceptions 'legitimations,' or sometimes 'symbols of justification'" (*The Sociological Imagination*, New York: Oxford University Press, 1959, p. 36). Whether we view the process of legitimation in the context of the formation of such collective conceptions, or in the context of calling upon them to justify action, the process is fundamentally that of mobilizing collective support to oppose those who challenge power. Power so supported is authority, and the process fits the general model of coalition formation.

18. "Motivational investment" and "availability," which jointly determine dependency at any point in time, are functionally related through time. This is implied in our balancing operations. While these two variables can be readily distinguished in the case of Dmg, they are too intimately fused in Dgm to be clearly separated. The values by which

a group sees a given role as "important" at time 2, evolve from felt scarcity in that role and similar roles at time 1.

19. F. Harary and R. Norman, *Graph Theory as a Mathematical Model in the Social Sciences*, Ann Arbor: Institute for Social Research, 1953. An effort to apply such a model to power relations can be found in John R. P. French, Jr., "A Formal The-ory of Social Power," *The Psychological Review*, 63 (May, 1956), pp. 181-194.

48
Human Capital and Social Capital

James S. Coleman

In *Foundations of Social Theory* (1990), a lengthy theoretical treatise written near the end of a long and varied sociological career, James S. Coleman (1926–1995) emerged as the most important spokesperson in sociology for rational choice theory, an orientation that has had a major impact in economics and political science. As with Homans' exchange theory, the starting point for Coleman's paradigm is the individual; he endorses a conceptual orientation known as "methodological individualism." The two elementary concepts in Coleman's theory are actors and resources. In this selection from the book, two key resources—human capital and social capital—are described. The former refers to the skills and knowledge an individual possesses, while the latter refers to social relations.

Probably the most important and most original development in the economics of education in the past thirty years has been the idea that the concept of physical capital, as embodied in tools, machines, and other productive equipment, can be extended to include human capital as well (see Schultz, 1961; Becker, 1964). Just as physical capital is created by making changes in materials so as to form tools that facilitate production, human capital is created by changing persons so as to give them skills and capabilities that make them able to act in new ways.

Social capital, in turn, is created when the relations among persons change in ways that facilitate action. Physical capital is wholly tangible, being embodied in observable material form; human capital is less tangible, being embodied in the skills and knowledge acquired by an individual; social capital is even less tangible, for it is embodied in the *relations* among persons. Physical capital and human capital facilitate productive activity, and social capital does so as well. For example, a group whose members manifest trustworthiness and place extensive trust in one another will be able to accomplish much more than a comparable group lacking that trustworthiness and trust.

The distinction between human capital and social capital can be exhibited by a diagram such as Figure 48-1, which represents the relations of three persons (A, B, and C); the human capital resides in the nodes, and the social capital resides in the lines connecting the nodes. Social capital and human capital are often complementary. For example, if B is a child and A is an adult who is a parent of B, then for A to further the cognitive development of B, there must be capital in both the node and the link. There must be human capital held by A and social capital in the relation between A and B.

Using the concept of social capital will uncover no processes that are different in fun-

Figure 48-1
Three-Person Structure: Human Capital in Nodes and Social Capital in Relations

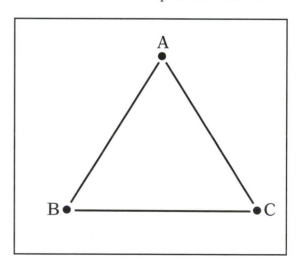

damental ways from those discussed in other chapters. This concept groups some of those processes together and blurs distinctions between types of social relations, distinctions that are important for other purposes. The value of the concept lies primarily in the fact that it identifies certain aspects of social structure by their function, just as the concept "chair" identifies certain physical objects by their function, disregarding differences in form, appearance, and construction. The function identified by the concept "social capital" is the value of those aspects of social structure to actors, as resources that can be used by the actors to realize their interests.

By identifying this function of certain aspects of social structure, the concept of social capital aids in both accounting for different outcomes at the level of individual actors and making the micro-to-macro transition without elaborating the social-structural details through which this occurs. For example, characterizing the clandestine study circles of South Korean radical students as constituting social capital that these students can use in their revolutionary activities is an assertion that the groups constitute a resource which aids in moving the students from individual protest to organized revolt. If a resource that accomplishes this task is held to be necessary in a theory of revolt . . . then the study circles can be grouped with other organizational structures, of different origins, which have fulfilled the same function for individuals with revolutionary goals in other contexts, such as the *comités d'action lycéen* of the French student revolt of 1968 or the workers' cells in czarist Russia described and advocated by Lenin (1973 [1902]).

It is true, of course, that for other purposes one wants to investigate the details of such organizational resources, to understand the elements that are critical to their usefulness as resources for a given purpose, and to examine how they came into being in a particular case. But the concept of social capital can allow showing how such resources can be combined with other resources to produce different system-level behavior or, in other cases, different outcomes for individuals. Whether social capital will come to be as useful a quantitative concept in social science as are the concepts of financial capital, physical capital, and human capital remains to be seen; its current value lies primarily in its usefulness for qualitative analyses of social systems and for those quantitative analyses that employ qualitative indicators.

. . . [T]he concept of social capital will be left unanalyzed (as it was in the brief descriptions given above as examples). In this chapter, however, I will examine just what it is about social relations that can constitute useful capital resources for individuals.

Obligations and Expectations

. . . [I]f A does something for B and trusts B to reciprocate in the future, this establishes an expectation in A and an obligation on the part of B to keep the trust. This obligation can be conceived of as a "credit slip" held by A to be redeemed by some performance by B. If A holds a large number of these credit slips from a number of persons with whom he has relations, then the analogy to financial capital is direct: The credit slips constitute a large body of credit on which A can draw if necessary—unless, of course, the placement of trust has been unwise, and the slips represent bad debts that will not be repaid. In some social structures (such as, for example, the neighborhoods discussed by Willmott and Young, 1967) it is said that people are "always doing things for each other." There are a large number of these credit slips outstanding, often on both sides of a relation (for these credit slips often appear to be not fungible across different areas of activity, so credit slips from B held by A and those from A held by B are not fully used to cancel each other out). . . . In other social structures where individuals are more self-sufficient, depending on each other less, there are fewer of these credit slips outstanding at any time.

Two elements are critical to this form of social capital: the level of trustworthiness of the social environment, which means that obligations will be repaid, and the actual extent of obligations held. Social structures differ in both of these dimensions, and actors within a particular structure differ in the second.

A case which illustrates the value of trustworthiness is the rotating credit association found in Southeast Asia and elsewhere. These associations are groups of friends and neighbors who typically meet monthly; each person contributes the same amount of money to a central fund, which is then given to one of the members (through bidding or by lot). After *n* months each of the *n* persons has made *n* contributions and received one payout. As Geertz (1962) points out, these associations serve as efficient institutions for amassing savings for small capital expenditures, an important aid to economic development. Without a high degree of trustworthiness among the members of the group, such a credit association could not exist— for a person who received a payout early in the sequence of meetings could abscond, leaving the others with a loss. One could not imagine such a rotating credit association operating successfully in urban areas marked by a high degree of social disorganization—or, in other words, by a lack of social capital.

Another situation in which extreme trustworthiness facilitates actions that would not otherwise be possible is that of heads of state. Various accounts of the experiences of heads of state suggest that for persons in this position it is extremely valuable to have an extension of one's self, an agent one can trust absolutely to act as one would in a given situation. Many heads of state have such a person, who may not occupy a formal position of power but may be a member of a personal staff. The fact that these persons are often old friends, or cronies, rather than persons who have distinguished themselves in some political activity, is derivative from this: The most important attribute of such a person is that trust can be placed in him, and this requirement often dictates choosing a long-term personal friend. Such persons often come to have enormous power due to their proximity to a head of state and the trust placed in them; and there are many recorded accounts of the use of that power. What is of interest here is the social capital this relation provides for the head of state, assuming that the trust is well placed. The trusted other is virtually an extension of self, allowing the head of state to expand his capacity for action.

Still another case that illustrates the importance of trustworthiness as a form of social capital is a system of mutual trust. The extreme example of such a system is a couple, each of whom places extensive trust in the other, whether they are deeply in love or not. For both members of such a couple, the relation has extraordinary psychological value. Each can confide in the other, can expose inner doubts, can be completely forthright with the other, can raise sensitive issues—all without fear of the other's misuse of the trust.

Differences in social structures with respect to the extent of outstanding obligations arise for a variety of reasons. These include, besides the general level of trustworthiness that leads obligations to be repaid, the actual needs that persons have for help, the existence of other sources of aid (such as government welfare services), the degree of affluence (which reduces the amount of aid needed from others), cultural differences in the tendency to lend aid and ask for aid (see Banfield, 1967), the degree of closure of social networks, the logistics of social contacts (see Festinger, Schachter, and Back, 1963), and other factors. Individuals in social structures with high levels of obligations outstanding at any time, whatever the source of those obligations, have greater social capital on which they can draw. The density of outstanding obligations means, in effect, that the overall usefulness of the tangible resources possessed by actors in that social structure is amplified by their availability to other actors when needed.

In a farming community such as . . . where one farmer got his hay baled by another and where farm tools are extensively borrowed and lent, the social capital allows each farmer to get his work done with less physical capital in the form of tools and equipment. Such a social structure is analogous to an industrial community in which bills of exchange (that is, debts) are passed around, serving as money and effectively reducing the financial capital necessary to carry out a given level of manufacturing activity. (See Ashton, 1945, for a description of this in Lancashire in the 1790s, before a centralized monetary system was well established in England.)

Individual actors in a social system also differ with respect to the extent of credit slips on which they can draw at any time. For example, in hierarchically structured extended family settings, a patriarch often holds an extraordinarily large set of such credit slips, which he can call in at any time to get done what he wants done. Another clear example occurs in villages in traditional settings that are highly stratified, where certain wealthy families, because of their wealth, have built up extensive credits on which they can call at any time. (It is the existence of such asymmetries that can make some families immune to sanctions that can be used to regulate the actions of others in the community. . . .)

Similarly, in a political setting such as a legislature, a legislator in a position that brings extra resources (such as the Speaker of the House of Representatives or the Majority Leader of the Senate in the U.S. Congress) can, by effective use of those resources, build up a set of credits from other legislators so that it becomes possible for him to get legislation passed that would otherwise be defeated. This concentration of obligations constitutes social capital that is useful not only for the powerful legislator, but also in increasing the level of action of the legislature. Thus those members of legislatures who have extensive credit slips should be more powerful than those who do not because they can use the credits to produce bloc voting on many issues. It is well recognized, for example, that in the U.S. Senate, some senators are members of what is called the Senate Club, and others are not. This in effect means that some senators are embedded in a system of credits and debts, and others (outside the Club) are not. It is also well recognized that those in the Club are more powerful than those outside it.

Another example showing asymmetry in the sets of obligations and expectations is the one . . . about the crisis in medical care in the United States due to liability suits. Traditionally physicians have been in control of events having literally life-and-death importance to patients, who in turn often felt unable to adequately compensate them for the extreme benefits they brought about. Part of a physician's payment was in the form of gratitude, deference, and high occupational prestige. These constituted a felt obligation to the physician, a form of social capital which inhibited patients dissatisfied with the outcome of their medical treatments from taking action against the physician.

But several factors have changed. One is that physicians' monopoly on medical knowledge has been lessened by an expansion of education. A second is a reduction in the likelihood that there is a personal relation between physician and patient, since a patient is less likely to use a family doctor or even a general practitioner and more likely to see specialists for particular medical problems. A third is the high income of many physicians, which reduces the perceived asymmetry between service and compensation. A fourth is the increased use of liability insurance, which transfers the financial cost of a lawsuit from physician to insurer. The combination of these and other factors has reduced the social capital that protected the physician from becoming a target when patients experienced undesirable medical outcomes.

***

Why do rational actors create obligations? Although some of the variation in the extent of outstanding obligations arises from social changes of the sort described above, some appears to arise from the intentional creation of obligation by a person who does something for another. For example, Turnbull (1972), who studied the Ik, a poverty-ridden tribe in Africa, describes an occasion when a man arrived home to find his neighbors, unasked, on the roof of his house fixing it. Despite his not wanting this aid, he was unable to induce them to stop. In this case and others there appears to be, not the creation of obligations through necessity, but a purposive creation of obligations. The giving of gifts has been interpreted in this light (see Mauss, 1954), as have the potlatches of the Kwakiutl tribe in the Pacific Northwest. In rural areas persons who do favors for others often seem to prefer that these favors not be repaid immediately, and those for whom a favor is done sometimes seem anxious to relieve themselves of the obligation.

Although the motives for freeing oneself from obligations may be readily understood (especially if the existence of obligations consumes one's attention), the motives for creating obligations toward oneself are less transparent. If there is a nonzero chance that the obligation will not be repaid, it would appear that rational persons would extend such credit only if they expect to receive something greater in return—just as a bank makes a loan only at sufficient interest to realize a profit after allowing for risk. The question then becomes whether there is anything about social obligations to make a rational person interested in establishing and maintaining such obligations on the part of others toward himself.

A possible answer is this: When I do a favor for you, this ordinarily occurs at a time when you have a need and involves no great cost to me. If I am rational and purely self-interested, I see that the importance to you of this favor is sufficiently great that you will be ready to repay me with a favor in my time of need that will benefit me more than this favor costs me—unless, of course, you are also in need at that time. This does not apply when the favor is merely the lending of money, since a unit of money holds about the same interest to a person over time.[1] When the favor involves services, expenditure of time, or some other nonfungible resource, however, or when it is of intrinsically more value to the recipient than to the donor (such as help with a task that can be done by two persons but not by one), this kind of mutually profitable exchange is quite possible. The profitability for the donor depends on the recipient's not repaying the favor until the donor is in need.

Thus creating obligations by doing favors can constitute a kind of insurance policy for which the premiums are paid in inexpensive currency and the benefit arrives as valuable currency. There may easily be a positive expected profit.

There is one more point: A rational, self-interested person may attempt to prevent others from doing favors for him or may attempt to relieve himself of an obligation at a time he chooses (that is, when repaying the favor costs him little), rather than when the donor is in need, because the call for his services may come at an inconvenient time (when repaying the obligation would be costly). Thus

in principle there can be a struggle between a person wanting to do a favor for another and the other not wanting to have the favor done for him or a struggle between a person attempting to repay a favor and his creditor attempting to prevent repayment.

Information Potential

An important form of social capital is the potential for information that inheres in social relations. Information is important in providing a basis for action. But acquisition of information is costly. The minimum it requires is attention, which is always in short supply. One means by which information can be acquired is to use social relations that are maintained for other purposes. Katz and Lazarsfeld (1955) show how this operates for women in several areas of life; for example, a woman who has an interest in being in style but not at the leading edge of fashion can use certain friends, who do stay on the leading edge, as sources of information. As another example, a person who is not deeply interested in current events but who is interested in being informed about important developments can save the time required to read a newspaper if he can get the information he wants from a friend who pays attention to such matters. A social scientist who is interested in being up to date on research in related fields can make use of his everyday interactions with colleagues to do so, if he can depend on them to be up to date in their fields.

All these are examples of social relations that constitute a form of social capital in providing information that facilitates action. The relations in this case are valuable for the information they provide, not for the credit slips they provide in the form of obligations that one holds for others' performance.

Norms and Effective Sanctions

. . . When an effective norm does exist, it constitutes a powerful, but sometimes fragile, form of social capital. Effective norms that inhibit crime in a city make it possible for women to walk freely outside at night and for old people to leave their homes without fear. Norms in a community that support and provide effective rewards for high achievement in school greatly facilitate the school's task. A prescriptive norm that constitutes an especially important form of social capital within a collectivity is the norm that one should forgo self-interests to act in the interests of the collectivity. A norm of this sort, reinforced by social support, status, honor, and other rewards, is the social capital which builds young nations (and which dissipates as they grow older), strengthens families by leading members to act selflessly in the family's interest, facilitates the development of nascent social movements from a small group of dedicated, inward-looking, and mutually rewarding persons, and in general leads persons to work for the public good. In some of these cases the norms are internalized; in others they are largely supported through external rewards for selfless actions and disapproval for selfish actions. But whether supported by internal or external sanctions, norms of this sort are important in overcoming the public-good problem that exists in conjoint collectivities.

As all these examples suggest, effective norms can constitute a powerful form of social capital. This social capital, however, like the forms described earlier, not only facilitates certain actions but also constrains others. Strong and effective norms about young persons' behavior in a community can keep them from having a good time. Norms which make it possible for women to walk alone at night also constrain the activities of criminals (and possibly of some noncriminals as well). Even prescriptive norms that reward certain actions, such as a norm which says that a boy who is a good athlete should go out for football, are in effect directing energy away from other activities. Effective norms in an area can reduce innovativeness in that area, can constrain not only deviant actions that harm others but also deviant actions that can benefit everyone. (See Merton, 1968, pp. 195–203, for a discussion of how this can come about.)

Authority Relations

If actor A has transferred rights of control of certain actions to another actor, B, then B has available social capital in the form of those rights of control. If a number of actors have transferred similar rights of control to B, then B has available an extensive body of social capital, which can be concentrated on certain activities. Of course, this puts extensive power in B's hands. What is not quite so straightforward is that the very concentration of these rights in a single actor increases the total social capital by overcoming (in principle, if not always entirely in fact) the free-rider problem experienced by individuals with similar interests but without a common authority. It appears, in fact, to be precisely the desire to bring into being the social capital needed to solve common problems that leads persons under certain circumstances to vest authority in a charismatic leader (as discussed . . . in Zablocki, 1980, and Scholem, 1973).

Appropriable Social Organization

Voluntary organizations are brought into being to further some purpose of those who initiate them. In a housing project built during World War II in a city in the eastern United States, there were many physical problems caused by poor construction, such as faulty plumbing, crumbling sidewalks, and other defects (Merton, n.d.). Residents organized to confront the builders and to address these problems in other ways. Later, when the problems were solved, the residents' organization remained active and constituted available social capital which improved the quality of life in the project. Residents had available to them resources that were seen as unavailable where they had lived before. (For example, despite the fact that there were *fewer* teenagers in the community, residents were *more* likely to express satisfaction concerning the availability of babysitters.)

Members of the New York Typographical Union who were monotype operators formed a social club called the Monotype Club (Lipset, Trow, and Coleman, 1956). Later, as employers looked for monotype operators and as monotype operators looked for jobs, both found this organization to be an effective employment referral service and utilized it for this purpose. Still later, when the Progressive Party came into power in the New

York Typographical Union, the Monotype Club served as an organizational resource for the ousted Independent Party. The Monotype Club subsequently served as an important source of social capital for the Independents, sustaining their party as an organized opposition while they were out of office.

In an example used earlier in this chapter, the study circles of South Korean student radicals were described as being groups of students who came from the same high school or hometown or church. In this case also, organization that was initiated for one purpose is appropriable for other purposes, constituting important social capital for the individuals who have available to them the organizational resources.

These examples illustrate the general point that organization brought into existence for one set of purposes can also aid others, thus constituting social capital that is available for use.[2] It may be that this form of social capital can be dissolved, with nothing left over, into elements that are discussed under other headings in this section, that is, obligations and expectations, information potential, norms, and authority relations. If so, listing this form of social capital is redundant. But the phenomenon of social organization being appropriated as existing social capital for new purposes is such a pervasive one that separate mention appears warranted.

Intentional Organization

A major use of the concept of social capital depends on its being a by-product of activities engaged in for other purposes. . . . [T]here is often little or no direct investment in social capital. There are, however, forms of social capital which are the direct result of investment by actors who have the aim of receiving a return on their investment.

The most prominent example is a business organization created by the owners of financial capital for the purpose of earning income for them. These organizations ordinarily take the form of authority structures composed of positions connected by obligations and expectations and occupied by persons. . . . In creating such an organization, an entrepreneur or capitalist transforms financial capital into physical capital in the form of buildings and tools, social capital in the form of the organization of positions, and human capital in the form of persons occupying positions. Like the other forms of capital, social capital requires investment in the designing of the structure of obligations and expectations, responsibility and authority, and norms (or rules) and sanctions which will bring about an effectively functioning organization.

Another form of intentional organization is a voluntary association which produces a public good. For example, a group of parents whose children attend a school forms a PTA chapter where one did not exist before. This organization constitutes social capital not only for the organizers but for the school, the students, and other parents. Even if the organization serves only the original purpose for which it is organized and is not appropriated for other purposes, as is the case for organizations described in an earlier section, it serves this purpose, by its very nature, for a wider range of actors than those who initiated it. Such an organization is, concretely, of the same sort as those described earlier. The PTA is the same kind of organization as the Monotype Club, the residents' association formed to deal with faulty plumbing, and the church groups of South Korean Youth. All are voluntary associations. As it functions, however, the organization creates two kinds of by-products as social capital. One is the by-product described in the preceding section, the appropriability of the organization for other purposes. A second is the by-product described here: Because the organization produces a public good, its creation by one subset of persons makes its benefits available to others as well, whether or not they participate. For example, the disciplinary standards promulgated by an active PTA change a school in ways that benefit nonparticipants as well as participants. . . .

Endnotes

1. It is interesting that, for persons whose interest in money fluctuates wildly over time, this sort of exchange is possible. In a rural county in West Virginia, the county clerk would lend money to the three town drunks when their need for money was great and then collect from them, with exorbitant

interest, when they received their welfare checks, when money was of less interest to them.

2. A classic instance of this is described by Sills (1957). The March of Dimes was originally dedicated to the elimination of polio. When Salk's vaccine virtually eradicated polio, the March of Dimes organization did not go out of existence but directed its efforts toward other diseases.

References

Ashton, T. S. 1945. The bill of exchange and private banks in Lancashire, 1790–1830. *Economic History Review* 15, nos. 1, 2:25–35.

Banfield, E. 1967. *The moral basis of a backward society*. New York: Free Press.

Becker, G. 1964. *Human capital*. New York: National Bureau of Economic Research, Columbia University Press.

Festinger, L., S. Schachter, and K. Back. 1963. *Social pressures in informal groups*. Stanford: Stanford University Press.

Geertz, C. 1962. The rotating credit association: a "middle rung" in development. *Economic Development and Cultural Change* 10:240–263.

Katz, E., and P. F. Lazarsfeld. 1955. *Personal influence*. New York: Free Press.

Lenin, V. I. 1973 (1902). *What is to be done?* Peking: Foreign Language Press.

Lipset, M., M. A. Trow, and J. S. Coleman. 1956. *Union democracy*. New York: Free Press.

Mauss, M. 1954. *The gift*. New York: Free Press.

Merton, R. K. 1968. *Social theory and social structure*. 3rd ed. New York: Free Press.

——. n.d. Study of World War II housing projects. Unpublished manuscript. Columbia University, Department of Sociology.

Scholem, G. 1973. *Sabbatai Sevi, the mystical messiah*. Princeton: Princeton University Press.

Schultz, T. 1961. Investment in human capital. *American Economic Review* 51 (March):1–17.

Sills, D. 1957. *The volunteers, means and ends in a national organization*. New York: Free Press.

Turnbull, C. 1972. *The mountain people*. New York: Simon and Schuster.

Willmott, P., and M. Young. 1967. *Family and class in a London suburb*. London: New English Library.

Zablocki, B. 1980. *Alienation and charisma*. New York: Free Press.

49

The Emergence of Cooperative Social Institutions

Michael Hechter

From a rational choice perspective, Michael Hechter (b. 1943) attempts in this essay to offer an account of the manner in which social institutions arise. Rejecting what he terms the "invisible hand" approach, which treats institutions as the spontaneous outcome of the actions of self-interested individuals in interaction with others, he opts for a "solidaristic" approach. Of the two variants of solidaristic explanation—the imposition of institutions by powerful rulers versus the voluntary construction of institutions by relatively equal individuals—Hechter turns to the latter, since it raises the more interesting theoretical issues. Not the least of these issues is the matter of the "free-rider problem," a major focus of attention in this selection.

The origin of social institutions is a very old concern in social theory. Currently it has re-emerged as one of the most intensely debated issues in social science. Among economists and rational choice theorists, there is growing awareness that most, if not all, of the social outcomes that are of interest to explain are at least partly a function of institutional constraints. Yet the role of institutions is negligible both in general equilibrium theory and in most neoclassical economic models. Among other social scientists, there is a burgeoning substantive interest in institutions ranging from social movements, to formal organizations, to states, and even international regimes.

This chapter discusses the two principal approaches to the problem of institutional genesis—*invisible-hand* and *solidaristic*. It further argues that the second of these is likely to afford us with a better means of attacking the problem than the first. Finally, one particular solidaristic explanation that holds promise for future research on institutional genesis is introduced.

The Concept of Social Institutions

Although the term *institution* is bandied about quite liberally in contemporary social science, no consensual definition of it has as yet emerged. The ambiguity of the term gives authors both the obligation and the license to adopt their favorite definition. At the most general level, I will take the existence of a social institution to be revealed by the appearance of *some regularity in collective behavior*. *Collective behavior* may be said to occur if different individuals behave similarly when placed in the same social situation;[1] *regularity*, for its part, indicates that this collective behavior endures over some long but indefinite period of time.

If institutions are revealed by the appearance of collective behavioral regularities, then one naturally wonders both about their origins and about the mechanisms responsible for their persistence. In institutionally rich environments, new institutions can arise from old ones through modification or diffusion processes (White, 1981; DiMaggio and Powell, 1983). Such solutions to the problem of institutional genesis are limited, however, because they are exogenous and thus beg the question of the prime mover.

What is most challenging to account for theoretically is just how institutions emerge out of anarchy, that is, from a state of nature. How, in other words, do institutions ever arise from a *noninstitutional* environment? Two types of explanations have been advanced to address this hoary old Hobbesian problem.

The *invisible-hand* approach to institutional genesis, advocated to a greater or lesser degree by Menger [1883] (1963), Hayek (1973; 1976), and Nozick (1974), among others, views the emergence of institutions as a spontaneous by-product of the voluntary actions of self-interested individuals who share *no common ends or values* (see

Hayek, 1976:111). In such accounts, existing social institutions are usually conceived as Pareto-efficient equilibria; therefore they are self-sustaining (because no one who is subject to them has an incentive to change them), rather than dependent on some third-party enforcement apparatus (like the state) whose existence, in turn, requires additional explanation.

Since invisible-hand arguments can offer an entirely endogenous explanation for the emergence of social institutions, they are to be admired for their parsimony and elegance (Nozick, 1974:18–22; Ullmann-Margalit, 1978). Their principal advantage is that they rely on fewer assumptions than do other kinds of explanations.

The alternative approach to the problem of institutional genesis rests on quite different premises. Rather than emerging spontaneously among self-interested actors each pursuing their own ends, institutions in this view are a product of *solidarity*. Solidarity can only arise among individuals who share some common end (Hechter, 1987). To attain this common end, actors must establish a set of obligations as well as a mechanism that enforces compliance to these obligations (Hobbes, [1651] 1968; Durkheim [1897] 1951; Blau, 1964:253; Hayek, 1976). From the solidaristic perspective, institutions persist not because they constitute self-enforcing equilibria, but because they are supported by consciously-designed controls.

There are two varieties of solidaristic explanations. On the one hand, institutions can be *imposed* upon a given population by some conqueror or overlord. Since it is easy to explain institutional emergence in the face of significant power differentials among individuals, this solution begs too many questions to be theoretically interesting (as Hobbes well understood). On the other hand, individuals with roughly equal power can create institutions *voluntarily*, in effect binding themselves to a joint project. This contractarian process is theoretically interesting precisely because it is such a problematic outcome.

Which approach is superior, the invisible-hand or solidaristic one? There is a great deal of debate in the literature on this question. Most of the advocates of invisible-hand explanations of institutional genesis rest their arguments on repeated game theory.

Yet, these arguments only suffice for the establishment and maintenance of *conventions* (Lewis, 1969)—such as the rule that we all drive on the right hand side of the road[2]—rather than for the establishment of *n*-person *cooperative institutions*. By cooperative institution, I refer to an institution, principally serving nonclosely related kin,[3] that enables those who are subject to it to reap a surplus by agreeing on a jointly maximizing strategy that is otherwise unavailable due to the absence or inappropriateness of markets.

There is an essential difference between conventions and cooperative institutions. Cooperation is the dominant strategy in conventions because there is no free-rider problem. Compliance with a convention provides its own private reward: for example, drivers who ignore conventional rules of the road take their own lives in hand. Hence, conventions indeed can be conceived of as equilibria. In cooperative institutions (which resemble Prisoner's Dilemmas), however, defection is the dominant strategy. Hence, these institutions can persist only by precluding free riders, or by assuring would-be cooperators that they are not liable to be exploited by defectors.

Contrary to the rhetoric of Taylor (1976), Hardin (1982), and Axelrod (1984), repeated game theory offers no adequate solution to the emergence of cooperation among *n* players of a Prisoner's Dilemma supergame (Hechter, 1990). The inadequacy of repeated game theory in this respect is due to two separate problems. In the first place, there are multiple equilibria in the supergame, some of which are efficient and some inefficient (Aumann, 1985).[4] Yet under most conditions it is difficult to determine which of these multiple equilibria will be realized. In the second place, unique cooperative solutions to the supergame rest on a most unrealistic assumption—that players are endowed with perfect monitoring capacity (Bendor and Mookherjee, 1987). This assumption limits the application of game-theoretic solutions to the evolution of cooperative institutions to the smallest of groups.[5]

In the wake of these current difficulties with the invisible-hand approach, it is best to consider the merits of solidaristic explanations, even though they require much stronger initial conditions. From a solidaristic point of view, the emergence of cooperative institutions requires individual agreement on some common end, acceptance of corporate obligations, and the establishment of formal controls to preclude free riding.

Can these admittedly strong initial conditions be explained on the basis of the typical self-interested behavioral assumptions of rational choice theory?[6] I believe that the answer to this question is a qualified *yes*. Using the relatively weak assumptions that are traditional in rational choice, it is indeed possible to explain the emergence of cooperative institutions on the basis of solidaristic logic. The remainder of this chapter sketches out the basic argument, and then suggests that the argument can be applied to several types of empirical situations.

A Solidaristic Approach to the Emergence of Cooperative Institutions

Briefly, the genesis of cooperative institutions depends on the conjunction of (1) individuals' *demands* to provide themselves with jointly-produced private (that is, excludable) goods, as well as on (2) these individuals' potential *control capacity*—that is, their opportunities either to dissuade each other from free riding, or to assure each other of their intent to cooperate. Both demand and control capacity are necessary for the emergence of cooperative institutions; without either, this kind of institutional genesis is doomed.

The demand for cooperative institutions arises from individuals' desires to consume jointly-produced private goods (hereafter termed *joint goods*) that cannot be obtained by following individual strategies. Cooperative institutions are generally formed to take advantage of positive externalities, such as increasing returns to scale, risk-sharing, and cost-sharing. The demand for joint goods is heightened by contextual events like wars, invasions, epidemics, and natural disasters, as well as by endogenous processes like rapid demographic growth. These events and processes are commonly experienced by a number of people, and on this account stimulate demand for goods that spread risk—such as the protection afforded by walls around a settlement, and the insurance provided the establishment of a mutual benefit society.

But the mere existence of demand for a joint good is insufficient to guarantee its production. One of the firmest conclusions of rational choice is that whereas the production of private goods is hardly problematic, in general public goods will not be produced at optimal levels, if they are produced at all. Whether a joint good is public or private is largely a function of its excludability from potential consumers. With respect to producers, both the protection afforded by town walls and the insurance offered by mutual benefit associations are *collective* goods, but with respect to consumers they are *private* goods in that these consumers (under certain conditions) can be readily excluded from them.

Whether or not a joint good is excludable is, at least in part, due to the control capacity of the potential producers of the good. This control capacity depends upon formal controls that must emerge endogenously. The establishment of these formal controls may be seen as a series of solutions to a three-tier free-rider problem. All three of these free-rider problems must be solved before a cooperative institution can emerge. Since the first two of these problems are already well-appreciated in the literature, this chapter focuses on the third of these.

The First Tier Free-Rider Problem: Design-Making

In the first place, at least one design or plan must be devised that promises to yield the joint good. Each plan must comprise a set of *production rules* that specify what must get done by whom in order to provide an adequate supply of the good.[7] Yet since these designs are themselves a collective good, who will devise them? Although X is eager to consume the joint good, X can spend her time more profitably by attempting to add to her resource endowment than by thinking up designs for newfangled institutions.

The solution to this first-order free-rider problem is the entrepreneurial one; it lies in the individuals' incentive to think up designs that—were their design implemented—would provide them with private benefits greatly exceeding the cost of design-making. For example, ambitious individuals would gamble by formulating plans whose adoption requires either expertise or resources that they alone can claim to have.

The Second Tier Free-Rider Problem: Establishment of an Initial Constitution

One particular design then must be selected by the relevant population. The desire to consume the joint good motivates individuals to make such a selection, for if they fail to do so, too little of the good will be produced. It is probable that each rational individual will prefer a realistic design that seems to offer the greatest amount of the good at the least (private) cost. These individual preferences must then be aggregated into a collective design. Under the conditions of the state of nature—that is, in the absence of any prior institutional framework, and in the absence of any significant resource imbalance among participants—agreement on a unanimity rule is likeliest among a relatively small group of rational egoists, because this kind of rule is most consistent with each member's private interest (Buchanan and Tullock, 1962).

The Third Tier Free-Rider Problem: Implementation of the Design

Even though all institution-builders want to consume the joint good, each rational actor will prefer to free ride on the others' contributions. This preference may not, however, characterize those contingent cooperators who would willingly contribute to the establishment of a cooperative institution if they were assured that others would do likewise (this is often known as the *assurance problem*). If there is no means of deterring free riders, then there will be suboptimal production of the joint good—either because everyone prefers to free ride, or because the assurance problem cannot be resolved to the satisfaction of contingent cooperators.[8]

Whatever its specific causes, suboptimal production of the joint good leads the group to unravel. In order to attain optimal production, formal controls that assure high levels of compliance with production (and distribution) rules by monitoring and sanctioning group members must be adopted.

Yet since these controls are themselves a collective good, their establishment has been difficult to explain from choice-theoretic premises. One solution (the solution I have been working on) flows from the *visibility* of the production and distribution of the joint good.

For a joint good to be maximally excludable, both individual production and distribution must be highly visible. In the absence of visibility, neither free riding (a production problem), nor overconsumption (a distribution problem) can be precluded. Production visibility is at a maximum when individual effort can be well-measured by output assessment. Distribution visibility, however, is at a maximum when individuals must draw measurable shares of the joint good publicly from some central store or repository.

Most (if not all) of the positive externalities of cooperative institutions rest on the advantages of pooling individual assets so that a common central store, or bank, is thereby established. The individual depositor expects to draw some net private benefit from this central store (either interest, or—most likely in the state of nature—access to a wholly different kind of good than that deposited, such as a share of the meat of a large game animal, or insurance against some loss).

Two examples should suffice to illustrate how control is attained in cooperative institutions. In hunting and gathering societies hunters pool individual inputs of time and labor in drives to kill large game that yield meat. Both the production and distribution of killed meat is highly visible to the other hunters. The effort that each hunter contributes to the drive is difficult to conceal: individual roles in the drive are agreed upon before it takes place, and whether a given person is performing his assigned role is relatively visible (although this is a less accurate way to judge his contribution than output assessment would provide). As for distribution, the meat that is produced by the drive is usually spatially concentrated—and thereby constitutes a central fund—for, given the technology of hunter-gatherers, the most efficient way to kill large animals is to stampede them into shallow arroyos or pits (Wheat, 1967; Lee, 1979).

In rotating credit associations (Hechter, 1987: Chap. 6), individuals pool a given amount of money (which is maximally visible because it is an archetypical output) for the right to draw upon the common store of money to increase their purchasing power. In this way the monetary contributions of individual participants generate what is in effect a credit line, access to which is highly visible to all other participants.

Once individual assets are pooled in a central place, however, another free-rider problem occurs: how is it possible to stop a depositor from taking more than her fair share, or from consuming the entire central fund? This is a question that faces all rational investors—would you be likely to deposit your paycheck in a bank that you believe will soon be robbed? Presumably, only if you had some assurance that your deposit is secure. *Hence it is rational for individuals to establish formal controls in cooperative institutions so as to preserve the integrity of their investment* (which, after all, is a private good). By establishing these controls, individuals inadvertently provide themselves with a collective good—namely, security of the common fund.

But who will monitor the depositors; who will sanction them; and how will the requisite sanctioning resources be produced? *All members* will take on the burden of monitoring in the initial cooperative institution. Since anyone who consumes more than their fair share of the common fund appropriates some of my own assets, I am motivated to try to get my own (augmented) investment back. There is no free-rider problem here. Whereas I can assume that other members also have an interest in getting their own investment back, I have no assurance that they won't take my share, split it among themselves, and claim that my share was never found. There is no guarantee that anyone else will look after my interests.

Likewise, *all members* will sanction the noncompliant depositor; no depositor has anything to gain by associating with a rule-breaker whose assets have already been stripped—and presumably much to lose (if it is discovered that the deviant has been helped, the helper herself is then subject to sanctioning).[9] Finally, the ultimate sanctioning resource is easily produced, for it lies entirely within the control of the members themselves—ostracism from the group.[10]

By-Products of Extant Cooperative Institutions: A Fourth Tier in Institutional Genesis

It is likely that the institutionalized group may come to produce different goods than those providing its initial rationale. This is because the group now has the immense comparative advantage that it is *already organized*[11] and therefore can produce new joint goods much more efficiently than can unorganized individuals.[12]

In certain situations, the group may even come to produce *public* (nonexcludable) goods. This can occur if members gain so much from the production of a public good that they are willing to provide it even to non-contributors.[13] In larger groups, this can also occur due to *agency* considerations. This will happen if the agent is not fully constrained by her principals, and if she can increase her own reputation by transforming some of the assets of the central fund into public goods.[14]

All told, this analysis suggests that cooperative institutions indeed can arise from the interaction of rational egoists in a state of nature. In such an environment, however, cooperative institutions will emerge only in a contractarian fashion. Without prior cooperative institutions, there can be no entrepreneurial route to new ones. This is why the earliest institutions tend to be of the "primitive communist" variety.[15] In institutionally rich environments where, for example, individual private property rights have been established, it is far simpler for these institutions to emerge via an entrepreneurial rather than a contractarian route on account of decision-making costs, and of the costs of specifying fully adequate contracts (Williamson, 1975; North, 1981).

This discussion of the emergence of cooperative institutions has two principal implications. If institutions emerge as a result of the demand for joint private goods, then *shifts in a variety of environmental and demographic conditions will heighten demand for certain kinds of joint goods and favor the emergence of institutions supplying these goods*.

Thus, the members of foraging societies tend to form local groups in the dry season—when the scarcity of water increases the benefits of cooperation among different nuclear families—but these groups disband when there is sufficient water to meet the subsistence needs of individual families (Johnson and Earle, 1987). Likewise, as markets penetrate into economically isolated territories this leads to the establishment of insurance institutions (Hechter, 1987). Finally, the rise of insecurity (due to the threat of invasion, piracy, and so forth) promotes the establishment of protective associations. Other kinds of shifts will diminish the demand for such institutions. Hence the growth of insurance markets in the late nineteenth century is associated with the decline of fraternal insurance institutions. If some public good-providing organization in a territory did not go through the first stage (that is, if it did not grow from the roots of some private good-producing institution), such evidence would contradict the thrust of this analysis.

Yet demand alone is insufficient to produce cooperative institutions: *both in their roles as producers and consumers, individuals must be highly visible to one another in order to reduce the severity of the free-rider and assurance problems*.

In the state of nature, bulky goods that must be cooperatively acquired are likely to promote both kinds of visibility. This is consistent with the finding that meat (at least some of which is often cooperatively acquired) is more widely shared among hunter-gatherers than other types of food (Kaplan and Hill, 1985). Irrigation systems provide a graphic example of a cooperative institution that develops to provide access to a bulky joint good. Wittfogel (1957:18), for example, notes that water is a distinctive resource in that it has a tendency to gather in bulk.[16] Further research into the visibility of

the production of different kinds of joint goods, and of the potential centricity of these goods, doubtless will provide a richer body of empirical implications for the genesis of cooperative institutions.

It should be emphasized that the analysis in this chapter is quite different from Mancur Olson's (1965) well-known explanation of the development of collective goods-seeking organizations like trade unions and farm organizations. Insofar as these groups sought to raise the wages of whole classes of workers, they aimed to produce a collective good. Given this, the optimal strategy for any given worker is to free ride and cash in on the (presumably successful) efforts of union organizers and their credulous followers. How, then, did these groups emerge? Olson's explanation is that the early trade unions (in the days before the passage of closed-shop legislation) could lure members only if they provided them with desirable selective incentives, including insurance. In Olson's account, therefore, insurance is considered to be the by-product of trade unions.

The problem with Olson's explanation is that, like formal controls, selective incentives are themselves a collective good. This means that they, too, have to be produced by rational egoists. How is it that a group aiming to provide a public good can attract any rational members at all, let alone manage to produce selective incentives? As the previous analysis shows, the rise of groups providing immanent joint goods entails no such liability. Since they are formed for the provision of *private* goods, there is no initial free-rider problem. To obtain their goods, members are led to adopt formal controls that make possible production of the goods. Once the goods have been produced, they can be used in a variety of ways. For example, there is no inherent reason why the members of an insurance group cannot convert their common assets into a strike fund and reconstitute themselves as a trade union. . . .

Endnotes

1. Consider an elevator having male and female passengers. If male passengers are observed to allow the females to exit first, this is a collective be-

havioral regularity. Whether this behavioral regularity is due to the presence of a norm or to explicit rules is beside the point.

2. For the purposes of this chapter, language itself may be considered to be a convention.

3. This restriction is due to the fact that the rise of institutions among close relations can be explained easily by evolutionary arguments based on genetic relatedness. Such reasoning is, however, generally insufficient to account for institutions whose scope surpasses the members of a nuclear family.

4. The problem of multiple equilibria is double-barrelled. On the one hand, cooperation may not emerge because some of these equilibria are inefficient. On the other hand, cooperation may not emerge even if the various equilibria are all efficient, since they are unlikely to be equally preferred by all the players or the game. This situation then leads to a noncooperative bargaining problem.

5. In the absence of perfect monitoring capacity, a player can never be certain of the moves that other players have taken in past plays of the game. Thus, she cannot infer that cooperation is ever rational.

6. This question is critical, for if we suspend self-interested behavioral assumptions—and allow individuals to have internalized values or some small but positive amount of altruism—then there is an all too easy way to overcome the assurance problem, and thereby to account for the emergence of cooperative institutions. This strategy is akin to invoking a *deus ex machina*, but there can be no theoretical justification for so doing.

7. I ignore the obvious complication that the initial production functions for the joint good will be estimates, and that disagreements may well result about the accuracy of these estimates.

8. There is a growing experimental literature on the use of provision points and money-back guarantees as means of resolving the assurance problem. Whereas there is evidence that some of these arrangements do, in fact, result in the production of greater public goods, each of them is imposed *exogenously* in the experiments. Hence these solutions to the free-rider and assurance problems are inconsistent with the premises of this analysis.

9. In more complex situations where there are alternative benefit-providing institutions, deviant actors often gain a negative reputation that makes them unsuitable for admission to any such institution. After other participants get their investment back, what is their incentive to ruin the deviant's reputation? Why should rational egoists be concerned about the fortunes of the participants in *other* institutions? This kind of problem is en-demic in academic hiring situations, where the members of sending departments often provide misleading information to receiving departments in hopes of getting rid of a troublesome colleague or a sub-par student. The only force that can counter this free-rider problem is the damage that such deceit might bring to the information provider in further repeat dealings. Hence, the less frequent the contact between the members of two academic departments, the less reliable the information supplied about potential colleagues and students, *ceteris paribus*. The multiplexity of ties between groups increases the probability of this intergroup sanctioning.

10. It should be noted that this solution to the emergence of cooperative institutions is practicable only in relatively small groups. In essence, the creation of a central store of resources commits participants to involvement in a repeated game. As such, many of the mechanisms that produce cooperation in the literature on repeated games (Taylor, 1976; Axelrod, 1984) are employed here to the same effect. The reader may wonder wherein this approach differs from the invisible-hand approach. Whereas repeated game theorists take the existence of the supergame (and sometimes the existence of a specific discount rate) as a given, this analysis explains how it is that rational egoists voluntarily commit themselves to social situations involving repeated exchange.

11. The connection between pre-existing organizations founded to produce joint private goods and public good-providing organizations often has been stressed in the literature on social movements (Oberschall, 1973; McAdam *et al.*, 1988). Thus in her analysis of the emergence of the contemporary women's movement, Evans (1980) locates its roots in informal networks of women who had come to know one another in the context of prior civil rights and New Left political organizations. Black churches (which offered insurance benefits) played an important crystallizing role in the development of the civil rights movement (Oberschall, 1973:126–27; McAdam, 1982; Morris, 1984). Fraternal-service groups played a similar role in the emergence of local anti-pornography movements (Curtis and Zurcher, 1973:56); and mosques played this kind of role in the early days of the Iranian Revolution (Snow and Marshall, 1984).

12. Naturally, this kind of an argument has its limits, otherwise all production would be concentrated in just one institution. For an interesting discussion of the limits of integration in firms, see Hart (1987).

13. Thus, to satisfy his desire to watch movies in the middle of the night, Howard Hughes bought a local Las Vegas station (Hardin, 1982).

14. For example, the agents of some American ethnically-based fraternal societies had political aspirations in their communities, and by judiciously investing these funds they could further these political aspirations (Stolarik, 1980). Likewise, the managers of large Minneapolis corporations are motivated to provide charitable donations in the community by the access to high prestige social circles that these donations uniquely provide (Galaskiewicz, 1985). The provision of public goods also can be a by-product of relatively homogeneous groups. In such groups, access to the joint good may be limited only to those members who contribute to specific public goods that are unrelated to the group's initial rationale. Thus some Pittsburgh fraternal associations expelled members who had committed crimes or treason, or who hired out as strikebreakers (Galey, 1977). This then explains how the self-interest of rational egoists can lead them to produce collective (and sometimes even public) goods.

15. In contrast, the Marxian explanation for primitive communism rests on questionable arguments about the absence of a surplus beyond that necessary for subsistence.

16. Clearly, the demand for a predictable water supply is insufficient to account for actual irrigation works, for many peoples who would have gained from it did not adopt such practices. Whether the adopters of irrigation had a visibility advantage over nonadoptors remains to be explored in further research.

References

Aumann, Robert J. (1985). "Repeated Games." Pp. 209–242 in George R. Feiwel, ed., *Issues in Contemporary Microeconomics and Welfare*. Albany, NY: State University of New York Press.

Axelrod, Robert. (1984). *The Evolution of Cooperation*. New York: Basic Books.

Bendor, Jonathan, and Dilip Mookherjee. (1987). "Institutional structure and the logic of ongoing collective action." *American Political Science Review*, 81(1):129–54.

Blau, Peter M. (1964). *Exchange and Power in Social Life*. New York: John Wiley.

Buchanan, James M. and Gordon Tullock. (1962). *The Calculus of Consent*. Ann Arbor: University of Michigan Press.

Curtis, Russell L. and Louis A. Zurcher, Jr. (1973). "Stable resources of protest movement: The multi-organizational field." *Social Forces*, 52(1):53–60.

DiMaggio, Paul J. and Walter W. Powell. (1983). "Institutional isomorphism." *American Sociological Review*, 48(2):147–160.

Durkheim, Emile. (1951). *Suicide*. New York: Free Press. [Originally published 1897.]

Evans, Sarah. (1980). *Personal Politics*. New York: Vintage Books.

Galaskiewicz, Joseph. (1985). *Social Organization of an Urban Grants Economy: A Study of Business Philanthropy and Nonprofit Organizations*. Orlando, FL: Academic Press.

Galey, Margaret E. (1977). "Ethnicity, fraternalism, social and mental health." *Ethnicity*, 4(1):19–53.

Hardin, Russell. (1982). *Collective Action*. Baltimore: Johns Hopkins University Press (for Resources for the Future).

Hart, Oliver. (1987). "Incomplete contracts and the theory of the firm." Paper presented at the Conference on Knowledge and Institutional Change, University of Minnesota.

Hayek, Friedrich A. (1973). *Law, Legislation and Liberty*, Vol. I. Chicago: University of Chicago Press.

——. (1976). *Law, Legislation and Liberty*, Vol. II. Chicago: University of Chicago Press.

Hechter, Michael. (1987). *Principles of Group Solidarity*. Berkeley and London: University of California Press.

——. (1990). "On the inadequacy of game theory for the resolution of real-world collective action problems." In M. Levi and K. S. Cook, eds., *The Limits of Rationality*. Chicago: University of Chicago Press. In press.

Hobbes, Thomas. (1968). *Leviathan*, edited by C. B. Macpherson. Harmondsworth, England: Penguin. [Originally published 1651.]

Johnson, Allen W. and Timothy Earle. (1987). *The Evolution of Human Societies*. Stanford: Stanford University Press.

Kaplan, Hillard and Kim Hill. (1985). "Food sharing among Ache foragers: Tests of explanatory hypotheses." *Current Anthropology*, 26(2):223–239.

Lee, Richard B. (1979). *The !Kung San*. Cambridge: Cambridge University Press.

Lewis, David. (1969). *Convention: A Philosophical Study*. Cambridge: Harvard University Press.

McAdam, Doug. (1982). *Political Process and the Development of Black Insurgency, 1930–1970*. Chicago: University of Chicago Press.

McAdam, Doug, John D. McCarthy, and Mayer N. Zald. (1988). "Social movements and collective behavior: Building micro-macro bridges." Pp. 695–738 in Neil J. Smelser, ed.,

Handbook of Sociology. Newbury Park, CA: Sage.

Menger, Carl. (1963). *Investigations into the Method of the Social Sciences with Special Reference to Economics*, edited by Louis Schneider. Translated by Francis J. Nock. Champaign-Urbana: University of Illinois Press. [Originally published 1883.]

Morris, Aldon. (1984). *The Origins of the Civil Rights Movement*. New York: Free Press.

North, Douglass C. (1981). *Structure and Change in Economic History*. New York: Norton.

Nozick, Robert. (1974). *Anarchy, State and Utopia*. New York: Basic Books.

Oberschall, Anthony. (1973). *Social Conflict and Social Movements*. Englewood Cliffs, N.J.: Prentice-Hall.

Olson, Mancur. (1965). *The Logic of Collective Action*. Cambridge: Harvard University Press.

Snow, David A. and Susan Marshall. (1984). "Cultural imperialism, social movements, and the Islamic revival." Pp. 131–152 in Louis Kriesberg, ed., *Social Movements, Conflicts and Change*, Vol. 7. Greenwich, CT: JAI Press.

Stolarik, M. Mark. (1980). "Slovak fraternal benefit societies." Pp. 130–145 in Scott Cummings, ed., *Urban Self-Help in America*. Port Washington, NY: Kennikat Press.

Taylor, Michael. (1976). *Anarchy and Cooperation*. London: John Wiley.

Ullman-Margalit, Edna. (1978). "Invisible hand explanations." *Synthese*, 39:263–91.

Wheat, J. B. (1967). "A Paleo-Indian bison kill." *Scientific American*, January.

White, Harrison C. (1981). "Where do markets come from?" *American Journal of Sociology*, 87(3):517–547.

Williamson, Oliver. (1975). *Markets and Hierarchies*. New York: Free Press.

Wittfogel, Karl A. (1957). *Oriental Despotism: A Comparative Study of Total Power*. New Haven: Yale University Press.

50
Persons

Harrison C. White

The fact that Harrison White (b. 1930) has two doctorates—one in theoretical physics and the other in sociology—is evident in his efforts to construct mathematical models of social relations. White's work is difficult to summarize, in part because he is admittedly eclectic and because he is not grounded in any one theoretical school. Indeed, part of the difficulty in locating his work vis-à-vis the classics and competing theory schools is that he operates at a remove from both the tradition and his contemporaries. To complicate things further, his sociological interests are wide ranging. Despite these difficulties, it is clear that he has been profoundly shaped by structuralist theories and can most appropriately be defined as a network theorist. Networks are viewed as operating in a middle space between individuals and groups on the one hand and the society at large on the other. In this passage from what some view as his most important work, *Identity and Control* (1992), he argues that identities and positions exist prior to persons, who emerge only through network contexts.

Persons come into existence and are formed as overlaps among identities from distinct network-populations. Identities and positions do prefigure persons, but persons emerge only as the contexts become more sophisticated. Persons build in terms of styles across distinct populations. Conversation prefigures personal identity.

. . . A network spreads through many nodes but it need not catch up all the nodes embedded in any given identity. A child as a person, itself a compound of identities, comes late in sequences of other disciplines of family and gang. Personhood never would have emerged in the child had it not also placed as a node in some other networks than the playground, in networks across some other populations as contexts. Conversely, a personal identity may touch on many networks but does not encompass all of any network. A personal identity presupposes distinct networks—not just in different locales but also with different tones. Consider, as illustration, games versus storytellings right on the playground.

Identities are the basis from which persons are constructed. Identities are triggered. They are contingent by-products from mismatch between embeddings of disciplines, on the one hand, through contingencies upon ecology and network histories on the other. Identities are as real—they function about the same in relation to environing social organization—however they fit as actors into the complex interlocking of gels and strands of social process and organization. But persons are special: for example, not all the sorts of actors considered can converse, despite all having identities.

Person should be a construct from the middle of the analysis, not a given boundary condition. Personhood has to be accounted for, which means specifying contexts where it may, where it will, and where it cannot enter. But in most present social science ""person" is instead taken as the unquestioned atom. This is an unacknowledged borrowing and transcription of the soul construct from Christian theology.[1] Before general theory in social science can be attained, "persons" have to be assimilated as being but particular embodiments of a class of socially constructed actors, and that not the only class.

Persons come to be generated only out of large-scale frictions among distinct network-populations. It is through common style that persons link across network populations. Ordinarily, persons and styles coexist, but the charismatic is a person purged of style. While style tends to reduce ambage at the expense of ambiguity, personhood tends to reduce ambiguity—to sustain orderly interpretive frames—at the cost of increased ambage.

Etiology of Persons

The emergence of identities from irregularities is traced even amidst the smooth life of the isolated island of Tikopeia by Firth. These are natural irregularities from storm or fishing upset, but also social irregularity from health degradation or randomly triggered brawl. Firth, in his reports (1957) across two generations concerning this tribe, isolated on a Melanesian atoll, weaves an account in which one sees persons emerging only dimly and partially in their own eyes. Persons become vivid and real only in consequences of and as by-product from bridging across to distinct populations, be they Firth's and our society, or Asian sailing-bark crews.

In the much more complex tribal spread across the hills of upper Burma, Leach (1954) painted a very similar picture of how persons emerged—and faded. They did so in sequentially invoking and ignoring two competing forms of social portrayal, *mayu* and *dama*, which appeared and then faded as a by-product of eddies of social action. Populations analytically distinct, though only partially segregated, were bridged by actors who maneuvered from one to the other according to political situation and thereby became persons.

Our access to other ages through what we call history is not usually sufficient to reconstruct social milieus and contexts in which then ordinary persons would have appeared. There are, however, exemplary studies which appear to support the conjecture about personhood; for examples, consult Tilly (1978, 1990) and his students on contentious assemblies, Bynum (1987) on medieval spiritual life, and M. Howell (1988) on medieval practical life. Usually there is not enough precision to establish or refute the conjecture that persons are by-products of interaction between populations.

But in our own day and cities, field work confirms these ideas. Personal identity can come from turbulences in early life which result from and carry over into several realms, of family, neighborhood, and the like. Willis (1977) gives a vivid characterization of this for working-class British teenagers. Many if not most of these youth participate for long periods in social scenes in which they never step outside routine role performances; so their personhood is never induced or invoked, despite inevitable chronic mismatches among alternate role performances and role complementarities.

All the earlier chapters on ties and disciplines and institutions may sound impersonal, and much too elaborate. But in fact our consciousnesses as persons result from and are caught up in style for these mazes. Each "I," in the common parlance, is a more-or-less rickety ensemble; it is firm and whole only temporarily as a facet of one particular constituent discipline energized in some situation and style. In a specific context we may recognize some particular self operating in one or another of the three species of discipline. But, overall, persons are aptly seen as walking wounded, who evolve out of stochastic processes of continuing bruisings and coalescences among networks and disciplines. Take an early example.

Luther comes from a period long known for its induction of person in the modern sense. The book *Young Man Luther* is unusual both in its impact, and in its authorship by a psychoanalyst (Erikson 1958). Historians have always re-created Luther, like other "world historical" figures, as a strain point at confluences of significant social tides. They do not agree on some preexisting uniqueness and strength of person but do join in a re-creation of the entourage. And specialists in theological history (Obermann 1981) are engaged in a revisionist debate as to the originality of Luther's ideas and of Luther's systematic formulation, as opposed to a revived perception of liveliness in late medieval nominalist theology preceding Luther. But they too will join in an "as-if" account of Luther's importance, minimally as an expression of incoming major cultural reformation.

Erik Erikson contributes a highly original view, of the importance of dynamics in young Luther's family constellation, which is fed into, rather than used to contradict, the historical and theological perspectives. Erikson's accomplishment illustrates one major theme: each social reality, of whatever scope, is caught up in and affected by other scopes. Erikson is convincing on Luther as being quite literally created as a person by cross-pressures of his immediate family life, as both interpreted and, simultaneously, concretely shaped by the late medieval theological and institutional context. The person as a pearl shaped in a family bivalve of turbulent flows: this could have been Erikson's subtitle.

Persons and Styles

The ordinary person is a late construct, by the standards of archaeological reconstruction of societies. As Nissen argues from the archaeological record of Mesopotamia, persons are like pottery in this respect. A lot of corporate actors evolve and reproduce as disciplines before there is pottery with its styles, and before persons are recognizable. Pottery provides not just an illustration of style, but what seems from an archaeological perspective to be the principal early vessel of style. Pottery came in relatively late, and it came in along with persons (Nissen 1988). Pottery combines the story aspects of style with physical substrate in transparent form. The correlation continues to this day (Dauber 1987).

Persons in seeking control cannot and do not attempt to deal severally with the enormous, the astronomical array of paths and influences upon them. Instead they come to deal with combinations as styles. Persons work with sets of perceptions both of their own and of others' situations, social and physical. Only some such sets prove able to reproduce themselves and thereby become objective constraints. Such sets are styles in that they exert constraints, like molecular disciplines but in more sophisticated context. Style goes with a patterning in physical space that survives turbulence and reproduces, and likewise for style in social spaces of ties or stories and of values or roles. Stories are generated as explanations along with the embeddings within habits that, all together, can define a style for an individual actor. A person and a style can define each other, and the same duality obtains up through larger social formations. Styles can have still smaller or much more encompassing concrete referents such as conversations and communities, respectively.

Individual actors watch one another within disciplines and social networks and imbibe patterns in how to maneuver and how to account in stories and values for the maneuvers. Thereby individuals acquire a style, as they jointly reproduce profiles through their mutually patterned actions. A style may come as a distinct pattern of combining and embedding disciplines, as well as personal actors into an overall network topology. Gearings for action, intentional and unintentional, rely on common styles as well as on profiles.

In Simmelian milieu of strangers on downtown streets, style is the only skim on the surface of chaotic social process. Styles are byproducts of turbulence in tangible structure and process, in institutions. Style and turbulence presuppose each other. They arise across many ranges of incident and network, and across the many levels mixed up in social organization. The social economy of different relations is not developed only or primarily at a level of individual dyads and actors.

Formations at higher scopes must be reaching down with contextual pressures as styles through any particular discipline to effect an orderliness of perception. And conversely from lower scopes, where for example, conversations as prototypes become elaborated into further disciplines or styles of perception. The three species of discipline—the commit interface, the select arena, and the mobilize council—are those which have proved robust to all these perception pressures, above and below.

Selves and Multiplex Ties

"Real selves" cannot be disentangled from "intimate ties," as we see in modern social contexts, which have been so concerned to create "privacy." The modern concept of friendship is wholly aside from tit-for-tat, from favor for help. Silver (1989, esp. p. 274; 1990) provides convincing argument and evidence for this evolution of friendship: he fixes the beginning as the Scot Enlightenment. Equate Silver's tie of friendship with a multiplex tie, the kind of overall tie that we take for granted as the basis for civil and civic life.

This overall tie presupposes a lack of concern with the detailed balancing of obligations found in traditional formations. There is no tangible, concrete mechanism perceived as concerned with enforcement of obligation. This kind of multiplex tie itself comes to seem a recent, modern innovation.

A tribal or feudal society does not know the luxury of a single, overall tie not built into concrete economy of obligation. Such social formations rather make use of relations each part of which is lucidly factored out by audience and occasion—as kinship, as village, whatever. This multiplex tie is a late and sophisticate construct, on this interpretation of evolution.

Yet the modern multiplex tie need not be fraught with fearsome potency from balanced duress in gaming. Romantic love is merely representative of extreme examples, not of medians in multiplexity. Some extreme examples, notably feud, can also be found in traditional formations.

What this overall tie can bring about is the person. By this argument, the person is a late construct in perception. "Self" becomes the creation as well as the creator of person, with multiplex tie as the occasion for perception of a self. The tie of marriage is an example.

The key is a multiplex tie that requires and builds to disparate populations. Elizabeth Bott (1957) emphasized this. She showed how to predict differences in marital personalities from underlying divergences in partners' interlock in their concrete social relations. Marital person was read by Bott from immediate context of social networks, which changed from couple to couple in London. A "joint" form of marriage relation was distinguished by Bott from segregated roles of domestic wife and "pub" husband. Only the joint-form, requiring straddling different populations, yielded persons.

The world of romantic love, discussed below, is a precursor and correlate of the joint-form marriage. Romantic love is induced by the same modern contexts in which attitudes become reified. Love is an induction of person, but as only a metastable state. Romantic love is so important because development of this sort of subtle, ambiguous, gamed bond of some duration is a main path to unique personal identity in Goffmanesque social contexts. Here is where the esoteric game theory which economists misplace onto "rational decision" might yield empirical insight.[2] Stable identities as persons are difficult to build; they are achieved

only in some social contexts; they are not pre-given analytic foci.

Community

Silver (1989, 1990) also argues that distinct identity as a person in the modern sense followed from rather than created a multiplex tie, the overall tie. Across levels of identities similar interpretation of multiplex tie should be possible. Persons are not the only constructions made out of identities. Identities are a much broader class than persons, or than facets of persons, or than any other entities that are embedded by any particular discipline.

For example, communities can be seen as built out of identities rather than persons, and as being only partial analogues of persons. Consider this analysis of the concept of community:

> We need to develop a conceptualization of community which allows us to penetrate beneath simple categories . . . to see a variable of social relations. . . . The relationship between community as a complex of social relationships and community as a complex of ideas and sentiments has been little explored (p. 107). . . . What is important about "sense of belonging" is . . . his modification of consideration of alternative courses of action on the basis of the communal relations to which he belongs. (Calhoun 1980, p. 110)

Then he continues, "The self-regulation of community is dependent on dense, multiplex bonds. . . . The crucial issue is the breakdown of the structure of hierarchical incorporation which knit local communities into the society as a whole" (p. 115). Recast Calhoun's point. Earlier forms of community had types of tie well defined and built into explicit disciplines, so that sense of community was not relevant. The development of multiplex tie from community to other actors is what induces and permits the appearance of community persona akin to the modern individual person, as signaler.

A large-scale exemplar of the signaling argument for identity is how "lost," "saved," and "liberated" communities are not successive stages, but rather alternative structural models:

Many scholars believed that community ties were now few in number, weak, narrowly specialized, transitory, and fragmented. . . . These scholars feared that community had been "lost.". . . Others argued that people gregariously form and retain communities in all social settings. . . . By the 1960s their "Community Saved" argument had had much the better of the debate empirically. . . . Both the "Lost" and the "Saved" arguments assume that a flourishing community can only be one that replicates the standard image of preindustrial communities: densely knit, tightly bounded, and mutually supportive villages. But such bucolic imagery not only disregards widespread preindustrial individualism, exploitation, cleavage, and mobility . . . but it also restricts the criteria. . . . Scholars who have avoided this mislabeling . . . argue that large-scale specialization and personal mobility have "Liberated" community—encouraging membership in multiple, interest-based communities predominantly composed of long-distance friendship ties . . . people are not so much antisocial or gregarious beings as they are *operators*. . . . Each model speaks to a different means of obtaining and retaining resources: direct use of formal organizations (Lost); membership in densely knit, all-encompassing, solidary groups (Saved); or selective use of specialized, diversified, sparsely knit social nets (Liberated) . . . all three models are likely to be reflected in current realities to some extent. (Wellman, Carrington, and Hall 1988, pp. 133–35)

These are alternatives for community identity, they constitute a story-set for it. This set of stories is in fact used both in common parlance and also simultaneously in professional jousts by scholarly analysts within their own world. The set of stories clusters around some value(s).

There is community as identity of personal sort at still larger scope and higher level. Identity acquires theophany, covenant, and law before gaining the most universal recognition, as for example Jehovah (Jahweh in Gottwald 1979, p. 94). All three of these aspects—pronouncement, reciprocal commitment, and rules—presuppose and can only be observed in social context. Social context is not opaque like the "insides" of persons, and so it is requisite for the three aspects even regarding a particular human person. All three aspects presuppose value. This is true even where the "actor" is least personal.

There is analogue to community at smaller scale. Ties are the detritus of discipline formations. Ties are fragments of what might have locked into disciplines, thus yielding identities enabled to generate social action. Within a discipline there are strong connections among the constituting entities, which may themselves be identities, so that other types of connection exist between identities. These connections are mutual pressures which come to fit together so as to support some transitive order, perhaps some personhood.

Modern Person From Love and Attitudes

The modern vision of social milieus is exemplified by Goffman's (1963, 1967, 1971) and Simmel's (1955) strangers. These are persons who are so little reinforced by siting in specific social structures as to have only shadowy existence, to be creatures mostly bracketed, to be abstract actors triggered into concreteness only through encounters. Turn back to romantic love.

This modern vision fits as well a province of romantic love, which at first sight seems so surely and purely a matter of one preexisting person intensely attuned to another. Perhaps. But in fact the two persons are meeting in the Small World. This Small World has been emerging since around the time a phenomenology of romantic love was spreading beyond troubadour circles (Bloch 1977).[3] It is just when persons are shadowy in their social sitings that intensely personal attractions are generated, as Swidler (1989) argued. But this modern vision also reminds us that an identity may have just one or two facets or personae (out of its corporate self) exposed to observation at a given time. These facets are cobbled together, by the identity, from different frames, perhaps spun together in stories.

Romances are outcomes of mutual searches among networks and groups which are keyed to occasions, to specific times marked by assemblages of persons as at acquaintance dances. Attention can only be given, in social as well as physical perception, to limited numbers of "contacts" at a time. Romantic acquaintanceship can only be pursued one "date" at a time. Romantic personages are a construct out of, a by-product of distinctive eddies and enclaves which emerge as by chance in a Small World in which "eligibility" itself, perceived active participation, is induced by the states of queues in what can be visualized as a system of stochastic social servers.

Romantic love is a colorful topic. The same truths can be argued about more everyday stuff of our life in Small World contexts. Attitudes are perhaps the most distinctive invention for modern contexts of social life. Substantial portions of time and cognitive attention are given to the adaptations and replenishment of hosts of notions on topics remarkably far removed from any tangible aspect of the actual living of the persons concerned.

Persons become unique in identities, yet must be validated as stereotypes. So today to some extent the person is the attitudes. Each set of attitudes can distinguish an identity.[4] . . . Each such set then can find it comfortable to recognize and define as persons other such combinations, variously alike, or compatible, or neither.

Modern democratic politics and its incessant stream of "news"— events made meaningful by episodic campaigns and elections—can be seen, in part, as contributing to the sustenance of personhood, to the creation of persons as distinctive combinations of attitudes which can be perceived as having meaningful continuity over time. Modern politics is a very inexpensive way to create the voters as civil persons, whatever the significance of the ostensible processes of decision and governance. Modern politics can be seen as a phenomenological by-product of the Small World. Milgram's (1977) unknown names as "targets" do not seem bizarre to us as civil beings in part because we have come to attend to and "know" remote names as politicians.

Politics is just an example. Sports is another, or rather each is a cascading modern family of examples. Persons are defined and define themselves most easily and inexpen-

sively, within the Small World which also yields romantic love, by what particular families of attitudes they penetrate into, as much as by particular attitudes upon topics apparently portentous enough that every person should indulge in a "holding." Trivial Pursuit is a parlor game emblematic of an age.

Endnotes

1. Christian theology worked out "soul" during centuries when a strikingly dual polity was emerging in its region, and this secular context helped shape and limit the construct. But the ultimate fixity of the soul, carried over to hobble social science, was a Pauline theological imperative.

2. It could be argued that the crippling of game theory is the worst effect of rational-choice theory. . . . At its introduction by von Neumann, game theory had the potential of refounding the theory of social action. Unfortunately, it devolved into the hands of economic theorists. Except in the work of Schelling, who eschews systematic theory or modeling, the results for many years were increasingly arid exercises. New developments may be afoot, but effective game theory has to concern the induction of identities and disciplines, of social organization.

3. There are no person-pheromones which signal one person as special to another; i.e. there is no doing ant societies (Wilson 1970) one better. A queueing system of stochastic servers (Kleinrock 1964; Riordan 1962) is a formal-modeling way to situate romantic love.

4. Combinatoric calculations show the number of possible combinations or sets to be astronomically larger than any human population. . . .

References

Bloch, R. Howard. *Medieval French Literature and Law.* Berkeley, CA: University of California Press, 1977.

Bott, Elizabeth. *Family and Social Network.* London: Tavistock, 1957.

Bynum, Carolyn. *Holy Feast and Holy Fast: The Religious Significance of Food to Medieval Women.* Berkeley, CA: University of California Press, 1987.

Calhoun, C. J. "Community: Toward a variable conceptualization for comparative research." *Social History* 5(1980): 105–129.

Dauber, Ken. "Claims, Identities and Multiple Logics." Department of Sociology, University of Arizona, September 25, 1987.

Erikson, Erik. *Young Man Luther.* New York: Norton, 1958.

Firth, Raymond. *We, The Tikopia.* London: Allen & Unwin, 1957.

Goffman, Erving. *Behavior in Public Places.* Glencoe, IL: Free Press, 1963.

——. *Interaction Ritual.* New York: Pantheon, 1967.

——. *Relations in Public.* New York: Harper, 1971.

Gottwald, Norman K. *The Tribes of Jahweh: A Sociology of the Religion of Liberated Israel, 1250–1050 B.C.E.* Maryknoll, NY: Orbis Books, 1979.

Howell, Nancy (Lee). "Understanding Simple Social Structure: Kinship Units and Ties." In Wellman, Barry, and S. D. Berkowitz, eds., *Social Structures: A Network Approach.* New York: Cambridge University Press, 1988.

Kleinrock, Leonard. *Communication Nets: Stochastic Message Flow and Delay.* New York: McGraw-Hill, 1964.

Leach, Edmund, R. *The Political Systems of Highland Burma.* Boston: Beacon, 1954.

Milgram, Stanley. *The Individual in a Social World.* Reading, MA: Addison-Wesley, 1977.

Nissen, Hans, J. *The Early History of the Ancient Near East: 9000–2000 B.C.* Translated by Elizabeth Lutzeier. Chicago: University of Chicago Press, 1988.

Obermann, Heiko. *Masters of the Reformation.* New York, Cambridge University, 1981.

Riordan, J. *Stochastic Service Systems.* New York: Wiley, 1962.

Silver, Allan. "Friendship and Trust as Moral Ideals: An Historical Approach." *European Journal of Sociology* 30(1989): 274–297.

——. "Friendship in Commercial Society: Eighteenth-Century Social Theory and Modern Society." *American Journal of Sociology* 91(1990): 1474–1504.

Simmel, Georg. *Conflict and the Web of Group-Affiliations.* Translated by K. Wolff and R. Bendix. Glencoe, IL: Free Press, 1955.

Swidler, Ann. Unpublished paper, 1989.

Tilly, Charles. *From Mobilization to Revolution.* Reading, MA: Addison-Wesley, 1978.

——. *Coercion, Capital and European States A.D. 990–1990.* Cambridge, MA: Blackwell, 1990.

Wellman, Barry, Peter J. Carrington, and Alan Hall. "Networks as Personal Communities." In Wellman, Barry, and S. D. Berkowitz, eds., *Social Structures: A Network Approach,* Chapter 6. New York: Cambridge University Press, 1988.

Willis, Paul. *Learning to Labour.* London: Gower, 1977.

Wilson, E. O. *Insect Societies.* Cambridge, MA: Harvard University Press, 1970.

51

Formulation of Exchange Theory

Peter Blau

Peter Blau (1918–2002), who was born in Vienna and emigrated to the United States during the Nazi era, was a key exponent of exchange theory for over three decades. During this time he attempted to go beyond the general propositional stage articulated by George Homans in order to focus on social structure. In this excerpt from *Structural Contexts of Opportunities* (1994), Blau builds on micro-level exchange theory while articulating an appreciation of both the difference between economic and social exchange and the factors that make the macro level different from the micro level. One of the issues he addresses is the paradoxical fact that social exchange both facilitates social bonding and gives rise to status differentiation.

A fundamental difference between social life in small isolated communities and that in large complex societies is the declining significance of the groups into which one is born and the growing significance of reciprocated choices for human relations. To be sure, the significance of ascribed positions has by no means disappeared in contemporary complex societies. Most people's closest relations are with their parents and children. Other ascribed positions continue to exert a major influence on social relations, notably one's kin and the ethnic group and social class into which one is born. Yet, even for quite close relatives, except one's immediate family, the extent of social interaction and the intimacy of the relation are not ascribed but depend on reciprocal choices. Larger ascribed affiliations, like ethnic and class background, affect the likelihood of choice but do not predeter-mine who selects whom as close associate, which depends on reciprocated choices.

Thus, ascribed as well as achieved positions govern probabilities of association, which are generally higher for ascribed than achieved affiliations, but they do not determine specific associates (with the exception of parents and children), let alone the extent of social interaction and the closeness of the relation. Their probabilistic influences on ingroup associations are similar to those of a community's population structure. The population distributions in a community also influence only the probabilities of ingroup and intergroup relations of various kinds, but the specific dyads within which these probabilities find expression depend on mutual choices.

Dependence on reciprocated choice implies that, if I want to associate with someone, I cannot realize my goal unless I make him interested in associating with me. For our social relation to persist once it has been established, both of us have to sustain an interest in its continuation. To determine what brings these conditions about is the objective of exchange theory, which analyzes the processes that establish reciprocity in social relations and sustain it, and which thereby dissects the dynamics of social interaction.

Structural conditions impose limits on the exchange relations that can develop. The population structure of an entire society or large community, however, is far removed from the daily social life of individuals and hence does not affect it directly but indirectly. Multilevel structural analysis traces these indirect limiting influences. It discloses how macro-structural conditions are transmitted to successive levels and which ones reach the lowest level on which direct social interaction and exchange occur. It may indicate, for example, that society's racial heterogeneity penetrates into small substructures or that it is reflected in segregation of different races in different suburbs and neighborhoods with much homogeneity within them. The former situation would make intergroup relations more likely than the latter, but neither would determine which specific social relations occur.

Many, if not most, human gratifications are obtained in relations with other human beings. Intellectual stimulation and relaxing conversation, sexual pleasures and the enchantment of love, academic recognition and a happy family life, satisfying the lust for power and the need for acceptance—all of these are contingent on eliciting responses from others. Exchange theory analyzes the mutual gratifications persons provide one another that sustain social relations.

***

The basic assumption of the theory of social exchange is that persons establish social associations because they expect them to be rewarding and that they continue social interaction and expand it because they experience it to be rewarding. This assumption that two parties associate with one another not owing to normative requirements but because they both expect rewards from doing so implies that the exchange of rewards is a starting mechanism of social relations that is not contingent on norms prescribing obligations. If a person is attracted to others because she expects associating with them to be rewarding, she will want to associate with them to obtain the expected rewards. For them to associate with her, they must be interested in doing so, which depends, according to the initial assumption, on their expecting such association to be rewarding to them. Consequently, for the first person to realize the rewards expected from the association with others, she must impress them as a desirable associate with whom interaction will be rewarding.

Individuals are often hesitant to take the first step for fear of rejection. A widely used early strategy is for people to impress others in whom they are interested with their outstanding qualities—their wit, charm, intelligence, knowledge of the arts—which implicitly promises that associating with them would be a rewarding experience. If the early steps are successful, they tend to become self-fulfilling prophecies. As each person puts his best foot forward, associating with him turns out to be an enjoyable experience. In due course, people start doing favors for one another. In a work situation, the more experienced may give their colleagues advice or help with a difficult job. Neighbors may lend one another tools. People who met

socially may issue invitations to dinner or a party.

Most people enjoy doing favors for others, usually without any thought of return, at least initially. Nevertheless, a person who benefits from an association is under an obligation to reciprocate. If the benefits are recurrent—whether involving merely the enjoyment of the other's company or getting frequently needed advice about one's work from a colleague—the self-imposed obligation to reciprocate is sustained by the interest in continuing to obtain the benefits. It is further reinforced by the fear of not seeming ungrateful. Even when there is no initial thought of return, failure to reciprocate when the occasion arises invites such an accusation, which will be experienced though it remains unspoken.

Imagine a neighbor lends you her lawn mower in the summer, but when she asks you next winter to borrow your snow blower you refuse. The neighbor and others who learn of your refusal undoubtedly will consider you ungrateful, and whether they do or not, you yourself will feel ungrateful and surely will be hesitant to ask to borrow her lawn mower again. The feelings and possible accusations of ingratitude indicate that favors freely given are not entirely free but create obligations in one's own mind to reciprocate as well as possible social pressures to discharge the obligations.

A fundamental distinction between social and economic exchange is that social exchange engenders diffuse obligations, whereas those in economic exchange are specified in an implicit or explicit contract. For economic transactions that are not immediately completed, like purchases in stores, the terms of the exchange are agreed upon in advance by both parties, and major agreements are formalized in a contract that specifies the precise nature of the obligations of both parties and when any outstanding debts are due. The favors in social exchange, by contrast, create diffuse obligations, to be discharged at some unspecified future date. If a couple give a dinner party, for instance, they have no agreement on when and where or even whether the guests will invite them back, though their relations may be weakened if they do not, or if they do so too late or too soon. The diffuseness of the obligations implies that large-scale social exchange is not likely to occur unless firm social bonds rooted in trust have been established.

In the absence of legal obligations to make a return for benefits received, the initial problem of new acquaintances is to prove themselves trustworthy in social exchange. This typically occurs as exchange relations evolve in a slow process, starting with minor transactions entailing little risk and requiring little trust. The mutual discharge of obligations and reciprocation profit both parties and prove them increasingly trustworthy as favors are regularly reciprocated. The growing mutual advantages gained from the association fortify their social bond. This may appear to be merely a by-product of social exchange, but it is, in fact, its most important product.

Implicit in discussions of social exchange is an element of rationality, if not calculation, which may give the impression that social exchange theory is simply a version of rational choice theory. However, this impression is misleading. To be sure, social exchange does imply some rational pursuit of rewards, but the prime benefit sought, once the friendship bond of mutual support and trust is clearly established, is the rewarding experience derived from the association itself. Any material benefits exchanged are incidental and of significance largely as tokens of the friendship.

✳✳✳

I conceptualize processes of social association as occurring in the relation between two persons. Accordingly, the exchange theory just presented analyzes exchange processes in dyads. . . . Ekeh (1974) has criticized my and Homans's (1961) exchange theory as individualistic, ignoring the difference between my concern with social structure and Homans's psychological reductionism. His criticism centers on the analysis of dyadic exchange. He contrasts the concept of restricted or two-party exchange unfavorably with Lévi-Strauss's (1949) generalized or multiparty exchange. Ekeh (1974: 62–65) considers the latter (multiparty) exchange

more Durkheimian, owing to its concern with structural integration, whereas he dismisses dyadic exchange as individualistic and thus lacking a structural focus.

There is good reason that I, as a structural sociologist, prefer restricted dyadic to generalized multiparty exchange. Generalized exchange refers to the prevailing practice that all members of a tribe or group freely provide benefits to other members without looking for any return from the person to whom the contribution is made. Since doing favors for others is socially expected, it is in effect a group norm. Conformity with this norm is the reason that all group members receive favors in the long run and solidarity is strengthened. My criticism of generalized exchange is that it is simply another name for conformity to group norms and consequently commits the tautological fallacy of explaining social conduct in terms of social norms demanding this conduct.[1] Generalized exchange thereby dispenses with the crucial insight of exchange theory that interpersonal relations are not contingent on social norms, because gradually expanding reciprocity supplies a mechanism for establishing and maintaining them and engendering trust to boot.

That my analysis of social exchange is confined to exchange processes that occur in dyads does not mean that the social context in which these processes occur can be ignored, since it does influence them. Actually, exchange processes are affected by several contexts of widening social circles. The most immediate social context is the groups to which the dyads belong, which exert two distinct influences on dyadic exchange.

First, a group's network structure defines the alternative opportunities for exchange relations various persons have and thereby affects the outcomes of persons in different network positions. (Exchange processes, in turn, may alter the network structure.) Experiments performed by Cook and her colleagues indicate that networks that provide alternative exchange partners to one person but not to others increase the bargaining power of this person in dyadic exchanges (see, for example, Cook, Gillmore, and Tamagishi 1983).

A second influence of the immediate social context is that it discourages failure to reciprocate for benefits received by social disapproval of such ingratitude. I realize that my reference to social disapproval, which implies social pressure, sounds as if I attributed exchange to group norms, for which I criticized the principle of generalized exchange. There is a major difference, however. If the practice of making a contribution freely to any group member without expecting a return from that member is explained by the cultural norm to do so, the *explicans* cannot explain the *explicandum*, because the two are redundant. But exchange is explained not by social pressures but by the returns it brings, including pleasant company or friendship as well as possibly tangible benefits. Social exchange, however, cannot prevail if trust, once established, is violated, and social disapproval discourages its violation. Social pressures do not explain—account for—reciprocal exchange, but they help to sustain it.

The influence of the wider social circles—the population structure of a neighborhood, community, or entire society—depends on the extent to which the population distributions of the encompassing social structure penetrate into the substructures of face-to-face groups. Many of the differences in society's population structure are the result of differences among rather than within substructures on successive levels. As a result, face-to-face groups are less differentiated than their encompassing social structures. Multilevel structural analysis discloses how much differentiation in various dimensions penetrates into the substructures of interpersonal relations. Greater homophily in segregated substructures promotes ingroup relations, but despite much segregation, some differentiation penetrates to the lowest level of interpersonal relations. Consequently, although ingroup relations prevail in daily social intercourse, intergroup relations also regularly occur.

The common occurrence of intergroup relations is revealed in a study by Marsden (1990) that applies my theoretical scheme to the egocentric face-to-face networks of a sample of the American population. He initially distinguishes a demand-side view of networks in terms of preferences for various kinds of associates from a supply-side view, like my theory's, in terms of opportunities for associating with diverse others. On the basis of previous research on the composition of families and work places, we know that families are more diverse in age and sex but less diverse in ethnic and religious affiliation than associates at work. Accordingly, Marsden hypothesizes more intergroup relations in respect to age and sex and fewer intergroup relations in respect to ethnic and religious affiliation between relatives than between fellow workers. The results support these hypotheses, which stipulate intergroup as well as ingroup relations even between close associates. Marsden concludes that my macro-structural opportunity theory is applicable to the study of the relations in microstructures, contrary to what I myself had stated.

I am pleased that the theory can be used in the investigation of face-to-face networks, which I had questioned. One should note, however, that confining network analysis to the supply-side approach would fail to take full advantage of the possibilities for analysis the small scope of these networks provides. In the study of large populations, analysis and research cannot proceed without ignoring the complexities of social life by having to aggregate specific observations into gross concepts and measures, like heterogeneity, intersection, or intergroup relations. The subtle processes that govern face-to-face relations are admittedly (but inevitably) obscured by such aggregations. The study of interpersonal relations and small networks can directly analyze these processes and thereby contribute to our understanding of them.

Imbalance in Exchange

A paradox of social exchange is that it gives rise to both social bonds between peers and differentiation of status. This was the case for the ceremonial exchange of gifts in nonliterate societies, and it is the case for exchange processes in advanced industrial societies. To start by exemplifying the former, the Kula ceremonial gift exchange of the Trobriand Islanders, as discussed by Malinowski (1961: 92), "provides every man within its ring with a few friends near at hand, and with some friendly allies in far away, dangerous, foreign districts." A few pages later he states that "among the natives of the Kula . . . wealth is the indispensable appanage of social rank" (p. 97). Probably the extreme case of the significance of social exchange for differentiation of status is the famous potlatch of the Kwakiutl, a feast of reckless spending in which "status in associations and clans, and rank of every kind, are determined by the war of property" (Mauss 1954: 35).

A contemporary case of status differentiation resulting from social exchange was observed in the office of a federal government agency responsible for the enforcement of certain laws. The duties of the agents involved investigating private firms by auditing their books and conducting interviews, determining any legal violations and the action to be taken, and negotiating a settlement with the employer or a top manager. The work was quite complex, and agents often encountered problems. When they did, they were expected to consult their supervisor, but they tended to be reluctant to do so for fear of adversely affecting their annual rating by their supervisor. Instead, they usually consulted colleagues. Whereas officially prohibited, this practice was widespread and evidently tolerated. Although agents worked on different cases, one could observe all day long pairs or small clusters of persons in deep discussions, most of which dealt with problems of their cases. Lunch periods were filled with such discussions.

The observation of these consultations originally gave me the idea of social exchange. To cite the central passage (Blau 1955: 108):[2]

A consultation can be considered an exchange of values; both participants gain something and both have to pay a price. The questioning agent is enabled to perform better than he could otherwise have done, without exposing his difficulties to the supervisor. By asking for advice, he implicitly pays his respect to the superior proficiency of his colleague. This acknowledgment of inferiority is the cost of receiving assistance. The consultant gains prestige, in return for which he is willing

to devote some time to the consultation and permit it to disrupt his own work. The following remark illustrates this: 'I like giving advice. It's flattering, I suppose, if you feel that the others come to you for advice.'

The principle of marginal utility applies to these exchanges. Although most agents liked being consulted, for those frequently asked for advice the gain in informal status of an additional consultation diminished and the cost in repeated interruptions of one's own work increased. As the most popular consultant said to me when asked about being consulted, "I never object, although sometimes it's annoying." The principle also applies to agents who frequently need advice, but in reverse, of course.

Repeated admissions of needing advice undermine one's self-confidence and standing in the group, particularly if an oft-interrupted consultant expresses some impatience or annoyance. To forestall such experiences, most agents establish partnerships of mutual consultation, reserving consulting the most expert colleagues for their most difficult problems. Since agents often have tentative solutions for their problems and need not so much an answer as assurance that theirs is correct, a colleague whose expertise is not superior to one's own can provide such support.

The most expert agents face a different dilemma: asking for advice or even for confirmation of their tentative solutions may well endanger their superior standing as experts. Making official decisions in a difficult case on one's own can easily raise doubts and questions in a person's mind, even an expert's. One way to cope with this situation is to stop going over it again and again in one's head and instead telling some colleagues about the interesting problems that have arisen in a given case and discussing how they might be solved, possibly over lunch if not in the office.

Such "thinking out loud" may well stimulate new associations and ideas one would not have come up with on one's own, particularly as the listeners are also experienced agents, who might raise objections if one is on the wrong track, and whose assent implicit in attentive listening and interested questions conveys approval. In contrast to asking for advice, telling colleagues about interesting problems in a case and how they might be solved enhances the respect of one's colleagues, though it is, in effect, a subtle form of asking colleagues to corroborate one's own provisional decisions.

***

To put the underlying principles of imbalanced and balanced exchange into general terms, rendering important services or providing valued benefactions is a claim to superior status. Reciprocation denies this claim, and excessive returns make a counterclaim, which can lead to a potlatch-like war of seeking to outdo one another to stay ahead. Failure to reciprocate by discharging one's obligations validates the claim and acknowledges the other's superiority in return for the benefits received and in the hope of continuing to receive them. Thus, the contingency that determines whether social exchanges lead to friendships between peers or superordination and subordination is whether benefits received are reciprocated or not. This, in turn, depends on whether one of the two parties has superior resources of the kind that are in contention (which was professional competence in the case of agents).[3]

In a seminal article, Emerson (1962) specified conditions in which balance in social exchange can be restored. I have slightly modified his scheme to conceptualize it as four alternatives to becoming dependent on a person's influence who has some services to offer that others need or want. First, they can give him something he needs or wants enough to reciprocate by satisfying their wishes, provided that they have resources that meet his needs. Second, they can obtain the needed benefits elsewhere, assuming that they have access to alternative sources of these benefits. These two possibilities, if recurring, result in reciprocal exchange relations between peers. Third, they can coerce him to give them what they want. This involves domination by force and is outside the purview of exchange. Fourth, they can resign themselves to do without what they

thought they needed, which is Diogenes' solution for remaining independent.

If none of these four alternatives is available, the others become dependent on the supplier of the needed services and must defer to her to reciprocate for the benefits received lest she lose interest in continuing to provide them. Deference implies not only paying respect to another's superior ability, implicit in asking her help, but also deferring to her wishes in everyday intercourse. Thus, the social interaction among colleagues or in other groups that involves imbalances in social exchange gives rise to differentiation in the power to influence as well as in prestige, which is reflected in a stratified structure of informal status.

The illustration of instrumental assistance in a work group may have left the misleading impression that most social exchange involves instrumental benefits. Much of the social interaction, even among co-workers and still more outside a work situation, is social intercourse engaged in for its own sake. Hechter (1987: 33) states that people often join groups to pursue joint goods or common objectives, and he stresses that their joint achievement and, particularly, the intrinsic gratifications obtained from social associations among fellow members are the sources of group solidarity.[4]

Workers who organize in order to bargain collectively with their employer for higher wages exemplify joint efforts to achieve a common objective. It is in the interest of the group as a whole if workers who devote more energy to and prove more adept in this endeavor are allowed to take the leading role in their organizing effort. Thus, superior status based on past services prompts other workers to acknowledge and submit to the leadership of the one who seems to be most effective in making contributions to organizing the nascent union. Informal leadership is legitimated by the social approval of the rest of the group, and this approval is the return for past services and for the future contributions the leader is expected to make to the welfare of the group by helping to organize them.[5]

This fictitious description may well be idealized, but it is not completely inaccurate for the initial stage of workers getting together on their own to organize themselves for joint bargaining. To be sure, it is not applicable to formal positions of leadership, particularly not to the impersonal power their incumbents exercise. Thus, the description is not intended to depict the leadership of large national unions; indeed, it is designed as a contrast to them. Once a union has become a large, formal organization and its leaders have become persons of great power, a handful of workers with a grievance cannot on their own decide upon a course of action if the powerful leader is opposed. All they can do is organize a wildcat strike informally, as workers originally did, but now against both the union leadership and management. The point of this illustration is that the interpersonal power that develops in face-to-face relations is fundamentally different from the impersonal power to dominate large numbers, even in the rare cases when the latter emerged from the former.[6]

Endnotes

1. Cultural theories that explain social patterns in terms of norms and values are prone to commit this tautology. It is the same fallacy as that of psychological explanations of behavior in terms of instincts to engage in such behavior.

2. As indicated by the publication date, this was written long before the women's movement called attention to the implicit bias involved in referring to some unspecified person always by the masculine pronoun instead of using either he/she or even s/he (which I find deplorable) or alternating between feminine and masculine pronouns, as I have done. . . .

3. This analysis applies to processes of differentiation in informal status among persons whose formal status is essentially the same.

4. The achievement of joint goods raises the well-known free-rider problem (that persons may benefit from public goods without contributing to their production), which Hechter considers to have solved by distinguishing partly excludable goods from public goods. The former are not available to the entire public but only to group members. His major illustration is that one cannot enjoy the sociability in a group without having become a member and thus a contributor to that

sociability. But this solution does not work for instrumental objectives, as indicated by the case next discussed in the text.

5. Workers who fail to contribute to the organizing efforts of the new union would also benefit from its success, which illustrates the criticism I made in the last sentence of the preceding footnote that Hechter's (1987) concept of partial excludability does not solve the freeloader problem for joint instrumental objectives.

6. I am particularly critical of the inference made by conservative social scientists that the elite's domination of society's economy and government is earned as a return for the great contributions they have made to society. It is the counterpart of the assumption that oligopolistic corporations achieved their position in free competition.

References

Blau, Peter M. 1955. *The Dynamics of Bureaucracy*. Chicago: University of Chicago Press.

Cook, Karen S., Mary R. Gillmore, and Toshio Tamagishi. 1983. "The Distribution of Power in Exchange Networks." *American Journal of Sociology* 89:275–305.

Ekeh, Peter P. 1974. *Social Exchange Theory*. Cambridge, Mass.: Harvard University.

Emerson, Richard M. 1962. "Power-Dependence Relations." *American Sociological Review* 27:31–41.

Hechter, Michael. 1987. *Principles of Group Solidarity*. Berkeley: University of California Press.

Homans, George C. 1961. *Social Behavior*. New York: Harcourt, Brace, & World.

Lévi-Strauss, Claude. 1949. *Les structures élémentaires de la parenté*. Paris: Press Universitaires de France.

Malinowski, Bronislaw. 1961 (1922). *Argonauts of the Western Pacific*. New York: Dutton.

Marsden, Peter V. 1990. "Network Diversity, Substructures, and Opportunities for Contact." Pp. 396–410 in C. Calhoun, M. W. Meyer, and W. R. Scott (eds.), *Structures of Power and Constraint*. Cambridge: University Press.

Mauss, Marcel. 1954 (1925). *The Gift*. Glencoe, Ill.: Free Press.

XII. Feminist Theory

52
Doing Gender

Candace West and
Don H. Zimmerman

Distinguishing between sex and gender, Candace West (b. 1942) and Don H. Zimmerman (b. 1937) borrow insights from both Erving Goffman and Harold Garfinkel in making the claim that gender is the product of social interaction. They begin by stressing the fact that although in everyday life sex and gender are intertwined, it is necessary to analytically distinguish them. Gender is socially constructed, and in this regard it is appropriate to speak about "doing gender," for it ought to be construed as "a routine accomplishment embedded in everyday interaction." Central to their efforts at theoretical rethinking is an emphasis on the display of gender (borrowing from Goffman), sex categorization (using the insights of Garfinkel's famous study on the sex reassignment of Agnes), and accountability.

Perspectives on Sex and Gender

In Western societies, the accepted cultural perspective on gender views women and men as naturally and unequivocally defined categories of being (Garfinkel 1967, pp. 116–18) with distinctive psychological and behavioral propensities that can be predicted from their reproductive functions. Competent adult members of these societies see differences between the two as fundamental and enduring—differences seemingly supported by the division of labor into women's and men's work and an often elaborate differentiation of feminine and masculine attitudes and behaviors that are prominent fea-

tures of social organization. Things are the way they are by virtue of the fact that men are men and women are women—a division perceived to be natural and rooted in biology, producing in turn profound psychological, behavioral, and social consequences. The structural arrangements of a society are presumed to be responsive to these differences.

Analyses of sex and gender in the social sciences, though less likely to accept uncritically the naive biological determinism of the view just presented, often retain a conception of sex-linked behaviors and traits as essential properties of individuals (for good reviews, see Hochschild 1973; Tresemer 1975; Thorne 1980; Henley 1985). The "sex differences approach" (Thorne 1980) is more commonly attributed to psychologists than to sociologists, but the survey researcher who determines the "gender" of respondents on the basis of the sound of their voices over the telephone is also making trait-oriented assumptions. Reducing gender to a fixed set of psychological traits or to a unitary "variable" precludes serious consideration of the ways it is used to structure distinct domains of social experience (Stacey and Thorne 1985, pp. 307–8).

Taking a different tack, role theory has attended to the social construction of gender categories, called "sex roles" or, more recently, "gender roles" and has analyzed how these are learned and enacted. Beginning with Linton (1936) and continuing through the works of Parsons (Parsons 1951; Parsons and Bales 1955) and Komarovsky (1946, 1950), role theory has emphasized the social and dynamic aspect of role construction and enactment (Thorne 1980; Connell 1983). But at the level of face-to-face interaction, the application of role theory to gender poses problems of its own (for good reviews and critiques, see Connell 1983, 1985; Kessler, Ashendon, Connell, and Dowsett 1985;

Lopata and Thorne 1978; Thorne 1980; Stacey and Thorne 1985). Roles are *situated* identities—assumed and relinquished as the situation demands—rather than *master identities* (Hughes 1945), such as sex category, that cut across situations. Unlike most roles, such as "nurse," "doctor," and "patient" or "professor" and "student," gender has no specific site or organizational context.

Moreover, many roles are already gender marked, so that special qualifiers—such as "female doctor" or "male nurse"—must be added to exceptions to the rule. Thorne (1980) observes that conceptualizing gender as a role makes it difficult to assess its influence on other roles and reduces its explanatory usefulness in discussions of power and inequality. Drawing on Rubin (1975), Thorne calls for a reconceptualization of women and men as distinct social groups, constituted in "concrete, historically changing—and generally unequal—social relationships" (Thorne 1980, p. 11).

We argue that gender is not a set of traits, nor a variable, nor a role, but the product of social doings of some sort. What then is the social doing of gender? It is more than the continuous creation of the meaning of gender through human actions (Gerson and Peiss 1985). We claim that gender itself is constituted through interaction.[1] To develop the implications of our claim, we turn to Goffman's (1976) account of "gender display." Our object here is to explore how gender might be exhibited or portrayed through interaction, and thus be seen as "natural," while it is being produced as a socially organized achievement.

Gender Display

Goffman contends that when human beings interact with others in their environment, they assume that each possesses an "essential nature"—a nature that can be discerned through the "natural signs given off or expressed by them" (1976, p. 75). Femininity and masculinity are regarded as "prototypes of essential expression—something that can be conveyed fleetingly in any social situation and yet something that strikes at the most basic characterization of the individual" (1976, p. 75). The means through which we provide such expressions are "perfunctory, conventionalized acts" (1976, p. 69), which convey to others our regard for them, indicate our alignment in an encounter, and tentatively establish the terms of contact for that social situation. But they are also regarded as expressive behavior, testimony to our "essential natures."

Goffman (1976, pp. 69–70) sees *displays* as highly conventionalized behaviors structured as two-part exchanges of the statement-reply type, in which the presence or absence of symmetry can establish deference or dominance. These rituals are viewed as distinct from but articulated with more consequential activities, such as performing tasks or engaging in discourse. Hence, we have what he terms the "scheduling" of displays at junctures in activities, such as the beginning or end, to avoid interfering with the activities themselves. Goffman (1976, p. 69) formulates *gender display* as follows:

> If gender be defined as the culturally established correlates of sex (whether in consequence of biology or learning), then gender display refers to conventionalized portrayals of these correlates.

These gendered expressions might reveal clues to the underlying, fundamental dimensions of the female and male, but they are, in Goffman's view, optional performances. Masculine courtesies may or may not be offered and, if offered, may or may not be declined (1976, p. 71). Moreover, human beings "themselves employ the term 'expression', and conduct themselves to fit their own notions of expressivity" (1976, p. 75). Gender depictions are less a consequence of our "essential sexual natures" than interactional portrayals of what we would like to convey about sexual natures, using conventionalized gestures. Our *human* nature gives us the ability to learn to produce and recognize masculine and feminine gender displays—"a capacity [we] have by virtue of being persons, not males and females" (1976, p. 76).

Upon first inspection, it would appear that Goffman's formulation offers an engaging sociological corrective to existing formulations of gender. In his view, gender is a socially scripted dramatization of the culture's *idealization* of feminine and masculine natures, played for an audience that is well schooled in the presentational idiom. To continue the metaphor, there are scheduled performances presented in special locations, and like plays, they constitute introductions to or time out from more serious activities.

There are fundamental equivocations in this perspective. By segregating gender display from the serious business of interaction, Goffman obscures the effects of gender on a wide range of human activities. Gender is not merely something that happens in the nooks and crannies of interaction, fitted in here and there and not interfering with the serious business of life. While it is plausible to contend that gender displays—construed as conventionalized expressions—are optional, it does not seem plausible to say that we have the option of being seen by others as female or male.

It is necessary to move beyond the notion of gender display to consider what is involved in doing gender as an ongoing activity embedded in everyday interaction. Toward this end, we return to the distinctions among sex, sex category, and gender introduced earlier.

Sex, Sex Category, and Gender

Garfinkel's (1967, pp. 118–40) case study of Agnes, a transsexual raised as a boy who adopted a female identity at age 17 and underwent a sex reassignment operation several years later, demonstrates how gender is created through interaction and at the same time structures interaction. Agnes, whom Garfinkel characterized as a "practical methodologist," developed a number of procedures for passing as a "normal, natural female" both prior to and after her surgery. She had the practical task of managing the fact that she possessed male genitalia and that she lacked the social resources a girl's biography would presumably provide in everyday interaction. In short, she needed to display herself as a woman, simultaneously learning what it was to be a woman. Of necessity, this full-time pursuit took place at a time when most people's gender would be well-accredited and routinized. Agnes had to consciously contrive what the vast majority of women do without thinking. She was not "faking" what "real" women do naturally. She was obliged to analyze and figure out how to act within socially structured circumstances and conceptions of femininity that women born with appropriate biological credentials come to take for granted early on. As in the case of others who must "pass," such as transvestites, Kabuki actors, or Dustin Hoffman's "Tootsie," Agnes's case makes visible what culture has made invisible—the accomplishment of gender.

Garfinkel's (1967) discussion of Agnes does not explicitly separate three analytically distinct, although empirically overlapping, concepts—sex, sex category, and gender.

Sex

Agnes did not possess the socially agreed upon biological criteria for classification as a member of the female *sex*. Still, Agnes regarded herself as a female, albeit a female with a penis, which a woman ought not to possess. The penis, she insisted, was a "mistake" in need of remedy (Garfinkel 1967, pp. 126–27, 131–32). Like other competent members of our culture, Agnes honored the notion that there *are* "essential" biological criteria that unequivocally distinguish females from males. However, if we move away from the commonsense viewpoint, we discover that the reliability of these criteria is not beyond question (Money and Brennan 1968; Money and Erhardt 1972; Money and Ogunro 1974; Money and Tucker 1975). Moreover, other cultures have acknowledged the existence of "cross-genders" (Blackwood 1984; Williams 1986) and the possibility of more than two sexes (Hill 1935; Martin and Voorhies 1975, pp. 84–107; but see also Cucchiari 1981, pp. 32–35).

More central to our argument is Kessler and McKenna's (1978, pp. 1–6) point that genitalia are conventionally hidden from public inspection in everyday life; yet we continue through our social rounds to "observe" a world of two naturally, normally sexed persons. It is the *presumption* that essential criteria exist and would or should be there if looked for that provides the basis for sex categorization. Drawing on Garfinkel, Kessler and McKenna argue that "female" and "male" are cultural events—products of what they term the "gender attribution process"—rather than some collection of traits, behaviors, or even physical attributes. Illustratively they cite the child who, viewing a picture of someone clad in a suit and a tie, contends, "It's a man, because he has a pee-pee" (Kessler and McKenna 1978, p. 154). Translation: "He must have a pee-pee [an essential characteristic] because I see the *insignia* of a suit and tie." Neither initial sex assignment (pronouncement at birth as a female or male) nor the actual existence of essential criteria for that assignment (possession of a clitoris and vagina or penis and testicles) has much—if anything—to do with the identification of sex category in everyday life. There, Kessler and McKenna note, we operate with a moral certainty of a world of two sexes. We do not think, "Most persons with penises are men, but some may not be" or "Most persons who dress as men have penises." Rather, we take it for granted that sex and sex category are congruent—that knowing the latter, we can deduce the rest.

Sex Categorization

Agnes's claim to the categorical status of female, which she sustained by appropriate identificatory displays and other characteristics, could be *discredited* before her transsexual operation if her possession of a penis became known and after by her surgically constructed genitalia (see Raymond 1979, pp. 37, 138). In this regard, Agnes had to be continually alert to actual or potential threats to the security of her sex category. Her problem was not so much living up to some prototype of essential femininity but preserving her categorization as female. This task was made easy for her by a very powerful resource, namely, the process of commonsense categorization in everyday life.

The categorization of members of society into indigenous categories such as "girl" or "boy," or "woman" or "man," operates in a distinctively social way. The act of categorization does not involve a positive test, in the sense of a well-defined set of criteria that must be explicitly satisfied prior to making an identification. Rather, the application of membership categories relies on an "if-can" test in everyday interaction (Sacks 1972, pp.

332–35). This test stipulates that if people *can be seen* as members of relevant categories, *then categorize them that way*. That is, use the category that seems appropriate, except in the presence of discrepant information or obvious features that would rule out its use. This procedure is quite in keeping with the attitude of everyday life, which has us take appearances at face value unless we have special reason to doubt (Schutz 1943; Garfinkel 1967, pp. 272–77; Bernstein 1986).[2] It should be added that it is precisely when we have special reason to doubt that the issue of applying rigorous criteria arises, but it is rare, outside legal or bureaucratic contexts, to encounter insistence on positive tests (Garfinkel 1967, pp. 262–83; Wilson 1970).

Agnes's initial resource was the predisposition of those she encountered to take her appearance (her figure, clothing, hair style, and so on) as the undoubted appearance of a normal female. Her further resource was our cultural perspective on the properties of "natural, normally sexed persons." Garfinkel (1967, pp. 122–28) notes that in everyday life, we live in a world of two—and only two—sexes. This arrangement has a moral status, in that we include ourselves and others in it as "essentially, originally, in the first place, always have been, always will be, once and for all, in the final analysis, either 'male' or 'female' " (Garfinkel 1967, p. 122).

Consider the following case:

This issue reminds me of a visit I made to a computer store a couple of years ago. The person who answered my questions was truly a *salesperson*. I could not categorize him/her as a woman or a man. What did I look for? (1) Facial hair: She/he was smooth skinned, but some men have little or no facial hair. (This varies by race, Native Americans and Blacks often have none.) (2) Breasts: She/he was wearing a loose shirt that hung from his/her shoulders. And, as many women who suffered through a 1950s' adolescence know to their shame, women are often flat-chested. (3) Shoulders: His/hers were small and round for a man, broad for a woman. (4) Hands: Long and slender fingers, knuckles a bit large for a woman, small for a man. (5) Voice: Middle range, unexpressive for a woman, not at all the exaggerated tones some gay males affect.

(6) His/her treatment of me: Gave off no signs that would let me know if I were of the same or different sex as this person. There were not even any signs that he/she knew his/her sex would be difficult to categorize and I wondered about that even as I did my best to hide these questions so I would not embarrass him/her while we talked of computer paper. I left still not knowing the sex of my salesperson, and was disturbed by that unanswered question (child of my culture that I am). (Diane Margolis, personal communication)

What can this case tell us about situations such as Agnes's (cf. Morris 1974; Richards 1983) or the process of sex categorization in general? First, we infer from this description that the computer salesclerk's identificatory display was ambiguous, since she or he was not dressed or adorned in an unequivocally female or male fashion. It is when such a display *fails* to provide grounds for categorization that factors such as facial hair or tone of voice are assessed to determine membership in a sex category. Second, beyond the fact that this incident could be recalled after "a couple of years," the customer was not only "disturbed" by the ambiguity of the salesclerk's category but also assumed that to acknowledge this ambiguity would be embarrassing to the salesclerk. Not only do we want to know the sex category of those around us (to see it at a glance, perhaps), but we presume that others are displaying it for us, in as decisive a fashion as they can.

Gender

Agnes attempted to be "120 percent female" (Garfinkel 1967, p. 129), that is, unquestionably in all ways and at all times feminine. She thought she could protect herself from disclosure before and after surgical intervention by comporting herself in a feminine manner, but she also could have given herself away by overdoing her performance. Sex categorization and the accomplishment of gender are not the same. Agnes's categorization could be secure or suspect, but did not depend on whether or not she lived up to some ideal conception of femininity. Women can be seen as unfeminine, but that does not make them "unfemale." Agnes faced an ongoing task of *being* a woman—something beyond style of dress (an identificatory display) or allowing men to light her cigarette (a gender display). Her problem was to produce configurations of behavior that would be seen by others as normative gender behavior.

Agnes's strategy of "secret apprenticeship," through which she learned expected feminine decorum by carefully attending to her fiancé's criticisms of other women, was one means of masking incompetencies and simultaneously acquiring the needed skills (Garfinkel 1967, pp. 146–147). It was through her fiancé that Agnes learned that sunbathing on the lawn in front of her apartment was "offensive" (because it put her on display to other men). She also learned from his critiques of other women that she should not insist on having things her way and that she should not offer her opinions or claim equality with men (Garfinkel 1967, pp. 147–148). (Like other women in our society, Agnes learned something about power in the course of her "education.")

Popular culture abounds with books and magazines that compile idealized depictions of relations between women and men. Those focused on the etiquette of dating or prevailing standards of feminine comportment are meant to be of practical help in these matters. However, the use of any such source *as a manual of procedure* requires the assumption that doing gender merely involves making use of discrete, well-defined bundles of behavior that can simply be plugged into interactional situations to produce recognizable enactments of masculinity and femininity. The man "does" being masculine by, for example, taking the woman's arm to guide her across a street, and she "does" being feminine by consenting to be guided and not initiating such behavior with a man.

Agnes could perhaps have used such sources as manuals, but, we contend, doing gender is not so easily regimented (Mithers 1982; Morris 1974). Such sources may list and describe the sorts of behaviors that mark or display gender, but they are necessarily incomplete (Garfinkel 1967, pp. 66–75; Wieder 1974, pp. 183–214; Zimmerman and Wieder 1970, pp. 285–98). And to be successful, marking or displaying gender must be finely fitted to situations and modified or transformed as the occasion demands. Doing gender consists of managing such occasions so that, whatever the particulars, the outcome is seen and seeable in context as gender-appropriate or, as the case may be, gender-*in*appropriate, that is, *accountable*.

Gender and Accountability

As Heritage (1984, pp. 136–37) notes, members of society regularly engage in "descriptive accountings of states of affairs to one another," and such accounts are both serious and consequential. These descriptions name, characterize, formulate, explain, excuse, excoriate, or merely take notice of some circumstance or activity and thus place it within some social framework (locating it relative to other activities, like and unlike).

Such descriptions are themselves accountable, and societal members orient to the fact that their activities are subject to comment. Actions are often designed with an eye to their accountability, that is, how they might look and how they might be characterized. The notion of accountability also encompasses those actions undertaken so that they are specifically unremarkable and thus not worthy of more than a passing remark, because they are seen to be in accord with culturally approved standards.

Heritage (1984, p. 179) observes that the process of rendering something accountable is interactional in character:

> [This] permits actors to design their actions in relation to their circumstances so as to permit others, by methodically taking account of circumstances, to recognize the action for what it is.

The key word here is *circumstances*. One circumstance that attends virtually all actions is the sex category of the actor. As Garfinkel (1967, p. 118) comments:

> [T]he work and socially structured occasions of sexual passing were obstinately unyielding to [Agnes's] attempts to routinize the grounds of daily activities. This obstinacy points to the *omnirelevance* of sexual status to affairs of daily life as an invariant but unnoticed background in the texture of relevances that compose

the changing actual scenes of everyday life, (italics added)

If sex category is omnirelevant (or even approaches being so), then a person engaged in virtually any activity may be held accountable for performance of that activity as a *woman* or a *man*, and their incumbency in one or the other sex category can be used to legitimate or discredit their other activities (Berger, Cohen, and Zelditch 1972; Berger, Conner, and Fisek 1974; Berger, Fisek, Norman, and Zelditch 1977; Humphreys and Berger 1981). Accordingly, virtually any activity can be assessed as to its womanly or manly nature. And note, to "do" gender is not always to live up to normative conceptions of femininity or masculinity; it is to engage in behavior *at the risk of gender assessment*. While it is individuals who do gender, the enterprise is fundamentally interactional and institutional in character, for accountability is a feature of social relationships and its idiom is drawn from the institutional arena in which those relationships are enacted. If this be the case, can we ever *not* do gender? Insofar as a society is partitioned by "essential" differences between women and men and placement in a sex category is both relevant and enforced, doing gender is unavoidable.

Endnotes

1. This is not to say that gender is a singular "thing," omnipresent in the same form historically or in every situation. Because normative conceptions of appropriate attitudes and activities for sex categories can vary across cultures and historical moments, the management of situated conduct in light of those expectations can take many different forms.

2. Bernstein (1986) reports an unusual case of espionage in which a man passing as a woman convinced a lover that he/she had given birth to "their" child, who, the lover thought, "looked like" him.

References

Berger, Joseph, Bernard P. Cohen, and Morris Zelditch, Jr. 1972. "Status Characteristics and Social Interaction." *American Sociological Review* 37:241–55.

Berger, Joseph, Thomas L. Conner, and M. Hamit Fisek, eds. 1974. *Expectation States*

Theory: A Theoretical Research Program. Cambridge: Winthrop.

Berger, Joseph, M. Hamit Fisek, Robert Z. Norman, and Morris Zelditch, Jr. 1977. *Status Characteristics and Social Interaction: An Expectation States Approach.* New York: Elsevier.

Bernstein, Richard. 1986. "France Jails 2 in Odd Case of Espionage." *New York Times* (May 11).

Blackwood, Evelyn. 1984. "Sexuality and Gender in Certain Native American Tribes: The Case of Cross-Gender Females." *Signs: Journal of Women in Culture and Society* 10:27–42.

Connell, R. W. 1983. *Which Way Is Up?* Sydney: Allen & Unwin.

——. 1985. "Theorizing Gender." *Sociology* 19:260–72.

Cucchiari, Salvatore. 1981. "The Gender Revolution and the Transition From Bisexual Horde to Patrilocal Band: The Origins of Gender Hierarchy." Pp. 31–79 in *Sexual Meanings: The Cultural Construction of Gender and Sexuality,* edited by S. B. Ortner and H. Whitehead. New York: Cambridge.

Garfinkel, Harold. 1967. *Studies in Ethnomethodology.* Englewood Cliffs, NJ: Prentice-Hall.

Gerson, Judith M., and Kathy Peiss. 1985. "Boundaries, Negotiation, Consciousness: Reconceptualizing Gender Relations." *Social Problems* 32:317–31.

Goffman 1976. "Gender Display." *Studies in the Anthropology of Visual Communication* 3:69–77.

Henley, Nancy M. 1985. "Psychology and Gender." *Signs: Journal of Women in Culture and Society* 11:101–119.

Heritage, John. 1984. *Garfinkel and Ethnomethodology.* Cambridge, England: Polity Press.

Hill, W. W. 1935. "The Status of the Hermaphrodite and Transvestite in Navaho Culture." *American Anthropologist* 37:273–79.

Hochschild, Arlie R. 1973. "A Review of Sex Roles Research." *American Journal of Sociology* 78:1011–29.

Hughes, Everett C. 1945. "Dilemmas and Contradictions of Status." *American Journal of Sociology* 50:353–59.

Humphreys, Paul, and Joseph Berger. 1981. "Theoretical Consequences of the Status Characteristics Formulation." *American Journal of Sociology* 86:953–83.

Kessler, Suzanne J., and Wendy McKenna. 1978. *Gender: An Ethnomethodological Approach.* New York: Wiley.

Kessler, S., D. J. Ashendon, R. W. Connell, and G. W. Dowsett. 1985. "Gender Relations in Secondary Schooling." *Sociology of Education* 58:34–48.

Komarovsky, Mirra. 1946. "Cultural Contradictions and Sex Roles." *American Journal of Sociology* 52:184–89.

——. 1950. "Functional Analysis of Sex Roles." *American Sociological Review* 15:508–16.

Linton, Ralph. 1936. *The Study of Man.* New York: Appleton-Century.

Lopata, Helen Z., and Barrie Thorne. 1978. "On the Term 'Sex Roles.' " *Signs: Journal of Women in Culture and Society* 3:718–21.

Martin, M. Kay, and Barbara Voorhies. 1975. *Female of the Species.* New York: Columbia University Press.

Mithers, Carol L. 1982. "My Life as a Man." *The Village Voice* 27 (October 5):1ff.

Money, John, and John G. Brennan. 1968. "Sexual Dimorphism in the Psychology of Female Transsexuals." *Journal of Nervous and Mental Disease* 147:487–99.

Money, John, and Charles Ogunro. 1974. "Behavioral Sexology: Ten Cases of Genetic Male Intersexuality with Impaired Prenatal and Pubertal Androgenization," *Archives of Sexual Behavior* 3:181–206.

Money, John, and Patricia Tucker. 1975. *Sexual Signatures.* Boston: Little, Brown.

Money, John, and Anke, A. Erhardt. 1972. *Man and Woman/Boy and Girl.* Baltimore: Johns Hopkins.

Morris, Jan. 1974. *Conundrum.* New York: Harcourt Brace Jovanovich.

Parsons, Talcott. 1951. *The Social System.* New York: Free Press.

Parsons, Talcott, and Robert F. Bales. 1955. *Family, Socialization and Interaction Process.* New York: Free Press.

Raymond, Janice G. 1979. *The Transsexual Empire.* Boston: Beacon.

Richards, Renee (with John Ames). 1983. *Second Serve: The Renee Richards Story.* New York: Stein and Day.

Rubin, Gayle. 1975. "The Traffic in Women: Notes on the 'Political Economy' of Sex." Pp. 157–210 in *Toward an Anthropology of Women,* edited by R. Reiter. New York: Monthly Review Press.

Sacks, Harvey. 1972. "On the Analyzability of Stories by Children." Pp. 325–45 in *Directions in Sociolinguistics,* edited by J. J. Gumperz and D. Hymes. New York: Holt, Rinehart & Winston.

Schutz, Alfred. 1943. "The Problem of Rationality in the Social World." *Economics* 10:130–49.

Stacey, Judith, and Barrie Thorne. 1985. "The Missing Feminist Revolution in Sociology." *Social Problems* 32:301–16.

Thorne, Barrie. 1980. "Gender . . . How Is It Best Conceptualized?" Unpublished manuscript.

Tresemer, David. 1975. "Assumptions Made About Gender Roles." Pp. 308–39 in *Another Voice: Feminist Perspectives on Social Life and Social Science*, edited by M. Millman and R. M. Kantex. New York: Anchor/Doubleday.

Wieder, D. Lawrence. 1974. *Language and Social Reality: The Case of Telling the Convict Code*. The Hague: Mouton.

Williams, Walter L. 1986. *The Spirit and the Flesh: Sexual Diversity in American Indian Culture*. Boston: Beacon.

Wilson, Thomas P. 1970. "Conceptions of Interaction and Forms of Sociological Explanation." *American Sociological Review* 35:697–710.

Zimmerman, Don H., and D. Lawrence Wieder. 1970. "Ethnomethodology and the Problem of Order: Comment on Denzin." Pp. 287–95 in *Understanding Everyday Life*, edited by J. Denzin. Chicago: Aldine.

Reprinted from *Gender & Society*, June 1987, with permission of Sage Publications. ✦

53
Subversive Bodily Acts

Judith Butler

Feminist theory in sociology has been open to the influence of thinkers from outside of the discipline. Judith Butler (b. 1957) is an emblematic example of a nonsociologist who has had a marked impact on feminist theory in sociology. Her writing is engaging, provocative, and clearly shaped by postmodernism, as this selection from her book *Gender Trouble* (1990) attests. Butler is intent on calling into question the taken-for-granted nature of gender categories as obdurate realities, illustrating instead their inherent fluidity and variability. As such, she encourages us to view gender as socially constructed, or as a performative accomplishment. In her discussion, Butler is particularly interested in transgressing boundaries—as seen, for example, in her treatment of female impersonators. In exploring the complex interrelationships that weave sex, gender, and sexuality, she calls for a reappreciation of the significance of the body.

> Garbo 'got in drag' whenever she took some heavy glamour part, whenever she melted in or out of a man's arms, whenever she simply let that heavenly-flexed neck . . . bear the weight of her thrown-back head. . . . How resplendent seems the art of acting! It is all *impersonation*, whether the sex underneath is true or not.
>
> —Parker Tyler, "The Garbo Image," quoted in Esther Newton, *Mother Camp*

Categories of true sex, discrete gender, and specific sexuality have constituted the stable point of reference for a great deal of feminist theory and politics. These constructs of identity serve as the points of epistemic departure from which theory emerges and politics itself is shaped. In the case of feminism, politics is ostensibly shaped to express the interests, the perspectives, of "women." But is there a political shape to "women," as it were, that precedes and prefigures the political elaboration of their interests and epistemic point of view? How is that identity shaped, and is it a political shaping that takes the very morphology and boundary of the sexed body as the ground, surface, or site of cultural inscription? What circumscribes that site as "the female body"? Is "the body" or "the sexed body" the firm foundation on which gender and systems of compulsory sexuality operate? Or is "the body" itself shaped by political forces with strategic interests in keeping that body bounded and constituted by the markers of sex?

The sex/gender distinction and the category of sex itself appear to presuppose a generalization of "the body" that preexists the acquisition of its sexed significance. This "body" often appears to be a passive medium that is signified by an inscription from a cultural source figured as "external" to that body. Any theory of the culturally constructed body, however, ought to question "the body" as a construct of suspect generality when it is figured as passive and prior to discourse. There are Christian and Cartesian precedents to such views which, prior to the emergence of vitalistic biologies in the nineteenth century, understand "the body" as so much inert matter, signifying nothing or, more specifically, signifying a profane void, the fallen state: deception, sin, the premonitional metaphorics of hell and the eternal feminine. There are many occasions in both Sartre's and Beauvoir's work where "the body" is figured as a mute facticity, anticipating some meaning that can be attributed only by a transcendent consciousness, understood in Cartesian terms as radically immaterial. But what establishes this dualism for us? What separates off "the body" as indifferent to signification, and signification itself as the act of a radically disembodied consciousness or, rather, the act that radically disembodies that consciousness? To what extent is that Cartesian dualism presupposed in phenomenology adapted to the structuralist frame in which mind/body is redescribed as culture/nature? With respect to gender discourse, to what extent do these problematic dualisms still operate within the very descriptions that are supposed to lead us out of that binarism and its implicit hierarchy? How are the contours of the body clearly marked as the taken-for-granted ground or surface upon which gender significations are inscribed, a mere facticity devoid of value, prior to significance?

Wittig suggests that a culturally specific epistemic *a priori* establishes the naturalness of "sex." But by what enigmatic means has "the body" been accepted as a *prima facie* given that admits of no genealogy? Even within Foucault's essay on the very theme of genealogy, the body is figured as a surface and the scene of a cultural inscription: "the body is the inscribed surface of events."[1] The task of genealogy, he claims, is "to expose a body totally imprinted by history." His sentence continues, however, by referring to the goal of "history"—here clearly understood on the model of Freud's "civilization"—as the "destruction of the body" (148). Forces and impulses with multiple directionalities are precisely that which history both destroys and preserves through the *entstehung* (historical event) of inscription. As "a volume in perpetual disintegration" (148), the body is always under siege, suffering destruction by the very terms of history. And history is the creation of values and meanings by a signifying practice that requires the subjection of the body. This corporeal destruction is necessary to produce the speaking subject and its significations. This is a body, described through the language of surface and force, weakened through a "single drama" of domination, inscription, and creation (150). This is not the *modus vivendi* of one kind of history rather than another, but is, for Foucault, "history" (148) in its essential and repressive gesture.

Although Foucault writes, "Nothing in man [*sic*]—not even his body—is sufficiently stable to serve as the basis for self-recognition or for understanding other men [*sic*]" (153), he nevertheless points to the constancy of cultural inscription as a "single drama" that acts on the body. If the creation of values, that historical mode of signification, requires the destruction of the body, much as the instrument of torture in Kafka's *In the Penal Colony* destroys the body on which it writes, then there must be a body

prior to that inscription, stable and self-identical, subject to that sacrificial destruction. In a sense, for Foucault, as for Nietzsche, cultural values emerge as the result of an inscription on the body, understood as a medium, indeed, a blank page; in order for this inscription to signify, however, that medium must itself be destroyed—that is, fully transvalued into a sublimated domain of values. Within the metaphorics of this notion of cultural values is the figure of history as a relentless writing instrument, and the body as the medium which must be destroyed and transfigured in order for "culture" to emerge.

By maintaining a body prior to its cultural inscription, Foucault appears to assume a materiality prior to signification and form. Because this distinction operates as essential to the task of genealogy as he defines it, the distinction itself is precluded as an object of genealogical investigation. Occasionally in his analysis of Herculine, Foucault subscribes to a prediscursive multiplicity of bodily forces that break through the surface of the body to disrupt the regulating practices of cultural coherence imposed upon that body by a power regime, understood as a vicissitude of "history." If the presumption of some kind of precategorial source of disruption is refused, is it still possible to give a genealogical account of the demarcation of the body as such as a signifying practice? This demarcation is not initiated by a reified history or by a subject. This marking is the result of a diffuse and active structuring of the social field. This signifying practice effects a social space for and of the body within certain regulatory grids of intelligibility.

Mary Douglas' *Purity and Danger* suggests that the very contours of "the body" are established through markings that seek to establish specific codes of cultural coherence. Any discourse that establishes the boundaries of the body serves the purpose of instating and naturalizing certain taboos regarding the appropriate limits, postures, and modes of exchange that define what it is that constitutes bodies:

ideas about separating, purifying, demarcating and punishing transgressions have as their main function to impose system on an inherently untidy experience. It is only by exaggerating the difference between within and without, above and below, male and female, with and against, that a semblance of order is created.[2]

Although Douglas clearly subscribes to a structuralist distinction between an inherently unruly nature and an order imposed by cultural means, the "untidiness" to which she refers can be redescribed as a region of *cultural* unruliness and disorder. Assuming the inevitably binary structure of the nature/culture distinction, Douglas cannot point toward an alternative configuration of culture in which such distinctions become malleable or proliferate beyond the binary frame. Her analysis, however, provides a possible point of departure for understanding the relationship by which social taboos institute and maintain the boundaries of the body as such. Her analysis suggests that what constitutes the limit of the body is never merely material, but that the surface, the skin, is systemically signified by taboos and anticipated transgressions; indeed, the boundaries of the body become, within her analysis, the limits of the social *per se*. A poststructuralist appropriation of her view might well understand the boundaries of the body as the limits of the socially *hegemonic*. In a variety of cultures, she maintains, there are

pollution powers which inhere in the structure of ideas itself and which punish a symbolic breaking of that which should be joined or joining of that which should be separate. It follows from this that pollution is a type of danger which is not likely to occur except where the lines of structure, cosmic or social, are clearly defined.

A polluting person is always in the wrong. He [sic] has developed some wrong condition or simply crossed over some line which should not have been crossed and this displacement unleashes danger for someone.[3]

In a sense, Simon Watney has identified the contemporary construction of "the Polluting person" as the person with AIDS in his *Policing Desire: AIDS, Pornography, and the Media*.[4] Not only is the illness figured as the "gay disease," but throughout the media's hysterical and homophobic response to the illness there is a tactical construction of a continuity between the polluted status of the homosexual by virtue of the boundary-trespass that *is* homosexuality and the disease as a specific modality of homosexual pollution. That the disease is transmitted through the exchange of bodily fluids suggests within the sensationalist graphics of homophobic signifying systems the dangers that permeable bodily boundaries present to the social order as such. Douglas remarks that "the body is a model that can stand for any bounded system. Its boundaries can represent any boundaries which are threatened or precarious."[5] And she asks a question which one might have expected to read in Foucault: "Why should bodily margins be thought to be specifically invested with power and danger?"[6]

Douglas suggests that all social systems are vulnerable at their margins, and that all margins are accordingly considered dangerous. If the body is synecdochal for the social system *per se* or a site in which open systems converge, then any kind of unregulated permeability constitutes a site of pollution and endangerment. Since anal and oral sex among men clearly establishes certain kinds of bodily permeabilities unsanctioned by the hegemonic order, male homosexuality would, within such a hegemonic point of view, constitute a site of danger and pollution, prior to and regardless of the cultural presence of AIDS. Similarly, the "polluted" status of lesbians, regardless of their low-risk status with respect to AIDS, brings into relief the dangers of their bodily exchanges. Significantly, being "outside" the hegemonic order does not signify being "in" a state of filthy and untidy nature. Paradoxically homosexuality is almost always conceived within the homophobic signifying economy as *both* uncivilized and unnatural.

The construction of stable bodily contours relies upon fixed sites of corporeal permeability and impermeability. Those sexual practices in both homosexual and heterosexual contexts that open surfaces and orifices to erotic signification or close down others effectively reinscribe the boundaries of the body along new cultural lines. Anal sex among men is an example as is the radical re-membering of the body in Wittig's *The Lesbian Body*. Douglas alludes to "a kind of sex pollution which expresses a desire to keep the body (physical and social) intact,"[7] suggesting that the naturalized notion of "the" body is itself a consequence of taboos that render that body discrete by virtue of its stable boundaries. Further, the rites of passage that govern various bodily orifices presuppose a heterosexual construction of gendered exchange, positions, and erotic possibilities. The deregulation of such exchanges accordingly disrupts the very boundaries that determine what it is to be a body at all. Indeed, the critical inquiry that traces the regulatory practices within which bodily contours are constructed constitutes precisely the genealogy of "the body" in its discreteness that might further radicalize Foucault's theory.[8]

Significantly, Kristeva's discussion of abjection in *The Powers of Horror* begins to suggest the uses of this structuralist notion of a boundary-constituting taboo for the purposes of constructing a discrete subject through exclusion.[9] The "abject" designates that which has been expelled from the body, discharged as excrement, literally rendered "Other." This appears as an expulsion of alien elements, but the alien is effectively established through this expulsion. The construction of the "not-me" as the abject establishes the boundaries of the body which are also the first contours of the subject. Kristeva writes:

> *nausea* makes me balk at that milk cream, separates me from the mother and father who proffer it. "I" want none of that element, sign of their desire; "I" do not want to listen, "I" do not assimilate it, "I" expel it. But since the food is not an "other" for "me," who am only in their desire, I expel *myself*, I spit *myself* out, I abject *myself* within the same motion through which "I" claim to establish myself.[10]

The boundary of the body as well as the distinction between internal and external is established through the ejection and transvaluation of something originally part of identity into a defiling otherness. As Iris

Young has suggested in her use of Kristeva to understand sexism, homophobia, and racism, the repudiation of bodies for their sex, sexuality, and/or color is an "expulsion" followed by a "repulsion" that founds and consolidates culturally hegemonic identities along sex/race/sexuality axes of differentiation.[11] Young's appropriation of Kristeva shows how the operation of repulsion can consolidate "identities" founded on the instituting of the "Other" or a set of Others through exclusion and domination. What constitutes through division the "inner" and "outer" worlds of the subject is a border and boundary tenuously maintained for the purposes of social regulation and control. The boundary between the inner and outer is confounded by those excremental passages in which the inner effectively becomes outer, and this excreting function becomes, as it were, the model by which other forms of identity-differentiation are accomplished. In effect, this is the mode by which Others become shit. For inner and outer worlds to remain utterly distinct, the entire surface of the body would have to achieve an impossible impermeability. This sealing of its surfaces would constitute the seamless boundary of the subject; but this enclosure would invariably be exploded by precisely that excremental filth that it fears.

Regardless of the compelling metaphorrs of the spatial distinction of inner and outer, they remain linguistic terms that facilitate and articulate a set of fantasies, feared and desired. "Inner" and "outer" make sense only with reference to a mediating boundary that strives for stability. And this stability, this coherence, is determined in large part by cultural orders that sanction the subject and compel its differentiation from the abject. Hence, "inner" and "outer" constitute a binary distinction that stabilizes and consolidates the coherent subject. When that subject is challenged, the meaning and necessity of the terms are subject to displacement. If the "inner world" no longer designates a topos, then the internal fixity of the self and, indeed, the internal locale of gender identity, become similarly suspect. The critical question is not *how* did that identity become *internalized*? as if internalization were a process or a mechanism that might be descriptively reconstructed. Rather, the question is: From what strategic position in public discourse and for what reasons has the trope of interiority and the disjunctive binary of inner/outer taken hold? In what language is "inner space" figured? What kind of figuration is it, and through what figure of the body is it signified? How does a body figure on its surface the very invisibility of its hidden depth?

From Interiority to Gender Performatives

In *Discipline and Punish* Foucault challenges the language of internalization as it operates in the service of the disciplinary regime of the subjection and subjectivation of criminals.[12] Although Foucault objected to what he understood to be the psychoanalytic belief in the "inner" truth of sex in *The History of Sexuality*, he turns to a criticism of the doctrine of internalization for separate purposes in the context of his history of criminology. In a sense, *Discipline and Punish* can be read as Foucault's effort to rewrite Nietzsche's doctrine of internalization in *On the Genealogy of Morals* on the model of *inscription*. In the context of prisoners, Foucault writes, the strategy has been not to enforce a repression of their desires, but to compel their bodies to signify the prohibitive law as their very essence, style, and necessity. That law is not literally internalized, but incorporated, with the consequence that bodies are produced which signify that law on and through the body; there the law is manifest as the essence of their selves, the meaning of their soul, their conscience, the law of their desire. In effect, the law is at once fully manifest and fully latent, for it never appears as external to the bodies it subjects and subjectivates. Foucault writes:

> It would be wrong to say that the soul is an illusion, or an ideological effect. On the contrary, it exists, it has a reality, it is produced permanently *around, on, within*, the body by the functioning of a power that is exercised on those that are punished (my emphasis).[13]

The figure of the interior soul understood as "within" the body is signified through its inscription *on* the body, even though its primary mode of signification is through its very absence, its potent invisibility. The effect of a structuring inner space is produced through the signification of a body as a vital and sacred enclosure. The soul is precisely what the body lacks; hence, the body presents itself as a signifying lack. That lack which *is* the body signifies the soul as that which cannot show. In this sense, then, the soul is a surface signification that contests and displaces the inner/outer distinction itself, a figure of interior psychic space inscribed *on* the body as a social signification that perpetually renounces itself as such. In Foucault's terms, the soul is not imprisoned by or within the body, as some Christian imagery would suggest, but "the soul is the prison of the body."[14]

The redescription of intrapsychic processes in terms of the surface politics of the body implies a corollary redescription of gender as the disciplinary production of the figures of fantasy through the play of presence and absence on the body's surface, the construction of the gendered body through a series of exclusions and denials, signifying absences. But what determines the manifest and latent text of the body politic? What is the prohibitive law that generates the corporeal stylization of gender, the fantasied and fantastic figuration of the body? We have already considered the incest taboo and the prior taboo against homosexuality as the generative moments of gender identity, the prohibitions that produce identity along the culturally intelligible grids of an idealized and compulsory heterosexuality. That disciplinary production of gender effects a false stabilization of gender in the interests of the heterosexual construction and regulation of sexuality within the reproductive domain. The construction of coherence conceals the gender discontinuities that run rampant within heterosexual, bisexual, and gay and lesbian contexts in which gender does not necessarily follow from sex, and desire, or sexuality generally, does not seem to follow from gender—indeed, where none of these dimensions of significant corporeality express or reflect one another. When the disorganization and disaggregation of the field of bodies disrupt the regulatory fiction of heterosexual coherence, it seems that the expressive model loses its descriptive force. That regulatory ideal is then exposed as a norm and a fiction that disguises itself as a developmental law regulating the sexual field that it purports to describe.

According to the understanding of identification as an enacted fantasy or incorporation, however, it is clear that coherence is desired, wished for, idealized, and that this idealization is an effect of a corporeal signification. In other words, acts, gestures, and desire produce the effect of an internal core or substance, but produce this *on the surface* of the body, through the play of signifying absences that suggest, but never reveal, the organizing principle of identity as a cause. Such acts, gestures, enactments, generally construed, are *performative* in the sense that the essence or identity that they otherwise purport to express are *fabrications* manufactured and sustained through corporeal signs and other discursive means. That the gendered body is performative suggests that it has no ontological status apart from the various acts which constitute its reality. This also suggests that if that reality is fabricated as an interior essence, that very interiority is an effect and function of a decidedly public and social discourse, the public regulation of fantasy through the surface politics of the body, the gender border control that differentiates inner from outer, and so institutes the "integrity" of the subject. In other words, acts and gestures, articulated and enacted desires create the illusion of an interior and organizing gender core, an illusion discursively maintained for the purposes of the regulation of sexuality within the obligatory frame of reproductive heterosexuality. If the "cause" of desire, gesture, and act can be localized within the "self" of the actor, then the political regulations and disciplinary practices which produce that ostensibly coherent gender are effectively displaced from view. The displacement of a political and discursive origin of gender identity onto a psychological "core" precludes an analysis of the political constitution of the gendered subject and its fabricated notions about the ineffable interiority of its sex or of its true identity.

If the inner truth of gender is a fabrication and if a true gender is a fantasy instituted and inscribed on the surface of bodies, then it seems that genders can be neither true nor false, but are only produced as the truth effects of a discourse of primary and stable identity. In *Mother Camp: Female Impersonators in America*, anthropologist Esther Newton suggests that the structure of impersonation reveals one of the key fabricating mechanisms through which the social construction of gender takes place.[15] I would suggest as well that drag fully subverts the distinction between inner and outer psychic space and effectively mocks both the expressive model of gender and the notion of a true gender identity. Newton writes:

> At its most complex, [drag] is a double inversion that says, "appearance is an illusion." Drag says [Newton's curious personification] "my 'outside' appearance is feminine, but my essence 'inside' [the body] is masculine." At the same time it symbolizes the opposite inversion; "my appearance 'outside' [my body, my gender] is masculine but my essence 'inside' [myself] is feminine."[16]

Both claims to truth contradict one another and so displace the entire enactment of gender significations from the discourse of truth and falsity.

The notion of an original or primary gender identity is often parodied within the cultural practices of drag, cross-dressing, and the sexual stylization of butch/femme identities. Within feminist theory, such parodic identities have been understood to be either degrading to women, in the case of drag and cross-dressing, or an uncritical appropriation of sex-role stereotyping from within the practice of heterosexuality, especially in the case of butch/femme lesbian identities. But the relation between the "imitation" and the "original" is, I think, more complicated than that critique generally allows. Moreover, it gives us a clue to the way in which the relationship between primary identification—that is, the original meanings accorded to gender—and subsequent gender experience might be reframed. The performance of drag plays upon the distinction between the anatomy of the performer and the gender that is being performed. But we are actually in the presence of three contingent dimensions of significant corporeality: anatomical sex, gender identity, and gender performance. If the anatomy of the performer is already distinct from the gender of the performer, and both of those are distinct from the gender of the performance, then the performance suggests a dissonance not only between sex and performance, but sex and gender, and gender and performance. As much as drag creates a unified picture of "woman" (what its critics often oppose), it also reveals the distinctness of those aspects of gendered experience which are falsely naturalized as a unity through the regulatory fiction of heterosexual coherence. *In imitating gender, drag implicitly reveals the imitative structure of gender itself—as well as its contingency.* Indeed, part of the pleasure, the giddiness of the performance is in the recognition of a radical contingency in the relation between sex and gender in the face of cultural configurations of causal unities that are regularly assumed to be natural and necessary. In the place of the law of heterosexual coherence, we see sex and gender denaturalized by means of a performance which avows their distinctness and dramatizes the cultural mechanism of their fabricated unity.

The notion of gender parody defended here does not assume that there is an original which such parodic identities imitate. Indeed, the parody is *of* the very notion of an original; just as the psychoanalytic notion of gender identification is constituted by a fantasy of a fantasy, the transfiguration of an Other who is always already a "figure" in that double sense, so gender parody reveals that the original identity after which gender fashions itself is an imitation without an origin. To be more precise, it is a production which, in effect—that is, in its effect—postures as an imitation. This perpetual displacement constitutes a fluidity of identities that suggests an openness to resignification and recontextualization; parodic proliferation deprives hegemonic culture and its critics of the claim to naturalized or essentialist gender identities. Although the gender meanings taken up in these parodic styles are

clearly part of hegemonic, misogynist culture, they are nevertheless denaturalized and mobilized through their parodic recontextualization. As imitations which effectively displace the meaning of the original, they imitate the myth of originality itself. In the place of an original identification which serves as a determining cause, gender identity might be reconceived as a personal/cultural history of received meanings subject to a set of imitative practices which refer laterally to other imitations and which, jointly, construct the illusion of a primary and interior gendered self or parody the mechanism of that construction.

According to Fredric Jameson's "Postmodernism and Consumer Society," the imitation that mocks the notion of an original is characteristic of pastiche rather than parody:

> Pastiche is, like parody, the imitation of a peculiar or unique style, the wearing of a stylistic mask, speech in a dead language: but it is a neutral practice of mimicry, without parody's ulterior motive, without the satirical impulse, without laughter, without that still latent feeling that there exists something *normal* compared to which what is being imitated is rather comic. Pastiche is blank parody, parody that has lost it humor.[17]

The loss of the sense of "the normal," however, can be its own occasion for laughter, especially when "the normal," "the original" is revealed to be a copy, and an inevitably failed one, an ideal that no one *can* embody. In this sense, laughter emerges in the realization that all along the original was derived.

Parody by itself is not subversive, and there must be a way to understand what makes certain kinds of parodic repetitions effectively disruptive, truly troubling, and which repetitions become domesticated and recirculated as instruments of cultural hegemony. A typology of actions would clearly not suffice, for parodic displacement, indeed, parodic laughter, depends on a context and reception in which subversive confusions can be fostered. What performance where will invert the inner/outer distinction and compel a radical rethinking of the psychological presuppositions of gender identity and sexuality? What performance where will compel a reconsideration of the *place* and stability of the masculine and the feminine? And what kind of gender performance will enact and reveal the performativity of gender itself in a way that destabilizes the naturalized categories of identity and desire. . . .

Endnotes

1. Michel Foucault, "Nietzsche, Genealogy, History," in *Language, Counter-Memory, Practice: Selected Essays and Interviews by Michel Foucault*, trans. Donald F. Bouchard and Sherry Simon, ed. Donald F. Bouchard (Ithaca: Cornell University Press, 1977), p. 148. References in the text are to this essay.

2. Mary Douglas, *Purity and Danger* (London, Boston, and Henley: Routledge and Kegan Paul, 1969), p. 4.

3. Ibid., p. 113.

4. Simon Watney, *Policing Desire: AIDS, Pornography, and the Media* (Minneapolis: University of Minnesota Press, 1988).

5. Douglas, *Purity and Danger*, p. 115.

6. Ibid., p. 121.

7. Ibid., p. 140.

8. Foucault's essay "A Preface to Transgression" (in *Language, Counter-Memory, Practice*) does provide an interesting juxtaposition with Douglas' notion of body boundaries constituted by incest taboos. Originally written in honor of Georges Bataille, this essay explores in part the metaphorical "dirt" of transgressive pleasures and the association of the forbidden orifice with the dirt-covered tomb. See pp. 46–48.

9. Kristeva discusses Mary Douglas' work in a short section of *The Powers of Horror: An Essay on Abjection*, trans. Leon Roudiez (New York: Columbia University Press, 1982), originally published as *Pouvoirs de l'horreur* (Paris: Éditions de Seuil, 1980). Assimilating Douglas' insights to her own

reformulation of Lacan, Kristeva writes, "Defilement is what is jettisoned from the *symbolic system*. It is what escapes that social rationality, that logical order on which a social aggregate is based, which then becomes differentiated from a temporary agglomeration of individuals and, in short, constitutes a *classification system* or *a structure*" (p. 65).

10. Ibid., p. 3.

11. Iris Marion Young, "Abjection and Oppression: Unconscious Dynamics of Racism, Sexism, and Homophobia," paper presented at the Society of Phenomenology and Existential Philosophy Meetings, Northwestern University, 1988. The paper will be published in the proceedings of the 1988 meetings by the State University of New York Press. It will also be included as part of a larger chapter in her forthcoming *The Politics of Difference*.

12. Parts of the following discussion were published in two different contexts, in my "Gender Trouble, Feminist Theory, and Psychoanalytic Discourse," in *Feminism/Postmodernism*, ed. Linda J. Nicholson (New York: Routledge, 1989) and "Performative Acts and Gender Constitution: An Essay in Phenomenology and Feminist Theory," *Theatre Journal*, Vol. 20, No. 3, Winter 1988.

13. Michel Foucault, *Discipline and Punish: The Birth of the Prison*, trans. Alan Sheridan (New York: Vintage, 1979), p. 29.

14. Ibid., p. 30.

15. See the chapter "Role Models" in Esther Newton, *Mother Camp: Female Impersonators in America* (Chicago: University of Chicago Press, 1972).

16. Ibid., p. 103.

17. Fredric Jameson, "Postmodernism and Consumer Society," in *The Anti-Aesthetic: Essays on Postmodern Culture*, ed. Hal Foster (Port Townsend, WA: Bay Press, 1983), p. 114.

54

Toward an Afrocentric Feminist Epistemology

Patricia Hill Collins

Patricia Hill Collins (b. 1948) is the most important advocate within sociology proper of what she terms in this essay, from her book *Black Feminist Thought* (1990), "an Afrocentric feminist epistemology." The essay begins with a critique of Eurocentric and masculinist thought, which, particularly in its positivist articulation (she contends), seeks to divorce the researcher from the object of investigation, enforce a notion of objectivity by preventing emotions from entering in, and promote a value-free research process. The remainder of the essay is devoted to sketching a black feminist epistemology as an alternative. Key to this approach is recognizing and appreciating the concrete experiences of daily life as the basis for meaning construction and the notion of understanding, not as an individual accomplishment, but as the result of the collective efforts resulting from sisterhood.

A small girl and her mother passed a statue depicting a European man who had barehandedly subdued a ferocious lion. The little girl stopped, looked puzzled and asked, 'Mama, something's wrong with that statue. Everybody knows that a man can't whip a lion.' 'But darling,' her mother replied, 'you must remember that the man made the statue.'

—As told by Katie G. Cannon

Black feminist thought, like all specialized thought, reflects the interests and standpoint of its creators. Tracing the origin and diffusion of any body of specialized thought reveals its affinity to the power of the group that created it (Mannheim 1936). Because elite white men and their representatives control structures of knowledge validation, white male interests pervade the thematic content of traditional scholarship. As a result, Black women's experiences with work, family, motherhood, political activism, and sexual politics have been routinely distorted in or excluded from traditional academic discourse.

Black feminist thought as specialized thought reflects the thematic content of African-American women's experiences. But because Black women have had to struggle against white male interpretations of the world in order to express a self-defined standpoint, Black feminist thought can best be viewed as subjugated knowledge. The suppression of Black women's efforts for self-definition in traditional sites of knowledge production has led African-American women to use alternative sites such as music, literature, daily conversations, and everyday behavior as important locations for articulating the core themes of a Black feminist consciousness.

Investigating the subjugated knowledge of subordinate groups—in this case a Black women's standpoint and Black feminist thought—requires more ingenuity than that needed to examine the standpoints and thought of dominant groups. I found my training as a social scientist inadequate to the task of studying the subjugated knowledge of a Black women's standpoint. This is because subordinate groups have long had to use alternative ways to create independent self-definitions and self-valuations and to rearticulate them through our own specialists. Like other subordinate groups, African-American women have not only developed a distinctive Black women's standpoint, but have done so by using alternative ways of producing and validating knowledge.

Epistemology is the study of the philosophical problems in concepts of knowledge

363

and truth. The techniques I use in this volume to rearticulate a Black women's standpoint and to further Black feminist thought may appear to violate some of the basic epistemological assumptions of my training as a social scientist. In choosing the core themes in Black feminist thought that merited investigation, I consulted established bodies of academic research. But I also searched my own experiences and those of African-American women I know for themes we thought were important. My use of language signals a different relationship to my material than that which currently prevails in social science literature. For example, I often use the pronoun "our" instead of "their" when referring to African-American women, a choice that embeds me in the group I am studying instead of distancing me from it. In addition, I occasionally place my own concrete experiences in the text. To support my analysis, I cite few statistics and instead rely on the voices of Black women from all walks of life. These conscious epistemological choices signal my attempts not only to explore the thematic content of Black feminist thought but to do so in a way that does not violate its basic epistemological framework.

One key epistemological concern facing Black women intellectuals is the question of what constitutes adequate justifications that a given knowledge claim, such as a fact or theory, is true. In producing the specialized knowledge of Black feminist thought, Black women intellectuals often encounter two distinct epistemologies: one representing elite white male interests and the other expressing Afrocentric feminist concerns. Epistemological choices about who to trust, what to believe, and why something is true are not benign academic issues. Instead, these concerns tap the fundamental question of which versions of truth will prevail and shape thought and action.

The Eurocentric, Masculinist Knowledge Validation Process

Institutions, paradigms, and other elements of the knowledge validation procedure controlled by elite white men constitute the Eurocentric masculinist knowledge validation process. The purpose of this process is to represent a white male standpoint. Although it reflects powerful white males interest, various dimensions of the process are not necessarily managed by white men themselves. Scholars, publishers, and other experts represent specific interests and credentialing processes, and their knowledge claims must satisfy the political and epistemological criteria of the contexts in which they reside (Kuhn 1962; Mulkay 1979).

Two political criteria influence the knowledge validation process. First, knowledge claims are evaluated by a community of experts whose members represent the standpoints of the groups from which they originate. Within the Eurocentric masculinist process this means that a scholar making a knowledge claim must convince a scholarly community controlled by white men that a given claim is justified. Second, each community of experts must maintain its credibility as defined by the larger group in which it is situated and from which it draws its basic, taken-for-granted knowledge. This means that scholarly communities that challenge basic beliefs held in the culture at large will be deemed less credible than those which support popular perspectives.

When white men control the knowledge validation process, both political criteria can work to suppress Black feminist thought. Given that the general culture shaping the taken-for-granted knowledge of the community of experts is permeated by widespread notions of Black and female inferiority, new knowledge claims that seem to violate these fundamental assumptions are likely to be viewed as anomalies (Kuhn 1962). Moreover, specialized thought challenging notions of Black and female inferiority is unlikely to be generated from within a white-male-controlled academic community because both the kinds of questions that could be asked and the explanations that would be found satisfying would necessarily reflect a basic lack of familiarity with Black women's reality. The experiences of African-American women scholars illustrate how individuals who wish to rearticulate a Black women's standpoint through Black feminist thought can be suppressed by a white-male-controlled knowledge validation process. Exclusion from basic literacy, quality educational experiences, and faculty and administrative positions has limited Black women's access to influential academic positions (Zinn et al. 1986). While Black women can produce knowledge claims that contest those advanced by the white male community, this community does not grant that Black women scholars have competing knowledge claims based in another knowledge validation process. As a consequence, any credentials controlled by white male academicians can be denied to Black women producing Black feminist thought on the grounds that it is not credible research.

Black women with academic credentials who seek to exert the authority that our status grants us to propose new knowledge claims about African-American women face pressures to use our authority to help legitimate a system that devalues and excludes the majority of Black women. When an outsider group—in this case, African-American women—recognizes that the insider group— namely, white men—requires special privileges from the larger society, a special problem arises of keeping the outsiders out and at the same time having them acknowledge the legitimacy of this procedure. Accepting a few "safe" outsiders addresses this legitimation problem (Berger and Luckmann 1966). One way of excluding the majority of Black women from the knowledge validation process is to permit a few Black women to acquire positions of authority in institutions that legitimate knowledge, and to encourage us to work within the taken-for-granted assumptions of Black female inferiority shared by the scholarly community and by the culture at large. Those Black women who accept these assumptions are likely to be rewarded by their institutions, often at significant personal cost. Those challenging the assumptions run the risk of being ostracized.

African-American women academicians who persist in trying to rearticulate a Black women's standpoint also face potential rejection of our knowledge claims on epistemological grounds. Just as the material realities of the powerful and the dominated produce separate standpoints, each group may also have distinctive epistemologies or theories of knowledge. Black women scholars may know that something is true but be unwilling or unable to legitimate our claims using Eurocentric, masculinist criteria for consistency with substantiated knowledge and criteria for methodological adequacy. For any body of knowledge, new knowledge claims must be consistent with an existing body of knowledge that the group controlling the interpretive context accepts as true. The methods used to validate knowledge claims must also be acceptable to the group controlling the knowledge validation process.

The criteria for the methodological adequacy of positivism illustrate the epistemological standards that Black women scholars would have to satisfy in legitimating Black feminist thought using a Eurocentric masculinist epistemology. While I describe Eurocentric masculinist approaches as a single process, many schools of thought or paradigms are subsumed under this one process. Moreover, my focus on positivism should be interpreted neither to mean that all dimensions of positivism are inherently problematic for Black women nor that nonpositivist frameworks are better. For example, most traditional frameworks that women of color internationally regard as oppressive to women are not positivist, and Eurocentric feminist critiques of positivism may have less political importance for women of color, especially those in traditional societies than they have for white feminists (Narayan 1989).

Positivist approaches aim to create scientific descriptions of reality by producing objective generalizations. Because researchers have widely differing values, experiences, and emotions, genuine science is thought to be unattainable unless all human characteristics except rationality are eliminated from the research process. By following strict methodological rules, scientists aim to distance themselves from the values, vested interests, and emotions generated by their class, race, sex, or unique situation. By decontextualizing themselves, they allegedly become detached observers and manipulators of nature (Jaggar 1983; Harding 1986). Moreover, this researcher decontextualization is paralleled by comparable efforts to remove the objects of study from their contexts. The result of this entire process is often the separation of information from meaning (Fausto-Sterling 1989).

Several requirements typify positivist methodological approaches. First, research methods generally require a distancing of the researcher from her or his "object" of study by defining the researcher as a "subject" with full human subjectivity and by objectifying the "object" of study (Keller 1985; Asante 1987; Hooks 1989). A second requirement is the absence of emotions from the research process (Hochschild 1975; Jaggar 1983). Third, ethics and values are deemed inappropriate in the research process, either as the reason for scientific inquiry or as part of the research process itself (Richards 1980; Haan et al. 1983). Finally, adversarial debates, whether written or oral, become the preferred method of ascertaining truth: the arguments that can withstand the greatest assault and survive intact become the strongest truths (Moulton 1983).

Such criteria ask African-American women to objectify ourselves, devalue our emotional life, displace our motivations for furthering knowledge about Black women, and confront in an adversarial relationship those with more social, economic and professional power. It therefore seems unlikely that Black women would use a positivist epistemological stance in rearticulating a Black women's standpoint. Black women are more likely to choose an alternative epistemology for assessing knowledge claims, one using different standards that are consistent with Black women's criteria for substantiated knowledge and with our criteria for methodological adequacy. If such an epistemology exists, what are its contours? Moreover, what is its role in the production of Black feminist thought?

The Contours of an Afrocentric Feminist Epistemology

Africanist analyses of the Black experience generally agree on the fundamental elements of an Afrocentric standpoint (Okanlawon 1972). Despite varying histories, Black societies reflect elements of a core African value system that existed prior to and independently of racial oppression (Jahn 1961;

Mbiti 1969; Diop 1974; Zahan 1979; Sobel 1979; Richards 1980, 1990; Asante 1987; Myers 1988). Moreover, as a result of colonialism, imperialism, slavery, apartheid, and other systems of racial domination, Black people share a common experience of oppression. These two factors foster shared Afrocentric values that permeate the family structure, religious institutions, culture, and community life of Blacks in varying parts of Africa, the Caribbean, South America, and North America (Walton 1971; Gayle 1971; Smitherman 1977; Shimkin et al. 1978; Walker 1980; Sudarkasa 1981; Thompson 1983; Mitchell and Lewter 1986; Asante 1987; Brown 1989). This Afrocentric consciousness permeates the shared history of people of African descent through the framework of a distinctive Afrocentric epistemology (Turner 1984).

Feminist scholars advance a similar argument by asserting that women share a history of gender oppression, primarily through sex/gender hierarchies (Eisenstein 1983; Hartsock 1983b; Andersen 1988). These experiences transcend divisions among women created by race, social class, religion, sexual orientation, and ethnicity and form the basis of a women's standpoint with a corresponding feminist consciousness and epistemology (Rosaldo 1974; D. Smith 1987; Hartsock 1983a; Jaggar 1983).

Because Black women have access to both the Afrocentric and the feminist standpoints, an alternative epistemology used to rearticulate a Black women's standpoint should reflect elements of both traditions. The search for the distinguishing features of an alternative epistemology used by African-American women reveals that values and ideas Africanist scholars identify as characteristically "Black" often bear remarkable resemblance to similar ideas claimed by feminist scholars as characteristically "female." This similarity suggests that the material conditions of race, class, and gender oppression can vary dramatically and yet generate some uniformity in the epistemologies of subordinate groups. Thus the significance of an Afrocentric feminist epistemology may lie in how such an epistemology enriches our understanding of how subordinate groups create knowledge that fosters resistance.

The parallels between the two conceptual schemes raise a question: Is the worldview of women of African descent more intensely infused with the overlapping feminine/Afrocentric standpoints than is the case for either African-American men or white women? While an Afrocentric feminist epistemology reflects elements of epistemologies used by African-Americans and women as groups, it also paradoxically demonstrates features that may be unique to Black women. On certain dimensions Black women may more closely resemble Black men; on others, white women; and on still others Black women may stand apart from both groups. Black women's both/and conceptual orientation, the act of being simultaneously a member of a group and yet standing apart from it, forms an integral part of Black women's consciousness. Black women negotiate these contradictions, a situation Bonnie Thornton Dill (1979) labels the "dialectics of Black womanhood," by using this both/and conceptual orientation.

Rather than emphasizing how a Black women's standpoint and its accompanying epistemology are different from those in Afrocentric and feminist analyses, I use Black women's experiences to examine points of contact between the two. Viewing an Afrocentric feminist epistemology in this way challenges additive analyses of oppression claiming that Black women have a more accurate view of oppression than do other groups. Such approaches suggest that oppression can be quantified and compared and that adding layers of oppression produces a potentially clearer standpoint (Spelman 1982). One implication of standpoint approaches is that the more subordinated the group, the purer the vision of the oppressed group. This is an outcome of the origins of standpoint approaches in Marxist social theory, itself an analysis of social structure rooted in Western either/or dichotomous thinking. Ironically, by quantifying and ranking human oppressions, standpoint theorists invoke criteria for methodological adequacy characteristic of positivism. Although it is tempting to claim that Black women are more oppressed than everyone else and therefore have the best standpoint from which to understand the mechanisms, processes, and effects of oppression, this simply may not be the case.

Like a Black women's standpoint, an Afrocentric feminist epistemology is rooted in the everyday experiences of African-American women. In spite of diversity that exists among women, what are the dimensions of an Afrocentric feminist epistemology?

Concrete Experience as a Criterion of Meaning

"My aunt used to say, 'A heap see, but a few know,'" remembers Carolyn Chase, a 31-year-old inner-city Black woman (Gwaltney 1980, 83). This saying depicts two types of knowing—knowledge and wisdom—and taps the first dimension of an Afrocentric feminist epistemology. Living life as Black women requires wisdom because knowledge about the dynamics of race, gender, and class oppression has been essential to Black women's survival. African-American women give such wisdom high credence in assessing knowledge.

Allusions to these two types of knowing pervade the words of a range of African-American women. Zilpha Elaw, a preacher of the mid-1800s, explains the tenacity of racism:

> The pride of a white skin is a bauble of great value with many in some parts of the United States, who readily sacrifice their intelligence to their prejudices, and possess more knowledge than wisdom. (Andrews 1986, 85)

In describing differences separating African-American and white women, Nancy White invokes a similar rule: "When you come right down to it, white women just think they are free. Black women *know* they ain't free" (Gwaltney 1980, 147). Geneva Smitherman, a college professor specializing in African-American linguistics, suggests that

> from a black perspective, written documents are limited in what they can teach about life and survival in the world. Blacks are quick to ridicule 'educated fools,'. . . they have 'book learning' but no

'mother wit,' knowledge, but not wisdom. (Smitherman 1977, 76)

Mabel Lincoln eloquently summarizes the distinction between knowledge and wisdom:

> To black people like me, a fool is funny— you know, people who love to break bad, people you can't tell anything to, folks that would take a shotgun to a roach. (Gwaltney 1980, 68)

African-American women need wisdom to know how to deal with the "educated fools" who would "take a shotgun to a roach." As members of a subordinate group, Black women cannot afford to be fools of any type, for our objectification as the Other denies us the protections that white skin, maleness, and wealth confer. This distinction between knowledge and wisdom, and the use of experience as the cutting edge dividing them, has been key to Black women's survival. In the context of race, gender, and class oppression, the distinction is essential. Knowledge without wisdom is adequate for the powerful, but wisdom is essential to the survival of the subordinate.

For most African-American women those individuals who have lived through the experiences about which they claim to be experts are more believable and credible than those who have merely read or thought about such experiences. Thus concrete experience as a criterion for credibility frequently is invoked by Black women when making knowledge claims. For instance, Hannah Nelson describes the importance personal experience has for her:

> Our speech is most directly personal, and every black person assumes that every other black person has a right to a personal opinion. In speaking of grave matters, your personal experience is considered very good evidence. With us, distant statistics are certainly not as important as the actual experience of a sober person. (Gwaltney 1980, 7)

Similarly, Ruth Shays uses her concrete experiences to challenge the idea that formal education is the only route to knowledge:

> I am the kind of person who doesn't have a lot of education, but both my mother and my father had good common sense.

> Now, I think that's all you need. I might not know how to use thirty-four words where three would do, but that does not mean that I don't know what I'm talking about. . . . I know what I'm talking about because I'm talking about myself. I'm talking about what I have lived. (Gwaltney 1980, 27, 33)

Implicit in Ms. Shays's self-assessment is a critique of the type of knowledge that obscures the truth, the "thirty-four words" that cover up a truth that can be expressed in three.

Even after substantial mastery of white masculinist epistemologies, many Black women scholars invoke our own concrete experiences and those of other African-American women in selecting topics for investigation and methodologies used. For example, Elsa Barkley Brown (1986) subtitles her essay on Black women's history, "how my mother taught me to be an historian in spite of my academic training." Similarly, Joyce Ladner (1972) maintains that growing up as a Black woman in the South gave her special insights in conducting her study of Black adolescent women. Lorraine Hansberry alludes to the potential epistemological significance of valuing the concrete:

> In certain peculiar ways, we have been conditioned to think not small—but tiny. And the thing, I think, which has strangled us most is the tendency to turn away from the world in search of the universe. That is chaos in science—can it be anything else in art? (1969, 134)

Experience as a criterion of meaning with practical images as its symbolic vehicles is a fundamental epistemological tenet in African-American thought systems (Mitchell and Lewter 1986). "Look at my arm!" Sojourner Truth proclaimed: "I have ploughed, and planted, and gathered into barns, and no man could head me! And ain't I a woman?" (Loewenberg and Bogin 1976, 235). By invoking concrete practical images from her own life to symbolize new meanings, Truth deconstructed the prevailing notions of woman. Stories, narratives, and Bible principles are selected for their applicability to the lived experiences of African-Americans and become symbolic representations of a whole wealth of experience. Bible tales are often told for the wisdom they express about everyday life, so their interpretation involves no need for scientific historical verification. The narrative method requires that the story be told, not torn apart in analysis, and trusted as core belief, not "admired as science" (Mitchell and Lewter 1986, 8).

June Jordan's essay about her mother's suicide illustrates the multiple levels of meaning that can occur when concrete experiences are used as a criterion of meaning. Jordan describes her mother, a woman who literally died trying to stand up, and the effect her mother's death had on her own work:

> I think all of this is really about women and work. Certainly this is all about me as a woman and my life work. I mean I am not sure my mother's suicide was something extraordinary. Perhaps most women must deal with a similar inheritance, the legacy of a woman whose death you cannot possibly pinpoint because she died so many, many times and because, even before she became your mother, the life of that woman was taken. . . . I came too late to help my mother to her feet. By way of everlasting thanks to all of the women who have helped me to stay alive I am working never to be late again. (Jordan 1985, 26)

While Jordan has knowledge about the concrete act of her mother's death, she also strives for wisdom concerning the meaning of that death.

Some feminist scholars offer a similar claim that women as a group are more likely than men to use concrete knowledge in assessing knowledge claims. For example, a substantial number of the 135 women in a study of women's cognitive development were "connected knowers" and were drawn to the sort of knowledge that emerges from first-hand observation (Belenky et al. 1986). Such women felt that because knowledge comes from experience, the best way of understanding another person's ideas was to develop empathy and share the experiences that led the person to form those ideas.

In valuing the concrete, African-American women invoke not only an Afrocentric tradition but a women's tradition as well. Some feminist theorists suggest that women

are socialized in complex relational nexuses where contextual rules versus abstract principles govern behavior (Chodorow 1978; Gilligan 1982). This socialization process is thought to stimulate characteristic ways of knowing (Hartsock 1983a; Belenky et al. 1986). These theorists suggest that women are more likely to experience two modes of knowing: one located in the body and the space it occupies and the other passing beyond it. Through their child-rearing and nurturing activities, women mediate these two modes and use the concrete experiences of their daily lives to assess more abstract knowledge claims (D. Smith 1987).

Although valuing the concrete may be more representative of women than men, social class differences among women may generate differential expression of this women's value. One study of working-class women's ways of knowing found that both white and African-American women rely on common sense and intuition (Luttrell 1989). These forms of knowledge allow for subjectivity between the knower and the known, rest in the women themselves (not in higher authorities), and are experienced directly in the world (not through abstractions).

Amanda King, a young African-American mother, describes how she used the concrete to assess the abstract and points out how difficult mediating these two modes of knowing can be:

> The leaders of the ROC [a labor union] lost their jobs too, but it just seemed like they were used to losing their jobs. . . . This was like a lifelong thing for them, to get out there and protest. They were like, what do you call them—intellectuals. . . . You got the ones that go to the university that are supposed to make all the speeches, they're the ones that are supposed to lead, you know, put this little revolution together, and then you got the little ones . . . that go to the factory everyday, they be the ones that have to fight. I had a child and I thought I don't have the time to be running around with these people. . . . I mean I understand some of that stuff they were talking about, like the bourgeoisie, the rich and the poor and all that, but I had surviving on my mind for me and my kid. (Byerly 1986, 198)

For Ms. King abstract ideals of class solidarity were mediated by the concrete experience of motherhood and the connectedness it involved.

In traditional African-American communities Black women find considerable institutional support for valuing concrete experience. Black women's centrality in families, churches, and other community organizations allows us to share our concrete knowledge of what it takes to be self-defined Black women with younger, less experienced sisters. "Sisterhood is not new to Black women," asserts Bonnie Thornton Dill, but "while Black women have fostered and encouraged sisterhood, we have not used it as the anvil to forge our political identities" (1983, 134). Though not expressed in explicitly political terms, this relationship of sisterhood among Black women can be seen as a model for a whole series of relationships African-American women have with one another (Gilkes 1985; Giddings 1988).

Given that Black churches and families are both woman-centered, Afrocentric institutions, African-American women traditionally have found considerable institutional support for this dimension of an Afrocentric feminist epistemology. While white women may value the concrete, it is questionable whether white families—particularly middle-class nuclear ones—and white community institutions provide comparable types of support. Similarly, while Black men are supported by Afrocentric institutions, they cannot participate in Black women's sisterhood. In terms of Black women's relationships with one another, African-American women may find it easier than others to recognize connectedness as a primary way of knowing, simply because we are encouraged to do so by a Black women's tradition of sisterhood.

References

Andersen, Margaret. 1988. *Thinking about Women: Sociological Perspectives on Sex and Gender*. 2d ed. New York: Macmillan.

Andrews, William L. 1986. *Sisters of the Spirit: Three Black Women's Autobiographies of the Nineteenth Century*. Bloomington: Indiana University Press.

Asante, Molefi Kete. 1987. *The Afrocentric Idea*. Philadelphia: Temple University Press.

Belenky, Mary Field, Blythe McVicker Clinchy, Nancy Rule Goldberger, and Jill Mattuck Tarule. 1986. *Women's Ways of Knowing*. New York: Basic Books.

Berger, Peter L. and Thomas Luckmann. 1966. *The Social Construction of Reality*. New York: Doubleday.

Brown, Elsa Barkley. 1986. *Hearing Our Mothers' Lives*. Atlanta: Fifteenth Anniversary of African-American and African Studies, Emory University. (unpublished)

——. 1989. "African-American Women's Quilting: A Framework for Conceptualizing and Teaching African-American Women's History." *Signs* 14(4): 921–29.

Byerly, Victoria. 1986. *Hard Times Cotton Mills Girls*. Ithaca, NY: Cornell University Press.

Chodorow, Nancy. 1978. *The Reproduction of Mothering*. Berkeley: University of California Press.

Dill, Bonnie Thornton. 1979. "The Dialectics of Black Womanhood." *Signs* 4(3): 543–55.

——. 1983. "Race, Class, and Gender: Prospects for an All-Inclusive Sisterhood." *Feminist Studies* 9(1): 131–50.

Diop, Cheikh. 1974. *The African Origin of Civilization: Myth or Reality*. New York: L. Hill.

Eisenstein, Hester. 1983. *Contemporary Feminist Thought*. Boston: G. K. Hall.

Fausto-Sterling, Anne. 1989. "Life in the XY Corral." *Women's Studies International Forum* 12(3): 319–31.

Gayle, Addison, ed. 1971. *The Black Aesthetic*. Garden City, NY: Doubleday.

Giddings, Paula. 1988. *In Search of Sisterhood: Delta Sigma Theta and the Challenge of the Black Sorority Movement*. New York: William Morrow.

Gilkes, Cheryl Townsend. 1985. "'Together and in Harness': Women's Traditions in the Sanctified Church." *Signs* 10(4): 678–99.

Gilligan, Carol. 1982. *In a Different Voice*. Cambridge, MA: Harvard University Press.

Gwaltney, John Langston. 1980. *Drylongso, A Self-Portrait of Black America*. New York: Vintage.

Haan, Norma, Robert Bellah, Paul Rabinow, and William Sullivan, eds. 1983. *Social Science as Moral Inquiry*. New York: Columbia University Press.

Hansberry, Lorraine. 1969. *To Be Young, Gifted and Black*. New York: Signet.

Harding, Sandra. 1986. *The Science Question in Feminism*. Ithaca, NY: Cornell University Press.

Hartsock, Nancy M. 1983a. "The Feminist Standpoint: Developing the Ground for a Specifically Feminist Historical Materialism." In *Discovering Reality*, edited by Sandra Harding and Merrill B. Hintikka, 283–310. Boston: D. Reidel.

——. 1983b. *Money, Sex and Power*. Boston: Northeastern University Press.

Hochschild, Arlie Russell. 1975. "The Sociology of Feeling and Emotion: Selected Possibilities." In *Another Voice: Feminist Perspectives on Social Life and Social Science*, edited by Marcia Millman and Rosabeth Kanter, 280–307. Garden City, NY: Anchor.

Hooks, Bell. 1989. *Talking Back: Thinking Feminist, Thinking Black*. Boston: South End Press.

Jaggar, Alison M. 1983. *Feminist Politics and Human Nature*. Totawa, NJ: Rowman & Allanheld.

Jahn, Janheinz. 1961. *Muntu: An Outline of Neo-African Culture*. London: Faber and Faber.

Jordan, June. 1985. *On Call*. Boston: South End Press.

Keller, Evelyn Fox. 1985. *Reflections on Gender and Science*. New Haven, CT: Yale University Press.

Kuhn, Thomas. 1962. *The Structure of Scientific Revolutions*. 2d ed. Chicago: University of Chicago Press.

Ladner, Joyce. 1972. *Tomorrow's Tomorrow*. Garden City, NY: Doubleday.

Loewenberg, Bert J., and Ruth Bogin, eds. 1976. *Black Women in Nineteenth-Century American Life*. University Park: Pennsylvania State University Press.

Luttrell, Wendy. 1989. "Working-Class Women's Ways of Knowing: Effects of Gender, Race, and Class." *Sociology of Education* 62(1): 33–46.

Mannheim, Karl. 1936. *Ideology and Utopia*. New York: Harcourt, Brace & World.

Mbiti, John S. 1969. *African Religions and Philosophy*. London: Heinemann.

Mitchell, Henry H., and Nicholas Cooper Lewter. 1986. *Soul Theology: The Heart of American Black Culture*. San Francisco: Harper & Row.

Moulton, Janice. 1983. "A Paradigm of Philosophy: The Adversary Method." In *Discovering Reality*, edited by Sandra Harding and Merrill B. Hintikka, 149–64. Boston: D. Reidel.

Mulkay, Michael. 1979. *Science and the Sociology of Knowledge*. Boston: Unwin Hyman.

Myers, Linda James. 1988. *Understanding an Afrocentric World View: Introduction to an Optimal Psychology*. Dubuque, IA: Kendall/Hunt.

Narayan, Uma. 1989. "The Project of Feminist Epistemology: Perspectives from a Nonwestern Feminist." In *Gender/Body/Knowledge: Feminist Reconstructions of Being and Knowing*, edited by Alison M. Jaggar and Susan R. Bordo, 256–69. New Brunswick, NJ: Rutgers University Press.

Okanlawon, Alexander. 1972. "Africanism—A Synthesis of the African World-View." *Black World* 21(9): 40–44, 92–97.

Richards, Dona. 1980. "European Mythology: The Ideology of 'Progress.' " In *Contemporary Black Thought*, edited by Molefi Kete Asante and Abdulai Sa. Vandi, 59–79. Beverly Hills, CA: Sage.

——. 1990. "The Implications of African-American Spirituality." In *African Culture: The Rhythm of Unity*, edited by Molefi Kete Asante and Kariamu Welsh Asante, 207–31. Trenton, NJ: Africa World Press.

Rosaldo, Michelle Z. 1974. "Women, Culture and Society: A Theoretical Overview." In *Woman, Culture and Society*, edited by Michelle Rosaldo and Louise Lamphere, 17–42. Stanford: Stanford University Press.

Shimkin, Demitri B., Edith M. Shimkin, and Dennis A. Frate, eds. 1978. *The Extended Family in Black Societies*. Chicago: Aldine.

Smith, Dorothy. 1987. *The Everyday World as Problematic*. Boston: Northeastern University Press.

Smitherman, Geneva. 1977. *Talkin and Testifyin: The Language of Black America*. Boston: Houghton Mifflin.

Sobel, Mechal. 1979. *Trabelin' On: The Slave Journey to an Afro-Baptist Faith*. Princeton: Princeton University Press.

Spelman, Elizabeth V. 1982. "Theories of Race and Gender: The Erasure of Black Women." *Quest* 5(4): 36–62.

Sudarkasa, Niara. 1981. "Interpreting the African Heritage in Afro-American Family Organization." In *Black Families*, edited by Harriette Pipes McAdoo, 37–53. Beverly Hills, CA: Sage.

Thompson, Robert Farris. 1983. *Flash of the Spirit: African and Afro-American Art and Philosophy*. New York: Vintage.

Turner, James E. 1984. "Foreword: Africana Studies and Epistemology: A Discourse in the Sociology of Knowledge." In *The Next Decade: Theoretical and Research Issues in Africana Studies*, edited by James E. Turner, v–xxv. Ithaca, NY: Cornell University Africana Studies and Research Center.

Walker, Sheila S. 1980. "African Gods in the Americas: The Black Religious Continuum." *Black Scholar* 11(8): 25–36.

Walton, Ortiz M. 1971. "Comparative Analysis of the African and Western Aesthetics." In *The Black Aesthetic*, edited by Addison Gayle, 154–64. Garden City, NY: Doubleday.

Zahan, Dominique. 1979. *The Religion, Spirituality, and Thought of Traditional Africa.* Chicago: University of Chicago Press.

Zinn, Maxine Baca, Lynn Weber Cannon, Elizabeth Higginbotham, and Bonnie Thornton Dill. 1986. "The Costs of Exclusionary Practices in Women's Studies." *Signs* 11(2): 290–303.

55
Sociology From Women's Experience: A Reaffirmation

Dorothy E. Smith

Dorothy E. Smith (b. 1926), trained at the University of California, Berkeley, was for years unknown to the larger sociological community because of the demands of raising a family coupled with the sexism of the discipline during the earlier years of her career. In recent years, however, she has been "discovered," and her argument on behalf of a sociological theory that begins with women's concrete experiences has had a significant impact on feminist thinking (its influence on the work of Patricia Hill Collins, for example, is obvious). This particular essay, published in the journal *Sociological Theory* in 1992, is the result of a symposium on her work. In it she is asked to reflect on the comments and criticisms of others and in the process to rearticulate her position. Central to her theory is the notion of "standpoint," which means that although her sociology begins with women's concrete experiences, it does not end there. Smith concludes with a discussion of her suspicions about political opposition beginning within the realm of social theory.

The discussion of my work by Pat Hill Collins, Bob Connell, and Charles Lemert is generous and very much appreciated. My difficulty in responding is that each develops a critique from a very different theoretical stance.[1] Lemert brings to bear his interest in what he describes as the sociological dilemma of the subject-object relation, and the postmodernist critique of modernity and its unitary subject. Pat Hill Collins draws on the tradition of critical theory, strikingly informed by her experience of and commitment to recovering the suppressed feminist thought of black women. Connell works within a Marxist tradition and with specific concerns about the relation of sociology to political practice. Also, each constructs her or his own straw Smith. Lemert reads the project of an inquiry *beginning from* women's experience as a sociology *of* women's *subjective* experience. Collins reads into my project her objective of creating a transformative knowledge. Connell confounds beginning from experience with individualism, and interprets my rather careful (and critical) explications of the conceptual practices of power as an abhorrence of abstractions in general.

In response I will clarify how I've understood and worked for a sociology beginning from women's experience. It is not, I insist, a totalizing theory. Rather it is a *method of inquiry*, always ongoing, opening things up, discovering. In addition, to reemphasize its character as inquiry relevant to the politics and practice of progressive struggle, whether of women or of other oppressed groups, this essay refers to some of the work being done from this approach.

Standpoint

The very intellectual successes of the women's movement have created their own contradictions. Though they follow from the powerful discovery of a world split apart— we learned to see, act, and speak from a ground in our experience as women—the intellectual achievements of feminism have woven texts over that original moment. Indeed Connell's question "If the 'standpoint of women' is not an extralocal abstraction, what would be?" reflects (as criticism) the distance between the theorizing of "standpoint" and what I thought I was talking about, working from, trying to build into a sociology.

My project is a sociology that begins in the actualities of women's experience. It builds on that earlier extraordinary moment, unlike anything I've experienced before or since, a giving birth to ourselves—slow, remorseless, painful, and powerful. It attempts to create a method of inquiry beginning from the site of being that we discovered as we learned to center ourselves as speaking, knowing subjects in our experience as women. When I first began this sociological project, I and others used notions such as "women's perspective," "women's experience," "women's standpoint" to express this singular move—the foundation of this phase of the women's movement. Particularly since Sandra Harding's (1986) study of *The Science Question in Feminism*, the concept of "standpoint" has been used to formalize such notions and subject them to a critique. Formalization is inevitable, but it also breaks connection with the original experience that sought expression in a variety of terms. My own attempts to express the project probably contribute to this process, though I wish they would not. Only when I encounter critiques, for example those of Lemert and of Harding herself, or Connell's version, which seems both to be correct and to miss the point altogether, do I become aware that in my own thinking I still rely on the original and extraordinary discovery. Can I explicate it better than I have, in this new context, where feminist theorizing has developed to such a sophisticated level and where even the notion of subject that we used to rely on (see Schutz 1962, for example) is called into question?

The experience, of course, was complex, individualized, various. It's hard to recall now that at that time we did not even have a language for our experiences of oppression as women. But we shared a method. We learned in consciousness-raising groups, through the writings of other women (I relied a great deal on the rich and marvelous poetry that feminists were writing at that time), in talk, and through an inner work that transformed our external and internal relationships. We explored *our experience as women* with other women—not that we necessarily agreed or shared our experiences.

In those early days, taking the standpoint of women transformed how we thought and worked, how we taught, the social relationships of the classroom, almost every aspect of our lives. Remaking sociology was a matter that arose out of practical demands. Established sociology distorted, turned things upside down, turned us into objects, wasn't much use. I thought we could have a sociology responding to people's lack of knowledge of how our everyday worlds are hooked into and shaped by social relations, organization, and powers beyond the scope of direct experience. The theorizing of "standpoint" within feminist discourse displaces the practical politics that the notion of "standpoint" originally captured. The concept is moved upstairs, so to speak, and is reduced to a purely discursive function.

In exploring our experiences we talked with, wrote to and for, women, beginning with what we shared as women, our sexed bodies. Here was and is the site of women's oppression, whether of violence, of rape, of lack of control over our choices to have children, through our connectedness to our children, or through childbirth and suckling. To declare this is not to formulate essentialism or biological determinism. Women's experience of oppression, whatever its form and focus, was grounded in male control, use, domination of our bodies. No transcendence for us. We were irremediably (as it seemed) defined by our bodies' relevance for and uses to men.

I emphasize this embodied ground of our experiencing as women. Much feminist theorizing since this original moment has taken up the standpoint in text-mediated discourse for which Descartes wrote the constitution. The Cartesian subject escapes the body, hence escaping the limitations of the local historical particularities of time, place, and relationship. When we began with our experiences as women, however, we were always returning to ourselves and to each other as subjects *in our bodies*.

I'm not talking about *reflecting* on our bodily existence or describing our bodily experience. The consciousness raising of this phase of the women's movement did not *reflect* on the body from a discursive standpoint. But the sexed body was always the common ground in relation to which we could find ourselves with each other *as women*, even if only to discover the depth of our differences. Of course our experiences in this mode were multiple and various, and as we sought in them a common ground, we also disagreed, sometimes bitterly—fierce fights and divisions were endemic. It was a lot of work to arrive at shared political projects. But what we could have in common was explored through experiences grounded in our sexed bodies, our women's bodies. Exploring the varieties of our experience returned us to the site of our bodily being to rediscover, remake ourselves, stripping away the inner and outer restraints and constraints. We sought our grounding in what was there for us when we took up the particularized, localized, *felt* experiencing of a subject who is not divorced from her bodily site of being.

I certainly think that other sociological transformations may be created from other sites of oppression, although I don't think (as Connell seems to do) that it is the oppositional which defines the standpoint. I am so bold as to believe that there's something distinctive about the standpoint of women as I've expressed and experienced it, and have tried to build it into a method of sociological inquiry. Its distinction is this: that the standpoint of women situates inquiry in the actualities of people's living, beginning with their experience of living, and understands that inquiry and its product are in and of the same actuality.

For me, then, the standpoint of women locates a place to begin inquiry before things have shifted upwards into the transcendent subject. Once you've gone up there, settled into text-mediated discourse, irremediably stuck on the reading side of the textual surface, you can't peek round it to find the other side where you're actually *doing* your reading. You can reflect back, but you're already committed to a standpoint other than that of actual people's experience.

I'm not arguing against abstractions, as Connell seems to think (this would indeed be a contradiction). And I'm not concerned merely with "discrediting" (Connell) or "deconstructing" (Collins) the relations of ruling. I'm concerned with examining and explicating how "abstractions" are put together, with concepts, knowledge, facticity, as socially organized practices. Making these processes visible also makes visible how we participate in and incorporate them into our own practices (see "The Politics and the Product" below). In explicating the so-

cial relations of knowledge, I am concerned also with redesigning them. My notion of an everyday world as problematic is just such an attempt—to redesign the social organization of our systematically developed knowledge of society.

Theorizing the standpoint of women contradicts the project I am addressing. Interpreting that project in those terms misinterprets it. All three critics argue that my project necessarily privileges a particular experience. Lemert, for example, asks whether I do not do "sociology with exceptional, if not exclusive, attention to one specific and gendered subjective experience of the actual world[.]" It's true that I begin with what I learned from my own experience of two worlds of consciousness and their relations (so, incidentally, did Descartes), but the formulation of a method of inquiry that I developed in fact works to make a space into which anyone's experience, however various, could become a beginning-place inquiry. "Anyone" could be an Afro- or Chinese or Caucasian Canadian, an individual from one of the First Nations, an old woman or man, a lesbian or a gay man, a member of the ruling class, or any other man.

I draw a contrast between beginning with the standpoint of women and standpoints constituted in text-mediated discourse. The categories that identify diversity (race, gender, class, age, and so forth) for Collins, oppositional sites for Connell, and fragmented identities for Lemert are categories of such discourse and of discursively embedded political organization and activism. To begin with the categories is to begin in discourse. Experiencing as a woman of color, as Himani Bannerji (1987) has pointed out, does not break down into experience as a woman and experience as a person of color. Roxana Ng (1990) has explored how the category "immigrant women" is constituted in the social relations of the Canadian state and labor market. The latter study in particular calls into question Haraway's (1985) derivation of identities from the discursive fragmentation of social categories (cited by Lemert). Are we really to be stuck with Althusser's (1971) condemnation of the subject to lasting dependency on being interpellated by "ideological state apparatuses"? Of course no one's citing Althusser these days, but Haraway follows the same path from discourse to subjectivity, from discursive category to identity. I want to go another way.

If I could think of a term other than "standpoint," I'd gladly shift, especially now that I've been caged in Harding's (1986) creation of the category of "standpoint theorists" and subjected to the violence of misinterpretation, replicated many times in journals and reviews, by those who speak of Hartsock and Smith but have read only Harding's version of us (or have read us through her version). My notion of standpoint doesn't privilege a knower. It does something rather different. It shifts the ground of knowing, the place where inquiry begins. Since knowledge is essentially socially organized, it can never be an act or an attribute of individual consciousness.

As I see it, the notion of standpoint works like this: Social scientific inquiry ordinarily begins from a standpoint in a text-mediated discourse or organization; it operates to claim a piece of the actual for the relations of ruling of which that discourse or organization is part; it proceeds from a concept or theory expressing those relations and it operates selectively in assembling observations of the world that are ordered discursively. The standpoint of women proposes a different *point d'appui:* It begins one step back before the Cartesian shift that forgets the body. The body isn't forgotten; hence the actual site of the body isn't forgotten. Inquiry starts with the knower who is actually located; she is active; she is at work; she is connected with particular other people in various ways; she thinks, laughs, desires, sorrows, sings, curses, loves just here; she reads here; she watches television. Activities, feelings, experiences, hook her into extended social relations linking her activities to those of other people and in ways beyond her knowing. Whereas a standpoint beginning in text-mediated discourse begins with the concepts or schema of that discourse and turns towards the actual to find its object, the standpoint of women never leaves the actual. The knowing subject is always located in a particular spatial and temporal site, a particular configuration of the everyday/everynight world. Inquiry is directed towards exploring and explicating what she does not know—the social relations and organization pervading her world but invisible in it.

A Method of Inquiry

Central to this particular sociology for women (I take for granted there's more than one) is a method of inquiry. The notion of a standpoint of women doesn't stand by itself as a theoretical construct; it is a place to begin inquiry. I argue that proceeding (and I emphasize the activity here) according to established methods of inquiry in sociology, beginning in discourse with *its* concepts, and relying on standard good social scientific methodologies produces people as objects. This is an effect of its methods of thinking and inquiry; it is not an effect of the sociologist's intentions. Sociologists' intentions may be as oppositional and as progressive as any of us could wish, but if they work with standard methods of thinking and inquiry, they import the relations of ruling into the texts they produce. (Note, as an aside, that this is not an issue of quantitative versus qualitative method.)

Hence the importance of the method of inquiry, as a method both of thinking about society and social relations, and of doing research—or, as I sometimes prefer to put it, of writing the social into discursive texts. Unlike sociologies that seek to generate a totalizing system, this sociology is always in the making. From different sites of women's experience, different social relations or different aspects of the same complex are brought into view and their organization is explicated. Far from being a dead end, as Connell suggests, it is a lively, unfolding, fascinating, and very productive method. I am not talking now about my own work, but am referring to the growing body of work, mostly in Canada, that is exploring contemporary social relations by using this approach, an enterprise that is ongoing and not exclusively mine. Those who have taken up such methods of inquiry have taken them in their own direction; there's no orthodoxy. From innovations made in different courses of inquiry, we learn how to do things that we didn't know how to do before, or we see flaws and problems in how we were working. I am struck by the extraordinary expansion of our grasp of how the relations of ruling are put together, and by the effectiveness with which this knowledge can be put to practical use in a variety of contexts.

So let me try to characterize this method of inquiry briefly:

1. The subject/knower of inquiry is not a transcendent subject but is situated in the actualities of her own living, in relations with others. Lemert is quite right when he says that "key to the position is the somewhat open term 'actual.' " Yes, it is a key, and it is not defined. I don't give it content because I use it like the arrow you see on maps of malls, which tells you, "You are here!" I want the term *actual* to be always directing us back to the "outside the text" in which living goes on and in which the text is being read. Of course the text is always in the actual, though we seem to feel that we can escape through the text, riding it like the magic carpet of legend. The "open" term *actual* reminds us of the actuality of the flying carpet, of us who are riding it, and of the ground below.

2. In this method, we're talking about the actual ongoing practices of actual individuals. This ontology is based on Marx and Engels's formulation in *The German Ideology*. Yet we're not concerned just with what individuals do. The sociology I'm proposing is interested in the social as people's ongoing concerting and coordinating of activities. Here I mark a shift away from the social as order or as rules or as meaning, to the social as actually happening and hence as investigatable. This notion owes much to ethnomethodology, except that I want to extend it to macro relations.

3. What I've called the standpoint of women locates us in bodily sites—local, actual, particular. The idea is not to reenact the theory/practice split and opt for practice, but to locate the knower in a lived world in which both theory and practice go on, in which theory is itself a practice, and in which the divide between the two can itself be brought under examination. The entry into text-mediated discourse and the relations of text-mediated discourse are themselves actual. They are the activity of people

together, happening, always now. Concepts, beliefs, ideas, knowledge, and so on (what Marxists know as consciousness) are included in this ontology. They are practices, they happen, they are ongoing, and they are integral to the concerting and coordinating of people's activities.

4. Inquiry and its product are forms of social organization. They enter into and may become constituents of social relations. Knowledge itself is not distinct from yet dependent on social practices and contexts, as Flax (quoted by Lemert) holds; rather, it is understood as socially organized. Hence the importance, for this sociology, of investigating social relations as a critique of its own practices as well as those of others. Designing a new organization for sociological knowledge is the project of a sociology for women, and of making the everyday/everynight world a problematic of inquiry.

5. Texts, text mediation, textuality, are central. The text is the bridge between the actual and the discursive. It is a material object that brings into actual contexts of reading a fixed form of meaning that can be and may be read in many other settings by many other people at the same time or at other times. It creates something like an escape hatch out of the actual and is foundational to any possibility of abstraction of whatever kind including this one written here. The preceding clauses can be read as a set of procedures for writing the social into texts, and hence for exploiting the power of the textual to analyze and isolate dimensions of organization that are fully embedded in the actualities of living. Of course that writing, that text, its reading, are always ongoing and in the actual. The act of reading is very deceitful in this respect; it conceals its particularity, its being in time and place.

6. Text-mediated relations are the forms in which power is generated and held in contemporary societies. Marx argued that economic relations are a specialization of interdependencies which were previously embedded in direct personal relationships, as in feudalism. With the emergence of money, markets, and capital, these relations become distinct, specialized, and autonomic. Similarly, in contemporary societies, the functions of organization and control

are increasingly vested in distinct, specialized, and (to some extent) autonomic forms of organization and relations mediated by texts. I've called these "the relations of ruling." The materiality of the text and its indefinite replicability create a peculiar ground in which it can seem that language, thought, culture, formal organization have their own being outside lived time and the actualities of people's living—other than as the latter become objects of action or investigation from within the textual. But from the viewpoint of this method of inquiry, the textual mediation of these relations and forms of organization has the miraculous effect of creating a join between the local and particular (on one hand) and the generalizing and generalized organization of the relations of ruling (on the other), hence making the latter investigatable in a new way.

From this very summary formulation of the method of inquiry, we return to issues raised by the critics. Lemert thematizes subjective and objective, representing what I'm doing as a sociology of women's, perhaps of anyone's, *subjective* experience. But the standpoint of women locates the knowing subject in the actual, before the differentiation between subjective and objective—a conceptualization of objectifying institutions. To respond to another issue Lemert raises, I do hold that texts or textual technologies are essential to the objectification both of organization and of knowledge, but not, as he seems to suggest, that texts necessarily result in objectification.

Lemert suggests that the postmodernist sealing off of an escape hatch out of text-mediated discourse is merely an issue of postmodernism's "willingness to tolerate the irony and uncertain possibilities of life in a world without comforting certitudes." I disagree. The issue, as far as I'm concerned, isn't comfort or tolerance for ambiguity or appreciation of irony. Rather it is an issue of the reliability and accuracy of the products of inquiry, beginning from the standpoint of women. The product I imagine is an explication, an unfolding, of how things actually are being put together, of actual ongoing social organization. I am also increasingly formulating the enterprise of inquiry as a kind of ongoing dialogue with society, with people,

in which the inquirer is always exposed to the discipline of the other—sometimes the other's direct response, but more often how people's activities are actually coordinated. The language of dominant discourse, to use Collins's term, is continually displaced and reworked in the process of trying to "get it right." It is necessarily destabilized because it is always open to being rewritten as it is disciplined by its engagement with the actual.

All three critics treat what I'm doing as derived from or as a synthesis of previous sociological theories. Collins is critical of my "grounding . . . work in sociological theories, yet refusing to embrace fully any one theoretical perspective," and describes it as eclecticism. Connell views it as "synthesis." But if we're talking about actual people and the actual ongoing concerting of activities, there's a common ground—a real world, if you like—to which we can refer. If you're seeking to learn how things actually are put together, that dialogue with the world constrains you. You or I draw on what is available in sociology that we can use in developing inquiry and methods of inquiry. This is neither synthesis nor eclecticism. Obviously I think of what I'm doing as sociology, and use what I've learned from sociology. But to situate the standpoint governing inquiry in the theoretical organization of sociological discourse contradicts the project of beginning from the standpoint of women "in real life" (to use Marx and Engels's phrase in *The German Ideology*).

If we are going to do a sociology that serves women, perhaps people in general, it is crucial to get it right. This objective makes no claim to a unitary, absolute, or final truth (hence Lemert's application of the Flax paradox doesn't apply). I've used the analogy of a map. We have maps, we use maps, we rely on maps in a perfectly ordinary and mundane way. I'm not aiming for the one truth. I'm aiming rather to produce sociological accounts and analyses that can have this kind of credence: Here is how you get from the Bloor-Bathurst intersection to Ossington on the subway line. The map extends my capacity to move about effectively in the city. It does not tell me everything about the subway system in Toronto (its technology, operations, organization), but it does tell me the sequence of stations and gives me some idea of the distance between them. I'd like to develop a sociology that would tie people's sites of experience and action into accounts of social organization and relations which have that ordinarily reliable kind of faithfulness to "how it works."[2]

The project of inquiry from the standpoint of women is always reflexive. Also, it is always about ourselves as inquirers—not just our personal selves, but our selves as participants. The metaphor of insider and outsider contains an ambiguity that I should be more watchful of, for I disagree with Collins's view and Connell's implication that there is an outside in society. They are directing our attention to issues of marginality, exclusion, suppressed and oppositional cultures and positions—being outside in that general sense. But as I've used the metaphor, I've wanted to stress that those outside positions are inside. In the sense I'm trying to capture, we are inside necessarily, and so there are no modes of investigation other than those beginning from within. This is as true of established sociology as of a sociology developing inquiry from women's standpoint. Established sociology has powerful ways of writing the social into the text, which produce society as seen from an Archimedean point. A sociology for women says: "You can't have that wish." There is no other way than beginning from the actual social relations in which we are participants. This fact can be concealed, but not avoided.

Therefore I'm in general agreement with Collins, who suggests that "assuming the language of dominant discourses, even using the language of objectified knowledge to critique its terms, weds the thinker to the relations of ruling supported by objectified knowledge." Yet my proposed critique is not just in language—one set of terms against another—but in an inquiry disciplined by its commitment to explore how things actually work, including language not as terms but as actual practice. Such inquiry explores "dominant discourses" and discovers, among other matters, how we may be implicated in those discourses. A sociology from the standpoint of women insists that there is no place outside; hence it must be an insider's

sociology. It may be Connell's failure to grasp my insistence on critique through inquiry which allows him to draw the odd conclusion that I make feminism as such "the principle of anarchy" outside and opposed to the patriarchal power structure. In the sense I mean "insider," there are no outsiders. We are all participants. We discover ourselves in exploring the relations in which we participate and that shape how we participate. The project locates itself in a dialectic between actual people located just as we are and social relations, in which we participate and to which we contribute, that have come to take on an existence and a power over against us.

The Politics and the Product

Connell makes a major and, in my view, unjustified shift from the feminist sociology I'm putting forward to a vaguely defined "oppositional mode of doing sociology." It is indeed true that my feminism is generally oppositional, but I'd have got nowhere if I'd stuck with the radical tradition of European sociology, as Connell suggests, which for the most part is embedded as deeply in the male-dominated standpoints of ruling as is American sociology.

Much of my earlier work as a feminist sociologist was in critical dialogue with the deeply masculine values of the Marxism that pervaded the activism of the 1960s, 1970s, and early 1980s. My critique of the ideological practice of sociology (Smith 1990a) is equally applicable to the thinking of the Marxist theorizing of that period and earlier. In fact, an original and much earlier version was directed primarily towards the Marxist thinking of that time. I came to see that the oppositional stance of Marxism did not preclude adopting a standpoint in the relations of ruling. Relevant here is the poststructuralist insight that the language and concepts of a discourse always speak more and other than our intentions. Though I address this effect quite differently, preserving an ontology of the actual and proposing to explore discourse as actual ongoing textually mediated relations among actual people, the point is the same. Marxists might have an oppositional intention, but in taking up modes of thinking, reasoning, inquiry, and explanation within the established discourses of social science, humanities, and philosophy, they have imported into their oppositional work a standpoint or standpoints within the relations of ruling. The thoroughly masculinist stance consolidated this approach. Whatever their intentions, the organization of the discourse drew the Marxists into relations that contradicted what they sought, perhaps even to the point of locating them in class relations on the side opposite that to which they claimed allegiance.

I do not suggest for one moment that Marxists were dishonest—only that they did not have methods of analysis, or perhaps a standpoint, from which such contradictions might become visible. Characteristically, the working class was other and object (analyses of women were always of their place in the working class). Characteristically, drawing on Lenin and Lukacs, Marxists viewed the working class as the political constituency of revolution, to be led by an "oppositional" intelligentsia. Characteristically, Althusser's theorizing empowered a "scientific" intelligentsia and, in a new day, recreated an ideology enabling a revolutionary intelligentsia to represent itself as the proper leaders of its constituency, the working class. Characteristically, the Marxist-Leninist organizations—at least those I was familiar with in Canada and the United States—were led by university-educated and mostly middle-class male members of the intelligentsia, while middle-class women and working-class women and men played various subordinate roles. When the feminist critique finally was launched internally, it precipitated the collapse of the movement in Canada.

Oppositional modes of doing sociology do not of themselves entail a shift of standpoint from the ruling relations. These relations are built into methods of thinking, reasoning, and inquiry that have been powerfully influential in Europe as well as in North America, and have invaded oppositional thinking, rather like a computer virus, on these two continents.

Opposition as such is not what I'm doing. Nor am I convinced, as Collins is, that knowledge as such can be transformative. She sees my work as failing when measured against her own objective, and indeed against her achievement (in *Black Feminist Thought* [1990]), of a transformed knowledge. Perhaps relations of dominance, such as those of white over nonwhite or of men over women, can be transformed through knowing them. The unyoking of black women's subjugated knowledge that has been Pat Hill Collins's own enterprise is surely empowering, but when we turn to the practice of change, how shall we proceed? Collins is concerned to transform the consciousness of the oppressed. My concern is with what we confront in transforming oppressive relations.

I've never seen resistance or opposition as beginning in theory, much less in sociology. Rather I've thought of "revolution" and organization for change as needing a division of labor in which the production of knowledge plays an essential, though not a leading, part. But the social organization of such knowledge must not reclaim the enterprise for the established relations of ruling. I want a sociology capable of exploring and mapping actual organization and relations that are invisible but active in the everyday/everynight sites where people take up resistance and struggle, capable of producing a knowledge that extends and expands their and our grasp of how things are put together and hence their and our ability to organize and act effectively.

Universities and colleges already are political; teaching in the social sciences and the humanities is a practical politics. Teaching the canon is patriarchal activism. I take this fact seriously. Of course I want a sociology for women to provide useful research services to organizations working for women's issues, but I want more as well.

I take the view that when we employ standard sociological methods of work, we inadvertently realign the issues that concern us with those of the relations of ruling. I want to build a sociology that opens up the social relations and forms of organization shaping our lives from the standpoint of women. You cannot get there directly from the kinds of applied participatory research that Connell recommends for me, though such a sociology would serve participatory research well. The long exclusion of women's knowledge and thought from universities and schools makes me very wary of proposals that would confine the focus of a sociology for women to immediate practical issues. Yes, I presuppose an "agentic professional," but I want her to be able to work very differently than she is able to with established sociological strategies of thinking and inquiry. I want her to know methods of inquiry beginning from a standpoint outside the relations of ruling and to be able to call on a sociological knowledge put together the same way.

Far from representing the limitations of the method of inquiry I propose, as Connell seems to suggest, my micro analyses of ideology open up the ways in which we social scientists participate as subjects in the orders of ruling. The latter aren't just literary matters or demonstrations of how the schemata of psychiatry generate accounts. An example is Adele Mueller's (1987) investigation showing how research on peasant women in the Third World, done by feminist researchers and theorized in the "women and development" discourse of the United States, is tied into the latter's development policies. The ideological organization I examined at the micro level in *The Conceptual Practices of Power* is shown to operate in the organization of relations of state, researchers, and the local realities of Third World woman. Gillian Walker (1990) also investigates ideological organization at the institutional level. She explores the process through which the concept of "family violence" was established as the conceptual organizer of state administrative and welfare practice, of the work of professionals, of the research and theoretical discourses concerned, and of the work of "transition houses."

This doesn't mean merely exploring relations in which intellectuals are active. The text-mediated relations of ruling are indeed pervasive. Alison Griffith and I (Griffith and Smith 1987), in the course of an inquiry into the work that mothers do in relation to their children's schooling, came to recognize in our own lives as single parents and in our talk with other mothers the pervasive organizing effect of a mothering discourse that was founded in North America in the 1920s and 1930s. I've written too about "feminin-

ity" as a text-mediated discourse in which women participate actively (Smith 1990b).

My research concern is to build an ordinary good knowledge of the text-mediated organization of power from the standpoint of women in contemporary capitalism. Not for one moment do I suggest that this is all there is to be done or indeed all that this method of inquiry makes possible, but it is powerfully relevant to making change in our kind of society. Work produced from this approach has been relevant and has been used in a variety of contexts of struggle for change, including collective bargaining, issues of racial inequality in Canada, pay and employment equity, environmental activism, social policy, and gay activism—very much the kind of knowledge that Australian "femocrats" would find useful in their bridging of the gap between women's experience outside the bureaucracy and their efforts to make change from within. Studies exploring specific contexts build a more general knowledge of how the ruling relations are put together and how to investigate them. Of special importance is an increasing knowledge of how textuality operates in the organization of power and of how concepts and ideology enter directly into the organization of ruling, replicating organizational controls across multiple sites.

People working from this approach have investigated the text-based organization of nursing and how it articulates the work of nurses on the ward with the new systems of financial accounting in health care (Campbell 1984); how public service systems of job descriptions organize gender-differentiated career lines (Cassin forthcoming; Reimer 1988); how the process of planning legislation and the operations of planning departments at municipal levels work to defeat local activists' opposition to development even when the activists win (Turner 1991); how government policies involving changing funding practices transform the accounting practices of community colleges and hence their internal systems of control over and use of teaching staff (McCoy 1991); how to reorganize the availability of treatment for people with AIDS and who are HIV-positive so as to make "possible" clinical knowledge widely available (G. Smith 1990);

the ideology of the "single parent" as organizer of multiple sites (parent-teacher contact, classroom, administration, newspaper features) in education (Griffith 1986); and the formation and practice of social work consciousness as an agent of ruling (De Montigny 1989). I have mentioned other issues earlier.

It is also possible to deploy this method of inquiry on topics other than the text-based relations of ruling, as demonstrated by Himani Bannerji's (1988) brilliant study of late nineteenth-century Bengali theater in the formation of ruling-class consciousness in colonial Bengal; by Ann Manicom's (1988) marvelous investigation of how teachers' work is shaped by the economic status of the homes of the children they teach; and by George Smith's (1991) investigation of the experience of gay students in high school, which explores through that experience the distinctive social organization of their oppression.

Fragmentary as these studies may seem, they teach us more and more about the complex and interwoven organization of the relations of ruling, and more and more about how institutional processes are coordinated and "run." Directly or indirectly, most of this work provides a knowledge of the processes and relations of ruling that at least some collectivities have found invaluable. And after all, there is a politics of inquiry that goes beyond direct service to organized struggles. We teach, and teaching sociology, as Sally Hacker (1990: 158) once told me, is essentially a political act, both in substance and in classroom practice.

Endnotes

1. My responses are based on drafts of the critical essays, not on the final versions.

2. Of course sociological maps could not be as representationally simple as subway system maps, though indeed the latter are highly artful and indeed are interesting and sophisticated as translators of properties of local spatial and social organizational relations to a visual text. It is also important epistemologically to recognize that quite different maps or diagrams could be produced to represent the same actuality. A diagram of the subway's electrical system would be quite different.

References

Althusser, Louis. 1971. "Ideology and Ideological State Apparatuses." Pp. 127–86 in *Lenin and Philosophy: Other Essays*. New York: Monthly Review Press.

Bannerji, Himani. 1987. "Introducing Racism: Notes towards an Anti-Racist Feminism." *Resources for Feminist Research* 16: 10–12.

———. 1988. "The Politics of Representation: A Study of Class and Class Struggle in the Political Theatre of West Bengal." PhD dissertation, University of Toronto.

Campbell, Marie. 1984. "Information Systems and Management of Hospital Nursing: A Study in the Social Organization of Knowledge." PhD dissertation, University of Toronto.

Cassin, A. Marguerite. Forthcoming. "Pay Equity and the Routine Production of Inequality." *Canadian Journal of Women and the Law.*

Collins, Patricia Hill. 1990. *Black Feminist Thought*. London: Unwin Hyman.

De Montigny, Gerald. 1989. "Accomplishing Professional Reality: An Ethnography of Social Workers' Practice." PhD dissertation, University of Toronto.

Griffith, Alison. 1986. "Reporting the Facts: Media Accounts of Single Parent Families." *Resources for Feminist Research* 15: 32–43.

Griffith, Alison and Dorothy E. Smith. 1987. "Constructing Cultural Knowledge: Mothering as Discourse." Pp. 87–103 in *Women and Education*, edited by J. Gaskell and A. McLaren. Calgary: Detselig.

Hacker, Sally. 1990. *Doing It the Hard Way: Investigations of Gender and Technology*, edited by Dorothy E. Smith and Susan Turn. Boston: Unwin Hyman.

Haraway, Donna. 1985. "A Manifesto for Cyborgs: Science, Technology, and Socialist Feminism in the 1980s." *Socialist Review* 15: 65–108.

Harding, Sandra. 1986. *The Science Question in Feminism*. Ithaca: Cornell University Press.

Manicom, Ann. 1988. "Constituting Class Relations: The Social Organization of Teachers' Work." PhD dissertation, University of Toronto.

McCoy, Liza. 1991. "Accounting as Interorganizational Organization." Paper presented at the annual meetings of the Society for the Study of Social Problems, Cincinnati.

Mueller, Adele. 1987. "Peasants and Professionals: The Social Organization of Women and Development Knowledge." PhD dissertation, University of Toronto.

Ng, Roxana. 1990. "Immigrant Women: The Construction of a Labour Market Category."

Canadian Journal of Women and the Law 4: 96–112.

Reimer, Marilee. 1988. "The Social Organization of the Labour Process: A Case Study of the Documentary Management of Clerical Labour in the Public Service." PhD dissertation, University of Toronto.

Schutz, Alfred. 1962. "On Multiple Realities." Pp. 207–59 in *Collected Papers*, Vol. 1. The Hague: Martinus Nijhoff.

Smith, Dorothy E. 1990a. *The Conceptual Practices of Power: A Feminist Sociology of Knowledge*. London: Routledge.

——. 1990b. *Texts, Facts, and Femininity: Exploring the Relations of Ruling*. London: Routledge.

Smith, George W. 1990. "Political Activist as Ethnographer." *Social Problems* 37: 401–21.

——. 1991. "The Ideology of 'Fag': Barriers to Education for Gay Students." Paper presented at the annual meetings of the Society for the Study of Social Problems, Cincinnati.

Turner, Susan M. 1991. "Rendering the Site Developable: Textual Organization in the Planning Process." Paper presented at the annual meetings of the Canadian Sociology and Anthropology Association, Kingston, Ontario.

Walker, Gillian. 1990. *Family Violence: The Politics of Conceptualization in the Women's Movement*. Toronto: University of Toronto Press.

56
Rethinking Freud on Women

Nancy Chodorow

Nancy Chodorow (b. 1944) is a feminist theorist who, rather than rejecting Freud's work (as many feminists have done on the grounds that it is inherently misogynistic), attempts to link Freud to feminist theorizing. She finds much to admire in Freud as a clinician, as a critic of the repressive cultural conditions of his times, and as a spokesperson for tolerance. She sees his ideas as having value for the present. Nevertheless, Chodorow is not an uncritical admirer of Freud, for she finds his understanding of women to be inadequate. Rather than an outright rejection, she calls for a reconsideration of his value to contemporary theory, and in so doing she draws on the object relations tradition in psychoanalysis, particularly on the work of two women who were psychoanalytic pioneers, Karen Horney and Melanie Klein.

When we think about Freud on women, we do not typically refer to the five approaches to woman as subject that I have delineated, but to Freud's conceptualization of female development or female sexuality—what I consider as theoretical woman in the developmental theory. We can also situate and relativize this explicit theoretical treatment of woman as subject in another way, in relation not to other accounts of woman as subject but to accounts of woman as object. I believe that Freud's writings offer a strong, consistent treatment of what we might consider to be woman in the male psyche: that is, woman as object, not subject.

Such a claim is in some ways self-evident: Freud was, after all, a man, and any account of women that he produced is, finally, an account of women viewed through the mind of a man. But I mean, rather, that Freud gave us, both explicitly and implicitly, psychodynamic accounts of how men view women (or certain women) as objects or others, and of what femininity and women mean in the masculine psyche. There is something intuitively more convincing in these accounts of woman as object in the male psyche than in those of woman as subject; indeed, they do not seem to have been widely criticized (for their accuracy as portrayals, in any case) in the psychoanalytic or feminist literature since Freud. The way that both male and female writers seem more or less to agree with and elaborate upon Freud's claims in this area—claims, for example, about male fetishism, masculine fear or contempt of women, and problems in men's heterosexual object choice and experience—is in striking contrast to the way that female writers especially, but also some male writers, have taken issue with almost everything Freud claims about women as subjects. I will return to the question of whether his view of woman as subject may also be a picture of woman's experience as seen or imagined by man, but that is not my concern in this discussion.

In examining Freud's explicit treatments of women as objects, one must acknowledge Karen Horney, who covers in her discussions of "The Flight from Womanhood" and "The Dread of Woman" most of what needs to be said on the subject of men's fear and contempt of women; and Melanie Klein, who in her early writings on the Oedipus complex also unpacks for us the prehistory of men's (and women's) fear and contempt of women and flight from femininity.[1] Insofar as Freud's discussions of male development and masculinity center on the masculine castration complex, it can be said that he is preoccupied, indeed obsessed, with the meaning in the male psyche of the female, of sexual difference, and of what marks this difference. Presence of the penis distinguishes the male, and "Nature has, as a precaution, attached . . . a portion of his narcissism to that particular organ."[2]

Freud discusses women as sex objects to men in "A Special Type of Choice of Object Made by Men" and "On the Universal Tendency to Debasement in the Sphere of Love" (in which his developmental account implies that this "universal" tendency is found exclusively in the male).[3] Men, he suggests, split women symbolically and erotically into mothers, or mothers and sisters, on the one hand, and prostitutes on the other. The former cannot be sexually desired, though they are supposed to be the kind of woman a man should marry; the latter, though they are maritally and socially forbidden, can be sexually desired. As long as a woman symbolizes the mother, she is a forbidden oedipal object, an indication of an attachment carried on too long. Fleeing to a woman who is or is like a prostitute protects the defensively constructed idea of the mother's sexual purity and denies oedipal desire. Alternatively, it equates the mother with a prostitute, thereby giving her son access to her along with his father. Psychically derived impotence follows the same line of reasoning: men become impotent with women who are like, or who represent psychically, their mothers. Freud here gives us the psychodynamics of a split long present in Western culture, literature, and social organization. Indeed, the wife must eventually reciprocate her husband's setting her up as an asexual mother, for "a marriage is not made secure until the wife has succeeded in making her husband her child as well and in acting as a mother to him."[4]

Some men do not stop with the simple expedient of separating sexual from asexual women; they must deny the female sexual constitution altogether. "Fetishism," claims Freud, is "a substitute . . . for a particular and quite special penis": that is, the penis that the mother was once thought to have.[5] All boys struggle with acknowledging females'— originally the mother's—castration. Fetishists resolve the struggle by disavowal or denial, creating a fetish that externally represents the maternal phallus and thus supports such disavowal.

Disavowal also enters the realm of mythology. Medusa's snakes condense signification on the one hand of the mature female external genitals and on the other of many penises, which in turn stand both for castration (because the one penis has been lost) and denial of castration (because there are many penises). Medusa's decapitated head, the castrated female genitals, evokes horror and even paralysis—a reminder of castra-

tion—in the man who looks at it, but this paralysis is also an erection, thereby asserting that the penis is still there. In this two-page vignette Freud captures the extreme horror at castration and at the fantasied potential destructiveness of women and the female genitals, which in other writings he glosses with milder words such as "contempt."[6]

The phallic mother is also important in female development; the girl, when she first learns about sexual difference, believes that her mother has a penis and that she will too when she grows up. For both sexes, the preoedipal mother is in Freud's view "phallic": that is, active. But the recognition of the mother's castration seems more permanently traumatic to the boy: "No male human being is spared the fright of castration at the sight of the female genital."[7] The girl is, finally, much more traumatized by a castration of her own. In Freud's view, a more drastic solution than fetishism to conflict over the mother's castration (fetishism, after all, still enables a heterosexual object choice with fetish added on as phallus) is homosexuality, in which the partner himself possesses the phallus directly.[8]

Like theoretical women and femininity itself, clinical women are presented as objects as well as subjects in Freud's writings. In the "Irma" dream several doctors inject, palpate, minutely examine, and try to cure Irma, who recalcitrantly and vindictively tries to undermine their efforts.[9] Servant women—Grusha, seen from behind as she bends over scrubbing the floor; the governesses Fräulein Peter and Fräulein Lina allowing their small charge to play with their genitals; and Lina, squeezing abscesses from her buttocks at night—play important roles in the formation of neurotic symptomatology in both the Wolf Man and the Rat Man and specify clinically and developmentally the class splits described in the "Contributions to the Psychology of Love."[10] Class here intertwines with gender and sexuality in the formation of male erotic desire.

Freud's perspective from within the male psyche toward both abstract woman and individual clinical women as object, and his ease of identification with men in this stance, produce what has seemed to many commentators a notable amorality in his views of male behavior. I am referring not so much to his giving up of the seduction hypothesis (it seems clear that Freud made his about-face for theoretical and social as well as evidential reasons, but that he was certainly at the same time well aware of the prevalence and negative impact of the sexual abuse of children and of incest) as I am to particular clinical cases. Freud barely notes that Dora's father gave her mother syphilis and that his illness may have affected his children's health as well. He condemns neither this father, who handed Dora over at the age of fourteen to a grown man, nor Herr K., who was willing to accept the gift and who tried to seduce her. The case of Paul Lorenz, the Rat Man, is presented with objectivity muted by empathy, and it is a masterful rendition of the phenomenology of obsessive neurosis. But Freud mentions only in passing, as interesting fact, that Lorenz may have seduced his sister and that he certainly felt free to seduce and use a range of other women—sometimes with drastic consequences, as he apparently drove one of them to suicide. In the case vignette of the "dear old uncle" who had the habit of taking the young daughters of friends for outings, arranging for their being stranded overnight, and masturbating them, Freud remarks only on the man's creation of symbolic equivalence between clean or dirty money and clean or dirty hands, and he queries the possible health consequences to the girls of the man's hands being dirty. But he does not even note, let alone comment forcefully on, the man's hands being used to masturbate the young daughters of friends in the first place.[11]

Freud's account of the male psyche represents women, and especially the mother, not only explicitly but implicitly, or latently, as object. In *Civilization and Its Discontents* he contrasts the "oceanic feeling" with longing for the father as the origin of religious feeling. This oceanic feeling—resonant with "limitless narcissism" and in contrast to which mature ego-feeling in later life seems a "shrunken residue"—is very clearly, though not stated as such, the original feeling of the infant with its mother. It is not longing for the mother, for lost narcissistic oneness, then, that generates religious need but longing for the father. This longing re-

sults from "infantile helplessness" in the face of fear.[12] As the account develops, it becomes clear that the fear Freud refers to is oedipal fear and fear of castration: precisely, the boy's fear of his father, merged with his love for him. What begins here as an impersonal oceanic feeling, held by generic human beings of both sexes, turns out to be contrasted with a specifically masculine relation to the father, which Freud thus sees emphatically as more important for the boy than the relation to the mother.

Even less explicitly acknowledged than the mother who signifies the limitless narcissism of childhood is the idealized mother, symbolized by her breast and her sometimes perfect love. In striking contrast to the devaluation and contempt for the mother that he displays elsewhere and to his minimizing of the importance of this early relation in *Civilization and Its Discontents*, Freud also claims that "sucking at the mother's breast is the starting-point of the whole of sexual life, the unmatched prototype of every later sexual satisfaction. . . . I can give you no idea of the important bearing of this first object upon the choice of every later object, of the profound effects it has in its transformations and substitutions in even the remotest regions of our sexual life."[13] Such sucking is ostensibly gender-free, but Freud later implies that the satisfaction and its sequelae may be gender-differentiated. It is hard to separate male wish-fulfillment from objective description of the female psyche when Freud tells us that "a mother is only brought unlimited satisfaction by her relation to a son; this is altogether the most perfect, the most free from ambivalence of all human relationships."[14]

In Freud's Pantheon, then, masculine images of the mother seem to oscillate between an Aphrodite—all mature heterosexual love and global eroticized giving, perhaps with a touch of narcissism, in love with her son and his penis—and someone who, like Hera, is more vengeful, strong and insistent, resentful of men and their betrayals. Not only is this latter mother herself castrated, but she castrates, or threatens to castrate, both her son and her daughter. In contrast to Jungian writing, Demeter—the mother who loves the daughter and mourns her loss—is nowhere to be found.[15]

In "The Taboo of Virginity" Freud suggests that women other than mothers—specifically, recently deflowered ex-virgins—might castrate a man or take his penis in revenge for their painful defloration.[16] In many cultures, therefore, the custom is *jus primae noctis:* the right of strong, powerful, older men to perform a bride's defloration. Having discussed at length elsewhere the girl's penis envy as well as her very problematic sexual socialization, Freud here suggests in passing that a virgin may indeed be hurt or resent her first experience of intercourse; a husband, who must live with his wife for some time, should be spared her revenge and anger. To build our sense of horror, Freud invokes the decapitating (castrating) Judith and Holofernes, but he is much more certain of the part male fantasy plays in the custom:

> Whenever primitive man has set up a taboo he fears some danger and it cannot be disputed that a generalized dread of women is expressed in all these rules of avoidance. The man is afraid of being weakened by the woman, infected with her femininity. . . . The effect which coitus has of discharging tensions and causing flaccidity may be the prototype of what the man fears.[17]

Even worse, it seems, than the impotence and lack of sexual desire that Freud suggests in the first two "Contributions to the Psychology of Love," is the possibility of total weakening and "infection" with femininity. The young, innocent husband must be protected against such a psychic threat. We must ask, in this context, if the imagined reaction of the girl is not almost entirely that of a man imagining how he would feel if reminded by intercourse of his lack of a penis.

Freud presents as objective truth a final version of woman as subject that is, like the resentment of defloration, really an extension of imaginings and beliefs held by the male psyche. He describes a variety of traits that characterize a woman and that he attributes entirely to penis envy and women's lack of a penis. These include shame about

her body, jealousy (arising directly from the envy itself), a lesser sense of justice (resulting from the weak female superego, a superego that never fully forms because the girl does not fear castration and does not therefore give up oedipal longings or internalize sexual prohibitions), and narcissism and vanity as the self-love that a man centers on his penis becomes defensively diffused throughout the female body. As Freud acknowledges, feminists in his time accused him of male bias in these views. He also points out—in possible contradiction to his resting his case on clinical findings—that these are "character-traits which critics of every epoch have brought up against women."[18] As cultural man, then, he seems to have borrowed a variety of masculine cultural attitudes toward women, whose origins he then coincidentally attributes to the process of female development.

***

We are thus led back to our place of beginning, the theory of femininity. At various points Freud claims that active and passive are our best approximations of masculine and feminine, but he in fact focuses much more on the distinction between phallically endowed and castrated: women, basically, are castrated men. I am not the first person to ask where his overwhelming preoccupation with the penis and castration—male organs and a threat to masculine body integrity, as Freud himself, along with later psychoanalytic commentators, verifies—comes from. We have good reason, from his own account, to think that such a preoccupation comes from the boy; that as Freud wonders about femininity, he is asking, as one commentator puts it, "What is femininity—*for men?*"[19] I have tried to sort out his approach to women as subjects, women as objects to their own subjectivity, and women as explicit and implicit objects in the male psyche. But we are left with this problem: what part of the Freudian construction of woman as subject is really constructed after the fact from the central conflict and trauma in Freud's theory of sexuality, based on an explicit and implicit male norm? Is he asking, as Horney suggests, how a man or boy would feel if he were someone without a penis?[20] Hence, woman as manifest subject becomes, possibly, a latent projection of man.

Freud claims, quite rightly, that his theory comes from clinical experience, and he supports it by drawing upon the writings of several women analysts. But the issue of clinical experience in early psychoanalysis is complicated. For one thing, the women analysts he cites—Deutsch, Lampl-de Groot, and Brunswick—were themselves analyzed by Freud, as was Marie Bonaparte, whose later theorizing on the connections of femininity, masochism, and passivity became Freudian orthodoxy on the psychology of women.[21] Like other analysands, these women analysts seem to have remained transferentially and in actuality attached. Lampl-de Groot, even as she provides the basis for a radically new theory, does not take issue with Freud's claim for the centrality of the female castration complex. Indeed, she reviews almost everything he has written before suggesting—modestly, on the basis of two cases—that there might possibly be something he left out. Deutsch and Anna Freud in their own writings give evidence that they wanted to please Freud by the kinds of theories they created, and they have more than once been taken to task on this account.

Moreover, as the biographical literature on psychoanalysts expands, we are becoming more aware of just how autobiographical the early writings often were. These first analysts, after all, did not have a lot of cases, and one knows—even as one doesn't know—oneself best. Freud makes it quite explicit that his theory of the Oedipus complex evolved from his own self-analysis. His *Interpretation of Dreams* stands as a classic account of psychoanalytic theory creation through self-analysis. We do not know about other occasions when he may have used himself as a case without acknowledging the fact. Other writings are not so candid. A biography of Deutsch and her own autobiography make clear the autobiographical basis, translated into fictive case accounts, of much of her theory of femininity, and among early women writers on women Deutsch is a leading defender and supporter of the theories of primary penis envy, narcissism, masochism and passivity. Elizabeth Young-Bruehl suggests that Freud's "Dissolution of the Oedipus Complex" and "Some Psychical Consequences of the Anatomical Distinction between the Sexes," as well as the earlier paper "A Child Is Being Beaten," come at least partially (and probably entirely in "A Child") from his analysis of his daughter Anna, whose own writings on beating fantasies and on altruism are themselves autobiographical: though presented fictively as cases. Both Deutsch and Anna Freud, in writings now available, affirm at some length their hatred and jealousy of mothers, who are all bad, and their idealization of fathers, who are virtually all good.[22]

Freud's "clinical experience" with women patients, then, from the end of World War I through the mid-1920s—just before his writings on femininity—involved those same women who wrote of themselves and of their own patients as they supported and helped to create his position. Did, and how did, his analysis of these young women followers—including Anna, the one nearest and dearest to him—affect his theory? How much were the autobiographical and theoretical understandings reflected in their writings on femininity affected by their analysis with Freud—a Freud who, as we know from his classic case reports, was not loath to offer his patients interpretations based on previously conceived theories? These understandings, translated by at least Deutsch and Anna Freud into fictive patient accounts as well as into theory, must have emerged at least partially from interpretations and reconstructions made by that very powerful and charismatic person who later used *their* writings as independent corroboration of his own position. They may well have been reflecting their own experience—there are certainly women with the particular configuration of love and hate for father and mother they describe, and women who for a variety of reasons express envy of or desire for a penis, or passive or masochistic sexual desires—but they cast their writings in universal terms, as characterizing femininity per se. And Freud, for theoretical reasons, used them that way as well.

The problem here is not the partially autobiographical basis of these early psychoanalytic writings. Though it is only recently that, under the name of countertransference, analysts have been publicly willing to open themselves as extensively to scrutiny, much early psychoanalytic theory (I do not speculate about psychoanalytic theory today) was autobiographically based, and in the case of the theory of femininity, as elsewhere, the opposition (Horney and Klein, for instance) almost certainly drew upon implicit autobiographical understandings as well.[23] I want to direct attention to the special complexities in the case of Freud's views on the psychology of women and the somewhat less than independently developed clinical and theoretical support he draws upon. We can only begin to untangle the convoluted interactions in theory creation here, but we are certainly thereby invited to rethink such theory.

Although Freud claimed that his understanding of women was "incomplete and fragmentary" and that the girl's attachment to her mother seemed "grey with age and shadowy,"[24] he nevertheless developed a broad-sweeping theory about femininity and treated and discussed many women clinically. For the most part we admire his clinical accounts, his forthright defense of hysterical women, and his condemnation of the conditions leading to repression and hysteria in women. We admire also his toleration and understanding of variations in sexual object choice and sexual subjectivity. Yet though we are still not able completely to evaluate his theory of femininity, most evaluations find it extremely problematic.

By contrast, Freud's understandings about male attitudes toward women and femininity do not seem at all fragmentary and incomplete. They are specific, informative, persuasive, precise; they cover, ingeniously, a variety of sexual, representational, and neurotic formations. They illuminate for us, with passion and empathy, masculine fantasies and conflicts. Rethinking Freud on women, then, leaves us with a normative theory of female psychology and sexuality, a rich account of masculinity as it defines itself in relation to women, and several potential openings toward more plural conceptions of gender and sexuality.

Endnotes

1. See Karen Horney, "The Flight from Womanhood: The Masculinity Complex in Women as Viewed by Men and by Women," and "The Dread of Women," both in *Feminine Psychology* (New York: Norton, 1967), 54–70, 133–46; and Melanie Klein, "Early Stages of the Oedipus Conflict," in *Love, Guilt and Reparation*, 186–98, as well as her post-Freudian writings such as "The Oedipus Conflict in the Light of Early Anxieties," in *Love, Guilt and Reparation*, 370–419, and "Envy and Gratitude," in *Envy and Gratitude* (New York: Delta, 1975), 176–235.

2. Freud, "Fetishism," *S.E.* 21:153. I have rearranged the structure of Freud's sentence to make it active and to fit into my own sentence, but I have not changed his words. The original phrase is, "the portion of his narcissism which Nature has, as a precaution, attached to that particular organ."

3. Freud, "A Special Type of Choice of Object Made by Men" and "On the Universal Tendency to Debasement in the Sphere of Love" are his first two "Contributions to the Psychology of Love" (*S.E.* 11:163–90).

4. Freud, "Femininity," 133–34.

5. Freud, "Fetishism," 152.

6. Freud, "Medusa's Head," *S.E.* 18:273–74.

7. Freud, "Fetishism," 154.

8. Kenneth Lewes, in *The Psychoanalytic Theory of Male Homosexuality* (New York: Simon and Schuster, 1988), 78, points out that all preoedipal children are psychically male homosexual, since they are imaged by Freud to be sexually phallic and sexually desirous of a phallic mother.

9. Freud, *The Interpretation of Dreams*, *S.E.* 4:96–121.

10. On Grusha, see Freud, *From the History of an Infantile Neurosis* ["The Wolf Man"], *S.E.* 17: 90–96. On Fräuleins Peter and Lina, see *Notes upon a Case of Obsessional Neurosis* ["The Rat Man"], *S.E.* 10:160–61.

11. "The Rat Man," 197–98.

12. Freud, *Civilization and Its Discontents*, *S.E.* 21:72, 68. On oneness in the early infantile relationship to the mother, see Freud, "On Narcissism: An Introduction," *S.E.* 14:67–102.

13. Freud, *Introductory Lectures*, 16:314.

14. Freud, "Femininity," 133.

15. See Carl J. Jung and Karoly Kerenyi, *Essays on a Science of Mythology: The Myth of the Divine Child and the Mysteries of Eleusis* (Princeton: Princeton Univ. Press, 1963); and Erich Neumann, *The Great Mother*, 2d ed. (Princeton:

Princeton Univ. Press, 1963). On Hera in the masculine psyche, see Philip Slater, *The Glory of Hera: Greek Mythology and the Greek Family* (Boston: Beacon Press, 1968).

16. Freud, "The Taboo of Virginity (Contributions to the Psychology of Love, III)," *S.E.* 11: 191–208.

17. Ibid., 198–99.

18. Freud, "Some Psychical Consequences," 257.

19. Shoshana Felman, "Rereading Femininity," *Yale French Studies* 62 (1981): 21. Felman also points out that accounts by women, like my account here, are really asking, "What does the question 'What is femininity—*for men?*' mean *for women?*"

20. Horney, "Flight from Womanhood," esp. 57–60 and 70.

21. Marie Bonaparte, *Female Sexuality* (New York: International Univ. Press, 1953).

22. . . .On the autobiographical bases of Deutsch's and Anna Freud's writings, see Helene Deutsch, *Confrontations with Myself* (New York: Norton, 1973); Paul Roazen, *Helene Deutsch* (New York: Anchor, 1985); Nellie Thompson, "Helene Deutsch: A Life in Theory," *Psychoanalytic Quarterly* 56 (1987): 317—53; and Young-Bruehl, *Anna Freud*. On Bonaparte, see Celia Bertin, *Marie Bonaparte* (New York: Harcourt Brace Jovanovich, 1982).

23. See Quinn, *A Mind of Her Own;* and Grosskurth, *Melanie Klein*.

24. Freud, "Femininity," 135, and "Female Sexuality," 226.

XIII. Critical Theory

57

Art in the Age of Mechanical Reproduction

Walter Benjamin
(translated by Harry Zohn)

Though associated with members of the Frankfurt School, Walter Benjamin (1892–1940) was an independent scholar without formal institutional affiliations. His thought was influenced by a wide range of intellectual currents, including the neo-Marxism of Theodor Adorno, the more traditional Marxism of Bertolt Brecht, the utopian theory of Ernst Bloch, and the mysticism of Gershom Scholem. First published in 1936, "Art in the Age of Mechanical Reproduction" is one of his most original and widely read works. In this essay, he seeks to explain the impact on art of the introduction of new technologies that allow for the easy reproduction of the work. This is most evident in photography and film. His argument is that in traditional cultures, art contained an aura, which he sees as linked to ritual. In the modern world, that aura is lost as a consequence of various modes of mechanical reproduction. Benjamin does not engage in a critique of this new development but instead seeks to articulate its implications for the society at large.

Preface

When Marx undertook his critique of the capitalistic mode of production, this mode was in its infancy. Marx directed his efforts in such a way as to give them prognostic value. He went back to the basic conditions underlying capitalistic production and through his presentation showed what could be expected of capitalism in the future. The result was that one could expect it not only to exploit the proletariat with increasing intensity, but ultimately to create conditions which would make it possible to abolish capitalism itself.

The transformation of the superstructure, which takes place far more slowly than that of the substructure, has taken more than half a century to manifest in all areas of culture the change in the conditions of production. Only today can it be indicated what form this has taken. Certain prognostic requirements should be met by these statements. However, theses about the art of the proletariat after its assumption of power or about the art of a classless society would have less bearing on these demands than theses about the developmental tendencies of art under present conditions of production. Their dialectic is no less noticeable in the superstructure than in the economy. It would therefore be wrong to underestimate the value of such theses as a weapon. They brush aside a number of outmoded concepts, such as creativity and genius, eternal value and mystery—concepts whose uncontrolled (and at present almost uncontrollable) application would lead to a processing of data in the Fascist sense. The concepts which are introduced into the theory of art in what follows differ from the more familiar terms in that they are completely useless for the purposes of Fascism. They are, on the other hand, useful for the formulation of revolutionary demands in the politics of art.

I

In principle a work of art has always been reproducible. Man-made artifacts could always be imitated by men. Replicas were made by pupils in practice of their craft, by masters for diffusing their works, and, finally, by third parties in the pursuit of gain. Mechanical reproduction of a work of art, however, represents something new. Historically, it advanced intermittently and in leaps at long intervals, but with accelerated intensity. The Greeks knew only two procedures of technically reproducing works of art: founding and stamping. Bronzes, terra cottas, and coins were the only art works which they could produce in quantity. All others were unique and could not be mechanically reproduced. With the woodcut graphic art became mechanically reproducible for the first time, long before script became reproducible by print. The enormous changes which printing, the mechanical reproduction of writing, has brought about in literature are a familiar story. However, within the phenomenon which we are here examining from the perspective of world history, print is merely a special, though particularly important, case. During the Middle Ages engraving and etching were added to the woodcut; at the beginning of the nineteenth century lithography made its appearance.

With lithography the technique of reproduction reached an essentially new stage. This much more direct process was distinguished by the tracing of the design on a stone rather than its incision on a block of wood or its etching on a copperplate and permitted graphic art for the first time to put its products on the market, not only in large numbers as hitherto, but also in daily changing forms. Lithography enabled graphic art to illustrate everyday life, and it began to keep pace with printing. But only a few decades after its invention, lithography was surpassed by photography. For the first time in the process of pictorial reproduction, photography freed the hand of the most important artistic functions which henceforth devolved only upon the eye looking into a lens. Since the eye perceives more swiftly than the hand can draw, the process of pictorial reproduction was accelerated so enormously that it could keep pace with speech. A film operator shooting a scene in the studio captures the images at the speed of an actor's speech. Just as lithography virtually implied the illustrated newspaper, so did photography foreshadow the sound film. The techni-

cal reproduction of sound was tackled at the end of the last century. These convergent endeavors made predictable a situation which Paul Valéry pointed up in this sentence: "Just as water, gas, and electricity are brought into our houses from far off to satisfy our needs in response to a minimal effort, so we shall be supplied with visual or auditory images, which will appear and disappear at a simple movement of the hand, hardly more than a sign" (*op. cit.*, p. 226). Around 1900 technical reproduction had reached a standard that not only permitted it to reproduce all transmitted works of art and thus to cause the most profound change in their impact upon the public; it also had captured a place of its own among the artistic processes For the study of this standard nothing is more revealing than the nature of the repercussions that these two different manifestations—the reproduction of works of art and the art of the film—have had on art in its traditional form.

II

Even the most perfect reproduction of a work of art is lacking in one element: its presence in time and space, its unique existence at the place where it happens to be. This unique existence of the work of art determined the history to which it was subject throughout the time of its existence. This includes the changes which it may have suffered in physical condition over the years as well as the various changes in its ownership. The traces of the first can be revealed only by chemical or physical analyses which it is impossible to perform on a reproduction; changes of ownership are subject to a tradition which must be traced from the situation of the original.

The presence of the original is the prerequisite to the concept of authenticity. Chemical analyses of the patina of a bronze can help to establish this, as does the proof that a given manuscript of the Middle Ages stems from an archive of the fifteenth century. The whole sphere of authenticity is outside technical—and of course, not only technical—reproducibility. . . . Confronted with its manual reproduction, which was usually branded as a forgery, the original preserved all its authority; not so *vis à vis* technical reproduction. The reason is twofold. First, process reproduction is more independent of the original than manual reproduction. For example, in photography, process reproduction can bring out those aspects of the original that are unattainable to the naked eye yet accessible to the lens, which is adjustable and chooses its angle at will. And photographic reproduction, with the aid of certain processes, such as enlargement or slow motion, can capture images which escape natural vision. Secondly, technical reproduction can put the copy of the original into situations which would be out of reach for the original itself. Above all, it enables the original to meet the beholder halfway, be it in the form of a photograph or a phonograph record. The cathedral leaves its locale to be received in the studio of a lover of art; the choral production, performed in an auditorium or in the open air, resounds in the drawing room.

The situations into which the product of mechanical reproduction can be brought may not touch the actual work of art, yet the quality of its presence is always depreciated. This holds not only for the art work but also, for instance, for a landscape which passes in review before the spectator in a movie. In the case of the art object, a most sensitive nucleus—namely, its authenticity—is interfered with whereas no natural object is vulnerable on that score. The authenticity of a thing is the essence of all that is transmissible from its beginning, ranging from its substantive duration to its testimony to the history which it has experienced. Since the historical testimony rests on the authenticity, the former, too, is jeopardized by reproduction when substantive duration ceases to matter. And what is really jeopardized when the historical testimony is affected is the authority of the object. . . .

One might subsume the eliminated element in the term "aura" and go on to say: that which withers in the age of mechanical reproduction is the aura of the work of art. This is a symptomatic process whose significance points beyond the realm of art. One might generalize by saying: the technique of reproduction detaches the reproduced object from the domain of tradition. By making

many reproductions it substitutes a plurality of copies for a unique existence. And in permitting the reproduction to meet the beholder or listener in his own particular situation, it reactivates the object reproduced. These two processes lead to a tremendous shattering of tradition which is the obverse of the contemporary crisis and renewal of mankind. Both processes are intimately connected with the contemporary mass movements. Their most powerful agent is the film. Its social significance, particularly in its most positive form, is inconceivable without its destructive, cathartic aspect, that is, the liquidation of the traditional value of the cultural heritage. This phenomenon is most palpable in the great historical films. It extends to ever new positions. In 1927 Abel Gance exclaimed enthusiastically: "Shakespeare, Rembrandt, Beethoven will make films . . . all legends, all mythologies and all myths, all founders of religion, and the very religions . . . await their exposed resurrection, and the heroes crowd each other at the gate."[1] Presumably without intending it, he issued an invitation to a far-reaching liquidation.

III

During long periods of history, the mode of human sense perception changes with humanity's entire mode of existence. The manner in which human sense perception is organized, the medium in which it is accomplished, is determined not only by nature but by historical circumstances as well. The fifth century, with its great shifts of population, saw the birth of the late Roman art industry and the Vienna Genesis, and there developed not only an art different from that of antiquity but also a new kind of perception. The scholars of the Viennese school, Riegl and Wickhoff, who resisted the weight of classical tradition under which these later art forms had been buried, were the first to draw conclusions from them concerning the organization of perception at the time. However far-reaching their insight, these scholars limited themselves to showing the significant, formal hallmark which characterized perception in late Roman times. They did not attempt—and, perhaps, saw no way—to show the social transformations expressed by these changes of perception. The conditions for an analogous insight are more favorable in the present. And if changes in the medium of contemporary perception can be comprehended as decay of the aura, it is possible to show its social causes.

The concept of aura which was proposed above with reference to historical objects may usefully be illustrated with reference to the aura of natural ones. We define the aura of the latter as the unique phenomenon of a distance, however close it may be. If, while resting on a summer afternoon, you follow with your eyes a mountain range on the horizon or a branch which casts its shadow over you, you experience the aura of those mountains, of that branch. This image makes it easy to comprehend the social bases of the contemporary decay of the aura. It rests on two circumstances, both of which are related to the increasing significance of the masses in contemporary life. Namely, the desire of contemporary masses to bring things "closer" spatially and humanly, which is just as ardent as their bent toward overcoming the uniqueness of every reality by accepting its reproduction. . . . Every day the urge grows stronger to get hold of an object at very close range by way of its likeness, its reproduction. Unmistakably, reproduction as offered by picture magazines and newsreels differs from the image seen by the unarmed eye. Uniqueness and permanence are as closely linked in the latter as are transitoriness and reproducibility in the former. To pry an object from its shell, to destroy its aura, is the mark of a perception whose "sense of the universal equality of things" has increased to such a degree that it extracts it even from a unique object by means of reproduction. Thus is manifested in the field of perception what in the theoretical sphere is noticeable in the increasing importance of statistics. The adjustment of reality to the masses and of the masses to reality is a process of unlimited scope, as much for thinking as for perception.

IV

The uniqueness of a work of art is inseparable from its being imbedded in the fabric of tradition. This tradition itself is thoroughly alive and extremely changeable. An ancient statue of Venus, for example, stood in a different traditional context with the Greeks, who made it an object of veneration, than with the clerics of the Middle Ages, who viewed it as an ominous idol. Both of them, however, were equally confronted with its uniqueness, that is, its aura. Originally the contextual integration of art in tradition found its expression in the cult. We know that the earliest art works originated in the service of a ritual—first the magical, then the religious kind. It is significant that the existence of the work of art with reference to its aura is never entirely separated from its ritual function. . . . In other words, the unique value of the "authentic" work of art has its basis in ritual, the location of its original use value. This ritualistic basis, however remote, is still recognizable as secularized ritual even in the most profane forms of the cult of beauty. . . . The secular cult of beauty, developed during the Renaissance and prevailing for three centuries, clearly showed that ritualistic basis in its decline and the first deep crisis which befell it. With the advent of the first truly revolutionary means of reproduction, photography, simultaneously with the rise of socialism, art sensed the approaching crisis which has become evident a century later. At the time, art reacted with the doctrine of *l'art pour l'art*, that is, with a theology of art. This gave rise to what might be called a negative theology in the form of the idea of "pure" art, which not only denied any social function of art but also any categorizing by subject matter. (In poetry, Mallarmé was the first to take this position.)

An analysis of art in the age of mechanical reproduction must do justice to these relationships, for they lead us to an all-important insight: for the first time in world history mechanical reproduction emancipates the work of art from its parasitical dependence on ritual. To a greater degree the work of art reproduced becomes the work of art designed for reproducibility. . . . From a photographic negative, for example, one can make any number of prints; to ask for the "authentic" print makes no sense. But the instant the criterion of authenticity ceases to be applicable to artistic production, the total function of art is reversed. Instead of being based on ritual, it begins to be based on another practice—politics.

V

Works of art are received and valued on different planes. Two polar types stand out: with one, the accent is on the cult value; with the other, on the exhibition value of the work. . . . Artistic production begins with ceremonial objects destined to serve in a cult. One may assume that what mattered was their existence, not their being on view. The elk portrayed by the man of the Stone Age on the walls of his cave was an instrument of magic. He did expose it to his fellow men, but in the main it was meant for the spirits. Today the cult value would seem to demand that the work of art remain hidden. Certain statues of gods are accessible only to the priest in the cella; certain Madonnas remain covered nearly all year round; certain sculptures on medieval cathedrals are invisible to the spectator on ground level. With the emancipation of the various art practices from ritual go increasing opportunities for the exhibition of their products. It is easier to exhibit a portrait bust that can be sent here and there than to exhibit the statue of a divinity that has its fixed place in the interior of a temple. The same holds for the painting as against the mosaic or fresco that preceded it. And even though the public presentability of a mass originally may have been just as great as that of a symphony, the latter originated at the moment when its public presentability promised to surpass that of the mass.

With the different methods of technical reproduction of a work of art, its fitness for exhibition increased to such an extent that the quantitative shift between its two poles turned into a qualitative transformation of its nature. This is comparable to the situation of the work of art in prehistoric times when, by the absolute emphasis on its cult value, it was, first and foremost, an instrument of magic. Only later did it come to be recognized as a work of art. In the same way today, by the absolute emphasis on its exhibition value the work of art becomes a creation with entirely new functions, among which the one we are conscious of, the artistic function, later may be recognized as incidental. . . . This much is certain: today photography and the film are the most serviceable exemplifications of this new function.

Endnote

1. Abel Gance, "Le Temps de l'image est venu," *L'Art cinématographique*, Vol. 2, pp. 94 f, Paris, 1927.

58
Philosophy and Critical Theory

Herbert Marcuse

Herbert Marcuse (1898–1979) was one of the key figures associated with the critical theory developed at the Frankfurt School between World Wars I and II. Like so many of his generation, Marcuse was forced to leave Germany because of the rise of Nazism. He settled in the United States, where he remained for the rest of his life, becoming in the process an influential thinker whose ideas were embraced in the 1960s by radical students active in the New Left. In this essay, originally published in 1937, Marcuse attempts to indicate the lineage of critical theory in German philosophy, especially in the traditions emerging out of Kant and Hegel. He depicts critical theory as preoccupied with the potential for human freedom, and as such it offers a critique of contemporary social conditions, not from the perspective of utopian thinking but with an eye to the actual potential for societal transformation.

From the beginning the critical theory of society was constantly involved in philosophical as well as social issues and controversies. At the time of its origin, in the thirties and forties of the nineteenth century, philosophy was the most advanced form of consciousness, and by comparison real conditions in Germany were backward. Criticism of the established order there began as a critique of that consciousness, because otherwise it would have confronted its object at an earlier and less advanced historical stage than that which had already attained reality in countries outside Germany. Once critical theory had recognized the responsibility of economic conditions for the totality of the established world and comprehended the social framework in which reality was organized, philosophy became superfluous as an independent scientific discipline dealing with the structure of reality. Furthermore, problems bearing on the potentialities of man and of reason could now be approached from the standpoint of economics.

Philosophy thus appears within the economic concepts of materialist theory, each of which is more than an economic concept of the sort employed by the academic discipline of economics. It is more due to the theory's claim to explain the totality of man and his world in terms of his social being. Yet it would be false on that account to reduce these concepts to philosophical ones. To the contrary, the philosophical contents relevant to the theory are to be educed from the economic structure. They refer to conditions that, when forgotten, threaten the theory as a whole.

In the conviction of its founders the critical theory of society is essentially linked with materialism. This does not mean that it thereby sets itself up as a philosophical system in opposition to other philosophical systems. The theory of society is an economic, not a philosophical, system. There are two basic elements linking materialism to correct social theory: concern with human happiness, and the conviction that it can be attained only through a transformation of the material conditions of existence. The actual course of the transformation and the fundamental measures to be taken in order to arrive at a rational organization of society are prescribed by analysis of economic and political conditions in the given historical situation. The subsequent construction of the new society cannot be the object of theory, for it is to occur as the free creation of the liberated individuals. When reason has been realized as the rational organization of mankind, philosophy is left without an object. For philosophy, to the extent that it has been, up to the present, more than an occupation or a discipline within the given division of labor, has drawn its life from reason's not yet being reality.

Reason is the fundamental category of philosophical thought, the only one by means of which it has bound itself to human destiny. Philosophy wanted to discover the ultimate and most general grounds of Being.

Under the name of reason it conceived the idea of an authentic Being in which all significant antitheses (of subject and object, essence and appearance, thought and being) were reconciled. Connected with this idea was the conviction that what exists is not immediately and already rational but must rather be brought to reason. Reason represents the highest potentiality of man and of existence; the two belong together. For when reason is accorded the status of substance, this means that at its highest level, as authentic reality, the world no longer stands opposed to the rational thought of men as mere material objectivity (*Gegenständlichkeit*). Rather, it is now comprehended by thought and defined as a concept (*Begriff*). That is, the external, antithetical character of material objectivity is overcome in a process through which the identity of subject and object is established as the rational, conceptual structure that is common to both. In its structure the world is considered accessible to reason, dependent on it, and dominated by it. In this form philosophy is idealism; it subsumes being under thought. But through this first thesis that made philosophy into rationalism and idealism it became critical philosophy as well. As the given world was bound up with rational thought and, indeed, ontologically dependent on it, all that contradicted reason or was not rational was posited as something that had to be overcome. Reason was established as a critical tribunal. In the philosophy of the bourgeois era reason took on the form of rational subjectivity. Man, the individual, was to examine and judge everything given by means of the power of his knowledge. Thus the concept of reason contains the concept of freedom as well. For such examination and judgment would be meaningless if man were not free to act in accordance with his insight and to bring what confronts him into accordance with reason.

> Philosophy teaches us that all properties of mind subsist only through freedom, that all are only means for freedom, and that all seek and produce only freedom. To speculative philosophy belongs the knowledge that freedom is that alone which is true of mind.[1]

Hegel was only drawing a conclusion from the entire philosophical tradition when he identified reason and freedom. Freedom is the "formal element" of rationality, the only form in which reason can be.[2]

With the concept of reason as freedom, philosophy seems to reach its limit. What remains outstanding to the realization of reason is not a philosophical task. Hegel saw the history of philosophy as having reached its definitive conclusion at this point. However, this meant for mankind not a better future but the bad present that this condition perpetuates. Kant had, of course, written essays on universal history with cosmopolitan intent, and on perpetual peace. But his transcendental philosophy aroused the belief that the realization of reason through factual transformation was unnecessary, since individuals could become rational and free within the established order. In its basic concepts this philosophy fell prey to the order of the bourgeois epoch. In a world without reason, reason is only the semblance of rationality; in a state of general unfreedom, freedom is only a semblance of being free. This semblance is generated by the internalization of idealism. Reason and freedom become tasks that the individual is to fulfill within himself, and he can do so regardless of external conditions. Freedom does not contradict necessity, but, to the contrary, necessarily presupposes it. Only he is free who recognizes the necessary as necessary, thereby overcoming its mere necessity and elevating it to the sphere of reason. This is equivalent to asserting that a person born crippled, who cannot be cured at the given state of medical science, overcomes this necessity when he gives reason and freedom scope within his crippled existence, i.e. if from the start he always posits his needs, goals, and actions only as the needs, goals, and actions of a cripple. Idealist rationalism canceled the given antithesis of freedom and necessity so that freedom can never trespass upon necessity. Rather, it modestly sets up house within necessity. Hegel once said that this suspension of necessity "transfigures necessity into freedom."[3]

Freedom, however, can be the truth of necessity only when necessity is already true "in itself." Idealist rationalism's attachment to the status quo is distinguished by its particular conception of the relation of freedom and necessity. This attachment is the price it had to pay for the truth of its knowledge. It is already given in the orientation of the subject of idealist philosophy. This subject is rational only insofar as it is entirely self-sufficient. All that is "other" is alien and external to this subject and as such primarily suspect. For something to be true, it must be certain. For it to be certain, it must be posited by the subject as its own achievement. This holds equally for the *fundamentum inconcussum* of Descartes and the synthetic a priori judgments of Kant. Self-sufficiency and independence of all that is other and alien is the sole guarantee of the subject's freedom. What is not dependent on any other person or thing, what possesses itself, is free. Having excludes the other. Relating to the other in such a way that the subject really reaches and is united with it (or him) counts as loss and dependence. When Hegel ascribed to reason, as authentic reality, movement that "remains within itself," he could invoke Aristotle. From the beginning, philosophy was sure that the highest mode of being was being-within-itself (*Beisichselbstsein*).

This identity in the determination of authentic reality points to a deeper identity, property. Something is authentic when it is self-reliant, can preserve itself, and is not dependent on anything else. For idealism this sort of being is attained when the subject has the world so that it cannot be deprived of it, that it disposes of it omnipresently, and that it appropriates it to the extent that in all otherness the subject is only with itself. However, the freedom attained by Descartes' *ego cogito*, Leibniz's monad, Kant's transcendental ego, Fichte's subject of original activity, and Hegel's world-spirit is not the freedom of pleasurable possession with which the Aristotelian God moved in his own happiness. It is rather the freedom of interminable, arduous labor. In the form that it assumed as authentic Being in modern philosophy, reason has to produce itself and its reality continuously in recalcitrant material. It exists only in this process. What reason is to accomplish is neither more nor less than the constitution of the world for the ego. Reason is supposed to create the universality and community in

which the rational subject participates with other rational subjects. It is the basis of the possibility that, beyond the encounter of merely self-sufficient monads, a common life develops in a common world. But even this achievement does not lead beyond what already exists. It changes nothing. For the constitution of the world has always been effected prior to the actual action of the individual; thus he can never take his most authentic achievement into his own hands. The same characteristic agitation, which fears really taking what is and making something else out of it, prevails in all aspects of this rationalism. Development is proclaimed, but true development is "not a transformation, or becoming something else."[4] For at its conclusion it arrives at nothing that did not already exist "in itself" at the beginning. The absence of concrete development appeared to this philosophy as the greatest benefit. Precisely at its maturest stage, the inner statics of all its apparently so dynamic concepts become manifest. . . .

Critical theory's interest in the liberation of mankind binds it to certain ancient truths. It is at one with philosophy in maintaining that man can be more than a manipulable subject in the production process of class society. To the extent that philosophy has nevertheless made its peace with man's determination by economic conditions, it has allied itself with repression. That is the bad materialism that underlies the edifice of idealism: the consolation that in the material world everything is in order as it is. (Even when it has not been the personal conviction of the philosopher, this consolation has arisen almost automatically as part of the mode of thought of bourgeois idealism and constitutes its ultimate affinity with its time.) The other premise of this materialism is that the mind is not to make its demands in this world, but is to orient itself toward another realm that does not conflict with the material world. The materialism of bourgeois practice can quite easily come to terms with this attitude. The bad materialism of philosophy is overcome in the materialist theory of society. The latter opposes not only the production relations that gave rise to bad materialism, but every form of production that dominates man instead of being dominated by him: this idealism underlies its materialism. Its constructive concepts, too, have a residue of abstractness as long as the reality toward which they are directed is not yet given. Here, however, abstractness results not from avoiding the status quo, but from orientation toward the future status of man. It cannot be supplanted by another, correct theory of the established order (as idealist abstractness was replaced by the critique of political economy). It cannot be succeeded by a new theory, but only by rational reality itself. The abyss between rational and present reality cannot be bridged by conceptual thought. In order to retain what is not yet present as a goal in the present, phantasy is required. The essential connection of phantasy with philosophy is evident from the function attributed to it by philosophers, especially Aristotle and Kant, under the title of "imagination." Owing to its unique capacity to "intuit" an object though the latter be not present and to create something new out of given material of cognition, imagination denotes a considerable degree of independence from the given, of freedom amid a world of unfreedom. In surpassing what is present, it can anticipate the future. It is true that when Kant characterizes this "fundamental faculty of the human soul" as the a priori basis of all knowledge,[5] this restriction to the a priori diverts once again from the future to what is always past. Imagination succumbs to the general degradation of phantasy. To free it for the construction of a more beautiful and happier world remains the prerogative of children and fools. True, in phantasy one can imagine anything. But critical theory does not envision an endless horizon of possibilities.

The freedom of imagination disappears to the extent that real freedom becomes a real possibility. The limits of phantasy are thus no longer universal laws of essence (as the last bourgeois theory of knowledge that took seriously the meaning of phantasy so defined them[6]), but technical limits in the strictest sense. They are prescribed by the level of technological development. What critical theory is engaged in is not the depiction of a future world, although the response of phantasy to such a challenge would not perhaps be quite as absurd as we are led to

believe. If phantasy were set free to answer, with precise reference to already existing technical material, the fundamental philosophical questions asked by Kant, all of sociology would be terrified at the utopian character of its answers. And yet the answers that phantasy could provide would be very close to the truth, certainly closer than those yielded by the rigorous conceptual analyses of philosophical anthropology. For it would determine what man is on the basis of what he really can be tomorrow. In replying to the question, "What may I hope?", it would point less to eternal bliss and inner freedom than to the already possible unfolding and fulfillment of needs and wants. In a situation where such a future is a real possibility, phantasy is an important instrument in the task of continually holding the goal up to view. Phantasy does not relate to the other cognitive faculties as illusion to truth (which in fact, when it plumes itself on being the only truth, can perceive the truth of the future only as illusion). Without phantasy, all philosophical knowledge remains in the grip of the present or the past and severed from the future, which is the only link between philosophy and the real history of mankind.

Strong emphasis on the role of phantasy seems to contradict the rigorously scientific character that critical theory has always made a criterion of its concepts. This demand for scientific objectivity has brought materialist theory into unusual accord with idealist rationalism. While the latter could pursue its concern with man only in abstraction from given facts, it attempted to undo this abstractness by associating itself with science. Science never seriously called use-value into question. In their anxiety about scientific objectivity, the Neo-Kantians are at one with Kant, as is Husserl with Descartes. How science was applied, whether its utility and productivity guaranteed its higher truth or were instead signs of general inhumanity—philosophy did not ask itself these questions. It was chiefly interested in the methodology of the sciences. The critical theory of society maintained primarily that the only task left for philosophy was elaborating the most general results of the sciences. It, too, took as its basis the viewpoint that science had sufficiently demonstrated its ability to serve the development of the productive forces and to open up new potentialities of a richer existence. But while the alliance between idealist philosophy and science was burdened from the beginning with sins engendered by the dependence of the sciences on established relations of domination, the critical theory of society presupposes the disengagement of science from this order. Thus the fateful fetishism of science is avoided here in principle. But this does not dispense the theory from a constant critique of scientific aims and methods which takes into account every new social situation. Scientific objectivity as such is never a sufficient guarantee of truth, especially in a situation where the truth speaks as strongly against the facts and is as well hidden behind them as today. Scientific predictability does not coincide with the futuristic mode in which the truth exists. Even the development of the productive forces and the evolution of technology know no uninterrupted progression from the old to the new society. For here, too, man himself is to determine progress: not "socialist" man, whose spiritual and moral regeneration is supposed to constitute the basis for planning the planners (a view that overlooks that "socialist" planning presupposes the disappearance of the abstract separation both of the subject from his activity and of the subject as universal from each individual subject), but the association of those men who bring about the transformation. Since what is to become of science and technology depends on them, science and technology cannot serve a priori as a conceptual model for critical theory.

Critical theory is, last but not least, critical of itself and of the social forces that make up its own basis. The philosophical element in the theory is a form of protest against the new "Economism," which would isolate the economic struggle and separate the economic from the political sphere. At an early stage, this view was countered with the criticism that the determining factors are the given situation of the entire society, the interrelationships of the various social strata, and relations of political power. The transformation of the economic structure must so reshape the organization of the entire society that, with the abolition of economic antagonisms between groups and individuals, the political sphere becomes to a great extent independent and determines the development of society. With the disappearance of the state, political relations would then become, in a hitherto unknown sense, general human relations: the organization of the administration of social wealth in the interest of liberated mankind. The materialist theory of society is originally a nineteenth-century theory. Representing its relation to rationalism as one of "inheritance," it conceived this inheritance as it manifested itself in the nineteenth century. Much has changed since then. At that time the theory had comprehended, on the deepest level, the possibility of a coming barbarity, but the latter did not appear to be as imminent as the "conservative" abolition of what the nineteenth century represented: conservative of what the culture of bourgeois society, for all its poverty and injustice, had accomplished nonetheless for the development and happiness of the individual. What had already been achieved and what still remained to be done was clear enough. The entire impetus of the theory came from this interest in the individual, and it was not necessary to discuss it philosophically. The situation of inheritance has changed in the meantime. It is not a part of the nineteenth century, but authoritarian barbarity, that now separates the previous reality of reason from the form intended by the theory. More and more, the culture that was to have been abolished recedes into the past. Overlaid by an actuality in which the complete sacrifice of the individual has become a pervasive and almost unquestioned fact of life, that culture has vanished to the point where studying and comprehending it is no longer a matter of spiteful pride, but of sorrow. Critical theory must concern itself to a hitherto unknown extent with the past—precisely insofar as it is concerned with the future.

In a different form, the situation confronting the theory of society in the nineteenth century is being repeated today. Once again real conditions fall beneath the general level of history. Fettering the productive forces and keeping down the standard of life is characteristic of even the economically most developed countries. The reflection cast by the truth of the future in the philosophy of the past provides indications of factors that point beyond today's anachronistic conditions. Thus critical theory is still linked to these truths. They appear in it as part of a process: that of bringing to consciousness potentialities that have emerged within the maturing historical situation. They are preserved in the economic and political concepts of critical theory.

Endnotes

1. Hegel, *Vorlesungen über die Philosophie der Geschichte* in *Werke*, 2d ed. (Berlin, 1840–47), IX, p. 22.

2. Hegel, *Vorlesungen über die Geschichte der Philosophie* in Werke, XIII, p. 34.

3. Hegel, *Enzyclopädie der philosophischen Wissenschaften*, par. 158, *op. cit.*, VI, p. 310.

4. Hegel, *Vorlesungen über die Geschichte der Philosophie, op. cit.*, p. 41.

5. Kant, *Kritik der reinen Vernunft*, *op. cit.*, p. 625.

6. Edmund Husserl, *Formale und transzendentale Logik* in *Jahrbuch für Philosophie*, X (Halle, 1929), p. 219.

59
Traditional and Critical Theory

Max Horkheimer

As the founding director of the Institute of Social Research, better known as the Frankfurt School, Max Horkheimer (1895–1973) was one of the key exponents of critical theory. Like his close associate Theodor Adorno (1903–1969), he lived in exile in the United States during World War II, but disliking American mass culture, both men returned to Germany after the war. In this 1937 essay, Horkheimer compares what he calls "traditional" theory and critical theory. What he has in mind regarding the former is positivist theory that, in attempting to offer a rigorously scientific account of social life—thus the interest in statistics in empirical research—seeks to divorce theory from ethics and praxis. Critical theory, by contrast, is reflexive theory that locates itself within social life as it seeks to comprehend the world in historical rather than naturalistic terms.

What is "theory"? The question seems a rather easy one for contemporary science. Theory for most researchers is the sum-total of propositions about a subject, the propositions being so linked with each other that a few are basic and the rest derive from these. The smaller the number of primary principles in comparison with the derivations, the more perfect the theory. The real validity of the theory depends on the derived propositions being consonant with the actual facts. If experience and theory contradict each other, one of the two must be reexamined. Either the scientist has failed to observe correctly or something is wrong with the principles of the theory. In relation to facts, therefore, a theory always remains a hypothesis. One must be ready to change it if its weaknesses begin to show as one works through

the material. Theory is stored-up knowledge, put in a form that makes it useful for the closest possible description of facts. Poincaré compares science to a library that must ceaselessly expand. Experimental physics is the librarian who takes care of acquisitions, that is, enriches knowledge by supplying new material. Mathematical physics—the theory of natural science in the strictest sense—keeps the catalogue; without the catalogue one would have no access to the library's rich contents. "That is the rôle of mathematical physics. It must direct generalisation, so as to increase what I have called just now the output of science."[1] The general goal of all theory is a universal systematic science, not limited to any particular subject matter but embracing all possible objects. The division of sciences is being broken down by deriving the principles for special areas from the same basic premises. The same conceptual apparatus which was elaborated for the analysis of inanimate nature is serving to classify animate nature as well, and anyone who has once mastered the use of it, that is, the rules for derivation, the symbols, the process of comparing derived propositions with observable fact, can use it at any time. But we are still rather far from such an ideal situation.

Such, in its broad lines, is the widely accepted idea of what theory is. Its origins supposedly coincide with the beginnings of modern philosophy. The third maxim in Descartes' scientific method is the decision

> to carry on my reflections in due order, commencing with objects that were the most simple and easy to understand, in order to rise little by little, or by degrees, to knowledge of the most complex, assuming an order, even if a fictitious one, among those which do not follow a natural sequence relative to one another.

The derivation as usually practiced in mathematics is to be applied to all science. The order in the world is captured by a deductive chain of thought.

> Those long chains of deductive reasoning, simple and easy as they are, of which geometricians make use in order to arrive at the most difficult demonstrations, had caused me to imagine that all those

things which fall under the cognizance of men might very likely be mutually related in the same fashion; and that, provided only that we abstain from receiving anything as true which is not so, and always retain the order which is necessary in order to deduce the one conclusion from the other, there can be nothing so remote that we cannot reach to it, nor so recondite that we cannot discover it.[2]

Depending on the logician's own general philosophical outlook, the most universal propositions from which the deduction begins are themselves regarded as experiential judgments, as inductions (as with John Stuart Mill), as evident insights (as in rationalist and phenomenological schools), or as arbitrary postulates (as in the modern axiomatic approach). In the most advanced logic of the present time, as represented by Husserl's *Logische Untersuchungen*, theory is defined "as an enclosed system of propositions for a science as a whole."[3] Theory in the fullest sense is "a systematically linked set of propositions, taking the form of a systematically unified deduction."[4] Science is "a certain totality of propositions . . . , emerging in one or other manner from theoretical work, in the systematic order of which propositions a certain totality of objects acquires definition."[5] The basic requirement which any theoretical system must satisfy is that all the parts should intermesh thoroughly and without friction. Harmony, which includes lack of contradictions, and the absence of superfluous, purely dogmatic elements which have no influence on the observable phenomena, are necessary conditions, according to Weyl.[6]

In so far as this traditional conception of theory shows a tendency, it is towards a purely mathematical system of symbols. As elements of the theory, as components of the propositions and conclusions, there are ever fewer names of experiential objects and ever more numerous mathematical symbols. Even the logical operations themselves have already been so rationalized that, in large areas of natural science at least, theory formation has become a matter of mathematical construction.

The sciences of man and society have attempted to follow the lead of the natural sciences with their great successes. The difference between those schools of social science which are more oriented to the investigation of facts and those which concentrate more on principles has nothing directly to do with the concept of theory as such. The assiduous collecting of facts in all the disciplines dealing with social life, the gathering of great masses of detail in connection with problems, the empirical inquiries, through careful questionnaires and other means, which are a major part of scholarly activity, especially in the Anglo-Saxon universities since Spencer's time—all this adds up to a pattern which is, outwardly, much like the rest of life in a society dominated by industrial production techniques. Such an approach seems quite different from the formulation of abstract principles and the analysis of basic concepts by an armchair scholar, which are typical, for example, of one sector of German sociology. Yet these divergences do not signify a structural difference in ways of thinking. In recent periods of contemporary society the so-called human studies (*Geisteswissenschaften*) have had but a fluctuating market value and must try to imitate the more prosperous natural sciences whose practical value is beyond question. . . .

We must go on now to add that there is a human activity which has society itself for its object.[7] The aim of this activity is not simply to eliminate one or other abuse, for it regards such abuses as necessarily connected with the way in which the social structure is organized. Although it itself emerges from the social structure, its purpose is not, either in its conscious intention or in its objective significance, the better functioning of any element in the structure. On the contrary, it is suspicious of the very categories of better, useful, appropriate, productive, and valuable, as these are understood in the present order, and refuses to take them as non-scientific presuppositions about which one can do nothing. The individual as a rule must simply accept the basic conditions of his existence as given and strive to fulfill them; he finds his satisfaction and praise in accomplishing as well as he can the tasks connected with his place in society and in courageously doing his duty despite all the sharp criticism he may choose to exercise in particular matters. But the critical attitude of which we are speaking is wholly distrustful of the rules of conduct with which society as presently constituted provides each of its members. The separation between individual and society in virtue of which the individual accepts as natural the limits prescribed for his activity is relativized in critical theory. The latter considers the overall framework which is conditioned by the blind interaction of individual activities (that is, the existent division of labor and the class distinctions) to be a function which originates in human action and therefore is a possible object of planful decision and rational determination of goals.

The two-sided character of the social totality in its present form becomes, for men who adopt the critical attitude, a conscious opposition. In recognizing the present form of economy and the whole culture which it generates to be the product of human work as well as the organization which mankind was capable of and has provided for itself in the present era, these men identify themselves with this totality and conceive it as will and reason. It is their own world. At the same time, however, they experience the fact that society is comparable to nonhuman natural processes, to pure mechanisms, because cultural forms which are supported by war and oppression are not the creations of a unified, self-conscious will. That world is not their own but the world of capital.

Previous history thus cannot really be understood; only the individuals and specific groups in it are intelligible, and even these not totally, since their internal dependence on an inhuman society means that even in their conscious action such individuals and groups are still in good measure mechanical functions. The identification, then, of men of critical mind with their society is marked by tension, and the tension characterizes all the concepts of the critical way of thinking. Thus, such thinkers interpret the economic categories of work, value, and productivity exactly as they are interpreted in the existing order, and they regard any other interpretation as pure idealism. But at the same time they consider it rank dishonesty simply to accept the interpretation; the critical acceptance of the categories which rule social life contains simultaneously their condemnation. This dialectical character of the self-interpretation of contemporary man is what, in the last analysis, also causes the obscurity of the Kantian critique of reason. Reason cannot become transparent to itself as long as men act as members of an organism which lacks reason. Organism as a naturally developing and declining unity cannot be a sort of model for society, but only a form of deadened existence from which society must emancipate itself. An attitude which aims at such an emancipation and at an alteration of society as a whole might well be of service in theoretical work carried on within reality as presently ordered. But it lacks the pragmatic character which attaches to traditional thought as a socially useful professional activity.

In traditional theoretical thinking, the genesis of particular objective facts, the practical application of the conceptual systems by which it grasps the facts, and the role of such systems in action, are all taken to be external to the theoretical thinking itself. This alienation, which finds expression in philosophical terminology as the separation of value and research, knowledge and action, and other polarities, protects the savant from the tensions we have indicated and provides an assured framework for his activity. Yet a kind of thinking which does not accept this framework seems to have the ground taken out from under it. If a theoretical procedure does not take the form of determining objective facts with the help of the simplest and most differentiated conceptual systems available, what can it be but an aimless intellectual game, half conceptual poetry, half impotent expression of states of mind? The investigation into the social conditioning of facts and theories may indeed be a research problem, perhaps even a whole field for theoretical work, but how can such studies be radically different from other specialized efforts? Research into ideologies, or sociology of knowledge, which has been taken over from the critical theory of society and established as a special discipline, is not opposed either in its aim or in its other ambitions to the usual activities that go on within classificatory science. . . .

How is critical thought related to experience? One might maintain that if such thought were not simply to classify but also to determine for itself the goals which classification serves, in other words its own fundamental direction, it would remain locked up within itself, as happened to idealist philosophy. If it did not take refuge in utopian fantasy, it would be reduced to the formalistic fighting of sham battles. The attempt legitimately to determine practical goals by thinking must always fail. If thought were not content with the role given to it in existent society, if it were not to engage in theory in the traditional sense of the word, it would necessarily have to return to illusions long since laid bare.

The fault in such reflections as these on the role of thought is that thinking is understood in a detachedly departmentalized and therefore spiritualist way, as it is today under existing conditions of the division of labor. In society as it is, the power of thought has never controlled itself but has always functioned as a nonindependent moment in the work process, and the latter has its own orientation and tendency. The work process enhances and develops human life through the conflicting movement of progressive and retrogressive periods. In the historical form in which society has existed, however, the full measure of goods produced for man's enjoyment has, at any particular stage, been given directly only to a small group of men. Such a state of affairs has found expression in thought, too, and left its mark on philosophy and religion. But from the beginning the desire to bring the same enjoyment to the majority has stirred in the depths of men's hearts; despite all the material appropriateness of class organization, each of its forms has finally proved inadequate. Slaves, vassals, and citizens have cast off their yoke. Now, inasmuch as every individual in modern times has been required to make his own the purposes of society as a whole and to recognize these in society, there is the possibility that men would become aware of and concentrate their attention upon the path which the social work process has taken without any definite theory behind it, as a result of disparate forces interacting, and with the despair of the masses acting as a decisive factor at major turning points. Thought does not spin such a possibility out of itself but rather becomes aware of its own proper function. In the course of history men have come to know their own activity and thus to recognize the contradiction that marks their existence. The bourgeois economy was concerned that the individual should maintain the life of society by taking care of his own personal happiness. Such an economy has within it, however, a dynamism which results in a fantastic degree of power for some, such as reminds us of the old Asiatic dynasties, and in material and intellectual weakness for many others. The original fruitfulness of the bourgeois organization of the life process is thus transformed into a paralyzing barrenness, and men by their own toil keep in existence a reality which enslaves them in ever greater degree.

Yet, as far as the role of experience is concerned, there is a difference between traditional and critical theory. The viewpoints which the latter derives from historical analysis as the goals of human activity, especially the idea of a reasonable organization of society that will meet the needs of the whole community, are immanent in human work but are not correctly grasped by individuals or by the common mind. A certain concern is also required if these tendencies are to be perceived and expressed. According to Marx and Engels such a concern is necessarily generated in the proletariat. Because of its situation in modern society the proletariat experiences the connection between work which puts ever more powerful instruments into men's hands in their struggle with nature, and the continuous renewal of an outmoded social organization. Unemployment, economic crises, militarization, terrorist regimes—in a word, the whole condition of the masses—are not due, for example, to limited technological possibilities, as might have been the case in earlier periods, but to the circumstances of production which are no longer suitable to our time. The application of an intellectual and physical means for the mastery of nature is hindered because in the prevailing circumstances these means are entrusted to special, mutually opposed interests. Production is not geared to the life of the whole community while heeding also the claims of individuals; it is geared to the power-backed claims of individuals while being concerned hardly at all with the life of the community. This is the inevitable result, in the present property system, of the principle that it is enough for individuals to look out for themselves. . . .

Even the critical theory, which stands in opposition to other theories, derives its statements about real relationships from basic universal concepts, as we have indicated, and therefore presents the relationships as necessary. Thus both kinds of theoretical structure are alike when it comes to logical necessity. But there is a difference as soon as we turn from logical to real necessity, the necessity involved in factual sequences. The biologist's statement that internal processes cause a plant to wither or that certain processes in the human organism lead to its destruction leaves untouched the question whether any influences can alter the character of these processes or change them totally. Even when an illness is said to be curable, the fact that the necessary curative measures are actually taken is regarded as purely extrinsic to the curability, a matter of technology and therefore nonessential as far as the theory as such is concerned. The necessity which rules society can be regarded as biological in the sense described, and the unique character of critical theory can therefore be called in question on the grounds that in biology as in other natural sciences particular sequences of events can be theoretically constructed just as they are in the critical theory of society. The development of society, in this view, would simply be a particular series of events, for the presentation of which conclusions from various other areas of research are used, just as a doctor in the course of an illness or a geologist dealing with the earth's prehistory has to apply various other disciplines. Society here would be the individual reality which is evaluated on the basis of theories in the special sciences.

However many valid analogies there may be between these different intellectual endeavors, there is nonetheless a decisive difference when it comes to the relation of subject and object and therefore to the necessity of the event being judged. The object with which the scientific specialist deals is not affected at all by his own theory. Subject and object are kept strictly apart. Even if it turns out that at a later point in time the objective event is influenced by human intervention, to science this is just another fact. The objective occurrence is independent of the theory, and this independence is part of its necessity: the observer as such can effect no change in the object. A consciously critical attitude, however, is part of the development of society: the construing of the course of history as the necessary product of an economic mechanism simultaneously contains both a protest against this order of things, a protest generated by the order itself, and the idea of self-determination for the human race, that is the idea of a state of affairs in which man's actions no longer flow from a mechanism but from his own decision. The judgment passed on the necessity inherent in the previous course of events implies here a struggle to change it from a blind to a meaningful necessity. If we think of the object of the theory in separation from the theory, we falsify it and fall into quietism or conformism. Every part of the theory presupposes the critique of the existing order and the struggle against it along lines determined by the theory itself.

The theoreticians of knowledge who started with physics had reason, even if they were not wholly right, to condemn the confusion of cause and operation of forces and to substitute the idea of condition or function for the idea of cause. For the kind of thinking which simply registers facts there are always only series of phenomena, never forces and counterforces; but this, of course, says something about this kind of thinking, not about nature. If such a method is applied to society, the result is statistics and descriptive sociology, and these can be important for many purposes, even for critical theory.

Endnotes

1. Henri Poincaré, *Science and Hypothesis*, tr. by W[illiam] J[ohn] G[reenstreet] (London: Walter Scott, 1905), p. 145.

2. Descartes, *Discourse on Method*, in *The Philosophical Works of Descartes*, tr. by Elizabeth S. Haldane and G. R. T. Ross (Cambridge: Cambridge University Press, 1931 . . .), Volume 1, p. 92.

3. Edmund Husserl, *Formale und transzendentale Logik* (Halle, 1929), p. 89.

4. Husserl, *op. cit.*, p. 79.

5. Husserl, *op. cit.*, p. 91.

6. Hermann Weyl, *Philosophie der Naturwissenschaft*, in *Handbuch der Philosophie*, Part 2 (Munich-Berlin, 1927), pp. 118ff.

7. In the following pages this activity is called "critical" activity. The term is used here less in the sense it has in the idealist critique of pure reason than in the sense it has in the dialectical critique of political economy. It points to an essential aspect of the dialectical theory of society.

60

On Systematically Distorted Communication

Jürgen Habermas

Jürgen Habermas (b. 1929) is the most important second-generation member of the Frankfurt School. Devising a brilliant synthesis of social theory influenced by Marx, Weber, Freud, Parsons, and others, he has created his own unique perspective as a latter-day defender of the ideals of the Enlightenment. Key to his work is an attempt to complement Marx's focus on the labor process with the notion of communicative practices. Of importance for the prospects of democracy, he believes, are situations characterized by "undistorted communication," which involves an ideal speech situation in which the participants interact as relative equals without coercion and with an open and tolerant willingness to listen to the arguments of others. In this essay from 1970, Habermas uses Freudian ideas to discuss some of the impediments that make realizing the ideal speech situation difficult.

1. Where difficulties of comprehension are the result of cultural, temporal, or social distance, we can say in principle what further information we would need in order to achieve understanding: we know that we must decipher the alphabet, become acquainted with lexicon and grammar, or uncover context-specific rules of application. In attempting to explain unclear or incomprehensible meaning-associations we are able to recognize, within the limits of normal communication, what it is that we do not—yet—know. However, this "hermeneutic" consciousness of translation difficulties proves to be inadequate when applied to systematically distorted communication. For in this case incomprehensibility results from a faulty organization of speech itself. Obvious examples are those clearly pathological speech disturbances to be observed, for example, among psychotics. But the more important occurrences of the pattern of systematically distorted communication are those which appear in speech which is not conspicuously pathological. This is what we encounter in the case of pseudocommunication, where the participants do not recognize any communication disturbances. Pseudocommunication produces a system of reciprocal misunderstandings which, due to the false assumption of consensus, are not recognized as such. Only a neutral observer notices that the participants do not understand one another. . . .

Freud dealt with the occurrence of systematically deformed communication in order to define the scope of specifically incomprehensible acts and utterances. He always envisaged the dream as the standard example of such phenomena. . . . He employed the insights gained from clinical phenomena as the key to the pseudonormality, that is to the hidden pathology, of collective behavior and entire social systems. In our discussion of psychoanalysis as a kind of linguistic analysis pertaining to systematically distorted communication, we shall first consider the example of neurotic symptoms.

Three criteria are available for defining the scope of specific incomprehensible acts and utterances. (a) On the level of language, distorted communication becomes noticeable because of the use of rules which deviate from the recognized system of linguistic rules. . . . Using dream texts, Freud examined, in particular, condensation, displacement, absence of grammaticalness, and the use of words with opposite meaning. (b) On the behavior level, the deformed language game appears in the form of rigidity and compulsory repetition. Stereotyped behavior patterns recur in situations involving stimuli which cause emotionally loaded reactions. . . . (c) If, finally, we consider the system of distorted communication as a whole, we are struck by the discrepancy between the levels of communication; the usual congruency between linguistic symbols, actions, and accompanying gestures has disintegrated. . . . There is a communication obstruction in the self between the ego, which is capable of speech and participates in intersubjectively established language-games, and that "inner foreign territory" (Freud), which is represented by a private or a primary linguistic symbolism.

2. Alfred Lorenzer has examined the analytical conversation between physician and patient from the standpoint of psychoanalysis as analysis of language.[1] He considers the process by which the meanings of specific incomprehensible manifestations are decoded as an understanding of scenes linked by analogy to those in which the symptoms occur. The purpose of analytical interpretation is to explain the incomprehensible meaning of the symptomatic manifestations. Where neuroses are involved, these manifestations are part of a deformed language-game in which the patient "acts": that is, he plays an incomprehensible scene by violating role-expectations in a strikingly stereotyped manner. The analyst tries to make the symptomatic scene understandable by associating it with analogous scenes in the situation of transference. The latter holds the key to the coded relation between the symptomatic scene, which the adult patient plays outside the doctor's office, and an original scene experienced in early childhood. In the transference situation the patient forces the doctor into the role of the conflict-defined primary reference person. The doctor, in the role of the reflective or critical participant, can interpret the transference situation as a repetition of early childhood experiences; he can thus construct a dictionary for the hidden idiosyncratic meanings of the symptoms. "Scenic understanding" is therefore based on the discovery that the patient behaves in the same way in his symptomatic scenes as he does in certain transference situations; such understanding aims at the reconstruction, confirmed by the patient in an act of self-reflection, of the original scene.

2.1. The reestablished original scene is typically a situation in which the child has once suffered and repulsed an unbearable conflict. This repulse is coupled with a process of desymbolization and the formation of a symptom. The child excludes the experience of the conflict-filled object from public communication (and at the same time makes it inaccessible to its own ego as well); it separates the conflict-laden portion of its memory of the object and, so to speak, desymbolizes the meaning of the relevant reference person. The gap which arises in the semantic field is then closed by employing an unquestionable symbol in place of the isolated symbolic content. This symbol, of course, strikes us as being a symptom, because it has gained private linguistic significance and can no longer be used according to the rules of public language. The analyst's scenic understanding establishes meaning equivalences between the elements of three patterns—the everyday scene, the transference scene, and the original scene—and solves the specific incomprehensibility of the symptom; thus it assists in achieving resymbolization, that is, the reentry of isolated symbolic contents into public communication. The latent meaning of the present situation becomes accessible when it is related to the unimpaired meaning of the original infantile scene. Scenic understanding makes it possible to "translate" the meaning of the pathologically frozen communication pattern which had been hitherto unconscious and inaccessible to public communication.

2.2. If we consider everyday interpretation within the range of ordinary language or translation from one language into another, or trained linguistic analysis in general, all of them leading to hermeneutic understanding of initially incomprehensible utterances, then scenic understanding differs from that hermeneutic understanding because of its explanatory power.[2] That is, the disclosure of the meaning of specific incomprehensible acts or utterances develops to the same extent as, in the course of reconstruction of the original scene, a clarification of the genesis of the faulty meaning is achieved. The What, the semantic content of a systematically distorted manifestation, cannot be "understood" if it is not possible at the same time to "explain" the Why, the origin of the symptomatic scene with reference to the initial circumstances which led to the systematic distortion itself. . . .

Scenic understanding—in contrast to hermeneutic understanding, or ordinary semantic analysis—cannot be conceived as being a mere application of communicative competence, free from theoretical guidance.

3. The theoretical propositions on which this special kind of language analysis is implicitly based can be elicited from three points of view. (1) The psychoanalyst has a preconception of the structure of nondistorted ordinary communication; (2) he attributes the systematic distortion of communication to the confusion of two developmentally following phases of prelinguistic and linguistic symbol-organization; and (3) to explain the origin of deformation he employs a theory of deviant socialization which includes the connection between patterns of interaction in early childhood and the formation of personality structures. I would like to consider these three aspects briefly.

3.1. The first set of theoretical propositions concerns the structural conditions that must be met if normal communication is to obtain.

(a) In the case of a nondeformed language-game there is a congruency on all three levels of communication. Linguistic expressions, expressions represented in actions, and those embodied in gestures do not contradict one another, but rather supplement one another by metacommunication. . . .

(b) Normal communication conforms to intersubjectively recognized rules; it is public. The communicated meanings are identical for all members of the language-community. Verbal utterances are constructed according to the valid system of grammatical rules and are conventionally applied to specific situations. For extra-verbal expressions, which are not grammatically organized, there is likewise a lexicon which varies socioculturally within certain limits.

(c) In the case of normal speech the speakers are aware of the categorical difference between subject and object. They differentiate between outer and inner speech and separate the private from the public world. The differentiation between being and appearance depends, moreover, on the distinction between the language-sign, its significative content (*significatum*), and the object which the symbol denotes (referent, *denotatum*). . . .

(d) In normal communication an intersubjectivity of mutual understanding, guaranteeing ego-identity, develops and is maintained in the relation between individuals who acknowledge one another. On the one hand, the analytic use of language allows the identification of objects (thus the categorization of particular items, the subordination of elements under classes, and the inclusion of sets). On the other hand, the reflexive use of language assures a relationship between the speaking subject and the language community which cannot be sufficiently presented by analytic operations.

. . . The relation between I (ego), you (alter ego), and we (ego and alter ego) is established only by an analytically paradoxical achievement: the speaking persons identify themselves at the same time with two incompatible dialogue roles and thereby ensure the identity of the I (ego) as well as of the group. The one being (ego) asserts his absolute nonidentity in relation to the other being (alter ego); at the same time, however, both recognize their identity inasmuch as each acknowledges the other as being an ego, that is, a nonreplaceable individual who can refer to himself as "I." Moreover, that which links them both is a mutual factor (we), a collectivity, which in turn asserts its individuality in relation to other groups. This means that the same paradoxical relationship is established on the level of intersubjectively linked collectives as holds between the individuals.

The specific feature of linguistic intersubjectivity exists in the fact that individuated persons communicate on the basis of it. In the reflexive use of language we present inalienably individual aspects in unavoidably general categories in such a way that we metacommunicatively comment upon and sometimes even revoke direct information (and confirm it only with reservations). We do this for the purpose of an indirect representation of the nonidentical aspects of the ego, aspects which are not sufficiently covered by the general determinations and yet cannot be manifestly represented other than by just these determinations. The analytical use of language is necessarily embedded in the reflexive use, because the inter-subjectivity of mutual understanding cannot be maintained without reciprocal self-representation on the part of the speaking subjects. Inasmuch as the speaker masters this indirect information on the metacommunicative level, he differentiates between essence and appearance. The understanding we come to about objects can be direct, but the subjectivity we encounter when we speak with one another remains, in direct information, only at the level of appearance. The categorical meaning of this kind of indirect communication, in which the indefinable individualized aspect of a person is expressed, and his claim upon individuality is maintained, is something we merely reify in the ontological concept of essence. In fact this essence exists only in its appearances.

(e) Finally, normal speech is distinguished by the fact that the sense of substance and causality, of space and time, is differentiated according to whether these categories are applied to the objects within a world or to the linguistically constituted world itself, which allows for the mutuality of speaking subjects. The interpretational schema, "substance," has a different meaning for the identity of items which can be clearly categorized analytically from that which it has for speaking and interacting subjects themselves, whose ego-identity, as has been shown, just cannot be grasped by analytically clear-cut operations. The interpretational schema of causality, when applied to observable events, leads to the concept of "cause"; when it is applied to an association of intentional actions it leads to the concept of "motive." In the same way "space" and "time" undergo a different schematism when viewed in regard to physically measurable properties of observable events from that which they undergo when viewed according to experienced interactions. . . .

3.2. The second set of postulates concerns the connection between two genetically successive phases of human symbol-organization.

(a) The archaic symbol-organization, which resists the transformation of its contents into grammatically regulated communication, can only be disclosed on the basis of the data of speech pathology and by

means of the analysis of dream material. . . . Freud had already noticed the lack of logical connections in his dream analyses. He draws attention particularly to the use of words with opposite meaning, a remnant on the linguistic level of the genetically earlier peculiarity of combining logically incompatible meanings. Prelinguistic symbols are emotionally loaded and remain fixed to particular scenes. There is no dissociation of linguistic symbol and bodily gesture. The connection to a particular context is so strong that the symbol cannot vary independently of actions. Although the palaeosymbols represent a prelinguistic basis for the intersubjectivity of mutual existence and shared action, they do not allow public communication in the strict sense of the word.

. . . Prelinguistic symbol-organization does not allow an analytically satisfying categorization of the objects experienced. Two types of deficiencies are found in the communication and thought disturbances of psychotics: namely "amorphous" and "fragmented" speech disorders.[3] In both cases the analytic operations of classification are disturbed. In the first, a fragmentation of structure is apparent which does not allow disintegrated single elements to be compiled into classes according to general criteria. In the second, an amorphous structure appears which does not allow aggregates of superficially similar and vaguely compiled things to be analyzed. . . . Animistic *Weltanschauungen*, for example, are formed in accordance with such primary classes.

(b) The symbol-organization described here, which precedes language genetically, is a theoretical construct. We cannot observe it anywhere. But the psychoanalytical decoding of systematically distorted communication presupposes such a construction, because that special type of semantic analysis introduced here as "scenic understanding" resolves confusions of ordinary speech by interpreting them either as forced regression back to an earlier level of communication, or as the breakthrough of the earlier form of communication into language. On the basis of the analyst's experience with neurotic patients, we can, as has been shown, recognize the function of psychoanalysis as language analysis, insofar as it allows separated symbolic contents, which lead to a private narrowing of public communication, to be reintegrated into common linguistic usage. The performance of the analyst in putting an end to the process of inhibition serves the purpose of resymbolization; inhibition itself can therefore be understood as a process linked to desymbolization. The defense mechanism of inhibition, which is analogous to flight, is revealed by the patient in his resistance to plausible interpretations made by the analyst. This mechanism is an operation carried on with and by language; otherwise it would not be possible to reverse the process of repulsion hermeneutically, i.e., precisely by means of a special type of semantic analysis. The fleeing ego, which has to submit to the demands of outer reality in a conflict situation, hides itself from itself by eliminating the symbolic representation of unwanted demands of instinct from the text of its everyday consciousness. By means of this censorship the representation of the prohibited object is excommunicated from public communication and banished to the archaic level of palaeosymbols. Moreover, the assumption that neurotic behavior is controlled by palaeosymbols, and only subsequently rationalized by a substitutive interpretation, offers an explanation for the characteristics of this behavior pattern: for its pseudocommunicative function, for its stereotyped and compulsive form, for its emotional load and expressive content, and, finally, for its rigid fixation upon particular situations.

If inhibition can be understood as desymbolization, then it follows that there must be a correspondingly linguistic interpretation for the complementary defense mechanism, which does not turn against the self but rather against outer reality, i.e., for projection and denial. While in the case of inhibition the language-game is deformed by the symptoms formed in place of the excommunicated symbols, the distortion in the case of this defense mechanism results directly from the uncontrolled penetration of palaeosymbolic derivatives into language. In this case the therapeutic type of language analysis doesn't aim at retransforming the desymbolized content into linguistically articulated meaning, but aims rather at a con-

sciously achieved communication of the intermingled prelinguistic elements.

In both cases the systematic distortion can be explained by the fact that palaeosymbolically fixed semantic contents have encysted themselves, like foreign bodies, into the grammatically regulated use of symbols. Language analysis has the duty of dissolving this syndrome, i.e., of isolating the two language levels. There is, however, a third case: the processes of the creative extension of language. In this case a genuine integration is accomplished. The palaeosymbolically fixed meaning-potential is then brought into the open and is thus made available for public communication. This transfer of semantic contents from the prelinguistic into the common stock of language widens the scope of communicative action as it diminishes that of unconsciously motivated action. The moment of success in the use of creative language is a moment of emancipation. . . .

3.3. Psychoanalysis, which interprets the specific incomprehensibility of systematically distorted communication, can no longer strictly speaking be conceived according to the translation model which applies to simple hermeneutic understanding or ordinary semantic analysis. For the obscurities which controlled "translation" from prelinguistic symbolism to language does away with are ones which arise not within the scope defined by a given language-system, but rather within language itself. Here it is the very structure of communication, hence the basis of all translation, that we are concerned with. Semantic analysis of this special type therefore needs a systematic preunderstanding which pertains to language and linguistic communication as such, while on the other hand our ordinary semantic analysis proceeds *ad hoc* from a traditionally determined pre-understanding which is tested and revised within the process of interpretation. The theoretical propositions deal, as described, with the preconditions of normal communication, with two levels of symbol organization, and with the mechanism of speech disorder. These theoretical assumptions can be organized in the structural model.

The constructions of "ego" and "id" interpret the analyst's experiences in his encountering the resistance of his patients. "Ego" is the instance which fulfils the function of reality-testing and of censorship. "Id" is the name given to those parts of the self that are isolated from the ego and whose representations become accessible in connection with the processes of repression and projection. The "id" is expressed indirectly by the symptoms which close the gap which develops in everyday language when desymbolization takes place; direct representation of the "id" is found in the illusory palaeosymbolic elements dragged into the language by projection and denial. Now, the same clinical experience which leads to the construction of an ego- and id-instance, shows also that the defense mechanisms usually work unconsciously. For this reason Freud introduced the category of "superego": an ego-foreign instance which is formed out of detached identifications with the expectations of primary reference persons. All three categories—ego, id, and superego—reflect fundamental experiences typical of a systematically distorted communication. The dimensions established by id and superego for the personality structure correspond to the dimensions of deformation of the intersubjectivity of mutual understanding in informal communication. So the structural model which Freud introduced as the categorical frame of metapsychology can be reduced to a theory of deviant communicative competence.[4]

4. I have chosen psychoanalysis as my example in order to differentiate between two types of interpretation and two forms of communication.

From the viewpoint of a logic of explanation, this example of the semantic analysis of specific incomprehensible manifestations is of interest because, in a unique way, it affords simultaneous hermeneutic understanding and causal explanation. The analyst's understanding owes its explanatory power—as we have seen—to the fact that the clarification of a systematically inaccessible meaning succeeds only to the extent to which the origin of the faulty or misleading meaning is explained. The reconstruction of the original scene makes both possible at the same time: the reconstruction leads to an understanding of the meaning of a deformed language-game and simultaneously explains

the origin of the deformation itself. Of course, the connection between semantic analysis and causal explanation doesn't become evident until one shows that the categorical framework of the theory used—in our case the Freudian metapsychology—is based on an at least implicitly underlying language theory. I have outlined only some of the assumptions which extend to the structure of normal communication and to the mechanisms of systematic distortion of communication. These assumptions have to be developed within the framework of a theory of communicative competence.

I can sum up my thesis as follows. The common semantic analysis of incomprehensible utterances, which leads to hermeneutic understanding, makes use of the non-analyzed communicative competence of a native speaker. On the other hand, the special type of semantic analysis which deals with manifestations of a systematically distorted communication and affords an explanatory understanding, presupposes a theory of communicative competence. It is only in virtue of an at least implicit hypothesis concerning the nature and the acquisition of communicative competence that explanatory power can be accorded to this (particular) semantic analysis.

Endnotes

1. A. Lorenzer, *Symbol und Verstehen im psychoanalytischen Prozess, Vorarbeiten zu einer Metatheorie der Psychoanalyse*, forthcoming, Suhrkamp Verlag: Frankfurt a. M. 1970.

2. Cf. S. Arieti, *The Intrapsychic Self*, Basic Books, New York 1967; also H. Werner and B. Kaplan, *Symbol Formation*, John Wiley, New York 1967; P. Watzlawick, J. H. Beavin, and D. D. Jackson, *Pragmatics in Human Communication*, W. W. Norton: New York 1967, esp. chs. 6 and 7.

3. See L. C. Wynne, "Denkstörung und Familienbeziehung bei Schizophrenen," *Psyche*, May 1965, pp. 82 ff.

4. For further elaboration see Jürgen Habermas, *Erkenntnis und Interesse*, Suhrkamp Verlag: Frankfurt a. M. 1968, chs. 10 and 11.

Reprinted from "On Systematically Distorted Communication," Jürgen Habermas, *Inquiry*, 13, 1970, pp. 205–218, by permission of The Taylor & Francis Group. ✦

XIV. Contemporary Theories of Modernity

61
Shame and Repugnance

Norbert Elias

Not too many years before his death, Norbert Elias (1897–1990) was "discovered" by sociology, and since then he has been viewed as one of the most important historical sociologists of the century. Another émigre who left Germany during the Hitler years, Elias published *The Civilizing Process* in 1939, just before the world plunged into war. The timing of its release sealed the fate of the book, as it would be read by only a few, and Elias would teach in England in relative obscurity for decades. This changed in the 1970s; since that time theorists have paid considerable attention to his work. The overarching focus of Elias' work is the way Western civilization has developed and in particular the varied ways that people have been transformed psychologically and behaviorally. Of particular concern to Elias are the ways that self-restraint has become a characteristic feature of the "civilized" person. This selection from *Power and Civility* (Part II of *The Civilizing Process*) offers insights into the ways in which the development of notions of shame and repugnance have been an integral part of this process.

No less characteristic of a civilizing process than "rationalization" is the peculiar moulding of the drive economy that we call "shame" and "repugnance" or "embarrassment". Both these, the strong spurt of rationalization and the (for a time) no less strong

advance of the threshold of shame and repugnance that becomes more and more perceptible in the make-up of Western men broadly speaking from the sixteenth century onwards, are different sides of the same transformation of the social personality structure. The feeling of shame is a specific excitation, a kind of anxiety which is automatically reproduced in the individual on certain occasions by force of habit. Considered superficially, it is fear of social degradation or, more generally, of other people's gestures of superiority. But it is a form of displeasure or fear which arises characteristically on those occasions when a person who fears lapsing into inferiority can avert this danger neither by direct physical means nor by any other form of attack. This defencelessness against the superiority of others, this total exposure to them does not arise directly from a threat from the physical superiority of others actually present, although it doubtless has its origins in physical compulsion, in the bodily inferiority of the child in face of its parents or teachers. In adults, however, this defencelessness results from the fact that the people whose superiority one fears are in accord with one's own superego, with the agency of self-constraint implanted in the individual by others on whom he was dependent, who possessed power and superiority over him. In keeping with this, the anxiety that we call "shame" is heavily veiled to the sight of others; however strong it may be, it is never directly expressed in noisy gestures. Shame takes on its particular coloration from the fact that the person feeling it has done or is about to do something through which he comes into contradiction with people to whom he is bound in one form or another, and with himself, with the sector of his consciousness by which he controls

414

himself. The conflict expressed in shame-fear is not merely a conflict of the individual with prevalent social opinion; the individual's behaviour has brought him into conflict with the part of himself that represents this social opinion. It is a conflict within his own personality; he himself recognizes himself as inferior. He fears the loss of the love or respect of others, to which he attaches or has attached value. Their attitude has precipitated an attitude within him that he automatically adopts towards himself. This is what makes him so defenceless against gestures of superiority by others which somehow trigger off this automatism within him.

This also explains why the fear of transgression of social prohibitions takes on more clearly the character of shame the more completely alien constraints have been turned into self-restraints by the structure of society, and the more comprehensive and differentiated the ring of self-restraints have become within which a person's conduct is enclosed. The inner tension, the excitement that is aroused whenever a person feels compelled to break out of this enclosure in any place, or when he has done so, varies in strength according to the gravity of the social prohibition and the degree of self-constraint. In ordinary life we call this excitement shame only in certain contexts and above all when it has a certain degree of strength; but in terms of its structure it is, despite its many nuances and degrees, always the same event. Like self-constraints, it is to be found in a less stable, less uniform and less all-embracing form even at simpler levels of social development. Like these constraints, tensions and fears of this kind emerge more clearly with every spurt of the civilizing process, and finally predominate over others—particularly the physical fear of others. They predominate the more, the larger the areas that are pacified, and the greater the importance in the moulding of people of the more even constraints that come to the fore in society when the representatives of the monopoly of physical violence normally only exercise their control as it were standing in the wings—the further, in a word, the civilization of conduct advances. Just as we can only speak of "reason" in con-

junction with advances of rationalization and the formation of functions demanding foresight and restraint, we can only speak of shame in conjunction with its sociogenesis, with spurts in which the shame-threshold advances or at least moves, and the structure and pattern of self-constraints are changed in a particular direction, reproducing themselves thenceforth in the same form over a greater or lesser period. Both rationalization and the advance of the shame and repugnance thresholds are expressions of a reduction in the direct physical fear of other beings, and of a consolidation of the automatic inner anxieties, the compulsions which the individual now exerts on himself. In both, the greater, more differentiated foresight and long-term view which become necessary in order that larger and larger groups of people may preserve their social existence in an increasing differentiated society, are equally expressed. It is not difficult to explain how these seemingly so different psychological changes are connected. Both, the intensification of shame like the increased rationalization, are different aspects of the growing split in the individual personality that occurs with the increasing division of functions; they are different aspects of the growing differentiation between drives and drive-controls, between "id" and "ego" or "super-ego" functions. The further this differentiation of individual self-steering advances, the more clearly that sector of the controlling functions which in a broader sense is called the "ego" and in a narrower the "super-ego", takes on a twofold function. On the one hand this sector forms the centre from which a person regulates his relations to other living and non-living beings, and on the other it forms the centre from which a person, partly consciously and partly quite automatically and unconsciously, controls his "inner life", his own affects and impulses. The layer of psychological functions which, in the course of the social transformation that has been described, is gradually differentiated from the drives, the ego or super-ego functions, has, in other words, a twofold task within the personality: they conduct at the same time a domestic policy and a foreign policy—which, moreover, are not always in harmony and often enough in contradiction. This explains the fact that in the same socio-historical period in which rationalization makes perceptible advances, an advance in the shame and repugnance threshold is also to be observed. It also explains the fact that here, as always—in accordance with the sociogenetic ground rule—a corresponding process is to be observed even today in the life of each individual child: the rationalization of conduct is an expression of the foreign policy of the same super-ego formation whose domestic policy is expressed in an advance of the shame threshold.

From here many large trains of thought lead off in different directions. It remains to be shown how this increased differentiation within the personality is manifested in a transformation of particular drives. Above all, it remains to be shown how it leads to a transformation of sexual impulses and an advance of shame feelings in the relations of men and women.[1] It must be enough here to indicate some of the main connections between the social processes described above and this advance of the frontier of shame and repugnance.

Even in the more recent history of the West itself, shame feelings have not always been built into the personality in the same way. To mention only one difference, the manner in which they are built in is not the same in a hierarchical society made up of estates as in the succeeding bourgeois industrial order.

The examples quoted earlier, above all those showing differences in the development of shame on the exposure of certain bodily parts,[2] give a certain impression of such changes. In courtly society shame on exposing certain parts is, in keeping with the structure of this society, still largely restricted within estate or hierarchical limits. Exposure in the presence of social inferiors, for example by the king in front of a minister, is placed under no very strict social prohibition, any more than the exposure of a man before the socially weaker and lower-ranking woman was in an earlier phase. Given his minimal functional dependence on those of lower rank, exposure as yet arouses no feeling of inferiority or shame; it can even be taken, as Della Casa states, as a sign of benevolence towards the inferior. Exposure by someone of lower rank before a superior, on the other hand, or even before people of equal rank, is banished more and more from social life as a sign of lack of respect; branded as an offence, it becomes invested with fear. And only when the walls between estates fall away, when the functional dependence of all on all increases and all members of society become several degrees more equal, does such exposure, except in certain narrower enclaves, become an offence in the presence of any other person. Only then is such behaviour so profoundly associated with fear in the individual from an early age, that the social character of the prohibition vanishes entirely from his consciousness, shame appearing as a command coming from within himself.

And the same is true of embarrassment. This is an inseparable counterpart of shame. Just as the latter arises when someone infringes the prohibitions of his own self and of society, the former occurs when something outside the individual impinges on his danger zone, on forms of behaviour, objects, inclinations which have early on been invested with fear by his surroundings until this fear—in the manner of a conditioned reflex—is reproduced automatically in him on certain occasions. Embarrassment is displeasure or anxiety which arises when another person threatens to breach, or breaches, society's prohibitions represented by one's own super-ego. And these feelings too become more diverse and comprehensive the more extensive and subtly differentiated the danger zone by which the conduct of the individual is regulated and moulded, the further the civilization of conduct advances.

It was shown earlier by a series of examples how, from the sixteenth century onwards, the frontier of shame and embarrassment gradually begins to advance more rapidly. Here, too, the chains of thought begin slowly to join up. This advance coincides with the accelerated courtization of the upper class. It is the time when the chains of dependence intersecting in the individual grow denser and longer, when more and more people are being bound more and more closely together and the compulsion to self-control is increasing. Like mutual dependence, mutual observation of people increases; sensibilities, and correspondingly prohibitions, become more differentiated; and equally more subtle, equally more manifold become the reasons for shame and for embarrassment aroused by the conduct of others.

It was pointed out above that with the advancing division of functions and the greater integration of people, the major contrasts between different classes and countries diminish, while the nuances, the varieties of their moulding within the framework of civilization multiply. Here one encounters a corresponding trend in the development of individual conduct and sentiment. The more the strong contrasts of individual conduct are tempered, the more the violent fluctuations of pleasure or displeasure are contained, moderated and changed by self-control, the greater becomes the sensitivity to shades or nuances of conduct, the more finely attuned people grow to minute gestures and forms, and the more complex becomes their experience of themselves and their world at levels which were previously hidden from consciousness through the veil of strong affects.

To clarify this by an obvious example, "primitive" people experience human and natural events within the relatively narrow circle which is vitally important to them—narrow, because their chains of dependence are relatively short—in a manner in which is in some respects far more differentiated than that of "civilized" people. The differentiation varies, depending on whether we are concerned with farmers or hunters or herdsmen, for example. But however this may be, it can be stated generally that, insofar as it is of vital importance to a group, the ability of primitive people to distinguish things in forest and field, whether it be a particular tree from another, or sounds, scents or movements, is more highly developed than in "civilized" people. But among more primitive people the natural sphere is still far more a danger zone; it is full of fears which more civilized men no longer know. This is decisive for what is or is not distinguished. The manner in which "nature" is experienced is fundamentally affected, slowly at the end of the Middle Ages and then more quickly from the sixteenth century onwards, by the pacifi-cation of larger and larger populated areas. Only now do forests, meadows and mountains gradually cease to be danger zones of the first order, from which anxiety and fear constantly intrude into individual life. And now, as the network of roads becomes, like social interdependence in general, more dense; as robber-knights and beasts of prey slowly disappear; as forest and field cease to be the scene of unbridled passions, of the savage pursuit of man and beast, wild joy and wild fear; as they are moulded more and more by intertwining peaceful activities, the production of goods, trade and transport; now, to pacified men a correspondingly pacified nature becomes visible, and in a new way. It becomes—in keeping with the mounting significance which the eye attains as the mediator of pleasure with the growing moderation of the affects—to a high degree an object of visual pleasure. In addition, people—more precisely the town-people for whom forest and field are no longer their everyday background but a place of relaxation—grow more sensitive and begin to see the open country in a more differentiated way, at a level which was previously screened off by danger and the play of unmoderated passions. They take pleasure in the harmony of colour and lines, become open to what is called the beauty of nature; their feelings are aroused by the changing shades and shapes of the clouds and the play of light on the leaves of a tree.

And, in the wake of this pacification, the sensitivity of people to social conduct is also changed. Now, inner fears grow in proportion to the decrease of outer ones—the fears of one sector of the personality for another. As a result of these inner tensions, people begin to experience each other in a more differentiated way which was precluded as long as they constantly faced serious and inescapable threats from outside. Now a major part of the tensions which were earlier discharged directly in combat between man and man, must be resolved as an inner tension in the struggle of the individual with himself. Social life ceases to be a danger zone in which feasting, dancing and noisy pleasure frequently and suddenly give way to rage, blows and murder, and becomes a different kind of danger zone if the individual cannot sufficiently restrain himself, if he touches sensitive spots, his own shame-frontier or the embarrassment-threshold of others. In a sense, the danger zone now passes through the self of every individual. Thus people become, in this respect too, sensitive to distinctions which previously scarcely entered consciousness. Just as nature now becomes, far more than earlier, a source of pleasure mediated by the eye, people too become a source of visual pleasure or, conversely, of visually aroused displeasure, of different degrees of repugnance. The direct fear inspired in men by men has diminished, and the inner fear mediated through the eye and through the super-ego is rising proportionately.

When the use of weapons in combat is an everyday occurrence, the small gesture of offering someone a knife at table (to recall one of the examples mentioned earlier) has no great importance. As the use of weapons is restricted more and more, as external and internal pressures make the expression of anger by physical attack increasingly difficult, people gradually become more sensitive to anything reminiscent of an attack. The very gesture of attack touches the danger zone; it becomes distressing to see a person passing someone else a knife with the point towards him.[3] And from the most highly sensitized small circles of high courtly society, for whom this sensitivity also represents a prestige value, a means of distinction cultivated for that very reason, this prohibition gradually spreads throughout the whole of civilized society. Thus aggressive associations, infused no doubt with others from the layer of elementary urges, combine with status tensions in arousing anxiety.

How the use of a knife is then gradually restricted and surrounded, as a danger zone, by a wall of prohibitions, has been shown through a number of examples. It is an open question how far, in the courtly aristocracy, the renunciation of physical violence remains an external compulsion, and how far it has already been converted into an inner constraint. Despite all restrictions, the use of the table knife, like that of the dagger, is still quite extensive. Just as the hunting and killing of animals is still a permitted and commonplace amusement for the lords of the earth, the carving of dead animals at table remains within the zone of the permitted and is as yet not felt as repugnant. Then, with the slow rise of bourgeois classes, in whom pacification and the generation of inner constraints by the very nature of their social functions is far more complete and binding, the cutting up of dead animals is pushed back further behind the scenes of social life (even if in particular countries, particularly England, as so often, some of the older customs survive incorporated in the new) and the use of the knife, indeed the mere holding of it, is avoided wherever it is not entirely indispensable. Sensitivity in this direction grows.

This is one example among many of particular aspects of the structural transformation of society that we denote by the catchword "civilization". Nowhere in human society is there a zero-point of fear of external powers, and nowhere a zero-point of automatic inner anxieties. Although they may be experienced as very different, they are finally inseparable. What takes place in the course of a civilizing process is not the disappearance of one and the emergence of the other. What changes is merely the proportion between the external and the self-activating fears, and their whole structure. People's fears of external powers diminish without ever disappearing; the never-absent, latent or actual anxieties arising from the tension between drives and drive-control functions become relatively stronger, more comprehensive and continuous. The documentation for the advance of the shame and embarrassment frontiers . . . consists in fact of nothing but particularly clear and simple examples of the direction and structure of a change in the human personality which could be demonstrated from many other aspects too. A very similar structure is exhibited, for example, by the transition from the medieval-Catholic to the Protestant super-ego formation. This, too, shows a pronounced shift towards the internalization of fears. And one thing certainly should not be overlooked in all this: the fact that today, as formerly, all forms of adult inner anxieties are bound up with the child's fears of others, of external powers.

Endnotes

1. This particular problem, important as it is, must be left aside for the time being. Its elucidation demands a description and an exact analysis of the changes which the structure of the family and the whole relationship of the sexes have undergone in the course of Western history. It demands, furthermore, a general study of changes in the upbringing of children and the development of adolescents. The material which has been collected to elucidate this aspect of the civilizing process, and the analyses it made possible have proved too extensive; they threatened to dislocate the framework of this study and will find their place in a further volume.

The same applies to the middle-class line of the civilizing process, the change it produced in bourgeois-urban classes and the non-courtly landed aristocracy. While this transformation of conduct and of the structure of psychological functions is certainly connected in these classes, too, with a specific historical restructuring of the *whole* Western social fabric, nevertheless—as already pointed out on a number of occasions—the non-courtly middle-class line of civilization follows a different pattern to the courtly one. Above all, the treatment of sexuality in the former is not the same as in the latter—partly because of a different family structure, and partly because of the different kind of foresight which middle-class professional functions demand. Something similar emerges if the civilizing transformation of Western religion is investigated. The change in religious feeling to which sociology has paid most attention hitherto, the increased inwardness and rationalization expressed in the various Puritan and Protestant movements, is obviously closely connected to certain changes in the situation and structure of the middle classes. The corresponding change in Catholicism, as shown, for example, in the formation of the power position of the Jesuits, appears to take place in closer touch with the absolutist central organs, in a manner favoured by the hierarchical and centralist structure of the Catholic Church. These problems, too, will only be solved when we have a more exact overall picture of the intertwining of the non-courtly, middle-class and the courtly lines of civilization, leaving aside for the time being the civilizing movement in worker and peasant strata which emerges more slowly and much later.

2. *The Civilizing Process*, vol. 1, pp. 207ff. On the general problem of shame feelings cf. *The Spectator* (1807), vol. 5, no. 373: "If I was put to define Modesty, I would call it, The reflection of an ingenuous Mind, either when a Man has committed an Action for which he censures himself, or fancies that he is exposed to the Censure of others." See also the observation there on the difference of shame feelings between men and women.

3. *The Civilizing Process*, vol. 1, pp. 122ff.

62
Spectacular Time

Guy Debord

The thought of French theorist Guy Debord (1931–1994) was shaped by Marx and subsequent Marxist thinkers, including Lucien Goldman and Henri Lefebvre. A political activist, he was one of the founding members of the Situationist International and an influential figure during the student revolts of May 1968. His major work, *The Society of the Spectacle* (1967), is actually a brief, aphoristic book devoted to specifying what he meant by spectacle and how this term can be seen as characterizing modern life. His central claim is that the spectacle refers to social relations mediated by images. The book contains 221 theses, ranging in length from a sentence to page-long paragraphs. The selection included here is devoted to what he refers to as "spectacular time." Time in contemporary capitalist society is seen as a commodity. If traditional societies could be seen in terms of cyclical time, today it has become "pseudo-cyclical." In these theses, Debord shifts between a focus on what spectacular time means for production and how it shapes modern patterns of consumption. The chapter ends with a fairly traditional Marxist assertion that this alienating type of time can be overcome in "the revolutionary project of realizing a classless society." Stripped of these Marxist claims, Debord's ideas have percolated into some currents of postmodernism.

> We have nothing of our own but time, which is enjoyed precisely by those who have no place to stay.
> —Baltasar Gracian, *L'Homme de cour*

147

The time of production, commodity-time, is an infinite accumulation of equivalent intervals. It is the abstraction of irreversible time, all of whose segments must prove on the chronometer their merely quantitative equality. This time is in reality exactly what it is in its *exchangeable* character. In this social domination by commodity-time, "time is everything, man is nothing; he is at most the carcass of time" (*Poverty of Philosophy*). This is time devalued, the complete inversion of time as "the field of human development."

148

The general time of human non-development also exists in the complementary form of *consumable* time which returns as *pseudo-cyclical* time to the daily life of the society based on this determined production.

149

Pseudo-cyclical time is actually no more than the *consumable disguise* of the commodity-time of production. It contains the essential properties of commodity-time, namely exchangeable homogeneous units and the suppression of the qualitative dimension. But being the by-product of this time which aims to retard concrete daily life and to keep it retarded, it must be charged with pseudo-valuations and appear in a sequence of falsely individualized moments.

150

Pseudo-cyclical time is the time of consumption of modern economic survival, of increased survival, where daily life continues to be deprived of decision and remains bound, no longer to the natural order, but to the pseudo-nature developed in alienated labor; and thus this time *naturally* reestablishes the ancient cyclical rhythm which regulated the survival of preindustrial societies. Pseudo-cyclical time leans on the natural remains of cyclical time and also uses it to compose new homologous combinations: day and night, work and weekly rest, the recurrence of vacations.

151

Pseudo-cyclical time is a time *transformed by industry*. The time which has its basis in the production of commodities is itself a consumable commodity which includes everything that previously (during the phase of dissolution of the old unitary society) was differentiated into private life, economic life, political life. All the consumable time of modern society comes to be treated as a raw material for varied new products which impose themselves on the market as uses of socially organized time. "A product which already exists in a form which makes it suitable for consumption can nevertheless in its turn become a raw material for another product" (*Capital*).

152

In its most advanced sector, concentrated capitalism orients itself towards the sale of "completely equipped" blocks of time, each one constituting a single unified commodity which integrates a number of diverse commodities. In the expanding economy of "services" and leisure, this gives rise to the formula of calculated payment in which "everything's included": spectacular environment, the collective pseudo-displacement of vacations, subscriptions to cultural consumption, and the sale of sociability itself in the form of "passionate conversations" and "meetings with personalities." This sort of spectacular commodity, which can obviously circulate only because of the increased poverty of the corresponding realities, just as obviously fits among the pilot-articles of modernized sales techniques by being payable on credit.

153

Consumable pseudo-cyclical time is spectacular time, both as the time of consumption of images in the narrow sense, and as the image of consumption of time in the broad sense. The time of image-consumption, the medium of all commodities, is inseparably the field where the instruments of the spectacle exert themselves fully, and also their goal, the location and main form of all specific consumption: it is known that the time-saving constantly sought by modern society, whether in the speed of vehicles or in the use of dried soups, is concretely translated for the population of the United States in the fact that the mere contemplation of television occupies it for an average of three to six hours a day. The social image of the consumption of time, in turn, is exclusively dominated by moments of leisure and vacation, moments presented *at a distance* and desirable by definition, like every spectacular commodity. Here this commodity is explicitly presented as the moment of real life, and the point is to wait for its cyclical return. But even in those very moments reserved for living, it is still the spectacle that is to be seen and reproduced, becoming ever more in-

tense. What was represented as genuine life reveals itself simply as more *genuinely spectacular* life.

154

The epoch which displays its time to itself as essentially the sudden return of multiple festivities is also an epoch without festivals. What was, in cyclical time, the moment of a community's participation in the luxurious expenditure of life is impossible for the society without community or luxury. When its vulgarized pseudo-festivals, parodies of the dialogue and the gift, incite a surplus of economic expenditure, they lead only to deception always compensated by the promise of a new deception. In the spectacle, the lower the use value of modern survival-time, the more highly it is exalted. The reality of time has been replaced by the *advertisement* of time.

155

While the consumption of cyclical time in ancient societies was consistent with the real labor of those societies, the pseudo-cyclical consumption of the developed economy is in contradiction with the abstract irreversible time of its production. While cyclical time was the time of immobile illusion, really lived, spectacular time is the time of self-changing reality, lived in illusion.

156

What is constantly new in the process of production of things is not found in consumption, which remains the expanded repetition of the same. In spectacular time, since dead labor continues to dominate living labor, the past dominates the present.

157

Another side of the deficiency of general historical life is that individual life as yet has no history. The pseudo-events which rush by in spectacular dramatizations have not been lived by those informed of them; moreover they are lost in the inflation of their hurried replacement at every throb of the spectacular machinery. Furthermore, what is really lived has no relation to the official irreversible time of society and is in direct opposition to the pseudo-cyclical rhythm of the consumable by-product of this time. This individual experience of separate daily life remains without language, without concept, without critical access to its own past which has been recorded nowhere. It is not communicated. It is not understood and is forgotten to the profit of the false spectacular memory of the unmemorable.

158

The spectacle, as the present social organization of the paralysis of history and memory, of the abandonment of history built on the foundation of historical time, is the *false consciousness of time*.

159

The preliminary condition required for propelling workers to the status of "free" producers and consumers of commodity time was *the violent expropriation of their own time*. The spectacular return of time became possible only after this first dispossession of the producer.

160

The irreducibly biological element which remains in labor, both in the dependence on the natural cycle of waking and sleep and in the existence of irreversible time in the expenditure of an individual life, is a mere *accessory* from the point of view of modern production; consequently, these elements are ignored in the official proclamations of the movement of production and in the consumable trophies which are the accessible translation of this incessant victory. The spectator's consciousness, immobilized in the falsified center of the movement of its world, no longer experiences its life as a passage toward self-realization and toward death. One who has renounced using his life can no longer admit his death. Life insurance advertisements suggest merely that he is guilty of dying without ensuring the regularity of the system after this economic loss; and the advertisement of the *American way of death* insists on his capacity to maintain in this encounter the greatest possible number of *appearances* of life. On all other fronts of the advertising onslaught, it is strictly forbidden to grow old. Even a "youth-capital," contrived for each and all and put to the most mediocre uses, could never acquire the durable and cumulative reality of financial capital. This social absence of death is identical to the social absence of life.

161

Time, as Hegel showed, is the *necessary* alienation, the environment where the subject realizes himself by losing himself, where he becomes other in order to become truly himself. Precisely the opposite is true in the dominant alienation, which is undergone by the producer of an *alien present*. In this *spatial alienation*, the society that radically separates the subject from the activity it takes from him, separates him first of all from his own time. It is this surmountable social alienation that has prohibited and petrified the possibilities and risks of the *living* alienation of time.

162

Under the visible *fashions* which disappear and reappear on the trivial surface of contemplated pseudo-cyclical time, the *grand style* of the age is always located in what is oriented by the obvious and secret necessity of revolution.

163

The natural basis of time, the actual experience of the flow of time, becomes human and social by existing *for man*. The restricted condition of human practice, labor at various stages, is what has humanized and also dehumanized time as cyclical and as separate irreversible time of economic production. The revolutionary project of realizing a classless society, a generalized historical life, is the project of a withering away of the social measure of tie, to the benefit of a playful model of irreversible time of individuals and groups, a model in which *independent federated times* are simultaneously present. It is the program of a total realization, within the context of time, of communism which suppressed all that exists independently of individuals.

164

The world already possesses the dream of a time whose consciousness it must now possess in order to actually live it.

63

The Reflexivity of Modernity

Anthony Giddens

The former director of the London School of Economics and Political Science and early on a key promoter of Prime Minister Tony Blair's New Labour platform as an instance of "the third way," Anthony Giddens (b. 1938) has taught at Cambridge University as well as in the United States. He is known for his insightful exegetical examinations of both the classical social theorists and contemporary approaches. In this passage from *The Consequences of Modernity* (1990), it is clear that his approach stakes out a position in opposition to postmodernists who have claimed that we have entered a new state of development beyond the modern. On the contrary, Giddens thinks we have entered "late modernity." As he sees it, part of the problem with the idea of postmodernity is that it fails to adequately appreciate how the modern project, although it does develop historically and changes over time, signifies a singular break with tradition. In other words, the stages of modernity are part of a larger whole. Here he focuses on the fact that modernity encourages a reflexivity that is quite unlike what is found in traditional society. He sketches out some of the implications of reflexivity, particularly as it becomes even more implicated in the way that the social system reproduces itself.

The Reflexivity of Modernity

Inherent in the idea of modernity is a contrast with tradition. As noted previously, many combinations of the modern and the traditional are to be found in concrete social settings. Indeed, some authors have argued that these are so tightly interlaced as to make any generalised comparison valueless. But such is surely not the case, as we can see by pursuing an enquiry into the relation between modernity and reflexivity.

There is a fundamental sense in which reflexivity is a defining characteristic of all human action. All human beings routinely "keep in touch" with the grounds of what they do as an integral element of doing it. I have called this elsewhere the "reflexive monitoring of action," using the phrase to draw attention to the chronic character of the processes involved.[1] Human action does not incorporate chains of aggregate interactions and reasons, but a consistent—and, as Erving Goffman above all has shown us, never-to-be-relaxed—monitoring of behaviour and its contexts. This is not the sense of reflexivity which is specifically connected with modernity, although it is the necessary basis of it.

In traditional cultures, the past is honoured and symbols are valued because they contain and perpetuate the experience of generations. Tradition is a mode of integrating the reflexive monitoring of action with the time-space organisation of the community. It is a means of handling time and space, which inserts any particular activity or experience within the continuity of past, present, and future, these in turn being structured by recurrent social practices. Tradition is not wholly static, because it has to be reinvented by each new generation as it takes over its cultural inheritance from those preceding it. Tradition does not so much resist change as pertain to a context in which there are few separated temporal and spatial markers in terms of which change can have any meaningful form.

In oral cultures, tradition is not known as such, even though these cultures are the most traditional of all. To understand tradition, as distinct from other modes of organising action and experience, demands cutting into time-space in ways which are only possible with the invention of writing. Writing expands the level of time-space distanciation and creates a perspective of past, present, and future in which the reflexive appropriation of knowledge can be set off from designated tradition. However, in pre-modern civilisations reflexivity is still largely limited to the reinterpretation and clarification of tradition, such that in the scales of time the side of the "past" is much more heavily weighed down than that of the "future."

Moreover, since literacy is the monopoly of the few, the routinisation of daily life remains bound up with tradition in the old sense.

With the advent of modernity, reflexivity takes on a different character. It is introduced into the very basis of system reproduction, such that thought and action are constantly refracted back upon one another. The routinisation of daily life has no intrinsic connections with the past at all, save in so far as what "was done before" happens to coincide with what can be defended in a principled way in the light of incoming knowledge. To sanction a practice because it is traditional will not do; tradition can be justified, but only in the light of knowledge which is not itself authenticated by tradition. Combined with the inertia of habit, this means that, even in the most modernised of modern societies, tradition continues to play a role. But this role is generally much less significant than is supposed by authors who focus attention upon the integration of tradition and modernity in the contemporary world. For justified tradition is tradition in sham clothing and receives its identity only from the reflexivity of the modern.

The reflexivity of modern social life consists in the fact that social practices are constantly examined and reformed in the light of incoming information about those very practices, thus constitutively altering their character. We should be clear about the nature of this phenomenon. All forms of social life are partly constituted by actors' knowledge of them. Knowing "how to go on" in Wittgenstein's sense is intrinsic to the conventions which are drawn upon and reproduced by human activity. In all cultures, social practices are routinely altered in the light of ongoing discoveries which feed into them. But only in the era of modernity is the revision of convention radicalised to apply (in principle) to all aspects of human life, including technological intervention into the material world. It is often said that modernity is marked by an appetite for the new, but this is not perhaps completely accurate. What is characteristic of modernity is not an embracing of the new for its own sake, but the presumption of wholesale reflexivity—

which of course includes reflection upon the nature of reflection itself.

Probably we are only now, in the late twentieth century, beginning to realise in a full sense how deeply unsettling this outlook is. For when the claims of reason replaced those of tradition, they appeared to offer a sense of certitude greater than that provided by preexisting dogma. But this idea only appears persuasive so long as we do not see that the reflexivity of modernity actually subverts reason, at any rate where reason is understood as the gaining of certain knowledge. Modernity is constituted in and through reflexively applied knowledge, but the equation of knowledge with certitude has turned out to be misconceived. We are abroad in a world which is thoroughly constituted through reflexively applied knowledge, but where at the same time we can never be sure that any given element of that knowledge will not be revised.

Even philosophers who most staunchly defend the claims of science to certitude, such as Karl Popper, acknowledge that, as he expresses it, "all science rests upon shifting sand."[2] In science, *nothing* is certain, and nothing can be proved, even if scientific endeavour provides us with the most dependable information about the world to which we can aspire. In the heart of the world of hard science, modernity floats free.

No knowledge under conditions of modernity *is* knowledge in the "old" sense, where "to know" is to be certain. This applies equally to the natural and the social sciences. In the case of social science, however, there are further considerations involved. We should recall at this point the observations made earlier about the reflexive components of sociology.

In the social sciences, to the unsettled character of all empirically based knowledge we have to add the "subversion" which comes from the reentry of social scientific discourse into the contexts it analyses. The reflection of which the social sciences are the formalised version (a specific genre of expert knowledge) is quite fundamental to the reflexivity of modernity as a whole.

Because of the close relation between the Enlightenment and advocacy of the claims of reason, natural science has usually been taken as the preeminent endeavour distinguishing the modern outlook from what went before. Even those who favour interpretative rather than naturalistic sociology have normally seen social science as the poor relation of the natural sciences, particularly given the scale of technological development consequent upon scientific discoveries. But the social sciences are actually more deeply implicated in modernity than is natural science, since the chronic revision of social practices in the light of knowledge about those practices is part of the very tissue of modern institutions.[3]

All the social sciences participate in this reflexive relation, although sociology has an especially central place. Take as an example the discourse of economics. Concepts like "capital," "investment," "markets," "industry," and many others, in their modern senses, were elaborated as part of the early development of economics as a distinct discipline in the eighteenth and early nineteenth centuries. These concepts, and empirical conclusions linked to them, were formulated in order to analyse changes involved in the emergence of modern institutions. But they could not, and did not, remain separated from the activities and events to which they related. They have become integral to what "modern economic life" actually is and inseparable from it. Modern economic activity would not be as it is were it not for the fact that all members of the population have mastered these concepts and an indefinite variety of others.

The lay individual cannot necessarily provide formal definitions of terms like "capital" or "investment," but everyone who, say, uses a savings account in a bank demonstrates an implicit and practical mastery of those notions. Concepts such as these, and the theories and empirical information linked to them, are not merely handy devices whereby agents are somehow more clearly able to understand their behaviour than they could do otherwise. They actively constitute what that behaviour is and inform the reasons for which it is undertaken. There cannot be a clear insulation between literature available to economists and that which is either read or filters through in other ways to interested parties in the population: business leaders, government officials, and members of the public. The economic environment is constantly being altered in the light of these inputs, thus creating a situation of continual mutual involvement between economic discourse and the activities to which it refers.

The pivotal position of sociology in the reflexivity of modernity comes from its role as the most generalised type of reflection upon modern social life. Let us consider an example at the "hard edge" of naturalistic sociology. The official statistics published by governments concerning, for instance, population, marriage and divorce, crime and delinquency, and so forth, seem to provide a means of studying social life with precision. To the pioneers of naturalistic sociology, such as Durkheim, these statistics represented hard data, in terms of which the relevant aspects of modern societies can be analysed more accurately than where such figures are lacking. Yet official statistics are not just analytical characteristics of social activity, but again enter constitutively into the social universe from which they are taken or counted up. From its inception, the collation of official statistics has been constitutive of state power and of many other modes of social organisation also. The coordinated administrative control achieved by modern governments is inseparable from the routine monitoring of "official data" in which all contemporary states engage.

The assembling of official statistics is itself a reflexive endeavour, permeated by the very findings of the social sciences that have utilised them. The practical work of coroners, for example, is the basis for the collection of suicide statistics. In the interpretation of causes/motives for death, however, coroners are guided by concepts and theories which purport to illuminate the nature of suicide. It would not be at all unusual to find a coroner who had read Durkheim.

Nor is the reflexivity of official statistics confined to the sphere of the state. Anyone in a Western country who embarks upon marriage today, for instance, knows that divorce rates are high (and may also, however imperfectly or partially, know a great deal more about the demography of marriage and the family). Knowledge of the high rate of divorce might affect the very decision to marry, as well as decisions about related considerations—provisions about property and so forth. Awareness of levels of divorce, moreover, is normally much more than just consciousness of a brute fact. It is theorised by the lay agent in ways pervaded by sociological thinking. Thus virtually everyone contemplating marriage has some idea of how family institutions have been changing, changes in the relative social position and power of men and women, alterations in sexual mores, etc.—all of which enter into processes of further change which they reflexively inform. Marriage and the family would not be what they are today were they not thoroughly "sociologised" and "psychologised."

The discourse of sociology and the concepts, theories, and findings of the other social sciences continually "circulate in and out" of what it is that they are about. In so doing they reflexively restructure their subject matter, which itself has learned to think sociologically. *Modernity is itself deeply and intrinsically sociological.* Much that is problematic in the position of the professional sociologist, as the purveyor of expert knowledge about social life, derives from the fact that she or he is at most one step ahead of enlightened lay practitioners of the discipline.

Hence the thesis that more knowledge about social life (even if that knowledge is as well buttressed empirically as it could possibly be) equals greater control over our fate is false. It is (arguably) true about the physical world, but not about the universe of social events. Expanding our understanding of the social world might produce a progressively more illuminating grasp of human institutions and, hence, increasing "technological" control over them, if it were the case either that social life were entirely separate from human knowledge about it or that knowledge could be filtered continuously into the reasons for social action, producing step-by-step increases in the "rationality" of behaviour in relation to specific needs.

Both conditions do in fact apply to many circumstances and contexts of social activity. But each falls well short of that totalising impact which the inheritance of Enlighten-

ment thought holds out as a goal. This is so because of the influence of four sets of factors.

One—factually very important but logically the least interesting, or at any rate the least difficult to handle analytically—is differential power. The appropriation of knowledge does not happen in a homogeneous fashion, but is often differentially available to those in power positions, who are able to place it in the service of sectional interests.

A second influence concerns the role of values. Changes in value orders are not independent of innovations in cognitive orientation created by shifting perspectives on the social world. If new knowledge could be brought to bear upon a transcendental rational basis of values, this situation would not apply. But there is no such rational basis of values, and shifts in outlook deriving from inputs of knowledge have a mobile relation to changes in value orientations.

The third factor is the impact of unintended consequences. No amount of accumulated knowledge about social life could encompass all circumstances of its implementation, even if such knowledge were wholly distinct from the environment to which it applied. If our knowledge about the social world simply got better and better, the scope of unintended consequences might become more and more confined and unwanted consequences rare. However, the reflexivity of modern social life blocks off this possibility and is itself the fourth influence involved. Although least discussed in relation to the limits of Enlightenment reason, it is certainly as significant as any of the others. The point is not that there is no stable social world to know, but that knowledge of that world contributes to its unstable or mutable character.

The reflexivity of modernity, which is directly involved with the continual generating of systematic self-knowledge, does not stabilise the relation between expert knowledge and knowledge applied in lay actions. Knowledge claimed by expert observers (in some part, and in many varying ways) rejoins its subject matter, thus (in principle, but also normally in practice) altering it. There is no parallel to this process in the natural sciences; it is not at all the same as where, in the field of microphysics the intervention of an observer changes what is being studied.

Endnotes

1. Anthony Giddens, *New Rules of Sociological Method* (London: Hutchinson, 1974).

2. Karl Popper, *Conjectures and Refutations* (London: Routledge, 1962), p. 34.

3. Anthony Giddens, *Constitution of Society* (Cambridge, Eng.: Polity, 1984), ch. 7.

64
Risk Society: Towards a New Modernity

Ulrich Beck

(translated by Mark Ritter)

Risk has become an increasingly consequential concept in the contemporary social sciences. It has been explored in intriguing ways by such diverse figures as Mary Douglas, Kai Erikson, Niklas Luhmann, and Anthony Giddens. One of the most ambitious attempts to link risk to the idea of a new stage of modernity is that undertaken by the German sociologist Ulrich Beck (b. 1944). Beck contends that in contrast to the early stage of modernity, the contemporary stage can be appropriately described as a "risk society." The thrust of his argument is captured in the pithy introduction to this excerpt from his book, *Risk Society*: "Poverty Is Hierarchic, Smog Is Democratic." Risk arises from the unintended negative consequences of industrialization, particularly ecological consequences. Thus, while nuclear power was promoted as a clean and safe alternative to such energy sources as coal, the disaster at Chernobyl and the near disaster at Three Mile Island highlight the fact that nuclear energy has the potential for creating catastrophic disasters. Though the idea of risk society involves more than ecological issues, it has served to advance the development of environmental sociology. As this selection reveals, Beck is also intent on articulating the concept of risk in terms of globalization theory. While seeking to analytically differentiate class positions from risk positions, he concludes with a discussion about how these two positions often overlap empirically.

Globalizing the Risks of Civilization

Reduced to a formula: *poverty is hierarchic, smog is democratic*. With the expansion of modernization risks—with the endangering of nature, health, nutrition, and so on—the social differences and limits are relativized. Very different consequences continue to be drawn from this. *Objectively,* however, risks display an *equalizing* effect within their scope and among those affected by them. It is precisely therein that their novel political power resides. In this sense risk societies are *not* exactly class societies; their risk positions cannot be understood as class positions, or their conflicts as class conflicts.

This becomes even clearer when one inspects the particular style, the particular distribution pattern of modernization risks. They possess an *inherent tendency towards globalization*. A universalization of hazards accompanies industrial production, independent of the place where they are produced: food chains connect practically everyone on earth to everyone else. They dip under borders. The acid content of the air is not only nibbling at sculptures and artistic treasures, it also long ago brought about the disintegration of modern customs barriers. Even in Canada the lakes have become acidified, and forests are dying even in the northern reaches of Scandinavia.

The globalization tendency brings about afflictions, which are once again unspecific in their generality. Where everything turns into a hazard, somehow nothing is dangerous anymore. Where there is no escape, people ultimately no longer want to think about it. This eschatological ecofatalism allows the pendulum of private and political moods to swing in *any* direction. The risk society shifts from hysteria to indifference and vice versa. Action belongs to yesterday anyway. Perhaps one can get at the omnipresent and everlasting pesticides with (in)sects?

The Boomerang Effect

Contained within the globalization and yet clearly differentiated from it is a distribution pattern of risks which contains a considerable amount of political explosive. Sooner or later the risks also catch up with those who produce or profit from them. Risks display a social *boomerang effect* in their diffusion: even the rich and powerful are not safe from them. The formerly "latent side effects" strike back even at the centers of

428

their production. The agents of modernization themselves are emphatically caught in the maelstrom of hazards that they unleash and profit from. This can happen in a multitude of ways.

Take the example of agriculture once again. In Germany, the consumption of artificial fertilizer grew from 143 to 378 kilograms per hectare over the period 1951 to 1983, and the use of agricultural chemicals rose from 25,000 to 35,000 tonnes between 1975 and 1983. The yields per hectare also rose, but not nearly as fast as the expense for fertilizer and pesticides. Yields doubled for grain and were 20 percent higher for potatoes. A disproportionately *small* increase of yields in relation to the use of fertilizer and chemicals contrasts with a disproportionately *large* increase in the natural destruction that is visible and painful to the farmer.

An outstanding index of this alarming development is the strong decrease in many wild plant and animal species. The "red lists" that serve as official "death certificates" to record these threats to existence are growing longer and longer.

> Of 680 plant species occurring in Greenland, 519 are endangered. The populations of bird species dependent on meadows, such as the white stork, the curlew, or the whinchat, are decreasing drastically; people are trying to preserve the last flocks in Bavaria through a 'meadow birds program' . . . The affected animals include ground nesting birds, animals at the top of food chains like predatory birds, owls and dragonflies, or those specialized in food which is becoming scarce, for instance large insects or flower nectar available through the whole growing season. (Rat der Sachverständigen für Umweltfragen 1985: 20)

Formerly "unseen secondary effects" thus become visible primary effects which endanger their causal production centers themselves. The production of modernization risks follows the *boomerang curve*. Intensive industrial agriculture, subsidized with billions, does not just cause the lead content in mothers' milk and children to rise dramatically in distant cities. It also frequently undermines the natural basis of agricultural production itself: the fertility of the soil declines, vitally important animals and plants disappear, and the danger of soil erosion grows.

The circularity of this social endangering can be generalized: under the roof of modernization risks, *perpetrator* and *victim* sooner or late become *identical*. In the worst, unthinkable case, a nuclear world war, this is evident; it also destroys the aggressor. Here it becomes clear that the Earth has become an ejector seat that no longer recognizes any distinctions between rich and poor, black and white, north and south or east and west. But the effect only exists when it occurs, and when it occurs, it no longer exists, because nothing exists any more. This apocalyptic threat therefore leaves behind no tangible traces *in the now* of its threat (Anders 1983). That is different in the ecological crisis. It undermines even the economic foundations of agriculture, and thus the food supply of the people themselves. Here effects are visible which make their mark not just in nature, but also in the pocketbooks of the wealth and the health of the powerful. From competent authorities, and not divided along party lines at all, one can hear quite shrill, apocalyptic sounds in this field.

Ecological Devaluation and Expropriation

The boomerang effect need not manifest itself as a direct threat to life; it can also affect secondary media, money, property and legitimation. It does not just strike back directly at the individual source; in a wholesale, egalitarian way it impairs everyone. The destruction of forests does not just cause bird species to disappear, but also makes the economic value of land and forest property shrink. Where a nuclear or coal-fired power plant is being built or planned, land prices fall. Urban and industrial areas, freeways and thoroughfares all pollute their vicinity. It may still be a matter of debate whether 7 percent of the land in Germany is already so polluted from these causes that in good conscience no agriculture should be carried out there, or whether this will not occur until some point in the near future. The principle, however, is the same: property is being devalued, it is undergoing a creeping *ecological expropriation*.

This effect can be generalized. The destruction and endangering of nature and the environment, news of toxic substances in foodstuffs and consumer articles, threatening—and worse yet, actual—chemical, toxic or reactor accidents have the effect of a creeping or galloping devaluation and expropriation of property rights. Through the unrestrained production of modernization risks, a policy of *making the Earth uninhabitable* is being conducted in continuing leaps and bounds, and sometimes in catastrophic intensification. What is being opposed as a "communist menace" is occurring as the sum of our own actions via the detour through a contaminated nature. On the battlefield of market opportunities, beyond the doctrinal wars of ideology, everyone is pursuing a "scorched Earth" policy against everyone else—with resounding but seldom lasting success.

What is contaminated or considered contaminated may belong to whomever you will—for the loss of social and economic value the distinction is inconsequential. Even if legal title to ownership is maintained, it will become useless and worthless. In the case of "ecological expropriation" we are thus concerned with a *social and economic expropriation while legal ownership continues*. This applies to foodstuffs as much as to the air, the soil and the water. It applies to everything that lives *in* them, and above all, to those who live *from* what lives in them. The talk of "residential toxins" makes it clear that everything that constitutes the culture of our everyday life can be included here.

The basic insight lying behind all this is as simple as possible: everything which threatens life on this Earth also threatens the property and commercial interests of those who live *from* the commodification of life and its requisites. In this way a genuine and systematically intensifying *contradiction* arises between the profit and property interests that advance the industrialization process and its frequently threatening consequences, which endanger and expropriate possessions and profits (not to mention the possession and profit of life).

With reactor accidents or chemical catastrophes, "blank spots" on the map arise again in the most advanced stage of civilization. They are monuments of what threatens us. Even toxic accidents, or suddenly discovered toxic waste dumps, transform housing estates into *toxic waste* estates and turn farmland into *waste*land. But there are many preliminary and insidious forms. The fish from the contaminated seas endanger not just the people who eat them, but *because of that*, also all the many people who make a living *from* fishing. During smog alerts the land dies temporarily. Entire industrial regions are transformed into eerie ghost towns. Such is the will of the boomerang effect: even the wheels of the polluting industries come to a halt. But not only theirs. *Smog cares not a jot about the polluter pays principle.* On a wholesale and egalitarian basis it strikes everyone, independently of his or her share in smog production. Thus, smog is certainly not an advertising factor for sanatoriums, certainly not a big seller. The legally established requirement to publicize effectively the maximum smog levels in the air at such establishments (like air and water temperatures) ought to turn the spa administrations and the resort industry into committed supporters of a pollution-fighting policy—even though they have so far advocated policies against setting standards.

Risk Positions Are Not Class Positions

In this way, with the globalization of risks a social dynamic is set in motion, which can no longer be composed of and understood in class categories. Ownership implies nonownership and thus a social relationship of tension and conflict, in which reciprocal social identities can continually evolve and solidify—"them up there, us down here." The situation is quite different for risk positions. Anyone affected by them is badly off, but deprives the others, the non-affected, of nothing. Expressed in an analogy, the "class" of the "affected" does not confront a "class" that is not affected. It confronts at most a "class" of not-yet-affected people. The escalating scarcity of health will drive even those still well off today (in health and well-being) into the ranks of the "soup kitchens" provided by insurance companies, tomorrow and the day after tomorrow into the pariah community of the invalid and the wounded.

The perplexity of authorities in the face of toxic accidents and toxic waste scandals, and the avalanche of legal, jurisdictional and compensation issues that is triggered each time, all speak a clear language. To wit, conflicts that arise around modernization risks occur around *systematic causes* that coincide with the motor of progress and profit. They relate to the scale and expansion of hazards and the ensuing demands of compensation and/or a fundamental change of course. In those conflicts what is at stake is the issue of whether we can continue the exploitation of nature (including our own), and thus, whether our concepts of "progress," "prosperity," "economic growth," or "scientific rationality" are still correct. In this sense, the conflicts that erupt here take on the character of *doctrinal struggles within civilization* over the proper road for modernity. In many respects, these resemble the doctrinal struggles of the Middle Ages more than the class conflicts of the nineteenth and early twentieth centuries.

Neither do industrial risks and destruction have any respect for national boundaries. They couple the life of a blade of grass in the Bavarian Forest ultimately to effective international agreements on fighting pollution. The *supra*-nationality of the movement of pollution can no longer be dealt with with by individual national efforts. The industrial countries must agree from now on to be distinguished according to their *national balances of emissions or immissions*. In other words, *international inequalities* are arising between different industrial nations with "active" "even," or "passive" balances of pollutants, or to put it more clearly, between "filthy countries" and those who have to clean up, inhale or pay for the filth of others with increasing deaths, expropriations and devaluations. The socialist "fraternal community" will also soon have to face up to this distinction and the sources of conflict in it.

Risk Position as Fate

The international intractability of modernization risks is matched by the way they spread. At least for the consumer, their invisibility hardly leaves a decision open. They are "piggy-back" problems which are inhaled or ingested *with* other things. They are the *stowaways of normal consumption*. They travel on the wind and in the water. They can be in anything and everything, and along with the absolute necessities of life—air to breathe, food, clothing, home furnishings—they pass through all the otherwise strictly controlled protective areas of modernity. Unlike wealth, which is attractive but can also be repellent, for which selection, purchase and decisions are always possible and necessary, risks and destruction steal in everywhere implicitly and unhindered by free(!) decisions. In this sense they bring about a new kind of risk *ascription* by civilization. This recalls in some respects the *status fate in medieval society*. Now there exists a kind of *risk fate in developed civilization*, into which one is born, which one cannot escape with any amount of achievement, with the "small difference" (that is the one with the big effect) that we are *all* confronted similarly by that fate.

In developed civilization, which had set out to remove ascriptions, to evolve privacy, and to free people from the constraints of nature and tradition, there is thus emerging a new global ascription of risks, against which individual decisions hardly exist for the simple reason that the toxins and pollutants are interwoven with the natural basis and the elementary life processes of the industrial world. The experience of this victimization by risks which is *closed to decisions* makes understandable much of the shock, the helpless rage and the "no future" feelings with which many people react ambivalently and with necessarily exploitative criticism to the latest achievements of technical civilization. Is it at all possible to create and maintain a critical distance towards things one cannot escape? Is it permissible to abandon a critical distance just *because* one cannot escape it, and to flee to the inevitable with scorn or cynicism, indifference or jubilation?

New International Inequalities

The worldwide equalization of risk positions must not deceive us about *new* social inequalities *within* the affliction by risk. These arise especially where risk positions and class positions overlap—also on an international scale. The proletariat of the global risk society settles beneath the smokestacks, next to the refineries and chemical factories in the industrial centers of the Third World. The "greatest industrial catastrophe in history" (*Der Spiegel*), the toxic accident in the Indian city of Bhopal, has raised this in the consciousness of the global public. Hazardous industries have been transferred to the low-wage countries of the Third World. This is no coincidence. There is a systematic "attraction" between extreme poverty and extreme risk. In the shunting yard where risks are distributed, stations in "underdeveloped provincial holes" enjoy special popularity. And one would have to be a naive fool to continue to assume that the responsible switchmen do not know what they are doing. More evidence for this is the attested "higher acceptance" of an unemployed provincial population of "new" (job-creating) technologies.

On the international scale it is emphatically true that material misery and blindness to hazards coincide.

A German development expert reports on the careless use of pesticides, in Sri Lanka, for instance. 'There they spread DDT around with bare hands, the people are powdered white.'

On the Antilles island of Trinidad (population 1.2 million) a total 120 deaths from pesticides were reported. "A farmer: 'If you don't feel sick after spraying, you haven't sprayed enough'" (*Der Spiegel* 1984, no. 50: 119).

For these people the complex installations of the chemical factories with their imposing pipes and tanks are expensive symbols of success. The death threat they contain, by contrast, remains largely invisible. For them, the fertilizers, pesticides and herbicides they produce signify above all emancipation from material need. They are prerequisites of the "green revolution," which, systematically supported by the Western industrial states, has raised food production by 30 percent, and in some Asian and Latin American countries by 40 percent over the past few years. The fact that every year "several hundred thousand tonnes of pesticide are sprayed . . . on cotton and rice fields, on tobacco and fruit plantations" (119) resides behind the tangible successes. In the competition between the visible threat of death from hunger and the invisible threat of death from toxic chemicals, the evident fight against material misery is victorious. *Without* the widespread use of chemical materials the yields of the land would sink and insects and spoilage would consume their part. *With* chemicals the poor countries of the periphery can build up their own stocks of foodstuffs, and gain a bit of independence from the power centers of the industrial world. The chemical factories in the Third World reinforce this impression of independence in production and from expensive imports. The struggle against hunger and autonomy forms the protective shield behind which the hazards, imperceptible in any case, are suppressed, minimized and, *by virtue of that*, amplified, diffused and eventually returned to the wealthy industrial countries via the food chain.

Safety and protection regulations are insufficiently developed, and where they do exist, they are often just so much paper. The "industrial naiveté" of the rural population, which often can neither read nor write, much less afford protective clothing, provides management with unimagined opportunities to legitimize the ways of dealing with risks that would be unthinkable in the more risk-conscious milieus of the industrial states. Management can issue strict safety regulations, knowing they will be enforceable and insist that they be obeyed. This way they keep their hands clean, and can shift responsibility for accidents and death to the people's cultural blindness to hazards, cheaply and in good conscience. When catastrophes do occur, the jungle of competing jurisdictions and the material interest of the poor countries offer good opportunities for a policy of minimization and obfuscation to limit the devastating consequences by selective defining the problem. Economic conditions of production, freed from the constraints of legitimation, attract industrial concerns life magnets, and combine with the particular interests of the countries in overcoming material poverty and gaining national autonomy into an explosive mixture, in the truest sense of the word. *The devil of hunger is fought with the Beelzebub of multiplying risks.* Particularly hazardous industries are transferred to the poor countries of the periphery. The poverty of the Third World is joined by horror at the unleashed destructive powers of the developed risk industry. The pictures and reports from Bhopal and Latin America speak a language of their own.

Villa Parisi

The dirtiest chemical town in the world is located in Brazil . . . Every year the slum residents have to redo their corrugated iron roofs, because the acidic rain eats them away. Anyone who lives here for some time develops rashes, 'alligator skin,' as the Brazilians say.

The worst affected are the residents of Villa Parisi, a slum of 15,000 people, most of whom have been able to build modest little houses of gray stone. Here they even sell gas masks in supermarkets. Most of the children have asthma, bronchitis, diseases of the nose and throat, and skin rashes.

In Villa Parisi, it's easy to find your way by smell. On one corner an open sewer is bubbling, on the other a slimy green stream runs. A smell like burnt chicken feathers indicates the steel works, while the odor of rotten eggs marks the chemical factory. An emission meter set up by the town's authorities failed in 1977, after one and a half years of service. It apparently could not withstand the pollution.

The history of the dirtiest town in the world began in 1954, when Pegropràs, the Brazilian oil company, selected the coastal marsh as the site for its refinery. Soon Cosipa, Brazil's largest steel concern, and Copegràs, a Brazilian-American fertilizer company, arrived, followed by multinationals like Fiat, Dow Chemical and Union Carbide. It was the boom phase of Brazilian capitalism. The military government invited foreign enterprises to produce environmentally harmful products there. 'Brazil can still afford to import pollution,' boasted Planning Minister Paulo Vellosa in 1972, the year of the environmental conference in Stockholm. Brazil's only ecological problem was poverty, he claimed.

'The main causes of disease are malnutrition, alcohol and cigarettes,' the spokesman for Pegropràs says. 'The people are already ill when they come from

Copataò,' agrees Paulo Figueiredo, boss of Union Carbide, 'and if they get worse, they blame it on us. That's simply illogical.' For years, the governor of São Paulo has been attempting to bring a fresh breeze into polluted Copataò. He fired thirteen officials of the lax environmental agency and employed computers to monitor emissions. But the minor fines of a few thousand dollars didn't bother the environmental violators.

The catastrophe happened on 25 February of this year. Through the sloppiness of Pegropràs, 700,000 liters of oil flowed into the swamp on which the pile buildings of Villa Soco stand. Within two minutes a fire storm raced through the favela. Over 500 people were burnt to death. The corpses of small children were never found. 'They just evaporated from the heat,' a Brazilian official said. (Der Spiegel 1984, no. 50: 110)

Bhopal

The birds fell from the skies. Water buffaloes, cows and dogs lay dead in the streets and fields—bloated after a few hours in the sun of Central Asia [*sic*]. And everywhere the asphyxiated people, curled up, foam at the lips, their cramped hands dug into the earth. There were 3000 of them by the end of last week and new victims were still being found; the authorities stopped counting. 20,000 people will probably go blind. As many as 200,000 were injured.

In the city of Bhopal an industrial apocalypse without parallel in history occurred last Sunday night and Monday morning. A toxic cloud escaped from a chemical factory and settled like a shroud over sixty-five thickly settled square kilometers; when it finally dissipated, the sickly sweet smell of decay was spreading. The city had turned into a battlefield, in the midst of peace. Hindus burned their dead on cremation pyres, twenty-five at a time. Soon there was a shortage of wood for the ritual cremation—thus kerosene flames licked around the corpses. The Moslem cemetery became too crowded. Earlier graves had to be opened, breaking the holy commandments of Islam. 'I know it's a sin to bury two people in a single grave,' one of the grave-diggers complains. 'May Allah forgive us. We're putting three, four and even more in.' (110)

In contrast to material poverty, however, the pauperization of the Third World through hazards is contagious for the wealthy. The multiplication of risks causes world society to contract into a community of danger. The boomerang effect strikes precisely those wealthy countries which had hoped to get rid of hazards by transferring them overseas, but then had to import cheaper foodstuffs. The pesticides return to their industrialized homeland in the fruit, cacao beans and tea leaves. The extreme international inequalities and the interconnections of the world markets move the poor neighborhoods in the peripheral countries to the doorsteps of the rich industrial centers. They become the breeding grounds of an international contamination, which—like the infectious diseases of the poor in the cramped medieval cities—does not spare even the wealthy neighborhoods of the world community.

Two Epochs, Two Cultures: On the Relationship Between the Perception and the Production of Risks

Inequalities in class and risk society can therefore overlap and condition one another; the latter can produce the former. The unequal distribution of social wealth offers almost impregnable defensive walls and justifications for the production of risks. Here a precise distinction must be made between the cultural and political *attention* to risks and their actual *diffusion*.

Class societies are societies where, across all the gaps between classes, the main concern is the visible satisfaction of material needs. Here, hunger and surplus or power and weakness confront each other. Misery needs no self-confirmation. It exists. Its directness and visibility correspond to the material evidence of wealth and power. The certainties of class societies are in this sense the certainties of a culture of *visibility*: emaciated hunger contrasts with plump satiety; palaces with hovels, splendors with rags.

These evident qualities of the tangible no longer hold in risk societies. What escapes perceptibility no longer coincides with the unreal, but can instead even possess a higher degree of hazardous reality. Immediate need competes with the known element of risk. The world of visible scarcity or surplus grows dim under the predominance of risk.

References

Anders, G. 1983. *Die atomare Bedrohung*. Munich.

Rat der Sachverständigen für Umweltfragen. 1985. *Sondergutachten Umweltprobleme der Landwertschaft*. Abridged, unpublished ms. Bonn.

XV. Structuralism, Poststructuralism, and Postmodernism

65

Structures and the Habitus

Pierre Bourdieu

Pierre Bourdieu (1930–2002) was the chair of sociology at the prestigious Collége de France, and from this position he commanded authority as one of the premier social theorists in the world. Influenced by both Marxism and structuralism, his work has built on these traditions while simultaneously serving as a corrective to the tendency in both paradigms to exhibit a lack of theoretical regard for the role of real-life actors. In this passage from *Outline of a Theory of Practice* (1977), Bourdieu discusses three of the terms that are of central importance to his own contributions to theory: structure, habitus, and practice. Structure refers to the external constraints that impinge on actors, practice to human agency, and habitus to the cognitive structures through which people orient themselves toward the world. Together they are used in an attempt to find a path between structuralism and extreme social constructionism.

The habitus, the durably installed generative principle of regulated improvisations, produces practices which tend to reproduce the regularities immanent in the objective conditions of the production of their generative principle, while adjusting to the demands inscribed as objective potentialities in the situation, as defined by the cognitive and motivating structures making up the habitus. It follows that these practices cannot be directly deduced either from the objective conditions, defined as the instantaneous sum of the stimuli which may appear to have directly triggered them, or from the conditions which produced the durable principle of their production. These practices can be accounted for only by relating the objective *structure* defining the social conditions of the production of the habitus which engendered them to the conditions in which this habitus is operating, that is, to the *conjuncture* which, short of a radical transformation, represents a particular state of this structure. In practice, it is the habitus, history turned into nature, i.e. denied as such, which accomplishes practically the relating of these two systems of relations, in and through the production of practice. The "unconscious" is never anything other than the forgetting of history which history itself produces by incorporating the objective structures it produces in the second natures of habitus:

> . . . in each of us, in varying proportions, there is part of yesterday's man; it is yesterday's man who inevitably predominates in us, since the present amounts to little compared with the long past in the course of which we were formed and from which we result. Yet we do not sense this man of the past, because he is inveterate in us; he makes up the unconscious part of ourselves. Consequently we are led to take no account of him, any more

than we take account of his legitimate demands. Conversely, we are very much aware of the most recent attainments of civilization, because, being recent, they have not yet had time to settle into our unconscious.[1]

Genesis amnesia is also encouraged (if not entailed) by the objectivist apprehension which, grasping the product of history as an *opus operatum*, a *fait accompli*, can only invoke the mysteries of pre-established harmony or the prodigies of conscious orchestration to account for what, apprehended in pure synchrony, appears as objective meaning, whether it be the internal coherence of works or institutions such as myths, rites, or bodies of law, or the objective co-ordination which the concordant or conflicting practices of the members of the same group or class at once manifest and presuppose (inasmuch as they imply a community of dispositions).

Each agent, wittingly or unwittingly, willy nilly, is a producer and reproducer of objective meaning. Because his actions and works are the product of a *modus operandi* of which he is not the producer and has no conscious mastery, they contain an "objective intention", as the Scholastics put it, which always outruns his conscious intentions. The schemes of thought and expression he has acquired are the basis for the intentionless invention of regulated improvisation. Endlessly overtaken by his own words, with which he maintains a relation of "carry and be carried", as Nicolaï Hartmann put it, the virtuoso finds in the *opus operatum* new triggers and new supports for the *modus operandi* from which they arise, so that his discourse continuously feeds off itself like a train bringing along its own rails.[2] If witticisms surprise their author no less than their audience, and impress as much by their retrospective necessity as by their novelty, the reason is that the *trouvaille* appears as the simple unearthing, at once accidental and irresistible, of a buried possibility. It is because subjects do not, strictly speaking, know what they are doing that what they do has more meaning than they know. The habitus is the universalizing mediation which causes an individual agent's practices, without either explicit reason or signifying

intent, to be none the less "sensible" and "reasonable". That part of practices which remains obscure in the eyes of their own producers is the aspect by which they are objectively adjusted to the structures of which the principle of their production is itself the product.[3]

One of the fundamental effects of the orchestration of habitus is the production of a commonsense world endowed with the *objectivity* secured by consensus on the meaning *(sens)* of practices and the world, in other words the harmonization of agents' experiences and the continuous reinforcement that each of them receives from the expression, individual or collective (in festivals, for example), improvised or programmed (commonplaces, sayings), of similar or identical experiences. The homogeneity of habitus is what—within the limits of the group of agents possessing the schemes (of production and interpretation) implied in their production—causes practices and works to be immediately intelligible and foreseeable, and hence taken for granted. This practical comprehension obviates the "intention" and "intentional transfer into the Other" dear to the phenomenologists, by dispensing, for the ordinary occasions of life, with close analysis of the nuances of another's practice and tacit or explicit inquiry ("What do you *mean*?") into his intentions. Automatic and impersonal, significant without intending to signify, ordinary practices lend themselves to an understanding no less automatic and impersonal: the picking up of the objective intention they express in no way implies "reactivation" of the "lived" intention of the agent who performs them.[4] "Communication of consciousnesses" presupposes community of "unconsciouses" (i.e. of linguistic and cultural competences). The deciphering of the objective intention of practices and works has nothing to do with the "reproduction" (*Nachbildung*, as the early Dilthey puts it) of lived experiences and the reconstitution, unnecessary and uncertain, of the personal singularities of an "intention" which is not their true origin.

The objective homogenizing of group or class habitus which results from the homogeneity of the conditions of existence is what enables practices to be objectively harmonized without any intentional calculation or conscious reference to a norm and mutually adjusted *in the absence of any direct interaction* or, *a fortiori,* explicit co-ordination.

> 'Imagine', Leibniz suggests, 'two clocks or watches in perfect agreement as to the time. This may occur in one of three ways. The first consists in mutual influence; the second is to appoint a skilful workman to correct them and synchronize them at all times; the third is to construct these clocks with such art and precision that one can be assured of their subsequent agreement.'[5]

So long as, retaining only the first or at a pinch the second hypothesis, one ignores the true principle of the conductorless orchestration which gives regularity, unity, and systematicity to the practices of a group or class, and this even in the absence of any spontaneous or externally imposed organization of individual projects, one is condemned to the naive artificialism which recognizes no other principle unifying a group's or class's ordinary or extraordinary action than the conscious co-ordination of a conspiracy.[6] If the practices of the members of the same group or class are more and better harmonized than the agents know or wish, it is because, as Leibniz puts it, "following only [his] own laws", each "nonetheless agrees with the other".[7] The habitus is precisely this immanent law, *lex insita,* laid down in each agent by his earliest upbringing, which is the precondition not only for the co-ordination of practices but also for practices of co-ordination, since the corrections and adjustments the agents themselves consciously carry out presuppose their mastery of a common code and since undertakings of collective mobilization cannot succeed without a minimum of concordance between the habitus of the mobilizing agents (e.g. prophet, party leader, etc.) and the dispositions of those whose aspirations and world-view they express.

So it is because they are the product of dispositions which, being the internalization of the same objective structures, are objectively concerted that the practices of the members of the same group or, in a differentiated society, the same class are endowed with an objective meaning that is at once unitary and systematic, transcending subjective intentions and conscious projects whether individual or collective.[8] To describe the process of objectification and orchestration in the language of *interaction* and mutual adjustment is to forget that the interaction itself owes its form to the objective structures which have produced the dispositions of the interacting agents and which allot them their relative positions in the interaction and elsewhere. Every confrontation between agents in fact brings together, in an *interaction* defined by the *objective structure* of the relation between the groups they belong to (e.g. a boss giving orders to a subordinate, colleagues discussing their pupils, academics taking part in a symposium), systems of dispositions (carried by "natural persons") such as a linguistic competence and a cultural competence and, through these habitus, all the objective structures of which they are the product, structures which are active only when *embodied* in a competence acquired in the course of a particular history (with the different types of bilingualism or pronunciation, for example, stemming from different modes of acquisition).[9]

Thus, when we speak of class habitus, we are insisting, against all forms of the occasionalist illusion which consists in directly relating practices to properties inscribed in the situation, that "interpersonal" relations are never, except in appearance, *individual-to-individual* relationships and that the truth of the interaction is never entirely contained in the interaction. This is what social psychology and interactionism or ethnomethodology forget when, reducing the objective structure of the relationship between the assembled individuals to the conjunctural structure of their interaction in a particular situation and group, they seek to explain everything that occurs in an experimental or observed interaction in terms of the experimentally controlled characteristics of the situation, such as the relative spatial positions of the participants or the nature of the channels used. In fact it is their present and past positions in the social structure that biological individuals carry with them, at all times and in all places, in the form of dispositions which are so many marks of *social position* and hence of the social distance between objective positions, that is, between social persons conjuncturally brought together (in physical space, which is not the same thing as social space) and correlatively, so many reminders of this distance and of the conduct required in order to "keep one's distance" or to manipulate it strategically, whether symbolically or actually, to reduce it (easier for the dominant than for the dominated), increase it, or simply maintain it (by not "letting oneself go", not "becoming familiar", in short, "standing on one's dignity", or on the other hand, refusing to "take liberties" and "put oneself forward", in short "knowing one's place" and staying there).

Even those forms of interaction seemingly most amenable to description in terms of "intentional transfer into the Other", such as sympathy, friendship, or love, are dominated (as class homogamy attests), through the harmony of habitus, that is to say, more precisely, the harmony of ethos and tastes—doubtless sensed in the imperceptible cues of body *hexis*—by the objective structure of the relations between social conditions. The illusion of mutual election or predestination arises from ignorance of the social conditions for the harmony of aesthetic tastes or ethical leanings, which is thereby perceived as evidence of the ineffable affinities which spring from it.

In short, the habitus, the product of history, produces individual and collective practices, and hence history, in accordance with the schemes engendered by history. The system of dispositions—a past which survives in the present and tends to perpetuate itself into the future by making itself present in practices structured according to its principles, an internal law relaying the continuous exercise of the law of external necessities (irreducible to immediate conjunctural constraints)—is the principle of the continuity and regularity which objectivism discerns in the social world without being able to give them a rational basis. And it is at the same time the principle of the transformations and regulated revolutions which neither the extrinsic and instantaneous determinisms of a mechanistic sociology nor the purely internal but equally punctual determination of voluntarist or spontaneist subjectivism are capable of accounting for.

It is just as true and just as untrue to say that collective actions produce the event or that they are its product. The conjuncture capable of transforming practices objectively co-ordinated because subordinated to partially or wholly identical objective necessities, into *collective action* (e.g. revolutionary action) is constituted in the dialectical relationship between, on the one hand, a *habitus,* understood as a system of lasting, transposable dispositions which, integrating past experiences, functions at every moment as a *matrix of perceptions, appreciations, and actions* and makes possible the achievement of infinitely diversified tasks, thanks to analogical transfers of schemes permitting the solution of similarly shaped problems, and thanks to the unceasing corrections of the results obtained, dialectically produced by those results, and on the other hand, an *objective event* which exerts its action of conditional stimulation calling for or demanding a determinate response, only on those who are disposed to constitute it as such because they are endowed with a determinate type of dispositions (which are amenable to reduplication and reinforcement by the "awakening of class consciousness", that is, by the direct or indirect possession of a discourse capable of securing symbolic mastery of the practically mastered principles of the class habitus). Without ever being totally co-ordinated, since they are the product of "causal series" characterized by different structural durations, the dispositions and the situations which combine synchronically to constitute a determinate conjuncture are never wholly independent, since they are engendered by the objective structures, that is, in the last analysis, by the economic bases of the social formation in question. The hysteresis of habitus, which is inherent in the social conditions of the reproduction of the structures in habitus, is doubtless one of the foundations of the structural lag between opportunities and the dispositions to grasp them which is the cause of missed opportunities and, in particular, of the frequently observed incapacity to think historical crises in categories of perception and thought other than those of the past, albeit a revolutionary past.

If one ignores the dialectical relationship between the objective structures and the cognitive and motivating structures which they produce and which tend to reproduce them, if one forgets that these objective structures are themselves products of historical practices and are constantly reproduced and transformed by historical practices whose productive principle is itself the product of the structures which it consequently tends to reproduce, then one is condemned to reduce the relationship between the different social agencies (*instances*), treated as "different translations of the same sentence"—in a Spinozist metaphor which contains the truth of the objectivist language of "articulation"—to the logical formula enabling any one of them to be derived from any other. The unifying principle of practices in different domains which objectivist analysis would assign to separate "sub-systems", such as matrimonial strategies, fertility strategies, or economic choices, is nothing other than the habitus, the locus of practical realization of the "articulation" of fields which objectivism (from Parsons to the structuralist readers of Marx) lays out side by side without securing the means of discovering the real principle of the structural homologies or relations of transformation objectively established between them (which is not to deny that the structures are objectivities irreducible to their manifestation in the habitus which they produce and which tend to reproduce them). So long as one accepts the canonic opposition which, endlessly reappearing in new forms throughout the history of social thought, nowadays pits "humanist" against "structuralist" readings of Marx, to declare diametrical opposition to subjectivism is not genuinely to *break* with it, but to fall into the fetishism of social laws to which objectivism consigns itself when in establishing between structure and practice the relation of the virtual to the actual, of the score to the performance, of essence to existence, it merely substitutes for the creative man of subjectivism a man subjugated to the dead laws of a natural history. And how could one underestimate the strength of the ideological couple subjectivism/objectivism when one sees that the critique of the *individual* considered as *ens realissimum* only leads to his being made an epiphenomenon of hypostatized structure, and that the well-founded assertion of the primacy of objective relations results in products of human action, the structures, being credited with the power to develop in accordance with their own laws and to determine and overdetermine other structures? Just as the opposition of language to speech as mere execution or even as a preconstructed object masks the opposition between the objective relations of the language and the dispositions making up linguistic competence, so the opposition between the structure and the individual against whom the structure has to be won and endlessly rewon stands in the way of construction of the dialectical relationship between the structure and the dispositions making up the habitus.

If the debate on the relationship between "culture" and "personality" which dominated a whole era of American anthropology now seems so artificial and sterile, it is because, amidst a host of logical and epistemological fallacies, it was organized around the relation between two complementary products of the same realist, substantialist representation of the scientific object. In its most exaggerated forms, the theory of "basic personality" tends to define personality as a miniature replica (obtained by "moulding") of the "culture", to be found in all members of the same society, except deviants. Cora Du Bois's celebrated analyses on the Alor Island natives provide a very typical example of the confusions and contradictions resulting from the theory that "culture" and personality can each be deduced from the other: determined to reconcile the anthropologist's conclusions, based on the postulate that the same influences produce the same basic personality, with her own clinical observations of four subjects who seem to her to be "highly individual characters", each "moulded by the specific factors in his individual fate", the psychoanalyst who struggles to find individual incarnations of the basic personality is condemned to recantations and contradictions.[10] Thus, she can see

Mangma as "the most typical" of the four ("his personality corresponds to the basic personality structure") after having written: "It is difficult to decide how typical Mangma is. I would venture to say that if he were typical, the society could not continue to exist." Ripalda, who is passive and has a strong super-ego, is "atypical." So is Fantan, who has "the strongest character formation, devoid of inhibitions toward women" (extreme heterosexual inhibition being the rule), and "differs from the other men as much as a city-slicker differs from a farmer". The fourth, Malekala, whose biography is typical at every point, is a well-known prophet who tried to start a revivalist movement, and his personality seems to resemble that of Ripalda, another sorcerer who, as we have seen, is described as atypical. All this is capped by the analyst's observation that "characters such as Mangma, Ripalda and Fantan can be found in any society". Anthony F. Wallace, from whom this critique is taken,[11] is no doubt right in pointing out that the notion of modal personality has the advantage of avoiding the illogicalities resulting from indifference to differences (and thus to statistics) usually implicit in recourse to the notion of basic personality. But what might pass for a mere refinement of the measuring and checking techniques used to test the validity of a theoretical construct amounts in fact to the substitution of one object for another: a system of hypotheses as to the *structure* of personality, conceived as a homeostatic system which changes by reinterpreting external pressures in accordance with its own logic, is replaced by a simple description of the central tendency in the distribution of the values of a variable or rather a combination of variables. Wallace thus comes to the tautological conclusion that in a population of Tuscarora Indians, the modal personality type defined by reference to twenty-seven variables is to be found in only 37 per cent of the subjects studied. The construction of a class *ethos* may, for example, make use of a reading of statistical regularities treated as *indices*, without the principle which unifies and explains these regularities being reducible to the regularities in which it manifests itself. In short, failing to see in the notion of "basic personality"

anything other than a way of pointing to a directly observable "datum", i.e. the "personality type" shared by the greatest number of members of a given society, the advocates of this notion cannot, in all logic, take issue with those who submit this theory to the test of statistical critique, in the name of the same realist representation of the scientific object.

The habitus is the product of the work of inculcation and appropriation necessary in order for those products of collective history, the objective structures (e.g. of language, economy, etc.) to succeed in reproducing themselves more or less completely, in the form of durable dispositions, in the organisms (which one can, if one wishes, call individuals) lastingly subjected to the same conditionings, and hence placed in the same material conditions of existence. Therefore sociology treats as identical all the biological individuals who, being the product of the same objective conditions, are the supports of the same habitus: social class, understood as a system of objective determinations, must be brought into relation not with the individual or with the "class" as a *population*, i.e. as an aggregate of enumerable, measurable biological individuals, but with the class habitus, the system of dispositions (partially) common to all products of the same structures. Though it is impossible for *all* members of the same class (or even two of them) to have had the same experiences, in the same order, it is certain that each member of the same class is more likely than any member of another class to have been confronted with the situations most frequent for the members of that class. The objective structures which science apprehends in the form of statistical regularities (e.g. employment rates, income curves, probabilities of access to secondary education, frequency of holidays, etc.) inculcate, through the direct or indirect but always convergent experiences which give a social environment its *physiognomy*, with its "closed doors", "dead ends", and limited "prospects", that "art of assessing likelihoods", as Leibniz put it, of anticipating the objective future, in short, the sense of reality or realities which is perhaps the best-concealed principle of their efficacy.

In order to define the relations between class, habitus and the organic individuality which can never entirely be removed from sociological discourse, inasmuch as, being given immediately to immediate perception (*intuitus personae*), it is also socially designated and recognized (name, legal identity, etc.) and is defined by a *social trajectory* strictly speaking irreducible to any other, the habitus could be considered as a subjective but not individual system of internalized structures, schemes of perception, conception, and action common to all members of the same group or class and constituting the precondition for all objectification and apperception: and the objective coordination of practices and the sharing of a worldview could be founded on the perfect impersonality and interchangeability of singular practices and views. But this would amount to regarding all the practices or representations produced in accordance with identical schemes as impersonal and substitutable, like singular intuitions of space which, according to Kant, reflect none of the peculiarities of the individual ego. In fact, it is in a relation of homology, of diversity within homogeneity reflecting the diversity within homogeneity characteristic of their social conditions of production, that the singular habitus of the different members of the same class are united; the homology of world-views implies the systematic differences which separate singular world-views, adopted from singular but concerted standpoints. Since the history of the individual is never anything other than a certain specification of the collective history of his group or class, *each individual system of dispositions* may be seen as a *structural variant* of all the other group or class habitus, expressing the difference between trajectories and positions inside or outside the class. "Personal" style, the particular stamp marking all the products of the same habitus, whether practices or works, is never more than a *deviation* in relation to the *style* of a period or class so that it relates back to the common style not only by its conformity—like Phidias, who, according to Hegel, had no "manner"—but also by the difference which makes the whole "manner".

The principle of these individual differences lies in the fact that, being the product of a chronologically ordered series of structuring determinations, the habitus, which at every moment structures in terms of the structuring experiences which produced it the structuring experiences which affect its structure, brings about a unique integration, dominated by the earliest experiences, of the experiences statistically common to the members of the same class. Thus, for example, the habitus acquired in the family underlies the structuring of school experiences (in particular the reception and assimilation of the specifically pedagogic message), and the habitus transformed by schooling, itself diversified, in turn underlies the structuring of all subsequent experiences (e.g. the reception and assimilation of the messages of the culture industry or work experiences), and so on, from restructuring to restructuring. Springing from the encounter in an integrative organism of relatively independent causal series, such as biological and social determiniams, the habitus makes coherence and necessity out of accident and contingency: for example, the equivalences it establishes between positions in the division of labour and positions in the division between the sexes are doubtless not peculiar to societies in which the division of labour and the division between the sexes coincide almost perfectly. In a class society, all the products of a given agent, by an essential *overdetermination*, speak inseparably and simultaneously of his class—or, more precisely, his position in the social structure and his rising or falling trajectory—and of his (or her) body—or, more precisely, all the properties, always socially qualified, of which he or she is the bearer—sexual properties of course, but also physical properties, praised, like strength or beauty, or stigmatized. . . .

Endnotes

1. E. Durkheim, *L'evolution pedogogique en France* (Paris: Alcan, 1938), p. 16.

2. R. Ruyer, *Paradoxes de la conscience et limites de l'antomatisme* (Paris: Albin Michel, 1966), p. 136.

3. This universalization has the same limits as the objective conditions of which the principle generating practices and works is the product. The ob-

jective conditions exercise simultaneously a universalizing effect and a particularizing effect, because they cannot homogenize the agents whom they determine and whom they constitute into an objective group, without distinguishing them from all the agents produced in different conditions.

4. One of the merits of subjectivism and moralism is that the analyses in which it condemns, as inauthentic, actions subject to the objective solicitations of the world (e.g. Heidegger on everyday existence and *"Das Man"* or Sartre on the "spirit of seriousness") demonstrate, *per absurdum*, the impossibility of the authentic existence that would gather all pregiven significations and objective determinations into a project of freedom. The *purely ethical* pursuit of authenticity is the privilege of the leisured thinker who can afford to dispense with the economy of thought which "inauthentic" conduct follows.

5. G. W. Leibniz, "Second éclaircissement du système de la communication des substances" (1696), in *Oeuvres philosophiques*, ed. P. Janet (Paris: de Lagrange, 1866), vol. II, p. 548.

6. Thus, ignorance of the surest but best-hidden foundation of group or class integration leads some (e.g. Aron, Dahl, etc.) to deny the unity of the dominant class with no proof than the impossibility of establishing empirically that the members of the dominant class have an explicit *policy*, expressly imposed by explicit co-ordination, and others (Sartre, for example) to see the awakening of class consciousness—a sort of revolutionary cogito bringing the class into existence by constituting it as a "class for itself"—as the only possible foundation of the unity of the dominated class.

7. Leibniz, "Second éclaircissement", p. 548.

8. Were such language not dangerous in another way, one would be tempted to say, against all form of subjectivist voluntarism, that class unity rests fundamentally on the "class unconscious". The awakening of "class consciousness" is not a primal act constituting the class in a blaze of freedom; its sole efficacy, as with all actions of primal symbolic reduplication, lies in the extent to which it brings to consciousness all that is implicitly assumed in the unconscious mode in the class habitus.

9. This takes us beyond the false opposition in which the theories of acculturation have allowed themselves to be trapped with, on the one hand, the *realism of the structure* which represents cultural or linguistic contact as contacts between cultures or languages, subject to generic laws (e.g. the law of the restructuring of borrowings) and specific laws (those established by analysis of the structures specific to the languages or cultures in contact) and on the other hand the *realism of the element*, which emphasizes the contacts between the *societies* (regarded as populations) involved or, at best, the structures of the relations between those societies (domination, etc.).

10. *The People of Alor* (Minneapolis: University of Minnesota Press, 1944).

11. *Culture and Personality* (New York: Random House, 1965), p. 86.

66
Advertising

Jean Baudrillard

Jean Baudrillard (1929–2007), a French social thinker, taught sociology at the University of Nanterre during the tumultuous days of 1968, when student revolts nearly toppled the government of Charles DeGaulle. In the aftermath of those events, Baudrillard left the university, turned from Marxism, and emerged as one of the most radical proponents of postmodernism. Central to his vision of contemporary social life was the notion that our cultures have been thoroughly saturated by the media and entertainment industries such that the differences between the real and the images, signs, and simulations have dissolved. The result was the emergence of what he referred to as "hyperreality." In this essay (published in 1968, at the beginning of his transition from Marxism to postmodernism) he explores from various angles the significance of advertising in shaping modern consumerism.

Discourse on Objects and Discourse-as-Object

Any analysis of the system *of* objects must ultimately imply an analysis of discourse about objects—that is to say, an analysis of promotional 'messages' (comprising image and discourse). For advertising is not simply an adjunct to the system of objects; it cannot be detached therefrom, nor can it be restricted to its 'proper' function (there is no such thing as advertising strictly confined to the supplying of information). Indeed, advertising is now an irremovable aspect of the system of objects precisely by virtue of its disproportionateness. This lack of proportion is the 'functional' apotheosis of the system. Advertising in its entirety constitutes a useless and unnecessary universe. It is pure connotation. It contributes nothing to production or to the direct practical application of things, yet it plays an integral part in the system of objects, not merely because it relates to consumption but also because it itself becomes an object to be consumed. A clear distinction must be drawn in connection with advertising's dual status as a discourse on the object and as an object in its own right. It is as a useless, unnecessary discourse that it comes to be consumable as a cultural object. What achieves autonomy and fulfilment through advertising is thus the whole system that I have been describing at the level of objects: the entire apparatus of personalization and imposed differentiation; of proliferation of the inessential and subordination of technical requirements to the requirements of production and consumption; of dysfunctionality and secondary functionality. Since its function is almost entirely secondary, and since both image and discourse play largely allegorical roles in it, advertising supplies us with the ideal object and casts a particularly revealing light upon the system of objects. And since, like all heavily connoted systems, it is self-referential,[1] we may safely rely on advertising to tell us what it is that we consume *through* objects.

Advertising in the Indicative and in the Imperative

Advertising sets itself the task of supplying information about particular products and promoting their sale. In principle this 'objective' function is still its fundamental purpose.[2] The supplying of information has nevertheless given way to persuasion—even to what Vance Packard calls 'hidden persuasion', the aim of which is a completely managed consumption. The supposed threat this poses of a totalitarian conditioning of man and his needs has provoked great alarm. Studies have shown, however, that advertising's pervasive power is not as great as had been supposed. A saturation point is in fact soon reached: competing messages tend to cancel each other out, and many claims fail to convince on account of their sheer excessiveness. Moreover, injunctions and exhortations give rise to all kinds of counter-motivations and resistances, whether rational or irrational, among them the refusal of passivity, the desire not to be 'taken over', negative reactions to hyperbole, to repetition, and so on. In short, the discourse of advertising is just as likely to dissuade as to persuade, and consumers, though not entirely immune, appear to exercise a good deal of discretion when it comes to the advertising message.

Having said this, let us not be misled by the *avowed* aim of that message; while advertising may well fail to sell the consumer on a particular brand—Omo, Simca or Frigidaire—it does sell him on something else, something much more fundamental to the global social order than Omo or Frigidaire—something, indeed for which such brand names are merely a cover. Just as the object's function may ultimately amount merely to the provision of a justification for the latent meanings that the object imposes, so in advertising (and all the more so inasmuch as it is the more purely connotative system) the product designated—that is, its denotation or description—tends to be merely an effective mask concealing a confused process of integration.

So even though we may be getting better and better at resisting advertising in the *imperative,* we are at the same time becoming ever more susceptible to advertising in the *indicative*—that is, to its actual *existence* as a product to be consumed at a secondary level, and as the clear *expression* of a culture. It is in this sense that we do indeed 'believe' in advertising: what we consume in this way is the luxury of a society that projects itself as an agency for dispensing goods and 'transcends itself' in a culture. We are thus taken over at one and the same time by an established agency and by that agency's self-image.

The Logic of Father Christmas

Those who pooh-pooh the ability of advertising and of the mass media in general to condition people have failed to grasp the peculiar logic upon which the media's efficacy reposes. For this is not a logic of propositions and proofs, but a logic of fables and of the willingness to go along with them. We do not believe in such fables, but we cleave to them nevertheless. Basically, the 'demonstration' of a product convinces no one, but

it does serve to rationalize its purchase, which in any case either precedes or overwhelms all rational motives. Without 'believing' in the product, therefore, *we believe in the advertising that tries to get us to believe in it.* We are for all the world like children in their attitude towards Father Christmas. Children hardly ever wonder whether Father Christmas exists or not, and they certainly never look upon getting presents as an effect of which that existence is the cause: rather, their belief in Father Christmas is a rationalizing confabulation designed to extend earliest infancy's miraculously gratifying relationship with the parents (and particularly with the mother) into a later stage of childhood. That miraculous relationship, though now in actuality past, is internalized in the form of a belief which is in effect an ideal extension of it. There is nothing artificial about the romance of Father Christmas, however, for it is based upon the shared interest that the two parties involved have in its preservation. Father Christmas himself is unimportant here, and the child only believes in him precisely because of that basic lack of significance. What children are actually consuming through this figure, fiction or cover story (which in a sense they continue to believe in even after they have ceased to do so) is the action of a magical parental solicitude and the care taken by the parents to continue colluding with their children's embrace of the fable. Christmas presents themselves serve merely to underwrite this compromise.[3]

Advertising functions in much the same way. Neither its rhetoric nor even the informational aspect of its discourse has a decisive effect on the buyer. What the individual does respond to, on the other hand, is advertising's underlying leitmotiv of protection and gratification, the intimation that its solicitations and attempts to persuade are the sign, indecipherable at the conscious level, that somewhere there is an agency (a social agency in the event, but one that refers directly to the image of the mother) which has taken it upon itself to inform him of his own desires, and to foresee and rationalize these desires to his own satisfaction. He thus no more 'believes' in advertising than the child believes in Father Christmas, but this in no way impedes his capacity to embrace an internalized infantile situation, and to act accordingly. Herein lies the very real effectiveness of advertising, founded on its obedience to a logic which, though not that of the conditioned reflex, is nonetheless very rigorous: a logic of belief and regression.[4] . . .

The Festival of Buying Power

This gratificatory, infantilizing function of advertising, which is the basis of our belief in it and hence of our collusion with the social entity, is equally well illustrated by its playful aspect. We are certainly susceptible to the reassurance advertising offers by supplying an image that is never negative, but we are equally affected by advertising as a fantastic manifestation of a society capable of swamping the mere necessity of products in superfluous images: advertising as a show (again, the most democratic of all), a game, a *mise en scène*. Advertising serves as a permanent display of the buying power, be it real or virtual, of society overall. Whether we partake of it personally or not, we all live and breathe this buying power. By virtue of advertising, too, the product exposes itself to our view and invites us to handle it; it is, in fact, eroticized—not just because of the explicitly sexual themes evoked[5] but also because the purchase itself, simple appropriation, is transformed into a manoeuvre, a scenario, a complicated dance which endows a purely practical transaction with all the traits of amorous dalliance: advances, rivalry, obscenity, flirtation, prostitution— even irony. The mechanics of buying (which is already libidinally charged) gives way to a complete eroticization of choosing and spending.[6] Our modern environment assails us relentlessly, especially in the cities, with its lights and its images, its incessant inducements to status-consciousness and narcissism, emotional involvement and obligatory relationships. We live in a cold-blooded carnival atmosphere, a formal yet electrifying ambience of empty sensual gratification wherein the actual process of buying and consuming is demonstrated, illuminated, mimicked—even frustrated—much as the sexual act is anticipated by dance. By means of advertising, as once upon a time by means of feasts, society puts itself on display and consumes its own image. An essential regulatory function is evident here. Like the dream, advertising defines and redirects an imaginary potentiality. Like the dream's, its practical character is strictly subjective and individual.[7] And, like the dream, advertising is devoid of all negativity and relativity: with never a sign too many nor a sign too few, it is essentially superlative and totally immanent in nature.[8] Our night-time dreams are uncaptioned, whereas the one that we live in our waking hours via the city's hoardings, in our newspapers and on our screens, is covered with captions, with multiple subtitling. Both, however, weave the most colourful of narratives from the most impoverished of raw materials, and just as the function of nocturnal dreams is to protect sleep, so likewise the prestige of advertising and consumption serves to ensure the spontaneous absorption of ambient social values and the regression of the individual into social consensus.

Festival, immanence, positivity—to use such terms amounts to saying that *in the first instance advertising is itself less a determinant of consumption than an object of consumption*. What would an object be today if it were not put on offer both in the mode of discourse and image (advertising) and in the mode of a range of models (choice)? It would be psychologically nonexistent. And what would modern citizens be if objects and products were not proposed to them in the twin dimensions of advertising and choice? They would not be *free*. We can understand the reactions of the two thousand West Germans polled by the Allenbach Demoscopic Institute: 60 percent expressed the view that there was too much advertising, yet when they were asked, 'Would you rather have too much advertising (Western style) or minimal—and only socially useful—advertising (as in the East)?', a majority favoured the first of these options, taking an excess of advertising as indicative not only of affluence but also of freedom—and hence of a basic value.[9] Such is the measure of the emotional and ideological collusion that advertising's spectacular mediation creates between the individual and society (whatever the structures of the latter may be). If all advertising were abolished, individuals would feel frustrated by the empty hoardings. Frustrated not merely by the lack of opportunity (even in an ironic way) for play, for dreaming, but also, more profoundly, by the feeling that they were no longer somehow 'being taken care of'. They would miss an environment thanks to which, in the absence of active social participation, they can at least partake of a travesty of the social entity and enjoy a warmer, more maternal and more vivid atmosphere. One of the first demands of man in his progression towards well-being is that his desires be attended to, that they be formulated and expressed in the form of images for his own contemplation (something which is a problem, or becomes a problem, in socialist countries). Advertising fills this function, which is futile, regressive and inessential—yet for that very reason even more profoundly necessary.

Gratification/Repression: A Two-Sided Agency

We need to discern the true imperative of advertising behind the gentle litany of the object: 'Look how the whole of society simply adapts itself to you and your desires. It is therefore only reasonable that you should become integrated into that society.' Persuasion is hidden, as Vance Packard says, but its aim is less the 'compulsion' to buy, or conditioning by means of objects, than the subscription to social consensus that this discourse urges: the object is a service, a personal relationship between society and you. Whether advertising is organized around the image of the mother or around the need to play, it always aims to foster *the same tendency to regress to a point anterior to real social processes*, such as work, production, the market, or value, which might disturb this magical integration: the object has not been bought by you, you have voiced a desire for it and all the engineers, technicians, and so on, have worked to gratify your desire. With the advent of industrial society the division of labour severs labour from its product. Advertising adds the finishing touch to this development by creating a radical split, at the moment of purchase, between *products* and consumer *goods;* by interpolating a vast maternal image between

labour and the product of labour, it causes that *product* no longer to be viewed as such (complete with its history, and so on), but purely and simply as a good, as an *object*. And even as it separates the producer and the consumer within the one individual, thanks to the material abstraction of a highly differentiated system of objects, advertising strives inversely to re-create the infantile confusion of the object with the desire for the object, to return the consumer to the stage at which the infant makes no distinction between its mother and what its mother gives it.

In reality advertising's careful omission of objective processes and the social history of objects is simply a way of making it easier, by means of the imagination as a social agency, to impose the *real* order of production and exploitation. This is where, behind the psychogogy of advertising, it behoves us to recognize the demagogy of a *political* discourse whose own tactics are founded on a splitting into two—on the splitting of social reality into a real agency and an image, with the first disappearing behind the second, becoming indecipherable and giving way to nothing more than a pattern of absorption into a material world. When advertising tells you, in effect, that 'society adapts itself totally to you, so integrate yourself totally into society', the reciprocity thus invoked is obviously fake: what adapts to you is an imaginary agency, whereas you are asked in exchange to adapt to an agency that is distinctly real. Via the armchair that 'weds the shape of your body', it is the entire technical and political order of society that weds *you* and takes you in hand. Society assumes a maternal *role* the better to preserve the rule of *constraint*.[10] The immense political role played by the diffusion of products and advertising techniques is here clearly evident: these mechanisms effectively replace earlier moral or political ideologies. Indeed, they go farther, for moral and political forms of integration were never unproblematical and always had to be buttressed by overt repression, whereas the new techniques manage to do without any such assistance: the consumer internalizes the agency of social control and its norms in the very process of consuming.

This effectiveness is reinforced by the status accorded the signs advertising manipulates and the process whereby these are 'read'.

Signs in advertising speak to us of objects, but they never (or scarcely ever) explain those objects from the standpoint of a *praxis:* they refer to objects as to a world that is absent. These signs are literally no more than a 'legend': they are there primarily for the purpose of being read. But while they do not refer to the real world, neither do they exactly replace that world: their function is to impose a specific activity, a specific kind of reading. If they did carry information, then a *full* reading, and a transition to the practical realm, would occur. But their role is a different one: to draw attention to the absence of what they designate. To this extent the reading of such signs is intransitive—organized in terms of a specific system of *satisfaction* which is, however, perpetually determined by the absence of reality, that is to say, by *frustration.*

The image creates a void, indicates an absence, and it is in this respect that it is 'evocative'. It is deceptive, however. It provokes a cathexis which it then immediately short-circuits at the level of reading. It focuses free-floating wishes upon an object which it masks as much as reveals. The image disappoints: *its function is at once to display and simultaneously to disabuse.* Looking is based on a presumption of contact; the image and its reading are based on a presumption of possession. Thus advertising offers neither a hallucinated satisfaction nor a practical mediation with the world. Rather, what it produces is dashed hopes: unfinished actions, continual initiatives followed by continual abandonments thereof, false dawnings of objects, false dawnings of desires. A whole psychodrama is quickly enacted when an image is read. In principle, this enables the reader to assume his passive role and be transformed into a consumer. In actuality, the sheer profusion of images works at the same time to counter any shift in the direction of reality, subtly to fuel feelings of guilt by means of continual frustration, and to arrest consciousness at the level of a phantasy of satisfaction. In the end the image and the reading of the image are by no means the shortest way to the object, merely the shortest way to another image. The signs of advertising thus follow upon one another like the transient images of hypnagogic states.

We must not forget that the image serves in this way to avoid reality and create frustration, for only thus can we grasp how it is that *the reality principle omitted from the image nevertheless effectively re-emerges therein as the continual repression of desire* (as the spectacularization, blocking and dashing of that desire and, ultimately, its regressive and visible transference onto an object). This is where the profound collusion between the advertising sign and the overall order of society becomes most evident: it is not in any mechanical sense that advertising conveys the values of society; rather, more subtly, it is in its ambiguous *presumptive* function—somewhere between possession and dispossession, at once a designation and an indication of absence—that the advertising sign 'inserts' the social order into its system of simultaneous determination by gratification on the one hand and repression on the other.[11]

Gratification, frustration—two indivisible aspects of social integration. Every advertising image is a key, a *legend*, and as such reduces the anxiety-provoking polysemy of the world. But in the name of intelligibility the image becomes impoverished, cursory; inasmuch as it is still susceptible of too many interpretations, its meaning is further narrowed by the addition of discourse—of a subtitle, as it were, which constitutes a second legend. And, by virtue of the way it is read, the image always refers only to other images. In the end advertising soothes people's consciousness by means of a controlled social semantics—controlled, ultimately, to the point of focusing on a single referent, namely the whole society itself. Society thus monopolizes all the roles. It conjures up a host of images whose meanings it immediately strives to limit. It generates an anxiety that it then seeks to calm. It fulfils and disappoints, mobilizes and demobilizes. Under the banner of advertising it institutes the reign of a freedom of desire, but desire is never truly liberated thereby (which would in fact entail the end of the social order): desire is liberated by the image only to the point where its emergence triggers the associated reflexes of anxiety and guilt. Primed by the image only to be defused by it, and made to feel guilty to boot, the nascent desire is co-opted by the agency of control. There is a profusion of freedom, but this freedom is imaginary; a continual mental orgy, but one which is stage-managed, a controlled regression in which all perversity is resolved in favour of order. If gratification is massive in consumer society, repression is equally massive—and both reach us together via the images and discourse of advertising, which activate the repressive reality principle at the very heart of the pleasure principle.

Endnotes

1. See Roland Barthes's account of the system of fashion: *Système de la mode* (Paris: Seuil, 1967).

2. We should not forget, however, that the earliest advertisements were for miracle cures, home remedies, and the like; they supplied information, therefore, but information only of the most tendentious kind.

3. One is reminded of the neutral substances or placebos that doctors sometimes prescribe for psychosomatic patients. Quite often these patients make just as good a recovery after the administration of such inactive elements as they do after taking real medicine. What is it that such patients derive or assimilate from the placebo? The answer is the idea of medicine *plus* the presence of the physician: the mother and the father simultaneously. Here too, then, belief facilitates the retrieval of an infantile situation, the result being the regressive resolution of a psychosomatic conflict.

4. Such an approach might well be extended to mass communications in general, though this is not the place to attempt it.

5. Some common leitmotivs (breasts, lips) should perhaps be deemed less erotic than 'nurturing' in character.

6. The literal meaning of the German word for advertising, *'die Werbung'*, is erotic exploration. *'Der umworbene Mensch'*, the person won over by advertising, can also mean a person who is sexually solicited.

7. Advertising campaigns designed to alter group behaviour or modify social structures (for example, those against alcohol abuse, dangerous driving, etc.) are notoriously ineffective. Advertising resists the (collective) reality principle. The only imperative that may be effective in this context is 'Give!'—for it is part of the reversible system of gratification.

8. Negative or ironic advertisements are mere antiphrasis—a well-known device, too, of the dream.

9. Naturally the existing political situation of the two Germanies must be taken into account, but there can be little doubt that the absence of advertising in the Western sense is a real contributing factor to West German prejudice against the East.

10. What is more, behind this system of gratification we may discern the reinforcement of all the structures of authority (planning, centralization, bureaucracy). Parties, States, power structures—all are able to strengthen their hegemony under cover of this immense mother-image which renders any real challenge to them less and less possible.

11. This account may also be applied to the system of objects, because the object too is ambiguous, because it is never *merely* an object but always at the same time *an indication of the absence of a human relationship* (just as the sign in advertising is an indication of the absence of a real object)—for these reasons, the object may likewise play a powerful integrative role. It is true, however, that the object's practical specificity means that the indication of the absence of the real is less marked in the case of the object than in that of the advertising sign.

67
Panopticism

Michel Foucault

Michel Foucault (1926–1984) is a central figure among poststructuralists. Like other French thinkers of his generation, he was profoundly affected by the events of 1968, as well as by his personal experiences with LSD, San Francisco's gay scene in the 1970s, and the advent of the AIDS epidemic (Foucault died of AIDS). Central to Foucault's vision was a concern for the connections between power and knowledge; with his interest in sexuality, he also wanted to understand the body in relation to power/knowledge. In *Discipline and Punish* (1975), he examines the transition in prisons in the late eighteenth and early nineteenth centuries, when torture and other cruel punishments were replaced by more rationalized forms of punishment. Whereas earlier writers have typically described this change as a move toward more humane forms of punishment, Foucault sees it as an example of the growing power of authorities. The Panopticon discussed in this selection from the book is the prime example of the wedding of knowledge and power into a new system of heightened surveillance and control.

Bentham's *Panopticon* is the architectural figure of this composition. We know the principle on which it was based: at the periphery, an annular building; at the centre, a tower; this tower is pierced with wide windows that open onto the inner side of the ring; the peripheric building is divided into cells, each of which extends the whole width of the building; they have two windows, one on the inside, corresponding to the windows of the tower; the other, on the outside, allows the light to cross the cell from one end to the other. All that is needed, then, is to place a supervisor in a central tower and to shut up in each cell a madman, a patient, a condemned man, a worker or a schoolboy. By the effect of backlighting, one can observe from the tower, standing out precisely against the light, the small captive shadows in the cells of the periphery. They are like so many cages, so many small theatres, in which each actor is alone, perfectly individualized and constantly visible. The panoptic mechanism arranges spatial unities that make it possible to see constantly and to recognize immediately. In short, it reverses the principle of the dungeon; or rather of its three functions—to enclose, to deprive of light and to hide—it preserves only the first and eliminates the other two. Full lighting and the eye of a supervisor capture better than darkness, which ultimately protected. Visibility is a trap.

To begin with, this made it possible—as a negative effect—to avoid those compact, swarming, howling masses that were to be found in places of confinement, those painted by Goya or described by Howard. Each individual, in his place, is securely confined to a cell from which he is seen from the front by the supervisor; but the side walls prevent him from coming into contact with his companions. He is seen, but he does not see; he is the object of information, never a subject in communication. The arrangement of his room, opposite the central tower, imposes on him an axial visibility; but the divisions of the ring, those separated cells, imply a lateral invisibility. And this invisibility is a guarantee of order. If the inmates are convicts, there is no danger of a plot, an attempt at collective escape, the planning of new crimes for the future, bad reciprocal influences; if they are patients, there is no danger of contagion; if they are madmen there is no risk of their committing violence upon one another; if they are schoolchildren, there is no copying, no chatter, no waste of time; if they are workers, there are no disorders, no theft, no coalitions, none of those distractions that slow down the rate of work, make it less perfect or cause accidents. The crowd, a compact mass, a locus of multiple exchanges, individualities merging together, a collective effect, is abolished and replaced by a collection of separated individualities. From the point of view of the guardian, it is replaced by a multiplicity that can be numbered and supervised; from the point of view of the inmates, by a sequestered and observed solitude (Bentham, 60–64).

Hence the major effect of the Panopticon: to induce in the inmate a state of conscious and permanent visibility that assures the automatic functioning of power. So to arrange things that the surveillance is permanent in its effects, even if it is discontinuous in its action; that the perfection of power should tend to render its actual exercise unnecessary; that this architectural apparatus should be a machine for creating and sustaining a power relation independent of the person who exercises it; in short, that the inmates should be caught up in a power situation of which they are themselves the bearers. To achieve this, it is at once too much and too little that the prisoner should be constantly observed by an inspector: too little, for what matters is that he knows himself to be observed; too much, because he has no need in fact of being so. In view of this, Bentham laid down the principle that power should be visible and unverifiable. Visible: the inmate will constantly have before his eyes the tall outline of the central tower from which he is spied upon. Unverifiable: the inmate must never know whether he is being looked at at any one moment, but he must be sure that he may always be so. In order to make the presence or absence of the inspector unverifiable, so that the prisoners, in their cells, cannot even see a shadow, Bentham envisaged not only venetian blinds on the windows of the central observation hall, but, on the inside, partitions that intersected the hall at right angles and, in order to pass from one quarter to the other, not doors but zig-zag openings; for the slightest noise, a gleam of light, a brightness in a half-opened door would betray the presence of the guardian.[1] The Panopticon is a machine for dissociating the see/being seen dyad: in the peripheric ring, one is totally seen, without ever seeing; in the central tower, one sees everything without ever being seen.[2]

It is an important mechanism, for it automatizes and disindividualizes power. Power has its principle not so much in a person as in a certain concerted distribution of bodies, surfaces, lights, gazes; in an arrangement whose internal mechanisms produce the relation in which individuals are caught

up. The ceremonies, the rituals, the marks by which the sovereign's surplus power was manifested are useless. There is a machinery that assures dissymmetry, disequilibrium, difference. Consequently, it does not matter who exercises power. Any individual, taken almost at random, can operate the machine: in the absence of the director, his family, his friends, his visitors, even his servants (Bentham, 45). Similarly, it does not matter what motive animates him: the curiosity of the indiscreet, the malice of a child, the thirst for knowledge of a philosopher who wishes to visit this museum of human nature, or the perversity of those who take pleasure in spying and punishing. The more numerous those anonymous and temporary observers are, the greater the risk for the inmate of being surprised and the greater his anxious awareness of being observed. The Panopticon is a marvellous machine which, whatever use one may wish to put it to, produces homogeneous effects of power.

A real subjection is born mechanically from a fictitious relation. So it is not necessary to use force to constrain the convict to good behaviour, the madman to calm, the worker to work, the schoolboy to application, the patient to the observation of the regulations. Bentham was surprised that panoptic institutions could be so light: there were no more bars, no more chains, no more heavy locks; all that was needed was that the separations should be clear and the openings well arranged. The heaviness of the old 'houses of security', with their fortress-like architecture, could be replaced by the simple, economic geometry of a 'house of certainty'. The efficiency of power, its constraining force have, in a sense, passed over to the other side—to the side of its surface of application. He who is subjected to a field of visibility, and who knows it, assumes responsibility for the constraints of power; he makes them play spontaneously upon himself; he inscribes in himself the power relation in which he simultaneously plays both roles; he becomes the principle of his own subjection. By this very fact, the external power may throw off its physical weight; it tends to the non-corporal; and, the more it approaches this limit, the more constant, profound and permanent are its effects: it is a perpetual victory that avoids any physical confrontation and which is always decided in advance.

Bentham does not say whether he was inspired, in his project, by Le Vaux's menagerie at Versailles: the first menagerie in which the different elements are not, as they traditionally were, distributed in a park (Loisel, 104–7). At the centre was an octagonal pavilion which, on the first floor, consisted of only a single room, the king's *salon;* on every side large windows looked out onto seven cages (the eighth side was reserved for the entrance), containing different species of animals. By Bentham's time, this menagerie had disappeared. But one finds in the programme of the Panopticon a similar concern with individualizing observation, with characterization and classification, with the analytical arrangement of space. The Panopticon is a royal menagerie; the animal is replaced by man, individual distribution by specific grouping and the king by the machinery of a furtive power. With this exception, the Panopticon also does the work of a naturalist. It makes it possible to draw up differences: among patients, to observe the symptoms of each individual, without the proximity of beds, the circulation of miasmas, the effects of contagion confusing the clinical tables; among schoolchildren, it makes it possible to observe performances (without there being any imitation or copying), to map aptitudes, to assess characters, to draw up rigorous classifications and, in relation to normal development, to distinguish 'laziness and stubbornness' from 'incurable imbecility'; among workers, it makes it possible to note the aptitudes of each worker, compare the time he takes to perform a task, and if they are paid by the day, to calculate their wages (Bentham, 60–64).

So much for the question of observation. But the Panopticon was also a laboratory; it could be used as a machine to carry out experiments, to alter behaviour, to train or correct individuals. To experiment with medicines and monitor their effects. To try out different punishments on prisoners, according to their crimes and character, and to seek the most effective ones. To teach different techniques simultaneously to the workers,

to decide which is the best. To try out pedagogical experiments—and in particular to take up once again the well-debated problem of secluded education, by using orphans. One would see what would happen when, in their sixteenth or eighteenth year, they were presented with other boys or girls; one could verify whether, as Helvetius thought, anyone could learn anything; one would follow 'the genealogy of every observable idea'; one could bring up different children according to different systems of thought, making certain children believe that two and two do not make four or that the moon is a cheese, then put them together when they are twenty or twenty-five years old; one would then have discussions that would be worth a great deal more than the sermons or lectures on which so much money is spent; one would have at least an opportunity of making discoveries in the domain of metaphysics. The Panopticon is a privileged place for experiments on men, and for analysing with complete certainty the transformations that may be obtained from them. The Panopticon may even provide an apparatus for supervising its own mechanisms. In this central tower, the director may spy on all the employees that he has under his orders: nurses, doctors, foremen, teachers, warders; he will be able to judge them continuously, alter their behaviour, impose upon them the methods he thinks best; and it will even be possible to observe the director himself. An inspector arriving unexpectedly at the centre of the Panopticon will be able to judge at a glance, without anything being concealed from him, how the entire establishment is functioning. And, in any case, enclosed as he is in the middle of this architectural mechanism, is not the director's own fate entirely bound up with it? The incompetent physician who has allowed contagion to spread, the incompetent prison governor or workshop manager will be the first victims of an epidemic or a revolt. " 'By every tie I could devise', said the master of the Panopticon, 'my own fate had been bound up by me with theirs' " (Bentham, 177). The Panopticon functions as a kind of laboratory of power. Thanks to its mechanisms of observation, it gains in efficiency and in the ability to penetrate into men's behaviour; knowledge follows the advances of power, discovering new objects of knowledge over all the surfaces on which power is exercised.

The plague-stricken town, the panoptic establishment—the differences are important. They mark, at a distance of a century and a half, the transformations of the disciplinary programme. In the first case, there is an exceptional situation: against an extraordinary evil, power is mobilized; it makes itself everywhere present and visible; it invents new mechanisms; it separates, it immobilizes, it partitions; it constructs for a time what is both a counter-city and the perfect society; it imposes an ideal functioning, but one that is reduced, in the final analysis, like the evil that it combats, to a simple dualism of life and death: that which moves brings death, and one kills that which moves. The Panopticon, on the other hand, must be understood as a generalizable model of functioning; a way of defining power relations in terms of the everyday life of men. No doubt Bentham presents it as a particular institution, closed in upon itself. Utopias, perfectly closed in upon themselves, are common enough. As opposed to the ruined prisons, littered with mechanisms of torture, to be seen in Piranese's engravings, the Panopticon presents a cruel, ingenious cage. The fact that it should have given rise, even in our own time, to so many variations, projected or realized, is evidence of the imaginary intensity that it has possessed for almost two hundred years. But the Panopticon must not be understood as a dream building: it is the diagram of a mechanism of power reduced to its ideal form; its functioning, abstracted from any obstacle, resistance or friction, must be represented as a pure architectural and optical system: it is in fact a figure of political technology that may and must be detached from any specific use.

It is polyvalent in its applications; it serves to reform prisoners, but also to treat patients, to instruct schoolchildren, to confine the insane, to supervise workers, to put beggars and idlers to work. It is a type of location of bodies in space, of distribution of individuals in relation to one another, of hierarchical organization, of disposition of centres and channels of power, of definition of the instruments and modes of intervention of power, which can be implemented in hospitals, workshops, schools, prisons. Whenever one is dealing with a multiplicity of individuals on whom a task or a particular form of behaviour must be imposed, the panoptic schema may be used. It is—necessary modifications apart—applicable 'to all establishments whatsoever, in which, within a space not too large to be covered or commanded by buildings, a number of persons are meant to be kept under inspection' (Bentham, 40; although Bentham takes the penitentiary house as his prime example, it is because it has many different functions to fulfil—safe custody, confinement, solitude, forced labour and instruction).

In each of its applications, it makes it possible to perfect the exercise of power. It does this in several ways: because it can reduce the number of those who exercise it, while increasing the number of those on whom it is exercised. Because it is possible to intervene at any moment and because the constant pressure acts even before the offences, mistakes or crimes have been committed. Because, in these conditions, its strength is that it never intervenes, it is exercised spontaneously and without noise, it constitutes a mechanism whose effects follow from one another. Because, without any physical instrument other than architecture and geometry, it acts directly on individuals; it gives 'power of mind over mind'. The panoptic schema makes any apparatus of power more intense: it assures its economy (in material, in personnel, in time); it assures its efficacity by its preventative character, its continuous functioning and its automatic mechanisms. It is a way of obtaining from power 'in hitherto unexampled quantity', 'a great and new instrument of government. . .; its great excellence consists in the great strength it is capable of giving to *any* institution it may be thought proper to apply it to' (Bentham, 66).

It's a case of 'it's easy once you've thought of it' in the political sphere. It can in fact be integrated into any function (education, medical treatment, production, punishment); it can increase the effect of this function, by being linked closely with it; it can constitute a mixed mechanism in which relations of power (and of knowledge) may be precisely adjusted, in the smallest detail, to the processes that are to be supervised; it can establish a direct proportion between 'surplus power' and 'surplus production'. In short, it arranges things in such a way that the exercise of power is not added on from the outside, like a rigid, heavy constraint, to the functions it invests, but is so subtly present in them as to increase their efficiency by itself increasing its own points of contact. The panoptic mechanism is not simply a hinge, a point of exchange between a mechanism of power and a function; it is a way of making power relations function in a function, and of making a function function through these power relations. Bentham's Preface to *Panopticon* opens with a list of the benefits to be obtained from his 'inspection-house': '*Morals reformed—health preserved—industry invigorated—instruction difused—public burthens lightened*—Economy seated, as it were, upon a rock—the gordian knot of the Poor-Laws not cut, but untied—all by a simple idea in architecture!' (Bentham, 39).

Furthermore, the arrangement of this machine is such that its enclosed nature does not preclude a permanent presence from the outside: we have seen that anyone may come and exercise in the central tower the functions of surveillance, and that, this being the case, he can gain a clear idea of the way in which the surveillance is practised. In fact, any panoptic institution, even if it is as rigorously closed as a penitentiary, may without difficulty be subjected to such irregular and constant inspections: and not only by the appointed inspectors, but also by the public; any member of society will have the right to come and see with his own eyes how the schools, hospitals, factories, prisons function. There is no risk, therefore, that the increase of power created by the panoptic machine may degenerate into tyranny; the disciplinary mechanism will be democratically controlled, since it will be constantly accessible 'to the great tribunal committee of the world'.[3] This Panopticon, subtly arranged so that an observer may observe, at a glance, so many different individuals, also enables everyone to come and observe any of the observers. The seeing machine was once a sort of dark room into which individuals spied; it has become a transparent building

in which the exercise of power may be supervised by society as a whole.

The panoptic schema, without disappearing as such or losing any of its properties, was destined to spread throughout the social body; its vocation was to become a generalized function. The plague-stricken town provided an exceptional disciplinary model: perfect, but absolutely violent; to the disease that brought death, power opposed its perpetual threat of death; life inside it was reduced to its simplest expression; it was, against the power of death, the meticulous exercise of the right of the sword. The Panopticon, on the other hand, has a role of amplification; although it arranges power, although it is intended to make it more economic and more effective, it does so not for power itself, nor for the immediate salvation of a threatened society: its aim is to strengthen the social forces—to increase production, to develop the economy, spread education, raise the level of public morality; to increase and multiply.

How is power to be strengthened in such a way that, far from impeding progress, far from weighing upon it with its rules and regulations, it actually facilitates such progress? What intensificator of power will be able at the same time to be a multiplicator of production? How will power, by increasing its forces, be able to increase those of society instead of confiscating them or impeding them? The Panopticon's solution to this problem is that the productive increase of power can be assured only if, on the one hand, it can be exercised continuously in the very foundations of society, in the subtlest possible way, and if, on the other hand, it functions outside these sudden, violent, discontinuous forms that are bound up with the exercise of sovereignty. The body of the king, with its strange material and physical presence, with the force that he himself deploys or transmits to some few others, is at the opposite extreme of this new physics of power represented by panopticism; the domain of panopticism is, on the contrary, that whole lower region, that region of irregular bodies, with their details, their multiple movements, their heterogeneous forces, their spatial relations; what are required are mechanisms that analyse distributions, gaps, series, combinations, and which use instruments that render visible, record, differentiate and compare: a physics of a relational and multiple power, which has its maximum intensity not in the person of the king, but in the bodies that can be individualized by these relations. At the theoretical level, Bentham defines another way of analysing the social body and the power relations that traverse it; in terms of practice, he defines a procedure of subordination of bodies and forces that must increase the utility of power while practising the economy of the prince. Panopticism is the general principle of a new 'political anatomy' whose object and end are not the relations of sovereignty but the relations of discipline.

The celebrated, transparent, circular cage, with its high tower, powerful and knowing, may have been for Bentham a project of a perfect disciplinary institution; but he also set out to show how one may 'unlock' the disciplines and get them to function in a diffused, multiple, polyvalent way throughout the whole social body. These disciplines, which the classical age had elaborated in specific, relatively enclosed places—barracks, schools, workshops—and whose total implementation had been imagined only at the limited and temporary scale of a plague-stricken town, Bentham dreamt of transforming into a network of mechanisms that would be everywhere and always alert, running through society without interruption in space or in time. The panoptic arrangement provides the formula for this generalization. It programmes, at the level of an elementary and easily transferable mechanism, the basic functioning of a society penetrated through and through with disciplinary mechanisms.

***

There are two images, then, of discipline. At one extreme, the discipline-blockade, the enclosed institution, established on the edges of society, turned inwards towards negative functions: arresting evil, breaking communications, suspending time. At the other extreme, with panopticism, is the discipline-mechanism: a functional mechanism that must improve the exercise of

power by making it lighter, more rapid, more effective, a design of subtle coercion for a society to come. The movement from one project to the other, from a schema of exceptional discipline to one of a generalized surveillance, rests on a historical transformation: the gradual extension of the mechanisms of discipline throughout the seventeenth and eighteenth centuries, their spread throughout the whole social body, the formation of what might be called in general the disciplinary society.

A whole disciplinary generalization—the Benthamite physics of power represents an acknowledgement of this—had operated throughout the classical age. The spread of disciplinary institutions, whose network was beginning to cover an ever larger surface and occupying above all a less and less marginal position, testifies to this: what was an islet, a privileged place, a circumstantial measure, or a singular model, became a general formula; the regulations characteristic of the Protestant and pious armies of William of Orange or of Gustavus Adolphus were transformed into regulations for all the armies of Europe; the model colleges of the Jesuits, or the schools of Batencour or Demia, following the example set by Sturm, provided the outlines for the general forms of educational discipline; the ordering of the naval and military hospitals provided the model for the entire reorganization of hospitals in the eighteenth century. . . .

Endnotes

1. In the *Postscript to the Panopticon*, 1791 [1843], Bentham adds dark inspection galleries painted in black around the inspector's lodge, each making it possible to observe two storeys of cells.

2. In his first version of the *Panopticon*, Bentham had also imagined an acoustic surveillance, operated by means of pipes leading from the cells to the central tower. In the *Postscript* he abandoned the idea, perhaps because he could not introduce into it the principle of dis-symmetry and prevent the prisoners from hearing the inspector as well as the inspector hearing them. Julius tried to develop a system of dis-symmetrical listening (Julius, 18).

3. Imagining this continuous flow of visitors entering the central tower by an underground passage and then observing the circular landscape of

the Panopticon, was Bentham aware of the Pan-
oramas that Barker was constructing at exactly
the same period (the first seems to have dated
from 1787) and in which the visitors, occupying
the central place, saw unfolding around them a
landscape, a city or a battle? The visitors occupied
exactly the place of the sovereign gaze.

References

Bentham, J., *Works*, ed. Bowring, IV, 1843.

Loisel, G., *Histoire des ménageries*, 11, 1912.

68

Postmodernity, or Living With Ambivalence

Zygmunt Bauman

Zygmunt Bauman (b. 1925), who has lived and taught in England for many years, witnessed as a Polish Jew the authoritarian regimes of both the Nazis and Communists as they one after the other ruled his native land, and he witnessed first-hand the potent threat of anti-Semitism. While some have seen these ideological movements as anomalies, repudiations of the general trends inherent in modernity, Bauman does not see them as accidents but rather as emblematic of the darker side of modernity. As this essay published in 1991 reveals, Bauman characterizes our postmodern condition in terms of the ambivalence we experience because the foundations or grand narratives of modernity have been called into question. Unlike more radical postmodernists, he does not think a complete break between the modern and postmodern has occurred, and he remains committed to the possibility that freedom and reason are realizable goals.

We could try to transform our contingency into our destiny.

—Agnes Heller

In one respect the social sciences born in the age of Enlightenment have not failed—writes Agnes Heller: 'they have indeed provided self-knowledge, and they never ceased providing self-knowledge of *modern* society, of a *contingent* society, of one society among many, *our society*'.[1] And yet, let us observe, this partial success was itself a failure, if judged by the standards of the social sciences' ambition. Whatever modern social sciences did, they did not deliver *on their promise;* instead, with no knowing and even less intending, they delivered something they did not promise; to put it bluntly, they were delivering a reasonable product all along under the false pretences of supplying something else altogether. . . . Awareness of contingency—of the contingency of the modern self, of the contingency of modern society—was not what they, their prophets, their apostles, their intended converts and aspiring beneficiaries bargained for. If one agrees with Heller that the social sciences, all their self-deception notwithstanding, did supply precious knowledge later to be appreciated as an insight into contingency, one must still insist that they did it while misconceiving the true nature of their business, or that they did it while trying to pass their products for something other than it was (thus remaining—knowingly or unknowingly—in breach of the official trading act. . . .): that they informed of *contingency* while believing themselves to narrate *necessity,* of particular *locality* while believing themselves to narrate *universality,* of tradition-bound interpretation while believing themselves to narrate the extraterritorial and extratemporal truth, of undecidability while believing themselves to narrate transparency, of the provisionality of the human condition while believing themselves to narrate the certainty of the world, of the *ambivalence* of man-made design while believing themselves to narrate the *order* of nature.

It was all these beliefs (false beliefs), and not their deliveries (useful deliveries) that made the social sciences, and the mentality from which they arose, and the power structure that contemplated itself in that mentality, *modern.* For most of its history, modernity lived in and through self-deception. Concealment of its own parochiality, conviction that whatever is not universal in its particularity is but not-yet-universal, that the project of universality may be incomplete, but remains most definitely on, was the core of that self-deception. It was perhaps thanks to that self-deception that modernity could deliver both the wondrous and the gruesome things that it did; in this, as in so many other cases, ignorance, so to speak, turned out to be a privilege. The question is: is the fading

456

of self-deception a final fulfilment, emancipation, or the end of modernity?

The distinctive feature of the belief in the truth of one's knowledge is not the conviction that the knowledge in question is satisfying, pleasing, useful, or otherwise worth holding to. Such a conviction does not require the belief in truth for support. More often than not, this conviction can be and is held without worry about authoritative confirmation that the belief in truth is sound. Where one cannot do without the 'well grounded concept of truth' is when it comes to tell others that they are in error and hence (1) ought or must change their minds, thus (2) confirming the superiority (read: right to command) of the holder of truth (read: the giver of command). The bid for truth as a claimed quality of knowledge arises therefore solely in the context of hegemony and proselytism; in the context of coexistence of autonomously sustained bodies of knowledge of which at least one refuses to coexist peacefully and respect the existing borders; in the context of plurality that is treated by at least one member as a vexing state to be rectified; in the context of a balance of forces under pressure to turn into asymmetry of power.

Truth is, in other words, a *social relation* (like *power, ownership* or *freedom*): an aspect of a hierarchy built of superiority-inferiority units; more precisely, an aspect of the hegemonic form of domination or of a bid for domination-through-hegemony. Modernity was, from its inception, such a form and such a bid. The part of the world that adopted modern civilization as its structural principle and constitutional value was bent on dominating the rest of the world by dissolving its alterity and assimilating the product of dissolution. The persevering alterity could not but be treated as a temporary nuisance; as an error, sooner or later bound to be supplanted by truth. The battle of order against chaos in wordly affairs was replicated by the war of truth against error on the plane of consciousness. The order bound to be installed and made universal was a *rational* order; the truth bound to be made triumphant was the *universal* (hence apodictic and obligatory) truth. Together, political order and true knowledge blended into a de-

sign for *certainty*. The rational-universal world of order and truth would know of no contingency and no ambivalence. The target of certainty and of absolute truth was indistinguishable from the crusading spirit and the project of domination.

While setting itself apart, making itself distinct so that it would be possible to reserve a position of command toward the rest of the *oikoumene*, modernity thought of itself as of the seed of future universality, as of an entity destined to replace all other entities and thus to abolish the very difference between them. It thought of the *differentiation* it perpetrated as of *universalization*. This was modernity's self-deception. This was, however, a self-deception bound to disclose itself even without outside help (there was, anyway, no 'outside' left, allowed the legitimacy to disclose anything); a self-deception that could last only as long as it worked toward that disclosure. The self-deception supplied the courage and the confidence to pursue that lonely work of universality that spawned ever more difference; to persevere in such a chase of uniformity as was bound to result in more ambivalence. The self-deception of modernity was pregnant with its self-disclosure.

It is perhaps the fruit of that pregnancy that Agnes Heller dubbed the 'death wish' that was to be found at the other end of the long march toward 'wish-fulfillment'; that was to be, as we tried to argue here, the latter's inescapable heir and successor. Awareness of contingency, though a prodigal child, was a fully legitimate offspring of blind self-confidence; it could not but be born of it and it could not be born of any other parent. The residents of the house of modernity had been continuously trained to feel at home under conditions of necessity and to feel unhappy at the face of contingency; contingency, they had been told, was that state of discomfort and anxiety from which one needed to escape by making oneself into a binding norm and thus doing away with difference. Present unhappiness is the realization that this is not to be, that the hope will not come true and hence one needs to learn to live without the hope that supplied the meaning—the only meaning—to life. As Richard Rorty observed: 'The vocabularies are, typically, parasitic on the hopes—in the sense that the principal function of the vocabularies is to tell stories about future outcomes which compensate for present sacrifices'[2]—and, let us add, give name to present sufferings; they narrate the present as *specific* suffering that needs a *concrete* sacrifice to cease be a suffering *as such*. We are unhappy today, as we have been left with the old vocabulary but without the hope that fed it with life juices. The rustle of desiccated, sapless words reminds us ceaselessly, obtrusively of the void that is where hope once was.

Having been trained to live in necessity, we have found ourselves living in contingency. And yet, being bound to live in contingency, we can, as Heller suggests, make 'an attempt to transform it into our destiny'. One makes something a destiny by embracing the fate: by an act of choice and the will to remain loyal to the choice made. Abandoning the vocabulary parasitic on the hope of (or determination for) universality, certainty and transparency is the first choice to be made; the first step on the road to emancipation. We cannot forget contingency any more; were it able to speak, contingency would repeat what Nietzsche wrote to his discoverer, friend and prophet Georg Brandes on 4 January 1889 (the day he finally withdrew from the concerns of mundane life): 'After you had discovered me, it was no trick to find me; the difficulty now is to lose me. . . .'[3] But we can transfer contingency from the vocabulary of dashed hopes into that of the opportunity, from the language of domination into that of emancipation. Heller writes:

> An individual has transformed his or her contingency into his or her destiny if this person has arrived at the consciousness of having made the best out of his or her practically infinite possibilities. A society has transformed its contingency into its destiny if the members of this society arrive at the awareness that they would prefer to live at no other place and at no other time than the here and now. . . .

The Antinomies of Postmodernity

The collapse of 'grand narratives' (as Lyotard put it)—the dissipation of trust in supra-individual and supra-communal courts of appeal—has been eyed by many observers with fear, as an invitation to the 'everything goes' situation, to universal permissiveness and hence, in the end, to the demise of all moral, and thus social, order. Mindful of Dostoyevsky's dictum 'If there is no God, everything is permitted', and of Durkheim's identification of asocial behaviour with the weakening of collective consensus, we have grown to believe that unless an awesome and incontestable authority—sacred or secular, political or philosophical—hangs over each and every human individual, then anarchy and universal carnage are likely to follow. This belief supported well the modern determination to install an artificial order: a project that made all spontaneity suspect until proven innocent, that proscribed everything not explicitly prescribed and identified ambivalence with chaos, with 'the end of civilization' as we know it and as it could be imagined. Perhaps the fear emanated from the suppressed knowledge that the project was doomed from the start; perhaps it was cultivated deliberately, since it served a useful role as an emotional bulwark against dissention; perhaps it was just a side-effect, an intellectual afterthought born of the sociopolitical practice of cultural crusade and enforced assimilation. One way or the other, modernity bent on the bulldozing of all unauthorized difference and all wayward life-patterns could not but gestate the horror of deviation and render deviation synonymous with diversity. As Adorno and Horkheimer commented, the lasting intellectual and emotional scar left by the philosophical project and political practice of modernity was the fear of the void, and the void was the absence of a universally binding, unambiguous and enforceable standard.

Of the popular fear of the void, of the anxiety born of the absence of clear instruction that leaves nothing to the harrowing necessity of choice, we know from the worried accounts narrated by intellectuals, the appointed or self-appointed interpreters of social experience. The narrators are never absent from their narration, though, and it is a hopeless task to try to sift out their presence from their stories. It may well be that at all times there was life outside philosophy, and that such life did not share the worries of the narrators; that it did quite well without being regimented by rationally proved and philosophically approved universal standards of truth, goodness and beauty. It may well be even that much of that life was liveable, orderly and moral *because* it was *not* tinkered with, manipulated and corrupted by the self-acclaimed agents of the 'universal ought'.[4] There is hardly any doubt, however, that one form of life can fare but badly without the prop of universally binding and apodictically valid standards: the form of life of the narrators themselves (more precisely, such form of life as contains the stories those narrators were telling through most of modern history).

It was that form of life first and foremost that lost its foundation once social powers abandoned their ecumenical ambitions, and felt therefore more than anyone else threatened by the fading out of universalistic expectations. As long as modern powers clung resolutely to their intention of constructing a better, reason-guided, and thus ultimately universal order, intellectuals had little difficulty in articulating their own claim to the crucial role in the process: universality was their domain and their field of expertise. As long as the modern powers insisted on the elimination of ambivalence as the measure of social improvement, intellectuals could consider their own work—the promotion of universally valid rationality—as a major vehicle and driving force of progress. As long as the modern powers continued to decry and banish and evict the Other, the different, the ambivalent—intellectuals could rely on mighty support for their authority of passing judgement and sorting out truth from falsity, knowledge from mere opinion. Like the adolescent hero of Cocteau's *Orphée*, convinced that the sun would not rise without his guitar and serenade, the intellectuals grew convinced that the fate of morality, civilized life and social order hangs on their solution of the problem of universality: on their clinching and final proof that the human 'ought' is unambiguous, and that its non-ambiguity has unshakeable and totally reliable foundations.

This conviction translated into two complementary beliefs: that there will be no good in the world *unless* its necessity has been proven; and that proving such a necessity, if and when accomplished, will have a similar effect on the world as that imputed to the legislative acts of a ruler: it will replace chaos with order and make the opaque transparent. Husserl was perhaps the last great philosopher of the modern era spurred into action by those twin beliefs. Appalled by the idea that whatever we see as truth may be founded but in beliefs, that our knowledge has merely a psychological grounding, that we might have adopted logic as a secure guide to correct thinking simply because this is how people happen on the whole to think, Husserl (like Descartes, Kant and other recognized giants of modern thought before him) made a gigantic effort to cut reason free from its worldly habitat (or was it prison?): to return it to where it belonged—a *transcendental*, out-worldly region, towering above the daily human bustle at a height at which it cannot be reached—neither glimpsed nor tarnished—from the lowly world of common daily experience. The latter could not be the domicile of reason, as it was precisely the world of the common and the ordinary and the spontaneous that was to be remade and reformed and transformed by the verdicts of reason. Only the few, capable of the formidable effort of transcendental reduction (an experience not unlike the shaman's trances, or forty days of desert meditation), can travel to those esoteric places where truth comes into view. For the time of their journey, they must forget—suspend and bracket out—the 'mere existing', so that they may become one with the transcendental subject—that thinking subject that thinks the truth because it does not think anything else, because it is free from its worldly interests and the common errors of the worldly way.

The world which Husserl left behind while embarking on his solitary expedition to the sources of certainty and truth took little note. This was a world of evil on the loose, of concentration camps and of growing stockpiles of bombs and poison gas. The most spectacular and lasting effect of absolute truth's last stand was not so much its *inconclusiveness*, stemming as some would say from the errors of design, but its utter *irrelevance* to the worldly fate of truth and goodness. The latter fate was decided far away from philosophers' desks, down in the world of daily life where struggles for political freedom raged and the limits of the state ambition to legislate social order, to define, to segregate, to organize, to constrain and to suppress were pushed forward and rolled backwards.

It seems that the more advanced is the cause of freedom at home the less demand there is for the services of explorers of distant lands where absolute truth is reputed to reside. When one's own truth seems secure and the truth of the other does not seem to be a challenge or a threat, truth can live well without sycophants assuring it of being 'the truest of them all' and the warlords determined to make sure that no one disagrees. Once the difference ceases to be a crime, it may be enjoyed at peace, and enjoyed for what it is, rather than for what it represents or what it is destined to become. Once the politicians abandon their search for empires, there is little demand for the philosophers' search for universality.[5] Empires of unconfined and unchallenged sovereignty, and the truth of unlimited and uncontested universality were the two arms with which modernity wished to remould the world according to the design of perfect order. Once the intention is no more, both arms find themselves without use.

In all probability the diversity of truths, standards of goodness and beauty does not grow once the intention is gone; neither does it become more resilient and stubborn than before; it only looks less alarming. It was, after all, the modern intention that made difference into an offence: *the* offence, the most mortal and least forgivable sin, to be precise. The pre-modern eye viewed difference with equanimity; as if it was in the pre-ordained order of things that they are and should remain different. Being unemotional, difference was also safely out of the cognitive focus. After a few centuries during which human diversity lived in hiding (a concealment enforced by the threat of exile) and it learned to be embarrassed about its stigma of iniquity, the postmodern eye (that is, the modern eye liberated from modern fears and inhibitions) views difference with zest and glee: difference is beautiful and no less good for that.

The appearance of sequence is, to be sure, itself an effect of the modern knack for neat divisions, clean breaks and pure substances. The postmodern celebration of difference and contingency has not displaced the modern lust for uniformity and certainty. Moreover, it is unlikely ever to do it; it has no capacity of doing so. Being what it is, postmodern mentality and practice cannot displace or eliminate or even marginalize anything. As it is always the case with the notoriously ambivalent (multi-final: opening more than one option, pointing to more than one line of future change) human condition, the gains of postmodernity are simultaneously its losses; what gives it its strength and attraction is also the source of its weakness and vulnerability.

There is no clean break or unambiguous sequence. Postmodernity is weak on exclusion. Having declared limits off limits, it cannot but include and incorporate modernity into the very diversity that is its distinctive mark. It cannot refuse admission lest it should lose its identity. (Paradoxically, refusal would be equivalent to the ceding of the whole real estate to the rejected applicant.) It cannot but admit the rights of a legitimate resident even to such a lodger as denies its right to admit residents and the right of other residents to share its accommodation. Modern mentality is a born litigant and an old hand in lawsuits. Postmodernity cannot defend its case in court, as there is no court whose authority it would recognize. It might be forced instead to follow the Christian injunction of offering another cheek to the assailant's blows. It certainly is doomed to a long and hard life of cohabitation with its sworn enemy as a room-mate.

To the modern determination to seek or enforce consensus, postmodern mentality may only respond with its habitual tolerance of dissent. This makes the antagonists' chances unequal, with the odds heavily on the side of the resolute and strong-willed. Tolerance is too wan a defence against willfulness and lack of scruples. By itself, tolerance remains a sitting target—an easy prey for the unscrupulous. It can repulse assaults only when reforged into solidarity: into the universal recognition that difference is one universality that is not open to negotiation and that attack against the universal right to be different is the only departure from universality that none of the solidary agents, however different, may tolerate otherwise than at its own, and all the other agents', peril.

And so the transformation of the *fate* into a *destiny*, of tolerance into solidarity, is not just a matter of moral perfection, but a condition of survival. Tolerance as 'mere tolerance' is moribund; it can survive only in the form of solidarity. It just would not do to rest satisfied that the other's difference does not confine or harm my own—as some differences, of some others, are most evidently bent on constraining and damaging. Survival in the world of contingency and diversity is possible only if each difference recognizes another difference as the necessary condition of the preservation of its own. Solidarity, unlike tolerance, its weaker version, means readiness to fight; and joining the battle for the sake of the other's difference, not one's own. Tolerance is ego-centred and contemplative; solidarity is socially oriented and militant.

Like all other human conditions, postmodern tolerance and diversity has its dangers and its fears. Its survival is not guaranteed—not by God's design, universal reason, laws of history, or any other supra-human force. In this respect, of course, the postmodern condition does not differ at all from all other conditions; it differs only by knowing about it, by its knowledge of living without guarantee, of being on its own. This makes it exceedingly anxiety-prone. And this also gives it a chance. . . .

Endnotes

1. Agnes Heller, 'From Hermeneutics in Social Science toward a Hermeneutics of Social Science', in *Theory and Society*, vol. 18 (1989), pp. 291–322. Other quotations from Heller that follow come from the same source.

2. Rorty, *Contingency, Irony and Solidarity*, p.86.

3. Quoted after Martin Heidegger, *What Is Called Thinking*, trans. F. D. Wieck and J. G. Gray (New York: Harper & Row, 1968), p. 53. Cf. also Shoshana Felman, *Writing and Madness*, trans.

Martha Noel Evans and author (Ithaca: Cornell University Press, 1985), p. 62.

4. It is a prominent feature of the postmodern mentality that these and similar doubts are more and more widely shared by intellectual observers. Suddenly a growing number of social scientists discover that normative regulation of daily life is often sustained through 'grass roots' initiative frequently of a heterodox ('deviationary' in official parlance) nature, and has to be protected against encroachments from above. Compare, for example, Michel de Certeau's analysis of *la peruque* [*The Practice of Everyday Life* (Berkeley: University of California Press, 1984), pp. 25ff] as the tool of defence of the self-regulated sphere of autonomy; or Hebdige's brilliant characterization of subculture (normally the object of officially inspired 'moral panics' and detracted as a hiccup of barbarism, as a product of disintegration of order) as a phenomenon which 'forms up in the space between surveillance and the evasion of surveillance' and 'translates the fact of being under scrutiny into the pleasure of being watched. It is a hiding in the light.' Subculture, in Hebdige's interpretation, is a 'declaration of independence, of otherness, of alien intent, a refusal of anonymity, of subordinate status. It is an *in*subordination. And at the same time it is also a confirmation of the fact of powerlessness, a celebration of impotence. Subcultures are both a play for attention and a refusal, once attention has been granted, to be read according to the book.' [*Hiding in the Light* (London: Routledge, 1988), p. 35.] Subculture is deliberate or semi-deliberate politics; it has its conscious or subconscious motive, programme and strategy. It often reaches its purpose: it gains attention, and then it is closely scrutinized so that its inner nature as a defence of autonomy can be gleaned. There are, however, much more massive though less vociferous and hence less visible territories of daily life that do not attract the obtrusive attention of the law-enforcing authorities and thus also the curiosity of intellectual commentators.

5. Emperor Shih Huang Ti, the hero of Borges's story, was credited with ordering the construction of the Chinese Wall *and* the burning of all the books that had been written before his time. He also boasted in his inscriptions that all things under his reign had the names that befitted them. And he decreed that his heirs should be called Second Emperor, Third Emperor, Fourth Emperor, and so on to infinity [Jorge Luis Borges, 'The Walls and the Books', in *Other Inquisitions*, 1937–1952, trans. Ruth L. C. Simms (New York: Washington Square Press, 1966), pp. 1–2.] The four decrees of Shih Huang Ti represent modern ambition at its fullest and most logically coherent. The Wall

guarded the perfect kingdom against interference by other coercive pressures; the destruction of books stopped infiltration of other ideas. With the kingdom secure on both fronts, no wonder all things finally received their right and proper names, and, starting with Shih Huang Ti's reign, future history was to be only more of the same.

69

Modern and Postmodern

Mike Featherstone

Mike Featherstone (b. 1946) is a British sociologist influenced by contemporary French postmodernist theory and by British cultural studies. As is the case with many postmodernists, he has focused considerable attention on consumption, in contrast to more Marxian inspired sociologists who have been primarily interested in production. In other words, the focus of attention has shifted from the factory to the shopping mall. Featherstone finds value in the idea of postmodernism but is acutely aware that many see it simply as a passing intellectual fashion and that much of postmodernist thought is written in such an opaque and convoluted style that it puts off many readers. Given the considerable confusion and contestation about what is meant by modernism and postmodernism, he offers (in this essay published in 1991) a thoughtful and nuanced analysis of the meaning of both terms.

Any reference to the term 'postmodernism' immediately exposes one to the risk of being accused of jumping on a bandwagon, of perpetuating a rather shallow and meaningless intellectual fad. One of the problems is that the term is at once fashionable yet irritatingly elusive to define. As the 'Modern-day Dictionary of Received Ideas' confirms, 'This word has no meaning. Use it as often as possible' (*Independent*, 24 December 1987). Over a decade earlier, in August 1975, another newspaper announced that 'postmodernism is dead', and that 'post-post-modernism is now the thing' (Palmer, 1977: 364). If postmodernism is an ephemeral fashion then some critics are clear as to who are responsible for its prominence: 'today's paid theorists surveying the field from their booklined studies in polytechnics and universities are obliged to invent movements because their careers—no less than those of miners and fishermen—depend on it. The more movements they can give names to, the more successful they will be' (Pawley, 1986). For other critics these strategies are not just internal moves within the intellectual and academic fields; they are clear indicators and barometers of the 'malaise at the heart of contemporary culture'. Hence 'It is not difficult to comprehend this cultural and aesthetic trend now known as Postmodernism—in art and architecture, music and film, drama and fiction—as a reflection of . . . the present wave of political reaction sweeping the Western world' (Gott, 1986). But it is all to easy to see postmodernism as a reactionary, mechanical reflection of social changes and to blame the academics and intellectuals for coining the term as part of their distinction games. Even though certain newspaper critics and para-intellectuals use the term in a cynical or dismissive manner, they confirm that postmodernism has sufficient appeal to interest a larger middle-class audience. Few other recent academic terms can claim to have enjoyed such popularity. Yet it is not merely an academic term, for it has gained impetus from artistic 'movements' and is also attracting wider public interest through its capacity to speak to some of the cultural changes we are currently going through.

Before we can look at the means of transmission and dissemination of the concept, we need a clearer notion of the range of phenomena which are generally included under the umbrella concept postmodernism. We therefore need to take account of the great interest and even excitement that it has generated, both inside and outside the academy, and to ask questions about the range of cultural objects, experiences and practices which theorists are adducing and labelling postmodern, before we can decide on its political pedigree or dismiss it as merely a short swing of the pendulum.

In the first place the broad range of artistic, intellectual and academic fields in which the term 'postmodernism' has been used, is striking. We have music (Cage, Stockhausen, Briers, Holloway, Tredici, Laurie Anderson);

art (Rauschenberg, Baselitz, Mach, Schnabel, Kiefer; some would also include Warhol and sixties pop art, and others Bacon); fiction (Vonnegut's *Slaughterhouse Five*, and the novels of Barth, Barthelme, Pynchon, Burroughs, Ballard, Doctorow); film (*Body Heat, The Wedding, Blue Velvet, Wetherby*); drama (The theatre of Artaud); photography (Sherman, Levine, Prince); architecture (Jencks, Venturi, Bolin); literary theory and criticism (Spanos, Hassan, Sontag, Fielder); philosophy (Lyotard, Derrida, Baudrillard, Vattimo, Rorty); anthropology (Clifford, Tyler, Marcus); sociology (Denzin); geography (Soja). The very names of those included and excluded in the list will doubtless strike some as controversial. To take the example of fiction, as Linda Hutcheon (1984: 2) argues, some would wish to include the novels of Garcia Marquez and even Cervantes under the heading of postmodernism and others would want to refer to them as neo-baroque and baroque. Scott Lash would want to regard Dada as postmodernism *avant la lettre* (Lash, 1988). There are those who work and write unaware of the term's existence and others who seek to thematize and actively promote it. Yet it can be argued that one of the functions of the interest in postmodernism on the part of critics, para-intellectuals, cultural intermediaries and academics has been to diffuse the term to wider audiences in different national and international contexts (this is one of the senses in which one can talk about the globalization of culture); and to increase the speed of interchange and circulation of the term between the various fields in the academy and the arts, which now want to, and have to, pay more attention to developments among their neighbours. In this sense it is possible that some greater agreement on the meaning of the term might eventually emerge as commentators in each particular field find it necessary to recapitulate and explain the multiplex history and usages of the term in order to educate new, academic audiences.

To work towards some preliminary sense of the meaning of postmodernism it is useful to identify the family of terms derived from 'the postmodern' and these can best be understood by contrasting them to those which derive from 'the modern'.

modern	postmodern
modernity	postmodernity
modernité	*postmodernité*
modernization	postmodernization
modernism	postmodernism

If 'the modern' and 'the postmodern' are the generic terms it is immediately apparent that the prefix 'post' signifies that which comes after, a break or rupture with the modern which is defined in counterdistinction to it. Yet the term 'postmodernism' is more strongly based on a negation of the modern, a perceived abandonment, break with or shift away from the definitive features of the modern, with the emphasis firmly on the sense of the relational move away. This would make the postmodern a relatively ill-defined term as we are only on the threshold of the alleged shift, and not in a position to regard the postmodern as a fully fledged positivity which can be defined comprehensively in its own right. Bearing this in mind we can take a closer look at the pairings.

Modernity-Postmodernity

This suggests the epochal meaning of the terms. Modernity is generally held to have come into being with the Renaissance and was defined in relation to Antiquity, as in the debate between the Ancients and the Moderns. From the point of view of late nineteenth- and early twentieth-century German sociological theory, from which we derive much of our current sense of the term, modernity is contrasted to the traditional order and implies the progressive economic and administrative rationalization and differentiation of the social world (Weber, Tönnies, Simmel): processes which brought into being the modern capitalist-industrial state and which were often viewed from a distinctly anti-modern perspective.

Consequently, to speak of postmodernity is to suggest an epochal shift or break from modernity involving the emergence of a new social totality with its own distinct organizing principles. It is this order of change that has been detected in the writing of Baudrillard, Lyotard, and to some extent, Jameson (Kellner, 1988). Both Baudrillard and Lyotard assume a movement towards a post-industrial age. Baudrillard (1983) stresses that new forms of technology and information become central to the shift from a productive to a reproductive social order in which simulations and models increasingly constitute the world so that the distinction between the real and appearance becomes erased. Lyotard (1984) talks about the postmodern society, or postmodern age, which is premised on the move to a post-industrial order. His specific interest is in the effects of the 'computerization of society' on knowledge and he argues that the loss of meaning in postmodernity should not be mourned, as it points to a replacement of narrative knowledge by a plurality of language games, and universalism by localism. Yet Lyotard, like many users of the family of terms, sometimes changes register from one term to the next and switches usages, preferring more recently to emphasize that the postmodern is to be regarded as part of the modern. For example, in 'Rules and Paradoxes and Svelte Appendix' he writes:

> "postmodern" is probably a very bad term because it conveys the idea of a historical "periodization". "Periodizing", however, is still a "classic" or "modern" ideal. "Postmodern" simply indicates a mood, or better a state of mind (Lyotard, 1986–7: 209).

The other interesting point to note about Lyotard's use of postmodernity in *The Postmodern Condition*, is that where he talks about the changes in knowledge accompanying the move to the post-industrial society he still conceives this as occurring within capitalism, adding weight to the argument of critics that the move to the postmodern society is under-theorized in Lyotard's work (see Kellner, 1988). Although the move is assumed at some points, it is easier to avoid the accusations of providing a grand narrative account of the move to postmodernity and the eclipse of grand narratives, by insisting on a more diffuse notion of 'mood' or 'state of mind'. Fredric Jameson (1984) has a more definite periodizing concept of the postmodern, yet he is reluctant to conceive of it as an epochal shift, rather postmodernism is the cultural dominant, or cultural logic, of the third great stage of capitalism,

late capitalism, which originates in the post World War Two era.

Lyotard's invocation of a postmodern mood or state of mind points us towards a second meaning of modernity-postmodernity. The French use of *modernité* points to the experience of modernity in which modernity is viewed as a quality of modern life inducing a sense of the discontinuity of time, the break with tradition, the feeling of novelty and sensitivity to the ephemeral, fleeting and contingent nature of the present (see Frisby, 1985a). This is the sense of being modern associated with Baudelaire which, as Foucault (1986: 40) argues, entails an ironical heroicization of the present: the modern man is the man who constantly tries to invent himself. It is this attempt to make sense of the experience of life in the new urban spaces and nascent consumer culture, which developed in the second half of the nineteenth century, which provided the impetus for the theories of modern everyday life in the work of Simmel, Kracauer and Benjamin discussed by David Frisby (1985b) in his *Fragments of Modernity*. The experience of modernity also forms the subject matter of Marshall Berman's (1982) book *All That is Solid Melts into Air* in which he looks at the visions and idioms accompanying the modernization process which he pulls together under the term 'modernism'. Berman discusses the modern sensibility that is manifest in a wide range of literary and intellectual figures from Rousseau and Goethe in the eighteenth century to Marx, Baudelaire, Pushkin and Dostoevsky in the nineteenth.

Apart from the confusing use of modernism to take in the whole of the experience and the culture that accompanied the modernization process, Berman and many of those who are currently trying to delineate the equivalent experience of postmodernity focus upon a particularly restrictive notion of experience: that which appears in literary sources and is so designated by intellectuals. But we have to raise the sociological objection against the literary intellectual's licence in interpretating the everyday, or in providing evidence about the everyday lives of ordinary people. Of course, some intellectuals may have articulated well the experience of the shocks and jolts of modernity. Yet we need to make the jump from modernity or postmodernity as a (relatively restricted) subjective experience to outlining the actual practices and activities which take place in the everyday lives of various groups. Certainly the descriptions of subjective experience may make sense within intellectual practices, and within aspects of the practices of particular audiences educated to interpret these sensibilities, but the assumption that one can make wider claims needs careful substantiation.

To take an example of the alleged experience of postmodernity (or *postmodernité*), we can refer to Jameson's (1984) account of the Bonaventura Hotel in Los Angeles. Jameson gives a fascinating interpretation of the experience of the new hyperspace of postmodern architecture, which, he argues, forces us to expand our sensorium and body. Yet we get little idea how individuals from different backgrounds actually experience the hotel, or better still, how they incorporate the experience into their day-to-day practices. Perhaps for them to interpret the experience as postmodern they need guidelines to make sense of things they may not fully notice, or view through inappropriate codes. Hence, if we want to understand the social generation and interpretation of the experience of postmodernity we need to have a place for the role of cultural entrepreneurs and intermediaries who have an interest in creating postmodern pedagogies to educate publics. The same can be said for two other features of postmodern culture identified by Jameson: the transformation of reality into images and the fragmentation of time into a series of perpetual presents. Here we can take an example which encompasses both features: the media, which tends to be central to many discussions of the postmodern sensibility (one thinks for example of Baudrillard's simulational world, where 'TV is the world'). Yet for all the alleged pluralism and sensitivity to the Other talked about by some theorists one finds little discussion of the actual experience and practice of watching television by different groups in different settings. On the contrary, theorists of the postmodern often talk of an ideal-type channel-hopping MTV (music

television) viewer who flips through different images at such speed that she/he is unable to chain the signifiers together into a meaningful narrative, he/she merely enjoys the multiphrenic intensities and sensations of the surface of the images. Evidence of the extent of such practices, and how they are integrated into, or influence, the day-to-day encounters between embodied persons is markedly lacking. Thus while learned references to the characteristic experiences of postmodernity are important we need to work from more systematic data and should not rely on the readings of intellectuals. In effect we should focus upon the actual cultural practices and changing power balances of those groups engaged in the production, classification, circulation and consumption of postmodern cultural goods, something which will be central to our discussion of postmodernism below.

Modernization-Postmodernization

On the face of it, both terms seem to sit unhappily amidst discussion of modernity-postmodernity, modernism-postmodernism. Modernization has been regularly used in the sociology of development to point to the effects of economic development on traditional social structures and values. Modernization theory is also used to refer to the stages of social development which are based upon industrialization, the growth of science and technology, the modern nation state, the capitalist world market, urbanization and other infrastructural elements. (In this usage it has strong affinities with the first sense of modernity we discussed above.) It is generally assumed, via a loose base-superstructure model, that certain cultural changes (secularization and the emergence of a modern identity which centres around self-development) will result from the modernization process. If we turn to postmodernization it is clear that a concomitant detailed outline of specific social processes and institutional changes has yet to be theorized. All we have is the possibility of deriving the term from those usages of postmodernity which refer to a new social order and epochal shift mentioned above. For example, Baudrillard's (1983) depiction of a postmodern simulational world is based upon the assumption that the development of commodity production coupled with information technology have led to the 'triumph of signifying culture' which then reverses the direction of determinism, so that social relations become saturated with shifting cultural signs to the extent that we can no longer speak of class or normativity and are faced by 'the end of the social'. Baudrillard, however, does not use the term 'postmodernization'.

Yet the term does have the merit of suggesting a process with degrees of implementation, rather than a fully fledged new social order or totality. One significant context for the utilization of the term 'postmodernization' is the field of urban studies and here we can point to the writings of Philip Cooke (1988) and Sharon Zukin (1988). For Cooke, postmodernization is an ideology and set of practices with spatial effects which have been notable in the British economy since 1976. Zukin also wants to use postmodernization to focus on the restructuring of socio-spatial relations by new patterns of investment and production in industry, services, labour markets and tele-communications. Yet, while Zukin sees postmodernization as a dynamic process comparable to modernization, both she and Cooke are reluctant to regard it as pointing to a new stage of society, for both see it as taking place within capitalism. This has the merit of focusing on processes of production as well as consumption and the spatial dimension of particular cultural practices (the redevelopment of downtowns and waterfronts, development of urban artistic and cultural centres, and the growth of the service class and gentrification) which accompany them.

Modernism-Postmodernism

As with the pairing modernity-postmodernity, we are again faced with a range of meanings. Common to them all is the centrality of culture. In the most restricted sense, modernism points to the styles we associate with the artistic movements which originated around the turn of the century and which have dominated the various arts until recently. Figures frequently cited are: Joyce, Yeats, Gide, Proust, Rilke, Kafka, Mann, Musil, Lawrence and Faulkner in literature; Rilke, Pound, Eliot, Lorca, Valery in poetry; Strindberg and Pirandello in drama; Matisse, Picasso, Braque, Cézanne and the Futurist, Expressionist, Dada and Surrealist movements in painting; Stravinsky, Schoenberg and Berg in music (see Bradbury and McFarlane, 1976). There is a good deal of debate about how far back into the nineteenth century modernism should be taken (some would want to go back to the bohemian avant-garde of the 1830s). The basic features of modernism can be summarized as: an aesthetic self-consciousness and reflexiveness; a rejection of narrative structure in favour of simultaneity and montage; an exploration of the paradoxical, ambiguous and uncertain open-ended nature of reality; and a rejection of the notion of an integrated personality in favour of an emphasis upon the de-structured, de-humanized subject (see Lunn, 1985: 34ff). One of the problems with trying to understand postmodernism in the arts is that many of these features are appropriated into various definitions of postmodernism. The problem with the term, as with the other related terms we have discussed, revolves around the question of when does a term defined oppositionally to, and feeding off, an established term start to signify something substantially different?

According to Kohler (1977) and Hassan (1985) the term 'postmodernism' was first used by Federico de Onis in the 1930s to indicate a minor reaction to modernism. The term became popular in the 1960s in New York when it was used by young artists, writers and critics such as Rauschenberg, Cage, Burroughs, Barthelme, Fielder, Hassan and Sontag to refer to a movement beyond the 'exhausted' high modernism which was rejected because of its institutionalization in the museum and the academy. It gained wider usage in architecture, the visual and performing arts, and music in the 1970s and 1980s and then was rapidly transmitted back and forth between Europe and the United States as the search for theoretical explanations and justifications of artistic postmodernism shifted to include wider discussions of postmodernity and drew in, and generated an interest in, theorists such as

Bell, Kristeva, Lyotard, Vattimo, Derrida, Foucault, Habermas, Baudrillard and Jameson (see Huyssen, 1984). Amongst the central features associated with postmodernism in the arts are: the effacement of the boundary between art and everyday life; the collapse of the hierarchal distinction between high and mass/popular culture; a stylistic promiscuity favouring eclecticism and the mixing of codes; parody, pastiche, irony, playfulness and the celebration of the surface 'depthlessness' of culture; the decline of the originality/genius of the artistic producer; and the assumption that art can only be repetition.

There is also a wider usage of the terms 'modernism' and 'postmodernism' which refers to broader cultural complexes: that is, modernism as the culture of modernity, and postmodernism as the emergent culture of postmodernity. Daniel Bell (1976) takes up this position in which he sees the fundamental cultural assumption of modernity, the ideal of the autonomous self-determining individual, as giving rise to the bourgeois entrepreneur in the economic realm and the artistic search for the untrammelled self (which finds its expression in modernism) in the cultural realm. For Bell modernism is a corrosive force, unleashing an adversarial culture which in conjunction with the hedonistic culture of mass consumption subverts traditional bourgeois values and the Puritan ethic. Bell's analysis is based on the notion of the disjunction of the three realms, the polity, culture and economy, so there is no sense in looking for a base-superstructural model in his work in which a shift in the economy or socio-economic order such as to the post-industrial society would give rise to a new culture of postmodernism. Rather, postmodernism is perceived as a heightening of the antinomian tendencies of modernism with desire, the instinctual, and pleasure unleashed to carry the logic of modernism to its furthest reaches exacerbating the structural tensions of society and disjunction of the realms (Bell, 1980). Jameson (1984) too uses postmodernism to refer to culture in the broader sense and talks about postmodernism as a cutural logic, or cultural dominant, which leads to the transformation of the cultural sphere in contemporary society. While

Jameson shows some reluctance in adopting the view of periodization which assumes a sudden shift and transformation of all aspects of culture, he follows Mandel (1975) and links the stages of modernism to monopoly capitalism and postmodernism to post-World War Two late capitalism. This suggests that he uses a form of the base-superstructural model. Yet he also goes part of the way along the same route as Baudrillard, without referring to him, to argue that postmodernism is based upon the central role of reproduction in the

> "de-centred global network" of present-day multinational capitalism which leads to a "prodigious expansion of culture throughout the social realm, to the point at which everything in our social life . . . can be said to have become "cultural" (Jameson, 1984: 85–7).

There is one further point that needs to be taken up from the work of Bell and Jameson before going on to look at the use of postmodernism as a cipher for fundamental cultural changes as well as the possible expansion of the significance of culture in contemporary Western societies. John O'Neill (1988) has argued that both Bell and Jameson adopt a nostalgic reaction to postmodernism, and are united against postmodernism in their 'will to order', their desire to renew the threatened social bond via religion (Bell) or the Marxist utopia (Jameson). Both have the merit or flaw, depending on where you stand, of wanting to totalize: to depict postmodernism in its degrees of connectedness and disjunction to the contemporary social order. They also want to judge postmodernism as negative; they have a distaste for it, a response which has not passed unnoticed on the part of those critics who welcome the playfulness and pluralistic, 'democratic' spirit of postmodernism, and would see Jameson (and by association, Bell) as nostalgically bemoaning the loss of authority of the intellectual aristocracy over the population (see Hutcheon, 1986–7; During, 1987).

For those who welcome postmodernism as a mode of critical analysis which opens up ironies, inter-textuality and paradoxes, attempts to devise a theory of postmodern society or postmodernity, or delineate the role of postmodernism within the social order, are essentially flawed efforts to totalize or systematize. In effect they are authoritarian grand narratives which are ripe for playful deconstruction. Critics are, for example, quick to point out this apparent inconsistency in Lyotard's *Postmodern Condition*. Kellner (1988), for example, argues that Lyotard's notion of postmodernity itself entails a master narrative, that we can't have a theory of the postmodern without one. It should be added that Lyotard (1988) has recently emphasized the need to move away from what he sees as the misunderstanding of his book as an example of totalizing reason. For those who take seriously the implications of postmodernism as a mode of critical theorizing or cultural analysis, the attempt to produce a sociological understanding must necessarily fail as it cannot avoid totalizations, systematizations and legitimation via the flawed grand narratives of modernity: science, humanism, Marxism, feminism etc. Sociological synthesis must be abandoned for playful deconstruction and the privileging of the aesthetic mode. A postmodern sociology so conceived would abandon its generalizing social science ambitions and instead parasitically play off the ironies, incoherences, inconsistencies and inter-textuality of sociological writings. There are, of course, lessons to be learned from a postmodern sociology: it focuses attention on the ways in which theories are built up, their hidden assumptions, and questions the theorist's authority to speak for 'the Other', who as many researchers are finding out, is now often actively disputing both the account and the authority of the academic theorist. Yet if we are to attempt to make sense of the emergence of postmodernism and the changes taking place in the culture of contemporary Western societies we need to move beyond the false oppositions of foundationalism and relativism, of single epistemology and plural ontology, and investigate specific social and cultural processes and the dynamics of the production of particular funds of knowledge. In effect we must relinquish the attractions of a postmodern sociology and work towards a sociological account of postmodernism. . . .

To follow such an approach would entail focusing on the interrelationship between three aspects or meanings of the culture of postmodernism. In the first place we can consider postmodernism in the arts and in the academic and intellectual fields. Here we could usefully employ the field approach of Bourdieu (1971, 1979) and focus upon the economy of symbolic goods: the conditions of supply and demand for such goods, the processes of competition and monopolization, and the struggles between established and outsiders. We could, for example, direct attention to the act of *naming* as an important strategy of groups engaged in struggles with other groups; the use of new terms by outsider groups who have an interest in destabilizing existing symbolic hierarchies to produce a classification of the field more in line with their own interests; the conditions which are breaking down the barriers between sub-fields of the arts and academic subjects; the conditions which dictate changes in the demand for particular types of cultural goods by various state agencies, consumers, audiences and publics.

To adequately deal with the last areas, indeed to adequately conceptualize all the above areas, would take us outside the specific analysis of particular artistic and intellectual fields and their interrelationship. Here we would need to consider postmodernism in terms of a second 'level' of culture, what is often called the cultural sphere, and consider the means of transmission and circulation to audiences and publics and the feedback effect of the audience response in generating further interest amongst intellectuals. To focus on this second area we need to look at artists, intellectuals and academics as specialists in symbolic production and consider their relationship to other symbolic specialists in the media, and those engaged in consumer culture, popular culture and fashion occupations. Here we need to focus on the emergence of what Bourdieu (1984) calls the 'new cultural intermediaries', who rapidly circulate information between formerly sealed-off areas of culture, and the emergence of new communication channels under conditions of intensified competition (Crane, 1987). We also need to consider the competition, changing balances of power and interdependences between specialists in symbolic production and economic specialists (cf. Elias, 1987) within conditions of a growth in the former group's power potential as producers and consumers accompanying the growth of mass and higher education in Western nations in the post-war era. We need to examine some of the processes of de-monopolization and de-hierarchization of previously established and legitimate cutural enclaves which has brought about a phase of cultural declassification in the Western world (DiMaggio, 1987). Finally, in addition to considering these changes on an intrasocietal level we need also to consider the processes of intensified competition on an intersocietal level which is shifting the balance of power away from Western intellectuals and artists and their right to speak for humanity, as well as the emergence of genuine global cultural questions through what Roland Robertson (1990) has called 'globalization'. These processes point to changes within the broader cultural sphere which are worthy of investigation in their own right; processes which, it can be argued, the concept of postmodernism has served to sensitize us to.

The concept of postmodernism is not, however, merely an empty sign which can be manipulated by artists, intellectuals and academics as part of the power struggles and interdependencies within their particular fields. Part of its appeal is that it speaks to the above changes and also purports to illuminate changes in the day-to-day experiences and cultural practices of broader groups in society. It is here that the evidence is weakest and the possibility of simply relabelling experiences as postmodern which were formerly granted little significance, is most obvious. It is here that we face the problem of an adequate definition of postmodernism and find a good deal of loose conceptual confusion with notions of 'the loss of a sense of historical past', 'schizoid culture', 'excremental culture', 'the replacement of reality by images', 'simulations', 'unchained signifiers' etc., multiplying. Scott Lash (1988) has endeavoured to move to a tighter definition of postmodernism as involving de-differentiation and the figural, which are held to be central to postmodern

regimes of signification; yet here too we possess little systematic evidence about day-to-day practices, and we need information in terms of the stock sociological questions 'who? when? where? how many?' if we are to impress colleagues that postmodernism is more than a fad. Yet there is also a sense in which postmodernism proceeds under its own steam, with the changes in the cultural sphere we have hinted at above, leading to the formation of new audiences and publics interested in postmodernism. Such audiences and publics may eventually adopt postmodern practices and become attuned to postmodern experiences under the guidance of pedagogues produced by cultural intermediaries and para-intellectuals. Such 'feed-back' could lead to postmodernism becoming translated into reality.

To summarize, there is, as yet, no agreed meaning to the term 'postmodern'—its derivatives, the family of terms which include postmodernity, *postmodernité*, postmodernization and postmodernism are often used in confusing and interchangeable ways. I have attempted to outline and discuss some of these meanings. Postmodernism is of interest to a wide range of artistic practices and social science and humanities disciplines because it directs our attention to changes taking place in contemporary culture. These can be understood in terms of (1) the artistic, intellectual and academic fields (changes in modes of theorization, presentation and dissemination of work which cannot be detached from changes in specific competitive struggles occurring in particular fields); (2) changes in the broader cultural sphere involving the modes of production, consumption and circulation of symbolic goods which can be related to broader shifts in the balance of power and interdependencies between groups and class fractions on both inter- and intra-societal levels; (3) changes in the everyday practices and experiences of different groups, who as a result of some of the processes referred to above, may be using regimes of signification in different ways and developing new means of orientation and identity structures. It is apparent that in recent years we have witnessed a dramatic upsurge of interest in the issue of culture. Culture, once on the periphery of social science disciplines, particularly in sociology, has now been thrust increasingly towards the centre of the field and some of the barriers between the social sciences and humanities are in the process of being dismantled (Featherstone, 1988). We can understand this in terms of two processes which must be interrelated: firstly, the way in which culture has shifted in the arsenal of social science concepts from something which is essentially explicable in terms of other factors to broader metacultural questions concerning the cultural underpinning, or 'deep' cultural coding, of the social (see Robertson, 1988); secondly, the way in which the culture of contemporary Western societies seems to be undergoing a series of major transformations which must be investigated in terms of intrasocietal, intersocietal and global processes. It should be apparent that this is one reason for the rise of interest in postmodernism, and a further reason why as cultural theorists and researchers we should be interested in it.

References

Baudrillard, J. (1983) *Simulations*. New York: Semiotext(e).

Bell, D. (1976) *The Cultural Contradictions of Capitalism*. London: Heinemann

——. (1980) 'Beyond Modernism, Beyond Self', in *Sociological Journeys*. London: Heinemann.

Berman, M. (1982) *All That Is Solid Melts Into Air*. New York: Simon and Schuster.

Bourdieu, P. (1971) 'Intellectual Field and Creative Project', in M. Young (ed.), *Knowledge and Control*. London: Collier-Macmillan.

——. (1979) 'The Production of Belief: Contribution to an Economy of Symbolic Goods', *Media, Culture and Society*, 2.

——. (1984) *Distinction: A Social Critique of the Judgement of Taste*, trans. R. Nice. London: Routledge & Kegan Paul.

Bradbury, M. and McFarlane, J. (eds.) (1976) *Modernism 1890–1930*. Harmondsworth: Penguin.

Cooke, P. (1988) 'Modernity, Postmodernity and the City', *Theory, Culture & Society*, 5(2–3).

Crane, D. (1987) *The Transformation of the Avant-Garde*. Chicago: Chicago University Press.

DiMaggio, P. (1987) 'Classification in Art', *American Sociological Review*, 52(4).

During, S. (1987) 'Postmodernism or Post-colonialism Today', *Textual Practice*, 1(1).

Elias, N. (1987) 'The Retreat of Sociologists into the Present', *Theory, Culture & Society*, 4(2–3).

Featherstone, M. (1988) 'Cultural Production, Consumption and the Development of the Cultural Sphere', paper presented at the Third German-American Sociological Theory Group Conference, Bremen.

Foucault, M. (1986) 'What is Enlightenment?', in P. Rabinow (ed.), *The Foucault Reader*. Harmondsworth: Penguin.

Frisby, D. (1985a) 'Georg Simmel, First Sociologist of Modernity', *Theory, Culture & Society*, 2(3).

——. (1985b) *Fragments of Modernity*. Oxford: Polity Press.

Gott, R. (1986) 'The Crisis of Contemporary Culture', *Guardian*, 1 December, p. 10.

Hassan, I. (1985) 'The Culture of Postmodernism', *Theory, Culture & Society*, 2(3).

Hutcheon, L. (1984) *Narcissistic Narrative: The Metafictional Paradox*. London: Methuen.

——. (1986–7) 'The Politics of Postmodernism', *Cultural Critique*, 5.

Huyssen, A. (1984) 'Mapping the Postmodern', *New German Critique*, 33: 5–52.

Jameson, F. (1984) 'Postmodernism: or the Cultural Logic of Late Capitalism', *New Left Review*, 146.

Kellner, D. (1988) 'Postmodernism as Social Theory: Some Challenges and Problems', *Theory, Culture & Society*, 5(2–3).

Kohler, M. (1977) 'Postmodernismus: Ein begriffsgeschichter Überblick', *America Studies*, 22(1).

Lash, S. (1988) 'Discourse or Figure? Postmodernism as a Regime of Signification', *Theory, Culture & Society*, 5(2–3).

Lunn, E. (1985) *Marxism and Modernism*. London: Verso.

Lyotard, J. F. (1984) *The Postmodern Condition*. Manchester: Manchester University Press.

——. (1986–7) 'Rules and Paradoxes or Svelte Appendix', *Cultural Critique*, 5.

——. (1988) 'Interview', *Theory, Culture & Society*, 5(2–3).

Mandel, E. (1975) *Late Capitalism*. London: New Left Books.

O'Neill, J. (1988) 'Religion and Postmodernism: The Durkheimian Bond in Bell and Jameson', *Theory, Culture & Society*, 5(2–3).

Palmer, R. E. (1977) 'Postmodernity and Hermeneutics', *Boundary 2*, 22.

Pawley, M. (1986) 'Architecture: All the History that Fits', *Guardian*, 3 December: 10.

Robertson, R. (1988) 'The Sociological Significance of Culture: Some General Considerations', *Theory, Culture & Society*, 5(1).

———. (1990) 'Mapping the Global Conditions', *Theory, Culture & Society*, 7(2–3).

Zukin, S. (1988) 'The Postmodern Debate over Urban Form', *Theory, Culture & Society*, 5(2–3).

XVI. World Systems and Globalization Theory

70

The Three Instances of Hegemony in the History of the Capitalist World-Economy

Immanuel Wallerstein

Immanuel Wallerstein (b. 1930) is the most influential exponent of world-systems theory. This macrosociological theory, rooted in the Marxist tradition, is intent on viewing capitalism as a worldwide system from a perspective that emphasizes the longue durée and the operation of long-term cycles of development. This means that rather than viewing capitalism as essentially arising during the nineteenth century's Industrial Revolution, Wallerstein seeks to trace its rise to dominance from 1450 forward, with his more recent writings examining what he sees as the gradual demise of the system. He contends that there have been only two world-systems in human history: the world empires of the ancient world and the modern capitalist world-economy that is undergirded by political and military domination. Indeed, he thinks it is a serious mistake to contend that capitalism can be understood solely in economic terms; it is at once an economic and a political system. In this essay,

Wallerstein discusses the conceptual salience of "hegemony" in making sense of the way the modern world-system links its core exploiting nations to the nations on the periphery and semi-periphery. He identifies three points at which hegemonic states rose to prominence and notes the significance that wars played in a process that resulted in a restructuring of international relations.

When one is dealing with a complex, continuously evolving, large-scale historical system, concepts that are used as shorthand descriptions for structural patterns are only useful to the degree one clearly lays out their purpose, circumscribes their applicability, and specifies the theoretical framework they presuppose and advance.

Let me therefore state some premises which I shall not argue at this point. If you are not willing to regard these premises as plausible, you will not find the way I elaborate and use the concept of hegemony very useful. I assume that there exists a concrete singular historical system which I shall call the "capitalist world-economy," whose temporal boundaries go from the long sixteenth century to the present. Its spatial boundaries originally included Europe (or most of it) plus Iberian America but they subsequently expanded to cover the entire globe. I assume this totality is a *system*, that is, that it has been relatively autonomous of external forces; or to put it another way, that its patterns are explicable largely in terms of its internal dynamics. I assume that it is a *historical* system, that is, that it was born, has developed, and will one day cease to exist (through disintegration or fundamental transformation). I assume lastly that it is the dynamics of the system itself that explain its historically changing characteristics. Hence, insofar as it is a system, it has structures and these structures manifest themselves in cyclical rhythms, that is, mechanisms which reflect and ensure repetitious patterns. But insofar as this system is historical, no rhythmic movement ever returns the system to an equilibrium point but instead moves the system along various continua which may be called the secular trends of this system. These trends eventually must culminate in the impossibility of containing further reparations of the structured dislocations by restorative mechanisms. Hence the system undergoes what some call "bifurcating turbulence" and others the "transformation of quantity into quality."

To these methodological or metaphysical premises, I must add a few substantive ones about the operations of the capitalist world-economy. Its mode of production is capitalist; that is, it is predicated on the endless accumulation of capital. Its structure is that of an axial social division of labor exhibiting a core/periphery tension based on unequal exchange. The political superstructure of this system is that of a set of so-called sovereign states defined by and constrained by their membership in an interstate network or system. The operational guidelines of this interstate system include the so-called balance of power, a mechanism designed to ensure that no single state ever has the capacity to transform this interstate system into a single world-empire whose boundaries would match that of the axial division of labor. There have of course been repeated attempts throughout the history of the capitalist world-economy to transform it in the direction of a world-empire, but these attempts have all been frustrated. However, there have also been repeated and quite different attempts by given states to achieve hegemony in the interstate system, and these attempts have in fact succeeded on three occasions, if only for relatively brief periods.

The thrust of hegemony is quite different from the thrust to world empire; indeed it is many ways almost its opposite. I will therefore (1) spell out what I mean by hegemony, (2) describe the analogies in the three purported instances, (3) seek to decipher the roots of the thrust to hegemony and suggest why the thrust to hegemony has succeeded three times but never lasted too long, and (4) draw inferences about what we may expect in the proximate future. The point of doing all this is not to erect a Procrustean category into which to fit complex historical reality but to illuminate what I believe to be one of the central processes of the modern world-system.

(1) Hegemony in the interstate system refers to that situation in which the ongoing rivalry between the so-called "great powers" is so unbalanced that one power can largely impose its rules and its wishes (at the very least by effective veto power) in the economic, political, military, diplomatic, and even cultural arenas. The material base of such power lies in the ability of enterprises domiciled in that power to operate more efficiently in all three major economic arenas—agro-industrial production, commerce, and finance. The edge in efficiency of which we are speaking is one so great that these enterprises can not only outbid enterprises domiciled in other great powers in the world market in general, but quite specifically in very many instances within the home markets of the rival powers themselves.

I mean this to be a relatively restrictive definition. It is not enough for one power's enterprises simply to have a larger share of the world market than any other or simply to have the most powerful military forces or the largest political role. I mean hegemony only to refer to situations in which the edge is so significant that allied major powers are *de facto* client states and opposed major powers feel relatively frustrated and highly defensive vis-à-vis the hegemonic power. And yet while I want to restrict my definition to instances where the margin or power differential is really great, I do not mean to suggest that there is ever any moment when a hegemonic power is omnipotent and capable of doing anything it wants. Omnipotence does not exist within the interstate system.

Hegemony therefore is not a state of being but rather one end of a fluid continuum which describes the rivalry relations of great powers to each other. At one end of this continuum is an almost even balance, a situation in which many powers exist, all somewhat equal in strength, and with no clear or continuous groupings. This is rare and unstable. In the great middle of this continuum, many powers exist, grouped more or less into two camps, but with several neutral or swing elements, and with neither side (nor *a fortiori* any single state) being able to impose its will on others. This is the statistically normal situation of rivalry within the interstate system. And at the other end lies the situation of hegemony, also rare and unstable.

At this point, you may see what it is I am describing but may wonder why I am bothering to give it a name and thereby focus attention upon it. It is because I suspect hegemony is not the result of a random reshuffling of the cards but is a phenomenon that emerges in specifiable circumstances and plays a significant role in the historical development of the capitalist world-economy.

(2) Using this restrictive definition, the only three instances of hegemony would be the United Provinces in the mid-seventeenth century, the United Kingdom in the mid-nineteenth, and the United States in the mid-twentieth. If one insists on dates, I would tentatively suggest as maximal bounding points: 1625–72, 1815–73, 1945–67. But of course, it would be a mistake to try to be too precise when our measuring instruments are both so complex and so crude.

I will suggest four areas in which it seems to me what happened in the three instances was analogous. To be sure, analogies are limited. And to be sure, since the capitalist world-economy is in my usage a single continuously evolving entity, it follows by definition that the overall structure was different at each of the three points in time. The differences were real, the outcome of the secular trends of the world-system. But the structural analogies were real as well, the reflection of the cyclical rhythms of this same system.

The first analogy has to do with the sequencing of achievement and loss of relative efficiencies in each of the three economic domains. What I believe occurred was that in each instance enterprises domiciled in the given power in question achieved their edge

Chart 70-1

Capitalist World-Economy

first in agro-industrial production, then in commerce, and then in finance.[1] I believe they lost their edge in this sequence as well (this process having begun but not yet having been completed in the third instance). Hegemony thus refers to that short interval in which there is *simultaneous* advantage in all three economic domains.

The second analogy has to do with the ideology and policy of the hegemonic power. Hegemonic powers during the period of their hegemony tended to be advocates of global "liberalism." They came forward as defenders of the principle of the free flow of the factors of production (goods, capital, and labor) throughout the world-economy. They were hostile in general to mercantilist restrictions on trade, including the existence of overseas colonies for the stronger countries. They extended this liberalism to a generalized endorsement of liberal parliamentary institutions (and a concurrent distaste for political change by violent means), political restraints on the arbitrariness of bureaucratic power, and civil liberties (and a concurrent open door to political exiles). They tended to provide a high standard of living for their national working classes, high by world standards of the time.

None of this should be exaggerated. Hegemonic powers regularly made exceptions to their anti-mercantilism, when it was in their interest to do so. Hegemonic powers regularly were willing to interfere with political processes in other states to ensure their own advantage. Hegemonic powers could be very repressive at home, if need be, to guarantee the national "consensus." The high working-class standard was steeply graded by internal ethnicity. Nevertheless, it is quite striking that liberalism as an ideology did flourish in these countries at precisely the moments of their hegemony, and to a significant extent only then and there.

The third analogy is in the pattern of global military power. Hegemonic powers were primarily sea (now sea/air) powers. In the long ascent to hegemony, they seemed very reluctant to develop their armies, discussing openly the potentially weakening drain on state revenues and manpower of becoming tied down in land wars. Yet each found finally that it had to develop a strong

land army as well to face up to a major land-based rival which seemed to be trying to transform the world-economy into a world-empire.

In each case, the hegemony was secured by a thirty-year-long world war. By a world war, I shall mean (again somewhat restrictively) a land-based war that involves (not necessarily continuously) almost all the major military powers of the epoch in warfare that is very destructive of land and population. To each hegemony is attached one of these wars. World War Alpha was the Thirty Years' War from 1618–48, when Dutch interests triumphed over Hapsburg in the world-economy. World War Beta was the Napoleonic Wars from 1792–1815, when British interests triumphed over French. World War Gamma was the long Euroasian wars from 1914–45 when U.S. interests triumphed over German.

While limited wars have been a constant of the operations of the interstate system of the capitalist world-economy (there having been scarcely any year when there was not some war some place within the system), world wars have been, by contrast, a rarity. In fact their rarity and the fact that the number and timing seem to have correlated with the achievement of hegemonic status by one power brings us to the fourth analogy.

If we look to those very long cycles that Rondo Cameron has dubbed "logistics," we can see that world wars and hegemony have been in fact related to them. There has been very little scholarly work done on these logistics. They have been most frequently discussed in the comparisons between the A–B sequences of 1100–1450 and 1450–1750. There are only a few discussions of the logistics that may exist after the latter point in time. But if we take the prime observation which has been used to define these logistics—secular inflation and deflation—the pattern seems in fact to have continued.

It therefore might be plausible to argue the existence of such (price) logistics up to today using the following dates: 1450–1730, with 1600–1650 as a flat peak; 1730–1897, with 1810–17 as a peak; and 1897 to ?, with an as yet uncertain peak. If there are such logistics, it turns out that the world war and the (subsequent) hegemonic era are located somewhere around (just before and after) the peak of the logistic. That is to say, these processes seem to be the product of the long competitive expansion which seemed to have resulted in a particular concentration of economic and political power.

The outcome of each world war included a major restructuring of the interstate system (Westphalia; the Concert of Europe; the U.N. and Bretton Woods) in a form consonant with the need for relative stability of the now hegemonic power. Furthermore, once the hegemonic position was eroded economically (the loss of the efficiency edge in agro-industrial production), and therefore hegemonic decline set in, one consequence seemed to be the erosion of the alliance network which the hegemonic power had created patiently, and ultimately a serious reshuffling of alliances.

In the long period following the era of hegemony, two powers seemed eventually to emerge as the "contenders for the succession"—England and France after Dutch hegemony; the U.S. and Germany after British; and now Japan and western Europe after U.S. Furthermore, the eventual winner of the contending pair seemed to use as a conscious part of its strategy the gentle turning of the old hegemonic power into its "junior partner"—the English vis-à-vis the Dutch, the U.S. vis-à-vis Great Britain . . . and now?

(3) Thus far I have been primarily descriptive. I realize that this description is vulnerable to technical criticism. My coding of the data may not agree with everyone else's. I think nonetheless that as an initial effort this coding is defensible and that I have therefore outlined a broad repetitive pattern in the functioning of the interstate question. The question now is how to interpret it. What is there in the functioning of a capitalist world-economy that gives rise to such a cyclical pattern in the interstate system?

I believe this pattern of the rise, temporary ascendancy, and fall of hegemonic powers in the interstate system is merely one aspect of the central role of the political machinery in the functioning of capitalism as a mode of production.

There are two myths about capitalism put forward by its central ideologues (and, strangely, largely accepted by its nineteenth-century critics). One is that it is defined by the free flow of the factors of production. The second is that it is defined by the non-interference of the political machinery in the "market." In fact, capitalism is defined by the *partially* free flow of the factors of production and by the *selective* interference of the political machinery in the "market." Hegemony is an instance of the latter.

What defines capitalism most fundamentally is the drive for the endless accumulation of capital. The interferences that are "selected" are those which advance this process of accumulation. There are however two problems about "interference." It has a cost, and therefore the benefit of any interference is only a benefit to the extent it exceeds this cost. Where the benefits are available without any "interference," this is obviously desirable, as it minimizes the "deduction." And secondly, interference is always in favor of one set of accumulators as against another set, and the latter will always seek to counter the former. These two considerations circumscribe the politics of hegemony in the interstate system.

The costs to a given entrepreneur of state "interference" are felt in two main ways. First, in financial terms, the state may levy direct taxes which affect the rate of profit by requiring the firm to make payments to the state, or indirect taxes, which may alter the rate of profit by affecting the competitiveness of a product. Secondly, the state may enact rules which govern flows of capital, labor, or goods, or may set minimum and/or maximum prices. While direct taxes always represent a cost to the entrepreneur, calculations concerning indirect taxes and state regulations are more complex, since they represent costs both to the entrepreneur and to (some of) his competitors. The chief concern in terms of individual accumulation is not the absolute cost of these measures, but the comparative cost. Costs, even if high, may be positively desirable from the standpoint of a given entrepreneur, if the state's actions involve still higher costs to some competitor. Absolute costs are only of concern if the loss to the entrepreneur is greater than the medium-run gain which is possible through greater competitiveness brought about by such state actions. It follows that absolute cost is of greatest concern to those entrepreneurs who would do best in open market competition in the absence of state interference.

In general, therefore, entrepreneurs are regularly seeking state interference in the market in multiple forms—subsidies, restraints of trade, tariffs (which are penalties for competitors of different nationality), guarantees, maxima for input prices and minima for output prices, etc. The intimidating effect of internal and external repression is also of direct economic benefit to entrepreneurs. To the extent that the ongoing process of competition and state interference leads to oligopolistic conditions within state boundaries, more and more attention is naturally paid to securing the same kind of oligopolistic conditions in the most important market, the world market.

The combination of the competitive thrust and constant state interference results in a continuing pressure towards the concentration of capital. The benefits of state interference inside and outside the state boundaries is cumulative. In political terms, this is reflected as expanding world power. The edge a rising power's economic enterprises have vis-à-vis those of a competitive rising power may be thin and therefore insecure. This is where the world wars come in. The thirty-year struggle may be very dramatic militarily and politically. But the profoundest effect may be economic. The winner's economic edge is expanded by the very process of the war itself, and the post-war interstate settlement is designed to encrust that greater edge and protect it against erosion.

A given state thus assumes its world "responsibilities" which are reflected in its diplomatic, military, political, ideological, and cultural stances. All conspire to reinforce the cooperative relationship of the entrepreneurial strata, the bureaucratic strata, and with some lag the working-class strata of the hegemonic power. This power may then be exercised in a "liberal" form—given the real diminution of political conflict within the state itself compared to earlier and later periods, and to the importance in the interstate

arena of delegitimizing the efforts of other state machineries to act against the economic superiorities of the hegemonic power.

The problem is that global liberalism, which is rational and cost effective, breeds its own demise. It makes it more difficult to retard the spread of technological expertise. Hence over time it is virtually inevitable that entrepreneurs coming along later will be able to enter the most profitable markets with the most advanced technologies and younger "plant," thus eating into the material base of the productivity edge of the hegemonic power.

Secondly, the internal political price of liberalism, needed to maintain uninterrupted production at a time of maximal global accumulation, is the creeping rise of real income of both the working strata and the cadres located in the hegemonic power. Over time, this must reduce the competitive advantage of the enterprises located in this state.

Once the clear productivity edge is lost, the structure cracks. As long as there is a hegemonic power, it can coordinate more or less the political responses of all states with core-like economic activities to all peripheral states, maximizing thereby the differentials of unequal exchange. But when hegemony is eroded, and especially when the world-economy is in a Kondratieff downturn, a scramble arises among the leading powers to maintain their shares of the smaller pie, which undermines their collective ability to extract surplus via unequal exchange. The rate of unequal exchange thereby diminishes (but never to zero) and creates further incentive to a reshuffling of alliance systems.

In the period leading to the peak of a logistic, which leads towards the creation of the momentary era of hegemony, the governing parable is that of the tortoise and the hare. It is not the state that leaps ahead politically and especially militarily that wins the race, but the one that plods along improving inch by inch its long-term competitiveness. This requires a firm but discreet and intelligent organization of the entrepreneurial effort by the state-machinery. Wars may be left to others, until the climactic world war when the hegemonic power must at least invest its resources to clinch its victory. Thereupon comes "world responsibility" with its benefits but also its (growing) costs. Thus the hegemony is sweet but brief.

(4) The inferences for today are obvious. We are in the immediate post-hegemonic phase of this third logistic of the capitalist world-economy. The U.S. has lost its productive edge but not yet its commercial and financial superiorities; its military and political power edge is no longer so overwhelming. Its abilities to dictate to its allies (western Europe and Japan), intimidate its foes, and overwhelm the weak (compare the Dominican Republic in 1965 with El Salvador today) are vastly impaired. We are in the beginnings of a major reshuffling of alliances.[2] Yet, of course, we are only at the beginning of all this. Great Britain began to decline in 1873, but it was only in 1982 that it was openly challenged by Argentina, a middle-ranking military power.

The major question is whether this third logistic will act itself out along the lines of the previous ones. The great difference of this third logistic from the first two is that the capitalist world-economy has now entered into a structural crisis as an historical system. The question is whether this fact will obliterate these cyclical processes. I do not believe it will obliterate them but rather that it will work itself out in part through them.[3]

We should not invest more in the concept of hegemony than is there. It is a way of organizing our perception of process, not an "essence" whose traits are to be described and whose eternal recurrences are to be demonstrated and then anticipated. A processual concept alerts us to the forces at play in the system and the likely nodes of conflict. It does not do more. But it also does not do less. The capitalist world-economy is not comprehensible unless we analyze clearly what are the political forms which it has engendered and how these forms relate to other realities. The interstate system is not some exogenous, God-given, variable which mysteriously restrains and interacts with the capitalist drive for the endless accumulation of capital. It is its expression at the level of the political arena.

Endnotes

1. I have described this in empirical detail for the first instance in *The Modern World-System, II: Mercantilism and the Consolidation of the European World-Economy, 1600–1750* (New York: Academic, 1980), ch. 2.

2. See my "North Atlanticism in Decline," *SAIS Review,* No. 4, Summer, 1982, 21–26.

3. For a debate about this, see the Conclusions of S. Amin, G. Arrighi, A. G. Frank, and I. Wallerstein, *Dynamics of Global Crisis* (New York: Monthly Review Press, 1982).

"The Three Instances of Hegemony in the History of the Capitalist World-Economy" by Immanuel Wallerstein, from *International Journal of Comparative Sociology* XXIV, 1–2, January-April 1983, pp. 100–08. Reprinted by permission of Brill Academic Publishers. ✦

71
Mapping the Global Condition

Roland Robertson

sense it represents the trend towards the consolidation and strengthening of the territorial state. . . . In another sense it represents a reordering in the priority of international and domestic realms. In the medieval period the world, or transnational, environment was primary, the domestic secondary. (Richard Rosencrance, 1986: 77)

Roland Robertson (b. 1938) is one of the most important theorists of globalization. He thinks that an adequate theory of globalization must go beyond rather than be merely subsumed under either world-systems theory or modernization theory. Robertson seeks to sketch out the contours of contemporary globalization, which is depicted in terms of the emergence of a compressed and united, but not integrated, system. He begins with the claim that globalization has been happening for some time but that the pace has dramatically accelerated in recent decades, thereby deepening and widening globalization's impact. In this effort aimed at "mapping the global condition," he articulates five stages of development: the germinal, which dates to the fifteenth century; the incipient, which commenced around 1750; the take-off phase, a half-century stage beginning about 1870; the "struggle-for-hegemony" phase; and finally the current "uncertainty" stage.

> Nothing will be done anymore, without the whole world meddling in it. (Paul Valéry in Lesourne, 1986: 103)

> We are on the road from the evening-glow of European philosophy to the dawn of world philosophy. (Karl Jaspers, 1957: 83–4)

> Insofar as [present realities] have brought us a global present without a common past [they] threaten to render all traditions and all particular past histories irrelevant. (Hannah Arendt, 1957: 541)

> The transformation of the medieval into the modern can be depicted in at least two different ways. In one

My primary concern here is to continue the discussion of the analytical and empirical aspects of globalization. I also want to raise some general questions about social theory. As far as the main issue is concerned, I set out the grounds for systematic analysis and interpretation of globalization since the mid-fifteenth century, indicating the major phases of globalization in recent world history and exploring some of the more salient aspects of the contemporary global circumstance from an analytical point of view. On the general-theoretical front I argue again that much of social theory is both a product of and an implicit reaction to, as opposed to a direct engagement with, the globalization process.

While there is rapidly growing interest in the issue of globalization, much of it is expressed very diffusely. It has become a widely used term in a number of theoretical, empirical and applied areas of intellectual inquiry, including the various 'policy sciences,' such as business studies and strategic studies. There is also a danger that 'globalization' will become an intellectual 'play zone,' a site for the expression of residual social-theoretical interests, interpretive indulgence, or the display of world-ideological preferences. I think we must take very seriously Immanuel Wallerstein's (1987: 309) contention that 'world-systems' analysis is not a theory about the world. 'It is a protest against the ways in which social scientific inquiry was structured for all of us at its inception in the middle of the nineteenth century.' Even though I do not, as I have said, subscribe to world-systems theory in the conventional sense of the term, primarily because of its economism, and am not pessimistic about the possibility of our being able to accomplish significant theoretical work *vis-à-vis* the world as a whole, I consider it to be of the utmost importance for us to realize fully that much of the conventional sociology which has developed since the first quarter of the twentieth century has been held in thrall by the virtually global institutionalization of the idea of the culturally cohesive and sequestered national society during the main phase of 'classical' sociology. Ironically, the global aspect of that phenomenon has received relatively little attention (Meyer, 1980).

Globalization and the Structuration of the World

The present discussion, in this and the following chapters, is a continuation of previous efforts to theorize the topic of globalization, a task made all the more difficult by the recent and continuing events in the territories of the old USSR, Eastern and Central Europe, China and elsewhere, which have disrupted virtually all of the conventional views concerning 'world order.' At the same time those events and the circumstances they have created make the analytical effort even more urgent. We have entered a phase of what appears to us in the 1990s to be great global uncertainty—so much so that the very idea of uncertainty promises to become globally institutionalized. Or, to put it in a very different way, there is an eerie relationship between postmodernist theories and the idea of postmodernity, on the one hand, and the geopolitical 'earthquakes' that we (the virtually *global we*) have recently experienced, on the other.

We need to enlarge our conception of 'world politics' in such a way as to facilitate systematic discussion, but not conflation, of the relationship between politics in the relatively narrow sense and the broad questions of 'meaning' which can only be grasped by wide-ranging, empirically sensitive interpretations of the global-human condition as a whole. Specifically, I argue that what is often called world politics has in the twentieth century hinged considerably upon the issue of the interpretation of and the response to

modernity, aspects of which were politically and internationally thematized as the standard of 'civilization' (Gong, 1984) during the late nineteenth and early twentieth centuries with particular reference to the inclusion of non-European (mainly Asian) societies in Eurocentric 'international society' (Bull and Watson, 1984).

Communism and 'democratic capitalism' have constituted alternative forms of acceptance of modernity (Parsons, 1964), although some would now argue that the recent and dramatic ebbing of communism can in part be attributed to its 'attempt to preserve the integrity of the premodern system' (Parsons, 1967: 484–5) by invoking 'socialism' as the central of a series of largely 'covert gestures of reconciliation . . . toward both the past and the future' (Parsons, 1967: 484).[1] On the other hand fascism and neofascism have, in spite of their original claims to the establishment of *new* societal and international 'orders' (as was explicitly the case with the primary Axis powers of World War II: Germany and Japan), been directly interested in *transcending or resolving* the problems of modernity. That issue has certainly not disappeared. The world politics of the global debate about modernity has rarely been considered of relevance to the latter and yet it is clear that, for example, conceptions of the past by the major belligerents in World War I illustrated a sharp contrast between 'the temporalities of the nations of each alliance system and underlying causes of resentment and misunderstanding' (Kern, 1983: 277), with the nations whose leaders considered themselves to be relatively deprived—notably Germany and Japan— being particularly concerned to confront the problem of modernity in political and military terms.[2] Sociologists and philosophers are familiar with many intellectual developments of the 1920s and 1930s, but these have not been linked to the broad domain of *Realpolitik*. It may well be that the Cold War that developed after the defeat of great-power Fascism constituted an interruption and partial freezing of the world-cultural politics of modernity and that with the ending of the Cold War as conventionally understood those politics will now be resumed in a situation of much greater global complexity, in the interrelated contexts of more intense globalization, the growing political presence of Islam, the discourse of postmodernity and 'the ethnic revival' (A.D. Smith, 1981), which itself may be considered as *an aspect of* the contemporary phase of globalization (Lechner, 1984).

Any attempt to theorize the general field of globalization must lay the grounds for relatively patterned discussion of the politics of the global-human condition, by attempting to indicate the structure of any viable discourse about the shape and 'meaning' of the world as a whole. I regard this as an urgent matter partly because much of the explicit intellectual interpretation of the global scene is being conducted by academics operating under the umbrella of 'cultural studies' with exceedingly little attention to the issue of global complexity and structural contingency, except for frequently invoked labels such as 'late capitalism,' 'disorganized capitalism,' or the salience of 'the transnational corporation.' This is not at all to say that the economic factor is unimportant, or that the 'textual,' 'power-knowledge,' or 'hegemonic' aspects of the 'world system' are of minor significance. Rather, I am insisting that both the economics and the culture of the global scene should be analytically connected to the general structural and actional features of the global field.

I maintain that what has come to be called globalization is, in spite of differing conceptions of that theme, best understood as indicating the problem of *the form* in terms of which the world becomes 'united,' but by no means integrated in naive functionalist mode (Robertson and Chirico, 1985). Globalization as a topic is, in other words, a conceptual entry to the problem of 'world order' in the most general sense—but, nevertheless, an entry which has no cognitive purchase without considerable discussion of historical and comparative matters. It is, moreover, a phenomenon which clearly requires what is conventionally called interdisciplinary treatment. Traditionally the general field of the study of the world as a whole has been approached via the discipline of international relations (or, more diffusely, international studies). That discipline (sometimes regarded as a subdiscipline of political

science) was consolidated during particular phases of the overall globalization process and is now being reconstituted in reference to developments in other disciplinary areas, including the humanities (Der Derian and Shapiro, 1989). Indeed, the first concentrated thrust into the study of the world as a whole on the part of sociologists, during the 1960s (discussed in Nettl and Robertson, 1968), was undertaken, as has been seen, mainly in terms of the idea of the sociology of international relations. There can be little doubt that to this day the majority of social scientists still think of 'extra-societal' matters in terms of 'international relations' (including variants thereof, such as transnational relations, nongovernmental relations, supranational relations, world politics and so on). Nonetheless that tendency is breaking down, in conjunction with considerable questioning of what Michael Mann (1986) has called the unitary conception of society. While there have been attempts to carve out a new discipline for the study of the world as a whole, including the long-historical making of the contemporary 'world system' (e.g. Bergesen, 1980), my position is that it is not so much that we need a new discipline in order to study the world as a whole but that social theory in the broadest sense—as a perspective which stretches across the social sciences and humanities (Giddens and Turner, 1987: 1) and even the natural sciences—should be refocused and expanded so as to make concern with 'the world' a central hermeneutic, and in such a way as to constrain empirical and comparative-historical research in the same direction.

Undoubtedly, as we have already seen, there *have* been various attempts in the history of social theory to move along such lines but the very structure of the globalization process has inhibited such efforts from taking off into a fully fledged research program, mostly notably during the crucial take-off period of globalization itself, 1870–1925. So we are led to the argument that exerting ourselves to develop *global* social theory is not merely an exercise demanded by the transparency of the processes rendering the contemporary world as a whole as a single place but also that our labors in that regard are crucial to the empirical understanding of the bases upon which the matrix of contemporary disciplinarity and interdisciplinarity rests. There has been an enormous amount of talk in recent years about self-reflexiveness, the critical-theoretic posture, and the like; but ironically much of that talk has been about as far removed from discussion of the real world—in the twofold sense of quotidian contemporary realities and differences *and* the concrete global circumstance—as it could be. Much of fashionable social theory has favored the abstract and, from a simplistic global perspective, 'the local' to the great neglect of the global and civilizational contours and bases of Western social theory itself. The distinction between the global and the local is becoming very complex and problematic, to the extent that we should now perhaps speak in such terms as the global institutionalization of the life-world and the localization of globality.

In the second half of the 1980s 'globalization' (and its problematic variant, 'internationalization') became a commonly used term in intellectual, business, media and other circles, in the process acquiring a number of meanings, with varying degrees of precision. This has been a source of frustration, but not necessarily a cause for surprise or alarm, to those of us who had sought earlier in the decade to establish a relatively strict definition of globalization as part of an attempt to come to terms systematically with major aspects of contemporary 'meaning and change' (Robertson, 1978). Nevertheless a stream of analysis and research *has* been developed around the general idea, if not always the actual concept, of globalization. It is my intention here to indicate some of the most pressing issues in this area—not so much by surveying and evaluating different approaches to the making of the contemporary world system, world society, the global ecumene, or whatever one chooses to call the late twentieth-century world as a whole; but rather by considering some relatively neglected analytical and historical themes.

I deal here with relatively recent aspects of globalization, although I want to emphasize as strongly as possible that in doing so I am not suggesting for a moment that moves and thrusts in the direction of global unicity are unique to relatively recent history. I also argue that globalization is intimately related to modernity and modernization, as well as to postmodernity and 'postmodernization' (in so far as the latter pair of motifs have definite analytical purchase). In attempting to justify that proposal I am by no means suggesting that work within the frame of 'the globalization paradigm' should be limited to the relatively recent past. All I am maintaining is that the concept of globalization *per se* is most clearly applicable to a particular series of relatively recent developments concerning *the concrete structuration of the world as a whole*. The term 'structuration' has been deliberately chosen. Although I will shortly consider some aspects of Anthony Giddens's work on 'the global scene,' I cannot address here the general problems which arise from the concept of structuration (Cohen, 1989; Bryant and Jary, 1991). I will say only that if the notion of structuration is to be of assistance to us analytically in the decades ahead it has to be moved out of its quasi-philosophical context, its confinement within the canonical discourses about subjectivity and objectivity, individual and society, and so on (Archer, 1988). It has to be made directly relevant to *the world* in which we live. It has to contribute to the understanding of how the global 'system' has been and continues to be *made*. It has to be focused on the production and reproduction of 'the world' as the most salient plausibility structure of our time (Wuthnow, 1978: 65). The same applies to the cultural-agency problematic which Margaret Archer (1988) has recently theorized.

Human history has been replete with ideas concerning the physical structure, the geography, the cosmic location and the spiritual and/or secular significance of the world (Wagar, 1971); movements and organizations concerned with the patterning and/or the unification of the world as a whole have intermittently appeared for at least the last two thousand years; and ideas about the relationship between the universal and the particular have been central to all of the major civilizations. Even something like what has recently been called 'the global-local nexus' (or the 'local-global nexus') was thematized as long ago as the second century BC when Polybius, in his *Universal History*, wrote with reference to the rise of the Roman empire: 'Formerly the things which happened in the world had no connection among themselves. . . . But since then all events are united in a common bundle' (Kohn, 1971: 121).[3] However, the crucial considerations are that it has not been until relatively recent times that it has been realistically thought that 'humanity is rapidly becoming, physically speaking, a single society' (Hobhouse, 1906: 331), and that it has not been until quite recently that considerable numbers of people living on various parts of the planet have spoken and acted in direct reference to the problem of the 'organization' of the entire, heliocentric world. It is in relation to this heavily contested problem of the concrete patterning and consciousness of the world, including resistance to globality, that I seek to center the concept and the discourse of globalization.

The world as a whole could, in theory, have become the reality which it now is in ways and along trajectories other than those that have actually obtained (Lechner, 1989). The world could, in principle, have been rendered as a 'singular system' (Moore, 1966) via the imperial hegemony of a single nation or a 'grand alliance' between two or more dynasties or nations; the victory of 'the universal proletariat'; the global triumph of a particular form of organized religion; the crystallization of 'the world spirit'; the yielding of nationalism to the ideal of 'free trade'; the success of the world-federalist movement; the worldwide triumph of a trading company; or in yet other ways. Some of these have in fact held sway at certain moments in world history. Indeed, in coming to terms analytically with the contemporary circumstance we have to acknowledge that some such possibilities are as old as world history in any meaningful sense of that phrase and have greatly contributed to the existence of the globalized world of the late twentieth century. Moreover, much of world history can be fruitfully considered as sequences of 'miniglobalization,' in the sense that, for example, historic empire formation involved the unification of previously sequestered territories and social entities. There have also been shifts in the opposite direction, as with the deunification of medieval Europe, of which Rosencrance (1986) has spoken—although the rise of the territorial state also promoted imperialism and thus conceptions of the world as a whole.

Nonetheless, when all is said and done no single possibility has, or so I claim, been more continuously prevalent than another. There may have been periods in world history when one such possibility was more of a 'globalizing force' than others—and that must certainly be a crucial aspect of the discussion of globalization in the long-historical mode—but we have not as a world-people moved into the present global-human circumstance along one or even a small cluster of these particular trajectories. Yet in the present climate of 'globality' there is a strong temptation for some to insist that the single world of our day can be accounted for in terms of one particular process or factor, such as 'Westernization,' 'imperialism' or, in the dynamic and diffuse sense, 'civilization.' As I argue more specifically in later chapters, the problem of globality is very likely to become a basis of major ideological and analytical cleavages of the twenty-first century, as the idea of 'the new world order' in its political, military and economic senses, not least because the connotations of that term as used in pre-Axis and Axis contexts are so negative. While I do not subscribe to the view that social theorists should at all costs attempt to be neutral about these and other matters, I am committed to the argument that one's moral stance should be realistic and that one should have no intrinsically vested interest in the attempt to map this or any other area of the human condition. More precisely, I argue that systematic comprehension of the structuration of world order is essential to the viability of any form of contemporary theory and that such comprehension must involve analytical separation of the factors that have facilitated the shift towards a single world—for example the spread of capitalism, Western imperialism and the development of a global media system—from the *general and global* agency-structure (and/or culture) theme. While the empirical relationship between the two sets of issues is of great importance (and, of course, complex), conflation of them leads us into all sorts of difficulties and inhibits our ability to come to terms with the basic but shifting terms of the contemporary world order, including the 'structure' of 'disorderliness.'

Thus we must return to the question of the actual form of recent and contemporary moves in the direction of global interdependence and global consciousness. In posing the basic question in this way we immediately confront the critical issue of the period during which the move towards the world as a singular system became more or less inexorable. If we think of the history of the world as consisting for a very long time in *the objectiveness* of a variety of different civilizations existing in varying degrees of separation from each other, our main task now is to consider the ways in which the world 'moved' from being merely 'in itself' to the problem or the possibility of its being 'for itself.' Before coming directly to that vital issue I must attend briefly to some basic analytical matters. This I do via the statement of Giddens (1987: 255–93) on 'Nation-States in the Global State System.'

Giddens makes much of the point that 'the development of the sovereignty of the modern state from its beginnings depends upon a reflexively monitored set of relations between states' (Giddens, 1987: 263). He argues that the period of treaty making following World War I 'was effectively the first point at which a reflexively monitored system of nation-states came to exist globally' (1987: 256). I fully concur with both the emphasis on the importance of the post-World War I period and Giddens's claim that 'if a new and formidably threatening pattern of war was established at this time, so was a new pattern of peace' (1987: 256). More generally, Giddens's argument that the development of the modern state has been guided by increasingly global norms concerning its sovereignty is, if not original, of great importance. However, he tends to conflate the issue of the homogenization of the state (in Hegel's sense)—what Giddens calls 'the universal scope of the nation-state' (1987: 264)—and the issue of relationships between states.

It is important to make a distinction between the diffusion of expectations concerning the external legitimacy and mode of operation of the state and the development of regulative norms concerning the relationships between states; while readily acknowledging that the issue of the powers and limits of the state has been *empirically* linked to the structuring of the relationships between states and, moreover, that it constitutes a crucial axis of globalization. James Der Derian (1989) has recently drawn attention to an important aspect of that theme by indicating the proximity of the formal 'Declaration of the Rights of Man' that sovereignty resides in the nation to Jeremy Bentham's declaration in the same year of 1789 that there was a need for a new word—'international'—which would express, in a more significant way, the branch of law which goes commonly under the name of the *law of nations* (Bentham, 1948: 326).

So while the two issues upon which I have been dwelling via Giddens's analysis undoubtedly have been and remain closely interdependent, it is crucial to keep them analytically apart in order that we may fully appreciate variations in the nature of the empirical connections between them. In sum, the problem of contingency arising from state sovereignty and the development of relational rules between sovereign units is not the same as the issue of the crystallization and diffusion of conceptions of national statehood (A.D. Smith, 1979). Nor is it the same as the development and spread of conceptions of the shape and meaning of 'international society' (Gong, 1984). The second set of matters is on a different 'level' than that addressed by Giddens.

My primary reason for emphasizing this matter is that it provides an immediate entry to what I consider the most pressing general problem in the contemporary discussion of globalization. Giddens's analysis is a good example of an attempt to move toward the global circumstance via the conventional concerns of sociological theory. While readily conceding that it was his specific, initial concern to talk about the modern nation state and the internal and external violence with which its development has been bound up, the fact remains that in spite of all of his talk about global matters at the end of his analysis, Giddens is restricted precisely by his having to center 'the current world system' within a discussion of 'the global *state* system' (Giddens, 1987: 276–7; emphasis added). Even though he eventually separates, in analytical terms, the nation-state system (with the ambiguity I have indicated) as the political aspect of the world system from the 'global information system' (as relating to 'symbolic orders/modes of discourse'); the 'world-capitalist economy' (as the economic dimension of the world system); and the 'world military order' (as concerning 'law/modes of sanction')—along lines reminiscent of approaches of the 1960s (Nettl and Robertson, 1968) and, ironically, of a general Parsonian, functional-imperative approach—Giddens ends up with a 'map' of what he reluctantly calls the world system, which is centered upon his conflated characterization of the rise of the modern state system. Giddens (1990) has of course expanded upon, and modified his thinking about what he now calls globalization, in relation to modernity and the idea of postmodernity. . . .

'Mapping' the world social-scientifically is, of course, a common procedure; it crystallized during the 1960s both with the diffusion of perceptions concerning the existence of the Third World and with polarized First (liberal-capitalist) and Second (industrializing-communist) Worlds. Ever since that period—the beginning of the current phase of contemporary, late twentieth-century globalization—there has proliferated a large number of different and, indeed, conflicting ideological and/or 'scientific' maps of the world-system of national societies, so much so that it is reasonable to say that the discourse of mapping is a vital ingredient of global-political culture, one which fuses geography (as in the use of North-South and East-West terminology) with political, economic, cultural and other forms of placement of nations on the global-international map. Much of this overall effort has resulted in significant work—for example Johan Galtung's *The True Worlds* (1980) and Peter Worsley's (1984) lengthy discussion of the cultures of 'the three worlds.' Indeed, the kind of work which has strongly reminded us of the major cleavages and discontinuities in the world as a whole is a significant antidote to those who now speak blithely in 'global village' terms of a single world. Nonetheless there can be no denying that the world is much more singular than it was as recently as, say, the 1950s. The crucial question remains of the basic form or structure in terms of which that shift has occurred. That that form has been *imposed* upon certain areas of the world is, of course, a crucial issue, but until the matter of form (more elaborately, structuration) is adequately thematized our ability to comprehend the dynamics of the making of the world as a whole will be severely limited.

A Minimal Phase Model of Globalization

I offer here what I call and advocate as a necessarily minimal model of globalization. This model does not make grand assertions about primary factors, major mechanisms, and so on. Rather, it indicates the major constraining tendencies which have been operating in relatively recent history as far as world order and the compression of the world in our time are concerned.

One of the most pressing tasks in this regard is to confront the issue of the undoubted salience of the unitary nation state—more diffusely, the national society—since about the mid-eighteenth century and at the same time to acknowledge its historical uniqueness, in a sense its abnormality (McNeill, 1986). The homogeneous nation state—homogeneous here in the sense of a culturally homogenized, administered citizenry (B. Anderson, 1983)—is a construction of a particular form of life. That we ourselves have been increasingly subject to its constraints does not mean that for analytical purposes it has to be accepted as *the* departure point for analyzing and understanding the world. This is why I have argued not merely that national societies should be regarded as constituting but one general reference point for the analysis of the global-human circumstance, but that we have to recognize even more than we do now that the prevalence of the national society in the twentieth century is an aspect of globalization (Robertson, 1989)—that the diffusion of *the idea of* the national society as a form of institutionalized societalism (Lechner, 1989) was central to the accelerated globalization which began to occur just over a hundred years ago. I have also argued more specifically that the two other major components of globalization have been, in addition to national systems and the system of international relations, conceptions of individuals and of humankind. It is in terms of the shifting relationships between and the 'upgrading' of these reference points that globalization has occurred in recent centuries. This pattern has certainly been greatly affected by and subject to all sorts of economic, political and other processes and actions; but my task here is to legitimize the need for an overall comprehension of the global circumstance.

I now propose, in skeletal terms, that the temporal-historical path to the present circumstance of a very high degree of global density and complexity can be delineated as follows:

Phase I: The Germinal Phase. Lasting in Europe from the early fifteenth until the mid-eighteenth century. Incipient growth of national communities and downplaying of the medieval 'transnational' system. Expanding scope of the Catholic church. Accentuation of concepts of the individual and of ideas about humanity. Heliocentric theory of the world and beginning of modern geography; spread of Gregorian calendar.

Phase II: The Incipient Phase. Lasting—mainly in Europe—from the mid-eighteenth century until the 1870s. Sharp shift towards the idea of the homogeneous, unitary state; crystallization of conceptions of formalized international relations, of standardized citizenly individuals and a more concrete conception of humankind. Sharp increases in legal conventions and agencies concerned with international and transnational regulation and communication. International exhibitions. Beginning of problem of 'admission' of non-European societies to 'international society.' Thematization of nationalism-internationalism issue.

Phase III: The Take-off Phase. Lasting from the 1870s until the mid-1920s. 'Take-off' here refers to a period during which the increasingly manifest globalizing tendencies of previous periods and

places gave way to a single, inexorable form centered upon the four reference points, and thus constraints, of national societies, generic individuals (but with a masculine bias), a single 'international society,' and an increasingly singular, but not unified conception of humankind. Early thematization of 'the problem of modernity.' Increasingly global conceptions of the 'correct outline' of an 'acceptable' national society; thematization of ideas concerning national and personal identities; inclusion of a number of non-European societies in 'international society'; international formalization and attempted implementation of ideas about humanity. Globalization of immigration restrictions. Very sharp increase in number and speed of global forms of communication. The first 'international novels.' Rise of ecumenical movement. Development of global competitions—for example the Olympics and Nobel prizes. Implementation of world time and near-global adoption of Gregorian calendar. First world war.

Phase IV: The Struggle-for-Hegemony Phase. Lasting from the mid-1920s until the late-1960s. Disputes and wars about the fragile terms of the dominant globalization process established by the end of the take-off period. Establishment of the League of Nations and then the United Nations. Principle of national independence established. Conflicting conceptions of modernity (Allies v. the Axis), followed by high point of the Cold War (conflict within 'the modern project'). Nature of and prospects for humanity sharply focused by the Holocaust and use of the atomic bomb. The crystallization of the Third World.

Phase V: The Uncertainty Phase. Beginning in the late 1960s and displaying crisis tendencies in the early 1990s. Heightening of global consciousness in late 1960s. Moon landing. Accentuation of 'post-materialist' values. End of the Cold War and manifest rise of the problem of 'rights' and widespread access to nuclear and thermonuclear weaponry. Number of global institutions and movements greatly increases. Sharp acceleration in means of global communication. Societies increasingly facing problems of multiculturality and polyethnicity. Conceptions of individuals rendered more complex by gender, sexual, ethnic and racial considerations. Civil rights become a global issue. International system more fluid—end of bipolarity. Concern with humankind as a species-community greatly enhanced, particularly via environmental movements. Arising of interest in world civil society and world citizenship, in spite of 'the ethnic revolution.' Consolidation of global media system, including rivalries about such. Islam as a deglobalizing/reglobalizing movement. Earth Summit in Rio de Janeiro.

This is merely an outline, with much detail and more rigorous analysis and interpretation of the shifting relationships between and the relative autonomization of each of the four major components to be worked out. Some of this is attempted in the following chapters. Clearly one of the most important empirical questions has to do with the extent to which the form of globalization which was set firmly in motion during the period 1870–1925 will 'hold' in the coming decades. In more theoretical vein, much more needs to be done to demonstrate the ways in which the selective responses of relevant collective actors, particularly societies, to globalization play a crucial part in the making of the world as a whole. Different forms of societal participation in the globalization process make a crucial difference to its precise form. My main point is that there is a general autonomy and 'logic' to the globalization process, which operates in *relative* independence of strictly societal and other more conventionally studied sociocultural processes. The global system is not simply an outcome of processes of basically intra-societal origin (*contra* Luhmann, 1982) or even a development of the inter-state system. Its making has been and continues to be much more complex than that.

Endnotes

1. It is of more than passing interest to note that in speaking of communism as a radical branch of one of 'the great "reform" movements of post-medieval Western history'—socialism—Talcott Parsons said in 1964 that 'it seems a safe prediction that Communism will, from its own internal dynamics, evolve in the direction of the restoration—or where it has yet not existed, the institution—of political democracy' (1964: 396–7). On

the other hand, Parsons insisted, problematically, that the *internationalism* of communism had made a crucial contribution to world order.

2. Ronald Inglehart (1990: 33) observes in the course of his empirical analysis of culture in advanced industrial societies 'that the publics of the three major Axis powers, Germany, Japan, and Italy, all tend to be underachievers in life satisfaction. The traumatic discrediting of their social and political systems that accompanied their defeat in World War II may have left a legacy of cynicism that their subsequent social change and economic success has still not entirely erased.'

3. I owe the precise phrases 'local-global nexus' and 'global-local nexus' to Chadwick Alger (1988).

References

Alger, C. (1988) 'Perceiving, analyzing and coping with the local-global nexus', *International Social Science Journal*, 117 (August).

Anderson, B. (1983) *Imagined Communities*. London: Verso.

Archer, M.S. (1988) *Culture and Agency: The Place of Culture in Social Theory*. Cambridge: Cambridge University Press.

Arendt, H. (1957) 'Karl Jaspers: citizen of the world', in P.A. Schlipp (ed.), *The Philosophy of Karl Jaspers*. La Salle, IL: Open Court.

Bentham, J. (1948) *The Principles of Morals and Legislation*. New York: Lafner.

Bergesen, A. (1980) 'From utilitarianism to globology: the shift from the individual to the world as a world as the primordial unit of analysis', in A. Bergesen (ed.), *Studies of the Modern World-System*. New York: Academic Press.

Bryant, C.G.A., and Jary, D. (1991) *Giddens's Theory of Structuration*. London: Routledge.

Bull, H. and Watson, A. (eds.) (1984) *The Expansion of International Society*. Oxford: Clarendon Press.

Cohen, I.J. (1989) *Structuration Theory: Anthony Giddens and the Constitution of Social Life*. New York: St Martin's Press.

Der Derian, J. (1989) 'The boundaries of knowledge and power in international relations', in J. Der Derian and M.J. Shapiro (eds.), *International/Intertextual Relations: Postmodern Readings of World Politics*. Lexington, MA: Lexington Books.

Der Derian, J., and Shapiro, J. (eds.) (1989) *International/Intertextual Relations: Postmodern Readings of World Politics*. Lexington, MA: Lexington Books.

Galtung, J. (1980) *The True Worlds: A Transnational Perspective*. New York: Free Press.

Giddens, A. (1987) *The Nation-State and Violence.* Berkeley: University of California Press.

Giddens, A. (1990) *The Consequences of Modernity.* Stanford, CA: Stanford University Press.

Giddens, A. and Turner, J. (1987) 'Introduction', in A Giddens and J. Turner (eds.), *Social Theory Today.* Stanford, CA: Stanford University Press.

Gong, G.W. (1984) *The Standard of 'Civilization' in International Society.* Oxford: Clarendon Press.

Hobhouse, L.T. (1906) *Morals in Evolution. A Study of Comparative Ethics*, Volume I. New York: Henry Holt.

Inglehart, R. (1990) *Culture Shift in Advanced Industrial Society.* Princeton, NJ: Princeton University Press.

Jaspers, K. (1957) 'Philosophical autobiography', in P.A. Schlipp (ed.), *The Philosophy of Karl Jaspers.* La Salle, IL: Open Court.

Kern, S. (1983) *The Culture of Time and Space, 1880–1918.* Cambridge, MA: Harvard University Press.

Kohn, 1971. (1971) 'Nationalism and internationalism', in W.W. Wager (ed.), *History and the Idea of Mankind.* Albuquerque: University of New Mexico Press.

Lechner, F.J. (1984) 'Ethnicity an d revitalization in the modern world system', *Sociological Focus*, 17 (3).

——. (1989) 'Cultural aspects of the modern world-system', in W.H. Swatos (ed.), *Religious Politics in Global and Comparative Perspective.* New York: Greenwood Press.

Lesourne, J.F. (1986) *World Perspectives: A European Assessment.* New York: Gordon & Breach.

Luhmann, N. (1982) 'The world society as a social system', *International Journal of General Systems*, 8.

Mann, Michael. (1986) *The Sources of Social Power: Volume I, A History of Power From the Beginning to AD 1760.* Cambridge: Cambridge University Press.

McNeill, W.H. (1986) *Polyethnicity and National Unity in World History.* Toronto: University of Toronto Press.

Meyer, J.W. (1980) 'The world polity and the authority of the nation-state', in A. Bergesend (ed.), *Studies of the Modern World System.* New York: Academic Press.

Moore, W.E. (1966) 'Global sociology: the world as a singular system', *American Journal of Sociology*, 71 (5).

Nettl, J.P. and Robertson, R. (1968) *International Systems and the Modernization of Societies: The Formation of National Goals and Attitudes.* New York: Basic Books.

Parsons, T. (1964) 'Communism and the West: the sociology of conflict', in A. Etzioni and E. Etzioni (eds.), *Social Change: Sources, Patterns and Consequence.* New York: Basic Books.

——. (1967) *Sociological Theory and Modern Society.* New York: Free Press.

Robertson, R. (1978) *Meaning and Change: Explorations in the Cultural Sociology of Modern Societies.* Oxford: Basil Blackwell.

——. (1989) 'Globalization, politics, and religion', in J.A. Beckford and T. Luckmann (eds.), *The Changing Face of Religion.* London: Sage.

Robertson, R., and Chirico, J. (1985) 'Humanity, globalization and worldwide religious resurgence: a theoretical exploration', *Sociological Analysis*, 46 (3).

Rosencrance, R. (1986) *The Rise of the Trading State: Commerce and Conquest in the Modern World.* New York: Basic Books.

Smith, A.D. (1979) *Nationalism in the Twentieth Century.* New York: New York University Press.

——. (1981) *The Ethnic Revival.* New York: Cambridge University Press.

Wagar, W.W. (ed.) (1971) *History and the Idea of Mankind.* Albuquerque: University of New Mexico Press.

Wallerstein, I. (1987) 'World-system analysis', in W.R. Thompson (ed.), *Contending Approaches to World System Analysis.* Stanford, CA: Stanford University Press.

Worsley, P. (1984) *The Three Worlds: Culture and Development.* London: Weidenfeld & Nicolson.

Wuthnow, R. (1978) 'Religious movements and the transition in world order', in J. Needleman and G. Baker (eds.), *Understanding the New Religions.* New York: Seabury Press.

72
Disjunction and Difference in the Global Cultural Economy

Arjun Appadurai

Despite differences among globalization theorists, there is a general consensus that globalization is a consequence of the reduction in the constraints of geography on economic, political, social, and cultural social arrangements—the result of a process that geographer David Harvey has called "time-space compression." While these various aspects of globalization are interconnected, they also need to be analytically distinguished. In this excerpt from *Modernity at Large* (1996), anthropologist Arjun Appadurai (b. 1949) focuses on globalization's cultural dimensions. More specifically, he is concerned with providing a framework intended to assist in our understanding of disjunctures in the global culture. He does so by defining five "dimensions of cultural flows," giving them the following distinctive names: ethnoscapes, mediascapes, technoscapes, financescapes, and ideoscapes.

It takes only the merest acquaintance with the facts of the modern world to note that it is now an interactive system in a sense that is strikingly new. Historians and sociologists, especially those concerned with translocal processes (Hodgson 1974) and the world systems associated with capitalism (Abu-Lughod 1989; Braudel 1981–84; Curtin 1984; Wallerstein 1974; Wolf 1982), have long been aware that the world has been a congeries of large-scale interactions for many centuries, Yet today's world involves interactions of a new order and intensity. Cultural transactions between social groups in the past have

generally been restricted, sometimes by the facts of geography and ecology, and at other times by active resistance to interactions with the Other (as in China for much of its history and in Japan before the Meiji Restoration). Where there have been sustained cultural transactions across large parts of the globe, they have usually involved the long-distance journey of commodities (and of the merchants most concerned with them) and of travelers and explorers of every type (Helms 1988; Schafer 1963). The two main forces for sustained cultural interaction before this century have been warfare (and the large-scale political systems sometimes generated by it) and religions of conversion, which have sometimes, as in the case of Islam, taken warfare as one of the legitimate instruments of their expansion. Thus, between travelers and merchants, pilgrims and conquerors, the world has seen much long-distance (and long-term) cultural traffic. This much seems self-evident.

But few will deny that given the problems of time, distance, and limited technologies for the command of resources across vast spaces, cultural dealings between socially and spatially separated groups have, until the past few centuries, been bridged at great cost and sustained over time only with great effort. The forces of cultural gravity seemed always to pull away from the formation of large-scale ecumenes, whether religious, commercial, or political, toward smaller-scale accretions of intimacy and interest.

Sometime in the past few centuries, the nature of this gravitational field seems to have changed. Partly because of the spirit of the expansion of Western maritime interests after 1500, and partly because of the relatively autonomous developments of large and aggressive social formations in the Americas (such as the Aztecs and the Incas), in Eurasia (such as the Mongols and their descendants, the Mughals and Ottomans), in island Southeast Asia (such as the Buginese), and in the kingdoms of precolonial Africa (such as Dahomey), an overlapping set of ecumenes began to emerge, in which congeries of money, commerce, conquest, and migration began to create durable cross-societal bonds. This process was accelerated by the technology transfers and innovations of the late eighteenth and nineteenth centuries (e.g., Bayly 1989), which created complex colonial orders centered on European capitals and spread throughout the non-European world. This intricate and overlapping set of Eurocolonial worlds (first Spanish and Portuguese, later principally English, French, and Dutch) set the basis for a permanent traffic in ideas of peoplehood and selfhood, which created the imagined communities (Anderson 1983) of recent nationalisms throughout the world.

With what Benedict Anderson has called "print capitalism," a new power was unleashed in the world, the power of mass literacy and its attendant large-scale production of projects of ethnic affinity that were remarkably free of the need for face-to-face communication or even of indirect communication between persons and groups. The act of reading things together set the stage for movements based on a paradox—the paradox of constructed primordialism. There is, of course, a great deal else that is involved in the story of colonialism and its dialectically generated nationalisms (Chatterjee 1986), but the issue of constructed ethnicities is surely a crucial strand in this tale.

But the revolution of print capitalism and the cultural affinities and dialogues unleashed by it were only modest precursors to the world we live in now. For in the past century, there has been a technological explosion, largely in the domain of transportation and information, that makes the interactions of a print-dominated world seem as hard-won and as easily erased as the print revolution made earlier forms of cultural traffic appear. For with the advent of the steamship, the automobile, the airplane, the camera, the computer, and the telephone, we have entered into an altogether new condition of neighborliness, even with those most distant from ourselves. Marshall McLuhan, among others, sought to theorize about this world as a "global village," but theories such as McLuhan s appear to have overestimated the communitarian implications of the new media order (McLuhan and Powers 1989). We are now aware that with media, each time we are tempted to speak of the global village, we must be reminded that media cre-

ate communities with "no sense of place" (Meyrowitz 1985). The world we live in now seems rhizomic (Deleuze and Guattari 1987), even schizophrenic, calling for theories of rootlessness, alienation, and psychological distance between individuals and groups on the one hand, and fantasies (or nightmares) of electronic propinquity on the other. Here, we are close to the central problematic of cultural processes in today's world.

Thus, the curiosity that recently drove Pico Iyer to Asia (1988) is in some ways the product of a confusion between some ineffable McDonaldization of the world and the much subtler play of indigenous trajectories of desire and fear with global flows of people and things. Indeed, Iyer's own impressions are testimony to the fact that, if *a* global cultural system is emerging, it is filled with ironies and resistances, sometimes camouflaged as passivity and a bottomless appetite in the Asian world for things Western.

Iyer's own account of the uncanny Philippine affinity for American popular music is rich testimony to the global culture of the hyperreal, for somehow Philippine renditions of American popular songs are both more widespread in the Philippines, and more disturbingly faithful to their originals, than they are in the United States today. An entire nation seems to have learned to mimic Kenny Rogers and the Lennon sisters, like a vast Asian Motown chorus. But *Americanization* is certainly a pallid term to apply to such a situation, for not only are there more Filipinos singing perfect renditions of some American songs (often from the American past) than there are Americans doing so, there is also, of course, the fact that the rest of their lives is not in complete synchrony with the referential world that first gave birth to these songs.

In a further globalizing twist on what Fredric Jameson has recently called "nostalgia for the present" (1989), these Filipinos look back to a world they have never lost. This is one of the central ironies of the politics of global cultural flows, especially in the arena of entertainment and leisure. It plays havoc with the hegemony of Eurochronology. American nostalgia feeds on Filipino desire represented as a hypercompetent reproduction. Here, we have nostalgia without memory. The paradox, of course, has its explanations, and they are historical; unpacked, they lay bare the story of the American missionization and political rape of the Philippines, one result of which has been the creation of a nation of make-believe Americans, who tolerated for so long a leading lady who played the piano while the slums of Manila expanded and decayed. Perhaps the most radical postmodernists would argue that this is hardly surprising because in the peculiar chronicities of late capitalism, pastiche and nostalgia are central modes of image production and reception. Americans themselves are hardly in the present anymore as they stumble into the mega-technologies of the twenty-first century garbed in the film-noir scenarios of sixties' chills, fifties' diners, forties' clothing, thirties' houses, twenties' dances, and so on ad infinitum.

As far as the United States is concerned, one might suggest that the issue is no longer one of nostalgia but of a social *imaginaire* built largely around reruns. Jameson was bold to link the politics of nostalgia to the postmodern commodity sensibility, and surely he was right (1983). The drug wars in Colombia recapitulate the tropical sweat of Vietnam, with Ollie North and his succession of masks—Jimmy Stewart concealing John Wayne concealing Spiro Agnew and all of them transmogrifying into Sylvester Stallone, who wins in Afghanistan—thus simultaneously fulfilling the secret American envy of Soviet imperialism and the rerun (this time with a happy ending) of the Vietnam War. The Rolling Stones, approaching their fifties, gyrate before eighteen-year-olds who do not appear to need the machinery of nostalgia to be sold on their parents' heroes. Paul McCartney is selling the Beatles to a new audience by hitching his oblique nostalgia to their desire for the new that smacks of the old. *Dragnet* is back in nineties' drag, and so is *Adam-12*, not to speak of *Batman* and *Mission Impossible*, all dressed up technologically but remarkably faithful to the atmospherics of their originals.

The past is now not a land to return to in a simple politics of memory. It has become a synchronic warehouse of cultural scenarios, a kind of temporal central casting, to which recourse can be taken as appropriate, depending on the movie to be made, the scene to be enacted, the hostages to be rescued. All this is par for the course, if you follow Jean Baudrillard or Jean-Francois Lyotard into a world of signs wholly unmoored from their social signifiers (all the world's a Disneyland). But I would like to suggest that the apparent increasing substitutability of whole periods and postures for one another, in the cultural styles of advanced capitalism, is tied to larger global forces, which have done much to show Americans that the past is usually another country. If your present is their future (as in much modernization theory and in many self-satisfied tourist fantasies), and their future is your past (as in the case of the Filipino virtuosos of American popular music), then your own past can be made to appear as simply a normalized modality of your present. Thus, although some anthropologists may continue to relegate their Others to temporal spaces that they do not themselves occupy (Fabian 1983), postindustrial cultural productions have entered a postnostalgic phase.

The crucial point, however, is that the United States is no longer the puppeteer of a world system of images but is only one node of a complex transnational construction of imaginary landscapes. The world we live in today is characterized by a new role for the imagination in social life. To grasp this new role, we need to bring together the old idea of images, especially mechanically produced images (in the Frankfurt School sense); the idea of the imagined community (in Anderson's sense); and the French idea of the imaginary (*imaginaire*) as a constructed landscape of collective aspirations, which is no more and no less real than the collective representations of Émile Durkheim, now mediated through the complex prism of modern media.

The image, the imagined, the imaginary—these are all terms that direct us to something critical and new in global cultural processes: *the imagination as a social practice.* No longer mere fantasy (opium for the masses whose real work is elsewhere), no longer simple escape (from a world defined principally by more concrete purposes and structures), no longer elite pastime (thus not relevant to the lives of ordinary people), and no longer mere contemplation (irrelevant for new forms of desire and subjectivity), the imagination has become an organized field of social practices, a form of work (in the sense of both labor and culturally organized practice), and a form of negotiation between sites of agency (individuals) and globally defined fields of possibility. This unleashing of the imagination links the play of pastiche (in some settings) to the terror and coercion of states and their competitors. The imagination is now central to all forms of agency, is itself a social fact, and is the key component of the new global order. But to make this claim meaningful, we must address some other issues.

Homogenization and Heterogenization

The central problem of today's global interactions is the tension between cultural homogenization and cultural heterogenization. A vast array of empirical facts could be brought to bear on the side of the homogenization argument, and much of it has come from the left end of the spectrum of media studies (Hamelink 1983; Mattelart 1983; Schiller 1976), and some from other perspectives (Gans 1985; Iyer 1988). Most often, the homogenization argument subspeciates into either an argument about Americanization or an argument about commoditization, and very often the two arguments are closely linked. What these arguments fail to consider is that at least as rapidly as forces from various metropolises are brought into new societies they tend to become indigenized in one or another way: this is true of music and housing styles as much as it is true of science and terrorism, spectacles and constitutions. The dynamics of such indigenization have just begun to be explored systemically (Barber 1987; Feld 1988; Hannerz 1987, 1989; Ivy 1988; Nicoll 1989; Yoshimoto 1989), and much more needs to be done. But it is worth noticing that for the people of Irian Jaya, Indonesianization may be more worrisome than Americanization, as Japanization may be for Koreans, Indianization for Sri Lankans, Vietnamization for the Cambodians, and Russianization for the people of

Soviet Armenia and the Baltic republics. Such a list of alternative fears to Americanization could be greatly expanded, but it is not a shapeless inventory: for polities of smaller scale, there is always a fear of cultural absorption by polities of larger scale, especially those that are nearby. One man's imagined community is another man's political prison.

This scalar dynamic, which has widespread global manifestations, is also tied to the relationship between nations and states, to which I shall return later. For the moment let us note that the simplification of these many forces (and fears) of homogenization can also be exploited by nation-states in relation to their own minorities, by posing global commoditization (or capitalism, or some other such external enemy) as more real than the threat of its own hegemonic strategies.

The new global cultural economy has to be seen as a complex, overlapping, disjunctive order that cannot any longer be understood in terms of existing center-periphery models (even those that might account for multiple centers and peripheries). Nor is it susceptible to simple models of push and pull (in terms of migration theory), or of surpluses and deficits (as in traditional models of balance of trade), or of consumers and producers (as in most neo-Marxist theories of development). Even the most complex and flexible theories of global development that have come out of the Marxist tradition (Amin 1980; Mandel 1978; Wallerstein 1974; Wolf 1982) are inadequately quirky and have failed to come to terms with what Scott Lash and John Urry have called disorganized capitalism (1987). The complexity of the current global economy has to do with certain fundamental disjunctures between economy, culture, and politics that we have only begun to theorize.[1]

I propose that an elementary framework for exploring such disjunctures is to look at the relationship among five dimensions of global cultural flows that can be termed (a) *ethnoscapes*, (b) *mediascapes*, (c) *technoscapes*, (d) *financescapes*, and (e) *ideoscapes*.[2] The suffix *-scape* allows us to point to the fluid, irregular shapes of these landscapes, shapes that characterize international capital as deeply as they do international clothing styles. These terms with the common suffix -scape also indicate that these are not objectively given relations that look the same from every angle of vision but, rather, that they are deeply perspectival constructs, inflected by the historical, linguistic, and political situatedness of different sorts of actors: nation-states, multinationals, diasporic communities, as well as subnational groupings and movements (whether religious, political, or economic), and even intimate face-to-face groups, such as villages, neighborhoods, and families. Indeed, the individual actor is the last locus of this perspectival set of landscapes, for these landscapes are eventually navigated by agents who both experience and constitute larger formations, in part from their own sense of what these landscapes offer.

These landscapes thus are the building blocks of what (extending Benedict Anderson) I would like to call *imagined worlds*, that is, the multiple worlds that are constituted by the historically situated imaginations of persons and groups spread around the globe. . . . An important fact of the world we live in today is that many persons on the globe live in such imagined worlds (and not just in imagined communities) and thus are able to contest and sometimes even subvert the imagined worlds of the official mind and of the entrepreneurial mentality that surround them.

By *ethnoscape*, I mean the landscape of persons who constitute the shifting world in which we live: tourists, immigrants, refugees, exiles, guest workers, and other moving groups and individuals constitute an essential feature of the world and appear to affect the politics of (and between) nations to a hitherto unprecedented degree. This is not to say that there are no relatively stable communities and networks of kinship, friendship, work, and leisure as well as of birth, residence, and other filial forms. But it is to say that the warp of these stabilities is everywhere shot through with the woof of human motion, as more persons and groups deal with the realities of having to move or the fantasies of wanting to move. What is more, both these realities and fantasies now function on larger scales, as men and women

from villages in India think not just of moving to Poona or Madras but of moving to Dubai and Houston, and refugees from Sri Lanka find themselves in South India as well as in Switzerland, just as the Hmong are driven to London as well as to Philadelphia. And as international capital shifts its needs, as production and technology generate different needs, as nation-states shift their policies on refugee populations, these moving groups can never afford to let their imaginations rest too long, even if they wish to.

By *technoscape*, I mean the global configuration, also ever fluid, of technology and the fact that technology, both high and low, both mechanical and informational, now moves at high speeds across various kinds of previously impervious boundaries. Many countries now are the roots of multinational enterprise: a huge steel complex in Libya may involve interests from India, China, Russia, and Japan, providing different components of new technological configurations. The odd distribution of technologies, and thus the peculiarities of these technoscapes, are increasingly driven not by any obvious economies of scale, of political control, or of market rationality but by increasingly complex relationships among money flows, political possibilities, and the availability of both un- and highly skilled labor. So, while India exports waiters and chauffeurs to Dubai and Sharjah, it also exports software engineers to the United States—indentured briefly to Tata-Burroughs or the World Bank, then laundered through the State Department to become wealthy resident aliens, who are in turn objects of seductive messages to invest their money and know-how in federal and state projects in India.

The global economy can still be described in terms of traditional indicators (as the World Bank continues to do) and studied in terms of traditional comparisons (as in Project Link at the University of Pennsylvania), but the complicated technoscapes (and the shifting ethnoscapes) that underlie these indicators and comparisons are further out of the reach of the queen of social sciences than ever before. How is one to make a meaningful comparison of wages in Japan and the United States or of real-estate costs in New

York and Tokyo, without taking sophisticated account of the very complex fiscal and investment flows that link the two economies through a global grid of currency speculation and capital transfer?

Thus it is useful to speak as well of *financescapes*, as the disposition of global capital is now a more mysterious, rapid, and difficult landscape to follow than ever before, as currency markets, national stock exchanges, and commodity speculations move megamonies through national turnstiles at blinding speed, with vast, absolute implications for small differences in percentage points and time units. But the critical point is that the global relationship among ethnoscapes, technoscapes, and financescapes is deeply disjunctive and profoundly unpredictable because each of these landscapes is subject to its own constraints and incentives (some political, some informational, and some technoenvironmental), at the same time as each acts as a constraint and a parameter for movements in the others. Thus, even an elementary model of global political economy must take into account the deeply disjunctive relationships among human movement, technological flow, and financial transfers.

Further refracting these disjunctures (which hardly form a simple, mechanical global infrastructure in any case) are what I call *mediascapes* and *ideoscapes*, which are closely related landscapes of images. *Mediascapes* refer both to the distribution of the electronic capabilities to produce and disseminate information (newspapers, magazines, television stations, and film-production studios), which are now available to a growing number of private and public interests throughout the world, and to the images of the world created by these media. These images involve many complicated inflections, depending on their mode (documentary or entertainment), their hardware (electronic or preelectronic), their audiences (local, national, or transnational), and the interests of those who own and control them. What is most important about these mediascapes is that they provide (especially in their television, film, and cassette forms) large and complex repertoires of images, narratives, and ethnoscapes to viewers throughout the world, in which the world of commodities and the world of news and politics are profoundly mixed. What this means is that many audiences around the world experience the media themselves as a complicated and interconnected repertoire of print, celluloid, electronic screens, and billboards. The lines between the realistic and the fictional landscapes they see are blurred, so that the farther away these audiences are from the direct experiences of metropolitan life, the more likely they are to construct imagined worlds that are chimerical, aesthetic, even fantastic objects, particularly if assessed by the criteria of some other perspective, some other imagined world.

Mediascapes, whether produced by private or state interests, tend to be image-centered, narrative-based accounts of strips of reality, and what they offer to those who experience and transform them is a series of elements (such as characters, plots, and textual forms) out of which scripts can be formed of imagined lives, their own as well as those of others living in other places. These scripts can and do get disaggregated into complex sets of metaphors by which people live (Lakoff and Johnson 1980) as they help to constitute narratives of the Other and protonarratives of possible lives, fantasies that could become prolegomena to the desire for acquisition and movement.

Ideoscapes are also concatenations of images, but they are often directly political and frequently have to do with the ideologies of states and the counterideologies of movements explicitly oriented to capturing state power or a piece of it. These ideoscapes are composed of elements of the Enlightenment worldview, which consists of a chain of ideas, terms, and images, including *freedom, welfare, rights, sovereignty, representation,* and the master term *democracy.* The master narrative of the Enlightenment (and its many variants in Britain, France, and the United States) was constructed with a certain internal logic and presupposed a certain relationship between reading, representation, and the public sphere. (For the dynamics of this process in the early history of the United States, see Warner 1990.) But the diaspora of these terms and images across the world, especially since the nineteenth century, has loosened the internal coherence that held them together in a Euro-American master narrative and provided instead a loosely structured synopticon of politics, in which different nation-states, as part of their evolution, have organized their political cultures around different keywords (e.g., Williams 1976).

As a result of the differential diaspora of these keywords, the political narratives that govern communication between elites and followers in different parts of the world involve problems of both a semantic and pragmatic nature: semantic to the extent that words (and their lexical equivalents) require careful translation from context to context in their global movements, and pragmatic to the extent that the use of these words by political actors and their audiences may be subject to very different sets of contextual conventions that mediate their translation into public politics. Such conventions are not only matters of the nature of political rhetoric: for example, what does the aging Chinese leadership mean when it refers to the dangers of hooliganism? What does the South Korean leadership mean when it speaks of discipline as the key to democratic industrial growth?

These conventions also involve the far more subtle question of what sets of communicative genres are valued in what way (newspapers versus cinema, for example) and what sorts of pragmatic genre conventions govern the collective readings of different kinds of text. So, while an Indian audience may be attentive to the resonances of a political speech in terms of some keywords and phrases reminiscent of Hindi cinema, a Korean audience may respond to the subtle codings of Buddhist or neo-Confucian rhetoric encoded in a political document. The very relationship of reading to hearing and seeing may vary in important ways that determine the morphology of these different ideoscapes as they shape themselves in different national and transnational contexts. This globally variable synaesthesia has hardly even been noted, but it demands urgent analysis. Thus *democracy* has clearly become a master term, with powerful echoes from Haiti and Poland to the former Soviet Union and China, but it sits at the center of a variety of ideoscapes, composed of distinctive pragmatic configurations of rough translations of other central terms from the vocabulary of the Enlightenment. This creates ever new terminological kaleidoscopes, as states (and the groups that seek to capture them) seek to pacify populations whose own ethnoscapes are in motion and whose mediascapes may create severe problems for the ideoscapes with which they are presented. The fluidity of ideoscapes is complicated in particular by the growing diasporas (both voluntary and involuntary) of intellectuals who continuously inject new meaning-streams into the discourse of democracy in different parts of the world.

This extended terminological discussion of the five terms I have coined sets the basis for a tentative formulation about the conditions under which current global flows occur: they occur in and through the growing disjunctures among ethnoscapes, technoscapes, financescapes, mediascapes, and ideoscapes. This formulation, the core of my model of global cultural flow, needs some explanation. First, people, machinery, money, images, and ideas now follow increasingly nonisomorphic paths; of course, at all periods in human history, there have been some disjunctures in the flows of these things, but the sheer speed, scale, and volume of each of these flows are now so great that the disjunctures have become central to the politics of global culture. The Japanese are notoriously hospitable to ideas and are stereotyped as inclined to export (all) and import (some) goods, but they are also notoriously closed to immigration, like the Swiss, the Swedes, and the Saudis. Yet the Swiss and the Saudis accept populations of guest workers, thus creating labor diasporas of Turks, Italians, and other circum-Mediterranean groups. Some such guest-worker groups maintain continuous contact with their home nations, like the Turks, but others, like high-level South Asian migrants, tend to desire lives in their new homes, raising anew the problem of reproduction in a deterritorialized context.

Deterritorialization, in general, is one of the central forces of the modern world because it brings laboring populations into the lower-class sectors and spaces of relatively wealthy societies, while sometimes creating exaggerated and intensified senses of criticism or attachment to politics in the home state. Deterritorialization, whether of Hindus, Sikhs, Palestinians, or Ukrainians, is now at the core of a variety of global fundamentalisms, including Islamic and Hindu fundamentalism. In the Hindu case, for example, it is clear that the overseas movement of Indians has been exploited by a variety of interests both within and outside India to create a complicated network of finances and religious identifications, by which the problem of cultural reproduction for Hindus abroad has become tied to the politics of Hindu fundamentalism at home.

At the same time, deterritorialization creates new markets for film companies, art impresarios, and travel agencies, which thrive on the need of the deterritorialized population for contact with its homeland. Naturally, these invented homelands, which constitute the mediascapes of deterritorialized groups, can often become sufficiently fantastic and one-sided that they provide the material for new ideoscapes in which ethnic conflicts can begin to erupt. The creation of Khalistan, an invented homeland of the deterritorialized Sikh population of England, Canada, and the United States, is one example of the bloody potential in such mediascapes as they interact with the internal colonialisms of the nation-state (e.g., Hechter 1975). The West Bank, Namibia, and Eritrea are other theaters for the enactment of the bloody negotiation between existing nation-states and various deterritorialized groupings.

It is in the fertile ground of deterritorialization, in which money, commodities, and persons are involved in ceaselessly chasing each other around the world, that the mediascapes and ideoscapes of the modern world find their fractured and fragmented counterpart. For the ideas and images produced by mass media often are only partial guides to the goods and experiences that deterritorialized populations transfer to one another. In Mira Nair's brilliant film *India Cabaret*, we see the multiple loops of this fractured deterritorialization as young women, barely competent in Bombay's metropolitan glitz, come to seek their fortunes as cabaret dancers and prostitutes in Bombay, entertaining men in clubs with dance formats derived wholly from the prurient dance sequences of Hindi films. These scenes in turn cater to ideas about Western and foreign women and their looseness, while they provide tawdry career alibis for these women. Some of these women come from Kerala, where cabaret clubs and the pornographic film industry have blossomed, partly in response to the purses and tastes of Keralites returned from the Middle East, where their diasporic lives away from women distort their very sense of what the relations between men and women might be. These tragedies of displacement could certainly be replayed in a more detailed analysis of the relations between the Japanese and German sex tours to Thailand and the tragedies of the sex trade in Bangkok, and in other similar loops that tie together fantasies about the Other, the conveniences and seductions of travel, the economics of global trade, and the brutal mobility fantasies that dominate gender politics in many parts of Asia and the world at large.

While far more could be said about the cultural politics of deterritorialization and the larger sociology of displacement that it expresses, it is appropriate at this juncture to bring in the role of the nation-state in the disjunctive global economy of culture today. The relationship between states and nations is everywhere an embattled one. It is possible to say that in many societies the nation and the state have become one another's projects. That is, while nations (or more properly groups with ideas about nationhood) seek to capture or co-opt states and state power, states simultaneously seek to capture and monopolize ideas about nationhood (Baruah 1986; Chatterjee 1986; Nandy 1989). In general, separatist transnational movements, including those that have included terror in their methods, exemplify nations in search of states. Sikhs, Tamil Sri Lankans, Basques, Moros, Quebecois—each of these represents imagined communities that seek to create states of their own or carve pieces out of existing states. States, on the other hand, are everywhere seeking to monopolize the moral resources of community, either by flatly claiming perfect coevality between nation and state, or by systematically museumizing and representing all the groups within them in a variety of heritage politics that seems remarkably uniform throughout the world (Handler 1988; Herzfeld 1982; McQueen 1988).

Here, national and international mediascapes are exploited by nation-states to pacify separatists or even the potential fissiparousness of all ideas of difference. Typically, contemporary nation-states do this by exercising taxonomic control over difference, by creating various kinds of international spectacle to domesticate difference, and by seducing small groups with the fantasy of self-display on some sort of global or cosmopolitan stage. One important new feature of global cultural politics, tied to the disjunctive relationships among the various landscapes discussed earlier, is that state and nation are at each other's throats, and the hyphen that links them is now less an icon of conjuncture than an index of disjuncture. This disjunctive relationship between nation and state has two levels: at the level of any given nation-state, it means that there is a battle of the imagination, with state and nation seeking to cannibalize one another. Here is the seedbed of brutal separatisms—majoritarianisms that seem to have appeared from nowhere and microidentities that have become political projects within the nation-state. At another level, this disjunctive relationship is deeply entangled with the global disjunctures discussed throughout this chapter: ideas of nationhood appear to be steadily increasing in scale and regularly crossing existing state boundaries, sometimes, as with the Kurds, because previous identities stretched across vast national spaces or, as with the Tamils in Sri Lanka, the dormant threads of a transnational diaspora have been activated to ignite the micropolitics of a nation-state.

In discussing the cultural politics that have subverted the hyphen that links the nation to the state, it is especially important not to forget the mooring of such politics in the irregularities that now characterize disorganized capital (Kothari 1989; Lash and Urry 1987). Because labor, finance, and technology are now so widely separated, the volatilities that underlie movements for na-

tionhood (as large as transnational Islam on the one hand, or as small as the movement of the Gurkhas for a separate state in Northeast India) grind against the vulnerabilities that characterize the relationships between states. States find themselves pressed to stay open by the forces of media, technology, and travel that have fueled consumerism throughout the world and have increased the craving, even in the non-Western world, for new commodities and spectacles. On the other hand, these very cravings can become caught up in new ethnoscapes, mediascapes, and, eventually, ideoscapes, such as democracy in China, that the state cannot tolerate as threats to its own control over ideas of nationhood and peoplehood. States throughout the world are under siege, especially where contests over the ideoscapes of democracy are fierce and fundamental, and where there are radical disjunctures between ideoscapes and technoscapes (as in the case of very small countries that lack contemporary technologies of production and information); or between ideoscapes and financescapes (as in countries such as Mexico or Brazil, where international lending influences national politics to a very large degree); or between ideoscapes and ethnoscapes (as in Beirut, where diasporic, local, and translocal filiations are suicidally at battle); or between ideoscapes and mediascapes (as in many countries in the Middle East and Asia) where the lifestyles represented on both national and international TV and cinema completely overwhelm and undermine the rhetoric of national politics. In the Indian case, the myth of the law-breaking hero has emerged to mediate this naked struggle between the pieties and realities of Indian politics, which has grown increasingly brutalized and corrupt (Vachani 1989).

The transnational movement of the martial arts, particularly through Asia, as mediated by the Hollywood and Hong Kong film industries (Zarilli 1995) is a rich illustration of the ways in which long-standing martial arts traditions, reformulated to meet the fantasies of contemporary (sometimes lumpen) youth populations, create new cultures of masculinity and violence, which are in turn the fuel for increased violence in national and international politics. Such violence is in turn the spur to an increasingly rapid and amoral arms trade that penetrates the entire world. The worldwide spread of the AK-47 and the Uzi, in films, in corporate and state security, in terror, and in police and military activity, is a reminder that apparently simple technical uniformities often conceal an increasingly complex set of loops, linking images of violence to aspirations for community in some imagined world.

Returning then to the ethnoscapes with which I began, the central paradox of ethnic politics in today's world is that primordia (whether of language or skin color or neighborhood or kinship) have become globalized. That is, sentiments, whose greatest force is in their ability to ignite intimacy into a political state and turn locality into a staging ground for identity, have become spread over vast and irregular spaces as groups move yet stay linked to one another through sophisticated media capabilities. This is not to deny that such primordia are often the product of invented traditions (Hobsbawm and Ranger 1983) or retrospective affiliations, but to emphasize that because of the disjunctive and unstable interplay of commerce, media, national policies, and consumer fantasies, ethnicity, once a genie contained in the bottle of some sort of locality (however large), has now become a global force, forever slipping in and through the cracks between states and borders.

But the relationship between the cultural and economic levels of this new set of global disjunctures is not a simple one-way street in which the terms of global cultural politics are set wholly by, or confined wholly within, the vicissitudes of international flows of technology, labor, and finance, demanding only a modest modification of existing neo-Marxist models of uneven development and state formation. There is a deeper change, itself driven by the disjunctures among all the landscapes I have discussed and constituted by their continuously fluid and uncertain interplay, that concerns the relationship between production and consumption in today's global economy. Here, I begin with Marx's famous (and often mined) view of the fetishism of the commodity and suggest that this fetishism has been replaced in the world

at large (now seeing the world as one large, interactive system, composed of many complex subsystems) by two mutually supportive descendants, the first of which I call production fetishism and the second, the fetishism of the consumer.

By *production fetishism* I mean an illusion created by contemporary transnational production loci that masks translocal capital, transnational earning flows, global management, and often faraway workers (engaged in various kinds of high-tech putting-out operations) in the idiom and spectacle of local (sometimes even worker) control, national productivity, and territorial sovereignty. To the extent that various kinds of free-trade zones have become the models for production at large, especially of high-tech commodities, production has itself become a fetish, obscuring not social relations as such but the relations of production, which are increasingly transnational. The locality (both in the sense of the local factory or site of production and in the extended sense of the nation-state) becomes a fetish that disguises the globally dispersed forces that actually drive the production process. This generates alienation (in Marx's sense) twice intensified, for its social sense is now compounded by a complicated spatial dynamic that is increasingly global.

As for the *fetishism of the consumer,* I mean to indicate here that the consumer has been transformed through commodity flows (and the mediascapes, especially of advertising, that accompany them) into a sign, both in Baudrillard's sense of a simulacrum that only asymptotically approaches the form of a real social agent, and in the sense of a mask for the real seat of agency, which is not the consumer but the producer and the many forces that constitute production. Global advertising is the key technology for the worldwide dissemination of a plethora of creative and culturally well-chosen ideas of consumer agency. These images of agency are increasingly distortions of a world of merchandising so subtle that the consumer is consistently helped to believe that he or she is an actor, where in fact he or she is at best a chooser.

The globalization of culture is not the same as its homogenization, but globalization involves the use of a variety of instruments of homogenization (armaments, advertising techniques, language hegemonies, and clothing styles) that are absorbed into local political and cultural economies, only to be repatriated as heterogeneous dialogues of national sovereignty, free enterprise, and fundamentalism in which the state plays an increasingly delicate role: too much openness to global flows, and the nation-state is threatened by revolt, as in the China syndrome; too little, and the state exits the international stage, as Burma, Albania, and North Korea in various ways have done. In general, the state has become the arbitrageur of this *repatriation of difference* (in the form of goods, signs, slogans, and styles). But this repatriation or export of the designs and commodities of difference continuously exacerbates the internal politics of majoritarianism and homogenization, which is most frequently played out in debates over heritage.

Thus the central feature of global culture today is the politics of the mutual effort of sameness and difference to cannibalize one another and thereby proclaim their successful hijacking of the twin Enlightenment ideas of the triumphantly universal and the resiliency particular. This mutual cannibalization shows its ugly face in riots, refugee flows, state-sponsored torture, and ethnocide (with or without state support). Its brighter side is in the expansion of many individual horizons of hope and fantasy, in the global spread of oral rehydration therapy and other low-tech instruments of well-being, in the susceptibility even of South Africa to the force of global opinion, in the inability of the Polish state to repress its own working classes, and in the growth of a wide range of progressive, transnational alliances. Examples of both sorts could be multiplied. The critical point is that both sides of the coin of global cultural process today are products of the infinitely varied mutual contest of sameness and difference on a stage characterized by radical disjunctures between different sorts of global flows and the uncertain landscapes created in and through these disjunctures.

References

Abu-Lughod, L. (1989) *Before European Hegemony: The World System A.D. 1250–1350*. New York: Oxford University Press.

Amin, S. (1980) *Class and Nation: Historically and in the Current Crisis*. New York and London: Monthly Review Press.

Anderson, B. (1983) *Imagined Communities: Reflections on the Origin and Spread of Nationalism*. London: Verso.

Barber, K. (1987) Popular Arts in Africa, *African Studies Review* 30 (3, September): 1–78.

Barrier, G. N. (Ed.) (1981) *The Census in British India: New Perspectives*. New Delhi: Manohar.

Barth, F. (Ed.) (1969) *Ethnic Groups and Boundaries*. Boston: Little, Brown.

Baruah, S. (1986) Immigration, Ethnic Conflict and Political Turmoil, Assam 1979–1985, *Asian Survey* 26 (11, November): 1184–1206.

Bayly, C. A. (1989) *Imperial Meridian: The British Empire and the World, 1780–1830*. London and New York: Longman.

Braudel, F. (1981–1984) *Civilization and Capitalism, 15th–18th Century* (3 vols.). London: Collins.

Chatterjee, P. (1986) *Nationalist Thought and the Colonial World: A Derivative Discourse?* London: Zed Books.

Curtin, P. (1984) *Cross-Cultural Trade in World History*. Cambridge: Cambridge University Press.

Deleuze, G., and F. Guattari (1987) *A Thousand Plateaus: Capitalism and Schizophrenia*. B. Massumi (trans.). Minneapolis: University of Minnesota Press.

Fabian, J. (1983) *Time and the Other: How Anthropology Makes Its Object*. New York: Columbia University Press.

Feld, S. (1988) Notes on World Beat, *Public Culture* 1 (1): 31–37.

Gans, E. (1985) *The End of a Culture: Toward a Generative Anthropology*. Berkeley: University of California Press.

Hamelink, C. (1983) *Cultural Autonomy in Global Communications*. New York: Longman.

Handler, R. (1988) *Nationalism and the Politics of Culture in Quebec*. Madison: University of Wisconsin Press.

Hannerz, U. (1987) The World in Creolization, *Africa* 57 (4): 546–59.

——. (1989) Notes on the Global Ecumene, *Public Culture* 1 (2, Spring): 66–75.

Hechter, M. (1975) *Internal Colonialism: The Celtic Fringe in British National Development, 4536–4966*. Berkeley: University of California Press.

Helms, M. W. (1988) *Ulysses' Sail: An Ethnographic Odyssey of Power, Knowledge,* and Geographical Distance. Princeton, N.J.: Princeton University Press.

Herzfeld, M. (1982) *Ours Once More: Folklore, Ideology and the Making of Modern Greece*. Austin: University of Texas Press.

Hobsbawm, E., and T. Ranger (Eds.) (1983) *The Invention of Tradition*. New York: Columbia University Press.

Hodgson, M. (1974) *The Venture of Islam, Conscience and History in a World Civilization*. (3 vols.) Chicago: University of Chicago Press.

Ivy, M. (1988) Tradition and Difference in the Japanese Mass Media, *Public Culture* 1 (1): 21–29.

Iyer, P. (1988) *Video Night in Kathmandu*. New York: Knopf.

Jameson, F. (1983) Postmodernism and Consumer Society. In H. Foster (Ed.) *The Anti-Aesthetic: Essays on Postmodern Culture*. Port Townsend, Wash.: Bay Press, 111–25.

———. (1989) *State Against Democracy: In Search of Humane Governance*. New York: New Horizons.

Kothari, R. (1989). *State against Democracy: In Search of Humane Alternatives*. Delhi: Ajanta Publications. New York: New Horizon Press.

Lakoff, G., and M. Johnson (1980) *Metaphors We Live By*. Chicago and London: University of Chicago Press.

Lash, S., and J. Urry (1987) *The End of Organized Capitalism*. Madison: University of Wisconsin Press.

Mandel, E. (1978) *Late Capitalism*. London: Verso.

Mattelart, A. (1983) *Transnationals and the Third World: The Struggle for Culture*. South Hadley, Mass.: Bergin and Garvey.

McLuhan M., and B. R. Powers. (1989) *The Global Village: Transformations in World, Life and Media in the 2ist Century*. New York: Oxford University Press.

McQueen, H. (1988) The Australian Stamp: Image, Design and Ideology, *Arena* 84 (Spring): 78–96.

Meyrowitz, J. (1985) *No Sense of Place: The Impact of Electronic Media on Social Behavior*. New York: Oxford University Press.

Nandy, A. (1989) The Political Culture of the Indian State, *Daedalus* 118 (4): 1–26.

Nicoll, F. (1989) My Trip to Alice, *Criticism, Heresy and Interpretation* 3: 21–32.

Schafer, E. (1963) *Golden Peaches of Samarkand: A Study of Vang Exotics*. Berkeley: University of California Press.

Schiller, H. (1976) *Communication and Cultural Domination*. White Plains, N.Y.: International Arts and Sciences.

Vachani, L. (1989) Narrative, Pleasure and Ideology in the Hindi Film: An Analysis of the Outsider Formula. M. A. Thesis, Annenberg School of Communication, University of Pennsylvania.

Wallerstein, I. (1974) *The Modern World System*. (2 Vols.) New York and London: Academic Press.

Warner, M. (1990) *The Letters of the Republic: Publication and the Public Sphere in Eighteenth-Century America*. Cambridge, Mass.: Harvard University Press.

Williams, R. (1976) *Keywords*. New York: Oxford University Press.

Wolf, E. (1982) *Europe and the People Without History*. Berkeley: University of California Press.

Yoshimoto, M. (1989) The Postmodern and Mass Images in Japan, *Public Culture* 1 (2) 8–25.

Zarilli, P (1995) Repositioning the Body: An Indian Martial Art and its Pan-Asian Society Publics. In C. A. Breckenridge (Ed.) *Consuming Modernity: Public Culture in a South Asian World*. Minneapolis: University of Minnesota Press.

73
Theorizing Globalization

Douglas Kellner

In a theoretical perspective on globalization shaped by critical theory, Douglas Kellner (b. 1943) attempts to link the cultural, economic, and political aspects of globalization in what he refers to as a dialectical framework. He is quite clear about the forces driving globalization. They are the interconnected impacts of technological developments—particularly regarding communication technologies and transport advances—and capitalism. Technology and capitalism do not, however, produce a deterministic outcome. Instead, globalization is construed as being both multidimensional and contested. This being the case, globalization needs to be theorized as inherently contradictory, the task being to offer a theoretical account of the tensions between homogenization and fragmentation (an instance of which Benjamin Barber has colorfully described as the tension between McWorld and Jihad). Kellner is interested in the prospects of a progressive political agenda aimed at promoting equality and democracy on a global scale. To that end, he examines the significance of the incipient global movement against capitalist globalization, specifically pointing to the 1999 protests against the World Trade Organization (WTO) in Seattle and subsequent organized protests around the world.

Globalization appears to be the buzzword of the 1990s, the primary attractor of books, articles, and heated debate, just as postmodernism was the most fashionable and debated topic of the 1980s. A wide and diverse range of social theorists are arguing that today's world is organized by accelerating globalization, which is strengthening the dominance of a world capitalist economic system, supplanting the primacy of the nation-state with transnational corporations and organizations, and eroding local cultures and traditions through a global culture.[1] Marxists, world-systems theorists, functionalists, Weberians, and other contemporary theorists are converging on the position that globalization is a distinguishing trend of the present moment.

Moreover, advocates of a postmodern break in history argue that developments in transnational capitalism are producing a new global historical configuration of post-Fordism, or postmodernism, as an emergent cultural logic of capitalism (Harvey 1989; Soja 1989; Jameson 1991; Gottdiener 1995). Others define the emergent global economy and culture as a "network society" grounded in new communications and information technology (Castells 1996, 1997, 1998). For others, globalization marks the triumph of capitalism and its market economy.[2] Some theorists see the emergence of a new transnational ruling elite and the universalization of consumerism (Sklair 2001), while others stress global fragmentation of "the clash of civilizations" (Huntington 1996). Driving "post" discourses into novel realms of theory and politics, Michael Hardt and Antonio Negri (2000) present the emergence of "Empire" as producing fresh forms of sovereignty, economy, culture, and political struggle that open the new millennium to an unforeseeable and unpredictable flow of novelties, surprises, and upheavals.

Indeed, globalization is one of the most hotly debated issues of the present era. For some, it is a cover concept for global capitalism and imperialism and is accordingly condemned as another form of the imposition of the logic of capital and the market on ever more regions of the world and spheres of life. For others, it is the continuation of modernization and a force of progress, increased wealth, freedom, democracy, and happiness. Its defenders present globalization as beneficial, generating fresh economic opportunities, political democratization, cultural diversity, and the opening to an exciting new world. Its critics see globalization as harmful, bringing about increased domination and control by the wealthier overdeveloped nations over the poor underdeveloped countries, thus increasing the hegemony of the "haves" over the "have-nots." In addition, supplementing the negative view, globalization critics assert that globalization produces an undermining of democracy, a cultural homogenization, and increased destruction of natural species and the environment.[3] Some imagine the globalization project—whether viewed positively or negatively—as inevitable and beyond human control and intervention, whereas others view it generating new conflicts and new spaces for struggle, distinguishing between globalization from above and globalization from below (Brecher, Costello, and Smith 2000). In this study, I sketch aspects of a critical theory of globalization that will discuss the fundamental transformations in the world economy, politics, and culture in a dialectical framework that distinguishes between progressive and emancipatory features and oppressive and negative attributes. This requires articulations of the contradictions and ambiguities of globalization and the ways that globalization both is imposed from above and yet can be contested and reconfigured from below. I argue that the key to understanding globalization is theorizing it as at once a product of technological revolution and the global restructuring of capitalism in which economic, technological, political, and cultural features are intertwined. From this perspective, one should avoid both technological and economic determinism and all one-sided optics of globalization in favor of a view that theorizes globalization as a highly complex, contradictory, and thus ambiguous set of institutions and social relations, as well as one involving flows of goods, services, ideas, technologies, cultural forms, and people (see Appadurai 1996).

Finally, I will raise the question of whether debates centered around the "post" (e.g., postmodernism, postindustrialism, post-Fordism, and so on) do or do not help elucidate the phenomenon of globalization. I argue in the affirmative, claiming that discourses of the "post" dramatize what is new, original, and different in our current situation, but that such discourses can be and are easily misused. For the discourse of postmodernity, for example, to have any force, it must be grounded in analysis of scientific and technological revolution and the global restructuring of capital, or it is just an empty buzzword (see Best and Kellner 1997, 2001). Thus, to properly theorize postmodernity one must articulate globalization and the roles of technoscience and new technologies in its construction. In turn, understanding how scientific and technological revolution and the global restructuring of capitalism are creating unique historical configurations of globalization helps one perceive the urgency and force of the discourse of the "post."

Globalization, Technological Revolution, and the Restructuring of Capitalism

For critical social theory, globalization involves both capitalist markets and sets of social relations *and* flows of commodities, capital, technology, ideas, forms of culture, and people across national boundaries via a global networked society (see Castells 1996, 1997, 1998; Held et al. 1999). The transmutations of technology and capital work together to create a new globalized and interconnected world. A technological revolution involving the creation of a computerized network of communication, transportation, and exchange is the presupposition of a globalized economy, along with the extension of a world capitalist market system that is absorbing ever more areas of the world and spheres of production, exchange, and consumption into its orbit. The technological revolution presupposes global computerized networks and the free movement of goods, information, and peoples across national boundaries. Hence, the Internet and global computer networks make possible globalization by producing a technological infrastructure for the global economy. Computerized networks, satellite-communication systems, and the software and hardware that link together and facilitate the global economy depend on breakthroughs in microphysics. Technoscience has generated transistors, increasingly powerful and sophisticated computer chips, integrated circuits, high-tech communication systems, and a technological revolution that provides an infrastructure for the global economy and society (see Gilder 1989, 2000; Kaku 1997; Best and Kellner 2001).

From this perspective, globalization cannot be understood without comprehending the scientific and technological revolutions and global restructuring of capital that are the motor and matrix of globalization. Many theorists of globalization, however, either fail to observe the fundamental importance of scientific and technological revolution and the new technologies that help spawn globalization or interpret the process in a technological determinist framework that occludes the economic dimensions of the imperatives and institutions of capitalism. Such one-sided optics fail to grasp the co-evolution of science, technology, and capitalism and the complex and highly ambiguous system of globalization that combines capitalism and democracy, technological mutations, and a turbulent mixture of costs and benefits, gains and losses.

In order to theorize the global network economy, one therefore needs to avoid the extremes of technological and economic determinism. Technological determinists frequently use the discourse of postindustrial or postmodern society to describe current developments. This discourse often produces an ideal-type distinction between a previous mode of industrial production, characterized by heavy industry, mass production and consumption, bureaucratic organization, and social conformity, and a new postindustrial society, characterized by "flexible production" or post-Fordism, in which new technologies serve as the demiurge to a new postmodernity (Harvey 1989).

For postmodern theorists such as Jean Baudrillard (1993), technologies of information and social reproduction (e.g., simulation) have permeated every aspect of society and created a new social environment. In the movement toward postmodernity, Baudrillard claims that humanity has left behind reality and modern conceptions, as well as the world of modernity. This postmodern adventure is marked by an implosion of technology and the human, which is generating a new posthuman species and postmodern world.[4] For other less extravagant theorists of the technological revolu-

tion, the human species is evolving into a novel, postindustrial technosociety, culture, and condition in which technology, knowledge, and information are the axial or organizing principles (Bell 1976).

There are positive and negative models of technological determinism. A positive discourse envisages new technologies as producing a new economy interpreted affirmatively as fabricating a fresh wealth of nations. On this affirmative view, globalization provides opportunities for small business and individual entrepreneurs, empowering excluded persons and social groups. Technophiles claim that new technologies also make possible increased democratization, communication, education, culture, entertainment, and other social benefits, thus generating a Utopia of social progress.

Few legitimating theories of the information and technological revolution, however, contextualize the structuring, implementation, marketing, and use of new technologies in the context of the vicissitudes of contemporary capitalism. The ideologues of the information society act as if technology were an autonomous force and either neglect to theorize the co-evolution of capital and technology or use the advancements of technology to legitimate market capitalism (i.e., Gilder 1989, 2000; Gates 1995, 1999; Friedman 1999). Theorists such as Kevin Kelly, the executive editor of *Wired*, think that humanity has entered a postcapitalist society that constitutes an original and innovative stage of history and economy at which previous categories do not apply.[5] Or, like Bill Gates (1995, 1999), defenders of the "new economy" imagine computer and information technologies producing a "friction-free capitalism," perceived as a highly creative form of capitalism that goes beyond its previous contradictions, forms, and limitations.

By contrast, a negative version of technological determinism portrays the new world system as constituted by a monolithic or homogenizing technological system of domination. German philosopher and Nazi supporter Martin Heidegger talked of the "complete Europeanisation of the earth and man" (Heidegger 1971:15), claiming that Western science and technology were creating a new organization or framework, which he called *Gestell* (or "enframing"), that was encompassing ever more realms of experience. French theorist Jacques Ellul (1964) depicted a totalitarian expansion of technology—what he called *la technique*—imposing its logic on ever more domains of life and human practices. More recently, a large number of technophobic critics have argued that new technologies and global cyberspace constitute a realm of alienation and reification in which humans are alienated from our bodies, other people, nature, tradition, and lived communities (Borgmann 1994, 1999; Slouka 1995; Stoll 1995; Shenk 1997; Virilio 1998).

In addition to technologically determinist and reductive postindustrial accounts of globalization, there are economic determinist discourses that view it primarily as the continuation of capitalism, rather than its restructuring through technological revolution. A large number of theorists conceive globalization simply as a process of the imposition of the logic of capital and neoliberalism on various parts of the world, rather than seeing the restructuring process and the enormous changes and transformations that scientific and technological revolution are producing in the networked economy and society. Capital-logic theorists, for instance, portray globalization primarily as the imposition of the logic of capital on the world economy, polity, and culture, often engaging in economic determinism, rather than seeing the complex new configurations of economy, technology, polity, and culture and the attendant forces of domination and resistance. In the same vein, some critical theorists depict globalization as the triumph of a globalized hegemony of market capitalism, where capital creates a homogeneous world culture of commercialization, commodification, administration, surveillance, and domination (Robins and Webster 1999).

From these economistic perspectives, globalization is merely a continuation of previous social tendencies—that is, the logic of capital and domination by corporate and commercial interests of the world economy and culture. Defenders of capitalism, by contrast, present globalization as the triumph of free markets, democracy, and individual freedom (Fukuyama 1992; Friedman 1999). Hence, both positive and negative versions of economic and technological determinism exist. Most theories of globalization, therefore, are reductive, undialectical, and one-sided, either failing to see the interaction between technological features of globalization and the global restructuring of capitalism or failing to articulate the complex relations between capitalism and democracy. Dominant discourses of globalization are thus one-sidedly for or against globalization, failing to grasp the contradictions and the conflicting costs and benefits, upsides and downsides, of the process. Hence, many current theories of globalization do not capture the novelty and ambiguity of the present moment, which involves both innovative forms of technology and economy and emergent conflicts and problems generated by the contradictions of globalization.

In particular, an economic determinism and reductionism that merely depicts globalization as the continuation of market capitalism fails to comprehend the emergent forms and modes of capitalism itself, which are based on novel developments in science, technology, culture, and everyday life. Likewise, technological determinism fails to note how the new technologies and new economy are part of a global restructuring of capitalism and are not autonomous forces that themselves are engendering a new society and economy that breaks with the previous mode of social organization. The postindustrial society is sometimes referred to as the "knowledge society" or "information society," in which knowledge and information are given more predominant roles than in earlier days (see the survey and critique in Webster 1995). It is now obvious that the knowledge and information sectors are increasingly important domains of our contemporary moment, and that the theories of Daniel Bell and other postindustrial theorists are thus not as ideological and far off the mark as many of his critics on the left once argued. In order to avoid the technological determinism and idealism of many forms of this theory, however, one should theorize the information or knowledge "revolution" as part and parcel of a new form of *technocapitalism* marked by a synthesis of capital and technology.

Some poststructuralist theories that stress the complexity of globalization exaggerate the disjunctions and autonomous flows of capital, technology, culture, people, and goods. Thus, a critical theory of globalization grounds globalization in a theory of capitalist restructuring and technological revolution. To paraphrase Max Horkheimer, whoever wants to talk about capitalism must talk about globalization, and it is impossible to theorize globalization without talking about the restructuring of capitalism. The term "technocapitalism" is useful to describe the synthesis of capital and technology in the present organization of society (Kellner 1989a). Unlike theories of postmodernity (e.g., Baudrillard's) or the knowledge and information society, which often argue that technology is *the* new organizing principle of society, the concept of technocapitalism points to both the increasingly important role of technology *and* the enduring primacy of capitalist relations of production. In an era of unrestrained capitalism, it would be difficult to deny that contemporary societies are still organized around production and capital accumulation and that capitalist imperatives continue to dominate production, distribution, and consumption, as well as other cultural, social, and political domains.[6] Workers remain exploited by capitalists, and capital persists as the hegemonic force—more so than ever after the collapse of communism.

Moreover, with the turn toward neoliberalism as a hegemonic ideology and practice, the market and its logic come to triumph over public goods, and the state is subservient to economic imperatives and logic. Yet the term "technocapitalism" points to a new configuration of capitalist society in which technical and scientific knowledge, computerization and automation of labor, and information technology and multimedia play a role in the process of production analogous to the function of human labor-power, mechanization of the labor process, and machines in an earlier era of capitalism. This process is generating novel modes of societal organization, forms of culture and everyday life, conflicts, and modes of struggle.

The emergence of innovative forms of technology, politics, culture, and economy marks a situation parallel to that confronted by the Frankfurt school in the 1930s. These German theorists, who left Nazi Germany, were forced to theorize the new configurations brought about by the transition from market to state-monopoly capitalism (Bronner and Kellner 1989; Kellner 1989a). In their now classic texts, the Frankfurt school analyzed: the emergent forms of social and economic organization, technology, and culture; the rise of giant corporations and cartels and the capitalist state in "organized capitalism," in both its fascist and "democratic" state capitalist forms; and the culture industries and mass culture that served as new modes of social control, powerful forms of ideology and domination, and novel configurations of culture and everyday life.

Today, critical theorists confront the challenge of theorizing the emergent forms of technocapitalism and novelties of the present era constructed by syntheses of technology and capital in the formation of a new stage of global capitalism. The notion of technocapitalism attempts to avoid technological or economic determinism by guiding theorists to perceive the interaction of capital and technology in the present moment. Capital is generating innovative forms of technology, just as its restructuring is producing novel configurations of a networked global economy, culture, and polity. In terms of political economy, the emergent postindustrial form of technocapitalism is characterized by a decline of the state and the increased power of the market, accompanied by the growing power of globalized transnational corporations and governmental bodies and the declining power of the nation-state and its institutions—which remain, however, extremely important players in the global economy, as the responses to the terror attacks of September 11 document.

Globalization is also constituted by a complex interconnection between capitalism and democracy that involves positive and negative features and both empowers and disempowers individuals and groups, undermining and yet creating potential for fresh types of democracy. Yet many theories of globalization present it as either primarily negative, a disaster for the human species, or positive, as bringing a wealth of products, ideas, and economic opportunities to a global arena. Hence, I would advocate development of a critical theory of globalization that would dialectically appraise its positive and negative features. A critical theory is sharply critical of globalization's oppressive effects and skeptical of legitimating ideological discourse, but it also recognizes the centrality of the phenomenon in the present age. And it affirms and promotes globalization's progressive features (such as the Internet, which, as I document below, makes possible a reconstruction of education and more democratic polity, as well as increasing the power of capital), while noting contradictions and ambiguities.

The Contradictions of Globalization

The terrorist acts on the United States on September 11 and the subsequent Terror War dramatically disclose the downsides of globalization—the ways that global flows of technology, goods, information, ideologies, and people can have destructive as well as productive effects. The disclosure of powerful anti-Western terrorist networks shows that globalization divides the world as it unifies, that it produces enemies as it incorporates participants. The events disclose explosive contradictions and conflicts at the heart of globalization and the fact that the technologies of information, communication, and transportation that facilitate globalization can also be used to undermine and attack it, to generate instruments of destruction as well as production.[7]

The experience of September 11 points to the objective ambiguity of globalization: that positive and negative sides are interconnected, that the institutions of the open society unlock the possibilities of destruction and violence as well as those of democracy, free trade, and cultural and social exchange. Once again, the interconnection and interdependency of the networked world was dramatically demonstrated, as terrorists from the Middle East brought local grievances from their region to attack key symbols of American power and the very infrastructure

of New York. Some saw terrorism as an expression of the dark side of globalization, while I would conceive it as part of the objective ambiguity of globalization that simultaneously creates friends and enemies, wealth and poverty, and growing divisions between the "haves" and "have-nots." Yet the downturning of the global economy, intensification of local and global political conflicts, repression of human rights and civil liberties, and general increase in fear and anxiety have certainly undermined the naive optimism of globaphiles who perceived globalization as a purely positive instrument of progress and well-being.

The use of powerful technologies as weapons of destruction also discloses current asymmetries of power and emergent forms of terrorism and war, as the new millennium has exploded into dangerous conflicts and interventions. As technologies of mass destruction become more available and dispersed, perilous instabilities have emerged that have elicited policing measures to stem the flow of movements of people and goods both across borders and internally. In particular, the U.S. Patriot Act has led to repressive measures that are replacing the spaces of the open and free information society with new forms of surveillance, policing, and repression.

Ultimately, however, the abhorrent terror acts by Osama bin Laden's network and the violent military response to the al-Qaeda terrorist acts by the Bush Administration may be an anomalous paroxysm, whereby a highly regressive premodern Islamic fundamentalism has clashed with an old-fashioned patriarchal and unilateralist Wild West militarism. It could be that such forms of terrorism, militarism, and state repression will be superseded by more rational forms of politics that globalize and criminalize terrorism and that do not sacrifice the benefits of the open society and economy in the name of security. Yet the events of September 11 may open a new era of Terror War that will lead to the kind of apocalyptic futurist world depicted by cyberpunk fiction (see Kellner forthcoming).

In any case, the events of September 11 have promoted a fury of reflection, theoretical debates, and political conflicts and upheaval that put the complex dynamics of globalization at the center of contemporary theory and politics. To those skeptical of the centrality of globalization to contemporary experience, it is now clear that we are living in a global world that is highly interconnected and vulnerable to passions and crises that can cross borders and can affect anyone or any region at any time. The events of September 11 also provide a test case to evaluate various theories of globalization and the contemporary era. In addition, they highlight some of the contradictions of globalization and the need to develop a highly complex and dialectical model to capture its conflicts, ambiguities, and contradictory effects.

Consequently, I want to argue that in order to properly theorize globalization, one needs to conceptualize several sets of contradictions generated by globalization's combination of technological revolution and restructuring of capital, which in turn generates tensions between capitalism and democracy and "haves" and "have-nots." Within the world economy, globalization involves the proliferation of the logic of capital, but also the spread of democracy in information, finance, investing, and the diffusion of technology (see Friedman 1999; Hardt and Negri 2000). Globalization is thus a contradictory amalgam of capitalism and democracy in which the logic of capital and the market system enter ever more arenas of global life, even as democracy spreads and more political regions and spaces of everyday life are being contested by democratic demands and forces. But the overall process is contradictory. Sometimes globalizing forces promote democracy and sometimes they inhibit it. Thus, both equating capitalism and democracy and simply opposing them are problematic. These tensions are especially evident, as I will argue, in the domain of the Internet and the expansion of new realms of technologically mediated communication, information, and politics.

The processes of globalization are highly turbulent and have generated new conflicts throughout the world. Benjamin Barber (1996) describes the strife between McWorld and Jihad, contrasting the homogenizing, commercialized, Americanized tendencies of the global economy and culture with traditional cultures, which are often resistant to globalization. Thomas Friedman (1999) makes a more benign distinction between what he calls the Lexus and the Olive Tree. The former symbolizes modernization, affluence and luxury, and Westernized consumption; the latter symbolizes roots, tradition, place, and stable community.

Barber's model oversimplifies present world divisions and conflicts and does not adequately present the contradictions within the West or the "Jihad" world, although he postulates a dialectical interpenetrating of both forces and sees both as opposed to democracy. His book does, however, point to problems and limitations of globalization, noting serious conflicts and opponents, unlike Thomas Friedman's harmonizing duality of *The Lexus and the Olive Tree* (1999), which suggests that both poles of capitalist luxury and premodern roots are parts of the globalization process. In an ode to globalization, Friedman assumes the dual victory of capitalism and democracy, á la Fukuyama, while Barber demonstrates contradictions and tensions between capitalism and democracy within the New World (Dis)Order, as well as the antidemocratic animus of Jihad.

Hence, Friedman (1999) is too uncritical of globalization, caught up in his own Lexus high-consumption lifestyle, failing to perceive the depth of the oppressive features of globalization and the breadth and extent of resistance and opposition to it. In particular, he fails to articulate contradictions between capitalism and democracy and the ways that globalization and its economic logic undermine democracy as well as circulating it. Likewise, he does not grasp the virulence of the premodern and Jihadist tendencies that he blithely identifies with the Olive Tree, or the reasons why many parts of the world so strongly resist globalization and the West.

Consequently, it is important to present globalization as a strange amalgam of both homogenizing forces of sameness and uniformity *and* heterogeneity, difference, and hybridity, as well as a contradictory mixture of democratizing and antidemocratizing tendencies. On the one hand, globalization unfolds a process of standardization in which a globalized mass culture circulates the globe, creating sameness and homogeneity everywhere. On the other hand, globalized culture makes possible unique appropriations and developments everywhere, thus encouraging hybridity, difference, and heterogeneity to proliferate.[8] Every local context involves its own appropriation and reworking of global products and signifies, thus encouraging difference, otherness, diversity, and variety (Luke and Luke 2000). Grasping that globalization embodies these contradictory tendencies at once—that it can be a force of both homogenization and heterogeneity—is crucial to articulating the contradictions of globalization and avoiding one-sided and reductive conceptions.

My intention is to present globalization as conflictual, contradictory, and open to resistance and democratic intervention and transformation, not just as a monolithic juggernaut of progress or domination, as in many discourses. This goal is advanced by distinguishing between "globalization from below" and the "globalization from above" of corporate capitalism and the capitalist state, a distinction that should help us to get a better sense of how globalization does or does not promote democratization.

"Globalization from below" refers to the ways in which marginalized individuals and social movements resist globalization and/or use its institutions and instruments to further democratization and social justice. While on one level globalization significantly increases the supremacy of big corporations and big government, it can also give power to groups and individuals who were previously left out of the democratic dialogue and terrain of political struggle. Such potentially positive effects of globalization include increased access to education for individuals excluded from entry to culture and knowledge and the possible opportunity for oppositional individuals and groups to participate in global culture and politics through access to global communication and media networks and to circulate local struggles and oppositional ideas through these media. The role of new technologies in social movements, political struggle, and everyday life forces social movements to reconsider their political strategies and goals and democratic theory to appraise how new

technologies do and do not promote democratization (Kellner 1997, 1999b), social justice, and other positive attributes. Indeed, the movements against capitalist globalization that I would endorse are those that oppose oppressive institutions of capitalist globalization such as the WTO, IMF, and certain transnational corporations and that are for positive values such as social justice, labor and human rights, and ecology.

In their magisterial book *Empire*, Hardt and Negri (2000) present contradictions within globalization in terms of an imperializing logic of "Empire" and an assortment of struggles by the "multitude," creating a contradictory and tension-filled situation. As in my conception, Hardt and Negri present globalization as a complex process that involves a multidimensional mixture of production and effects of the global economy and capitalist market system, new technologies and media, expanded judicial and legal modes of governance, and emergent modes of power, sovereignty, and resistance.[9] Combining poststructuralism with "autonomous Marxism," Hardt and Negri stress political openings and possibilities of struggle within *Empire* in an optimistic and buoyant text that envisages progressive democratization and self-valorization in the turbulent process of the restructuring of capital.

Many theorists, by contrast, have argued that one of the trends of globalization is depoliticization of publics, the decline of the nation-state, and the end of traditional politics (Boggs 2000). While I would agree that globalization is promoted by tremendously powerful economic forces and that it often undermines democratic movements and decision making, I would also argue that there are openings and possibilities for a globalization from below that inflects globalization for positive and progressive ends, and that globalization can thus help promote as well as undermine democracy.[10] Globalization involves both a disorganization and reorganization of capitalism, a tremendous restructuring process, which creates openings for progressive social change and intervention. In a more fluid and open economic and political system, oppositional forces can gain concessions, win victories, and effect progressive changes. During the 1970s, new social movements, new nongovernmental organizations (NGOs), and new forms of struggle and solidarity emerged that have been expanding to the present day (Hardt and Negri 2000; Burbach 2001; Foran forthcoming).

The present conjuncture, I would suggest, is marked by a conflict between growing centralization and organization of power and wealth in the hands of the few and opposing processes exhibiting a fragmentation of power that is more plural, multiple, and open to contestation than was previously the case. As the following analysis will suggest, both tendencies are observable; it is up to individuals and groups to find openings for political intervention and social transformation. Thus, rather than just denouncing globalization or engaging in celebration and legitimation, a critical theory of globalization reproaches those aspects that are oppressive while seizing upon opportunities to fight domination and exploitation and to promote democratization, justice, and a progressive reconstruction of the polity, society, and culture.

Against capitalist globalization from above, there have been a significant eruption of forces and subcultures of resistance that have attempted to preserve specific forms of culture and society against globalization and homogenization and to create alternative forces of society and culture, thus exhibiting resistance and globalization from below. Most dramatically, peasant and guerrilla movements in Latin America, labor unions, students, and environmentalists throughout the world, and a variety of other groups and movements have resisted capitalist globalization and attacks on previous rights and benefits.[11] Several dozen people's organizations from around the world have protested World Trade Organization (WTO) policies, and a backlash against globalization is visible everywhere. Politicians who once championed trade agreements like the General Agreement on Tariffs and Trade (GATT) and the North American Free Trade Agreement (NAFTA) are now often quiet about these arrangements. At the 1996 annual Davos World Economic Forum, its founder and managing director presented a warning entitled "Start Taking the Backlash Against Globalization Seriously." Reports surfaced that major representatives of the capitalist system expressed fear that capitalism was getting too mean and predatory, that it needs a kinder and gentler state to ensure order and harmony, and that the welfare state might make a come-back (see *New York Times* 1996:A15).[12] One should take such reports with the proverbial grain of salt, but they do express fissures and openings in the system for critical discourse and intervention.

Indeed, by 1999, the theme of the annual Davos conference centered around making globalization work for poor countries and minimizing the differences between the "haves" and the "have-nots." The growing divisions between rich and poor were worrying some globalizers, as was the wave of crises in Asian, Latin American, and other developing countries. In James Flanigan's report in the *Los Angeles Times* (Flanigan 1999), the "main theme" is to "spread the wealth. In a world frightened by glaring imbalances and the weakness of economies from Indonesia to Russia, the talk is no longer of a new world economy getting stronger but of ways to 'keep the engine going' " (p. A13). In particular, the globalizers were attempting to keep economies growing in the more developed countries and capital flowing to developing nations. U.S. Vice President Al Gore called on all countries to spur economic growth, and he proposed a new U.S.-led initiative to eliminate the debt burdens of developing countries. South African President Nelson Mandela asked: "Is globalization only for the powerful? Does it offer nothing to the men, women and children who are ravaged by the violence of poverty?" (ibid.).

The Global Movement Against Capitalist Globalization

No clear answer emerged to Mandela's question as the new millennium opened, and with the global economic recession and the Terror War erupting in 2001, the situation of many developing countries has worsened. Yet as part of the backlash against globalization over the past years, a number of theorists have argued that the proliferation of difference and the move to more local discourses and practices define the contemporary scene. In this view, theory and politics should shift from the level of globalization and its accompanying, often totalizing, macrodimensions in order to focus on the local, the specific, the particular, the heterogeneous, and the microlevel of everyday experience. An array of theories associated with poststructuralism, postmodernism, feminism, and multiculturalism focuses on difference, otherness, marginality, the personal, the particular, and the concrete over more general theory and politics that aim at more global or universal conditions.[13] Likewise, a broad spectrum of subcultures of resistance have focused their attention on the local level, organizing struggles around identity issues such as gender, race, sexual preference, and youth subculture.

It can be argued that such dichotomies as those between the global and the local express contradictions and tensions between crucial constitutive forces of the present moment, and that it is therefore a mistake to reject focus on one side in favor of exclusive concern with the other (Cvetkovich and Kellner 1997). Hence, an important challenge for a critical theory of globalization is to think through the relationships between the global and the local by observing how global forces influence and even structure an increasing number of local situations. This requires analysis of how local forces mediate the global, inflecting global forces to diverse ends and conditions and producing unique configurations of the local and the global as the matrix for thought and action in the contemporary world (see Luke and Luke 2000).

Globalization is thus necessarily complex and challenging to both critical theories and radical democratic politics. However, many people operate with binary concepts of the global and the local and promote one or the other side of the equation as the solution to the world's problems. For globalists, globalization is the solution and underdevelopment, backwardness, and provincialism are the problems. For localists, globalization is the problem and localization is the solution. Less simplistically, however, it is the mix that

matters, and whether global or local solutions are most fitting depends on the conditions in the distinctive context that one is addressing and the specific solutions and policies being proposed.

For instance, the Internet can be used to promote capitalist globalization or struggles against it. One of the more instructive examples of the use of the Internet to foster movements against the excesses of corporate capitalism occurred in the protests in Seattle and throughout the world against the World Trade Organization (WTO) meeting in December 1999. Behind these actions lay a global protest movement, using the Internet to organize resistance to the WTO and capitalist globalization while championing democratization. Many Web sites contained anti-WTO material, and numerous mailing lists used the Internet to distribute critical material and to organize the protest. This resulted in the mobilization of caravans from all over the United States to take protestors, many of whom had never met and had been recruited through the Internet, to Seattle. There were also significant numbers of international participants in Seattle, which exhibited labor, environmentalist, feminist, anticapitalist, animal rights, anarchist, and other groups organized to protest aspects of globalization and form new alliances and solidarities for future struggles. In addition, protests occurred throughout the world, and a proliferation of material against the extremely secret WTO spread throughout the Internet.[14]

Furthermore, the Internet provided critical coverage of the event, documentation of the various groups' protests, and debate over the WTO and globalization. Whereas the mainstream media presented the protests as "antitrade," featuring the incidents of anarchist violence against property while minimizing police violence against demonstrators, the Internet provided pictures, eyewitness accounts, and reports of police brutality and the generally peaceful and non-violent nature of the protests. While the mainstream media framed the protests negatively and privileged suspect spokespeople such as Patrick Buchanan as critics of globalization, the Internet provided multiple representations of the demonstrations, advanced reflective discussion of the WTO and globalization, and presented a diversity of critical perspectives.

The Seattle protests had some immediate consequences. The day after the demonstrators made good on their promise to shut down the WTO negotiations, Bill Clinton gave a speech endorsing the concept of labor rights enforceable by trade sanctions, thus effectively making impossible any agreement and consensus during the Seattle meetings. In addition, at the World Economic Forum in Davos a month later, there was much discussion of how concessions on labor and the environment were necessary if consensus over globalization and free trade were to be possible. Importantly, the issue of overcoming divisions between the information-rich and poor and improving the lot of the disenfranchised and oppressed—bringing the benefits of globalization to these groups—were also seriously discussed at the meeting and in the media.

More significantly, many activists were energized by the new alliances, solidarities, and militancy and continued to cultivate an antiglobalization movement. The Seattle demonstrations were followed by struggles in April 2000 in Washington, DC, to protest the World Bank and the International Monetary Fund (IMF), and later in the year against capitalist globalization in Prague and Melbourne. In April 2001, an extremely large and militant protest erupted against the Free Trade Area of the Americas summit in Quebec City, and in summer 2001 a large demonstration took place in Genoa.

In May 2002, a surprisingly large demonstration took place in Washington, DC, against capitalist globalization and for peace and justice, and it was apparent that a new worldwide movement was in the making, uniting diverse opponents of capitalist globalization throughout the world. The anticorporate globalization movement favored globalization from below, which would protect the environment, labor rights, national cultures, democratization, and other goods from the ravages of uncontrolled capitalist globalization (Brecher, Costello, and Smith 2000; Steger 2002).

Initially, the incipient antiglobalization movement was precisely that—antiglobali-

zation. The movement itself, however, was increasingly global, was linking together diverse movements into global solidarity networks, and was using the Internet and instruments of globalization to advance its struggles. Moreover, many opponents of capitalist globalization recognized the need for a global movement to have a positive vision and to stand for such things as social justice, equality, labor, civil liberties and human rights, and a sustainable environmentalism. Accordingly, the anticapitalist globalization movement began advocating common values and visions, and began referring to itself in positive terms, like the social justice movement.

In particular, the movement against capitalist globalization used the Internet to organize mass demonstrations and to disseminate information to the world concerning the policies of the institutions of capitalist globalization. The events made clear that protestors were not against globalization per se, but opposed neoliberal and capitalist globalization, rejecting specific policies and institutions that produce intensified exploitation of labor, environmental devastation, growing divisions among the social classes, and the undermining of democracy. The emerging antiglobalization-from-above movements are contextualizing these problems in the framework of a restructuring of capitalism on a worldwide basis for maximum profit with zero accountability and have made clear the need for democratization, regulation, rules, and globalization in the interests of people, not profit.

The new movements against capitalist globalization have placed the issues of global justice and environmental destruction squarely in the center of important political concerns of our time. Hence, whereas the mainstream media failed to vigorously debate or even report on globalization until the eruption of a vigorous antiglobalization movement and rarely, if ever, critically discussed the activities of the WTO, the World Bank, and the IMF, there is now a widely circulating critical discourse and controversy over these institutions. Stung by criticisms, representatives of the World Bank in particular are pledging reform, and pressures are mounting concerning proper and improper roles for the major global institutions, highlighting their limitations and deficiencies and the need for reforms such as debt relief for overburdened developing countries to solve some of their fiscal and social problems.

Opposing capital's globalization from above, cyberactivists have thus been promoting globalization from below, developing networks of solidarity and propagating oppositional ideas and movements throughout the planet. Opposing the capitalist international of transnational corporate-led globalization, a Fifth International—to use Waterman's (1992) phrase—of computer-mediated activism is emerging that is qualitatively different from the party-based socialist and communist internationals. Such networking links labor, feminist, ecological, peace, and other anticapitalist groups, providing the basis for a new politics of alliance and solidarity to overcome the limitations of postmodern identity politics (see Dyer-Witheford 1999; Burbach 2001; Best and Kellner 2001).

Of course, right-wing and reactionary forces have used the Internet to promote their political agendas as well. In a short time, one can easily access an exotic witch's brew of Web sites maintained by the Ku Klux Klan and myriad neo-Nazi assemblages, including the Aryan Nation and various militia groups. Internet discussion lists also disperse these views, and right-wing extremists are aggressively active on many computer forums as well as radio programs and stations, public-access television programs, fax campaigns, video, and even rock-music productions. These organizations are hardly harmless, having carried out terrorism of various sorts from church burnings to the bombings of public buildings. Adopting quasi-Leninist discourse and tactics for ultralight causes, these groups have successfully recruited working-class members devastated by the developments of global capitalism, which has resulted in widespread unemployment in traditional forms of industrial, agricultural, and unskilled labor. Moreover, extremist Web sites have influenced alienated middle-class youth as well (a 1999 HBO documentary on *Hate on the Internet* provides a disturbing number of examples of how extremist Web sites influenced disaffected youth to commit hate crimes).

Indeed, a recent twist in the saga of technopolitics seems to be that allegedly "terrorist" groups are now increasingly using the Internet and Web sites to promote their causes. An article in the *Los Angeles Times* (2001:A1, A14) reports that groups like Hamas use their Web site to post reports of acts of terror against Israel, rather than calling newspapers or broadcasting outlets. A wide range of groups labeled as "terrorist" reportedly use e-mail, listserves, and Web sites to further their struggles—causes including Hezbollah and Hamas, the Maoist group Shining Path in Peru, and a variety of other groups throughout Asia and elsewhere. For instance, the Tamil Tigers, a liberation movement in Sri Lanka, offers position papers, daily news, and free e-mail service. According to the *Times*, experts are still unclear about "whether the ability to communicate online worldwide is prompting an increase or a decrease in terrorist acts." There have been widespread discussions of how bin Laden's al-Qaeda network used the Internet to plan the September 11 terrorist attacks on the United States, how the group communicated with each other, got funds and purchased airline tickets via the Internet, and used flight simulations to practice their hijacking. In the contemporary era, the Internet can thus be used for a diversity of political projects and goals ranging from education, to business, to political organization and debate, to terrorism.

Moreover, different political groups are engaging in cyberwar as an adjunct to their political battles. Israeli hackers have repeatedly attacked the Web sites of Hezbollah, while pro-Palestine hackers have reportedly placed militant demands and slogans on the Web sites of Israel's army, foreign ministry, and parliament. Pakistani and Indian computer hackers have waged similar cyberbattles against the Web sites of opposing forces in the bloody struggle over Kashmir, while rebel forces in the Philippines have taunted government troops with cell phone calls and messages and have attacked government Web sites.

The examples in this section suggest how technopolitics makes possible a refiguring of politics, a refocusing of politics on everyday life, and the use of the tools and techniques of new computer and communication technology to expand the field and domain of politics. In this conjuncture, the ideas of Guy Debord and the Situationist International are especially relevant, with their stress on the construction of situations, the use of technology, media of communication, and cultural forms to promote a revolution of everyday life and to increase the realm of freedom, community, and empowerment.[15] To some extent, the new technologies *are* revolutionary and *do* constitute a revolution of everyday life, but it is often a revolution that promotes and disseminates the capitalist consumer society and involves new modes of fetishism, enslavement, and domination yet to be clearly perceived and theorized.

Concluding Comments

The Internet is thus a contested terrain, used by left, right, and center to promote their own agendas and interests. The political battles of the future may well be fought in the streets, factories, parliaments, and other sites of past struggle, but politics is already mediated by broadcast, computer, and information technologies and will increasingly be so in the future. Those interested in the politics and culture of the future should therefore be clear on the important role of the new public spheres and intervene accordingly, while critical pedagogues have the responsibility of teaching students the skills that will enable them to participate in the politics and struggles of the present and future.

And so, to paraphrase Foucault, wherever there is globalization from above—globalization as the imposition of capitalist logic—there can be resistance and struggle. The possibilities of globalization from below result from transnational alliances between groups fighting for better wages and working conditions, social and political justice, environmental protection, and more democracy and freedom worldwide. In addition, a renewed emphasis on local and grassroots movements has put dominant economic

forces on the defensive in their own backyards, and the broadcasting media and the Internet have often called attention to oppressive and destructive corporate policies on the local level, putting national and even transnational pressure for reform upon major corporations. Moreover, proliferating media and the Internet make possible a greater circulation of struggles and new alliances and solidarities that can connect resistant forces that oppose capitalist and corporate-state elite forms of globalization from above (Dyer-Witheford 1999).

In a certain sense, the phenomena of globalization replicates the history of the United States and most so-called capitalist democracies in which tension between capitalism and democracy has been the defining feature of the conflicts of the past 200 years. In analyzing the development of education in the United States, Samuel Bowles and Herbert Gintis (1986) and Aronowitz and Giroux (1986) have analyzed the conflicts between corporate logic and democracy in schooling, Robert McChesney (1995 and 1997), myself (Kellner 1990, 1992, 2001, forthcoming), and others have articulated the contradictions between capitalism and democracy in the media and public sphere, and Joshua Cohen and Joel Rogers (1983) and many others argue that contradictions between capitalism and democracy are defining features of U.S. polity and history.

On a global terrain, Hardt and Negri (2000) have stressed the openings and possibilities for democratic transformative struggle within globalization, or what they call "Empire." I argue that similar arguments can be made in which globalization is not conceived merely as the triumph of capitalism and democracy working together, as it was in the classical theories of Milton Friedman or more recently in Francis Fukuyama. Nor should globalization be depicted solely as the triumph of capital, as in many despairing antiglobalization theories. Rather, one should see that globalization unleashes conflicts between capitalism and democracy and, in its restructuring processes, creates new openings for struggle, resistance, and democratic transformation.

I would also suggest that the model of Marx and Engels, as deployed in the "Communist Manifesto," could be usefully employed to analyze the contradictions of globalization (Marx and Engels 1978:469ff). From the historical materialist optic, capitalism was interpreted as the greatest, most progressive force in history for Marx and Engels, destroying a retrograde feudalism, authoritarian patriarchy, backwardness and provincialism in favor of a market society, global cosmopolitanism, and constant revolutionizing of the forces of production. Yet capitalism was also presented in the Marxian theory as a major disaster for the human race, condemning a large part of the race to alienated labor and regions of the world to colonialist exploitation and generating conflicts between classes and nations, the consequences of which the contemporary era continues to suffer.

Marx deployed a similar dialectical and historical model in his later analyses of imperialism, arguing, for instance, in his writings on British imperialism in India that British colonialism was a great productive and progressive force in India at the same time as it was highly destructive (Marx and Engels 1978:653ff). A similar dialectical and critical model can be used today that articulates the progressive elements of globalization in conjunction with its more oppressive features, deploying the categories of negation and critique, while sublating (*Aufhebung*) the positive features. Moreover, a dialectical and transdisciplinary model is necessary to capture the complexity and multidimensionality of globalization today, one that brings together in theorizing globalization, the economy, technology, polity, society, and culture, articulating the interplay of these elements and avoiding any form of determinism or reductivism.

Theorizing globalization dialectically and critically requires that we analyze both continuities and discontinuities with the past, specifying what is a continuation of past histories and what is new and original in the present moment. To elucidate the latter, I believe that the discourse of the postmodern is useful in dramatizing the changes and novelties of the mode of globalization. The concept of the postmodern can signal that which is fresh and original, calling attention to topics and phenomena that require novel theo-

rization and intense critical thought and inquiry. Hence, although Manuel Castells (1996, 1997, 1998) does the most detailed analysis of new technologies and the rise of what he calls a networked society, by refusing to link his analyses with the problematic of the postmodern, he cuts himself off from theoretical resources that enable theorists to articulate the novelties of the present that are unique and different from the previous mode of social organization.[16] Consequently, although there is admittedly a lot of mystification in the discourse of the postmodern, it signals emphatically the shifts and ruptures in our era—the novelties and originalities—and dramatizes the mutations in culture, subjectivities, and theory that Castells and other theorists of globalization or the information society gloss over. The discourse of the postmodern in relation to analysis of contemporary culture and society is just jargon, however, unless it is rooted in analysis of the global restructuring of capitalism and analysis of the scientific-technological revolution that is part and parcel of it (see Best and Kellner 1997, 2001).

As I have argued in this study, the term "globalization" is often used as a code word that stands for a tremendous diversity of issues and problems and serves as a front for a variety of theoretical and political positions. While it can function as a legitimating ideology to cover and sanitize ugly realities, a critical globalization theory can inflect the discourse to point precisely to these deplorable phenomena and can elucidate a series of contemporary problems and conflicts. In view of the different concepts and functions of globalization discourse, it is important to note that the concept of globalization is a theoretical construct that varies according to the assumptions and commitments of the theory in question. Seeing the term as a construct helps rob it of its force of nature as a sign of an inexorable triumph of market forces and the hegemony of capital, or, as the extreme right fears, of a rapidly encroaching world government. While the term can both describe and legitimate capitalist transnationalism and supranational government institutions, a critical theory of globalization does not buy into ideological valorizations and affirms difference, hybridity, resistance, and democratic self-determination against forms of global domination and subordination.

Globalization should thus be seen as a contested terrain, with opposing forces attempting to use its institutions, technologies, media, and forms for their own purposes. There are certainly negative aspects to globalization that strengthen elite economic and political forces over and against the underlying population. However, as I suggest above, there are also positive possibilities. Other beneficial openings include the opportunity for greater democratization, increased education and health care, and new possibilities within the global economy that provide entry to members of races, regions, and classes previously excluded from mainstream economics, politics, and culture within the modern corporate order.

Furthermore, there is Utopian potential in the new technologies, as well as the possibility for increased domination and the hegemony of capital. While the first generation of computers were large mainframe systems controlled by big government and big business, later generations of personal computers and networks have created a more decentralized situation in which ever more individuals own their own computers and use them for their own projects and goals. A new generation of wireless communication could enable areas of the world that do not even have electricity to participate in the communication and information revolution of the emergent global era. This would require, of course, something like a Marshall Plan for the developing world, which would necessitate help with disseminating technologies that would also address problems of world hunger, disease, illiteracy, and poverty.

In relation to education, the spread and distribution of information and communication technology signifies the possibility of openings of opportunities for research and interaction not previously accessible to students who did not have the privilege of access to major research libraries or institutions. Although it has its problems and limitations, the Internet makes available more information and knowledge to more people than any previous institution in history. Moreover, the Internet enables individuals to participate in discussions and to circulate their ideas and work in ways that were previously closed off to many excluded groups and individuals.

A progressive reconstruction of education that is done in the interests of democratization would demand access to new technologies for all, helping to overcome the so-called digital divide and divisions of the "haves" and "have-nots" as well as teaching information literacy to provide the skills necessary to participate in the emerging cybersociety (see Kellner 2000). Expanding democratic and multicultural reconstruction of education thus forces educators and citizens to confront the challenge of the digital divide, in which there are divisions between information and technology "haves" and "have-nots," just as there are class, gender, and race divisions in every sphere of the existing constellations of society and culture. Although the latest surveys of the digital divide indicate that the key indicators are class and education and not race and gender, making computers a significant force of democratization of education and society will nonetheless require significant investment and programs to assure that everyone receives the training, literacies, and tools necessary to properly function in a high-tech global economy and culture.[17]

Hence, a critical theory of globalization presents globalization as a product of capitalism and democracy, as a set of forces imposed from above in conjunction with resistance from below. In this optic, globalization generates new conflicts, new struggles, and new crises, which can be seen in part as resistance to capitalist logic. In the light of the neo-liberal projects to dismantle the welfare state, colonize the public sphere, and control globalization, it is up to citizens and activists to create new public spheres, politics, and pedagogies, to use the new technologies to discuss what kinds of society people today want, and to oppose the society against which people resist and struggle. This involves, minimally, demands for more education, health care, welfare, and benefits from the state and a struggle to create a more democratic and egalitarian society. But one cannot expect that generous corporations and a beneficent state are going to make available to citizens the bounties and benefits of the globalized new information economy. Rather, it is up to individuals and groups to promote democratization and progressive social change.

Thus, in opposition to the globalization from above of corporate capitalism, I would advocate a globalization from below, one which supports individuals and groups using the new technologies to create a more multicultural, egalitarian, democratic, and ecological world. Of course, the new technologies might exacerbate existing inequalities in the current class, gender, race, and regional configurations of power and give the major corporate forces powerful new tools to advance their interests. In this situation, it is up to people of good will to devise strategies to use the new technologies to promote democratization and social justice. For as the new technologies become ever more central to every domain of everyday life, developing an oppositional technopolitics in the new public spheres will become more and more important (see Kellner 1995a, 1995b, 1997, 2000). Changes in the economy, politics, and social life demand a constant reconceptualization of politics and social change in the light of globalization and the technological revolution, requiring new thinking as a response to ever-changing historical conditions.

Endnotes

1. Attempts to chart the globalization of capital, decline of the nation-state, and rise of a new global culture include the essays in Featherstone (1990), Giddens (1990), Robertson (1991), King (1991), Bird et al. (1993), Gilroy (1993), Arrighi (1994), Lash and Urry (1994), Grewal and Kaplan (1994), Wark (1994), Featherstone, Lash, and Robertson (1995), Axford (1995), Held (1995), Waters (1995), Hirst and Thompson (1996), Axtmann (1998), Albrow (1996), Cvetkovich and Kellner (1997), Kellner (1998), Friedman (1999), Held et al. (1999), Hardt and Negri (2000), Lechner and Boli (2000), Steger (2002), and Stiglitz (2002).

2. See apologists such as Fukuyama (1992) and Friedman (1999), who perceive this process as positive, while others, such as Mander and Goldsmith (1996), Eisenstein (1998), and Robins and Webster (1999) portray it as negative.

3. What appeared at the first stage of academic and popular discourses of globalization in the 1990s tended to be dichotomized into celebratory globophilia and dismissive globophobia. See Best and Kellner (2001). There was also a tendency on the part of some theorists to exaggerate the novelties of globalization, and on the part of others to dismiss these claims by arguing that globalization has been going on for centuries and not that much is new and different. For an excellent delineation and critique of academic discourses on globalization, see Steger (2002).

4. See Baudrillard (1993) and the analyses in Kellner (1989b, 1994).

5. See Kelly (1994, 1998) and the critique in Best and Kellner (1999).

6. In his extreme postmodern stage, Baudrillard (1993) argued that "simulation" had replaced production as the organizing principle of contemporary societies, marking "the end of political economy" (p. 955). See the critique in Kellner (1989b). In general, I am trying to mediate the economic determinism in some neo-Marxian and other theories of globalization and the technological determinism found in Baudrillard and others.

7. I am not able, in the framework of this paper, to theorize the alarming expansion of war and militarism in the post-September 11 environment. For my theorizing of war and militarism, see Kellner (2002, forthcoming).

8. For example, as Ritzer (1996) argues, McDonald's imposes not only a similar cuisine all over the world, but circulates processes of what he calls "McDonaldization" that involve a production/consumption model of efficiency, technological rationality, calculability, predictability, and control. Yet, as Watson et al. (1997) argue, McDonald's has various cultural meanings in diverse local contexts, as well as different products, organization, and effects. However, the latter source goes too far toward stressing heterogeneity, downplaying the cultural power of McDonald's as a force of a homogenizing globalization and Western corporate logic and system; see Kellner (1999a, 2003).

9. While I find *Empire* an extremely impressive and massively productive text, I am not sure what is gained by using the word "Empire" rather than the concepts of global capital and political economy. While Hardt and Negri (2000) combine categories of Marxism and critical social theory with poststructuralist discourse derived from Foucault and Deleuze and Guattari, they frequently favor the latter, often mystifying and obscuring the object of analysis. I am also not as confident as are they that the "multitude" replaces traditional concepts of the working class and other modern polit-

ical subjects, movements, and actors, and I find their emphasis on nomads, "New Barbarians," and the poor as replacement categories problematical. Nor am I clear on exactly what forms their poststructuralist politics would take. The same problem is evident, I believe, in an earlier decade's provocative and post-Marxist text by Laclau and Mouffe (1985), who valorized new social movements, radical democracy, and a postsocialist politics without providing many concrete examples or proposals for struggle in the present conjuncture.

10. I am thus trying to mediate in this paper between those who claim that globalization simply undermines democracy and those, such as Friedman (1999), who claim that globalization promotes democratization. I should also note that in distinguishing between globalization from above and globalization from below, I do not want to say that one is good and the other is bad in relation to democracy. As Friedman shows, capitalist corporations and global forces might very well promote democratization in many arenas of the world, and globalization from below might promote special interests or reactionary goals, so I criticize theorizing globalization in binary terms as primarily "good" or "bad." While critics of globalization simply see it as the reproduction of capitalism, its champions, like Friedman, do not perceive how globalization undercuts democracy. Likewise, Friedman does not engage the role of new social movements, dissident groups, or the "have-nots" in promoting democratization. Nor do concerns for social justice, equality, and participatory democracy play a role in his book.

11. On resistance by labor to globalization, see Moody (1997); on resistance by environmentalists and other social movements, see the studies in Mander and Goldsmith (1996). I provide examples below from several domains.

12. Friedman (1999:267ff) notes that George Soros was the star of Davos in 1995, when the triumph of global capital was being celebrated, but that the next year Russian Communist Party leader Gennadi A. Zyuganov was a major media focus when unrestrained globalization was being questioned. Friedman does not point out that this was a result of a growing recognition that divisions between "haves" and "have-nots" were becoming too scandalous and that predatory capitalism was becoming too brutal and ferocious.

13. Such positions are associated with the postmodern theories of Foucault, Lyotard, and Rorty and have been taken up by a wide range of feminists, multiculturalists, and others. On these theorists and postmodern politics, see Best and Kellner (1991, 1997, 2001) and the valorization

and critique of postmodern politics in Hardt and Negri (2000) and Burbach (2001).

14. As a December 1 *ABC News* story titled "Networked Protests" put it, "Disparate groups from the Direct Action Network to the AFL-CIO to various environmental and human rights groups have organized rallies and protests online, allowing for a global reach that would have been unthinkable just five years ago." As early as March, activists were hitting the news groups and list-serves—strings of e-mail messages people use as a kind of long-term chat—to organize protests and rallies.

In addition, while the organizers demanded that the protesters agree not to engage in violent action, one Web site urged WTO protesters to help tie up the WTO's Web servers, and another group produced an anti-WTO Web site that replicated the look of the official site (see RTMark's Web site, <http://gatt.org/>; the same group produced a replica of George W. Bush's site with satirical and critical material, winning the wrath of the Bush campaign). For compelling accounts of the anti-WTO demonstrations in Seattle and an acute analysis of the issues involved, see Hawkens (2000) and Klein (2000).

15. On the importance of the ideas of Debord and the Situationist International to make sense of the present conjuncture, see Best and Kellner (1997: chap. 3); on the new forms of the interactive consumer society, see Best and Kellner (2001).

16. Castells claims that Harvey (1989) and Lash (1990) say about as much about the postmodern as needs to be said (Castells 1996:26ff). With due respect to their excellent work, I believe that no two theorists or books exhaust the problematic of the postmodern, which involves mutations in theory, culture, society, politics, science, philosophy, and almost every other domain of experience and is thus inexhaustible (Best and Kellner 1997, 2001). Yet one should be careful in using postmodern discourse to avoid the mystifying elements, a point made in the books just noted as well as in Hardt and Negri (2000).

17. "Digital divide" has emerged as the buzz word for perceived divisions between information technology "haves" and "have-nots" in the current economy and society. A U.S. Department of Commerce report released in July 1999 claimed that the digital divide is dramatically escalating in relation to race, and the Clinton Administration and media picked up on this theme (U.S. Department of Commerce, NTIA 1999). A critique of the data involved in the report emerged, claiming that it was outdated; more recent studies by Stanford University, Cheskin Research, ACNieison, and the Forester Institute claim that education and class are more significant factors than race in con-

structing the divide (see Cyberatlas for a collection of reports and statistics on the divide).

In any case, it is clear that there is a gaping division between information-technology "haves" and "have-nots," that this is a major challenge to developing an egalitarian and democratic society, and that something needs to be done about the problem. My contribution involves the argument that empowering the "have-nots" requires the dissemination of new literacies, thus empowering groups and individuals previously excluded from economic opportunities and sociopolitical participation (see Kellner 2000).

References

Albrow, Martin. 1996. *The Global Age.* Cambridge, England: Polity Press.

Appadurai, Arjun. 1996. *Modernity at Large.* Minneapolis, MN: University of Minnesota Press.

Aronowitz, Stanley, and Henry Giroux. 1985. *Education Under Siege.* New York: Bergin and Garvey.

Aronson, Ronald. 1983. *The Dialectics of Disaster.* London, England: Verso.

Arrighi, Giovanni. 1994. *The Long Twentieth Century.* London, England, and New York: Verso.

Axford, Barrie. 1995. *The Global System.* Cambridge, England: Polity Press.

Axtmann, Roland, ed. 1998. *Globalization in European Context.* London, England: Cassells.

Barber, Benjamin. 1996. *Jihad vs. McWorld: How Globalism and Tribalism Are Reshaping the World.* New York: Times Books.

Baudrillard, Jean. 1993. *Symbolic Exchange and Death.* London, England: Sage.

Bell, Daniel. 1976. *The Coming of Post-Industrial Society.* New York: Basic Books.

Best, Steven, and Douglas Kellner. 1991. *Postmodern Theory: Critical Interrogations.* London, England, and New York: Macmillan and Guilford.

——. 1997. *The Postmodern Turn.* London, England, and New York: Routledge and Guilford Press.

——. 1999. "Kevin Kelly's Complexity Theory: The Politics and Ideology of Self-Organizing Systems." *Organization and Environment* 12:141–62.

——. 2001. *The Postmodern Adventure.* London, England, and New York: Routledge and Guilford Press.

Bird, Jon, Barry Curtis, Tim Putnam, and Lisa Tickner, eds. 1993. *Mapping the Futures: Local Cultures, Global Change.* London, England, and New York: Routledge.

Boggs, Carl. 2000. *The End of Politics.* New York: Guilford Press.

Borgmann, Albert. 1994. *Across the Postmodern Divide.* Chicago, IL: University of Chicago Press.

——. 1999. *Holding Onto Reality.* Chicago, IL: University of Chicago Press.

Bowles, Samuel, and Herbert Gintis. 1986. *On Democracy.* New York: Basic Books.

Brecher, Jeremy, and Tim Costello. 1994. *Global Village or Global Pillage: Economic Reconstruction From the Bottom Up.* Boston, MA: South End Press.

Brecher, Jeremy, Tim Costello, and Brendan Smith. 2000. *Globalization From Below.* Boston, MA: South End Press.

Bronner, Stephen Eric, and Douglas Kellner, eds. 1989. *Critical Theory and Society: A Reader.* New York: Routledge.

Burbach, Roger. 2001. *Globalization and Postmodern Politics: From Zapatistas to High-Tech Robber Barons.* London, England: Pluto Press.

Castells, Manuel. 1996. *The Information Age: Economy, Society, and Culture. Vol. 1, The Rise of the Network Society.* Oxford, England: Blackwell.

——. 1997. *The Information Age: Economy, Society, and Culture. Vol. 2, The Power of Identity.* Oxford, England: Blackwell.

——. 1998. *The Information Age: Economy, Society, and Culture. Vol. 3, End of Millennium.* Oxford, England: Blackwell.

Cohen, Joshua, and Joel Rogers. 1983. *On Democracy.* New York: Penguin.

Cvetkovich, Ann, and Douglas Kellner. 1997. *Articulating the Global and the Local: Globalization and Cultural Studies.* Boulder, CO: Westview Press. Cyberatlas, <http://cyberatlas.internet.com/big-picture/demographics>.

Drew, Jesse. 1998. "Global Communications in the Post-Industrial Age: A Study of the Communications Strategies of U.S. Labor Organizations." Ph.D. dissertation, University of Texas.

Dyer-Witheford, Nick. 1999. *Cyber-Marx: Cycles and Circuits of Struggle in High-Technology Capitalism.* Urbana and Chicago, IL: University of Illinois Press.

Eisenstein, Zillah. 1998. *Global Obscenities: Patriarchy, Capitalism, and the Lure of Cyberfantasy.* New York: New York University Press.

Ellul, Jacques. 1964. *The Technological Society.* New York: Knopf.

Featherstone, Mike, ed. 1990. *Global Culture: Nationalism, Globalization, and Modernity*. London, England: Sage.

Featherstone, Mike, Scott Lash, and Roland Robertson, eds. 1995. *Global Modernities*. London, England: Sage.

Flanigan, James. 1999. *Los Angeles Times*, February 19.

Foran, John, ed. Forthcoming. *The Future of Revolutions: Rethinking Radical Change in the Age of Globalization*. London, England: Zed Books.

Fredericks, Howard. 1994. "North American NGO Networking Against NAFTA: The Use of Computer Communications in Cross-Border Coalition Building." XVII International Congress of the Latin American Studies Association, pp. 1–24.

Friedman, Thomas. 1999. *The Lexus and the Olive Tree*. New York: Farrar Straus Giroux.

Fukuyama, Francis. 1992. *The End of History and the Last Man*. New York: Free Press.

Gates, Bill. 1995. *The Road Ahead*. New York: Viking.

——. 1999. *Business@the Speed of Thought*. New York: Viking.

Giddens, Anthony. 1990. *Consequences of Modernity*. Cambridge, England: Polity Press; Palo Alto, CA: Stanford University Press.

Gilder, George. 1989. *Microcosm*. New York: Simon and Schuster.

——. 2000. *Telecosm*. New York: Simon and Schuster.

Gilroy, Paul. 1993. *The Black Atlantic: Modernity and Double Consciousness*. Cambridge, MA: Harvard University Press.

Gottdiener, Mark. 1995. *Postmodern Semiotics*. Oxford, England: Blackwell.

Grewal, Inderpal, and Caren Kaplan, eds. 1994. *Scattered Hegemonies: Postmodernity and Transnational Feminist Practices*. Minneapolis, MN: University of Minnesota Press.

Hardt, Michael, and Antonio Negri. *Empire*. 2000. Cambridge, MA: Harvard University Press.

Harvey, David. 1989. *The Condition of Postmodernity*. Cambridge, MA: Blackwell.

Hawkens, Paul. 2000. "What Really Happened at the Battle of Seattle." <http://www.purefood.org/Corp/PaulHawken.cfm>.

Heidegger, Martin. 1971. *The Question Concerning Technology*. New York: Harper and Row.

Held, David. 1995. *Democracy and the Global Order*. Cambridge, England: Polity Press; Palo Alto, CA: Stanford University Press.

Held, David, Anthony McGrew, David Goldblatt, and Jonathan Perraton. 1999. *Global Transformations*. Cambridge, England: Polity Press; Palo Alto, CA: Stanford University Press.

Hirst, Paul, and Grahame Thompson. 1996. *Globalization in Question*. Cambridge, England: Polity Press.

Huntington, Samuel. 1996. *The Clash of Civilizations and the Remaking of World Order*. New York: Simon and Schuster.

Jameson, Fredric. 1991. *Postmodernism, or the Cultural Logic of Late Capitalism*. Durham, NC: Duke University Press.

Kaku, Michio. 1997. *Visions: How Science Will Revolutionize the 21st Century*. New York: Anchor Books.

Kellner, Douglas. 1989a. *Critical Theory, Marxism, and Modernity*. Cambridge, England: Polity Press; Baltimore, MD: Johns Hopkins University Press.

——. 1989b. *Jean Baudrillard: From Marxism to Postmodernism and Beyond*. Cambridge, England: Polity Press; Palo Alto, CA: Stanford University Press.

——. 1990. *Television and the Crisis of Democracy*. Boulder, CO: Westview Press.

——. 1992. *The Persian Gulf TV War*. Boulder, CO: Westview Press.

——, ed. 1994. *Jean Baudrillard: A Critical Reader*. Oxford, England: Basil Blackwell.

——. 1995a. *Media Culture*. London, England, and New York: Routledge.

——. 1995b. "Intellectuals and New Technologies." *Media, Culture, and Society* 17:201–17.

——. 1997. "Intellectuals, the New Public Spheres, and Technopolitics." *New Political Science* 41–42:169–88.

——. 1998. "Multiple Literacies and Critical Pedagogy in a Multicultural Society." *Educational Theory* 48:103–22.

——. 1999a. "Theorizing McDonaldization: A Multiperspectivist Approach." Pp. 186–206 in *Resisting McDonaldization*, edited by Barry Smart. London: Sage Publications.

——. 1999b. "Globalization from Below? Toward a Radical Democratic Technopolitics." *Angelaki* 4:101–13.

——. 2000. "New Technologies/New Literacies: Reconstructing Education for the New Millennium." *Teaching Education* 11:245–65.

——. 2001. *Grand Theft 2000*. Lanham, MD: Rowman and Littlefield.

——. 2002. "Postmodern War in the Age of Bush II." *New Political Science* 24(1):57–72.

——. 2003. *Media Spectacle*. London, England, and New York: Routledge.

——. Forthcoming. "September 11, Terror War, and the New Barbarism." Available online at

<http://www.gseis.ucla.edu/faculty/kellner/papers/septllkell.htm>.

Kelly, Kevin. 1994. *Out of Control: The New Biology of Machines, Social Systems, and the Economic World*. New York: Addison Wesley.

———. 1998. *New Rules for the New Economy*. New York: Viking.

King, Anthony D., ed. 1991. *Culture, Globalization, and the World-System: Contemporary Conditions for the Representation of Identity*. Binghamton, NY: SUNY Art Department.

Klein, Naomi. 2000. "Were the DC and Seattle Protests Unfocused, or Are Critics Missing the Point?" *The Nation* online, July 10. <http://past.thenation.com/cgi-bin/framizer.cgi?url=:http://past.thenation.com/issue/000710/0710klein.shtml>.

Laclau, Ernesto, and Chantel Mouffe. 1985. *Hegemony and Socialist Strategy: Toward a Radical Democratic Politics*. London, England: Verso.

Lash, Scott. 1990. *Sociology of Postmodernism*. London and New York: Routledge.

Lash, Scott, and John Urry. 1994. *Economies of Signs and Space*. London, England: Sage.

Latouche, Serge. 1996. *The Westernization of the World*. Cambridge, England: Polity Press.

Lechner, Frank X, and John Boli. 2000. *The Globalization Reader*. Maiden, MA, and Oxford, UK: Blackwell.

Luke, Allan, and Carmen Luke. 2000. "A Situated Perspective on Cultural Globalization." Pp. 275–98 in *Globalization and Education*, edited by Nicholas Burbules and Carlos Torres. London, England, and New York: Routledge.

Mander, Jerry, and Edward Goldsmith. 1996. *The Case Against the Global Economy*. San Francisco, CA: Sierra Club Books.

Marx, Karl, and Frederick Engels. 1978. *The Marx-Engels Reader*. 2d ed. Edited by Robert C. Tucker. New York: W. W. Norton.

McChesney, Robert. 1995. *Telecommunications, Mass Media, and Democracy: The Battle for the Control of U.S. Broadcasting, 1928–1935*. New York and Oxford: Oxford University Press.

———. 1997. *Corporate Media and the Threat to Democracy*. New York: Seven Stories Press.

Moody, Kim. 1988. *An Injury to One*. London, England: Verso.

———. 1997. "Towards an International Social-Movement Unionism." *New Left Review* 225:52–72.

Polyani, Karl. [1944] 1957. *The Great Transformation*. Boston, MA: Beacon Press.

Ritzer, George. 1996. *The McDonaldization of Society*. Thousand Oaks, CA: Pine Forge Press.

Robertson, Roland. 1991. *Globalization*. London, England: Sage.

Robins, Kevin, and Frank Webster. 1999. *Times of the Technoculture*. London, England, and New York: Routledge.

Shenk, David. 1997. *Data Smog: Surviving the Information Glut*. New York: HarperCollins.

Sklair, Leslie. 2001. *The Transnational Capitalist Class*. Cambridge: Blackwell.

Slouka, Mark. 1995. *War of the Worlds*. New York: Harper and Row.

Soja, Edward. 1989. *Postmodern Geographies*. London, England: Verso.

Steger, Manfred. 2002. *Globalism: The New Market Ideology*. Lanham, MD: Rowman and Littlefield.

Stiglitz, Joseph E. 2002. *Globalization and Its Discontents*. New York: Norton.

Stoll, Clifford. 1995. *Silicon Snake Oil: Second Thoughts on the Information Highway*. New York: Doubleday.

U.S. Department of Commerce, National Telecommunications and Information Administration (NTIA). 1999. "Falling Through the Net: Defining the Digital Divide." <http://www.ntia.doc.gov/ntiahome/fttn99/contents.html> (last accessed 29 June 2002).

Virilio, Paul. 1998. *The Virilio Reader*. Edited by James Der Derian. Maiden, MA, and Oxford, England: Blackwell Publishers.

Wark, McKenzie. 1994. *Virtual Geography: Living With Global Media Events*. Bloomington and Indianapolis, IN: Indiana University Press.

Waterman, Peter. 1992. "International Labour Communication by Computer: The Fifth International?" Working Paper Series 129, Institute of Social Studies, The Hague.

Waters, Malcolm. 1995. *Globalization*. London, England: Routledge.

Watson, James L., ed. 1997. *Golden Arches East: McDonalds in East Asia*. Palo Alto, CA: Stanford University Press.

Webster, Frank. 1995. *Theories of the Information Society*. London, England, and New York: Routledge.

Reprinted from "Theorizing Globalization," by Douglas Kellner, *Sociological Theory*, Vol. 20, No. 3 (Nov., 2002), pp. 285–305. Reprinted by permission of American Sociological Association. ✦

74

An Outline of a General Sociology of the Body

Bryan S. Turner

According to Cambridge University social theorist Bryan Turner (b. 1945), the body has been a neglected feature of social theory, a consequence of the impact of the Cartesian mind-body dualism on major thinkers ranging from Weber to Parsons. Turner offers a critique of the discipline's general failure to develop a satisfactory sociology of the body. He then notes that various subareas of sociology today are showing a growing interest in the body, particularly in the sociology of medicine, in studies of mass consumption, in feminist research, and in studies on sexuality and sexual practices. Building on these research projects, Turner seeks to offer a theoretical account of embodiment as a social project. He contends that a proper social theory of the body would lay the groundwork for an ambitious research agenda with the capacity to offer a phenomenology of corporeal sensibility, a preconceived notion of agency, a new understanding of interconnectedness and mutual dependency, and an understanding of the role of social institutions—particularly political institutions—in both protecting and controlling bodies. All of this begins, according to Turner, with an appreciation of the "ontological frailty" of people, who, he concurs with Heidegger, are "beings unto death."

Introduction

In this chapter my aim is to link the sociology of the body to broader concerns with ethics and politics, and in particular to ground the study of human rights in the sociology of embodiment (Turner, 1993, 1997a).

The analytic goal is to produce an ethics of embodiment by way of an overview of the recent sociology of the body. This chapter is also driven by a criticism of recent trends in sociology which I refer to as "decorative." Much modern sociology can be regarded as decorative because it is, amongst other things, merely a description of the cultural representation of the body, and as a result it fails to engage with the politics of the body; for example, with the question of torture. The argument is that there is an important connection between the sociology and phenomenology of the "lived body," the politics of the body, and the ethics of embodiment. As a critique of decorative sociology, this chapter is polemical, because I want to defend the notion of a foundational sociology of the body that will permit us to deal with major human issues (ageing, death, violence, pain, and torture) and major human emotions such as love and resentment. In this sense, one benchmark of an adequate sociology of the body is Elaine Scarry's *The Body in Pain* (1985).

The three key elements of this foundational theory are the notion that as human beings we are characterized by ontological frailty, and that as social beings we inhabit a world which is politically and socially precarious. Although I start with the issue of ontological frailty, it is also evident that we are always and already social; that is, we are produced by and bound up in preexisting social reality of human interconnectedness and interdependency. This theoretical framework is derived from Martin Heidegger's philosophical criticism of metaphysics (Heidegger, 1958), the philosophical anthropology of Arnold Gehlen (1980), and from the sociology of knowledge of Peter Berger and Thomas Luckmann (1966). This chapter, while presenting a general overview of the contemporary sociology of the body, also develops a foundationalist perspective which is critical of the consequences rather than the intentions of so-called structuralist or anti-humanist interpretations of the body; that is, from the social theories that claim to be inspired by the work of Michel Foucault (Jones and Porter, 1994).

The Sociology of the Body

There is therefore in contemporary social theory a strong movement toward an elaboration of the sociology of the body, ranging from the postmodern debate (Baudrillard, 1993) to calls for "rematerializing the human in the social sciences of religion" (McGuire, 1990). Although the early work on the sociology of the body was orchestrated by a feminist analysis of gender, sexuality, and the body, in recent years the study of cyborgs and the new biology has begun to re-focus debate. The early interest in the military use of cyborgs (Levidow and Robins, 1989) has expanded into research on the interconnections between the body and computers in the fields of political surveillance, medicine, and the environment (Featherstone and Burrows, 1995). However, as I have already indicated, one limitation with existing social theory of the body is that it fails to move beyond the notion of cultural representation and social construction to a genuine understanding of social reciprocity, which is the core issue in any sociological perspective. Analysis of the representation of the body has not moved beyond a set of ritualistic claims about the socially constructed nature of the body. A general outline of the theory of the body requires the following:

1. An elaborate understanding of the basic notion of embodiment, which would be a method of systematically exploring the complexity of the body in terms of its corporality, sensibility, and objectivity.

2. An embodied notion of social agency in the theory of social action and a comprehensive view of how the body-image functions in social space.

3. A genuinely sociological appreciation of the reciprocity of social bodies over time—that is, an understanding of the collective nature of embodiment.

4. A thoroughly historical sense of the body and its cultural formation.

5. A political understanding of the body in relation to governance, with special reference to what we might term corporeal citizenship, namely the sexual regulation and surveillance of bodies by state legislation on reproductive technology, abortion, adoption, and parenting.

I conceive of these areas of analysis in terms of a hierarchy: from the nature of embodiment, which addresses the question of social existence; to the nature of the social actor; to the social and political level of exchange and reciprocity; and to the most general level of historical, cultural formations. These theoretical objectives may be satisfied by recent developments in Actor Network Theory (Law, 1992; Latour, 1993). Some earlier developments of ANT were concerned to understand the place of the material world in social interaction, but more recently this interest has been extended to the body. ANT has two important components. First, for methodological rather than ontological reasons, it dissolves the distinction between human and nonhuman agency by defining an "actant" as any entity which has the capacity to do things. Second, entities or actants are able to accomplish things because they are parts of networks, which involve complex linkages between the natural, social, and cultural worlds (Latour, 1993). Bodies never act in isolation to do things; they are always parts of networks which involve other bodies, technologies, and cultural phenomena. Social action can never be reduced to a simple list of forces; what is brought about in the world is an effect of multiple networks.

In my attempt to develop a sociology of the body, this notion of network is partly satisfied by what I mean by "interconnectedness," and the inspiration for this position is not so much ANT as Spinoza. As interpreted through the work of Gilles Deleuze, I read Spinoza as saying that bodies exist in a material environment which is fundamentally responsive. Actions always lead to counter-actions and adjustments, and so the evolutionary process is "networky." In a famous example, Spinoza considered the evolution of the fly and the spider. Their evolutionary "fate" is bound together, despite the fact that spiders prey on flies and not vice versa. The frailty of embodiment cannot be understood outside the notion that in our bio-sociocultural world we are always interconnected. These propositions lead us into a debate about radical ecology which is beyond the scope of this chapter. Suffice it to say that a Spinozian view of social embodiment is one method of counteracting the individualism and instrumentalism of the Cartesian legacy.

The Cartesian legacy emphasized not only individualism but mastery over the environment, and the dominance of cognitive faculties. By contrast, Spinoza, with his emphasis on the body and the mutual dependency between all beings in their environment, offered a more adequate basis for a sociology of embodiment. The spirit of capitalism is often defined as individualistic, ascetic, rationalist, and disciplined. Perhaps we should regard Cartesianism as an adjunct of Hobbesian social contract theory and argue that the culture of capitalism was a strange mixture of Hobbesian norms of political conduct, Cartesian psychology, and Protestant sectarian values. Cartesianism accepted the mind/body division, individualism, secularist rationality, empiricism, and a definition of science as instrumental rationalism. This ensemble was perhaps best described by Weber as "an ethic of world mastery" in *The Protestant Ethic and the Spirit of Capitalism* (1930). The sociology of the body has criticized the entire mind/body dualism and questioned the empiricist foundation of the natural sciences as the legacy of Descartes. Contemporary sociology has embraced the idea of embodiment as a more adequate approach to the necessary interconnectedness of mental, physical, and social life. Such a position can be summarized ironically under the slogan "I eat, therefore I am." Such positions draw on a common distinction in European languages between the objective body, the subjective body, and lived experience. Many of these developments implicitly or explicitly appeal to Spinoza's ethics and politics as an alternative to Cartesian mind/body dualism, notions of world mastery and instrumental reason. Spinoza rejected mind/body dualism in favor of parallelism (mind and body are intimately interconnected, but also operate in an environment). He developed a social contract theory which placed responsibility on the sovereign to promote common welfare, preached civic tolerance of difference and diversity, rejected transcendental personal monotheism, and came close to pantheism. His philosophy has influenced contemporary radical ecologism. Since everything is connected with everything else, responsibility is collective, not individual. That "all things are connected" is the basic principle of ecology.

Contemporary interest in Spinoza is thus a consequence of a general dissatisfaction with the legacy of Descartes's rational actor, which was the foundation of nineteenth-century social science models of reality and which survived into contemporary theory via Weber's sociology of action and Talcott Parsons's general theory of voluntaristic social action in the 1950s. The phenomenological tradition has attempted to provide a more sustained notion of the relationship between the objective instrumental body and the subjective living body, which is captured in the distinction in the German between *Körper* and *Leib* (Honneth and Joas, 1988). The notion of embodiment suggests that all of the fundamental processes of conception, perception, evaluation, and judgment are connected to the fact that human beings are embodied social agents. It is not the case simply that human beings have a body, but they are involved in the development of their bodies over their own lifecycle; in this respect, they are bodies. The body is not a passive site on which social messages are inscribed; it is an active component of social ontology. It is not sufficient to argue that the body is represented in culture or that it provides a series of models of cultural representation. It is a sensual-practical actant which shapes and produces culture. While one can talk about an objective body, as sociologists we need to concentrate on corporeality or bodiliness as the experientiality of the body. The human body has to be understood as both sensory and sensual.

The nature of corporeality and embodiment leads directly into the question of the self and the social actor. The characterization of the social actor has been an issue which has dominated the entire development of the social sciences, involving as it does questions about the rationality of social action, the importance or otherwise of effective and emotional elements, and the role of symbol and culture in the constitution of the social self. This question has to be cast in a distinctively historical context; that is, we do not have to decide on an essentialist definition of the social actor but, rather, we are obliged to explore historical setting of the corporeality of the social self. Recent writing on the body has indeed associated the emergence of the debate about the body with the growing importance of the postmodern or reflexive self in high modernity. For example, Anthony Synnott has asserted that "the body is also, and primarily, the self. We are all embodied" (1993: 1) and, in a similar fashion, Chris Shilling, following the approach of Anthony Giddens (1991) to contemporary forms of intimacy, also argues that the project of the self in modern society is in fact the project of the body: "there is a tendency for the body to become increasingly central to the modern person's sense of self-identity" (Shilling, 1993: 1).

The transformation of medical technology has made possible the construction of the human body as a personal project through cosmetic surgery, organ transplants, and transsexual surgery. In addition, there is the whole panoply of dieting regimes, health farms, sports science, and nutritional science, which are focused on the development of the aesthetic, thin body. Both Synnott and Shilling have noted that modern sensibility and subjectivity are focused on the body as a representation of the self, such that the body is in contemporary society a mirror of the soul. This involves a profound process of secularization whereby the diet is transformed from a discipline of the soul into a mechanism for the expression of sexuality, which is in turn the focus of modern selfhood (Turner, 1984). Whereas traditional forms of diet subordinated desire in the interests of the salvation of the soul, in contemporary consumer society the diet assumes an entirely different meaning and focus, namely as an elaboration or amplification of sexuality. The project of the self is intimately bound up with these historical transformations of the nature of the body, its role in culture, and its location in the public

sphere. Although sociologists have invested much effort into understanding cosmetic surgery as a technique for refashioning the self through body transformations, there is an important system of rehabilitation in contemporary medicine and social work which contributes to both rebuilding the self and to normalizing the body (Seymour, 1998).

However, the claim made by Giddens (1991) and adopted by Shilling that high modernity is marked by the development of self-reflexivity is a problematic historical claim. The history of self-reflexivity has to be traced to the transformation of confessional practice in the twelfth century (Morris, 1987), through the growth of Christian disciplines and spiritual manuals in the Reformation, to the Protestant tradition of piety and to the Protestant diary, and to the Counter-Reformation's elaboration of baroque mentalities. In particular, the seventeenth century had a very distinctive conception of the person as a construct or artifice, as the product of social intervention and cultural organization. The individual as a creation of social and historical arrangements, was revisable. The idea that the world is a stage and all the people merely players perfectly expressed this view. What is significant about contemporary society is the fact that the possibility of the body/self as a project is now open to a mass audience, being no longer the goal or ideal of an elite court group or high bourgeois culture. Dieting, jogging, the workout, mass sport, and physical education have all brought the idea of the perfect body to a mass audience. In this sense, Giddens's claims about self-reflexivity and the democratization of love are certainly plausible in that the quest for personal satisfaction through the body beautiful is now a mass ideal.

It is clear that in a society dominated by personal consumption there will be a close connection between self conception, body-image, and consumer icons. The adornment of the body plays a central role in mass consumerism and advertising. The significance of Pasi Falk's approach to *The Consuming Body* (Falk, 1994) is to connect the emergence of the modern self with the idea of consumption. Following the work of Colin

Campbell (1987) on the relationship between romanticism and consumerism, Falk argues that the sense of the self in contemporary society is profoundly connected with the idea of unlimited personal consumption (of food, signs, and goods). I consume, therefore I am. The modern advertising industry has of course elaborated the whole idea of the consuming self as the ideal form of the modern person.

Sociology is, however, not simply an analysis of representational meanings, but a science or discipline of action, interaction, and exchange. We need to understand the body in the processes of action and interaction at the level of everyday reciprocities and exchange. Falk's approach to eating and consumption provides us with an important way of developing the notion of social solidarity from an analysis of the consuming body. One might note that the very word "sociology" comes from the Latin *socius*, meaning friendship or companionship; sociology is a science of the reciprocities that define and produce friendship and companionship. Companionship is in literal terms a community based upon the sharing of bread, and we might usefully understand sociology as an analysis of the eucharistic community; that is, an enquiry into forms of solidarity based upon the reciprocity of (already and always social) bodies in a context of shared eating. While sociologists have typically grounded social solidarity in the idea of shared values, there may be a more primitive notion of community; that is, an eating community. Here again, the mouth is a particularly interesting feature of the human body, being the site of an ambiguous set of practices which include eating and biting, kissing and shouting, sucking and talking. There is an important relationship between words and food, because words and food are crucial means of reciprocity and exchange. The argument about self formation is now connected, through a discussion of eating, with the formation of society itself as an eating community.

There is an important historical contrast between the ritual meal of primitive society and the individuated forms of eating and consumption in modern society, which points to an analytically significant contrast between communion with exchange. The hearth was the institution that created the foundation of classical Roman society; the hearth was the focal point where the family was gathered in ritualistic activities, which in turn created fundamental social bonds. The gods of the family hearth were particularistic deities of the social group. It was the eating community and the ritual meal which provided the ground-work for the formation of society as such. In Christianity, the ritual meal has been converted into a formal communion with God through the ritual consumption of the body and blood of Christ. Just as the affective bond between mother and child is formed through female lactation, so the intimate emotional bond at the base of society is formed by shared consumption of food around a ritualized pattern of eating. For Falk, the transformation taking place in modern society is thus away from the collective rituals of eating to the privatized meal. Here again, the history of society is linked to the history of the body; that is, to the transformation of taste taking place in the reorganization of eating.

The communal bonds of the ritual meal are eventually, through the processes of modernization, replaced by privatized forms of consumption in modern society, but this historical transformation is also one from the open body/closed self to the closed body/open self of modern society. In primitive society, the self is underdeveloped but by contrast the body is open, whereas in contemporary society the self is overdeveloped and correspondingly the body is closed. This open/closed body distinction is thus mapped on to a notion of collective and individualized patterns of eating. The modern consumption of food is not only shaped by commercial transformations of eating in the restaurant but also by the application of science through dietetics and nutrition to the production of effective and efficient means of eating.

In a recent study of the impact of Fordism and Taylorism on the food industry, George Ritzer (1993) has analyzed McDonaldization as an illustration of Weber's theory of rationalization and disenchantment. McDonalds operates with a limited menu, precise measurements of food, and standardized systems of delivery in order to achieve efficiency, profitability, and reliability. McDonaldization removes all surprises from life; its production methods remove the unpredictable from eating, including the risk of food poisoning. The short, hasty lunch undertaken at McDonalds is thus the opposite of the orgiastic ritual meal of the primitive hoard. The gap between the traditional family meal, with its bourgeois civility and conviviality, and the privatized lunch at McDonalds perhaps beautifully captures the distinction between the traditional life-world and the rational system of modern industrial society.

Embodiment, Politics, and Society

The contemporary sociology of the body has the following limitations and characteristics. It is often difficult to see what is sociological about much sociology of the body, and it is often narrowly focused on the representational and cultural dimensions of the body. It has an unclear or absent notion of embodiment, and it is not systematically related to other features of sociological investigation, such as politics and ethics. The ironic consequence of the emphasis on the body as cultural representation is that the phenomenal body disappears from consideration and there is no attention paid to the body as lived experience. The concentration on the cultural signs of the body obscures or precludes attention to the phenomenal and experiential body of the everyday world of eating, sleeping, and working. The body only becomes a focus of attention in everyday life when it begins to fail and to give rise to pain and discomfort through ageing and disease; at other times, it is out of sight (Leder, 1990).

The notion that the human body is socially constructed is to some extent driven by the feminist political aspiration to deny that women are determined by anatomy. "Femininity" and the "female" are regarded as social categories which are produced by the hegemonic effect of a heterosexual regime. Radical feminist politics has assumed structuralism and/or epistemological relativism to attack patriarchal assumptions about an essential nature of women. While such a position is compelling, as an exclusionary theoretical strategy it paradoxically denies the materiality of embodiment. Let us consider childbirth. Generally speaking, women experience "discomfort" from childbirth, but the lived-experience of birthing cannot be addressed by structuralism. There is a phenomenology of the life-world as a lived experience, about which cultural relativism and structuralism have no interest or purchase. To adopt an interest in the sensual experience of birthing is not to rule out an equally important focus on the history of male control over birthing and the profession of the midwife.

Second, women give birth to children for the obvious reason that they have the appropriate reproductive organs. The strong claim that bodies are socially constructed has to reject the proposition that the bodies of men and women can be differentiated by their reproductive organs. There is, however, a weaker version of social constructionism, which would argue that the difference between men and women is shaped or influenced by cultural practices, such as the activities of medical specialists. This weak version of social constructionism would not be incompatible with the phenomenology of women's birthing pains. In short, weak cultural relativism in epistemological terms is not necessarily incompatible with what I want to call, following Vattimo, a "hermeneutic ontology." Such a position has already been developed in the writing of Peter Berger and Thomas Luckmann, in their classical *The Social Construction of Reality* (1966), where they developed a constructivist sociology of knowledge (from writers such as Karl Mannheim and Alfred Schutz) with a foundationalist ontology taken from the philosophical anthropology of Arnold Gehlen (1980, 1988). Because human beings are, to quote Nietzsche, "unfinished animals," they have to socially construct the "real world." The limitations of human biology require social construction, in which social institutions become crucial for providing an habitual background to deliberative social action (Berger and Luckmann, 1965).

Let us consider some strong objections to my examples. Obviously the recognition of pain varies considerably with culture, class, and gender. Indeed, it may be important to distinguish between suffering which is highly variable across cultures and pain which is not. While suffering involves loss of self-respect and social regard as a result of abuse, we may define pain as the distress of the body following injury, disease, and so forth. Although the discomforts associated with birthing may be variable by culture, in most historical circumstances pain is an adjunct of giving birth. Suffering may or may not be associated with birth, depending on the social attitudes which surround mothering. In the case of illegitimate offspring, suffering normally follows from the stigmatization of conception out of wedlock. My attempt to reconcile these conflicting philosophical positions (in particular, weak constructionism and social phenomenology) would also recognize, for example, that the symptoms of menstruation are highly variable between cultures. As Margaret Lock's research (1998) shows the presence of menstrual hot flashes differs greatly between ageing women in America and Japan, but it is still the case that women mature and eventually cease reproduction. Both men and women experience the physical effects of the menopause, but in many societies there is no vocabulary by which such events can be defined or recognized (Hepworth and Featherstone, 1998).

This view of the relationship between culture and experience is compatible with the fact that, historically, our understanding of anatomy is the product of religious and moral values, and that anatomical sections were not simply the product of empirical observation. Such sections revealed different pictures of the interior of the body, because the eye perceives through the curtain of social values (Cunningham, 1997). Nevertheless, men cannot reproduce through a vaginal delivery, because they do not have the appropriate anatomical equipment. Other examples could be explored indefinitely. As Margot Lyon (1997) has argued, while breathing and breath have major cultural significance (as indications of the soul), respiration is necessary to existence. It can be partly controlled through breathing exercises, but the absence of respiration results

ultimately and for all practical purposes in the end of life. Respiration is a good illustration, therefore, of Mauss's notion of "techniques of the body," because, while it is an aspect of learned behavior that is culturally specific, it requires a common anatomy (Mauss, 1973). Another example can be taken from social gerontology. Ageing is culturally variable and the notion of stages of ageing is an effect of power relations, but ageing is a physical process over which neither society nor individuals have final control (Turner, 1995).

It is time to attempt a definition of embodiment, or at least to list its necessary components. First, in line with Norbert Elias's notion of the social as process (Elias, 1978), it is important not to reify the term, but to treat embodiment as processual phenomena, namely the social processes of embodying. Embodiment is the effect or consequences of ongoing practices of what we might call "corporealization." In this respect, it requires the learning or mastery of bodily techniques—walking, sitting, dancing, eating, and so forth. Embodiment is the ensemble of corporeal practices which produce and give "a body" its place in everyday life. Embodiment locates or places particular bodies within a social habitus. In this respect, embodiment could be readily described in terms of Pierre Bourdieu's notions of practice, disposition, and habitus (Bourdieu, 1984, 1990). Embodiment is an accomplishment by which a social actor embraces a set of dispositions, practices, and strategies and, as a result, comfortably occupies a unique habitus. Second, embodiment is about the production of a sensuous and practical presence in the life-world. Embodiment is the lived-experience of the sensual or subjective body, and it is in this sense very close to the notion of practice (praxis) in the early philosophical anthropology of Karl Marx, as outlined in the so-called Paris Manuscripts. The sensual, lived body is a practical accomplishment in the context of everyday social relations, but it is also the active shaping of the lived world by embodied practices. Third, embodiment is a social project in the sense that it takes place in a life-world that is already social. Embodiment is not an isolated project; it is located within a social and historical world of interconnected social actors, within a network. The phenomenology of the lived body is not grounded in any individualistic assumptions; on the contrary, it treats the body as necessarily a social product. Finally, while it is the process of making and becoming a body, it is also the project of making a self. Embodiment and enselfment are mutually dependent and self-reinforcing projects. The self involves a corporeal project within a specific social nexus, where the continuous but constantly disrupted self requires successful embodiment, a social habitus, and memory (Becker, 1997).

Although embodiment is a social project which is routinely accomplished (with comfort or ease), it also has its own specificity. My embodiment is uniquely accomplished within wholly routine and predictable contexts. We can express this paradox of particularity and uniformity in terms of the relationship between sociology and ontology in a formulation taken from the introduction to Heidegger's *The Question of Being* (1958). On the horizontal plane of sociology, an individual is routinely defined by a series of social roles which specify his or her standardized position in the public world of the economy and society. There is also an ontological plane that forms a vertical axis, which is defined by the person's finite and unique embodiment. The horizontal social plane is the precarious world of the social system; the vertical plane is the world of embodied frailty. In this sense, we might argue that sociological (horizontal) analysis is concerned with understanding the contingent and arbitrary characteristics of social being, while philosophical (vertical) analysis attempts to grasp the necessities of our human being. This formulation can be taken as a response to Foucault's claim that "[a]ll of my analyses are against the idea of universal necessities in human existence. They show the arbitrariness of institutions" (Gutman et al., 1988: 11). The horizontal plane of social relations is indeed arbitrary; it is also precarious. The institutions of ageing have been radically transformed in the late twentieth century, and the traditional system of gerontocracy no longer holds sway. However, on the vertical plane of human existence there are certain necessities which are concerned with ageing, decay, and death. The relationship between the phenomenology of death and the institutions of death and bereavement is contingent, but death is, for all practical purposes, certain.

By ontological frailty, I mean that human beings of necessity have a propensity to disease and sickness, that we are beings unto death, and that our ageing bodies set up a tension between the body as lived-experience, the objective body, and the body image which, through the life cycle, involves us in existential discomfort (Turner, 1995). As a result of these conditions, human beings at all stages are involved in various relationships of dependency. We are, in the language of Nietzsche, the unfinished animal. This fragility of the embodied self is important for any sociological understanding of the dependency of the self on embodied continuity. In the passage of the life-cycle, the self is constantly disrupted and challenged by the trauma and crisis of illness and sickness (Becker, 1997). By societal and political precariousness, I include the inability of political institutions to protect and serve the interests of individuals, the failure of social institutions to cope with social change, the inability of social institutions to reconcile the conflict of collective and individual interests, and finally the problems for society in terms of equity to cope with generational exchanges (Turner, 1998b). The argument from ontological frailty might suggest an individualist or even utilitarian paradigm. However, by the notion of interconnectedness it indicates that human beings are always and already social. They are deeply involved socially through language and socialization.

References

Aries, P. and Bèjin, A. (eds.) 1985: *Western Sexuality: Practice and Precept in Past and Present Times*. Oxford: Blackwell.

Armstrong, D. 1983: *Political Anatomy of the Body: Medical Knowledge in Britain in the Twentieth Century*. Cambridge: Cambridge University Press.

Barbalet, J. 1998: *Emotion, Social Theory and Social Structure*. Cambridge: Cambridge University Press.

Barker, F. 1984: *The Tremulous Private Body: Essay on Subjection*. London and New York: Methuen.

Baudrillard, J. 1993: *Symbolic Exchange and Death*. London: Sage.

Becker, G. 1997: *Disrupted Lives*. Berkeley: University of California Press.

Bell, R. M. 1985: *Holy Anorexia*. Chicago and London: University of Chicago Press.

Berger, P. L. and Luckmann, T. 1965: Arnold Gehlen and the theory of institutions. *Social Research*, 32(1), 110–15.

——, —— 1966: *The Social Construction of Reality*. Garden City, NY: Doubleday.

Bourdieu, P. 1984: *Distinction*. London: Routledge and Kegan Paul.

—— 1990: *The Logic of Practice*. Cambridge: Polity Press.

Brumberg, J. J. 1988: *Fasting Girls: The Emergence of Anorexia Nervosa as a Modern Disease*. Cambridge, MA: Harvard University Press.

Cadden, J. 1993: *Meanings of Sex Difference in the Middle Ages: Medicine, Science and Culture*. Cambridge: Cambridge University Press.

Campbell, C. 1987: *The Romantic Ethic and the Spirit of Modern Consumerism*. Oxford: Blackwell.

Coren, S. 1992: *Lefthander: Everything You Need to Know about Left-handedness*. London: John Murray.

Cranny-Francis, A. 1995: *The Body in the Text*. Carlton: Melbourne University Press.

Crownfield, D. (ed.) 1992: *Body/Text in Julia Kristeva: Religion, Women and Psychoanalysis*. New York: State University of New York Press.

Cunningham, A. 1997: *The Anatomical Renaissance. The Resurrection of the Anatomical Projects of the Ancients*. Aldershot: Scolar Press.

Douglas, M. 1966: *Purity and Danger: An Analysis of Concepts of Pollution and Taboo*. Harmondsworth: Penguin.

—— 1970: *Natural Symbols: Explorations in Cosmology*. London: Barrie and Rockliff.

Downey, G. L. and Dumit, J. (eds.) 1997: *Cyborgs and Citadels. Anthropological Interventions in Emerging Sciences and Technologies*. Sante Fe, New Mexico: School of American Research Press.

Dreyfus, H. L. 1991: *Being-in-the-World*. Cambridge, MA: The MIT Press.

Elias, N. 1978: *The Civilising Process*. Vol. 1. Oxford: Blackwell.

Falk, P. 1994: *The Consuming Body*. London: Sage.

Featherstone, M. and Burrows, R. (eds.) 1995: *Cyberspace/Cyberbodies/Cyberpunk. Cultures of Technological Embodiment*. London: Sage.

—— and Turner, B. S. 1995: *Body & Society*: An Introduction. *Body & Society*, 1(1), 1–12.

Feher, M. (ed.), with Naddaf, R. and Tazi, N. 1989: *Fragments for a History of the Human Body*. New York: Zone (3 vols). I

Foucault, M. 1981: *The History of Sexuality*. Vol. 1: *An Introduction*. Harmondsworth: Penguin.

—— 1987: *The History of Sexuality*. Vol. 2: *The Use of Pleasure*. Harmondsworth: Penguin.

—— 1988: *The History of Sexuality*. Vol. 3: *The Care of the Self*. Harmondsworth: Penguin.

Gaines, J. and Herzog, C. (eds.) 1990: *Fabrications: Costume and the Female Body*. New York and London: Routledge.

Gehlen, A. 1980: *Man in the Age of Technology*. New York: Columbia University.

—— 1988: *Man. His Nature and Place in the World*. New York: Columbia University.

Giddens, A. 1991: *Modernity and Self-Identity: Self and Society in the Late Modern Age*. Cambridge: Polity Press.

Gutman, H., Hutton, P., and Martin, L. (eds.) 1988: *Technologies of the Self*. London: Tavistock.

Heidegger, M. 1958: *The Question of Being*. New York: Twayne.

Hepworth, M. and Featherstone, M. 1998: "The Male Menopause: Lay Accounts and the Cultural Reconstruction of Midlife." In S. Nettleton and J. Watson (eds.), *The Body in Everyday Life*. London: Routledge, 276–301.

Hertz, R. 1960: *Death and the Right Hand*. London: Cohen and West.

Honneth, A. and Joas, H. 1988: *Social Action and Human Nature*. Cambridge: Cambridge University Press.

hooks, b. 1984: *Feminist Theory, from Margin to Center*. Boston: South End Press.

Husserl, E. 1991: *Cartesian Meditations: An Introduction to Phenomenology*. Dordrecht: Kluwer.

Jones, C. and Porter, R. (eds.) 1994: *Reassessing Foucault. Power, Medicine and the Body*. London and New York: Routledge.

Johnson, D. 1983: *Body*. Boston: Beacon Press

Kantorowicz, E. H. 1957: *The King's Two Bodies*. Princeton, NJ: Princeton University.

Lacqueur, T. 1990: *Making Sex. Body and Gender from the Greeks to Freud*. Cambridge, MA: Harvard University Press.

Latour, B. 1993: *We Have Never Been Modern*. Hemel Hempstead: Harvester Wheatsheaf.

Law, J. 1992: "Notes on the Theory of the Actor-Network—Orderings, Strategy and Heterogeneity." *Social Practice*, 5(4), 379–93.

Leder, D. 1990: *The Absent Body*. Chicago: University of Chicago Press

Levidow, L. and Robins, K. 1989: *Cyborgs Worlds: The Military Information Society*. London: Free Association Books.

Lock, M. 1998: "Anomalous Ageing: Managing the Postmenopausal Body." *Body & Society*, 4(1), 35–61.

Lyon, M. L. 1997: "The Material Body, Social Processes and Emotions: Techniques of the Body Revisited." *Body & Society*, 3(1), 83–101.

McGuire, M. B. 1990: "Religion and the Body: Rematerializing the Human Body in the Social Sciences of Religion." *Journal for the Scientific Study of Religion*, 29(3), 283–96.

Marin, L. 1988: *Portrait of the King*. London: Macmillan.

Martin, E. 1987: *The Woman in the Body: A Cultural Analysis of Reproduction*. Milton Keynes: Open University Press.

Martin, L. H., Gutman, H., and Hutton, P. H. (eds.) 1988: *Technologies of the Self: A Seminar with Michel Foucault*. London: Tavistock.

Mauss, M. 1973: "Techniques of the Body." *Economy & Society*, 2, 70–88.

Merleau-Ponty, M. 1962: *Phenomenology of Perception*. London: Routledge and Kegan Paul.

Miles, M. R. 1986: "The Virgin's One Bare Breast: Female Nudity and Religious Meaning in Tuscan Early Renaissance Culture." In S. R. Suleiman (ed.), *The Female Body in Western Culture: Contemporary Perspectives*. Cambridge, MA: Harvard University Press, 193–208.

Moi, T. (ed.) 1987: *French Feminist Thought. A Reader*. Oxford: Blackwell.

Morris, C. 1987: *The Discovery of the Individual 1105–1200*. Toronto: University of Toronto Press.

Morris, D. B. 1996: "About Suffering: Voice, Genre and Moral Community." *Daedalus*, 125, 25–45.

Nettleton, S. and Watson, J. (eds.) 1998: *The Body in Everyday Life*. London: Routledge.

O'Neill, J. 1985: *Five Bodies: The Human Shape of Modern Society*. Ithaca and London: Cornell University Press.

—— 1989: *The Communicative Body*. Evanston, IL: Northwestern University Press.

Petersen, A. and Bunton, R. (eds.) 1997: *Foucault, Health and Medicine*. London: Routledge.

Porter, D. (ed.) 1997: *Social Medicine and Medical Sociology in the Twentieth Century*. Amsterdam-Atlanta: Editions Rodopi.

Pouchelle, M. C. 1990: *The Body and Surgery in the Middle Ages*. New Brunswick, NJ: Rutgers University Press.

Ritzer, G. 1993: *The McDonaldization of Society*. London: Sage.

Rousselle, A. 1988: *Porneia: On Desire and the Body in Antiquity*. Oxford: Blackwell.

Scarry, E. 1985: *The Body in Pain. The Making and Unmaking of the World*. New York: Oxford University Press.

Schilder, P. 1964: *The Image and Appearance of the Human Body*. New York: John Wiley.

Schutz, A. 1962–1996: *Collected Papers: Alfred Schutz, 1899–1959*. Ed. M. Natanson. The Hague: Martinus Nijhoff.

Sennett, R. 1994: *Flesh and Stone. The Body and the City in Western Civilization*. New York: W. W. Norton.

Seymour, W. 1998: *Remaking the Body. Rehabilitation and Change*. St. Leonards: Allen & Unwin.

Shilling, C. 1993: *The Body and Social Theory*. London: Sage.

Synnott, A. 1993: *The Body Social: Symbolism, Sex and Society*. London: Routledge.

Turner, B. S. 1984: *The Body and Society: Explorations in Social Theory*. Oxford: Blackwell.

—— 1987: *Medical Power and Social Knowledge*. London: Sage.

—— 1992: *Regulating Bodies: Essays in Medical Sociology*. London: Routledge.

—— 1993: "Outline of a Theory of Human Rights." *Sociology*, 27(3), 489–512.

—— 1994: "Preface to Pasi Falk." *The Consuming Body*. London: Sage, vii–xvii.

—— 1995: "Aging and Edentity: Some Reflections on the Somatization of the Self." In M. Featherstone and A. Wemick (eds.), *Images of Aging. Cultural Representations of Later Life*. London: Routledge, 245–262.

—— 1997a: "A Neo-Hobbesian Theory of Human Rights: A Reply to Malcolm Waters." *Sociology*, 31(3), 565–571.

—— 1997b: "What Is the Sociology of the Body?" *Body & Society*, 3(1),103–7.

—— 1997c: "From Governmentality to Risk, Some Reflections on Foucault's Contribution to Medical Sociology." In A. Petersen and R. Bunton (eds.), *Foucault, Health and Medicine*. London: Routledge, ix–xxi.

—— 1998a: "Foreword to Wendy Seymour." *Remaking the Body*. St. Leonards: Allen & Unwin, v–viii.

—— 1998b: "Forgetfulness and Frailty. Otherness and Rights in Contemporary Social Theory." In C. Rojek and B. S. Turner (eds.), *The*

Politics of Jean-Francois Lyotard. Justice and Political Theory. London: Routledge, 25–42.

Vattimo, G. 1988: *The End of Modernity.* Cambridge: Polity Press.

—— 1993: *The Adventure of Difference. Philosophy after Nietzsche and Heidegger.* Cambridge: Polity Press.

Weber, M. 1930: *The Protestant Ethic and the Spirit of Capitalism.* London: George Allen and Unwin.

Wolfflin, H. 1950: *Principles of Art History. The Problem of the Development of Style in Later Art.* New York: Dover.

XVII. New Directions/ Creative Syntheses

75
The Subject and Societal Movements

Alain Touraine
(translated by Noal Mellott)

Alain Touraine (b. 1925) is a French social theorist and public intellectual rooted in the democratic socialist tradition. His overarching theoretical project has sought to position his work in contrast to functionalism and as a manifestation of a post-Marxist theory that builds on the Marxist tradition while transcending its limitations and problems. His work represents a unique blend of Marxist and non-Marxist sources. This project has variously been called "sociology of action" and "the self-production of society." Unlike theorists such as Anthony Giddens, who have attempted to link agency and structure in a coherent theoretical framework, Touraine tends to pay little attention to structure per se, treating action as antecedent to structure, which is therefore constitutive of action. In this aspect his work is not entirely distinctive. However, as this essay on social movements illustrates, his concern with collective rather than individual action does serve to distinguish his contribution to theory from those of most theoretical currents. Like resource mobilization theorists, he views contemporary social movements as rational responses to various types of discontent on the part of the subordinated sectors of society. Touraine goes beyond resource mobilization by arguing that pro-gressive social movements contain transformative potential; if successful, they can change the course of social development. In this regard, they can be conceived as subjects of history.

It is initially essential to distinguish three types of collective action. The first type of collective action involves social demands, and occurs at the level of organizations; and the second involves political crisis and occurs at the level of institutions and decision-making centers. The third, which is increasingly important and with which I am concerned, is one that responds to conditions in a deinstitutionalized society in which common beliefs no longer unify and where the Self is fractured. These conditions give rise to societal movements that involve the personal and collective struggle for the unification of the Subject. In contrast with collective action involving social demands, which are based on economic calculation, or those involving political crisis, which lead to political demands, a societal movement relies on a collective determination to acquire a fundamental cultural resource, such as knowledge, recognition, a model of morality, and, most especially, the will to become a Subject.

To make this more concrete, in collective actions involving social demands or under a political crisis, the language is political, even though the collective action may occur in an industry, firm, hospital, university or neighborhood. For example, whenever a recession throws people out of work and lowers wages, a population may rise up with strong demands, but they have few chances of raising consciousness by fostering an understanding of the situation or even an ideology. The actors' consciousness focuses on their own situation, on calculations for proving the validity of their claims, justifying demands about living standards or the strain of their work, or making comparisons with people in other socioeconomic categories. There is no reference to power relationships, or to the society's basic cultural orientations. Nor is there a reference to a social Subject, or to conflictive relations about the social uses of a cultural model, or to shared cultural orientations.

The Distinctiveness of Societal Movements

Just as the sociology of rational choice and interests has diligently studied social demands, and functionalist sociology has dwelled on institutions in crises, the third type of collective action requires analyses that center attention on how actors aim to change a society's key cultural models and how they are managed. Such a movement is recognizable because it brings together three characteristics: a conflict between social actors contending over the social relations whereby a society reproduces itself; a positive reference to the cultural values at stake in the conflict; and an idea as to how the Subject is joined to the societal movement.

It is never easy to detect whether a collective action contains a societal movement, with long-lasting consequences. The long, massive strike of May 1968 (with its demonstration on May 13, for which a million persons turned out) appeared at the time to have been a political crisis with only short-term effects. Yet a quarter of a century afterwards, there is no denying that it changed society and introduced cultural themes into politics. Therefore, we must consider it to have been a major societal movement with continuing consequences.

A societal movement is based on neither an economic calculation nor political pressure. It relies on the will to acquire a fundamental cultural resource (knowledge, a model of morality such as socialism or equality) and on the will to become a Subject. This will is not expressed in a vacuum—not in the solitude of a personal experience but in social relations and in a way that respects and advances personal and collective freedoms.

Societal movements criticize social relations involving inequality, domination, and power, but they go beyond that in appealing to an ethics of collective responsibility.

Many sociologists have concentrated on how societal movements mobilize resources. This approach is useful insofar as a movement's orientations can be reduced to the collective pursuit of individual interests. But why does the pursuit of individual interests spawn collective action? This question is especially pertinent given the strong temptation to be a free-rider, as Olson (1965) pointed out in his now classical analysis. This we might consider to be a sociology of resource mobilization, and involves actors and their objectives. Also, by focusing on societal movements, I am also not considering rebellions, namely actions taken against suffering, poverty, or slavery. Rebellions are defined by what they reject—by what they designate as unbearable—whereas societal movements have a positive orientation and accompany political, cultural, or social objectives. A rebellion is centered on its own suffering, whereas, in a societal movement, we find both conflict and hope.

In considering the role of hope, idealism, and an altered conscience, which are the seeds of societal movements, I can refer to some concrete examples. These would include: the popular movements that put an end to apartheid in South Africa; the Polish and Czech solidarity movements that prepared the fall of the Soviet system; the Tiananmen uprising; ongoing student actions in Korea, Taiwan, and Iran; and, also, as I indicated, the French student movement of May 1968. Societal movements are the real place where liberation and liberty join together. Although the public (sometimes with the help of the media) have recognized the importance of these movements, sociology has usually resisted interpreting them, except in the most reductionist of ways. A main emphasis in sociology since Olson's (1965) earlier work has been to state that such movements involve the rational pursuit of ends. This implies that many or most stay out of the conflict so they can benefit from those who take risks without taking risks themselves. But how can we explain that so many men and women have taken risks—

have fought and made sacrifices in the hope of achieving goals, a hope in which they themselves could not believe?

As I have defined societal movements as those that are transformative, and infused by shared energy, they involve subjective elements. Although it must be recognized that societal movements, such as the ones I have mentioned, accompany anti-social and sometimes destructive behaviors, it is important not to attach too much importance to such behaviors. The active Subject that lies within the societal movement and its concrete expressions has helped to erode the state's logic of power and the reproduction of inequality within the state, and, thereby, societal movements have further global consequences.

Two ways of thinking have obscured the very idea of a social movement. The first, which has always prevailed in France, only considers anything having to do with the state's power as important. Accordingly, only political actions have a broad scope, whereas social actions are always confined in narrow bounds. This, I believe, stems from historical features in France, and the fact that the French demanded, early on, a political democracy but have lagged behind in building a social democracy. The preference of the people in France, and in other Latin countries, for revolutionary radicalism stems from the strong bonds that, in these lands, united the state with the traditional oligarchy and, even more, with the Catholic Church. This has set the revolutionary tone of politics, a tone that has often had (and can still have) ringing effects. As a consequence, so many observers enthusiastically saluted the long workers' strike in May 1968 but scorned the students' cultural movement, which they qualified *as petit bourgeois*.

The second way of thinking that has obscured the nature of social movements seems the opposite of the foregoing. It is based on completely splitting the social apart from the political system. It is then easy to show how, in order to attain its objectives or grow, a political action must mobilize social resources but without a connection with the objectives or conceptions of social actors. This way of thinking is just as political as the first, but it endows politics with a different meaning. From this vantage point, social action is subordinate to political action, which aims specifically at acquiring or maintaining power. Such thinkers see social movements nearly everywhere, since, constantly (especially in democracies), politicians strengthen their hand by presenting themselves as the only actors capable of responding to social pressure. The extreme form of this is Leninism, which, by assigning the political vanguard the central role, places directly under its control movements or organizations, which are soon reduced to being relay mechanisms for the party.

The idea of a societal movement is different from these two conceptions. Above all else, it asserts that, under certain circumstances at least, social actors can define a central social cause and oppose opponents in the name of dominant cultural values, while also defending their particular interests. To talk about a societal movement is to affirm that social actors have pre-eminence over political authorities. This entails the idea of representative democracy and, in particular, of social democracy, wherein the party is the union's political muscle. To detect societal movements means inquiring into the conditions under which, at the level of conflicting social relations, actions emerge that have a general scope and are capable of commanding political actors and resources instead of being used by them.

In contrast with political conceptions of a revolutionary or a strategic sort, for which only political action can broaden the scope of demands that are always particularistic, the idea of a societal movement is based on the idea that there exists a central conflict. This is particularly the case in the contemporary world, which we could describe as postindustrial, computerized, and information-based. As I analyze the current situation, social conflicts in our society pit the Subject against the triumph of the marketplace and technology and also against authoritarian communitarian (exclusive) powers. For me, this cultural conflict seems as central as the economic conflict was in industrial society or the political conflict was during the first centuries of the modern era. If we reject the idea of a social movement from the start or use this phrase to refer only to demands or to reactions in a political crisis, we keep ourselves from corroborating, or even understanding, it.

Societal Movements and the Subject

A societal movement exists only if it combines a social conflict with a cultural cause defined with reference to a Subject. The Subject has assumed religious and political forms, and even taken on the form of a class or nation. I would like to argue that the Subject can emerge "finally as it is in itself"—as the personal Subject—only in our type of society. In all societies, however, the Subject reveals itself through moral values that oppose the social order. A societal movement defends a way of putting moral values to use that is different from the one its social opponent defends and tries to impose. Moral references and the consciousness of direct conflict with a social opponent who is defined by its way of appropriating common values and cultural resources are two inseparable aspects of a societal movement. This reference to morals should not be confused with claims based on needs or working conditions. Such claims back up demands for modifying the ratio of costs to benefits, whereas the moral discourse of a societal movement refers to freedom, a cause, fairness, justice, and the respect for fundamental rights.

Specifically, as we pass from the depiction of the working-class movement as a reaction to capitalism's contradictions to the image of a working-class movement with a cause that is both defensive and offensive, we see the growing importance of freedom, justice, and social rights. But we must go much further to detect and then understand contemporary societal movements during this transition period involving the postindustrial society. We must give up defining the social actor objectively as a socioeconomic category, because a societal movement does not aim at changing the relative positions of individuals on a scale of revenue or power. It seeks, instead, to rally a dominated, alienated, "fragmented" Subject. In this sense, the word "consciousness" must be used not to refer to the consciousness that a class or nation develops of its own situation but to emphasize the emergence of the actor.

But how does the actor constitute its own self? This question lies at the heart of a sociology that has stopped analyzing systems in order to understand the Subject. For some sociologists, reflection of the Subject upon itself leads it to seek a principle of order and control over the prevailing disorder and arbitrariness. For others, the Subject can assert itself only by referring to common values, a general interest. Sociologists of the first sort are often called "liberals"; those of the second, "communitarians." The first try to discover rules, procedures, and laws; the second, the contents, or substantial definition, of the Good. But the two are not so clearly or fully opposed as it seems, since laws transcribe a conception of the Good, and procedures never stay neutral whenever social interests come into play. The opposition between liberals and communitarians is played out within an objectivist conception of society, even though this conception is more traditional among communitarians (who may be traditionalists or even Tocquevillians). Quite different are those sociologists, such as Habermas (1989) or Taylor (1989), who, in contrast with both liberals and communitarians, assign a central place to the construction of the Subject. What must be added to their different approaches is the idea that the Subject constitutes itself only through social conflict.

Every societal movement has two sides: the one, Utopian; the other, ideological. As Utopian, the actor identifies the self in terms of the Subject's rights. As ideological, the actor concentrates on the struggle with a social opponent. Without a doubt, the class struggle is ideological. It emphasizes social conflict more than shared issues. On the other hand, the student movements of 1964 and 1968 in France were so Utopian that they defined their opponent in excessively vague terms. Even though every societal movement is lopsided, stressing Utopian or ideological aspects at the expense of the other, a societal movement requires both.

In contemporary social thought, we see two conceptions of individualism opposing each other. The one defends the multiplicity of choices offered to the large majority of individuals by our society of consumption and mass communications. For it, the market is the place of freedom, since it takes the place of the power of faith, doctrine, or established hierarchies. Opposite this conception, the second argues for the idea of a personal and collective Subject capable of endowing its situations and experiences with a general meaning. The first conception refers to freedom of choice; the second to autonomy and meaningful life experiences. These two conceptions form the grounds for social movements that, though opposite, both defend the individual.

Nothing sheds a brighter light on the Subject than the analysis of societal movements, because both the Subject and movements involve a moral principle about social relations. A societal movement cannot be reduced to moral protest; nor can the Subject be reduced to the pursuit of individual interests or pleasure. The Subject cannot be separated from a societal movement. They form two sides of a single reality. We thus see how much the idea of the Subject differs from that of conscience, especially when the latter, as classically formulated, means self-control or skeptical self-detachment (as in the case of Montaigne). The Subject is neither a being, nor a place, nor an autonomous space and time. It is a call to protest and to self-assertion.

A societal movement only exists if it succeeds in defining a conflictual social relation and the broad, societal issues underlying this conflict. It thus links together the assertion of an identity, a definition of the opponent, and an understanding of the issues that underlie contention. Can we draw the conclusion that a societal movement is more thoughtful, better controlled, and more responsible than protest or crisis behavior? Not at all. The degree of violence of a collective action has nothing to do with its nature. The violence depends on whether or not there is room for negotiations. A societal movement may assume a revolutionary form; but it stops being a movement only if it loses its autonomy and becomes a social resource in the hands of political leaders whose objectives are quite different from those of the original movement.

At this point, a historical question crops up: can societal movements still exist in societies under the sway of the market economy? Or does the marketplace tend to eliminate what I have called the system of historical action and, consequently, replace societal movements with simple demands or occasional political crises? Many postmodernists, reflecting on the contemporary global economy, contend that hyper-industrialized societies that have moved beyond historicity can only experience chaos or make adjustments to limited, controlled change. Clearly, this pessimistic view is shortsighted and ignores the human capacity for reflection and for possessing an historical awareness. I take the view that societal movements emerge in all types of societies, and, in particular, they emerge in those endowed with historicity—capable of cognitively, economically, and morally investing in themselves. For that reason, contemporary neoliberalism, even on a near global scale, does not preclude societal movements.

Societal Movements and Democracy

One of the reasons why I have analyzed societal movements for such a long time is that I felt it necessary to radically and intellectually criticize revolutionary actions and ideologies, which, from the Reign of Terror to Leninism, have always resulted in essentially totalitarian governments or even in fascism. My central thesis is that we cannot separate the forming of social actors and, therefore, of societal movements from the autonomy of the issues underlying their actions—hence from the political mediation that constitutes democracy's central, indispensable element. The Subject, societal movements, and democracy are as inseparable as historical necessity, revolutionary action, and totalitarianism, which represent their darker side. Societal movements, of whatever sort, bear them within democratic aspirations. They seek to give a voice to those who have no voice and bring them into political and economic decision-making. In contrast, revolutionary actors dream of cultural, ethnic, political, or social purification, of a unified and transparent society, of creating a new mankind, and of eradicating whatever counters a unanimity that soon has no other reason for being than to organize political support for a totalitarian power.

This general conception leads us, as sociologists, to maintain that the presence of a societal movement is linked neither to a revolutionary situation nor to the force of an ideological discourse or line of politics. Rather, it is linked to the actor's capacity for working out a praxis—to a commitment to societal conflict and the defense of societal values, i.e. values that cannot be reduced to interests and, consequently, that cannot lead to the annihilation of one's opponent. A movement's meaning lies neither in the situation where the movement forms nor in the consciousness that ideologists ascribe to it or impose on it. The meaning is in its ability to undertake a certain type of action and place social conflict and issues on a certain level. In opposition to an "economicist" tradition often linked to Marxism, I have constantly defended the idea of a societal movement and a historical actor. In my first study of the working-class movement (Touraine, 1965), I stated that this movement was defending workers' autonomy. We would be caricaturing the study of the consciousness of social movements were we to reduce it to its most ideological forms. In effect, the latter often lie the furthest from praxis; and when they do not, the movement has, in fact, turned into an authoritarian or totalitarian anti-movement. All forms of absolute ideological mobilization—the identification of a social actor with God, Reason, History or the Nation—entail the destruction of societal movements. The latter are open to conflict, debate, and democracy, whereas ideological movements risk replacing plurality with unanimity, conflict with homogeneity, and participation with manipulation. Revolutionary intellectuals and leaders, demagogues and fundamentalists, are the active agents in the destruction of social movements. How can this escape our notice at the end of a century teeming with neo-communitarian movements, the most powerful of which call for a theocratic society?

Nowadays, given the globalization of the economy, we see arising, on the one hand, societal movements for minority rights, immigrant rights, and, more generally, human rights, but we are also witnessing anti-movements, which are giving birth to sects and cults in democratic lands and to new totalitarian movements on a national, ethnic, or religious basis. Here I am using a notion that many commentators—without giving it much thought—have avoided because they wish to ignore the difficulties of comparing the Nazi and communist systems with contemporary nationalist and religious fundamentalist movements. Is it so hard to admit that each totalitarian system, despite its specific aspects, belongs to a general type? Recourse to a "faith," whether Islam, Christianity, or Hinduism, leads to religious warfare, which communism and the revolutionary Mexican system, despite their violently anti-religious campaigns, avoided. Beyond the specific aspects of each totalitarian system, all of them share one characteristic, namely an absolute political power that speaks in the name of a people (a particular historical, national, or cultural group) and an assertion of absolute superiority (as being representative of a reality above politics and the economy). A totalitarian system is always popular, national, and doctrinaire. It subordinates social practices to a power that claims to incarnate the idea that a people represent and defends a faith, race, class, history, or territory.

Obviously, totalitarianism destroys democracy, but it also annihilates social, cultural, and historical movements and actors. It reduces historicity by using economic or cultural resources for constructing a closed mythical identity, itself reduced in practice to the justification of an absolute power. The idea of a people has always been a disguise for an absolutist state. It is no accident that the totalitarian, then authoritarian, governments in the communist countries dependent on the Soviet Union chose to call themselves "people's republics. Totalitarianism is the central problem of the twentieth century. In like manner, when political activists reject elections or bring excessive moral or material pressure to bear on those who do not share their point of view, they destroy the social movement for which they claim to be speaking. They act like demagogues (or Red Guards) rather than like the vanguard leading a class, nation or socioeconomic category. In short, a societal movement is praxis and not just a consciousness, and is fully linked to the affirmation that there is no societal movement without democracy, and vice versa.

Social Movements in a Non-Democratic Situation

An objection immediately comes to mind. Does this vision not focus solely on developed lands, where modernization is self-sustaining? Does it not overlook situations where democracy does not exist, because of the arbitrary power imposed by a national or foreign state or an oligarchy interested in speculation and social power more than in economic rationality? This is such an important objection that the answers to it serve to guide the analysis of social movements. It calls for two complementary answers.

The first answer is that there can be no development without popular societal movements and democracy. Development results from combining three major factors: the abundance and quality of investment; the distribution of the fruits of growth; and public consciousness of the political unit. In effect, nation and modernization cannot be separated, since a developed economy is a dense, coherent, convergent network of exchanges, transactions, and interactions among all societal sectors. More simply, development supposes a ruling elite accumulating resources and making long-term decisions; but it also requires redistributive and leveling forces, universal participation in the process of modernization, and the reduction of social and cultural privileges. These forces, born out of popular mobilization, have recourse to political institutions. Instead of saying, as many do, that development is a condition for democracy, I contend that democracy is a condition for development. The inability of the Soviet Union to really develop and its increasing paralysis provided evidence in support of this. But is the fast growth of China and of other lands in Asia, or elsewhere, not counter-evidence? We must answer no. In China, we observe the breakup of a totalitarian system and, in the coastal provinces, the rapid growth of a market economy under the leadership of decision-making centers located abroad. This breakup has positive effects, especially coming as it does after the Cultural Revolution's

destructive violence. But if social movements do not form, if democracy is not born, the historical process under way in China will disintegrate into a new authoritarianism or else into chaos. The Soviet Union's former satellites and former Yugoslavia, too, are looking for a way between democratic development and regression into authoritarianism. Such regression has had tragic consequences in Serbia and has negatively affected Romania and several other ex-Soviet countries. Meanwhile, the communists . . . come back in Poland, Hungary, Bulgaria, and Lithuania, and their success in elections in Russia and elsewhere, cannot—at present—be interpreted as a defeat for democracy and modernization.

Self-sustaining growth is a worthy objective, but this conception must be broadened to take into account other factors. When the dominant mode of development is of a domestic sort, there is a risk that authoritarian agencies will attempt to control the people or reduce them to mere resources. And when the dominant mode of development is of a market sort, social movements inevitably disintegrate into a multitude of pressure groups whose demands make social inequality worse. Can social movements exist in non-democratic situations? Let us push these questions even further. Are there democratic elements, hence movements, whose actions tend toward a despotic or market model instead of a democratic one?

This second answer takes us back to the analysis of the Subject, which can assert itself only through struggling against both the marketplace and commodified community. This means that the Subject arises as a form of opposition and liberation within the world of the marketplace and within the universe of the community. Indeed, societal movements, like the Subject itself, arise within a mode of development or even in forms of social power.

The major historical case is that of collective movements in authoritarian societies ruled by a despotic power, a national oligarchy, or a foreign colonial power. In this case, movements are forced to combine the defense of the oppressed and the demands for democracy with a revolutionary action for destroying the powers that be. Even in democratic lands, the working-class movement has always borne its share of violence in reaction to the violence of employers or governments. The strategy of a collective movement and of its leaders consists in combining actions for breaking with the existing order with democratic actions—the "logic" of the struggle against the powers that be with actions for defending freedom and, thus, political consciousness. This combination often fails. For instance, the labor movement has sometimes been an instrument, lacking autonomy, in the service of a new political power; and, sometimes, it has only defended relatively privileged socioeconomic categories. But these failures, however many times they have happened, must not keep us from realizing that a cultural, historical, or societal movement was present, despite the non-democratic outcome. True, the Algerian national movement has led to a military dictatorship that quells popular opposition. Nonetheless, it was an anticolonial movement for national liberation. Nor does the horror of the Reign of Terror detract from the events of June 1789 that introduced democracy in France. A movement is never purely democratic, nor does a revolution ever entirely lack democratic contents.

Despair or Hope?

We would weaken the idea of a societal movement were we to reduce it to naming a particular—more ideal than real—type of collective action. It is a concept or theoretical formulation. The idea of a societal movement (and, more broadly, of a social movement) forces us to give up the too easy quests of conservative thought, which looks for factors of integration, and of revolutionary thought, which denounces a system of domination as incapable of being either restrained or reformed.

This idea also protects us against the fragmentation that menaces collective action and, indeed, all aspects of social life. On the one hand, social movements seem to be less focused on being interest groups currently than on efforts for defending social integration from "social fractures" and ruptures of social bonds. The theme of exclusion, which

has replaced exploitation, contains this idea. On the other hand, "identity movements" are abounding, in the United States where women, homosexuals, African Americans, and ethnic or national communities are asserting cultural autonomy while also fighting against discrimination, but also in countries obsessed with ideas of purity and homogeneity. The increasing separation between these two types of collective action, which are foreign to each other, is not just a given fact. It is a reality as pathological as the wider separation between the world of instrumentality and the world of identity, a separation that entails the collapse of social and especially political mediation between the economy and cultures.

There is a risk of too easily defining the idea of a societal movement only in terms of its twofold refusal of communitarianism and of economic globalization, and also some risk of considering any pressure group or identity movement as a significant societal movement. It is also important for sociologists to look for such movements underneath extreme ideologies where they are often hidden. Let us take two opposite examples. In Algeria (and other Islamic countries, Egypt in particular), there are political groups that use Islam to attain power and construct a fundamentally anti-modern, Iranian type of society. To survive, they use the techniques of modernity. However, we should not forget that this also gives expression to an uprooted population, to young people without jobs who use the *trabendo* (black market), or sports, as a means of forcing open the doors of the society of consumption. Those who oppose lay reactions to the dangerous politics of religious mobilization are right up to a point, but they are wrong in that they fail to see that many movements draw their force from the culture and society they defend because they feel threatened. The second example is the 1995 strike in the French public services. The events that took place then cannot be reduced to a defense of vested interests or privileges. They manifested a popular rejection of an economic policy that subordinated all of social life to deficit reduction, considered to be the key for developing a single European currency (which, in and of itself, is supposed to bring prosperity and jobs for all).

Let us try to clear up, at least a little, our confusion by recalling the "natural history" of any movement. It starts when the denunciation of misery goes along with a moral appeal to the dignity of everyone and the solidarity of all. Only thereafter is the opponent identified; and the conflict becomes central, before being institutionalized—as the organized social movement turns into a political force or party, which intervenes in economic and social policy-making. This ultimate phase usually accompanies a return to ideological discourses that, cut off from strategic actions, call for a return either to open conflict or to the denunciation of misery. In each phase, this history may be interrupted. This natural history teaches us useful lessons, even if these are too general to account for the wide diversity of historical situations. But these lessons are of less use for understanding the present than is a historical reflection that pays more attention to the effects of demodernization.

How could the split between the economic and cultural worlds not affect societal movements? The "civil/civic" movements of the seventeenth and eighteenth centuries worked for the creation of a national, republican political order. The working-class movement has drawn its strength from its consciousness that it was a means of progress, that it was pulling society "history-wise" through its struggle against the irrationality of capitalistic profit-seeking. These movements were borne by collective actors, which we label as social classes because they were defined by their political, economic, or social situations. This linkage between an objective meaning and a consciousness necessarily tears apart in the current situation of demodernization. Such movements are becoming increasingly moral, while fighting an opponent that is defined less as a power or class than as an agent of "dehumanization" and of domination through globalized networks of production, consumption, and communication. In this very concrete sense, the identity between the Subject and social movements compels recognition. In industrialized nations particularly, movements are less and less instrumental but more and more expressive.

The awareness of exclusion has spread with poverty, segregation, and joblessness. The societal movement against exclusion is arising out of the efforts of persons who, working in humanitarian organizations, increasingly think and act in terms not of the crisis of capitalism but of the conditions for the destruction or creation of the individual as Subject. There is no evidence that, in France, the leaders of the 1995 protests will be the forerunners of a movement that will organize, undertake a strategic action, and change into a party (as environmentalists have done in Germany). These groups, associations, and movements seem to be constituting themselves as historical, independent actors who mobilize volunteers, who actively use and criticize the media, but who critically stand aloof from a political system that, in their eyes, is subject to the constraints of the international economy. Meanwhile, the weak and threatened sectors of the vast middle class are organizing political actions for defending their vested interests. More diffuse, "everyday" movements— which are also more enthusiastic and more generous—are undertaking exemplary actions, decrying the denial of truth and justice, and combining the personal with collective solidarity. How can we not see in them the already constituted force of a new societal movement? To do so fits into a broader reflection on the conditions for political action and, therefore, for social control over both globalization and technological revolutions, in particular over the effects directly bearing on personality and culture.

Neither liberals nor revolutionaries believe in the capacity of social actions for producing their history through their cultural orientations and social conflicts. In contrast, I maintain that we should recognize the importance of demands for a sense of identity or of strategies for pressing demands. But only the idea of a societal movement enables us to recognize the existence of actions combining a fundamental social conflict with the pursuit of societal objectives (such as modernization, social integration or the respect for human rights) defined in concrete situations and social relations. The idea of a societal movement is not satisfied with completing a sociology that is mainly oriented toward the quest for social integration. It associates integration with conflict and, as a consequence, takes the central place in analyzing the social organization and social change. It is indispensable for any political sociology.

I am not insisting on placing the idea of the Subject at the center of analysis in order to "desocialize" societal movements, i.e. to separate them from the conflictual social relations where they have their origins. On the contrary, this insistence is intended to distinguish a societal movement from the political instruments and ideological apparatuses that keep us from seeing that a societal movement always appeals to the Subject's liberty. These appeals are not situated in the social vacuum of natural law, but in the social relations of domination, property, and power. A societal movement is thus both a struggle for and a struggle against.

Societal movements are important not just because they reveal the contradictions within modem societies, which is defined by their historicity, by the concentration of the means for changing society, and by the distance between the rulers and ruled. What best defines a societal movement is the linkage it establishes between cultural orientations and a social conflict bearing demands that are political and societal. If a societal movement does not form, all these elements separate from each other and, doing so, degrade. On the one hand, cultural orientations, when they are split off from social and political conflicts, turn into moral principles of belonging or of exclusion, mechanisms of cultural control, and norms of social conformity. On the other hand, political conflicts, when they are split off from societal movements, are reduced to struggles for power. Finally, demands, left to themselves, tend to reinforce established inequalities, since the most powerful and influential have the most vested interests to defend and are best equipped to press demands. We thus see a juxtaposition of pressure groups; movements of rejection that comprise categories defined as minorities, deviants or foreigners; and a communitarian populism that appeals to an indeterminate people against leaders

and intellectuals. Each of these aspects of social or political life could, it initially seems, be studied by itself, but that is impossible. All collective actions bear evidence of an absent or disintegrated societal movement.

Societal movements do not always exist; but they do represent a hypothesis that must be worked out in order to understand contemporary collective life. Sociological positivism that takes as starting point not social relations and historicity but principles of order (whether based on personal interests or communitarian values) provides poor explanations that are insufficient because positivists place nothing between the individual and society. In actual fact, however, neither the individual nor society exists as principles that can be isolated from social relations and processes that constantly join order with change, and integration with conflict.

Our need for these concepts and principles of analysis is all the greater now, in that we are living in a "fragmented" society that has been deprived of a consciousness of itself. Under these conditions, issues and actors of historical change are obscure, and discourses and ideologies lag behind practices or become artificially radicalized practices. Our societies are not just hypermodern; they lack meaning, since they suffer from the dissociation of practices from consciousness, and of acts from discourses. Nowadays, the center of society is an empty field where are scattered the remains of past combats and old discourses, which have become second-hand merchandise acquired by the merchants of power and ideologies. For this reason, the idea of a societal movement must be defended because it interprets this emptiness and gives a coherent meaning to all the behaviors, contradictory with each other, that originate in the disappearance and breakup or breakdown of the former social movements.

References

Habermas, J. (1989) *The Structural Transformation of the Public Sphere.* Cambridge, MA: MIT Press.

Olson, M. (1965) *The Logic of Collective Action.* Cambridge, MA: Harvard University Press.

Taylor, C (1996) *Philosophical Arguments*. Cambridge: Cambridge University Press.

Touraine, A. (1965) *Sociologie de l'action*. Paris: Seuil.

76

Interaction Ritual Theory

Randall Collins

Randall Collins (b. 1941) established his theoretical career by articulating a formal theory of conflict (see #37). However, recently he has developed a new theoretical orientation that he calls "interaction ritual theory" (IR). This approach offers a creative appreciation and utilization of two particular theorists: from the classics, Émile Durkheim, and from more recent vintage, Erving Goffman (whom Collins elsewhere has referred to as the most important theorist of the second half of the twentieth century). In this chapter from *Interaction Ritual Chains* (2004), Collins lays out the programmatic features of this theoretical approach, which begins with the claim that the starting point of such a theory is the situation, not the individual. In this respect, he follows Goffman in the first section of this excerpt to make claim to the analytical utility of such a position. In the second section, Durkheim comes into focus as Collins presents his case for the significance of interaction ritual for sociological theory in general. He stresses that IR offers a theory of social dynamics and moreover provides a social psychological account that is sensitive to both cognition and the emotions.

A theory of interaction ritual is the key to microsociology, and microsociology is the key to much that is larger. The small scale, the here-and-now of face-to-face interaction, is the scene of action and the site of social actors. If we are going to find the agency of social life, it will be here. Here reside the energy of movement and change, the glue of solidarity, and the conservatism of stasis. Here is where intentionality and consciousness find their places; here, too, is the site of the emotional and unconscious aspects of human interaction. In whatever idiom, here

is the empirical/experiential location for our social psychology, our symbolic or strategic interaction, our existential phenomenology or ethnomethodology, our arena of bargaining, games, exchange, or rational choice. Such theoretical positions may already seem to be extremely micro, intimate, and small scale. Yet we shall see they are for the most part not micro enough; some are mere glosses over what happens on the micro-interactional level. If we develop a sufficiently powerful theory on the micro-level, it will unlock some secrets of large-scale macrosociological changes as well.

Let us begin with two orienting points. First, the center of microsociological explanation is not the individual but the situation. Second, the term "ritual" is used in a confusing variety of ways; I must show what I will mean by it and why this approach yields the desired explanatory results.

Situation Rather Than Individual as Starting Point

Selecting an analytical starting point is a matter of strategic choice on the part of the theorist. But it is not merely an unreasoning *de gustibus non disputandum est*. I will attempt to show why we get more by starting with the situation and developing the individual, than by starting with individuals; and we get emphatically more than by the usual route of skipping from the individual to the action or cognition that ostensibly belongs to him or her and bypassing the situation entirely.

A theory of interaction ritual (IR) and interaction ritual chains is above all a theory of situations. It is a theory of momentary encounters among human bodies charged up with emotions and consciousness because they have gone through chains of previous encounters. What we mean by the social actor, the human individual, is a quasi-enduring, quasi-transient flux in time and space. Although we valorize and heroize this individual, we ought to recognize that this way of looking at things, this keyhole through which we peer at the universe, is the product of particular religious, political, and cultural trends of recent centuries. It is an ideology of how we regard it proper to think about ourselves and others, part of the folk idiom, not the most useful analytical starting point for microsociology.

This is not to say that the individual does not exist. But an individual is not simply a body, even though a body is an ingredient that individuals get constructed out of. My analytical strategy (and that of the founder of interaction ritual analysis, Erving Goffman) is to start with the dynamics of situations; from this we can derive almost everything that we want to know about individuals, as a moving precipitate across situations.

Here we might pause for a counterargument. Do we not know that the individual is unique, precisely because we can follow him or her across situations, and precisely because he or she acts in a familiar, distinctively recognizable pattern even as circumstances change? Let us disentangle what is valid from what is misleading in this statement. The argument assumes a hypothetical fact, that individuals are constant even as situations change; to what extent this is true remains to be shown. We are prone to accept it, without further examination, as "something everybody knows" because it is drummed into us as a moral principle: everyone is unique, be yourself, don't give in to social pressure, to your own self be true—these are slogans trumpeted by every mouthpiece from preachers' homilies to advertising campaigns, echoing everywhere from popular culture to the avant-garde marching-orders of modernist and hypermodernist artists and intellectuals. As sociologists, our task is not to go with the flow of taken-for-granted belief—(although doing just this is what makes a successful popular writer)—but to view it in a sociological light, to see what social circumstances created this moral belief and this hegemony of social categories at this particular historical juncture. The problem, in Goffman's terms, is to discover the social sources of the cult of the individual.

Having said this, I am going to agree that under contemporary social conditions, very likely most individuals are unique. But this is not the result of enduring individual essences. The uniqueness of the individual is something that we can derive from the theory of IR chains. Individuals are unique to

just the extent that their pathways through interactional chains, their mix of situations across time, differ from other persons' pathways. If we reify the individual, we have an ideology, a secular version of the Christian doctrine of the eternal soul, but we cut off the possibility of explaining how individual uniquenesses are molded in a chain of encounters across time.

In a strong sense, the individual is the interaction ritual chain. The individual is the precipitate of past interactional situations and an ingredient of each new situation. An ingredient, not the determinant, because a situation is an emergent property. A situation is not merely the result of the individual who comes into it, nor even of a combination of individuals (although it is that, too). Situations have laws or processes of their own; and that is what IR theory is about.

Goffman concluded: "not men and their moments, but moments and their men." In gender-neutral language: not individuals and their interactions, but interactions and their individuals; not persons and their passions, but passions and their persons. "Every dog will have its day" is more accurately "every day will have its dog." Incidents shape their incumbents, however momentary they may be; encounters make their encountees. It is games that make sports heroes, politics that makes politicians into charismatic leaders, although the entire weight of record-keeping, news-story-writing, award-giving, speech-making, and advertising hype goes against understanding how this comes about. To see the common realities of everyday life sociologically requires a gestalt shift, a reversal of perspectives. Breaking such deeply ingrained conventional frames is not easy to do; but the more we can discipline ourselves to think everything through the sociology of the situation, the more we will understand why we do what we do.

Let us advance to a more subtle source of confusion. Am I proclaiming, on the micro-level, the primacy of structure over agency? Is the structure of the interaction all-determining, bringing to naught the possibility of active agency? Not at all. The agency/structure rhetoric is a conceptual morass, entangling several distinctions and modes of rhetorical force. Agency/structure confuses the distinction of micro/macro, which is the local here-and-now vis-à-vis the interconnections among local situations into a larger swath of time and space, with the distinction between what is active and what is not. The latter distinction leads us to questions about energy and action; but energy and action are always local, always processes of real human beings doing something in a situation. It is also true that the action of one locality can spill over into another, that one situation can be carried over into other situations elsewhere. The extent of that spillover is part of what we mean by macro-patterns. It is acceptable, as a way of speaking, to refer to the action of a mass of investors in creating a run on the stock market, or of the breakdown of an army's logistics in setting off a revolutionary crisis, but this is a shorthand for the observable realities (i.e., what would be witnessed by a micro-sociologist on the spot). This way of speaking makes it seem as if there is agency on the macro-level, but that is inaccurate, because we are taken in by a figure of speech. Agency, if we are going to use that term, is always micro; structure concatenates it into macro.

But although the terms "micro" and "agency" can be lined up at one pole, they are not identical. There is structure at every level. Micro-situations are structures, that is to say, relationships among parts. Local encounters, micro-situations, have both agency and structure. The error to avoid is identifying agency with the individual, even on the micro-level. I have just argued that we will get much further if we avoid reifying the individual, that we should see individuals as transient fluxes charged up by situations. Agency, which I would prefer to describe as the energy appearing in human bodies and emotions and as the intensity and focus of human consciousness, arises in interactions in local, face-to-face situations, or as precipitates of chains of situations. Yes, human individuals also sometimes act when they are alone, although they generally do so because their minds and bodies are charged with results of past situational encounters, and their solitary action is social insofar as it aims at and comes from communicating with other persons and thus is situated by where it falls in an IR chain.

On the balance, I am not much in favor of the terminology of "agency" and "structure." "Micro" and "macro" are sufficient for us to chart the continuum from local to inter-local connections. The energizing and the relational aspects of interactions, however, are tightly connected. Perhaps the best we might say is that the local structure of interaction is what generates and shapes the energy of the situation. That energy can leave traces, carrying over to further situations because individuals bodily resonate with emotions, which trail off in time but may linger long enough to charge up a subsequent encounter, bringing yet further chains of consequences. Another drawback of the term "agency" is that it carries the rhetorical burden of connoting moral responsibility; it brings us back to the glorification (and condemnation) of the individual, just the moralizing gestalt that we need to break out from if we are to advance an explanatory microsociology. We need to see this from a different angle. Instead of agency, I will devote theoretical attention to emotions and emotional energy, as changing intensities heated up or cooled down by the pressure-cooker of interaction rituals. Instead of emphasizing structure, or taking the other tack of backgrounding it as merely a foil for agency, I will get on with the business of showing how IRs work. . . .

The Significance of Interaction Ritual for General Sociological Theory

The Durkheimian model addresses the central questions of social theory; and it has implications that extend to all corners of contemporary microsociology. It asks the basic question: What holds society together? And it answers the question with a mechanism of social rituals. Furthermore, it answers it with a mechanism that varies in intensity: society is held together to just the extent that rituals are effectively carried out, and during those periods of time when the effects of those rituals are still fresh in people's minds and reverberating in their emotions. Society is held together more intensely at some moments than at others. And the "society" that is held together is no abstract unity of a social system, but is just those groups of people assembled in particular places who feel solidarity with each other through the effects of ritual participation and ritually charged symbolism. The total population of France, or the United States, or anywhere else one might consider, consists of pockets of solidarity of different degrees of intensity. A population can be washed by waves of national solidarity on occasion, but these are particular and rather special ritually based events, subject to the same processes of ritual mobilization as more local pockets of solidarity.

This means that the Durkheimian model is entirely compatible with a view of stratification and group conflict. Indeed, it provides key mechanisms for just how stratification and conflict operate. Rephrase the question as, What holds society together as a pattern of stratified and conflicting groups? The answer is social rituals, operating to create and sustain solidarity within those groups. We can elaborate a more complicated answer, and later chapters will do so. Among those complications are these: that some groups have more resources for carrying out their rituals than others, so that some groups have more solidarity and thus can lord it over those who have less; and that these ritually privileged groups have more impressive symbols and fill their members with more emotional energy. We may examine more fine-grained processes of stratification: looking inside the very group that is brought together by participating in a ritual, we can see that some individuals are more privileged than others, by being nearer to the center of the ritual than others. Rituals thus have a double stratifying effect: between ritual insiders and outsiders; and, inside the ritual, between ritual leaders and ritual followers. Rituals are thus key mechanisms, and we might say key weapons, in processes of conflict and domination.

Durkheim famously argued that the utilitarian, economic dimension of life is not basic, but depends upon precontractual solidarity; that rituals provide the basis for a situation of social trust and shared symbolic meanings through which economic exchanges can be carried out. Here I am mak-

ing a similar argument with regard to social conflict: conflict is not the primordial condition of social life, a Hobbesian war of all against all, but is analytically derivative of social solidarity. That is to say, effective conflict is not really possible without the mechanisms of social ritual, which generate the alliances and the energies of the partisans, as well as their most effective weapons in dominating others. And the goals of conflict, the things that people fight over, are formed by these patterns of social rituals. The flashpoints of conflict, the incidents that set off overt struggle, almost always come from the precedence of symbols and the social sentiments they embody. All this is to say that social conflict, which I and many other theorists have argued is the major process structuring social life, especially on the macro-level of large-scale structures (Collins 1975; Mann 1986–93), requires for its explanation a Durkheimian microsociology of interaction rituals.

The central mechanism of interaction ritual theory is that occasions that combine a high degree of mutual focus of attention, that is, a high degree of intersubjectivity, together with a high degree of emotional entrainment—through bodily synchronization, mutual stimulation/arousal of participants' nervous systems—result in feelings of membership that are attached to cognitive symbols; and result also in the emotional energy of individual participants, giving them feelings of confidence, enthusiasm, and desire for action in what they consider a morally proper path. These moments of high degree of ritual intensity are high points of experience. They are high points of collective experience, the key moments of history, the times when significant things happen. These are moments that tear up old social structures or leave them behind, and shape new social structures. As Durkheim notes, these are moments like the French Revolution in the summer of 1789. We could add, they are moments like the key events of the Civil Rights movement in the 1960s; like the collapse of communist regimes in 1989 and 1991; and to a degree of significance that can be ascertained only in the future, as in the national mobilization in the United States following September 11, 2001. These examples are drawn from large-scale ritual mobilizations, and examples of a smaller scale could be drawn as we narrow our attention to smaller arenas of social action.

Interaction ritual theory is a theory of social dynamics, not merely of statics. Among social theorists there is a tendency to regard ritual analysis as conservative, a worship of traditions laid down in the past, a mechanism for reproducing social structure as it always existed. True enough, ritual analysis has often been used in this vein; and even theories like Bourdieu's, which combine Durkheim with Marx, see a mutually supporting interplay between the cultural or symbolic order and the order of economic power. For Bourdieu, ritual reproduces the cultural and therefore the economic fields. . . . But this is to miss the transformative power of ritual mobilization. Intense ritual experience creates new symbolic objects and generates energies that fuel the major social changes. Interactional ritual is a mechanism of change. As long as there are potential occasions for ritual mobilization, there is the possibility for sudden and abrupt periods of change. Ritual can be repetitive and conservatizing, but it also provides the occasions on which changes break through.

In this respect IR theory mediates between postmodernist and similar theories that posit ubiquitous situational flux of meanings and identities, and a culturalist view that fixed scripts or repertoires are repeatedly called upon. The contrast is articulated by Lamont (2000, 243–44, 271), who provides evidence that there are "cultural and structural conditions that lead individuals to use some criteria of evaluation rather than others." The argument is parallel to my use of IR theory, which pushes the argument at a more micro-situational level: that the operative structural conditions are those that make up the ingredients of interaction ritual; and that cultural repertoires are created in particular kind of IRs, and fade out in others. To show the conditions under which ritual operates in one direction or the other is a principal topic of this book.

Intense moments of interaction ritual are high points not only for groups but also for individual lives. These are the events that we remember, that give meaning to our per-sonal biographies, and sometimes to obsessive attempts to repeat them: whether participating in some great collective event such as a big political demonstration; or as spectator at some storied moment of popular entertainment or sports; or a personal encounter ranging from a sexual experience, to a strongly bonding friendly exchange, to a humiliating insult; the social atmosphere of an alcohol binge, a drug high, or a gambling victory; a bitter argument or an occasion of violence. Where these moments have a high degree of focused awareness and a peak of shared emotion, these personal experiences, too, can be crystalized in personal symbols, and kept alive in symbolic replays for greater or lesser expanses of one's life. These are the significant formative experiences that shape individuals; if the patterns endure, we are apt to call them personalities; if we disapprove of them we call them addictions. But this usage too easily reifies what is an ongoing flow of situations. The movement of individuals from one situation to another in what I call interaction ritual chains is an up-and-down of variation in the intensity of interaction rituals; shifts in behavior, in feeling and thought occur just as the situations shift. To be a constant personality is to be on an even keel where the kinds of interaction rituals flow constantly from one situation to the next. Here again, IR theory points up the dynamics of human lives, their possibility for dramatic shifts in direction.

IR theory provides a theory of individual motivation from one situation to the next. Emotional energy is what individuals seek; situations are attractive or unattractive to them to the extent that the interaction ritual is successful in providing emotional energy. This gives us a dynamic microsociology, in which we trace situations and their pull or push for individuals who come into them. Note the emphasis: the analytical starting point is the situation, and how it shapes individuals; situations generate and regenerate the emotions and the symbolism that charge up individuals and send them from one situation to another.

Interaction ritual is a full-scale social psychology, not only of emotions and situational behavior, but of cognition. Rituals generate symbols; experience in rituals inculcates those symbols in individual minds and memories. IR provides an explanation of variations in beliefs. Beliefs are not necessarily constant, but situationally fluctuate, as a number of theorists have argued and as researchers have demonstrated (Swider 1986; Lamont 2000). What IR theory adds to contemporary cultural theory in this regard is that what people think they believe at a given moment is dependent upon the kind of interaction ritual taking place in that situation: people may genuinely and sincerely feel the beliefs they express at the moment they express them, especially when the conversational situation calls out a higher degree of emotional emphasis; but this does not mean that they act on these beliefs, or that they have a sincere feeling about them in other everyday interactions where the ritual focus is different. IR theory gives the conditions under which beliefs become salient, by rising and falling in emotional loading. Everyday life is the experience of moving through a chain of interaction rituals, charging up some symbols with emotional significance and leaving others to fade. IR theory leads us into a theory of the momentary flow of internal mental life, an explanation of subjectivity as well as intersubjectivity.

Durkheim held that the individual consciousness is a portion of the collective consciousness. This is tantamount to saying that the individual is socialized from the outside, by social experience carried within. This is surely true, as most social scientists would agree, as far as early childhood socialization is concerned. The argument of IR theory carries this further: we are constantly being socialized by our interactional experiences throughout our lives. But not in a unidirectional and homogeneous way; it is intense interaction rituals that generate the most powerful emotional energy and the most vivid symbols, and it is these that are internalized. Contrary to an implication of Freudian theory and others that stress early childhood experience, socialization once laid down does not endure forever; emotional energies and symbolic meanings fade if they are not renewed. IR theory is not a model of a wind-up doll, programmed early in life, which ever after walks through the pattern once laid down. It is a theory of moment-to-moment motivation, situation by situation. Thus it has high theoretical ambitions: to explain what any individual will do, at any moment in time; what he or she will feel, think, and say

Viewed in the abstract, this may seem like an impossibly high ambition. But consider: there are considerable theoretical resources available for this task. We have Durkheimian theory, which yields an explicit model of what produces sentiments of group membership; of symbols that formulate social values, and through which humans think; and of emotional energies that animate individuals. This theory is cast in terms of conditions of varying strength, so that we can tell which situations will generate higher or lower levels of solidarity, respect for symbols, and emotional energy And this model is of wide applicability: it fits not only the great collective events of religion and politics, as Durkheim himself pointed out, but it can be brought to bear on the level of everyday life situation by Goffman's line of application. More and more details of how to apply the Durkheimian ritual theory to everyday life situations are becoming available, as I will attempt to show in later chapters, by drawing on such resources as Meadian symbolic interactionist theory of thinking as internalized conversation, along with contemporary research on conversation and on emotions, and on the ethnography of everyday life. The totality of social life is the totality of situations that people go through in their everyday lives; we have a powerful and wide-ranging model that explains what will happen in those situations. An offshoot of this situational microsociology is the internalization of social life in individuals' subjective experience: the sociology of thinking and feeling.

Why not follow this theoretical research program as far as it will go? Some intellectuals have philosophical commitments that hold them back from taking this path; we do not want a theory that explains everything, and we construct arguments to rule out the possibility of any such a theory succeeding. There are lines of metatheory, going back to Max Weber and to his Neo-Kantian predecessors, which hold that the territory of social science is the realm of human meanings and human freedom, *Geisteszuissenschaft* as opposed to *Naturwissenschaft,* a realm in which deterministic explanations do not apply. But such arguments are hardly conclusive: they try to lay out in advance and by conceptual definition what we can and cannot find along particular lines of investigation. Social theory and research moves along pragmatically, in the real flow of intellectual history; philosophers and metatheorists cannot legislate what we will not be able to explain in the future.

The program of interaction ritual theory is to take the intellectual tools that we have, and to apply them: to all situations, all emotions, all symbols, all thinking, all subjectivity and intersubjectivity. Intellectual life is an exciting adventure when we try to push it as far as we can. There is surely more emotional energy in exploration than in conservatively standing pat and trying to avoid extending our understanding beyond the boundaries set up by intellectual taboos. IR theory, as an intellectual enterprise, is a set of symbolic representations riding on its surge of emotional energy; it is the intellec-tual version of effervescence that gave elan to Durkheim and his research group, to Goffman and his followers, and to today's sociologists of emotion and process in everyday life. What I attempt to show in this book is some vistas that open up as we ride this intellectual movement into the future.

References

Collins, Randall. 1975. *Conflict Sociology: Toward an Exploratory Science.* New York: Academic Press.

Lamont, Michèle. 2000. *The Dignity of Working Men: Morality and the Boundaries of Race, Class, and Immigration.* New York and Cambridge, MA: Russell Sage Foundation and Harvard University Press.

Mann, Michael. 1986–93. *The Sources of Social Power,* 3 vols. Cambridge: Cambridge University Press.

Swidler, Ann. 1986. "Culture in Action." *American Sociological Review,* 51(2): 111–125.

77

Materials for an Exploratory Theory of the Network Society

Manuel Castells

Manuel Castells (b. 1942) is one of the foremost contemporary theorists of urbanization, globalization, and the impact of technology on contemporary social life. In his most recent work, he argues that we have entered an Information Age characterized by a global network society predicated in large part on advances in informational technologies. In this essay, Castells notes that although networks are not new forms of organization, a situation has emerged in recent decades wherein a network society comes to constitute the characteristic social structure of the new society. This transformation has made possible greater flexibility and decentralization of power compared to the preceding era of industrial society. The impact of network society is far-reaching, extending not simply to the realm of economic production but also filtering into patterns of consumption, power relations, the ways individuals experience the world, interpersonal relationships, and culture. In short, what he outlines is a reframing of sociological theory in an effort to capture the most significant technological and social changes of the past four decades.

Introduction

The network society is a specific form of social structure tentatively identified by empirical research as being characteristic of the Information Age. By social structure I understand the organizational arrangements of humans in relationships of production/consumption, experience, and power,

as expressed in meaningful interaction framed by culture. By Information Age I refer to a historical period in which human societies perform their activities in a technological paradigm constituted around microelectronics-based information/communication technologies, and genetic engineering. It replaces/subsumes the technological paradigm of the Industrial Age, organized primarily around the production and distribution of energy. . . .

The Network Society: An Overview

In the last two decades of the twentieth century a related set of social transformations has taken place around the world. While cultures, institutions, and historical trajectories introduce a great deal of diversity in the actual manifestations of each one of these transformations, it can be shown that, overall, the vast majority of societies are affected in a fundamental way by these transformations. All together they constitute a new type of social structure that I call the network society for reasons that hopefully will become apparent. I shall summarize below the main features of these transformations, in a sequential order that does not imply hierarchy of causation in any way.

We have entered *a new technological paradigm*, centred around microelectronics-based, information/communication technologies, and genetic engineering. In this sense what is characteristic of the network society is not the critical role of knowledge and information, because knowledge and information were central in all societies. Thus, we should abandon the notion of "Information Society," which I have myself used some times, as unspecific and misleading. What is new in our age is a new set of information technologies. I contend they represent a greater change in the history of technology than the technologies associated with the Industrial Revolution, or with the previous Information Revolution (printing). Furthermore, we are only at the beginning of this technological revolution, as the Internet becomes a universal tool of interactive communication, as we shift from computer-centred technologies to network-diffused technologies, as we make progress in nanotechnology (and thus in the diffusion capacity of information devices), and, even more importantly, as we unleash the biology revolution, making possible for the first time, the design and manipulation of living organisms, including human parts. What is also characteristic of this technological paradigm is the use of knowledge-based, information technologies to enhance and accelerate the production of knowledge and information, in a self-expanding, virtual circle. Because information processing is at the source of life, and of social action, every domain of our eco-social system is thereby transformed.

We live in a *new economy*, characterized by three fundamental features. First, it is *informational*, that is, the capacity of generating knowledge and processing/managing information determine the productivity and competitiveness of all kinds of economic units, be they firms, regions, or countries. While it took two decades for the new technological system to yield its productivity dividend, we are now observing substantial productivity growth in the most advanced economies and sectors, in spite of the difficulty in measuring informational productivity with the categories of the industrial era.

Second, this new economy is *global* in the precise sense that its core, strategic activities, have the capacity to work as a unit on a planetary scale in real time or chosen time. By core activities I mean financial markets, science and technology, international trade of goods and services, advanced business services, multinational production firms and their ancillary networks, communication media, and highly skilled speciality labour. Most jobs are in fact not global, but all economies are under the influence of the movements of their globalized core. Globalization is highly selective. It proceeds by linking up all that, according to dominant interests, has value anywhere in the planet, and discarding anything (people, firms, territories, resources) which has no value or becomes devalued, in a variable geometry of creative destruction and destructive creation of value.

Third, the new economy is *networked*. At the heart of the connectivity of the global economy and of the flexibility of informa-

tional production, there is a new form of economic organization, the *network enterprise*. This is not a network of enterprises. It is a network made from either firms or segments of firms, and/or from internal segmentation of firms. Large corporations are internally de-centralized as networks. Small and medium businesses are connected in networks. These networks connect among themselves on specific business projects, and switch to another network as soon as the project is finished. Major corporations work in a strategy of changing alliances and partnerships, specific to a given product, process, time, and space. Furthermore, these co-operations are based increasingly on sharing of information. These are information networks, which, in the limit, link up suppliers and customers through one firm, with this firm being essentially an intermediary of supply and demand, collecting a fee for its ability to process information.

The unit of this production process is not the firm, but the business project. The firm continues to be the legal unit of capital accumulation. But since the value of the firm ultimately depends on its valuation in the stock market, the unit of capital accumulation (the firm) itself becomes a node in a global network of financial flows. In this economy, the dominant layer is the global financial market, where all earnings from all activities and countries end up being traded. This global financial market works only partly according to market rules. It is shaped and moved by information turbulences of various origins, processed and transmitted almost instantly by tele-communicated, information systems, in the absence of the institutional regulation of global capital flows.

This new economy (informational, global, networked) is certainly capitalist. Indeed, for the first time in history, the whole planet is capitalist, for all practical purposes (except North Korea, but not Cuba or Myanmar, and certainly not China). But it is a new brand of capitalism, in which rules for investment, accumulation, and reward, have substantially changed (see Giddens and Hutton 2000). Besides, since nothing authorizes capitalism as eternal, it is essential to focus on the characteristics of the new economy because it may well outlast the mode of production where it was born, once capitalism comes under decisive challenge and/or plunges into a structural crisis derived from its internal contradictions (after all, statism died from its self-inflicted flaws).

Work and employment are substantially transformed in/by the new economy. But, against a persistent myth, there is no mass unemployment as a consequence of new information technologies. The empirical record is conclusive on this matter (Carnoy 2000). Yet, there is a serious unemployment problem in Europe, unrelated to technology, and there are dramatic problems of under-employment in the developing world, caused by economic and institutional backwardness, including the insufficient diffusion and inefficient use of information technologies. There is a decisive transformation of work and employment. Induced by globalization, and the network enterprise, and facilitated by information/communication technologies, the most important transformation in employment patterns concerns the development of flexible work, as the predominant form of working arrangements. Part-time work, temporary work, self-employment, work by contract, informal or semi-formal labour arrangements, and relentless occupational mobility, are the key features of the new labour market. Feminization of paid labour leads to the rise of the "flexible woman," gradually replacing the "organization man," as the harbinger of the new type of worker. The key transformation is the individualization of labour, reversing the process of socialization of production characteristic of the industrial era, still at the roots of our current system of industrial relations.

The work process is interconnected between firms, regions, and countries, in a stepped up spatial division of labour, in which networks of locations are more important than hierarchies of places. Labour is fundamentally divided in two categories: self-programmable labour, and generic labour. Self-programmable labour is equipped with the ability to retrain itself, and adapt to new tasks, new processes and new sources of information, as technology, demand, and management speed up their rate of change.

Generic labour, by contrast, is exchangeable and disposable, and co-exists in the same circuits with machines and with unskilled labour from around the world. Beyond the realm of employable labour, legions of discarded, devalued people form the growing planet of the irrelevant, from where perverse connections are made, by fringe capitalist business, through to the booming, global criminal economy. Because of this structural divide in terms of informational capacities, and because of the individualization of the reward system, in the absence of a determined public policy aimed at correcting structural trends, we have witnessed in the last 20 years a dramatic surge of inequality, social polarization, and social exclusion in the world at large, and in most countries, particularly, among advanced societies, in the USA and in the UK (see UNDP 1999; Hutton 1996; Castells 2000, for sources).

Shifting to the *cultural realm*, we see the emergence of a similar pattern of networking, flexibility, and ephemeral symbolic communication, in a culture organized primarily around an integrated system of electronic media, obviously including the Internet. Cultural expressions of all kinds are increasingly enclosed in or shaped by this electronic hypertext. But the new media system is not characterized by one-way, undifferentiated messages through a limited number of channels that constituted the world of mass media. And it is not a global village. Media are extraordinarily diverse, and send targeted messages to specific segments of audiences responding to specific moods of audiences. They are increasingly inclusive, bridging from one another, from network TV to cable TV or satellite TV, radio, VCR, video, portable devices, and the Internet. The whole set is coming together in the multimedia system, computer-operated by the digitalized set-top box that opens up hundreds of channels of interactive communication, reaching from the global from the local. While there is oligopolistic concentration of multimedia groups, there is, at the same time, market segmentation, and the rise of an interactive audience, superseding the uniformity of the mass audience. Because of the inclusiveness and flexibility of this system of symbolic exchange, most cultural expressions are enclosed in it, thus inducing the formation of what I call a culture of "real virtuality." Our symbolic environment is, by and large, structured by this flexible, inclusive hypertext, in which many people surf each day. The virtuality of this text is in fact a fundamental dimension of reality, providing the symbols and icons from which we think and thus exist.

This growing enclosure of communication in the space of a flexible, interactive, electronic hypertext does not only concern culture. It has a fundamental effect on *politics*. In almost all countries, media have become the space of politics. To an overwhelming extent people receive their information, on the basis of which they form their political opinion and structure their behaviour, through the media and particularly television and radio. Media politics needs to convey very simple messages. The simplest message is an image. The simplest, individualized image is a person. Political competition increasingly revolves around the personalization of politics. The most effective political weapons are negative messages. The most effective negative message is character assassination of opponents' personalities, and/or of their supporting organizations. Political marketing is an essential means to win political competition, including, in the information age, media presence, media advertising, telephone banks, targeted mailing, image making and unmaking. Thus, politics becomes a very expensive business, way beyond the means of traditional sources of political financing, at a time when citizens resist giving more of their tax money to politicians. Thus, parties and leaders use access to power as ways to obtain resources for their trade. Political corruption becomes a systemic feature of information age politics. Since character assassination needs some substance from time to time, systemic political corruption provides ample opportunity, as a market of intermediaries is created to leak and counter-leak damaging information. The politics of scandal takes centre stage in political competition, in close interaction with the media system, and with the co-operation of judges and prosecutors, the new stars of our political soap operas. Politics becomes a horse race, and a tragicomedy motivated by greed, backstage manoeuvres, betrayals, and, often, sex and violence—a genre increasingly indistinguishable from TV scripts.

As with all historical transformations, the emergence of a new social structure is linked to a redefinition of the material foundations of our life, of *time and space*, as Giddens (1984), Lash and Urry (1994), Thrift (1990), and Harvey (1990), among others, have argued. I propose the hypothesis that two emergent social forms of time and space characterize the network society, while coexisting with prior forms of time and space. These are timeless time and the space of flows. In contrast to the rhythm of biological time characteristic of most of human existence, and to clock time characterizing the industrial age, timeless time is defined by the use of new information/communication technologies in a relentless effort to annihilate time. On the one hand, time is compressed (as in split second global financial transactions, or in the attempt to fight "instant wars"), and on the other hand, time is de-sequenced, including past, present, and future occurring in a random sequence (as in the electronic hypertext or in the blurring of life-cycle patterns, both in work and parenting).

The space of flows refers to the technological and organizational possibility of organizing the simultaneity of social practices without geographical contiguity. Most dominant functions in our societies (financial markets, transnational production networks, media systems, etc.) are organized around the space of flows. And so do an increasing number of alternative social practices (such as social movements) and personal interaction networks. However, the space of flows does include a territorial dimension, as it requires a technological infrastructure that operates from certain locations, and as it connects functions and people located in specific places. Yet, the meaning and function of the space of flows depend on the flows processed within the networks, by contrast with the space of places, in which meaning, function, and locality are closely interrelated.

The central power-holding institution of human history, *the state*, is also undergoing a process of dramatic transformation. On the one hand, its sovereignty is called into question by global flows of wealth, communication, and information. On the other hand, its legitimacy is undermined by the politics of scandal and its dependence on media politics. The weakening of its power and credibility induce people to build their own systems of defence and representation around their identities, further de-legitimizing the state. However, the state does not disappear. It adapts and transforms itself. On the one hand, it builds partnerships between nation-states and shares sovereignty to retain influence. The European Union is the most obvious case, but around the world there is a decisive shift of power toward multi-national and transnational institutions, such as NATO, IMF/World Bank, United Nations agencies, World Trade Organization, regional trade associations, and the like. On the other hand, to regain legitimacy, most states have engaged in a process of devolution of power, decentralizing responsibilities and resources to nationalities, regions, and local governments, often extending this de-centralization to non-governmental organizations. The international arena is also witnessing a proliferation of influential, resourceful non-governmental organizations that interact with governments, and multinational political institutions. Thus, overall the new state is not any longer a nation-state. The state in the information age is a network state, a state made out of a complex web of power-sharing, and negotiated decision-making between international, multinational, national, regional, local, and non-governmental, political institutions.

There are two common trends in these processes of transformation that, together, signal a new historical landscape. First, none of them could have taken place without new information/communication technologies. Thus, while technology is not the cause of the transformation, it is indeed the indispensable medium. And in fact, it is what constitutes the historical novelty of this multidimensional transformation. Second, all processes are enacted by organizational forms that are built upon networks, or to be more specific, upon information networks.

Thus, to analyse the emerging social structure in theoretically meaningful terms, we have to define what information networks are, and elaborate on their strategic role in fostering and shaping current processes of social transformation.

Social Structure and Social Morphology: From Networks to Information Networks

A network is a set of interconnected nodes. A node is the point where the curve intersects itself. Networks are very old forms of social organization. But they have taken on a new life in the Information Age by becoming information networks, powered by new information technologies. Indeed, networks had traditionally a major advantage and a major problem, in contrast to other configurations of social morphology, such as centralized hierarchies. On the one hand, they are the most flexible and adaptable forms of organization, able to evolve with their environment and with the evolution of the nodes that compose the network. On the other hand, they have considerable difficulty in co-ordinating functions, in focusing resources on specific goals, in managing the complexity of a given task beyond a certain size of the network. Thus, while they were the natural forms of social expression, they were generally outperformed as tools of instrumentality. For most of human history, and unlike biological evolution, networks were outperformed by organizations able to master resources around centrally defined goals, achieved through the implementation of tasks in rationalized, vertical chains of command and control. But for the first time, the introduction of new information/communication technologies allows networks to keep their flexibility and adaptability, thus asserting their evolutionary nature. While, at the same time, these technologies allow for co-ordination and management of complexity, in an interactive system which features feedback effects, and communication patterns from anywhere to everywhere within the networks. It follows an unprecedented combination of flexibility and task implementation, of co-ordinated decision making, and de-centralized execution, which provide a superior social morphology for all human action.

Networks de-centre performance and share decision-making. By definition, a network has no centre. It works on a binary logic: inclusion/exclusion. All there is in the network is useful and necessary for the existence of the network. What is not in the network does not exist from the network's perspective, and thus must be either ignored (if it is not relevant to the network's task), or eliminated (if it is competing in goals or in performance). If a node in the network ceases to perform a useful function it is phased out from the network, and the network rearranges itself as cells do in biological processes. Some nodes are more important than others, but they all need each other as long as they are within the network. And no nodal domination is systemic. Nodes increase their importance by absorbing more information and processing it more efficiently. If they decline in their performance, other nodes take over their tasks. Thus, the relevance, and relative weight of nodes does not come from their specific features, but from their ability to be trusted by the network with an extra share of information. In this sense, the main nodes are not centres, but switchers, following a networking logic rather than a command logic, in their function vis-à-vis the overall structure.

Networks, as social forms, are value-free or neutral. They can equally kill or kiss: nothing personal. They process the goals they are programmed to perform. All goals contradictory to the programmed goals will be fought off by the network components. In this sense, a network is an automaton. But, who programmes the network? Who decides the rules that the automaton will follow? Social actors, naturally. Thus, there is a social struggle to assign goals to the network. But once the network is programmed, it imposes its logic to all its members (actors). Actors will have to play their strategies within the rules of the network. To assign different goals to the programme of the network (in contrast to perfect the programme within the same set of goals), actors will have to challenge the

network from the outside and in fact destroy it by building an alternative network around alternative values. Or else, building a defensive, non-network structure (a commune) which does not allow connections outside its own set of values. Networks may communicate, if they are compatible in their goals. But for this they need actors who possess compatible access codes to operate the switches. They are the switchers or power-holders in our society (as in the connections between media and politics, financial markets and technology, science and the military, and drug traffic and global finance through money laundering).

The speed and shape of structural transformations in our society, ushering in a new form of social organization, come from the widespread introduction of information networks as the predominant organizational form. Why now? The answer lies in the simultaneous availability of new, flexible information technologies and a set of historical events, which came together by accident, around the late 1960s and 1970s. These events include the restructuring of capitalism with its emphasis on deregulation and liberalization; the failed restructuring of statism unable to adapt itself to informationalism; the influence of libertarian ideology arising from the countercultural social movements of the 1960s; and the development of a new media system, enclosing cultural expressions in a global/local, interactive hypertext. All processes, interacting with each other, favoured the adoption of information networks as a most efficient form of organization. Once introduced, and powered by information technology, information networks, through competition, gradually eliminate other organizational forms, rooted in a different social logic. In this sense, they tend to assert the predominance of social morphology over social action. Let me clarify the meaning of this statement by entering into the heart of the argument, that is, by examining how specifically the introduction of information networks into the social structure accounts for the set of observable transformations as presented in the preceding section. Or, in other words, how and why information networks constitute the backbone of the network society.

The Role of Information Networks in Shaping Relationships of Production, Consumption, Power, Experience, and Culture

Information networks, as defined above, contribute, to a large extent, to the transformation of social structure in the information age. To be sure, this multidimensional transformation has other sources that interact with the specific effect of information networks, as mentioned above. Yet, in this analysis, I will focus on the specificity of the interaction between this new social morphology and the evolution of social structure. I will be as parsimonious as possible, trying to avoid repetition of arguments and observations already presented in this text.

A social structure is transformed when there is simultaneous and systemic transformation of relationships of production/consumption, power, and experience, ultimately leading to a transformation of culture. Information networks play a substantial role in the set of transformations I have analysed in my work and summarized here. This is how and why.

Relationships of Production

Although I suppose information networks will shape, eventually, other modes of production, for the time being we can only assess their effect in the capitalist mode of production. Networks change the two terms of the relationship (capital, labour) and their relationship. They transform capital by organizing its circulation in global networks and making it the dominant sphere of capital the one where value, from whichever origin, increases (or decreases) and is ultimately realized. Global financial markets are information networks. They constitute themselves into a collective "capitalist," independent from any specific capitalist (but not indifferent to), and activated by rules that are only partly market rules. In this sense, capital in the Information Age has become a human-made automaton, which, through mediations, imposes its structural determination on relationships of production. More specifically, global financial markets and their management networks constitute an automated network, governed by interactions between its multiple nodes, propelled by a combination of market logic, information turbulences, and actors' strategies and bets (see Castells 2000).

Relationships between capital and labour (all kinds of capital, all kinds of labour) are organized around the network enterprise form of production. This network enterprise is also globalized at its core, through telecommunications and transportation networks. Thus, the work process is globally integrated, but labour tends to be locally fragmented. There is simultaneous integration of production and specification of labour's contribution to the production process. Value in the production process depends essentially on the position occupied by each specific labour or each specific firm in the value chain. The rule is individualization of the relationship between capital and labour. In a growing number of cases, self-employment, or payment in stocks, leads to workers becoming holders of their own capital; however, any individual capital is submitted to the movements of the global automaton. As labour comes to be defined by a network of production and individualized in its relationship to capital, the critical cleavage within labour becomes that between networked labour and switched-off labour which ultimately becomes non-labour. Within networked labour, it is the capacity to contribute to the value-producing chain that determines the individual bargaining position. Thus labour's informational capacity, by ensuring the possibility of strategic positioning in the network, leads to a second, fundamental cleavage, between self-programmable labour and generic labour. For self-programmable labour, its individual interest is better served by enhancing its role in performing the goals of the network, thus establishing competition between labour and co-operation between capital (the network enterprize) as the structural rule of the game. Indeed game theory and rational choice theory seem to be adequate intellectual tools to understand socio-economic behaviour in the networked economy. While for generic labour, its strategy is survival: the key issue becomes not be degraded to the realm of discarded or devalued labour, either by automation or globalization, or both.

In the last analysis, the networking of relationships of production leads to the blurring of class relationships. This does not preclude exploitation, social differentiation and social resistance. But production-based, social classes, as constituted, and enacted in the Industrial Age, cease to exist in the network society.

Relationships of Consumption

Relationships of consumption (that is, the culturally meaningful, differential appropriation of the product) are determined by the interplay between relationships of production and culture. Who does what, in a given value production system, determines who gets what. What is valued as appropriation is framed by culture. The networking of production relationships, and the consequent individualization of labour, leads on the one hand to increasing differentiation and thus inequality in consumption. It also leads to social polarization and social exclusion following the opposition between self-programmable labour and generic labour, and between labour and devalued labour. The ability of networks to connect valuable labour and territories, and to discard dispensable labour and territories, so enhancing their performance through reconfiguration, leads to cumulative growth and cumulative decline. The winner-takes-all system is, in the consumption sphere, the expression of value creation by/in the networks.

On the other hand, the fragmentation of culture, and the individualization of positions in relationships of production, lead jointly to a growing diversification of consumption patterns. Mass consumption was predicated upon standardized production, stable relationships of production, and a mass culture organized around predictable senders and identifiable sets of values. In a world of networks, self-programmable individuals constantly redefine their life styles and thus their consumption patterns; while generic labour just strives for survival.

As culture is similarly fragmented and constantly recombined in the networks of a

kaleidoscopic hypertext, consumption patterns follow the variable geometry of symbolic appropriation. Thus, in the interplay between relationships of production and cultural framing, relationships of production define levels of consumption, and culture induces consumption patterns and life styles.

Relationships of Power

The most direct impact of information networks on social structure concerns power relationships. Historically, power was embedded in organizations and institutions, organized around a hierarchy of centres. Networks dissolve centres, they disorganize hierarchy, and make materially impossible the exercise of hierarchical power without processing instructions in the network, according to the network's morphological rules. Thus, contemporary information networks of capital, production, trade, science, communication, human rights, and crime, bypass the nation-state, which, by and large, has stopped being a sovereign entity, as I argued above. A similar process, in different ways, takes place in other hierarchical organizations that used to embody power ("power apparatuses" in the old Marxist terminology), such as churches, schools, hospitals, bureaucracies of all kinds. Just to illustrate this diversity, churches see their privilege as senders of belief called into question by the ubiquitous sending and receiving of messages in the interactive hypertext. While religions are flourishing, churches have to enter the new media world in order to promote their gospel. So doing, they survive, and even prosper, but they open themselves up to constant challenges to their authority. In a sense, they are secularized by their co-existence with profanity in the hypertext, except when/if they anchor themselves in fundamentalism by refusing to bend to the network, thus building self-contained, cultural communes.

The state reacts to its bypassing by information networks, by transforming itself into a network state. So doing, its former centres fade away as centres becoming nodes of power-sharing, and forming institutional networks. Thus, in the war against Yugoslavia, in spite of US military hegemony, decision-making was shared in various degrees by NATO governments, including regular video-conferences between the leaders of the main countries where key decisions were taken. This example goes beyond the former instances of traditional military alliances, by introducing joint war-making in real time. NATO was reinforced by NATO's state members, when these states, including the USA, entered the new world of shared sovereignty. But individual states became weakened in their autonomous decision-making. The network became the unit.

Thus, while there are still power relationships in society, the bypassing of centres by flows of information circulating in networks creates a new, fundamental hierarchy: the power of flows takes precedence over the flows of power.

Relationships of Experience

If power relationships are the ones most directly affected by the prevailing networking logic, the role of networks in the transformation of relationships of experience is more subtle. I will not force the logic of the analysis. I do not believe that we must see networks everywhere for the sake of coherence. Yet, I think it could be intriguing to elaborate tentatively on the links between networking and the transformation of relationships of experience.

This transformation, empirically speaking, revolves around the crisis of patriarchalism, and its far-reaching consequences for family, sexuality and personality. The fundamental source of this crisis is women's cultural revolution, and men's resistance to reverse their millennial privileges. Additional sources are the feminization of labour markets (undermining male domination in the family and in society at large), the revolution in reproductive technology, the self-centring of culture, the individualization of life patterns and the weakening of the state's authority to enforce patriarchalism. What networks have to do with all this?

There is one direct connection between the networking of work and the individualization of labour, and the mass incorporation of women to paid labour, under conditions of structural discrimination. Thus, new social relationships of production, translate into a good fit between the "flexible woman" (forced to flexibility to cope with her multiple roles) and the network enterprise. Networks of information and global communication are also critical in diffusing alternative life styles, role models and, more importantly, critical information, for instance about self-control of biological reproduction. Then, there is an additional, meaningful connection. The disintegration of the patriarchal family does not [leave] people, and children, isolated. They reconfigure life-sharing forms through networking. This is particularly true of women and their children, relying on a form of sociability and solidarity tested by millennia of living "underground." But also men, and men and women after going their own ways, come to rely on networks (sometimes around children of multiple marriages) to both survive and re-invent forms of togetherness. This trend shifts the basis of interpersonal relationships from nuclei to networks: networks of individuals and their children—which, by the way, are also individuals. What is left of families are transformed in partnerships which are nodes of networks. Sexuality is decoupled from the family, and transformed into consumption/images, stimulated and simulated from the electronic hypertext. The body, as proposed by Giddens some time ago, becomes an expression of identity (1991). It is individualized and consumed in sexual networks. At the level of personality, the process of socialization becomes customized, individualized, and made out of composite models. The autonomous ability to reprogramme one's own personality, in interaction with an environment of networks, becomes the crucial feature for psychological balance, replacing the strengthening of a set personality, embedded in established values. In this "risk society" (Beck 1992), the management of anxiety is the most useful personal skill. Two conflicting modes of interpersonal interaction emerge: on the one hand, self-reliant communes, anchored in their non-negotiable sets of beliefs; and on the other hand, networks of ever shifting individuals.

These are social networks, not information networks. So, in a way, they are a fundamental part of our societies, but not necessarily a feature of the network society—unless we extend the meaning of the concept beyond what I propose: information networks-based social structure. However, as communication technology, biological technology, transgender networking, and networks of individuals develop in parallel, as key elements of social practice, they are interacting, and influencing each other. Thus, the Internet is becoming a very instrumental tool of management of new forms of life, including the building of on-line communities of support and collective learning.

I see, however, a much stronger connection between networks and relationships of experience through the cultural transformations induced by communication networks, as experience becomes practice by its rooting in cultural codes.

Networks and Cultural Transformation

Culture was historically produced by symbolic interaction in a given space/time. With time being annihilated and space becoming a space of flows, where all symbols coexist without reference to experience, culture becomes the culture of real virtuality. It takes the form of an interactive network in the electronic hypertext, mixing everything, and voiding the meaning of any specific message out of this context, except that is for fundamental, non-communicable values external to the hypertext. So, culture is unified in the hypertext but interpreted individually (in line with the "interactive audience" school of thought in media theory). Culture is constructed by the actor, self-produced and self-consumed. Thus, because there are few common codes, there is systemic misunderstanding. It is this structurally induced cacophony that is celebrated as postmodernity. However, there is one common language, the language of the hypertext. Cultural expressions left out of the hypertext are purely individual experiences. The hypertext is the vehicle of communication, thus the provider of shared cultural codes. But these codes are formal, voided of specific meaning. Their only shared meaning is to be a node, or a blip, in the network of communication flows. Their communicative power comes from their capacity to be interpreted and rearranged in a multi-vocality of meanings, de-pending on the receiver, and on the interactor. Any assigned meaning becomes instantly obsolete, reprocessed by a myriad of different views and alternative codes. The fragmentation of culture and the recurrent circularity of the hypertext, leads to the individualization of cultural meaning in the communication networks. The networking of production, the differentiation of consumption, the decentring of power, and the individualization of experience are reflected, amplified, and codified by the fragmentation of meaning in the broken mirror of the electronic hypertext—where the only shared meaning is the meaning of sharing the network.

Conclusion: Social Change in the Network Society

Social structures are sets of organizational regularities historically produced by social actors, and constantly challenged, and ultimately transformed by deliberate social action. The network society is no exception to this sociological law. Yet, the characteristics of specific social structures impose constraints on the characteristics of their transformation process. Thus, the recurrence and flexibility of information networks, their embedded ability to bypass, ignore or eliminate instructions alien to their programmed goals, make social change in the network society a very tricky task. This is because, apparently, nothing must be changed—any new input can theoretically be added to the network, like free expression in the global media system. Yet, the price for the addition is to accept implicitly the programmed goal of the network, its ancillary language and operating procedures. Thus, my hypothesis is that there is little chance of social change within a given network, or network of networks. Understanding by social change, the transformation of the programme of the network, to assign to the network a new goal, following a different set of values and beliefs. This is in contrast to reprogramming the network by adding instructions compatible with the overarching goal.

Because of the capacity of the network to find new avenues of performance by switching off any non-compatible node, I think social change, under these circumstances, happens primarily through two mechanisms, both external to dominant networks. The first is the denial of the networking logic through the affirmation of values that cannot be processed in any network, only obeyed and followed. This is what I call cultural communes, that are not necessarily linked to fundamentalism, but which are always centred around their self-contained meaning. The second is alternative networks, that is networks built around alternative projects, which compete, from network to network, to build bridges of communication to other networks in society, in opposition to the codes of the currently dominant networks. Religious, national, territorial, and ethnic communes are examples of the first type of challenge. Ecologism, feminism, human rights movements are examples of alternative networks. All use the Internet and electronic media hypertext, as dominant networks do. This is not what makes them networks or communes. The critical divide lies in the communicability or non-communicability of their codes beyond their specific self-definition. The fundamental dilemma in the network society is that political institutions are not the site of power any longer. The real power is the power of instrumental flows, and cultural codes, embedded in networks. Therefore, the assault to these immaterial power sites, from outside their logic, requires either the anchoring in eternal values, or the projection of alternative, communicative codes that expand through networking of alternative networks. That social change proceeds through one way or another will make the difference between fragmented communalism and new history making.

Bibliography

Arquilla, John and Rondfeldt, David. 1999. *The Emergence of Noopolitik*. Santa Monica, CA: Rand, National Defense Research Institute.

Barber, Benjamin. 1995. *Jihad vs. McWorld*. New York: Times Books.

Beck, Ulrich. 1992. *Risk Society: Towards a New Modernity*. London: Sage.

Calhoun, Craig (ed.). 1994. *Social Theory and the Politics of Identity*. Oxford: Blackwell.

Carnoy, Martin. 2000. *Work, Family and Community in the Information Age*. New York: Russell Sage.

Castells, Manuel. 2000. "Information Technology and Global Capitalism," in A. Giddens and W. Hutton (eds.), *On the Edge*. London: Jonathan Cape.

Croteau, David and Hoynes, William. 1997. *Media/Society: Industries, Images, and Audiences*. Thousand Oaks, CA: Pine Forge Press.

De Kerckhove, Derrick. 1997. *"Connected Intelligence."* Toronto: Somerville House.

Dutton, William H. 1999. *Society on the Line: Information Politics in the Digital Age*. Oxford: Oxford University Press.

Giddens, Anthony. 1984. *The Constitution of Society: Outline of a Theory of Structuration*. Cambridge: Polity Press.

——. 1991. *Modernity and Self-Identity: Self and Society in the Late Modern Age*. Stanford: Stanford University Press.

Giddens, Anthony, and Hutton, Will (eds.). 2000. *On the Edge*. London: Jonathan Cape.

Graham, Stephen, and Marvin, Simon. 1996. *Telecommunications and the City: Electronic Spaces, Urban Places*. London: Routledge.

Hage, Jerald, and Powers, Charles. 1992. *Postindustrial Lives: Roles and Relationships in the 21st Century*. London: Sage.

Hall, Peter (Sir). 1998. *Cities in Civilization*. New York, Pantheon.

Harvey, David. 1990. *The Condition of Postmodernity*. Oxford: Blackwell.

Held, David, and Mc Grew, Anthony, Goldblatt, David, and Perraton, Jonathan. 1999. *Global Transformations: Politics, Economics, and Culture*. Stanford: Stanford University Press.

Hutton, Will. 1996 [1995]. *The State We're In*. London: Jonathan Cape.

Lash, Scott, and Urry, John. 1994. *Economies of Signs and Space*. London: Sage.

Lyon, David. 1999. *Postmodernity*. Buckingham: Open University Press.

Mansell, Robin, and Silverstone, Roger (eds.). 1996. *Communication by Design: The Politics of Information and Communication Technologies*. Oxford: Oxford University Press.

Scott, Allen. 1998. *Regions and the World Economy. The Coming Shape of Global Production, Competition, and Political Order*. New York: Oxford University Press.

Subirats, Marina. 1998. "Con diferencia: las mujeres frente al reto de la autonomia." Barcelona: Icaria.

Thrift, Nigel J. 1990. "The Making of Capitalism in Time Consciousness," in J. Hassard (ed.), *The Sociology of Time*. London: Macmillan.

Touraine, Alain. 1993 [1973]. *Production de la societé*. Paris: Seuil.

——. 1997. *Pourrons-nous vivre ensemble? Egaux et differents*. Paris: Fayard.

Turkle, Sherry. 1995. *Life on the Screen, Identity in the Age of Internet*. New York: Simon and Schuster.

United Nations Development Programme. 1999. *1999 Human Development Report: Globalization With a Human Face*. New York: UNDP-United Nations.

Webster, Juliet. 1996. *Shaping Women's Work: Gender, Employment, and Information Technology*. London: Longman.

Wellman, Barry (ed.). 1999. *Networks in the Global Village*. Boulder, CO: Westview Press.

78

Mobile Sociology

John Urry

John Urry (b. 1946) is a British theorist whose sociological interests have been varied. His theoretical contributions have always been located within and shaped by a variety of concrete research projects. His early work focused on power, while subsequent work has examined urban and regional development, changes in the nature of contemporary capitalism, and the increasing significance of consumerism and tourism. More recently, he has turned his attention to complexity theory. Urry describes "Mobile Sociology" as a manifesto that urges greater appreciation of "diverse mobilities of peoples, objects, images, information, and wastes." In focusing attention on movement and fluidity, his argument bears a resemblance to that of Arjun Appadurai. What makes his essay distinctive is that it calls for further reflection on the very notion of society, which has been since sociology's formative period its presumed central object of inquiry. Picking up on Margaret Thatcher's infamous remark that "there is no such thing as society," he enters into a discussion of what we mean by society, in the process urging a greater self-reflexivity on the part of theorists.

> At the present moment of history the network of social relations spreads over the whole world, without any absolute solution of continuity. This gives rise to the difficulty . . . of defining what is meant by the term 'society' . . . If we say that our subject is the study and comparison of human societies we ought to be able to say what are the unit entities with which we are concerned.
> (A. R. Radcliffe-Brown 1952: 193)

A *self does* not amount to much, but no self is an island; each exists in a fabric of relations that is now more complex and mobile than ever before.
> (J-F Lyotard 1984: 15)

Introduction

In this article I outline some categories relevant for developing sociology as a 'discipline' as we enter the next century. I argue for a sociology concerned with the diverse mobilities of peoples, objects, images, information, and wastes; and of the complex interdependencies between, and social consequences of, these diverse mobilities.

Elsewhere I have shown how mobilities are transforming the historic subject-matter of sociology which within the 'west' has focused upon individual societies and their generic characteristics (Urry 2000). In *Sociology Beyond Societies* I develop a 'post-societal' agenda for sociology elaborating how various global 'networks and flows' undermine endogenous social structures that possess the power to reproduce themselves. New rules of sociological method are necessitated by the apparently declining powers of national societies since it is they that have historically provided the intellectual and organizational context for sociology. Some of the diverse mobilities that are materially transforming the 'social as society' into the 'social as mobility' include imaginative travel, movements of images and information, virtual travel, object travel and corporeal travel (see Urry 2000: ch. 3). The consequence of such diverse mobilities is to produce what Beck terms the growth of 'inner mobility' for which coming and going, being both here and there at the same time, has become much more globally normal (1999: 75–6).

In this article I show how mobilities criss-crossing societal borders in new temporal-spatial patterns constitute a novel agenda for sociology, of mobility. Much twentieth-century sociology has been based upon the study of occupational, income, educational and social mobility. This literature regarded society as a uniform surface and failed to register the geographical intersections of region, city and place, with the social categories of class, gender and ethnicity. Further, there are crucial flows of people within, but especially beyond, the territory of each society, and these flows relate to many different desires, for work, housing, leisure, religion, family relationships, criminal gain, asylum seeking and so on. Moreover, not only people are mobile, but so too are many 'objects', 'images', 'informations' and 'wastes'. Mobility is thus to be understood in a horizontal rather than a vertical sense, and it applies to a variety of actants and not just to humans.

Bauman's vertical metaphor of 'gardening' to characterize modern societies is pertinent here (1987). He suggests that a gardening state has replaced earlier 'gamekeeper' states that were not involved in giving society an overall shape and were uninterested in detail. By contrast the gardening state presumes exceptional concern with pattern, regularity and ordering, with what is growing and with what should be weeded out. Legislators have been central to careful tendering by the gardening state, with using their reason to determine what is, and is not, productive of order. The social sciences have been part of that application of reason to society through facilitating the husbandry of societal resources, identifying what is and what is not to be cultivated and determining what are the exact conditions of growth of particular plants.

However, the new global order appears to involve a return to the gamekeeper state and away from that of the gardener. The gamekeeper was concerned with regulating mobilities, with ensuring that there was sufficient stock for hunting in a particular site but not with the detailed cultivation of each animal in each particular place. Animals roamed around and beyond the estate, like the roaming hybrids that currently wander in and especially across national borders. States are increasingly unable or unwilling to garden their society, only to regulate the conditions of their stock so that on the day of the hunt there is appropriate stock available for the hunter. As Beck has recently argued: 'capital, culture, technology' and politics merrily come together to roam *beyond* the regulatory power of the national state' (1999: 107).

The former East European societies were 'gardening' societies. Following the Second World War, the individual societies of central and eastern Europe constructed exceptionally strong frontiers both from the 'West' and especially from each other. Cultural communication into and out of such societies was exceptionally difficult. The Cold War chilled culture as well as politics. So although such societies were internationally linked via the hegemony of the USSR, there was a parallel emphasis upon cultural involution and the reinforcement of strongly reinforced national networks. It constituted an interesting social laboratory based upon the concept of 'society'.

But what happened was that regional frontiers of each society were transgressed, they were got around through various fluid-like movements. The attempt to freeze the peoples and cultures of 'Eastern Europe' could not be sustained. The Berlin Wall was of course the most dramatic example of this attempted gardening the people of a society. But through the 1960s, forms of communication and later of leisure travel noticeably increased. Both peoples and objects especially began to flow across the carefully constructed borders, often involving what has been termed the 'invisible hand of the smuggler' (Braun et al. 1996: 1). Objects of the 'West' became used and talked about in multiple informal ways, helping the citizens of such societies to form new bases of personal identity, new ways of collectively remembering and new images of self and society. Many citizens went to inordinate lengths to learn about and to acquire objects that were immutable in their western-ness. Thus these societies became surrounded by hordes of 'animals' (consumer goods, images, western ideas and so on) which increasingly crossed into and over the land that had been so carefully husbanded. Their populations chased after the animals and trampled underfoot the carefully tended plants (another kind of 'animal farm'! See Urry 2000: ch. 2).

In the next section I consider 'sociology' and 'society' in more detail, before turning briefly to global networks and fluids. I consider how notions of complexity can analyse intensely mobile hybrids that roam across the globe and help to create a self-reproducing global order. I conclude with some observations about the implications of this mobile order for 'sociology', the science of 'society'.

'There Is No Such Thing as Society'

When former British Prime Minister Margaret Thatcher famously declared that 'there is no such thing as society', sociologists led the charge to critique her claim. They declared that there are obviously societies and that Thatcher's claim indicated the wrongness of her policies based upon trying to reduce the societal to the interests of 'individual men and women and their families'. However, the riposte to Thatcher from the sociological community was not fully justified since it is actually unclear just what is meant by 'society'. Although there is something 'more' in social life than 'individual men and women and their families', exactly what this surplus amounts to is not so obvious (see Albertsen and Diken 1999: ch. 2, for extensive discussion).

Sociological discourse has indeed been premised upon 'society' as its object of study (Billig 1995: 52–3; Hewitt 1997: Urry 2000: ch. 1). This was especially so from the 1920s onwards as sociology was institutionalized, especially within the American academy. MacIver and Page's standard *Society: An Introductory Analysis* argues that sociology is ' "about" social relationships, the network of relationships we call society' (1950: v). The radical Gouldner in *The Coming Crisis of Western Sociology* talks of 'Academic Sociology's emphasis on the potency of society and the subordination of men [sic] to it' (1972: 52). Wallerstein summarizes the overall situation: 'no concept is more pervasive in modern social science than society' (1987: 315; note that the major exception to this is Luhmann's analysis of autopeitic systems, see 1990: ch. 1; 1995). This construction of the discourse of sociology around the concept of society in part stemmed from the apparent autonomy of American society throughout the twentieth century and is thus to universalize the American societal experience.

However, what most of these formulations neglect to specify is how 'society' connects to the system of nations and nation-states. Billig argues that: 'the "society" which lies at the heart of sociology's self-definition is created in the image of the nation-state' (1995: 53). Interestingly American-based theories of society have frequently ignored the 'nationalist' basis of American and indeed of all western societies. They have typically viewed nationalism as surplus to society that only needs deployment in situations of 'hot' extremism, situations which supposedly do not describe societies of the 'west' (Billig 1995: 52–4).

In theorizing society, sovereignty, national citizenship and social governmentality lie at its core. Each 'society' is a sovereign social entity with a nation-state that organizes the rights and duties of each societal member or citizen. Most major sets of social relationships flow within the territorial boundaries of the society. The state possesses a monopoly of jurisdiction or governmentality over members living within the territory or region of the society. Economy, politics, culture, classes, gender and so on are societally structured. In combination they constitute a clustering or a 'social structure'. Such a structure organizes and regulates the life-chances of each member of the society in question.

This societal structure is not only material but also cultural, so that its members believe they share some common identity that is bound up in part with the territory that the society occupies or lays claim to. And *contra* the argument of much sociology, central to most such societies is a vernacular nationalism that articulates the identities of each society through its mundane differences from the other. These include the waving of celebratory flags, singing national anthems, flying flags on public buildings, identifying with one's own sports-heroes, being addressed in the media as a member of a given society, celebrating independence day and so on (Billig 1995),

However, societies are never entirely self-reproducing entities. Sociology has a tendency to treat what is 'outside' the society as an unexamined environment. But no society, even in the heyday of the nation-state earlier this century, has been separate from the very system of such states and from the notion of national identity that mobilizes sovereign societies. As Calhoun points out: 'No nation-state ever existed entirely unto itself' (1997: 118; Wallerstein 1991: 77). It is through this interdependence that societies are constituted as partially self-regulating entities, significantly defined by their banal or vernacular differences from each other.

Over the past two centuries this conception of society has been central to North American and West-European notions of what it is to possess the rights and duties of social citizenship. To be human meant that one is a member or citizen of a particular society. Historically and conceptually there has been a strong connection between the idea of humanness and of membership of a society. Society here means that ordered through a nation-state, with clear territorial and citizenship boundaries and a system of governance over its particular citizens. Conceptually and historically there has been an indivisible duality, of citizens and societies. Rose characterizes this model as government from 'the social point of view' (1996: 328; see Marshall and Bottomore 1992). There is a nationalisation of social responsibility' with societal governmentality effected through new forms of expertise, particularly that of sociology as the science of such societies and of the appropriate forms of social citizenship (Knorr Cetina 1997).

In this account 'society' and its characteristic social divisions of especially social class are strongly interconnected with the 'nation-state'. Mann shows that societies, nations and states have been historically intertwined (1993: 737). They developed together and should not be conceptualized as billiard balls existing only in external relations with one another. Mann evocatively talks of the sheer patterned messiness of the social world and of the mutually reinforcing intersections of class and nation, as societies developed their 'collective powers' especially over nature.

Sociology as a specific academic practice was the product of this particular historical moment, of an emergent industrial capitalism in Western Europe and North America. It took for granted the success of modern societies in their spectacular overcoming of nature. Sociology specialized in describing and explaining the character of these modern societies based upon industries that enabled and utilized dramatic new forms of energy and resulting patterns of social life. As such sociology adopted one or other versions of a tradition-modernity divide that implied that a revolutionary change had occurred in North Atlantic rim societies between 1700–1900. These modern societies were presumed to be qualitatively different from the past. Sociology was thus based upon the acceptance and enhancement of the presumed division of academic labour stemming from the Durkheimian identification of the region of the social to be investigated and explained autonomously (Durkheim 1952 [1897]). Until recently this academic division between a world of natural facts and one of social facts made good sense as a strategy of professionalization for sociology. This sphere was parallel to, but did not challenge or confront, those physical sciences that dealt with an apparently distinct and analysable nature (see Macnaghten and Urry 1998).

Each society was sovereign, based upon a social governmentality. The concerns of each society were to be dealt with through national policies, especially from the 1930s onwards through a Keynesian welfare state that could identify and respond to the risks of organized capitalism (Lash and Urry 1987; 1994). These risks were seen as principally located *within* the geographical borders and temporal frames of each society. And solutions were devised and implemented within such societal frontiers. National societies were based upon a concept of the citizen who owed duties to, and received rights from, their society through the core institutions of the nation-state. This 'societal' model applied to the dozen or so societies of the North Atlantic rim. Most of the rest of the world was subject to domination by these societies of the North Atlantic rim.

In the next section I consider further this system which contemporary changes have put into question and which suggest that Thatcher was right when she said there is no such thing as society. But that there may not be such a thing as society is not because of the power of individual human subjects, but because of their weakness in the face of 'inhuman' fluid and mobile processes of globalization. Wallerstein points out that: 'What is fundamentally wrong with the concept of society is that it reifies and therefore crystallizes social phenomena whose real significance lies not in their solidity but precisely in their fluidity and malleability' (1991: 71).

Global Networks and Fluids

A useful starting point here is Mann's description of the contemporary world

> Today, we live in a global society. It is not a unitary society, . . . nor is it an ideological community or a state, but it is a single power network. Shock waves reverberate around it, casting down empires, transporting massive quantities of people, materials and messages, and finally, threatening the ecosystem and atmosphere of the planet. (1993: 11)

He makes a number of points here: there is no unified global society but there are exceptional levels of global interdependence; unpredictable shock waves spill out 'chaotically' from one part to the system as a whole; there are not just 'societies' but massively powerful 'empires' roaming the globe; and there is mass mobility of peoples, objects and dangerous human wastes.

What then are appropriate metaphors to make sense of these transformations? Mol and Law argue that there are three distinct metaphors of space or social topologies, regions, networks and fluids (1994; Urry 2000: ch. 2). First, there are *regions* in which objects are clustered together and boundaries are drawn around each particular regional cluster. Second, there are *networks* in which relative distance is a function of the relations between the components comprising the network—the invariant outcome is delivered across the entire network that often crosses regional boundaries. And third, there is the metaphor of the *fluid* that flows: 'neither boundaries nor relations mark the difference between one place and another. Instead, sometimes boundaries come and go, allow leakage or disappear altogether, while relations transform themselves without fracture. Sometimes, then, social space behaves like a fluid' (Mol and Law 1994: 643).

The sociological concept of society is based upon the metaphor of a region,

namely that 'objects are clustered together and boundaries are drawn around each particular cluster' (Mol and Law 1994: 643). And one way to study globalization is through seeing it involved in inter-regional competition with 'society'. Globalization could be viewed as the replacing of one region, the bounded nation-state-society of the 'west', with another, that of global economy and culture. And as both economy and culture are increasingly globalized, so the old dominant region of society appears to become relatively less powerful. In the fight between these two regions it looks as though the global region will win out and defeat the societal region (see Robertson 1992).

But this is only one way of understanding globalization. Globalization can also be viewed not as one larger region replacing the smaller region of each society, but as involving alternative metaphors of *network* and *fluid* (Mol and Law 1994; Waters 1995; Albrow 1996; Castells 1996, 1997; Eade 1997; Held et al. 1999; Beck 1999). The globalization literature has described the wide variety of new *machines and technologies* that dramatically compress or shrink time-space. These technologies carry people, information, money, images and risks, and flow within and across national societies in increasingly brief moments of time. Such technologies do not derive directly and uniquely from human Intentions and actions. They are intricately interconnected with machines, texts, objects and other technologies. The appropriate metaphor to capture these intersections of peoples and objects is not that of a vertical structure that typically involves a centre, a concentration of power, vertical hierarchy and a formal or informal constitution. Castells argues, by contrast, that we should employ the metaphor of network, 'the unit is the network' (1996: 198).

> Networks constitute the new social morphology of our societies, and the diffusion of networking logic substantially modifies the operation and outcomes in processes of production, experience, power and culture . . . the network society, characterized by the pre-eminence of social morphology over social action. (Castells 1996: 469)

Castells defines a network as a set of interconnected nodes, the distance between social positions are shorter where such positions constitute nodes within a network as opposed to those which lie outside the particular network. Networks are to be viewed as dynamic open structures, so long as they are able to effect communication with new nodes and to innovate (Castells 1996: 470–1). Much economic geography has detailed the apparently increased significance of such networks within the contemporary economy, at the intra-firm level, at the inter-firm and inter-organizational level and at the firm-community levels (see Amin and Thrift 1992; Cooke and Morgan 1993; Messner 1997).

Network here does not mean purely *social* networks since the 'convergence of social evolution and information technologies has created a new material basis for the performance of activities throughout the social structure. This material basis, built in networks, earmarks dominant social processes, thus shaping social structure itself' (Castells 1996: 471). Networks thus produce complex and enduring connections across space and through time between peoples and things (see Murdoch 1995: 745). They spread across time and space which is hugely important, since according to Law, if 'left to their own devices *human actions and words do not spread very far at all*' (1994: 24). Different networks possess different reaches or abilities to bring home distant events, places or people, to overcome the friction of regional space within appropriate periods of time (Emirbayer and Sheller 1999: 748). This requires mobilizing, stabilizing and combining peoples, actions or events elsewhere into a stable network, an immutable mobile (Latour 1987). Accountancy, for example, is particularly effective at reducing the variety of activities in distant regions to a common set of figures, the flows of information, that can be instantaneously translated back to other parts of the network and especially to its control and command headquarters (Murdoch 1995: 749).

By contrast with the immutable mobiles of accountancy, Mol and Law show how the networks and flows involved in the measurement of haemoglobin levels are less secure

(1994: 647–50). They ask how it is possible to produce regional maps of such comparative haemoglobin levels—analogous to accountants producing regional maps of the relative profitability of different plants of a global company. They argue that this requires a network constituted across many different regions, comprising appropriate technologies, measuring machines and people with suitable medical and technical skills. However, such a network is problematic to establish because in parts of the world there are inadequate numbers of machines to undertake appropriate measurement and, even where they do exist, they may not be appropriately maintained (see Messner 1997, more generally on network failure). Where a successful network does get established across a number of regions, this transforms the configurations of space and time that are no longer 'regional'. In a network established for measuring haemoglobin levels, two hospitals can be proximate although they are geographically hundreds of kilometres apart from each other. They constitute nodes within that particular set of networked flows.

There are two further aspects of networks to distinguish here, namely, scapes and flows. *Scapes* are the networks of machines, technologies, organizations, texts and actors that constitute various interconnected nodes along which *flows* can be relayed. Such scapes reconfigure the dimensions of time and space. Once particular scapes have been established, then individuals and especially corporations within each society will normally try to become connected to them through being constituted as nodes within that particular network. They will seek to develop their own hub airport or at least have regular flights to such airports; they will wish their local schools to be plugged into the internet; they will try to attract satellite broadcasting; they may even seek to reprocess nuclear waste products, and so on. Between certain nodes along some scapes extraordinary amounts of information may flow, of financial, economic, scientific and news data and images, into which some groups are extremely well plugged-in while others are effectively excluded. What becomes significant is what Brunn and

Leinbach term 'relative' as opposed to 'absolute' location (1991: xvii). This creates novel inequalities of flow as opposed to the inequalities of stasis. Graham and Marvin maintain that what is involved here is a rewarping of time and space by advanced telecommunication and transportation structures, as scapes pass by some areas and connect other areas along information and transport rich 'tunnels' (1996: 60). Social and spatial distances are no longer homologous (Beck 1999: 104).

So far I have talked rather generally of global networks criss-crossing the regional borders of society, thus bringing out some aspects of contemporary 'de-territorialization' (Lefebvre 1991: 346-8). These notions will now be made more precise by distinguishing between two different kinds of such networks, *global networks* and what I will call *global fluids*.

Numerous 'global' enterprises, such as American Express, McDonalds, Coca Cola, Disney, Sony, BA and so on, are organized on the basis of a *global network* (see Ritzer 1992; 1995; 1997). Such a network of technologies, skills, texts and brands ensures that more or less the same product is delivered in more or less the same way in every country in which the enterprise operates. Such products are produced in predictable, calculable, routinized and standardized environments. These companies have produced enormously effective networks based upon immutable mobiles with few Tailings'. Such networks depend upon allocating a very large proportion of resources to branding, advertising, quality control, staff training and the internalization of the corporate image, all of which cross societal boundaries in standardized patterns so maintaining constancy. Distance is measured in terms of the time taken to get to the next McDonalds, the next Disney park, the next BA hub airport and so on, that is, from one node in this global network to the next. Such global networks can also be found within oppositional organizations such as Greenpeace. Like other global players it devotes much attention to developing and sustaining its brand identity throughout the world. Greenpeace's brand identity has 'such an iconic status that it is a world-wide symbol of ecological virtue quite above and beyond the actual practical successes of the organization' within particular societies (Szerszynski 1997: 46).

Second, there are *global fluids*, the heterogeneous, uneven and unpredictable mobilities of people, information, objects, money, images and risks, that move chaotically across regions in strikingly faster and unpredictable shapes. Such global fluids (as opposed to networks) demonstrate (see Deleuze and Guattari 1986, 1988; Lefebvre 1991; Mol and Law 1994; Auge 1995; Kaplan 1996; Shields 1997) no clear point of departure or arrival, just de-territorialized movement or mobility (rhizomatic rather than arboreal). They are relational in that they productively effect relations between the spatially varying features of a scape that would otherwise remain functionless. Fluids move in particular directions at certain speeds but with no necessary end-state or purpose. They possess different properties of viscosity and, as with blood, can be thicker or thinner and hence move in different shapes at different speeds. They move according to certain temporalities, over each minute, day, week, year and so on. Most importantly, fluids do not always keep within the scape—they may move outside or escape like white blood corpuscles through the 'wall' of the blood vessel into tinier and tinier capillaries; hence their power is diffused through these various fluids into very many often minute capillary-like relations of domination/subordination. Different fluids spatially intersect in the 'empty meeting grounds' of the non-places of modernity, such as motels, airports, service stations, the internet, international hotels, cable television, expense account restaurants and so on.

I have thus set out some characteristics of global networks and fluids. Because these are inhuman hybrids, conceptions of agency that specifically focus upon the capacities of humans to attribute meaning or sense or to follow a social rule are inappropriate. This is not to suggest that humans do not do such things, not to suggest that human do not exert agency. But they only do so in circumstances which are not of their own making; and it is those circumstances—the enduring and increasingly intimate relations of subjects *and* objects—that are of paramount significance. This means that the human and physical worlds are elaborately intertwined and cannot be analysed separately from each other, as society and as nature, or humans and objects. Also agency is not a question of humans acting independently of objects in terms of their unique capacities to attribute meaning or to follow rules. If then there is not autonomous realm of human agency, so there should not be thought of as a distinct level of *social* reality that is the unique outcome of humans acting in and through their specific powers. Various writers have tried to develop the thesis of the dialectic of individuals making society and society making individuals (Berger and Luckmann 1967). But such a dialectic would only be only plausible if we mean by society something trivial, that is pure social interactions abstracted from the networks of intricate relationships with the inhuman. Since almost all social entities do involve networks of connections between humans and these other components, so there are no uniquely *human* societies as such. Societies are necessarily hybrids.

More generally, Laclau and Mouffe show the impossibility of society as a valid object of discourse (1985). What we can ask stitches a 'society' together when inhuman networks criss-cross it in strikingly new ways at ever-faster speeds? The classic philosophical-sociological debates as to the respective virtues of methodological individualism versus holism, or in their later manifestations, structurationism versus the dualism of structure, are unhelpful here. They do not deal with the complex consequences of diverse mobilities; the intersecting sensuous relations of humans with diverse objects; the timed and spaced quality of relations stretching across societal borders; and the complex and unpredictable intersections of many 'regions, networks and flows'. To describe these as either 'structure' or as 'agency' does injustice to the complexity of such relations. Luhmann summarizes: 'There can be no "intersubjectivity" on the basis of the subject' (1995: xli). The ordering of social life is contingent, unpredictable, irreducible to human subjects and is only made possible by extra-somatic assets (as opposed to the pure sociality of baboon

society: Law 1994). Knorr Cetina outlines the necessity of analysing 'sociality with objects' (1997).

In the next section I consider whether notions of 'complexity' can illuminate such inhuman, mobile intersecting hybrids—is complexity the basis of 'post-social' knowledge?

Complex Mobilities

The 'complex' nature of both physical and social systems means that they are characterized by a very large number of elements that interact physically and informationally over time and result in positive and negative feedback loops (see Byrne 1998; Cilliers 1998; Wallerstein 1998; Thrift 1999, on recent social science applications of chaos/complexity theory). Such systems interact dissipatively with their environment and have a history that evolves irreversibly through time. Emergent, unintended and non-linear consequences are generated within such systems, consequences that are patterned but unpredictable, distant in time and/or space from where they originate and involving potential system bifurcation.

In the physical sciences complexity theory uses mathematical formulae and computer algorithms to characterize the enormously large number of iterative events. In certain experiments, the analysis of increases in the reproduction patterns of gypsy moths showed, through resulting changes in population size, dramatic non-linear changes in the quality of the system. Changes in the parameter resulted in transformations in the system; in certain contexts, order generates chaos. The more complex the system the more likely it is that small fluctuations will be critical (see Prigogine and Stengers 1984).

This iterative character of systems has been insufficiently interrogated within sociology (although see Mingers 1995; Eve, Horsfall, Lee 1997). Partly this is because of the presumed a-temporal character of the social world, rather than the seeing of all social hybrids as necessarily historical (as are physical hybrids; see Adam 1990). But it has also stemmed from the baleful consequences of the divide between structure and agency. In sociological thought the millions of individual iterative actions are largely subsumed under the notion of 'structure' (such as the class structure, or the structure of gender relations or social structure) which is seen as 'ordered' and reproduced through continuous iteration. The concept of structure solves the problem of iteration for sociology. However, social systems do change and sociology then draws upon the concept of agency to argue that some sets of agents can on occasions manage to escape such a structure and effect change in it. If social systems change then this is seen to result from agency.

Certain authors have however seen the limitations of this formulation, including those that emphasize the performativity of gender through the stylized repetition of actions over time (Butler 1990). Giddens develops the 'duality of structure' to account for the recursive character of social life (1984). Now recursive is like iteration; and Giddens undoubtedly advances the ways in which we understand how 'structures' are both drawn on, and are the outcome of, countless iterative actions by knowledgeable agents. However, Giddens insufficiently examines the 'complex' character of these iterative processes, of how order can generate chaos, unpredictability and non-linearity. So although there is recurrence, such recurrent actions may produce non-equilibrium, non-linearity and, if the parameters change dramatically, a sudden branching of the social world. And this is the crucial point; such complex change may have nothing necessarily to do with agents actually seeking to change that world. The agents may simply keep carrying out the same recurrent actions or what they conceive to be the same actions. But it is through iteration over time that they may generate unexpected, unpredictable and chaotic outcomes, often the very opposite of what the human agents involved may seek to realize. Moreover, of course, agents are not just humans but will be a variety of human and non-human actants that constitute the typical mobile, roaming hybrids (where states at best 'regulate the game' rather than 'tend the garden'; see Urry 2000: ch. 8).

One social science example of complexity thinking is Marx's analysis of the unfolding 'contradictions' of capitalism (see Elster 1978). Marx argues that individual capitalists seek to maximize their profits and hence pay their particular workers as little as possible or make them work increasingly long hours. This 'exploitation' of the workforce will continue unless states, or collective actions by trade unions, prevent it, or workers die prematurely. The consequences of such endlessly repeated actions reproduces the capitalist system since substantial profits are generated, so offsetting what Marx hypothesized as the law of the declining rate of profit. The realization of such profits has the effect of reproducing the class relations of capital and wage-labour integral to the ordering of the capitalist system.

However, the very process of sustaining order through each capitalist exploiting their particular workers, results in three system contradictions, of over-production, of an increasingly revolutionary workforce and the smashing down of Chinese walls and the internationalization of the proletariat. Thus the outcomes of capitalist order are, over time and millions of iterations, the opposite of what capitalists appeared to be reproducing through exploiting their local workforce. Millions of iterations produce chaos out of order, non-linear changes and a potentially catastrophic branching of the capitalist system (see Reed and Harvey 1992). Much sociology has sought to explain why these predictions have not materialized. However, Marx's inability to predict social revolution can be regarded by contemporary theory as comprehensible since relatively small perturbations in the system can produce a very different branching of the social world from what he envisaged a century or so ago.

Moreover, Marx's analysis brings out the key significance of *local* forms of information, and more generally of what Kwa terms a baroque rather than a romantic conception of complex wholes (1998). Cilliers describes how any emergent complex system is the result of a rich interaction of simple elements each of which 'only respond [s] to the limited information each is presented with' (1998: 5). Thus, according to Marx, each capitalist operates under conditions that are far from equilibrium; they can only respond to 'local' sources of information since relevant information carries across only a limited temporal and spatial range. Moreover, local struggles by groups of workers against the conditions of their exploitation had the longer-term effect, through complex iteration, of reproducing the capitalist system, albeit in a quite different form. In the end such struggles prevented such an exploitation of the workforce that social revolution of the sort Marx predicted would have resulted. The struggles of workers, based upon local knowledge, had the effect of re-establishing social order, but at a higher 'social welfare' level.

Capitalism, we now know, has indeed broken down many Chinese walls and has gone global. Can complexity provide some illumination into such a global capitalism? Is an emergent level of the 'global' developing that is recursively self-producing, where its outputs constitute inputs into an autopoietic circular system of 'global' objects, identities, institutions and social practices. And if there is, what are its complex properties, how are chaos and order combined in the global? First, we can note that billions of individual actions occur, each of which is based upon exceptionally localized forms of information. Most people most of the time act iteratively in terms of local information, knowing almost nothing about the global connections or implications of what they are doing. However, these local actions do not remain simply local since they are captured, represented, marketed, circulated and generalized elsewhere. They are carried along the scapes and flows of the emerging global world, transporting ideas, people, images, monies and technologies to potentially everywhere. Indeed such actions may jump the scapes, since they are fluid-like and difficult to keep within particular channels (such as the internet jumping from military to road protestor communications).

The consequences for the global level are non-linear, large-scale, unpredictable and partially ungovernable (baroque rather than romantic: see Kwa 1998). Small causes at certain places produce massive consequences elsewhere. Consider a pile of sand; if an extra grain of sand is placed on top it may stay there or it may cause a small avalanche. The system is self-organized but the effects of local changes can vary enormously (Cilliers 1998: 97). The heap will maintain itself at the critical height and we cannot know in advance what will happen to any individual action or what its consequence will be for the pile of sand.

The emergent global order is one of constant disorder and disequilibrium. The following are some recent examples of where millions of actions based upon local knowledge have, through iteration, resulted in unpredictable and non-linear consequences at the emergent global level (see Urry 2000: ch. 2 on each of these). For US military communications in the event of a nuclear war there developed the arpanet/internet, but which has then provided a scape which has generated extraordinary flows of image, information and non-military communications throughout the world (internet use has grown faster than any previous new technology). In 1989 there was the almost instantaneous collapse of all of 'communist' Eastern Europe, once it was seen that the particular local centre of the Kremlin was unable and unwilling to prevent such an occurrence. The apparently 'rational' decision of millions of individual people to exercise their right to drive has resulted in carbon gas discharges that threaten the long-term survival of the planet (even where most motorists are aware of such consequences). And omnipotent consumerism has almost everywhere generated religious fundamentalism. Barber apocalyptically describes the emergent global order as being locked in a major conflict between the consumerist 'McWorld' on the one hand, and the identity politics of the 'Jihad', on the other (1996). There is a 'new world disorder' in which McWorld and Jihad depend upon, and globally reinforce, each other.

There is a kind of spiralling global disequilibrium that threatens existing public spheres, civil society and democratic forms. There are of course forms of global governance designed to dampen down some of these forms of disequilibrium, but mostly they are based upon national governments acting within particular *local* contexts. Baker has elaborated on how the relationship between the centre and the periphery, or what he calls the 'centriphery', functions to create both order and turbulence in social life (1993). He suggests that the centriphery functions as an attractor, which is defined as the space to which the trajectory of any particular system is over time attracted (Byrne 1998: 26–9; Cilliers 1998: 96–7). In this case the centriphery is a dynamic pattern that is repeated at many different levels, involving flows of energy, information and ideas that simultaneously create both centres and peripheries. The trajectory of social systems is irreversibly attracted to the centriphery.

Baker further argues that

> Today, particular multinational industries center vast amounts of human activity, locating specific aspects of their enterprise in different continents. In each of these cases, the exchange of goods and services binds and lubricates a dynamic relationship between the center and the periphery. As centering progresses, it deepens the periphery. . . . Because centering and peripheralizing involve the transformation of energy and information and, thus, the creation of entropy, the process is irreversible. (1993: 140)

A specific form taken by the strange attractor of the centriphery is that of 'glocalization', whereby there is a parallel irreversible process of globalization-deepening-localization-deepening-globalization and so on. Both are bound together through a dynamic relationship, as huge flows of resources move backwards and forwards between the global and the local. Neither the global nor the local can exist without the other. They develop in a symbiotic, irreversible and unstable set of relationships, in which each gets transformed through billions of world-wide iterations. Small perturbations in the system can result in unpredictable and chaotic branching of such a system, as has happened with what Imken terms the 'non-linear, asymmetrical, chaotically-assembled . . . new artificial life-form of the global telecommunications *Matrix*' (Imken 1999: 92).

Conclusion

I have thus illustrated how 'complexity' systems can assist in the analysis of mobile hybrids. How though does this leave 'sociol-ogy' which would seem to be cast adrift once we leave the relatively safe boundaries of bounded societies. Most of the tentative certainties that sociology has cautiously erected would appear to dissolve with the structure of feeling entailed by complexity. These developments seem to imply a post-disciplinary social/ cultural/political science with no particular space or role for individual disciplines (see Sayer 1999). Why should 'sociology' analyse these intersecting complex mobilities that have travelled onto the intellectual stage in such a powerful fashion (see Thrift 1999, on the new *complex* 'structure of feeling' within the academy, management science and 'new age')?

First, most other disciplines are subject to extensive forms of discursive normalization, monitoring and policing that make them poor candidates for post-disciplinary reconfiguration. Indeed theories, methods and data may be literally expelled from such disciplines since they are viewed as too 'social' and outside the concerns of that particular policed discipline (see Urry 1995: ch. 2). There are many examples of how sociology provides a place of temporary intellectual dwelling for those marginalized by discursive normalization in adjacent disciplines. Moreover, sociology's discursive formation has often demonstrated a relative lack of hierarchy, a somewhat unpoliced character, an inability to resist intellectual invasions, an awareness that all human practice is socially organized, a potential to identify the social powers of objects and nature, and an increasing awareness of spatial and temporal processes. While all these wreak havoc with any remaining notion of society *tout court*, sociology could develop a new agenda for a discipline that is losing its central concept of human 'society'. It is a discipline organized around networks, mobility and horizontal fluidities. More generally, Diken advocates the 'more "mobile" theorizing' that will be necessary to deal with emerging hybrid entities, as well as with so-called societies (1998: 248).

Dogan and Pahre show the importance of 'intellectual mobility' for innovation in the social sciences (1990). Their extensive research demonstrates that innovation does not principally result from those scholars who are firmly entrenched within disciplines, nor from those practising rather general 'interdisciplinary' or 'post-disciplinary' studies. Rather innovation results from academic mobility across clear disciplinary borders, a mobility that generates 'creative marginality'. It is this marginality, resulting from scholars moving from the centre to the periphery of their discipline and then crossing its frontiers that produces new productive hybridities in the social sciences. These can constitute institutionalized sub-fields (such as medical sociology) or more informal networks (such as historical sociology; see Dogan and Pahre 1990: ch. 21). This creative marginality results from complex, overlapping and disjunctive processes of migration, processes which can occur across disciplinary and/or geographical and/or social borders (in the case of the 'Frankfurt School' it was all three; Dogan and Pahre 1990: 73–4). Intellectual mobilities are good for the social sciences, so it would seem (see Diken 1998, as well). Sociology has often been the beneficiary of the 'creative marginality' of such creative 'in-migrants'.

Further, most important developments in sociology have at least indirectly stemmed from social movements with 'emancipatory interests' fuelling a new or reconfigured social analysis. Examples of such mobilized groupings which at different historical moments have included the working class, farmers, the professions, urban protest movements, student's movement, women's movement, immigrant groups, environmental NGOs, gay and lesbian movement, 'disabled' groups and so on. The emancipatory interests of these groupings are not always directly reflected within sociology; more they have had a complex and refracted impact. But in that sense, sociology has been 'parasitic' upon these movements, thus demonstrating how the 'cognitive practices' of such movements have helped to constitute 'public spaces for thinking new thoughts, activating new actors, generating new ideas' within societies (Eyerman and Jamison 1991: 161; Urry 1995: ch. 2). Societies were organized through debate occurring within a relatively delimited national, public sphere. The information and knowledge produced by its universities centrally formed those debates and delimited possible outcomes. Disciplines were particularly implicated in contributing knowledge to such a public sphere, and indeed in constituting that sphere as part of a national civil society (Cohen and Arato 1992; Emirbayer and Sheller 1999).

However, the increasingly mediatized nature of contemporary civil societies transforms all of this. It is not so much that the mass media reflects what goes on elsewhere, so much as what happens in and through the media *is* what happens elsewhere. The sphere of public life that provided the context for knowledge produced within the academy is now increasingly mediatized (see Dahlgren 1995). Thrift describes the cosmopolitan mediatization of complexity science, especially as organized in and through the Sante Fe Institute (Thrift 1999). Debate is concerned as much with image, meaning, and emotion, as it is with written texts, cognition and science. The global economy of signs, of globally circulating information and images, is transforming the public sphere into an increasingly denationalized, visual and emotional public stage (Urry 2000: ch. 7; Knorr Cetina 1997).

And on that mediated public stage, many social groupings are appearing, developing partially, imperfectly and contingently, a kind of globalizing civil society. This is summarized within the World Order Models Project. Falk documents the widespread growth of trans-national citizens associations, world-wide shifts towards democratization and non-violence, huge difficulties for national states in maintaining popularity and legitimacy, and the more general growth of diverse global trends (1995; and see Archibugi, Held, Kohler 1998). Falk concludes that: 'Such cumulative developments are facilitating the birth and growth of global civil society' (Falk 1995: 35). And it is this set of social transformations that could constitute the social base for the sociology of mobilities I have elaborated in this article. The social basis of a 'global civil society' and its emancipatory interests may result in a 'sociology of mobilities' of the sort I have outlined here, as we move chaotically into the next century.

References

Adam, B. 1990 *Time and Social Theory*, Cambridge: Polity.

Albertsen, N. and Diken, B. 1999 *Moving Ontologies/Mobile Sociologies*, mimeo, Sociology Dept., Lancaster University.

Albrow, M. 1996 *The Global Age*, Cambridge: Polity.

Amin, A. and Thrift, N. 1992 'Neo-Marshallian nodes in global networks', *International Journal of Urban and Regional Research* 16: 571–87.

Archibugi, D., Held, D. and Kohler, M. (eds.) 1998 *Re-Imagining Political Community*, Cambridge: Polity.

Auge, M. 1995 *Non-Places*, London: Verso.

Baker, P. 1993 'Chaos, order, and sociological theory', *Sociological Inquiry* 63: 123–49.

Barber, B. 1996 *Jihad vs McWorld*, New York: Ballantine.

Bauman, Z. 1987 *Legislators and Interpreters*, Cambridge: Polity.

Beck, U. 1999 *What Is Globalization?* Cambridge: Polity.

Berger, P. and Luckmann, T. 1967 *The Social Construction of Reality*, London: Allen Lane.

Billig, M. 1995 *Banal Nationalism*, London: Sage.

Braun, R., Dessewfly, T., Scheppele, K., Smejkalova, J., Wessely, A., Zentai, V. 1996 *Culture without Frontiers*, Internationales Forschungszentrum Kulturwissenschaten, Vienna: Research Grant Proposal.

Brunn, S. and Leinbach, R. (eds.) 1991 *Collapsing Space and Time: Geographic Aspects of Communications and Information*, London: HarperCollins.

Butler, J. 1990 *Gender Trouble*, New York: Routledge.

Byrne, D. 1998 *Complexity Theory and the Social Sciences*, London: Routledge.

Calhoun, C. 1997 *Nationalism*, Buckingham: Open University Press.

Castells, M. 1996 *The Rise of the Network Society*, Oxford: Blackwell.

——. 1997 *The Power of Identity*, Oxford: Blackwell.

Cilliers, P. 1998 *Complexity and Post-modernism*, London: Routledge.

Cohen, J. and Arato, A. 1992 *Civil Society and Political Theory*, Cambridge: MIT Press.

Cooke, P. and Morgan, K. 1993 'The John Urry network paradigm: new departures in corporate and regional development', *Environment and Planning D. Society and Space* 11: 543–64.

Dahlgren, P. 1995 *Television and the Public Sphere*, London: Sage.

Deleuze, G. and Guattari, F. 1986 *Nomadology*, New York: Semiotext(e).

——. 1988 *A Thousand Plateaus. Capitalism and Schizophrenia*, London: Athlone Press.

Diken, B. 1998 *Strangers, Ambivalence and Social Theory*, Aldershot: Ashgate.

Dogan, M. and Pahre, R. 1990 *Creative Marginality*, Boulder: Westview Press.

Durkheim, E. [1897] 1952 *Suicide*, London: Routledge.

Eade, J. (ed.) 1997 *Living the Global City*, London: Routledge.

Elster, J. 1978 *Logic and Society*, Chichester: Wiley.

Emirbayer, M. and Sheller, M. 1999 'Publics in history', *Theory and Society* 28: 145–97.

Eve, R., Horstall, S. and Lee, M. (eds.) 1997 *Chaos, Complexity, and Sociology*, California: Sage.

Eyerman, R. and Jamison, A. 1991 *Social Movements. A Cognitive Approach*, Cambridge: Polity.

Falk, R. 1995 *On Human Governance*, Cambridge: Polity.

Giddens, A. 1984 *The Constitution of Society*, Cambridge: Polity.

Gouldner, A. 1972 *The Coming Crisis of Western Sociology*, London: Heinemann.

Graham, S. and Marvin, S. 1996 *Telecommunications and the City*, London: Routledge.

Held, D., McGrew, A., Goldblatt, D. and Perraton, J. 1999 *Global Transformations*, Cambridge: Polity.

Hewitt, R. 1997 *The Possibilities of Society*, Albany: SUNY Press.

Imken, O. 1999 'The convergence of virtual and actual in the Global Matrix', in M. Crang, P. Crang, J. May (eds.), *Virtual Geographies*, London: Routledge.

Kaplan, C. 1996 *Questions of Travel*, Durham, US: Duke University Press.

Knorr Cetina, K. 1997 'Sociality with objects', *Theory, Culture and Society* 14: 1–30.

Kwa, C. 1998 'Romantic and baroque conceptions of complex wholes in the sciences', mimeo, University of Amsterdam.

Ladau, E. and Mouffe, C. 1985 *Hegemony and Socialist Strategy*, London: Verso.

Lash, S. and Urry, J. 1987 *The End of Organized Capitalism*, Cambridge: Polity.

—— 1994 *Economies of Signs and Space*, London: Sage.

Latour, B. 1987 *Science in Action*, Milton Keynes: Open University Press.

Law, J. 1994 *Organizing Modernity*, Oxford: Basil Blackwell.

Lefebvre, H. 1991 *The Production of Space*, Oxford: Blackwell.

Luhmann, N. 1990 *Essays on Self Reference*, New York: Columbia University Press.

—— 1995 *Social Systems,* Stanford: Stanford University Press.

Lyotard, J-F. 1984 *The Postmodern Condition,* Manchester: Manchester University Press.

MacIver, R. and Page, C. 1950 *Society: An Introductory Analysis,* London: Macmillan.

Macnaghten, P. and Urry, J. 1998 *Contested Natures,* London: Sage.

Mann, M. 1993 *The Sources of Social Power: Vol. 2.* Cambridge: Cambridge University Press.

Marshall, T. H. and Bottomore, T. 1992 *Citizenship and Social Class,* London: Pluto.

Messner, D. 1997 *The Network Society: Economic Development and International Competitiveness as Problems of Social Governance,* London: Cass.

Mingers, J. 1995 *Self Producing Systems,* New York: Plenum.

Mol, A. and Law, J. 1994 'Regions, networks and fluids: anaemia and social topology', *Social Studies of Science* 24: 641–71.

Murdoch, J. 1995 'Actor-networks and the evolution of economic forms: combining description and explanation in theories of regulation, flexible specialization, and networks', *Environment and Planning A,* 27: 731–57.

Prigogine, I. and Stengers, L. 1984 *Order out of Chaos,* New York: Bantam.

Radcliffe-Brown, R. 1952 *Structure and Function in Primitive Society,* London: Cohen and West.

Reed, M. and Harvey, D. 1992 'The new science and the old: complexity and realism in the social sciences', *Journal for the Theory of Social Behaviour* 22: 353–80.

Ritzer, G. 1992 *The McDonaldization of Society,* London: Pine Forge.

—— 1995 *Expressing America,* London: Pine Forge.

—— 1997 ' "McDisneyization" and "post-tourism": complementary perspectives on contemporary tourism', in C. Rojek and J. Urry (eds.), *Touring Cultures,* London: Routledge.

Robertson, R. 1992 *Globalization,* London: Sage.

Rose, N. 1996 'Reconfiguring the territory of government', *Economy and Society* 25: 327–56.

Sayer, A. 1999 'Long live postdisciplinary studies'. *Sociology and the curse of disciplinary parochialism/imperialism',* British Sociological Association Conference, Glasgow, April.

Shields, R. 1997 'Flow as a new paradigm', *Space and Culture* 1: 1–4.

Szerszynski, B. 1997 'The varieties of ecological piety', *Worldviews: Environment, Culture, Religion* 1: 37–55.

Thrift, N. 1999 'The place of complexity', *Theory, Culture and Society* 16: 31–70.

Urry, J. 1995 *Consuming Places,* London: Routledge.

—— 2000 *Sociology Beyond Societies,* London: Sage.

Wallerstein, I. 1987 'World-systems analysis', in J. Turner and A. Giddens (eds.), *Social Theory Today,* Cambridge: Polity.

—— 1991 *Unthinking Social Science,* Cambridge: Polity.

—— 1998 'The heritage of sociology, the promise of social science', *Presidential Address, 14th World Congress of Sociology,* Montreal, July.

Waters, M. 1995 *Globalization,* London: Routledge.